Moody's Handbook of Dividend Achievers

1995

SUZANNE WITTEBORT, *Associate Director*

DANNY A. ZOTTOLI, JR., *Publisher*

HOWARD G. KIEDAISCH, *Managing Director*

Editors

MONICA D. GARRETT   SAMUEL A. YOUNG

Business Analysts

BRAD A. ARMBRUSTER   JEFFREY A. LONG
PAUL O. ELIZONDO   THOMAS J. MALLIS
MICHAEL A. GOLDEN   STACY K. MUNN
ANDREW HERRNSTEIN   SEAN POLLAND

Moody's Investors Service

a company of
The Dun & Bradstreet Corporation

TABLE OF CONTENTS

Page

COMPANY REPORTS   Arranged Alphabetically

Moody's
DIVIDEND ACHIEVERS

In 1979, Moody's introduced a study of companies that have increased their payment of cash dividends annually for at least the past ten consecutive calendar years. Moody's has dubbed these distinctive companies Dividend Achievers.

Each year, Moody's compiles its list of Dividend Achievers from more than 10,000 companies in its U.S. equity database, which includes firms listed on the New York and American Stock Exchanges and those actively traded on the Nasdaq over-the-counter market.

Moody's Dividend Achievers list is based on the concept that certain equity investments can provide a rising cash return over the long run, while offering the additional benefit of potential price appreciation. Annual total return, income plus price appreciation, for some stocks may compare favorably with some fixed-income alternatives, particularly during times of low interest rates. In addition, dividends can also serve as signals from companies' managements about the future. When boards increase dividends they're saying, in effect, that they believe that future earnings will be able to sustain the higher payouts.

Moody's 1995 survey has identified 332 companies that have increased their per-share cash dividends annually for at least the past ten consecutive calendar years. This year's list features fourteen new additions that reached the ten-year mark in 1994. They include five of the "Baby Bell" regional operating companies spun off from AT&T Corp. on January 1, 1984.

Altogether, of the 13,200 publicly-held issues (including mutual funds and small-cap companies) tracked by Moody's, 1,960, or approximately 15%, increased their dividends in 1994—up from 1,717 in 1993 and the greatest number since 1984.

The list of Dividend Achievers follows, ranked by average annual compound dividend growth rate over the ten-year period of 1984-94. The list includes the exchange on which each stock is traded, its ten-year dividend growth rate, and the number of consecutive calendar years in which the company has paid out a higher per-share cash dividend.

W. H. Brady Co. heads our list of 1995 Dividend Achievers with an annual compound dividend growth rate over ten years of 39.7% W.H. Brady Co. is an international coated film and industrial identification products company. The second-highest growth rate, 31.1%, belongs to *Arthur J. Gallagher & Co.*, an international insurance brokerage and risk-management services firm with offices in five countries. *Progressive Corp.*, one of the nation's largest providers of private passenger automobile insurance through independent agents, achieved a dividend growth rate of 29.5%. The fourth-highest growth rate, 28.5%, belongs to *Wal-Mart Stores, Inc.*, operator of 2,256 discount department stores and 428 Sam's Wholesale Clubs in 49 states, Puerto Rico and Canada. *Cintas Corp.*, a designer and manufacturer of rental uniforms for small businesses and large corporations, has the fifth-highest growth rate at 27.5%

For 51 consecutive years, *Winn-Dixie Stores, Inc.* has increased its annual dividends. Winn-Dixie, the fifth-largest retail-food chain in the nation, has supermarkets in 14 states. *Ohio Casualty Corp.*, the parent company for several insurance companies, has increased its annual dividend for 49 consecutive years. *Texas Utilities Co.* has increased its annual dividend for 48 years in row. *Central & South West Corp.*, a Dallas-based utility holding company, boasts 44 straight years of increased dividends. Each of the following companies has increased its dividend for 43 consecutive years: *Aon Corp.* and *Torchmark Corp.*, insurance and financial services holding companies; *The Dun & Bradstreet Corp.*, the world's largest marketer of information software and services for business decision-making; *SCANA Corp.*, a Columbia, S.C.-based energy holding company, and *Tambrands Corp.*, a manufacturer of personal-care products.

RANKING THE 1995 DIVIDEND ACHIEVERS

Companies are listed by the ten-year average annual compound growth rate of their dividends.

Rank	Company	Growth Rate %	No. of Yrs.
1.	[2] Brady (W.H.) Co. (NA)	39.7	10
2.	Gallagher (Arthur J.) & Co. (NY)	31.3	10
3.	[1] Progressive Corp. (NY)	29.5	25
4.	[1] Wal-Mart Stores, Inc. (NY)	28.5	13
5.	[2] Cintas Corp. (NA)	27.5	12
6.	MacNeal Schwendler Corp. (AM)	24.9	11
7.	[2] TCA Cable TV, Inc. (NA)	24.8	12
8.	[1] Sysco Corp. (NY)	23.1	18
9.	[1] Hasbro Inc. (AM)	23.0	13
10.	First Northern Savings Bank (NA)	22.9	10
11.	[1] Ennis Business Forms, Inc. (NY)	22.6	18
12.	[1] Philip Morris Inc. (NY)	21.4	26
13.	[1] Merck & Co. (NY)	21.2	11
14.	[1] WMX Technologies (NY)	20.6	18
15.	[1] Crompton & Knowles Corp. (NY)	20.5	18
16.	[2] Wausau Paper Mills Co. (NA)	20.2	10
17.	[1] UST Inc. (NY)	20.1	24
18.	[2] Eaton Vance Corp. (NA)	19.6	13
	[1] Golden West Financial Corp. (NY)	19.6	11
20.	[1] Wrigley (Wm.) Jr. Co. (NY)	19.2	14
21.	[1] GEICO Corp. (NY)	19.0	17
	[1] Hartford Steam Boiler Insp. (NY)	19.0	29
23.	[1] Family Dollar Stores, Inc. (NY)	18.8	18
24.	National Penn Bancshares (NA)	18.7	11
	[1] Pall Corp. (NY)	18.7	14
26.	[1] Bard (C.R.), Inc. (NY)	18.6	23
27.	[1] Valspar Corp. (NY)	17.9	16
28.	[1] Abbott Laboratories (NY)	17.8	22
	[1] Circuit City Stores, Inc. (NY)	17.8	14
30.	[1] Albertson's Inc. (NY)	17.7	23
	[1] Temple-Inland Inc. (NY)	17.7	10
32.	[1] Bemis Co., Inc. (NY)	17.5	11
33.	[1] Lockheed Corp. (NY)	17.4	10
34.	[1] Anheuser-Busch Cos., Inc. (NY)	17.1	20
	[1] Cooper Tire & Rubber Co. (NY)	17.1	15
36.	[2] Wilmington Trust Co. (NA)	17.0	13
37.	[1] State Street Boston Corp. (NY)	16.9	14
38.	[1] Flightsafety International (NY)	16.8	18
	[1] Rubbermaid, Inc. (NY)	16.8	40
40.	Tompkins County Trust Co. (NA)	16.6	12
41.	[1] Hillenbrand Industries, Inc. (NY)	16.2	24
42.	[2] Fifth Third Bancorp (NA)	15.7	22
	[2] Liqui-Box Corp. (NA)	15.7	16
	[1] Premier Industrial Corp. (NY)	15.7	20
45.	[1] Block (H. & R.), Inc. (NY)	15.6	31
	[1] Conagra, Inc. (NY)	15.6	17
	[1] Harland (John H.) Co. (NY)	15.6	42
	[1] Smucker (J.M.) Co. (NY)	15.6	19
49.	[1] Great Lakes Chemical Corp. (NY)	15.5	21
50.	First Empire State Corp. (AM)	15.4	14
51.	[1] Leggett & Platt, Inc. (NY)	15.2	25
	[1] Tootsie Roll Industries, Inc. (NY)	15.2	31
53.	[1] Bristol-Myers Squibb Co. (NY)	15.0	22
	[1] Medtronic, Inc. (NY)	15.0	17
55.	[2] General Binding Corp. (NA)	14.9	19
	[1] Pitney Bowes Inc. (NY)	14.9	11
	Superior Surgical Mfg. Co. (AM)	14.9	11
58.	[2] Sigma Aldrich Corp. (NA)	14.8	13
59.	[1] Firstar Corp. (NY)	14.7	16
	[1] Sara Lee Corp. (NY)	14.7	18
61.	[1] Banc One Corp. (NY)	14.6	24
	[1] Hannaford Bros. Co. (NY)	14.6	23
63.	[1] Campbell Soup Co. (NY)	14.5	12
64.	[1] AFLAC Inc. (NY)	14.4	12
	[2] Bruno's, Inc. (NA)	14.4	20
	[1] Hormel Foods Corp. (NY)	14.4	27
	[1] Johnson & Johnson (NY)	14.4	32
	[2] Nordstrom, Inc. (NA)	14.4	21
69.	[1] Automatic Data Processing (NY)	14.3	19
	[1] Giant Food Inc. (AM)	14.3	14
	[1] Quaker Oats Co. (NY)	14.3	28
	[1] Teleflex, Inc. (NY)	14.3	17
73.	[1] Deluxe Corp. (NY)	14.1	34
	[1] Heinz (H.J.) Co. (NY)	14.1	31
	[1] Legg Mason, Inc. (NY)	14.1	11
	[1] Torchmark Corp. (NY)	14.1	43
77.	[2] Cincinnati Financial Corp. (NA)	14.0	34
	[1] Walgreen Co. (NY)	14.0	19
79.	[1] Avery Dennison Corp. (NY)	13.9	19
	[1] Nucor Corp. (NY)	13.9	22
	[1] Pepsico, Inc. (NY)	13.9	23
82.	[1] Air Products & Chemicals (NY)	13.7	12
	[2] Kelly Services, Inc. (NA)	13.7	23
	[1] Stanhome Inc. (NY)	13.7	11
85.	[1] Harcourt General (NY)	13.6	27
86.	[2] First Hawaiian Inc. (NA)	13.5	12
87.	[1] First Union Corp. (NY)	13.4	17
	[1] General Mills, Inc. (NY)	13.4	30
89.	[2] Kimball International (NA)	13.3	11
90.	Bowl America Inc. (AM)	13.2	22
	[2] Central Fidelity Banks, Inc. (NA)	13.2	14
	[1] Illinois Tool Works, Inc. (NY)	13.2	32
	[1] Lilly (Eli) & Co. (NY)	13.2	27
	[1] NBD Bancorp, Inc. (NY)	13.2	28
	[1] Sonoco Products Co. (NY)	13.2	11
96.	American Precision Inds. (NY)	13.0	14
	[2] Apogee Enterprises Inc. (NA)	13.0	20
	AVEMCO Corp. (NY)	13.0	19
	[1] Coca-Cola Co. (The) (NY)	13.0	32
	[1] Crawford & Co. (NY)	13.0	14
101.	[1] Dean Foods Co. (NY)	12.9	22
	[1] Flowers Industries, Inc. (NY)	12.9	22
103.	[2] RPM Inc. (NA)	12.8	21
104.	[1] Interpublic Group of Cos. (NY)	12.7	13
	[1] Kellogg Co. (NY)	12.7	38
	[1] Wachovia Corp. (NY)	12.7	17

Rank	Company	Growth Rate %	No. of Yrs.	Rank	Company	Growth Rate %	No. of Yrs.
	[1] Warner-Lambert Co. (NY)	12.7	42	165.	[1] AMP Inc. (NY)	10.1	42
108.	[2] Old Kent Financial Corp. (NA)	12.6	14		Stepan Co. (AM)	10.1	28
	[2] U.S. Bancorp (Portland, OR) (NA)	12.6	35		[1] UtiliCorp United Inc. (NY)	10.1	37
110.	[1] Clorox Co. (NY)	12.4	18	168.	[1] Bandag Inc. (NY)	10.0	18
	[1] Fleetwood Enterprises, Inc. (NY)	12.4	12		[1] May Department Stores Co. (NY)	10.0	19
	[1] Kimberly-Clark Corp. (NY)	12.4	21	170.	[1] American General Corp. (NY)	9.9	11
	[1] Wallace Computer Svcs. (NY)	12.4	23		[1] Ameritech Corp. (NY)	9.9	10
114.	[1] Baxter International Inc. (NY)	12.3	38		Betz Laboratories, Inc. (NY)	9.9	29
	[1] NationsBank Corp. (NY)	12.3	17		[1] Keystone International (NY)	9.9	23
	[1] PPG Industries, Inc. (NY)	12.3	23		[1] Weis Markets Inc. (NY)	9.9	20
117.	Bancorp Hawaii, Inc. (NY)	12.2	17		[2] Weyco Group, Inc. (NA)	9.9	14
118.	[1] Gillette Co. (The) (NY)	12.1	17	176.	[1] Becton, Dickinson & Co. (NY)	9.8	22
	[1] Hubbell, Inc. (NY)	12.1	34		[1] Chubb Corp. (NY)	9.8	30
120.	[2] Huntington Bancshares, Inc. (NA)	12.0	28		[2] Marshall & Ilsley Corp. (NA)	9.8	21
121.	Compass Bancshares, Inc. (NA)	11.9	11	179.	[1] Dover Corp. (NY)	9.7	39
122.	[1] First of America Corp. (NY)	11.8	11		[1] Grainger (W.W.), Inc. (NY)	9.7	23
	[2] Strawbridge & Clothier (NA)	11.8	11		[1] Loral Corp. (NY)	9.7	18
124.	[1] Hershey Foods Corp. (NY)	11.7	21		[1] V.F. Corp. (NY)	9.7	22
	[1] Keycorp (NY)	11.7	29	183.	[1] Dayton-Hudson Corp. (NY)	9.6	23
126.	Black Hills Corp. (NY)	11.6	14	184.	[1] Diebold, Inc. (NY)	9.5	41
	[1] Intl. Flavors & Fragrances (NY)	11.6	33		[1] Marsh & McLennan Cos. (NY)	9.5	33
	[1] Pep Boys (NY)	11.6	17	186.	Amer. Heritage Life Invest. (NY)	9.4	25
	[2] SouthTrust Corp. (NA)	11.6	25		[1] AmSouth Bancorporation (NY)	9.4	24
130.	[1] Archer Daniels Midland Co. (NY)	11.4	20		[1] National Service Industries (NY)	9.4	33
	[1] Bankers Trust NY Corp. (NY)	11.4	16	189.	[1] First Virginia Banks, Inc. (NY)	9.3	18
	[1] Jefferson Pilot Corp. (NY)	11.4	27		Oshawa Group Ltd. (NA)	9.3	16
	[1] Sherwin Williams Co. (NY)	11.4	15	191.	[1] Church & Dwight Co. Inc. (NY)	9.2	21
134.	[2] Fuller (H.B.) Co. (NA)	11.3	27		[1] Colgate-Palmolive Co. (NY)	9.2	32
	[2] Golden Enterprises, Inc. (NA)	11.3	17	193.	[1] Donnelley (R.R.) & Sons Co. (NY)	9.1	25
	[1] Luby's Cafeterias, Inc. (NY)	11.3	21		[1] K Mart Corp. (NY)	9.1	30
137.	[1] General Electric Co. (NY)	11.2	19		[1] Rohm & Haas Co. (NY)	9.1	17
138.	[1] Lee Enterprises, Inc. (NY)	11.1	34	196.	[2] Regions Financial Corp. (NA)	9.0	23
139.	[1] Dun & Bradstreet Corp. (NY)	11.0	43	197.	[2] Mine Safety Appliances Co. (NA)	8.9	24
	Mercantile Bankshares Corp. (NA)	11.0	18	198.	[2] American National Ins. Co. (NA)	8.8	21
	[1] Pfizer Inc. (NY)	11.0	27	199.	[1] Stanley Works (NY)	8.7	27
	[1] SUPERVALU Inc. (NY)	11.0	22	200.	[1] Bell Atlantic Corp. (NY)	8.6	10
143.	[2] CCB Financial Corp. (NA)	10.9	30	201.	ReliaStar Financial Corp. (NY)	8.5	23
	[2] Mark Twain Bancshares (NA)	10.9	24	202.	Citizens Banking (NA)	8.4	11
145.	[1] Anthony Industries, Inc. (NY)	10.8	16		FirstMerit Corp. (NA)	8.4	12
	[1] EG&G Inc. (NY)	10.8	21		New Plan Realty Trust (NY)	8.4	13
	[2] Nordson Corp. (NA)	10.8	13		[1] SBC Communications Inc. (NY)	8.4	10
148.	[1] Hunt Manufacturing Co. (NY)	10.7	27	206.	[1] American Home Products (NY)	8.3	42
	[1] Masco Corp. (NY)	10.7	36		[1] Star Banc Corp. (NY)	8.3	23
	[1] McDonald's Corp. (NY)	10.7	18		[1] Tambrands, Inc. (NY)	8.3	43
	[1] Millipore Corp. (NY)	10.7	24	209.	[1] ALLTEL Corp. (NY)	8.2	34
152.	[2] Block Drug Co., Inc. (NA)	10.6	23		[1] La-Z-Boy Chair Co. (NY)	8.2	13
153.	[1] Comerica, Inc. (NY)	10.5	11		[1] Monsanto Co. (NY)	8.2	22
	[1] Morgan (J.P.) & Co., Inc. (NY)	10.5	18		[1] Witco Corp. (NY)	8.2	22
	Myers Industries (AM)	10.5	18	213.	[2] Ohio Casualty Corp. (NA)	8.1	49
	RLI Corp. (NY)	10.5	18	214.	[2] Pentair, Inc. (NA)	8.0	18
157.	[1] American Business Products (NY)	10.4	37		[1] Providian Corp. (NY)	8.0	25
	[1] American Water Works Co. (NY)	10.4	19	216.	[1] American Brands, Inc. (NY)	7.9	27
	[2] First Tennessee National (NA)	10.4	17		[2] Haverty Furniture Cos., Inc. (NA)	7.9	20
	[2] Quaker Chemical Corp. (NA)	10.4	23		[1] Rockwell International Corp. (NY)	7.9	18
	[2] SAFECO Corp. (NA)	10.4	19	219.	[1] Lowe's Companies, Inc. (NY)	7.8	17
162.	[1] General Re (NY)	10.3	18		[1] Procter & Gamble Co. (NY)	7.8	41
163.	American Recreation Centers (NA)	10.2	27		[1] Universal Corp. (NY)	7.8	24
	[1] Southern National Corp. (NY)	10.2	23	222.	[1] NYNEX Corp. (NY)	7.7	10

Rank	Company	Growth Rate %	No. of Yrs.	Rank	Company	Growth Rate %	No. of Yrs.
	[1] U.S. West Inc. (NY)	7.7	10	278.	Clarcor Inc. (NY)	5.3	14
224.	[1] Gannett Co., Inc. (NY)	7.6	23		[1] Northern States Power Co. (NY)	5.3	19
	[1] Martin Marietta Corp. (NY)	7.6	23		[1] St. Joseph Light & Power Co. (NY)	5.3	14
	[1] NACCO Industries Inc. (NY)	7.6	11	281.	Mobile Gas Service Corp. (NA)	5.2	17
	North Carolina Natural Gas (NY)	7.6	16	282.	[1] California Water Service Co. (NY)	5.1	27
	[1] Raytheon Co. (NY)	7.6	10	283.	Northwestern Public Service (NY)	5.0	11
229.	[1] Louisiana-Pacific Corp. (NY)	7.5	18	284.	[2] American Filtrona Corp. (NA)	4.7	24
	[1] Minnesota Mining & Mfg. (NY)	7.5	36		[1] Duke Power Co. (NY)	4.7	19
	[1] ServiceMaster L.P. (NY)	7.5	24		[1] Minn. Power & Light Co. (NY)	4.7	24
	[1] Telephone & Data Systems (AM)	7.5	20		SJW Corp. (AM)	4.7	28
	Washington R.E.I.T. (AM)	7.5	33	288.	[1] Carlisle Cos. Inc. (NY)	4.4	18
234.	[1] Honeywell Inc. (NY)	7.4	19	289.	[1] Central Louisiana Electric (NY)	4.3	13
	Trustmark Corp. (NA)	7.4	21		[1] Engelhard Corp. (NY)	4.3	13
236.	[1] Emerson Electric Co. (NY)	7.3	38		[1] Questar Corp. (NY)	4.3	15
	[1] Potlatch Corp. (NY)	7.3	11		[1] WPL Holdings (NY)	4.3	22
238.	[2] Commerce Bancshares, Inc. (NA)	7.2	26	293.	[2] Nash-Finch Co. (NA)	4.1	25
	Home Beneficial Corp. (NA)	7.2	31		[1] San Diego Gas & Electric Co. (NY)	4.1	18
	Valley Resources Inc. (AM)	7.2	14	295.	Gorman-Rupp Co. (AM)	4.0	22
241.	[1] Lincoln National Corp. (NY)	6.9	11		[1] Hawaiian Electric Inds., Inc. (NY)	4.0	31
	Pratt & Lambert United (NY)	6.9	16		[2] Middlesex Water Co. (NA)	4.0	22
243.	[1] Houghton Mifflin Co. (NY)	6.8	12		[2] Tennant Co. (NA)	4.0	22
	[1] USLIFE Corp. (NY)	6.8	21		[1] WPS Resources Corp. (NY)	4.0	36
245.	[1] Piedmont Natural Gas Co. (NY)	6.7	15	300.	[1] Dominion Resources Inc. (NY)	3.9	19
246.	[1] Consolidated Edison Co. (NY)	6.6	20		[1] Florida Progress Corp. (NY)	3.9	42
	EnergyNorth, Inc. (NY)	6.6	11		[2] United Cities Gas Co. (NA)	3.9	13
248.	[1] Angelica Corp. (NY)	6.5	22	303.	Southern Calif. Water Co. (NY)	3.8	41
	[2] Boatmen's Bancshares, Inc. (NA)	6.5	14		[1] Washington Gas Light Co. (NY)	3.8	18
	[1] Du Pont (E.I.) De Nemours (NY)	6.5	12		[1] Western Resources, Inc. (NY)	3.8	20
	[1] McGraw Hill Cos., Inc. (NY)	6.5	21	306.	[1] Helmerich & Payne, Inc. (NY)	3.7	18
	[1] Old Republic Intl. Corp. (NY)	6.5	13	307.	[1] Frontier Corp. (NY)	3.6	35
	[1] Wisconsin Energy Corp. (NY)	6.5	33		[1] Household International, Inc. (NY)	3.6	42
254.	[1] GTE Corp. (NY)	6.4	24		Public Service Co. of NC (Ny)	3.6	26
255.	[1] Aon Corp. (NY)	6.3	43		[1] WICOR Inc. (NY)	3.6	11
	[1] TECO Energy, Inc. (NY)	6.3	35	311.	[1] Union Electric Co. (NY)	3.4	19
	[1] Winn Dixie Stores, Inc. (NY)	6.3	51	312.	[1] Century Tele. Enterprises (NY)	3.3	21
258.	[1] Central & Southwest Corp. (NY)	6.2	44		[1] Chemed Corp. (NY)	3.3	24
	[2] Consumers Water Co. (The) (NA)	6.2	37		[1] KU Energy Corp. (NY)	3.3	13
	Energen Corp. (NY)	6.2	12	315.	[1] SCANA Corp. (NY)	3.2	43
	[2] United Carolina Bancshares (NA)	6.2	14	316.	[1] PP&L Resources, Inc. (NY)	3.1	18
262.	[2] Kenan Transport (NA)	6.1	11		[1] TRW, Inc. (NY)	3.1	23
	[1] National Fuel Gas Co. (NY)	6.1	23	318.	[1] Brooklyn Union Gas Co. (NY)	3.0	18
264.	[1] Consolidated Natural Gas (NY)	6.0	30	319.	[1] Texas Utilities Co. (NY)	2.9	48
	[1] Republic New York Corp. (NY)	6.0	19	320.	[1] LG&E Energy Corp. (NY)	2.8	40
266.	[1] Indiana Energy, Inc. (NY)	5.9	19		[2] Otter Tail Power Co. (NA)	2.8	19
267.	Federal Realty Invest. Trust (NY)	5.8	27	322.	[2] Madison Gas & Electric (NA)	2.7	19
	[1] Southern Indiana Gas & Elec. (NY)	5.8	35	323.	[2] Northwest Natural Gas Co. (NA)	2.6	38
269.	[1] Bay State Gas Co. (NY)	5.7	10	324.	[1] Orange & Rockland Utilities (NY)	2.5	19
	[1] Exxon Corp. (NY)	5.7	12	325.	[1] Atlantic Energy, Inc. (NY)	2.4	42
271.	[1] Alco Standard Corp. (NY)	5.5	30		[1] Green Mountain Power Corp. (NY)	2.4	20
	Frisch's Restaurants, Inc. (AM)	5.5	11	327.	[1] ABM Industries (NY)	2.3	30
	[1] Peoples Energy Corp. (NY)	5.5	11		[1] Allegheny Power System (NY)	2.3	34
	[1] Potomac Electric Power Co. (NY)	5.5	18		[1] CIPSCO Inc. (NY)	2.3	10
275.	[1] CSX Corp. (NY)	5.4	14	330.	Colonial Gas Co. (NA)	2.2	14
	[1] Johnson Controls, Inc. (NY)	5.4	19	331.	[1] BCE, Inc. (NY)	2.1	23
	Wesco Financial Corp. (AM)	5.4	23	332.	[2] Connecticut Water Service (NA)	1.5	19

[1] Moody's Handbook of Common Stocks. [2] Moody's Handbook of Nasdaq Stocks.
(NY) New York Stock Exchange. (NA) Nasdaq Stock Market. (AM) American Stock Exchange.

THE LONGEST RECORDS OF DIVIDEND ACHIEVEMENT

The following Dividend Achievers boast the longest records of consecutive annual dividend increases.

Rank	Company	No. of Yrs.	Rank	Company	No. of Yrs.
1.	Winn-Dixie Stores, Inc.	51		Southern California Water Co.	41
2.	Ohio Casualty Corp.	49	20.	LG&E Energy Corp.	40
3.	Texas Utilities Co.	48		Rubbermaid, Inc.	40
4.	Central & Southwest Corp.	44	22.	Dover Corp.	39
5.	Aon Corp.	43	23.	Baxter International Inc.	38
	Dun & Bradstreet Corp. (The)	43		Emerson Electric Co.	38
	SCANA Corp.	43		Kellogg Co.	38
	Tambrands, Inc.	43		Northwest Natural Gas Co.	38
	Torchmark Corp.	43	27.	American Business Products Inc.	37
10.	American Home Products Corp.	42		Consumers Water Co.	37
	AMP Inc.	42		UtiliCorp United Inc.	37
	Atlantic Energy, Inc.	42	30.	Masco Corp.	36
	Florida Progress Corp.	42		Minnesota Mining & Manufacturing Co.	36
	Harland (John H.) Co.	42		WPS Resources Corp.	36
	Household International, Inc.	42	33.	Frontier Corp.	35
	Warner-Lambert Co.	42		Southern Indiana Gas & Electric Co.	35
17.	Diebold, Inc.	41		TECO Energy, Inc.	35
	Procter & Gamble Co.	41		U.S. Bancorp (Portland, OR)	35

DIVIDEND ACHIEVER NAME CHANGES

The following companies have changed their names in the last year.

Old Name	New Name
First Bancorporation of Ohio	FirstMerit Corp.
George A. Hormel & Company	Hormel Foods Corp.
McGraw Hill, Inc.	McGraw Hill Companies, Inc.
NWNL Companies, Inc.	ReliaStar Financial Corp.
Pennsylvania Power & Light Co.	PP&L Resources, Inc.
Rochester Telephone Corp.	Frontier Corp.

DIVIDEND ACHIEVER ARRIVALS AND DEPARTURES

The following companies, which recorded ten consecutive years of dividend increases in 1994, mark their debut as Dividend Achievers.

Ameritech Corporation	Lockheed Corp.
Bay State Gas Company	NYNEX Corp.
Bell Atlantic Corporation	Raytheon Company
Brady (W.H.) Co.	SBC Communications Inc.
CIPSCO Inc.	Temple-Inland Inc.
First Northern Savings Bank	U.S. West Inc.
Gallagher (Arthur J.) & Co.	Wausau Paper Mills Co.

DIVIDEND ACHIEVER ARRIVALS AND DEPARTURES (CONT.)

According to Moody's records, the following former Dividend Achievers did not increase their dividends in 1994 and dropped from the list.

Atlanta Gas Light Co.
Ball Corp.
Empire District Electric Co.
FPL Group, Inc.
General Host Corp.
Glatfelter (P.H.) Co.
Great Western Financial Corp.
Jostens, Inc.

LaBatt (John) Ltd.
Lance, Inc.
Longs Drug Stores Corp.
Melville Corp.
Pacific Telecom, Inc.
Rite Aid Corp.
SCE Corp.

The following former Dividend Achiever companies have been merged or acquired.

BB&T Financial Corp.
Dibrell Brothers, Inc.

Syntex Corp.
Valley Bancorporation

WAITING IN THE WINGS...

The following companies have increased their dividends for nine consecutive years and are among those Moody's is tracking for possible inclusion in the 1996 edition.

Federal National Mortgage Association
Health Care Property Investors, Inc.
Roto-Rooter Inc.

SunTrust Banks, Inc.
UNITIL Corp.
Watts Industries, Inc.

TOP 20 RETURNS ON EQUITY

Rank	Company	Return on Equity %	Rank	Company	Return on Equity %
1.	Tambrands, Inc.	109.4	11.	Philip Morris, Inc.	37.0
2.	UST Inc.	107.1	12.	American Home Products Corp.	35.9
3.	Coca-Cola Co. (The)	48.8	13.	Gallagher (Arthur J.) & Co.	35.7
4.	Dun & Bradstreet Corp. (The)	47.7	14.	Gillette Co. (The)	34.6
5.	ServiceMaster L.P.	45.5	15.	Wrigley (Wm.) Jr. Co.	33.5
6.	Quaker Oats Co.	42.7	16.	Bristol-Myers Squibb Co.	32.3
7.	General Mills, Inc.	40.8	17.	Colgate-Palmolive Co.	31.8
8.	Kellogg Co.	39.0	18.	Campbell Soup Co.	31.7
9.	Warner-Lambert Co.	38.2	19.	Pfizer Inc.	30.0
10.	Abbott Laboratories	37.5	20.	Ennis Business Forms, Inc.	28.9

TOP 20 RETURNS ON ASSETS

Rank	Company	Return on Assets %	Rank	Company	Return on Assets %
1.	UST Inc.	52.3	12.	Liqui-Box Corp.	14.9
2.	Wrigley (Wm.) Jr. Co.	23.6	13.	Bristol-Myers Squibb Co.	14.3
	Ennis Business Forms, Inc.	23.6		Medtronic, Inc.	14.3
4.	Tambrands Inc.	19.7	15.	Merck & Co.	13.7
5.	Premier Industrial Corp.	19.1	16.	Betz Laboratories, Inc.	13.2
6.	Abbott Laboratories	17.8		Great Lakes Chemical Corp.	13.2
7.	Coca-Cola Co. (The)	17.1	18.	Luby's Cafeterias, Inc.	13.0
8.	Bandag Inc.	16.1		Sigma Aldrich Corp.	13.0
9.	Kellogg Co.	15.8	20.	Rubbermaid, Inc.	12.9
10.	International Flavors & Fragrances	15.4		Washington R.E.I.T.	12.9
11.	Block (H. & R.), Inc.	15.3			

TOP 20 AVERAGE YIELDS

Rank	Company	Average Yield %	Rank	Company	Average Yield %
1.	Texas Utilities Co.	8.5		Minnesota Power & Light Co.	7.0
2.	Green Mountain Power Corp.	7.8	14.	The Consumers Water Co.	6.9
3.	BCE, Inc.	7.6	15.	Florida Progress Corp.	6.8
4.	Potomac Electric Power Co.	7.4		Union Electric Co.	6.8
5.	Orange & Rockland Utilities Inc.	7.3	17.	Central & South West Corp.	6.7
	PP&L Resources, Inc.	7.3	18.	Western Resources, Inc.	6.6
7.	Consolidated Edison Co. of NY, Inc.	7.2	19.	Black Hills Corp.	6.5
	San Diego Gas & Electric Co.	7.2		Connecticut Water Service, Inc.	6.5
9.	Allegheny Power System, Inc.	7.1		Peoples Energy Corp.	6.5
	CIPSCO Inc.	7.1		St. Joseph Light & Power Co.	6.5
	Frontier Corp.	7.1		WPL Holdings	6.5
12.	Hawaiian Electric Industries, Inc.	7.0			

HIGHEST PRICE/EARNINGS RATIOS

Rank	Company	P/E Ratio	Rank	Company	P/E Ratio
1.	Church & Dwight Co. Inc.	66.5	11.	Harcourt General, Inc.	29.6
2.	Sara Lee Corp.	51.0	12.	Coca-Cola Co. (The)	29.5
3.	Alco Standard Corporation	47.9	13.	Millipore Corp.	28.3
4.	SUPERVALU Inc.	45.1	14.	Telephone & Data Systems, Inc.	28.1
5.	Wesco Financial Corp.	44.7	15.	General Mills, Inc.	27.5
6.	Helmerich & Payne, Inc.	40.9	16.	Cintas Corp.	27.3
7.	Dayton-Hudson Corp.	34.5		Gillette Co. (The)	27.3
8.	Engelhard Corp.	30.8	18.	Block (H. & R.), Inc.	26.3
	Medtronic, Inc.	30.8	19.	Flowers Industries, Inc.	25.7
10.	Federal Realty Investment Trust	30.3	20.	Universal Corp.	25.4

LOWEST PRICE/EARNINGS RATIOS

Rank	Company	P/E Ratio	Rank	Company	P/E Ratio
1.	Bell Atlantic Corporation	7.4	11.	Boatmen's Bancshares, Inc.	8.9
2.	Bankers Trust NY Corp.	7.5		NationsBank Corporation	8.9
3.	Keycorp	8.0	13.	BCE, Inc.	9.0
4.	Martin Marietta Corp.	8.4		Comerica, Inc.	9.0
	Republic New York Corp.	8.4		USLIFE Corporation	9.0
6.	NBD Bancorp, Inc.	8.6	16.	First of America Corp.	9.1
7.	American Brands, Inc.	8.7	17.	CCB Financial Corp.	9.2
	Bancorp Hawaii, Inc.	8.7		Firstar Corp.	9.2
	First Union Corp.	8.7	19.	PP&L Resources, Inc.	9.3
	Old Kent Financial Corp.	8.7		Southern National Corp.	9.3

HIGHEST LONG-TERM PRICE SCORES

Definitions of price scores may be found on page 16a.

Rank	Company	Price Score	Rank	Company	Price Score
1.	Lowe's Companies, Inc.	204.8	11.	Engelhard Corp.	130.7
2.	Nucor Corp.	174.8	12.	Mark Twain Bancshares	129.9
3.	Wrigley (Wm.) Jr. Co.	144.6	13.	Alco Standard Corporation	129.8
4.	Medtronic, Inc.	142.5	14.	Coca-Cola Co. (The)	129.5
5.	Gillette Co. (The)	140.8	15.	Eaton Vance Corp.	129.2
6.	Loral Corp.	139.8	16.	Tompkins County Trust Co.	128.4
7.	Progressive Corp.	139.2		Wesco Financial Corp.	128.4
8.	Pep Boys - Manny, Moe & Jack	137.9	18.	First Tennessee National Corp.	128.3
9.	Diebold, Inc.	134.8	19.	Nordson Corp.	128.1
10.	AFLAC Inc.	134.6	20.	Leggett & Platt, Inc.	127.7

HIGHEST SHORT-TERM PRICE SCORES

Definitions of price scores may be found on page 16a.

Rank	Company	Price Score	Rank	Company	Price Score
1.	Medtronic, Inc.	124.5	11.	Walgreen Co.	110.8
2.	Becton, Dickinson & Co.	114.3	12.	American Home Products Corp.	110.6
3.	Archer Daniels Midland Co.	113.7		Campbell Soup Co.	110.6
	Lilly (Eli) & Co.	113.7	14.	Johnson & Johnson	110.3
5.	Baxter International	112.5	15.	Abbott Laboratories	110.2
	Merck & Co.	112.5	16.	Pall Corp.	110.1
7.	Pfizer Inc.	112.4	17.	Bruno's, Inc.	110.0
8.	Household International, Inc.	111.7	18.	Avery Dennison Corp.	109.4
9.	Coca-Cola Co. (The)	111.6	19.	General Re	109.1
10.	Kelly Services, Inc.	110.9	20.	McDonald's Corp.	108.8

TOP 1994 TOTAL RETURNS

The following Dividend Achievers earned investors total returns—stock-price appreciation plus dividends—of more than 10% in 1994.

Rank	Company	Total Return %	Rank	Company	Total Return %
1.	Archer Daniels Midland Co.	43.29	28.	General Re Corp.	17.21
2.	Medtronic, Inc.	36.38	29.	Coca-Cola Co. (The)	17.15
3.	Beckton, Dickinson & Co.	36.34	30.	Alco Standard Corporation	16.46
4.	ABM Industries	32.95	31.	Chemed Corp.	16.11
5.	Pentair, Inc.	31.73	32.	Century Telephone Enterprises	15.81
6.	Nordstrom, Inc.	28.44	33.	Lilly (Eli) & Co.	14.74
7.	Gillette Co. (The)	27.19	34.	Pfizer Inc.	14.68
8.	General Binding Corp.	26.38	35.	Brady (W.H.) Co.	14.44
9.	International Flavors & Fragrances	24.83	36.	Citizens Banking Corp.	14.28
10.	Johnson & Johnson	24.52	37.	Jefferson Pilot Corp.	14.25
11.	Avery Dennison Corp.	24.22	38.	Merck & Co.	14.23
12.	Trustmark Corp.	23.50	39.	Hormel Foods Corp.	14.12
13.	American Precision Inds. Inc.	23.00	40.	Mark Twain Bancshares	13.98
14.	Millipore Corp.	22.39	41.	Wrigley (Wm.) Jr. Co.	13.94
15.	Conagra, Inc.	21.32	42.	AFLAC Inc.	13.84
16.	Quaker Chemical Corp.	21.06	43.	Illinois Tool Works, Inc.	13.56
17.	AMP Inc.	20.57	44.	Nordson Corp.	12.67
18.	United Carolina Bancshares	20.19	45.	Abbott Laboratories	12.62
19.	Du Pont (E.I.) De Nemours	20.09	46.	Clorox Co.	11.95
20.	Baxter International	20.05	47.	Southern National Corp.	11.92
21.	Flightsafety International	19.84	48.	Proctor & Gamble Co.	11.09
22.	Hannaford Brothers Co.	19.79	49.	RPM, Inc.	10.96
23.	American Brands, Inc.	18.77	50.	Bandag Inc.	10.52
24.	Pep Boys - Manny, Moe & Jack	18.72		Carlisle Companies, Inc.	10.52
25.	Warner-Lambert Co.	17.69	52.	Ameritech Corp.	10.21
26.	Household International, Inc.	17.53		First Tennessee National Corp.	10.21
27.	Lowe's Companies, Inc.	17.38	54.	Campbell Soup Co.	10.05

ADVERTISING
* Interpublic Group of Companies, Inc.

AIRCRAFT & AEROSPACE
* Rockwell International Corp.

AMUSEMENTS
Bowl America Inc.
Hasbro, Inc.
* Stanhome, Inc.

APPAREL
* Angelica Corp.
Superior Surgical Manufacturing. Co.
* VF Corp.

AUTOMOBILE PARTS
Clarcor Inc.
* Myers Industries, Inc.

BANKS - MAJOR
* Bankers Trust New York Corp.
* Morgan (J.P.) & Co., Inc.

BANKS - MID-ATLANTIC
* Central Fidelity Banks, Inc.
* First Virginia Banks, Inc.
* Marshall & Ilsley Corp.
* Mercantile Bankshares Corp.
* National Penn Bancshares, Co.

BANKS - MIDWEST
* Banc One Corp.
* Boatmen's Bancshares, Inc.
* Citizens Banking
* Comerica, Inc.
Commerce Bancshares, Inc.
* Fifth Third Bancorp
* First of America Corp.
* FirstMerit Corp.
* Firstar Corp.
* KeyCorp
* Mark Twain Bancshares, Inc.
* NBD Bancorp, Inc.
* Old Kent Financial Corp.
* Star Banc Corp.

BANKS - NORTHEAST
* First Empire State Corp.
First Northern Savings Bank
* Huntington Bancshares, Inc.
Republic New York Corp.
* State Street Boston Corp.
Tompkins Trust Company
* Wilmington Trust Corporation

BANKS - SOUTH
* AmSouth Bancorporation
* CCB Financial Corp.
* Compass Bancshares, Inc.
* First Tennessee National Corp.
* First Union Corp.
* NationsBank Corporation
* Regions Financial Corp.
* Southern National Corp.
* Southtrust Corp.
* Trustmark Corp.

* United Carolina Bancshares Corporation
* Wachovia Corp.

BANKS - WEST
* Bancorp Hawaii, Inc.
* First Hawaiian, Inc.
* U.S. Bancorp (Portland, Ore.)

BREWING
* Anheuser-Busch Companies, Inc.

BUILDING MATERIALS & EQUIPMENT
Apogee Enterprises, Inc.

CANDY & GUM
* Hershey Foods Corporation
Tootsie Roll Industries, Inc.
* Wrigley (Wm.) Jr. Co.

CHEMICALS
* Air Products & Chemicals, Inc.
Betz Laboratories Inc.
Brady (W.H.) Co.
* Chemed Corp.
* Crompton & Knowles Corp.
* Du Pont (E.I.) de Nemours & Company
* Engelhard Corporation
* Fuller (H.B.) Co.
Great Lakes Chemical Corp.
* Monsanto Company
* PPG Industries, Inc.
Quaker Chemical Corp.
Rohm & Haas Co.
Sigma-Aldrich Corporation
Stepan Co.
* Witco Corp.

COMPUTERS-COMPONENTS & PERIPHERAL EQUIPMENT
MacNeal-Schwendler Corp.

COMPUTERS - MAJOR
* Honeywell Inc.

COMPUTERS - SERVICES
Automatic Data Processing, Inc.

CONGLOMERATES
Carlisle Companies, Inc.
Hillenbrand Industries, Inc.
* Minnesota Mining & Manufacturing Co.
* TRW Inc.

COSMETICS & TOILETRIES
* Gillette Co.
* International Flavors & Fragrances, Inc.
* Tambrands, Inc.

DEFENSE SYSTEMS & EQUIPMENT
* Lockheed Corp.
Loral Corporation
* Martin Marietta Corp.
Raytheon Co.

DRUGS
* American Home Products Corp.
Block Drug Co. Inc.
* Bristol-Myers Squibb Co.

* Lilly (Eli) & Co.
* Merck & Co., Inc.
* Pfizer Inc.
* Warner-Lambert Co.

ELECTRIC POWER - CENTRAL & SOUTHEASTERN REGIONS
* Central Louisiana Electric Company, Inc.
* CIPSCO Inc.
* Duke Power Co.
* Florida Progress Corp.
* KU Energy Corporation
* LG&E Energy Corp.
* Madison Gas & Electric Co.
* Minnesota Power & Light Co.
* St. Joeseph Light & Power Co.
* SCANA Corp.
* Southern Indiana Gas & Electric Co.
* TECO Energy, Inc.
* Wisconsin Energy Corp.
* UtiliCorp United Inc.
* WPL Holdings, Inc.
* WPS Resources Corporation

ELECTRIC POWER - NORTHEASTERN REGION
* Allegheny Power System, Inc.
* Consolidated Edison Co. of New York, Inc.
* Dominion Resources, Inc.
* Green Mountain Power Corp.
* Orange & Rockland Utilities, Inc.
* Potomac Electric Power Co.
* PP&L Resources, Inc.

ELECTRIC POWER - WESTERN REGION
Black Hills Corp.
* Central & South West Corp.
* Hawaiian Electric Industries, Inc.
* Northern States Power Co. (Minn.)
* Northwestern Public Service Co.
* Otter Tail Power Co.
* San Diego Gas & Electric Co.
* Texas Utilities Co.
* Union Electric Co.

ELECTRICAL EQUIPMENT
* AMP, Inc.
* Emerson Electric Co.
* General Electric Co.
* Hubbell Inc.

ELECTRIC COMPONENTS
American Precision Industries, Inc.
* EG&G, Inc.
* Premier Industrial Corp.

ENGINEERING & CONSTRUCTION
* Masco Corp.

FINANCE
* Household International, Inc.

FINANCIAL SERVICES
* Eaton Vance Corp.

FOOD - GRAIN & AGRICULTURE
Archer Daniels Midland Co.
* ConAgra, Inc.

FOOD PROCESSING
* Campbell Soup Company
* Dean Foods Co.
* Flowers Industries, Inc.
* General Mills, Inc.
* Golden Enterprises, Inc.
* Heinz (H.J.) Co.
* Hormel Foods Corp.
* Kellogg Co.
* Quaker Oats Co.
* Sara Lee Corp.
* The Smucker (J.M.) Co.

FOOD WHOLESALERS
* Nash Finch Company
* SUPERVALU Inc.
* Sysco Corporation

FOREST PRODUCTS
* Louisiana-Pacific Corp.
* Potlatch Corp.

FURNITURE & FIXTURES
Kimball International
* La-Z-Boy Chair Co.
Leggett & Platt, Inc.

GROCERY CHAINS
* Albertson's Inc.
Bruno's, Inc.
* Giant Food Inc.
* Hannaford Bros. Co.
* Weis Markets, Inc.
* Winn-Dixie Stores, Inc.

HARDWARE & TOOLS
* Illinois Tool Works Inc.
* The Stanley Works

INSURANCE - BROKERAGE
Gallagher (Arthur J.) & Co.
* Marsh & McLennan Companies, Inc.
* Torchmark Corp.

INSURANCE - COMBINED
* American General Corp.
* Aon Corp.
* Cincinnati Financial Corp.
Crawford & Co.
* Jefferson-Pilot Corp.
* Lincoln National Corp.
* Old Republic International Corp.
The Progressive Corp.
SAFECO Corp.

INSURANCE - LIFE
* AFLAC Inc.
* American Heritage Life Investment Corp.
  American National Insurance Co.
  Home Beneficial Corp.
* Providian Corp.
* ReliaStar Financial Corp.
* USLIFE Corp.

INSURANCE - PROPERTY & CASUALTY
  Avemco Corp.
* The Chubb Corp.
  GEICO Corp.
* General Re Corp.
* Hartford Steam Boiler Inspection & Insurance Co.
* Ohio Casualty Corp.
* RLI Corp.

MACHINERY & EQUIPMENT
  Dover Corp.
  NACCO Industries Inc.
* Nordson Corporation
  Tennant Co.

MAINTENANCE & SECURITY SERVICES
  ABM Industries, Inc.

MEASURING & CONTROL INSTRUMENTS
  Gorman-Rupp Co.
* Johnson Controls, Inc.
* Keystone International, Inc.
* Millipore Corp.
* Teleflex, Inc.

MEDICAL & DENTAL EQUIPMENT & SUPPLIES
* Abbott Laboratories
* Bard (C.R.), Inc.
* Baxter International Inc.
* Becton, Dickinson & Co.
* Johnson & Johnson
* Medtronic, Inc.
* Mine Safety Appliances Co.

MOBILE HOMES
  Fleetwood Enterprises

NATURAL GAS
* Consolidated Natural Gas Co.
  EnergyNorth, Inc.
* National Fuel Gas Co.
* North Carolina Natural Gas Corp.
* Peoples Energy Corp.
* Valley Resources, Inc.

NATURAL GAS - DISTRIBUTORS
* Bay State Gas
* Brooklyn Union Gas Co.
* Colonial Gas Co.
* Energen Corp.
* Indiana Energy, Inc.
* Mobile Gas Service Corp.
* Northwest Natural Gas Co.
* Piedmont Natural Gas Co., Inc.
* Public Service Co. of North Carolina, Inc.
* Questar Corp.
* United Cities Gas Company
* The Washington Gas Light Co.
* WICOR, Inc.

NEWSPAPERS
* Gannett Co., Inc.
  Lee Enterprises, Inc.

OFFICE EQUIPMENT & SUPPLIES
* American Business Products, Inc.
* Avery Dennison Corp.
* Diebold, Inc.
  Ennis Business Forms, Inc.
  General Binding Corp.
  Hunt Manufacturing Co.
* Pitney Bowes Inc.
  Wallace Computer Services, Inc.

OIL
* Atlantic Energy, Inc.
* Exxon Corp.

OIL SERVICE & EQUIPMENT
  Helmerich & Payne, Inc.

PAINTS & RELATED PRODUCTS
  Pratt & Lambert, Inc.
* RPM Inc.
* Sherwin-Williams Co.
  The Valspar Corp.

PAPER
* Bemis Co., Inc.
* Kimberly-Clark Corp.
* Pentair, Inc.
* Sonoco Products Co.
* Temple-Inland Inc.
  Wausau Paper Mill Co.

PLASTICS & PLASTIC PRODUCTS
* American Filtrona Corp.
* Liqui-Box Corp.
* Rubbermaid, Inc.

POLLUTION CONTROL
* Pall Corp.
* WMX Technologies Inc.

PRINTING & ENGRAVING
* Alco Standard Corp.
  Deluxe Corp.
* Donnelley (R. R.) & Sons Co.
* Harland (John H.) Co.

PUBLISHING
* Houghton Mifflin Co.
* McGraw-Hill Companies, Inc.

RAILROADS
* CSX Corporation

REAL ESTATE INVESTMENT TRUSTS
* Federal Realty Investment Trust
  New Plan Realty Trust
* Washington Real Estate Investment Trust

RECREATION
* American Recreation Centers, Inc.
  Anthony Industries, inc.

RESTAURANTS
  Frisch's Restaurants, Inc.
* Luby's Cafeterias, Inc.
* McDonald's Corp.

RETAIL DEPARTMENT STORES
* Dayton Hudson Corp.
* May Department Stores Co.
* Strawbridge & Clothier

RETAIL - DISCOUNT & VARIETY STORES
Family Dollar Stores, Inc.
* K Mart Corp.
Wal-Mart Stores, Inc.

RETAIL - DRUG STORES
* Walgreen Co.

RETAIL - SPECIALTY STORES
Circuit City Stores, Inc.
* Harcourt General, Inc.
Haverty Furniture Companies, Inc.
* Lowe's Companies, Inc.
Nordstrom, Inc.
* Pep Boys-Manny, Moe & Jack

SAVINGS & LOAN
Golden West Financial Corp.
Wesco Financial Corp.

SECURITIES BROKERAGE
Legg Mason, Inc.

SERVICES
* Block (H & R), Inc.
Cintas Corporation
The Dun & Bradstreet Corp.
FlightSafety International, Inc.
Kelly Services, Inc.
* National Service Industries, Inc.
* ServiceMaster Limited Partnership

SHOE MANUFACTURING
Weyco Group, Inc.

SOAPS & CLEANERS
* Church & Dwight Co., Inc.
* Clorox Co.
* Colgate-Palmolive Co.
* Procter & Gamble Co.

SOFT DRINKS
* The Coca-Cola Co.
* Pepsico, Inc.

STEEL
* Nucor Corp.

TELECOMMUNICATIONS
* ALLTEL Corp.
* Ameritech Corporation
* BCE Inc.
* Bell Atlantic Corporation
* Century Telephone Enterprises, Inc.
* Frontier Corp.
* GTE Corp.
* NYNEX Corporation
* SBC Communications Inc.
* Telephone & Data Systems, Inc.
* U S West Inc.

TELEVISION & RADIO BROADCASTING
TCA Cable TV, Inc.

TIRES & RUBBER GOODS
* Bandag, Inc.
Cooper Tire & Rubber Co.

TOBACCO
* American Brands, Inc.
* Philip Morris Companies, Inc.
* Universal Corp.
* UST, Inc.

TRUCKING
Kenan Transport Co.

WATER COMPANIES
* American Water Works Company, Inc.
* California Water Service Co.
* Connecticut Water Service, Inc.
* Consumers Water Co.
* Middlesex Water Company
SJW Corp.
Southern California Water Co.

WHOLESALERS - DISTRIBUTORS - JOBBERS
Grainger (W.W.), Inc.
Oshawa Group Ltd.

*Designates companies offering dividend reinvestment plans

HOW TO USE THIS BOOK

Moody's Handbook of Dividend Achievers is a compact, easy-to-use reference for people who recognize that investing wisely in stocks with increasing annual dividend payments can be a profitable endeavor. This valuable investment tool provides basic financial and business information on 331 companies that have increased their dividends consistently over the past 10 years. The presentation of background information plus current and historical data provides the answers to three basic questions:

1. What does the company do?
   (See H)
2. How has it done in the past?
   (See B, D, E, G, J, K)
3. How is it doing now?
   (See D, E, F, G, I)

The following common terms are used throughout the *Moody's Handbook of Dividend Achievers:*

A. CAPSULE STOCK INFORMATION – Shown are the stock symbol, plus the approximate yield afforded by the indicated dividend based on a recent price, and the price/earnings ratio, based on the most recent four quarters' earnings.

B. LONG-TERM PRICE CHART – The chart illustrates the pattern of monthly stock price movements, fully adjusted for stock dividends and splits. Monthly stock trading volume is also included.

C. PRICE SCORES – Below each company's price/volume chart are *Moody's Price Scores*. These are two basic measures of the stock's performance. Each stock is measured against the New York Stock Exchange Composite Index. A score of 100 indicates that the stock did as well as the New York Stock Exchange Composite Index during the time period. A score of less than 100 means that the stock did not do as well; a score of more than 100 means that the stock outperformed the NYSE Composite Index.

Thus, *Moody's Price Scores* allow the user to make easy, across-the-board comparisons of various stocks' historical price performance. All stocks, regardless of exchange, are measured against the NYSE Composite Index so that their scores may be compared with any other stock.

The *7 YEAR PRICE SCORE* mirrors the common stock's price growth over the previous 7 years. The higher the price score, the better the relative performance. It is based on the ratio of the latest 12-month average price to the current 7-year average. This ratio is then put on an index basis in which the same ratio for the market as a whole (the New York Stock Exchange Composite Index) is taken as 100.

The *12 MONTH PRICE SCORE* is a similar measurement but for a shorter period of time. It indicates the recent vigor or sluggishness of a stock's price movement. It is based on the ratio of the latest 2-month average price to the current 12-month average. As was done for the Long-Term Price Score, this ratio is also indexed to the same ratio for the market as a whole.

In both cases, all prices are adjusted for all stock dividends and splits.

D. INTERIM EARNINGS (Per Share) – This figure essentially is what has been reported by the company. Figures are reported before extraordinary items, discontinued operations and cummulative effects of accounting changes (unless otherwise noted).

E. INTERIM DIVIDENDS (Per Share) – The cash dividends are the actual dollar amounts declared by the company. No adjustments have been made for stock dividends and splits. **Ex-Dividend Date:** a stockholder must purchase the stock prior to this date in order to be entitled to the dividend. The **Record Date** indicates the date on which the shareholder had to have been a holder of record in order to have qualified for the dividend. The **Payable Date** indicates the date the company paid or intends to pay the dividend. The cash amount shown in the first column is followed by a letter (example "Q" for quarterly) to indicate the frequency of the dividend.

Indicated Dividend is the annualized rate (fully adjusted) of the latest regular cash dividend. An asterisk appears next to the indicated dividends of companies that have dividend reinvestment programs.

F. CAPITALIZATION – These are certain items in the company's capital account. Both

ILLUSTRATIVE INC.

	YIELD	2.2%
	P/E RATIO	16.1

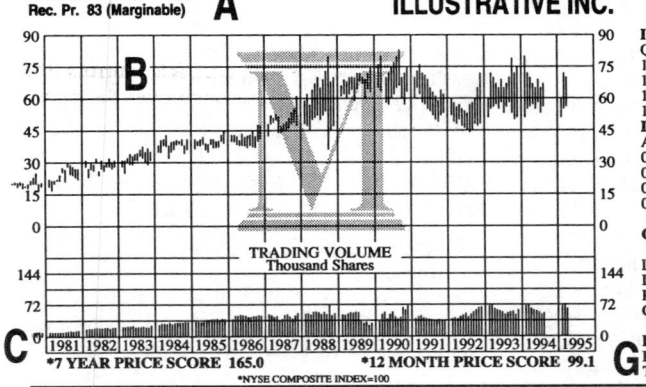

B

C

	1981	1982	1983	1984	1985	1986	1987	1988	1989	1990	1991	1992	1993	1994	1995

TRADING VOLUME
Thousand Shares

*7 YEAR PRICE SCORE 165.0   ***12 MONTH PRICE SCORE 99.1**
*NYSE COMPOSITE INDEX=100

INTERIM EARNINGS (Per Share):

Qtr.	3/31	6/30	9/30	12/31
1992	0.91	1.02	1.10	1.60
1993	0.96	1.07	1.15	1.97
1994	1.08	1.05	1.21	1.10
1995	1.02	...	...	...

D

INTERIM DIVIDENDS (Per Share):

Amt.	Decl.	Ex.	Rec.	Pay.
0.45Q	3/3/94	3/17	3/26	4/14
0.45Q	6/6/94	6/19/94	6/27/94	7/14/94
0.45Q	9/19/94	9/26/94	10/10/94	11/13/94
0.45Q	12/25/94	1/2/95	1/21/95	2/7/95

E

Indicated Div.: $1.80

CAPITALIZATION (12/31/94):

	($000)	(%)
Long-Term Debt	260,000	22.5
Def. Inc. Taxes	16,000	1.4
Preferred Stock	3,000	0.3
Common Surplus	875,000	75.8
Total	1,154,000	100.0

F

DIVIDEND ACHIEVER STATUS:
Rank: 25   1984-94 Growth Rate: 15.0%
Total Years of Dividend Growth: 20

G

RECENT DEVELOPMENTS: For the quarter ended 3/31/95 net income per share was $1.02 compared with $1.08 last year. For the quarter ended 12/31/94, net sales were $3.7 billion compared with $3.4 billion last year. Net income was $185.4 million or $4.44 per share versus $178 million or $5.15 per share a year ago. Increased sales were due in part to an overall acceptance of Company's new products. The start-up costs of these new products limited net income growth. For the fourth quarter ended 12/31/94, net income fell to $58.0 million or $1.10 per share compared with $59.5 million or $1.97 per share a year ago. Sales totaled $860.0 million, up 4% from $825.0 million a year ago. Sales and earnings in foreign markets advanced 17% and 20%, respectively over the year earlier results. During the fourth quarter, the Company introduced a new drug product for hypertension, called which has had a favorable market impact.

I

H
BUSINESS

ILLUSTRATIVE INC. is engaged in the research, manufacture and marketing of ethical pharmaceuticals, proprietary drugs and other products used in human and animal health care. It also provides medical services and manufactures medical instruments. Products are distributed in the U.S. and most free-world countries. Major products include tranquilizers, amphetamines, specialty antibiotics and vaccines; animals health products include vaccines and feed additives; medical services include a full range of pathology services. Sales (operating income) in 1994 were as follows: pharmaceutical products, 55% (48%); medical services and instruments 20% (18%); industrial products, 7% (8%); and others, 18% (26%).

ANNUAL EARNINGS AND DIVIDENDS PER SHARE

	1994	1993	1992	1991	1990	1989	1988
Earnings Per Share	5.15	4.63	5.10	4.00	4.16	4.10	3.70
Dividends Per Share	1.55	1.36	1.32	1.23	1.16	1.06	0.96
Dividend Payout %	30.1	29.4	25.9	30.7	27.9	25.6	25.9

J

ANNUAL FINANCIAL DATA

RECORD OF EARNINGS (IN MILLIONS):

Net Sales	3,675.0	3,400.0	3,214.2	2,526.3	2,500.6	2,234.8	2,116.5
Costs and Expenses	3,200.2	3,100.0	2,900.1	2,399.1	2,210.4	2,074.3	1,937.4
Depreciation	20.0	18.0	19.0	17.4	15.3	16.4	12.3
Operating Profit	455.0	282.0	295.1	109.4	274.9	144.1	166.8
Income Before Taxes	242.4	230.0	220.1	123.6	251.3	133.6	118.7
Income Taxes	57.0	52.0	75.1	70.2	84.0	41.1	38.1
Net Income	185.4	178.0	145.5	53.3	167.3	92.5	80.6
Aver. Com. Shs. (000)	36,000	17,500	17,000	15,250	15,200	14,530	14,500

K

BALANCE SHEET (IN MILLIONS):

Cash, Securities, Etc.	380.0	350.0	310.6	270.3	290.4	282.0	279.5
Receivables	140.0	120.0	125.0	120.9	130.3	126.3	120.3
Inventories	250.0	230.0	220.2	206.5	200.6	202.4	190.6
Gross Property	1,600.0	1,500.9	1,000.7	1,100.0	1,004.5	980.6	902.5
Depreciation Reserve	513.1	510.1	500.1	510.1	475.0	450.3	470.1
Long-Term Debt	260.0	249.0	229.4	300.5	296.1	301.6	322.3
Net Stockholders' Equity	875.0	540.0	530.1	523.7	518.2	504.6	501.4
Total Assets	2,800.0	2,700.0	2,432.0	2,031.6	1,963.4	1,825.4	1,612.0
Total Current Assets	1,960.0	1,400.0	1,021.4	926.2	700.1	626.3	650.0
Total Current Liabs.	973.0	470.0	426.5	400.1	296.4	251.4	225.3
Net Working Capital	987.0	930.0	594.9	526.1	403.7	374.9	424.7
Yr.-End Com. Shs. (000)	35,000	16,500	16,000	15,063	15,047	14,490	14,500

STATISTICAL RECORD:

Operating Profit Margin %	12.4	8.3	9.2	4.3	11.0	6.4	7.0
Book Value Per Share	25.00	32.73	33.13	34.53	34.31	34.80	37.12
Return on Equity %	21.2	33.0	27.4	10.2	32.3	18.3	16.1
Return on Assets %	6.6	6.6	5.9	2.6	8.5	5.1	5.0
Average Yield %	2.3	2.3	2.1	1.7	1.7	2.1	1.8
P/E Ratio	16.5-9.5	15.6-9.5	15.2-9.4	21.1-14.9	18.0-14.4	19.8-9.3	16.6-11.7
Price Range	85-49	72-44	77½-48	84½-59½	75-59¾	81-38	61½-43¼

Statistics are as originally reported.

OFFICERS:
V. Martinez, Chmn.
S.R. Fogle, Vice Chmn.
S.D. Johnson, Pres. & C.E.O.
S.S. Stephens, V.P.-Fin
Y. Cohen, Secretary
S. Mankovich, Treas.

INCORPORATED: DE, June, 1929

PRINCIPAL OFFICE: 99 Church St., New York, NY 10007

TELEPHONE NUMBER: (212) 885-2160

NO. OF EMPLOYEES: 24,000 (approx.)

ANNUAL MEETING: In July

SHAREHOLDERS: 15,500

INSTITUTIONAL HOLDINGS:
No. of Institutions: 15
Shares Held: 5,700,675

L

REGISTRAR(S): First National Bank of N.Y.

TRANSFER AGENT(S): First National Bank of N.Y.

the dollar amounts and their respective percentages are given.

Long-term Debt is the total amount of debt owed by the company due beyond one year.

Capital Lease Obligations is shown as a separate caption when displayed on the balance sheet as such.

Deferred Income Taxes represents the company's tax liability arising from accelerated depreciation and investment tax credit.

Preferred Stock and/or Preference Stock is the sum of equity issues, exclusive of common stock, whose holders have a prior claim, ahead of the common shareholders, to the income of the company while it continues to operate and to its assets in the event of dissolution.

Minority Interest in this instance is a capital item reflecting the share of ownership by an outside party in a consolidated subsidiary of the company.

Common and Surplus is the sum of the stated or par value of the common stock, plus additional paid-in capital and retained earnings less the dollar amount of treasury shares.

G. DIVIDEND ACHIEVER STATUS – The company's rank among the dividend achievers is given. Also included is the company's average annual compound dividend growth rate for the latest 10 year period and the number of consecutive calendar years the cash payment increased.

H. COMPANY BUSINESS – This is what a company does: its products or services, its markets and production facilities.

I. RECENT DEVELOPMENTS – This paragraph focuses on the current position of an individual company. In addition to analysis of recently released sales and earnings figures, items covered include, where applicable (if available), new product introductions, capital expenditures, expanded operations, acquisitions, labor developments, equity or debt financing, the rate of incoming orders, the level of backlog and other operating statistics.

J. ANNUAL EARNINGS AND DIVIDENDS PER SHARE – These figures are fully adjusted for all stock dividends and stock splits.

Earnings Per Share are as reported by the company except for adjustment for certain items as footnoted.

Dividends Per Share represent the sum of all cash payments on a calendar year basis. Any fiscal year ending prior to June 30, for example, is shown with dividends for the prior calendar year.

Dividend Payout % is the percentage of cash paid out of **Earnings Per Share**.

K. ANNUAL FINANCIAL DATA – Here is pertinent earnings and balance sheet information essential to analyzing a Company's performance. The comparisons, each year shown as originally reported, provide the necessary historical perspective to intelligently review the various operating and financial trends.

RECORD OF EARNINGS:

Net Sales is the total income from operations; non-operating revenues are excluded.

Revenues is the total income from operations including non-operating revenues.

Costs and Expenses are the total of all costs related to the operation of the business – including cost of sales, selling, and general and administrative expenses. Excluded items are depreciation, interest and non-operating expenses.

Depreciation includes all non-cash charges such as depletion and amortization as well as depreciation.

Operating Profit is the profit remaining after deducting depreciation as well as all operating costs and expenses from the company's net sales and revenues. The figure is *before* interest expenses, extraordinary gains and charges, and income and expense items of a non-operating nature.

Income Before Taxes is the remaining income *after* deducting all costs, expenses, property charges, interest, etc. but *before* deducting income taxes.

Income Taxes are as reported by the company and include both the amount of current taxes actually paid out and the amount deferred.

Minority Interest in the income statement is that portion of *profits* of a consolidated subsidiary that is allocated to a minority owner of that subsidiary who shares in the results of its operations.

Net Income is as reported by the company, before extraordinary gains and losses.

Average Common Shares is the weighted average number of shares including common equivalent shares outstanding during the year, as reported by the company.

BALANCE SHEET:

Cash and Securities comprise unrestricted cash and temporary investments in marketable securities, such as U.S. Government securities, certificates of deposit and short-term investments.

Receivables are all accounts due from customers, etc., shown as current assets.

Inventories are the sum of the raw materials, work-in-process and finished goods as valued by the company.

Gross Property is total fixed assets, including all property, land, plants, buildings, equipment, fixtures, etc.

Depreciation Reserve is the accumulation of annual charges to income representing a computed decline in the value of an asset due to wear and tear or obsolescence.

Long-term Debt is the total long-term debt (due beyond one year) reported by the company, including bonds, capital lease obligations, notes, mortgages, debentures, etc.

Stockholders' Equity is the sum of all capital stock accounts – stated values of preferred and common stock, paid-in capital, earned surplus (retained earnings), etc., net of all treasury stock.

Total Assets represent the sum of all tangible and intangible assets as reported.

Total Current Assets are all of the company's short-term assets such as cash, marketable securities, inventories, etc., as reported.

Total Current Liabilities are all of the obligations of the company due within one year, as reported.

Net Working Capital is derived by subtracting Current Liabilities from Current Assets.

Year-end Common Shares are the number of shares outstanding as of the date of the company's annual report, exclusive of treasury stock and adjusted for subsequent stock dividends and splits.

STATISTICAL RECORD:

Operating Profit Margin is the amount of operating profit derived from net sales or revenues.

Book Value Per Share is calculated by taking the aggregate dollar value of tangible assets as carried on the Company's books and dividing it by the outstanding shares of common stock at year end. This figure is fully adjusted for all stock dividends and splits. Book value for Banks and Public Utilities is as reported by the company.

Return on Equity, a measure of profitability, is the ratio of net income to net stockholders' equity, expressed as a percentage.

Return on Assets is the ratio of net income to total assets, expressed as a percentage.

Average Yield is the ratio (expressed as a percentage) of the annual dividend to the mean price of the common stock (average of the high and low for the year). Both prices and dividends are for calendar years.

Price/Earnings Ratio is shown as a range. The figures are calculated by dividing the stock's highest price for the year and its lowest price by the year's earnings per share. Prices are for calendar years.

L. ADDITIONAL INFORMATION on each stock includes the officers of the company, date of incorporation, its address, telephone number, annual meeting date, the number of employees, the number of stockholders, institutional holdings, registrar and transfer agent.

INSTITUTIONAL HOLDINGS – indicates the number of investment companies, insurance companies, bank trust and college endowment funds holding the stock and the total number of shares held as last reported.

ABBREVIATIONS AND SYMBOLS

d	Deficit
E	Extra
M	Monthly
N.M.	Not Meaningful
OTC	Over-The-Counter Market
P.F.	Pro Forma
Q	Quarterly
r	Revised
S	Semi-annual
Sp	Special Dividend

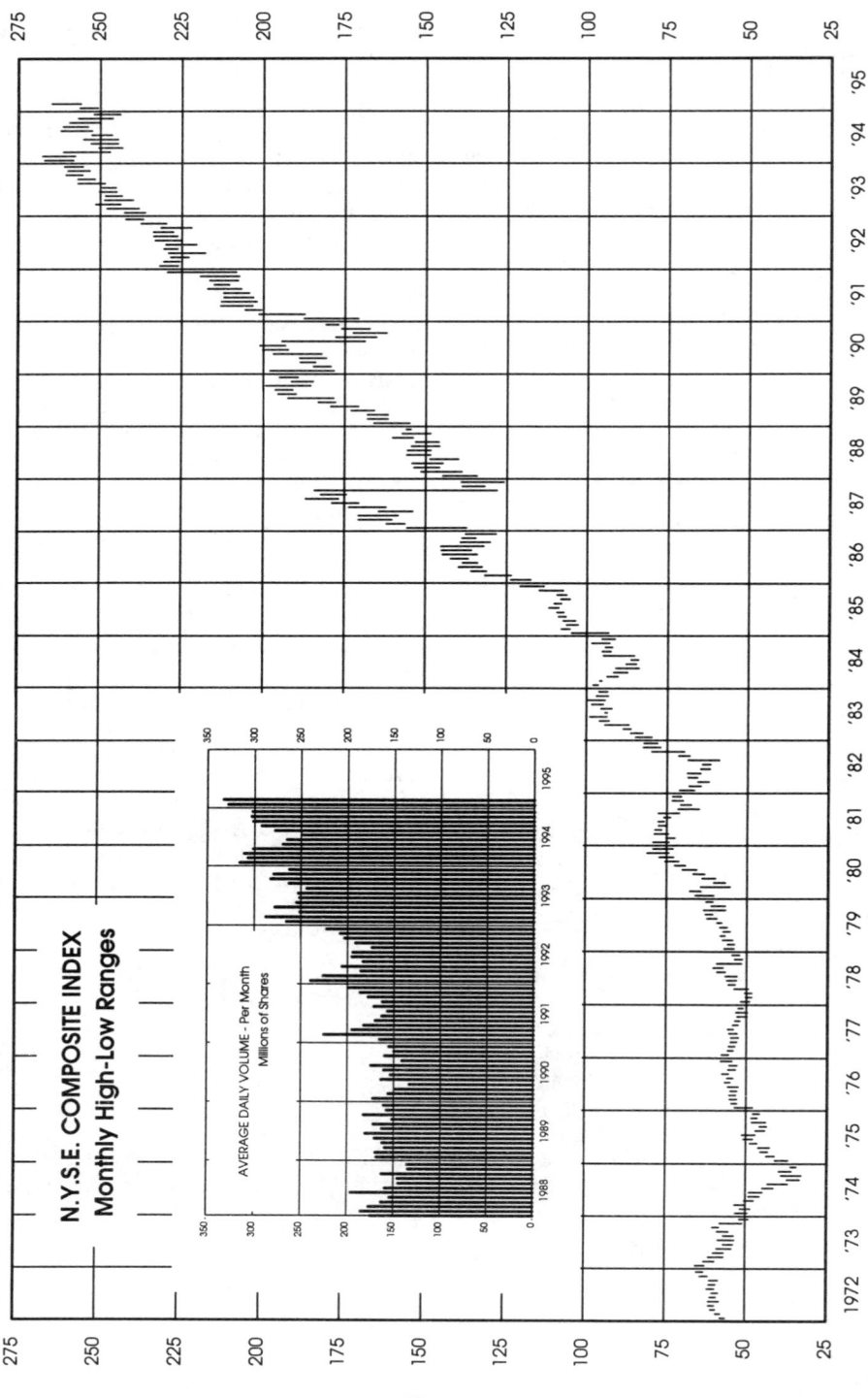

N.Y.S.E. COMPOSITE INDEX
Monthly High-Low Ranges

AVERAGE DAILY VOLUME - Per Month
Millions of Shares

20a

NYS SYMBOL ABT
Rec. Pr. 39⅜

ABBOTT LABORATORIES

YIELD 2.1%
P/E RATIO 20.3

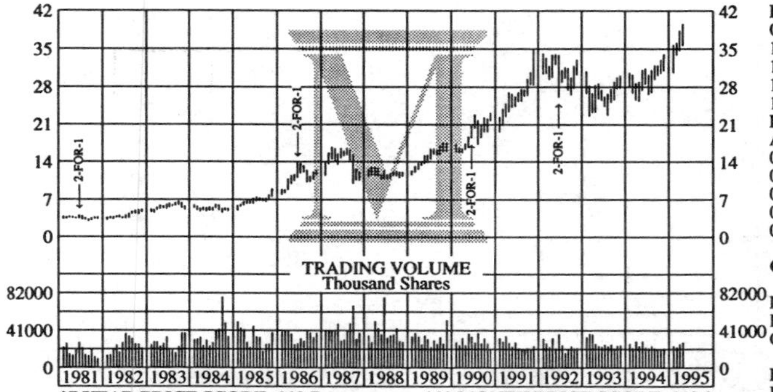

*7 YEAR PRICE SCORE 110.7 *12 MONTH PRICE SCORE 110.2
*NYSE COMPOSITE INDEX=100

INTERIM EARNINGS (Per Share):

Qtr.	Mar.	June	Sept.	Dec.
1992	0.35	0.37	0.33	0.42
1993	0.41	0.42	0.38	0.48
1994	0.45	0.46	0.43	0.53
1995	0.52	...	...	...

INTERIM DIVIDENDS (Per Share):

Amt.	Decl.	Ex.	Rec.	Pay.
0.19Q	2/11/94	4/11/94	4/15/94	5/15/94
0.19Q	6/10	7/11	7/15	8/15
0.19Q	9/9	10/7	10/14	11/15
0.19Q	12/9	1/9/95	1/13/95	2/15/95
0.21Q	2/10/95	4/7	4/14	5/15

*Indicated div.: $0.84**

CAPITALIZATION (12/31/94):

	($000)	(%)
Long-Term Debt	287,091	6.5
Deferred Income Tax	55,597	1.3
Common & Surplus	4,049,400	92.2
Total	4,392,088	100.0

DIVIDEND ACHIEVER STATUS:
Rank: 28 1984-94 Growth Rate: 17.8%
Total Years of Dividend Growth: 22

RECENT DEVELOPMENTS: For the year ended 12/31/94, net income increased 8.4% to $1.52 billion compared with $1.40 billion a year ago. Sales were up 9% to $9.16 billion from $8.41 billion. Prior-year results included a pre-tax gain of $70 million. All four of the Company's core businesses (pharmaceuticals, nutritionals, diagnostics and hospital products) contributed to the improved sales and earnings. Gains were particularly strong in the worldwide pharmaceutical operations, led by the success of Biaxin.

PROSPECTS: Growth is being driven by the worldwide pharmaceutical business. In January, the Food and Drug Administration recommended approval of Abbott's Sevoflurane, a new inhalation anesthetic. Demand for this type of anesthetic is increasing due to cost pressures, growth in outpatient procedures and advancements in clinical specialties. Sales of Hytrin are being propelled by indications for benign prostatic hyperplasia, a common disease for men over 50.

BUSINESS

ABBOTT LABORATORIES principal business is the discovery, development, manufacture, and sale of a broad and diversified line of human health care products and services. Pharmaceutical and nutritional products include a broad line of adult and pediatric pharmaceuticals, nutritional vitamins, and hematinics; personal care products, agricultural and chemical products, and bulk pharmaceuticals. Hospital and laboratory products include diagnostic systems; intravenous and irrigating fluids and related administration equipment; venipuncture products, anesthetics, critical care equipment; and other specialty products.

BUSINESS LINE ANALYSIS

(12/31/94)	Rev(%)	Inc($000)
Pharmac & Nutritional	4,951	62.9
Hospital & Laboratory	4,205	37.1
Total	9,156	100.0

ANNUAL EARNINGS AND DIVIDENDS PER SHARE

	1994	1993	1992	1991	1990	1989	1988
Earnings Per Share	**1.87**	**1.69**	**1.47**	[2] **1.27**	**1.11**	**0.97**	**0.84**
Dividends Per Share	**0.74**	**0.66**	[1] **0.577**	**0.48**	[3] **0.403**	**0.338**	**0.29**
Dividend Payout %	**39.6**	**39.1**	**39.3**	**37.6**	**36.3**	**35.1**	**34.5**

[1] 2-for-1 stk. split, 6/1/92 [2] Before extraord. item & acctg. chg. [3] 2-for-1 stk. split, 5/31/90

ANNUAL FINANCIAL DATA

	1994	1993	1992	1991	1990	1989	1988
RECORD OF EARNINGS (IN MILLIONS):							
Total Revenues	9,156.0	8,407.8	7,851.9	6,876.6	6,158.7	5,379.8	4,937.0
Costs and Expenses	6,501.3	5,999.8	5,898.1	4,940.5	4,396.8	3,851.3	3,564.1
Depreciation & Amort	510.5	484.1	427.8	379.0	355.9	307.3	270.9
Operating Earnings	2,144.2	1,924.0	1,526.0	1,557.0	1,406.0	1,221.1	1,102.0
Earnings Before Taxes	2,166.7	1,943.2	1,738.8	1,544.2	1,350.7	1,194.2	1,055.5
Income Taxes	650.0	544.1	499.7	455.5	385.0	334.4	303.4
Net Income	1,516.7	1,399.1	1,239.1	[1] 1,088.7	965.8	859.8	752.0
Aver. Shs. Outstg. (000)	812,236	828,988	844,122	854,062	870,098	893,288	903,052
[1] Before extra. item cr$128,182,000.							
BALANCE SHEET (IN MILLIONS):							
Cash and Cash Equivalents	315.3	378.8	258.2	146.2	53.2	48.7	582.6
Receivables, Net	1,468.5	1,336.2	1,244.4	1,150.9	1,070.2	892.7	781.8
Inventories	1,018.2	940.5	863.8	815.4	777.6	696.0	611.3
Gross Property	7,053.6	6,221.1	5,497.1	4,785.2	4,257.6	3,626.8	3,289.7
Accumulated Depreciation	3,132.8	2,710.2	2,397.9	2,123.1	1,881.8	1,536.6	1,337.1
Long-Term Debt	287.1	306.8	110.0	125.1	134.8	146.7	349.3
Net Stockholders' Equity	4,049.4	3,674.9	3,347.6	3,203.0	2,833.6	2,726.4	2,464.6
Total Assets	8,523.7	7,688.6	6,941.2	6,255.3	5,563.2	4,851.6	4,825.1
Total Current Assets	3,876.3	3,585.5	3,231.7	2,891.1	2,461.2	2,102.8	2,353.0
Total Current Liabilities	3,475.9	3,094.9	2,782.5	2,229.3	2,001.2	1,383.6	1,439.7
Net Working Capital	400.5	490.6	449.2	661.7	460.1	719.2	913.3
Year End Shs Outstg (000)	803,280	821,130	836,052	850,529	858,281	884,959	899,382
STATISTICAL RECORD:							
Operating Profit Margin %	23.4	22.9	19.4	22.6	22.8	22.7	22.3
Book Value Per Share	5.04	4.48	4.00	3.77	3.30	3.08	2.74
Return on Equity %	37.5	38.1	37.0	34.0	34.1	31.5	30.5
Return on Assets %	17.8	18.2	17.9	17.4	17.4	17.7	15.6
Average Yield %	2.5	2.5	1.9	1.8	2.1	2.3	2.4
P/E Ratio	18.2-13.6	18.3-13.4	23.3-17.8	27.5-15.5	20.9-14.1	18.2-12.0	15.6-12.8
Price Range	34-25⅝	30⅞-22⅝	34¼-26⅛	34⅞-19⅝	23¼-15⅝	17⅝-11⅝	13⅛-10¾

Statistics are as originally reported.

OFFICERS:
D.L. Burnham, Chmn. & C.E.O.
T.R. Hodgson, Pres. & C.O.O.
G.P. Coughlan, Sr. V.P.-Finance & C.F.O.
J.M. De Lasa, Sr. V.P., Sec. & Gen. Couns.

INCORPORATED: IL, Mar., 1900

PRINCIPAL OFFICE: 100 Abbott Park Road, Abbott Park, IL 60064-3500

TELEPHONE NUMBER: (708) 937-6100
FAX: (708) 937-1511
NO. OF EMPLOYEES: 49,464
ANNUAL MEETING: In April
SHAREHOLDERS: 86,324
INSTITUTIONAL HOLDINGS:
No. of Institutions: 910
Shares Held: 416,437,759

REGISTRAR(S): First National Bank of Boston, Shareholder Services Division, Boston, MA

TRANSFER AGENT(S): First National Bank of Boston, Shareholder Services Division, Boston, MA

NYS SYMBOL ABM
Rec. Pr. 23⅛

ABM INDUSTRIES, INC.

YIELD 2.6%
P/E RATIO 13.7

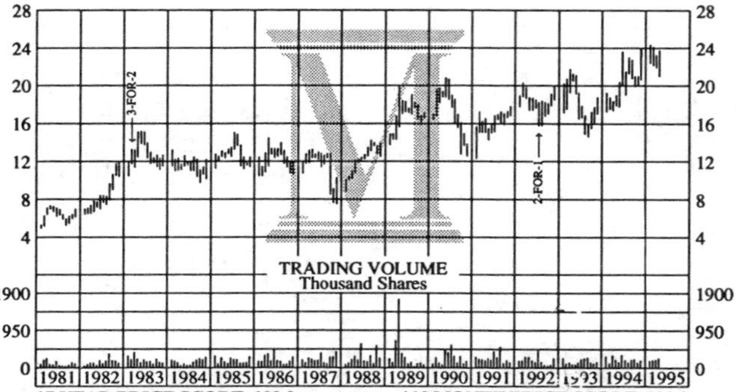

*7 YEAR PRICE SCORE 102.0 *12 MONTH PRICE SCORE 103.2

*NYSE COMPOSITE INDEX=100

INTERIM EARNINGS (Per Share):

Qtr.	Jan.	Apr.	July	Oct.
1991-92	0.26	0.34	0.39	0.45
1992-93	0.28	0.31	0.39	0.47
1993-94	0.31	0.36	0.45	0.53
1994-95	0.35	...	...	...

INTERIM DIVIDENDS (Per Share):

Amt.	Decl.	Ex.	Rec.	Pay.
0.13Q	3/15/94	4/11/94	4/15/94	5/4/94
0.13Q	6/22	7/11	7/15	8/3
0.13Q	9/20	10/7	10/14	11/3
0.15Q	12/20	1/9/95	1/16/95	2/3/95
0.15Q	3/21/95	4/7	4/13	5/3

Indicated div.: $0.60

CAPITALIZATION (10/31/94):

	($000)	(%)
Long-Term Debt	25,254	16.2
Redeemable Pfd Stock	6,400	4.1
Common & Surplus	124,331	79.7
Total	155,985	100.0

DIVIDEND ACHIEVER STATUS:
Rank: 327 1984-94 Growth Rate: 2.3%
Total Years of Dividend Growth: 30

RECENT DEVELOPMENTS: For the fiscal year ended 10/31/94, net income rose 20.0% to $15.2 million from $12.6 million in 1993. Revenues for the year were up 14.4% to $884.6 million from $773.3 million the previous year. Acquisitions throughout the year provided a boost to revenues. In addition, ABM was able to increase its market share by further penetrating certain markets. ABM experienced particularly strong activity in the New York market and improved results in California.

PROSPECTS: ABM believes that overall office building vacancy has bottomed out and the Company is well-positioned to benefit from any improvement in that market. Results continue to benefit from the co-marketing of ABM's services. Further revenue growth will be supported by increasing use of contracted janitorial services by managers seeking cost-effective alternatives to in-house services. Margins are benefiting from revenue growth.

BUSINESS

ABM INDUSTRIES, INC. is engaged in the business of providing commercial, industrial and institutional janitorial, window cleaning and building maintenance services. The Company is also engaged in the business of air conditioning, heating equipment, elevator and escallator installation, repair and servicing; lighting and outdoor signage installation and maintenance; parking facility operations; building security services; and janitorial supplies and equipment sales. Amtech group offers a wide range of mechanical, electrical and elevator services to retail and commercial businesses.

REVENUES

(10/31/94)	(000)	(%)
Janitorial Services	492	55.0
Amtech Services	229	25.6
Other Services	174	19.4
Total	895	100.0

ANNUAL EARNINGS AND DIVIDENDS PER SHARE

	10/31/94	10/31/93	10/31/92	10/31/91	10/31/90	10/31/89	10/31/88
Earnings Per Share	**1.65**	**1.45**	**1.43**	**1.37**	**[2] 1.24**	**1.13**	**0.93**
Dividends Per Share	**0.515**	**0.50**	**[1] 0.49**	**0.473**	**0.47**	**0.463**	**0.458**
Dividend Payout %	**31.2**	**34.5**	**34.3**	**34.6**	**37.9**	**41.1**	**49.5**

[1] 2-for-1 stk. split, 7/31/92 [2] Before extraord. item

ANNUAL FINANCIAL DATA

	10/31/94	10/31/93	10/31/92	10/31/91	10/31/90	10/31/89	10/31/88
RECORD OF EARNINGS (IN THOUSANDS):							
Total Revenues	884,633	773,312	760,097	745,721	679,128	638,362	581,667
Costs and Expenses	846,815	743,748	730,985	717,052	658,903	614,265	560,427
Depreciation & Amort	9,300	7,158	6,634	6,970	7,019	6,778	7,348
Operating Profit	28,518	22,406	22,478	21,699	13,206	17,319	13,892
Income Bef Income Taxes	25,059	20,242	20,417	18,578	10,539	14,592	...
Income Taxes	9,890	7,596	8,425	7,478	4,237	5,864	5,579
Net Income	15,169	12,646	11,992	11,100	[1] 6,302	8,728	7,100
Aver. Shs. Outstg.	8,908	8,646	8,397	8,146	7,950	8	7,688
[1] Before extra. item cr$1,387,000.							
BALANCE SHEET (IN THOUSANDS):							
Cash and Cash Equivalents	7,368	1,688	2,365	2,484	1,608	2,504	3,455
Receivables, Net	152,426	138,868	130,469	119,869	110,377	103,652	92,514
Inventories	17,420	16,288	13,802	13,343	12,590	10,534	10,190
Gross Property	56,902	50,838	47,275	46,488	47,760	45,260	43,014
Accumulated Depreciation	37,083	33,795	32,266	30,893	31,545	29,648	26,425
Long-Term Debt	25,254	20,937	15,435	9,477	20,005	20,032	14,036
Net Stockholders' Equity	130,731	116,588	100,825	89,554	79,558	69,389	61,918
Total Assets	299,470	268,140	226,340	211,652	201,696	189,983	172,018
Total Current Assets	189,442	166,933	153,721	141,598	132,383	121,977	111,341
Total Current Liabilities	99,277	90,320	78,535	80,119	66,453	63,625	66,054
Net Working Capital	90,165	76,613	75,186	61,479	65,930	58,352	45,287
Year End Shares Outstg	9,049	8,778	8,514	8,260	8,040	7,854	7,654
STATISTICAL RECORD:							
Operating Profit Margin %	3.2	2.9	3.0	2.9	1.9	2.7	2.4
Book Value Per Share	6.96	5.97	8.02	7.11	5.89	5.13	4.82
Return on Equity %	12.2	11.5	11.9	12.4	7.9	12.6	11.5
Return on Assets %	5.1	4.7	5.3	5.2	3.1	4.6	4.1
Average Yield %	2.5	2.7	2.7	3.1	2.8	2.8	4.0
P/E Ratio	14.5-10.5	15.0-10.1	14.2-11.0	13.1-9.1	26.1-15.8	17.7-12.3	15.5-9.6
Price Range	23⅞-17¼	21¾-14⅝	20⅜-15¾	17⅞-12⅜	20⅞-12⅝	19⅞-13¾	14¼-8⅞

Statistics are as originally reported.

OFFICERS:
S.J. Rosenberg, Chmn.
W.W. Steele, Pres. & C.E.O.
H.H. Kahn, V.P., Gen. Counsel & Sec.
D.H. Hebble, V.P. & C.F.O.

INCORPORATED: CA, Apr., 1955; reincorp., DE, Mar., 1985

PRINCIPAL OFFICE: 50 Fremont Street, Suite 2600, San Francisco, CA 94105-2230

TELEPHONE NUMBER: (415) 597-4500

FAX: (415) 597-7160

NO. OF EMPLOYEES: 42,000 (approx.)

ANNUAL MEETING: In March

SHAREHOLDERS: 3,600 (approx.)

INSTITUTIONAL HOLDINGS:
No. of Institutions: 47
Shares Held: 2,114,632

REGISTRAR(S): Chemical Bank Trust Co.-California, San Francisco, CA

TRANSFER AGENT(S): Chemical Bank Trust Co.-California, San Francisco, CA

NYS SYMBOL AFL
Rec. Pr. 40

AFLAC INC.

YIELD 1.3%
P/E RATIO 13.3

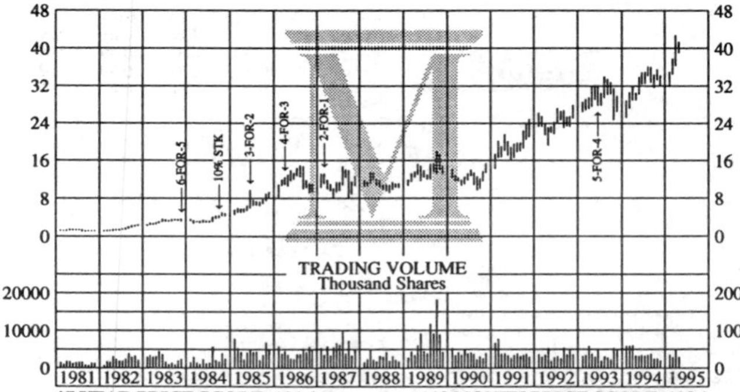

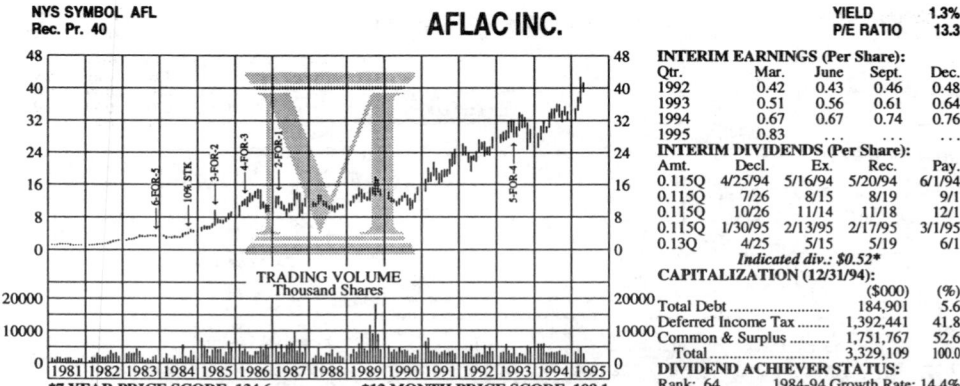

***7 YEAR PRICE SCORE 134.6** ***12 MONTH PRICE SCORE 108.1**

*NYSE COMPOSITE INDEX=100

INTERIM EARNINGS (Per Share):

Qtr.	Mar.	June	Sept.	Dec.
1992	0.42	0.43	0.46	0.48
1993	0.51	0.56	0.61	0.64
1994	0.67	0.67	0.74	0.76
1995	0.83	...	...	...

INTERIM DIVIDENDS (Per Share):

Amt.	Decl.	Ex.	Rec.	Pay.
0.115Q	4/25/94	5/16/94	5/20/94	6/1/94
0.115Q	7/26	8/15	8/19	9/1
0.115Q	10/26	11/14	11/18	12/1
0.115Q	1/30/95	2/13/95	2/17/95	3/1/95
0.13Q	4/25	5/15	5/19	6/1

Indicated div.: $0.52*

CAPITALIZATION (12/31/94):

	($000)	(%)
Total Debt	184,901	5.6
Deferred Income Tax	1,392,441	41.8
Common & Surplus	1,751,767	52.6
Total	3,329,109	100.0

DIVIDEND ACHIEVER STATUS:
Rank: 64 1984-94 Growth Rate: 14.4%
Total Years of Dividend Growth: 12

RECENT DEVELOPMENTS: For the quarter ended 12/31/94, net income was $77.4 million compared with $66.9 million a year ago, an increase of 15.8%. Total revenues jumped 22.6% to $1.64 billion from $1.33 billion for the comparable quarter in 1993. Premiums, principally for supplemental health insurance, increased 23.1% to $1.38 billion from $1.12 billion for the year-earlier quarter. Net investment income was $226.3 million, up 22.1% from $185.3 million in the 1993 quarter.

PROSPECTS: The Company's insurance operations are well-positioned to obtain future growth opportunities in the United States and Japan. All Japanese citizens are covered by either government-provided or employee-sponsored health plans. Fallout from these plans produces large coverage gaps and AFL fills those gaps with supplemental health insurance. AFLAC anticipates business will grow once health care reform is instituted in the US.

BUSINESS

AFLAC INC. is an international insurance organization whose principal subsidiary is American Family Life Assurance Company of Columbus. In addition to life, and health & accident insurance, AFL has pioneered cancer-expense and intensive-care insurance coverage. AFLAC Japan is the fourth-largest life insurer in Japan in terms of policies in force and new policies sold. The Broadcast Group encompasses seven television stations located in the Midwest and Southeast United States. AFLAC's subsidiary Communicorp specializes in printing, advertising, audio-visuals, sales incentives, business meetings and mailings.

BUSINESS LINE ANALYSIS

(12/31/94)	Rev(%)	Inc(%)
Insurance	97.9	97.7
Broadcast-U.S.	1.3	2.3
Corp. & other U.S. Opers	0.8	0.0
Total	100.0	100.0

ANNUAL EARNINGS AND DIVIDENDS PER SHARE

	1994	1993	1992	1991	1990	1989	1988
Earnings Per Share	**2.84**	**2.32**	**1.79**	**1.46**	**1.15**	**0.80**	**1.08**
Dividends Per Share	**0.445**	**[1] 0.388**	**0.344**	**0.296**	**0.264**	**0.232**	**0.20**
Dividend Payout %	**15.7**	**16.7**	**19.2**	**20.3**	**22.9**	**29.0**	**18.5**

[1] 5-for-4 stk. split, 6/15/93

ANNUAL FINANCIAL DATA

	1994	1993	1992	1991	1990	1989	1988
RECORD OF EARNINGS (IN MILLIONS):							
Insurance Premiums	5,180.7	4,225.4	3,369.2	2,765.3	2,259.1	2,033.2	1,959.7
Total Interest Income	838.8	689.3	533.2	431.3	341.0	295.7	262.0
Total Revenues	6,110.8	5,000.6	3,986.5	3,282.7	2,678.4	2,438.2	2,324.6
Benefits & Claims	4,256.5	3,423.3	2,692.4	2,188.8	1,759.2	1,561.1	1,518.0
Earn Bef Income Taxes	504.3	428.4	324.5	264.7	216.4	178.0	199.1
Income Taxes	211.5	184.5	141.2	116.0	99.2	97.2	90.2
Net Income	292.8	[1] 243.9	183.4	148.7	117.2	80.8	108.9
Aver. Shs. Outstg. (000)	103,101	105,201	102,544	101,980	101,719	101,420	101,219
[1] Before acctg. change cr$11,438,000.							
BALANCE SHEET (IN MILLIONS):							
Cash	17.6	23.4	36.1	46.3	26.4	24.0	20.1
Fixed Maturities	15,530.7	12,137.8	9,095.9	7,678.2	5,922.4	4,632.4	4,207.5
Eq Secur Available for Sale	84.4	82.1	68.3	61.2	55.1	49.4	112.6
Mtge Loans on Real Estate	25.1	57.5	85.3	85.4	80.0	35.1	...
Total Assets	20,287.1	15,442.7	11,901.4	10,144.5	8,034.8	6,515.4	6,073.8
Benefits and Claims	16,006.6	12,065.5	9,263.0	7,799.3	6,149.2	4,865.6	4,523.6
Net Stockholders' Equity	1,751.8	1,365.6	1,081.9	923.5	791.0	702.2	642.4
Year End Shs Outstg (000)	99,636	103,471	82,412	81,735	101,814	101,578	101,319
STATISTICAL RECORD:							
Book Value Per Share	17.58	13.20	13.13	11.30	7.77	6.91	6.34
Return on Equity %	16.7	17.9	16.9	16.1	14.8	11.5	17.0
Return on Assets %	1.4	1.6	1.5	1.5	1.5	1.2	1.8
Average Yield %	1.5	1.3	1.5	1.5	2.1	1.6	1.7
P/E Ratio	12.7-8.9	14.7-10.7	15.6-10.8	17.0-9.8	13.4-8.5	22.5-13.4	12.6-8.6
Price Range	36⅛-25¼	34-24¾	27⅞-19¼	24⅞-14¼	15⅝-9¾	18-10¾	13⅝-9¼

Statistics are as originally reported.

OFFICERS:
P.S. Amos, Chmn.
D.P. Amos, Pres. & C.E.O.
K. Cloninger, III, Exec. V.P. & C.F.O.
N.P. Foster, Exec. V.P.-Corp. Fin.

PRINCIPAL OFFICE: 1932 Wynnton Road, Columbus, GA 31999

TELEPHONE NUMBER: (706) 323-3431
FAX: (706) 324-6330
NO. OF EMPLOYEES: 4,000
ANNUAL MEETING: In May
SHAREHOLDERS: 34,628 approx.
INSTITUTIONAL HOLDINGS:
No. of Institutions: 248
Shares Held: 56,245,932

REGISTRAR(S): Columbus Bank & Trust Co., Columbus, GA

TRANSFER AGENT(S): At Company's Office

NYS SYMBOL APD
Rec. Pr. 51⅛

AIR PRODUCTS & CHEMICALS, INC.

YIELD 1.9%
P/E RATIO 23.6

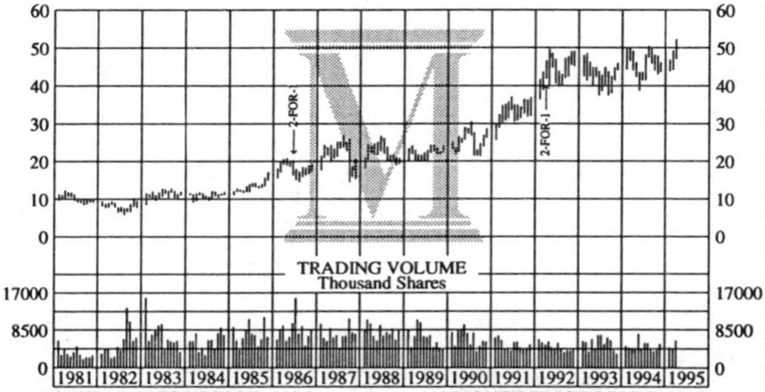

*7 YEAR PRICE SCORE 110.1 *12 MONTH PRICE SCORE 101.7

*NYSE COMPOSITE INDEX=100

INTERIM EARNINGS (Per Share):

Qtr.	Dec.	Mar.	June	Sept.
1991-92	0.57	0.65	0.60	0.63
1992-93	0.61	0.66	0.62	d0.13
1993-94	0.66	0.12	0.58	0.70
1994-95	0.77	...	...	...

INTERIM DIVIDENDS (Per Share):

Amt.	Decl.	Ex.	Rec.	Pay.
0.245Q	6/16/94	6/28/94	7/5/94	8/12/94
0.245Q	9/15	9/27	10/3	11/14
0.245Q	11/18	12/27	1/3/95	2/13/95
0.245Q	3/16/95	3/28/95	4/3	5/12

*Indicated div.: $0.98**

CAPITALIZATION (9/30/94):

	($000)	(%)
Long-Term Debt	891,900	25.1
Cap. Lease Oblig.	30,600	0.9
Deferred Income Tax	423,500	11.9
Common & Surplus	2,206,400	62.1
Total	3,552,400	100.0

DIVIDEND ACHIEVER STATUS:
Rank: 82 1984-94 Growth Rate: 13.7%
Total Years of Dividend Growth: 12

RECENT DEVELOPMENTS: For the quarter ended 12/31/94, net income was $86.7 million compared with income of $75.1 million, before the cumulative effect of an accounting change in the equivalent 1993 period. Net sales rose by 11% to $920.8 million from $827.3 million in the corresponding period of the previous year. The industrial gas and chemical sectors increased operating income by 17% and 54%, respectively. Each benefited from increased product volume and higher margins.

PROSPECTS: During the second quarter, the Company will convert its ammonia capacity, which accounted for $8.0 million in operating income during the first quarter of fiscal 1995, into hydrogen production, thereby ending APD's operations in the commodity ammonia business. The environmental and energy systems business should continue its to improve revenue on the strength of American Ref-Fuel, Inc. the Company's joint venture with Browning Ferris Industries, Inc.

BUSINESS

AIR PRODUCTS & CHEMICALS, INC. is a supplier of industrial gases and related equipment, specialty and intermediate chemicals, and environmental and energy systems. The industrial gases segment produces and distributes industrial gases such as oxygen, nitrogen, argon, and hydrogen as well as a variety of medical and specialty gases. The equipment and technology segment supplies cryogenic and gas processing equipment. The chemicals segment produces polymer products, polyurethane intermediates and additives, and aminos and specialty additives. The environmental and energy segment owns and operates waste-to-energy and cogeneration facilities.

REVENUES

(09/30/94)	Rev(%)	Inc(%)
Industrial Gases	56.5	76.6
Chemicals	33.9	23.0
Environmental & Energy	1.9	(6.0)
Equipment & Technology	7.7	6.4
Total	100.0	100.0

ANNUAL EARNINGS AND DIVIDENDS PER SHARE

	9/30/94	9/30/93	9/30/92	9/30/91	9/30/90	9/30/89	9/30/88
Earnings Per Share	**2.06**	**1.76**	**[1] 2.45**	**2.23**	**2.08**	**2.02**	**1.95**
Dividends Per Share	**0.95**	**0.89**	**[2] 0.825**	**0.75**	**0.69**	**0.63**	**0.55**
Dividend Payout %	**46.1**	**50.6**	**33.7**	**33.7**	**33.3**	**31.2**	**28.2**

[1] Before extraord. item [2] 2-for-1 stk. split, 3/10/92

ANNUAL FINANCIAL DATA

	9/30/94	9/30/93	9/30/92	9/30/91	9/30/90	9/30/89	9/30/88
RECORD OF EARNINGS (IN MILLIONS):							
Total Revenues	3,483.8	3,355.5	3,226.1	2,959.1	2,913.3	2,670.4	2,445.2
Costs and Expenses	2,644.9	2,640.5	2,405.4	2,202.5	2,202.4	2,001.1	1,811.1
Depreciation	352.8	345.7	340.2	319.1	303.2	281.2	257.6
Operating Income	486.1	369.3	480.5	437.5	407.7	388.1	376.5
Income Bef Income Taxes	325.3	300.8	407.0	362.6	336.8	321.5	303.7
Income Taxes	91.8	99.9	130.0	113.7	106.9	99.4	89.9
Net Income	247.8	200.9	[1] 277.0	248.9	229.9	222.1	213.7
Aver. Shs. Outstg. (000)	113,600	113,900	113,000	112,000	110,800	109,882	109,716
[1] Before extra. item dr$6,000,000.							
BALANCE SHEET (IN MILLIONS):							
Cash and Cash Equivalents	99.9	238.4	116.8	104.4	74.4	49.5	36.2
Receivables, Net	662.0	576.7	535.2	477.8	473.6	437.6	375.5
Inventories	292.4	293.6	310.6	283.3	282.2	291.1	240.2
Gross Property	6,519.5	5,952.8	5,784.5	5,332.2	5,010.2	4,441.9	4,085.8
Accumulated Depreciation	3,526.9	3,247.2	3,038.8	2,709.6	2,525.1	2,224.3	2,024.1
Long-Term Debt	891.9	985.6	956.2	944.6	953.9	853.7	667.9
Capital Lease Obligations	30.6	30.8	...	...	...	...	...
Net Stockholders' Equity	2,206.4	2,101.9	2,097.7	1,841.3	1,688.4	1,444.9	1,272.2
Total Assets	5,036.2	4,761.5	4,547.8	4,283.5	3,971.1	3,441.6	3,064.3
Total Current Assets	1,177.7	1,196.3	1,054.3	957.2	908.9	832.8	691.1
Total Current Liabilities	1,076.4	874.0	719.3	784.5	623.0	494.5	516.8
Net Working Capital	101.3	322.3	335.0	172.7	285.9	338.3	174.3
Year End Shs Outstg (000)	113,408	114,152	113,366	112,400	111,400	110,172	109,708
STATISTICAL RECORD:							
Operating Profit Margin %	14.0	11.0	14.9	14.8	14.0	14.5	15.4
Book Value Per Share	18.86	17.85	17.87	15.81	14.67	12.64	11.26
Return on Equity %	10.6	9.6	13.2	13.5	13.6	15.4	16.8
Return on Assets %	4.6	4.2	6.1	5.8	5.8	6.5	7.0
Average Yield %	2.1	2.1	1.9	2.4	2.7	2.8	2.4
P/E Ratio	24.5-18.8	27.6-21.3	20.2-14.9	16.7-11.5	14.7-10.3	12.1-9.9	13.7-9.4
Price Range	50⅜-38¾	48½-37½	49½-36½	37⅛-25⅝	30½-21½	24⅜-20	26¾-18¼

Statistics are as originally reported.

OFFICERS:
H.A. Wagner, Chmn., C.E.O. & Pres.
G.A. White, Sr. V.P.-Fin.
J.H. Agger, V.P., Gen. Couns. & Sec.
D.H. Kelly, V.P. & Treas.

INCORPORATED: MI, Oct., 1940; reincorp., DE, Jun., 1961

PRINCIPAL OFFICE: 7201 Hamilton Blvd., Allentown, PA 18195-1501

TELEPHONE NUMBER: (610) 481-4911

NO. OF EMPLOYEES: 13,300 approx.

ANNUAL MEETING: In January

SHAREHOLDERS: 11,765

INSTITUTIONAL HOLDINGS:
No. of Institutions: 376
Shares Held: 39,415,564

REGISTRAR(S): Mellon Securities Trust Co., Pittsburgh, PA

TRANSFER AGENT(S): Mellon Securities Trust Co., Pittsburgh, PA

ALBERTSON'S INC.

YIELD 1.8%
P/E RATIO 18.0

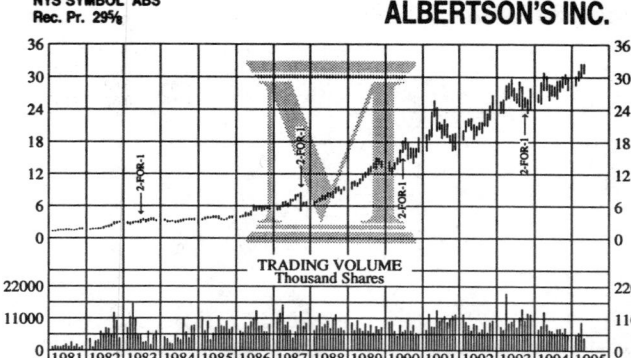

TRADING VOLUME
Thousand Shares

*7 YEAR PRICE SCORE 121.1   *12 MONTH PRICE SCORE 102.4
*NYSE COMPOSITE INDEX=100

INTERIM EARNINGS (Per Share):

Qtr.	Apr.	July	Oct.	Jan.
1991-92	0.22	0.22	0.23	0.31
1992-93	0.12	0.25	0.27	0.40
1993-94	0.29	0.30	0.25	0.50
1994-95	0.34	0.37	0.37	0.57

INTERIM DIVIDENDS (Per Share):

Amt.	Decl.	Ex.	Rec.	Pay.
0.11Q	3/7/94	5/2/94	5/6/94	5/25/94
0.11Q	5/27	8/1	8/5	8/25
0.11Q	9/6	10/31	11/4	11/25
0.11Q	12/5	1/30/95	2/3/95	2/25/95
0.13Q	3/6/95	5/1	5/5	5/25

Indicated div.: $0.52*

CAPITALIZATION (2/2/95):

	($000)	(%)
Long-Term Debt	382,775	17.4
Cap. Lease Oblig.	129,573	5.9
Deferred Income Tax	2,017	0.1
Common & Surplus	1,687,893	76.6
Total	2,202,258	100.0

DIVIDEND ACHIEVER STATUS:
Rank: 30   1984-94 Growth Rate: 17.7%
Total Years of Dividend Growth: 23

RECENT DEVELOPMENTS: For the year ended 2/2/95, earnings before the cumulative effect of an accounting change for postretirement benefits was $417.4 million compared with net income of $339.7 million a year earlier. Sales for the year improved 5.4% to $11.89 billion from $11.28 billion the year before. The increase in sales reflects identical store sales increases, the continued expansion of net square footage in retail locations, inflation and the purchase of 74 Jewel Osco stores from April 1992.

PROSPECTS: Albertson's is concentrating on increasing sales in existing stores and developing programs to reduce expenses. A $2.6 billion capital expenditure program will focus on building new stores, remodeling existing stores, and expanding its distribution system. ABS is also boosting its efforts to increase sales in existing stores and reduce expenses as a percentage of sales, mainly through improvements in information technology, including new computerized pharmacies and electronic payment systems.

BUSINESS

ALBERTSON'S INC. is the fourth-largest retail food-drug chain in the United States. As of 2/2/95, the Company operated 720 stores in 19 western, midwestern and southern states. The Company operates stores in three different formats: Combination food-drug, conventional, and warehouse. Combination food-drug units, averaging 55,000 square feet, consist of grocery, general merchandise, and meat and produce departments, along with pharmacy, lobby/video, floral, and bakery service departments. The grocery warehouse stores are full-line, mass-merchandise markets. Retail operations are supported by 11 Company-owned distribution centers.

QUARTERLY DATA

(2/2/95)($000)	Rev	Inc
1st Quarter	2,909,808	68,151
2nd Quarter	2,987,680	93,677
3rd Quarter	2,928,012	94,326
4th Quarter	3,069,121	144,211

ANNUAL EARNINGS AND DIVIDENDS PER SHARE

	2/2/95	2/3/94	1/28/93	1/30/92	1/31/91	2/1/90	2/2/89
Earnings Per Share	1.65	1.34	1.04	0.97	0.88	0.74	0.61
Dividends Per Share	0.42	0.34	0.31	0.27	0.23	0.185	0.135
Dividend Payout %	25.5	25.4	29.8	27.8	26.3	25.3	22.1

ANNUAL FINANCIAL DATA

RECORD OF EARNINGS (IN MILLIONS):

	2/2/95	2/3/94	1/28/93	1/30/92	1/31/91	2/1/90	2/2/89
Total Revenues	11,894.6	11,283.7	10,173.7	8,680.5	8,218.6	7,422.7	6,773.1
Costs and Expenses	10,933.9	10,457.7	9,524.2	8,133.5	7,720.8	6,997.1	6,426.8
Depreciation & Amort	226.5	196.4	171.7	132.8	122.2	105.9	85.7
Operating Profit	734.2	629.6	477.8	414.2	375.6	319.6	260.6
Earn Bef Income Taxes	678.7	552.2	443.7	406.4	366.0	309.8	257.0
Income Taxes	261.3	212.5	167.6	148.6	132.2	113.2	94.4
Net Income	①417.4	339.7	②276.1	257.8	233.8	196.6	162.5
Aver. Shs. Outstg. (000)	253,633	254,227	264,418	266,338	267,554	268,272	266,424

① Bef. acctg. change dr$17,006,000.   ② Bef. acctg. change dr$6,858,000.

BALANCE SHEET (IN MILLIONS):

	2/2/95	2/3/94	1/28/93	1/30/92	1/31/91	2/1/90	2/2/89
Cash and Cash Equivalents	50.2	62.5	39.5	34.4	23.4	43.7	81.6
Receivables, Net	109.3	174.5	130.9	93.0	79.7	69.2	69.2
Inventories	948.6	871.7	830.1	613.2	562.7	544.7	432.3
Gross Property	3,496.3	3,109.2	2,727.3	2,166.2	1,959.4	1,745.2	1,477.9
Accumulated Depreciation	1,186.9	1,027.3	882.3	773.5	691.0	598.5	518.2
Long-Term Debt	382.8	554.1	404.5	52.5	56.1	111.5	64.0
Capital Lease Obligations	129.6	110.9	103.8	99.2	103.0	106.9	113.0
Net Stockholders' Equity	1,687.9	1,389.4	1,388.4	1,199.5	1,087.9	929.5	800.5
Total Assets	3,621.7	3,294.9	2,945.6	2,216.2	2,013.5	1,862.7	1,591.0
Total Current Assets	1,189.6	1,122.2	1,013.5	751.3	677.4	668.1	592.0
Total Current Liabilities	1,095.4	990.1	813.0	652.2	585.6	555.0	488.4
Net Working Capital	94.2	132.2	200.5	99.0	91.8	113.1	103.6
Year End Shs Outstg (000)	253,984	253,407	264,659	264,261	267,640	267,840	267,716

STATISTICAL RECORD:

	2/2/95	2/3/94	1/28/93	1/30/92	1/31/91	2/1/90	2/2/89
Operating Profit Margin %	6.2	5.6	4.7	4.8	4.6	4.3	3.8
Book Value Per Share	6.65	5.48	5.25	4.54	4.06	3.47	2.99
Return on Equity %	24.7	24.4	19.9	21.5	21.5	21.1	20.3
Return on Assets %	11.5	10.3	9.4	11.6	11.6	10.6	10.2
Average Yield %	1.5	1.3	2.4	1.3	1.5	1.5	1.7
P/E Ratio	18.7-15.2	22.2-17.4	25.7-17.7	26.5-16.9	21.4-13.9	20.4-12.3	16.0-9.8
Price Range	30⅞-25⅛	29¾-23⅜	26¼-18⅜	25¾-16⅜	18⅞-12¼	15⅛-9⅛	9¾-6

Statistics are as originally reported.

OFFICERS:
G.G. Michael, Chmn. & C.E.O.
J.B. Carley, Pres. & C.O.O.
A.C. Olson, Sr. V.P.-Fin. & C.F.O.

INCORPORATED: DE, Apr., 1969

PRINCIPAL OFFICE: 250 Parkcenter Blvd.
P.O. Box 20, Boise, ID 83726

TELEPHONE NUMBER: (208) 385-6200
FAX: (208) 385-6539
NO. OF EMPLOYEES: 76,000 (approx.)
ANNUAL MEETING: In May
SHAREHOLDERS: 17,000 (approx.)
INSTITUTIONAL HOLDINGS:
No. of Institutions: 400
Shares Held: 47,122,545

REGISTRAR(S): Chemical Trust Co. of California, San Francisco, CA 94111

TRANSFER AGENT(S): Chemical Trust Co. of California, San Francisco, CA 94111

NYS SYMBOL ASN
Rec. Pr. 70⅞

ALCO STANDARD CORP.

YIELD 1.5%
P/E RATIO 47.9

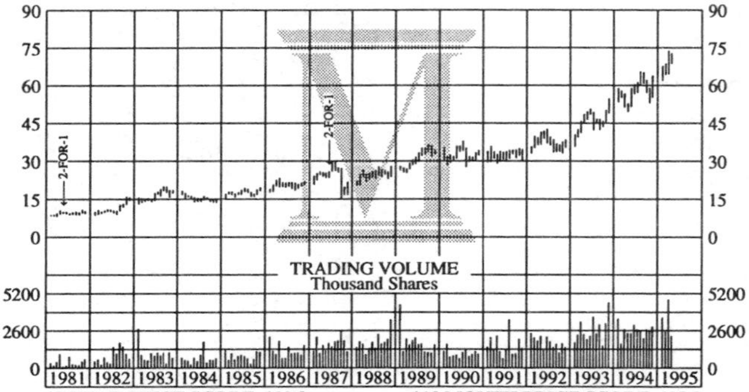

***7 YEAR PRICE SCORE 129.8** ***12 MONTH PRICE SCORE 108.0**

*NYSE COMPOSITE INDEX=100

INTERIM EARNINGS (Per Share):

Qtr.	Dec.	Mar.	June	Sept.
1991-92	0.43	0.52	0.58	0.69
1992-93	----------------	d0.04	----------------	
1993-94	0.60	0.64	d0.95	0.83
1994-95	0.77	0.83	...	...

INTERIM DIVIDENDS (Per Share):

Amt.	Decl.	Ex.	Rec.	Pay.
0.25Q	2/4/94	2/15/94	2/22/94	3/10/94
0.25Q	5/3	5/17	5/23	6/10
0.25Q	8/9	8/16	8/22	9/10
0.26Q	11/11	11/15	11/21	12/10
0.26Q	1/27/95	2/14/95	2/21/95	3/10/95

*Indicated div.: $1.04**

CAPITALIZATION (9/30/94):

	($000)	(%)
Long-Term Debt	340,771	19.6
Deferred Income Tax	32,192	1.8
Preferred Stock	199,912	11.5
Common & Surplus	1,167,232	67.1
Total	1,740,107	100.0

DIVIDEND ACHIEVER STATUS:
Rank: 271 1984-94 Growth Rate: 5.5%
Total Years of Dividend Growth: 30

RECENT DEVELOPMENTS: For the quarter ended 12/31/94, ASN reported net income of $45.5 million, a 42.7% increase compared with net income of $31.9 million in 1993. Revenues for the quarter were up 13.5% to $2.18 billion from $1.92 billion the year before. Revenue from Alco Office Products rose 27.7% to $636.1 million, reflecting internal growth as well as a number of acquisitions made in the past year. Unisource revenues were $1.55 billion for the first quarter, up 8.5%, reflecting price and volume increases.

PROSPECTS: ASN continues to realize operational benefits from the $175 million restructuring program at Unisource, scheduled for completion in September 1996. Alco Office Products continues to expand its market share through an aggressive acquisition program, with a goal of acquiring $400 million in annualized revenue this year. AOP has also initiated a three-year program to build a uniform information technology system that should change its organization to a more efficient network.

BUSINESS

ALCO STANDARD CORP. is a distribution and service company with operations in paper distributing and converting, office products distribution and aviation and industrial services. The Company has three business groups. Paper Corporation of America markets and distributes paper, plastic and disposable products for office, industrial and food service use. Alco Office Products (AOP) sells, leases and rents photocopiers, facsimile machines, micrographic equipment, typewriters and other automated office equipment and provides equipment service and supplies. ASN is a major dealer of Canon, Ricoh and Sharp copiers and fax machines. In 1993, the Company dissolved a German joint venture by selling its interest in IMMOS, a Munich-based office products network.

BUSINESS LINE ANALYSIS

(09/30/94)	Rev(%)	Inc(%)
Unisource	72.0	44.9
Alco Office Products	28.0	55.1
Total	100.0	100.0

ANNUAL EARNINGS AND DIVIDENDS PER SHARE

	9/30/94	9/30/93	9/30/92	9/30/91	9/30/90	9/30/89	9/30/88
Earnings Per Share	**1.10**	**[1] d0.04**	**[1] 2.22**	**[1] 1.95**	**[1] 2.19**	**[1] 2.68**	**[1] 2.12**
Dividends Per Share	**1.01**	**0.97**	**0.93**	**0.89**	**0.85**	**0.78**	**0.70**
Dividend Payout %	**91.8**	**...**	**41.9**	**45.6**	**38.8**	**29.1**	**33.0**

[1] Before disc. oper.

ANNUAL FINANCIAL DATA

RECORD OF EARNINGS (IN MILLIONS):							
Total Revenues	7,996.1	6,444.6	4,925.1	4,758.2	4,320.4	4,145.9	3,816.9
Costs and Expenses	7,553.5	[1] 6,178.6	4,644.0	4,492.2	4,075.4	3,918.4	3,618.8
Depreciation & Amort	96.8	...	64.1	68.5	54.6	50.6	47.5
Operating Profit	345.8	266.0	217.0	197.5	190.4	177.0	150.6
Inc Fr Cont Opers Bef Taxes	156.8	24.6	172.5	144.2	145.2	148.8	131.9
Income Taxes	86.2	17.0	68.3	56.3	54.3	32.6	30.7
Net Income	70.6	[2] 7.6	[3] 104.2	[4] 87.9	[5] 90.9	[6] 116.2	[7] 100.0
Aver. Shs. Outstg. (000)	53,729	47,396	46,876	44,574	41,523	43,309	47,195

[1] Incl. Dep. [2] Before disc. op. dr$7,515,000. [3] Before disc. op. dr$8,455,000. [4] Before disc. op. cr$29,715,000. [5] Before disc. op. cr$15,268,000. [6] Before disc. op. cr$54,550,000. [7] Before disc. op. cr$10,006,000.

BALANCE SHEET (IN MILLIONS):							
Cash and Cash Equivalents	53.4	36.5	24.4	120.1	27.5	37.8	37.0
Receivables, Net	915.5	855.7	659.2	559.2	547.0	482.5	468.0
Inventories	610.0	592.0	460.2	365.9	361.2	324.0	315.9
Gross Property	653.7	596.9	545.0	460.7	521.6	463.9	421.4
Accumulated Depreciation	299.8	260.6	250.6	216.8	230.3	194.1	171.2
Long-Term Debt	340.8	590.2	472.0	291.0	237.6	165.6	170.5
Net Stockholders' Equity	1,367.1	1,045.6	860.4	821.2	690.6	601.8	668.7
Total Assets	3,502.3	3,348.9	2,444.8	2,020.6	1,738.1	1,478.7	1,399.0
Total Current Assets	1,710.5	1,576.7	1,183.5	1,078.9	957.9	865.7	838.6
Total Current Liabilities	1,056.9	1,020.2	687.5	562.9	570.1	535.7	443.2
Net Working Capital	653.5	556.6	496.0	516.0	387.8	330.0	395.4
Year End Shs Outstg (000)	54,448	46,964	45,949	44,638	40,887	40,280	48,640

STATISTICAL RECORD:							
Operating Profit Margin %	4.3	4.1	4.4	4.2	4.4	4.3	3.9
Book Value Per Share	7.71	2.72	7.69	10.19	10.08	9.39	10.75
Return on Equity %	5.2	0.7	12.1	10.7	13.2	19.3	14.9
Return on Assets %	2.0	0.2	4.3	4.3	5.2	7.9	7.1
Average Yield %	1.7	...	2.5	2.7	2.6	2.5	2.9
P/E Ratio	59.5-45.0	...	19.2-14.9	18.4-14.9	17.3-12.6	13.7-9.5	13.2-9.6
Price Range	65½-49½	54¾-35¾	42⅝-33⅛	35⅞-29	37⅞-27⅝	36⅝-25⅜	28-20¼

Statistics are as originally reported.

OFFICERS:
R.B. Mundt, Chmn.
W.F. Drake, Jr., Vice-Chmn.
J.E. Stuart, Pres. & C.E.O.
K.E. Dinkelacker, Exec. V.P. & C.F.O.

INCORPORATED: OH, Nov., 1952

PRINCIPAL OFFICE: 825 Duportail Rd., Wayne, PA 19087-5589

TELEPHONE NUMBER: (610) 296-8000
FAX: (610) 296-8419
NO. OF EMPLOYEES: 30,600
ANNUAL MEETING: In January
SHAREHOLDERS: 14,404
INSTITUTIONAL HOLDINGS:
No. of Institutions: 228
Shares Held: 23,941,688

REGISTRAR(S): National City Bank, Cleveland, OH 44114

TRANSFER AGENT(S): National City Bank, Cleveland, OH 44114

ALLEGHENY POWER SYSTEM, INC.

YIELD 7.0%
P/E RATIO 15.8

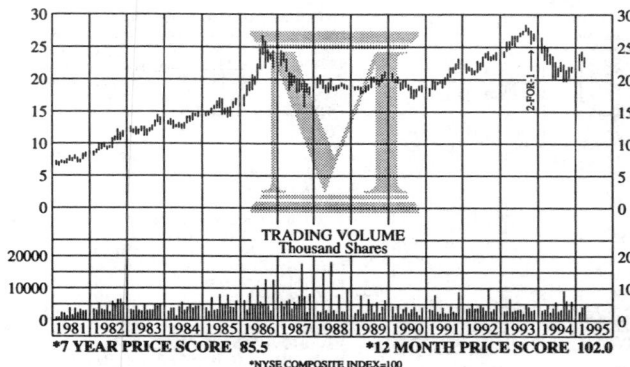

INTERIM EARNINGS (Per Share):

Qtr.	Mar.	June	Sept.	Dec.
1991	0.56	0.39	0.44	0.42
1992	0.62	0.39	0.39	0.44
1993	0.60	0.39	0.47	0.42
1994	0.67	0.37	0.44	0.38

INTERIM DIVIDENDS (Per Share):

Amt.	Decl.	Ex.	Rec.	Pay.
0.41Q	3/3/94	3/8/94	3/14/94	3/31/94
0.41Q	6/2	6/7	6/13	6/30
0.41Q	9/8	9/12	9/16	9/30
0.41Q	12/1	12/6	12/12	12/30
0.41Q	3/2/95	3/7/95	3/13/95	3/31/95

Indicated div.: $1.64*

CAPITALIZATION (12/31/94):

	($000)	(%)
Long-Term Debt	2,178,472	38.3
Deferred Income Tax	1,130,131	19.8
Preferred Stock.................	325,286	5.7
Common & Surplus	2,059,304	36.2
Total	5,693,193	100.0

DIVIDEND ACHIEVER STATUS:
Rank: 327   1984-94 Growth Rate: 2.3%
Total Years of Dividend Growth: 34

TRADING VOLUME
Thousand Shares

*7 YEAR PRICE SCORE 85.5   *12 MONTH PRICE SCORE 102.0

*NYSE COMPOSITE INDEX=100

RECENT DEVELOPMENTS: For the quarter ended 12/31/94, income before an accounting adjustment was $45.8 million compared with net income of $49.3 million in the same period of 1993. Income for the 1994 quarter includes a net charge of $5.3 million from the write-off of assets. Revenues increased slightly to $582.8 million. The increase in revenues was the result of increased sales to commercial and industrial customers, partially offset by decreased sales to nonaffiliated utilities and residential customers.

PROSPECTS: AYP has rate cases outstanding in several of its service territories, primarily to recover expenses related to compliance with the Clean Air Act. Meanwhile, regulators in Pennsylvania have granted West Penn Power about $57.3 million in additional revenues on an annual basis and a return on equity of 11.5%. AYP's efforts to consolidate its businesses and realign management are expected to provide significant cost savings and operating efficiencies.

BUSINESS

ALLEGHENY POWER SYSTEM, INC. furnishes electricity in western Pennsylvania, northern West Virginia, western Maryland and small adjoining sections of Ohio and Virginia. Monongahela Power Co., Potomac Edison Co., and West Penn Power Co., its subsidiaries, serve 1.3 million customers in an area of 29,100 square miles with a population of 2.9 million. The service areas contain heavy industry, particularly iron and steel operations and bituminous coal mining.

REVENUES

(12/31/94)	($000)	(%)
Residential	863,700	35.2
Commercial	459,300	18.7
Industrial...................	728,000	29.7
Nonaffiliated Utilities	331,600	13.5
Other........................	69,100	2.9
Total	2,451,700	100.0

ANNUAL EARNINGS AND DIVIDENDS PER SHARE

	1994	1993	1992	1991	1990	1989	1988
Earnings Per Share	1.86	1.88	1.83	1.81	1.81	1.86	1.98
Dividends Per Share	1.64	①1.63	1.605	1.585	1.58	1.55	1.51
Dividend Payout %	88.2	86.7	87.7	87.8	87.5	83.3	76.3

① Adj. for 2-for-1 stk. split, 11/19/93

ANNUAL FINANCIAL DATA

RECORD OF EARNINGS (IN MILLIONS):

Total Revenues	2,451.7	2,331.5	2,306.7	2,282.2	2,301.9	2,260.7	2,170.5
Depreciation	223.9	210.4	197.8	189.7	180.9	172.3	165.7
Maintenance	241.9	231.2	210.9	204.2	182.0	185.5	166.6
Operating Income	388.1	374.6	356.1	349.5	341.5	337.3	350.6
Interest Expense	156.4	154.3	145.8	142.3	138.2	134.3	134.9
Net Income	①219.8	215.8	203.5	194.0	191.4	194.9	205.1
Aver. Shs. Outstg. (000)	118,272	114,937	111,226	107,548	106,102	104,786	103,460

① Before acctg. change cr$43,446,000.

BALANCE SHEET (IN MILLIONS):

Gross Plant	7,586.8	7,176.8	6,679.9	6,255.7	5,986.2	5,721.5	5,493.0
Accumulated Depreciation	2,529.4	2,388.8	2,240.0	2,093.7	1,946.1	1,807.1	1,680.2
Prop., Plant & Equip, Net	5,057.4	4,788.1	4,439.9	4,162.0	4,040.1	3,914.4	3,812.9
Long-term Debt	2,178.5	2,038.0	1,951.6	1,747.6	1,642.2	1,578.4	1,586.1
Net Stockholders' Equity	2,384.6	2,232.3	2,105.9	1,950.0	1,897.9	1,848.2	1,790.7
Total Assets	6,362.2	5,949.2	5,039.3	4,855.0	4,561.3	4,433.3	4,334.4
Year End Shs Outstg (000)	119,293	117,664	113,898	108,452	106,984	105,578	104,268

STATISTICAL RECORD:

Book Value Per Share	17.14	16.49	15.92	15.40	15.12	14.85	14.48
Op. Inc/Net Pl %	7.7	7.8	8.0	8.4	8.5	8.6	9.2
Dep/Gr. Pl %	3.0	2.9	3.0	3.0	3.0	3.0	3.0
Accum. Dep/Gr. Pl %	33.3	33.3	33.5	33.5	32.5	31.6	30.6
Return on Equity %	9.3	9.8	9.8	10.1	10.2	10.7	11.7
Average Yield %	7.1	6.3	7.1	7.8	8.3	7.9	7.8
P/E Ratio	14.2-10.6	15.2-12.5	13.3-11.3	12.9-9.7	11.7-9.4	11.4-9.6	10.5-9.1
Price Range	26½-19¾	28½-23½	24⅜-20¾	23¼-17½	21⅛-17	21¼-17⅞	20¾-18

Statistics are as originally reported.

NYS SYMBOL AT
Rec. Pr. 24⅞

ALLTEL CORP.

YIELD 3.9%
P/E RATIO 17.0

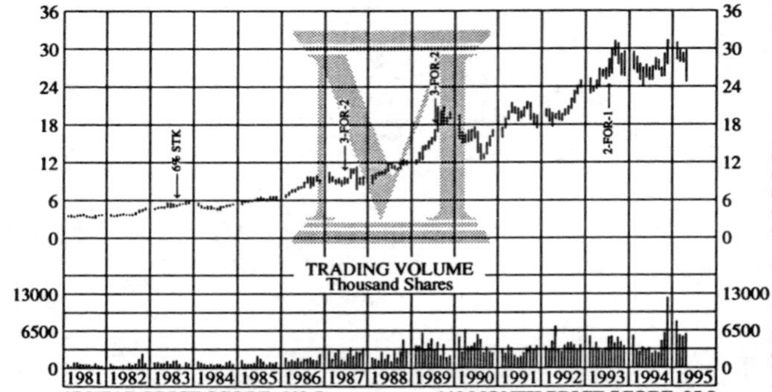
36
30
24
18
12
6
0
6% STK
3-FOR-2
3-FOR-2
2-FOR-1
TRADING VOLUME
Thousand Shares
13000
6500
0
1981 1982 1983 1984 1985 1986 1987 1988 1989 1990 1991 1992 1993 1994 1995

*7 YEAR PRICE SCORE 112.5 *12 MONTH PRICE SCORE 95.8

*NYSE COMPOSITE INDEX=100

INTERIM EARNINGS (Per Share):

Qtr.	Mar.	June	Sept.	Dec.
1992	0.27	0.32	0.32	0.34
1993	0.34	0.34	0.35	0.36
1994	0.38	0.40	0.42	0.23
1995	0.41	...	...	...

INTERIM DIVIDENDS (Per Share):

Amt.	Decl.	Ex.	Rec.	Pay.
0.22Q	4/21/94	5/27/94	6/3/94	7/5/94
0.22Q	7/21	8/29	9/2	10/3
0.24Q	10/24	11/30	12/6	1/3/95
0.24Q	1/26/95	2/17/95	2/24/95	4/3
0.24Q	4/20	6/8	6/12	7/3

*Indicated div.: $0.96**

CAPITALIZATION (12/31/94):

	($000)	(%)
Long-Term Debt	1,846,150	47.4
Deferred Income Tax	416,546	10.7
Preferred Stock	17,149	0.4
Common & Surplus	1,616,049	41.5
Total	3,895,894	100.0

DIVIDEND ACHIEVER STATUS:
Rank: 209 1984-94 Growth Rate: 8.2%
Total Years of Dividend Growth: 34

RECENT DEVELOPMENTS: For the year ended 12/31/94, net income increased 16% to $304.0 million from $262.0 million in 1993. Revenues advanced 26% to $2.96 billion. The results exclude an after-tax write-down of $32 million on certain assets of the information services subsidiary. The improved results were attributed to strong performances in ALLTEL's telephone, information services, product distribution and cellular businesses. Fourth quarter 1994 revenues rose 18% to $772.4 million.

PROSPECTS: The outlook for continued growth is positive. Cellular operations are making increasingly important contributions to ATE's financial performance. ALLTEL Mobile communications and BellSouth Mobility have signed an agreement that would create a partnership comprising cellular properties owned by the two companies in five markets. The partnership, pending receipt of necessary regulatory approvals and other conditions, will extend ATE's reach into a number of strong Sun Belt markets.

BUSINESS

ALLTEL CORPORATION provides telephone service to nearly 1.2 million customers in twenty-five states and has subsidiaries or investments in companies that provide cellular telephone service, information services, communications products and other related services. The Company's cellular operations serve 6.8 million "pops" (one gauge of potential customers) in twenty-one states. ALLTEL distributes equipment nationwide through two subsidiaries: ALLTEL Supply Inc., a supplier of telecommunications equipment, and HWC Distributing Corp., one of the nation's largest master distributors of special wire and cable products. Systematics, Inc., is a provider of data processing management, applications software and consulting services for banks and other financial institutions.

ANNUAL EARNINGS AND DIVIDENDS PER SHARE

	1994	1993	1992	1991	1990	1989	1988
Earnings Per Share	**1.43**	**1.39**	**1.22**	**1.17**	**1.17**	**1.16**	**0.97**
Dividends Per Share	**0.88**	**[1] 0.80**	**0.74**	**0.70**	**0.64**	**[2] 0.575**	**0.506**
Dividend Payout %	**61.5**	**57.6**	**60.7**	**59.8**	**54.5**	**49.6**	**52.2**

[1] 2-for-1 stk. split, 7/12/93 [2] 3-for-2 stk. split, 7/14/89

ANNUAL FINANCIAL DATA

	1994	1993	1992	1991	1990	1989	1988
RECORD OF EARNINGS (IN MILLIONS):							
Total Revenues	2,961.7	2,342.1	2,092.1	1,747.8	1,573.8	1,225.6	1,068.5
Costs and Expenses	1,965.9	1,550.6	[1] 1,404.8	[1] 1,181.9	[1] 1,031.2	[1] 772.7	[1] 663.9
Depreciation & Amort	362.0	272.4	...	...	...	...	...
Operating Income	633.9	519.0	442.7	348.9	350.5	287.7	250.0
Income Bef Income Taxes	436.5	449.9	357.3	282.3	283.7	220.2	191.8
Income Taxes	164.8	187.9	128.7	93.3	90.9	66.3	66.8
Net Income	271.8	262.0	228.6	189.0	192.8	153.9	125.0
Aver. Shs. Outstg. (000)	190,037	187,665	185,672	160,096	162,446	130,816	126,082
[1] Incl. Dep.							
BALANCE SHEET (IN MILLIONS):							
Cash and Cash Equivalents	26.1	7.9	30.4	50.4	42.4	29.1	36.1
Receivables, Net	533.2	379.7	257.3	219.1	222.0	189.3	171.1
Inventories	94.5	22.3	20.5	19.0	19.0	21.3	23.5
Gross Property	4,696.8	4,234.8	3,297.4	2,913.5	2,759.4	2,485.7	2,394.8
Accumulated Depreciation	1,733.6	1,558.4	1,235.4	1,088.1	1,004.6	871.2	842.3
Long-Term Debt	1,846.2	1,596.0	1,018.2	992.3	905.2	799.0	675.1
Net Stockholders' Equity	1,633.2	1,563.3	1,314.0	1,093.0	1,028.8	920.2	817.3
Total Assets	4,689.5	4,201.8	3,068.3	2,724.2	2,554.2	2,310.7	2,118.2
Total Current Assets	668.4	425.5	320.8	298.5	293.3	249.2	238.6
Total Current Liabilities	605.6	608.6	451.5	360.5	343.3	321.6	314.3
Net Working Capital	62.8	d183.1	d130.7	d62.0	d50.0	d72.4	d75.7
Year End Shs Outstg (000)	187,981	187,458	184,678	158,438	158,438	132,542	126,934
STATISTICAL RECORD:							
Book Value Per Share	8.56	5.53	4.86	4.58	4.60	4.85	5.14
Return on Equity %	16.7	16.9	17.5	17.5	19.0	17.2	15.8
Average Yield %	3.2	3.0	3.5	3.7	4.0	3.5	4.8
P/E Ratio	21.9-16.8	22.5-16.5	20.5-14.4	18.5-13.6	16.8-10.6	18.1-10.0	13.0-8.9
Price Range	31⅜-24	31¼-22⅞	25-17⅝	21⅝-15⅞	19⅝-12⅜	21-11⅝	12⅝-8⅝

Statistics are as originally reported.

OFFICERS:
J.T. Ford, Chmn. & C.E.O.
F.X. Frantz, Sr. V.P., Gen. Couns. & Sec.
J.M. Green, Treas.

INCORPORATED: OH, Jun., 1960; reincorp., DE, 1990

PRINCIPAL OFFICE:

TELEPHONE NUMBER:

NO. OF EMPLOYEES: 16,363

ANNUAL MEETING: In April

SHAREHOLDERS: 93,000 approx.

INSTITUTIONAL HOLDINGS:
No. of Institutions: 282
Shares Held: 71,035,064

REGISTRAR(S): Society National Bank, Cleveland, OH

TRANSFER AGENT(S): Society National Bank, Cleveland, OH

AMERICAN BRANDS INC.

INTERIM EARNINGS (Per Share):

Qtr.	Mar.	June	Sept.	Dec.
1991	1.06	0.90	0.91	1.04
1992	1.18	0.98	0.98	1.15
1993	1.22	0.75	0.42	0.91
1994	0.74	0.81	0.75	2.34

INTERIM DIVIDENDS (Per Share):

Amt.	Decl.	Ex.	Rec.	Pay.
0.50Q	10/25/94	10/28/94	11/3/94	12/1/94
0.50Q	10/25	10/28	11/3	12/1
0.50Q	10/25	10/28	11/3	12/1
0.50Q	1/31/95	2/2/95	2/8/95	3/1/95
0.50Q	4/25	5/2	5/8	6/1

Indicated div.: $2.00*

CAPITALIZATION (12/31/94):

	($000)	(%)
Long-Term Debt	1,512,100	24.1
Deferred Income Tax	133,000	2.1
Preferred Stock	15,700	0.2
Common & Surplus	4,621,800	73.6
Total	6,282,600	100.0

DIVIDEND ACHIEVER STATUS:

Rank: 216   1984-94 Growth Rate: 7.9%
Total Years of Dividend Growth: 27

RECENT DEVELOPMENTS: For the year ended 12/31/94, income from continuing operations rose to $885.1 million from $541.2 million in 1993. Total revenue increased by 4% to $13.15 billion from $12.63 billion in the year before. On 12/22/94, the Company completed the sale of American Tobacco Co. for approximately $1.00 billion. The $578.0 million pre-tax gain on the sale of was partially offset by a $245.0 million pre-tax charge for the anticipated disposition of other nonstrategic businesses.

PROSPECTS: The disposition of American Tobacco and the planned sale of the Franklin Life Insurance business affirm the Company's focus upon other consumer-related markets including hardware and home improvement, office products and golf and leisure. The sale of American Tobacco does not meet the accounting definition of a discontinued operation; therefore, future revenue and earnings will be considerably lower on a comparative basis to 1994.

BUSINESS

AMERICAN BRANDS, INC. is a global consumer products holding company. Tobacco includes Gallaher Ltd., the leading cigarette producer in the U.K. Distilled spirits include Jim Beam Brands Co. and the U.K.-based Whyte & Mackay Distillers Ltd. Life insurance is marketed through the Franklin group of companies. ACCO World Corp. manufactures and markets office supplies. Hardware and Home Improvement operates through MasterBrand Industries. Specialty Businesses include golf and leisure equipment and optical goods.

BUSINESS LINE ANALYSIS

(12/31/94)	Rev(%)	Inc(%)
Tobacco Products	53.4	48.6
Distilled Spirits	11.0	20.8
Hardware & Home Improvement Products	11.0	16.6
Golf & Leisure Products	4.4	6.9
Office Products	9.1	7.0
Other Businesses	11.1	.1
Total	100.0	100.0

ANNUAL EARNINGS AND DIVIDENDS PER SHARE

	1994	1993	1992	1991	1990	1989	1988
Earnings Per Share	4.38	3.30	4.29	3.91	① 2.99	3.26	③ 2.72
Dividends Per Share	1.992	1.97	1.805	1.593	② 1.405	1.255	1.13
Dividend Payout %	45.5	59.7	42.1	40.7	47.0	38.6	41.5

① Per primary shrare ② 2-for-1 stk. split, 10/25/90 ③ Before disc. oper.

ANNUAL FINANCIAL DATA

RECORD OF EARNINGS (IN MILLIONS):

	1994	1993	1992	1991	1990	1989	1988
Total Revenues	26,293.0	13,701.4	27,316.2	14,063.8	13,780.9	11,921.4	11,980.0
Costs and Expenses	③ 11,737.8	12,199.9	11,986.8	12,349.6	11,923.2	10,317.6	10,454.2
Depreciation & Amort	...	308.9	304.1	281.2	250.5	206.0	211.9
Operating Income	1,312.4	1,397.9	1,755.0	1,630.8	1,607.2	1,397.8	1,313.9
Inc From Cont Opers	1,351.2	...	...	...	596.0	630.8	540.8
Income Taxes	466.1	407.9	514.3	431.9	451.5	431.6	443.4
Net Income	734.1	② 668.2	883.8	806.1	596.0	630.8	580.0
Aver. Shs. Outstg. (000)	201,600	201,800	204,000	202,600	194,451	189,153	193,400

① Incl. Dep. ② Before acctg. change dr$198,400,000.

BALANCE SHEET (IN MILLIONS):

	1994	1993	1992	1991	1990	1989	1988
Cash and Cash Equivalents	110.1	141.6	140.2	128.5	154.0	149.3	115.7
Receivables, Net	1,067.9	1,342.7	1,354.2	1,434.6	1,493.1	1,175.6	1,217.8
Inventories	2,015.7	2,043.2	1,810.2	2,141.0	2,032.6	1,675.0	1,815.9
Gross Property	2,228.7	2,690.7	2,514.2	2,542.4	2,430.5	1,991.1	1,933.4
Accumulated Depreciation	1,016.0	1,218.6	1,107.8	1,070.0	959.0	803.0	768.0
Long-Term Debt	1,512.1	2,492.4	2,406.8	2,555.1	2,433.8	1,717.4	2,359.2
Net Stockholders' Equity	4,637.5	4,271.4	4,301.6	4,316.9	3,790.0	3,101.5	2,660.7
Total Assets	9,794.4	16,339.0	14,963.0	15,115.5	13,835.2	11,394.2	12,200.6
Total Current Assets	4,670.9	3,913.3	3,680.7	4,060.9	3,963.9	3,095.3	3,235.0
Total Current Liabilities	3,115.5	5,890.0	5,231.1	5,379.1	4,910.4	4,012.1	3,520.0
Net Working Capital	1,555.4	d1,976.7	d1,550.4	d1,318.2	d946.5	d916.8	d285.0
Year End Shs Outstg (000)	201,211	201,744	202,577	203,918	200,357	189,412	186,800

STATISTICAL RECORD:

	1994	1993	1992	1991	1990	1989	1988
Operating Profit Margin %	5.0	10.2	6.4	11.6	11.7	11.7	11.0
Book Value Per Share	5.33	2.64	5.39	3.87	2.83	5.34	2.14
Return on Equity %	19.1	15.6	20.5	19.3	16.3	21.3	23.0
Return on Assets %	9.0	4.1	5.9	5.3	4.3	5.5	4.8
Average Yield %	5.9	5.7	4.1	3.8	3.9	3.5	4.0
P/E Ratio	8.8-6.7	12.3-8.6	11.6-9.1	12.2-9.1	13.9-10.3	12.6-9.4	13.2-7.8
Price Range	38⅜-29⅜	40⅝-28½	49⅞-39	47⅝-35⅝	41⅝-30⅞	41-30⅝	35⅞-21⅛

Statistics are as originally reported.

OFFICERS:
T.C. Hays, Chmn. & C.E.O.
J.T. Ludes, Pres. & C.O.O.
D.L. Bauerlein, Jr., Sr. V.P. & C.F.O.
L.F. Fernous, Jr., V.P. & Sec.
INCORPORATED: DE, 1985
PRINCIPAL OFFICE: 1700 East Putnam Ave.
P.O. Box 811, Old Greenwich, CT 06870

TELEPHONE NUMBER: (203) 698-5000
FAX: (203) 637-2580
NO. OF EMPLOYEES: 34,820
ANNUAL MEETING: In May
SHAREHOLDERS: 59,740 common
INSTITUTIONAL HOLDINGS:
No. of Institutions: 560
Shares Held: 107,756,454

REGISTRAR(S): First Chicago Trust Co. of New York, New York, NY 10008

TRANSFER AGENT(S): First Chicago Trust Co. of New York, New York, NY 10008

AMERICAN BUSINESS PRODUCTS, INC.

YIELD 3.2%
P/E RATIO 14.3

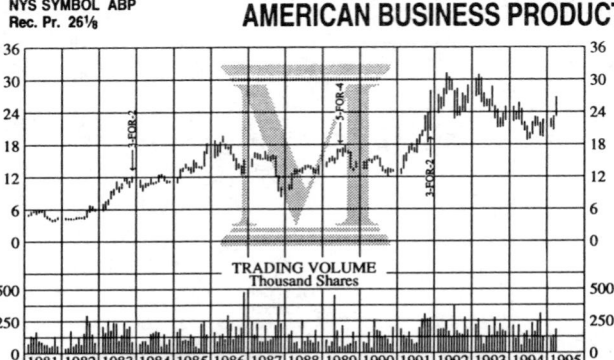

*7 YEAR PRICE SCORE 91.7   *12 MONTH PRICE SCORE 104.2
*NYSE COMPOSITE INDEX=100

INTERIM EARNINGS (Per Share):

Qtr.	Mar.	June	Sept.	Dec.
1991	0.37	0.33	0.39	0.46
1992	0.43	0.63	0.43	0.43
1993	0.44	0.34	0.34	0.45
1994	0.40	0.41	0.42	0.60

INTERIM DIVIDENDS (Per Share):

Amt.	Decl.	Ex.	Rec.	Pay.
0.20Q	2/9/94	2/23/94	3/1/94	3/15/94
0.20Q	4/28	5/25	6/1	6/15
0.20Q	7/27	8/26	9/1	9/15
0.20Q	10/26	11/25	12/1	12/15
0.21Q	2/8/95	2/23/95	3/1/95	3/15/95

Indicated div.: $0.84*

CAPITALIZATION (12/31/94):

	($000)	(%)
Long-Term Debt	75,144	35.3
Common & Surplus	137,481	64.7
Total	212,625	100.0

DIVIDEND ACHIEVER STATUS:
Rank: 157   1984-94 Growth Rate: 10.4%
Total Years of Dividend Growth: 37

RECENT DEVELOPMENTS: Income, before the cumulative effect of an accounting change, was $19.5 million for the year ended 12/31/94, or 17% higher than 1993's income of $16.7 million. Net sales rose 16% to $563.1 million from $486.1 million in 1993, marking the 56th consecutive year of higher sales. For the three months ended 12/31/94, net income was $6.4 million compared with $4.8 million in the corresponding 1993 period. Net sales increased 8% to $144.9 million from $133.5 million in the same period of 1993.

PROSPECTS: Operating results will continue to benefit from an improving economy in the U.S. The Company should be able to maintain its margins, due to streamlining efforts and efficiency gains, despite continued higher paper costs. Also, a new manufacturing facility for Discount Labels, ABP's fastest growing subsidiary, will help prepare this subsidiary for growth over the next few years. ABP expects sales of Discount Labels to double in the next three years.

BUSINESS

AMERICAN BUSINESS PRODUCTS, INC. is a leading manufacturer and distributor of labels, business forms, envelopes and supplies used to manage information more efficiently. ABP's product line consists of three segments: business supplies printing, book manufacturing, and specialty extrusion coating and laminating. Business supplies and products consist primarily of business forms, labels and specialty mailers and envelopes. Book manufacturing includes production of hard and soft covered books, catalogs, and brochures. Specialty extrusion coating and laminating applies plastic coatings to rolls of paper, film, or fabric.

BUSINESS LINE ANALYSIS

(12/31/94)	Rev(%)	Inc(%)
Business Supplies......		
Printing............	76.2	79.3
Book Manufacturing .	8.8	13.9
Extrusion Coating &..		
Laminating	15.0	21.6
Corporate...................	0.0	(14.8)
Total	100.0	100.0

ANNUAL EARNINGS AND DIVIDENDS PER SHARE

	1994	1993	1992	1991	1990	1989	1988
Earnings Per Share	1.83	1.56	1.83	1.55	1.33	1.27	1.21
Dividends Per Share	0.80	0.75	① 0.70	0.627	0.587	⑤ 0.523	0.469
Dividend Payout %	43.7	48.1	38.3	40.3	44.0	41.3	38.7

① Bef acctg chge ② 3-for-2 stk. split, 12/17/91 ⑤ 5-for-4 stk. split, 6/89

ANNUAL FINANCIAL DATA

RECORD OF EARNINGS (IN THOUSANDS):

	1994	1993	1992	1991	1990	1989	1988
Total Revenues	563,133	486,139	463,470	446,533	398,794	387,140	358,242
Costs and Expenses	505,014	439,348	419,760	403,060	363,366	354,068	327,537
Depreciation & Amort	17,391	14,661	11,809	10,953	9,650	8,806	7,632
Operating Profit	40,728	32,130	31,901	32,520	25,778	24,266	23,073
Income Bef Income Taxes	33,007	26,643	30,487	26,736	22,465	22,101	21,510
Income Taxes	13,479	9,960	10,905	10,248	8,197	8,484	8,500
Net Income	① 19,528	16,683	② 19,582	16,488	14,268	13,617	13,010
Aver. Shs. Outstg.	10,684	10,683	10,691	10,671	10,718	10,728	10,712

① Before acctg. change dr$605,000. ② Before acctg. change dr$12,449,000.

BALANCE SHEET (IN THOUSANDS):

	1994	1993	1992	1991	1990	1989	1988
Cash and Cash Equivalents	25,997	30,151	30,025	25,256	20,092	13,522	7,421
Receivables, Net	72,536	65,000	53,671	52,871	51,789	49,546	49,158
Inventories	51,929	45,687	37,272	37,384	35,147	31,713	34,205
Gross Property	185,639	176,220	149,466	135,922	130,058	115,739	105,758
Accumulated Depreciation	93,199	81,772	71,540	62,572	58,018	52,972	47,561
Long-Term Debt	75,144	85,580	40,005	41,673	43,339	11,277	8,858
Net Stockholders' Equity	137,481	127,093	118,819	119,783	109,875	103,264	95,145
Total Assets	312,101	302,192	237,238	218,086	207,003	164,140	152,257
Total Current Assets	152,712	141,768	121,938	115,735	107,418	95,088	90,987
Total Current Liabilities	63,419	55,330	44,509	42,809	39,825	36,451	35,983
Net Working Capital	89,293	86,438	77,429	72,926	67,593	58,637	55,004
Year End Shares Outstg	10,663	10,682	10,686	10,683	10,656	10,740	10,715

STATISTICAL RECORD:

	1994	1993	1992	1991	1990	1989	1988
Operating Profit Margin %	7.2	6.6	6.9	7.3	6.5	6.3	6.4
Book Value Per Share	9.71	8.63	9.50	9.49	8.49	9.37	8.82
Return on Equity %	14.2	13.1	16.5	13.8	13.0	13.2	13.7
Return on Assets %	6.3	5.5	8.3	7.6	6.9	8.3	8.5
Average Yield %	3.6	2.9	2.6	3.1	4.2	3.4	3.9
P/E Ratio	14.1-10.2	19.9-13.5	17.1-12.4	18.1-8.1	11.9-9.1	14.2-10.2	11.8-8.0
Price Range	25¾-18¾	31-21⅛	31¼-22¾	28-12½	15⅞-12⅛		18-13	14¼-9⅝

Statistics are as originally reported.

OFFICERS:
T.R. Carmody, Chmn. & C.E.O.
R.W. Gundeck, Pres. & C.O.O.
W.C. Downer, V.P.-Fin.
D.M. Gray, Sec.

INCORPORATED: GA, Apr., 1986

PRINCIPAL OFFICE: 2100 RiverEdge Pkwy. Suite 1200, Atlanta, GA 30328

TELEPHONE NUMBER: (404) 953-8300
FAX: (404) 952-2343
NO. OF EMPLOYEES: 4,152
ANNUAL MEETING: In April
SHAREHOLDERS: 3,240
INSTITUTIONAL HOLDINGS:
No. of Institutions: 69
Shares Held: 2,968,138

REGISTRAR(S): Wachovia Bank of NC, N.A., Winston-Salem, NC

TRANSFER AGENT(S): Wachovia Bank of NC, N.A., Winston-Salem, NC

AMERICAN FILTRONA CORP.

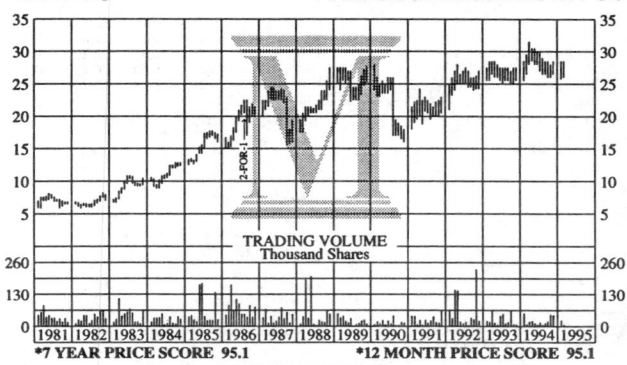

INTERIM EARNINGS (Per Share):

Qtr.	Mar.	June	Sept.	Dec.
1991	0.43	0.58	0.46	0.49
1992	0.30	0.39	0.41	d0.77
1993	0.38	0.43	0.55	0.60
1994	0.46	0.43	0.49	0.70

INTERIM DIVIDENDS (Per Share):

Amt.	Decl.	Ex.	Rec.	Pay.
0.24Q	1/26/94	2/4/94	2/10/94	2/25/94
0.24Q	4/26	5/4	5/10	5/25
0.25Q	7/27	8/4	8/10	8/25
0.25Q	10/25	11/4	11/10	11/25
0.25Q	1/25/95	2/6/95	2/10/95	2/24/95

Indicated div.: $1.00*

CAPITALIZATION (12/31/94):

	($000)	(%)
Long-Term Debt	1,300	1.6
Deferred Income Tax	151	0.2
Common & Surplus	78,365	98.2
Total	79,816	100.0

DIVIDEND ACHIEVER STATUS:
Rank: 284   1984-94 Growth Rate: 4.7%
Total Years of Dividend Growth: 24

TRADING VOLUME
Thousand Shares

1981 1982 1983 1984 1985 1986 1987 1988 1989 1990 1991 1992 1993 1994 1995

*7 YEAR PRICE SCORE 95.1   ***12 MONTH PRICE SCORE 95.1**

*NYSE COMPOSITE INDEX=100

RECENT DEVELOPMENTS: For the twelve months ended 12/31/94, income from continuing operations increased 16.4% to $7.8 million from $6.7 million in 1993. Income from continuing operations in 1994 excluded a $3.8 million gain on the sale of discontinued operations. Total revenues were up 14.2% to $150.2 million, compared with $131.5 million the previous year. Net sales grew 13.9% to $149.2 million from $130.9 million. Investment income was $1.0 million, up 70% from $611,000 the prior year. Sales of bonded fiber products jumped 10% to $56 million reflecting higher sales in writing instrument components, medical diagnostic test kit components, and tobacco filters. Plastic product sales increased 17% to $93 million due to continued strength in AFIL's plastic extrusion operations, modest gains in packaging materials, and the addition of the Tri-Lite Plastic companies in mid-1994.

BUSINESS

AMERICAN FILTRONA CORPO-RATION develops and manufactures various fiber products in the United States and Canada and industrial filtration products in the United States and Ireland. The Company's principal products are: fiber filters for cigarettes and cigars, fiber ink reservoirs, tips and wicks for writing instruments; a variety of plastic products, converted from plastic resins and films and used in food packaging, lighting fixtures, signs and displays and many other applications; and filters and filtration systems primarily for protecting industrial equipment from contaminents.

BUSINESS LINE ANALYSIS

(12/31/94)	Rev(%)	Inc(%)
Bonded Fibers	37.5	41.1
Plastic Products	62.5	58.9
Total	100.0	100.0

ANNUAL EARNINGS AND DIVIDENDS PER SHARE

	1994	1993	1992	1991	1990	1989	1988
Earnings Per Share	2.08	1.96	0.33	1.96	1.87	2.08	1.68
Dividends Per Share	0.98	0.95	0.94	0.92	0.88	0.83	0.78
Dividend Payout %	47.1	48.5	N.M.	46.9	47.1	39.9	46.4

ANNUAL FINANCIAL DATA

RECORD OF EARNINGS (IN THOUSANDS):

	1994	1993	1992	1991	1990	1989	1988
Total Revenues	150,191	131,532	145,423	145,861	145,414	148,236	135,859
Costs and Expenses	133,279	117,141	131,912	130,423	129,985	131,924	122,821
Depreciation & Amort	4,681	3,910	4,549	4,032	4,306	3,715	3,310
Operating Profit	29,990	26,112	32,388	33,685	32,792	32,639	29,329
Income Bef Income Taxes	12,231	10,480	2,462	11,406	11,124	12,597	9,727
Income Taxes	4,425	3,775	1,250	4,100	4,175	4,900	3,600
Net Income	⚊7,806	⚋6,705	1,212	7,306	6,949	7,697	6,127
Aver. Shs. Outstg.	3,749	3,728	3,716	3,719	3,716	3,716	3,658

⚊ Before disc. op. cr$3,954,859. ⚋ Before disc. op. cr$611,288.

BALANCE SHEET (IN THOUSANDS):

	1994	1993	1992	1991	1990	1989	1988
Cash and Cash Equivalents	30,522	24,276	18,211	18,977	14,083	7,677	14,655
Receivables, Net	17,350	14,139	14,406	14,751	15,301	17,165	13,430
Inventories	17,107	11,475	15,366	13,614	15,310	15,084	15,664
Gross Property	58,167	47,208	54,095	51,193	48,577	46,414	46,377
Accumulated Depreciation	32,171	28,688	30,676	27,755	25,567	22,122	26,367
Long-Term Debt	1,300	...	...	...	...	500	1,000
Net Stockholders' Equity	78,365	70,966	67,421	70,354	66,397	62,511	57,130
Total Assets	100,494	87,094	83,068	86,070	82,869	80,198	73,994
Total Current Assets	66,327	61,402	49,730	49,360	46,056	41,482	45,233
Total Current Liabilities	19,311	13,182	11,351	12,700	13,647	14,206	13,237
Net Working Capital	47,016	48,220	38,379	36,660	32,410	27,276	31,996
Year End Shares Outstg	3,736	3,739	3,718	3,707	3,714	3,709	3,671

STATISTICAL RECORD:

	1994	1993	1992	1991	1990	1989	1988
Operating Profit Margin %	8.1	8.0	6.2	7.8	7.6	8.5	7.2
Book Value Per Share	19.52	17.82	16.35	16.59	15.42	14.26	13.48
Return on Equity %	10.0	9.4	1.8	10.4	10.5	12.3	10.7
Return on Assets %	7.8	7.7	1.5	8.5	8.4	9.6	8.3
Average Yield %	3.4	3.6	3.8	4.4	4.0	3.3	3.5
P/E Ratio	15.1-12.3	15.8-13.9	84.8-63.6	12.4-9.2	15.0-8.6	13.3-10.7	16.4-10.4
Price Range	31½-25½	28½-25	28-21	24¼-18	28-16	27¾-22¼	27½-17½

Statistics are as originally reported.

OFFICERS:
J.L. Morgan, Chmn. & C.E.O.
L.C. Drozeski, Jr., Pres. & C.O.O.
J.D. Barlow, Jr., V.P.-Fin. & Treas.
A.B. Gibbs, Sec.

INCORPORATED: NY, 1954; reincorp., VA, 1971

PRINCIPAL OFFICE: 3951 Westerre Parkway Suite 300, Richmond, VA 23233

TELEPHONE NUMBER: (804) 346-2400

FAX: (804) 346-0164

NO. OF EMPLOYEES: 1,100 (approx.)

ANNUAL MEETING: In April

SHAREHOLDERS: 1,200 (approx.)

INSTITUTIONAL HOLDINGS:
No. of Institutions: 28
Shares Held: 899,700

REGISTRAR(S): Wachovia Bank of North Carolina, N.A., P.O. Box 3001, Winston-Salem, NC 27102

TRANSFER AGENT(S): Wachovia Bank of North Carolina, N.A., P.O. Box 3001, Winston-Salem, NC 27102

AMERICAN GENERAL CORP.

YIELD 3.9%
P/E RATIO 13.0

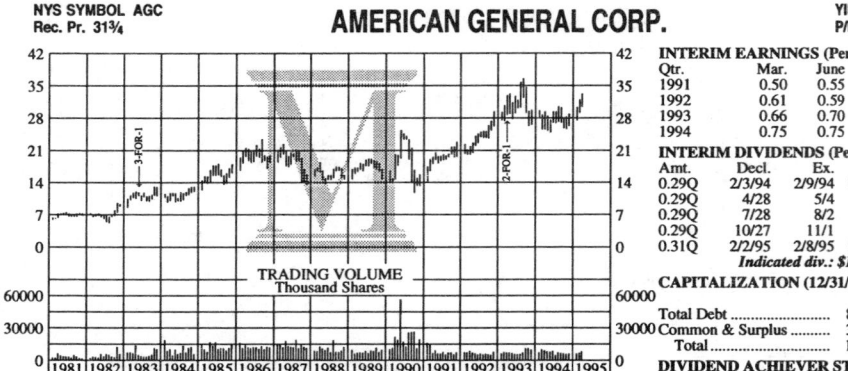

7 YEAR PRICE SCORE 105.5   **12 MONTH PRICE SCORE 106.2**
*NYSE COMPOSITE INDEX=100

TRADING VOLUME
Thousand Shares

INTERIM EARNINGS (Per Share):

Qtr.	Mar.	June	Sept.	Dec.
1991	0.50	0.55	0.53	0.55
1992	0.61	0.59	0.63	0.62
1993	0.66	0.70	0.55	d0.76
1994	0.75	0.75	0.77	0.18

INTERIM DIVIDENDS (Per Share):

Amt.	Decl.	Ex.	Rec.	Pay.
0.29Q	2/3/94	2/9/94	2/15/94	3/1/94
0.29Q	4/28	5/4	5/10	6/1
0.29Q	7/28	8/2	8/8	9/1
0.29Q	10/27	11/1	11/7	12/1
0.31Q	2/2/95	2/8/95	2/14/95	3/1/95

Indicated div.: $1.24*

CAPITALIZATION (12/31/94):

	($000)	(%)
Total Debt	8,926,000	72.1
Common & Surplus	3,457,000	27.9
Total	12,383,000	100.0

DIVIDEND ACHIEVER STATUS:
Rank: 170   1984-94 Growth Rate: 9.9%
Total Years of Dividend Growth: 11

RECENT DEVELOPMENTS: For the quarter ended 3/31/95, net income jumped 8.7% to $175.0 million from $161.0 million in the prior-year quarter. Revenues and deposits totaled $2.52 billion, up 21.3% from $2.08 billion in the corresponding 1994 quarter. First quarter 1995 results included operations of The Franklin Life Insurance Western National Corp. The retirement annuities segment reported a modest increase in earnings to $54.0 million from $53.0 million the year before.

PROSPECTS: In the consumer finance segment, private label credit cards and other retailer development efforts have encouraged new growth potential. The life insurance segment earnings have increased substantially due to AGC's recent acquisition of The Franklin Life Insurance Company. AGC is benefiting from a favorable response to VALIC's new Portfolio Director variable annuity product and Portfolio Optimizer asset allocation service.

BUSINESS

AMERICAN GENERAL CORP., with assets of $55.7 billion at 3/31/95, is one of the nation's largest consumer financial service organizations. It is a leading provider of retirement annuities, consumer loans, and life insurance. Variable Annuity Life Insurance Co., AGC's retirement annuity company, which contributed 22% of 1994 revenues, is a leading provider of retirement plans for teachers and other employees of not-for-profit organizations. The consumer finance companies, 40%, offer a wide range of credit-related products and services. The life insurance segment, 38%, emphasizes the sale and service of both traditional and interest-sensitive life insurance and annuities.

REVENUES

(12/31/94)	($000)	(%)
Prems & oth		
Consideration	1,210,000	24.2
Net Investment		
Income	2,493,000	49.7
Finance Charges	1,248,000	24.9
Other	62,000	1.2
Total	5,013,000	100.0

ANNUAL EARNINGS AND DIVIDENDS PER SHARE

	1994	1993	1992	1991	1990	1989	1988
Earnings Per Share	2.45	1.15	2.45	2.13	2.35	② 1.67	② 1.61
Dividends Per Share	1.16	1.238	① 1.04	1.00	1.398	0.75	0.70
Dividend Payout %	47.3	N.M.	42.5	47.1	59.6	44.9	43.5

① 2-for-1 stk split,03/01/93 ② Before disc. oper.

ANNUAL FINANCIAL DATA

RECORD OF EARNINGS (IN MILLIONS):

	1994	1993	1992	1991	1990	1989	1988
Insurance Premiums	1,210.0	1,252.0	1,213.0	1,168.0	1,154.0	1,160.0	1,140.0
Total Interest Income	2,493.0	2,437.0	2,327.0	2,178.0	2,095.0	1,919.0	1,727.0
Total Revenues	4,841.0	4,829.0	4,602.0	4,395.0	4,481.0	4,227.0	3,823.0
Ins Policyholder Bens	2,224.0	2,311.0	2,198.0	2,065.0	1,868.0	1,780.0	1,626.0
Inc Bef Income Tax Exp	802.0	602.0	775.0	678.0	836.0	603.0	534.0
Income Taxes	289.0	352.0	242.0	198.0	274.0	190.0	121.0
Net Income	513.0	① 250.0	533.0	480.0	562.0	② 413.0	③ 413.0
Aver. Shs. Outstg. (000)	209,403	216,579	217,455	225,362	238,584	245,730	268,126

① Before acctg. change dr$46,000,000. ② Before disc. op. cr$51,000,000. ③ Before disc. op. cr$29,000,000.

BALANCE SHEET (IN MILLIONS):

	1994	1993	1992	1991	1990	1989	1988
Cash	45.0	6.0	17.0	39.0	91.0	108.0	119.0
Fixed Maturities	25,700.0	26,479.0	21,308.0	17,913.0	15,584.0	13,810.0	12,474.0
Equity Securities	224.0	233.0	390.0	438.0	353.0	1,383.0	1,120.0
Policy Loans	1,197.0	1,156.0	1,081.0	1,039.0	1,002.0	971.0	936.0
Mtge Loans on Real Estate	2,651.0	3,032.0	3,703.0	4,247.0	4,702.0	4,341.0	3,979.0
Total Assets	46,295.0	43,982.0	39,742.0	36,105.0	33,808.0	32,062.0	30,422.0
Benefits and Claims	29,623.0	27,239.0	24,736.0	22,071.0	19,942.0	17,832.0	16,047.0
Net Stockholders' Equity	3,457.0	5,137.0	4,616.0	4,329.0	4,153.0	4,110.0	4,319.0
Year End Shs Outstg (000)	203,052	214,158	216,257	217,662	222,550	219,544	247,602

STATISTICAL RECORD:

	1994	1993	1992	1991	1990	1989	1988
Book Value Per Share	17.03	23.99	21.34	19.89	18.59	18.63	17.34
Return on Equity %	14.8	4.9	11.5	11.1	13.6	10.1	9.6
Return on Assets %	1.1	0.6	1.3	1.3	1.7	1.3	1.4
Average Yield %	4.2	3.9	4.2	5.4	7.5	4.4	4.3
P/E Ratio	12.4-10.2	31.7-22.8	12.0-8.2	10.7-6.6	10.8-5.0	11.5-8.0	11.5-8.5
Price Range	30½-24⅞	36½-26¼	29⅜-20⅛	22⅞-14	25⅜-11¾	19¼-14¾	18½-13¾

Statistics are as originally reported.

OFFICERS:
H.S. Hooks, Chmn. & C.E.O.
R.M. Devlin, Vice-Chmn.
J.R. Tuerff, Pres.
A.P. Young, Sr. V.P. & C.F.O.
J.L. Gleaves, V.P. & Treas.

INCORPORATED: TX, Jul., 1980

PRINCIPAL OFFICE: 2929 Allen Parkway, Houston, TX 77019-2155

TELEPHONE NUMBER: (713) 522-1111

NO. OF EMPLOYEES: 14,200 (approx.)

ANNUAL MEETING: In April

SHAREHOLDERS: 28,809

INSTITUTIONAL HOLDINGS:
No. of Institutions: 374
Shares Held: 75,841,412

REGISTRAR(S): First Chicago Trust Co. of New York, New York, NY 10008

TRANSFER AGENT(S): First Chicago Trust Co. of New York, New York, NY 10008

NYS SYMBOL AHL
Rec. Pr. 18⅜

AMERICAN HERITAGE LIFE INVESTMENT CORP.

YIELD 3.6%
P/E RATIO 10.7

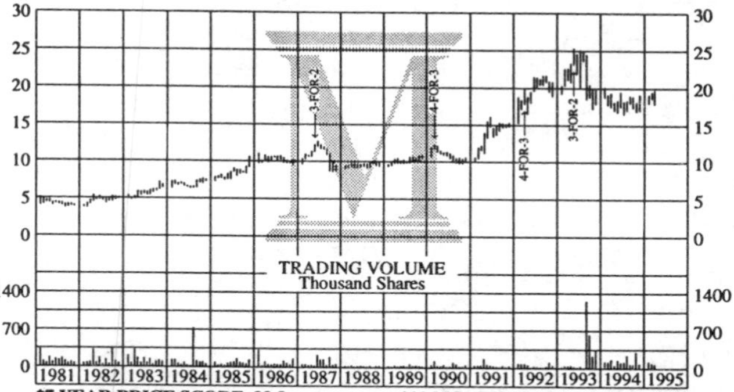

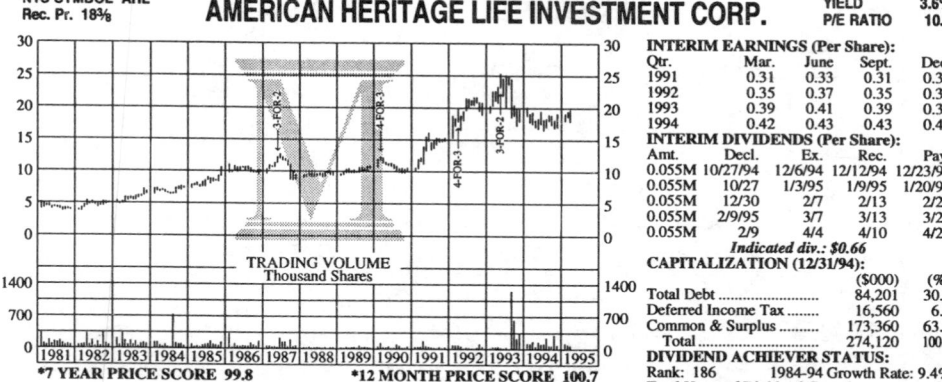

30
25
20
15
10
5
0
3-FOR-2
4-FOR-3
4-FOR-3
3-FOR-2
TRADING VOLUME
Thousand Shares
1400
700
0
1981
1982
1983
1984
1985
1986
1987
1988
1989
1990
1991
1992
1993
1994
1995

*7 YEAR PRICE SCORE 99.8 *12 MONTH PRICE SCORE 100.7

*NYSE COMPOSITE INDEX=100

INTERIM EARNINGS (Per Share):

Qtr.	Mar.	June	Sept.	Dec.
1991	0.31	0.33	0.31	0.31
1992	0.35	0.37	0.35	0.35
1993	0.39	0.41	0.39	0.39
1994	0.42	0.43	0.43	0.43

INTERIM DIVIDENDS (Per Share):

Amt.	Decl.	Ex.	Rec.	Pay.
0.055M	10/27/94	12/6/94	12/12/94	12/23/94
0.055M	10/27	1/3/95	1/9/95	1/20/95
0.055M	12/30	2/7	2/13	2/24
0.055M	2/9/95	3/7	3/13	3/24
0.055M	2/9	4/4	4/10	4/21

Indicated div.: $0.66

CAPITALIZATION (12/31/94):

	($000)	(%)
Total Debt	84,201	30.7
Deferred Income Tax	16,560	6.0
Common & Surplus	173,360	63.3
Total	274,120	100.0

DIVIDEND ACHIEVER STATUS:
Rank: 186 1984-94 Growth Rate: 9.4%
Total Years of Dividend Growth: 25

RECENT DEVELOPMENTS: For the year ended 12/31/94, net earnings rose 19.9% to $23.6 million, or $1.71 per share, compared with $19.7 million, or $1.59 per share, in 1993. Net investment income rose 4.4% to $66.7 million from $63.9 million a year earlier. Total insurance revenues, including group and credit premium equivalents, were up 8.5% to $445.5 million from $410.4 million the prior year. Earnings from operations climbed 17.9% to $22.3 million from $18.9 million. The Company reported net realized investment gains of $1.3 million compared with $770,000 in 1993. For the quarter ended 12/31/94, AHL reported a 10.9% increase in net earnings to $6.0 million from $5.4 million in the comparable 1993 period. Insurance revenues advanced 12.6% to $116.9 million from $103.8 million.

BUSINESS

AMERICAN HERITAGE LIFE INVESTMENT CORPORATION is a holding company whose principal subsidiary is American Heritage Life Insurance Company. The insurance company is licensed in 49 states, Puerto Rico, The District of Columbia and the U.S. Virgin Islands and markets ordinary life, individual accident and health and annuities, group life and group accident and health, and credit life and credit accident and health insurance, through licensed agents and brokers. In addition, First Colonial Insurance Company, a subsidiary of American Heritage Life Insurance Company, markets credit property insurance and is currently licensed in twelve states.

BUSINESS LINE ANALYSIS

(12/31/94)	Rev (%)	Inc (%)
Ordinary	49.4	57.2
Group	18.8	16.3
Credit	31.8	25.8
Real Invest Gains	0.0	0.7
Total	100.0	100.0

ANNUAL EARNINGS AND DIVIDENDS PER SHARE

	1994	1993	1992	1991	1990	1989	1988
Earnings Per Share	**1.71**	**1.59**	**1.42**	**1.27**	**1.10**	**[4] 0.97**	**0.91**
Dividends Per Share	**0.64**	**[1] 0.587**	**[2] 0.558**	**0.53**	**[3] 0.50**	**0.436**	**0.421**
Dividend Payout %	**37.4**	**36.9**	**39.3**	**41.7**	**45.5**	**44.9**	**46.5**

[1] 3-for-2 stk split, 05/21/93 [2] 33.3% stk div, 3/2/92 [3] 33% stk div, 2/26/90 [4] Before extraord. item

ANNUAL FINANCIAL DATA

	1994	1993	1992	1991	1990	1989	1988
RECORD OF EARNINGS (IN MILLIONS):							
Insurance Premiums	230.6	227.4	212.1	195.9	178.0	163.2	197.7
Total Interest Income	66.7	63.9	59.7	54.5	43.4	38.9	33.1
Total Revenues	299.3	292.4	272.0	250.5	220.8	201.6	231.0
Benefits & Claims	146.1	159.3	155.7	147.7	128.1	121.2	160.7
Earn Bef Income Taxes	34.7	28.9	24.2	22.0	18.7	16.6	...
Income Taxes	11.0	9.2	7.3	6.9	5.7	4.9	4.1
Net Income	23.6	19.7	16.9	15.1	13.1	[1] 11.6	11.0
Aver. Shs. Outstg. (000)	13,855	12,399	11,903	11,860	11,898	11,975	12,044
[1] Before extra. item cr$3,316,000.							
BALANCE SHEET (IN MILLIONS):							
Cash	19.5	19.0	18.1	15.2	13.2	8.3	6.4
Fixed Maturities	412.7	443.3	365.4	332.3	297.8	266.6	224.3
Common Stocks	52.5	54.9	87.6	54.4	33.7	36.4	30.9
Policy Loans	351.2	334.7	292.5	247.9	207.3	111.8	72.7
Mtge Loans on Real Estate	20.6	17.9	14.0	15.1	16.8	17.0	16.2
Total Assets	1,179.3	1,138.6	1,017.0	892.6	780.6	610.9	510.8
Benefits and Claims	874.0	818.9	745.6	684.9	615.4	446.5	355.0
Net Stockholders' Equity	173.4	183.9	148.0	131.1	114.1	109.3	101.8
Year End Shs Outstg (000)	13,860	13,834	7,927	11,835	11,855	11,985	11,977
STATISTICAL RECORD:							
Book Value Per Share	12.51	13.30	18.67	11.08	9.63	9.12	8.50
Return on Equity %	13.6	10.7	11.4	11.5	11.5	10.6	10.8
Return on Assets %	2.0	1.7	1.7	1.7	1.7	1.9	2.2
Average Yield %	3.5	2.8	3.0	4.1	4.5	4.3	4.4
P/E Ratio	11.8-9.6	16.0-10.8	15.2-10.7	12.7-7.9	11.1-8.9	11.3-9.7	11.1-9.9
Price Range	20⅛-16½	25⅜-17¼	21⅝-15¼	16⅛-10	12¼-9¾	11-9⅜	10⅛-9

Statistics are as originally reported.

OFFICERS:
T.O. Douglas, Chmn., Pres. & C.E.O.
C.R. Morehead, Exec. V.P., Treas. & C.F.O.
W.M. Heekin, Sr. V.P., Sec. & Gen. Couns.

INCORPORATED: FL, Sep., 1968

PRINCIPAL OFFICE: 1776 American Heritage Life Drive, Jacksonville, FL 32224

TELEPHONE NUMBER: (904) 354-1776

NO. OF EMPLOYEES: 507

ANNUAL MEETING: In April

SHAREHOLDERS: 8,900 (approx.)

INSTITUTIONAL HOLDINGS:
No. of Institutions: 35
Shares Held: 1,344,369

REGISTRAR(S): Barnett Bank Trust Co., Jacksonville, FL

TRANSFER AGENT(S): Barnett Banks Trust Co., Jacksonville, FL

AMERICAN HOME PRODUCTS CORP.

YIELD 3.9%
P/E RATIO 15.5

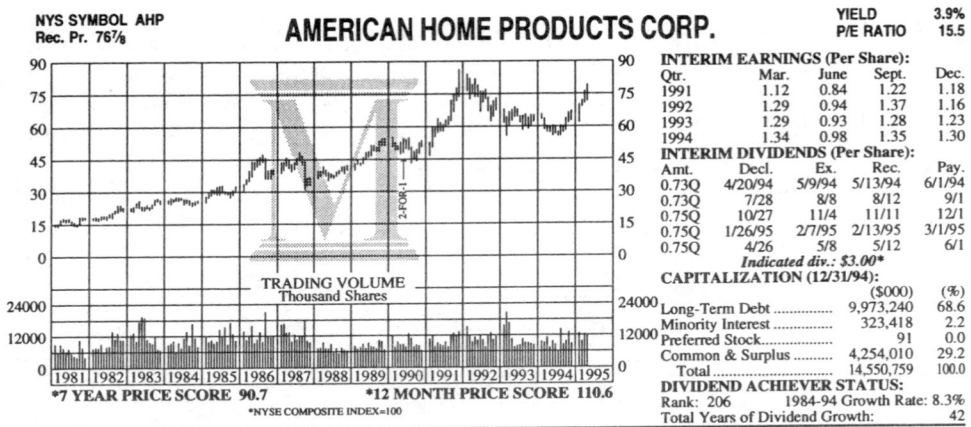

*7 YEAR PRICE SCORE 90.7   *12 MONTH PRICE SCORE 110.6
*NYSE COMPOSITE INDEX=100

INTERIM EARNINGS (Per Share):

Qtr.	Mar.	June	Sept.	Dec.
1991	1.12	0.84	1.22	1.18
1992	1.29	0.94	1.37	1.16
1993	1.29	0.93	1.28	1.23
1994	1.34	0.98	1.35	1.30

INTERIM DIVIDENDS (Per Share):

Amt.	Decl.	Ex.	Rec.	Pay.
0.73Q	4/20/94	5/9/94	5/13/94	6/1/94
0.73Q	7/28	8/8	8/12	9/1
0.75Q	10/27	11/4	11/11	12/1
0.75Q	1/26/95	2/7/95	2/13/95	3/1/95
0.75Q	4/26	5/8	5/12	6/1

Indicated div.: $3.00

CAPITALIZATION (12/31/94):

	($000)	(%)
Long-Term Debt	9,973,240	68.6
Minority Interest	323,418	2.2
Preferred Stock	91	0.0
Common & Surplus	4,254,010	29.2
Total	14,550,759	100.0

DIVIDEND ACHIEVER STATUS:
Rank: 206   1984-94 Growth Rate: 8.3%
Total Years of Dividend Growth: 42

RECENT DEVELOPMENTS: For the year ended 12/31/94, net income increased 4% to $1.53 billion compared with $1.47 billion a year ago. Sales were up 8% to $8.97 billion from $8.30 billion. The acquisition of American Cyanamid, acquired on 11/21/94 in a transaction valued at $9.7 billion, made a significant contribution to sales growth. In January, AHP entered into a definitive agreement to sell its South American oral-health business to Colgate-Palmolive.

PROSPECTS: The acquisition of American Cyanamid has substantially increased the Company's debt leverage and fixed charges. However, management is taking advantage of opportunities for market synergies and cost reduction. The merger has made AHP a stronger competitor in the domestic and international pharmaceutical markets, as well as enhancing research efforts. R&D expenditures should amount to more than $1 billion in 1995.

BUSINESS

AMERICAN HOME PRODUCTS CORPORATION is a leading manufacturer of health care products such as prescription drugs, medical devices, supplies and instrumentation, and over-the-counter medications. The Company also markets food and consumer products in the U.S. and Canada. Prescription drug subsidiaries include: Wyeth-Ayerst Labs, A.H. Robins Company, Sherwood Medical, Corometrics Medical Systems, Fort Dodge Laboratories and Whitehall Labs. Food Products include: American Home Foods producing Chef Boy-ar-dee, Gulden's Mustard, and Pam.

BUSINESS LINE ANALYSIS

(12/31/94)	Rev(%)	Inc(%)
United States	65.9	66.3
Canada & Latin America	11.4	13.3
Europe & Africa	15.9	14.8
Asia & Australia	6.8	5.6
Total	100.0	100.0

ANNUAL EARNINGS AND DIVIDENDS PER SHARE

	1994	1993	1992	1991	1990	1989	1988
Earnings Per Share	4.97	4.73	☐ 3.66	4.36	3.92	3.54	3.19
Dividends Per Share	2.94	2.86	2.66	2.375	2.15	1.95	1.80
Dividend Payout %	59.2	60.5	72.7	54.5	54.8	55.2	56.4

☐ Before acctg. chg.

ANNUAL FINANCIAL DATA

RECORD OF EARNINGS (IN MILLIONS):

Total Revenues	8,966.2	8,304.9	7,873.7	7,079.4	6,775.2	6,747.0	5,530.6
Costs and Expenses	6,482.2	6,068.1	5,757.3	5,195.2	5,079.8	5,037.9	4,040.5
Depreciation & Amort	306.2	241.1	210.2	167.2	179.8	168.2	141.7
Operating Profit	2,994.9	2,658.4	2,458.6	1,717.0	1,515.7	1,541.0	1,348.5
Inc Bef Fed & Fgn Tax on Income	2,029.8	1,992.7	1,724.1	1,759.8	1,828.3	1,414.3	1,348.5
Income Taxes	501.5	523.4	573.3	384.5	597.7	312.2	416.3
Net Income	1,528.3	1,469.3	☐1,150.7	1,375.3	1,230.6	1,102.2	932.2
Aver. Shs. Outstg. (000)	307,413	310,668	314,201	315,726	314,066	311,644	298,358

☐ Before acctg. change cr$310,104,000.

BALANCE SHEET (IN MILLIONS):

Cash and Cash Equivalents	1,944.2	2,220.3	1,982.4	2,064.6	1,788.5	1,207.8	758.7
Receivables, Net	2,380.7	1,389.6	1,250.5	1,024.2	1,021.4	1,197.6	957.2
Inventories	2,246.2	958.9	944.6	842.0	795.9	892.1	735.1
Gross Property	5,458.1	3,460.4	3,056.9	2,659.2	2,532.8	2,453.2	2,061.6
Accumulated Depreciation	1,646.1	1,400.6	1,279.1	1,182.4	1,095.4	971.5	752.3
Long-Term Debt	9,973.2	859.3	601.9	104.7	776.6	1,895.8	. . .
Net Stockholders' Equity	4,254.1	3,876.5	3,562.6	3,300.5	2,675.2	1,970.0	2,975.7
Total Assets	21,674.8	7,687.4	7,141.4	5,938.8	5,637.1	5,681.5	4,610.7
Total Current Assets	7,821.2	4,807.7	4,552.1	4,119.1	3,826.1	3,532.8	2,576.2
Total Current Liabilities	4,618.1	1,584.4	1,492.7	1,270.1	1,028.7	1,108.9	866.0
Net Working Capital	3,203.2	3,223.3	3,059.4	2,848.9	2,797.4	2,423.9	1,710.2
Year End Shs Outstg (000)	305,981	310,326	313,048	315,623	314,028	312,532	292,236

STATISTICAL RECORD:

Operating Profit Margin %	24.3	24.0	24.2	24.3	22.4	22.8	24.4
Return on Equity %	35.9	37.9	32.3	41.7	46.0	55.9	31.3
Return on Assets %	7.1	19.1	16.1	23.2	21.8	19.4	20.2
Average Yield %	4.8	4.6	3.6	3.6	4.4	4.1	4.6
P/E Ratio	13.5-11.1	14.6-11.7	23.0-17.0	19.8-10.7	14.1-11.0	15.5-11.3	13.3-11.1
Price Range	67¼-55⅜	69-55½	84¼-62¼	86¼-46½	55⅛-43	54¾-39⅞	42½-35¼

Statistics are as originally reported.

OFFICERS:
J.R. Stafford, Chmn., C.E.O. & Pres.
J.R. Considine, V.P.-Fin.
R.E. Parker, Treas.
C.G. Emerling, Sec.

INCORPORATED: DE, Feb., 1926

PRINCIPAL OFFICE: 5 Giralda Farms, Madison, NJ 07940-0874

TELEPHONE NUMBER: (201) 660-5000
FAX: (201) 660-5771
NO. OF EMPLOYEES: 74,009
ANNUAL MEETING: In April
SHAREHOLDERS: 70,371
INSTITUTIONAL HOLDINGS:
No. of Institutions: 959
Shares Held: 197,401,271

REGISTRAR(S): Chemical Bank, New York, NY

TRANSFER AGENT(S): Chemical Bank, New York, NY

NASDAQ SYMBOL ANAT
Rec. Pr. 63¾

AMERICAN NATIONAL INSURANCE CO.

YIELD 3.7%
P/E RATIO 9.7

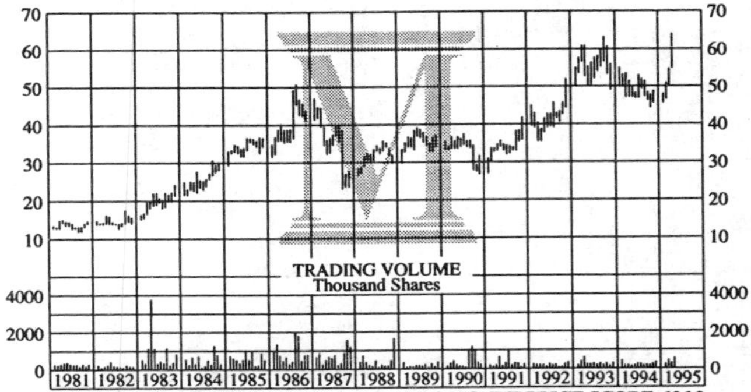

70
60
50
40
30
20
10
TRADING VOLUME
Thousand Shares
4000
2000
0
1981
1982
1983
1984
1985
1986
1987
1988
1989
1990
1991
1992
1993
1994
1995

***7 YEAR PRICE SCORE 99.6** ***12 MONTH PRICE SCORE 106.9**

*NYSE COMPOSITE INDEX=100

INTERIM EARNINGS (Per Share):

Qtr.	Mar.	June	Sept.	Dec.
1992	1.51	1.24	1.62	2.00
1993	1.95	2.06	1.20	1.80
1994	1.37	2.02	2.11	2.85
1995	1.71	...	...	...

INTERIM DIVIDENDS (Per Share):

Amt.	Decl.	Ex.	Rec.	Pay.
0.55Q	4/29/94	5/27/94	6/3/94	6/17/94
0.55Q	7/28	8/29	9/2	9/16
0.59Q	10/27	11/28	12/2	12/16
0.59Q	2/23/95	2/27/95	3/3/95	3/17/95
0.59Q	4/28	5/26	6/2	6/16

Indicated div.: $2.36

CAPITALIZATION (12/31/94):

	($000)	(%)
Total Debt	12,423	0.5
Deferred Income Tax	146,289	6.6
Common & Surplus	2,072,308	92.9
Total	2,231,020	100.0

DIVIDEND ACHIEVER STATUS:
Rank: 198 1984-94 Growth Rate: 8.8%
Total Years of Dividend Growth: 21

RECENT DEVELOPMENTS: For the year ended 12/31/94, net income was $215.1 million, up 16.0% from $185.6 million for the prior year. Revenues rose 5.0% to $1.40 billion from $1.33 billion a year earlier. The 1994 net gain from the sale of investments was $59.2 million compared with a gain of $35.8 million in 1993. Sales of life insurance for 1994 totaled $9.52 billion, a gain of 4.1% over $9.15 billion reported the year before. Operating income increased 4.2% to $155.9 million from $149.7 million in 1993. For the quarter ended 12/31/94, net income jumped 45.7% to $69.3 million from $47.6 million for the corresponding quarter in 1993. Revenues were $361.7 million compared with $325.4 million in the 1993 quarter, an increase of 11.2%. Operating income increased 13.3% to $50.5 millilon from $44.6 million in the prior-year quarter.

BUSINESS

AMERICAN NATIONAL INSURANCE COMPANY is licensed to do business in 49 states, the District of Columbia, Puerto Rico, Guam, American Samoa and Western Europe. The Company offers a broad line of insurance coverages including: life, health, disability and annuities; group life and health; personal lines property and casualty and credit insurance. The Company also offers a variety of mutual funds for sale through its licensed representatives. In addition to ANAT, the family of companies includes: Standard Life and Accident Insurance Co., American National Life Insurance Co. of Texas, American National Property and Casualty Co., Garden State Life Insurance Co. and Securities Management and Research, Inc., manager and distributor for the American National group of funds.

BUSINESS LINE ANALYSIS

(12/31/94)	Rev(%)	Inc(%)
Individual Life	43.2	71.3
Indiv Accident & Health	19.8	9.9
Annuities	2.4	0.0
Group Life & Health	13.5	6.6
Credit Insurance	3.1	1.3
Property & Casualty	18.0	10.9
Total	100.0	100.0

ANNUAL EARNINGS AND DIVIDENDS PER SHARE

	1994	1993	1992	1991	1990	1989	1988
Earnings Per Share	**8.35**	**7.00**	**[1] 6.68**	**4.76**	**3.96**	**3.59**	**3.33**
Dividends Per Share	**2.24**	**2.08**	**1.92**	**1.76**	**1.63**	**1.51**	**1.42**
Dividend Payout %	**26.8**	**29.7**	**28.7**	**37.0**	**41.2**	**42.1**	**42.6**

[1] Before acctg. chg.

ANNUAL FINANCIAL DATA

	1994	1993	1992	1991	1990	1989	1988
RECORD OF EARNINGS (IN MILLIONS):							
Insurance Premiums	876.0	863.9	843.5	779.9	697.6	646.3	581.8
Total Interest Income	333.3	312.2	313.2	312.3	303.8	291.9	279.1
Total Revenues	1,395.4	1,329.0	1,318.1	1,197.4	1,100.3	1,031.9	933.7
Ins Policyholder Bens	670.8	653.1	667.9	611.6	582.9	543.3	486.6
Gain Fr Opers Bef Fed Inc Taxes	315.9	289.1	253.6	184.9	158.9	148.6	135.5
Income Taxes	100.8	103.6	85.0	58.9	50.1	47.2	41.2
Net Income	215.1	185.5	168.6	126.0	108.7	101.4	94.2
Aver. Shs. Outstg. (000)	26,479	26,479	26,479	26,481	27,477	28,258	...
BALANCE SHEET (IN MILLIONS):							
Cash	2.9	16.7	14.3	13.4	18.6	15.5	10.9
Fixed Maturities	2,577.8	2,031.1	1,897.3	1,834.3	1,849.4	1,742.3	1,732.6
Com Stocks, At Market	623.7	673.0	602.0	733.0	534.0	615.8	468.6
Policy Loans	300.1	301.1	304.3	309.6	309.8	285.5	287.8
Mtge Loans on Real Estate	930.8	915.7	850.1	856.1	769.5	703.4	673.6
Total Assets	5,961.2	5,450.9	5,164.5	5,076.7	4,754.2	4,516.1	4,303.3
Benefits and Claims	3,519.8	3,068.9	2,911.1	2,876.0	2,794.0	2,547.2	2,486.9
Net Stockholders' Equity	2,072.3	1,961.7	1,856.7	1,777.5	1,607.0	1,617.0	1,522.8
Year End Shs Outstg (000)	26,479	26,479	26,479	26,479	26,504	28,162	28,267
STATISTICAL RECORD:							
Book Value Per Share	78.26	74.09	70.12	67.13	60.63	57.42	53.87
Return on Equity %	10.4	9.5	9.1	7.1	6.8	6.3	6.2
Return on Assets %	3.6	3.4	3.3	2.5	2.3	2.2	2.2
Average Yield %	4.5	3.7	4.4	5.1	5.1	4.4	4.6
P/E Ratio	6.8-5.4	9.0-7.0	8.2-5.6	8.8-5.7	9.5-6.8	10.9-8.3	10.7-8.0
Price Range	55-44¼	63¼-49	52-35½	41¾-27	37½-26¾	39¼-29¾	35¾-26½

Statistics are as originally reported.

OFFICERS:
R.L. Moody, Chmn. & C.E.O.
O.C. Clay, Pres.
V.E. Soler, Jr., V.P., Sec. & Treas.

INCORPORATED: TX, Mar., 1905

PRINCIPAL OFFICE: One Moody Plaza, Galveston, TX 77550

TELEPHONE NUMBER: (409) 763-4661

FAX: (409) 766-6502

NO. OF EMPLOYEES:

ANNUAL MEETING: In April

SHAREHOLDERS: N.A.

INSTITUTIONAL HOLDINGS:
No. of Institutions: 85
Shares Held: 20,915,780

REGISTRAR(S): Boatmen's Trust Co., St.Louis, MO 63101

TRANSFER AGENT(S): Boatmen's Trust Co., St. Louis, MO 63101

AMERICAN PRECISION INDUSTRIES INC.

YIELD	2.8%
P/E RATIO	17.4

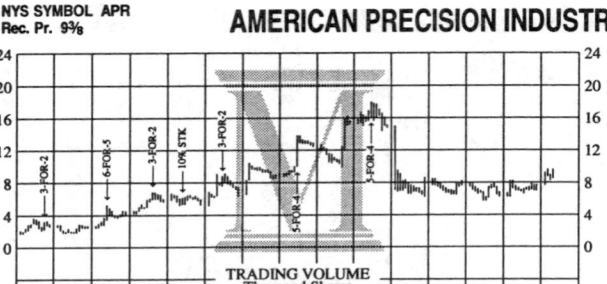

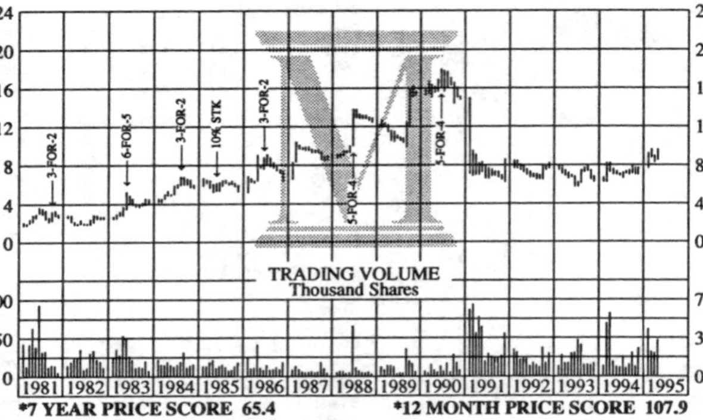

TRADING VOLUME
Thousand Shares

1981 | 1982 | 1983 | 1984 | 1985 | 1986 | 1987 | 1988 | 1989 | 1990 | 1991 | 1992 | 1993 | 1994 | 1995

*7 YEAR PRICE SCORE 65.4   *12 MONTH PRICE SCORE 107.9
*NYSE COMPOSITE INDEX=100

INTERIM EARNINGS (Per Share):

Qtr.	Mar.	July	Sept.	Dec.
1993	0.08	0.06	0.07	0.08
1994	0.10	0.12	0.13	0.14
1995	0.15	...	...	...

INTERIM DIVIDENDS (Per Share):

Amt.	Decl.	Ex.	Rec.	Pay.
0.0625Q	4/25/94	6/20/94	6/24/94	7/13/94
0.0625Q	7/26	9/19	9/23	10/12
0.0625Q	12/16	12/19	12/23	1/11/95
0.0625Q	2/27/95	3/20/95	3/24/95	4/12
0.065Q	4/28	6/21	6/23	7/12

Indicated div.: $0.26

CAPITALIZATION (12/30/94):

	($000)	(%)
Long-Term Debt	2,472	7.4
Common & Surplus	30,905	92.6
Total	33,377	100.0

DIVIDEND ACHIEVER STATUS:
Rank: 96   1984-94 Growth Rate: 13.0%
Total Years of Dividend Growth: 14

RECENT DEVELOPMENTS: For the year ended 12/30/94, net earnings increased 67.4% to $3.4 million from $2.1 million in 1993. Revenues for the twelve-month period advanced 27.1% to $65.3 million, compared with $51.3 million the previous year. Net sales were up 27.6% to $64.9 million from $50.9 million. However, investment income slid 22.5% to $369,000 from $476,000 a year earlier. A stronger emphasis on product development, sales and marketing was instrumen-

tal in the Company's improved performance. Each operating unit contributed to revenue and earnings growth. Results were also enhanced by the addition of Harowe Servo Controls, acquired in June 1994. APR expects to acquire the assets and business of Gettys Corporation by mid-1996. The Company has already assumed responsibility for the day-to-day management of Gettys.

BUSINESS

AMERICAN PRECISION INDUS-TRIES, INC. and its subsidiaries conduct operations in two major industrial classifications, namely Industrial Process Equipment, which includes the Heat Transfer Group, and Electronics Products, comprised of the Electronic Components and Motion Control Groups. The Industrial Process Equipment segment produces and sells heat transfer products for cooling oil, air, and other gases; steam condensing; vapor recovery; and many other processing requirements. The Electronics Products segment produces and sells an extensive line of quality inductors used in electronic circuits to satisfy various filtering requirements used in telecommunications, aerospace, avionics, industrial, computer, diagnostic medical equipment and military/defense applications; and electro-magnetic components used in the continous starting, stopping and cycling of equipment.

BUSINESS LINE ANALYSIS

(12/31/94)	Rev(%)	Inc(%)
Heat Transfer.............	51.0	69.0
Motion Technology ...	30.1	7.9
Electronic Components..........	18.3	23.1
General Corporate	0.6	0.0
Total	100.0	100.0

ANNUAL EARNINGS AND DIVIDENDS PER SHARE

	12/30/94	12/31/93	1/1/93	1/3/92	12/28/90	12/29/89	12/30/88
Earnings Per Share	0.49	0.29	0.34	0.50	0.46	0.62	0.49
Dividends Per Share	0.245	0.23	0.21	0.19	0.17	0.148	0.132
Dividend Payout %	50.0	79.3	61.8	38.0	37.0	23.9	26.9

ANNUAL FINANCIAL DATA

RECORD OF EARNINGS (IN THOUSANDS):

Total Revenues	65,265	51,334	51,295	51,453	48,640	52,379	49,731
Costs and Expenses	57,465	46,230	45,760	44,150	42,165	44,327	42,338
Deprec & Amortzation	2,275	1,712	1,531	1,382	1,358	1,050	1,167
Operating Profit	6,413	3,994	4,097	5,921	5,663	7,002	6,226
Earn Bef Income Taxes	5,305	3,148	3,711	5,522	4,852	6,905	5,464
Income Taxes	1,874	1,098	1,324	1,887	1,506	2,406	1,893
Net Income	3,431	2,050	2,387	3,635	3,346	4,499	3,571
Aver. Shs. Outstg.	7,062	7,057	7,104	7,251	7,344	7,304	7,281

BALANCE SHEET (IN THOUSANDS):

Cash and Cash Equivalents	3,841	6,508	5,457	5,011	3,987	4,863	3,905
Receivables, Net	10,555	7,082	7,814	6,712	7,350	8,267	7,585
Inventories	8,827	6,369	5,808	6,140	5,881	5,670	5,647
Gross Property	26,656	23,438	21,736	20,235	19,136	17,631	14,513
Accumulated Depreciation	16,454	15,085	13,536	12,246	10,960	9,889	9,544
Long-Term Debt	2,472	2,663	3,039	4,110	4,683	5,559	4,135
Net Stockholders' Equity	30,905	29,212	28,712	28,068	27,695	25,713	22,071
Total Assets	44,469	37,332	33,896	33,931	34,718	34,488	28,929
Total Current Assets	24,238	20,598	19,803	19,381	18,939	20,377	18,863
Total Current Liabilities	10,916	5,457	4,974	4,102	4,423	5,088	4,656
Net Working Capital	13,322	15,141	14,829	15,279	14,516	15,289	14,207
Year End Shares Outstg	7,064	7,058	7,055	7,117	7,362	7,317	7,306

STATISTICAL RECORD:

Operating Profit Margin %	8.5	6.6	7.8	11.5	10.5	13.4	12.5
Book Value Per Share	4.06	4.14	4.07	3.94	3.76	3.51	3.02
Return on Equity %	11.1	7.0	8.3	13.0	12.1	17.5	16.2
Return on Assets %	7.7	5.5	7.0	10.7	9.6	13.0	12.3
Average Yield %	3.4	3.3	2.8	1.8	1.1	1.1	1.2
P/E Ratio	16.8-12.8	27.6-19.8	25.0-19.1	30.0-12.5	39.1-31.3	26.2-15.9	28.1-17.9
Price Range	8¼-6¼	8-5¾	8½-6½	15-6¼	18-14⅜	16¼-9⅞	13¾-8¾

Statistics are as originally reported.

OFFICERS:
R.J. Fierle, Chmn.
K. Wiedenhaupt, Pres.
J.W. Bingel, Pres.-Electronic Components Group
J.M. Murray, V.P.-Fin. & Treas.
J.J. Tanous, Esq., Sec.
INCORPORATED: DE, Dec., 1986
PRINCIPAL OFFICE: 2777 Walden Ave., Buffalo, NY 14225

TELEPHONE NUMBER: (716) 684-9700
NO. OF EMPLOYEES: 847
ANNUAL MEETING: In April
SHAREHOLDERS: 1,074
INSTITUTIONAL HOLDINGS:
No. of Institutions: 21
Shares Held: 1,107,795

REGISTRAR(S): Society National Bank, Cleveland, OH

TRANSFER AGENT(S): Society National Bank, Cleveland, OH

AMERICAN RECREATION CENTERS, INC.

YIELD 3.3%
P/E RATIO 24.6

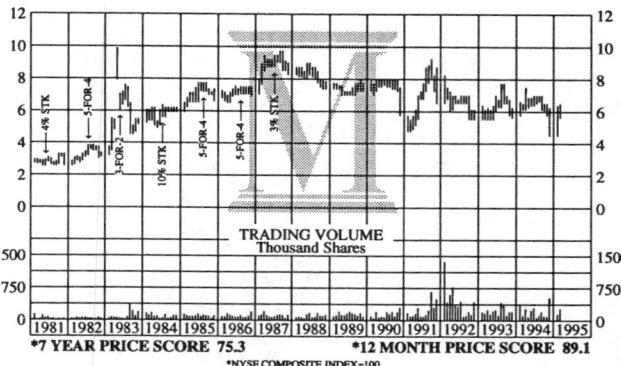

TRADING VOLUME
Thousand Shares

1981 1982 1983 1984 1985 1986 1987 1988 1989 1990 1991 1992 1993 1994 1995

*7 YEAR PRICE SCORE 75.3　　***12 MONTH PRICE SCORE 89.1**

*NYSE COMPOSITE INDEX=100

INTERIM EARNINGS (Per Share):

Qtr.	Aug.	Nov.	Feb.	May
1991-92	0.07	0.18	0.14	0.21
1992-93	0.03	0.09	0.12	0.14
1993-94	0.03	Nil	0.18	0.17
1994-95	0.11	d0.16	0.18	...

INTERIM DIVIDENDS (Per Share):

Amt.	Decl.	Ex.	Rec.	Pay.
0.055Q	1/12/94	3/14/94	3/18/94	4/8/94
0.06Q	5/17	6/13	6/17	7/11
0.06Q	7/20	9/12	9/16	10/10
0.06Q	11/9	12/12	12/16	1/10/95
0.06Q	1/12/95	3/13/95	3/17/95	4/10

Indicated div.: $0.24*

CAPITALIZATION (5/25/94):

	($000)	(%)
Long-Term Debt	29,125	40.4
Deferred Income Tax	8,122	11.3
Minority Interest	5,936	8.2
Common & Surplus	28,880	40.1
Total	72,063	100.0

DIVIDEND ACHIEVER STATUS:
Rank: 163　　1984-94 Growth Rate: 10.2%
Total Years of Dividend Growth: 27

RECENT DEVELOPMENTS: For the three months ended 2/22/95, net income remained flat with the comparable prior-year period at $893,000. Earnings for the third quarter of fiscal 1995 included an after-tax gain of $325,000, or $0.06 per share, from the sale of Luck Lanes in San Pablo, CA. Operating revenues totaled $22.1 million, an increase of 4.5% over $21.1 million in the same period last year. Operating income for AMRC's bowling operations rose 8.8% to $2.5 million on a sales increase of 15.3% to $12.7 million. Bowling results benefited from acquisition growth, as comparable bowls dropped nearly 2% for the quarter. AMRC's bowling operations are facing weak economic conditions in some markets and smoking-related issues at others. Direct marketing operations reported an operating loss as revenues declined 6.1% to $9.2 million.

BUSINESS

AMERICAN RECREATION CENTERS, INC. is an industry leader in both bowling and specialty direct marketing industries. The Company's bowling division operates 39 bowling centers, with 21 in California, 7 in Texas, 6 in Wisconsin, three in Oklahoma, and one each in Kentucky and Missouri. The Company owns a majority-interest in The Right Start, Inc., one of the nation's leading direct marketers of top-quality products for infants and children through age 5.

BUSINESS LINE ANALYSIS

(5/25/94)	Rev(%)	Inc(%)
Bowling	40.8	37.3
Direct Marketing	57.6	61.9
Other	1.6	0.8
Total	100.0	100.0

ANNUAL EARNINGS AND DIVIDENDS PER SHARE

	5/25/94	5/26/93	5/27/92	5/29/91	5/30/90	5/31/89	5/25/88
Earnings Per Share	0.38	0.38	0.60	0.52	0.31	0.17	① 0.24
Dividends Per Share	0.21	0.19	0.17	0.148	0.13	0.125	② 0.117
Dividend Payout %	55.3	50.0	28.3	28.5	41.9	73.5	48.8

① Before acctg. chg. ② 3% stk div, 7/87

ANNUAL FINANCIAL DATA

RECORD OF EARNINGS (IN THOUSANDS):

Total Revenues	97,136	81,110	65,258	57,025	47,114	38,356	24,071
Costs and Expenses	87,238	71,780	57,509	48,886	40,819	34,302	20,030
Depreciation & Amort	3,790	3,226	2,427	2,638	2,078	1,652	1,486
Operating Income	6,108	6,104	5,322	5,501	4,217	2,402	2,555
Inc Bef Income Taxes & Minor Interst	3,433	3,695	5,091	4,160	2,281	1,411	1,857
Income Taxes	1,204	1,314	1,767	1,616	779	600	800
Net Income	1,889	1,841	2,986	2,544	1,502	811	① 1,057
Aver. Shs. Outstg.	4,940	4,889	4,920	...	...	...	...

① Before acctg. change cr$923,000.

BALANCE SHEET (IN THOUSANDS):

Cash and Cash Equivalents	7,218	7,907	14,347	3,495	2,216	1,080	2,498
Receivables, Net	1,417	938	976	644	550	882	803
Inventories	5,478	5,574	2,480	2,361	2,217	1,014	...
Gross Property	79,110	71,949	62,057	58,865	54,022	51,593	45,825
Accumulated Depreciation	25,142	21,681	19,037	19,127	16,798	15,208	14,139
Long-Term Debt	29,125	28,500	24,899	22,847	20,480	17,261	15,136
Net Stockholders' Equity	28,880	27,170	26,377	23,727	22,990	22,175	21,160
Total Assets	84,013	80,029	72,866	61,208	56,605	51,893	45,969
Total Current Assets	17,871	17,803	19,893	9,017	6,638	4,309	4,762
Total Current Liabilities	11,950	12,761	10,774	8,750	8,263	7,092	5,393
Net Working Capital	5,921	5,042	9,119	267	d1,625	d2,783	d631
Year End Shares Outstg	5,004	4,886	4,924	4,920	4,907	4,907	4,341

STATISTICAL RECORD:

Operating Profit Margin %	6.3	7.5	8.2	9.6	9.0	6.3	10.6
Book Value Per Share	5.77	5.56	5.36	4.82	4.69	4.52	4.87
Return on Equity %	6.5	6.8	11.3	10.7	6.5	3.7	5.0
Return on Assets %	2.2	2.3	4.1	4.2	2.7	1.6	2.3
Average Yield %	3.2	2.8	2.4	2.2	1.7	1.5	1.4
P/E Ratio	20.4-14.5	21.7-14.5	15.4-7.9	15.4-11.1	25.8-22.6	52.9-43.4	40.6-29.2
Price Range	7¾-5½	8¼-5½	9¼-4¾	8-5¾	8-7	9-7⅜	9¾-7

Statistics are as originally reported.

OFFICERS:
R. Feuchter, Chmn.
R.A. Crist, Pres. & C.E.O.
K.B. Wagner, V.P., Treas. & Asst. Sec.
G.G. Davis, III, V.P.-Legal & Sec.

INCORPORATED: CA, Apr., 1959

PRINCIPAL OFFICE: 11171 Sun Center Drive
Suite 120, Rancho Cordova, CA 95670

TELEPHONE NUMBER: (916) 852-8005
FAX: (916) 852-8004
NO. OF EMPLOYEES: 1,300 (approx.)
ANNUAL MEETING: In September
SHAREHOLDERS: 4,100 (approx.)
INSTITUTIONAL HOLDINGS:
No. of Institutions: 12
Shares Held: 544,084

REGISTRAR(S):

TRANSFER AGENT(S): First Interstate Bank
of California, Los Angeles, CA

NYS SYMBOL AWK
Rec. Pr. 29⅝

AMERICAN WATER WORKS CO., INC.

YIELD 4.3%
P/E RATIO 12.7

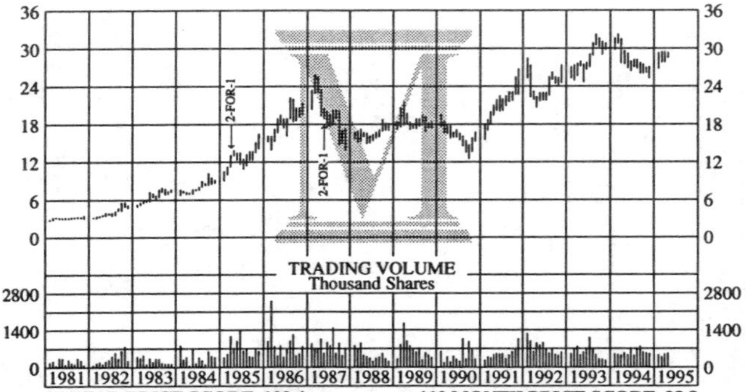

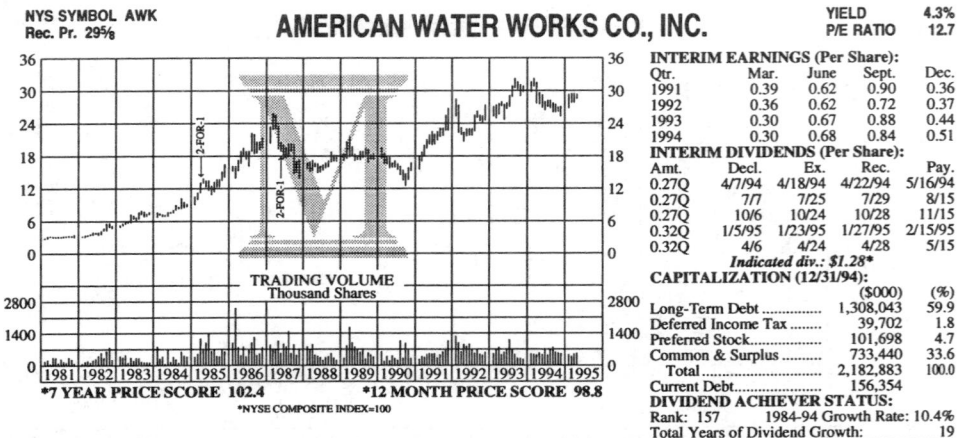

2-FOR-1
2-FOR-1
TRADING VOLUME
Thousand Shares

*7 YEAR PRICE SCORE 102.4 *12 MONTH PRICE SCORE 98.8

*NYSE COMPOSITE INDEX=100

INTERIM EARNINGS (Per Share):

Qtr.	Mar.	June	Sept.	Dec.
1991	0.39	0.62	0.90	0.36
1992	0.36	0.62	0.72	0.37
1993	0.30	0.67	0.88	0.44
1994	0.30	0.68	0.84	0.51

INTERIM DIVIDENDS (Per Share):

Amt.	Decl.	Ex.	Rec.	Pay.
0.27Q	4/7/94	4/18/94	4/22/94	5/16/94
0.27Q	7/7	7/25	7/29	8/15
0.27Q	10/6	10/24	10/28	11/15
0.32Q	1/5/95	1/23/95	1/27/95	2/15/95
0.32Q	4/6	4/24	4/28	5/15

*Indicated div.: $1.28**

CAPITALIZATION (12/31/94):

	($000)	(%)
Long-Term Debt	1,308,043	59.9
Deferred Income Tax	39,702	1.8
Preferred Stock	101,698	4.7
Common & Surplus	733,440	33.6
Total	2,182,883	100.0
Current Debt	156,354	

DIVIDEND ACHIEVER STATUS:
Rank: 157 1984-94 Growth Rate: 10.4%
Total Years of Dividend Growth: 19

RECENT DEVELOPMENTS: For the year ended 12/31/94, net income increased to $74.7 million from $71.4 million in the previous year. Net revenue was $770.2 million compared with $717.5 million in the prior year. For the quarter ended 12/31/94, net income rose 22% to $16.7 million from $13.7 million in the corresponding 1993 period. Revenue was $187.6 million, a 3% boost from $182.0 million in the prior-year quarter. Net income growth outpaced revenue growth.

PROSPECTS: The Company continues to look for opportunities to purchase new water operations that will add value and build on the geographic diversity of its operations. AWK currently has six subsidiary companies with rate cases in progress, which would contribute about $44 million in revenues if approved. Continuing regionalization of water supply systems would benefit AWK, which has been positioning its operations for just such an event.

BUSINESS

AMERICAN WATER WORKS is engaged in the ownership of companies providing water supply service. The Company and its subsidiaries constitute the American Water System, which has been functioning for 46 years. The American Water Works Service Company, a subsidiary, provides professional and staff services to affiliated companies. In 1986, AWK established American Commonwealth Management Services Company to provide management services to water and sewer systems. Its 23 subsidiary operating companies provide water service to more than 6.0 million customers in 700 communities in 21 states.

REVENUES

(12/31/94)	($000)	(%)
Residential	431,225	56.0
Commercial	169,532	22.0
Industrial	53,049	6.9
Public & Other Service	90,436	11.7
Other Water	6,502	0.8
Wastewater Service	13,933	1.8
Authority Management Fees	5,564	0.8
Total	770,241	100.0

ANNUAL EARNINGS AND DIVIDENDS PER SHARE

	1994	1993	1992	1991	1990	1989	1988
Earnings Per Share	**2.34**	**2.29**	**2.07**	**2.27**	**1.85**	**1.56**	**1.84**
Dividends Per Share	**1.08**	**1.00**	**0.925**	**0.86**	**0.80**	**0.74**	**0.68**
Dividend Payout %	**46.2**	**43.7**	**44.7**	**37.9**	**43.2**	**47.4**	**37.0**

ANNUAL FINANCIAL DATA

	1994	1993	1992	1991	1990	1989	1988
RECORD OF EARNINGS (IN MILLIONS):							
Total Revenues	770.2	717.5	657.4	633.0	570.7	527.5	511.9
Depreciation & Amort	72.9	66.8	58.4	52.1	47.0	39.7	35.5
Prov for Fed Inc Taxes	42.2	40.5	31.4	32.1	25.1	22.7	26.7
Operating Income	182.8	172.5	164.5	166.1	147.2	128.7	128.9
Interest Expense	106.7	95.7	93.7	91.8	89.6	80.7	70.3
Net Income	78.7	75.4	68.2	73.6	57.1	48.3	56.9
Aver. Shs. Outstg. (000)	31,918	31,139	30,943	30,731	30,535	30,462	30,462
BALANCE SHEET (IN MILLIONS):							
Gross Plant	3,238.6	2,990.7	26.2	25.4	21.6	19.9	19.3
Accumulated Depreciation	535.1	484.2	406.2	371.5	338.5	309.0	283.1
Prop, Plant & Equip, Net	2,703.4	2,506.4	d380.0	d346.1	d316.9	d289.1	d263.8
Long-term Debt	1,308.0	1,187.4	944.1	948.0	799.7	775.3	684.3
Net Stockholders' Equity	835.1	759.8	719.1	675.5	569.8	537.9	521.6
Total Assets	3,206.7	2,994.0	d148.0	d142.8	d126.9	d115.0	d96.0
Year End Shs Outstg (000)	32,659	31,244	31,035	30,794	30,618	30,462	30,462
STATISTICAL RECORD:							
Book Value Per Share	21.76	20.25	18.91	17.74	16.31	15.27	14.45
Op. Inc/Net Pl %	6.8	6.9	7.5	8.2	7.7	7.4	8.2
Dep/Gr. Pl %	2.3	2.2	222.4	205.0	217.9	199.7	184.4
Accum. Dep/Gr. Pl %	16.5	16.2	1547.6	1463.1	1567.4	1553.3	1468.8
Return on Equity %	10.5	11.2	10.9	12.5	10.6	9.5	11.8
Average Yield %	3.8	3.5	3.8	4.1	5.0	3.9	4.0
P/E Ratio	13.8-10.8	14.1-10.8	13.8-10.0	11.8-6.8	10.6-6.8	13.8-10.7	10.2-8.1
Price Range	32¼-25¼	32¼-24⅝	28½-20⅝	26¾-15½	19⅝-12½	21½-16¾	18¾-14⅞

Statistics are as originally reported.

OFFICERS:
M.W. Lewis, Chmn.
N.G. Harris, Vice-Chmn.
G.W. Johnstone, Pres. & C.E.O.
J.J. Barr, V.P., C.F.O. & Treas.

INCORPORATED: DE, Aug., 1936

PRINCIPAL OFFICE: 1025 Laurel Oak Road, Voorhees, NJ 08043

TELEPHONE NUMBER: (609) 346-8200

NO. OF EMPLOYEES: 3,992

ANNUAL MEETING: In May

SHAREHOLDERS: 28,761 (common); 1,007 (5% pref.); 293 (5% pfd.).

INSTITUTIONAL HOLDINGS:
No. of Institutions: 124
Shares Held: 14,952,546

REGISTRAR(S): First National Bank of Boston, Shareholder Services Division, Boston, MA

TRANSFER AGENT(S): First National Bank of Boston, Shareholder Services Division, Boston, MA

NYS SYMBOL AIT
Rec. Pr. 44⅞

AMERITECH CORPORATION

YIELD 4.5%
P/E RATIO 14.5

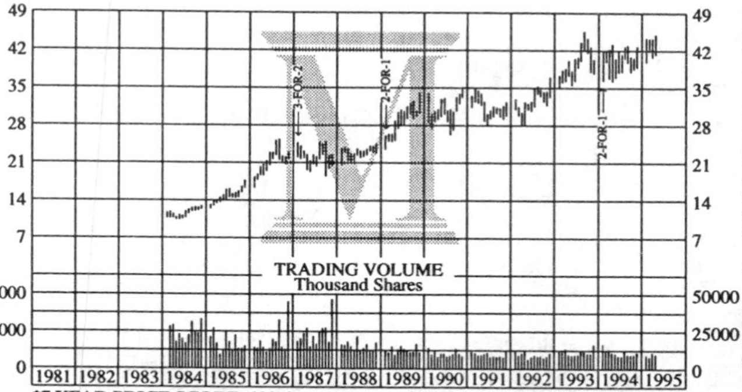

49
42
35
28
21
14
7
3-FOR-2
2-FOR-1
2-FOR-1
TRADING VOLUME
Thousand Shares
50000
25000
0
1981 1982 1983 1984 1985 1986 1987 1988 1989 1990 1991 1992 1993 1994 1995

*7 YEAR PRICE SCORE 102.6 *12 MONTH PRICE SCORE 98.9

*NYSE COMPOSITE INDEX=100

INTERIM EARNINGS (Per Share):

Qtr.	Mar.	June	Sept.	Dec.
1992	0.63	0.64	0.62	0.63
1993	0.56	0.72	0.78	0.73
1994	0.08	0.81	0.46	0.78
1995	1.05	...	...	...

INTERIM DIVIDENDS (Per Share):

Amt.	Decl.	Ex.	Rec.	Pay.
0.48Q	3/15/94	3/25/94	3/31/94	5/2/94
0.48Q	6/15	6/24	6/30	8/1
0.48Q	9/21	9/26	9/30	11/1
0.50Q	12/21	12/23	12/30	2/1/95
0.50Q	3/15/95	3/27/95	3/31/95	5/1

*Indicated div.: $2.00**

CAPITALIZATION (12/31/94):

	($000)	(%)
Long-Term Debt	4,362,300	40.5
Cap. Lease Oblig.	85,600	0.8
Deferred Income Tax	255,800	2.4
Common & Surplus	6,055,100	56.3
Total	10,758,800	100.0

DIVIDEND ACHIEVER STATUS:
Rank: 170 1984-94 Growth Rate: 9.9%
Total Years of Dividend Growth: 10

RECENT DEVELOPMENTS: For the year ended 12/31/94, income was $1.17 billion compared with $1.51 billion, including a gain, in 1993. Results for 1994 included after-tax charges of $455.8 million for work-force reductions, $61.3 million to reduce certain asset values, but did not include an extraordinary non-cash after-tax charge of $2.23 billion for an accounting change. Revenues grew 5.9% to $12.57 billion. The number of cellular customers in 1994 rose 51% to 439,000.

PROSPECTS: In an effort to improve its long-term competitiveness, AIT will expand its portfolio of interactive services. AIT received authorization to start building an interactive video network that will eventually reach up to 6 million customers. Policymakers in Wisconsin, Indiana, Michigan and Ohio have approved plans that will regulate prices instead of profits. Under an employee-reduction plan, 11,500 employees will leave AIT by August 1995.

BUSINESS

AMERITECH CORPORATION (formerly American Information Technologies Corp.) is one of seven regional holding companies divested by AT&T on January 1, 1984. It is the parent company of subsidiaries comprising the Ameritech Bell Group and the Ameritech Information Systems, which provide advanced communications and information products and services to more than 12 million residential and business customers in the Great Lakes region, through the Bell companies serving Illinois, Indiana, Michigan, Ohio and Wisconsin. The Information Systems also sells Ameritech Bell Company network products and services to meet the communication and information needs of government and institutional customers.

QUARTERLY DATA

(12/31/94)	REV($000)	INC($000)
1st Quarter	3,033,900	43,800
2nd Quarter	3,184,400	446,600
3rd Quarter	3,170,000	250,900
4th Quarter	3,181,200	(1,804,900)
TOTAL	12,569,500	(1,063,000)

ANNUAL EARNINGS AND DIVIDENDS PER SHARE

	1994	1993	1992	1991	1990	1989	1988
Earnings Per Share	**2.13**	**2.78**	**2.51**	**2.20**	**2.37**	**2.30**	**2.28**
Dividends Per Share	**1.92**	1 **1.84**	**1.76**	**1.70**	**1.58**	2 **1.46**	**1.35**
Dividend Payout %	**90.1**	**66.2**	**70.1**	**77.4**	**66.8**	**63.6**	**59.3**

1 Adj for 2-for-1 stk split, 01/24/94 2 2-for-1 stk split, 1/23/89

ANNUAL FINANCIAL DATA

	1994	1993	1992	1991	1990	1989	1988
RECORD OF EARNINGS (IN MILLIONS):							
Total Revenues	12,569.5	11,710.4	11,153.0	10,818.4	10,662.5	10,211.3	9,903.3
Costs and Expenses	8,335.5	6,990.1	6,777.7	6,921.7	6,648.7	6,260.0	6,013.7
Depreciation & Amort	2,204.7	2,162.1	2,031.3	1,914.7	1,824.8	1,796.6	1,757.4
Operating Profit	2,029.3	2,558.2	2,344.0	1,982.0	2,189.0	2,154.7	2,132.2
Income Bef Income Taxes	1,741.4	2,222.5	1,973.7	1,656.4	1,810.5	1,784.9	1,818.6
Income Taxes	571.0	709.7	627.7	490.9	556.7	546.7	581.2
Net Income	1 1,170.4	1,512.8	2 1,346.0	1,165.5	1,253.8	1,238.2	1,237.4
Aver. Shs. Outstg. (000)	549,200	544,100	536,600	531,000	530,600	539,400	544,400

1 Before extra. item dr$2,234,000,000. 2 Before acctg. change dr$1,746,400,000.

	1994	1993	1992	1991	1990	1989	1988
BALANCE SHEET (IN MILLIONS):							
Cash and Cash Equivalents	73.7	155.9	92.4	25.3	119.2	520.2	353.5
Receivables, Net	2,300.0	2,068.9	1,952.3	1,981.7	1,824.2	1,705.4	1,642.6
Inventories	203.7	133.7	177.6	193.6	206.4	206.2	161.1
Gross Property	29,545.7	29,117.4	28,370.1	27,157.6	26,369.9	25,092.4	24,224.1
Accumulated Depreciation	16,091.2	11,751.3	11,035.4	10,171.5	9,717.7	8,796.9	8,146.6
Long-Term Debt	4,362.3	4,090.4	4,586.1	4,964.4	5,074.4	5,069.3	4,487.2
Net Stockholders' Equity	6,055.1	7,844.6	6,992.2	8,097.0	7,732.4	7,685.9	7,843.5
Total Assets	19,317.3	23,427.7	22,817.7	22,289.7	21,715.1	19,833.0	19,163.0
Total Current Assets	2,890.6	2,626.7	2,519.2	2,526.1	2,478.0	2,771.0	2,374.4
Total Current Liabilities	5,156.1	5,685.3	5,239.1	5,072.0	4,606.9	3,227.2	2,953.8
Net Working Capital	d2,265.5	d3,058.6	d2,719.9	d2,545.9	d2,128.9	d456.2	d579.4
Year End Shs Outstg (000)	551,462	546,643	540,344	533,266	528,652	540,382	538,394
STATISTICAL RECORD:							
Book Value Per Share	10.98	14.35	12.94	15.18	14.63	14.22	14.57
Return on Equity %	19.3	19.3	19.3	14.4	16.2	16.1	15.8
Average Yield %	4.8	4.6	5.4	5.4	5.2	5.1	6.0
P/E Ratio	20.2-17.0	16.4-12.6	14.7-11.2	15.9-12.7	14.7-11.1	14.9-10.2	10.8-9.0
Price Range	43⅛-36¼	45⅝-35	37-28⅛	34⅞-27⅞	34⅞-26¼	34⅛-23½	24½-20½

Statistics are as originally reported.

OFFICERS:
R.C. Notebaert, Chmn., Pres. & C.E.O.
R.H. Brown, Vice-Chmn.
L.J. Rutigliano, Vice-Chmn.
J.A. Edwardson, Exec. V.P. & C.F.O.
R.W. Pehlke, V.P. & Treas.

PRINCIPAL OFFICE: 30 South Wacker Drive, Chicago, IL 60606

TELEPHONE NUMBER: (312) 750-5000
FAX: (312) 207-1601
NO. OF EMPLOYEES: 67,192
ANNUAL MEETING: In April
SHAREHOLDERS: 956,338
INSTITUTIONAL HOLDINGS:
No. of Institutions: 808
Shares Held: 198,998,553

REGISTRAR(S): Chemical Bank, New York, NY

TRANSFER AGENT(S): American Transtech, Inc., Jacksonville, FL

NYS SYMBOL AMP
Rec. Pr. 38½

AMP, INC.

YIELD	2.4%
P/E RATIO	23.2

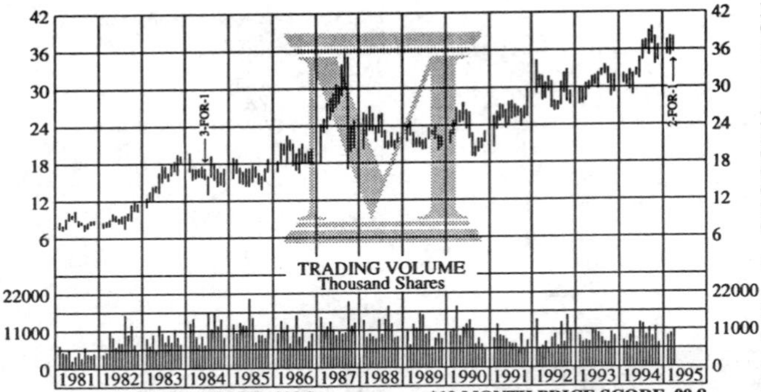

***7 YEAR PRICE SCORE 108.0** ***12 MONTH PRICE SCORE 99.8**

*NYSE COMPOSITE INDEX=100

INTERIM EARNINGS (Per Share):

Qtr.	Mar.	June	Sept.	Dec.
1991	0.33	0.31	0.29	0.30
1992	0.33	0.34	0.37	0.33
1993	0.35	0.36	0.37	0.34
1994	0.38	0.46	0.44	0.48

INTERIM DIVIDENDS (Per Share):

Amt.	Decl.	Ex.	Rec.	Pay.
0.21Q	4/27/94	5/3/94	5/9/94	6/1/94
0.21Q	7/27	8/2	8/8	9/1
0.21Q	10/26	11/1	11/7	12/1
2-for-1	1/25/95	3/2/95	2/6/95	3/1/95
0.23Q	1/25	1/31	2/6	3/1

Indicated div.: $0.92*

CAPITALIZATION (12/31/94):

	($000)	(%)
Long-Term Debt	211,244	8.1
Deferred Income Tax	48,921	1.9
Common & Surplus	2,334,415	90.0
Total	2,594,580	100.0

DIVIDEND ACHIEVER STATUS:
Rank: 165 1984-94 Growth Rate: 10.1%
Total Years of Dividend Growth: 42

RECENT DEVELOPMENTS: For the year ended 12/31/94, net income improved 24% to $369.0 million from $296.7 million in 1993. Net sales were $4.03 billion compared with $3.45 billion the year before. AMP benefited from the global economic recovery and favorable exchange rates that contributed an estimated $60.0 million to net income. U.S. sales increased 15%, spurred by sales to the automotive, communications and industrial/commercial equipment markets.

PROSPECTS: The electrical/electronic markets that AMP serves have good prospects as economic growth continues throughout the world. The Company continues its Journey to Excellence program to accelerate productivity, quality and service improvement efforts and AMP's product/market diversification program, and intensified acquisition/alliance activities. The program has contributed to sales, capital spending, quality and ratings and subsidiary growth.

BUSINESS

AMP INC. is a producer of electrical and electronic connection devices and switching and programming devices, sold throughout many diverse markets. Over 100,000 types and sizes of terminals, splices, connectors, cable assemblies, switches, touch screen data entry systems and related applications tooling (52,000 machines and many millions of tools) are supplied to more than 200,000 electrical and electronic equipment manufacturers, and tens of thousands of customers who install and maintain that equipment. The Company has over 175 facilities in the U.S. and 36 other countries.

BUSINESS LINE ANALYSIS

(12/31/94)	Rev(%)	Inc(%)
United States	45.7	48.3
Europe	28.4	31.7
Asia/Pacific	20.9	16.7
Americas	5.0	3.3
Total	100.0	100.0

ANNUAL EARNINGS AND DIVIDENDS PER SHARE

	1994	1993	1992	1991	1990	1989	1988
Earnings Per Share	**1.76**	**1.42**	**1.38**	**1.23**	**1.35**	**1.31**	**1.48**
Dividends Per Share	**[1] 0.84**	**0.80**	**0.76**	**0.72**	**0.68**	**0.60**	**0.50**
Dividend Payout %	**47.7**	**56.5**	**55.3**	**58.8**	**50.4**	**45.6**	**33.8**

[1] Adj. for 2-for-1 stk. split, 3/1/95.

ANNUAL FINANCIAL DATA

	1994	1993	1992	1991	1990	1989	1988
RECORD OF EARNINGS (IN MILLIONS):							
Total Revenues	4,027.5	3,450.6	3,337.1	3,095.0	3,043.6	2,796.6	2,669.7
Costs and Expenses	3,080.9	2,643.6	2,515.8	2,370.0	2,338.1	2,141.7	1,981.3
Depreciation & Amort	299.7	282.2	288.0	255.2	217.7	180.3	158.5
Income From Operations	646.8	524.8	533.3	469.8	487.8	474.6	529.9
Income Bef Income Taxes	594.3	485.9	479.1	423.6	462.0	455.3	529.2
Income Taxes	224.9	189.3	188.8	163.9	174.9	174.4	210.1
Net Income	369.4	296.7	290.3	259.7	287.1	280.9	319.1
Aver. Shs. Outstg. (000)	209,600	209,796	210,992	211,766	212,624	213,432	215,738
BALANCE SHEET (IN MILLIONS):							
Cash and Cash Equivalents	395.4	387.5	478.0	451.0	460.2	334.2	331.6
Receivables, Net	953.5	713.7	646.2	670.9	627.0	576.2	517.6
Inventories	581.1	459.3	435.1	440.6	481.7	494.8	481.6
Gross Property	3,451.4	2,954.9	2,715.2	2,550.4	2,303.3	1,927.5	1,749.5
Accumulated Depreciation	1,980.2	1,709.8	1,536.5	1,370.2	1,181.8	973.8	855.0
Long-Term Debt	211.2	131.0	42.9	53.0	61.1	69.5	82.8
Net Stockholders' Equity	2,334.4	2,056.4	1,943.3	1,913.0	1,792.8	1,625.4	1,521.3
Total Assets	3,770.9	3,117.9	3,005.1	3,006.9	2,928.6	2,529.8	2,375.5
Total Current Assets	2,011.8	1,644.4	1,614.1	1,616.4	1,618.4	1,437.2	1,363.1
Total Current Liabilities	1,011.3	752.4	845.5	888.4	953.2	725.5	662.2
Net Working Capital	1,000.5	892.0	768.7	728.0	665.2	711.7	700.9
Year End Shs Outstg (000)	209,636	209,812	209,860	212,068	211,902	212,980	214,890
STATISTICAL RECORD:							
Operating Profit Margin %	16.1	15.2	16.0	15.2	16.0	17.0	19.8
Book Value Per Share	11.14	9.80	9.26	9.02	8.46	7.63	7.08
Return on Equity %	15.8	14.4	14.9	13.6	16.0	17.3	21.0
Return on Assets %	9.8	9.5	9.7	8.6	9.8	11.1	13.4
Average Yield %	4.9	5.2	5.0	5.7	5.8	5.4	4.2
P/E Ratio	22.6-16.4	23.8-19.4	24.9-19.1	24.5-16.7	20.5-14.1	18.8-15.2	18.3-13.7
Price Range	39⅝-28⅞	33⅝-27⅜	34⅜-26⅜	30-20½	27⅝-18⅞	24⅝-20	27⅛-20¼

Statistics are as originally reported.

OFFICERS:
J.E. Marley, Chmn.
W.J. Hudson, Pres. & C.E.O.
R.M. Ripp, V.P. & C.F.O.
D. Henschel, Sec.

INCORPORATED: NJ, Sep., 1941; reincorp., PA, Apr., 1989

PRINCIPAL OFFICE: P.O. Box 3608, Harrisburg, PA 17105-3608

TELEPHONE NUMBER: (717) 564-0100

FAX: (717) 780-6130

NO. OF EMPLOYEES: 30,400

ANNUAL MEETING: In April

SHAREHOLDERS: 9,050

INSTITUTIONAL HOLDINGS:
No. of Institutions: 539
Shares Held: 81,799,667

REGISTRAR(S): Manufacturers Hanover Trust Co., New York, NY

TRANSFER AGENT(S): Manufacturers Hanover Trust Co., New York, NY
Continental Stock Transfer & Trust Co., New York, NY

NYS SYMBOL ASO
Rec. Pr. 31⅞

AMSOUTH BANCORPORATION

YIELD 4.8%
P/E RATIO 13.6

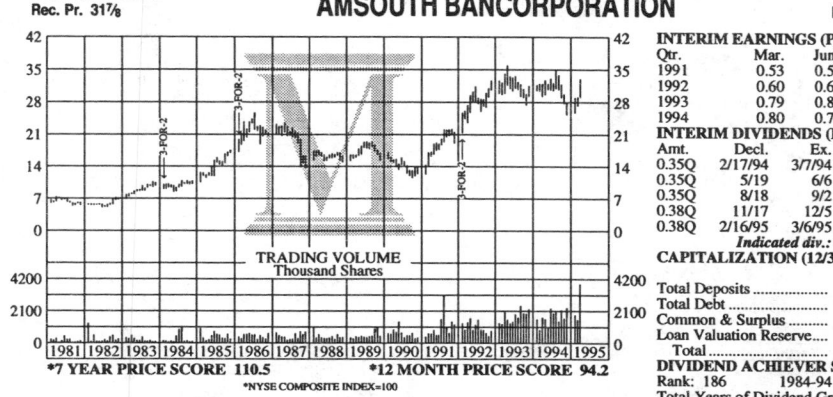

*7 YEAR PRICE SCORE 110.5   *12 MONTH PRICE SCORE 94.2

*NYSE COMPOSITE INDEX=100

TRADING VOLUME
Thousand Shares

INTERIM EARNINGS (Per Share):

Qtr.	Mar.	June	Sept.	Dec.
1991	0.53	0.57	0.53	0.54
1992	0.60	0.62	0.66	0.67
1993	0.79	0.80	0.80	0.80
1994	0.80	0.78	0.71	0.02

INTERIM DIVIDENDS (Per Share):

Amt.	Decl.	Ex.	Rec.	Pay.
0.35Q	2/17/94	3/7/94	3/11/94	4/1/94
0.35Q	5/19	6/6	6/10	7/1
0.35Q	8/18	9/2	9/9	10/1
0.38Q	11/17	12/5	12/9	1/3/95
0.38Q	2/16/95	3/6/95	3/10/95	4/1

Indicated div.: $1.52*

CAPITALIZATION (12/31/94):

	($000)	(%)
Total Deposits	13,067,062	77.8
Total Debt	2,254,987	13.4
Common & Surplus	1,310,458	7.8
Loan Valuation Reserve	171,167	1.0
Total	16,803,674	100.0

DIVIDEND ACHIEVER STATUS:
Rank: 186   1984-94 Growth Rate: 9.4%
Total Years of Dividend Growth: 24

RECENT DEVELOPMENTS: For the year ended 12/31/94, net income totaled $127.3 million, down 13.2% from the $146.7 million earned in 1993. Net interest income rose 13.5% to $537.2 million, but noninterest revenue fell 12.3% from a year earlier to $179.0 million. Noninterest expense grew 14% to $522.9 million. The provision for loan losses was increased to $30.1 million from $28.0 million. Loan growth was strong; as loans, net of unearned income, moved up 33.8% to $11.43 billion.

PROSPECTS: The Company's efforts to focus on rebuilding earnings momentum has resulted in the decision to sell its mortgage servicing business. ASO expects to reduce staff levels and improve efficiency ratios once this sale is completed. The Company will continue to originate mortgage loans through its branch-banking network. Loan growth is impressive. Complementing the solid loan growth are 17,000 new customers, netted through product promotion campaigns.

BUSINESS

AMSOUTH BANCORPORATION is headquartered in Birmingham, Alabama and as of 12/31/94, had assets of $16.8 billion. The Company operates 309 banking offices in four southeastern states and 53 mortgage banking offices in nine southeastern states. Bank affiliates are AmSouth Bank N.A., AmSouth Bank of Florida, AmSouth Bank of Tennessee, AmSouth Bank of Georgia and AmSouth Bank of Walker, Alabama. Bank-related affiliates include: AmSouth Mortgage Company, Inc., AmSouth Investment Services, and AmSouth Leasing Corp.

LOAN DISTRIBUTION

(12/31/94)	($000)	(%)
Commercial	2,699,315	23.5
Commercial Real Est Mtges	1,370,877	11.9
Real Estate Construction	540,722	4.7
Residential First Mtges	4,275,570	37.2
Other Residential Mtges	632,073	5.5
Dealer Indirect	886,872	7.7
Other Consumer	1,090,692	9.5
Total	11,496,121	100.0

ANNUAL EARNINGS AND DIVIDENDS PER SHARE

	1994	1993	1992	1991	1990	1989	1988
Earnings Per Share	2.25	3.10	2.55	2.17	2.17	1.73	2.20
Dividends Per Share	1.40	1.16	① 1.04	0.96	0.933	0.88	0.827
Dividend Payout %	62.2	37.4	40.8	44.2	42.9	50.8	37.6

① 3-for-2 stk split, 1/16/92

ANNUAL FINANCIAL DATA

RECORD OF EARNINGS (IN MILLIONS):

Total Interest Income	1,047.7	777.0	673.7	745.3	773.3	771.4	679.2
Total Interest Expense	480.4	314.9	297.7	426.5	491.9	509.5	428.6
Net Interest Income	567.3	462.1	376.0	318.9	281.4	261.9	250.6
Credit Loss Provision	30.1	19.0	36.6	41.5	31.1	43.3	18.8
Net Income	127.3	146.2	102.0	80.4	76.7	63.2	79.8
Aver. Shs. Outstg. (000)	56,527	47,153	40,006	36,970	35,274	36,413	36,320

BALANCE SHEET (IN MILLIONS):

Cash & Due From Banks	616.6	577.0	528.9	502.1	563.4	450.8	467.0
Loans & Lse Financing, Net	11,258.7	7,812.1	5,902.8	5,478.7	5,561.9	5,536.9	5,241.7
Total Domestic Deposits	13,067.1	9,567.9	7,428.6	7,372.7	7,066.9	6,672.4	6,510.9
Long-term Debt	386.1	163.1	136.2	139.0	128.7	130.6	131.3
Net Stockholders' Equity	1,310.5	1,090.0	782.8	715.7	588.5	560.7	533.4
Total Assets	16,778.0	12,547.9	9,750.7	9,459.3	8,706.1	8,565.4	8,312.9
Year End Shs Outstg (000)	58,056	49,516	40,192	39,791	35,130	36,174	36,347

STATISTICAL RECORD:

Return on Assets %	0.76	1.17	1.05	0.85	0.88	0.74	0.96
Return on Equity %	9.70	13.40	13.00	11.20	13.00	11.30	15.00
Book Value Per Share	22.57	22.01	19.48	17.99	16.75	15.50	14.68
Average Yield %	4.6	3.7	3.9	5.6	6.5	5.1	5.1
P/E Ratio	15.5-11.3	11.6-8.8	12.8-8.4	10.2-5.7	7.9-5.3	11.2-8.7	8.0-6.8
Price Range	34⅞-25⅜	35⅞-27⅜	32⅝-21⅜	22⅛-12⅜	17⅛-11½	19⅜-15⅛	17⅝-14⅞

Statistics are as originally reported.

OFFICERS:
J.W. Woods, Chmn. & C.E.O.
C.D. Ritter, Pres. & C.O.O.
K.M. Hudak, Sr. Exec. V.P. & C.F.O.

INCORPORATED: DE, Nov., 1970

PRINCIPAL OFFICE: Amsouth Sonat Tower
1900 Fifth Avenue North, Birmingham, AL
35203

TELEPHONE NUMBER: (205) 320-7151

NO. OF EMPLOYEES: 5,858

ANNUAL MEETING: In April

SHAREHOLDERS: 14,674

INSTITUTIONAL HOLDINGS:
No. of Institutions: 156
Shares Held: 20,340,822

REGISTRAR(S): Registrar & Transfer Co.,
Cranford, NJ 07016

TRANSFER AGENT(S): Registrar & Transfer
Co., Cranford, NJ 07016
AmSouth Bank, N.A., Birmingham, AL
35202

ANGELICA CORP.

YIELD 3.8%
P/E RATIO 17.3

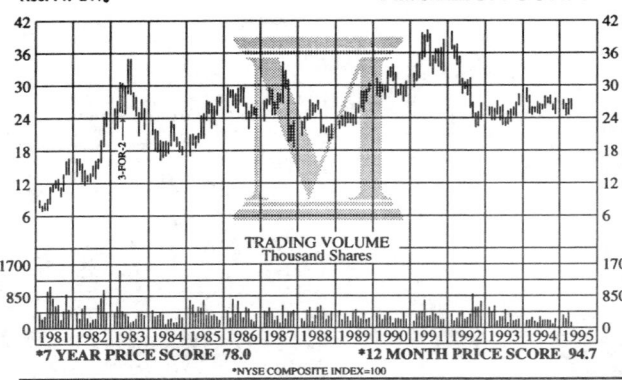

INTERIM EARNINGS (Per Share):

Qtr.	Apr.	July	Oct.	Jan.
1992-93	0.54	0.41	0.42	0.13
1993-94	0.28	0.26	0.43	0.26
1994-95	0.35	0.35	0.46	0.28

INTERIM DIVIDENDS (Per Share):

Amt.	Decl.	Ex.	Rec.	Pay.
0.235Q	2/23/94	3/9/94	3/15/94	4/1/94
0.235Q	5/24	6/9	6/15	7/1
0.235Q	9/1	9/9	9/15	10/1
0.235Q	11/30	12/9	12/15	1/1/95
0.235Q	3/1/95	3/9/95	3/15/95	4/1

Indicated div.: $0.94*

CAPITALIZATION (1/28/95):

	($000)	(%)
Long-Term Debt	69,683	25.8
Deferred Income Tax	3,476	1.3
Common & Surplus	196,660	72.9
Total	269,819	100.0

DIVIDEND ACHIEVER STATUS:
Rank: 248   1984-94 Growth Rate: 6.5%
Total Years of Dividend Growth: 22

TRADING VOLUME
Thousand Shares

*7 YEAR PRICE SCORE 78.0   *12 MONTH PRICE SCORE 94.7
*NYSE COMPOSITE INDEX=100

RECENT DEVELOPMENTS: For the fiscal year ended 1/28/95, net income increased 17.2% to $13.1 million from $11.2 million in fiscal 1994. Revenues were up 10.7% to $472.8 million, compared with $427.1 million the prior year. AGL's rental services segment posted a 6% rise in earnings on a 13.6% increase in revenues. Sales and earnings in the Life Retail Stores segment grew 21.4% and 52.0%, respectively, as same store sales were up 8.6%.

PROSPECTS: The same trend of many hospitals sending its employees to retail stores for uniform needs that is boosting results in the Life Retail Stores segment, is hurting results in the Manufacturing and Marketing segment. AGL's future results will benefit from the acquisition of a uniform manufacturing business in Dallas, TX, and a privately-owned chain of four retail uniform stores in Portland, OR. AGL also recently acquired two laundry businesses.

BUSINESS

ANGELICA CORP. provides rental and laundry services of textiles and garments primarily to health care institutions; manufactures and markets uniforms for institutions and businesses; and operates a national chain of retail uniform and shoe stores. Principal markets are: health services, including hospitals, nurses and other health care professionals; hospitality, including hotels and restaurants; commerce, including retailers and transportation companies; industry, including manufacturers, food processors and high technology companies. AGL operates directly in Canada and the U.K. through Angelica International, Ltd.

BUSINESS LINE ANALYSIS

(1/28/95)	Rev(%)	Inc(%)
Rental services	49.7	60.3
Manufacturing & marketing	36.3	21.0
Retail Sales	14.0	18.7
Total	100.0	100.0

ANNUAL EARNINGS AND DIVIDENDS PER SHARE

	1/28/95	1/29/94	1/30/93	2/1/92	1/26/91	1/27/90	1/28/89
Earnings Per Share	1.44	1.23	① 1.50	2.43	2.37	2.06	1.79
Dividends Per Share	0.94	0.925	0.92	0.88	0.82	0.76	0.72
Dividend Payout %	65.3	75.6	64.7	36.2	34.6	36.9	40.2

① Before acctg. chg.

ANNUAL FINANCIAL DATA

RECORD OF EARNINGS (IN THOUSANDS):

Total Revenues	472,832	427,128	430,797	434,471	413,635	368,752	328,134
Costs and Expenses	427,297	385,237	385,770	377,300	360,213	323,171	290,252
Depreciation	13,297	12,872	12,578	11,743	10,313	9,360	8,513
Income From Operations	32,238	29,019	32,449	45,428	43,109	36,221	29,369
Income Bef Income Taxes	21,254	18,060	22,253	36,518	35,910	31,236	27,062
Income Taxes	8,183	6,909	8,450	13,848	13,814	12,022	10,420
Net Income	13,071	11,151	① 13,803	22,670	22,096	19,214	16,642
Aver. Shs. Outstg.	9,107	9,089	9,217	9,345	9,330	9,327	9,299

① Before acctg. change cr$1,984,000.

BALANCE SHEET (IN THOUSANDS):

Cash and Cash Equivalents	2,211	2,020	2,746	6,121	2,038	6,887	2,457
Receivables, Net	69,071	68,247	66,507	67,311	68,118	61,821	53,510
Inventories	105,827	104,570	102,596	100,027	97,509	83,625	73,447
Gross Property	202,879	189,905	181,587	173,203	153,684	135,201	115,502
Accumulated Depreciation	105,229	95,937	86,709	76,387	67,882	61,072	54,827
Long-Term Debt	69,683	72,255	78,175	80,506	57,782	50,588	19,013
Net Stockholders' Equity	196,660	191,993	189,209	190,303	175,684	161,134	149,712
Total Assets	353,548	332,861	326,657	335,173	316,439	279,168	232,883
Total Current Assets	219,917	210,255	204,878	210,762	205,339	183,796	156,058
Total Current Liabilities	69,183	53,067	43,749	50,383	70,375	53,724	51,840
Net Working Capital	150,734	157,188	161,129	160,379	134,964	130,072	104,218
Year End Shares Outstg	9,119	9,086	9,064	9,316	9,286	9,284	9,306

STATISTICAL RECORD:

Operating Profit Margin %	6.8	6.8	7.5	10.5	10.4	9.8	9.0
Book Value Per Share	20.77	20.49	20.19	19.85	18.45	17.01	15.73
Return on Equity %	6.6	5.8	7.3	11.9	12.6	11.9	11.1
Return on Assets %	3.7	3.4	4.2	6.8	7.0	6.9	7.1
Average Yield %	3.5	3.6	3.0	2.5	2.7	2.9	3.1
P/E Ratio	20.5-17.0	23.1-18.3	26.7-14.8	16.6-12.2	14.3-11.4	14.7-10.7	15.3-11.0
Price Range	29½-24½	28⅜-22½	40-22¼	40¼-29⅝	33⅞-27	30⅜-22	27⅜-19⅝

Statistics are as originally reported.

OFFICERS:
L.J. Young, Chmn., Pres. & C.E.O.
T.M. Armstrong, Sr. V.P.-Fin. & Admin. & C.F.O.
J. Witter, V.P., Gen. Counsel & Sec.
T.M. Degnan, Treas.

INCORPORATED: MO, Mar., 1968

PRINCIPAL OFFICE: 424 South Woods Mill Rd., Chesterfield, MO 63017-3406

TELEPHONE NUMBER: (314) 854-3800

NO. OF EMPLOYEES: 9,800 (approx.)

ANNUAL MEETING: In May

SHAREHOLDERS: 1,710

INSTITUTIONAL HOLDINGS:
No. of Institutions: 98
Shares Held: 7,612,102

REGISTRAR(S): Boatmen's Trust Co., St.Louis, MO 63101

TRANSFER AGENT(S): Boatmen's Trust Co., St. Louis, MO 63101

ANHEUSER-BUSCH COS., INC.

YIELD 2.7%
P/E RATIO 15.1

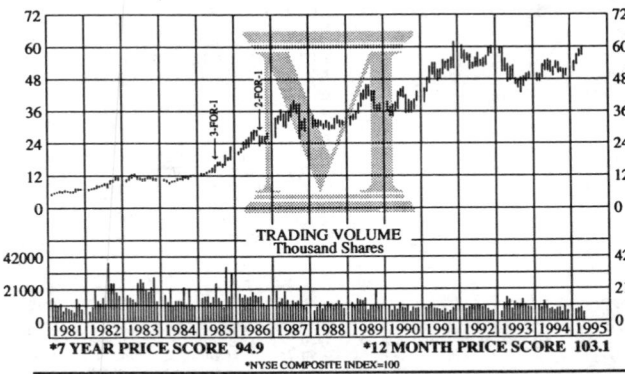

TRADING VOLUME
Thousand Shares

| 1981 | 1982 | 1983 | 1984 | 1985 | 1986 | 1987 | 1988 | 1989 | 1990 | 1991 | 1992 | 1993 | 1994 | 1995 |

*7 YEAR PRICE SCORE 94.9   *12 MONTH PRICE SCORE 103.1
*NYSE COMPOSITE INDEX=100

INTERIM EARNINGS (Per Share):

Qtr.	Mar.	June	Sept.	Dec.
1991	0.70	1.00	1.01	0.55
1992	0.77	1.10	1.12	0.61
1993	0.69	1.12	d0.28	0.62
1994	0.76	1.21	1.26	0.68

INTERIM DIVIDENDS (Per Share):

Amt.	Decl.	Ex.	Rec.	Pay.
0.36Q	4/27/94	5/3/94	5/9/94	6/9/94
0.40Q	7/27	8/3	8/9	9/9
0.40Q	10/26	11/3	11/9	12/9
0.40Q	12/14	2/3/95	2/9/95	3/9/95
0.40Q	4/26/95	5/3	5/9	6/9

*Indicated div.: $1.60**

CAPITALIZATION (12/31/94):

	($000)	(%)
Long-Term Debt	3,078,400	35.2
Deferred Income Tax	1,258,200	14.4
Common & Surplus	4,415,500	50.4
Total	8,752,100	100.0

DIVIDEND ACHIEVER STATUS:
Rank: 34   1984-94 Growth Rate: 17.1%
Total Years of Dividend Growth: 20

RECENT DEVELOPMENTS: For the year ended 12/31/94, net income was a record $1.03 billion compared with $594.5 million, including a $565.0 million restructuring charge, in 1993. Net sales advanced 5% to $12.05 billion. BUD attributed the record numbers to the following factors: increased beer sales volume, improved product mix and cost benefits resulting from a program initiated in 1993. Beer sales volume increased 1.4% to a record 88.5 million barrels.

PROSPECTS: BUD should continue to benefit from strong sales of its ice-brewed products. BUD plans to enhance premium brand volume growth through increased marketing initiatives, new product introductions, and selective price increases. Meanwhile, international growth will be supported by a proposed investment in the Zhongde Brewery of China. BUD has also signed a contract-brewing arrangement with Kirin Brewery of Japan for the production of Kirin Ice.

BUSINESS

ANHEUSER-BUSCH is a diversified corporation whose chief subsidiary is Anheuser-Busch, Inc., the world's largest brewer. In 1994, BUD accounted for about 44.7% of industry sales, including imports. Brands include Budweiser, Bud Light, Bud Dry, Michelob, Michelob Light, Michelob Dry, Michelob Classic Dark, Mich, Busch, Busch Light, Natural Light. BUD is also the country's second-largest producer of fresh baked goods and the second largest theme park operator. BUD also engages in container manufacturing and recycling, malt and rice production, international beer marketing, non-beer beverages, snack foods, family entertainment, real estate development, major league baseball, stadium ownership, creative services, railcar repair and transportation services.

ANNUAL EARNINGS AND DIVIDENDS PER SHARE

	1994	1993	1992	1991	1990	1989	1988
Earnings Per Share	3.91	2.17	①3.48	3.26	2.96	2.68	2.45
Dividends Per Share	1.52	1.36	1.20	1.06	0.94	0.80	0.66
Dividend Payout %	38.9	62.7	34.5	32.5	31.8	29.9	26.9

① Before acctg. chg.

ANNUAL FINANCIAL DATA

RECORD OF EARNINGS (IN MILLIONS):

	1994	1993	1992	1991	1990	1989	1988
Total Revenues	12,053.8	11,505.3	11,393.7	10,996.3	10,743.6	9,481.3	8,924.1
Costs and Expenses	9,527.2	9,685.1	9,051.0	8,740.7	8,648.9	7,742.3	7,301.0
Depreciation & Amort	627.5	608.3	567.0	534.1	495.7	410.3	359.0
Operating Income	1,899.1	1,211.9	1,775.7	1,721.5	1,599.0	1,328.7	1,264.1
Income Bef Income Taxes	1,707.1	1,050.4	1,615.2	1,520.6	1,352.1	1,226.7	1,160.1
Income Taxes	675.0	455.9	621.0	580.8	509.7	459.5	444.2
Net Income	1,032.1	594.5	①994.2	939.8	842.4	767.2	715.9
Aver. Shs. Outstg. (000)	264,100	274,300	285,800	287,900	284,600	286,200	292,200

① Before acctg. change dr$76,700,000.

BALANCE SHEET (IN MILLIONS):

	1994	1993	1992	1991	1990	1989	1988
Cash and Cash Equivalents	156.4	127.4	215.0	97.3	95.3	36.4	63.9
Receivables, Net	784.6	751.1	649.8	654.8	562.6	527.8	463.1
Inventories	624.8	626.7	660.7	635.6	567.2	531.7	512.2
Gross Property	12,224.1	11,727.1	11,385.1	10,589.6	10,016.7	9,187.9	7,643.0
Accumulated Depreciation	4,676.4	4,230.0	3,861.4	3,393.1	2,952.9	2,516.6	2,175.3
Long-Term Debt	3,078.4	3,031.7	2,642.5	2,644.9	3,147.1	3,307.3	1,615.3
Net Stockholders' Equity	4,415.5	4,255.5	4,620.4	4,438.1	3,679.1	3,099.9	3,102.9
Total Assets	11,045.4	10,880.3	10,537.9	9,986.5	9,634.3	9,025.7	7,109.8
Total Current Assets	1,861.6	1,795.2	1,815.8	1,627.7	1,426.3	1,276.9	1,194.3
Total Current Liabilities	1,669.0	1,815.6	1,459.8	1,402.8	1,411.9	1,302.6	1,179.1
Net Working Capital	192.6	d20.4	356.0	224.9	14.4	d25.7	15.2
Year End Shs Outstg (000)	257,300	267,037	278,402	285,052	282,306	282,988	283,406

STATISTICAL RECORD:

	1994	1993	1992	1991	1990	1989	1988
Operating Profit Margin %	15.8	10.5	15.6	15.7	14.9	14.0	14.2
Book Value Per Share	15.28	14.08	14.78	13.75	11.14	9.06	10.58
Return on Equity %	23.4	14.0	21.5	21.2	22.9	24.7	23.1
Return on Assets %	9.3	5.5	9.4	9.4	8.7	8.5	10.1
Average Yield %	3.0	2.6	2.1	2.1	2.4	2.1	2.1
P/E Ratio	14.2-12.1	27.8-19.8	17.5-14.9	19.0-12.0	15.3-11.5	17.2-11.4	14.0-11.8
Price Range	55⅜-47⅛	60¼-43	60¾-51¾	62-39¼	45¼-34	46-30⅝	34⅜-29

Statistics are as originally reported.

OFFICERS:
A.A. Busch, III, Chmn. & Pres.
J. Iglesias, Chmn. & Sr. V.P.-Europe,
Anheuser-Busch Europe, Inc.
J.E. Ritter, E.V.P., C.F.O. & Ch. Adm. Off.
J.G. Brown, V.P. & Sec.

INCORPORATED: DE, Apr., 1979

PRINCIPAL OFFICE: One Busch Place, St. Louis, MO 63118

TELEPHONE NUMBER: (314) 577-2000

NO. OF EMPLOYEES: 42,622

ANNUAL MEETING: In April

SHAREHOLDERS: 66,001

INSTITUTIONAL HOLDINGS:
No. of Institutions: 679
Shares Held: 157,016,195

REGISTRAR(S): Boatmen's Trust Co.,
St.Louis, MO 63101

TRANSFER AGENT(S): Boatmen's Trust Co.,
St. Louis, MO 63101

ANTHONY INDUSTRIES, INC.

YIELD	2.8%
P/E RATIO	12.9

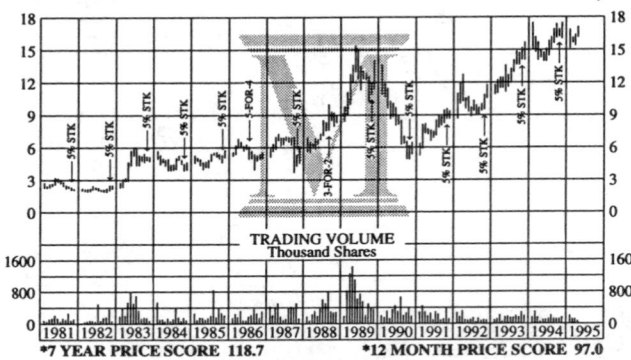

INTERIM EARNINGS (Per Share):

Qtr.	Mar.	June	Sept.	Dec.
1992	0.06	0.28	0.28	0.19
1993	0.08	0.38	0.35	0.66
1994	0.04	0.42	0.38	0.25
1995	0.17	...	...	...

INTERIM DIVIDENDS (Per Share):

Amt.	Decl.	Ex.	Rec.	Pay.
5%	11/17/94	11/25/94	12/1/94	12/29/94
5%	11/17	11/25	12/1	12/29
0.11Q	11/17	12/22	12/29	1/3/95
0.11Q	2/15/95	3/6/95	3/10/95	4/4
0.11Q	5/4	6/6	6/9	7/6

Indicated div.: $0.44

CAPITALIZATION (12/31/94):

	($000)	(%)
Long-Term Debt	109,921	52.6
Common & Surplus	98,996	47.4
Total	208,917	100.0

TRADING VOLUME
Thousand Shares

1981 1982 1983 1984 1985 1986 1987 1988 1989 1990 1991 1992 1993 1994 1995

DIVIDEND ACHIEVER STATUS:
Rank: 145   1984-94 Growth Rate: 10.8%
Total Years of Dividend Growth: 16

*7 YEAR PRICE SCORE 118.7   ***12 MONTH PRICE SCORE 97.0**
*NYSE COMPOSITE INDEX=100

RECENT DEVELOPMENTS: For the year ended 12/31/94, net income increased 17.2% to $13.0 million from $11.1 million in the previous year. Sales were up 16.4% to $502.4 million. The improved results reflect strong demand for Anthony's in-line skates, snowboards and full-suspension mountain bicycles. The Feb. 1995 acquisition of Dana Design Ltd. enhances ANT's position in the high-end backpack market. ANT has also acquired the assets of Wilderness Experience.

PROSPECTS: Earnings growth is being driven by broad-based improvements. Demand for leisure and recreation products remains strong, particularly for in-line skates, snowboards and full-suspension mountain bicycles. Results benefit from improved manufacturing efficiencies and new product introductions at the worldwide Shakespeare fishing tackle and Stearns active water sports businesses. Brand expansion remains a key strategy in these two businesses.

BUSINESS

ANTHONY INDUSTRIES is organized into two industry segments. The recreational products segment includes alpine and nordic skis and ski apparel; athletic jackets, imprintable shirts and bowling shirts; personal flotation devices; construction of residential concrete swimming pools, swimming pool equipment, pool covers; and the manufacture and sale of rods, reels and other fishing tackle items. The industrial products segment consists of the manufacture and sale of extruded monofilament used by the paperweaving industry and for cutting line, fishing line and sewing thread; fiberglass marine antennas and light poles; and laminated and coated paperboard products.

BUSINESS LINE ANALYSIS

(12/31/94)	Rev(%)	Inc(%)
Recreational Products	66.1	48.9
Industrial Products	33.9	51.1
Total	100.0	100.0

ANNUAL EARNINGS AND DIVIDENDS PER SHARE

	1994	1993	1992	1991	1990	1989	1988
Earnings Per Share	1.09	0.99	0.81	0.63	⑥ 0.27	1.36	1.22
Dividends Per Share	① 0.419	② 0.399	③ 0.38	④ 0.362	⑥ 0.345	⑦ 0.328	⑧ 0.246
Dividend Payout %	38.4	40.3	51.7	63.5	N.M.	24.1	22.3

① 5% stk div,12/94 ② 5% stk div, 12/93 ③ 5% stk div,11/24/92 ④ 5% stk div, 24.1 ⑤
Before extraord. item ⑥ 5% stk div, 11/27/90 ⑦ 5% stk div, 12/89 ⑧ 3-for-2 split, 9/88

ANNUAL FINANCIAL DATA

RECORD OF EARNINGS (IN THOUSANDS):

	1994	1993	1992	1991	1990	1989	1988
Total Revenues	504,022	432,945	403,206	371,596	377,958	382,999	309,077
Costs and Expenses	467,574	401,142	373,865	344,224	355,216	345,827	281,745
Depreciation & Amort	8,634	9,083	9,653	9,786	9,508	7,997	5,757
Operating Profit	27,814	22,720	19,688	17,586	13,234	29,175	21,575
Income Bef Income Taxes	20,333	16,961	12,911	10,680	4,468	21,309	16,136
Income Taxes	7,300	5,840	4,390	4,075	1,745	7,885	5,810
Net Income	13,033	11,121	8,521	6,605	⑫ 2,723	13,424	...
Aver. Shs. Outstg.	11,919	11,236	11,081	11,026	10,828	10,395	...

⑫ Before extra. item dr$988,000.

BALANCE SHEET (IN THOUSANDS):

Cash and Cash Equivalents	7,700	5,860	2,123	3,069	2,599	2,765	3,696
Receivables, Net	119,082	96,448	85,470	75,919	73,262	66,899	60,374
Inventories	101,742	82,375	77,448	70,610	68,371	70,188	55,282
Gross Property	131,459	122,085	113,755	108,510	105,356	97,519	83,765
Accumulated Depreciation	79,095	71,991	65,446	58,491	50,988	49,048	42,377
Long-Term Debt	109,921	87,271	68,525	43,451	53,750	7,169	11,711
Net Stockholders' Equity	98,996	88,656	83,598	80,663	78,137	78,134	62,937
Total Assets	304,414	257,279	236,200	221,650	220,551	209,809	179,927
Total Current Assets	232,848	187,756	168,916	152,439	147,017	143,663	124,102
Total Current Liabilities	82,602	69,976	73,095	87,197	78,754	78,580	70,234
Net Working Capital	150,246	117,780	95,821	65,242	68,263	65,083	53,868
Year End Shares Outstg	11,842	11,212	11,110	11,021	11,086	10,508	...

STATISTICAL RECORD:

Operating Profit Margin %	5.5	5.2	4.9	4.7	3.5	7.6	7.0
Book Value Per Share	7.02	6.50	6.14	5.90	5.59	6.08	...
Return on Equity %	13.2	12.5	10.2	8.2	3.5	17.2	16.4
Return on Assets %	4.3	4.3	3.6	3.0	1.2	6.4	5.7
Average Yield %	2.7	3.0	3.6	4.9	3.7	2.8	3.2
P/E Ratio	16.1-12.7	16.8-11.6	17.5-11.8	16.0-8.8	54.5-19.5	11.9-6.5	...
Price Range	17½-13⅞	15¾-10⅞	12¾-8⅝	9⅝-5¼	13⅝-4⅞	15⅜-8⅜	10-5½

Statistics are as originally reported.

OFFICERS:
B.I. Forester, Chairman & C.E.O.
R.M. Rodstein, President & C.O.O.
J.J. Rangel, Sr. V.P.-Finance
M.E. Lane, V.P. & Treas.

INCORPORATED: DE, Sep., 1959

PRINCIPAL OFFICE: 4900 South Eastern Ave., Suite 200, Los Angeles, CA 90040

TELEPHONE NUMBER: (213) 724-2800

NO. OF EMPLOYEES: 3,700 approx.

ANNUAL MEETING: In May

SHAREHOLDERS: 1,893

INSTITUTIONAL HOLDINGS:
No. of Institutions: 44
Shares Held: 3,059,366 (Adj.)

REGISTRAR(S): Harris Trust Co. of N.Y., New York, NY 10005

TRANSFER AGENT(S): Harris Trust Co. of N.Y., New York, NY 10005

NYS SYMBOL AOC
Rec. Pr. 37¼

AON CORP.

YIELD 3.7%
P/E RATIO 12.1

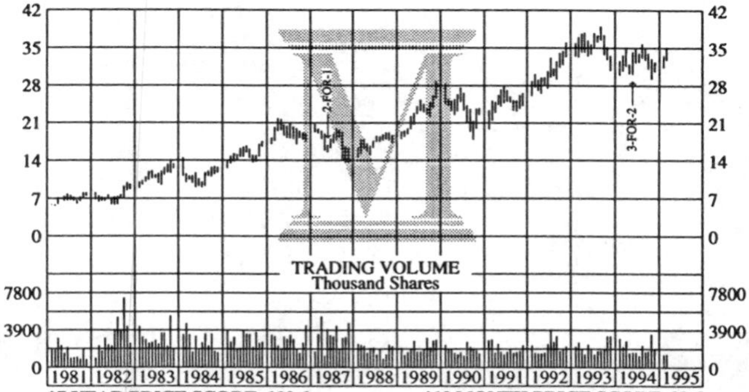

*7 YEAR PRICE SCORE 100.6 *12 MONTH PRICE SCORE 99.6

*NYSE COMPOSITE INDEX=100

INTERIM EARNINGS (Per Share):

Qtr.	Mar.	June	Sept.	Dec.
1991	0.61	0.63	0.65	0.59
1992	0.73	0.65	0.62	d0.03
1993	0.79	0.69	0.67	0.67
1994	0.88	0.77	0.76	0.74

INTERIM DIVIDENDS (Per Share):

Amt.	Decl.	Ex.	Rec.	Pay.
0.32Q	7/15/94	7/27/94	8/2/94	8/15/94
0.32Q	9/16	10/26	11/1	11/14
0.32Q	1/20/95	2/3/95	2/9/95	2/23/95
10%	2/15	3/9	3/15	3/27
0.34Q	3/17	4/26	5/2	5/15

*Indicated div.: $1.36**

CAPITALIZATION (12/31/94):

	($000)	(%)
Total Debt	739,400	24.3
Preferred Stock	61,100	2.0
Common & Surplus	2,246,300	73.7
Total	3,046,800	100.0

DIVIDEND ACHIEVER STATUS:
Rank: 255 1984-94 Growth Rate: 6.3%
Total Years of Dividend Growth: 43

RECENT DEVELOPMENTS: For the quarter ended 12/31/94, net income rose 10.4% to $86.0 million from $77.9 million for the comparable quarter in 1993. Total revenue was $1.08 billion compared with $977.3 million the year before, an increase of 10.5%. Revenues from insurance brokerage and consulting, life insurance and accident and health insurance services increased 20.9%, 4.9% and 8.6%, respectively. Revenues from premiums and policy fees grew 7.5% to $503.0 million.

PROSPECTS: The reinsurance and wholesale brokerage operations are producing excellent results reflecting good internal growth. The capital accumulation life products are reporting robust revenue growth in variable annuities; however, higher interest rates and adjusted crediting rates have caused capital accumulation spreads to narrow. AOC will continue to focus on expense management and to seek improved efficiencies related to integration activities.

BUSINESS

AON CORPORATION is an insurance holding company with more than $17.0 billion in assets. The retail brokerage arm of AOC, Rollins Hudig Hall Group, is the world's fourth-largest brokerage and consulting firm. Aon Specialty Group markets specialty insurance products and services for associations and affinity groups. Nicholson Leslie places wholesale and reinsurance buisness in the London and international markets. Aon Risk Services serves the alternative markets. The employee benefits needs of commercial clients are met through Godwins International.

REVENUES

(12/31/94)	($000)	(%)
Insur Brokerage & Consult	1,422,100	34.2
Life	946,900	22.8
Accident & Health	1,296,600	31.2
Specialty Prop & Casualty	315,600	7.6
Corporate & Other	175,700	4.2
Total	4,156,900	100.0

ANNUAL EARNINGS AND DIVIDENDS PER SHARE

	1994	1993	1992	1991	1990	1989	1988
Earnings Per Share	**3.14**	**[1] 2.81**	**[2] 1.93**	**2.47**	**2.41**	**2.36**	**2.12**
Dividends Per Share	**1.26**	**1.18**	**1.11**	**1.05**	**0.99**	**0.91**	**0.84**
Dividend Payout %	**40.1**	**41.9**	**57.4**	**42.6**	**41.3**	**38.7**	**39.6**

Note: 10% stk.div., 3/27/95. [1] 3-for-2 split, 5/16/94 [2] Before acctg. chg.

ANNUAL FINANCIAL DATA

	1994	1993	1992	1991	1990	1989	1988
RECORD OF EARNINGS (IN MILLIONS):							
Insurance Premiums	1,933.7	1,823.0	1,826.3	1,734.0	1,558.7	1,396.5	1,939.2
Total Interest Income	759.5	745.2	737.0	712.8	660.6	589.8	503.4
Total Revenues	4,156.9	3,844.8	3,336.5	2,930.9	2,626.4	2,324.7	2,732.4
Benefits to Policyholders	1,304.9	1,267.3	1,305.6	1,247.0	1,104.5	957.6	1,444.4
Income Before Income Tax	537.6	479.1	290.5	331.5	325.2	314.1	278.4
Income Taxes	177.6	155.3	84.3	89.5	86.2	81.7	74.0
Net Income	360.0	323.8	[1] 206.2	242.0	239.0	232.4	179.5
Aver. Shs. Outstg. (000)	116,795	117,005	115,374	107,666	109,127	108,298	106,143
[1] Before acctg. change dr$79,600,000.							
BALANCE SHEET (IN MILLIONS):							
Cash	508.8	163.8	87.7	38.1	74.1	31.9	18.0
Fixed Maturities	7,144.1	7,053.4	6,732.1	6,253.5	5,367.7	4,343.5	3,920.2
Policy Loans	214.9	207.3	204.5	193.9	178.3	162.7	146.7
Mtge Loans on Real Estate	567.5	557.1	592.3	657.7	715.6	721.1	677.4
Total Assets	17,921.9	16,279.1	14,289.8	11,633.2	10,432.2	9,156.4	8,266.0
Benefits and Claims	9,310.4	8,776.3	7,759.2	7,341.8	6,832.5	5,566.9	5,186.7
Net Stockholders' Equity	2,307.4	2,287.8	2,103.9	1,775.0	1,457.6	1,422.4	1,284.8
Year End Shs Outstg (000)	118,501	110,061	109,985	107,699	107,430	107,366	108,758
STATISTICAL RECORD:							
Book Value Per Share	18.96	20.66	18.99	16.45	13.56	13.24	11.52
Return on Equity %	15.9	14.2	9.8	13.6	16.4	16.3	14.3
Return on Assets %	2.0	2.0	1.4	2.1	2.3	2.5	2.2
Average Yield %	3.9	3.4	3.6	4.4	4.3	3.9	5.0
P/E Ratio	12.5-10.2	15.3-12.1	20.5-14.9	12.4-8.8	13.0-8.2	13.5-8.4	9.9-7.6
Price Range	35¾-29¼	39-30⅞	36-26⅛	27⅞-19⅞	28⅜-17⅞	28⅞-18	19⅛-14⅝

Statistics are as originally reported.

OFFICERS:
P.G. Ryan, Chmn., Pres. & C.E.O.
H.N. Medvin, Exec. V.P., C.F.O. & Treas.
A.F. Quern, Sr. V.P. & Corp. Sec.

INCORPORATED: IL, Oct., 1949

PRINCIPAL OFFICE: 123 North Wacker Drive, Chicago, IL 60606

TELEPHONE NUMBER: (312) 701-3000

NO. OF EMPLOYEES: 18,000 (approx.)

ANNUAL MEETING: In April

SHAREHOLDERS: 14,000 (approx.)

INSTITUTIONAL HOLDINGS:
No. of Institutions: 275
Shares Held: 32,458,566

REGISTRAR(S): First Chicago Trust Co. of New York, New York, NY 10008

TRANSFER AGENT(S): First Chicago Trust Co. of New York, New York, NY 10008

NASDAQ SYMBOL APOG
Rec. Pr. 17

APOGEE ENTERPRISES, INC.

YIELD 1.9%
P/E RATIO 17.5

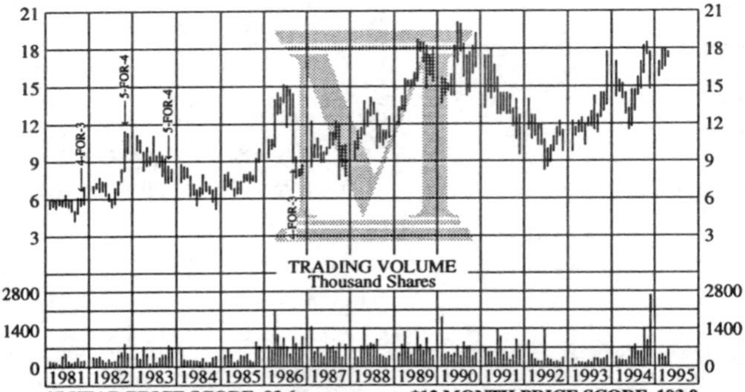

21
18
15
12
9
6
3
2800
1400
0
4-FOR-3
5-FOR-4
5-FOR-4
4-FOR-3
TRADING VOLUME
Thousand Shares
1981 1982 1983 1984 1985 1986 1987 1988 1989 1990 1991 1992 1993 1994 1995

*7 YEAR PRICE SCORE 93.6 *12 MONTH PRICE SCORE 103.9

*NYSE COMPOSITE INDEX=100

INTERIM EARNINGS (Per Share):

Qtr.	May	Aug.	Nov.	Feb.
1991-92	0.20	0.29	0.02	0.12
1992-93	0.02	0.15	0.15	0.02
1993-94	0.07	0.18	0.22	d0.22
1994-95	0.19	0.32	0.28	0.18

INTERIM DIVIDENDS (Per Share):

Amt.	Decl.	Ex.	Rec.	Pay.
0.075Q	4/26/94	5/4/94	5/10/94	5/26/94
0.075Q	7/29	8/10	8/16	9/1
0.08Q	10/20	10/26	11/1	11/17
0.08Q	1/17/95	1/25/95	1/31/95	2/16/95
0.08Q	4/24	5/3	5/9	5/25

Indicated div.: $0.32

CAPITALIZATION (2/25/95):

	($000)	(%)
Long-Term Debt	80,566	39.0
Minority Interest	1,427	0.7
Common & Surplus	124,629	60.3
Total	206,622	100.0

DIVIDEND ACHIEVER STATUS:
Rank: 96 1984-94 Growth Rate: 13.0%
Total Years of Dividend Growth: 20

RECENT DEVELOPMENTS: For the fiscal year ended 2/25/95, APOG reported net income of $13.1 million compared with $3.3 million the previous year. Prior-year results included restructuring charges of $5.2 million and were before an accounting credit of $525,000. Net sales advanced 9.9% to $756.5 million from $688.2 million. Operating profit for APOG's building products and services operations was $4.4 million compared with a $14.5 million loss the prior year. Meanwhile, sales grew 9.2% to $508 million. Automotive glass operations posted an 11.7% sales increase to $249.0 million, while operating income rose slightly. Operating profit growth was limited by ongoing price competition, expenditures for state-of-the-art information systems and support, and expanded marketing initiatives. Backlog at fiscal year-end slid 10.1% due to a focus on selecting jobs with greater margin potential.

BUSINESS

APOGEE ENTERPRISES INC. maintains operations in the fabrication, installation and distribution of glass and aluminum. Its products and services include glass, windows and curtainwall for commercial and institutional construction and remodeling markets; curtainwall installation at major high-rise construction sites; design, manufacture and installation of institutional and government security systems; metal and glass coating services; fabrication, sale and installation of automotive glass; and such consumer-oriented products as venetian blinds, shutters, picture frame glass and computer anti-glare screens. For the year ended 2/25/95, building products and services accounted for 67.1% of sales and 18.1% of operating income.

ANNUAL EARNINGS AND DIVIDENDS PER SHARE

	2/25/95	2/26/94	2/27/93	2/29/92	3/2/91	3/3/90	2/25/89
Earnings Per Share	**0.97**	**0.25**	**0.34**	**0.63**	**1.25**	**1.04**	**1.00**
Dividends Per Share	**0.305**	**0.285**	**0.265**	**0.255**	**0.23**	**0.19**	**0.155**
Dividend Payout %	**31.4**	**N.M.**	**77.9**	**40.5**	**18.4**	**18.3**	**15.5**

ANNUAL FINANCIAL DATA

	2/25/95	2/26/94	2/27/93	2/29/92	3/2/91	3/3/90	2/25/89
RECORD OF EARNINGS (IN THOUSANDS):							
Total Revenues	756,549	688,233	572,450	596,281	599,525	589,657	433,740
Costs and Expenses	732,287	665,451	550,971	560,727	552,949	545,483	400,619
Depreciation & Amort	15,131	15,724	15,110	16,305	13,309	12,141	8,987
Operating Income	24,262	9,352	8,244	16,720	30,232	30,399	24,269
Income Bef Income Taxes	20,127	6,617	6,450	15,750	28,842	23,375	21,634
Income Taxes	8,101	2,634	1,936	7,245	11,825	9,280	8,213
Net Income	13,050	[1] 3,308	4,514	8,505	17,017	14,095	13,421
Aver. Shs. Outstg.	13,501	13,289	13,293	13,512	13,630	13,566	13,447
[1] Before acctg. change cr$525,000.							
BALANCE SHEET (IN THOUSANDS):							
Cash and Cash Equivalents	2,894	10,824	8,908	18,742	20,468	12,189	2,990
Receivables, Net	165,099	153,051	114,902	102,703	98,402	102,744	88,093
Inventories	54,559	52,732	40,189	39,489	39,531	37,010	34,127
Gross Property	161,694	141,410	132,261	126,922	117,961	107,289	93,284
Accumulated Depreciation	86,666	76,493	66,133	56,341	46,469	37,434	28,598
Long-Term Debt	80,566	35,688	28,419	25,267	29,398	41,366	46,277
Net Stockholders' Equity	124,629	114,063	112,335	113,781	109,050	95,754	83,871
Total Assets	361,928	306,188	251,456	249,509	250,343	244,103	207,686
Total Current Assets	256,820	221,286	169,029	166,376	162,676	154,845	126,881
Total Current Liabilities	135,719	140,846	99,787	101,011	102,492	94,948	71,767
Net Working Capital	121,101	80,440	69,242	65,365	60,184	59,897	55,114
Year End Shares Outstg	13,443	13,312	13,177	13,461	13,477	13,467	13,414
STATISTICAL RECORD:							
Operating Profit Margin %	3.2	1.4	1.4	2.8	5.0	5.2	5.6
Book Value Per Share	9.27	8.42	8.15	8.04	7.72	6.72	5.80
Return on Equity %	10.5	2.9	4.0	7.5	15.6	14.7	16.0
Return on Assets %	3.6	1.1	1.8	3.4	6.8	5.8	6.5
Average Yield %	2.0	2.1	2.4	1.9	1.4	1.2	1.3
P/E Ratio	19.1-11.9	71.0-39.0	41.2-24.3	28.6-15.1	16.1-10.9	18.0-11.4	14.1-9.0
Price Range	18½-11½	17¾-9¾	14-8¼	18-9½	20⅛-13⅝	18¾-11⅞	14⅛-9

Statistics are as originally reported.

OFFICERS:
D.W. Goldfus, Chmn. & C.E.O.
G.K. Anderson, Pres.
W.G. Gardner, C.F.O., Treas. & Sec.

INCORPORATED: MN, Jul., 1949

PRINCIPAL OFFICE: 7900 Xerxes Ave S. Suite 1800, Minneapolis, MN 55431-1159

TELEPHONE NUMBER: (612) 835-1874

FAX: (612) 835-3196

NO. OF EMPLOYEES: 6,200

ANNUAL MEETING: In June

SHAREHOLDERS: 5,100 (approx.)

INSTITUTIONAL HOLDINGS:
No. of Institutions: 58
Shares Held: 5,446,824

REGISTRAR(S): American Stock Transfer Co., 40 Wall St., 46th Floor, New York, NY 10005

TRANSFER AGENT(S): American Stock Transfer Co., 40 Wall St., 46th Floor, New York, NY 10005

ARCHER DANIELS MIDLAND CO.

YIELD 0.5%
P/E RATIO 11.1

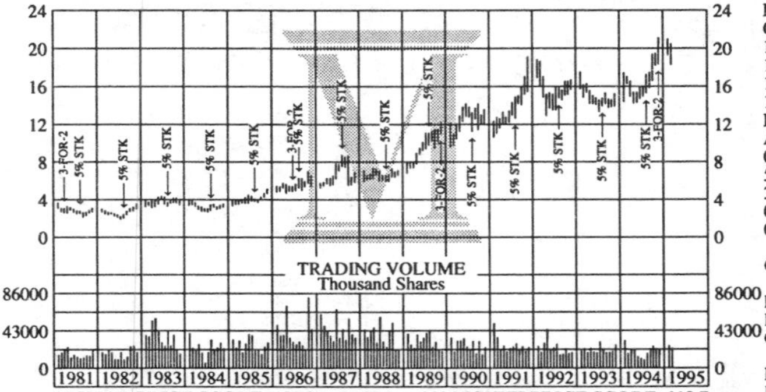

INTERIM EARNINGS (Per Share):

Qtr.	Sept.	Dec.	Mar.	June
1991-92	0.37	0.38	0.31	0.40
1992-93	0.37	0.46	0.38	0.35
1993-94	0.13	0.28	0.25	0.73
1994-95	0.30	0.43	...	...

INTERIM DIVIDENDS (Per Share):

Amt.	Decl.	Ex.	Rec.	Pay.
0.025Q	7/21/94	8/1/94	8/5/94	8/29/94
5%	7/21	8/16	8/22	9/19
3-for-2	10/20	12/6	11/4	12/5
0.025Q	10/20	10/31	11/4	11/28
0.025Q	1/23/95	1/30/95	2/3/95	2/27/95

Indicated div.: $0.10

CAPITALIZATION (6/30/94):

	($000)	(%)
Long-Term Debt	2,021,417	26.9
Deferred Income Tax	432,396	5.8
Common & Surplus	5,045,421	67.3
Total	7,499,234	100.0

DIVIDEND ACHIEVER STATUS:
Rank: 130   1984-94 Growth Rate: 14.4%
Total Years of Dividend Growth: 20

TRADING VOLUME
Thousand Shares

*7 YEAR PRICE SCORE 108.9   *12 MONTH PRICE SCORE 113.7
*NYSE COMPOSITE INDEX=100

RECENT DEVELOPMENTS: For the quarter ended 12/31/94, net income was $220.1 million versus $146.1 million a year earlier. Net sales and other operating income increased 14.2% to $3.22 billion, due primarily to volume increases and recent acquisitions. Sales of oilseed products rose 14% due to increased volume as a result of strong demand for vegetable oils and meal products. Sales of corn products increased 8% due to increased average selling prices.

PROSPECTS: The Company's two main businesses, soybean processing and wheat milling, should continue to benefit from strong margin growth in the near term. Additionally, ADM is concentrating on vertically integrating its business into high-technology areas, such as vitamin production. Meanwhile, it is expected that corn and gasoline prices will remain the major influences on ethanol earnings instead of government legislation.

BUSINESS

ARCHER DANIELS MIDLAND COMPANY is engaged in the business of processing and merchandising agricultural commodities. It is one of the largest domestic processors of oil seeds and of vegetable oil. ADM is one of the largest flour millers and corn refiners in the U.S. Corn syrups, high fructose syrups, glucose, corn starches and ethyl alcohol (ethanol) are products of the corn wet milling operations. Other operations include storage of grain, shelling of peanuts, production of consumer food products and formula feeds, production of alt products and refining of sugar. ADM Investor Services provides ADM and other commercial firms with commodity hedging services and is a futures commission merchant.

BUSINESS LINE ANALYSIS

(6/30/94)	Rev(%)	Inc(%)
United states	73.5	91.9
Foreign	26.5	8.1
Total	100.0	100.0

ANNUAL EARNINGS AND DIVIDENDS PER SHARE

	6/30/94	6/30/93	6/30/92	6/30/91	6/30/90	6/30/89	6/30/88
Earnings Per Share	0.93	① 1.05	0.93	0.86	0.89	0.79	0.65
Dividends Per Share	0.073	0.064	0.060	0.058	0.055	0.039	0.033
Dividend Payout %	7.8	6.1	6.5	6.7	6.2	4.9	5.1

Note: Adj. for all splits up to 12/94. ① Before acctg. chg.

ANNUAL FINANCIAL DATA

RECORD OF EARNINGS (IN MILLIONS):

Total Revenues	11,374.4	9,811.4	9,231.5	8,468.2	7,751.3	7,928.8	6,798.4
Costs and Expenses	10,253.5	8,744.7	8,189.5	7,589.8	6,828.8	7,086.0	6,073.5
Depreciation & Amort	354.5	328.5	293.7	261.4	248.1	220.5	184.0
Earnings From Operations	766.4	738.2	748.3	617.0	674.4	622.3	540.9
Earn Bef Income Taxes	738.3	746.0	759.6	718.0	753.2	667.7	571.9
Income Taxes	254.2	211.5	255.8	251.3	269.6	243.1	218.9
Net Income	484.1	① 534.5	503.8	466.7	483.5	424.7	353.1
Aver. Shs. Outstg. (000)	346,864	359,914	360,877	362,127	360,860	357,496	363,717

① Before acctg. change cr$33,018,000.

BALANCE SHEET (IN MILLIONS):

Cash and Cash Equivalents	1,335.5	1,868.3	1,403.5	890.5	829.5	841.9	644.4
Receivables, Net	1,041.8	824.9	696.8	639.0	632.9	510.9	637.8
Inventories	1,422.1	1,131.8	1,025.0	917.5	771.2	695.0	773.7
Gross Property	6,661.0	6,001.7	5,548.1	4,831.9	3,977.7	3,281.6	2,851.9
Accumulated Depreciation	3,122.5	2,786.8	2,488.0	2,136.3	1,845.9	1,449.3	1,190.7
Long-Term Debt	2,021.4	2,039.1	1,562.5	980.3	750.9	690.1	692.9
Net Stockholders' Equity	5,045.4	4,883.3	4,492.4	3,922.3	3,573.2	3,033.5	2,630.5
Total Assets	8,746.9	8,404.1	7,524.5	6,260.6	5,450.0	4,728.3	4,397.6
Total Current Assets	3,910.8	3,921.7	3,213.4	2,531.6	2,303.8	2,105.7	2,118.8
Total Current Liabilities	1,127.0	960.2	936.8	856.9	676.3	618.5	710.1
Net Working Capital	2,783.8	2,961.5	2,276.6	1,674.7	1,627.5	1,487.2	1,408.7
Year End Shs Outstg (000)	328,039	359,914	359,944	359,934	344,905	344,905	356,726

STATISTICAL RECORD:

Operating Profit Margin %	6.7	7.5	8.1	7.3	8.7	7.8	8.0
Book Value Per Share	15.38	13.57	12.48	10.90	10.36	8.80	7.37
Return on Equity %	9.6	10.9	11.2	11.9	13.5	14.0	13.4
Return on Assets %	5.5	6.4	6.7	7.5	8.9	9.0	8.0
Average Yield %	0.3	0.3	0.3	0.3	0.3	0.3	0.3
P/E Ratio	30.4-22.8	25-19.0	30.4-20.8	33.4-18.6	23.9-16.0	23.3-13.0	16.9-13.7
Price Range	28¼-21¼	26¼-20	28¼-19⅜	28¾-16	21¼-14¼	18⅜-10¼	11-8⅞

Statistics are as originally reported.

OFFICERS:
D.O. Andreas, Chmn. & C.E.O.
M.D. Andreas, Vice-Chmn. & Exec. V.P.
J.R. Randall, Pres.
R.P. Reising, V.P., Sec. & General Counsel
D.J. Schmalz, V.P., Contr. & C.F.O.

INCORPORATED: DE, May, 1923

PRINCIPAL OFFICE: 4666 Faries Pkwy. Box 1470, Decatur, IL 62525

TELEPHONE NUMBER: (217) 424-5200

NO. OF EMPLOYEES: 16,013

ANNUAL MEETING: In October

SHAREHOLDERS: 33,940

INSTITUTIONAL HOLDINGS:
No. of Institutions: 543
Shares Held: 156,418,958

REGISTRAR(S): Harris Trust & Savings Bank, Chicago, IL

TRANSFER AGENT(S): Harris Trust & Savings Bank, Chicago, IL

ATLANTIC ENERGY, INC.

YIELD 8.5%
P/E RATIO 12.9

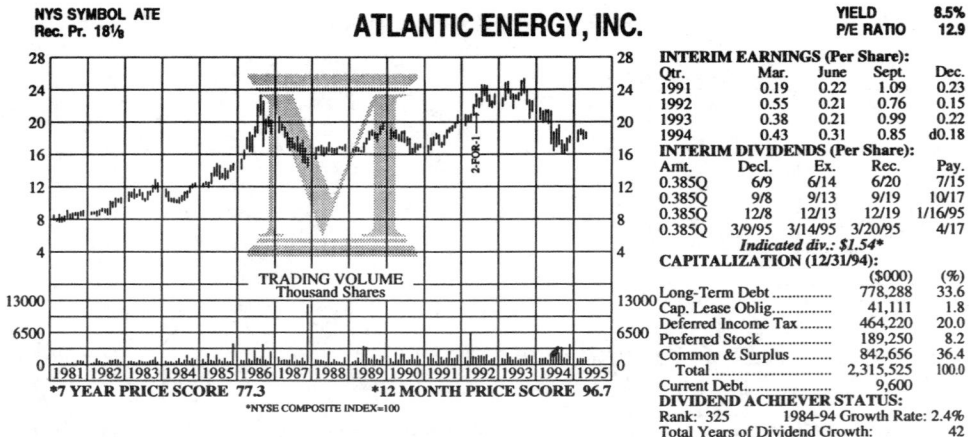

INTERIM EARNINGS (Per Share):

Qtr.	Mar.	June	Sept.	Dec.
1991	0.19	0.22	1.09	0.23
1992	0.55	0.21	0.76	0.15
1993	0.38	0.21	0.99	0.22
1994	0.43	0.31	0.85	d0.18

INTERIM DIVIDENDS (Per Share):

Amt.	Decl.	Ex.	Rec.	Pay.
0.385Q	6/9	6/14	6/20	7/15
0.385Q	9/8	9/13	9/19	10/17
0.385Q	12/8	12/13	12/19	1/16/95
0.385Q	3/9/95	3/14/95	3/20/95	4/17

*Indicated div.: $1.54**

CAPITALIZATION (12/31/94):

	($000)	(%)
Long-Term Debt	778,288	33.6
Cap. Lease Oblig.	41,111	1.8
Deferred Income Tax	464,220	20.0
Preferred Stock	189,250	8.2
Common & Surplus	842,656	36.4
Total	2,315,525	100.0

Current Debt.................. 9,600

DIVIDEND ACHIEVER STATUS:
Rank: 325   1984-94 Growth Rate: 2.4%
Total Years of Dividend Growth: 42

RECENT DEVELOPMENTS: For the year ended 12/31/94, net income was $76.1 million, down 20.1% from $95.3 million reported in 1993. The 1994 results included non-recurring charges of $20.4 million after tax, primarily for Atlantic City Electric Co.'s employee-reduction program. Revenues for the year were $913.0 million, up 5.5%. Total energy sales were up 1.3%. Net loss including the aforementioned charge for the quarter ended 12/31/94 slid 16.8% to $9.9 million.

PROSPECTS: Stronger economic conditions and successful cost-cutting efforts may offset some of the negative effects of increased competition. Atlantic City Electric's rates are high by national and regional norms. Consequently, ATE is facing stiff competition from nonutility electric generators. The heavy competition is likely to remain and have an adverse effect on ATE's ability to retain large customers. Cost-cutting efforts are continuing.

BUSINESS

ATLANTIC ENERGY, INC. provides electric service to the southern third of New Jersey. Tourism plays a major part in the eastern shore economy, while commercial and light industrial customers are situated in the western section of the service area. Farming and agriculture are significant in the south and west. Electric revenues are derived 48% residential, 38% commercial, and 14% industrial and other customers. Other subsidiaries include Atlantic Southern Properties, Inc. which owns, develops and manages commercial real estate; Atlantic Generation, Inc.; ATE Investment, Inc.; Atlantic Energy Technology, Inc. and Deepwater Operating Company.

ANNUAL EARNINGS AND DIVIDENDS PER SHARE

	1994	1993	1992	1991	1990	1989	1988
Earnings Per Share	1.41	1.80	1.67	1.75	1.51	1.87	1.84
Dividends Per Share	1.54	1.53	☐ 1.51	1.49	1.46	1.41	1.385
Dividend Payout %	N.M.	85.0	90.4	85.4	96.7	75.4	75.3

☐ 2-for-1 stk split, 5/15/92

ANNUAL FINANCIAL DATA

RECORD OF EARNINGS (IN MILLIONS):

Total Revenues	913.0	865.7	816.8	778.0	716.8	705.0	675.9
Depreciation & Amort	73.3	68.0	69.4	66.0	62.1	58.5	54.8
Maintenance	37.6	45.4	49.8	52.0	52.4	55.2	59.6
Prov for Fed Inc Taxes	42.5	45.3	37.1	36.2	26.9	22.9	26.5
Operating Income	153.5	159.6	137.2	144.9	124.6	134.7	122.8
Interest Expense	55.7	59.6	1.3	51.7	54.2	50.5	49.4
Net Income	76.1	95.3	86.2	85.6	68.9	81.0	72.2
Aver. Shs. Outstg. (000)	54,149	52,888	51,592	49,008	45,590	43,268	39,186

BALANCE SHEET (IN MILLIONS):

Gross Plant	2,526.1	2,417.0	2,296.6	2,190.6	2,042.1	1,861.5	1,725.3
Accumulated Depreciation	726.0	668.8	599.1	545.8	504.2	459.2	419.2
Prop, Plant & Equip, Net	1,800.1	1,748.1	1,697.5	1,644.8	1,537.9	1,402.2	1,306.1
Long-term Debt	819.4	810.5	680.1	617.9	632.9	638.9	545.5
Net Stockholders' Equity	1,031.9	1,049.7	1,022.2	986.5	822.4	756.8	658.0
Total Assets	2,545.6	2,487.5	2,220.2	2,151.4	2,006.0	1,864.5	1,660.3
Year End Shs Outstg (000)	54,155	53,507	52,199	50,896	45,952	45,092	40,024

STATISTICAL RECORD:

Book Value Per Share	15.56	15.62	15.17	14.84	14.36	14.27	13.58
Op. Inc/Net Pl %	8.5	9.1	8.1	8.8	8.1	9.6	9.4
Dep/Gr. Pl %	2.9	2.8	3.0	3.0	3.0	3.1	3.2
Accum. Dep/Gr. Pl %	28.7	27.7	26.1	24.9	24.7	24.7	24.3
Return on Equity %	8.6	10.9	10.4	10.8	9.8	11.8	12.4
Average Yield %	8.2	6.7	6.8	8.1	8.3	7.8	8.4
P/E Ratio	15.4-11.3	14.1-11.3	14.7-11.7	12.1-9.2	12.7-10.6	10.6-8.7	9.5-8.4
Price Range	21¾-16	25⅜-20⅜	24⅝-19½	21-16	19¼-16	19⅞-16¼	17½-15⅜

Statistics are as originally reported.

QUARTERLY DATA

(12/31/94) ($000)	Rev	Inc
1st Quarter	232,098	39,712
2nd Quarter	205,822	30,427
3rd Quarter	272,708	58,431
4th Quarter	202,410	24,969

OFFICERS:
E.D. Huggard, Chmn.
J.L. Jacobs, Pres. & C.E.O.
J.G. Salomone, V.P., Sec. & Treas.

INCORPORATED: NJ, Aug., 1986

PRINCIPAL OFFICE: 6801 Black Horse Pike, Pleasantville, NJ 08232

TELEPHONE NUMBER: (609) 645-4500
FAX: (609) 645-4100
NO. OF EMPLOYEES: 1,794
ANNUAL MEETING:
SHAREHOLDERS: 48,850
INSTITUTIONAL HOLDINGS:
No. of Institutions: 117
Shares Held: 10,199,095

REGISTRAR(S): At Company's Office

TRANSFER AGENT(S): At Company's Office

NYS SYMBOL AUD
Rec. Pr. 64⅛

AUTOMATIC DATA PROCESSING INC.

YIELD 0.9%
P/E RATIO 24.0

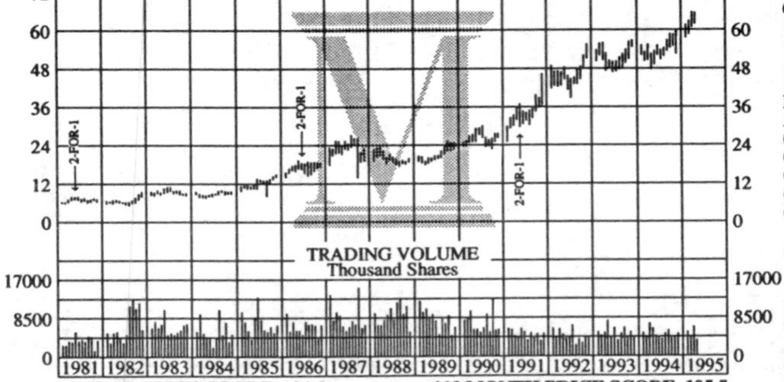

2-FOR-1
2-FOR-1
2-FOR-1
TRADING VOLUME
Thousand Shares

*7 YEAR PRICE SCORE 124.6 *12 MONTH PRICE SCORE 105.5

*NYSE COMPOSITE INDEX=100

INTERIM EARNINGS (Per Share):

Qtr.	Sept.	Dec.	Mar.	June
1991-92	0.33	0.44	0.57	0.50
1992-93	----------	2.08	----------	
1993-94	0.42	0.57	0.74	0.64
1994-95	0.49	0.67	0.87	...

INTERIM DIVIDENDS (Per Share):

Amt.	Decl.	Ex.	Rec.	Pay.
0.13Q	1/24/94	3/8/94	3/14/94	4/1/94
0.15Q	5/23	6/7	6/13	7/1
0.15Q	8/15	9/12	9/16	10/1
0.15Q	11/15	12/12	12/16	1/1/95
0.15Q	1/23/95	3/13/95	3/17/95	4/1

Indicated div.: $0.60

CAPITALIZATION (6/30/94):

	($000)	(%)
Long-Term Debt	372,959	17.8
Deferred Income Tax	33,553	1.6
Common & Surplus	1,691,251	80.6
Total	2,097,763	100.0

DIVIDEND ACHIEVER STATUS:
Rank: 69 1984-94 Growth Rate: 14.3%
Total Years of Dividend Growth: 19

RECENT DEVELOPMENTS: For the quarter ended 12/31/94, net income rose to $94.9 million, an 18.4% increase from $80.2 million reported in the same period last year. Revenues climbed 16.4% to $672.6 million from $577.7 million in the prior year, sparked by 14% and 30% gains in the Employer and Dealer Services divisions, respectively. Dealer Services' growth included internal growth of more than 15% and the effect of several small acquisitions. Brokerage Services revenues increased 6% for the quarter.

PROSPECTS: The Company is continuing its focus on the Employer Services division by attempting to accelerate automation, develop new products and migrate new technologies. Earnings from this group will be enhanced by new client sales, improved client retention rates and increased payroll processing services. Dealer Services will benefit from a healthy automotive industry and increased customer traffic in auto dealerships.

BUSINESS

AUTOMATIC DATA PROCESSING, INC. is the largest independent company in the United States dedicated exclusively to providing computerized transaction processing, recordkeeping, data communications, and information services. The Company services about 250,000 clients in nearly every segment of business, industry, and government for the collection of data, data processing and data dissemination. The Company primarily operates out of nine business services that include: Employer, Brokerage, Dealer, Automotive, Claims, Interactive Business, ADP Credit Corp., Network Services and International operations.

QUARTERLY DATA

(06/30/94) ($000)	Rev	Inc
1st Quarter	551,983	53,710
2nd Quarter	577,661	80,180
3rd Quarter	674,405	104,990
4th Quarter	664,917	90,440

ANNUAL EARNINGS AND DIVIDENDS PER SHARE

	6/30/94	6/30/93	6/30/92	6/30/91	6/30/90	6/30/89	6/30/88
Earnings Per Share	2.37	2.08	1.84	1.63	1.44	1.27	1.10
Dividends Per Share	0.56	0.49	0.43	[1] 0.375	0.325	0.28	0.24
Dividend Payout %	23.6	23.6	23.4	23.0	22.6	22.1	21.8

[1] Adj. for 2-for-1 stk. split, 5/1/91

ANNUAL FINANCIAL DATA

RECORD OF EARNINGS (IN MILLIONS):							
Total Revenues	2,469.0	2,223.4	1,940.6	1,771.8	1,714.0	1,677.7	1,549.2
Costs and Expenses	1,853.5	1,676.8	1,470.6	1,349.5	1,303.2	1,266.1	1,171.5
Depreciation & Amort	148.3	140.2	116.1	114.5	113.5	123.6	107.0
Operating Profit	628.0	538.8	465.3	405.4	387.4	377.5	344.2
Earn Bef Income Taxes	446.3	386.6	341.6	299.6	285.3	271.8	255.0
Income Taxes	112.2	92.4	85.4	71.9	73.6	84.2	84.7
Net Income	[1] 334.1	294.2	256.2	227.7	211.7	187.6	170.3
Aver. Shs. Outstg. (000)	140,890	141,327	139,045	139,936	147,168	148,448	155,118
[1] Before acctg. change dr$4,800,000.							
BALANCE SHEET (IN MILLIONS):							
Cash and Cash Equivalents	590.6	368.2	413.5	320.2	396.3	372.8	390.8
Receivables, Net	298.1	294.3	243.6	225.4	262.0	240.7	206.7
Gross Property	1,001.3	911.9	943.3	909.9	914.5	915.1	882.3
Accumulated Depreciation	605.4	550.7	586.7	537.6	514.2	482.3	460.0
Long-Term Debt	373.0	347.6	333.2	49.1	82.1	259.9	244.7
Net Stockholders' Equity	1,691.3	1,494.5	1,296.7	1,052.6	1,127.0	949.5	982.3
Total Assets	2,705.6	2,439.4	2,169.3	1,564.9	1,692.3	1,679.3	1,653.5
Total Current Assets	985.4	771.3	733.7	621.8	735.1	728.4	688.3
Total Current Liabilities	478.2	416.3	367.0	322.3	382.2	376.6	338.7
Net Working Capital	507.2	355.0	366.8	299.5	352.9	351.8	349.6
Yr End Com Shs Outstg (000)	140,699	141,119	140,151	138,227	147,652	145,504	154,512
STATISTICAL RECORD:							
Operating Profit Margin %	18.9	18.3	18.2	17.4	17.4	17.4	17.6
Book Value Per Share	7.69	6.51	5.29	5.75	6.27	5.05	4.96
Return on Equity %	19.8	19.7	19.8	21.6	18.8	19.8	17.3
Return on Assets %	12.3	12.1	11.8	14.5	12.5	11.2	10.3
Average Yield %	1.0	0.9	0.9	1.1	1.2	1.3	1.2
P/E Ratio	24.3-20.1	27.3-22.5	30.2-21.1	28.5-15.3	20.9-15.7	20.1-14.2	21.5-15.8
Price Range	57½-47⅝	56⅞-46⅞	55⅝-38¾	46⅜-25	30⅛-22⅝	25⅜-17⅞	23⅝-17⅜

Statistics are as originally reported.

OFFICERS:
J.S. Weston, Chmn. & C.E.O.
A.F. Weinbach, Pres. & C.O.O.
F.D. Anderson, Jr., V.P. & C.F.O.
J.B. Pirret, V.P. & Treas.

INCORPORATED: DE, Jun., 1961

PRINCIPAL OFFICE: One ADP Blvd., Roseland, NJ 07068-1728

TELEPHONE NUMBER: (201) 994-5000

NO. OF EMPLOYEES: 22,000 (approx.)

ANNUAL MEETING: In November

SHAREHOLDERS: 22,935

INSTITUTIONAL HOLDINGS:
No. of Institutions: 540
Shares Held: 98,543,171

REGISTRAR(S): Chemical Bank, New York, NY

TRANSFER AGENT(S): Chemical Bank, New York, NY

NYS SYMBOL AVE
Rec. Pr. 17⅞

AVEMCO CORP.

YIELD 2.5%
P/E RATIO 14.9

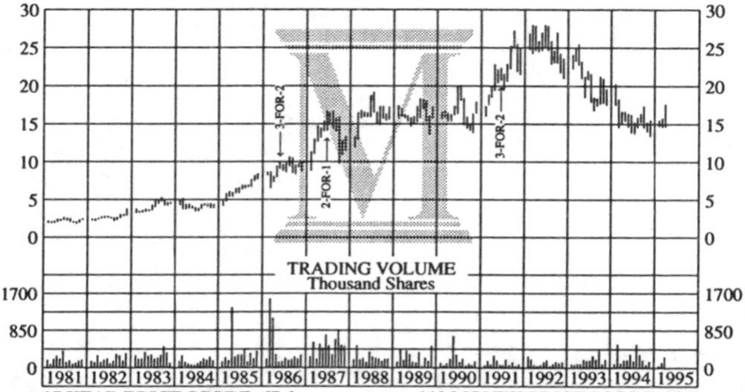

3-FOR-2
2-FOR-1
3-FOR-2
TRADING VOLUME
Thousand Shares
30
25
20
15
10
5
0
1700
850
0
1981
1982
1983
1984
1985
1986
1987
1988
1989
1990
1991
1992
1993
1994
1995

***7 YEAR PRICE SCORE 67.6** ***12 MONTH PRICE SCORE 98.6**

*NYSE COMPOSITE INDEX=100

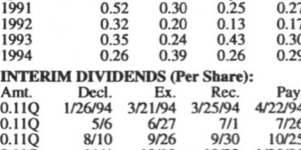

INTERIM EARNINGS (Per Share):

Qtr.	Mar.	June	Sept.	Dec.
1991	0.52	0.30	0.25	0.27
1992	0.32	0.20	0.13	0.17
1993	0.35	0.24	0.43	0.30
1994	0.26	0.39	0.26	0.29

INTERIM DIVIDENDS (Per Share):

Amt.	Decl.	Ex.	Rec.	Pay.
0.11Q	1/26/94	3/21/94	3/25/94	4/22/94
0.11Q	5/6	6/27	7/1	7/26
0.11Q	8/10	9/26	9/30	10/25
0.11Q	11/4	12/19	12/23	1/20/95
0.11Q	2/8/95	3/27/95	3/31/95	4/25

Indicated div.: $0.44

CAPITALIZATION (12/31/94):

	($000)	(%)
Total Debt	54,600	49.5
Common & Surplus	55,610	50.5
Total	110,210	100.0

DIVIDEND ACHIEVER STATUS:
Rank: 96 1984-94 Growth Rate: 13.0%
Total Years of Dividend Growth: 19

RECENT DEVELOPMENTS: For the year ended 12/31/94, net earnings decreased 25.9% to $10.8 million from $14.6 million, before a credit from accounting changes of $943,000, in 1993. Revenues for the twelve-month period were up slightly to $104.6 million, compared with $103.9 million the previous year. The Company reported nominal realized investment losses of $0.02 per share in 1994 compared with realized investment gains of $0.58 per share in 1993. Gross premiums written for all lines of business grew 10% to $90.6 million. AVE's statutory loss ratio was 61.3% versus 66.2% the prior year. The Company ended 1994 with an underwriting ratio of 89.9% compared with 95.6% in 1993. For the quarter ended 12/31/94, net earnings slid 7.3% to $2.6 million from $2.8 million in the comparable 1993 period. Revenues were up 1.1% to $25.5 million, compared with $25.2 million a year earlier.

BUSINESS

AVEMCO CORPORATION, a Delaware Corporation, is an insurance holding company organized in 1959, that coordinates the activities of its subsidiaries and provides them with management, business planning, human resource, marketing and financial services. The subsidiaries of the the Company are engaged in the business of providing specialty property and casualty insurance products and services, principally involving general aviation. Insurance products are distributed on a direct basis, through exclusive agents and through independent agents and brokers. AVEMCO Insurance Company (AIC), the largest of the AVEMCO Group subsidiaries, is the hub of the Group's insurance activities. AIC serves both as a direct writer of insurance and as the reinsurer for the major portion of the business produced and managed by other members of the AVEMCO Group. Other subsidiaries include National Aviation Underwriters, Inc., Eastern Aviation and Marine Underwriters, Inc., Matterhorn Bank Programs, Inc., Loss Management Services, Inc., Brooks-Shettle Company, MEDEX Assistance Corporaiton, and The Wheatley Group, Ltd.

ANNUAL EARNINGS AND DIVIDENDS PER SHARE

	1994	1993	1992	1991	1990	1989	1988
Earnings Per Share	**1.20**	**1.33**	**0.82**	**1.34**	**1.06**	**1.03**	**1.36**
Dividends Per Share	**0.44**	**0.41**	**0.40**	**[1] 0.347**	**0.273**	**0.257**	**0.207**
Dividend Payout %	**36.7**	**30.8**	**48.8**	**25.9**	**25.8**	**24.8**	**15.2**

[1] 3-for-2 stk split,06/17/91

ANNUAL FINANCIAL DATA

	1994	1993	1992	1991	1990	1989	1988
RECORD OF EARNINGS (IN THOUSANDS):							
Insurance Premiums	75,518	62,702	57,385	51,874	53,792	66,028	85,561
Total Interest Income	8,245	9,004	9,218	9,332	9,774	10,780	9,381
Total Revenues	104,590	103,901	86,923	84,540	79,257	93,299	106,405
Earn Bef Income Taxes	13,539	18,853	10,787	18,777	14,851	16,645	24,781
Income Taxes	2,706	4,224	1,184	3,367	2,396	3,014	6,259
Net Income	10,833	[1] 14,629	9,603	15,410	12,455	13,631	18,411
Aver. Shs. Outstg.	9,019	11,041	11,734	11,511	11,726	13,197	13,628
[1] Before acctg. change cr$943,000.							
BALANCE SHEET (IN THOUSANDS):							
Cash	5,191	2,918	2,358	983	346	366	1,006
Fixed Maturities	104,489	113,887	121,723	120,383	108,331	103,358	95,001
Equity Securities, At Mkt	21,619	16,721	21,971	22,816	28,835	36,667	31,877
Total Assets	205,192	210,693	203,158	194,065	184,543	191,213	202,918
Benefits and Claims	68,203	76,517	51,117	49,279	55,672	62,202	71,207
Net Stockholders' Equity	55,610	53,930	89,215	84,065	68,720	75,922	84,019
Year End Shares Outstg	8,850	9,109	11,493	11,417	11,098	11,927	13,238
STATISTICAL RECORD:							
Return on Equity %	19.5	27.1	10.8	18.3	18.1	18.0	21.9
Book Value Per Share	6.28	5.92	7.76	7.36	6.19	6.37	6.35
Average Yield %	2.6	1.9	1.6	1.6	1.6	1.6	1.3
P/E Ratio	16.9-11.1	19.2-12.6	34.1-25.6	20.3-11.9	19.0-13.1	17.8-13.2	14.1-8.7
Price Range	20¼-13⅜	25½-16¾	28-21	27¼-16	20⅛-13⅞	18⅜-13⅝	19⅛-11⅞

Statistics are as originally reported.

OFFICERS:
W.P. Condon, Chmn. & C.E.O.
J.F. Shettle, Jr., Pres. & C.O.O.
J.R. Yuska, Sr. V.P. & C.F.O.
T.H. Chero, Sr. V.P. & Sec.
T.E. Lentz, Treas.

INCORPORATED: DE, Nov., 1959

PRINCIPAL OFFICE: 411 Aviation Way, Frederick, MD 21701

TELEPHONE NUMBER: (301) 694-5700

FAX: (301) 694-4242

NO. OF EMPLOYEES: 428

ANNUAL MEETING: In May

SHAREHOLDERS: 3,500 approx.

INSTITUTIONAL HOLDINGS:
No. of Institutions: 51
Shares Held: 8,166,020

REGISTRAR(S): Chemical Bank, New York, NY

TRANSFER AGENT(S): Chemical Bank, New York, NY

NYS SYMBOL AVY
Rec. Pr. 42¼

AVERY DENNISON CORP.

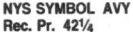

YIELD 2.6%
P/E RATIO 19.5

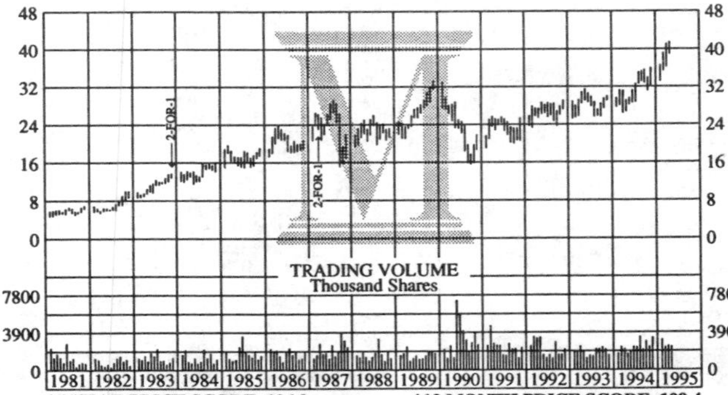

48
40
32
24
16
8
0
2-FOR-1
2-FOR-1
TRADING VOLUME
Thousand Shares
7800
3900
0
1981 1982 1983 1984 1985 1986 1987 1988 1989 1990 1991 1992 1993 1994 1995

*7 YEAR PRICE SCORE 106.3 *12 MONTH PRICE SCORE 109.4

*NYSE COMPOSITE INDEX=100

INTERIM EARNINGS (Per Share):

Qtr.	Mar.	June	Sept.	Jan.
1993	0.38	0.39	0.33	0.34
1994	0.45	0.50	0.50	0.52
1995	0.65	...	...	...

INTERIM DIVIDENDS (Per Share):

Amt.	Decl.	Ex.	Rec.	Pay.
0.24Q	4/29/94	5/25/94	6/1/94	6/15/94
0.24Q	7/28	8/31	9/7	9/21
0.27Q	10/27	12/1	12/7	12/21
0.27Q	1/26/95	2/23/95	3/1/95	3/15/95
0.27Q	4/27	6/1	6/7	6/21

*Indicated div.: $1.08**

CAPITALIZATION (12/31/94):

	($000)	(%)
Long-Term Debt	440,000	37.6
Common & Surplus	729,000	62.4
Total	1,169,000	100.0

DIVIDEND ACHIEVER STATUS:
Rank: 79 1984-94 Growth Rate: 13.9%
Total Years of Dividend Growth: 19

RECENT DEVELOPMENTS: For the year ended 12/31/94, net income was $109.4 million, a 30% increase from $83.3 million, before the cumulative effect of an accounting change, in the previous year. Net sales rose to $2.86 billion versus $2.61 billion in the year before. The pressure-sensitive adhesives and materials sector drove the boost in earnings and the subsequent increase of net income. Operations in the U.S. and abroad improved over the prior year.

PROSPECTS: Cost reductions, realignment of operations and expanding production capacity are all part of an ongoing capital expenditure plan. AVY is pushing into new markets and developing new product lines to take advantage of improving global economies, especially in the United States and Europe. Growth should continue in the pressure-sensitive adhesives and materials unit, which drove the revenue and earnings surge of the prior year.

BUSINESS

AVERY DENNISON CORP. was formed through the merger of Avery International Corp. (a California-based manufacturer of self adhesive base materials, labels, tapes, office products and specialty chemicals) and Dennison Manufacturing Co. (a Massachusetts-based manufacturer serving worldwide markets for stationery and office products, systems for identification and control and package decoration systems). Businesses from both companies continue to operate separately. The Company's operating groups are as follows: Materials North America, Materials Europe, Automotive & Graphic Systems Divisions, Specialty Tape Divisions, Chemical Divisions, Converting Europe, Label Divisions N.A., Soabar Products and Fastener Divisions and Office Products Group.

REVENUES

(12/31/94)	($000)	(%)
Adhesives & Materials	1,526,900	53.4
Office Products	805,800	28.2
Converted Products	614,700	21.5
Intersector	(103,600)	(3.6)
Divested Operations	12,900	0.5
Net Sales	2,856,700	100.0

ANNUAL EARNINGS AND DIVIDENDS PER SHARE

	12/31/94	1/1/94	1/2/93	1/4/92	12/31/90	11/30/89	11/30/88
Earnings Per Share	**1.97**	**1.44**	**1.33**	**1.02**	**0.10**	**1.96**	**1.77**
Dividends Per Share	**0.99**	**0.90**	**0.82**	**0.76**	**0.64**	**0.54**	**0.515**
Dividend Payout %	**50.3**	**62.5**	**61.7**	**74.5**	**N.M.**	**27.6**	**29.1**

ANNUAL FINANCIAL DATA

	12/31/94	1/1/94	1/2/93	1/4/92	12/31/90	11/30/89	11/30/88
RECORD OF EARNINGS (IN MILLIONS):							
Total Revenues	2,856.7	2,608.7	2,622.9	2,545.1	2,590.2	1,732.4	1,582.0
Costs and Expenses	2,538.3	2,337.9	2,356.5	2,319.7	2,453.8	1,520.5	1,385.2
Depreciation & Amort	102.5	95.4	93.9	83.1	80.8	50.3	45.1
Operating Profit	215.9	175.4	172.5	142.3	55.6	161.6	151.7
Inc Bef Taxes on Income	172.9	132.2	130.2	104.8	15.6	139.1	127.8
Income Taxes	63.5	48.9	50.1	41.8	9.7	52.6	50.1
Net Income	109.4	[1] 83.3	80.1	63.0	5.9	86.5	77.7
Aver. Shs. Outstg. (000)	55,600	58,000	60,400	61,900	62,000	44,200	44,000
[1] Before acctg. change cr$1,100,000.							
BALANCE SHEET (IN MILLIONS):							
Cash and Cash Equivalents	3.1	5.8	3.9	5.3	6.5	3.1	5.9
Receivables, Net	450.9	411.2	415.4	423.8	491.5	298.6	281.4
Inventories	206.4	184.1	225.1	253.1	325.0	193.8	202.2
Gross Property	1,532.3	1,412.7	1,399.2	1,420.7	1,395.7	758.3	711.9
Accumulated Depreciation	700.7	654.2	619.3	606.5	574.0	279.3	249.3
Long-Term Debt	440.0	402.1	334.8	329.5	376.0	213.2	214.7
Net Stockholders' Equity	729.0	719.1	802.6	825.0	846.3	538.6	509.4
Total Assets	1,763.1	1,639.0	1,684.0	1,740.4	1,890.3	1,142.1	1,119.1
Total Current Assets	676.9	614.6	661.3	700.5	846.8	505.7	502.5
Total Current Liabilities	554.1	473.0	438.7	474.5	548.0	324.1	329.6
Net Working Capital	122.8	141.6	222.6	226.0	298.8	181.6	172.9
Year End Shs Outstg (000)	53,550	56,194	58,875	61,253	61,980	44,232	44,081
STATISTICAL RECORD:							
Operating Profit Margin %	7.6	6.7	6.6	5.6	2.1	9.3	9.6
Book Value Per Share	11.23	10.50	11.29	11.07	11.21	9.10	8.45
Return on Equity %	15.0	11.6	10.0	7.6	0.7	16.1	15.3
Return on Assets %	6.2	5.1	4.8	3.6	0.3	7.6	6.9
Average Yield %	3.2	3.2	3.1	3.4	2.6	2.0	2.3
P/E Ratio	18.3-13.4	21.9-17.4	21.9-17.5	25.2-18.6	N.M	17.0-10.7	14.7-10.9
Price Range	36-26⅜	31½-25⅛	29⅛-23¼	25¾-19	33-15½	33¼-21	26-19¼

Statistics are as originally reported.

OFFICERS:
C.D. Miller, Chmn. & C.E.O.
P.M. Neal, Pres. & C.O.O.
R.G. Jenkins, Sr. V.P.-Finance & C.F.O.
W.H. Smith, V.P. & Treas.
R.G. Van Schoonenberg, V.P., Gen. Counsel & Sec.

INCORPORATED: DE, Sep., 1946

PRINCIPAL OFFICE: 150 N. Orange Grove Blvd., Pasadena, CA 91103-7090

TELEPHONE NUMBER: (818) 304-2000

NO. OF EMPLOYEES: 15,400 (approx.)

ANNUAL MEETING: In April

SHAREHOLDERS: 9,594

INSTITUTIONAL HOLDINGS:
No. of Institutions: 305
Shares Held: 36,484,468

REGISTRAR(S): Security Pacific National Bank, Los Angeles, CA 90060

TRANSFER AGENT(S): Security Pacific National Bank, Los Angeles, CA 90060

NYS SYMBOL ONE
Rec. Pr. 30¾

BANC ONE CORP.

YIELD 4.4%
P/E RATIO 12.6

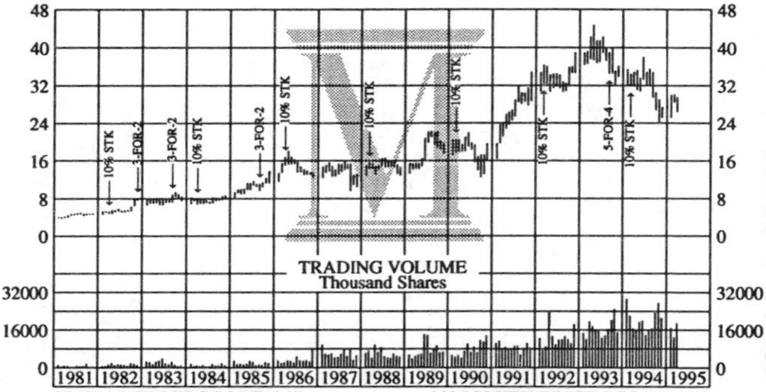

*7 YEAR PRICE SCORE 96.9 *12 MONTH PRICE SCORE 90.0

*NYSE COMPOSITE INDEX=100

INTERIM EARNINGS (Per Share):

Qtr.	Mar.	June	Sept.	Dec.
1991	0.55	0.58	0.58	0.62
1992	0.67	0.67	0.64	0.65
1993	0.77	0.73	0.82	0.53
1994	0.81	0.81	0.68	0.15

INTERIM DIVIDENDS (Per Share):

Amt.	Decl.	Ex.	Rec.	Pay.
0.31Q	4/19/94	6/9/94	6/15/94	6/30/94
0.31Q	7/19	9/9	9/15	9/30
0.31Q	10/18	12/9	12/15	1/2/95
0.34Q	1/24/95	3/9/95	3/15/95	3/31
0.34Q	4/18	6/13	6/15	6/30

Indicated div.: $1.36*

CAPITALIZATION (12/31/94):

	($000)	(%)
Total Deposits	68,090,054	77.3
Total Debt	11,488,217	13.1
Preferred Stock	249,900	0.3
Common & Surplus	7,314,960	8.3
Loan Valuation Reserve	897,180	1.0
Total	88,040,311	100.0

DIVIDEND ACHIEVER STATUS:
Rank: 61 1984-94 Growth Rate: 14.6%
Total Years of Dividend Growth: 24

RECENT DEVELOPMENTS: For the twelve months ended 12/31/94, income was $1.01 billion compared with $1.17 billion for 1993. Prior-year results were restated to reflect the acquisition of Liberty National Bancorp. Net interest income, on a fully-taxable equivalent basis, was $4.3 billion, down from $4.4 billion a year earlier. The net interest margin declined to 5.46% from 6.19%. Average earning assets increased by 11% to $78.3 billion from $70.6 billion.

PROSPECTS: The Company plans to reduce its workforce by 8.6% or 4,300 employees and close 100 branches in the Midwest. Solid loan demand is creating a competitive loan-pricing environment in the banking industry. However, the net interest margin is likely to be adversely affected by higher short-term interest rates. In August 1994, ONE acquired Liberty National Bancorp, a $5.3 billion multi-bank holding company headquartered in Louisville, KY.

BUSINESS

BANC ONE CORP. is an $88.9 billion bank holding company. In terms of assets, it ranks as the second-largest banking organization in Indiana and in Ohio and the third-largest in Wisconsin and Texas. The Company operates 69 affiliate banking organizations with 1,418 offices in Illinois, Indiana, Kentucky, Michigan, Ohio, Colorado, Arizona, Texas, West Virginia, Utah and Wisconsin. In addition, Banc One also operates affiliates that engage in data processing, venture capital, merchant banking, trust, investment management, brokerage, equipment leasing, consumer finance and insurance.

LOAN DISTRIBUTION

(12/31/94)	($000)	(%)
Comm, Finl & Agricultural	16,619,186	26.8
Commercial Real Estate	5,571,296	9.0
Construction Real Estate	2,195,003	3.5
Residential Real Estate	11,273,689	18.2
Consumer	19,070,286	30.7
Credit Card	5,924,383	9.6
Leases	1,339,069	2.2
Total	61,992,912	100.0

ANNUAL EARNINGS AND DIVIDENDS PER SHARE

	1994	1993	1992	1991	1990	1989	1988
Earnings Per Share	**2.42**	**2.93**	**2.62**	**2.33**	**2.01**	**1.83**	**1.72**
Dividends Per Share	**[1] 1.24**	**[2] 1.03**	**[3] 0.82**	**0.75**	**[4] 0.67**	**0.61**	**[5] 0.56**
Dividend Payout %	**51.2**	**35.2**	**31.3**	**32.2**	**33.3**	**33.3**	**32.6**

[1] 10% stk div, 3/4/94 [2] 5-for-4 stk split, 9/1/93 [3] 10% stk div, 2/10/92 [4] 10% stk div, 3/2/90 [5] 10% stk div, 3/88

ANNUAL FINANCIAL DATA

	1994	1993	1992	1991	1990	1989	1988
RECORD OF EARNINGS (IN MILLIONS):							
Total Interest Income	6,437.5	5,735.1	4,829.1	3,309.6	2,801.6	2,651.1	2,271.5
Total Interest Expense	2,248.8	1,645.0	1,664.2	1,538.9	1,560.6	1,534.7	1,211.0
Net Interest Income	4,188.6	4,090.1	3,165.0	1,770.7	1,240.9	1,116.3	1,060.5
Credit Loss Provision	242.3	368.5	510.5	424.4	300.3	197.5	183.4
Net Income	1,005.1	[1] 1,120.6	781.3	529.5	423.4	[2] 348.2	340.2
Aver. Shs. Outstg. (000)	407,380	376,828	290,204	220,823	209,356	196,804	195,733

[1] Before acctg. change cr$19,391,000. [2] Before acctg. change cr$14,626,000.

	1994	1993	1992	1991	1990	1989	1988
BALANCE SHEET (IN MILLIONS):							
Cash & Due From Banks	5,073.4	4,757.5	4,095.0	2,924.7	1,881.3	1,687.8	1,610.4
US Government Securities	...	...	7,713.4	4,446.0	3,094.4	2,937.6	1,258.9
Tax-exempt Securities	...	...	1,495.3	1,385.4	1,310.3	1,249.2	1,364.8
Loans & Lse Financing, Net	61,095.7	52,927.5	37,995.4	29,658.7	20,043.1	17,658.3	17,087.4
Total Domestic Deposits	68,090.1	60,943.2	48,464.7	37,057.0	22,316.0	20,952.2	19,501.8
Long-term Debt	1,866.4	1,701.7	1,197.5	703.1	581.0	371.6	378.9
Net Stockholders' Equity	7,564.9	7,033.6	5,213.5	3,814.1	2,899.5	2,279.2	2,040.8
Total Assets	88,922.6	79,918.6	61,417.4	46,293.1	30,336.0	26,552.2	25,273.7
Year End Shs Outstg (000)	396,986	380,687	290,102	230,750	218,398	198,014	195,482
STATISTICAL RECORD:							
Return on Assets %	1.13	1.40	1.27	1.14	1.40	1.31	1.35
Return on Equity %	13.30	15.90	15.00	13.90	14.60	15.30	16.70
Book Value Per Share	18.43	17.82	17.08	15.36	13.17	11.39	10.31
Average Yield %	4.0	2.7	2.4	2.9	3.9	3.4	3.1
P/E Ratio	15.7-10.0	15.3-11.0	14.8-11.7	15.0-7.1	10.9-6.2	12.6-7.6	9.7-7.5
Price Range	38-24⅛	44¾-32¼	38⅞-30⅝	34⅞-16½	21⅞-12½	22¼-13⅜	16⅝-12⅞

Statistics are as originally reported.

OFFICERS:
J.B. McCoy, Chmn. & C.E.O.
D.L. McWhorter, Pres. & C.O.O.
G.R. Meiling, Treas.
F.L. Cullen, C.F.O.

INCORPORATED: DE, Oct., 1967

PRINCIPAL OFFICE: 100 East Broad St., Columbus, OH 43271

TELEPHONE NUMBER: (614) 248-5944

NO. OF EMPLOYEES: 48,800 (approx.)

ANNUAL MEETING: In April

SHAREHOLDERS: 82,256

INSTITUTIONAL HOLDINGS:
No. of Institutions: 668
Shares Held: 181,426,942 (adj.)

REGISTRAR(S): Bank One, Indianapolis, N.A.,, Indianapolis, IN

TRANSFER AGENT(S): Bank One, Indianapolis, N.A.,, Indianapolis, IN

NYS SYMBOL BOH
Rec. Pr. 27⅝

BANCORP HAWAII, INC.

YIELD 3.8%
P/E RATIO 8.7

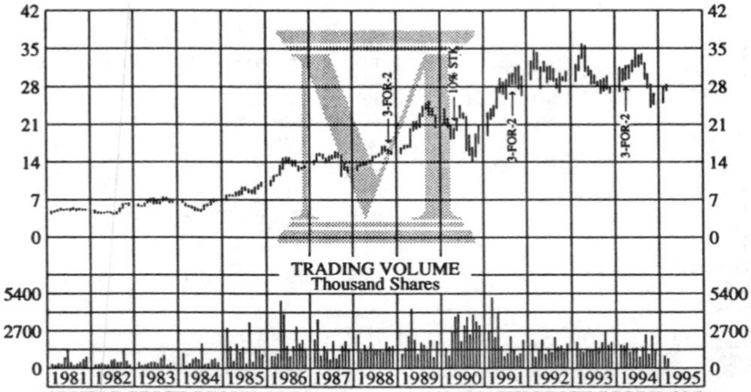

*7 YEAR PRICE SCORE 98.7 *12 MONTH PRICE SCORE 89.1

*NYSE COMPOSITE INDEX=100

INTERIM EARNINGS (Per Share):

Qtr.	Mar.	June	Sept.	Dec.
1991	0.96	1.01	1.02	1.07
1992	1.08	1.13	1.12	0.79
1993	0.77	0.79	0.70	0.83
1994	0.80	0.79	0.75	0.41

INTERIM DIVIDENDS (Per Share):

Amt.	Decl.	Ex.	Rec.	Pay.
50%	1/27/94	3/16/94	2/17/94	3/15/94
0.26Q	4/28	5/16	5/20	6/14
0.26Q	7/27	8/12	8/18	9/15
0.26Q	10/27	11/15	11/21	12/14
0.26Q	1/26/95	2/14/95	2/21/95	3/14/95

Indicated div.: $1.04*

CAPITALIZATION (12/31/94):

	($000)	(%)
Total Deposits	7,115,054	57.2
Total Debt	4,201,825	33.8
Common & Surplus	966,788	7.8
Loan Valuation Reserve	148,508	1.2
Total	12,432,175	100.0

DIVIDEND ACHIEVER STATUS:
Rank: 117 1984-94 Growth Rate: 12.2%
Total Years of Dividend Growth: 17

RECENT DEVELOPMENTS: For the year ended 12/31/94, net income decreased 11.2% to $117.7 million from $132.6 million in 1993. Total interest income was $813.0 million compared with $802.6 million the previous year. However, net interest income decreased 3.8% to $449.3 million from $467.2 million. Non-interest income fell 3.3% to $148.3 million from $153.3 million. Total non-performing assets dropped 22.7% to $53.2 million. The Company's reserve for loan losses at year-end totaled $148.5 million, up 18.5% from $125.3 million a year earlier. Return on average assets was 0.93% and return on average equity was 12.13%. As of 12/31/94, total assets grew 1.0% to $12.6 billion. BOH was challenged by a sluggish economy resulting from several interest rate hikes. For the quarter ended 12/31/94, net income fell 51.7% to $17.2 million from $35.7 million.

BUSINESS

BANCORP HAWAII, INC. has more than 115 offices throughout Hawaii, Asia and the Pacific. Its principal subsidiaries are the state's largest commercial bank, Bank of Hawaii; thrift holding company, Bancorp Pacific, Inc.; Arizona commercial bank, First National Bank of Arizona; and securities brokerage firm, Bancorp Investment Group, Ltd. The state's largest trust company, Hawaiian Trust Company, Ltd., along with leasing subsidiary Bancorp Leasing of Hawaii are subsidiaries of Bank of Hawaii. Bank of Hawaii has locations in Hawaii, the West and South Pacific, Taipei, Tokyo, Hong Kong, Singapore, Seoul, Manila, Cebu, Davao, New York and Nassau.

LOANS DISTRIBUTION

(12/31/94)	($000)	(%)
Commercial & Industrial	1,830,803	23.2
Construction loans	130,971	1.7
Mortgage loans	4,113,783	52.1
Installment	741,612	9.4
Foreign loans	696,734	8.8
Lease financing	378,090	4.8
Total	7,891,993	100.0

ANNUAL EARNINGS AND DIVIDENDS PER SHARE

	1994	1993	1992	1991	1990	1989	1988
Earnings Per Share	**2.75**	**3.09**	**2.75**	**2.69**	**2.42**	**2.15**	**3.18**
Dividends Per Share	**[1] 1.04**	**0.905**	**[2] 0.845**	**[3] 0.782**	**[4] 0.704**	**0.591**	**[5] 0.779**
Dividend Payout %	**37.8**	**29.3**	**30.8**	**29.0**	**28.8**	**27.0**	**36.7**

[1] 3-for-2 split, 3/94 [2] Bef. acctg. chge. [3] 3-for-2 stk split,09/16/91 [3] 10% stk div, 5/4/90 [5] 50% stk div, 11/88

ANNUAL FINANCIAL DATA

RECORD OF EARNINGS (IN MILLIONS):	1994	1993	1992	1991	1990	1989	1988
Total Interest Income	813.0	808.8	827.2	929.0	871.0	685.4	519.7
Total Interest Expense	363.7	335.4	386.5	521.1	521.0	399.1	278.1
Net Interest Income	449.3	473.4	440.7	407.9	350.1	286.3	241.6
Credit Loss Provision	21.9	54.2	50.1	29.6	28.0	20.9	30.9
Net Income	117.7	132.6	[1] 116.8	112.7	95.7	79.9	74.9
Aver. Shs. Outstg. (000)	42,825	42,968	42,528	41,846	39,504	37,076	35,310

[1] Before acctg. change cr$10,762,000.

BALANCE SHEET (IN MILLIONS):	1994	1993	1992	1991	1990	1989	1988
Cash & Non-int Bearing Deps	508.8	395.3	393.6	485.9	488.9	409.7	381.6
Loans & Lse Financing, Net	7,599.5	6,983.1	6,691.7	6,517.2	6,286.1	4,806.3	4,014.1
Total Domestic Deposits	5,964.2	6,170.8	6,726.3	7,882.7	7,692.7	5,950.1	4,981.8
Total Foreign Deposits	1,150.8	834.2	1,164.2	783.5	1,092.3	1,074.1	679.7
Long-term Debt	861.6	378.2	119.4	75.5	117.1	47.6	36.7
Net Stockholders' Equity	966.8	938.1	828.3	724.0	630.3	482.7	400.0
Total Assets	12,586.4	12,462.1	12,713.1	11,409.3	10,698.5	8,317.1	6,634.7
Year End Shs Outstg (000)	41,851	42,638	42,084	41,504	27,314	22,544	32,709
STATISTICAL RECORD:							
Return on Assets %	0.94	1.06	0.92	0.99	0.89	0.96	1.13
Return on Equity %	12.20	14.10	14.10	15.60	15.20	16.50	18.70
Book Value Per Share	23.10	22.00	19.68	17.44	23.07	21.41	12.23
Average Yield %	3.5	2.9	2.7	3.1	3.7	2.9	5.3
P/E Ratio	12.6-8.8	11.6-8.6	12.6-9.8	11.8-7.0	10.1-5.8	11.7-7.2	8.0-5.9
Price Range	34¾-24⅛	35⅞-26⅝	34⅝-26⅞	31⅞-18⅞	24½-14	25¼-15½	17-12½

Statistics are as originally reported.

OFFICERS:
L.M. Johnson, Chmn. & C.E.O.
R.J. Dahl, Pres.
D.A. Houle, Sr. V.P., Treas. & C.F.O.
R.E. Miyashiro, V.P. & Sec.

INCORPORATED: HI, Aug., 1971

PRINCIPAL OFFICE: Financial Plaza of The Pacific 130 Merchant Street, Honolulu, HI 96813

TELEPHONE NUMBER: (808) 537-8111

FAX: (808) 521-7602

NO. OF EMPLOYEES: 4,488

ANNUAL MEETING: In April

SHAREHOLDERS:

INSTITUTIONAL HOLDINGS:
No. of Institutions: 191
Shares Held: 17,580,635

REGISTRAR(S): Hawaiian Trust Co. Ltd., Honolulu, HI 96802
The Bank of New York, New York, NY

TRANSFER AGENT(S): Hawaiian Trust Co., Ltd., Honolulu, HI 96802
The Bank of New York, New York, NY

BANDAG, INC.

YIELD 1.3%
P/E RATIO 23.8

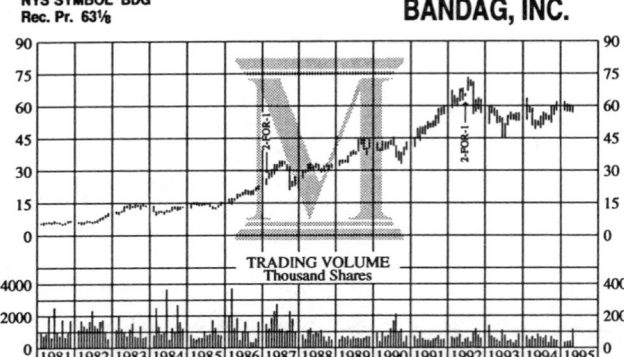

INTERIM EARNINGS (Per Share):

Qtr.	Mar.	June	Sept.	Dec.
1992	0.59	0.77	0.81	0.81
1993	0.51	0.70	0.83	0.84
1994	0.57	0.79	1.11	1.04
1995	0.75	...	...	...

INTERIM DIVIDENDS (Per Share):

Amt.	Decl.	Ex.	Rec.	Pay.
0.175Q	5/5/94	6/15/94	6/21/94	7/21/94
0.175Q	8/9	9/14	9/20	10/20
0.20Q	11/15	12/14	12/20	1/20/95
0.20Q	3/13/95	3/20/95	3/24/95	4/21
0.20Q	5/9	6/16	6/20	7/20

Indicated div.: $0.80*

CAPITALIZATION (12/31/94):

	($000)	(%)
Deferred Income Tax	22,545	4.9
Common & Surplus	434,049	95.1
Total	456,594	100.0

DIVIDEND ACHIEVER STATUS:
Rank: 168   1984-94 Growth Rate: 10.0%
Total Years of Dividend Growth: 18

TRADING VOLUME
Thousand Shares

*7 YEAR PRICE SCORE 95.4   *12 MONTH PRICE SCORE 98.4

*NYSE COMPOSITE INDEX=100

RECENT DEVELOPMENTS: For the quarter ended 12/31/94, net income jumped 20% to $27.6 million compared with $23.0 million for the same period last year. Sales rose 15% to $183.6 million from $160.4 million in the corresponding period. For the twelve months ended 12/31/94, net income advanced 19% to $94.0 million compared with $78.7 million for the same period a year ago. Revenues increased to $650.6 million from $590.2 million last year.

PROSPECTS: Bandag's European operations are leading the way with higher unit volume and profits. This is being accomplished through the elimination of exclusive territories and repositioning other franchises. In addition, an improving European economy and weak dollar are adding to earnings. Due to higher rubber prices and the fact that prices for new tires appear to be stabilizing at high levels, demand for retread tires is expected to strengthen.

BUSINESS

BANDAG, INCORPORATED engages in the manufacture of precured tread rubber, equipment, and supplies primarily for the retreading of truck and bus tires by a 'cold' bonding reaction. The Company also does some custom processing of rubber compounds and sells retread tires. Revenues are also generated by more than 1,200 franchised dealers in the U.S. as well as other foreign countries who are licensed to produce and market cold process retreads utilizing the Bandag process. The Company also operates Bandag ETA, a nationwide emergency roadside service.

BUSINESS LINE ANALYSIS

(12/31/94)	Rev(%)	Inc(%)
United States	64.0	83.0
Western Europe	17.0	4.5
Other	19.0	12.5
Total	100.0	100.0

ANNUAL EARNINGS AND DIVIDENDS PER SHARE

	1994	1993	1992	1991	1990	1989	1988
Earnings Per Share	3.51	2.88	2.99	2.86	2.75	2.61	2.34
Dividends Per Share	0.70	① 0.65	0.60	0.55	0.50	0.45	0.40
Dividend Payout %	19.9	22.6	20.1	19.2	18.2	17.2	17.1

① 2-for-1 stk split,06/10/92

ANNUAL FINANCIAL DATA

RECORD OF EARNINGS (IN THOUSANDS):

Total Revenues	665,692	601,059	602,388	593,917	595,853	535,159	498,109
Costs and Expenses	478,403	440,596	441,894	440,807	445,288	390,425	365,907
Depreciation & Amort	35,328	33,322	27,550	21,813	18,964	15,515	14,178
Operating Profit	151,961	127,141	132,944	131,297	131,601	129,219	118,024
Earn Bef Income Taxes	149,835	124,975	130,746	128,385	128,102	123,322	112,851
Income Taxes	55,841	46,241	47,723	48,786	49,319	47,395	43,096
Net Income	93,994	78,734	①83,023	79,599	78,783	75,927	69,755
Aver. Shs. Outstg.	26,801	27,337	27,743	27,842	28,632	29,076	29,830

① Before acctg. change dr$220,000.

BALANCE SHEET (IN THOUSANDS):

Cash and Cash Equivalents	83,383	83,047	36,767	37,183	11,321	4,869	7,018
Receivables, Net	199,287	181,716	187,286	199,663	186,376	162,564	158,461
Inventories	51,154	43,133	53,471	51,460	57,815	57,422	42,819
Gross Property	359,731	320,142	291,917	237,510	211,163	177,860	152,290
Accumulated Depreciation	207,973	173,521	149,622	126,410	113,168	92,739	80,082
Net Stockholders' Equity	434,049	413,092	334,610	297,052	235,953	212,793	158,121
Total Assets	582,146	550,731	469,239	442,157	392,166	347,247	314,761
Total Current Assets	344,879	316,141	284,593	293,746	260,160	228,749	212,238
Total Current Liabilities	113,300	102,542	115,633	117,617	126,241	107,355	128,198
Net Working Capital	231,579	213,599	168,960	176,129	133,919	121,394	84,040
Year End Shares Outstg	26,801	27,152	27,292	27,737	27,732	28,960	29,277

STATISTICAL RECORD:

Operating Profit Margin %	22.8	21.2	22.1	22.1	22.1	24.1	23.7
Return on Equity %	21.7	19.1	24.8	26.8	33.4	35.7	44.1
Return on Assets %	16.1	14.3	17.7	18.0	20.1	21.9	22.2
Average Yield %	1.2	1.2	0.9	1.1	1.3	1.2	1.3
P/E Ratio	18.1-14.0	20.9-15.5	24.5-18.7	21.0-14.2	16.5-12.0	17.1-12.3	14.4-11.3
Price Range	63½-49⅛	60¼-44¾	73¼-56	60-40¾	45½-33	44⅝-32⅛	33¾-26⅜

Statistics are as originally reported.

OFFICERS:
M.G. Carver, Chmn., C.E.O. & Pres.
T.E. Dvorchak, Sr. V.P. & C.F.O.
W.W. Heidbreder, V.P.-Legal & Tax Admin. & Sec.
L.A. Carver, Treas.

INCORPORATED: IA, Dec., 1957

PRINCIPAL OFFICE: 2905 North Highway 61, Muscatine, IA 52761-5886

TELEPHONE NUMBER: (319) 262-1400

FAX: (319) 262-1284

NO. OF EMPLOYEES: 2,502

ANNUAL MEETING: In May

SHAREHOLDERS: 4,529

INSTITUTIONAL HOLDINGS:
No. of Institutions: 160
Shares Held: 6,498,019

REGISTRAR(S): First National Bank of Boston, Shareholder Services Division, Boston, MA

TRANSFER AGENT(S): First National Bank of Boston, Shareholder Services Division, Boston, MA

BANKERS TRUST NEW YORK CORP.

YIELD	7.5%
P/E RATIO	7.5

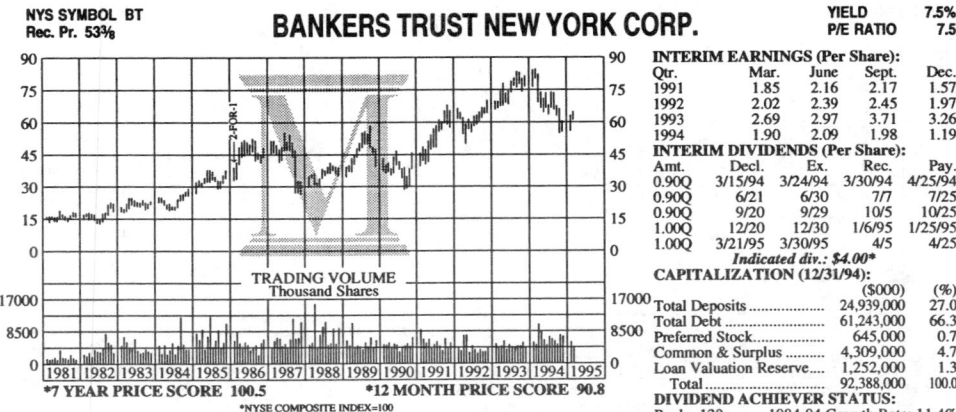

7 YEAR PRICE SCORE 100.5   **12 MONTH PRICE SCORE 90.8**

*NYSE COMPOSITE INDEX=100

INTERIM EARNINGS (Per Share):

Qtr.	Mar.	June	Sept.	Dec.
1991	1.85	2.16	2.17	1.57
1992	2.02	2.39	2.45	1.97
1993	2.69	2.97	3.71	3.26
1994	1.90	2.09	1.98	1.19

INTERIM DIVIDENDS (Per Share):

Amt.	Decl.	Ex.	Rec.	Pay.
0.90Q	3/15/94	3/24/94	3/30/94	4/25/94
0.90Q	6/21	6/30	7/7	7/25
0.90Q	9/20	9/29	10/5	10/25
1.00Q	12/20	12/30	1/6/95	1/25/95
1.00Q	3/21/95	3/30/95	4/5	4/25

*Indicated div.: $4.00**

CAPITALIZATION (12/31/94):

	($000)	(%)
Total Deposits	24,939,000	27.0
Total Debt	61,243,000	66.3
Preferred Stock	645,000	0.7
Common & Surplus	4,309,000	4.7
Loan Valuation Reserve	1,252,000	1.3
Total	92,388,000	100.0

DIVIDEND ACHIEVER STATUS:
Rank: 130   1984-94 Growth Rate: 11.4%
Total Years of Dividend Growth: 16

RECENT DEVELOPMENTS: For the year ended 12/31/94, net income was $615 million, down significantly from the $1.07 billion earned in 1993. The decline in earnings was attributed to unsettled market conditions. Net interest revenue was $1.17 billion, down 10.8% from $1.31 billion a year ago. Noninterest revenue fell to $2.47 billion or 26.5% from the $3.36 billion earned in 1993. Results were hammered by a $1.17 billion drop in trading revenue to $465 million.

PROSPECTS: In reclassifying $423 million in derivative contracts as receivables in the loan account, BT expects to leverage the effects of these contracts by charging anticipated losses to the allowance for credit losses instead of to net income. In September 1994, civil lawsuits were filed against the Company by Gibson Greetings Inc. and Procter & Gamble claiming BT misrepresented the risks associated with derivative products.

BUSINESS

BANKERS TRUST NEW YORK CORP. is a bank holding company whose principal subsidiary is Bankers Trust Company. As of 12/31/94, BT had consolidated assets of $97 billion, making it one of the largest bank holding companies in the United States. Bankers Trust is a commercial bank, providing banking and trust services to financial institutions, governments, and individuals of high net worth.

LOAN DISTRIBUTION

(12/31/94)	($000)	(%)
Commercial &		
Industrial	2,218,000	17.6
Financial Institutions	2,221,000	17.6
Real Estate		
Construction	234,000	1.9
Real Estate Mortgage	1,126,000	8.9
Other Domestic	1,044,000	8.3
International	5,760,000	45.7
Total	12,603,000	100.0

ANNUAL EARNINGS AND DIVIDENDS PER SHARE

	1994	1993	1992	1991	1990	1989	1988
Earnings Per Share	7.17	12.40	8.82	7.75	7.80	d12.10	8.09
Dividends Per Share	3.60	3.12	2.80	2.54	2.33	2.08	1.86
Dividend Payout %	50.2	25.2	31.7	32.8	29.9	...	23.0

ANNUAL FINANCIAL DATA

RECORD OF EARNINGS (IN MILLIONS):

	1994	1993	1992	1991	1990	1989	1988
Total Interest Income	5,030.0	4,436.0	4,219.0	4,322.0	5,592.0	6,220.0	4,590.0
Total Interest Expense	3,858.0	3,122.0	3,072.0	3,585.0	4,799.0	4,446.0	3,265.0
Net Interest Income	1,172.0	1,314.0	1,147.0	737.0	793.0	1,774.0	1,325.0
Credit Loss Provision	25.0	93.0	225.0	238.0	194.0	1,877.0	50.0
Net Income	615.0	① 1,070.0	761.0	667.0	665.0	d980.0	648.0
Aver. Shs. Outstg. (000)	82,000	84,000	83,000	82,000	81,000	82,000	80,000

① Before acctg. change dr$75,000,000.

BALANCE SHEET (IN MILLIONS):

	1994	1993	1992	1991	1990	1989	1988
Cash & Due From Banks	1,985.0	1,750.0	1,384.0	1,747.0	4,149.0	3,331.0	3,618.0
Loans & Lse Financing, Net	11,249.0	13,876.0	15,698.0	15,241.0	19,305.0	18,421.0	22,801.0
Total Domestic Deposits	9,054.0	10,305.0	10,188.0	9,181.0	13,099.0	13,195.0	13,284.0
Total Foreign Deposits	15,885.0	12,471.0	14,883.0	13,653.0	15,489.0	13,025.0	19,206.0
Long-term Debt	6,455.0	5,597.0	3,992.0	3,081.0	2,650.0	2,435.0	2,450.0
Net Stockholders' Equity	4,954.0	4,784.0	3,809.0	3,412.0	3,024.0	2,386.0	3,498.0
Total Assets	97,016.0	92,082.0	72,448.0	63,959.0	63,596.0	55,658.0	57,943.0
Year End Shs Outstg (000)	78,000	81,000	83,000	82,000	81,000	81,000	81,000

STATISTICAL RECORD:

	1994	1993	1992	1991	1990	1989	1988
Return on Assets %	0.63	1.16	1.05	1.04	1.05	...	1.12
Return on Equity %	12.40	22.40	20.00	19.50	22.00	...	18.50
Book Value Per Share	55.24	52.89	39.87	35.51	31.16	26.37	43.19
Average Yield %	5.2	4.2	4.7	4.7	6.2	4.5	5.2
P/E Ratio	11.8-7.6	6.7-5.3	8.0-5.7	8.9-5.2	6.0-3.7	...	5.1-3.7
Price Range	84⅝-54¾	83½-65¾	70⅛-50	68-39½	46¾-28½	58¼-34½	41¼-29⅝

Statistics are as originally reported.

OFFICERS:
C.S. Sanford, Chmn. & C.E.O.
G.J. Vojta, Vice-Chmn.
E.B. Shanks, Jr., Pres.
T.T. Yates, Exec. V.P., C.F.O. & Contr.
J.T. Byrne, Jr., Sr. V.P. & Sec.
INCORPORATED: NY, May, 1965
PRINCIPAL OFFICE: 280 Park Avenue, New York, NY 10017

TELEPHONE NUMBER: (212) 250-2500
NO. OF EMPLOYEES: 14,529
ANNUAL MEETING: In April
SHAREHOLDERS: 21,973 (approx.)
INSTITUTIONAL HOLDINGS:
No. of Institutions: 504
Shares Held: 64,050,719

REGISTRAR(S): Bankers Trust Company, New York, NY 10015

TRANSFER AGENT(S): Bankers Trust Company of California, New York, NY 10017

BARD (C.R.), INC.

YIELD 2.1%
P/E RATIO 20.1

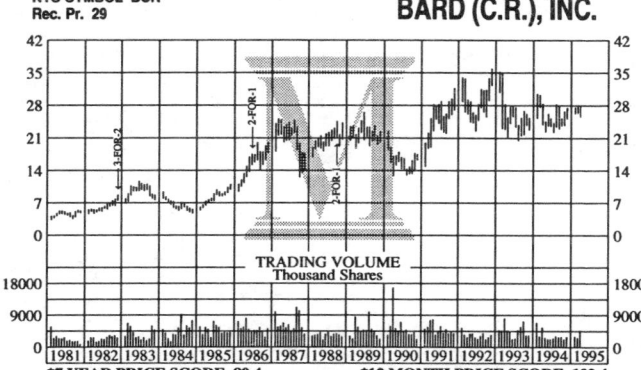

TRADING VOLUME
Thousand Shares

| 1981 | 1982 | 1983 | 1984 | 1985 | 1986 | 1987 | 1988 | 1989 | 1990 | 1991 | 1992 | 1993 | 1994 | 1995 |

*7 YEAR PRICE SCORE 89.4   *12 MONTH PRICE SCORE 102.4
*NYSE COMPOSITE INDEX=100

INTERIM EARNINGS (Per Share):

Qtr.	Mar.	June	Sept.	Dec.
1991	0.26	0.27	0.26	0.29
1992	0.32	0.34	0.36	0.40
1993	0.51	0.39	d0.48	0.77
1994	0.44	0.45	0.44	0.11

INTERIM DIVIDENDS (Per Share):

Amt.	Decl.	Ex.	Rec.	Pay.
0.14Q	1/12/94	1/18/94	1/24/94	2/4/94
0.14Q	4/20	4/26	5/2	5/13
0.15Q	7/13	7/19	7/25	8/5
0.15Q	10/12	10/18	10/24	11/4
0.15Q	12/14	1/17/95	1/23/95	2/3/95

*Indicated div.: $0.60**

CAPITALIZATION (12/31/94):

	($000)	(%)
Long-Term Debt	78,300	15.1
Common & Surplus	439,800	84.9
Total	518,100	100.0

DIVIDEND ACHIEVER STATUS:
Rank: 26   1984-94 Growth Rate: 18.6%
Total Years of Dividend Growth: 23

RECENT DEVELOPMENTS: For the year ended 12/31/94, net income increased 20.4% to $74.9 million from $62.1 million the prior year. Sales were up 4.9% to $1.02 billion, compared with $970.8 million in 1993. Earnings included non-recurring charges of $16.9 million in 1994 and $26.0 million in 1993. Gross margin improved to 51.2% from 50.9% due to cost-reduction programs and a more favorable product mix. Research and development expenditures rose 5% to $69.8 million.

PROSPECTS: BCR's earnings will be pressured by increased competition between medical device manufacturers in a market of declining patient procedures and hospital device expenditures. In addition, the trend toward consolidation of buying groups and hospital partnerships continues to place pressure on prices. However, urological sales will benefit from the international rollout of Contigen, a treatment for urinary incontinence.

BUSINESS

BARD (C.R.), INC. is a multinational developer, manufacturer and marketer of health care products. The Company engages in the design, manufacture, packaging, distribution and sale of medical, surgical, diagnostic and patient-care devices. Bard holds strong positions in cardiovascular, urological, surgical and general health care products. BCR products are marketed worldwide to hospitals, individual health care professionals, extended care facilities, alternate site facilities and the home, employing a combination of direct delivery and medical specialty distributors. Hospitals, physicians and nursing homes purchase approximately 90% of the Company's products. The Cardiovascular Group accounted for 36% of 1994 sales; Surgical, 35%; and Urological, 29%.

BUSINESS LINE ANALYSIS

(12/31/94)	Rev(%)	Inc(%)
United States	74.4	63.9
Foreign	25.6	36.1
Total	100.0	100.0

ANNUAL EARNINGS AND DIVIDENDS PER SHARE

	1994	1993	1992	1991	1990	1989	1988
Earnings Per Share	1.44	1.19	1.42	1.08	0.76	1.18	1.38
Dividends Per Share	0.58	0.54	0.50	0.46	0.42	0.36	0.28
Dividend Payout %	40.3	45.4	35.2	42.6	55.3	30.5	20.3

ANNUAL FINANCIAL DATA

RECORD OF EARNINGS (IN MILLIONS):

	1994	1993	1992	1991	1990	1989	1988
Total Revenues	1,018.2	970.8	990.2	876.0	785.3	777.8	757.5
Costs and Expenses	827.9	806.8	832.2	753.5	691.0	637.9	605.6
Depreciation & Amort	39.6	35.5	35.6	29.5	27.5	24.0	23.5
Operating Income	150.7	128.5	122.4	93.0	66.8	115.9	128.4
Income Before Taxes	103.0	98.9	107.0	76.9	58.5	103.2	123.8
Income Taxes	28.1	36.8	32.0	19.7	18.2	37.8	45.1
Net Income	74.9	①62.1	75.0	57.2	40.3	65.4	78.7
Aver. Shs. Outstg. (000)	52,005	52,197	52,197	52,909	53,063	53,266	55,419	57,047
① Before acctg. change dr$6,100,000.							

BALANCE SHEET (IN MILLIONS):

	1994	1993	1992	1991	1990	1989	1988
Cash and Cash Equivalents	34.2	75.0	49.8	33.8	19.9	11.1	24.3
Receivables, Net	187.3	167.3	178.8	157.2	143.0	131.2	132.9
Inventories	199.2	173.5	181.8	176.6	171.8	155.1	151.0
Gross Property	312.3	260.9	253.0	244.4	230.5	217.7	196.8
Accumulated Depreciation	112.4	92.0	90.2	86.8	83.0	78.1	66.0
Long-Term Debt	78.3	68.5	68.6	68.9	69.8	70.3	41.2
Net Stockholders' Equity	439.8	383.1	392.4	365.7	342.2	333.6	328.6
Total Assets	958.4	798.6	712.5	657.6	612.8	562.6	531.0
Total Current Assets	428.0	421.5	416.9	373.9	341.4	304.8	314.2
Total Current Liabilities	364.6	264.3	215.0	189.9	170.8	123.0	127.7
Net Working Capital	63.4	157.2	201.9	184.0	170.6	181.8	186.5
Year End Shs Outstg (000)	52,048	52,098	52,839	53,019	53,044	54,517	61,362

STATISTICAL RECORD:

	1994	1993	1992	1991	1990	1989	1988
Operating Profit Margin %	14.8	13.2	12.4	10.6	8.5	14.9	17.0
Book Value Per Share	3.35	4.49	5.94	5.81	5.30	5.00	5.13
Return on Equity %	17.0	16.2	19.1	15.6	11.8	19.6	24.0
Return on Assets %	7.8	7.8	10.5	8.7	6.6	11.6	14.8
Average Yield %	2.2	1.9	1.7	2.0	2.4	1.6	1.3
P/E Ratio	21.2-15.5	29.6-17.2	25.3-15.8	29.4-13.8	29.6-16.9	22.5-15.9	17.8-12.2
Price Range	30½-22¼	35¼-20½	35⅞-22½	31¾-14⅞	22½-12⅞	26½-18¾	24⅝-16⅞

Statistics are as originally reported.

OFFICERS:
W.H. Longfield, Pres. & C.E.O.
W.C. Bopp, Sr. V.P. & C.F.O.
R.A. Flink, V.P., Gen. Coun. & Sec.
E.L. Parker, V.P. & Treas.

INCORPORATED: NJ, Feb., 1972

PRINCIPAL OFFICE: 730 Central Ave., Murray Hill, NJ 07974

TELEPHONE NUMBER: (908) 277-8000

NO. OF EMPLOYEES: 8,650 (approx.)

ANNUAL MEETING: In April

SHAREHOLDERS: 7,985 (approx.)

INSTITUTIONAL HOLDINGS:
No. of Institutions: 295
Shares Held: 34,048,183

REGISTRAR(S): First Chicago Trust Co. of New York, New York, NY 10008

TRANSFER AGENT(S): First Chicago Trust Co. of New York, New York, NY 10008

BAXTER INTERNATIONAL INC.

YIELD 3.1%
P/E RATIO 16.0

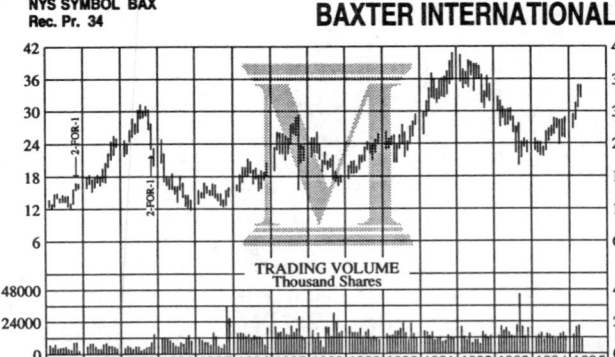

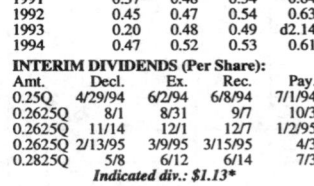

TRADING VOLUME
Thousand Shares

| 1981 | 1982 | 1983 | 1984 | 1985 | 1986 | 1987 | 1988 | 1989 | 1990 | 1991 | 1992 | 1993 | 1994 | 1995 |

*7 YEAR PRICE SCORE 84.8   *12 MONTH PRICE SCORE 112.5
*NYSE COMPOSITE INDEX=100

INTERIM EARNINGS (Per Share):

Qtr.	Mar.	June	Sept.	Dec.
1991	0.37	0.48	0.54	0.64
1992	0.45	0.47	0.54	0.63
1993	0.20	0.48	0.49	d2.14
1994	0.47	0.52	0.53	0.61

INTERIM DIVIDENDS (Per Share):

Amt.	Decl.	Ex.	Rec.	Pay.
0.25Q	4/29/94	6/2/94	6/8/94	7/1/94
0.2625Q	8/1	8/31	9/7	10/3
0.2625Q	11/14	12/1	12/7	1/2/95
0.2625Q	2/13/95	3/9/95	3/15/95	4/3
0.2825Q	5/8	6/12	6/14	7/3

Indicated div.: $1.13*

CAPITALIZATION (12/31/94):

	($000)	(%)
Long-Term Debt	2,341,000	38.6
Common & Surplus	3,720,000	61.4
Total	6,061,000	100.0

DIVIDEND ACHIEVER STATUS:
Rank: 114   1984-94 Growth Rate: 12.3%
Total Years of Dividend Growth: 38

RECENT DEVELOPMENTS: For the year ended 12/31/94, net income amounted to $596 million compared with a loss of $268 million in 1993. The prior-year loss included pre-tax charges of $1.03 billion associated with restructuring and litigation charges. Sales were up 4.4% to $9.32 billion from $8.88 billion a year earlier. Baxter completed the sale of its diagnostic-products manufacturing business to Bain Capital for approximately $415 million.

PROSPECTS: The Company is generating strong cash flows from operations. Cash flow will be used to repurchase stock and reduce debt levels. Baxter is performing well in a difficult healthcare environment. Competition for patients among healthcare providers is becoming more intense. Trends toward consolidation in the Company's customer base and competitors is expected to continue. These conditions are inhibiting BAX's ability to increase prices.

BUSINESS

BAXTER INTERNATIONAL INC. is engaged in the development, distribution, and manufacture of a diversified line of products, systems and services used primarily in the healthcare field. The Medical Specialties segment develops and markets specialized medical products used for cardiac care, dialysis therapy, diagnostic testing, and blood processing. The Medical/Laboratory Products and Distribution segment manufactures and markets products for educational and government laboratories, industrial research and development facilities, and manufacturing facilities. The Company distributes and manufactures a broad range of products to hospitals, other health care providers and clinical laboratories. Medical specialties was responsible for 38% of sales in 1994 and Medical/laboratory products and distribution, 62%.

REVENUES

(12/31/94)	($000)	(%)
Medical Specialties ...	3,557	38.1
Medical/Laboratory Prods.	5,767	61.9
Total	9,324	100.0

ANNUAL EARNINGS AND DIVIDENDS PER SHARE

	1994	1993	1992	1991	1990	1989	1988
Earnings Per Share	2.13	d0.97	① 1.99	2.03	d0.05	1.50	1.31
Dividends Per Share	1.012	0.965	② 0.83	0.715	0.62	0.545	0.485
Dividend Payout %	47.5	...	41.7	35.2	...	36.3	37.0

① Before disc. oper. ② Bef discont opers

ANNUAL FINANCIAL DATA

RECORD OF EARNINGS (IN MILLIONS):

	1994	1993	1992	1991	1990	1989	1988
Total Revenues	9,324.0	8,879.0	8,471.0	8,921.0	8,100.0	7,399.0	6,861.0
Costs and Expenses	8,234.0	8,573.0	7,359.0	7,765.0	7,671.0	6,565.0	6,125.0
Depreciation & Amort	524.0	494.0	447.0	427.0	383.0	368.0	335.0
Operating Profit	1,366.0	1,276.0	1,362.0	1,088.0	362.0	766.0	668.0
Income Bef Income Taxes	801.0	d330.0	753.0	805.0	105.0	637.0	518.0
Income Taxes	205.0	cr62.0	192.0	214.0	65.0	191.0	130.0
Net Income	596.0	① d268.0	② 561.0	591.0	40.0	446.0	388.0
Aver. Shs. Outstg. (000)	280,000	277,000	279,000	280,000	253,000	282,000	277,000

① Before acctg. change cr$70,000,000. ② Before disc. op. cr$45,000,000; and acctg. chg dr$165,000,000.

BALANCE SHEET (IN MILLIONS):

	1994	1993	1992	1991	1990	1989	1988
Cash and Cash Equivalents	471.0	479.0	32.0	328.0	40.0	67.0	201.0
Receivables, Net	2,187.0	2,017.0	1,799.0	1,939.0	1,743.0	1,743.0	1,437.0
Inventories	1,537.0	1,772.0	1,632.0	1,596.0	1,532.0	1,502.0	1,512.0
Gross Property	4,431.0	4,491.0	4,209.0	3,966.0	3,526.0	3,151.0	2,935.0
Accumulated Depreciation	1,869.0	1,836.0	1,562.0	1,511.0	1,357.0	1,048.0	911.0
Long-Term Debt	2,341.0	2,800.0	2,433.0	2,249.0	1,729.0	2,052.0	2,246.0
Net Stockholders' Equity	3,720.0	3,185.0	3,795.0	4,373.0	4,092.0	4,246.0	4,041.0
Total Assets	10,002.0	10,545.0	9,155.0	9,340.0	8,517.0	8,503.0	8,550.0
Total Current Assets	4,340.0	4,422.0	3,589.0	4,004.0	3,443.0	3,424.0	3,323.0
Total Current Liabilities	2,766.0	2,933.0	2,368.0	2,357.0	2,324.0	1,859.0	1,886.0
Net Working Capital	1,574.0	1,489.0	1,221.0	1,647.0	1,119.0	1,565.0	1,437.0
Year End Shs Outstg (000)	282,000	277,000	279,000	279,000	279,000	249,000	246,000

STATISTICAL RECORD:

	1994	1993	1992	1991	1990	1989	1988
Operating Profit Margin %	11.0	2.7	12.3	12.2	4.5	10.4	9.7
Book Value Per Share	5.07	2.51	4.68	5.49	4.28	2.96	1.59
Return on Equity %	16.0	...	14.8	13.5	1.0	10.5	9.8
Return on Assets %	6.0	...	6.1	6.3	0.5	5.2	4.5
Average Yield %	4.0	3.7	2.3	2.2	2.5	2.5	2.3
P/E Ratio	13.6-10.2	...	20.4-15.3	20.1-12.6	...	17.3-11.7	19.9-12.4
Price Range	28⅞-21⅝	32¾-20	40½-30½	40⅞-25⅝	29½-20½	25⅞-17½	26¼-16¼

Statistics are as originally reported.

OFFICERS:
W.B. Graham, Senior Chmn.
V.R. Loucks, Jr., Chmn. & C.E.O.
H.M. Jansen Kraemer, Jr., Sr. V.P. & C.F.O.
L.D. Damron, Treas.

INCORPORATED: DE, Oct., 1931

PRINCIPAL OFFICE: One Baxter Parkway, Deerfield, IL 60015

TELEPHONE NUMBER: (708) 948-2000

FAX: (708) 948-3948

NO. OF EMPLOYEES:

ANNUAL MEETING: In May

SHAREHOLDERS:

INSTITUTIONAL HOLDINGS:
No. of Institutions: 654
Shares Held: 179,728,242

REGISTRAR(S): First Chicago Trust Co. of New York, New York, NY 10008

TRANSFER AGENT(S): First Chicago Trust Co. of New York, New York, NY 10008

NYS SYMBOL BGC
Rec. Pr. 24¼

BAY STATE GAS CO.

YIELD 6.0%
P/E RATIO 13.9

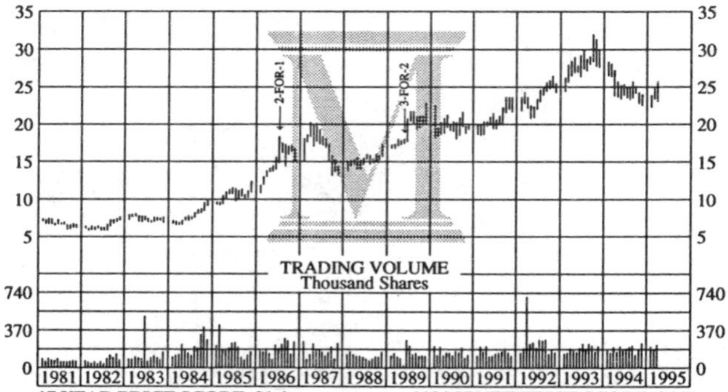

***7 YEAR PRICE SCORE 91.4** ***12 MONTH PRICE SCORE 96.7**

*NYSE COMPOSITE INDEX=100

INTERIM EARNINGS (Per Share):

Qtr.	Dec.	Mar.	June	Sept.
1991-92	0.91	1.44	d0.22	d0.53
1992-93		1.75		
1993-94	0.91	1.75	d0.24	d0.54
1994-95	0.78	...	...	...

INTERIM DIVIDENDS (Per Share):

Amt.	Decl.	Ex.	Rec.	Pay.
0.355Q	1/27/94	2/8/94	2/14/94	3/1/94
0.365Q	4/28	5/12	5/18	6/1
0.365Q	7/28	8/12	8/18	9/1
0.365Q	10/27	11/9	11/16	12/1
0.365Q	1/26/95	2/9/95	2/15/95	3/1/95

Indicated div.: $1.46*

CAPITALIZATION (9/30/94):

	($000)	(%)
Long-Term Debt	191,000	39.7
Deferred Income Tax	69,198	14.4
Preferred Stock	5,293	1.1
Common & Surplus	215,389	44.8
Total	480,880	100.0
Current Debt	37,750	

DIVIDEND ACHIEVER STATUS:
Rank: 269 1984-94 Growth Rate: 5.7%
Total Years of Dividend Growth: 10

RECENT DEVELOPMENTS: For the quarter ended 12/31/94, net income fell to $10.5 million compared with $11.8 million in the same period a year earlier. Revenues declined to $115.8 million from $136.1 million a year ago. Weather, which was 12.5% warmer than the year-earlier period, was the primary contributor to lower gas revenues and earnings. The negative effect of the weather was partially offset by a 6.7% decline in operating and maintenance expenses.

PROSPECTS: The restructuring of the natural gas industry will provide many opportunities for Bay State in the future. However, short-term earnings may be squeezed by lower conversion rates from heating oil to gas. Growth in earnings is likely due to increased residential construction in BGC's service territory, a low residential heating penetration rate of 37%, and a rebounding economy. Additionally, BGC's has low operating costs.

BUSINESS

BAY STATE GAS COMPANY is the largest independent natural gas distributor in New England. Bay State Gas serves Brockton, Springfield, Lawrence and 57 surrounding towns and cities in Massachusetts. Northern Utilities, Inc., a wholly-owned subsidiary, serves the Portsmouth area of New Hampshire and the Portland and Lewiston areas of Maine. The Company also supplies wholesale gas to other utilities in Massachusetts and neighboring states. Another subsidiary, Granite State Gas Transmission, Inc. owns and operates interstate gas pipelines in New England. In addition, Bay State Gas invests in cogeneration opportunities and is active in the retail sale of propane and home improvement products.

QUARTERLY DATA

(9/30/94)($000)	Rev	Inc
1st Quarter	136,137	11,798
2nd Quarter	205,589	22,819
3rd Quarter	64,781	(3,037)
4th Quarter	44,712	(7,095)

ANNUAL EARNINGS AND DIVIDENDS PER SHARE

	9/30/94	9/30/93	9/30/92	9/30/91	9/30/90	9/30/89	9/30/88
Earnings Per Share	**1.85**	**1.75**	**1.41**	**1.32**	**1.78**	**1.81**	**1.72**
Dividends Per Share	**1.45**	**1.41**	**1.37**	**1.325**	**1.26**	**[1] 1.18**	**1.093**
Dividend Payout %	**78.4**	**80.6**	**97.2**	**N.M.**	**70.8**	**65.2**	**63.6**

[1] 3-for-2 stk split, 5/89

ANNUAL FINANCIAL DATA

	9/30/94	9/30/93	9/30/92	9/30/91	9/30/90	9/30/89	9/30/88
RECORD OF EARNINGS (IN THOUSANDS):							
Total Revenues	451,219	400,408	360,378	337,961	359,527	302,365	270,188
Maintenance	8,275	8,155	8,461	9,036	9,861	8,434	8,991
Operating Income	39,350	34,566	31,161	27,442	29,859	27,888	24,256
Interest Expense	14,946	12,899	12,781	12,085	10,952	10,945	9,315
Net Income	24,485	22,807	18,363	15,817	20,185	18,159	15,870
Aver. Shs. Outstg.	13,086	12,721	11,714	10,598	10,336	9,405	9,031
BALANCE SHEET (IN THOUSANDS):							
Gross Plant	630,878	583,479	542,914	481,730	434,258	392,125	364,521
Accumulated Depreciation	163,023	141,011	126,911	113,800	104,656	95,195	87,515
Prop, Plant & Equip, Net	467,855	442,468	416,003	367,930	329,602	296,930	277,006
Long-term Debt	191,000	176,000	120,839	137,360	99,910	115,207	97,171
Net Stockholders' Equity	220,682	205,480	207,544	166,719	160,684	152,505	108,981
Total Assets	620,728	563,000	498,930	452,153	403,430	364,987	330,818
Year End Shares Outstg	13,290	12,890	12,550	10,736	10,425	10,272	9,075
STATISTICAL RECORD:							
Book Value Per Share	16.21	15.52	14.90	13.60	13.42	12.81	11.34
Op. Inc/Net Pl %	8.4	7.8	7.5	7.5	9.1	9.4	8.8
Dep/Gr. Pl %	3.7	3.6	3.0	3.0	2.9	3.0	3.1
Accum. Dep/Gr. Pl %	25.8	24.2	23.4	23.6	24.1	24.3	24.0
Return on Equity %	11.2	11.3	9.7	10.6	14.2	13.5	15.0
Average Yield %	5.7	5.0	5.8	6.3	6.2	6.0	7.0
P/E Ratio	15.3-12.2	18.3-13.9	18.8-14.7	17.9-14.0	12.6-10.1	12.6-9.3	10.1-8.1
Price Range	28⅜-22½	32-24⅜	26½-20¾	23⅝-18½	22½-18	22⅞-16¾	17⅜-13⅞

Statistics are as originally reported.

OFFICERS:
C.H. Tenney, II, Chmn.
R.A. Young, Pres. & C.E.O.
T.W. Sherman, Exec. V.P., C.F.O. & Treas.

INCORPORATED: MA, Nov., 1974

PRINCIPAL OFFICE: 300 Friberg Parkway, Westborough, MA 01581

TELEPHONE NUMBER: (508) 836-7000

NO. OF EMPLOYEES: 1,072

ANNUAL MEETING: In January

SHAREHOLDERS: 11,674

INSTITUTIONAL HOLDINGS:
No. of Institutions: 40
Shares Held: 2,784,170

REGISTRAR(S): First National Bank of Boston, Shareholder Services Division, Boston, MA

TRANSFER AGENT(S): First National Bank of Boston, Shareholder Services Division, Boston, MA

NYS SYMBOL BCE
Rec. Pr. 31¾

BCE INC.

YIELD 8.6%
P/E RATIO 9.0

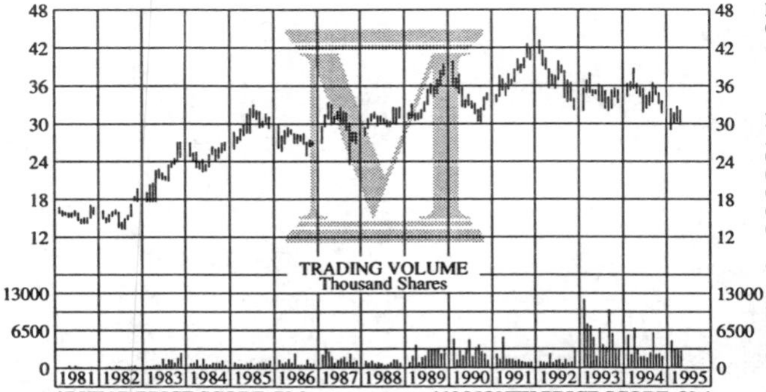

*7 YEAR PRICE SCORE 79.0 *12 MONTH PRICE SCORE 89.4
*NYSE COMPOSITE INDEX=100

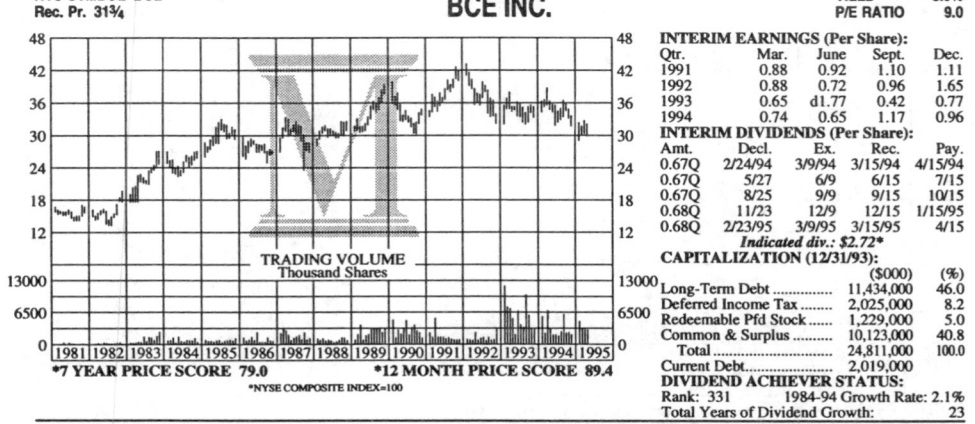

INTERIM EARNINGS (Per Share):

Qtr.	Mar.	June	Sept.	Dec.
1991	0.88	0.92	1.10	1.11
1992	0.88	0.72	0.96	1.65
1993	0.65	d1.77	0.42	0.77
1994	0.74	0.65	1.17	0.96

INTERIM DIVIDENDS (Per Share):

Amt.	Decl.	Ex.	Rec.	Pay.
0.67Q	2/24/94	3/9/94	3/15/94	4/15/94
0.67Q	5/27	6/9	6/15	7/15
0.67Q	8/25	9/9	9/15	10/15
0.68Q	11/23	12/9	12/15	1/15/95
0.68Q	2/23/95	3/9/95	3/15/95	4/15

*Indicated div.: $2.72**

CAPITALIZATION (12/31/93):

	($000)	(%)
Long-Term Debt	11,434,000	46.0
Deferred Income Tax	2,025,000	8.2
Redeemable Pfd Stock	1,229,000	5.0
Common & Surplus	10,123,000	40.8
Total	24,811,000	100.0
Current Debt	2,019,000	

DIVIDEND ACHIEVER STATUS:
Rank: 331 1984-94 Growth Rate: 2.1%
Total Years of Dividend Growth: 23

RECENT DEVELOPMENTS: For the year ended 12/31/94, income from continuing operations was $1.18 billion compared with $159.0 million in 1993. Revenues increased 9.3% to $21.67 billion. The 1994 results include a third-quarter gain of $151 million. The strong performance was attributed primarily to improved results at Northern Telecom (NT). NT is benefiting from strong growth in international markets and in wireless systems.

PROSPECTS: Long-term growth prospects will be heavily dependent on BCE's ability to offset the negative effects of regulatory changes. New regulatory guidelines will increase competitive pressures. Meanwhile, BCE's results are being pressured by long-distance market share loss and greater expenses. Margins for Northern Telecom are improving due to growth in international markets, wireless communications and switching products.

BUSINESS

BCE INC. provides telecommunications services and manufactures and supplies telecommunications equipment. Its Bell Canada subsidiary is Canada's largest supplier of telecommunications services, providing advanced voice, data, and image communications to some seven million customers. BCE owns 52.8% of Northern Telecom Ltd., a leading global supplier of fully-digital telecommunications systems; and 65.5%, BCE Mobile Communications, a provider of cellular telephone and paging systems. Montreal Trustco Inc., wholly owned by BCE, markets financial and trust services. BCE owns 70% of Bell-Northern development. Investments are administered by BCE Telecom.

REVENUES

(12/31/94)	($000)	(%)
Canadian Telecom	8,868,000	40.9
Telecom Equipment Manufac.	12,137,000	56.1
International Telecom	138,000	0.6
Directories	518,000	2.4
Total	21,661,000	100.0

ANNUAL EARNINGS AND DIVIDENDS PER SHARE

	1994	1993	1992	1991	1990	1989	1988
Earnings Per Share	3.52	0.21	4.21	[1] 4.01	[2] 3.50	[3] 3.91	2.96
Dividends Per Share	2.68	2.64	2.60	2.56	2.52	2.48	2.44
Dividend Payout %	76.1	N.M.	61.8	63.8	72.0	63.7	82.4

[1] In Canadian dollars [2] Canadian dollars [3] Before disc. oper.

ANNUAL FINANCIAL DATA

	1994	1993	1992	1991	1990	1989	1988
RECORD OF EARNINGS (IN MILLIONS):							
Total Revenues	21,670.0	19,827.0	21,270.0	19,884.0	18,373.0	16,681.0	15,253.0
Depreciation	2,700.0	2,471.0	2,328.0	2,219.0	2,018.0	1,813.0	1,601.0
Operating Profit	2,810.0	1,167.0	3,542.0	3,381.0	...	...	...
Interest Expense	1,211.0	1,222.0	1,099.0	1,033.0	911.0	830.0	720.0
Net Income	1,178.0	[1] 159.0	1,390.0	1,329.0	1,147.0	[2] 1,201.0	887.0
Aver. Shs. Outstg. (000)	308,800	307,000	307,600	307,649	303,813	297,508	285,427

[1] Before disc. op. dr$815,000,000. [2] Before disc. op. dr$440,000,000.

	1994	1993	1992	1991	1990	1989	1988
BALANCE SHEET (IN MILLIONS):							
Gross Plant	36,708.0	35,165.0	33,428.0	31,520.0	29,087.0	26,946.0	26,715.0
Accumulated Depreciation	14,551.0	12,857.0	12,044.0	11,469.0	10,513.0	9,655.0	8,763.0
Prop, Plant & Equip, Net	22,157.0	22,308.0	21,384.0	20,051.0	18,574.0	17,291.0	17,952.0
Long-term Debt	11,434.0	10,449.0	8,613.0	7,971.0	7,431.0	7,005.0	7,448.0
Net Stockholders' Equity	11,352.0	10,923.0	12,307.0	11,959.0	11,325.0	10,406.0	9,369.0
Total Assets	38,092.0	36,708.0	48,312.0	45,704.0	41,987.0	39,261.0	28,069.0
Year End Shs Outstg (000)	309,290	308,162	305,347	310,292	305,412	302,052	289,546
STATISTICAL RECORD:							
Book Value Per Share	32.73	31.46	36.28	34.60	33.04	31.61	32.31
Op. Inc/Net Pl %	15.8	6.1	17.3	16.4	16.5	15.8	12.1
Accum. Dep/Gr. Pl %	39.6	36.6	36.0	36.4	36.1	35.8	32.8
Return on Equity %	10.4	1.6	12.5	12.4	11.4	12.6	9.5
Average Yield %	7.6	7.5	6.9	6.7	7.2	7.1	8.0
P/E Ratio	11-9	N.M	10.3-7.6	10.6-8.3	11.4-8.6	10.1-7.8	10.6-9.1
Price Range	38¾-31⅝	38-32	43¼-32⅛	42⅝-33⅜	40-30¼	39⅜-30½	32⅝-28⅛

Statistics are as originally reported.

OFFICERS:
L.R. Wilson, Chmn., Pres. & C.E.O.
R.E. Osborne, Exec. V.P. & C.F.O.
C.A. Labarge, V.P. & Treas.

INCORPORATED: CN, 1970

PRINCIPAL OFFICE: 1000 rue de La Gauchetiere Ouest Bureau 3700, Montreal

TELEPHONE NUMBER: (514) 397-7267
FAX: (514) 397-7157
NO. OF EMPLOYEES: 116,000
ANNUAL MEETING: In May
SHAREHOLDERS: 224,874; 336 preferred.
INSTITUTIONAL HOLDINGS:
No. of Institutions: 211
Shares Held: 24,371,471

REGISTRAR(S): The Royal Bank of Scotland, PLC, London, England

TRANSFER AGENT(S): Royal Trust Co., London, England

NYS SYMBOL BDX
Rec. Pr. 54¾

BECTON, DICKINSON & CO.

YIELD 1.5%
P/E RATIO 17.2

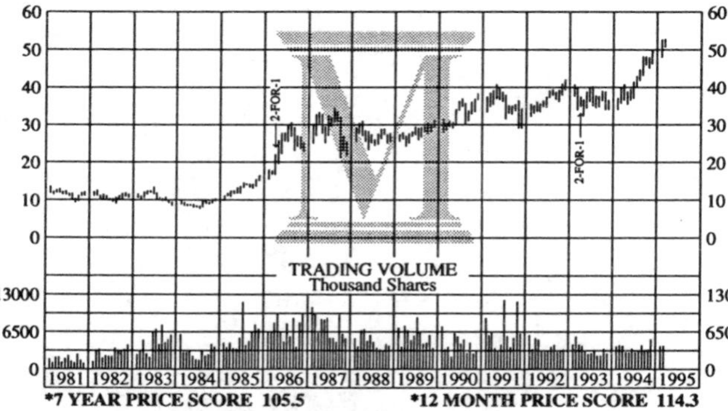

2-FOR-1
2-FOR-1
TRADING VOLUME
Thousand Shares
1981 1982 1983 1984 1985 1986 1987 1988 1989 1990 1991 1992 1993 1994 1995

*7 YEAR PRICE SCORE 105.5 *12 MONTH PRICE SCORE 114.3

*NYSE COMPOSITE INDEX=100

INTERIM EARNINGS (Per Share):

Qtr.	Dec.	Mar.	June	Sept.
1991-92	0.28	0.66	0.72	0.93
1992-93		2.71		
1993-94	0.33	0.76	0.78	1.18
1994-95	0.46	...	...	...

INTERIM DIVIDENDS (Per Share):

Amt.	Decl.	Ex.	Rec.	Pay.
0.185Q	1/25/94	3/4/94	3/10/94	3/31/94
0.185Q	5/24	6/3	6/9	6/30
0.185Q	7/26	9/2	9/9	9/30
0.205Q	11/22	12/13	12/19	1/3/95
0.205Q	1/24/95	3/6/95	3/10/95	3/31

*Indicated div.: $0.82**

CAPITALIZATION (9/30/94):

	($000)	(%)
Long-Term Debt	669,157	31.1
Preferred Stock	56,331	2.6
Common & Surplus	1,425,363	66.3
Total	2,150,851	100.0

DIVIDEND ACHIEVER STATUS:
Rank: 176 1984-94 Growth Rate: 9.8%
Total Years of Dividend Growth: 22

RECENT DEVELOPMENTS: For the quarter ended 12/31/94, net income increased 30.5% to $33.5 million compared with $25.7 million in the corresponding 1993 period. Sales were up 7.1% to $593.5 million from $554.1 million. The earnings growth was partly attributable to ongoing efforts to improve gross margin through cost-reduction programs. Operating results were also enhanced by a stronger product mix. Medical revenue growth was driven by international operations.

PROSPECTS: Improved efficiencies are enabling the Company to operate in a more competitive environment, which is characterized by hospital consolidations and pricing pressures. These conditions persist despite the diminished threat of legislative action. Cash flows from operations will be used for potential acquisitions, debt reduction and share repurchases. In the next few years, BDX should benefit from increasing demand around the world.

BUSINESS

BECTON, DICKINSON & COMPANY manufactures products for use by health care professionals, medical research institutions, industry and the general public. Products are manufactured at both domestic and foreign locations for sale worldwide. The medical segment includes diabetes care products, intravenous and cardiovascular catheters, operating room supplies, suction products, elastic support products, surgical blades, examination gloves, thermometers and contract packaging services. Products in the diagnostic segment include blood collection products, laboratory ware and suppliers, manual and instrumented microbiology products. In 1994, foreign operations represented 44% of total sales and 31% of operating income.

BUSINESS LINE ANALYSIS

(9/30/94)	Rev (%)	Inc ($000)
Medical Supply & Devices	55.5	274,498
Diagnostic Systems	44.5	110,989
Total	100.0	385,487

ANNUAL EARNINGS AND DIVIDENDS PER SHARE

	9/30/94	9/30/93	9/30/92	9/30/91	9/30/90	9/30/89	9/30/88
Earnings Per Share	**3.05**	**[1] 2.71**	**2.58**	**2.43**	**2.34**	**[3] 2.00**	**[3] 1.85**
Dividends Per Share	**0.74**	**[2] 0.66**	**0.60**	**0.58**	**0.54**	**0.50**	**0.43**
Dividend Payout %	**24.3**	**30.4**	**23.3**	**23.9**	**23.1**	**25.0**	**23.3**

[1] Before acctg. chg. [2] 2-for-1 stk split,03/01/93 [3] Before disc. oper.

ANNUAL FINANCIAL DATA

RECORD OF EARNINGS (IN MILLIONS):							
Total Revenues	2,559.5	2,465.4	2,365.3	2,172.2	2,012.7	1,811.5	1,709.4
Costs and Expenses	2,000.2	1,978.3	1,867.1	1,708.5	1,571.5	1,433.7	1,361.1
Depreciation & Amort	203.7	189.8	169.6	149.9	135.7	121.9	109.2
Operating Income	325.0	270.4	328.6	313.7	305.5	255.8	239.0
Income Bef Income Taxes	296.2	222.9	269.5	267.3	274.1	227.8	206.3
Income Taxes	69.0	10.1	68.7	77.5	91.9	69.8	57.4
Net Income	227.2	[1] 212.8	200.8	189.8	182.3	[2] 158.0	[3] 148.9
Aver. Shs. Outstg. (000)	73,333	76,930	77,028	77,096	77,320	79,172	80,802

[1] Before acctg. change dr$141,057,000. [2] Before disc. op. cr$55,594,000. [3] Before disc. op. cr$13,087,000.

BALANCE SHEET (IN MILLIONS):							
Cash and Cash Equivalents	178.8	64.9	100.5	84.3	72.9	95.1	123.5
Receivables, Net	589.9	557.8	585.1	468.0	422.2	361.0	339.4
Inventories	420.0	445.9	453.4	406.3	397.6	355.2	356.4
Gross Property	2,479.9	2,363.9	2,294.8	2,097.2	1,924.0	1,655.7	1,434.6
Accumulated Depreciation	1,103.6	960.8	865.3	745.8	647.9	555.1	509.1
Long-Term Debt	669.2	680.6	685.1	739.1	649.3	516.0	500.0
Net Stockholders' Equity	1,481.7	1,457.0	1,694.2	1,461.9	1,335.3	1,071.5	959.8
Total Assets	3,159.5	3,087.6	3,177.7	2,780.0	2,593.5	2,270.1	2,067.5
Total Current Assets	1,326.6	1,150.7	1,221.2	1,031.6	961.9	868.6	883.0
Total Current Liabilities	678.3	636.1	713.3	531.3	573.8	567.8	715.0
Net Working Capital	648.2	514.7	507.9	500.3	388.1	300.9	168.0
Year End Shs Outstg (000)	70,278	74,727	75,960	75,482	75,283	76,555	78,886

STATISTICAL RECORD:							
Operating Profit Margin %	12.7	11.0	13.9	14.4	15.2	14.1	14.0
Book Value Per Share	17.18	15.83	18.58	16.65	14.96	11.88	10.20
Return on Equity %	15.3	14.6	11.8	13.0	13.6	14.7	15.5
Return on Assets %	7.2	6.9	6.3	6.8	7.0	7.0	7.2
Average Yield %	1.8	2.2	1.6	1.7	1.6	1.8	1.6
P/E Ratio	16.4-11.1	15.0-12.0	16.4-12.5	16.8-11.9	16.4-11.9	15.6-12.1	16.8-12.6
Price Range	49⅞-34	40¾-32⅝	42⅛-32¼	40¾-29	38⅜-27⅞	31⅛-24¼	31⅛-23¼

Statistics are as originally reported.

OFFICERS:
C. Castellini, Chmn., Pres. & C.E.O.
J.W. Galiardo, Vice-Chmn. & Gen. Couns.
A.J. Battaglia, Group Pres.
R.A. Reynolds, V.P.-Fin. & Contr.

INCORPORATED: NJ, Nov., 1906

PRINCIPAL OFFICE: One Becton Dr., Franklin Lakes, NJ 07417-1880

TELEPHONE NUMBER: (201) 847-6800

NO. OF EMPLOYEES: 18,600 (approx.)

ANNUAL MEETING: In February

SHAREHOLDERS: 7,586 (approx.)

INSTITUTIONAL HOLDINGS:
No. of Institutions: 362
Shares Held: 29,789,460

REGISTRAR(S): First Chicago Trust Co. of New York, New York, NY 10008

TRANSFER AGENT(S): First Chicago Trust Co. of New York, New York, NY 10008

NYS SYMBOL BEL
Rec. Pr. 56

BELL ATLANTIC CORP.

YIELD 5.0%
P/E RATIO 7.4

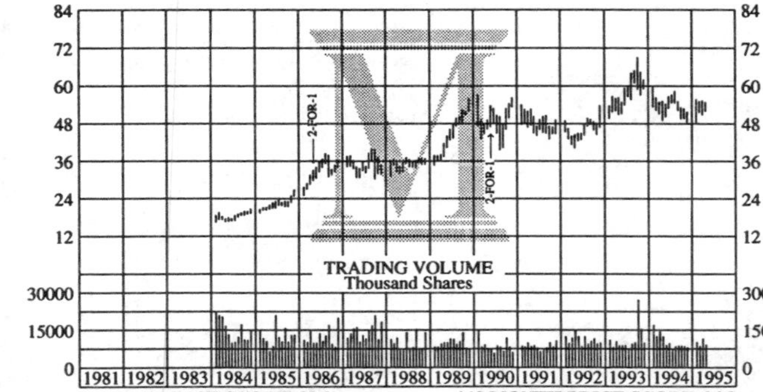

TRADING VOLUME
Thousand Shares
2-FOR-1
2-FOR-1
1981 1982 1983 1984 1985 1986 1987 1988 1989 1990 1991 1992 1993 1994 1995

*7 YEAR PRICE SCORE 90.9 *12 MONTH PRICE SCORE 94.8

*NYSE COMPOSITE INDEX=100

INTERIM EARNINGS (Per Share):

Qtr.	Mar.	June	Sept.	Dec.
1991	0.91	0.91	0.98	0.68
1992	0.81	0.74	0.91	0.76
1993	0.85	0.88	0.89	0.77
1994	0.91	0.95	0.63	0.72

INTERIM DIVIDENDS (Per Share):

Amt.	Decl.	Ex.	Rec.	Pay.
0.69Q	3/22/94	4/5/94	4/11/94	5/2/94
0.69Q	6/28	7/5	7/11	8/1
0.69Q	8/23	10/4	10/11	11/1
0.69Q	11/22	1/4/95	1/10/95	2/1/95
0.70Q	3/28/95	4/4	4/10	5/1

*Indicated div.: $2.80**

CAPITALIZATION (12/31/94):

	($000)	(%)
Long-Term Debt	6,805,700	47.1
Deferred Income Tax	1,482,400	10.2
Redeemable Pfd Stock	85,000	0.6
Common & Surplus	6,081,300	42.1
Total	14,454,400	100.0

DIVIDEND ACHIEVER STATUS:
Rank: 200 1984-94 Growth Rate: 8.6%
Total Years of Dividend Growth: 10

RECENT DEVELOPMENTS: For the year ended 12/31/94, income before extraordinary charges was $1.40 billion compared with $1.48 billion in 1993. Extraordinary charges in 1994 totaled $2.16 billion, reflecting accounting changes, workforce reductions and the write-down of assets and investments. Revenues totaled $13.79 billion, up 4.9%. Fourth quarter net income was $314.9 million versus $337.2 million, before extraordinary charges, in the same period of 1993.

PROSPECTS: BEL and Nynex Corp. have agreed to merge their wireless operations to create a nationwide cellular network. If approved, the merger is expected to be completed in mid-1995. BEL and NYNEX also formed partnerships with U S WEST and AirTouch to bid jointly for personal communications services in areas where the four companies do not already have wireless operations. Improved economic conditions and cost-cutting efforts bode well for 1995's results.

BUSINESS

BELL ATLANTIC CORPORATION is a holding company for seven telephone subsidiaries: New Jersey Bell Telephone Co.; The Bell Telephone Co. of Pennsylvania; The Chesapeake and Potomac Telephone Co., The Chesapeake and Potomac Telephone Co. of Maryland, Virginia, and West Virginia (collectively referred to as C & P Companies); and the Diamond State Telephone Co. The business of the Company encompasses two segments: Communications and Related Services, and Financial and Real Estate Services. The Communications and Related Services segment provides wireless communications products, including cellular service, servicing computers and computer networking. Financial and Real Estate engages in lease financing of commercial, industrial and high technology equipment.

QUARTERLY DATA

(12/31/94)	Rev($000)	Inc($000)
1st Quarter	3,419,600	748,800
2nd Quarter	3,430,000	797,500
3rd Quarter	3,455,300	591,000
4th Quarter	3,486,500	667,300

ANNUAL EARNINGS AND DIVIDENDS PER SHARE

	1994	1993	1992	1991	1990	1989	1988
Earnings Per Share	3.21	3.39	[1] 3.23	[2] 3.41	3.38	2.71	3.32
Dividends Per Share	2.74	2.66	2.58	2.48	2.32	2.16	2.01
Dividend Payout %	85.4	78.5	79.9	72.7	68.6	79.6	60.5

[1] Before extraord. item [2] Before acctg. chg.

ANNUAL FINANCIAL DATA

	1994	1993	1992	1991	1990	1989	1988
RECORD OF EARNINGS (IN MILLIONS):							
Total Revenues	13,791.4	12,990.2	12,647.0	12,279.7	12,298.0	11,448.6	10,880.1
Costs and Expenses	8,334.7	7,647.5	7,723.4	7,455.6	7,311.2	7,015.9	6,281.6
Depreciation & Amort	2,652.1	2,545.1	2,417.4	2,298.7	2,377.2	2,419.9	2,354.0
Operating Income	2,804.6	2,797.6	2,506.2	2,525.4	2,609.6	2,012.8	2,244.5
Inc Bef Inc Taxes, Extraord Item, & Acctg Chg	2,286.8	2,273.6	2,025.7	1,996.4	1,982.1	1,545.5	1,846.8
Income Taxes	884.9	792.0	643.5	664.8	669.6	471.0	530.0
Net Income	[1] 1,401.9	[2] 1,481.6	[3] 1,382.2	d222.7	1,312.5	1,074.5	1,316.8
Aver. Shs. Outstg. (000)	437,200	436,300	433,000	394,800	393,600	396,000	396,100

[1] Before extra. item dr$2,156,700,000. [2] Before extra. item dr$58,400,000. [3] Before extra. item dr$41,600,000.

	1994	1993	1992	1991	1990	1989	1988
BALANCE SHEET (IN MILLIONS):							
Cash and Cash Equivalents	142.9	154.6	329.7	245.3	109.7	443.1	301.6
Receivables, Net	2,328.1	2,762.3	2,628.8	2,587.6	2,685.2	2,401.3	2,122.5
Inventories	274.6	250.9	266.0	293.3	357.9	278.7	316.5
Gross Property	33,745.8	32,329.9	31,046.2	31,847.9	30,783.5	29,312.2	27,569.7
Accumulated Depreciation	16,807.7	11,964.0	10,716.2	11,886.1	11,336.4	10,438.1	9,395.8
Long-Term Debt	6,805.7	7,206.2	7,348.2	7,959.5	8,171.1	7,720.6	6,557.2
Net Stockholders' Equity	6,166.3	8,224.4	7,816.3	7,831.3	8,930.0	8,590.6	9,176.7
Total Assets	24,271.8	29,544.2	28,099.5	27,881.6	27,998.5	26,219.7	24,729.2
Total Current Assets	3,783.3	3,870.8	3,991.3	3,849.4	3,827.6	3,768.9	3,206.4
Total Current Liabilities	5,576.7	6,123.9	5,872.2	5,175.2	5,965.0	5,053.0	4,265.2
Net Working Capital	d1,793.4	d2,253.1	d1,880.9	d1,325.8	d2,137.4	d1,284.1	d1,058.8
Year End Shs Outstg (000)	436,186	436,080	433,969	396,051	393,191	394,455	394,031
STATISTICAL RECORD:							
Book Value Per Share	13.94	18.86	18.01	19.77	22.71	21.78	23.29
Return on Equity %	23.1	18.0	17.7	...	14.7	12.5	14.3
Average Yield %	5.1	4.5	5.5	5.1	4.8	4.8	5.9
P/E Ratio	18.6-15.1	20.4-14.6	16.7-12.5	15.9-12.6	16.9-11.7	20.7-12.8	11.2-9.4
Price Range	59⅝-48⅜	69⅛-49⅝	53⅞-40¼	54⅛-43	57⅛-39½	56⅛-34¾	37¼-31⅛

Statistics are as originally reported.

OFFICERS:
R.W. Smith, Chmn. & C.E.O.
J.G. Cullen, President
W.O. Albertini, V.P. & C.F.O.
J.H. Dickerson, Jr., V.P.-Fin. & Contr.
B.L. Connor, V.P. & Treas.

PRINCIPAL OFFICE: 1717 Arch Street, Philadelphia, PA 19103

TELEPHONE NUMBER: (215) 963-6333
NO. OF EMPLOYEES: 22,705
ANNUAL MEETING: In April
SHAREHOLDERS: 500,550
INSTITUTIONAL HOLDINGS:
No. of Institutions: 586
Shares Held: 114,691,905

REGISTRAR(S): Chemical Bank, New York, NY

TRANSFER AGENT(S): American Transtech Inc., Jacksonville, FL

BEMIS CO., INC.

YIELD 2.3%
P/E RATIO 17.9

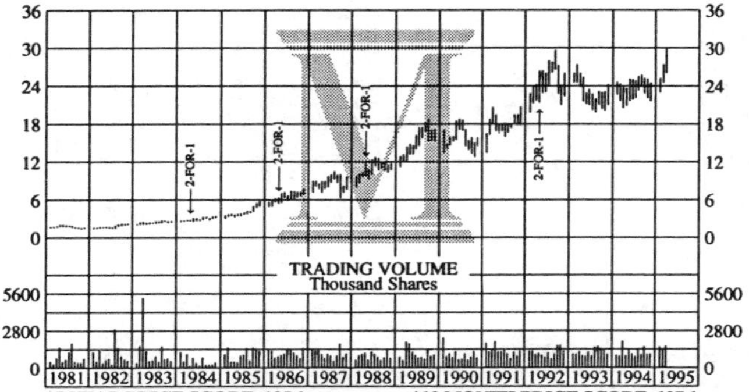

TRADING VOLUME
Thousand Shares

| 1981 | 1982 | 1983 | 1984 | 1985 | 1986 | 1987 | 1988 | 1989 | 1990 | 1991 | 1992 | 1993 | 1994 | 1995 |

*7 YEAR PRICE SCORE 105.1   *12 MONTH PRICE SCORE 107.1

*NYSE COMPOSITE INDEX=100

INTERIM EARNINGS (Per Share):

Qtr.	Mar.	June	Sept.	Dec.
1991	0.16	0.26	0.27	0.35
1992	0.21	0.30	0.28	0.32
1993	0.21	0.30	0.02	0.36
1994	0.26	0.36	0.35	0.43

INTERIM DIVIDENDS (Per Share):

Amt.	Decl.	Ex.	Rec.	Pay.
0.135Q	2/3/94	2/9/94	2/15/94	3/1/94
0.135Q	5/5	5/16	5/20	6/1
0.135Q	8/4	8/15	8/19	9/1
0.135Q	10/20	11/14	11/18	12/1
0.16Q	2/2/95	2/8/95	2/14/95	3/1/95

Indicated div.: $0.64

CAPITALIZATION (12/31/94):

	($000)	(%)
Long-Term Debt	171,728	26.3
Deferred Income Tax	40,013	6.1
Minority Interest	23,930	3.7
Common & Surplus	418,027	63.9
Total	653,698	100.0

DIVIDEND ACHIEVER STATUS:
Rank: 32   1984-94 Growth Rate: 17.5%
Total Years of Dividend Growth: 11

RECENT DEVELOPMENTS: Net income for the year ended 12/31/94 rose 58.0% to $72.8 million from $46.1 million, before a $1.7 million accounting charge, in 1993. Revenues for the twelve month period advanced 15.5% to $1.39 billion, compared with $1.20 billion the previous year. Earnings before taxes climbed 58.8% to $118.1 million from $74.4 million. The cost of goods sold increased to 77.5% of sales from 77.0%. Volume growth is being driven by the addition of new accounts.

PROSPECTS: Overall profitability is being enhanced by higher unit volume, continued penetration of key markets, and improved efficiencies. BMS's ongoing capital expenditure program will help improve margins as the Company's operating performance becomes further refined. In addition, BMS is successfully reducing the adverse impact of higher raw material prices on profitability through its own selling price increases.

BUSINESS

BEMIS COMPANY, INC. is a major manufacturer of flexible packaging and specialty coated and graphics products. Flexible packaging products include coated and laminated films, polyethylene packaging, packaging machinery, multi-wall paper bags and consumer-size paper packaging, and specialty containers. Specialty coated and graphics products include pressure-sensitive materials, non-woven products, and rotogravure cylinders. The primary market for BMS' products is the food industry, which accounts for about 70% of sales. Other markets include chemicals, agribusiness, pharmaceuticals, printing and graphic arts, and a variety of other industrial end uses.

BUSINESS LINE ANALYSIS

(12/31/94)	Rev(%)	Inc(%)
Flexible Packaging		
Prod	70.2	71.1
Special Coat &		
Graph Prod	29.8	28.9
Total	100.0	100.0

ANNUAL EARNINGS AND DIVIDENDS PER SHARE

	1994	1993	1992	1991	1990	1989	1988
Earnings Per Share	1.40	0.89	① 1.11	1.03	0.99	0.90	0.74
Dividends Per Share	0.54	0.50	② 0.46	0.42	0.36	0.30	③ 0.22
Dividend Payout %	38.6	56.2	41.4	40.8	36.4	33.3	29.7

① Before acctg. chg. ② 2-for-1 stk split, 4/1/92 ③ 100% stk. div., 3/88.

ANNUAL FINANCIAL DATA

RECORD OF EARNINGS (IN MILLIONS):

	1994	1993	1992	1991	1990	1989	1988
Total Revenues	1,390.5	1,203.5	1,181.3	1,141.6	1,128.2	1,076.7	1,069.1
Costs and Expenses	1,209.6	1,054.8	1,033.4	999.0	991.2	946.3	951.6
Depreciation & Amort	51.8	47.0	48.3	47.1	42.3	36.8	34.0
Operating Profit	142.2	115.8	115.6	108.8	110.0	105.8	96.0
Income Bef Income Taxes	118.1	74.4	90.3	84.9	81.7	75.9	65.4
Income Taxes	45.3	28.3	33.0	31.9	30.8	28.9	25.8
Net Income	72.8	① 46.1	② 57.3	53.0	50.9	47.0	39.6
Aver. Shs. Outstg. (000)	51,953	51,767	51,840	51,530	51,402	52,146	53,490

① Before acctg. change dr$1,746,000. ② Before acctg. change dr$274,000.

BALANCE SHEET (IN MILLIONS):

	1994	1993	1992	1991	1990	1989	1988
Cash and Cash Equivalents	12.7	8.9	0.1	1.4	9.2	1.4	1.2
Receivables, Net	197.2	161.7	166.1	156.8	168.9	151.4	148.3
Inventories	168.2	127.1	128.9	131.3	144.6	113.9	135.8
Gross Property	722.5	676.6	665.9	614.9	597.7	523.8	462.9
Accumulated Depreciation	261.1	261.7	275.2	245.0	227.3	200.2	180.6
Long-Term Debt	171.7	123.2	131.1	128.9	171.1	109.6	119.6
Net Stockholders' Equity	418.0	370.5	361.0	329.2	295.6	266.0	237.4
Total Assets	923.3	789.8	742.7	714.9	756.5	631.6	595.0
Total Current Assets	418.9	337.0	314.6	307.8	344.1	286.4	302.5
Total Current Liabilities	210.8	184.2	160.6	167.1	193.9	171.3	166.3
Net Working Capital	208.1	152.8	154.0	140.6	150.2	115.1	136.3
Year End Shs Outstg (000)	51,211	51,201	51,152	50,986	50,918	50,890	50,098

STATISTICAL RECORD:

	1994	1993	1992	1991	1990	1989	1988
Operating Profit Margin %	9.3	8.4	8.4	8.4	8.4	8.7	7.8
Book Value Per Share	7.58	6.75	6.55	5.94	5.26	5.13	4.64
Return on Equity %	17.4	12.4	15.9	16.1	17.2	17.7	16.7
Return on Assets %	7.9	5.8	7.7	7.4	6.7	7.4	6.7
Average Yield %	2.3	2.1	1.9	2.5	2.3	2.0	2.1
P/E Ratio	18.4-14.6	30.8-22.3	26.7-17.8	20.1-13.1	18.9-13.0	20.8-12.5	17.2-10.8
Price Range	25¾-20½	27⅜-19⅞	29⅝-19¾	20¾-13½	18¾-12⅞	18¾-11¼	12¾-8

Statistics are as originally reported.

OFFICERS:
J.H. Roe, Pres. & C.E.O.
S.W. Johnson, Sr. V.P., Sec. & Gen. Counsel
B.R. Field, III, Sr. V.P., C.F.O. & Treas.
INCORPORATED: MO, May, 1885
PRINCIPAL OFFICE: 222 South 9th Street Suite 2300, Minneapolis, MN 55402-4099

TELEPHONE NUMBER: (612) 376-3000
NO. OF EMPLOYEES: 8,120
ANNUAL MEETING: In May
SHAREHOLDERS: 5,602
INSTITUTIONAL HOLDINGS:
No. of Institutions: 143
Shares Held: 10,125,225

REGISTRAR(S): Norwest Bank Minnesota, N.A., South St. Paul, MN

TRANSFER AGENT(S): Norwest Bank Minnesota, N.A., South St. Paul, MN

BETZ LABORATORIES INC.

YIELD 3.4%
P/E RATIO 17.5

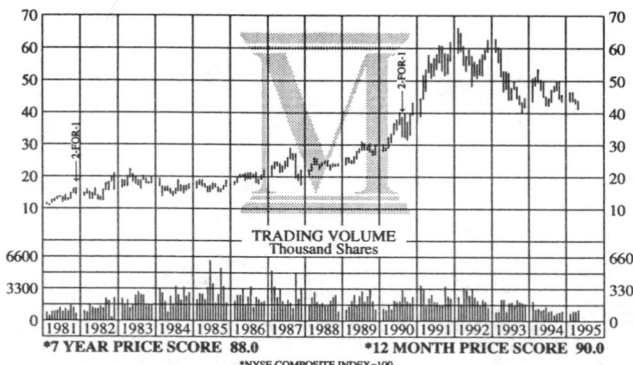

INTERIM EARNINGS (Per Share):

Qtr.	Mar.	June	Sept.	Dec.
1992	0.66	0.67	0.71	0.67
1993	0.62	0.61	0.58	0.24
1994	0.61	0.64	0.65	0.53
1995	0.63	....	....	....

INTERIM DIVIDENDS (Per Share):

Amt.	Decl.	Ex.	Rec.	Pay.
0.35Q	4/14/94	4/22/94	4/28/94	5/12/94
0.36Q	6/9	7/22	7/28	8/11
0.36Q	8/11	10/21	10/27	11/10
0.36Q	12/8	1/20/95	1/26/95	2/9/95
0.36Q	4/13/95	4/21	4/27	5/11

Indicated div.: $1.44

CAPITALIZATION (12/31/94):

	($000)	(%)
Long-Term Debt	96,500	23.0
Preferred Stock.................	98,433	23.4
Common & Surplus	225,525	53.6
Total	420,458	100.0

DIVIDEND ACHIEVER STATUS:
Rank: 170   1984-94 Growth Rate: 9.9%
Total Years of Dividend Growth: 29

TRADING VOLUME
Thousand Shares

*7 YEAR PRICE SCORE 88.0   *12 MONTH PRICE SCORE 90.0

*NYSE COMPOSITE INDEX=100

RECENT DEVELOPMENTS: For the twelve months ended 12/31/94, net income increased 15.4% to $73.2 million from $63.4 million in 1993. Results for 1993 included a restructuring charge of $16.2 million and were before an accounting credit of $3.6 million. Sales for the year advanced 3.4% to $708.3 million, compared with $684.9 million the prior year. For the quarter ended 12/31/94, net income more than doubled to $16.4 million from $7.8 million in the corresponding 1993 period. Sales were up 4.1% to $175.3 million, compared with $168.4 million a year earlier. The Company's foreign operations performed well, posting double-digit sales volume gains in Canada, the Carribean, Australia and Korea. This growth was spurred by an improved European economy and strong new account activity to the paper industry. Domestic operations reported modest growth.

BUSINESS

BETZ LABORATORIES INC. produces and sells specialty chemical products for the treatment of water and wastewater and process systems operating in a wide variety of industrial and commercial applications, with particular emphasis on the chemical, petroleum refining, paper and steel industries. Betz also provides technical and laboratory services necessary to utilize Betz products effectively. The Company's products are used chiefly in boilers, water and steam pipes, cooling systems, heat exchangers, air conditioning equipment, water cooled production equipment, pulp and paper mill systems, industrial and municipal intake water and waste effluent, and settling basins and lagoons. The virtue of these products is that they control corrosion, scale formation, foam formation and fouling. The Company also produces formulated biocides to control the growth of plant and animal life in water used in industrial cooling systems and in water used as a carrier in pulp and paper production; as well as polymers used as retention aids and flocculants in the paper and mining industries and in industrial and municipal water and waste treatment and pollution abatement.

ANNUAL EARNINGS AND DIVIDENDS PER SHARE

	1994	1993	1992	1991	1990	1989	1988
Earnings Per Share	2.43	2.05	2.71	2.47	2.12	1.77	1.58
Dividends Per Share	1.42	1.38	1.30	1.16	① 1.01	0.89	0.80
Dividend Payout %	58.4	67.3	48.0	47.0	47.0	50.3	50.6

① 100% stk div, 8/9/90

ANNUAL FINANCIAL DATA

RECORD OF EARNINGS (IN THOUSANDS):

	1994	1993	1992	1991	1990	1989	1988
Total Revenues	708,286	684,872	706,972	665,565	596,805	516,669	447,580
Costs and Expenses	545,670	541,503	536,825	512,701	462,820	403,306	348,631
Depreciation & Amort	45,111	42,083	38,883	33,827	29,869	25,902	22,974
Operating Earnings	117,505	101,286	131,264	119,037	104,116	87,461	75,976
Earn Bef Income Taxes	120,944	104,070	134,171	123,810	107,399	90,920	78,803
Income Taxes	47,773	40,691	52,124	48,286	41,925	35,060	30,418
Net Income	73,171	① 63,379	82,047	75,524	65,474	55,860	48,385
Aver. Shs. Outstg.	28,108	28,576	28,474	28,547	28,512	30,224	30,747

① Before acctg. change cr$2,141,000.

BALANCE SHEET (IN THOUSANDS):

	1994	1993	1992	1991	1990	1989	1988
Cash and Cash Equivalents	43,926	43,921	46,363	59,009	39,781	29,325	8,499
Receivables, Net	121,660	102,882	106,073	93,164	86,191	76,019	67,555
Inventories	39,624	37,346	34,991	35,820	38,442	31,436	34,828
Gross Property	600,536	554,623	509,776	451,694	403,360	344,719	296,598
Accumulated Depreciation	291,588	253,881	221,405	197,064	169,909	143,254	121,629
Long-Term Debt	96,500	97,500	98,000	98,500	99,000	99,500	...
Net Stockholders' Equity	323,958	299,319	297,689	258,932	220,705	183,454	230,574
Total Assets	555,498	521,129	510,617	475,844	427,356	369,227	318,534
Total Current Assets	229,876	208,635	202,492	200,805	176,374	145,465	120,364
Total Current Liabilities	98,673	92,041	84,137	88,003	77,386	56,793	59,615
Net Working Capital	131,203	116,594	118,355	112,802	98,988	88,672	60,749
Year End Shs Outstg	27,865	28,127	28,520	28,468	28,416	28,428	30,876

STATISTICAL RECORD:

	1994	1993	1992	1991	1990	1989	1988
Operating Profit Margin %	16.6	14.8	18.6	17.9	17.4	16.9	17.0
Book Value Per Share	7.86	6.95	6.78	5.41	4.41	2.57	7.12
Return on Equity %	22.6	21.2	27.6	29.2	29.7	30.4	21.0
Return on Assets %	13.2	12.2	16.1	15.9	15.3	15.1	15.2
Average Yield %	3.0	2.7	2.3	2.3	2.8	3.2	3.4
P/E Ratio	22.1-17.4	30.7-19.5	24.4-17.8	25.1-15.7	20.4-13.1	17.8-13.4	16.7-13.1
Price Range	53⅝-42¼	62⅞-40	66¼-48¼	62-38¾	43¼-27¾	31¼-23⅝	26¼-20⅝

Statistics are as originally reported.

OFFICERS:
J.F. McCaughan, Chmn. & C.E.O.
W.R. Cook, Pres. & C.O.O.
R.D. Voncanon, V.P.-Fin. & Treas.
W.C. Brafford, V.P., Sec. & Gen. Coun.

INCORPORATED: PA, Feb., 1957

PRINCIPAL OFFICE: 4636 Somerton Rd., Trevose, PA 19053

TELEPHONE NUMBER: (215) 355-3300

FAX: (215) 953-5544

NO. OF EMPLOYEES: 1,266

ANNUAL MEETING: In April

SHAREHOLDERS: 1,710 (approx.)

INSTITUTIONAL HOLDINGS:
No. of Institutions: Not Available
Shares Held: Not Available

REGISTRAR(S): Mellon Bank East, Pittsburgh, PA 15230

TRANSFER AGENT(S): Mellon Bank East, Pittsburgh, PA 15230

NYS SYMBOL BKH
Rec. Pr. 21¼

BLACK HILLS CORP.

YIELD 6.3%
P/E RATIO 12.7

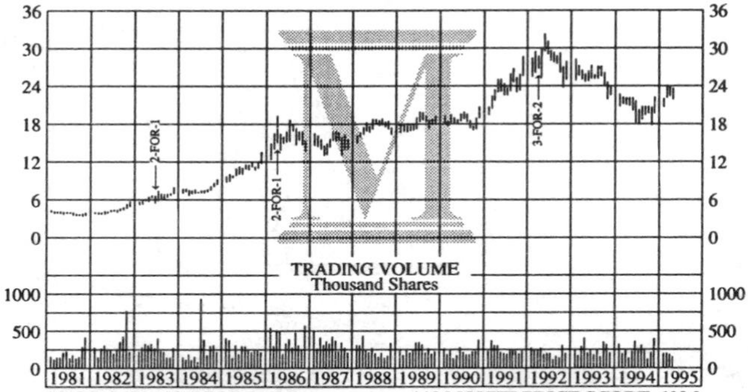

***7 YEAR PRICE SCORE 78.8** ***12 MONTH PRICE SCORE 103.9**

*NYSE COMPOSITE INDEX=100

INTERIM EARNINGS (Per Share):

Qtr.	Mar.	June	Sept.	Dec.
1991	0.49	0.31	0.51	0.35
1992	0.41	0.41	0.46	0.45
1993	0.45	0.33	0.44	0.44
1994	0.41	0.31	0.49	0.46

INTERIM DIVIDENDS (Per Share):

Amt.	Decl.	Ex.	Rec.	Pay.
0.33Q	4/28/94	5/9/94	5/13/94	6/1/94
0.33Q	7/20	8/8	8/12	9/1
0.33Q	10/26	11/4	11/10	12/1
0.335Q	1/30/95	2/6/95	2/10/95	3/1/95
0.335Q	4/27	5/8	5/12	6/1

*Indicated div.: $1.34**

CAPITALIZATION (12/31/94):

	($000)	(%)
Long-Term Debt	128,925	36.9
Deferred Income Tax	45,474	13.0
Common & Surplus	175,410	50.1
Total	349,809	100.0
Current Debt	2,144	

DIVIDEND ACHIEVER STATUS:
Rank: 126 1984-94 Growth Rate: 11.6%
Total Years of Dividend Growth: 14

RECENT DEVELOPMENTS: For the twelve months ended 12/31/94, net income was $23.8 million, up 3.7% from the previous year's income of $22.9 million. Operating income increased 2.6% to $38.8 million from $37.8 million. The decrease in operating income from the coal mining segment to $11.8 million from $12.4 million partially offset operating gains reported in BKH's electric and oil and gas segments. This was attributed to the Wyodak Plant being out of service for five weeks of scheduled maintenance. The Company realized a gain to net income of $1.7 million in 1994 pertaining to settlement agreements with PacifiCorp. Revenues were $145.4 million for 1994, a 4.1% increase over $139.4 million for 1993.

BUSINESS

THE BLACK HILLS CORPORATION operates an electric public utility under the assumed name of Black Hills Power and Light Company, and in addition is engaged in coal mining through Wyodak Resources, and is into oil and gas production through Western Production. Black Hills Power is engaged in the generation, purchase, transmission, distribution, and sale of electric power and energy in 11 counties in western South Dakota, northeastern Wyoming, and southeastern Montana. The population of this area is approximately 165,000. Principal industries in the territory served are cattle and sheep raising, farming, milling, meat packing, lumbering, the production of cement, mineral mining, wood products, gold jewelry, and the refining of oil. Wyodak Resources is engaged in the mining and sale of sub-bituminous coal. The coal mining operation is located approximately five miles east of Gillette, Wyoming. Western Production is an oil and gas producing and operating company based in Wyoming.

REVENUES

(12/31/94)	($000)	(%)
Electric	104,756	72.0
Coal Mining	28,594	19.7
Oil & Gas Production	12,052	8.3
Total	145,402	100.0

ANNUAL EARNINGS AND DIVIDENDS PER SHARE

	1994	1993	1992	1991	1990	1989	1988
Earnings Per Share	**1.66**	**1.66**	**1.73**	**1.66**	**1.67**	**[2] 1.60**	**1.53**
Dividends Per Share	**1.32**	**1.28**	**[1] 1.24**	**1.173**	**1.093**	**1.013**	**0.933**
Dividend Payout %	**79.5**	**77.1**	**71.7**	**70.7**	**65.3**	**63.3**	**60.9**

[1] 3-for-2 stk split, 3/3/92 [2] Before disc. oper.

ANNUAL FINANCIAL DATA

	1994	1993	1992	1991	1990	1989	1988
RECORD OF EARNINGS (IN THOUSANDS):							
Total Revenues	145,402	139,373	135,343	133,373	127,498	120,004	283,868
Deprec, Depl & Amort	17,676	16,051	13,860	12,012	9,930	9,484	10,054
Maintenance	...	6,869	6,513	6,729	6,088	6,784	7,069
Total Operating Income	38,754	37,786	36,349	35,467	29,474	27,682	26,754
Interest Expense	6,356	8,088	8,587	7,824	4,756	4,267	4,230
Net Income	23,805	22,946	23,638	22,681	22,938	[1] 21,957	[2] 21,166
Aver. Shs. Outstg.	14,339	13,811	13,689	13,675	13,675	13,676	13,665
[1] Before disc. op. dr$861,000. [2] Before disc. op. cr$1,248,000.							
BALANCE SHEET (IN THOUSANDS):							
Gross Plant	516,799	425,893	391,218	369,303	333,917	310,018	312,987
Accumulated Depreciation	156,046	144,492	132,890	122,574	111,111	101,591	93,245
Prop, Plant & Equip, Net	360,753	281,401	258,328	246,729	222,806	208,427	219,742
Long-term Debt	128,925	85,274	88,816	92,982	78,978	78,939	85,096
Net Stockholders' Equity	175,410	168,089	149,158	141,963	135,329	127,338	120,100
Total Assets	436,877	352,853	330,202	314,180	290,234	267,819	281,286
Year End Shares Outstg	14,386	14,270	13,701	13,675	13,675	13,676	13,650
STATISTICAL RECORD:							
Book Value Per Share	12.19	11.78	10.89	10.38	9.90	9.31	8.80
Op. Inc/Net Pl %	10.7	13.4	14.1	14.4	13.2	13.3	12.2
Dep/Gr. Pl %	3.4	3.8	3.5	3.3	3.0	3.1	3.2
Accum. Dep/Gr. Pl %	30.2	33.9	34.0	33.2	33.3	32.8	29.8
Return on Equity %	13.6	13.7	15.8	16.0	16.9	17.2	17.6
Average Yield %	6.5	5.1	4.4	4.9	5.8	5.6	5.5
P/E Ratio	13.7-10.7	17.0-13.2	18.6-13.7	17.2-11.7	12.3-10.1	12.4-10.4	12.3-9.8
Price Range	22¾-17¾	28¼-21⅞	32¼-23¾	28⅝-19⅜	20⅝-17	19⅞-16⅝	18⅞-15

Statistics are as originally reported.

OFFICERS:
D.P. Landguth, Chmn., Pres. & C.E.O.
E.E. Hoyt, Pres. & C.O.O.
D.E. Clement, Sr. V.P.-Fin.
R.R. Basham, Treas. & Sec.

INCORPORATED: SD, Aug., 1941

PRINCIPAL OFFICE: 625 Ninth St., Rapid City, SD 57709

TELEPHONE NUMBER: (605) 348-1700

FAX: (605) 348-4748

NO. OF EMPLOYEES: 356

ANNUAL MEETING: In May

SHAREHOLDERS: 6,951 common

INSTITUTIONAL HOLDINGS:
No. of Institutions: 83
Shares Held: 3,580,576

REGISTRAR(S): Chemical Bank, New York, NY

TRANSFER AGENT(S): Chemical Bank, New York, NY

BLOCK DRUG CO., INC.

YIELD 3.0%
P/E RATIO 15.2

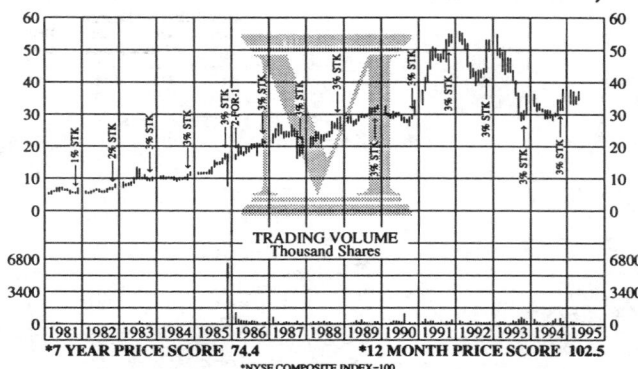

INTERIM EARNINGS (Per Share):

Qtr.	June	Sept.	Dec.	Mar.
1991-92	0.76	0.77	0.73	0.79
1992-93	----------------	3.16	-----------------	
1993-94	0.83	0.57	0.56	0.54
1994-95	0.61	0.63	0.61	...

INTERIM DIVIDENDS (Per Share):

Amt.	Decl.	Ex.	Rec.	Pay.
0.26Q	6/7/94	6/14/94	6/20/94	7/1/94
0.26Q	8/2	8/26	9/1	10/3
0.27Q	10/25	11/25	12/1	1/3/95
3%	10/25	11/25	12/1	1/3
0.27Q	1/24/95	2/23/95	3/1/95	4/3

Indicated div.: $1.08

CAPITALIZATION (3/31/94):

	($000)	(%)
Long-Term Debt	17,880	3.3
Deferred Income Tax	11,424	2.1
Common & Surplus	515,121	94.6
Total	544,425	100.0

DIVIDEND ACHIEVER STATUS:
Rank: 152   1984-94 Growth Rate: 10.6%
Total Years of Dividend Growth: 23

TRADING VOLUME
Thousand Shares

1981 1982 1983 1984 1985 1986 1987 1988 1989 1990 1991 1992 1993 1994 1995

*7 YEAR PRICE SCORE 74.4   ***12 MONTH PRICE SCORE 102.5**
*NYSE COMPOSITE INDEX=100

RECENT DEVELOPMENTS: For the quarter ended 12/31/94, net income was $12.2 million, up 12.5% from $10.9 million for the year before. Net sales climbed 5.1% to $163.6 million from $155.6 million for the corresponding quarter in 1993. For the nine months ended 12/31/94, net income slipped 2.1% to $36.5 million from $37.3 million for the same period in 1993. Net sales were $489.5 million compared with $459.7 million for the year-earlier period, an increase of 6.5%. For the quarter ended 9/30/94, net income increased 14.6% to $12.4 million in the comparable period of 1993. Revenues advanced 8% to $165.9 million compared with $153.5 million a year ago. The Company announced that it had reached an agreement in principal to acquire the assets of Goody's Pharmaceuticals, Inc. of Winston-Salem, North Carolina.

BUSINESS

BLOCK DRUG CO., INC. develops, manufactures and markets three categories of products: dental products, including consumer oral hygiene and professional dental products; consumer products, including proprietary over the counter products and household products; and ethical pharmaceuticals. Denture cleansers and adhesives, specialty toothpastes and toothpastes are the key products that comprise the consumer oral hygiene segment. These products include POLIDENT, DENTU-CREME and their line extensions, SUPER POLI-GRIP, WERNET'S and SUPER WERNET'S, SENSODYNE and PROMISE. Block is a leading manufacturer and marketer of professional dental products for use in chairside patient treatment and dental office infection control. Block's personal care products include: NYTOL Sleep-Aid Tablets, TEGRIN Medicated Shampoos and BC Headache Powder. Household products include 2000 FLUSHES, X-14 brand names. Pharmaceutical products and ethical nonprescription products are manufactured and marketed by Reed & Carnrick. The Division markets products in several medical categories including dermatology, gastroenterology, cardiovascular disease and proctology.

ANNUAL EARNINGS AND DIVIDENDS PER SHARE

	3/31/94	3/31/93	3/31/92	3/31/91	3/31/90	3/31/89	3/31/88
Earnings Per Share	2.45	3.16	3.03	2.80	2.41	2.27	1.97
Dividends Per Share	1.032	①0.964	②0.748	③0.636	④0.565	⑤0.497	⑥0.45
Dividend Payout %	42.1	30.5	24.7	22.6	23.6	22.0	22.8

Note: 3%stk.div.1/3/95. ①3% stk div,11/24/92 ②3% stk div,11/25/91 ③3% stk div, 11/27/90 ④3% stk div, 1/2/90 ⑤3% stk div, 1/3/89 ⑥3% stk div, 1/88

ANNUAL FINANCIAL DATA

RECORD OF EARNINGS (IN THOUSANDS):

Total Revenues	636,666	651,316	585,260	530,854	453,014	424,303	369,102
Costs and Expenses	565,013	561,944	506,252	452,321	388,600	365,757	320,667
Depreciation & Amort	14,539	11,659	10,554	7,388	5,638	5,157	
Operating Profit	431,071	444,863	403,746	371,950	313,289	296,404	257,200
Income Bef Income Taxes	57,114	77,713	68,454	69,062	57,026	52,908	43,278
Income Taxes	9,262	16,167	11,187	15,852	10,886	9,413	5,330
Net Income	47,852	61,546	57,267	53,210	46,140	43,495	37,948
Aver. Shs. Outstg.	19,544	19,504	19,490	19,606	19,796	19,781	19,790

BALANCE SHEET (IN THOUSANDS):

Cash and Cash Equivalents	28,234	32,910	30,541	28,793	32,308	32,090	25,146
Receivables, Net	97,814	95,743	87,775	76,735	59,452	54,688	51,120
Inventories	88,986	96,458	89,223	81,214	69,138	68,555	55,135
Gross Property	289,414	259,801	228,007	192,936	152,247	116,354	101,286
Accumulated Depreciation	81,940	70,550	65,567	56,655	46,885	41,888	38,149
Long-Term Debt	17,880	19,160	19,435	19,459	19,660	12,117	17,887
Net Stockholders' Equity	515,121	485,298	446,550	398,736	352,013	311,993	275,979
Total Assets	771,068	726,497	649,608	550,735	460,268	417,748	356,260
Total Current Assets	249,113	254,839	236,173	206,246	179,530	170,447	143,393
Total Current Liabilities	216,476	203,636	166,610	117,626	76,035	81,812	52,475
Net Working Capital	32,637	51,203	69,563	88,620	103,315	88,635	90,918
Year End Shares Outstg	19,529	19,513	18,929	19,463	19,802	19,789	19,774

STATISTICAL RECORD:

Operating Profit Margin %	9.0	11.9	11.7	13.0	12.6	12.5	11.7
Book Value Per Share	25.26	23.72	22.67	19.59	16.94	14.83	13.20
Return on Equity %	9.3	12.7	12.8	13.3	13.1	13.9	13.8
Return on Assets %	6.2	8.5	8.8	9.7	10.0	10.4	10.7
Average Yield %	2.3	1.8	1.7	2.0	1.9	2.0	2.0
P/E Ratio	23.1-11.8	18.2-12.7	19.3-11.5	13.1-10.0	14.5-11.6	13.8-9.2	14.6-8.7
Price Range	56½-28⅞	57½-40	56¾-33⅞	35½-27⅛	33¾-27⅛	30¼-20⅛	28-16⅝

Statistics are as originally reported.

OFFICERS:
L. Block, Sr. Chmn.
J.A. Block, Chmn.
T.R. Block, Pres. & Treas.
M. Kopp, Sr. V.P. & C.F.O.

INCORPORATED: NJ, Mar., 1970

PRINCIPAL OFFICE: 257 Cornelison Avenue, Jersey City, NJ 07302-9988

TELEPHONE NUMBER: (201) 434-3000

NO. OF EMPLOYEES: 3,501

ANNUAL MEETING: In March

SHAREHOLDERS: 564 Cl. A (approx.); 5 Cl. B (approx.)

INSTITUTIONAL HOLDINGS:
No. of Institutions: 83
Shares Held: 5,114,172

REGISTRAR(S):

TRANSFER AGENT(S): American Stock Transfer & Trust Co., 40 Wall Street, New York, NY 10005

BLOCK (H. & R.), INC.

YIELD 3.1%
P/E RATIO 26.3

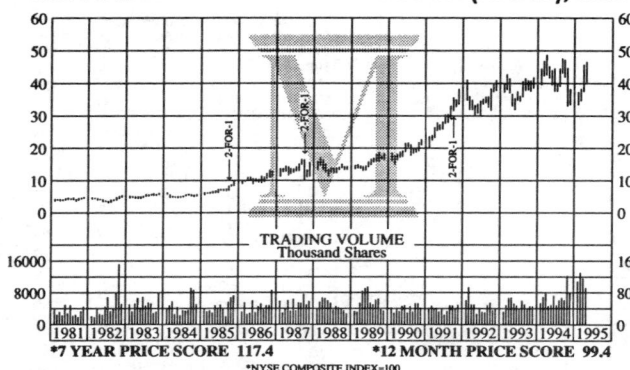

INTERIM EARNINGS (Per Share):

Qtr.	July	Oct.	Jan.	Apr.
1991-92	d0.05	d0.03	0.05	1.52
1992-93	---------------	1.68	---------------	
1993-94	d0.08	d0.04	d0.17	1.83
1994-95	d0.03	d0.01	0.08	...

INTERIM DIVIDENDS (Per Share):

Amt.	Decl.	Ex.	Rec.	Pay.
0.28Q	2/28/94	3/4/94	3/10/94	4/1/94
0.28Q	5/27	6/6	6/10	7/1
0.3125Q	6/22	9/6	9/12	10/3
0.3125Q	11/30	12/7	12/13	1/3/95
0.3125Q	2/28/95	3/7/95	3/13/95	4/3

*Indicated div.: $1.25**

CAPITALIZATION (4/30/94):

	($000)	(%)
Common & Surplus	707,875	100.0
Total	707,875	100.0

DIVIDEND ACHIEVER STATUS:
Rank: 45   1984-94 Growth Rate: 15.6%
Total Years of Dividend Growth: 31

RECENT DEVELOPMENTS: For the quarter ended 10/31/94, HRB reported a loss from continuing operations of $1.3 million compared with a loss of $4.2 million for the corresponding quarter in 1993. Revenues were $172.9 million, up 31.7% from $131.2 million for the year-ago quarter. H&R Block Tax Services, Inc. increased revenues 5.4% to $27.7 million resulting from greater tax preparation fees in Australia during its tax filing period.

PROSPECTS: CompuServe Inc., HRB's computer services subsidiary, has begun new ventures with the entertainment industry, offering the first-ever download of an unreleased full-length song and a wide array of video clips from major movies. Block Financial Corporation will likely report a loss from operations and start-up businesses in the 1995 third quarter resulting from the decision to not participate in Refund Anticipation Loans made during the 1995 tax season.

BUSINESS

H&R BLOCK, INC., is a diversified personal services company providing services in two industry areas. H&R Block Tax Services, Inc., offers tax return preparation and electronic filing services. CompuServe Inc., provides communications and information services to personal computer owners worldwide through CompuServe Information Service. For the fiscal year ended 4/30/94, revenues (operating profit) were derived from: tax operations, 61.1%, (64.2%); computer services, 34.8% (33%); financial services, 3.4% (2.8%) and other, 0.7% (0%). The temporary services unit Interim Services, Inc. was sold in January 1994, through a public stock offering.

ANNUAL EARNINGS AND DIVIDENDS PER SHARE

	4/30/94	4/30/93	4/30/92	4/30/91	4/30/90	4/30/89	4/30/88
Earnings Per Share	1.54	1.68	1.49	1.31	1.15	0.95	0.86
Dividends Per Share	1.152	1.03	① 0.805	0.675	0.55	0.46	② 0.388
Dividend Payout %	74.8	61.3	54.0	33.8	47.8	48.4	45.1

① 2-for-1 stk split,10/02/91   ② 2-for-1 stk split, 10/87

ANNUAL FINANCIAL DATA

RECORD OF EARNINGS (IN MILLIONS):

Total Revenues	1,238.7	1,525.3	1,370.7	1,190.8	1,052.7	899.6	794.1
Costs and Expenses	898.4	1,175.4	1,062.2	932.2	822.9	712.1	628.9
Depreciation & Amort	57.1	54.7	44.3	33.0	29.2	25.9	24.9
Operating Profit	471.0	439.0	384.9	334.0	295.8	239.2	211.2
Earn Bef Taxes on Income	283.2	295.3	264.3	225.6	200.5	161.6	140.3
Income Taxes	119.2	114.6	102.0	85.5	77.0	61.4	52.5
Net Income	① 164.0	180.7	162.3	140.1	123.5	100.2	87.9
Aver. Shs. Outstg. (000)	106,769	107,644	109,154	107,194	107,124	105,726	102,568

① Before disc. op. cr$36,533,000.

BALANCE SHEET (IN MILLIONS):

Cash and Cash Equivalents	514.4	334.8	274.3	228.2	239.8	252.0	210.9
Receivables, Net	165.9	228.7	271.9	392.4	369.0	315.8	208.4
Gross Property	357.7	320.8	261.0	233.0	210.5	192.4	169.0
Accumulated Depreciation	192.5	172.4	137.5	124.7	113.4	99.5	82.8
Long-Term Debt	...	...	...	...	4.9	4.7	4.7
Net Stockholders' Equity	707.9	650.5	613.7	573.6	503.3	445.9	373.7
Total Assets	1,074.7	1,005.8	962.7	1,035.8	941.5	826.4	676.5
Total Current Assets	699.8	589.9	568.0	648.0	642.2	595.5	440.1
Total Current Liabilities	336.2	329.9	327.8	437.3	411.8	356.7	285.4
Net Working Capital	363.6	260.0	240.2	210.6	230.4	238.8	154.7
Year End Shs Outstg (000)	106,149	106,355	106,598	106,496	105,628	105,011	101,364

STATISTICAL RECORD:

Operating Profit Margin %	22.9	19.4	19.3	18.9	19.0	18.0	17.7
Book Value Per Share	5.97	4.93	4.61	4.28	3.99	3.56	2.98
Return on Equity %	23.2	27.8	26.4	24.4	24.5	22.5	23.5
Return on Assets %	15.3	18.0	16.9	13.5	13.1	12.1	13.0
Average Yield %	3.1	2.8	2.8	3.6	3.5	3.2	2.9
P/E Ratio	27.8-20.7	24.5-17.9	25.7-13.4	17.4-11.5	16.3-11.4	18.2-12.0	19.3-11.6
Price Range	42¾-31⅛	41⅛-30⅛	38¼-20	22¾-15	18¾-13⅛	17¼-11⅜	16⅝-10

Statistics are as originally reported.

OFFICERS:
H.W. Bloch, Chmn.
T.M. Bloch, Pres. & C.E.O.
W.P. Anderson, V.P.-Corp. Devel. & C.F.O.
O. Wenich, V.P., Corp. Contr. & Treas.
J.H. Ingraham, Asst. V.P.-Legal & Sec.

INCORPORATED: MO, 1955

PRINCIPAL OFFICE: 4410 Main Street, Kansas City, MO 64111

TELEPHONE NUMBER: (816) 753-6900

FAX: (816) 753-8628

NO. OF EMPLOYEES: 3,400

ANNUAL MEETING: In September

SHAREHOLDERS: 33,457

INSTITUTIONAL HOLDINGS:
No. of Institutions: 557
Shares Held: 77,049,315

REGISTRAR(S): Boatmen's Trust Co., St.Louis, MO 63101

TRANSFER AGENT(S): Boatmen's Trust Co., St. Louis, MO 63101

NASDAQ SYMBOL BOAT
Rec. Pr. 30⅛

BOATMEN'S BANCSHARES, INC.

YIELD 4.5%
P/E RATIO 8.9

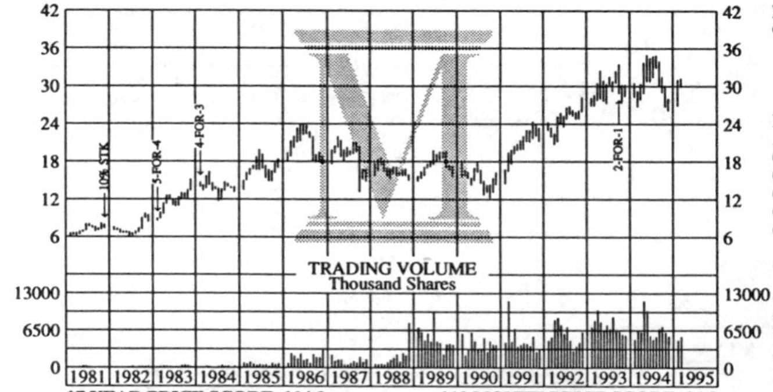

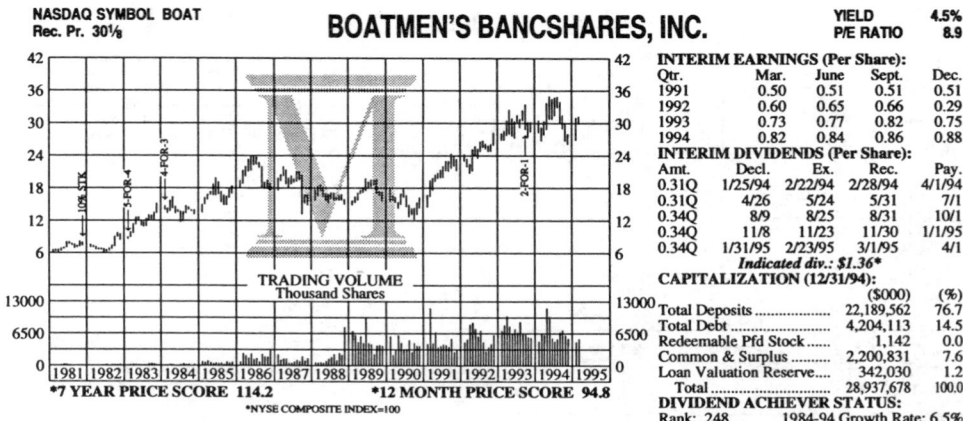

*7 YEAR PRICE SCORE 114.2 *12 MONTH PRICE SCORE 94.8

*NYSE COMPOSITE INDEX=100

INTERIM EARNINGS (Per Share):

Qtr.	Mar.	June	Sept.	Dec.
1991	0.50	0.51	0.51	0.51
1992	0.60	0.65	0.66	0.29
1993	0.73	0.77	0.82	0.75
1994	0.82	0.84	0.86	0.88

INTERIM DIVIDENDS (Per Share):

Amt.	Decl.	Ex.	Rec.	Pay.
0.31Q	1/25/94	2/22/94	2/28/94	4/1/94
0.31Q	4/26	5/24	5/31	7/1
0.34Q	8/9	8/25	8/31	10/1
0.34Q	11/8	11/23	11/30	1/1/95
0.34Q	1/31/95	2/23/95	3/1/95	4/1

*Indicated div.: $1.36**

CAPITALIZATION (12/31/94):

	($000)	(%)
Total Deposits	22,189,562	76.7
Total Debt	4,204,113	14.5
Redeemable Pfd Stock	1,142	0.0
Common & Surplus	2,200,831	7.6
Loan Valuation Reserve	342,030	1.2
Total	28,937,678	100.0

DIVIDEND ACHIEVER STATUS:
Rank: 248 1984-94 Growth Rate: 6.5%
Total Years of Dividend Growth: 14

RECENT DEVELOPMENTS: Net income for the year ended 12/31/94 was $355.3 million, up 11.9% from the $317.4 million reported for 1993. Earnings benefited from an increase in both interest and noninterest income and stronger credit quality as evidenced in a lower loan loss provision. Net interest income moved up 5.1% to $1.02 billion from $974.5 million. Interest and fees on loans totaled $1.27 billion versus $1.12 billion the year before. Noninterest income advanced to $526.5 million from $500.4 million, paced by a 27% gain in credit card income. Investment banking income fell 13.7% to $30.7 million. The provision for loan losses was significantly lowered to $24.3 million from $60.3 million a year earlier. Noninterest expense totaled $252.4 million versus $245.2 million in 1993. Excluding purchase acquisitions, noninterest expense rose only 1.6% in 1994.

BUSINESS

BOATMEN'S BANCSHARES, INC. is the largest bank holding company in Missouri. The Corporation's principal office is located in St. Louis, Missouri where its largest subsidiary, The Boatmen's National Bank of St. Louis, is located. The Corporation owns directly substantially all of the capital stock of 51 subsidiary banks, a trust company, a mortgage banking company, a credit life insurance company and an insurance agency. Boatmen's currently operates approximately 400 locations in Arkansas, Illinois, Iowa, Kansas, Missouri, New Mexico, Oklahoma, Tennessee, and Texas. The business of the Corporation consists primarily of the ownership, supervision and control of its subsidiaries. The Corporation provides its subsidiaries with advice, counsel and specialized services in various fields of financial and banking policy operations. The Corporation also engages in negotiations designed to lead to the acquisition of other banks and closely-related businesses.

ANNUAL EARNINGS AND DIVIDENDS PER SHARE

	1994	1993	1992	1991	1990	1989	1988
Earnings Per Share	3.40	3.07	2.26	2.04	1.95	1.86	1.00
Dividends Per Share	1.27	[1] 1.15	1.09	1.07	1.06	1.015	1.00
Dividend Payout %	37.4	37.5	48.3	52.6	54.4	54.6	99.5

[1] 2-for-1 stk split,10/04/93

ANNUAL FINANCIAL DATA

	1994	1993	1992	1991	1990	1989	1988
RECORD OF EARNINGS (IN MILLIONS):							
Total Interest Income	1,767.7	1,613.6	1,566.1	1,315.8	1,293.9	1,267.1	1,180.0
Total Interest Expense	743.7	632.0	718.7	753.3	808.9	804.8	710.8
Net Interest Income	1,023.9	981.6	847.5	562.5	485.0	462.3	469.1
Credit Loss Provision	24.3	60.2	134.6	88.5	69.2	69.4	87.4
Net Income	355.3	317.4	215.5	150.1	135.2	129.2	69.8
Aver. Shs. Outstg. (000)	106,400	104,100	95,530	73,774	69,359	68,360	66,868
BALANCE SHEET (IN MILLIONS):							
Cash & Due From Banks	1,885.5	1,608.1	1,700.4	1,400.7	1,788.9	1,237.9	1,570.3
Loans & Lse Financing, Net	16,138.4	14,484.8	12,340.8	9,520.3	9,032.1	8,811.5	8,757.1
Total Domestic Deposits	22,189.6	20,909.0	18,987.8	13,477.2	13,665.6	10,851.3	11,223.8
Long-term Debt	515.1	486.3	380.1	238.1	204.7	214.1	220.5
Net Stockholders' Equity	2,202.0	2,134.4	1,794.5	1,344.6	1,148.3	1,087.4	1,031.8
Total Assets	28,927.2	26,654.0	23,386.7	17,634.7	17,468.5	14,542.4	14,675.8
Year End Shs Outstg (000)	104,322	104,126	96,556	75,954	69,382	69,315	67,262
STATISTICAL RECORD:							
Return on Assets %	1.23	1.19	0.92	0.85	0.77	0.89	0.48
Return on Equity %	16.10	14.90	12.00	11.20	11.80	11.90	6.80
Book Value Per Share	21.10	20.49	18.57	17.69	16.53	15.67	14.86
Average Yield %	4.2	3.8	4.4	5.5	7.0	5.9	5.9
P/E Ratio	10.3-7.7	10.9-8.8	12.5-9.2	11.9-7.1	9.2-6.3	10.6-8.0	18.6-15.0
Price Range	35-26⅛	33½-26⅞	28¼-20¾	24⅜-14½	17⅞-12¼	19¾-14⅞	18⅝-15

Statistics are as originally reported.

OFFICERS:
A.B. Craig, III., Chmn. & C.E.O.
G.L. Curl, Vice-Chmn.
J.P. MacCarthy, Vice-Chmn.
S.B. Hayes, III., Pres.
J.W. Kienker, Exec. V.P. & C.F.O.

INCORPORATED: MO, Jun., 1946

PRINCIPAL OFFICE: One Boatmen's Plaza
800 Market Street, St. Louis, MO 63101

TELEPHONE NUMBER: (314) 466-6000
FAX: (314) 466-6027
NO. OF EMPLOYEES: 14,169
ANNUAL MEETING: In April
SHAREHOLDERS: 29,695 (approx.)
INSTITUTIONAL HOLDINGS:
No. of Institutions: 417
Shares Held: 50,761,929

REGISTRAR(S): Boatmen's Trust Co., St.Louis, MO 63101

TRANSFER AGENT(S): Boatmen's Trust Co., St. Louis, MO 63101

BOWL AMERICA INC.

YIELD 4.8%
P/E RATIO 11.9

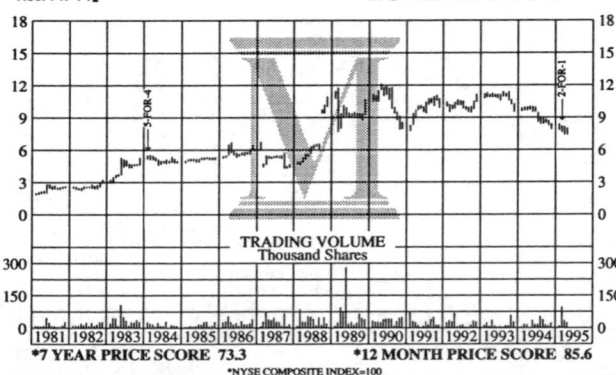

TRADING VOLUME
Thousand Shares

| 1981 | 1982 | 1983 | 1984 | 1985 | 1986 | 1987 | 1988 | 1989 | 1990 | 1991 | 1992 | 1993 | 1994 | 1995 |

*7 YEAR PRICE SCORE 73.3 ***12 MONTH PRICE SCORE 85.6**
*NYSE COMPOSITE INDEX=100

INTERIM EARNINGS (Per Share):

Qtr.	Sept.	Dec.	Mar.	June
1993-94	-------	0.67	-------	
1994-95	d0.03	0.37	...	...

INTERIM DIVIDENDS (Per Share):

Amt.	Decl.	Ex.	Rec.	Pay.
0.18Q	6/23/94	7/8/94	7/14/94	8/10/94
0.18Q	9/27	10/4	10/11	11/16
0.18Q	12/6	1/11/95	1/18/95	2/15/95
100%	12/6	2/16	1/18	2/15
0.09Q	3/28/95	4/12	4/19	5/17

Indicated div.: $0.36

CAPITALIZATION (7/3/94):

	($000)	(%)
Deferred Income Tax	1,035	3.3
Common & Surplus	29,948	96.7
Total	30,983	100.0

DIVIDEND ACHIEVER STATUS:
Rank: 90   1984-94 Growth Rate: 13.2%
Total Years of Dividend Growth: 22

RECENT DEVELOPMENTS: For the second quarter ended 12/31/94, net income decreased 14% to $1.1 million compared with $1.2 million for the same quarter in 1993. The Company attributed the decline to unseasonably mild weather, which allowed people to spend more time outdoors. The weather for the third quarter is expected to be more harsh, therefore tournament activity should increase. Reve-

nues increased 7.2% to $8.1 million for the second quarter versus $7.6 million for the comparable quarter of 1993. Of the 26 Bowl America locations, the Company's center in Gaithersburg is the most active. However, Gaithersburg reported lower earnings due to higher expenses attributed to the establishment of 24 hour operations and expanding the diner business.

BUSINESS

BOWL AMERICA INC. and its subsidiaries are engaged in the operation of 14 bowling centers in the greater metropolitan area of Washington, D.C., three bowling centers in the greater metropolitan area of Baltimore, Maryland, two bowling centers in the greater metropolitan area of Orlando, Florida, three bowling centers in the greater metropolitan area of Richmond, Virginia, and three bowling centers in the greater metropolitan area of Jacksonville, Florida. These 25 centers contain a total of 936 lanes. Additionally, the Company recently opened a new 48-lane center in Gaithersburg, Maryland. Hence, there are now 26 bowling centers comprised of 984 lanes. The Company has also incorported food and beverage services into each bowling center. In 1994, food and beverage sales represented approximately 30% of operating revenues. The remaining 70% of operating revenues was accounted for by fees for bowling and related services. On October 31, 1958, the Company acquired entire stock of Shirley Tenpin Bowl, Inc. for 200,000 shares. In July 1970, the Company acquired Lynwood Bowl, located in Woodbridge, Virginia.

ANNUAL EARNINGS AND DIVIDENDS PER SHARE

	7/3/94	6/27/93	6/28/92	6/30/91	7/1/90	7/2/89	7/3/88
Earnings Per Share	0.66	0.68	0.65	0.72	0.76	0.71	0.60
Dividends Per Share	① 0.36	0.34	0.33	0.32	0.30	0.27	0.25
Dividend Payout %	54.5	50.0	50.0	44.4	39.5	38.0	41.7

① 100%stk.div.2/15/95.

ANNUAL FINANCIAL DATA

RECORD OF EARNINGS (IN THOUSANDS):

Total Revenues	28,171	27,300	26,846	27,363	27,339	25,803	23,650
Costs and Expenses	20,854	20,180	19,682	19,632	19,188	18,175	17,168
Depreciation & Amort	1,715	1,416	1,243	1,086	1,126	1,097	1,015
Operating Profit	5,602	5,704	5,920	6,645	7,025	6,532	5,467
Earn Bef Prov for Inc Taxes	6,082	6,324	5,912	6,624	6,987	6,489	5,419
Income Taxes	2,265	2,350	2,195	2,485	2,640	2,421	2,022
Net Income	3,817	3,974	3,717	4,139	4,347	4,068	3,397
Aver. Shs. Outstg.	5,761	5,784	5,785	5,754	5,749	5,741	5,723

BALANCE SHEET (IN THOUSANDS):

Cash and Cash Equivalents	8,470	9,633	9,635	10,586	9,653	9,273	5,935
Receivables, Net	...	507	...	...	...	...	79
Inventories	586	635	497	510	549	537	446
Gross Property	39,515	34,461	32,195	29,723	27,395	24,147	23,551
Accumulated Depreciation	17,066	15,740	14,909	14,626	13,781	12,853	11,866
Long-Term Debt	...	...	...	...	132	203	140
Net Stockholders' Equity	29,948	28,452	26,474	24,482	22,064	19,501	16,820
Total Assets	33,550	31,611	29,471	28,289	25,564	22,879	19,659
Total Current Assets	9,430	11,444	10,665	11,663	10,597	10,184	6,718
Total Current Liabilities	2,567	2,124	2,071	2,911	2,587	2,504	2,045
Net Working Capital	6,863	9,319	8,594	8,752	8,009	7,680	4,673
Year End Shares Outstg	5,752	5,780	5,786	5,749	5,749	5,756	3,820

STATISTICAL RECORD:

Operating Profit Margin %	19.9	20.9	22.1	24.3	25.7	25.3	23.1
Book Value Per Share	5.21	4.92	4.58	4.26	3.84	3.39	4.40
Return on Equity %	12.7	14.0	14.0	16.9	19.7	20.9	20.2
Return on Assets %	11.4	12.6	12.6	14.6	17.0	17.8	17.3
Average Yield %	4.0	3.2	3.1	3.4	3.0	2.8	3.5
P/E Ratio	15.0-11.8	16.6-13.9	17.2-14.7	15.5-10.8	16.1-10.4	16.5-10.9	18.5-7.8
Price Range	10-7⅛	11⅜-9½	11⅛-9½	11⅛-7¾	12⅛-7⅛	11¾-7¾	11-4⅝

Statistics are as originally reported.

OFFICERS:
L.H. Goldberg, Pres.
R.E. Macklin, Sr. V.P. & Treas.
Dr. H. Katzman, Sr. V.P. & Sec.

INCORPORATED: MD, Jul., 1958

PRINCIPAL OFFICE: 6446 Edsall Road, Alexandria, VA 22312

TELEPHONE NUMBER: (703) 941-6300

NO. OF EMPLOYEES: 800 (approx.)

ANNUAL MEETING: In December

SHAREHOLDERS: 618 Cl. A; Cl. B, 33 (approx.)

INSTITUTIONAL HOLDINGS:
No. of Institutions: 20
Shares Held: 495,435

REGISTRAR(S): First American Bank of Washington, Washington, DC 20005

TRANSFER AGENT(S): First American Bank of Washington, Washington, DC 20005

BRADY (W.H.) CO.

YIELD 1.3%
P/E RATIO 18.0

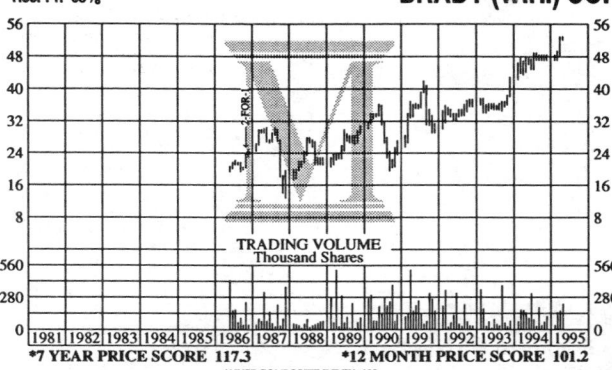

INTERIM EARNINGS (Per Share):

Qtr.	Oct.	Jan.	Apr.	July
1991-92	0.44	0.44	0.52	d0.22
1992-93	0.48	0.48	0.56	0.81
1993-94	0.59	0.53	0.76	0.67
1994-95	0.70	0.83	1.30	...

INTERIM DIVIDENDS (Per Share):

Amt.	Decl.	Ex.	Rec.	Pay.
0.17Q	3/25/94	4/4/94	4/8/94	4/29/94
0.17Q	6/6	7/1	7/8	7/29
0.20Q	9/23	10/3	10/10	10/31
0.20Q	11/22	12/30	1/6/95	1/31/95
0.20Q	2/21/95	4/3/95	4/7	4/28

Indicated div.: $0.80

CAPITALIZATION (7/31/94):

	($000)	(%)
Long-Term Debt	1,855	1.3
Preferred Stock	2,855	1.9
Common & Surplus	142,274	96.8
Total	146,984	100.0

DIVIDEND ACHIEVER STATUS:
Rank: 1   1984-94 Growth Rate: 39.7%
Total Years of Dividend Growth: 10

TRADING VOLUME
Thousand Shares

*7 YEAR PRICE SCORE 117.3   *12 MONTH PRICE SCORE 101.2
*NYSE COMPOSITE INDEX=100

RECENT DEVELOPMENTS: Net income for the second quarter of fiscal 1995 ended 1/31/95 was $6.1 million or $0.83 per share, up 58% over 1994's second-quarter net income of $3.9 million or $0.53 per share. Net sales for the second quarter were $78.9 million, up 23% from the previous year's sales of $64.1 million. Operating income advanced 59% to $9.7 million compared with $6.1 million in the corresponding period of 1993. Record-level sales were aided by all of the Company's operating groups posting sales increases. Sales were especially strong in Europe, due in part to increased demand for printing systems and label and tape consumables. The Company announced on 2/1/95 that it was selling its medical products unit, Brady Medical Products, Company to B. Braun Medical Inc.

BUSINESS

W.H. BRADY CO. develops, manufactures and sells a broad range of stock and customized products employing its knowledge of surface chemistry, principally in adhesives, coatings and graphics technologies. Brady's products include over 30,000 stock items and a wide variety of custom items, which are used primarily to identify, inform or instruct, including pressure sensitive identification, labeling and marketing systems for electrical wires and pipes; self-bonding nameplates, faceplates, and control panels; safety and instructional signs; specialized tapes used in audio, video and computer applications; and pressure sensitive wound care products.

REVENUES

(7/31/94)	($000)	(%)
United States	161,024	62.9
Europe	64,634	25.3
Other	30,183	11.8
Total	255,841	100.0

ANNUAL EARNINGS AND DIVIDENDS PER SHARE

	7/31/94	7/31/93	7/31/92	7/31/91	7/31/90	7/31/89	7/31/88
Earnings Per Share	2.55	2.33	[1] 1.16	2.14	2.09	[2] 1.31	1.36
Dividends Per Share	0.71	0.62	0.57	0.50	0.42	0.31	0.25
Dividend Payout %	27.8	26.6	49.1	23.4	20.0	23.7	18.4

[1] Before acctg. chg. [2] Before extraord. item & acctg. chg.

ANNUAL FINANCIAL DATA

RECORD OF EARNINGS (IN THOUSANDS):

Total Revenues	255,841	242,970	235,965	211,063	191,161	174,174	153,016
Costs and Expenses	216,931	207,473	211,880	183,431	162,450	152,661	130,912
Depreciation & Amort	9,435	10,173	8,744	7,478	6,453	6,884	6,255
Operating Income	29,475	25,324	15,341	20,154	22,258	14,629	15,849
Income Bef Income Taxes	29,902	25,829	15,361	22,451	25,616	16,653	17,273
Income Taxes	11,362	8,973	6,972	7,054	10,606	6,778	6,968
Net Income	18,540	16,856	[1] 8,389	15,397	15,010	[2] 9,875	10,305
Aver. Shs. Outstg.	7,226	7,195	7,176	7,158	7,151	7,457	7,490

[1] Before acctg. change dr$3,334,000. [2] Before extra. item cr$4,625,000; and acctg. chg cr$1,233,000.

BALANCE SHEET (IN THOUSANDS):

Cash and Cash Equivalents	66,107	42,366	28,519	35,991	38,384	27,506	20,049
Receivables, Net	32,308	30,522	30,851	26,144	25,185	22,874	21,307
Inventories	23,737	22,731	22,007	19,702	17,681	13,944	11,966
Gross Property	116,635	114,746	118,829	99,821	87,875	79,282	75,279
Accumulated Depreciation	52,292	47,384	47,362	40,433	35,500	30,658	27,808
Long-Term Debt	1,855	1,978	2,524	1,982	3,298	3,637	3,086
Net Stockholders' Equity	145,129	128,068	119,771	115,260	103,784	89,443	84,987
Total Assets	202,509	179,899	173,054	156,812	147,197	129,890	117,201
Total Current Assets	131,763	105,644	94,641	96,084	94,037	77,082	61,027
Total Current Liabilities	31,740	27,703	28,548	25,201	26,240	24,026	18,535
Net Working Capital	100,023	77,941	66,093	70,883	67,797	53,056	42,492
Year End Shares Outstg	7,246	7,206	7,180	7,165	7,156	7,150	7,490

STATISTICAL RECORD:

Operating Profit Margin %	11.5	10.4	6.5	9.5	11.6	8.4	10.4
Book Value Per Share	19.63	17.38	16.28	15.69	14.10	12.11	10.96
Return on Equity %	12.8	13.2	7.0	13.4	14.5	11.0	12.1
Return on Assets %	9.2	9.4	4.8	9.8	10.2	7.6	8.8
Average Yield %	1.6	1.7	1.7	1.5	1.5	1.2	1.1
P/E Ratio	9.8-8.5	9.4-7.5	29.3-23.4	10.0-6.1	8.9-4.8	23.7-15.6	20.6-12.7
Price Range	49-42¼	43-34	37½-30	42-25½	36¼-19½	31-20½	28-17¼

Statistics are as originally reported.

OFFICERS:
K.M. Hudson, Pres. & C.E.O.
D.P. DeLuca, Sr. V.P.-Fin., C.F.O. & Treas.
P.J. Lettenberger, Sec.

INCORPORATED: WI, 1939

PRINCIPAL OFFICE: 727 West Glendale Avenue P.O Box 571, Milwaukee, WI 53201

TELEPHONE NUMBER: (414) 332-8100
FAX: (414) 332-0861
NO. OF EMPLOYEES: 1,900 (approx.)
ANNUAL MEETING: In November
SHAREHOLDERS: 304 (cl A); 2 (Cl B).
INSTITUTIONAL HOLDINGS:
No. of Institutions: 51
Shares Held: 3,069,263

REGISTRAR(S):

TRANSFER AGENT(S): First Wisconsin Trust Co., Milwaukee, WI

BRISTOL-MYERS SQUIBB CO.

YIELD 4.7%
P/E RATIO 17.6

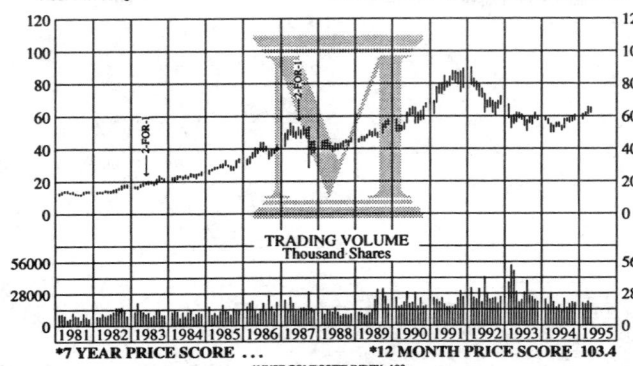

INTERIM EARNINGS (Per Share):

Qtr.	Mar.	June	Sept.	Dec.
1991	0.94	0.94	1.08	0.98
1992	1.03	0.92	1.10	d0.08
1993	1.11	1.01	1.18	0.50
1994	1.14	1.07	1.22	0.19

INTERIM DIVIDENDS (Per Share):

Amt.	Decl.	Ex.	Rec.	Pay.
0.73Q	3/1/94	3/25/94	4/1/94	5/1/94
0.73Q	6/6	6/27	7/1	8/1
0.73Q	9/12	10/3	10/7	11/1
0.74Q	12/6	12/30	1/6/95	2/1/95
0.74Q	3/7/95	4/3/95	4/7	5/1

Indicated div.: $2.96*

CAPITALIZATION (12/31/94):

	($000)	(%)
Long-Term Debt	644,000	10.1
Common & Surplus	5,704,000	89.9
Total	6,348,000	100.0

TRADING VOLUME
Thousand Shares

DIVIDEND ACHIEVER STATUS:
Rank: 53   1984-94 Growth Rate: 15.0%
Total Years of Dividend Growth: 22

*7 YEAR PRICE SCORE ...   *12 MONTH PRICE SCORE 103.4
*NYSE COMPOSITE INDEX=100

RECENT DEVELOPMENTS: For the year ended 12/31/94, net income declined 6% to $1.84 billion compared with $1.96 billion a year ago. Sales rose 5% to $11.98 billion from $11.41 billion. Earnings included special charges of $488 million after taxes ($0.96 per share) in 1994 and $310 million ($0.60 per share) in 1993. The special charges in both years were associated with breast implant liability claims related to a discontinued subsidiary.

PROSPECTS: Capoten sales will continue to benefit from new indications for the treatment of diabetes and heart dysfunction. Pharmaceutical sales will also receive a boost from the FDA's approval of Serzone, a treatment for depression. This product will be less expensive and is believed to eliminate certain side effects associated with Eli Lilly's Prozac.

BUSINESS

BRISTOL-MYERS SQUIBB is involved in health, pharmaceutical, and medical related areas. Pharmaceutical Products, 58% of 1994 sales, include prescription medicines, mainly cardiovascular drugs and antibiotics, anti-cancer and central nervous systems drugs, diagnostic agents and other pharmaceutical products. Medical Devices, include orthopedic implants, ostomy care and wound management products, surgical instruments and other medical devices. Nonprescription Health Products, include infant formulas and other nutritional products, analgesics, vitamins, cough/cold remedies and skin care products. Toiletries and Beauty Aids, include hair care preparations, haircoloring, and deodorants.

BUSINESS LINE ANALYSIS

(12/31/94)	Rev(%)	Inc(%)
Pharmaceutical		
Products	58.2	86.0
Medical Devices	14.1	(9.7)
Nonprescrip Health		
Prods	17.1	17.3
Toiletries & Beauty		
Aids	10.6	6.4
Total	100.0	100.0

ANNUAL EARNINGS AND DIVIDENDS PER SHARE

	1994	1993	1992	1991	1990	1989	1988
Earnings Per Share	3.62	3.80 ①	②2.97	3.95	3.33	1.43	2.88
Dividends Per Share	2.92	2.88	2.76	2.40	2.12	2.00	1.68
Dividend Payout %	80.7	75.8	92.9	60.8	63.7	N.M.	58.3

① Before disc. oper. ② Before acctg. chg.

ANNUAL FINANCIAL DATA

RECORD OF EARNINGS (IN MILLIONS):

	1994	1993	1992	1991	1990	1989	1988
Total Revenues	11,984.0	11,413.0	11,156.0	11,159.0	10,300.0	9,189.0	5,973.0
Costs and Expenses	9,185.0	8,702.0	8,901.0	8,147.0	7,667.0	7,910.0	4,656.0
Depreciation & Amort	328.0	308.0	295.0	246.0	244.0	196.0	128.0
Operating Profit	4,329.0	4,031.0	3,933.0	3,759.0	3,270.0	2,727.0	1,583.0
Earn Bef Income Taxes	2,555.0	2,571.0	1,987.0	2,887.0	2,524.0	1,277.0	1,285.0
Income Taxes	713.0	612.0	449.0	831.0	776.0	530.0	456.0
Net Income	1,842.0	1,959.0	①1,538.0	2,056.0	1,748.0	747.0	829.0
Aver. Shs. Outstg. (000)	509,000	515,000	518,000	521,000	525,000	523,000	288,000

① Before disc. op. cr$670,000,000; and acctg. chg dr$246,000,000.

BALANCE SHEET (IN MILLIONS):

	1994	1993	1992	1991	1990	1989	1988
Cash and Cash Equivalents	2,423.0	2,729.0	2,385.0	1,583.0	1,958.0	2,282.0	1,710.0
Receivables, Net	2,043.0	1,859.0	1,984.0	1,971.0	1,776.0	1,578.0	946.0
Inventories	1,397.0	1,322.0	1,490.0	1,451.0	1,366.0	1,139.0	689.0
Gross Property	5,836.0	5,236.0	5,032.0	4,718.0	4,271.0	3,804.0	2,078.0
Accumulated Depreciation	2,170.0	1,862.0	1,891.0	1,782.0	1,640.0	1,454.0	828.0
Long-Term Debt	644.0	588.0	176.0	135.0	231.0	237.0	215.0
Net Stockholders' Equity	5,704.0	5,940.0	6,020.0	5,795.0	5,418.0	5,084.0	3,547.0
Total Assets	12,910.0	12,101.0	10,804.0	9,416.0	9,215.0	8,497.0	5,191.0
Total Current Assets	6,710.0	6,570.0	6,621.0	5,567.0	5,670.0	5,552.0	3,566.0
Total Current Liabilities	4,274.0	3,065.0	3,300.0	2,752.0	2,821.0	2,659.0	1,164.0
Net Working Capital	2,436.0	3,505.0	3,321.0	2,815.0	2,849.0	2,893.0	2,402.0
Year End Shs Outstg (000)	507,000	512,000	518,000	520,000	524,000	525,000	288,000

STATISTICAL RECORD:

	1994	1993	1992	1991	1990	1989	1988
Operating Profit Margin %	20.6	21.1	17.6	24.8	23.2	11.8	19.9
Book Value Per Share	9.40	11.23	11.33	10.82	9.97	9.26	11.62
Return on Equity %	32.3	33.0	25.5	35.5	32.3	14.7	23.4
Return on Assets %	14.3	16.2	14.2	21.8	19.0	8.8	16.0
Average Yield %	5.3	4.9	3.7	3.2	3.6	3.9	4.0
P/E Ratio	16.9-13.8	17.7-13.4	30.3-20.2	22.6-15.5	20.4-15.2	40.6-30.8	16.1-13.2
Price Range	61-50	67¼-50⅞	90⅛-60	89⅜-61⅛	68-50½		58-44 46½-38⅛

Statistics are as originally reported.

OFFICERS:
R.L. Gelb, Chmn.
C.A. Heimbold, Jr., Pres. & C.E.O.
M.E. Autera, Exec. Vic-Pres. & C.F.O.
H.M. Bains, Jr., Treasurer
P.D. Kasa, Secretary
F.S. Schiff, Controller
INCORPORATED: DE, Aug., 1933
PRINCIPAL OFFICE: 345 Park Ave., New York, NY 10154-0037

TELEPHONE NUMBER: (212) 546-4000

NO. OF EMPLOYEES: 6,732

ANNUAL MEETING: In May

SHAREHOLDERS: 158,239 common

INSTITUTIONAL HOLDINGS:
No. of Institutions: 1,238
Shares Held: 245,088,427

REGISTRAR(S): Chemical Bank, New York, NY

TRANSFER AGENT(S): Chemical Bank, New York, NY

NYS SYMBOL BU
Rec. Pr. 23¾

BROOKLYN UNION GAS CO.

YIELD 5.9%
P/E RATIO 12.7

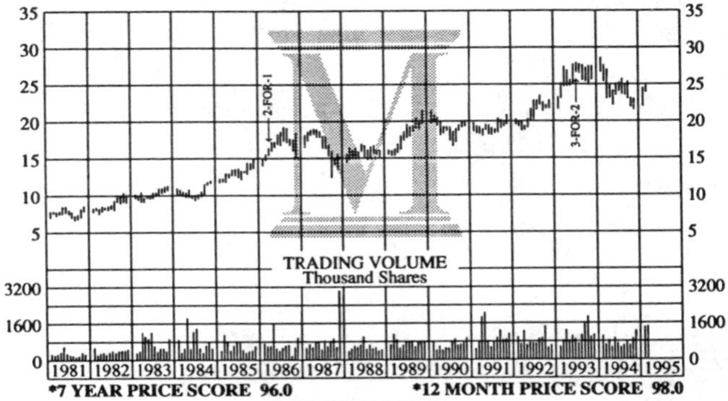

35
30
25
20
15
10
5
2-FOR-1
3-FOR-2
TRADING VOLUME
Thousand Shares
3200
1600
0
1981 1982 1983 1984 1985 1986 1987 1988 1989 1990 1991 1992 1993 1994 1995

*7 YEAR PRICE SCORE 96.0 *12 MONTH PRICE SCORE 98.0

*NYSE COMPOSITE INDEX=100

INTERIM EARNINGS (Per Share):

Qtr.	Dec.	Mar.	June	Sept.
1991-92	0.85	1.35	d0.12	d0.71
1992-93	----------	1.73	----------	
1993-94	0.90	1.57	d0.16	d0.44
1994-95	0.90	...	...	...

INTERIM DIVIDENDS (Per Share):

Amt.	Decl.	Ex.	Rec.	Pay.
0.3375Q	3/23/94	3/28/94	4/4/94	5/1/94
0.3375Q	6/22	6/28	7/5	8/1
0.3375Q	9/29	10/4	10/11	11/1
0.3475Q	12/21	12/27	1/3/95	2/1/95
0.3475Q	3/22/95	3/29/95	4/4	5/1

*Indicated div.: $1.39**

CAPITALIZATION (9/30/94):

	($000)	(%)
Long-Term Debt	701,377	40.4
Deferred Income Tax	252,316	14.6
Redeemable Pfd Stock	7,200	0.4
Common & Surplus	774,236	44.6
Total	1,735,129	100.0

DIVIDEND ACHIEVER STATUS:
Rank: 318 1984-94 Growth Rate: 3.0%
Total Years of Dividend Growth: 18

RECENT DEVELOPMENTS: For the quarter ended 12/31/94, net income was $42.8 million compared with $42.2 million last year. Revenues were $358.3 million, down 4% from $371.5 million a year earlier. Weather normalization in the regulated gas distribution business and hedging strategies in the gas exploration and production business significantly offset the effect on earnings of warm weather and low wellhead gas prices.

PROSPECTS: The Public Service Commission aproved a new three-year rate settlement to increase revenues by $31.3 million. The agreement allows an 11% return on common equity. Under the agreement the Company will be permitted to retain 100% of any earnings from incentives earned on a 12% ROE and retain 50% of any earnings thereafter. The Company is attempting to diversify operations through cogeneration and exploration projects.

BUSINESS

BROOKLYN UNION GAS is a natural gas distribution company with diversified businesses in gas exploration and production, propane distribution and gas-cogeneration projects. BU distributes natural gas in New York City's boroughs of Brooklyn, Queens and Staten Island with a service area covering 187 square miles and containing 1,122,000 accounts. Gas exploration, production and interstate marketing are conducted through Fuel Resources Inc., a wholly-owned subsidiary. This segment owns gas-lease interests in the Gulf of Mexico and has gas properties in the mid-continent region. The Company is also involved in gas cogeneration projects and equipment sales.

ANNUAL EARNINGS AND DIVIDENDS PER SHARE

	9/30/94	9/30/93	9/30/92	9/30/91	9/30/90	9/30/89	9/30/88
Earnings Per Share	1.85	1.73	1.35	1.45	1.43	1.68	1.66
Dividends Per Share	1.35	[1] 1.31	1.293	1.267	1.227	1.187	1.147
Dividend Payout %	75.7	76.0	96.0	87.2	86.0	70.6	69.1

[1] 3-for-2 stk split,07/21/93

ANNUAL FINANCIAL DATA

	9/30/94	9/30/93	9/30/92	9/30/91	9/30/90	9/30/89	9/30/88
RECORD OF EARNINGS (IN MILLIONS):							
Total Revenues	1,338.6	1,205.5	1,074.9	990.5	993.9	969.2	898.7
Maintenance	54.3	54.7	53.0	51.8	50.4	57.7	56.8
Prov for Fed Inc Taxes	40.7	41.5	29.2	26.7	19.0	26.4	26.4
Operating Income	134.3	123.1	98.4	95.5	93.3	98.0	90.0
Interest Expense	51.2	48.1	42.1	40.5	45.1	41.7	38.4
Net Income	87.4	76.6	59.9	61.8	56.4	64.3	61.7
Aver. Shs. Outstg. (000)	46,980	44,042	42,883	39,894	36,798	35,790	34,687
BALANCE SHEET (IN MILLIONS):							
Gross Plant	1,876.1	1,729.2	1,614.6	1,504.1	1,381.5	1,282.5	1,211.0
Accumulated Depreciation	470.8	423.7	385.9	352.8	318.8	293.1	314.5
Prop, Plant & Equip, Net	1,405.3	1,305.5	1,228.7	1,151.3	1,062.7	989.4	896.5
Long-term Debt	701.4	689.3	682.0	685.4	534.1	553.2	445.0
Net Stockholders' Equity	781.4	728.6	640.1	652.0	555.9	531.1	497.9
Total Assets	2,029.1	1,897.8	1,748.0	1,717.5	1,460.7	1,445.7	1,257.3
Year End Shs Outstg (000)	47,590	46,380	43,452	42,280	37,305	36,290	35,226
STATISTICAL RECORD:							
Book Value Per Share	16.27	15.55	14.55	14.37	13.68	13.36	12.77
Op. Inc/Net Pl %	9.6	9.4	8.0	8.3	8.8	9.9	10.0
Dep/Gr. Pl %	3.7	3.7	4.6	2.8	2.8	2.8	2.7
Accum. Dep/Gr. Pl %	25.1	24.5	23.9	23.5	23.1	22.9	26.0
Return on Equity %	11.3	10.6	9.5	10.2	11.1	13.3	13.7
Average Yield %	5.5	5.3	6.1	6.5	6.4	6.4	7.3
P/E Ratio	15.5-11.6	16.1-12.5	17.4-13.8	14.4-12.4	15.0-11.6	12.8-9.2	10.2-8.7
Price Range	28⅝-21½	27⅞-21⅝	23½-18⅝	20⅞-18	21½-16⅝	21½-15⅜	16⅞-14⅜

Statistics are as originally reported.

OFFICERS:
R.B. Catell, Pres. & C.E.O.
V.D. Enright, Sr. V.P. & C.F.O.
R.R. Wieczorek, V.P., Sec. & Treas.

INCORPORATED: NY, Sep., 1895

PRINCIPAL OFFICE: One MetroTech Center, Brooklyn, NY 11201-3850

TELEPHONE NUMBER: (718) 403-2000

FAX: (718) 852-8221

NO. OF EMPLOYEES: 3,506

ANNUAL MEETING: In February

SHAREHOLDERS: 35,233

INSTITUTIONAL HOLDINGS:
No. of Institutions: 159
Shares Held: 13,188,734

REGISTRAR(S): First Chicago Trust Co. of New York, New Jersey, NJ

TRANSFER AGENT(S): First Chicago Trust Co. of New York, New Jersey, NJ

NASDAQ SYMBOL BRNO
Rec. Pr. 10⅜

BRUNO'S, INC.

YIELD 2.5%
P/E RATIO 17.0

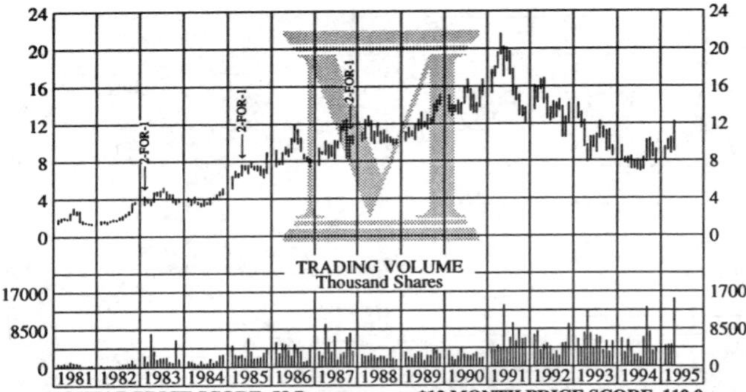

24
20
16
12
8
4
0
2-FOR-1
2-FOR-1
2-FOR-1
TRADING VOLUME
Thousand Shares
17000
8500
0
1981 1982 1983 1984 1985 1986 1987 1988 1989 1990 1991 1992 1993 1994 1995

*7 YEAR PRICE SCORE 58.7 *12 MONTH PRICE SCORE 110.0

*NYSE COMPOSITE INDEX=100

INTERIM EARNINGS (Per Share):

Qtr.	Sept.	Dec.	Apr.	June
1991-92	0.17	0.23	0.19	0.10
1992-93		0.60		
1993-94	0.12	0.12	0.12	0.16
1994-95	0.15	0.18	...	...

INTERIM DIVIDENDS (Per Share):

Amt.	Decl.	Ex.	Rec.	Pay.
0.06Q	5/2/94	5/9/94	5/13/94	5/27/94
0.065Q	7/25	8/1	8/5	8/19
0.065Q	10/17	10/24	10/28	11/10
0.065Q	1/18/95	2/6/95	2/10/95	2/24/95
0.065Q	5/1	5/8	5/12	5/26

Indicated div.: $0.26

CAPITALIZATION (7/2/94):

	($000)	(%)
Long-Term Debt	276,015	35.9
Cap. Lease Oblig.	20,445	2.7
Deferred Income Tax	51,136	6.6
Common & Surplus	421,354	54.8
Total	768,950	100.0

DIVIDEND ACHIEVER STATUS:
Rank: 64 1984-94 Growth Rate: 14.4%
Total Years of Dividend Growth: 20

RECENT DEVELOPMENTS: For the 14 weeks ended 12/31/94, net income was $14.1 million compared with $9.3 million a year earlier. Net sales increased 2.1% to $784.1 million from $768.2 million the year before. Same-store sales increased 1.6%. Results were aided by effective marketing and merchandising initiatives and expense controls. As a percentage of sales, gross margin increased to 23.6% from 22.5% a year earlier. Operating, selling and administrative expenses were flat at 18.1%. For the 26 weeks ended 12/31/94, net income was $25.6 million compared with $18.5 million the year before. Prior-year's results were before an extraordinary charge of $3.3 million related to the redemption of the Company's convertible subordinated debentures. Net sales advanced 2.0% to $1.44 billion from $1.41 billion a year earlier. Gross margin increased to 23.7% of sales from 22.8% the year before.

BUSINESS

BRUNO'S INCORPORATED is a leading regional supermarket retailer operating in the southeastern United States. Bruno's operates a total of 255 supermarkets and combination food and drug stores in Alabama, Georgia, Florida, Mississippi, Tennessee and South Carolina. Bruno's also operates seven liquor stores in Florida which are adjacent to supermarkets operated by Bruno's. The Company operates conventional, discount and warehouse supermarkets and combination food and drug stores of various sizes, primarily under five separate store formats. Bruno's 81 Food World supermarkets offer a wide selection of brand-name merchandise in a modern format that includes expanded specialty departments. Bruno's 30 Food Fair supermarkets are designed to operate with a lower overhead and competitive pricing in areas that will not support the volume necessary for a larger supermarket. Bruno's 51 Food Max stores are large "superwarehouse" stores emphasizing an open warehouse appearance with modern decor. Bruno's 14 Bruno's Food and Pharmacy stores are located in markets with suburban shoppers who appreciate "one-stop shopping" and a wide variety of merchandise. Bruno's 57 Piggly Wiggly stores are conventional supermarkets.

ANNUAL EARNINGS AND DIVIDENDS PER SHARE

	7/2/94	7/3/93	6/27/92	6/29/91	6/30/90	7/1/89	7/2/88
Earnings Per Share	**0.52**	**0.60**	**[1] 0.69**	**0.82**	**[2] 0.74**	**[3] 0.59**	**[2] 0.53**
Dividends Per Share	**0.25**	**0.23**	**0.21**	**0.19**	**0.16**	**0.13**	**[4] 0.10**
Dividend Payout %	**48.1**	**38.3**	**30.4**	**23.2**	**21.6**	**22.0**	**18.9**

[1] Before disc. oper. [2] Before extraord. item [3] Before extraord. item & acctg. chg. [4] 2-for-1 stk split, 11/87

ANNUAL FINANCIAL DATA

RECORD OF EARNINGS (IN MILLIONS):							
Total Revenues	2,834.7	2,872.3	2,657.8	2,618.2	2,394.8	2,134.1	1,982.3
Costs and Expenses	2,697.7	2,732.4	2,507.3	2,460.3	2,249.3	2,008.3	1,867.0
Depreciation & Amort	52.3	48.7	44.3	41.7	36.4	32.4	29.1
Operating Profit	84.7	91.2	106.3	116.2	109.2	93.4	86.1
Income Bef Income Taxes	68.8	73.4	87.1	105.2	95.9	75.2	67.1
Income Taxes	28.2	26.5	30.8	38.5	35.8	27.4	24.4
Net Income	37.3	46.9	43.4	66.7	[1] 60.1	[2] 47.8	[3] 42.8
Aver. Shs. Outstg. (000)	78,088	78,717	81,874	81,661	81,580	81,529	81,447

[1] Before extra. item dr$2,039,000. [2] Before extra. item dr$1,151,000. [3] Before extra. item dr$2,019,000.

BALANCE SHEET (IN MILLIONS):							
Cash and Cash Equivalents	30.3	20.1	19.5	15.7	40.9	23.3	34.9
Receivables, Net	36.2	26.7	39.5	38.4	23.8	23.5	12.1
Inventories	255.0	259.2	236.7	214.8	203.8	182.6	151.4
Gross Property	774.8	738.4	633.2	565.4	487.3	428.6	378.9
Accumulated Depreciation	234.7	194.5	165.4	134.2	109.3	85.7	64.7
Long-Term Debt	276.0	246.4	148.0	150.2	152.7	102.8	124.8
Capital Lease Obligations	20.4	22.7	24.2	25.5	27.4	29.0	30.5
Net Stockholders' Equity	421.4	402.7	422.4	390.2	337.1	290.7	249.7
Total Assets	927.2	916.9	834.7	773.2	728.1	660.7	591.8
Total Current Assets	330.7	313.9	303.2	277.8	276.5	237.3	204.2
Total Current Liabilities	156.3	196.4	192.2	156.2	158.4	187.5	140.0
Net Working Capital	174.4	117.5	111.0	121.5	118.2	49.8	64.1
Year End Shs Outstg (000)	78,090	78,047	81,890	81,768	81,589	81,553	81,491
STATISTICAL RECORD:							
Operating Profit Margin %	3.0	3.2	4.0	4.4	4.6	4.4	4.3
Book Value Per Share	4.86	4.60	4.61	4.19	3.52	2.92	2.39
Return on Equity %	8.9	11.6	10.3	17.1	17.8	16.4	17.1
Return on Assets %	4.0	5.1	5.2	8.6	8.3	7.2	7.2
Average Yield %	2.9	2.1	1.5	1.1	1.1	1.0	0.9
P/E Ratio	20.0-13.2	23.8-13.1	24.5-15.2	26.4-14.8	22.6-17.4	25.6-17.2	24.3-18.2
Price Range	10⅜-6⅞	14¼-7⅞	16⅞-10½	21⅝-12⅛	16¾-12⅞	15⅛-10⅛	12⅞-9⅝

Statistics are as originally reported.

OFFICERS:
R.G. Bruno, Chmn. & C.E.O.
P.F. Garrison, Pres. & C.O.O.
G.J. Griffin, Exec. V.P. & C.F.O.
R.M. Conley, Sec. & Corp. Couns.

INCORPORATED: AL, Apr., 1959

PRINCIPAL OFFICE: 800 Lakeshore Parkway, Birmingham, AL 35211

TELEPHONE NUMBER: (205) 940-9400

NO. OF EMPLOYEES: 11,084 (full-time); 16,136 (part-time).

ANNUAL MEETING: In October

SHAREHOLDERS: 8,077

INSTITUTIONAL HOLDINGS:
No. of Institutions: 214
Shares Held: 18,297,876

REGISTRAR(S):

TRANSFER AGENT(S): AmSouth Bank, N.A., Birmingham, AL 35202

CALIFORNIA WATER SERVICE CO.

YIELD 6.4%
P/E RATIO 13.0

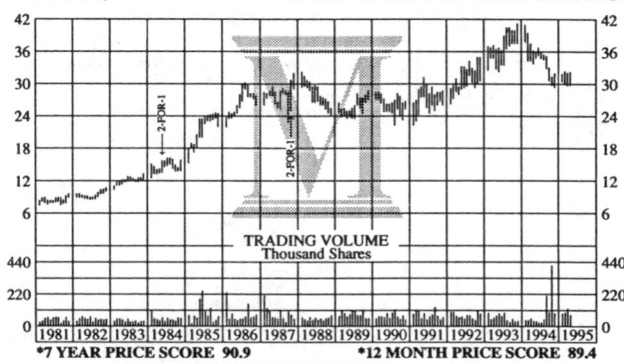

INTERIM EARNINGS (Per Share):

Qtr.	Mar.	June	Sept.	Dec.
1991	0.28	0.36	0.58	1.20
1992	0.31	0.63	0.74	0.50
1993	0.17	0.82	1.09	0.62
1994	0.24	0.71	0.92	0.49

INTERIM DIVIDENDS (Per Share):

Amt.	Decl.	Ex.	Rec.	Pay.
0.495Q	4/20/94	4/25/94	5/1/94	5/15/94
0.495Q	7/20	7/26	8/1	8/15
0.495Q	10/19	10/26	11/1	11/15
0.51Q	1/25/95	1/31/95	2/6/95	2/15/95
0.51Q	4/19	4/25	5/1	5/15

Indicated div.: $2.04

CAPITALIZATION (12/31/94):

	($000)	(%)
Long-Term Debt	128,944	44.1
Deferred Income Tax	15,710	5.3
Preferred Stock	3,475	1.2
Common & Surplus	144,447	49.4
Total	292,576	100.0
Current Debt	7,000	

DIVIDEND ACHIEVER STATUS:
Rank: 282   1984–94 Growth Rate: 5.1%
Total Years of Dividend Growth: 27

RECENT DEVELOPMENTS: For the year ended 12/31/94, net income declined to $14.4 million, a 7% drop from $15.5 million earned in the previous year. Operating revenue improved by 4% to $157.3 million from $151.7 million in the year before. A 7% surge in operating expenses to $131.8 million from $123.9 million offset the increased revenue. Net income for the fourth quarter was $3.1 million compared with $3.6 million in the same period of the previous year.

PROSPECTS: The favorable effect of rate increases and beneficial weather conditions should drive the Company's revenues higher. Additionally, short-term results should benefit from a $21.6 million construction project. However, the net effect of certain increasing operating expenses raises the specter of lower earnings if those expenses can not be maintained. CWT is also expanding its customer base by acquisitions and secured contracts.

BUSINESS

CALIFORNIA WATER SERVICE COMPANY is a public utility water company that owns and operates 20 water systems serving 38 cities and communities in California with an estimated population of more than 1,400,000. The sole business of the Company consists of the production, purchase, storage, purification, distribution and sale of water for domestic, industrial, public, and irrigation uses, and for fire protection. The Company has 362,000 customers located from Chico in the north to the Palos Verdes Peninsula in southern California. The Company also operates and manages several city-owned systems. Annual water production totals nearly 100 billion gallons with 55% derived from purchased surface sources and 45% pumped from more than 500 Company-owned wells.

REVENUES

(12/31/94)	($000)	(%)
Residential	114,751	73.0
Business	27,023	17.2
Industrial	5,478	3.5
Public Authorities	7,995	5.1
Other	2,024	1.2
Total	157,271	100.0

ANNUAL EARNINGS AND DIVIDENDS PER SHARE

	1994	1993	1992	1991	1990	1989	1988
Earnings Per Share	2.44	2.70	2.18	2.42	2.50	2.40	2.45
Dividends Per Share	1.98	1.92	1.86	1.80	1.74	1.68	1.60
Dividend Payout %	81.1	71.1	85.3	74.4	69.6	70.0	65.3

ANNUAL FINANCIAL DATA

RECORD OF EARNINGS (IN THOUSANDS):

	1994	1993	1992	1991	1990	1989	1988
Total Revenues	157,271	151,716	139,805	127,176	124,387	117,488	113,755
Depreciation	10,958	10,304	9,412	8,795	8,222	7,841	7,357
Maintenance	7,855	7,250	6,965	7,175	6,998	7,042	6,135
Net Operating Income	25,505	27,855	23,774	24,321	23,370	22,338	22,490
Interest Expense	11,384	12,627	11,414	10,777	9,657	9,236	8,634
Net Income	14,408	15,501	12,529	13,928	14,366	13,772	14,074
Aver. Shs. Outstg.	5,838	5,689	5,689	5,689	5,689	5,684	5,654

BALANCE SHEET (IN THOUSANDS):

Gross Plant	559,180	533,213	507,151	474,370	442,017	417,573	393,086
Accumulated Depreciation	151,285	141,510	132,538	124,433	116,608	109,771	103,723
Prop, Plant & Equip, Net	407,895	391,703	374,613	349,937	325,409	307,802	289,363
Long-term Debt	128,944	129,608	122,069	103,505	104,905	86,012	86,959
Net Stockholders' Equity	147,922	127,474	123,049	121,254	117,719	113,404	108,910
Total Assets	464,228	446,619	403,448	393,609	369,055	339,348	313,561
Year End Shares Outstg	6,247	5,689	5,689	5,689	5,689	5,689	5,672

STATISTICAL RECORD:

Book Value Per Share	23.12	21.80	21.02	20.70	20.08	19.32	18.59
Op. Inc/Net Pl %	6.3	7.1	6.3	7.0	7.2	7.3	7.8
Dep/Gr. Pl %	2.0	1.9	1.9	1.9	1.9	1.9	1.9
Accum. Dep/Gr. Pl %	27.1	26.5	26.1	26.2	26.4	26.3	26.4
Return on Equity %	9.7	12.2	10.2	11.5	12.2	12.1	12.9
Average Yield %	5.6	5.2	6.1	6.7	6.9	6.4	5.7
P/E Ratio	16.8-12.0	15.3-11.9	16.1-12.0	12.9-9.2	11.4-8.9	12.0-9.8	13.2-9.8
Price Range	41-29⅜	41¼-32¼	35-26¼	31¼-22¼	28½-22¼	28¾-23½	32¼-24

Statistics are as originally reported.

OFFICERS:
C.H. Stump, Chmn.
D.L. Houck, Pres. & C.E.O.
H.C. Ulrich, V.P., C.F.O. & Treas.
H.M. Kasley, Sec. & Legal Counsel

INCORPORATED: CA, Dec., 1926

PRINCIPAL OFFICE: 1720 North First Street, San Jose, CA 95112

TELEPHONE NUMBER: (408) 451-8200
FAX: (408) 437-9185
NO. OF EMPLOYEES: 624
ANNUAL MEETING: In April
SHAREHOLDERS: 5,500
INSTITUTIONAL HOLDINGS:
No. of Institutions: 50
Shares Held: 668,550

REGISTRAR(S): First National Bank of Boston, Shareholder Services Division, Boston, MA

TRANSFER AGENT(S): First National Bank of Boston, Shareholder Services Division, Boston, MA

CAMPBELL SOUP CO.

YIELD 2.6%
P/E RATIO 17.3

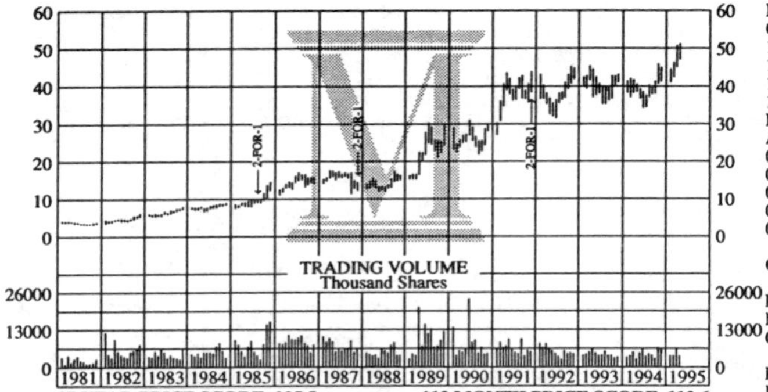

TRADING VOLUME
Thousand Shares

| 1981 | 1982 | 1983 | 1984 | 1985 | 1986 | 1987 | 1988 | 1989 | 1990 | 1991 | 1992 | 1993 | 1994 | 1995 |

*7 YEAR PRICE SCORE 105.5   *12 MONTH PRICE SCORE 110.6
*NYSE COMPOSITE INDEX=100

INTERIM EARNINGS (Per Share):

Qtr.	Oct.	Jan.	Apr.	July
1991-92	0.51	0.64	0.36	0.44
1992-93	0.62	d0.46	0.43	0.48
1993-94	0.66	0.81	0.47	0.57
1994-95	0.79	0.93	...	...

INTERIM DIVIDENDS (Per Share):

Amt.	Decl.	Ex.	Rec.	Pay.
0.28Q	3/24/94	3/31/94	4/7/94	4/29/94
0.28Q	6/23	6/30	7/7	8/1
0.28Q	9/22	9/30	10/6	10/31
0.31Q	11/17	12/30	1/6/95	1/31/95
0.31Q	3/23/95	4/3/95	4/7	4/28

Indicated div.: $1.24*

CAPITALIZATION (7/31/94):

	($000)	(%)
Long-Term Debt	560,000	21.0
Minority Interest	121,000	4.5
Common & Surplus	1,989,000	74.5
Total	2,670,000	100.0

DIVIDEND ACHIEVER STATUS:
Rank: 63   1984-94 Growth Rate: 14.5%
Total Years of Dividend Growth: 12

RECENT DEVELOPMENTS: For the quarter ended 1/29/95, net income was $231 million compared with $203 million a year earlier. Net sales advanced 7.7% to $2.04 billion from $1.89 billion the year before. Operating earnings in the U.S. rose 9% to $272 million on sales of $1.22 billion, up 5.2% from a year earlier. Strong volume gains were recorded by 'Swanson' traditional frozen dinners, canned poultry and broth, 'Great Start' breakfasts, 'Prego' spaghetti sauce, and 'V8' juice. International grocery earnings rose 13% to $40 million.

PROSPECTS: The Company has launched a series of marketing initiatives, including a new soup advertising campaign, in an effort to increase per-capita consumption among retail consumers. A strategic focus on brand power and cost controls should help profitability. Meanwhile, several strategic acquisitions within the International Group should help the Company capitalize on growing demand in the Pacific Rim market.

BUSINESS

CAMPBELL SOUP CO. is a major manufacturer of prepared convenience foods. It is also involved in the fresh foods, refrigerated foods, candy and mail order businesses. Famous brand names include Campbell's, Pepperidge Farm, Swanson, V-8, Franco-American and Mrs. Paul's. Products sold by CPB under these brand names include: canned foods such as ready-to-serve soups, juices, gravies, pasta, meat and vegetables; frozen foods such as dinners, breakfasts and entrees; plus other items including pickles and relishes, various condiments, chocolate, salads and confectionary items.

BUSINESS LINE ANALYSIS

(7/31/94)	Rev(%)	Inc(%)
Campbell U.S.A.	58.7	73.0
Campbell Biscuit &		
Bakery	18.3	14.3
Campbell		
International	23.0	12.7
Total	100.0	100.0

ANNUAL EARNINGS AND DIVIDENDS PER SHARE

	7/31/94	8/1/93	8/2/92	7/28/91	7/29/90	7/30/89	7/31/88
Earnings Per Share	2.51	① 1.02	1.95	1.58	0.02	0.05	0.94
Dividends Per Share	1.12	0.97	② 0.76	0.71	0.50	0.46	0.42
Dividend Payout %	45.0	95.0	39.0	36.7	N.M.	N.M.	44.9

① Before acctg. chg.   ② 2-for-1 stk split, 12/24/91

ANNUAL FINANCIAL DATA

RECORD OF EARNINGS (IN MILLIONS):

Total Revenues	6,690.0	6,586.2	6,263.2	6,204.1	6,205.8	5,672.1	4,868.9
Costs and Expenses	5,367.0	5,722.4	5,138.9	5,206.1	5,043.1	4,584.9	4,194.1
Depreciation & Amort	255.0	242.2	216.2	208.6	200.9	192.3	170.9
Operating Profit	1,146.0	1,043.4	967.8	845.7	676.4	599.6	510.2
Earnings Before Taxes	963.0	519.8	799.3	667.4	179.4	106.5	388.6
Income Taxes	333.0	262.6	308.8	265.9	175.0	93.4	147.0
Net Income	630.0	① 257.2	490.5	401.5	4.4	13.1	② 241.6
Aver. Shs. Outstg. (000)	251,000	251,900	251,700	254,000	259,200	258,600	258,800

① Before acctg. change dr$249,000,000.   ② Before acctg. change cr$32,500,000.

BALANCE SHEET (IN MILLIONS):

Cash and Cash Equivalents	96.0	69.5	117.7	191.7	103.2	147.1	120.8
Receivables, Net	578.0	646.3	577.1	527.4	624.5	538.0	486.9
Inventories	786.0	804.2	717.9	706.7	819.8	816.0	664.7
Gross Property	3,848.0	3,584.9	3,209.0	2,921.9	2,734.9	2,543.0	2,539.7
Accumulated Depreciation	1,447.0	1,320.5	1,243.2	1,131.5	1,017.2	1,002.4	1,030.8
Long-Term Debt	560.0	461.9	693.3	772.6	805.8	629.2	525.8
Net Stockholders' Equity	1,989.0	1,704.0	2,027.6	1,793.4	1,691.8	1,778.3	1,895.0
Total Assets	4,952.0	4,897.4	3,909.2	3,744.4	3,766.6	3,609.0	3,368.4
Total Current Assets	1,601.0	1,686.0	1,501.6	1,518.5	1,665.5	1,601.5	1,362.9
Total Current Liabilities	1,665.0	1,850.1	1,006.0	995.8	1,095.8	960.6	725.3
Net Working Capital	d64.0	d164.1	495.6	522.7	569.7	640.9	637.6
Year End Shs Outstg (000)	248,319	251,706	251,168	254,008	258,538	259,158	258,076

STATISTICAL RECORD:

Operating Profit Margin %	16.0	9.4	14.5	12.7	15.5	15.8	10.3
Book Value Per Share	5.83	4.40	6.31	5.35	5.06	5.06	5.42
Return on Equity %	31.7	15.1	24.2	22.4	0.3	0.7	12.7
Return on Assets %	12.7	5.3	12.5	10.7	0.1	0.4	7.2
Average Yield %	2.3	2.4	2.0	2.0	1.9	2.0	2.8
P/E Ratio	18.3-13.6	44.5-34.6	23.2-16.2	27.8-17.2	N.M	N.M	19.0-12.9
Price Range	46-34¼	45⅜-35¼	45¼-31½	43⅞-27⅛	31-21⅞	30⅜-15¼	17⅝-12

Statistics are as originally reported.

OFFICERS:
D.W. Johnson, Chmn., Pres. & C.E.O.
B. Dorrance, Vice-Chmn.
F.E. Weise III, Sr. V.P. Finance & C.F.O.
B.E. Edgerton, V.P. & Treas.

PRINCIPAL OFFICE: Campbell Place, Camden, NJ 08103-1799

TELEPHONE NUMBER: (609) 342-4800
FAX: (609) 342-3878
NO. OF EMPLOYEES: 44,378
ANNUAL MEETING: In November
SHAREHOLDERS: 43,000
INSTITUTIONAL HOLDINGS:
No. of Institutions: 488
Shares Held: 62,841,636

REGISTRAR(S): First Chicago Trust Co. of N.Y., New York, NY

TRANSFER AGENT(S): First Chicago Trust Co. of N.Y., New York, NY

NYS SYMBOL CSL
Rec. Pr. 38¾

CARLISLE COS., INC.

YIELD 2.1%
P/E RATIO 16.8

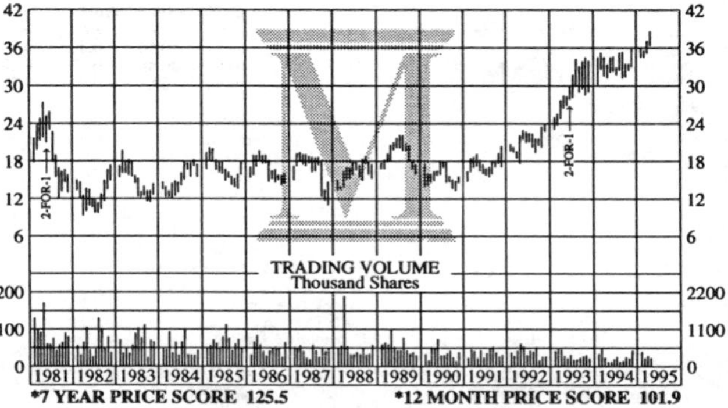

TRADING VOLUME
Thousand Shares
2-FOR-1
2-FOR-1
1981 1982 1983 1984 1985 1986 1987 1988 1989 1990 1991 1992 1993 1994 1995

*7 YEAR PRICE SCORE 125.5 *12 MONTH PRICE SCORE 101.9

*NYSE COMPOSITE INDEX=100

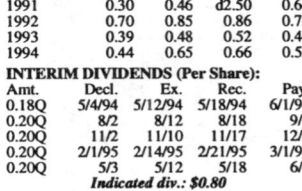

INTERIM EARNINGS (Per Share):

Qtr.	Mar.	June	Sept.	Dec.
1991	0.30	0.46	d2.50	0.64
1992	0.70	0.85	0.86	0.75
1993	0.39	0.48	0.52	0.44
1994	0.44	0.65	0.66	0.55

INTERIM DIVIDENDS (Per Share):

Amt.	Decl.	Ex.	Rec.	Pay.
0.18Q	5/4/94	5/12/94	5/18/94	6/1/94
0.20Q	8/2	8/12	8/18	9/1
0.20Q	11/2	11/10	11/17	12/1
0.20Q	2/1/95	2/14/95	2/21/95	3/1/95
0.20Q	5/3	5/12	5/18	6/1

Indicated div.: $0.80

CAPITALIZATION (12/31/94):

	($000)	(%)
Long-Term Debt	67,498	21.4
Common & Surplus	247,850	78.6
Total	315,348	100.0

DIVIDEND ACHIEVER STATUS:
Rank: 288 1984-94 Growth Rate: 4.4%
Total Years of Dividend Growth: 18

RECENT DEVELOPMENTS: For the quarter ended 12/31/94, net income jumped 22% to $8.5 million compared with $6.9 million in the corresponding period of 1993. Revenues were $170.0 million, up 12%. Revenues and earnings were boosted by the Construction Materials segment reporting a sales increase of 15%, the Transporation Products segment's sales rising 10%, and the General Industry segment reporting a sales increase of 10%.

PROSPECTS: The outlook for Carlisle is positive, but the continuation of double digit revenue growth may slow due to higher interest rates. In addition, production levels for the domestic automotive industry are starting to ebb, which will slow unit sales of custom-molded rubber, plastic products, and heavy-duty brake linings. Improved operating margins, expansion into new markets, and recent acquisitions should lead to increased profitability for the Company.

BUSINESS

CARLISLE COMPANIES, INC. produces and sells a diverse line of products for industry, primarily of rubber, plastic and metal content. The Construction Materials segment (41.7% of 1994 sales and 50.1% of operating income) produces elastomeric membranes, adhesives and related products for roofing systems and water barrier applications. Transportation products (28.9%, 19.3%) consist of manufactured rubber and plastic products for the automotive market, brake lining for heavy-duty trucks and off-road vehicles and specialty friction and brakes systems for construction equipment. The General Industry sector (29.4%, 30.6%) produces molded plastic foodservice products and small pneumatic tires.

ANNUAL EARNINGS AND DIVIDENDS PER SHARE

	1994	1993	1992	1991	1990	1989	1988
Earnings Per Share	**2.30**	**1.83**	**[1] 3.16**	**[1] 0.86**	**2.86**	**3.34**	**2.16**
Dividends Per Share	**0.76**	**[2] 0.70**	**0.66**	**0.63**	**0.61**	**0.59**	**0.57**
Dividend Payout %	**41.8**	**38.2**	**33.0**	**N.M.**	**42.7**	**35.3**	**52.8**

[1] Before disc. oper. [2] 2-for-1 stk split, 6/1/93

ANNUAL FINANCIAL DATA

	1994	1993	1992	1991	1990	1989	1988
RECORD OF EARNINGS (IN THOUSANDS):							
Total Revenues	692,650	611,270	528,052	500,771	621,064	553,678	567,386
Costs and Expenses	609,267	541,718	467,985	466,702	560,526	500,907	514,875
Depreciation & Amort	21,940	20,688	18,806	19,427	23,028	21,743	24,392
Operating Profit	73,376	60,029	51,985	43,765	51,204	45,129	51,126
Earn Bef Income Taxes	58,791	46,912	39,720	10,561	36,659	43,538	28,592
Income Taxes	23,223	18,534	15,492	4,007	13,931	16,545	11,208
Net Income	35,568	28,378	[1] 24,228	[2] 6,554	22,728	26,993	17,384
Aver. Shs. Outstg.	15,480	15,478	15,337	15,268	15,906	16,158	16,130

[1] Before disc. op. cr$471,000. [2] Before disc. op. dr$14,989,000.

	1994	1993	1992	1991	1990	1989	1988
BALANCE SHEET (IN THOUSANDS):							
Cash and Cash Equivalents	70,972	51,802	90,605	14,412	17,623	24,081	32,291
Receivables, Net	99,412	91,158	71,822	75,354	100,095	93,622	93,710
Inventories	74,937	64,976	49,973	53,380	79,114	67,475	56,494
Gross Property	341,945	318,794	282,996	280,353	296,756	256,108	238,297
Accumulated Depreciation	183,707	176,565	160,945	155,361	173,244	155,255	145,015
Long-Term Debt	67,498	59,548	69,098	48,623	44,501	17,417	21,703
Net Stockholders' Equity	247,850	220,523	204,202	190,088	207,461	208,707	191,031
Total Assets	485,283	420,363	383,528	355,711	373,977	337,855	325,380
Total Current Assets	273,243	236,679	237,226	197,452	212,793	203,019	199,642
Total Current Liabilities	108,574	92,205	75,138	82,134	91,984	86,675	83,427
Net Working Capital	164,669	144,474	162,088	115,318	120,809	116,344	116,215
Year End Shares Outstg	15,413	15,253	15,291	15,254	15,206	16,140	16,106
STATISTICAL RECORD:							
Operating Profit Margin %	8.9	8.0	7.8	2.9	6.0	5.6	5.0
Book Value Per Share	14.89	13.42	12.74	12.34	13.32	12.65	11.62
Return on Equity %	14.4	12.9	11.9	3.4	11.0	12.9	9.1
Return on Assets %	7.3	6.8	6.3	1.8	6.1	8.0	5.3
Average Yield %	2.3	3.6	6.4	7.1	7.7	6.2	7.1
P/E Ratio	15.7-13.2	18.9-12.6	15.0-11.2	47.4-34.6	12.7-9.4	13.3-9.6	17.5-12.4
Price Range	36⅛-30¼	34½-23⅛	23¾-17⅝	20⅜-14⅞	18⅛-13⅜	22¼-16	18⅞-13⅜

Statistics are as originally reported.

OFFICERS:
S.P. Munn, Chmn., Pres. & C.E.O.
D.J. Hall, Exec. V.P., Treas. & C.F.O.
S.C. Selbach, V.P., Sec. & Gen. Counsel.

INCORPORATED: DE, Sep., 1917; reincorp., DE, May, 1986

PRINCIPAL OFFICE: 250 South Clinton Street Suite 201, Syracuse, NY 13202-1258

TELEPHONE NUMBER: (315) 474-2500

FAX: (315) 474-2008

NO. OF EMPLOYEES: 4,588

ANNUAL MEETING: In April

SHAREHOLDERS: 2,350

INSTITUTIONAL HOLDINGS:
No. of Institutions: 68
Shares Held: 3,423,956

REGISTRAR(S): Harris Trust & Savings Bank, Chicago, IL

TRANSFER AGENT(S): Harris Trust & Savings Bank, Chicago, IL

CCB FINANCIAL CORP.

YIELD 3.4%
P/E RATIO 9.2

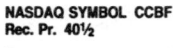

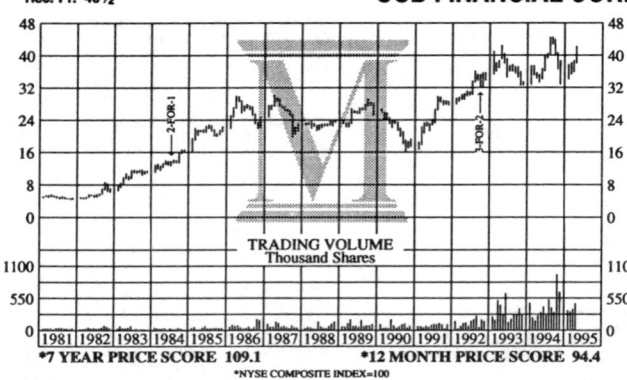

TRADING VOLUME
Thousand Shares

| 1981 | 1982 | 1983 | 1984 | 1985 | 1986 | 1987 | 1988 | 1989 | 1990 | 1991 | 1992 | 1993 | 1994 | 1995 |

*7 YEAR PRICE SCORE 109.1   *12 MONTH PRICE SCORE 94.4
*NYSE COMPOSITE INDEX=100

INTERIM EARNINGS (Per Share):

Qtr.	Mar.	June	Sept.	Dec.
1992	0.65	0.99	0.84	0.82
1993	0.81	0.83	0.83	1.03
1994	0.89	1.02	1.07	1.08
1995	1.21	...	...	...

INTERIM DIVIDENDS (Per Share):

Amt.	Decl.	Ex.	Rec.	Pay.
0.32Q	4/20/94	6/9/94	6/15/94	7/1/94
0.34Q	7/19	9/9	9/15	10/3
0.34Q	10/18	12/9	12/15	1/3/95
0.34Q	1/17/95	3/9/95	3/15/95	4/3
0.34Q	4/18	6/13	6/15	7/3

*Indicated div.: $1.36**

CAPITALIZATION (12/31/94):

	($000)	(%)
Total Deposits	3,032,171	86.5
Total Debt	188,580	5.4
Common & Surplus	251,391	7.2
Loan Valuation Reserve	31,283	0.9
Total	3,503,424	100.0

DIVIDEND ACHIEVER STATUS:
Rank: 143   1984-94 Growth Rate: 10.9%
Total Years of Dividend Growth: 30

RECENT DEVELOPMENTS: On March 16, 1995, CCB Financial and Security Capital Bancorp announced that shareholders approved the merger of Security Capital into CCBF. The resulting corporation will have $4.7 billion in assets and 150 offices in North Carolina. The transaction is expected to close in May 1995. For the year ended 12/31/94, the Company reported net income of $38.5 million, an increase of 31.7% from income, before accounting method changes, of $29.2 million in 1993. Net interest income surged 23.4% to $150.0 million from $121.5 million. Results were attributed to strong loan demand. Other income was $40.5 million, a modest 3.8% increase from $39.1 million a year earlier. Other expenses rose 12.6% to $118.9 million from $105.6 million. The provision for loan losses was increased 38.2% to $8.9 million from $6.5 million in 1993. The return on average assets and equity was 1.16% and 14.90%, respectively.

BUSINESS

CCB FINANCIAL CORPORATION is the bank holding company for Central Carolina Bank and Trust Company, CCB Savings Bank of Lenoir, Inc., SSB, Citizens Savings, SSB and Graham Savings Bank, Inc., SSB. The subsidiary banks conduct a general banking business, offering complete service in the commercial and retail banking, savings and trust fields through 112 offices located primarily in the Piedmont section of North Carolina. The principal activities of the subsidiary banks include the extension of commercial credit and installment lending, in addition to custodian and safekeeping of securities, safe deposits, night depositories and electronic data processing. CCBF also maintains a complete trust department. For corporations, such services include acting as registrar, transfer agent and dividend paying agent for securities, and as trustee for pension and profit-sharing plans. Portfolio management services and investment advice are also available to corporate customers. Non-banking activities through a wholly-owned subsidiary, Southland Associates Inc., include traditional real estate and insurance sales activities as well as real estate development.

ANNUAL EARNINGS AND DIVIDENDS PER SHARE

	1994	1993	1992	1991	1990	1989	1988
Earnings Per Share	4.06	3.50	3.30	2.81	②2.70	②2.78	2.63
Dividends Per Share	1.30	①1.22	1.11	1.03	0.973	0.92	0.847
Dividend Payout %	32.0	34.9	33.6	36.6	36.0	33.1	32.2

① 3-for-2 stk split,10/02/92 ② Per primary share

ANNUAL FINANCIAL DATA

RECORD OF EARNINGS (IN MILLIONS):

	1994	1993	1992	1991	1990	1989	1988
Total Interest Income	440.7	346.1	169.7	188.2	196.2	188.1	156.8
Total Interest Expense	97.0	73.8	70.6	96.0	110.1	108.6	83.6
Net Interest Income	343.8	272.3	99.1	92.1	86.1	79.5	73.2
Credit Loss Provision	8.9	6.5	6.0	7.4	6.3	4.9	3.5
Net Income	38.5	①29.2	25.3	21.5	20.5	21.0	19.7
Aver. Shs. Outstg. (000)	9,485	8,345	7,664	7,628	7,599	7,559	7,520

① Before acctg. change dr$1,371,234.

BALANCE SHEET (IN MILLIONS):

	1994	1993	1992	1991	1990	1989	1988
Cash & Due From Banks	173.2	191.3	129.0	159.6	141.2	140.6	143.0
US Government Securities	...	508.8	388.8	297.5	321.7	296.1	238.7
States & Political Subdiviss	...	50.3	43.6	55.7	62.8	63.8	59.1
Loans & Lse Financing, Net	2,477.2	2,132.5	1,502.1	1,427.1	1,363.1	1,288.6	1,187.3
Total Domestic Deposits	3,032.2	2,816.8	2,028.5	1,885.6	1,845.1	1,736.3	1,558.5
Long-term Debt	77.0	78.7	27.7	25.6	25.7	29.3	30.0
Net Stockholders' Equity	251.4	251.0	189.8	169.8	154.9	141.9	126.8
Total Assets	3,548.2	3,257.6	2,312.2	2,158.2	2,102.2	1,983.8	1,794.9
Year End Shs Outstg (000)	9,109	9,517	7,779	7,640	7,598	7,599	7,523

STATISTICAL RECORD:

	1994	1993	1992	1991	1990	1989	1988
Return on Assets %	1.08	0.90	1.10	0.99	0.98	1.06	1.10
Return on Equity %	15.30	11.60	13.30	12.60	13.20	14.80	15.60
Book Value Per Share	27.60	26.37	24.40	22.23	20.38	18.67	16.85
Average Yield %	3.4	3.3	3.5	4.4	4.5	3.6	3.7
P/E Ratio	11.0-8.1	12.1-9.3	10.9-8.4	10.6-5.9	10.0-6.0	10.5-8.0	9.1-8.1
Price Range	44½-32¾	42½-32½	36⅛-27⅛	29⅞-16⅝	26⅞-16½	29⅛-22⅛	24-21⅜

Statistics are as originally reported.

OFFICERS:
W.L. Burns, Jr., Chmn.
E.C. Roessler, Pres. & C.E.O.

INCORPORATED: NC, Nov., 1982

PRINCIPAL OFFICE: 111 Corcoran Street
P.O. Box 931, Durham, NC 27702

TELEPHONE NUMBER: (919) 683-7777
FAX: (919) 683-7254
NO. OF EMPLOYEES: 1,538
ANNUAL MEETING: In April
SHAREHOLDERS: 4,039
INSTITUTIONAL HOLDINGS:
No. of Institutions: 71
Shares Held: 3,317,909

REGISTRAR(S):

TRANSFER AGENT(S): First Union National
Bank of N.C., Charlotte, NC

NASDAQ SYMBOL CFBS
Rec. Pr. 29

CENTRAL FIDELITY BANKS, INC.

YIELD 4.1%
P/E RATIO 13.4

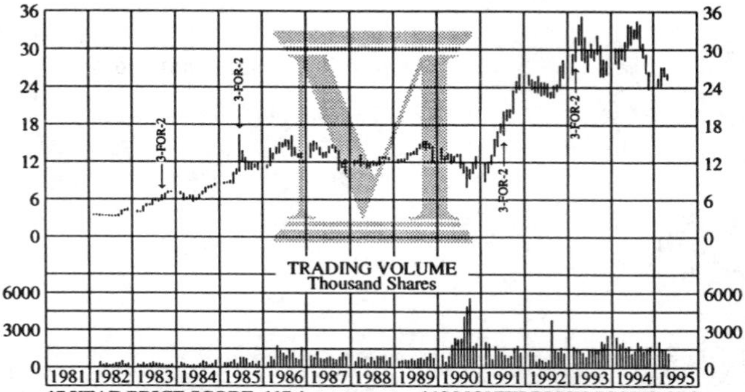

*7 YEAR PRICE SCORE 117.4 *12 MONTH PRICE SCORE 85.3

*NYSE COMPOSITE INDEX=100

INTERIM EARNINGS (Per Share):

Qtr.	Mar.	June	Sept.	Dec.
1991	0.45	0.47	0.48	0.46
1992	0.48	0.60	0.58	0.58
1993	0.63	0.68	0.69	0.66
1994	0.75	0.76	0.70	d0.04

INTERIM DIVIDENDS (Per Share):

Amt.	Decl.	Ex.	Rec.	Pay.
0.28Q	5/11/94	6/13/94	6/17/94	7/1/94
0.28Q	7/13	9/12	9/16	10/1
0.28Q	11/10	12/12	12/16	1/3/95
0.28Q	1/11/95	3/13/95	3/17/95	4/1
0.30Q	5/10	6/14	6/16	7/1

Indicated div.: $1.20

CAPITALIZATION (12/31/94):

	($000)	(%)
Total Deposits	7,227,244	72.1
Total Debt	2,059,475	20.6
Common & Surplus	623,072	6.2
Loan Valuation Reserve	110,000	1.1
Total	10,019,791	100.0

DIVIDEND ACHIEVER STATUS:
Rank: 90 1984-94 Growth Rate: 13.2%
Total Years of Dividend Growth: 14

RECENT DEVELOPMENTS: Net income fell 17.5% for the year ended 12/31/94 to $84.9 million from $102.9 million in 1993. Net interest income advanced a modest 3.4% to $335.1 million from $324.3 million, growth was attributable to a 7.5% jump in average earning assets. Noninterest income plummeted 53.6% to $58.4 million from $125.8 million a year earlier. Results included a $28.7 million loss from the sale of approximately $470 million of fixed-rate securities while the prior year's noninterest income included a $50.6 million gain on investment securities transactions. The provision for loan losses was reduced to $24.4 million from $79.5 million, a reduction of 69.4%. Noninterest expense increased 9.8% to $245.2 million from $223.3 million in 1993. Total loans rose 25.2% or $1.1 billion to an average of $5.3 billion over 1993. Total assets were $10.05 billion versus $9.66 billion and total deposits advanced 8.6% to $7.23 billion.

BUSINESS

CENTRAL FIDELITY BANKS, INC., with assets of $10.0 billion, is a bank holding company headquartered in Richmond, Virginia. Through its primary subsidiary Central Fidelity Bank and six other bank-related subsidiaries the Company serves only Virginia markets operating 230 branch offices, including 29 full-service supermarket locations. CFBS provides a wide variety of financial services including trust and fiduciary services, annuities, private-label mutual funds, insurance and mortgage banking to a broad customer base of individuals, corporations, institutions and governments. Limited international banking services are offered to Virginia-based companies primarily for foreign trade financing.

LOAN DISTRIBUTION

(12/31/94)	($000)	(%)
Commercial & Commercial	1,879,499	32.6
Real Estate		
Construction	305,457	5.3
Residential Real Estate	1,556,243	27.0
Consumer Second Mortgage	552,301	9.6
Installment	871,115	15.1
Bank Card	605,292	10.5
Total	5,769,907	100.0

ANNUAL EARNINGS AND DIVIDENDS PER SHARE

	1994	1993	1992	1991	1990	1989	1988
Earnings Per Share	**2.17**	**2.66**	**2.25**	**1.87**	**1.65**	**1.57**	**1.42**
Dividends Per Share	**1.09**	**1.06**	**[1] 0.787**	**[2] 0.711**	**0.587**	**0.533**	**0.498**
Dividend Payout %	**50.2**	**39.9**	**35.0**	**38.1**	**35.6**	**34.0**	**35.0**

[1] 3-for-2 stk split,02/23/93 [2] 3-for-2 stk split,07/02/91

ANNUAL FINANCIAL DATA

	1994	1993	1992	1991	1990	1989	1988
RECORD OF EARNINGS (IN MILLIONS):							
Total Interest Income	665.8	614.0	580.2	560.0	534.3	482.7	400.1
Total Interest Expense	330.7	289.7	285.7	319.4	326.1	286.3	229.9
Net Interest Income	335.1	324.3	294.5	240.6	208.2	196.4	170.2
Credit Loss Provision	24.4	79.5	99.8	49.8	45.0	17.2	17.1
Net Income	84.9	102.9	78.5	60.4	55.8	54.4	49.5
Aver. Shs. Outstg. (000)	39,164	38,737	34,963	32,396	33,843	34,698	34,844
BALANCE SHEET (IN MILLIONS):							
Cash & Due From Banks	274.8	264.5	280.8	265.7	316.0	244.9	230.7
US Government Securities	2,516.8	3,193.4	...	...	...	...	...
State & Municipal Secur	142.5	171.0	...	...	...	...	...
Loans & Lse Financing, Net	5,659.9	4,669.7	3,851.6	3,558.2	3,516.5	3,493.8	3,179.5
Total Domestic Deposits	7,227.2	6,656.0	6,672.5	5,178.0	4,532.8	4,142.3	3,744.5
Long-term Debt	158.6	159.9	167.8	22.7	27.0	31.3	36.0
Net Stockholders' Equity	623.1	726.1	603.9	429.4	381.6	378.5	342.9
Total Assets	10,054.2	9,662.3	8,712.3	6,805.8	6,172.7	5,335.2	4,731.4
Year End Shs Outstg (000)	39,324	39,023	38,432	32,716	32,254	34,737	34,711
STATISTICAL RECORD:							
Return on Assets %	0.84	1.07	0.90	0.89	0.90	1.02	1.05
Return on Equity %	13.60	14.20	13.00	14.10	14.60	14.40	14.40
Book Value Per Share	15.84	18.61	15.71	13.13	11.83	10.90	9.88
Average Yield %	3.7	3.5	3.1	4.1	5.2	3.9	4.1
P/E Ratio	15.9-10.9	13.3-9.7	12.6-9.9	14.0-4.7	8.8-4.8	9.8-7.6	9.2-7.7
Price Range	34½-23¾	35¼-25¾	28⅜-22⅜	26⅛-8⅞	14½-8	15⅜-11⅞	13⅛-11

Statistics are as originally reported.

OFFICERS:
L.N. Miller, Jr., Chmn. & Pres.
C.W. Tysinger, Treas.
W.N. Stoyko, Sec. & Corp. Counsel

INCORPORATED: VA, Dec., 1978

PRINCIPAL OFFICE: 1021 East Cary Street
P.O. Box 27602, Richmond, VA 23261

TELEPHONE NUMBER: (804) 697-6836

NO. OF EMPLOYEES: 3,500 (approx.)

ANNUAL MEETING: In May

SHAREHOLDERS: 14,724

INSTITUTIONAL HOLDINGS:
No. of Institutions: 145
Shares Held: 13,361,810

REGISTRAR(S): Central Fidelity Bank, Richmond, VA 23261

TRANSFER AGENT(S): Central Fidelity Bank, Richmond, VA 23261

CENTRAL LOUISIANA ELECTRIC CO., INC.

YIELD 6.6%
P/E RATIO 11.8

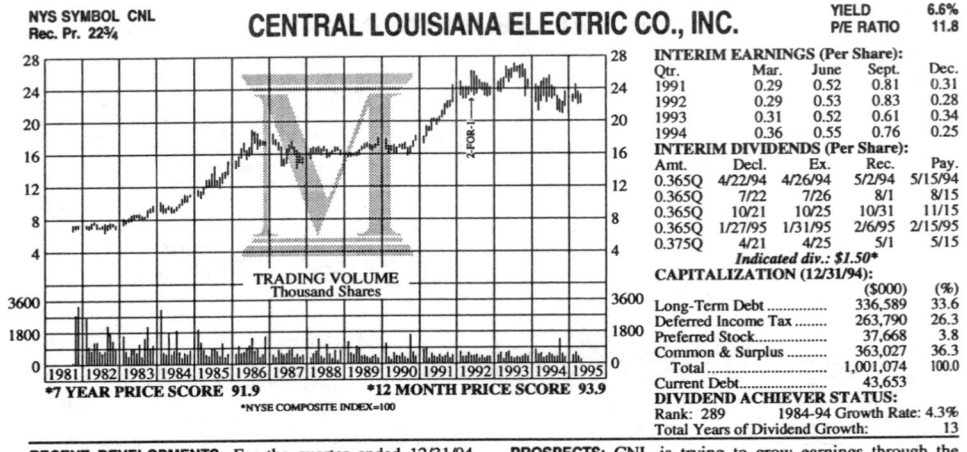

INTERIM EARNINGS (Per Share):

Qtr.	Mar.	June	Sept.	Dec.
1991	0.29	0.52	0.81	0.31
1992	0.29	0.53	0.83	0.28
1993	0.31	0.52	0.61	0.34
1994	0.36	0.55	0.76	0.25

INTERIM DIVIDENDS (Per Share):

Amt.	Decl.	Ex.	Rec.	Pay.
0.365Q	4/22/94	4/26/94	5/2/94	5/15/94
0.365Q	7/22	7/26	8/1	8/15
0.365Q	10/21	10/25	10/31	11/15
0.365Q	1/27/95	1/31/95	2/6/95	2/15/95
0.375Q	4/21	4/25	5/1	5/15

*Indicated div.: $1.50**

CAPITALIZATION (12/31/94):

	($000)	(%)
Long-Term Debt	336,589	33.6
Deferred Income Tax	263,790	26.3
Preferred Stock	37,668	3.8
Common & Surplus	363,027	36.3
Total	1,001,074	100.0
Current Debt	43,653	

DIVIDEND ACHIEVER STATUS:
Rank: 289   1984-94 Growth Rate: 4.3%
Total Years of Dividend Growth: 13

TRADING VOLUME Thousand Shares

*7 YEAR PRICE SCORE 91.9   *12 MONTH PRICE SCORE 93.9

*NYSE COMPOSITE INDEX=100

RECENT DEVELOPMENTS: For the quarter ended 12/31/94, net income was $6.1 million, down 25% from $8.1 million in the corresponding 1993 period. Revenues dropped 7% to $81.9 million. For the quarter, sales to residential customers were down because of milder weather. For the twelve months ended 12/31/94, net income was $45.0 million compared with $41.8 million in the same period a year ago. Revenues were down slightly to $379.6 million from $382.4 million last year.

PROSPECTS: CNL is trying to grow earnings through the acquisition of two co-ops, Teche Electric Cooperative, Inc. and Washington Tammany Cooperative, Inc. If the proposals are accepted by the co-ops these transactions would increase CNL's customer base by about 8,800 and 30,600 customers, respectively. Earnings will benefit from restructuring activities, reducing capital expenditures and emphasizing business development.

BUSINESS

CENTRAL LOUISIANA ELECTRIC CO., INC. renders electric service to approximately 214,000 customers in 62 communities and contiguous rural areas in the State of Louisiana. In November of 1981, CNL was spun off from its holding Company, Celeron. Revenues are derived: 44.5% residential, 19.1% commercial, 21.6% industrial, and 14.8% other. The Company owns or jointly owns four steam-electric generating stations, which have an aggregate capacity of 1,686,000 kilowatts. Generating sources are: 44% coal and lignites, 38% natural gas and 18% purchased power.

ANNUAL EARNINGS AND DIVIDENDS PER SHARE

	1994	1993	1992	1991	1990	1989	1988
Earnings Per Share	1.92	1.78	1.93	1.92	1.85	1.78	1.80
Dividends Per Share	1.45	1.41	[1] 1.37	1.325	1.265	1.205	1.145
Dividend Payout %	75.5	79.2	71.0	69.0	68.4	67.9	63.8

[1] 2-for-1 stk split, 5/26/92

ANNUAL FINANCIAL DATA

RECORD OF EARNINGS (IN MILLIONS):

	1994	1993	1992	1991	1990	1989	1988
Total Revenues	379.6	382.4	351.6	337.3	334.0	316.5	301.1
Depreciation	40.1	37.3	34.8	34.0	32.9	31.8	30.4
Maintenance	24.7	25.0	26.2	25.8	22.0	21.5	20.0
Operating Income	70.4	64.7	70.4	73.1	73.5	75.0	71.4
Interest Expense	26.4	25.8	27.9	30.6	31.7	32.6	30.5
Net Income	45.0	41.8	45.2	44.9	42.5	41.5	43.1
Aver. Shs. Outstg. (000)	22,415	22,350	22,280	22,362	22,494	22,471	22,438

BALANCE SHEET (IN MILLIONS):

	1994	1993	1992	1991	1990	1989	1988
Gross Plant	1,322.6	1,274.8	1,235.6	1,178.3	1,129.3	1,087.8	1,043.7
Accumulated Depreciation	410.5	379.8	356.7	327.2	301.0	274.1	246.0
Prop, Plant & Equip, Net	912.1	895.0	879.0	851.0	828.2	813.7	797.7
Long-term Debt	336.6	351.1	310.8	387.4	314.7	255.8	297.6
Net Stockholders' Equity	400.7	390.8	381.5	374.2	337.2	324.3	331.7
Total Assets	1,178.2	1,161.6	978.2	971.6	918.8	916.0	888.8
Year End Shs Outstg (000)	23,842	22,382	22,306	22,242	22,499	22,482	22,448

STATISTICAL RECORD:

	1994	1993	1992	1991	1990	1989	1988
Book Value Per Share	15.23	15.75	15.38	14.84	14.33	13.74	13.12
Op. Inc/Net Pl %	7.7	7.2	8.0	8.6	8.9	9.0	8.9
Dep/Gr. Pl %	3.0	2.9	2.8	2.9	2.9	2.9	2.9
Accum. Dep/Gr. Pl %	31.0	29.8	28.9	27.8	26.7	25.2	23.6
Return on Equity %	11.4	10.9	12.1	12.4	13.2	13.4	13.6
Average Yield %	6.2	5.6	5.6	6.3	7.4	7.2	7.1
P/E Ratio	13.3-10.9	15.2-12.9	13.6-11.8	12.8-9.0	9.9-8.5	10.1-8.8	9.4-8.5
Price Range	25⅝-20⅞	27⅛-23	26¼-22¾	24½-17¼	18¼-15¾	18-15⅝	17-15⅜

Statistics are as originally reported.

OFFICERS:
G.L. Nesbitt, Pres. & C.E.O.
D.M. Eppler, V.P.-Fin.
M.P. Prudhomme, Sec. & Treas.

PRINCIPAL OFFICE: 2030 Donahue Ferry Rd, Pineville, LA 71360

TELEPHONE NUMBER: (318) 484-7400
NO. OF EMPLOYEES:
ANNUAL MEETING: In April
SHAREHOLDERS: 12,835
INSTITUTIONAL HOLDINGS:
No. of Institutions: 127
Shares Held: 8,555,611

REGISTRAR(S): First Chicago Trust Company of N.Y., Jersey City, NJ

TRANSFER AGENT(S): First Chicago Trust Company of N.Y., Jersey City, NJ

CENTRAL & SOUTH WEST CORP.

YIELD 6.9%
P/E RATIO 12.0

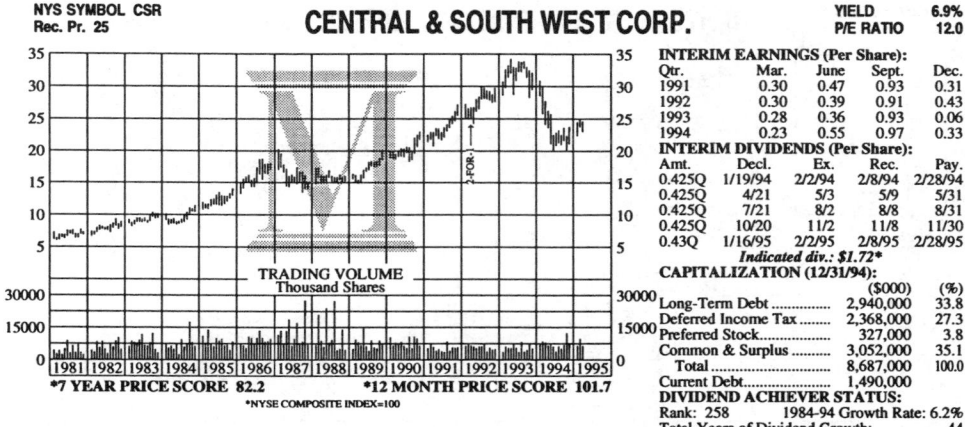

INTERIM EARNINGS (Per Share):

Qtr.	Mar.	June	Sept.	Dec.
1991	0.30	0.47	0.93	0.31
1992	0.30	0.39	0.91	0.43
1993	0.28	0.36	0.93	0.06
1994	0.23	0.55	0.97	0.33

INTERIM DIVIDENDS (Per Share):

Amt.	Decl.	Ex.	Rec.	Pay.
0.425Q	1/19/94	2/2/94	2/8/94	2/28/94
0.425Q	4/21	5/3	5/9	5/31
0.425Q	7/21	8/2	8/8	8/31
0.425Q	10/20	11/2	11/8	11/30
0.43Q	1/16/95	2/2/95	2/8/95	2/28/95

*Indicated div.: $1.72**

CAPITALIZATION (12/31/94):

	($000)	(%)
Long-Term Debt	2,940,000	33.8
Deferred Income Tax	2,368,000	27.3
Preferred Stock	327,000	3.8
Common & Surplus	3,052,000	35.1
Total	8,687,000	100.0

Current Debt.............................. 1,490,000

DIVIDEND ACHIEVER STATUS:
Rank: 258   1984-94 Growth Rate: 6.2%
Total Years of Dividend Growth: 44

*7 YEAR PRICE SCORE 82.2   ***12 MONTH PRICE SCORE 101.7**

TRADING VOLUME
Thousand Shares

*NYSE COMPOSITE INDEX=100

RECENT DEVELOPMENTS: For the quarter ended 12/31/94, net income was $68.0 million compared with a restated loss of $42.0 million for the same period of 1993. Revenues were $800.0 million, slipping 5.1%. Industrial and commercial kilowatthour sales of electricity increased 2.0% and 3.6%, respectively. Residential kilowatthour sales rose 1.1%. For the twelve-month period ended 12/31/94, net income jumped to $412.0 million from restated income of $327.0 million.

PROSPECTS: CSR's proposal to acquire El Paso Electric Company is in jeopardy. The Public Utility Commission of Texas' ruling on the acquisition noted that the proposed merger fails to provide sufficient revenue and adequate rate-making treatment for CSR. The ruling is being appealed by CSR. Earnings should be positively boosted by a 3.5% year-over-year kilowatt-hour sales growth rate in the Company's residential and industrial markets.

BUSINESS

CENTRAL & SOUTH WEST CORPORATION is a public utility holding company with four electric subsidiary companies: Central Power and Light Company, Public Service Company of Oklahoma, Southwestern Electric Power Company and West Texas Utilities Company. These four subsidiaries provide electricity to more than 4 million people in a 152,000 square mile area that encompasses parts of Texas, Oklahoma, Louisiana and Arkansas. CSR also owns five other subsidiaries. Transok, Inc., is an intrastate natural-gas gathering and transmission company. Central and South West Services, Inc., performs financial, engineering and electronic data processing services for the Corporation and its subsidiaries. The Company's other three subsidiaries are diversification ventures which include CSW Credit, Inc., CSW Leasing, Inc. and CSW Energy, Inc.

REVENUES

(12/31/94)	($000)	(%)
Residential	1,156,000	31.9
Commercial	836,000	23.1
Industrial	733,000	20.2
Sales for Resale	204,000	5.6
Other Electric	136,000	3.8
Gas & Other	558,000	15.4
Total	3,623,000	100.0

ANNUAL EARNINGS AND DIVIDENDS PER SHARE

	1994	1993	1992	1991	1990	1989	1988
Earnings Per Share	2.08	1.63	2.03	2.00	1.89	1.63	1.72
Dividends Per Share	1.70	1.62	① 1.54	1.46	1.38	1.30	1.22
Dividend Payout %	81.7	99.4	75.9	73.2	72.8	80.0	71.1

① 2-for-1 stk split, 3/9/92

ANNUAL FINANCIAL DATA

RECORD OF EARNINGS (IN MILLIONS):

Total Revenues	3,623.0	3,687.0	3,289.0	3,047.0	2,744.0	2,549.0	2,512.0
Depreciation & Amort.	356.0	366.0	308.0	291.0	283.0	277.0	254.0
Maintenance	176.0	197.0	170.0	181.0	164.0	155.0	133.0
Prov for Fed Inc Taxes	193.0	140.0	159.0	182.0	192.0	158.0	122.0
Operating Income	594.0	457.0	591.0	566.0	493.0	492.0	459.0
Interest Expense	293.0	269.0	266.0	270.0	322.0	275.0	225.0
Net Income	412.0	291.0	404.0	401.0	386.0	337.0	356.0
Aver. Shs. Outstg. (000)	189,300	188,400	188,300	188,300	188,200	188,400	189,200

① Before acctg. change cr$46,000,000.

BALANCE SHEET (IN MILLIONS):

Gross Plant	11,868.0	11,357.0	11,190.0	10,788.0	10,251.0	9,634.0	9,370.0
Accumulated Depreciation	3,870.0	3,550.0	3,287.0	2,986.0	2,701.0	2,448.0	2,219.0
Prop, Plant & Equip, Net	7,998.0	7,807.0	7,903.0	7,802.0	7,550.0	7,186.0	7,151.0
Long-term Debt	2,940.0	2,749.0	2,647.0	2,518.0	2,513.0	2,537.0	2,514.0
Net Stockholders' Equity	3,379.0	3,280.0	3,294.0	3,223.0	3,137.0	3,044.0	2,990.0
Total Assets	10,909.0	10,623.0	9,829.0	9,396.0	9,074.0	8,347.0	8,110.0
Year End Shs Outstg (000)	190,600	188,405	188,371	188,274	188,204	188,190	188,722

STATISTICAL RECORD:

Book Value Per Share	16.01	15.55	15.54	15.05	14.57	14.07	13.75
Op. Inc/Net Pl %	7.4	5.9	7.5	7.3	6.5	6.8	6.4
Dep/Gr. Pl %	3.0	2.9	2.8	2.7	2.8	2.9	2.7
Accum. Dep/Gr. Pl %	32.6	31.3	29.4	27.7	26.3	25.4	23.7
Return on Equity %	12.3	8.7	12.6	12.8	12.7	11.5	12.3
Average Yield %	6.7	5.2	5.7	6.1	6.7	7.4	7.6
P/E Ratio	14.8-9.7	24.6-20.3	14.8-11.9	13.7-10.4	12.2-9.7	12.3-9.1	10.2-8.6
Price Range	30⅞-20⅛	34¼-28¼	30-24¼	27¼-20¾	23-18⅜	20⅛-14⅞	17⅜-14¾

Statistics are as originally reported.

OFFICERS:
E.R. Brooks, Chmn., Pres. & C.E.O.
G.D. Rosilier, Sr. V.P. & C.F.O.
S.J. McDonnell, Treas.
F.L. Frawley, Corp. Sec. & Senior Attorney

INCORPORATED: DE, Jul., 1925

PRINCIPAL OFFICE: 1616 Woodall Rodgers Frwy, Dallas, TX 75202

TELEPHONE NUMBER: (214) 754-1000
FAX: (214) 754-1033
NO. OF EMPLOYEES: 8,055
ANNUAL MEETING: In April
SHAREHOLDERS: 74,000 (approx.)
INSTITUTIONAL HOLDINGS:
No. of Institutions: 515
Shares Held: 84,521,064

REGISTRAR(S): Central & South West Services, Inc., Dallas, TX

TRANSFER AGENT(S): Central & South West Services, Inc., Dallas, TX

CENTURY TELEPHONE ENTERPRISES, INC.

YIELD 1.1%
P/E RATIO 15.5

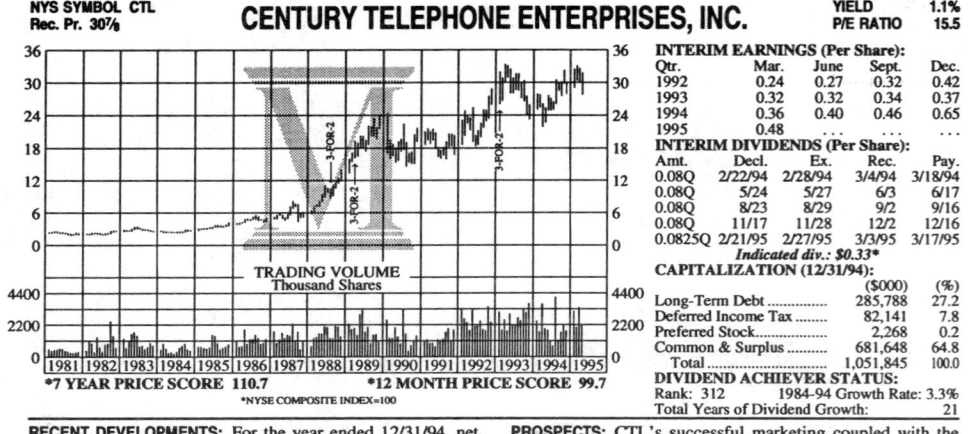

TRADING VOLUME
Thousand Shares

| 1981 | 1982 | 1983 | 1984 | 1985 | 1986 | 1987 | 1988 | 1989 | 1990 | 1991 | 1992 | 1993 | 1994 | 1995 |

*7 YEAR PRICE SCORE 110.7   *12 MONTH PRICE SCORE 99.7
*NYSE COMPOSITE INDEX=100

INTERIM EARNINGS (Per Share):

Qtr.	Mar.	June	Sept.	Dec.
1992	0.24	0.27	0.32	0.42
1993	0.32	0.32	0.34	0.37
1994	0.36	0.40	0.46	0.65
1995	0.48	...	...	...

INTERIM DIVIDENDS (Per Share):

Amt.	Decl.	Ex.	Rec.	Pay.
0.08Q	2/22/94	2/28/94	3/4/94	3/18/94
0.08Q	5/24	5/27	6/3	6/17
0.08Q	8/23	8/29	9/2	9/16
0.08Q	11/17	11/28	12/2	12/16
0.0825Q	2/21/95	2/27/95	3/3/95	3/17/95

*Indicated div.: $0.33**

CAPITALIZATION (12/31/94):

	($000)	(%)
Long-Term Debt	285,788	27.2
Deferred Income Tax	82,141	7.8
Preferred Stock	2,268	0.2
Common & Surplus	681,648	64.8
Total	1,051,845	100.0

DIVIDEND ACHIEVER STATUS:
Rank: 312   1984-94 Growth Rate: 3.3%
Total Years of Dividend Growth: 21

RECENT DEVELOPMENTS: For the year ended 12/31/94, net income increased 45.3% to $100.2 million from $69.0 million in 1993. Revenues grew 24.7% to $540.2 million. Gains on sales of assets contributed $8.2 million of the increase in net income. Telephone revenues increased 11.8% and operating income advanced 20.1%. Mobile communications revenues grew 78% and operating income increased 217.4%.

PROSPECTS: CTL's successful marketing coupled with the likelihood of further selective acquisitions bode well for future results. However, growth for 1995 will likely fall short of 1994's rapid pace. CTL signed a letter of intent to acquire the wireline cellular license for a northeastern Michigan market that has a population of approximately 130,000 from United States Cellular Corp.

BUSINESS

CENTURY TELEPHONE ENTERPRISES, INC. is a regional diversified telecommunications company that is primarily engaged in providing traditional telephone services and mobile communications services. Century's 34 telephone subsidiaries service more than 454,963 telephone access lines in 14 states. Century Cellunet, Inc. provides mobile communications services. Century Business Communications, Inc. offers mailing, direct marketing and creative services, database management, workflow analysis and systems consultation. Century Telecommunications, Inc. provides long-distance service and operator services on a regional basis. Century Area Long Lines, Inc. provides long-distance service in certain Century operating areas. Interactive Communications, Inc. provides interactive information services.

REVENUES

(12/31/94)	Rev($000)	(%)
Telephone	389,438	72.1
Mobile Communications	150,802	27.9
Total	540,240	100.0

ANNUAL EARNINGS AND DIVIDENDS PER SHARE

	1994	1993	1992	1991	1990	1989	1988
Earnings Per Share	1.88	[1] 1.35	[1] 1.25	0.80	0.67	0.51	0.58
Dividends Per Share	0.32	0.31	[2] 0.293	0.287	0.28	[3] 0.272	[4] 0.264
Dividend Payout %	17.0	23.0	23.4	35.8	41.6	53.7	45.5

[1] Before acctg. chg. [2] 3-for-2 stk split,01/04/93 [3] 3-for-2 stk split, 3/89 [4] 3-for-2 stock split, 8/88.

ANNUAL FINANCIAL DATA

RECORD OF EARNINGS (IN MILLIONS):

	1994	1993	1992	1991	1990	1989	1988
Total Revenues	691.0	513.7	411.6	321.0	276.2	232.6	193.7
Costs and Expenses	[1] 276.4	231.9	184.2	153.7	140.6	124.9	102.0
Depreciation & Amort	...	76.5	62.9	52.2	47.1	41.2	35.6
Operating Income	169.4	124.8	109.6	75.1	61.1	47.2	46.5
Inc Bef Inc Taxes & Cum Effect Of Acctg Chgs	161.5	106.3	92.6	57.5	48.5	32.9	34.4
Income Taxes	61.3	37.3	32.6	20.1	17.4	10.7	11.1
Net Income	100.2	69.0	[2] 60.0	37.4	31.1	22.2	23.4
Aver. Shs. Outstg. (000)	53,400	51,206	48,500	47,305	46,142	43,451	40,532

[1] Incl. Dep. [2] Before acctg. change dr$15,668,000.

BALANCE SHEET (IN MILLIONS):

	1994	1993	1992	1991	1990	1989	1988
Cash and Cash Equivalents	7.2	9.8	9.8	11.6	32.6	44.0	16.5
Receivables, Net	64.0	56.2	42.5	44.4	28.0	24.9	18.0
Inventories	7.1	4.4	4.5	3.8	4.0	5.4	5.6
Gross Property	1,314.2	1,170.4	1,004.4	796.1	734.8	695.8	580.0
Accumulated Depreciation	367.1	342.7	328.5	261.1	243.9	221.7	179.2
Long-Term Debt	285.8	460.9	391.9	254.8	230.7	257.7	180.1
Net Stockholders' Equity	683.9	532.2	407.6	345.9	310.6	282.0	184.6
Total Assets	1,643.3	1,319.4	1,040.5	764.5	706.4	691.6	497.8
Total Current Assets	81.2	72.5	60.1	61.3	65.9	75.6	40.7
Total Current Liabilities	286.7	179.2	120.7	76.0	83.2	67.9	64.1
Net Working Capital	d205.4	d106.7	d60.6	d14.7	d17.3	7.7	d23.5
Year End Shs Outstg (000)	53,574	51,295	48,897	47,047	46,251	45,782	40,625

STATISTICAL RECORD:

	1994	1993	1992	1991	1990	1989	1988
Book Value Per Share	4.48	4.57	3.88	4.91	4.33	3.77	3.66
Return on Equity %	14.7	13.0	14.7	10.8	10.0	7.9	12.9
Average Yield %	1.2	1.1	1.2	1.5	1.4	1.5	2.7
P/E Ratio	17.2-11.6	24.7-17.2	23.1-14.7	27.0-19.8	36.4-21.8	47.1-26.2	24.6-10.1
Price Range	32¼-21⅞	33⅜-23¼	28⅞-18⅜	21⅝-15⅞	24⅜-14⅝	24-13⅜	14-5¾

Statistics are as originally reported.

OFFICERS:
C.M. Williams, Chmn.
G.F. Post, III, Vice-Chmn., Pres. & C.E.O.
R.S. Ewing, Jr., Sr. V.P. & C.F.O.
H.P. Perry, Sr. V.P., Gen. Counsel & Sec.

INCORPORATED: LA, Apr., 1968

PRINCIPAL OFFICE: 100 Century Park Drive, Monroe, LA 71203

TELEPHONE NUMBER: (318) 388-9500
FAX: (318) 388-9562
NO. OF EMPLOYEES: 2,800 (approx.)
ANNUAL MEETING: In April
SHAREHOLDERS: 5,900 (approx.)
INSTITUTIONAL HOLDINGS:
No. of Institutions: 275
Shares Held: 41,019,868

REGISTRAR(S): Society National Bank, Dallas, TX

TRANSFER AGENT(S): Society National Bank, Dallas, TX

NYS SYMBOL CHE
Rec. Pr. 32½

CHEMED CORP.

YIELD 6.3%
P/E RATIO 17.1

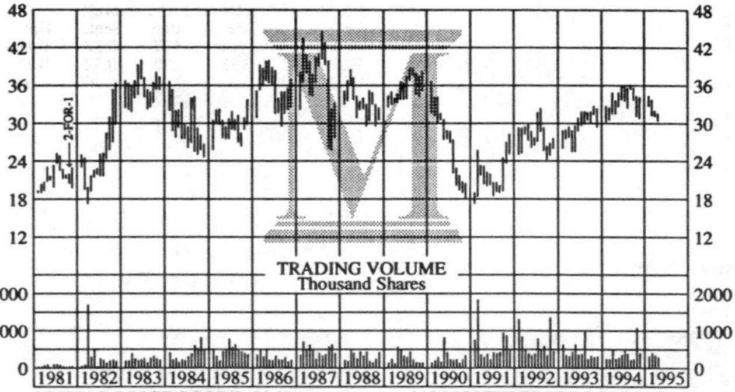

***7 YEAR PRICE SCORE 93.9** ***12 MONTH PRICE SCORE 88.5**

*NYSE COMPOSITE INDEX=100

INTERIM EARNINGS (Per Share):

Qtr.	Mar.	June	Sept.	Dec.
1991	0.04	0.21	0.41	0.45
1992	0.32	0.44	0.37	0.33
1993	0.42	0.50	0.43	0.41
1994	0.58	0.58	0.37	0.37

INTERIM DIVIDENDS (Per Share):

Amt.	Decl.	Ex.	Rec.	Pay.
0.51Q	5/16/94	5/23/94	5/27/94	6/10/94
0.51Q	8/4	8/15	8/19	9/9
0.51Q	11/3	11/17	11/23	12/9
0.51Q	2/2/95	2/15/95	2/22/95	3/10/95
0.51Q	5/15	5/22	5/26	6/9

Indicated div.: $2.04*

CAPITALIZATION (12/31/94):

	($000)	(%)
Long-Term Debt	92,133	28.6
Deferred Income Tax	7,606	2.4
Minority Interest	36,194	11.2
Common & Surplus	186,320	57.8
Total	322,253	100.0

DIVIDEND ACHIEVER STATUS:

Rank: 312 1984-94 Growth Rate: 3.3%

Total Years of Dividend Growth: 24

RECENT DEVELOPMENTS: For the year ended 12/31/94, income from continuing operations was $14.5 million compared with $14.8 million in the previous year. Income excluded earnings the Company realized upon the sale of some investments, including 1.6 million shares of Omnicare, Inc. and equity earnings in Omnicare through 11/30/94. Revenues rose by 23% to $645.0 million from $525.1 million in the previous year.

PROSPECTS: CHE continues to strengthen its position in growing markets. The Veratex Group is targeting physician buying groups and large dealer chains that have formed as a result of healthcare reform and managed-care programs. Roto-Rooter and Patient Care, Inc., have shown strong revenue growth and should continue to perform well. Meanwhile, cost-cutting measures are improving earnings for National Sanitary Supply Company.

BUSINESS

CHEMED CORPORATION maintains strategic positions in medical and dental supply manufacturing and distribution for the private-practice market, home healthcare services, hospice care, and pharmacy management for the long-term-care market; plumbing, drain cleaning, and residential appliance and air conditioning repair; and sanitary maintenance products and services. CHE owns 59% of Roto-Rooter Inc., a provider of sewer and drain cleaning services; 87% of National Sanitary Supply Co., the largest distributor of sanitary maintenance supplies in the U.S.; 26% of Omnicare, Inc., a long-term pharmacy services affiliate and 100% of The Veratex Group, a medical and dental supply company. In January 1994, the Company acquired Patient Care, Inc., a home-healthcare services provider.

BUSINESS LINE ANALYSIS

(12/31/94)	Rev(%)	Inc(%)
National Sanitary Supply	47.8	29.9
Roto-Rooter	26.7	46.3
Veratex	14.8	15.7
Patient Care	10.7	8.1
Total	100.0	100.0

ANNUAL EARNINGS AND DIVIDENDS PER SHARE

	1994	1993	1992	1991	1990	1989	1988
Earnings Per Share	1.47	1.75	[1] 1.45	[1] 1.10	1.60	2.61	[1] [2] 2.23
Dividends Per Share	2.04	2.01	2.00	1.97	1.96	1.84	1.72
Dividend Payout %	N.M.	N.M.	N.M.	N.M.	N.M.	70.5	77.1

[1] Before disc. oper. [2] Before extraord. item

ANNUAL FINANCIAL DATA

RECORD OF EARNINGS (IN THOUSANDS):	1994	1993	1992	1991	1990	1989	1988
Total Revenues	645,027	525,093	400,962	352,282	599,379	591,824	500,647
Costs and Expenses	606,935	493,113	379,434	336,883	555,263	533,888	450,646
Depreciation & Amort	15,807	13,123	9,234	8,101	9,485	8,431	7,048
Income From Operations	27,406	23,163	15,180	9,500	34,631	49,505	42,953
Income Bef Income Taxes	29,774	27,930	22,184	18,022	29,615	43,227	36,406
Income Taxes	10,954	9,278	6,531	5,405	10,361	15,228	13,725
Net Income	[1] 14,532	[2] 14,843	[3] 12,506	[4] 11,037	16,554	26,182	[5] 20,649
Aver. Shs. Outstg.	9,856	9,778	9,803	10,059	10,371	10,042	9,280

[1] Before disc. op. cr$29,390,000. [2] Before disc. op. cr$2,986,000; and acctg. chg cr$1,651,000. [3] Before disc. op. cr$3,145,000. [4] Before disc. op. cr$41,930,000. [5] Before disc. op. cr$1,335,000; and extra. item cr$472,000; and acctg. chg cr$1,664,000.

BALANCE SHEET (IN THOUSANDS):	1994	1993	1992	1991	1990	1989	1988
Cash and Cash Equivalents	24,239	15,815	47,704	83,044	1,418	6,545	4,361
Receivables, Net	87,562	63,977	59,576	45,350	81,011	82,696	78,232
Inventories	60,273	54,745	47,581	29,584	55,066	55,216	54,562
Gross Property	117,491	127,262	89,726	67,524	119,573	116,388	105,438
Accumulated Depreciation	40,375	33,952	26,854	23,133	53,577	50,574	44,336
Long-Term Debt	92,133	98,059	103,778	77,928	82,151	85,834	90,405
Net Stockholders' Equity	186,320	137,151	133,511	139,407	112,531	120,774	111,244
Total Assets	505,483	452,805	404,944	364,335	327,545	335,321	322,679
Total Current Assets	183,319	145,214	161,886	163,363	143,852	150,488	143,329
Total Current Liabilities	142,666	127,649	103,957	84,700	94,085	87,980	83,056
Net Working Capital	40,653	17,565	57,929	78,663	49,767	62,508	60,273
Year End Shares Outstg	9,865	9,799	9,759	9,903	10,189	10,262	9,381

STATISTICAL RECORD:	1994	1993	1992	1991	1990	1989	1988
Operating Profit Margin %	4.2	4.4	3.8	2.7	5.8	8.4	8.6
Book Value Per Share	5.24	2.05	4.46	7.58	5.68	6.30	6.08
Return on Equity %	7.8	10.8	9.4	7.9	14.7	21.7	18.6
Return on Assets %	2.9	3.3	3.1	3.0	5.1	7.8	6.4
Average Yield %	6.1	6.9	7.1	8.7	7.2	5.2	5.1
P/E Ratio	24.6-20.6	18.7-14.6	22.3-16.7	25.7-15.7	22.9-11.3	14.8-12.5	17.3-13.2
Price Range	36⅛-30¼	32¾-25½	32⅜-24¼	28¼-17¼	36⅝-18	38¾-32½	38½-29½

Statistics are as originally reported.

OFFICERS:
E.L. Hutton, Chmn. & C.E.O.
K.J. McNamara, Pres.
T.S. O'Toole, Exec. V.P. & Treas.
N.C. Dallob, V.P. & Sec.

INCORPORATED: DE, Apr., 1970

PRINCIPAL OFFICE: 2600 Chemed Center 255 East Fifth Street, Cincinnati, OH 45202-4726

TELEPHONE NUMBER: (513) 762-6900

NO. OF EMPLOYEES: 6,602

ANNUAL MEETING: In May

SHAREHOLDERS: 5,703

INSTITUTIONAL HOLDINGS:
No. of Institutions: 109
Shares Held: 3,506,986

REGISTRAR(S): Mellon Bank, N.A., Pittsburgh, PA

TRANSFER AGENT(S): Mellon Bank, N.A., Pittsburgh, PA

NYS SYMBOL CB
Rec. Pr. 85⅛

CHUBB CORP.

YIELD 2.3%
P/E RATIO 14.2

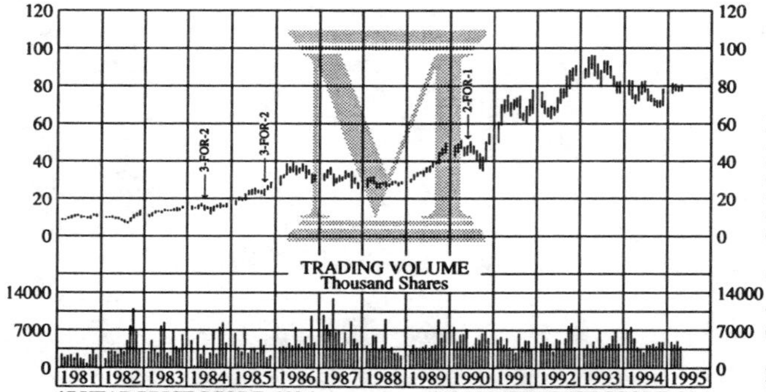

*7 YEAR PRICE SCORE 102.1 *12 MONTH PRICE SCORE 98.4

*NYSE COMPOSITE INDEX=100

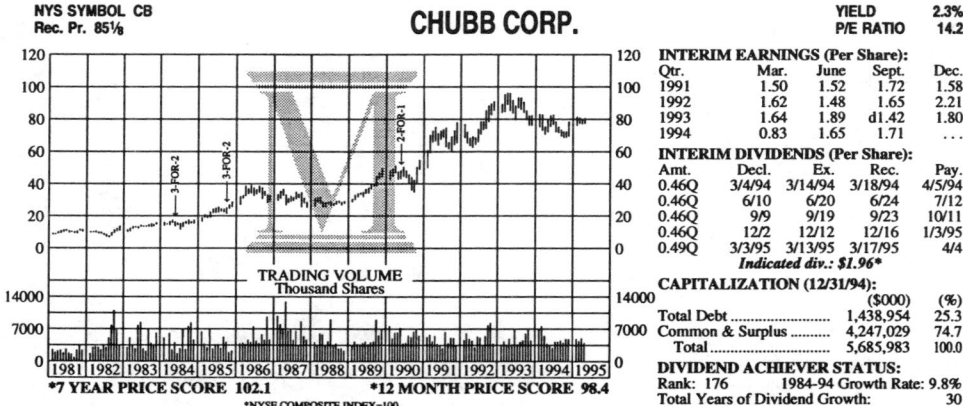

INTERIM EARNINGS (Per Share):

Qtr.	Mar.	June	Sept.	Dec.
1991	1.50	1.52	1.72	1.58
1992	1.62	1.48	1.65	2.21
1993	1.64	1.89	d1.42	1.80
1994	0.83	1.65	1.71	...

INTERIM DIVIDENDS (Per Share):

Amt.	Decl.	Ex.	Rec.	Pay.
0.46Q	3/4/94	3/14/94	3/18/94	4/5/94
0.46Q	6/10	6/20	6/24	7/12
0.46Q	9/9	9/19	9/23	10/11
0.46Q	12/2	12/12	12/16	1/3/95
0.49Q	3/3/95	3/13/95	3/17/95	4/4

*Indicated div.: $1.96**

CAPITALIZATION (12/31/94):

	($000)	(%)
Total Debt	1,438,954	25.3
Common & Surplus	4,247,029	74.7
Total	5,685,983	100.0

DIVIDEND ACHIEVER STATUS:
Rank: 176 1984-94 Growth Rate: 9.8%
Total Years of Dividend Growth: 30

RECENT DEVELOPMENTS: For the quarter ended 3/31/95, net income more than doubled to $146.7 million from $73.2 million in the year-earlier quarter. Net income for the current quarter included an after-tax charge of $6.5 million resulting from an accounting change. Property and casualty net premiums written rose 7.5% to $981.9 million from $913.0 million for the comparable quarter in 1994.

PROSPECTS: The property and casualty business segment is reporting only slight increases in premiums but is showing significant improvements in underwriting operations. The life and health business segment has not responded to CB's attempts to market life and health products through its traditional property and casualty distribution systems. The real estate business segment is expected to continue to report losses.

BUSINESS

THE CHUBB CORPORATION offers commercial and personal property and casualty insurance. It also maintains operations in life and health insurance, and real estate development. Chubb's clients are located in North America, South America, Europe, and the Pacific Rim. The Corporation operates over 100 offices and it ranks in the top 25 among diversified financial service organizations in the United States. For the year ended 12/31/94, property and casualty accounted for 78.4% of total revenues (net of realized gains); life and health insurance contributed 17.4%; and real estate, 4.3%.

ANNUAL EARNINGS AND DIVIDENDS PER SHARE

	1994	1993	1992	1991	1990	1989	1988
Earnings Per Share	**5.95**	**7.86**	**6.96**	**6.32**	**6.07**	**4.91**	**4.43**
Dividends Per Share	**1.81**	**1.69**	**1.57**	**1.44**	**[1] 1.28**	**1.14**	**1.045**
Dividend Payout %	**30.4**	**43.2**	**22.6**	**22.8**	**21.1**	**23.2**	**23.6**

[1] 2-for-1 stk split. 5/30/90

ANNUAL FINANCIAL DATA

	1994	1993	1992	1991	1990	1989	1988
RECORD OF EARNINGS (IN MILLIONS):							
Insurance Premiums	4,612.6	4,306.1	3,852.5	3,671.2	3,398.1	3,190.0	3,299.1
Total Interest Income	892.1	1,033.0	938.4	701.0	674.5	611.3	526.2
Total Revenues	5,709.5	5,499.7	4,940.8	4,513.2	4,247.5	4,022.6	3,980.5
Ins Claims & Policyholders' Bens	3,271.6	3,548.5	2,689.1	2,468.9	2,296.9	2,211.2	2,312.6
Inc Bef Fed & Fgn Income Tax	639.4	344.5	748.4	683.7	645.7	552.3	...
Income Taxes	110.9	0.3	131.3	131.7	123.6	131.5	97.3
Net Income	528.5	[1] 344.2	617.1	552.0	522.1	420.8	359.6
Aver. Shs. Outstg. (000)	90,450	90,549	90,094	88,638	87,364	87,243	84,860
[1] Before acctg. change dr$20,000,000.							
BALANCE SHEET (IN MILLIONS):							
Cash	5.6	4.6	6.7	9.8	11.7	10.3	6.8
Fixed Maturities	10,722.7	10,186.5	9,737.8	8,392.4	7,220.7	6,845.5	6,119.6
Equity Securities	642.2	930.0	738.2	1,143.3	857.7	860.2	664.1
Policy & Mortgage Loans	202.7	194.3	165.3	151.3	133.4	118.2	106.2
Mortgage Loans	...	...	27.6	35.9	37.1	42.9	47.6
Total Assets	20,723.1	19,436.9	15,019.2	13,774.7	12,267.7	11,178.6	9,741.2
Benefits and Claims	13,955.3	12,861.9	8,900.8	8,186.8	7,560.6	6,907.6	6,176.0
Net Stockholders' Equity	4,247.0	4,196.1	3,954.4	3,541.6	2,882.6	2,603.7	2,254.8
Year End Shs Outstg (000)	86,821	87,709	87,520	86,938	81,912	84,432	81,216
STATISTICAL RECORD:							
Return on Equity %	12.4	8.2	15.6	15.6	18.1	16.2	15.9
Book Value Per Share	48.92	47.84	45.18	40.74	35.19	30.84	27.76
Average Yield %	2.4	2.0	2.0	2.3	2.9	2.9	3.6
P/E Ratio	14.0-11.5	24.6-19.4	13.1-9.0	12.3-7.9	9.0-5.7	10.1-5.9	7.4-6.0
Price Range	83⅛-68⅝	96⅜-76	91-62⅜	78-50	54¾-34⅝	49¾-28⅞	31¾-25⅝

Statistics are as originally reported.

OFFICERS:
D.R. O'Hare, Chmn. & Pres.
P. Chubb, III, Vice-Chmn.
M.J. O,Neill, Jr., V.P. & Sec.
H.G. Gulick, V.P. & Sec.
P.J. Sempier, V.P. & Treas.

INCORPORATED: NJ, Jun., 1967

PRINCIPAL OFFICE: 15 Mountain View Road P.O. Box 1615, Warren, NJ 07061-1615

TELEPHONE NUMBER: (908) 903-2000

FAX: (908) 903-2003

NO. OF EMPLOYEES: 10,500 (approx.)

ANNUAL MEETING: In April

SHAREHOLDERS: 9,025 (approx.)

INSTITUTIONAL HOLDINGS:
No. of Institutions: 604
Shares Held: 60,145,750

REGISTRAR(S): First Chicago Trust Co. of New York, New York, NY 10008

TRANSFER AGENT(S): First Chicago Trust Co. of New York, New York, NY 10008

CHURCH & DWIGHT CO., INC.

YIELD 2.1%
P/E RATIO 66.5

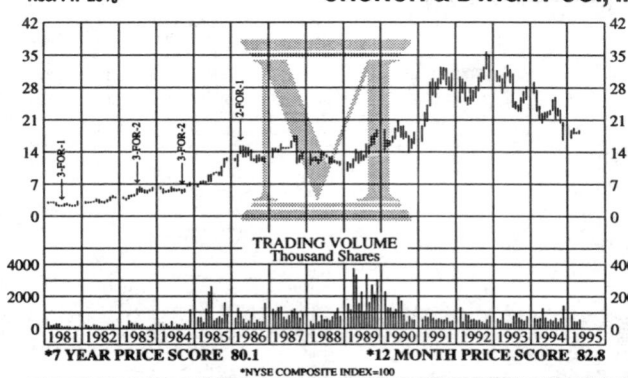

INTERIM EARNINGS (Per Share):

Qtr.	Mar.	June	Sept.	Dec.
1991	0.33	0.29	0.38	0.32
1992	0.22	0.36	0.46	0.41
1993	0.30	0.32	0.48	0.36
1994	0.12	0.32	d0.01	d0.12

INTERIM DIVIDENDS (Per Share):

Amt.	Decl.	Ex.	Rec.	Pay.
0.11Q	4/28/94	5/10/94	5/16/94	6/1/94
0.11Q	7/28	8/11	8/17	9/1
0.11Q	10/27	11/7	11/14	12/1
0.11Q	1/26/95	2/6/95	2/10/95	3/1/95
0.11Q	4/27	5/10	5/16	6/1

Indicated div.: $0.44*

CAPITALIZATION (12/31/94):

	($000)	(%)
Long-Term Debt	7,500	4.1
Deferred Income Tax	19,994	11.0
Common & Surplus	153,941	84.9
Total	181,435	100.0

TRADING VOLUME
Thousand Shares

*7 YEAR PRICE SCORE 80.1   *12 MONTH PRICE SCORE 82.8
*NYSE COMPOSITE INDEX=100

DIVIDEND ACHIEVER STATUS:
Rank: 191   1984-94 Growth Rate: 9.2%
Total Years of Dividend Growth: 21

RECENT DEVELOPMENTS: For the year ended 12/31/94, income before accounting changes dropped 79.3% to $6.1 million from $29.5 million the year before. Net sales were $491.0 million, down 3.3% from $507.7 million a year earlier. For the quarter ended 12/31/94, the Company incurred a loss of $2.4 million compared with an income of $7.2 million for the year-ago quarter. Net sales fell 6.4% to $116.3 million from $124.3 million in the 1993 quarter.

PROSPECTS: The Company hopes to capitalize on increased demand for baking soda products with new initiatives such as its introduction of an anti-perspirant. Growth will continue to be marginal as a result of increased price competition. In response, CHD is restructuring its liquid detergent segment; however, advertising and promotional costs will remain high.

BUSINESS

CHURCH & DWIGHT is the world's leading producer of sodium bicarbonate, popularly known as baking soda. The Company sells its products, primarily under the Arm & Hammer trademark, to consumers through supermarkets, drug stores and mass merchandisers and to industrial customers and distributors. CHD operates two business divisions. Consumer Products (80% of 1994 sales) produces Arm & Hammer products such as baking soda, carpet and room deodorizers, dental care products and laundry products. Specialty Products (20%) produces sodium bicarbonate and related products for the food, pharmaceuticals, animal feed and industrial markets.

ANNUAL EARNINGS AND DIVIDENDS PER SHARE

	1994	1993	1992	1991	1990	1989	1988
Earnings Per Share	0.31	1.46	1.45	1.34	① 1.13	0.42	0.75
Dividends Per Share	0.44	0.42	0.38	0.34	0.30	0.26	0.23
Dividend Payout %	N.M.	28.8	26.2	25.4	26.5	61.9	30.7

① Before extraord. item

ANNUAL FINANCIAL DATA

RECORD OF EARNINGS (IN THOUSANDS):

Total Revenues	491,048	507,651	516,438	485,487	428,547	387,641	346,779
Costs and Expenses	② 489,574	461,406	460,117	433,945	384,179	347,353	310,082
Deprec, Depl & Depreciation	...	10,622	11,547	11,209	10,525	10,111	9,734
Income From Operations	1,474	35,623	44,774	40,333	33,843	30,176	26,963
Income Bef Income Taxes	9,732	47,796	47,150	42,000	38,973	17,056	24,928
Income Taxes	3,615	18,310	17,647	15,525	15,767	8,408	8,454
Net Income	6,117	② 29,486	29,503	26,475	③ 23,206	8,648	16,474
Aver. Shs. Outstg.	19,706	20,223	20,338	19,831	20,455	20,728	21,985

① Incl. Dep. ② Before acctg. change cr$2,447,000. ③ Before extra. item dr$724,000.

BALANCE SHEET (IN THOUSANDS):

Cash and Cash Equivalents	7,635	9,581	25,596	8,705	45,704	43,321	25,906
Receivables, Net	56,331	56,499	45,597	48,439	42,326	38,348	38,965
Inventories	54,683	52,739	45,603	54,710	40,290	34,864	43,160
Gross Property	222,372	196,443	191,223	178,336	161,559	155,032	159,662
Accumulated Depreciation	83,912	74,248	70,686	64,608	58,502	52,829	48,212
Long-Term Debt	7,500	7,644	7,744	7,811	29,635	52,193	55,586
Net Stockholders' Equity	153,941	169,367	159,051	139,154	118,701	111,556	112,030
Total Assets	295,587	281,741	262,347	244,997	253,480	244,856	243,996
Total Current Assets	124,312	123,453	123,558	116,587	133,318	129,809	112,721
Total Current Liabilities	99,776	68,812	76,581	78,681	84,022	59,840	51,117
Net Working Capital	24,536	54,641	46,977	37,906	49,296	69,969	61,604
Year End Shares Outstg	19,527	20,079	20,335	20,300	20,222	20,712	20,959

STATISTICAL RECORD:

Operating Profit Margin %	0.3	7.0	8.7	8.3	7.9	7.8	7.8
Book Value Per Share	7.70	8.26	7.62	6.64	5.67	5.18	4.97
Return on Equity %	4.0	17.4	18.5	19.0	19.5	7.8	14.7
Return on Assets %	2.1	10.5	11.2	10.8	9.2	3.5	6.8
Average Yield %	1.9	1.5	1.3	1.4	1.7	1.8	1.8
P/E Ratio	94.4-53.6	22.5-15.7	24.7-16.7	24.3-12.1	18.5-12.2	44.9-23.2	18.7-14.7
Price Range	29¼-16⅝	32⅞-22¼	35¾-24¼	32½-16¼	20⅞-13¾	18⅞-9¾	14-11

Statistics are as originally reported.

OFFICERS:
D.C. Minton, Chmn. & C.E.O.
M.A. Bilawsky, V.P., Gen. Couns. & Sec.
A.P. Deasey, V.P.-Fin. & C.F.O.
M.A. Pickus, V.P. & Treas.

INCORPORATED: DE, 1925

PRINCIPAL OFFICE: 469 North Harrison St., Princeton, NJ 08543-5297

TELEPHONE NUMBER: (609) 683-5900

FAX: (609) 497-7177

NO. OF EMPLOYEES: 1,028

ANNUAL MEETING: In May

SHAREHOLDERS: 10,700 (approx.)

INSTITUTIONAL HOLDINGS:
No. of Institutions: 116
Shares Held: 9,026,349

REGISTRAR(S): Chemical Bank, New York, NY

TRANSFER AGENT(S): Chemical Bank, New York, NY

CINCINNATI FINANCIAL CORP.

YIELD 2.4%
P/E RATIO 14.3

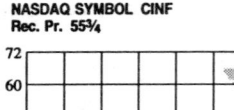

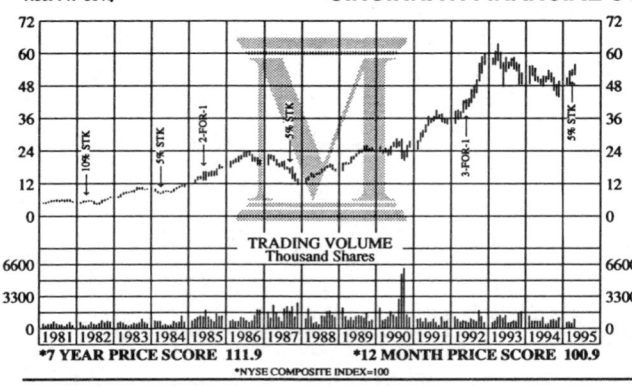

TRADING VOLUME
Thousand Shares

1981|1982|1983|1984|1985|1986|1987|1988|1989|1990|1991|1992|1993|1994|1995

*7 YEAR PRICE SCORE 111.9   *12 MONTH PRICE SCORE 100.9

*NYSE COMPOSITE INDEX=100

INTERIM EARNINGS (Per Share):

Qtr.	Mar.	June	Sept.	Dec.
1991	0.85	0.88	0.60	0.60
1992	1.03	0.99	0.67	0.70
1993	1.11	1.21	0.71	0.90
1994	0.94	1.14	0.92	0.90

INTERIM DIVIDENDS (Per Share):

Amt.	Decl.	Ex.	Rec.	Pay.
0.32Q	5/20/94	6/13/94	6/17/94	7/15/94
0.32Q	8/26	9/12	9/16	10/14
0.32Q	11/18	12/12	12/16	1/16/95
0.34Q	2/6/95	3/13/95	3/17/95	4/14
5%	2/4	3/13	3/17	4/28

Indicated div.: $1.36*

CAPITALIZATION (12/31/94):

	($000)	(%)
Total Debt	209,116	8.9
Deferred Income Tax	195,447	8.3
Common & Surplus	1,940,047	82.8
Total	2,344,610	100.0

DIVIDEND ACHIEVER STATUS:
Rank: 77   1984-94 Growth Rate: 14.0%
Total Years of Dividend Growth: 34

RECENT DEVELOPMENTS: For the year ended 12/31/94, net income was $201.2 million compared with net income of $202.2 million, before an accounting change, the year before. Net realized capital gains were $12.7 million in 1994 versus $33.5 million in 1993. Revenues were $1.51 billion, a gain of 4.9% over $1.44 billion a year earlier. Gross written premiums climbed 5.8% to $326.5 million and investment income rose 9.7% to $262.6 million for the current fiscal year. The combined loss and expense ratio was 100.6%, up from 100.1% a year earlier. For the quarter ended 12/31/94, net income fell 2.1% to $46.1 million from $47.1 million in the prior-year quarter. Net realized capital losses were $7.7 million compared with net realized capital gains of $1.5 million for the same period in 1993. Revenues rose 3.4% to $372.3 million from $359.9 million for the comparable quarter in 1993.

BUSINESS

CINCINNATI FINANCIAL CORP. has six subsidiary companies, operating principally in the field of insurance. The Cincinnati Insurance Company and the Cincinnati Casualty Company market property and casualty insurance, the Company's main business. Life, health and accident insurance is marketed by the Cincinnati Life Insurance Company. CFC Investment Company supports insurance subsidiaries through leasing, financing and real estate investments.

REVENUES

(12/31/94)	$000	(%)
Property/Casualty	(5,703)	(2.3)
Life/Health	(1,691)	(0.7)
Investment Income	244,347	98.0
Realized Gain on		
Invest	19,557	7.8
Other	5,874	2.4
Gen. Corporate		
expenses	(13,056)	(5.2)
Total	249,328	100.0

ANNUAL EARNINGS AND DIVIDENDS PER SHARE

	1994	1993	1992	1991	1990	1989	1988
Earnings Per Share	3.91	3.94	3.39	2.94	2.61	2.33	2.57
Dividends Per Share	1.24	1.10	① 1.00	0.883	0.79	0.687	0.567
Dividend Payout %	31.7	27.9	29.5	30.1	30.3	29.4	22.1

Note: 5%stk.div.4/28/95.   ① 3-for-1 stk split, 5/18/92

ANNUAL FINANCIAL DATA

RECORD OF EARNINGS (IN MILLIONS):

	1994	1993	1992	1991	1990	1989	1988
Insurance Premiums	1,219.0	1,140.8	1,038.8	947.6	871.2	813.3	768.4
Total Interest Income	262.6	239.4	218.9	193.2	167.4	149.3	130.9
Total Revenues	1,512.5	1,442.2	1,304.2	1,161.1	1,048.9	974.4	909.6
Ins Losses & Policyholder Bens	900.8	832.5	766.1	679.9	620.7	577.4	504.9
Income Bef Income Taxes	249.3	267.0	209.2	177.1	149.8	133.2	155.1
Income Taxes	48.1	64.8	37.9	30.9	20.8	18.7	22.2
Net Income	201.2	216.0	171.3	146.3	129.0	114.5	128.7
Aver. Shs. Outstg. (000)	54,805	54,669	53,671	52,296	51,896	51,566	51,008

BALANCE SHEET (IN MILLIONS):

	1994	1993	1992	1991	1990	1989	1988
Cash	48.3	48.1	50.0	57.2	39.5	35.1	23.9
Fixed Matur, At Amortized Cost	1,943.1	1,759.7	1,635.9	1,421.5	1,180.7	1,098.4	1,014.8
Eq Secur, At Mkt Value	2,230.2	2,318.8	1,972.3	1,604.7	1,049.3	1,100.2	798.8
Total Assets	4,734.3	4,602.3	4,098.7	3,436.0	2,589.6	2,552.0	2,117.4
Benefits and Claims	2,304.5	2,110.5	1,791.3	1,571.2	1,353.8	1,227.3	1,063.6
Net Stockholders' Equity	1,940.0	1,947.3	1,713.8	1,441.4	1,006.9	1,020.3	815.6
Year End Shs Outstg (000)	52,939	52,821	52,464	52,063	51,720	51,296	51,071

STATISTICAL RECORD:

	1994	1993	1992	1991	1990	1989	1988
Book Value Per Share	36.65	36.87	32.67	27.69	19.47	19.89	15.97
Return on Equity %	10.4	10.4	10.0	10.1	12.8	11.2	15.8
Return on Assets %	4.3	4.4	4.2	4.3	5.0	4.5	6.1
Average Yield %	2.5	2.0	2.1	2.8	3.2	3.2	3.6
P/E Ratio	14.9-11.7	17.0-12.7	18.5-10.5	13.9-8.8	11.5-8.2	11.8-7.5	7.9-5.1
Price Range	55½-43¾	63⅝-47⅝	59¾-34	39-24⅝	28½-20½	26¼-16¾	19⅜-12½

Statistics are as originally reported.

OFFICERS:
J.J. Schiff, Jr., Chmn.
W.H. Zimmer, Vice-Chmn.
R.B. Morgan, Pres. & C.E.O.
R.J. Driehaus, V.P.-Fin. & Treas.
V.H. Beckman, Sec.

INCORPORATED: DE, Sep., 1968

PRINCIPAL OFFICE: P.O. Box 145496, Cincinnati, OH 45250-5496

TELEPHONE NUMBER: (513) 870-2000

FAX: (513) 870-0609

NO. OF EMPLOYEES: 2,110

ANNUAL MEETING: In April

SHAREHOLDERS: 9,340 (approx.)

INSTITUTIONAL HOLDINGS:
No. of Institutions: 170
Shares Held: 16,778,760

REGISTRAR(S):

TRANSFER AGENT(S): At Company's Office

CINTAS CORP.

YIELD 0.6%
P/E RATIO 27.3

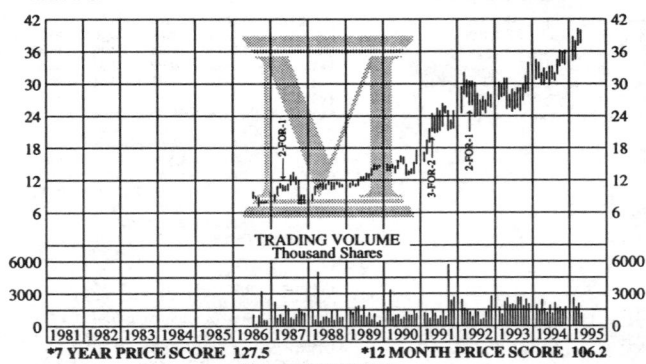

INTERIM EARNINGS (Per Share):

Qtr.	Aug.	Nov.	Feb.	May
1991-92	0.14	0.21	0.20	0.24
1992-93	------------------ 0.97 ------------------			
1993-94	0.23	0.29	0.28	0.32
1994-95	0.29	0.34	0.33	...

INTERIM DIVIDENDS (Per Share):

Amt.	Decl.	Ex.	Rec.	Pay.
0.17A	2/17/94	3/7/94	3/11/94	4/5/94
0.20A	2/15/95	3/6/95	3/10/95	4/3/95
	Indicated div.: $0.20			

CAPITALIZATION (5/31/94):

	($000)	(%)
Long-Term Debt	84,184	20.5
Deferred Income Tax	16,312	4.0
Common & Surplus	309,652	75.5
Total	410,148	100.0

DIVIDEND ACHIEVER STATUS:
Rank: 5   1984-94 Growth Rate: 27.5%
Total Years of Dividend Growth: 12

*7 YEAR PRICE SCORE 127.5   *12 MONTH PRICE SCORE 106.2

*NYSE COMPOSITE INDEX=100

RECENT DEVELOPMENTS: For the quarter ended 2/28/95, net income was $15.3 million compared with $13.1 million in the corresponding 1994 quarter, an increase of 17.3%. Revenues totaled $151.2 million, a gain of 16.9% over $129.4 million for the year-earlier quarter. During the quarter, the Company acquired all of the outstanding stock of Cadet Uniform Services, Ltd., a uniform rental company in Toronto, thereby increasing its ownership from 20% to 100%. Cadet services approximately 3,000 customers from two plants in Toronto, Ontario. For the nine months ended 2/28/95, net income increased 20.6% to $44.8 million from $37.2 million for the same period in 1994. Revenues reached $444.8 million, up 16.6% from $381.4 million for the prior-year period.

BUSINESS

CINTAS CORPORATION provides a highly-specialized service to businesses of all types—from small service companies to major corporations. The Company designs, manufactures and implements corporate identity uniform programs throughout the United States. Currently, the Company occupies 100 facilities located in 33 states and the province of Ontario, Canada. The Company operates processing plants that house administrative, sales and service personnel and the necessary equipment involved in the cleaning of uniforms and bulk items. Branch operations provide administrative, sales and service functions. The Company operates three distribution facilities and has three manufacturing plants, two of which produce trousers and one producing uniform shirts. The Company owns or leases approximately 2,050 vehicles.

REVENUES

(5/31/94)	($000)	(%)
Net Rentals	464,922	88.9
Net Sales	58,294	11.1
Total	523,216	100.0

ANNUAL EARNINGS AND DIVIDENDS PER SHARE

	5/31/94	5/31/93	5/31/92	5/31/91	5/31/90	5/31/89	5/31/88
Earnings Per Share	1.12	0.97	① 0.79	0.74	0.63	0.53	0.44
Dividends Per Share	0.17	0.14	② 0.095	③ 0.075	0.055	0.045	0.03
Dividend Payout %	15.2	14.4	12.0	10.2	8.8	8.6	6.9

① Before acctg. chg.   ② 2-for-1 stk split, 4/3/92   ③ 3-for-2 stk split, 4/3/91

ANNUAL FINANCIAL DATA

RECORD OF EARNINGS (IN THOUSANDS):

Total Revenues	523,216	452,722	401,563	322,479	284,536	243,619	204,513
Costs and Expenses	408,520	352,648	319,006	255,953	229,251	196,767	166,012
Depreciation	24,271	23,149	19,359	16,402	12,258	10,050	8,246
Operating Profit	209,871	183,068	158,268	129,016	112,815	96,114	82,027
Income Bef Income Taxes	85,451	71,303	58,206	48,777	41,626	34,810	27,672
Income Taxes	33,281	26,430	21,716	17,345	15,020	12,752	10,521
Net Income	52,170	44,873	① 36,490	31,432	26,606	22,058	17,151
Aver. Shs. Outstg.	46,706	46,411	46,145	42,876	42,476	41,768	39,636

① Before acctg. change cr$2,705,000.

BALANCE SHEET (IN THOUSANDS):

Cash and Cash Equivalents	60,782	54,969	22,912	18,439	30,374	30,134	18,914
Receivables, Net	56,347	48,075	40,721	35,261	31,841	27,038	22,154
Inventories	29,059	21,452	25,165	23,209	19,847	17,865	19,866
Gross Property	288,402	263,053	240,462	197,255	144,984	110,849	87,377
Accumulated Depreciation	95,899	82,206	67,507	44,689	33,668	27,920	22,779
Long-Term Debt	84,184	103,611	67,790	58,919	43,568	36,874	48,565
Net Stockholders' Equity	309,652	264,914	225,864	185,632	157,441	133,882	94,382
Total Assets	501,632	454,165	361,261	305,822	254,162	213,640	179,892
Total Current Assets	221,453	187,133	138,729	117,524	115,385	104,708	86,267
Total Current Liabilities	91,484	65,176	51,910	53,368	46,797	37,888	33,101
Net Working Capital	129,969	121,957	86,819	64,156	68,588	66,820	53,166
Year End Shares Outstg	46,801	46,579	46,190	43,421	42,518	42,426	39,825

STATISTICAL RECORD:

Operating Profit Margin %	17.3	17.0	15.7	15.5	15.1	15.1	14.8
Book Value Per Share	6.62	5.69	4.89	4.28	3.70	3.16	2.37
Return on Equity %	16.8	16.9	16.2	16.9	16.9	16.5	18.2
Return on Assets %	10.4	9.9	10.1	10.3	10.5	10.3	9.5
Average Yield %	0.6	0.5	0.5	0.5	0.4	0.5	0.3
P/E Ratio	30.4-22.1	33.1-24.5	33.4-19.5	23.8-17.4	23.8-16.9	22.6-15.6	30.7-17.3
Price Range	34-24¾	32⅛-23¾	26⅜-15⅜	17⅝-12⅞	15-10⅝	11¾-8⅛	13½-7⅝

Statistics are as originally reported.

OFFICERS:
R.T. Farmer, Chmn. & C.E.O.
R.J. Kohlhepp, Pres. & C.O.O.
D.T. Jeanmougin, Sr. V.P.-Fin.
K.L. Carnahan, Treas.
INCORPORATED: OH, 1968; reincorp., WA, Dec., 1986
PRINCIPAL OFFICE: 6800 Cintas Boulevard P.O. Box 625737, Cincinnati, OH 45262-5737

TELEPHONE NUMBER: (513) 459-1200
FAX: (513) 573-4130
NO. OF EMPLOYEES: 8,581
ANNUAL MEETING: In October
SHAREHOLDERS: 1,600 (approx.)
INSTITUTIONAL HOLDINGS:
No. of Institutions: 233
Shares Held: 19,036,188

REGISTRAR(S): Fifth Third Bank, Cincinnati, OH 45263

TRANSFER AGENT(S): Fifth Third Bank, Cincinnati, OH 45263

NYS SYMBOL CIP
Rec. Pr. 29⅜

CIPSCO INC.

YIELD 7.1%
P/E RATIO 12.1

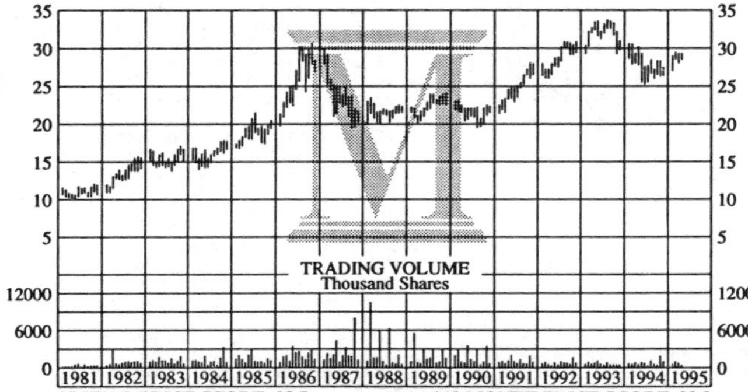

35
30
25
20
15
10
5
TRADING VOLUME
Thousand Shares
12000
6000
0
1981
1982
1983
1984
1985
1986
1987
1988
1989
1990
1991
1992
1993
1994
1995

*7 YEAR PRICE SCORE 88.7 *12 MONTH PRICE SCORE 98.8

*NYSE COMPOSITE INDEX=100

INTERIM EARNINGS (Per Share):

Qtr.	Mar.	June	Sept.	Dec.
1992	0.35	0.48	0.89	0.40
1993	0.49	0.37	1.18	0.47
1994	0.40	0.57	1.00	0.48
1995	0.37	...	...	...

INTERIM DIVIDENDS (Per Share):

Amt.	Decl.	Ex.	Rec.	Pay.
0.50Q	4/27/94	5/12/94	5/18/94	6/10/94
0.50Q	8/2	8/12	8/18	9/10
0.50Q	10/4	11/14	11/18	12/10
0.50Q	2/7/95	2/13/95	2/17/95	3/10/95
0.51Q	4/26	5/12	5/18	6/10

Indicated div.: $2.04*

CAPITALIZATION (12/31/94):

	($000)	(%)
Long-Term Debt	459,619	29.5
Deferred Income Tax	368,667	23.7
Preferred Stock	80,000	5.2
Common & Surplus	647,613	41.6
Total	1,555,899	100.0

DIVIDEND ACHIEVER STATUS:
Rank: 327 1984-94 Growth Rate: 2.3%
Total Years of Dividend Growth: 10

RECENT DEVELOPMENTS: For the quarter ended 12/31/94, net income was $16.4 million, up 2%. Revenues declined 3.9% to $200.2 million compared with $208.5 million a year earlier. For the twelve months ended 12/31/94, net income slipped to $84.0 million from $85.5 million in 1993. Kilowatthour sales to industrial customers increased 5%, but were offset by a decline in sales to residential customers, due to temperatures that were 11% milder than in 1993.

PROSPECTS: CIPSCO is on a cost-cutting binge, reducing overhead expense through the reduction of personnel. Approximately 13-15% of the workforce will be eliminated. Earnings will be pressured downward in the near-term, due to cost-cutting charges taken. It is unlikely CIP will need to request higher rates over the next several years. Most of the Company's capital expenditures will be for normal maintenance and upkeep of existing plant and equipment.

BUSINESS

CIPSCO Inc. (formerly Central Illinois Public Service Co.) is a holding company engaged in generation, transmission and distribution of electricity and the distribution of natural gas to a 20,000 square mile service area in central and southern Illinois. Electric service is provided to about 316,000 customers and natural gas service to about 164,000 customers. The service areas have a diversified industrial base, abundant coal and other mineral resources, highly productive agricultural lands, and a skilled labor force.

REVENUES

(12/31/94)	($000)	(%)
Residential	213,377	30.6
Commercial	178,723	25.6
Industrial	118,917	17.0
Public authorities & othe	13,799	2.0
Power supply agreements	78,613	11.3
Interchange sales(econom)	71,779	10.3
Cooperatives & municipals	22,250	3.2
Total	697,458	100.0

ANNUAL EARNINGS AND DIVIDENDS PER SHARE

	1994	1993	1992	1991	1990	1989	1988
Earnings Per Share	**2.46**	**2.51**	**2.13**	**2.11**	**1.92**	**1.91**	**2.35**
Dividends Per Share	**1.99**	**1.95**	**1.91**	**1.87**	**1.83**	**1.79**	**1.75**
Dividend Payout %	**80.9**	**78.9**	**89.7**	**88.6**	**95.3**	**93.7**	**74.5**

ANNUAL FINANCIAL DATA

	1994	1993	1992	1991	1990	1989	1988
RECORD OF EARNINGS (IN MILLIONS):							
Total Revenues	844.6	844.8	739.9	722.1	600.8	604.7	616.2
Depreciation	81.1	78.1	74.2	69.5	67.0	65.1	62.8
Maintenance	65.2	61.2	64.1	66.8	65.9	58.9	56.8
Income Taxes	...	...	...	...	33.1	39.4	45.8
Operating Income	165.3	170.7	143.0	154.8	97.1	109.4	116.1
Interest Expense	32.3	32.8	32.8	39.4	41.0	41.2	40.5
Net Income	84.0	85.5	72.5	72.1	65.8	71.2	80.1
Aver. Shs. Outstg. (000)	34,107	34,108	34,108	34,169	34,172	34,172	34,172
BALANCE SHEET (IN MILLIONS):							
Gross Plant	2,517.1	2,441.6	2,357.3	2,234.0	2,132.1	2,064.0	2,017.9
Accumulated Depreciation	1,077.5	1,020.1	961.4	900.6	846.2	788.4	736.1
Prop, Plant & Equip, Net	1,439.6	1,421.5	1,395.8	1,333.4	1,285.9	1,275.6	1,281.8
Long-term Debt	459.6	474.3	493.7	496.4	496.3	496.3	496.2
Net Stockholders' Equity	727.6	714.3	681.6	690.9	687.0	686.1	684.6
Total Assets	1,777.4	1,757.8	1,733.1	1,754.3	1,722.3	1,716.4	1,677.6
Year End Shs Outstg (000)	34,070	34,108	34,108	34,108	34,172	34,172	34,172
STATISTICAL RECORD:							
Book Value Per Share	19.01	18.60	18.08	17.86	17.62	17.52	17.38
Op. Inc/Net Pl %	11.5	12.0	10.2	11.6	7.6	8.6	9.1
Dep/Gr. Pl %	3.2	3.2	3.1	3.1	3.1	3.2	3.1
Accum. Dep/Gr. Pl %	42.8	41.8	40.8	40.3	39.7	38.2	36.5
Return on Equity %	11.5	12.0	10.6	10.7	9.9	10.7	12.2
Average Yield %	7.1	6.2	6.7	7.6	8.6	8.1	8.1
P/E Ratio	12.4-10.3	13.4-11.7	14.5-12.2	13.3-10.1	12.1-10.2	12.6-10.5	10.0-8.5
Price Range	30⅝-25¼	33¾-29¼	30⅞-26	28⅛-21⅜	23¼-19½	24⅛-20⅛	23½-19⅞

Statistics are as originally reported.

OFFICERS:
C.L. Greenwalt, Pres. & C.E.O.
R.W. Jackson, Sr. V.P. & Sec.
J.G. Bachman, V.P. & C.O.O.
J.C. Fiaush, Controller

INCORPORATED: IL, Jul., 1990

PRINCIPAL OFFICE: 607 E Adams St, Springfield, IL 62739

TELEPHONE NUMBER: (217) 523-3600

NO. OF EMPLOYEES: 2,592

ANNUAL MEETING: In April

SHAREHOLDERS: 42,790

INSTITUTIONAL HOLDINGS:
No. of Institutions: 133
Shares Held: 9,460,003

REGISTRAR(S): Harris Trust & Savings Bank, Chicago, IL

TRANSFER AGENT(S): Harris Trust & Savings Bank, Chicago, IL

NYS SYMBOL CC
Rec. Pr. 28⅜

CIRCUIT CITY STORES, INC.

YIELD 0.4%
P/E RATIO 16.5

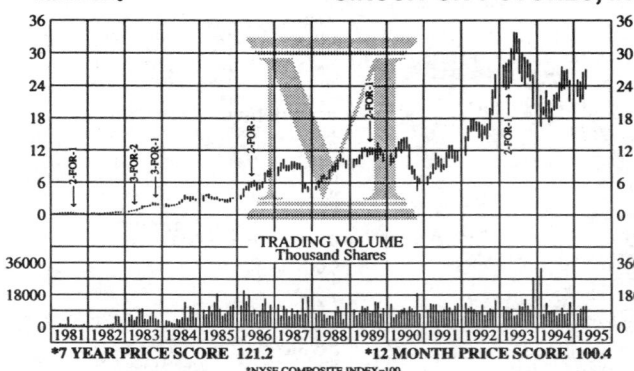

TRADING VOLUME
Thousand Shares

| 1981 | 1982 | 1983 | 1984 | 1985 | 1986 | 1987 | 1988 | 1989 | 1990 | 1991 | 1992 | 1993 | 1994 | 1995 |

*7 YEAR PRICE SCORE 121.2   *12 MONTH PRICE SCORE 100.4

*NYSE COMPOSITE INDEX=100

INTERIM EARNINGS (Per Share):

Qtr.	May	Aug.	Nov.	Feb.
1991-92	0.08	0.19	0.09	0.46
1992-93	-------------- 1.15 --------------			
1993-94	0.18	0.29	0.20	0.70
1994-95	0.20	0.37	0.29	0.86

INTERIM DIVIDENDS (Per Share):

Amt.	Decl.	Ex.	Rec.	Pay.
0.02Q	3/15/94	3/25/94	3/31/94	4/15/94
0.025Q	6/14	6/24	6/30	7/15
0.025Q	9/15	9/26	9/30	10/14
0.025Q	12/15	12/23	12/30	1/16/95
0.025Q	3/15/95	3/24/95	3/30/95	4/14

Indicated div.: $0.10

CAPITALIZATION (2/28/94):

	($000)	(%)
Long-Term Debt	29,648	4.0
Common & Surplus	710,392	96.0
Total	740,040	100.0

DIVIDEND ACHIEVER STATUS:
Rank: 28   1984-94 Growth Rate: 8.4%
Total Years of Dividend Growth: 14

RECENT DEVELOPMENTS: For the quarter ended 11/30/94, net income was $28.4 million compared with $19.5 million in the prior-year period. Total revenues advanced 38.0% to $1.41 billion. Comparable store sales rose 19%. Gross profit margin decreased to 23.9% of sales from 25.8% a year ago due to increased competitive activity and a greater percentage of computers and music software in the sales mix.

PROSPECTS: Circuit City will continue to face intense competition within the consumer electronics industry; however, the Company should benefit from several new marketing programs that emphasize low prices. CC should also benefit from a product mix that includes more home office and music software offerings. Store expansions should help growth as CC plans to open 180 Superstores and 20 stores for smaller trade areas over a three-year period.

BUSINESS

CIRCUIT CITY STORES, INC. is the nation's largest specialty retailer of brand name electronic equipment and consumer appliances including video cassette recorders, cameras, stereo systems, compact disc players, telephones, microwave ovens, washers, dryers, refrigerators, and ranges. It operates 301 Circuit City Superstores, four Circuit City stores, five consumer electronics-only stores and 36 Impulse Stores located in California, Nevada, Arizona and Mid-Atlantic and Southern States. The Circuit City Stores offer a full line of merchandise except major appliances. Circuit City Superstores sells a broader selection of the same line of merchandise including major appliances. The Impulse Stores sell smaller electronic products.

QUARTERLY DATA

(2/28/94)($000)	Rev	Inc
1st Quarter	798,950	17,230
2nd Quarter................	906,678	27,967
3rd Quarter	1,018,051	19,640
4th Quarter................	1,406,736	67,743

ANNUAL EARNINGS AND DIVIDENDS PER SHARE

	2/28/95	2/28/94	2/28/93	2/29/92	2/28/91	2/28/90	2/28/89
Earnings Per Share	1.72	1.36	1.15	0.83	① 0.61	0.85	0.76
Dividends Per Share	0.09	② 0.075	0.055	0.05	0.045	③ 0.035	0.025
Dividend Payout %	5.2	5.5	5.5	6.1	7.4	4.1	3.3

① Before acctg. chg. ② 2-for-1 stk. split, 3/93 ③ 2-for-1 stk. split, 7/89.

ANNUAL FINANCIAL DATA

RECORD OF EARNINGS (IN MILLIONS):

Total Revenues	5,582.9	4,130.4	3,269.8	2,790.2	2,366.9	2,096.6	1,721.5
Costs and Expenses	5,237.4	3,861.6	3,049.0	2,621.4	2,234.6	1,937.8	1,581.6
Depreciation & Amort	66.9	55.0	41.7	35.7	29.1	21.9	17.0
Gross Profit	1,385.0	1,105.7	923.7	809.3	689.7	619.1	501.9
Earn Bef Income Taxes	268.6	209.0	175.3	124.1	91.4	128.1	114.5
Income Taxes	100.7	76.6	65.0	45.9	34.8	50.0	45.0
Net Income	167.9	132.4	110.3	78.2	① 56.7	78.1	69.5
Aver. Shs. Outstg. (000)	97,369	97,000	97,000	96,140	95,000	93,080	92,136	91,084

① Before acctg. change dr$53,500,000.

BALANCE SHEET (IN MILLIONS):

Cash and Cash Equivalents	47.0	75.2	141.4	71.5	25.2	91.7	46.1
Receivables, Net	264.6	189.0	120.4	93.5	26.6	9.7	11.6
Inventories	1,036.7	721.3	515.8	420.1	389.8	331.2	302.6
Gross Property	① 593.0	636.6	516.5	437.2	443.9	320.3	255.9
Accumulated Depreciation	...	198.5	145.7	117.9	88.4	70.3	49.9
Long-Term Debt	178.6	29.6	82.4	85.4	94.4	93.9	94.7
Net Stockholders' Equity	877.5	710.4	575.5	448.0	366.9	359.3	273.6
Total Assets	2,004.0	1,554.7	1,262.9	999.6	874.1	713.7	587.5
Total Current Assets	1,387.2	997.0	790.9	597.4	450.4	442.2	366.9
Total Current Liabilities	706.1	546.3	373.0	279.0	261.0	222.2	192.2
Net Working Capital	681.1	450.7	417.9	318.4	189.4	220.0	174.7
Year End Shs Outstg (000)	96,476	96,080	95,670	93,866	92,680	91,722	90,468

① Net of accumulated depreciation.

STATISTICAL RECORD:

Operating Profit Margin %	5.0	5.2	5.5	4.8	4.4	6.5	7.1
Book Value Per Share	9.10	7.39	6.02	4.77	3.96	3.92	3.02
Return on Equity %	19.1	18.6	19.2	17.5	15.4	21.7	25.4
Return on Assets %	8.4	8.5	8.7	7.8	6.5	10.9	11.8
Average Yield %	0.4	0.3	0.3	0.5	0.5	0.3	0.3
P/E Ratio	16.0-9.6	24.9-14.5	22.7-9.7	15.9-6.9	23.8-7.4	15.9-10.4	15.0-6.1
Price Range	27½-16½	33⅞-19¾	26⅛-11⅛	13-5⅝	14½-4⅛	13½-8⅞	11⅜-4⅜

Statistics are as originally reported.

OFFICERS:
R.L. Sharp, Chmn., Pres. & C.E.O.
A.L. Wurtzel, Vice-Chmn.
M.T. Chalifoux, Sr. V.P., C.F.O. & Corp. Sec.
P.J. Dunn, Treas.

INCORPORATED: VA, Sep., 1949

PRINCIPAL OFFICE: 9950 Mayland Drive, Richmond, VA 23233-1464

TELEPHONE NUMBER: (804) 527-4000

NO. OF EMPLOYEES: 14,400 hourly; 9,300 on commission basis

ANNUAL MEETING: In June

SHAREHOLDERS: 7,800 (approx.)

INSTITUTIONAL HOLDINGS:
No. of Institutions: 364
Shares Held: 72,267,888

REGISTRAR(S): Mellon Securities Trust Company, Pittsburgh, PA

TRANSFER AGENT(S): Mellon Securities Trust Company Pittsburgh, PA

CITIZENS BANKING CORP.

YIELD 3.2%
P/E RATIO 13.5

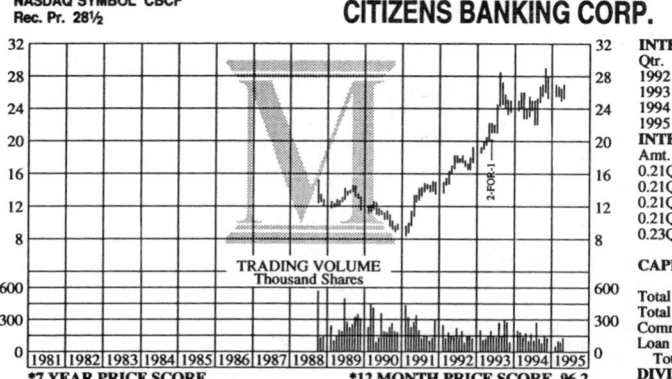

INTERIM EARNINGS (Per Share):

Qtr.	Mar.	June	Sept.	Dec.
1992	0.41	0.39	0.40	0.60
1993	0.46	0.47	0.46	0.50
1994	0.43	0.50	0.54	0.56
1995	0.51	...	...	...

INTERIM DIVIDENDS (Per Share):

Amt.	Decl.	Ex.	Rec.	Pay.
0.21Q	4/19/94	4/25/94	4/29/94	5/11/94
0.21Q	7/21	7/26	8/1	8/10
0.21Q	10/21	10/25	10/31	11/9
0.21Q	1/20/95	1/25/95	1/31/95	2/9/95
0.23Q	4/18	4/24	4/28	5/10

*Indicated div.: $0.92**

CAPITALIZATION (12/31/94):

	($000)	(%)
Total Deposits	2,252,318	83.8
Total Debt	151,680	5.7
Common & Surplus	258,730	9.6
Loan Valuation Reserve	24,714	0.9
Total	2,687,442	100.0

TRADING VOLUME Thousand Shares

| 1981 | 1982 | 1983 | 1984 | 1985 | 1986 | 1987 | 1988 | 1989 | 1990 | 1991 | 1992 | 1993 | 1994 | 1995 |

*7 YEAR PRICE SCORE ...   *12 MONTH PRICE SCORE 96.2

*NYSE COMPOSITE INDEX=100

DIVIDEND ACHIEVER STATUS:
Rank: 202   1984-94 Growth Rate: 8.4%
Total Years of Dividend Growth: 11

RECENT DEVELOPMENTS: For the year ended 12/31/94, net income rose 14.1% to $29.4 million from the previous year's $25.8 million. The improvement was partly related to the increase in interest income, which gained 8.1% to $180.0 million versus the past year's $166.4 million. Noninterest income of $33.7 million was a 10.5% jump from the 1993 figure of $30.5 million. The return on average assets of 1.09% was a leap from 1.02%. Net loans for CBCF were $1.79 billion, up 1.9% from last year's $1.76 billion. Deposits and book value per share remained flat at $2.25 billion and $18.31 per share, respectively. The Company expects to purchase four Michigan banks of Banc One Corporation for $115.0 million during the first quarter of 1995.

BUSINESS

CITIZENS BANKING CORPORATION is a bank holding company headquartered in Flint, Michigan, and is the parent of Citizens Commercial & Savings Bank, Flint; Second National Bank of Saginaw; Second National Bank of Bay City; National Bank of Royal Oak; State Bank of Standish; Grayling State Bank; Century Life Insurance Company of Michigan, a credit life reinsurance company, and Commercial National Bank, Berwyn, Illinois.

LOANS DISTRIBUTION

(12/31/94)	($000)	(%)
Commercial	748,318	41.2
Consumer		
Installment	581,252	32.0
Real Estate-		
Construction	24,947	1.4
Real Estate-Mortgage	384,401	21.1
Lease Financing	77,303	4.3
Total	1,816,221	100.0

ANNUAL EARNINGS AND DIVIDENDS PER SHARE

	1994	1993	1992	1991	1990	1989	1988
Earnings Per Share	2.03	1.88	② 1.80	1.62	1.51	1.43	1.34
Dividends Per Share	0.82	① 0.745	③ 0.69	0.645	0.60	0.555	0.495
Dividend Payout %	40.4	39.6	38.4	39.9	39.7	38.8	36.9

① 2-for-1 stk split,05/13/93 ② Before acctg. chg. ③ Bef acctg chge

ANNUAL FINANCIAL DATA

RECORD OF EARNINGS (IN MILLIONS):

	1994	1993	1992	1991	1990	1989	1988
Total Interest Income	180.0	166.5	178.8	210.6	221.0	219.1	197.8
Total Interest Expense	61.6	62.1	78.8	111.4	122.9	122.4	107.4
Net Interest Income	118.4	104.3	100.0	99.2	98.1	96.7	90.4
Credit Loss Provision	5.3	5.6	6.3	6.1	5.6	7.5	5.7
Net Income	29.4	25.8	① 23.5	21.1	20.1	19.1	18.0
Aver. Shs. Outstg. (000)	14,463	13,724	13,292	13,167	13,300	13,394	13,440
① Before acctg. change dr$12,905,000.							

BALANCE SHEET (IN MILLIONS):

	1994	1993	1992	1991	1990	1989	1988
Cash & Due From Banks	132.1	113.3	121.4	122.9	121.3	132.1	131.4
Loans & Lse Financing, Net	1,791.5	1,757.6	1,538.0	1,512.4	1,536.3	1,479.3	1,420.0
Total Domestic Deposits	2,252.3	2,246.8	2,086.1	2,064.0	2,018.3	1,954.8	1,935.5
Long-term Debt	5.2	10.9	15.1	20.4	43.3	33.0	19.6
Net Stockholders' Equity	258.7	255.2	219.3	218.2	205.9	196.6	185.1
Total Assets	2,703.8	2,714.1	2,498.8	2,492.6	2,425.2	2,392.6	2,354.1
Year End Shs Outstg (000)	14,128	14,115	13,377	13,079	13,124	13,392	13,406

STATISTICAL RECORD:

	1994	1993	1992	1991	1990	1989	1988
Return on Assets %	1.09	0.95	0.94	0.85	0.83	0.80	0.76
Return on Equity %	11.40	10.10	10.70	9.70	9.80	9.70	9.70
Book Value Per Share	18.31	18.08	16.39	16.68	15.69	14.68	13.80
Average Yield %	3.2	3.2	4.2	5.5	5.6	4.2	3.6
P/E Ratio	14.3-10.8	15.2-9.8	10.9-7.7	9.5-5.2	8.4-5.9	10.2-8.0	11.4-9.0
Price Range	29-22	28½-18½	19¼-13⅝	15⅛-8⅜	12⅝-8⅞	14⅝-11½	15¼-12⅛

Statistics are as originally reported.

OFFICERS:
C.R. Weeks, Jr., Chmn. & C.E.O.
J.W. Ennest, Vice-Chmn., C.F.O. & Treas.
D.A. Thomas, Jr., Vice-Chmn.
R.J. Vitito, Pres.
T.W. Gallagher, Sr. V.P., Sec. & Gen. Couns.
INCORPORATED: MI, 1982
PRINCIPAL OFFICE: One Citizens Banking Center, Flint, MI 48502

TELEPHONE NUMBER: (810) 766-7500
NO. OF EMPLOYEES: 1,604
ANNUAL MEETING: In April
SHAREHOLDERS: 6,700 (approx.)
INSTITUTIONAL HOLDINGS:
No. of Institutions: 26
Shares Held: 1,385,170

REGISTRAR(S): Mellon Securities Trust Co., Pittsburgh, PA

TRANSFER AGENT(S): Mellon Securities Trust Co., Pittsburgh, PA

CLARCOR INC.

YIELD 3.0%
P/E RATIO 18.4

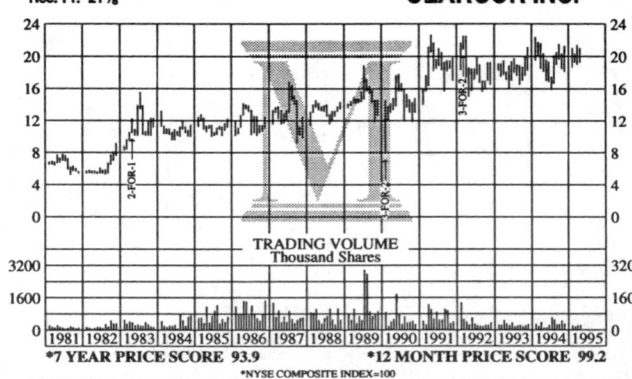

TRADING VOLUME
Thousand Shares

1981 1982 1983 1984 1985 1986 1987 1988 1989 1990 1991 1992 1993 1994 1995

*7 YEAR PRICE SCORE 93.9   ***12 MONTH PRICE SCORE 99.2**
*NYSE COMPOSITE INDEX=100

INTERIM EARNINGS (Per Share):

Qtr.	Feb.	Mar.	Aug.	Nov.
1991-92	0.20	0.29	0.34	0.27
1992-93	0.21	0.19	0.34	0.42
1993-94	0.23	0.28	0.40	0.48

INTERIM DIVIDENDS (Per Share):

Amt.	Decl.	Ex.	Rec.	Pay.
0.155Q	4/4/94	4/11/94	4/15/94	4/29/94
0.155Q	6/30	7/11	7/15	7/29
0.1575Q	8/3	10/7	10/14	10/28
0.1575Q	12/14	1/9/95	1/13/95	1/27/95
0.1575Q	3/31/95	4/7	4/14	4/28

Indicated div.: $0.63

CAPITALIZATION (11/30/94):

	($000)	(%)
Long-Term Debt	17,013	12.1
Deferred Income Tax	5,686	4.1
Minority Interest	171	0.1
Common & Surplus	117,462	83.7
Total	140,332	100.0

DIVIDEND ACHIEVER STATUS:
Rank: 278   1984-94 Growth Rate: 5.3%
Total Years of Dividend Growth: 14

RECENT DEVELOPMENTS: For the year ended 11/30/94, income was $20.6 million versus $17.3 million for 1993. Income was taken before a gain of $630,000 from the cumulative effect of an accounting change. The Company gained $3.2 million on the sale of stock in an affiliate. Yet, the Company expensed $2.8 million in write-offs, thereby largely offsetting gains. Operating profit for the year

increased 11.3% to $32.4 million from $29.1 million a year earlier. The Filtration Products Group gained 28% to achieve total net sales of $199.8 million. This performance contributed much to overall sales, since the group comprises nearly 75% of the Company's total net sales. The Consumer Products Group rose to $70.3 million from $69.1 million.

BUSINESS

CLARCOR INC. is a manufacturer of filtration products and consumer products. The Filtration Products Group includes five individual companies which provide filtration and purification systems for over-the-road trucking, off-road trucking, off-road construction, farming and mining equipment and railroad industries, food and beverage processing, and general industrial markets. The Consumer Products Group manufactures custom-decorated metal and plastic lithographed containers, composite and paperboard containers, collapsible tubes, promotional products and engineered plastic closures. The precision products group will be divested.

BUSINESS LINE ANALYSIS

(11/30/94)	Rev(%)	Inc(%)
Filtration Products	74.0	82.2
Consumer Products	26.0	17.8
Total	100.0	100.0

ANNUAL EARNINGS AND DIVIDENDS PER SHARE

	11/30/94	11/30/93	11/30/92	11/30/91	11/30/90	11/30/89	11/30/88
Earnings Per Share	1.39	1.16	①1.10	⑤1.24	1.37	③0.47	1.15
Dividends Per Share	0.622	0.61	②0.60	④0.55	⑤0.52	0.48	0.453
Dividend Payout %	44.7	52.6	54.5	44.4	37.9	N.M.	39.4

① Before acctg. chg. ② Bef acctg chge ③ Before disc. oper. ④ 3-for-2 stk split,02/18/92 ⑤ 3-for-2 stk split, 1/12/90

ANNUAL FINANCIAL DATA

RECORD OF EARNINGS (IN THOUSANDS):

Total Revenues	270,123	225,319	188,625	179,538	214,710	204,112	202,337
Costs and Expenses	230,465	189,957	155,615	143,687	173,122	177,011	164,279
Depreciation & Amort	7,292	6,295	5,380	4,998	7,801	7,117	6,287
Operating Profit	32,366	29,067	27,630	30,853	33,787	19,984	31,771
Earn Bef Income Taxes	32,560	27,078	25,305	28,543	32,556	18,969	33,106
Income Taxes	11,935	9,827	8,796	10,068	12,151	11,028	12,508
Net Income	21,255	17,251	14,139	①18,475	20,405	②7,941	20,598
Aver. Shs. Outstg.	14,814	14,838	14,973	14,873	14,843	17,040	17,926

① Before disc. op. cr$297,000. ② Before disc. op. dr$824,000.

BALANCE SHEET (IN THOUSANDS):

Cash and Cash Equivalents	19,567	13,838	15,051	9,629	14,810	4,815	20,852
Receivables, Net	45,699	44,152	52,019	35,677	31,951	27,239	27,102
Inventories	30,258	26,996	25,007	28,417	23,855	23,715	20,629
Gross Property	121,659	112,254	95,182	113,923	104,714	102,805	95,701
Accumulated Depreciation	69,044	64,618	59,598	68,211	61,966	58,582	53,638
Long-Term Debt	17,013	24,617	29,325	35,834	35,810	32,634	1,116
Net Stockholders' Equity	117,462	104,641	99,551	95,662	82,689	72,662	125,012
Total Assets	188,448	169,896	161,255	157,999	144,127	131,009	143,842
Total Current Assets	98,450	86,161	93,627	75,207	72,623	58,019	70,028
Total Current Liabilities	39,461	33,288	25,272	20,570	20,758	21,405	14,244
Net Working Capital	58,989	52,873	68,355	54,637	51,865	36,614	55,784
Year End Shares Outstg	14,761	14,819	14,986	14,908	14,846	15,045	17,900

STATISTICAL RECORD:

Operating Profit Margin %	12.0	12.9	14.6	17.2	15.7	9.8	15.7
Book Value Per Share	6.93	6.00	5.79	5.03	4.13	3.33	5.46
Return on Equity %	17.6	16.5	16.6	19.3	24.7	10.9	16.5
Return on Assets %	10.9	10.2	10.2	11.7	14.2	6.1	14.3
Average Yield %	3.3	3.3	3.2	3.0	4.0	3.1	3.5
P/E Ratio	16.1-11.4	18.2-13.8	20.5-13.6	18.2-11.3	13.0-5.7	40.2-25.0	12.6-9.9
Price Range	22⅜-15⅞	21⅛-16	22½-15	22⅝-14	17⅞-7⅞	18⅞-11¾	14½-11⅜

Statistics are as originally reported.

OFFICERS:
L.E. Gloyd, Chmn., Pres. & C.E.O.
B.A. Klein, V.P.-Fin. & C.F.O.
W.F. Knese, V.P., Treas. & Contr.
M.C. Arne, V.P. & Sec.

INCORPORATED: DE, 1969

PRINCIPAL OFFICE: 2323 Sixth Street P.O. Box 7007, Rockford, IL 61125

TELEPHONE NUMBER: (815) 962-8867

FAX: (815) 962-0417

NO. OF EMPLOYEES: 2,211 (approx.)

ANNUAL MEETING: In March

SHAREHOLDERS: 1,900

INSTITUTIONAL HOLDINGS:
No. of Institutions: 79
Shares Held: 6,901,285

REGISTRAR(S): First Chicago Trust Co. of New York, New York, NY 10008

TRANSFER AGENT(S): First Chicago Trust Co. of New York, New York, NY 10008

NYS SYMBOL CLX
Rec. Pr. 57⅞

CLOROX CO.

YIELD 3.3%
P/E RATIO 15.8

*7 YEAR PRICE SCORE 104.3   *12 MONTH PRICE SCORE 104.1
*NYSE COMPOSITE INDEX=100

TRADING VOLUME
Thousand Shares

INTERIM EARNINGS (Per Share):

Qtr.	Sept.	Dec.	Mar.	June
1991-92	0.81	0.47	0.72	0.22
1992-93	---------- 3.07 ----------			
1993-94	0.85	0.57	0.93	1.00
1994-95	1.00	0.64	1.02	...

INTERIM DIVIDENDS (Per Share):

Amt.	Decl.	Ex.	Rec.	Pay.
0.45Q	3/16/94	4/25/94	4/29/94	5/13/94
0.48Q	7/19	7/25	7/29	8/15
0.48Q	9/21	10/24	10/28	11/15
0.48Q	1/18/95	1/23/95	1/27/95	2/15/95
0.48Q	3/15	4/24	4/28	5/15

Indicated div.: $1.92*

CAPITALIZATION (6/30/94):

	($000)	(%)
Long-Term Debt	279,275	21.1
Deferred Income Tax	133,045	10.1
Common & Surplus	909,417	68.8
Total	1,321,737	100.0

DIVIDEND ACHIEVER STATUS:

Rank: 110   1984-94 Growth Rate: 12.4%
Total Years of Dividend Growth: 18

RECENT DEVELOPMENTS: For the quarter ended 12/31/94, net income rose 11.5% to $34.1 million from $30.6 million for the comparable quarter in 1993. Net sales were $414.5 million, up 11.8% from $370.8 million for the year-earlier quarter. Worldwide shipments increased substantially, setting a record for the quarter and included a 16.0% jump in domestic shipments.

PROSPECTS: New product introductions and line extensions are expected to remain at a high level and will help fuel future growth. Although these developments will require increased investment spending and competition will remain intense, CLX will continue to focus on cutting an additional $25 million in operating expenses by the end of fiscal 1996. International shipments, especially to the growing Asia/Pacific and Latin American regions, should continue to increase.

BUSINESS

THE CLOROX COMPANY is a diversified international company whose principal business is to develop, manufacture and market consumer products sold in grocery stores and other retail outlets. In addition, many of these products are sold to food service customers such as schools, hotels and restaurants. Major consumer products include: Clorox liquid bleach; Clorox 2 dry bleach; Clorox Pre-Wash and Clorox Detergent. Other name brands are: Formula 409 spray cleaner, Soft Scrub liquid cleanser, Pine-Sol cleaners, Kingsford charcoal briquets, Hidden Valley Ranch salad dressing, and Combat insecticides.

QUARTERLY DATA

(6/30/94)($000)	Rev	Inc
1st Quarter	449,744	78,378
2nd Quarter	370,844	30,586
3rd Quarter	481,928	49,515
4th Quarter................	534,433	53,578

ANNUAL EARNINGS AND DIVIDENDS PER SHARE

	6/30/94	6/30/93	6/30/92	6/30/91	6/30/90	6/30/89	6/30/88
Earnings Per Share	3.35	①3.07	②2.17	0.98	2.80	①2.63	2.46
Dividends Per Share	1.86	1.77	1.65	1.53	1.39	1.19	1.00
Dividend Payout %	55.5	57.6	76.0	N.M.	49.6	45.2	40.7

① Before disc. oper. ② Before acctg. chg.

ANNUAL FINANCIAL DATA

RECORD OF EARNINGS (IN MILLIONS):

Total Revenues	1,836.9	1,634.2	1,717.0	1,646.5	1,484.0	1,356.3	1,259.9
Costs and Expenses	1,511.0	1,254.2	1,371.3	1,446.7	1,217.4	1,104.9	1,015.2
Depreciation & Amort	94.1	83.6	89.6	87.0	50.1	44.7	37.5
Operating Profit	346.6	338.8	300.8	285.4	216.6	243.9	240.1
Earn Bef Income Taxes	306.6	275.2	210.9	86.2	243.6	229.7	211.8
Income Taxes	126.6	107.3	93.1	33.4	90.0	84.1	79.2
Net Income	①180.0	②167.9	③117.8	52.7	153.6	④145.6	132.6
Aver. Shs. Outstg. (000)	53,800	54,698	54,366	54,063	54,873	55,333	53,927

① Before disc. op. cr$32,064,000. ② Before disc. op. dr$867,000. ③ Before acctg. change dr$19,061,000. ④ Before disc. op. dr$21,416,000.

BALANCE SHEET (IN MILLIONS):

Cash and Cash Equivalents	115.9	71.2	69.0	113.9	124.6	233.3	259.3
Receivables, Net	268.4	246.0	226.7	219.5	151.5	143.4	139.3
Inventories	105.9	105.9	110.5	116.3	128.1	110.6	97.4
Gross Property	850.5	814.3	865.4	760.6	712.4	572.1	523.2
Accumulated Depreciation	317.9	276.2	283.9	238.8	194.9	161.2	147.3
Long-Term Debt	279.3	254.7	262.3	406.8	7.5	7.1	29.2
Net Stockholders' Equity	909.4	879.3	813.7	784.3	810.5	786.2	712.9
Total Assets	1,697.6	1,649.2	1,614.8	1,602.7	1,137.7	1,213.1	1,156.0
Total Current Assets	504.3	531.8	418.3	466.8	418.4	614.8	504.3
Total Current Liabilities	375.8	371.6	421.5	348.4	225.6	330.8	314.4
Net Working Capital	128.4	160.2	d3.2	118.4	192.8	284.1	189.9
Year End Shs Outstg (000)	53,372	54,850	54,545	54,196	54,032	55,398	54,044

STATISTICAL RECORD:

Operating Profit Margin %	16.4	18.1	14.9	6.9	14.6	15.2	16.5
Book Value Per Share	7.30	7.57	6.13	5.36	13.12	12.39	9.50
Return on Equity %	19.8	19.1	14.5	6.7	19.0	18.5	18.6
Return on Assets %	10.6	10.2	7.3	3.3	13.5	12.0	11.5
Average Yield %	3.5	3.6	3.6	4.0	3.6	3.2	3.3
P/E Ratio	16.6-14.0	18.0-14.3	24.0-18.2	43.2-35.7	16.2-11.5	16.9-11.5	13.7-10.6
Price Range	55¾-47	55⅜-44	52-39½	42⅜-35	45⅜-32⅛	44½-30⅛	33¾-26⅛

Statistics are as originally reported.

OFFICERS:

G.C. Sullivan, Chmn., Pres. & C.E.O.
E.A. Cutter, Sr. V.P., Gen. Counsel & Sec.
W.F. Ausfahl, Group V.P. & C.F.O.
K.M. Rose, V.P. & Treas.

INCORPORATED: DE, 1986

PRINCIPAL OFFICE: 1221 Broadway, Oakland, CA 94612-1888

TELEPHONE NUMBER: (510) 271-7000

NO. OF EMPLOYEES: 4,850 (approx.)

ANNUAL MEETING: October

SHAREHOLDERS: 23,000

INSTITUTIONAL HOLDINGS:
No. of Institutions: 420
Shares Held: 27,141,567

REGISTRAR(S): First Chicago Trust Co. of New York, New York, NY 10008

TRANSFER AGENT(S): First Chicago Trust Co. of New York, New York, NY 10008

NYS SYMBOL KO
Rec. Pr. 59⅞

COCA-COLA CO.

YIELD 1.5%
P/E RATIO 28.8

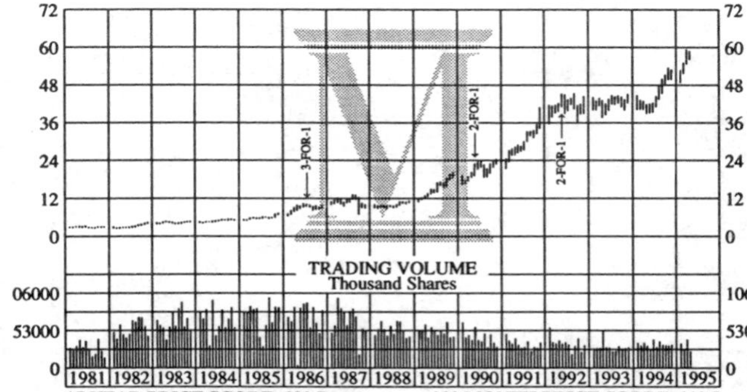

***7 YEAR PRICE SCORE 130.7** ***12 MONTH PRICE SCORE 110.5**
*NYSE COMPOSITE INDEX=100

INTERIM EARNINGS (Per Share):

Qtr.	Mar.	June	Sept.	Dec.
1992	0.29	0.43	0.41	0.30
1993	0.35	0.52	0.48	0.36
1994	0.40	0.59	0.55	0.44
1995	0.50	...	...	...

INTERIM DIVIDENDS (Per Share):

Amt.	Decl.	Ex.	Rec.	Pay.
0.195Q	4/21/94	6/9/94	6/15/94	7/1/94
0.195Q	7/21	9/9	9/15	10/1
0.195Q	10/20	11/25	12/1	12/15
0.22Q	2/16/95	3/9/95	3/15/95	4/1/95
0.22Q	4/20	6/13	6/15	7/1

Indicated div.: $0.88*

CAPITALIZATION (12/31/94):

	($000)	(%)
Long-Term Debt	1,426,000	20.9
Deferred Income Tax	180,000	2.6
Common & Surplus	5,235,000	76.5
Total	6,841,000	100.0

DIVIDEND ACHIEVER STATUS:
Rank: 96 1984-94 Growth Rate: 13.0%
Total Years of Dividend Growth: 32

RECENT DEVELOPMENTS: For the year ended 12/31/94, net income surged 17% to a record $2.55 billion from $2.19 billion in the previous year. Revenues advanced 16% to $16.17 billion. International and domestic unit case volume rose 11% and 7%, respectively, from the prior year. Gross profit grew 14% to $10.00 billion, reflecting increased investments in bottlers, which have lower gross margins than KO's core business.

PROSPECTS: The Company will continue to emphasize global marketing programs to boost overall sales. Near-term earnings growth should continue with the aid of a strong advertising campaign for Sprite, and the ongoing international rollout of 16-oz. glass and 20-oz. plastic contour bottles for Coca-Cola. Long term, KO is planning to invest $1 billion a year in the fast-growing markets of China and India.

BUSINESS

COCA-COLA CO. is the world's largest producer and distributor of soft drinks, soft drink concentrates and syrups. Principal soft drink products are: Coca-Cola, Coca-Cola Classic , Diet Coke, Fanta, Sprite, plus other assorted diet and caffeine-free versions. Coca-Cola Foods markets and processes citrus and other fruit juices and fruit drink products, primarily orange juice. Popular brands include Minute Maid and Hi-C. In 1994, soft drinks USA accounted for 22% of sales (18% of operating profit); soft drinks international, 67% (79%); and foods, 11% (3%). Coca-Cola holds an approximate 44% interest in Coca-Cola Enterprises, Inc., a soft drink bottling concern.

ANNUAL EARNINGS AND DIVIDENDS PER SHARE

	1994	1993	1992	1991	1990	1989	1988
Earnings Per Share	**1.98**	**1.68**	**[1] 1.43**	**1.21**	**1.02**	**[4] 0.89**	**0.72**
Dividends Per Share	**0.78**	**0.68**	**[2] 0.56**	**0.48**	**[3] 0.40**	**0.34**	**0.30**
Dividend Payout %	**39.4**	**40.5**	**39.2**	**39.5**	**39.2**	**40.1**	**42.1**

[1] Before acctg. chg. [2] 2-for-1 stk split, 5/12/92 [3] Adj for 2-for-1 stk split, 5/11/90 [4] Before disc. oper.

ANNUAL FINANCIAL DATA

RECORD OF EARNINGS (IN MILLIONS):							
Total Revenues	16,172.0	13,957.0	13,073.9	11,571.6	10,236.4	8,965.8	8,337.8
Costs and Expenses	12,053.0	10,495.0	9,981.8	8,991.1	8,040.9	7,056.2	6,569.8
Depreciation & Amort	411.0	360.0	321.9	261.4	243.9	183.8	169.8
Operating Income	3,708.0	3,102.0	2,770.1	2,319.0	1,951.6	1,725.8	1,598.3
Income Bef Income Taxes	3,728.0	3,185.0	2,746.1	2,383.3	2,014.4	1,764.3	1,582.1
Income Taxes	1,174.0	997.0	862.3	765.3	632.5	571.5	537.4
Net Income	2,554.0	[1] 2,188.0	[2] 1,883.8	1,618.0	1,381.9	[3] 1,192.8	1,044.7
Aver. Shs. Outstg. (000)	1,290,000	1,302,000	1,316,758	1,332,944	1,337,140	1,383,962	1,458,448

[1] Before acctg. change dr$12,000,000. [2] Before acctg. change dr$219,433,000. [3] Before disc. op. cr$530,986,000.

BALANCE SHEET (IN MILLIONS):							
Cash and Cash Equivalents	3,735.0	3,206.0	3,223.9	3,256.5	2,925.3	2,806.3	2,134.1
Receivables, Net	1,525.0	1,243.0	1,085.6	969.6	951.7	820.4	784.0
Inventories	1,047.0	1,049.0	1,018.6	987.8	982.3	789.1	778.8
Gross Property	6,157.0	5,596.0	5,242.9	4,444.6	3,785.7	3,294.7	2,908.9
Accumulated Depreciation	2,077.0	1,867.0	1,716.6	1,554.8	1,400.2	1,273.5	1,149.8
Long-Term Debt	1,426.0	1,428.0	1,120.1	985.3	535.9	548.7	761.1
Net Stockholders' Equity	5,235.0	4,584.0	3,888.4	4,425.8	3,849.2	3,485.5	3,345.3
Total Assets	14,975.0	13,085.0	12,132.4	11,292.1	9,994.8	9,094.8	7,902.1
Total Current Assets	6,307.0	5,498.0	5,328.1	5,213.9	4,859.4	4,415.8	3,696.9
Total Current Liabilities	6,177.0	5,171.0	5,303.2	4,117.6	4,296.5	3,657.9	2,868.9
Net Working Capital	130.0	327.0	24.9	1,096.3	562.9	757.9	828.0
Year End Shs Outstg (000)	1,275,933	1,297,453	1,306,771	1,328,960	1,336,478	1,348,060	1,419,156
STATISTICAL RECORD:							
Operating Profit Margin %	22.9	22.2	21.2	20.0	19.1	19.2	19.2
Book Value Per Share	3.59	3.11	2.68	3.10	2.62	2.19	2.11
Return on Equity %	48.8	47.7	48.4	36.6	35.9	34.2	31.2
Return on Assets %	17.1	16.7	15.5	14.3	13.8	13.1	13.2
Average Yield %	1.7	1.6	1.4	1.5	2.0	2.2	3.0
P/E Ratio	27.0-19.6	26.9-22.3	31.7-24.9	33.8-17.7	24.0-16.1	23.8-12.8	15.8-12.2
Price Range	53½-38⅞	45⅛-37½	45⅜-35⅝	40⅞-21⅜	24½-16⅜	20¼-10⅞	11⅜-8¾

Statistics are as originally reported.

OFFICERS:
R.C. Goizueta, Chmn. & C.E.O.
J.L. Stahl, Sr. V.P. & C.F.O.
D.M. Taggart, V.P. & Treas.
S.E. Shaw, Sec.

INCORPORATED: DE, Sep., 1919

PRINCIPAL OFFICE: One Coca-Cola Plaza, N.W., Atlanta, GA 30313-2499

TELEPHONE NUMBER: (404) 676-2121

NO. OF EMPLOYEES: 33,000 (approx.)

ANNUAL MEETING: In April

SHAREHOLDERS: 179,165 (of record)

INSTITUTIONAL HOLDINGS:
No. of Institutions: 1,165
Shares Held: 792,650,299

REGISTRAR(S): First Chicago Trust Co. of New York, New York, NY 10008

TRANSFER AGENT(S): First Chicago Trust Co. of New York, New York, NY 10008

COLGATE-PALMOLIVE CO.

YIELD 2.3%
P/E RATIO 18.7

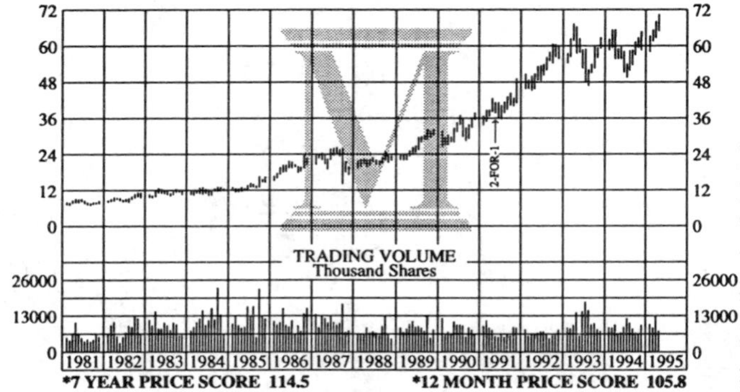

7 YEAR PRICE SCORE 114.5 **12 MONTH PRICE SCORE 105.8**
*NYSE COMPOSITE INDEX=100

INTERIM EARNINGS (Per Share):

Qtr.	Mar.	June	Sept.	Dec.
1991	0.65	0.66	d1.13	0.58
1992	0.74	0.75	0.78	0.66
1993	0.85	0.86	0.89	0.78
1994	0.98	0.93	1.00	0.91

INTERIM DIVIDENDS (Per Share):

Amt.	Decl.	Ex.	Rec.	Pay.
0.36Q	3/17/94	4/19/94	4/25/94	5/16/94
0.41Q	7/14	7/19	7/25	8/15
0.41Q	10/13	10/19	10/25	11/15
0.41Q	1/12/95	1/19/95	1/25/95	2/15/95
0.41Q	3/9	4/19	4/25	5/15

Indicated div.: $1.64

CAPITALIZATION (12/31/94):

	($000)	(%)
Long-Term Debt	1,751,500	45.3
Deferred Income Tax	295,400	7.6
Preferred Stock	408,400	10.6
Common & Surplus	1,414,500	36.5
Total	3,869,800	100.0

DIVIDEND ACHIEVER STATUS:
Rank: 191   1984-94 Growth Rate: 9.2%
Total Years of Dividend Growth: 32

RECENT DEVELOPMENTS: For the quarter ended 12/31/94, net income increased 12.3% to $137.1 million from $122.1 million the year before. Sales in North America declined less than 3.0% while sales for the Hill's Pet Nutrition business improved by 18.0%. Net sales were $2.00 billion compared with $1.84 billion a year ago, an increase of 8.5%. Led by strong gains in Latin America, Asia/Africa and Hill's Pet Nutrition.

PROSPECTS: CL's presence in both developed and developing markets outside the U.S. will allow the Company to take advantage of growth opportunities, especially in the Latin America and Asia/Africa markets. Despite recent downstocking by retailers, the Company's strategy of shifting the product mix to higher-margin products and continued new product activity should enhance domestic profitability over the long term.

BUSINESS

COLGATE-PALMOLIVE is a worldwide manufacturer and marketer of consumer products. The Company operates two segments. Oral, Personal and Household Care products, 83.3% of total revenues in 1994, consists of toothpastes, toothbrushes, soaps, shampoos, baby products, deodorants, detergents, cleaners, shave products and other similar items. Specialty Marketing, 16.7% of 1994 revenues, consists of pet dietary care products, crystal tableware, and portable fuel for warming food. Principal global trademarks include Colgate, Palmolive, Ajax, Fab, and Science Diet, in addition to various regional tradenames. The Company acquired Mennen Co. toiletries in 1992.

ANNUAL EARNINGS AND DIVIDENDS PER SHARE

	1994	1993	1992	1991	1990	1989	1988
Earnings Per Share	3.82	3.38	2.92	0.77	2.28	1.98	☑1.11
Dividends Per Share	1.54	1.34	1.15	☐1.02	0.90	0.78	☑0.74
Dividend Payout %	40.3	39.7	50.2	N.M.	39.5	39.3	71.2

☐ 2-for-1 stk split,05/16/91 ☑ Before disc. oper. ☑ Excludes $0.05 special dividend

ANNUAL FINANCIAL DATA

RECORD OF EARNINGS (IN MILLIONS):

	1994	1993	1992	1991	1990	1989	1988
Total Revenues	7,587.9	7,141.3	7,007.2	6,060.3	5,691.3	5,038.8	4,734.3
Costs and Expenses	6,303.4	5,977.4	6,016.1	5,632.5	5,010.4	4,506.3	4,347.8
Depreciation & Amort	235.1	209.6	192.5	146.2	126.2	97.0	82.0
Operating Profit	3,674.6	3,411.4	3,298.8	2,764.0	2,570.3	2,195.8	304.5
Income Bef Income Taxes	879.9	836.2	727.9	217.9	511.4	447.0	250.2
Income Taxes	299.7	288.1	250.9	93.0	190.4	166.9	97.6
Net Income	580.2	☐548.1	477.0	124.9	321.0	280.0	☑152.7
Aver. Shs. Outstg. (000)	146,200	155,900	156,500	135,300	132,200	135,804	136,762

☐ Before acctg. change dr$358,200,000. ☑ Before disc. op. cr$165,134,000.

BALANCE SHEET (IN MILLIONS):

Cash and Cash Equivalents	217.5	211.2	220.5	245.4	276.4	524.2	365.5
Receivables, Net	1,049.6	988.3	876.5	744.2	665.7	600.9	589.3
Inventories	713.9	678.0	695.6	675.9	692.4	590.7	629.7
Gross Property	3,103.4	2,820.2	2,582.4	2,360.6	2,124.3	1,728.7	1,636.3
Accumulated Depreciation	1,115.3	1,053.9	985.6	965.7	761.9	623.2	614.7
Long-Term Debt	1,751.5	1,532.4	946.5	850.8	1,068.4	1,059.5	674.3
Net Stockholders' Equity	1,822.9	1,875.0	2,619.8	1,866.3	1,363.6	1,123.2	1,150.6
Total Assets	6,142.4	5,761.2	5,434.1	4,510.6	4,157.9	3,536.5	3,217.6
Total Current Assets	2,177.7	2,070.4	1,995.1	1,857.7	1,812.7	1,896.9	1,782.8
Total Current Liabilities	1,529.2	1,394.0	1,359.5	1,261.7	1,296.7	989.4	1,071.9
Net Working Capital	648.5	676.4	635.6	596.0	516.0	907.5	710.9
Year End Shs Outstg (000)	144,404	149,257	137,268	123,128	95,267	94,509	138,138

STATISTICAL RECORD:

Operating Profit Margin %	13.8	13.4	11.4	4.6	9.7	8.6	6.4
Book Value Per Share	12.62	12.40	16.21	12.54	10.12	8.39	8.24
Return on Equity %	31.8	29.2	18.2	6.7	23.5	24.9	13.3
Return on Assets %	9.4	9.5	8.8	2.8	7.7	7.9	4.7
Average Yield %	2.7	2.4	2.2	2.5	2.8	2.9	3.6
P/E Ratio	17.1-13.0	19.9-13.8	20.8-15.5	63.8-43.7	16.6-11.6	16.4-11.2	22.3-17.3
Price Range	65⅜-49½	67¼-46¾	60⅝-45⅛	49⅛-33⅝	37¾-26⅜	32½-22⅛	24¾-19¼

Statistics are as originally reported.

OFFICERS:
R. Mark, Chmn. & C.E.O.
W.S. Shanahan, Pres. & C.O.O.
R.M. Agate, Sr. Exec. V.P. & C.F.O.
A.D. Hendry, S.V.P., Gen. Coun. & Sec.
V.P. Fin. & Treas., B.J. Heidtke

INCORPORATED: DE, Jul., 1923

PRINCIPAL OFFICE: 300 Park Ave., New York, NY 10022-7499

TELEPHONE NUMBER: (212) 310-2000

NO. OF EMPLOYEES: 32,800 (approx.)

ANNUAL MEETING: In May

SHAREHOLDERS: 40,300

INSTITUTIONAL HOLDINGS:
No. of Institutions: 763
Shares Held: 89,606,164

REGISTRAR(S): First Chicago Trust Co. of New York, New York, NY 10008

TRANSFER AGENT(S): First Chicago Trust Co. of New York, New York, NY 10008

NASDAQ SYMBOL CGES
Rec. Pr. 19

COLONIAL GAS CO.

YIELD 6.7%
P/E RATIO 13.9

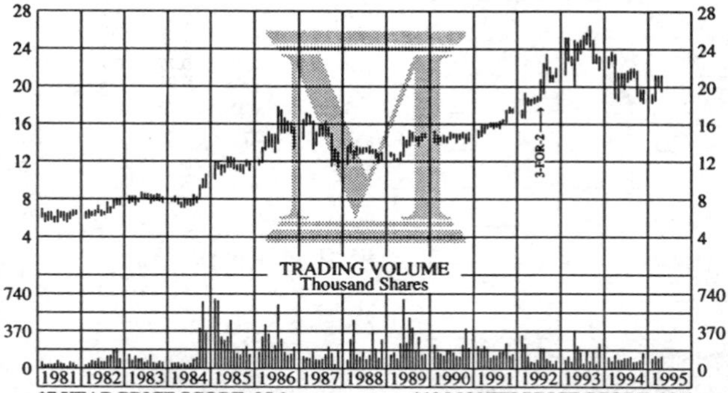

*7 YEAR PRICE SCORE 95.1 *12 MONTH PRICE SCORE 95.6

*NYSE COMPOSITE INDEX=100

INTERIM EARNINGS (Per Share):

Qtr.	Mar.	June	Sept.	Dec.
1991	1.33	d0.58	d0.50	0.85
1992	1.65	d0.47	d0.51	0.71
1993	1.53	d0.41	d0.47	0.87
1994	1.79	d0.41	d0.59	0.58

INTERIM DIVIDENDS (Per Share):

Amt.	Decl.	Ex.	Rec.	Pay.
0.315Q	4/20/94	5/25/94	6/1/94	6/15/94
0.315Q	8/9	8/26	9/1	9/15
0.315Q	11/17	11/25	12/1	12/15
0.315Q	2/14/95	2/23/95	3/1/95	3/15/95
0.32Q	4/19	5/25	6/1	6/15

*Indicated div.: $1.28**

CAPITALIZATION (12/31/94):

	($000)	(%)
Long-Term Debt	77,923	34.7
Cap. Lease Oblig.	2,237	1.0
Deferred Income Tax	45,437	20.2
Common & Surplus	99,175	44.1
Total	224,772	100.0
Current Debt	58,661	

DIVIDEND ACHIEVER STATUS:
Rank: 330 1984-94 Growth Rate: 2.2%
Total Years of Dividend Growth: 14

RECENT DEVELOPMENTS: For the year ended 12/31/94, net income declined 8.4% to $11.0 million from $12.0 million for the 1993 period. The Company incurred a restructuring charge in the 1994 fourth quarter of $3.2 million. The charge was comprised of $2.5 million for the cost of an early retirement program and $600,000 million in costs pertaining to the shutdown of two retail appliance stores. Operating revenues were stable at $166.2 million. Operating margin progressed 4.6% to $78.8 million from $75.3 million. This was attributed to a 3.8% fall in the cost of gas sold to $87.4 million from $90.9 million. The Company's customer base grew 3.4% and 1994 was the first full year of the implementation of the 4.9% rate increase.

BUSINESS

COLONIAL GAS COMPANY is primarily a regulated natural gas distribution utility. The Company serves 132,000 utility customers in 24 municipalities located northwest of Boston and on Cape Cod. Through its wholly-owned energy trucking subsidiary, Trangas Inc., the Company also provides over-the-road transportation of liquefied natural gas ('LNG'), propane and other commodities. The Company's combined natural gas distribution service areas in the Merrimack Valley region northwest of Boston and on Cape Cod cover approximately 622 square miles with a year-round population of approximately 500,000, which increases by approximately 350,000 during the summer tourist season on Cape Cod.

REVENUES

(12/31/94)	($000)	(%)
Residential	104,812	63.0
Commercial & Industrial	56,358	33.9
Non-firm Sales	2,429	1.6
Transportation	1,210	0.7
Non-firm Transportation	401	0.2
Other	1,049	0.6
Total	166,259	100.0

ANNUAL EARNINGS AND DIVIDENDS PER SHARE

	1994	1993	1992	1991	1990	1989	1988
Earnings Per Share	**1.36**	**1.52**	**1.38**	**1.11**	**0.82**	**1.44**	**1.20**
Dividends Per Share	**1.255**	**1.235**	[1] **1.213**	**1.193**	**1.167**	**1.14**	**1.113**
Dividend Payout %	**92.3**	**81.3**	**87.9**	**N.M.**	**N.M.**	**79.2**	**92.8**

[1] 3-for-2 stk split, 7/30/92

ANNUAL FINANCIAL DATA

	1994	1993	1992	1991	1990	1989	1988
RECORD OF EARNINGS (IN THOUSANDS):							
Total Revenues	178,325	173,819	154,853	137,719	134,298	139,892	124,428
Depreciation	9,235	6,831	5,914	5,488	5,129	4,726	4,388
Maintenance	5,996	5,631	5,477	5,124	5,235	5,335	4,994
Prov for Fed Inc Taxes	4,806	6,111	5,390	3,803	1,651	2,562	3,191
Interest Expense	8,409	8,141	7,466	8,141	8,445	8,217	7,369
Net Income	11,009	12,022	10,643	8,317	5,695	8,917	[1] 7,283
Aver. Shs. Outstg.	8,119	7,931	7,728	7,529	6,963	6,200	6,065
[1] Before acctg. change cr$2,014,000.							
BALANCE SHEET (IN THOUSANDS):							
Gross Plant	293,585	267,719	244,920	220,187	205,341	189,474	177,421
Accumulated Depreciation	65,473	57,857	52,700	48,127	43,823	39,964	36,499
Prop, Plant & Equip, Net	228,112	209,862	192,220	172,060	161,518	149,510	140,922
Long-term Debt	80,160	90,581	94,341	54,248	68,837	74,226	60,559
Net Stockholders' Equity	99,175	94,283	87,771	82,221	80,109	66,568	63,027
Total Assets	334,885	315,930	306,790	267,990	241,663	237,680	212,386
Year End Shares Outstg	8,227	8,030	7,844	7,625	7,449	6,267	6,140
STATISTICAL RECORD:							
Book Value Per Share	11.71	11.39	10.83	10.42	10.38	10.18	9.81
Dep/Gr. Pl %	3.1	2.6	2.4	2.5	2.5	2.5	2.5
Accum. Dep/Gr. Pl %	22.3	21.6	21.5	21.9	21.3	21.1	20.6
Return on Equity %	11.1	12.8	12.1	10.1	7.1	13.4	11.6
Average Yield %	6.0	5.3	6.0	7.4	8.0	8.3	8.7
P/E Ratio	17.5-13.4	17.4-13.2	17.0-12.0	16.1-13.1	18.8-16.9	10.7-8.3	11.7-9.7
Price Range	23¾-18¼	26½-20	23½-16⅝	17⅞-14½	15⅜-13⅞	15⅜-12	14-11⅝

Statistics are as originally reported.

OFFICERS:
F.L. Putnam, Jr., Chmn. & Sr. Exec. Officer
F.L. Putnam, III, Pres. & C.E.O.
N. Stravropoulos, Exec. V.P.-Fin.&Mktg. & C.F.O.

INCORPORATED: MA, Jul., 1981

PRINCIPAL OFFICE: 40 Market Street, Lowell, MA 01852

TELEPHONE NUMBER: (508) 458-3171

NO. OF EMPLOYEES: 407 full-time; 52 part-time

ANNUAL MEETING: In April

SHAREHOLDERS: 15,000

INSTITUTIONAL HOLDINGS:
No. of Institutions: 37
Shares Held: 989,730

REGISTRAR(S):

TRANSFER AGENT(S): First National Bank of Boston, Shareholder Services Division, Boston, MA

NYS SYMBOL CMA
Rec. Pr. 29½

COMERICA, INC.

YIELD 4.3%
P/E RATIO 9.0

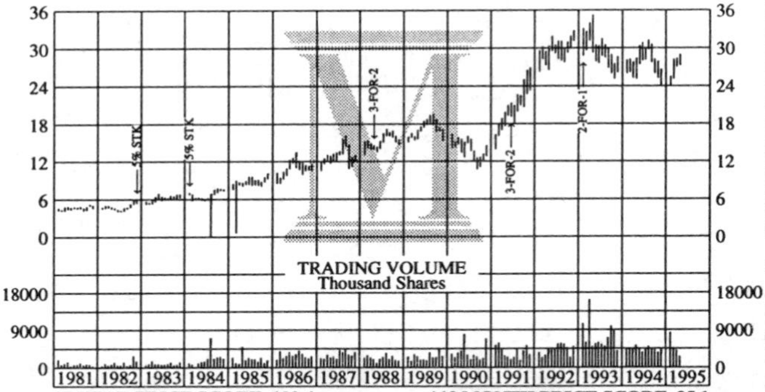

*7 YEAR PRICE SCORE 102.4 *12 MONTH PRICE SCORE 95.1

*NYSE COMPOSITE INDEX=100

INTERIM EARNINGS (Per Share):

Qtr.	Mar.	June	Sept.	Dec.
1991	0.62	0.64	0.60	0.66
1992	0.68	d0.14	0.71	0.72
1993	0.69	0.70	0.70	0.76
1994	0.79	0.83	0.84	0.82

INTERIM DIVIDENDS (Per Share):

Amt.	Decl.	Ex.	Rec.	Pay.
0.28Q	1/21/94	3/9/94	3/15/94	4/1/94
0.32Q	5/20	6/9	6/15	7/1
0.32Q	7/18	9/9	9/15	10/3
0.32Q	11/18	12/9	12/15	1/2/95
0.32Q	1/20/95	3/9/95	3/15/95	4/1

Indicated div.: $1.28*

CAPITALIZATION (12/31/94):

	($000)	(%)
Total Deposits	22,432,316	67.1
Total Debt	8,303,351	24.8
Common & Surplus	2,391,780	7.1
Loan Valuation Reserve	326,195	1.0
Total	33,453,642	100.0

DIVIDEND ACHIEVER STATUS:

Rank: 153 1984-94 Growth Rate: 10.5%
Total Years of Dividend Growth: 11

RECENT DEVELOPMENTS: For the year ended 12/31/94, net income was $387.2 million, up 13.7% from the $340.6 million earned in 1993. The Company cited solid loan growth and improved asset quality as the reasons for higher earnings. Net interest income was up to $1.23 billion from $1.13 billion. Noninterest income was $466.6 million compared with $462.5 million a year ago. The provision for loan losses declined 18.8% to $56 million from $69 million.

PROSPECTS: Earnings are benefiting from cost-management programs, increased loan activity and stabilizing margins. Credit quality continues to improve as nonperforming assets and charge-offs are spiraling downward. The Company announced plans to acquire University Bank and Trust Co. for $73 million. University Bank, based in Palo Alto, CA, has assets of $422 million.

BUSINESS

COMERICA, INC. is one of the largest bank holding companies in Michigan and the parent of Comerica Bank-Detroit. At 12/31/94, the Company had assets of approximately $33.4 billion and, in addition to Michigan, operates banks in Illinois, California, Florida and Texas. On June 18, 1992, Comerica merged with Manufacturers National Corp. The banks offer individuals, businesses and governmental agencies a full line of commercial banking services. At 12/31/94, the loan portfolio was classified as follows: commercial loans, 47.9%; commercial mortgage, 13.8%; construction, 1.9%; residential mortgage, 11%; consumer, 19%; lease finance, 1% and international, 5.4%.

ANNUAL EARNINGS AND DIVIDENDS PER SHARE

	1994	1993	1992	1991	1990	1989	1988
Earnings Per Share	**3.28**	**2.85**	**1.92**	**[2] 2.52**	**[4] 2.52**	**1.55**	**2.26**
Dividends Per Share	**1.20**	**1.045**	**[1] 0.94**	**[3] 0.904**	**0.85**	**0.733**	**0.60**
Dividend Payout %	**36.6**	**36.7**	**49.0**	**35.9**	**33.8**	**47.3**	**26.5**

[1] 2-for-1 stk split,01/05/93 [2] chg. to reflect 3-for-2- stk split 6/91 [3] 3-for-2 stk split,06/20/91 [4] Per primary share

ANNUAL FINANCIAL DATA

	1994	1993	1992	1991	1990	1989	1988
RECORD OF EARNINGS (IN MILLIONS):							
Total Interest Income	2,091.9	1,782.9	1,869.7	1,219.0	1,165.8	1,116.5	919.2
Total Interest Expense	861.8	649.3	783.9	624.4	673.6	669.1	523.3
Net Interest Income	1,230.1	1,133.5	1,085.9	594.7	492.1	447.4	395.9
Credit Loss Provision	56.0	69.0	113.4	57.9	57.2	103.1	38.7
Net Income	387.2	340.6	226.0	153.4	128.5	77.6	112.0
Aver. Shs. Outstg. (000)	118,160	119,569	56,858	59,484	49,598	47,501	46,862
BALANCE SHEET (IN MILLIONS):							
Cash & Due From Banks	1,822.3	1,600.7	1,485.5	765.8	627.9	675.1	640.4
Loans & Lse Financing, Net	21,883.1	18,801.3	17,509.6	9,090.1	8,178.2	7,704.9	6,790.2
Total Domestic Deposits	19,998.8	19,582.1	19,496.8	11,427.7	10,724.7	9,743.6	9,141.3
Total Foreign Deposits	2,433.5	1,367.8	897.9	13.3	29.8	139.1	108.5
Long-term Debt	4,097.9	1,460.6	737.0	244.3	263.8	274.3	275.7
Net Stockholders' Equity	2,391.8	2,181.7	2,029.4	1,052.1	791.2	704.8	668.4
Total Assets	33,429.9	30,294.9	26,586.8	14,450.8	13,300.4	12,149.5	11,145.5
Year End Shs Outstg (000)	116,912	114,871	57,438	62,320	50,006	49,371	47,115
STATISTICAL RECORD:							
Return on Assets %	1.16	1.12	0.85	1.06	0.97	0.64	1.01
Return on Equity %	16.20	15.60	11.10	14.60	16.20	11.00	16.80
Book Value Per Share	20.46	18.99	17.34	16.28	15.07	13.51	12.72
Average Yield %	4.3	3.5	3.2	4.4	6.3	4.2	4.0
P/E Ratio	9.5-7.4	12.4-8.8	17.1-13.7	10.7-5.5	6.5-4.3	12.7-9.8	7.6-5.8
Price Range	31¼-24⅛	35¼-25⅛	32¾-26¼	26⅞-13⅞	16⅜-10¾	19⅝-15⅛	17⅛-13

Statistics are as originally reported.

OFFICERS:
E.A. Miller, Chmn. & C.E.O.
J.D. Lewis, Vice-Chmn.
M.T. Monahan, Pres.
P.H. Martzowka, Exec. V.P. & C.F.O.
J.D. Dart, Exec. V.P., Gen. Couns. & Corp. Sec.

INCORPORATED: DE, 1972

PRINCIPAL OFFICE: Comerica Tower at Detroit Center, Detroit, MI 48226

TELEPHONE NUMBER: (313) 222-3300

NO. OF EMPLOYEES: 11,239

ANNUAL MEETING: In May

SHAREHOLDERS: 14,420 (approx.)

INSTITUTIONAL HOLDINGS:
No. of Institutions: 352
Shares Held: 66,957,814

REGISTRAR(S): Norwest Bank Minnesota, N.A., South St. Paul, MN

TRANSFER AGENT(S): Norwest Bank Minnesota, N.A., South St. Paul, MN

NASDAQ SYMBOL CBSH
Rec. Pr. 31½

COMMERCE BANCSHARES, INC.

YIELD 2.3%
P/E RATIO 11.0

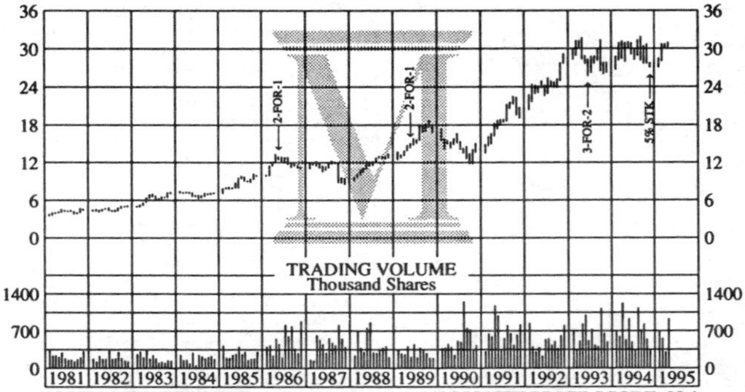

***7 YEAR PRICE SCORE 115.1** ***12 MONTH PRICE SCORE 98.1**

*NYSE COMPOSITE INDEX=100

INTERIM EARNINGS (Per Share):

Qtr.	Mar.	June	Sept.	Dec.
1991	0.49	0.49	0.51	0.51
1992	0.54	0.60	0.60	0.58
1993		2.60		
1994	0.66	0.72	0.75	0.72

INTERIM DIVIDENDS (Per Share):

Amt.	Decl.	Ex.	Rec.	Pay.
0.17Q	8/5/94	9/7/94	9/13/94	9/30/94
0.17Q	10/7	11/25	12/1	12/15
5%	12/2	12/6	12/12	12/29
0.18Q	2/3/95	3/2/95	3/8/95	3/31/95
0.18Q	4/19	6/6	6/9	6/30

Indicated div.: $0.72

CAPITALIZATION (12/31/94):

	($000)	(%)
Total Deposits	6,990,430	86.3
Total Debt	297,134	3.6
Common & Surplus	728,198	9.0
Loan Valuation Reserve	87,179	1.1
Total	8,102,941	100.0

DIVIDEND ACHIEVER STATUS:
Rank: 238 1984-94 Growth Rate: 7.2%
Total Years of Dividend Growth: 26

RECENT DEVELOPMENTS: For the year ended 12/31/94, net income was $96.1 million versus $86.9 million in 1993, an increase of 10.6%. Net interest income rose 10.6% to $314.6 million from $284.5 million. Results benefited from a 4.6% increase in average interest-earning assets to $7.12 billion. Net loans were up 10.2% for the year to $4.43 billion. Noninterest income of $121.4 million due to a $5.1 million decrease in gains on securities transactions and a $910,000 drop in gains on the sale of loans and foreclosed assets. The provision for loan losses was lowered by almost 49% to $5.8 million. Net charge-offs were $7.4 million, up from $6.4 million a year earlier. Other expense moved up to $282.1 million from $257.3 million. The increase was attributed to a 7.2% rise in salaries and employee benefits; a 44% jump in advertising expenses and a 17% increase in other operating expenses.

BUSINESS

COMMERCE BANCSHARES, INC. is a registered bank holding which presently owns or controls all of the outstanding capital stock of 14 banking institutions, all located in Missouri with the exception of Commerce Bank of Omaha N.A., which is located in Nebraska and is limited in its activities to the issuance of credit cards. The company also owns 6 nonbanking subsidiaries which are engaged in owning real estate and leasing the same to the Company's banking subsidiaries, underwriting credit life and credit accident and health insurance, selling property and casualty insurance, providing venture capital through a small business investment corporation, mortage banking, and providing discount brokerage services. COMMERCE BANCSHARES now ranks as the third largest multi-bank holding company in the state of Missouri.

LOAN DISTRIBUTION

(12/31/94)	($000)	(%)
Business	1,393,979	31.5
Real Estate-Construction	127,948	2.9
Real Estate-Business	586,769	13.2
Real Estate-Personal	813,134	18.3
Consumer	1,120,366	25.3
Credit card	390,466	8.8
Total	4,432,662	100.0

ANNUAL EARNINGS AND DIVIDENDS PER SHARE

	1994	1993	1992	1991	1990	1989	1988
Earnings Per Share	**2.85**	**2.60**	**2.32**	**2.00**	**[3] 1.91**	**1.98**	**2.34**
Dividends Per Share	**[1] 0.65**	**[2] 0.55**	**0.50**	**0.48**	**0.44**	**[4] 0.40**	**0.37**
Dividend Payout %	**22.8**	**21.2**	**21.6**	**24.0**	**23.0**	**20.2**	**15.8**

[1] 5% stk. div. 12/29/94 [2] 3-for-2 stk split, 5/28/93 [3] Before acctg. chg. [4] 2-for-1 stk split, 5/3/89.

ANNUAL FINANCIAL DATA

	1994	1993	1992	1991	1990	1989	1988
RECORD OF EARNINGS (IN MILLIONS):							
Total Interest Income	500.3	460.4	450.6	508.8	526.9	498.3	414.7
Total Interest Expense	185.7	175.9	202.9	286.2	314.6	291.8	234.1
Net Interest Income	314.6	284.5	247.7	222.7	212.3	206.5	180.6
Credit Loss Provision	5.8	11.4	19.1	19.0	15.1	15.7	9.2
Net Income	96.1	86.9	71.7	59.8	[1] 57.5	59.0	49.0
Aver. Shs. Outstg. (000)	33,712	31,665	29,396	28,265	28,596	28,361	29,922
[1] Before acctg. change cr$2,000,000.							
BALANCE SHEET (IN MILLIONS):							
Cash & Due From Banks	565.8	534.8	550.7	586.4	756.0	546.5	477.0
Loans & Lse Financing, Net	4,345.5	3,938.2	3,610.3	3,266.5	3,221.1	3,193.3	2,953.7
Total Domestic Deposits	6,990.4	6,839.5	6,458.7	5,850.4	5,764.4	4,987.9	4,683.4
Long-term Debt	6.5	6.9	7.3	38.1	39.3	10.4	15.5
Net Stockholders' Equity	728.2	712.6	603.7	507.3	457.8	398.0	379.2
Total Assets	8,035.6	8,047.4	7,541.6	6,765.4	6,709.1	5,829.2	5,444.0
Year End Shs Outstg (000)	33,569	31,784	29,719	28,108	27,903	27,254	29,090
STATISTICAL RECORD:							
Return on Assets %	1.20	1.08	0.95	0.88	0.86	1.01	0.90
Return on Equity %	13.20	12.20	11.90	11.80	12.60	14.80	12.90
Book Value Per Share	21.69	22.42	20.31	18.05	16.41	14.60	13.04
Average Yield %	2.2	2.9	2.0	2.7	3.0	2.6	3.3
P/E Ratio	11.2-9.3	11.6-9.4	12.0-8.4	10.6-6.4	8.6-5.8	9.0-6.0	8.2-5.5
Price Range	31⅞-26⅝	31¾-25¾	29¼-20⅜	22½-13½	17⅜-11¾	18¾-12½	13⅜-9

Statistics are as originally reported.

OFFICERS:
D.W. Kemper, Chmn., Pres. & C.E.O.
J.G. Himmel, Sr. V.P., Sec. & General Counsel
C.E. Templer, Treas. & Contr.

INCORPORATED: MO, Aug., 1966

PRINCIPAL OFFICE: 1000 Walnut, Kansas City, MO 64106

TELEPHONE NUMBER: (816) 234-2000

NO. OF EMPLOYEES: 4,167 (full-time); 595 (part-time)

ANNUAL MEETING: In April

SHAREHOLDERS: 5,786

INSTITUTIONAL HOLDINGS:
No. of Institutions: 103
Shares Held: 12,099,285

REGISTRAR(S): First Chicago Trust Co. of New York, New York, NY 10008

TRANSFER AGENT(S): First Chicago Trust Co. of New York, New York, NY 10008

COMPASS BANCSHARES INC.

YIELD 4.3%
P/E RATIO 9.6

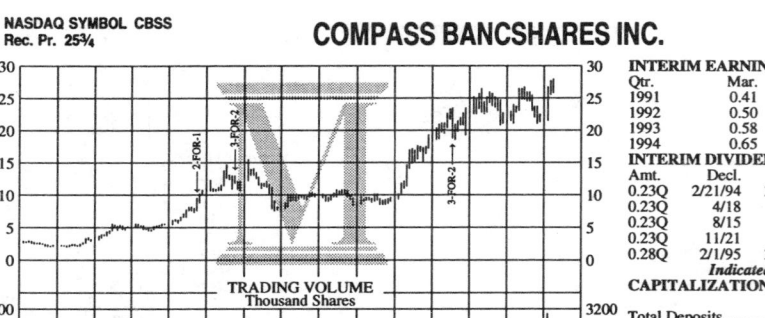

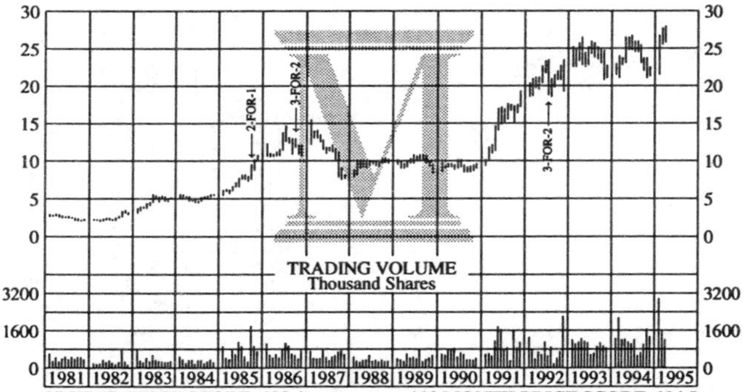

INTERIM EARNINGS (Per Share):

Qtr.	Mar.	June	Sept.	Dec.
1991	0.41	0.45	0.46	0.48
1992	0.50	0.52	0.52	0.54
1993	0.58	0.60	0.60	0.61
1994	0.65	0.66	0.67	0.71

INTERIM DIVIDENDS (Per Share):

Amt.	Decl.	Ex.	Rec.	Pay.
0.23Q	2/21/94	3/9/94	3/15/94	4/1/94
0.23Q	4/18	6/9	6/15	7/1
0.23Q	8/15	9/9	9/15	10/1
0.23Q	11/21	12/9	12/15	1/2/95
0.28Q	2/1/95	3/9/95	3/15/95	4/1

Indicated div.: $1.12*

CAPITALIZATION (12/31/94):

	($000)	(%)
Total Deposits	7,062,404	76.8
Total Debt	1,421,964	15.5
Common & Surplus	600,613	6.5
Loan Valuation Reserve	107,183	1.2
Total	9,192,164	100.0

DIVIDEND ACHIEVER STATUS:
Rank: 121 1984-94 Growth Rate: 11.9%
Total Years of Dividend Growth: 11

TRADING VOLUME
Thousand Shares

*7 YEAR PRICE SCORE 123.4   *12 MONTH PRICE SCORE 104.5
*NYSE COMPOSITE INDEX=100

RECENT DEVELOPMENTS: In March of 1995, the Company purchased 10 offices and $151 million in assets of San Antonio, TX-based Southwest Bankers, Inc. For the year ended 12/31/94, net income rose 11.1% to a record $99.7 million from $89.7 million for 1993. Return on assets was 1.24% and return on equity equaled 17.35%. Loans grew 11% while total deposits advanced 26% from the prior year. During the fourth quarter of 1994, the Company acquired 22 offices and $885 million in deposits of First Heights Bank, fsb in Houston, Texas. Net interest income moved up slightly to $331.4 million from $329.0 million. Noninterest income declined by 17.0% to $85.6 million from $103.2 million. Results were adversely affected by a $2.5 million loss on trading activities and an $8.2 million loss on securities purchases from a common trust fund. Noninterest expense was $262.0 million versus $257.7 million a year earlier.

BUSINESS

COMPASS BANCSHARES INC. is a $9.1 billion bank holding company with offices in Alabama, Texas and Florida. The Company conducts general banking and trust operations at 90 locations in 47 communities in Alabama. Compass Bank-Houston conducts a general commercial banking business from 38 locations in Houston, Texas and Compass Bank-Dallas conducts a general commercial banking business from 21 banking offices in Dallas and Collin Counties, Texas. River Oaks Trust Company offers a full range of trust services to customers in Texas through its offices in Houston and Dallas. Compass Bank, N.A. conducts a general commercial banking business with five branches in Pensacola and Gulf Breeze, Florida. Compass Bank-Florida conducts business from 18 locations in Jacksonville, Florida and 6 locations in Ft. Walton Beach, Florida. Central Bank of the South primarily provides cash management services to commercial customers of the subsidiary banks.

ANNUAL EARNINGS AND DIVIDENDS PER SHARE

	1994	1993	1992	1991	1990	1989	1988
Earnings Per Share	2.68	2.39	2.08	1.80	1.56	1.30	1.27
Dividends Per Share	0.88	0.736	① 0.646	0.573	0.529	0.502	0.46
Dividend Payout %	32.8	30.8	31.1	31.9	33.9	39.3	36.1

① 3-for-2 stk split, 7/6/92

ANNUAL FINANCIAL DATA

RECORD OF EARNINGS (IN MILLIONS):

	1994	1993	1992	1991	1990	1989	1988
Total Interest Income	577.7	522.6	516.7	496.5	454.6	423.1	351.2
Total Interest Expense	246.4	197.3	218.0	267.3	282.0	277.8	215.3
Net Interest Income	331.4	325.3	298.7	229.2	172.6	145.4	135.9
Credit Loss Provision	3.4	36.0	50.0	35.3	20.6	18.4	12.4
Net Income	99.7	89.3	74.4	59.4	48.9	41.9	41.0
Aver. Shs. Outstg. (000)	37,197	36,721	34,790	32,102	31,344	32,288	32,273

BALANCE SHEET (IN MILLIONS):

Cash & Due From Banks	483.3	279.6	321.0	289.1	224.7	248.4	272.5
Loans & Lse Financing, Net	5,654.3	5,038.5	4,361.2	3,548.5	3,068.9	2,804.0	2,557.0
Total Domestic Deposits	7,062.4	5,552.8	5,104.5	4,518.7	3,522.9	3,238.6	2,809.9
Long-term Debt	484.9	325.4	203.9	7.1	1.9	2.8	3.7
Net Stockholders' Equity	600.6	545.6	488.5	417.1	331.7	307.3	284.2
Total Assets	9,123.3	7,252.3	6,736.0	6,121.9	4,914.8	4,518.7	4,108.9
Year End Shs Outstg (000)	36,972	36,462	34,788	31,647	31,130	31,938	32,174

STATISTICAL RECORD:

Return on Assets %	1.09	1.23	1.10	0.97	0.99	0.93	1.00
Return on Equity %	16.60	16.40	15.20	14.20	14.70	13.60	14.40
Book Value Per Share	16.25	14.96	13.38	12.45	10.66	9.62	8.83
Average Yield %	3.7	3.1	3.1	4.0	5.7	5.2	5.0
P/E Ratio	10.0-7.8	11.1-8.7	11.3-8.9	10.8-5.2	6.5-5.4	8.4-6.4	8.2-6.2
Price Range	26¾-21	26½-20¾	23½-18½	19⅜-9⅜	10⅛-8½	10⅞-8⅜	10⅜-7⅞

Statistics are as originally reported.

OFFICERS:
D.P. Jones, Jr., Chmn. & C.E.O.
J.W. Powell, Gen. Couns. & Sec.
G.R. Hegel, C.F.O.

INCORPORATED: AL, 1970; reincorp., DE, 1970

PRINCIPAL OFFICE: 15 South 20th Street P O Box 10566, Birmingham, AL 35233

TELEPHONE NUMBER: (205) 933-3000

NO. OF EMPLOYEES: 4,000 (approx.)

ANNUAL MEETING: In April

SHAREHOLDERS: 6,221

INSTITUTIONAL HOLDINGS:
No. of Institutions: 42
Shares Held: 4,814,457

REGISTRAR(S):

TRANSFER AGENT(S): First National Bank of Boston, Shareholder Services Division, Boston, MA

NYS SYMBOL CAG
Rec. Pr. 33⅜

CONAGRA, INC.

YIELD 2.5%
P/E RATIO 16.9

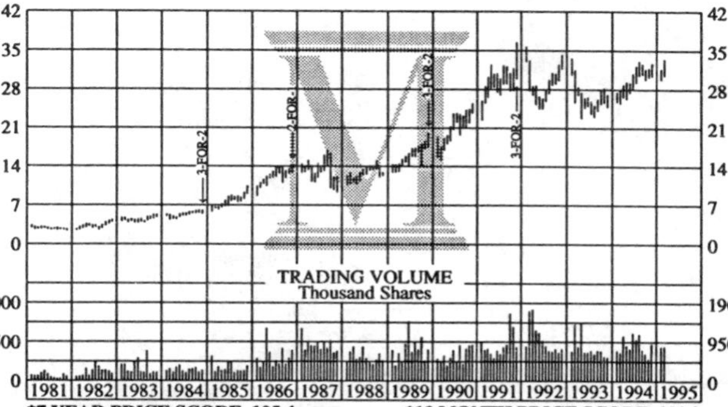

***7 YEAR PRICE SCORE 105.4** ***12 MONTH PRICE SCORE 101.9**

*NYSE COMPOSITE INDEX=100

INTERIM EARNINGS (Per Share):

Qtr.	Aug.	Nov.	Feb.	May
1992-93	0.28	0.53	0.38	0.39
1993-94	0.27	0.56	0.43	0.55
1994-95	0.31	0.63	0.49	...

INTERIM DIVIDENDS (Per Share):

Amt.	Decl.	Ex.	Rec.	Pay.
0.18Q	12/7/93	1/31/94	2/4/94	3/1/94
0.18Q	4/8/94	5/2	5/6	6/1
0.18Q	7/7	8/1	8/5	9/1
0.2075Q	9/22	10/31	11/4	12/1
0.2075Q	12/1	1/30/95	2/3/95	3/1/95

Indicated div.: $0.83*

CAPITALIZATION (5/29/94):

	($000)	(%)
Long-Term Debt	2,206,800	46.1
Redeemable Pfd Stock	355,600	7.4
Common & Surplus	2,226,900	46.5
Total	4,789,300	100.0

DIVIDEND ACHIEVER STATUS:
Rank: 45 1984-94 Growth Rate: 11.9%
Total Years of Dividend Growth: 17

RECENT DEVELOPMENTS: For the 13 weeks ended 11/27/94, net income was $149.9 million compared with $134.0 million a year ago. Net sales declined 1.0% to $6.29 billion. The Grocery Products segment posted unit volume growth and an operating profit gain in the quarter, aided by the acquisition of Marie Callender's frozen foods. The Meat Products segment experienced improved margins in U.S. fresh beef and pork products; however, beef earnings fell in Australia due to poor industry conditions.

PROSPECTS: Conagra plans to divest a number of non-core businesses, including several specialty retailing businesses and a pet accessories business, in an effort to focus more on its core food and agri-businesses. In the meantime, CAG should continue to experience cost savings as a result of a streamlined distribution system. Also, the acquisition of Marie Callender's will provide CAG with a premium, frozen food product line to add to its existing brand lineup.

BUSINESS

CONAGRA, INC. is a diversified, international food company that operates in three industry segments: Prepared Foods is comprised of branded shelf-stable & frozen foods; branded processed meats, chicken and turkey products; seafood products; and pet & home sewing accessories. Major brands include: Healthy Choice, Armour, and Wesson. Trading and Processing consists of commodities; animal feeds; food ingredients; seasonings; and processed products for domestic and international food industry customers. Agri-Products includes crop protection chemicals; fertilizers; and health care products for livestock.

BUSINESS LINE ANALYSIS

(5/29/94)	Rev(%)	Inc(%)
Agri-Products	12.6	8.6
Trading & Processing	10.8	10.5
Prepared Foods	77.6	80.9
Total	100.0	100.0

ANNUAL EARNINGS AND DIVIDENDS PER SHARE

	5/29/94	5/30/93	5/31/92	5/26/91	5/28/90	5/28/89	5/29/88
Earnings Per Share	**1.81**	**[1] 1.58**	**1.50**	**1.42**	**1.25**	**1.09**	**0.86**
Dividends Per Share	**0.747**	**0.645**	**0.48**	**0.415**	**[2] 0.357**	**0.309**	**0.268**
Dividend Payout %	**41.2**	**40.8**	**32.0**	**29.2**	**28.6**	**28.4**	**31.1**

[1] Before acctg. chg. [2] 3-for-2 stock split paid 12/1/89

ANNUAL FINANCIAL DATA

	5/29/94	5/30/93	5/31/92	5/26/91	5/28/90	5/28/89	5/29/88
RECORD OF EARNINGS (IN MILLIONS):							
Total Revenues	23,512.2	21,519.1	21,219.0	19,504.7	15,501.2	11,340.4	9,475.0
Costs and Expenses	22,174.8	20,306.0	20,012.0	18,464.3	14,862.1	10,794.3	9,088.4
Depreciation & Amort	368.4	348.7	319.3	250.8	129.7	101.7	89.5
Operating Profit	969.0	864.4	887.7	789.6	503.3	444.5	297.0
Income Bef Income Taxes	720.0	631.4	587.7	515.2	356.9	312.2	240.1
Income Taxes	282.9	239.9	215.3	204.0	125.2	114.3	85.4
Net Income	437.1	[1] 391.5	372.4	311.2	231.7	197.9	154.7
Aver. Shs. Outstg. (000)	228,500	233,000	231,900	205,350	184,785	180,831	178,173
[1] Before acctg. change dr$121,200,000.							
BALANCE SHEET (IN MILLIONS):							
Cash and Cash Equivalents	452.4	447.0	535.9	966.5	333.5	607.0	167.8
Receivables, Net	1,589.6	1,421.4	1,290.4	1,228.9	1,305.8	1,099.9	755.9
Inventories	2,884.4	2,439.2	2,373.9	2,019.8	1,648.8	1,383.1	1,096.1
Gross Property	4,150.4	3,719.0	3,364.3	2,740.1	1,703.5	1,397.7	1,166.6
Accumulated Depreciation	1,564.1	1,330.8	1,087.5	798.6	668.9	572.2	470.5
Long-Term Debt	2,206.8	2,159.2	2,124.4	2,093.0	635.4	560.1	489.9
Net Stockholders' Equity	2,582.5	2,410.4	2,588.3	2,173.5	1,098.0	958.2	824.0
Total Assets	10,721.8	9,988.7	9,758.7	9,420.3	4,804.2	4,278.2	3,042.9
Total Current Assets	5,143.3	4,486.7	4,371.2	4,342.9	3,347.8	3,160.4	2,076.2
Total Current Liabilities	4,752.8	4,272.6	4,081.3	4,087.4	2,967.5	2,651.5	1,636.1
Net Working Capital	390.5	214.1	289.9	255.5	380.3	508.9	440.1
Year End Shs Outstg (000)	248,195	251,710	231,963	209,511	184,094	180,917	175,545
STATISTICAL RECORD:							
Operating Profit Margin %	4.1	4.0	4.2	4.0	3.3	3.9	3.1
Book Value Per Share	9.86	9.02	9.62	8.67	5.95	5.25	4.64
Return on Equity %	19.6	19.1	16.7	17.1	21.1	20.8	19.0
Return on Assets %	4.1	3.9	3.8	3.3	4.8	4.6	5.1
Average Yield %	2.7	2.1	1.6	2.0	2.2	2.4	2.1
P/E Ratio	18.6-12.6	22.6-15.5	24.3-14.9	18.0-10.7	16.1-10.3	13.9-9.6	19.6-10.8
Price Range	33⅝-22¾	35¾-24½	36½-22⅜	25½-15⅛	20⅛-12⅞	15⅛-10½	16⅞-9¼

Statistics are as originally reported.

OFFICERS:
P.B. Fletcher, Chmn. & C.E.O.
J.D. Watkins, Pres. & C.O.O.
S.L. Key, Exec. V.P. & C.F.O.
L.B. Thomas, S.V.P. & Sec.

INCORPORATED: DE, Jan., 1976

PRINCIPAL OFFICE: One ConAgra Dr., Omaha, NE 68102-5001

TELEPHONE NUMBER: (402) 595-4000

NO. OF EMPLOYEES: 87,309 (approx.)

ANNUAL MEETING: In September

SHAREHOLDERS: 19,813 (approx.)

INSTITUTIONAL HOLDINGS:
No. of Institutions: 357
Shares Held: 85,136,668

REGISTRAR(S): Manufacturers Hanover Trust Co., New York, NY

TRANSFER AGENT(S): Manufacturers Hanover Trust Co., New York, NY

CONNECTICUT WATER SERVICE, INC.

YIELD 6.9%
P/E RATIO 11.8

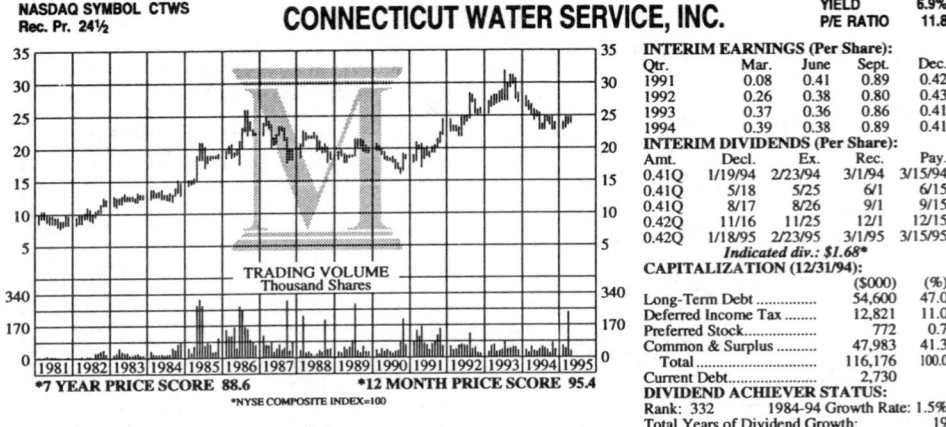

TRADING VOLUME
Thousand Shares

1981 1982 1983 1984 1985 1986 1987 1988 1989 1990 1991 1992 1993 1994 1995

*7 YEAR PRICE SCORE 88.6   ***12 MONTH PRICE SCORE 95.4**
*NYSE COMPOSITE INDEX=100

INTERIM EARNINGS (Per Share):

Qtr.	Mar.	June	Sept.	Dec.
1991	0.08	0.41	0.89	0.42
1992	0.26	0.38	0.80	0.43
1993	0.37	0.36	0.86	0.41
1994	0.39	0.38	0.89	0.41

INTERIM DIVIDENDS (Per Share):

Amt.	Decl.	Ex.	Rec.	Pay.
0.41Q	1/19/94	2/23/94	3/1/94	3/15/94
0.41Q	5/18	5/25	6/1	6/15
0.41Q	8/17	8/26	9/1	9/15
0.42Q	11/16	11/25	12/1	12/15
0.42Q	1/18/95	2/23/95	3/1/95	3/15/95

Indicated div.: $1.68*

CAPITALIZATION (12/31/94):

	($000)	(%)
Long-Term Debt	54,600	47.0
Deferred Income Tax	12,821	11.0
Preferred Stock	772	0.7
Common & Surplus	47,983	41.3
Total	116,176	100.0
Current Debt	2,730	

DIVIDEND ACHIEVER STATUS:
Rank: 332   1984-94 Growth Rate: 1.5%
Total Years of Dividend Growth: 19

RECENT DEVELOPMENTS: For the year ended 12/31/94, net income was $5.9 million compared with $5.6 million in previous year. Operating revenues were $38.1 million and remained flat from the year before. CTWS reduced its interest and debt expense by $398,000 for its corporate bonds and its preferred stock dividend by $217,000 as a result of refinancing completed in 1993. Additionally, other income and

deductions rose by $26,000 during the quarter. However, these gains were partially offset by a $328,000 decline in operating income. Residential and commercial consumption both dropped by approximately 1% from the prior year while industrial consumption climbed by 5% year-over-year. Meanwhile, revenues from fire protection increased by $75,000 from the prior year.

BUSINESS

CONNECTICUT WATER SERVICE, INC. is the parent company of The Connecticut Water Company, which supplies water to approximately 60,000 customers for residential, commercial, industrial and municipal purposes throughout 31 towns in the state of Connecticut. The Connecticut Water Company operates through three, non-contiguous operating regions. The Company represents the second largest investor-owned water system in the state of Connecticut in terms of operating revenues and utility plant investment. The area served has an estimated population of 209,000. The Connecticut Water Company's water system consists of some 950 miles of water main with reservoir storage capacity of approximately 6.8 billion gallons. The safe dependable yield from the Connecticut Water Company's 78 active wells and 20 reservoirs is approximately 39 million gallons per day. Water supply sources vary among the regions, but from the systems as a whole, about 55% of the total dependable yield comes from reservoirs and 45% from wells.

ANNUAL EARNINGS AND DIVIDENDS PER SHARE

	1994	1993	1992	1991	1990	1989	1988
Earnings Per Share	2.08	2.00	1.87	1.80	1.30	1.71	1.86
Dividends Per Share	1.65	1.64	1.61	1.60	1.57	1.56	1.53
Dividend Payout %	79.3	82.0	86.1	88.9	N.M.	91.2	82.3

ANNUAL FINANCIAL DATA

RECORD OF EARNINGS (IN THOUSANDS):

	1994	1993	1992	1991	1990	1989	1988
Total Revenues	38,129	38,131	37,190	37,372	32,301	29,804	28,378
Depreciation	3,236	3,037	2,912	2,877	2,748	2,491	2,201
Maintenance	1,970	1,793	1,474	1,834	1,578	1,261	1,211
Income Taxes	3,769	3,710	3,163	2,834	1,851	1,693	2,272
Utility Operating Income	9,655	9,983	10,033	10,402	8,712	8,773	8,086
Interest Expense	3,940	4,338	4,872	5,321	5,650	5,206	4,401
Net Income	5,880	5,567	5,149	4,877	2,983	3,721	3,966
Aver. Shs. Outstg.	2,812	2,769	2,729	2,686	2,272	2,148	2,117

BALANCE SHEET (IN THOUSANDS):

	1994	1993	1992	1991	1990	1989	1988
Gross Plant	183,242	177,698	172,241	168,451	163,567	155,294	143,113
Accumulated Depreciation	42,458	40,130	36,544	33,319	30,464	27,854	25,484
Prop, Plant & Equip, Net	140,784	137,568	135,697	135,132	133,103	127,440	117,629
Long-term Debt	54,600	51,600	51,600	52,412	52,953	54,067	49,243
Net Stockholders' Equity	48,755	48,908	46,910	45,359	44,894	38,075	34,371
Total Assets	171,241	163,080	149,696	148,625	145,379	140,555	129,790
Year End Shares Outstg	2,871	2,790	2,751	2,711	2,668	2,168	2,132

STATISTICAL RECORD:

	1994	1993	1992	1991	1990	1989	1988
Book Value Per Share	16.71	16.19	15.68	15.30	15.05	15.27	15.05
Op. Inc/Net Pl %	6.9	7.3	7.4	7.7	6.5	6.9	6.9
Dep/Gr. Pl %	1.7	1.7	1.7	1.7	1.7	1.6	1.5
Accum. Dep/Gr. Pl %	23.2	22.6	21.2	19.8	18.6	17.9	17.8
Return on Equity %	12.1	12.1	11.7	11.5	7.3	11.0	12.1
Average Yield %	6.5	5.7	6.4	7.7	8.5	7.9	7.6
P/E Ratio	13.5-10.9	15.9-12.6	15.2-11.6	13.6-9.4	16.0-12.3	12.6-10.4	12.2-9.5
Price Range	28-22¾	31⅞-25¼	28½-21¾	24½-17	20¾-16	21½-17¾	22¾-17¾

Statistics are as originally reported.

OFFICERS:
M.T. Chiaraluce, Pres. & C.E.O.
B.L. Lenz, V.P.-Fin. & Acctg. & Treas.
P.J. Bancroft, Asst. Treas. & Contr.
M.F. Halloran, Asst. Sec.

INCORPORATED: CT, Feb., 1956

PRINCIPAL OFFICE: 93 West Main Street, Clinton, CT 06413

TELEPHONE NUMBER: (203) 669-8636
FAX: (203) 669-9326
NO. OF EMPLOYEES: 164
ANNUAL MEETING: In April
SHAREHOLDERS: 5,252
INSTITUTIONAL HOLDINGS:
No. of Institutions: 24
Shares Held: 453,210

REGISTRAR(S):

TRANSFER AGENT(S): State Street Bank & Trust Co., Boston, MA 02266

NYS SYMBOL ED
Rec. Pr. 28½

CONSOLIDATED EDISON CO. OF NEW YORK, INC.

YIELD 7.2%
P/E RATIO 9.6

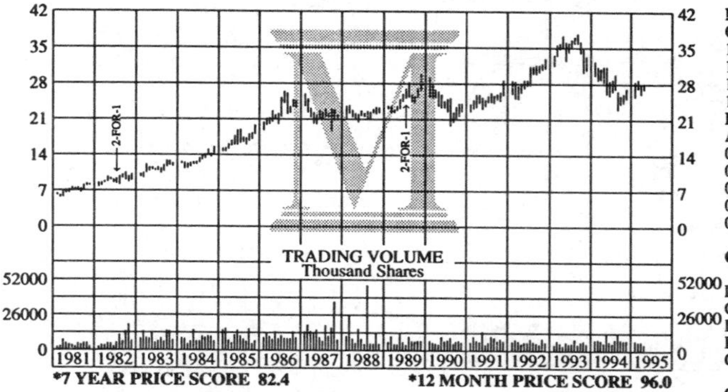

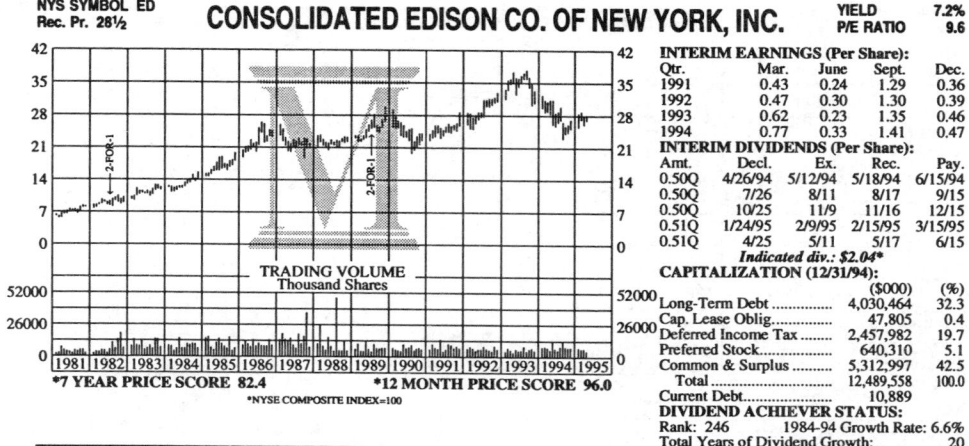

***7 YEAR PRICE SCORE 82.4** ***12 MONTH PRICE SCORE 96.0**

*NYSE COMPOSITE INDEX=100

INTERIM EARNINGS (Per Share):

Qtr.	Mar.	June	Sept.	Dec.
1991	0.43	0.24	1.29	0.36
1992	0.47	0.30	1.30	0.39
1993	0.62	0.23	1.35	0.46
1994	0.77	0.33	1.41	0.47

INTERIM DIVIDENDS (Per Share):

Amt.	Decl.	Ex.	Rec.	Pay.
0.50Q	4/26/94	5/12/94	5/18/94	6/15/94
0.50Q	7/26	8/11	8/17	9/15
0.50Q	10/25	11/9	11/16	12/15
0.51Q	1/24/95	2/9/95	2/15/95	3/15/95
0.51Q	4/25	5/11	5/17	6/15

Indicated div.: $2.04*

CAPITALIZATION (12/31/94):

	($000)	(%)
Long-Term Debt	4,030,464	32.3
Cap. Lease Oblig.	47,805	0.4
Deferred Income Tax	2,457,982	19.7
Preferred Stock	640,310	5.1
Common & Surplus	5,312,997	42.5
Total	12,489,558	100.0
Current Debt	10,889	

DIVIDEND ACHIEVER STATUS:
Rank: 246 1984-94 Growth Rate: 6.6%
Total Years of Dividend Growth: 20

RECENT DEVELOPMENTS: For the year ended 12/31/94, net income increased 11.5% to $734.3 million from $658.5 million in 1993. Revenues rose 1.7% to $6.37 billion. The increase in earnings for 1994 was attributed primarily to performance incentives under an electric rate agreement and cost-containment efforts. Electric sales, excluding sales to other utilities, increased 2.0%, gas sales rose 3.9%, and steam sales were up 4.4%.

PROSPECTS: Uncertainty regarding a pending rate case clouds earnings prospects. The utility has filed for electric rate increases of nearly $400 million over three years. Meanwhile, the commission's staff has proposed a reduction of $251 million. The staff recommended the disallowance of purchased-power costs from Sithe Energies. Competitive pressures for ED are lessened due to the small percentage of electric revenues that come from industrial customers.

BUSINESS

CONSOLIDATED EDISON CO. OF NEW YORK, INC. supplies electricity, gas, and steam to New York City's five boroughs and sections of Westchester County. The Company is one of the largest operating utilities in the country. Manufacturing is important, but the area is predominantly service oriented. Stability of the service area is the outstanding feature.

BUSINESS LINE ANALYSIS

(12/31/94)	Rev(%)	Inc(%)
Electric	80.7	85.1
Gas	14.0	11.3
Steam	5.3	3.6
Total	100.0	100.0

ANNUAL EARNINGS AND DIVIDENDS PER SHARE

	1994	1993	1992	1991	1990	1989	1988
Earnings Per Share	2.98	2.66	2.46	2.32	2.34	2.49	2.47
Dividends Per Share	2.00	1.94	1.90	1.86	1.82	[1] 1.72	1.60
Dividend Payout %	67.1	72.9	77.2	80.2	77.8	69.1	64.9

[1] 2-for-1 stk split, 06/30/89

ANNUAL FINANCIAL DATA

	1994	1993	1992	1991	1990	1989	1988
RECORD OF EARNINGS (IN MILLIONS):							
Total Revenues	6,373.1	6,265.4	5,932.9	5,873.1	5,738.9	5,550.6	5,108.8
Depreciation & Amort	422.4	403.7	380.9	359.8	342.8	324.9	308.1
Maintenance	506.2	570.8	529.0	520.9	509.5	483.1	447.2
Operating Income	1,036.2	951.1	880.4	813.1	800.8	783.7	773.2
Interest Expense	305.2	298.1	291.6	289.7	255.3	235.6	212.5
Net Income	734.3	658.5	604.1	566.9	571.5	606.1	599.3
Aver. Shs. Outstg. (000)	234,754	233,981	231,129	228,283	228,189	228,065	227,937
BALANCE SHEET (IN MILLIONS):							
Gross Plant	14,389.9	13,750.9	13,190.6	12,520.7	11,922.0	11,365.7	10,867.7
Accumulated Depreciation	3,828.6	3,594.8	3,461.0	3,257.7	3,106.8	2,954.4	2,797.0
Prop, Plant & Equip, Net	10,561.2	10,156.2	9,729.7	9,263.0	8,815.2	8,411.2	8,070.7
Long-term Debt	4,078.3	3,694.2	3,546.5	3,420.2	3,370.8	3,150.0	2,889.4
Net Stockholders' Equity	5,953.3	5,709.3	5,528.1	5,241.2	5,138.0	5,021.1	4,847.4
Total Assets	13,728.4	13,483.5	11,596.1	11,107.9	10,685.6	10,349.5	9,551.7
Year End Shs Outstg (000)	234,905	234,373	233,932	228,326	228,232	228,151	227,993
STATISTICAL RECORD:							
Book Value Per Share	22.62	21.63	20.89	20.18	19.73	19.21	18.44
Op. Inc/Net Pl %	9.8	9.4	9.0	8.8	9.1	9.3	9.6
Dep/Gr. Pl %	2.9	2.9	2.9	2.9	2.9	2.9	2.8
Accum. Dep/Gr. Pl %	26.6	26.1	26.2	26.0	26.1	26.0	25.7
Return on Equity %	12.5	11.7	11.1	10.9	11.2	12.2	12.5
Average Yield %	7.2	5.7	6.6	7.3	7.4	6.6	7.3
P/E Ratio	10.9-7.7	14.2-11.4	13.4-10.2	12.4-9.7	12.5-8.4	12.0-8.9	9.7-8.3
Price Range	32⅜-23	37¾-30¼	32⅞-25	28¾-22½	29¼-19¾	29⅞-22¼	23¾-20⅜

Statistics are as originally reported.

OFFICERS:
E.R. McGrath, Chmn., Pres. & C.E.O.
R.J. McCann, Exec. V.P. & C.F.O.
J.F. Cioffi, Treas.
A.M. Bankston, Sec.

INCORPORATED: NY, Nov., 1884

PRINCIPAL OFFICE: Four Irving Place, New York, NY 10003

TELEPHONE NUMBER: (212) 460-4600
NO. OF EMPLOYEES: 17,097
ANNUAL MEETING: In May
SHAREHOLDERS: 159,632 (common); preferred, 13,708
INSTITUTIONAL HOLDINGS:
No. of Institutions: 412
Shares Held: 67,912,394

REGISTRAR(S): Chemical Bank, New York, NY

TRANSFER AGENT(S): At Company's Office

NYS SYMBOL CNG
Rec. Pr. 38¾

CONSOLIDATED NATURAL GAS CO.

YIELD 5.0%
P/E RATIO 19.7

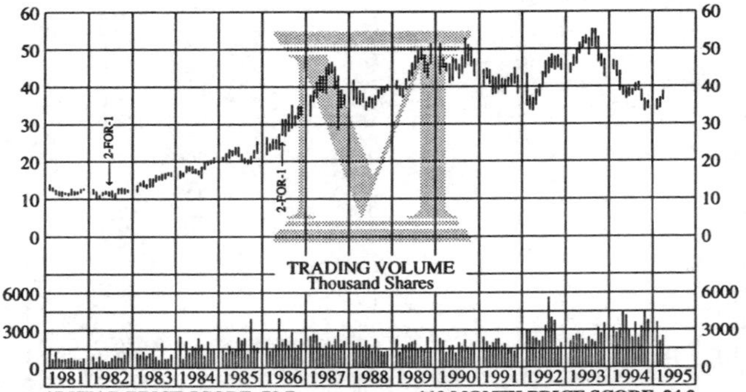

*7 YEAR PRICE SCORE 72.7 *12 MONTH PRICE SCORE 94.0

*NYSE COMPOSITE INDEX=100

INTERIM EARNINGS (Per Share):

Qtr.	Mar.	June	Sept.	Dec.
1991	1.17	d0.06	d0.26	1.10
1992	1.27	0.01	d0.15	1.05
1993	1.36	0.07	d0.32	0.93
1994	1.41	0.03	d0.26	0.79

INTERIM DIVIDENDS (Per Share):

Amt.	Decl.	Ex.	Rec.	Pay.
0.485Q	3/8/94	4/11/94	4/15/94	5/16/94
0.485Q	6/14	7/11	7/15	8/15
0.485Q	9/13	10/7	10/14	11/15
0.485Q	12/13	1/9/95	1/13/95	2/15/95
0.485Q	3/14/95	4/7	4/14	5/15

*Indicated div.: $1.94**

CAPITALIZATION (12/31/94):

	($000)	(%)
Long-Term Debt	1,151,973	27.9
Deferred Income Tax	791,862	19.2
Common & Surplus	2,184,334	52.9
Total	4,128,169	100.0
Current Debt	444,000	

DIVIDEND ACHIEVER STATUS:
Rank: 264 1984-94 Growth Rate: 6.0%
Total Years of Dividend Growth: 30

RECENT DEVELOPMENTS: For the year ended 12/31/94, net income was $183.2 million compared with $188.5 million in 1993. Total operating revenues were $3.04 billion, down 5% from the year before. The Company cited the following factors for the poor results: warmer weather in CNG's gas distribution serice areas, lower wellhead prices, lower gas and oil production, and higher operating and capital costs. Gas Distribution reported operating income of $159.0 million compared with $166.9 million a year earlier.

PROSPECTS: Warm weather in the Company's distribution service areas combined with sharply lower natural gas prices have weakened results significantly. Due to this, along with higher operating and capital costs, CNG implemented new rates for many of its customers in late 1994. These rate increases should aid earnings in 1995. Also, CNG plans to concentrate on its nonregulated businesses for future growth while keeping intact its strong position in regulated segments.

BUSINESS

CONSOLIDATED NATURAL GAS operates a pipeline subsidiary and distribution subsidiaries serving Ohio, Pennsylvania, Virginia, West Virginia, New York and the northeast U.S. Exploration and production operations are conducted through CNG Producing Co., in the Gulf of Mexico and southern and western U.S., and Canada and CNG Development Co., in the Appalachian area. Other operations include gas by-products and oil production.

REVENUES

(12/31/94)	($000)	(%)
Regulated Gas Sales	1,679,235	69.9
Nonregulated Gas Sales	723,626	30.1
Total Gas Sales	2,402,861	100.0

ANNUAL EARNINGS AND DIVIDENDS PER SHARE

	1994	1993	1992	1991	1990	1989	1988
Earnings Per Share	**1.97**	**2.03**	**2.19**	**1.94**	**1.91**	**2.20**	**2.34**
Dividends Per Share	**1.94**	**1.92**	**1.90**	**1.88**	**1.84**	**1.76**	**1.64**
Dividend Payout %	**98.4**	**94.6**	**86.8**	**96.9**	**96.3**	**80.0**	**70.1**

ANNUAL FINANCIAL DATA

	1994	1993	1992	1991	1990	1989	1988
RECORD OF EARNINGS (IN MILLIONS):							
Total Revenues	5,438.9	3,725.9	2,802.9	2,844.0	2,995.1	2,801.9	2,467.8
Depreciation & Amort	279.3	294.6	287.8	284.7	281.8	275.2	242.6
Maintenance	89.2	87.2	79.1	72.9	62.8	60.8	57.5
Interest Expense	87.5	79.5	83.4	87.8	92.9	77.9	62.8
Net Income	183.2	[1] 188.5	195.0	168.6	163.8	181.8	192.9
Aver. Shs. Outstg. (000)	93,000	92,808	89,128	86,837	85,683	82,492	82,498
[1] Before acctg. change cr$17,422,000.							
BALANCE SHEET (IN MILLIONS):							
Gross Plant	7,677.0	7,346.0	7,087.1	6,749.2	6,433.5	5,559.4	5,080.9
Accumulated Depreciation	3,650.3	3,429.8	3,212.2	3,010.8	2,820.8	2,205.9	2,067.5
Prop, Plant & Equip, Net	4,026.6	3,916.3	3,874.9	3,738.4	3,612.8	3,353.4	3,013.4
Long-term Debt	1,152.0	1,158.6	1,112.0	1,159.1	1,128.5	890.6	661.6
Net Stockholders' Equity	2,184.3	2,176.4	2,132.8	1,889.8	1,844.6	1,671.9	1,634.8
Total Assets	5,518.7	5,409.6	5,241.8	5,011.1	5,006.0	4,601.2	4,109.4
Year End Shs Outstg (000)	93,028	92,934	92,557	87,322	86,327	82,526	82,421
STATISTICAL RECORD:							
Book Value Per Share	23.48	23.42	23.04	21.64	21.37	20.26	19.83
Dep/Gr. Pl %	3.6	4.0	4.1	4.2	4.4	4.9	4.8
Accum. Dep/Gr. Pl %	47.5	46.7	45.3	44.6	43.8	39.7	40.7
Return on Equity %	8.4	8.7	9.1	8.9	8.9	10.9	11.8
Average Yield %	4.8	3.9	4.6	4.5	3.9	4.0	4.3
P/E Ratio	23.9-16.9	27.3-21.0	22.2-15.3	23.2-19.5	27.7-21.5	23.4-16.9	17.8-14.4
Price Range	47-33⅜	55⅝-42⅝	48⅝-33½	45-37⅞	52⅞-41	51½-37⅛	41¾-33¾

Statistics are as originally reported.

OFFICERS:
G.A. Davidson, Jr., Chmn. & C.E.O.
L.D. Johnson, Vice-Chmn. & C.F.O.
D.M. Westfall, Sr. V.P.-Financial
D.J. Dzuricky, V.P. & Treas.
L.J. McKeown, Sec.

INCORPORATED: DE, Jul., 1942

PRINCIPAL OFFICE:

TELEPHONE NUMBER:

NO. OF EMPLOYEES: 7,566

ANNUAL MEETING: In May

SHAREHOLDERS: 40,828

INSTITUTIONAL HOLDINGS:
No. of Institutions: 441
Shares Held: 41,760,472

REGISTRAR(S): Society National Bank, Cleveland, OH

TRANSFER AGENT(S): Society National Bank, Cleveland, OH

CONSUMERS WATER CO.

YIELD 7.8%
P/E RATIO 12.4

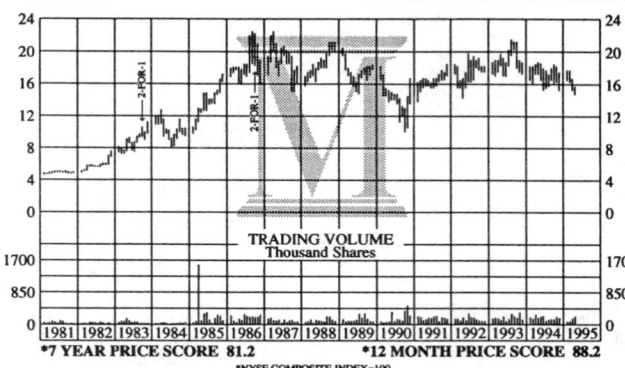

INTERIM EARNINGS (Per Share):

Qtr.	Mar.	June	Sept.	Dec.
1992	0.16	0.32	0.39	0.27
1993	0.25	0.20	0.50	0.60
1994	0.14	0.31	0.40	0.37

INTERIM DIVIDENDS (Per Share):

Amt.	Decl.	Ex.	Rec.	Pay.
0.29Q	7/15/94	8/4/94	8/10/94	8/25/94
0.295Q	9/12	11/4	11/10	11/25
0.295Q	12/7	2/6/95	2/10/95	2/24/95
0.295Q	4/5/95	5/4	5/10	5/25

*Indicated div.: $1.18**

CAPITALIZATION (12/31/94):

	($000)	(%)
Long-Term Debt	130,038	50.5
Deferred Income Tax	25,619	9.9
Preferred Stock	1,069	0.4
Common & Surplus	100,928	39.2
Total	257,654	100.0
Current Debt	29,816	

DIVIDEND ACHIEVER STATUS:
Rank: 258   1984-94 Growth Rate: 6.2%
Total Years of Dividend Growth: 37

RECENT DEVELOPMENTS: For the year ended 12/31/94, net income from continuing operations was $10.0 million compared with $12.0 million the year before. CONW's revenues climbed by 5% to $93.3 million from $89.1 million in the prior year. Improved revenues were primarily the result of higher sales at C/P Utility Services Company and rate increases. Throughout 1994, the Company's utilities processed ten rate cases, which should increase water revenues by more than $5.6 million per year. During the year, approved rate increases accounted for an additional $3.9 million in revenues, which helped to offset a loss of $2.3 million in revenues from the sales of the Washington Court House Division of the Company's Ohio Water Service Co. Additionally, sales at C/P Utility Services improved by 18%, or $2.0 million year-over-year.

BUSINESS

CONSUMERS WATER CO. is a holding company that owns and operates water utilities and a utility services company. Consumers currently owns eleven utilities in six states that serve the water and wastewater needs of over 218,000 customers. Consumers' utility services company provides operational and technical services primarily to water utilities and industrial clients. In Illinois, the Consumers Illinois Water Company operates six divisions serving 61,141 customers; in Ohio, The Ohio Water Service Company, with seven divisions serves 76,649 customers; in Pennsylvania, three different water companies serve 36,968 customers; in New Jersey, The Garden State Water Company with three divisions and the California Water Company serve 28,415 customers; in Maine, The Maine Water Company, with four divisions and the Camden and Rockland Water Company serve 9,780 customers. CONW also has locations in Connecticut, Florida and New Hampshire.

ANNUAL EARNINGS AND DIVIDENDS PER SHARE

	1994	1993	1992	1991	1990	1989	1988
Earnings Per Share	1.22	1.63	1.14	①1.46	①1.21	1.15	1.59
Dividends Per Share	1.165	1.145	1.125	1.105	1.085	1.05	0.98
Dividend Payout %	95.5	70.2	98.7	75.7	89.7	91.3	61.6

① Before disc. oper.

ANNUAL FINANCIAL DATA

RECORD OF EARNINGS (IN THOUSANDS):

Total Revenues	93,337	89,084	89,615	85,205	67,349	87,098	87,891
Depreciation & Amort	8,993	7,994	7,694	6,358	5,994	6,017	5,763
Prov for Fed Inc Taxes	4,623	4,128	4,182	3,091	3,204	3,018	3,528
Operating Income	24,436	22,845	23,146	20,569	20,389	20,922	20,631
Interest Expense	11,076	11,127	11,128	11,307	12,182	12,058	9,633
Net Income	10,000	①12,003	8,022	②9,418	③7,346	6,883	9,421
Aver. Shs. Outstg.	8,161	7,320	7,007	6,429	6,025	5,959	5,898

① Before disc. op. dr$6,084,000. ② Before disc. op. cr$1,800,000. ③ Before disc. op. dr$9,292,000.

BALANCE SHEET (IN THOUSANDS):

Gross Plant	419,521	382,005	362,667	336,885	315,750	312,657	288,448
Accumulated Depreciation	70,267	64,460	61,354	56,631	53,598	55,420	50,969
Prop, Plant & Equip, Net	349,254	317,545	301,313	280,254	262,152	257,237	237,479
Long-term Debt	130,038	124,050	119,832	101,410	105,420	99,958	89,146
Net Stockholders' Equity	101,997	98,007	85,321	81,173	65,099	72,588	70,967
Total Assets	401,380	371,657	343,569	315,154	302,550	302,045	282,561
Year End Shares Outstg	8,260	8,041	7,130	6,892	6,060	5,982	5,914

STATISTICAL RECORD:

Book Value Per Share	12.22	12.06	11.82	11.62	10.56	11.95	11.81
Op. Inc/Net Pl %	7.0	7.2	7.7	7.3	7.8	8.1	8.7
Accum. Dep/Gr. Pl %	16.7	16.9	16.9	16.8	17.0	17.7	17.7
Return on Equity %	9.8	12.2	9.4	11.6	11.3	9.5	13.3
Average Yield %	6.9	5.9	6.6	6.9	7.7	6.0	5.3
P/E Ratio	15.4-12.5	13.2-10.4	17.3-12.5	12.7-9.4	15.1-8.3	17.8-12.8	13.4-9.9
Price Range	18¾-15¼	21½-17	19¾-14¼	18½-13¾	18¼-10	20½-14¾	21¼-15¾

Statistics are as originally reported.

REVENUES

(12/31/94)	($000)	(%)
Water Utility	80,376	86.1
Other Operations	12,961	13.9
Total	93,337	100.0

OFFICERS:
D.R. Hastings, II, Chmn.
P.L. Haynes, Pres. & C.E.O.
J.F. Isacke, Sr. V.P. & C.F.O.
B.R. Mullany, V.P. & Sec.

INCORPORATED: ME, Feb., 1926

PRINCIPAL OFFICE: Three Canal Plaza, Portland, ME 04101

TELEPHONE NUMBER: (207) 773-6438

NO. OF EMPLOYEES: 640

ANNUAL MEETING: In May

SHAREHOLDERS: 6,000 (approx.)

INSTITUTIONAL HOLDINGS:
No. of Institutions: 41
Shares Held: 1,318,187

REGISTRAR(S): Continental Stock Transfer & Trust Co., New York, NY

TRANSFER AGENT(S): Continental Stock Transfer & Trust Co., New York, NY

NYS SYMBOL CTB
Rec. Pr. 28¾

COOPER TIRE & RUBBER CO.

YIELD 0.8%
P/E RATIO 18.7

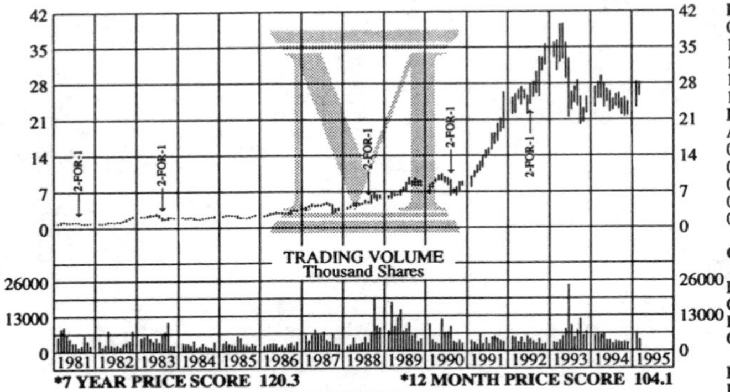

*7 YEAR PRICE SCORE 120.3 *12 MONTH PRICE SCORE 104.1

*NYSE COMPOSITE INDEX=100

INTERIM EARNINGS (Per Share):

Qtr.	Mar.	June	Sept.	Dec.
1991	0.15	0.24	0.27	0.31
1992	0.25	0.32	0.38	0.41
1993	0.30	0.29	0.30	0.33
1994	0.32	0.33	0.42	0.47

INTERIM DIVIDENDS (Per Share):

Amt.	Decl.	Ex.	Rec.	Pay.
0.055Q	2/14/94	3/1/94	3/7/94	3/31/94
0.055Q	5/4	5/27	6/3	6/30
0.06Q	7/18	8/29	9/2	9/30
0.06Q	11/10	11/18	11/25	12/19
0.06Q	2/14/95	2/28/95	3/6/95	3/31/95

Indicated div.: $0.24

CAPITALIZATION (12/31/94):

	($000)	(%)
Long-Term Debt	28,477	3.9
Cap. Lease Oblig.	5,137	0.7
Deferred Income Tax	29,737	4.1
Common & Surplus	662,077	91.3
Total	725,428	100.0

DIVIDEND ACHIEVER STATUS:
Rank: 34 1984-94 Growth Rate: 17.1%
Total Years of Dividend Growth: 15

RECENT DEVELOPMENTS: For the quarter ended 12/31/94, net income jumped 40% to $39.1 million compared with $27.8 million for the comparable period in 1993. Revenues rose 23% to $362.5 million. Industry demand for tires and rubber products pushed earnings higher. For the year ended 12/31/94, net income was $128.5 million versus $102.2 million in 1993. Revenues advanced 18% to $1.41 billion from $1.19 billion for the corresponding period a year ago.

PROSPECTS: Cooper is well positioned to capitalize on the increasing age of automobiles in North America, through the growing consumer acceptance of its tires. Higher industrial demand for engineered rubber products should drive revenues and earnings growth higher. Meanwhile, in spite of the recent high level in shipments of replacement tires, earnings growth may slow down as the effects of the recent increase in raw materials costs are felt.

BUSINESS

COOPER TIRE & RUBBER CO. specializes in the manufacturing and marketing of rubber products for consumers and industrial users. Products include automobile and truck tires, inner tubes, vibration control products, hose and tubing, automotive body sealing products and specialty seating components. CTB markets its products nationally and internationally through well-established channels of distribution. Represented among its customers are automobile manufacturing companies, independent distributors and dealers, oil companies, large retail chains and industrial manufacturers.

QUARTERLY DATA

(12/31/94)($000)	Rev	Inc
1st Quarter	329,132	26,506
2nd Quarter	329,339	27,459
3rd Quarter	383,456	35,454
4th Quarter	361,316	39,100

ANNUAL EARNINGS AND DIVIDENDS PER SHARE

	1994	1993	1992	1991	1990	1989	1988
Earnings Per Share	**1.54**	**1.22**	**[1] 1.30**	**0.96**	**0.81**	**0.71**	**0.50**
Dividends Per Share	**0.23**	**0.20**	**[2] 0.17**	**0.13**	**[3] 0.105**	**0.086**	**0.07**
Dividend Payout %	**14.9**	**16.4**	**13.1**	**13.5**	**13.0**	**12.1**	**14.0**

[1] Before acctg. chg. [2] 2-for-1 stk split, 7/1/92 [3] 2-for-1 stk split, 8/20/90

ANNUAL FINANCIAL DATA

	1994	1993	1992	1991	1990	1989	1988
RECORD OF EARNINGS (IN MILLIONS):							
Total Revenues	1,405.5	1,194.2	1,176.0	1,001.6	896.8	869.6	750.9
Costs and Expenses	1,139.1	981.3	966.0	840.6	759.6	749.2	661.6
Depreciation & Amort	55.6	46.4	38.1	32.0	27.6	23.4	19.9
Operating Profit	279.5	228.9	230.6	180.9	156.8	142.3	109.3
Income Bef Income Taxes	208.1	164.3	169.8	124.5	104.9	92.6	64.9
Income Taxes	79.6	62.0	61.7	45.0	38.4	34.4	23.9
Net Income	128.5	102.2	[1] 108.2	79.4	66.5	58.2	41.1
Aver. Shs. Outstg. (000)	83,623	83,350	83,357	82,738	82,391	82,077	81,583
[1] Before acctg. change dr$64,960,000.							
BALANCE SHEET (IN MILLIONS):							
Cash and Cash Equivalents	103.3	25.8	55.1	24.4	10.1	49.6	38.7
Receivables, Net	221.2	182.2	181.2	152.7	127.0	126.4	120.4
Inventories	116.5	111.1	75.0	78.0	121.4	70.7	67.9
Gross Property	880.6	807.2	700.6	596.5	520.9	426.3	356.4
Accumulated Depreciation	331.0	279.3	240.2	207.9	186.1	163.8	143.4
Long-Term Debt	28.5	38.7	48.1	47.5	85.3	60.4	62.3
Capital Lease Obligations	5.1	...	...	6.0	5.8	6.7	7.6
Net Stockholders' Equity	662.1	550.2	471.5	439.6	369.0	310.1	257.8
Total Assets	1,039.7	889.6	796.9	670.6	616.5	519.9	442.6
Total Current Assets	454.7	332.0	314.7	261.7	267.8	249.2	229.2
Total Current Liabilities	151.6	127.2	139.6	117.4	100.5	98.9	86.1
Net Working Capital	303.1	204.9	175.2	144.3	167.3	150.3	143.1
Year End Shs Outstg (000)	83,634	83,582	83,511	82,962	82,519	82,259	81,821
STATISTICAL RECORD:							
Operating Profit Margin %	15.0	14.0	14.6	12.9	12.2	11.2	9.2
Book Value Per Share	7.92	6.58	5.65	5.30	4.47	3.77	3.15
Return on Equity %	19.4	18.6	22.9	18.1	18.0	18.8	15.9
Return on Assets %	12.4	11.5	13.6	11.8	10.8	11.2	9.3
Average Yield %	0.9	0.7	0.6	0.8	1.3	1.1	1.3
P/E Ratio	19.2-14.0	32.5-16.4	27.4-17.0	27.5-8.2	13.0-7.7	13.7-7.9	13.8-7.0
Price Range	29½-21⅝	39⅝-20	35⅝-22⅛	26⅜-7⅞	10½-6¼	9¾-5⅝	6⅞-3½

Statistics are as originally reported.

OFFICERS:
P.W. Rooney, Chmn., Pres. & C.E.O.
J.A. Reinhardt, Exec. V.P. & C.F.O.
W.C. Hattendorf, V.P. & Treas.
S.C. Kaiman, Sec.

INCORPORATED: DE, Mar., 1930

PRINCIPAL OFFICE: 701 Lima Avenue, Findlay, OH 45840

TELEPHONE NUMBER: (419) 423-1321

FAX: (419) 424-4108

NO. OF EMPLOYEES: 7,815

ANNUAL MEETING: In May

SHAREHOLDERS: 7,623

INSTITUTIONAL HOLDINGS:
No. of Institutions: 196
Shares Held: 29,306,681

REGISTRAR(S): Society National Bank, Cleveland, OH

TRANSFER AGENT(S): Society National Bank, Cleveland, OH

NYS SYMBOL CRD B
Rec. Pr. 16⅜

CRAWFORD & CO.

YIELD 3.3%
P/E RATIO 14.4

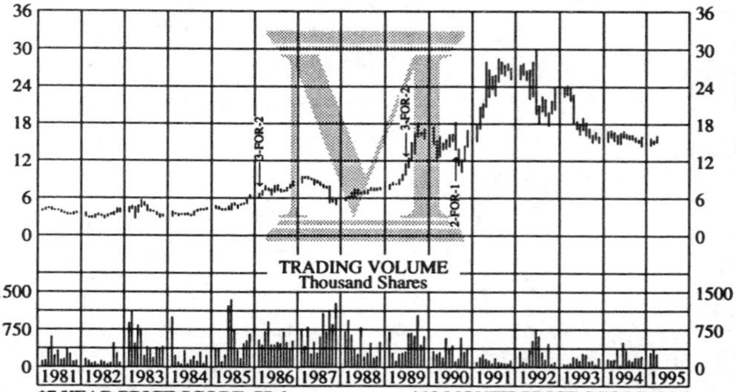

TRADING VOLUME
Thousand Shares

*7 YEAR PRICE SCORE 77.6   *12 MONTH PRICE SCORE 94.6
*NYSE COMPOSITE INDEX=100

INTERIM EARNINGS (Per Share):

Qtr.	Mar.	June	Sept.	Dec.
1991	0.24	0.28	0.28	0.25
1992	0.26	0.25	0.31	0.31
1993	0.26	0.27	0.28	0.25
1994	0.28	0.29	0.30	0.27

INTERIM DIVIDENDS (Per Share):

Amt.	Decl.	Ex.	Rec.	Pay.
0.125Q	1/26/94	2/3/94	2/9/94	2/18/94
0.125Q	4/27	5/5	5/11	5/20
0.125Q	7/27	8/4	8/10	8/19
0.125Q	10/26	11/4	11/10	11/21
0.135Q	2/1/95	2/9/95	2/15/95	2/24/95

Indicated div.: $0.54

CAPITALIZATION (12/31/94):

	($000)	(%)
Long-Term Debt	9,962	4.2
Deferred Income Tax	14,720	6.2
Common & Surplus	213,153	89.6
Total	237,835	100.0

DIVIDEND ACHIEVER STATUS:
Rank: 96   1984-94 Growth Rate: 13.0%
Total Years of Dividend Growth: 14

RECENT DEVELOPMENTS: For the quarter ended 12/31/94, net income was $9.3 million compared with $8.9 million a year earlier, an increase of 4.1%. Revenues climbed 3.3% to $142.1 million from $137.6 million for the same quarter in 1993. The improvement in revenues resulted from claims services to insurance companies, which increased nearly 16% over the 1993 quarter. However, this improvement was partially offset by lower revenues in claims services to the corporate or self-insured market and in the healthcare management segment.

PROSPECTS: CRD's claims administration services stand to perform well against strong competition in this market segment. While the health-care delivery system in the U.S. is still undergoing change, CRB believes the lack of health care reform legislation this year portends a future environment in which the private sector, rather than regulatory agencies, plays the dominant role. The acquisitions in the U.K. should strengthen revenues.

BUSINESS

CRAWFORD & CO. is a diversified services firm organized into three business units: Risk Management Services (RMS), Healthcare Managment (HCM) and Claims Services. RMS primarily fulfills corporate market needs by providing risk management and claims adjusting services including risk management information systems and services through the subsidiary, Crawford Risk Sciences Group. HCM offers a full range of managed care services for both the corporate and insurance markets. Claims Service is responsible for handling claims support to the insurance industry through the complete investigation, evaluation, disposition and management of losses.

REVENUES

(12/31/94)	($000)	(%)
U.S. Operations	541,969	92.2
Foreign Operations....	45,812	7.8
Total	587,781	100.0

ANNUAL EARNINGS AND DIVIDENDS PER SHARE

	1994	1993	1992	1991	1990	1989	1988
Earnings Per Share	1.14	1.06	1.13	1.05	0.91	0.79	0.54
Dividends Per Share	0.50	0.44	0.40	0.35	① 0.32	② 0.26	0.214
Dividend Payout %	43.9	41.5	35.4	33.3	35.2	32.9	39.6

① 2-for-1 stk split, 07/90   ② 3-for-2 stk split, 6/89

ANNUAL FINANCIAL DATA

RECORD OF EARNINGS (IN THOUSANDS):

	1994	1993	1992	1991	1990	1989	1988
Total Revenues	587,781	576,298	597,745	538,027	449,225	374,029	294,349
Costs and Expenses	504,818	495,669	514,113	460,728	388,188	320,770	253,263
Depreciation & Amort	14,912	15,779	16,715	15,607	10,461	9,306	10,646
Operating Profit	186,577	186,958	184,341	170,346	141,693	110,940	84,894
Income Bef Income Taxes	68,051	64,850	66,917	61,692	50,576	43,953	30,440
Income Taxes	27,450	26,800	26,500	24,250	18,450	16,250	11,600
Net Income	40,601	38,050	40,417	37,442	32,126	27,703	18,840
Aver. Shs. Outstg.	35,723	35,984	35,835	35,656	35,395	35,218	35,092

BALANCE SHEET (IN THOUSANDS):

Cash and Cash Equivalents	57,734	69,291	57,065	53,509	34,061	59,142	45,909
Receivables, Net	164,543	142,614	155,420	143,297	136,065	100,354	80,707
Gross Property	112,513	99,415	98,560	100,659	86,198	68,179	65,780
Accumulated Depreciation	75,065	62,979	56,925	52,512	41,014	37,822	36,000
Long-Term Debt	9,962	734	1,806	2,489	9,280	1,240	1,474
Net Stockholders' Equity	213,153	207,813	191,069	165,543	140,791	119,378	99,789
Total Assets	362,894	316,759	304,045	292,512	271,128	200,883	165,335
Total Current Assets	243,639	248,739	228,705	210,509	186,300	163,198	128,891
Total Current Liabilities	117,619	95,552	108,564	120,160	117,502	77,637	55,912
Net Working Capital	126,020	153,187	120,141	90,349	68,798	85,561	72,979
Year End Shares Outstg	35,029	36,030	35,904	35,720	35,543	35,304	35,134

STATISTICAL RECORD:

Book Value Per Share	6.09	5.77	5.32	4.63	3.96	3.38	2.84
Return on Equity %	19.0	18.3	21.2	22.6	22.8	23.2	18.9
Return on Assets %	11.2	12.0	13.3	12.8	11.9	13.8	11.4
Average Yield %	3.2	2.2	1.7	1.6	2.3	2.0	3.2
P/E Ratio	14.9-12.6	22.9-14.2	26.5-15.6	27.1-14.4	20.1-11.1	22.9-9.3	14.4-10.4
Price Range	17-14⅜	24¼-15	30-17⅝	28½-15⅛	18¼-10⅛	18⅛-7⅜	7¾-5⅝

Statistics are as originally reported.

OFFICERS:
F.L. Minix, Chmn. & C.E.O.
D.A. Smith, Pres. & C.F.O.
J.F. Osten, V.P., Gen. Couns. & Sec.

INCORPORATED: GA, May, 1943

PRINCIPAL OFFICE: 5620 Glenridge Drive.
N.E., Atlanta, GA 30342

TELEPHONE NUMBER: (404) 256-0830
NO. OF EMPLOYEES: 7,896
ANNUAL MEETING: In April
SHAREHOLDERS: 1,447 (cl. A); 1,233 (cl. B)
INSTITUTIONAL HOLDINGS:
No. of Institutions: 57
Shares Held: 13,813,437

REGISTRAR(S): Trust Company Bank,
Atlanta, GA

TRANSFER AGENT(S): Trust Company Bank,
Atlanta, GA

CROMPTON & KNOWLES CORP.

YIELD 2.9%
P/E RATIO 16.4

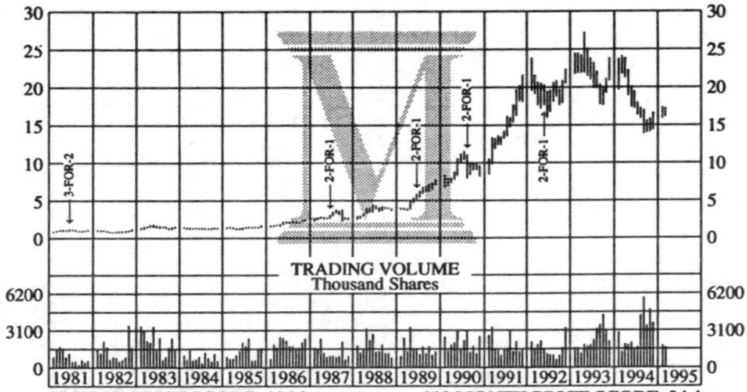

TRADING VOLUME
Thousand Shares

| 1981 | 1982 | 1983 | 1984 | 1985 | 1986 | 1987 | 1988 | 1989 | 1990 | 1991 | 1992 | 1993 | 1994 | 1995 |

*7 YEAR PRICE SCORE 106.0   *12 MONTH PRICE SCORE 94.4
*NYSE COMPOSITE INDEX=100

INTERIM EARNINGS (Per Share):

Qtr.	Mar.	June	Sept.	Dec.
1992	0.20	0.26	0.20	0.21
1993	0.24	0.30	0.22	0.24
1994	0.25	0.31	0.20	0.24

INTERIM DIVIDENDS (Per Share):

Amt.	Decl.	Ex.	Rec.	Pay.
0.10Q	1/25/94	2/7/94	2/11/94	2/25/94
0.12Q	4/11	5/2	5/6	5/27
0.12Q	7/20	8/1	8/5	8/26
0.12Q	10/19	10/31	11/4	11/25
0.12Q	1/25/95	2/8/95	2/10/95	2/24/95

Indicated div.: $0.48*

CAPITALIZATION (12/31/94):

	($000)	(%)
Long-Term Debt	54,000	19.0
Deferred Income Tax	6,681	2.3
Common & Surplus	223,907	78.7
Total	284,588	100.0

DIVIDEND ACHIEVER STATUS:
Rank: 15   1984-94 Growth Rate: 20.5%
Total Years of Dividend Growth: 18

RECENT DEVELOPMENTS: For the year ended 12/31/94, net income was $50.9 million, down slightly from $52.0 million earned in the previous year. Sales increased by 6% to $589.8 million from $558.3 million in the year before. Key domestic dye markets remained depressed throughout the year as a result of lagging apparel sales, therby reducing specialty chemicals sales by 6%. However, the sales of specialty process equipment and controls increased by 30%.

PROSPECTS: CNK has acquired McNeil Akron Repiquet S.a.r.l., a French plastics and rubber extrusion business, in an attempt to establish a more prominent market presence in Europe. In addition to a production facility, the acquisition will include local sales and service operations. The acquired business, with approximately $10.0 million in annual sales, will immediately boost market share. With the May 1994 acquisition of Egan Plastics Machinery, an additional $35 million in annualized sales should be realized in 1995.

BUSINESS

CROMPTON & KNOWLES CORP. produces specialty chemicals and equipment, which it markets in North America, Europe, Latin America and Asia. The specialty chemicals business is one of America's largest dye producers and a major participant in the specialty food and pharmaceutical ingredients business. Through this segment the Company also produces organic intermediates, flavors and food colors. CNK's other core business, specialty process equipment and controls, manufactures extrusion systems and related electronic controls for industries such as plastics and packaging.

BUSINESS LINE ANALYSIS

(12/31/94)	Rev(%)	Inc($000)
Specialty chemicals...	66.7	60,783
Specialty process equip...		
& controls...	33.3	31,195
Total...	100.0	91,978

ANNUAL EARNINGS AND DIVIDENDS PER SHARE

	12/31/94	12/25/93	12/26/92	12/28/91	12/29/90	12/30/89	12/31/88
Earnings Per Share	1.00	1.00	① 0.87	0.73	0.61	0.50	② 0.36
Dividends Per Share	0.46	0.38	0.305	0.248	0.197	0.145	0.108
Dividend Payout %	46.0	38.0	35.1	33.9	32.2	29.0	30.2

① Before acctg. chg. & extraord. loss ② Before disc. oper.

ANNUAL FINANCIAL DATA

RECORD OF EARNINGS (IN THOUSANDS):

Total Revenues	589,757	558,348	517,718	450,228	390,032	355,817	289,787
Costs and Expenses	495,365	463,911	433,340	378,478	330,643	306,902	254,611
Depreciation & Amort	13,298	12,076	11,635	10,028	7,984	6,474	5,280
Operating Profit	81,094	82,361	72,743	61,722	51,405	42,441	29,896
Earn Bef Income Taxes	79,969	82,473	68,337	56,600	47,260	38,588	26,943
Income Taxes	29,053	30,515	25,072	20,659	17,250	14,087	10,098
Net Income	50,916	51,958	① 43,265	35,941	30,010	24,501	② 16,845
Aver. Shs. Outstg.	51,152	52,176	49,967	49,317	49,270	49,064	47,239

① Before extra. item dr$3,000,000. ② Before disc. op. dr$1,517,000.

BALANCE SHEET (IN THOUSANDS):

Cash and Cash Equivalents	1,832	9,284	2,441	8,483	11,320	4,863	7,677
Receivables, Net	81,859	84,482	74,759	56,666	49,518	40,311	38,707
Inventories	157,356	113,932	115,688	111,108	95,111	69,583	63,082
Gross Property	202,796	173,312	163,114	134,823	123,481	90,677	78,798
Accumulated Depreciation	85,691	73,387	64,287	54,669	46,772	39,830	35,113
Long-Term Debt	54,000	14,000	24,000	76,118	70,330	41,213	44,594
Net Stockholders' Equity	223,907	239,996	211,452	140,763	117,565	98,901	81,921
Total Assets	432,328	363,246	350,715	308,562	282,644	217,850	205,642
Total Current Assets	260,657	220,396	207,383	185,235	164,442	127,216	120,584
Total Current Liabilities	139,042	95,439	102,593	85,712	88,340	71,068	72,352
Net Working Capital	121,615	124,957	104,790	99,523	76,102	56,148	48,232
Year End Shares Outstg	48,657	51,292	51,082	47,908	47,554	49,064	46,860

STATISTICAL RECORD:

Operating Profit Margin %	13.8	14.8	14.1	13.7	13.2	11.9	10.3
Book Value Per Share	3.71	4.03	3.46	2.26	1.83	1.45	1.14
Return on Equity %	22.7	21.6	20.5	25.5	25.5	24.8	20.6
Return on Assets %	11.8	14.3	12.3	11.6	10.6	11.2	8.2
Average Yield %	2.4	1.7	1.5	1.6	2.1	2.5	3.1
P/E Ratio	24.1-13.9	27.3-17.6	27.4-18.4	29.6-11.6	19.1-11.1	15.8-7.5	12.5-6.9
Price Range	24⅛-13⅞	27¼-17⅜	23⅞-16	21⅝-8½	11⅝-6¾	7⅞-3¾	4½-2½

Statistics are as originally reported.

OFFICERS:
V.A. Calarco, Chmn., Pres. & C.E.O.
C.J. Marsden, V.P.-Fin. & C.F.O.

INCORPORATED: MA, Feb., 1900

PRINCIPAL OFFICE: One Station Place Metro Center, Stamford, CT 06902

TELEPHONE NUMBER: (203) 353-5400
FAX: (203) 353-5424
NO. OF EMPLOYEES: 2,352
ANNUAL MEETING: In April
SHAREHOLDERS: 4,800 (approx.)
INSTITUTIONAL HOLDINGS:
No. of Institutions: 142
Shares Held: 24,084,494

REGISTRAR(S): Chase Manhattan Bank, N.A., New York, NY 10031

TRANSFER AGENT(S): Chase Manhattan Bank, N.A., New York, NY 10031

NYS SYMBOL CSX
Rec. Pr. 78⅞

CSX CORP.

YIELD 2.2%
P/E RATIO 12.7

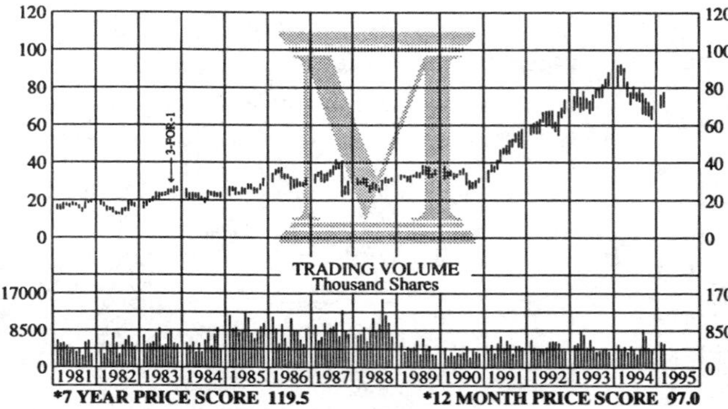
120
100
80
60
40
20
0
3-FOR-1
TRADING VOLUME
Thousand Shares
17000
8500
0
1981
1982
1983
1984
1985
1986
1987
1988
1989
1990
1991
1992
1993
1994
1995

***7 YEAR PRICE SCORE 119.5** ***12 MONTH PRICE SCORE 97.0**

*NYSE COMPOSITE INDEX=100

INTERIM EARNINGS (Per Share):

Qtr.	Mar.	June	Sept.	Dec.
1992	0.60	d3.13	1.25	1.47
1993	d0.09	1.48	0.61	1.46
1994	0.71	1.55	1.68	2.29

INTERIM DIVIDENDS (Per Share):

Amt.	Decl.	Ex.	Rec.	Pay.
0.44Q	2/9/94	2/18/94	2/25/94	3/15/94
0.44Q	5/3	5/19	5/25	6/15
0.44Q	7/13	8/19	8/25	9/15
0.44Q	10/12	11/18	11/25	12/15
0.44Q	2/8/95	2/17/95	2/24/95	3/15/95

Indicated Div.: $1.76*

CAPITALIZATION (12/30/94):

	($000)	(%)
Long-Term Debt	2,618,000	29.4
Deferred Income Tax	2,570,000	28.8
Common & Surplus	3,731,000	41.8
Total	8,919,000	100.0

DIVIDEND ACHIEVER STATUS:
Rank: 275 1984-94 Growth Rate: 5.4%
Total Years of Dividend Growth: 14

RECENT DEVELOPMENTS: For the year ended 12/31/94, net earnings were a record $652.0 million compared with $359.0 million in the previous year. Included in the 1994 results was the rail unit's $42.0 million after-tax gain ($0.40 per share) on the 1988 south Florida track sale. Revenues rose 7% to a record $9.61 billion. Income from operations was $1.23 billion versus $913.0 million the year before. The Company stated that cost-cutting initiatives and improved operating efficiencies led to the record results.

PROSPECTS: Given the positive effects of CSX's productivity and expense-reduction improvements, near-term earnings should continue to rise. Meanwhile, CSX Transportation Inc. will benefit from increased automotive and metal shipments, while the need for utility companies to replenish low stockpiles should boost coal shipments. The Intermodal unit should increase its market share with new business, as transcontinental traffic volume continues to grow.

BUSINESS

CSX CORPORATION is an international, multimodal transportation company with interests in rail freight, ocean container shipping, intermodal carriage, barging, trucking, warehousing and distribution. The rail system, CSX Transportation Inc., operates in 20 states, the District of Columbia and Ontario, Canada. Service is provided over 18,905 route-miles using a fleet of 2,810 locomotives. Sea-Land Services Inc., the ocean-container shipping unit, has a fleet of 83 vessels and serves 100 ports in 70 countries and territories. American Commercial Lines Inc. provides inland marine operations through its barging unit, American Commercial Barge Line Company (ACBL). Non-transportation interests include CSX Real Property Inc. and two resort properties.

REVENUES

(12/31/94)	($000)	(%)
Transportation	9,410	97.9
Non-transportation	198	2.1
Total	9,608	100.0

ANNUAL EARNINGS AND DIVIDENDS PER SHARE

	12/30/94	12/31/93	12/31/92	12/31/91	12/31/90	12/31/89	12/31/88
Earnings Per Share	**6.23**	**3.46**	**0.19**	**[1] d0.75**	**[2] 3.63**	**[2] 4.09**	**d0.33**
Dividends Per Share	**1.76**	**1.58**	**1.52**	**1.43**	**1.40**	**1.28**	**1.29**
Dividend Payout %	**28.3**	**45.7**	**N.M.**	**...**	**38.6**	**31.3**	**...**

[1] Before acctg. chg. [2] Before disc. oper.

ANNUAL FINANCIAL DATA

	12/30/94	12/31/93	12/31/92	12/31/91	12/31/90	12/31/89	12/31/88
RECORD OF EARNINGS (IN MILLIONS):							
Total Revenues	9,608.0	8,940.0	8,734.0	8,636.0	8,205.0	7,745.0	7,592.0
Operating Expenses	7,799.0	7,455.0	7,941.0	8,036.0	6,917.0	6,429.0	6,954.0
Depreciation	577.0	572.0	527.0	501.0	473.0	447.0	467.0
Operating Income	1,232.0	913.0	266.0	99.0	815.0	869.0	171.0
Earn Bef Income Taxes	1,006.0	633.0	d7.0	d113.0	537.0	692.0	d60.0
Income Taxes	354.0	274.0	cr27.0	cr37.0	172.0	265.0	cr22.0
Net Income	652.0	359.0	20.0	[1] d76.0	[2] 365.0	[3] 427.0	[4] d38.0
Aver. Shs. Outstg. (000)	104,652	104,000	103,000	100,000	98,000	101,000	146,000

[1] Before acctg. change dr$196,000,000. [2] Before disc. op. cr$51,000,000. [3] Before disc. op. cr$25,000,000. [4] Before disc. op. cr$185,000,000.

	12/30/94	12/31/93	12/31/92	12/31/91	12/31/90	12/31/89	12/31/88
BALANCE SHEET (IN MILLIONS):							
Cash and Cash Equivalents	535.0	499.0	530.0	465.0	609.0	591.0	625.0
Receivables, Net	857.0	776.0	605.0	728.0	728.0	645.0	896.0
Gross Property	16,315.0	15,853.0	15,702.0	15,176.0	14,927.0	14,262.0	14,048.0
Accumulated Depreciation	5,271.0	5,065.0	5,066.0	4,999.0	4,936.0	4,610.0	4,417.0
Long-Term Debt	2,618.0	3,133.0	3,245.0	2,804.0	3,025.0	2,727.0	3,032.0
Prop, Plant & Equip, Net	11,044.0	10,788.0	10,636.0	10,177.0	9,991.0	9,652.0	9,631.0
Net Stockholders' Equity	3,731.0	3,180.0	2,975.0	3,182.0	3,541.0	3,397.0	3,392.0
Total Assets	14,026.0	13,688.0	13,313.0	13,036.0	13,027.0	12,582.0	13,406.0
Total Current Assets	1,665.0	1,571.0	1,421.0	1,535.0	1,725.0	1,711.0	2,435.0
Total Current Liabilities	2,505.0	2,275.0	2,280.0	2,477.0	2,303.0	2,331.0	3,061.0
Net Working Capital	d840.0	d704.0	d859.0	d942.0	d578.0	d620.0	d626.0
Year End Shs Outstg (000)	104,722,000	104,000	103,000	102,000	99,000	98,000	107,000
STATISTICAL RECORD:							
Operating Profit Margin %	12.8	10.2	3.0	1.1	9.9	11.2	2.3
Book Value Per Share	0.04	30.58	28.88	31.20	35.77	33.13	30.30
Return on Equity %	17.5	11.3	0.7	...	10.3	12.6	...
Return on Assets %	4.6	2.6	0.2	...	2.8	3.4	...
Average Yield %	2.3	2.0	2.4	3.3	4.4	3.7	4.5
P/E Ratio	14.8-10.1	25.5-19.2	N.M	...	10.5-7.2	9.4-7.3	...
Price Range	92⅜-63⅛	88⅛-66⅜	73⅝-54½	58-29¾	38⅛-26	38⅝-29¾	32½-24⅜

Statistics are as originally reported.

OFFICERS:
J.W. Snow, Chmn., Pres. & C.E.O.
J. Ermer, Sr. V.P.-Fin.
A.A. Rudnick, V.P., Sec. & Gen. Coun.
W.H. Sparrow, V.P. & Treas.

INCORPORATED: VA, 1980

PRINCIPAL OFFICE: One James Cntr 901 E Cary St, Richmond, VA 23219

TELEPHONE NUMBER: (804) 782-1400
FAX: (804) 782-1409
NO. OF EMPLOYEES: 46,747
ANNUAL MEETING: In May
SHAREHOLDERS: 57,267 Common.
INSTITUTIONAL HOLDINGS:
No. of Institutions: 581
Shares Held: 64,285,681

REGISTRAR(S): Harris Trust Co., Chicago, IL

TRANSFER AGENT(S): Harris Trust Co., Chicago, IL

DAYTON-HUDSON CORP.

YIELD 2.6%
P/E RATIO 34.5

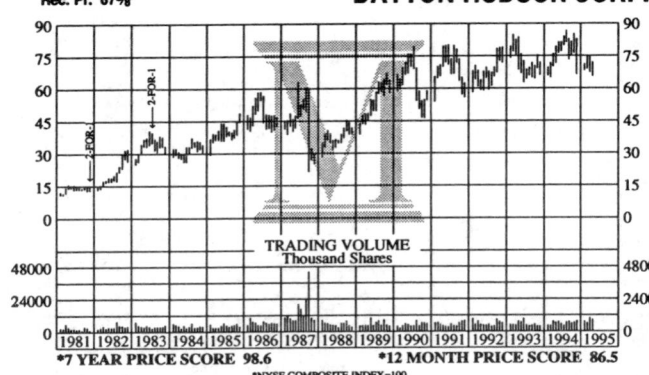

TRADING VOLUME
Thousand Shares

*7 YEAR PRICE SCORE 98.6
*12 MONTH PRICE SCORE 86.5

*NYSE COMPOSITE INDEX=100

INTERIM EARNINGS (Per Share):

Qtr.	Apr.	July	Oct.	Jan.
1992-93	----------	5.02	----------	
1993-94	0.35	0.28	0.54	3.81
1994-95	0.48	0.62	0.86	3.62

INTERIM DIVIDENDS (Per Share):

Amt.	Decl.	Ex.	Rec.	Pay.
0.42Q	4/13/94	5/16/94	5/20/94	6/10/94
0.42Q	6/8	8/15	8/20	9/10
0.42Q	10/12	11/14	11/20	12/10
0.42Q	1/11/95	2/13/95	2/20/95	3/10/95
0.44Q	4/12	5/15	5/20	6/10

Indicated div.: $1.76

CAPITALIZATION (1/28/95):

	($000)	(%)
Long-Term Debt	4,369,000	55.4
Cap. Lease Oblig.	119,000	1.5
Redeemable Pfd Stock	360,000	4.5
Common & Surplus	3,043,000	38.6
Total	7,891,000	100.0

DIVIDEND ACHIEVER STATUS:
Rank: 183   1984-94 Growth Rate: 9.6%
Total Years of Dividend Growth: 23

RECENT DEVELOPMENTS: For the fiscal year ended 1/28/95, net income increased to $434 million from $375 million the year before. Revenues amounted to $21.31 billion compared with $19.23 billion in the prior fiscal year. Despite continued inflation of retail prices at each of the Company's operating divisions, a 5% increase in comparable-store revenues was realized. Target stores reported revenue growth of 16% while Mervyn's and DSD showed revenue growth of 3% from the prior year.

PROSPECTS: The Company's efforts to improve inventory management through an everyday low-price strategy and a more fashion-oriented product mix have begun to aid results at Mervyn's. DH will continue to monitor costs by reducing advertising expenses and improving distribution efficiency and productivity. During fiscal 1995, DH plans to invest $1.3 billion in new stores (60 - 70), remodels and other capital support, including the upgrading of distribution and operational systems.

BUSINESS

DAYTON HUDSON is a diversified general merchandise retailer. Target is a national discount store chain offering low prices with stores selling hardlines and fashion softgoods; Mervyn's is a moderate-priced department store chain specializing in trend-right active and casual apparel and home softlines. The Department Store Division, operates three groups of full-service, full-line department stores under the names of Dayton's stores, Hudson's stores and Marshall Field Stores, offering moderate to better merchandise. As of 1/29/95, DH operated 960 stores including 611 Target, 286 Mervyn's, and 63 department stores.

BUSINESS LINE ANALYSIS

(1/29/95)	Rev(%)	Inc(%)
Target	63.8	60.6
Mervyn's	21.4	17.1
Department Stores	14.8	22.3
Total	100.0	100.0

ANNUAL EARNINGS AND DIVIDENDS PER SHARE

	1/28/95	1/29/94	1/30/93	2/1/92	2/2/91	2/3/90	1/28/89
Earnings Per Share	5.77	4.99	5.02	3.86	① 5.41	5.37	3.45
Dividends Per Share	1.68	1.60	1.52	1.44	1.32	1.12	1.02
Dividend Payout %	29.1	32.1	30.3	37.3	24.4	20.9	29.6

① Before acctg. chg.

ANNUAL FINANCIAL DATA

RECORD OF EARNINGS (IN MILLIONS):

Total Revenues	21,311.0	19,233.0	17,927.0	16,115.0	14,739.0	13,644.0	12,204.0
Costs and Expenses	19,640.0	17,682.0	16,420.0	14,835.0	13,386.0	12,384.0	11,224.0
Depreciation	531.0	498.0	459.0	410.0	369.0	315.0	290.0
Operating Profit	1,140.0	1,053.0	1,048.0	870.0	984.0	945.0	690.0
Earn Bef Income Taxes	714.0	607.0	611.0	472.0	659.0	678.0	472.0
Income Taxes	280.0	232.0	228.0	171.0	249.0	268.0	185.0
Net Income	434.0	375.0	383.0	301.0	① 410.0	410.0	287.0
Aver. Shs. Outstg. (000)	72,000	72,000	72,000	72,000	72,000	71,000	76,000	83,000

① Before acctg. change cr$2,000,000.

BALANCE SHEET (IN MILLIONS):

Cash and Cash Equivalents	147.0	321.0	117.0	96.0	92.0	103.0	53.0
Receivables, Net	1,810.0	1,536.0	1,514.0	1,430.0	1,407.0	1,138.0	1,223.0
Inventories	2,777.0	2,497.0	2,618.0	2,381.0	2,016.0	1,827.0	1,669.0
Gross Property	9,009.0	8,283.0	7,760.0	6,961.0	6,133.0	4,873.0	4,706.0
Accumulated Depreciation	2,624.0	2,336.0	2,197.0	1,859.0	1,608.0	1,350.0	1,220.0
Long-Term Debt	4,369.0	4,279.0	4,330.0	4,227.0	3,682.0	2,510.0	2,383.0
Capital Lease Obligations	119.0	...	...	...	...	...	...
Net Stockholders' Equity	3,403.0	3,105.0	2,860.0	2,608.0	2,427.0	2,132.0	1,861.0
Total Assets	11,697.0	10,778.0	10,337.0	9,485.0	8,524.0	6,684.0	6,523.0
Total Current Assets	4,959.0	4,511.0	4,414.0	4,032.0	3,658.0	3,107.0	2,981.0
Total Current Liabilities	3,390.0	3,075.0	2,964.0	2,580.0	2,422.0	2,195.0	2,003.0
Net Working Capital	1,569.0	1,436.0	1,450.0	1,452.0	1,236.0	912.0	978.0
Year End Shs Outstg (000)	72,000	72,000	71,000	71,000	71,000	71,000	78,000

STATISTICAL RECORD:

Operating Profit Margin %	5.3	5.5	5.8	5.4	6.7	6.9	5.7
Book Value Per Share	42.26	38.01	35.01	31.42	28.85	24.69	23.86
Return on Equity %	14.3	13.7	15.4	13.5	20.0	23.4	15.4
Return on Assets %	3.7	3.5	3.7	3.2	4.8	6.1	4.4
Average Yield %	2.2	2.2	2.2	2.1	2.1	2.1	2.8
P/E Ratio	15.1-11.2	17.0-12.6	15.8-11.6	20.8-13.9	14.7-8.5	12.5-7.2	13.2-8.2
Price Range	86⅞-64⅞	85-62⅝	79¼-58	80¼-53¾	79½-46¼	67-38¾	45½-28¼

Statistics are as originally reported.

OFFICERS:
K.A. Macke, Chmn. & C.E.O.
S.E. Watson, Pres.
D.A. Scovanner, Sr. V.P. & C.F.O.
J.T. Hale, Sr. V.P., Gen. Couns. & Sec.

INCORPORATED: MN, 1902

PRINCIPAL OFFICE: 777 Nicollet Mall, Minneapolis, MN 55402

TELEPHONE NUMBER: (612) 370-6948
FAX: (612) 370-5502
NO. OF EMPLOYEES: 174,000
ANNUAL MEETING: In May
SHAREHOLDERS: 11,707
INSTITUTIONAL HOLDINGS:
No. of Institutions: 437
Shares Held: 58,126,626

REGISTRAR(S): First Chicago Trust Co. of New York, New York, NY 10008

TRANSFER AGENT(S): First Chicago Trust Co. of New York, New York, NY 10008

DEAN FOODS CO.

YIELD 2.5%
P/E RATIO 13.8

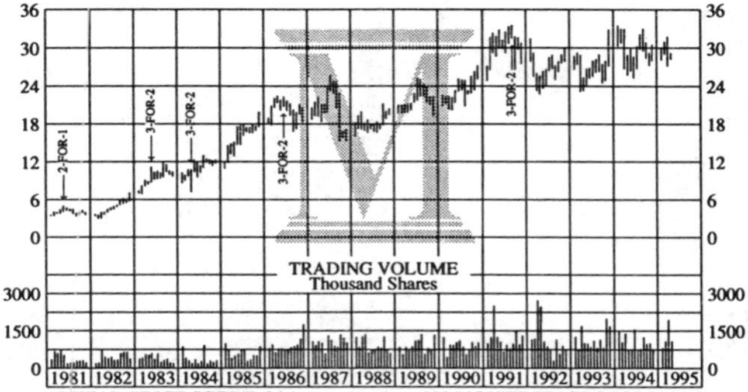

TRADING VOLUME
Thousand Shares

| 1981 | 1982 | 1983 | 1984 | 1985 | 1986 | 1987 | 1988 | 1989 | 1990 | 1991 | 1992 | 1993 | 1994 | 1995 |

*7 YEAR PRICE SCORE 94.1   *12 MONTH PRICE SCORE 94.4
*NYSE COMPOSITE INDEX=100

INTERIM EARNINGS (Per Share):

Qtr.	Aug.	Nov.	Feb.	May
1991-92	0.42	0.39	0.33	0.39
1992-93	0.39	0.43	0.41	0.50
1993-94	0.27	0.44	0.46	0.61
1994-95	0.43	0.50	0.43	...

INTERIM DIVIDENDS (Per Share):

Amt.	Decl.	Ex.	Rec.	Pay.
0.16Q	3/29/94	5/16/94	5/20/94	6/15/94
0.17Q	7/25	8/15	8/19	9/15
0.17Q	10/6	11/14	11/18	12/15
0.17Q	1/30/95	2/13/95	2/17/95	3/15/95
0.17Q	3/28	5/15	5/19	6/15

Indicated div.: $0.68

CAPITALIZATION (5/29/94):

	($000)	(%)
Long-Term Debt	136,150	18.8
Deferred Income Tax	63,410	8.8
Common & Surplus	524,774	72.4
Total	724,334	100.0

DIVIDEND ACHIEVER STATUS:
Rank: 101   1984-94 Growth Rate: 12.9%
Total Years of Dividend Growth: 22

RECENT DEVELOPMENTS: For the quarter ended 2/26/95 net income was $17.2 million, down 6.9% from the $18.4 million earned in the comparable 1994 quarter. The Company attributed results to increased interest costs, higher income taxes and lower earnings from ice cream operations. Sales advanced 7.0% to $665.9 million from $662.9 million in the prior-year period. Ice cream operations were hurt by tight margins and costs associated with entry into new markets and the introduction of Guilt Free, a new non-fat, no sugar added ice cream.

PROSPECTS: Despite the Company's failure to acquire Curtice-Burns Foods, Inc., DF will continue to seek strategic acquisitions in the future that complement its existing businesses. Meanwhile, it is expected that DF's dairy operations will benefit from adequate milk supplies and more stable raw milk costs by mid-1995. Despite lower canned vegetable pricing caused by an abundant corn crop in the Midwest, DF should manage to offset the low prices with its wide variety of product line offerings, which now includes Birds Eye frozen vegetables.

BUSINESS

DEAN FOODS CO. is a food processor and distributor engaged primarily in two business segments: Dairy Products and Specialty Food Products. The dairy products segment includes: fluid milk and related dairy products; ice cream and natural cheeses such as aged cheddar. The specialty food products segment includes: canned and frozen vegetables; pickles; relishes and salad dressings; non-dairy creamers; sauces; puddings; dips and salads. DF also operates a transportation business which concentrates on refrigerated and frozen cartage.

BUSINESS LINE ANALYSIS

(5/29/94)	Rev(%)	Inc(%)
Dairy Products	61.1	53.4
Specialty Food Products	38.9	46.6
Total	100.0	100.0

ANNUAL EARNINGS AND DIVIDENDS PER SHARE

	5/29/94	5/30/93	5/31/92	5/26/91	5/27/90	5/28/89	5/29/88
Earnings Per Share	1.78	1.73	1.53	1.79	1.53	1.52	1.07
Dividends Per Share	0.66	0.62	0.506	① 0.453	0.41	0.37	0.333
Dividend Payout %	37.0	35.8	33.1	25.3	26.9	24.3	31.3
3-for-2 stk. split							

ANNUAL FINANCIAL DATA

RECORD OF EARNINGS (IN MILLIONS):

Total Revenues	2,431.2	2,274.3	2,289.4	2,158.0	1,987.5	1,683.6	1,551.8
Costs and Expenses	2,236.5	2,094.4	2,112.5	1,975.1	1,837.6	1,555.2	1,424.4
Depreciation & Amort	61.9	54.0	50.3	47.0	38.6	32.0	35.7
Operating Profit	132.8	126.0	126.6	135.9	111.3	96.4	91.7
Income Before Taxes	118.3	114.8	105.5	124.3	102.1	101.8	76.5
Income Taxes	47.6	46.4	43.5	51.8	40.8	41.4	33.8
Net Income	① 70.8	68.4	62.0	72.5	61.2	60.4	42.8
① Before acctg. change cr$1,179,000.							

BALANCE SHEET (IN MILLIONS):

Cash and Cash Equivalents	11.0	41.6	34.0	44.1	43.5	70.0	53.8
Receivables, Net	169.4	146.5	152.5	151.6	140.6	121.4	111.2
Inventories	233.3	179.0	204.3	174.5	164.9	112.0	91.8
Gross Property	906.4	770.9	694.2	624.5	561.7	452.0	392.8
Accumulated Depreciation	363.2	327.1	278.4	248.6	224.6	198.0	181.1
Long-Term Debt	136.2	151.1	155.5	150.0	146.6	84.2	48.9
Net Stockholders' Equity	524.8	476.3	430.4	416.6	362.8	293.2	265.7
Total Assets	1,109.2	892.8	893.5	817.0	744.8	586.7	499.2
Total Current Assets	460.2	406.1	433.3	399.5	372.4	320.2	270.3
Total Current Liabilities	367.3	207.7	213.4	201.0	189.6	163.7	139.9
Net Working Capital	92.9	198.4	219.9	198.4	182.9	156.5	130.4
Year End Shs Outstg (000)	39,789	39,689	39,604	40,709	40,623	39,458	40,269

STATISTICAL RECORD:

Operating Profit Margin %	5.5	5.5	5.5	6.3	5.6	5.7	5.9
Book Value Per Share	10.64	11.11	10.00	9.36	8.16	7.26	6.42
Return on Equity %	13.5	14.4	14.4	17.4	16.9	20.6	16.1
Return on Assets %	6.4	7.7	6.9	8.9	8.2	10.3	8.6
Average Yield %	2.4	2.3	1.7	1.9	1.8	2.0	1.6
P/E Ratio	18.2-12.8	18.2-13.2	21.9-16.3	15.2-11.2	16.5-12.6	14.0-10.5	23.9-14.1
Price Range	32⅞-23⅛	31½-22¾	33½-24⅞	27¼-20⅛	25¼-19¼	21¼-16	25⅝-15⅛

Statistics are as originally reported.

OFFICERS:
H.M. Dean, Chmn. & C.E.O.
T.L. Rose, Pres. & C.O.O.
E.A. Blanchard, V.P., Sec. & Gen. Counsel

INCORPORATED: DE, May, 1968

PRINCIPAL OFFICE: 3600 North River Road, Franklin Park, IL 60131

TELEPHONE NUMBER: (312) 625-6200
FAX: (708) 671-8741
NO. OF EMPLOYEES: 12,100 (approx.)
ANNUAL MEETING: In October
SHAREHOLDERS: 8,936
INSTITUTIONAL HOLDINGS:
No. of Institutions: 158
Shares Held: 14,383,490

REGISTRAR(S): Harris Trust & Savings Bank, Chicago, IL

TRANSFER AGENT(S): Harris Trust & Savings Bank, Chicago, IL

DELUXE CORP.

YIELD 4.8%
P/E RATIO 18.4

TRADING VOLUME
Thousand Shares

*7 YEAR PRICE SCORE 67.6   *12 MONTH PRICE SCORE 97.1
*NYSE COMPOSITE INDEX=100

INTERIM EARNINGS (Per Share):

Qtr.	Mar.	June	Sept.	Dec.
1992	0.58	0.57	0.60	0.67
1993	0.62	0.03	0.45	0.61
1994	0.46	0.36	0.40	0.49
1995	0.41	...	...	...

INTERIM DIVIDENDS (Per Share):

Amt.	Decl.	Ex.	Rec.	Pay.
0.36Q	5/9/94	5/17/94	5/23/94	6/6/94
0.37Q	8/13	8/19	8/25	9/6
0.37Q	11/11	11/15	11/21	12/5
0.37Q	2/6/95	2/14/95	2/21/95	3/6/95
0.37Q	5/8	4/26	5/2	6/5

Indicated div.: $1.48

CAPITALIZATION (12/31/94):

	($000)	(%)
Long-Term Debt	110,867	11.5
Deferred Income Tax	40,552	4.2
Common & Surplus	814,393	84.3
Total	965,812	100.0

DIVIDEND ACHIEVER STATUS:

Rank: 73   1984-94 Growth Rate: 14.1%
Total Years of Dividend Growth: 34

RECENT DEVELOPMENTS: For the year ended 12/31/94, net income was $140.9 million compared with $141.9 million in the previous year. Included in 1994 results include a $10.0 million pretax credit and 1993 results include a $49.0 million pretax charge, both related to closing 16 check printing facilities. Sales were a record $1.75 billion, up 11% from $1.58 billion the year before. Despite a 2% increase in financial institution check orders, revenues for this segment declined 5% from a year ago.

PROSPECTS: The Company continues to diversify its business as long-term opportunities in the traditional check-market diminish. Recent acquisitions include a collection services company, a direct banking software company, and a credit card processing company. Also, even though institutional check-printing revenues are declining, the profitability of this business will benefit from cost reductions and improved efficiencies from plant restructuring.

BUSINESS

DELUXE CORPORATION specializes in the production and sale of checks, deposit tickets, and related forms for use by banks and their depositors. The Company has three business segments: Payment Systems provides check printing, electronic funds transfer, ATM card services, new account verification services, and credit reporting services; Business Systems manufactures and supplies computer and business forms, record keeping systems, and related office products; and Consumer Specialty Products manufactures and distributes greeting cards, gift wrap, stationery, and other products for household use. The Company has more than 85 printing plants located throughout the country to provide service to customers in all 50 states.

BUSINESS LINE ANALYSIS

(12/31/94)	Rev(%)	Inc($000)
Payment Systems	61.9	219,159
Business Systems	19.2	15
Consumer Specialty Prods	18.9	24,485
Total	100.0	243,659

ANNUAL EARNINGS AND DIVIDENDS PER SHARE

	1994	1993	1992	1991	1990	1989	1988
Earnings Per Share	1.71	1.71	2.42	2.18	2.03	1.79	1.68
Dividends Per Share	1.46	1.42	1.34	1.22	1.10	0.98	0.86
Dividend Payout %	85.4	83.0	55.4	56.0	54.2	54.7	51.2

ANNUAL FINANCIAL DATA

RECORD OF EARNINGS (IN MILLIONS):

	1994	1993	1992	1991	1990	1989	1988
Total Revenues	1,747.9	1,581.8	1,534.4	1,474.5	1,413.6	1,315.8	1,196.0
Costs and Expenses	1,417.8	1,277.6	1,145.5	1,110.5	1,088.0	1,027.1	931.1
Depreciation & Amort	86.4	72.3	66.6	76.0	51.0	44.9	38.1
Income From Operations	243.7	231.8	322.2	288.0	274.6	243.8	226.8
Income Bef Income Taxes	240.9	235.9	324.8	295.5	282.5	246.3	226.6
Income Taxes	100.0	94.1	122.0	112.6	110.3	93.7	83.3
Net Income	140.9	141.9	202.8	182.9	172.2	152.6	143.4
Aver. Shs. Outstg. (000)	82,400	82,936	83,861	84,005	84,638	85,346	85,255
BALANCE SHEET (IN MILLIONS):							
Cash and Cash Equivalents	78.2	221.8	380.9	317.3	114.5	45.0	22.0
Receivables, Net	195.5	178.1	141.3	111.7	125.1	126.8	110.2
Inventories	104.0	85.3	65.1	68.0	71.9	62.9	62.5
Gross Property	869.7	779.9	729.9	687.4	640.0	600.5	527.5
Accumulated Depreciation	407.9	378.3	340.8	314.2	283.9	254.6	225.5
Long-Term Debt	110.9	110.8	115.5	110.6	11.9	10.2	10.9
Net Stockholders' Equity	814.4	801.2	829.8	748.0	675.8	630.6	567.7
Total Assets	1,256.3	1,252.0	1,199.6	1,099.1	923.9	847.0	786.1
Total Current Assets	420.9	522.4	611.2	539.0	344.3	262.7	219.9
Total Current Liabilities	290.5	297.9	224.4	208.0	199.3	167.8	167.1
Net Working Capital	130.4	224.5	386.9	330.9	145.0	94.8	52.8
Year End Shs Outstg (000)	82,375	82,549	83,797	83,938	84,075	85,212	85,365
STATISTICAL RECORD:							
Operating Profit Margin %	13.9	14.7	21.0	19.5	19.4	18.5	19.0
Book Value Per Share	5.90	6.15	7.77	6.93	5.88	5.23	4.29
Return on Equity %	17.3	17.7	24.4	24.5	25.5	24.2	25.3
Return on Assets %	11.2	11.3	16.9	16.6	18.6	18.0	18.2
Average Yield %	4.6	3.6	3.1	3.0	3.5	3.3	3.5
P/E Ratio	22.2-15.0	28.0-18.6	20.2-15.8	22.2-15.0	17.7-13.1	20.0-13.4	16.9-12.5
Price Range	38-25⅝	47⅞-31¾	49-38⅛	48½-32⅝	35⅞-26⅝	35¾-24	28⅜-21

Statistics are as originally reported.

OFFICERS:
H.V. Haverty, Chmn., Pres. & C.E.O.
C.M. Osborne, Sr. V.P. & C.F.O.
J.H. LeFevre, Sr. V.P. & Sec.

INCORPORATED: MN, Mar., 1920

PRINCIPAL OFFICE: 1080 West County Road F, Shoreview, MN 55126-8201

TELEPHONE NUMBER: (612) 483-7111
FAX: (612) 481-4163
NO. OF EMPLOYEES: 18,000 (approx.)
ANNUAL MEETING: In May
SHAREHOLDERS: 22,436
INSTITUTIONAL HOLDINGS:
No. of Institutions: 377
Shares Held: 48,100,949

REGISTRAR(S): The Bank of New York, New York, NY

TRANSFER AGENT(S): The Bank of New York, New York, NY

DIEBOLD, INC.

YIELD 2.4%
P/E RATIO 19.1

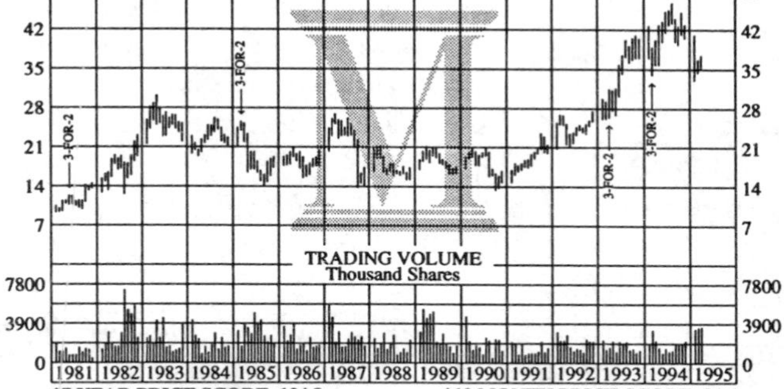

7 YEAR PRICE SCORE 134.8   **12 MONTH PRICE SCORE 84.6**
*NYSE COMPOSITE INDEX=100

INTERIM EARNINGS (Per Share):

Qtr.	Mar.	June	Sept.	Dec.
1992	0.21	0.29	0.37	0.50
1993	0.28	0.39	0.42	0.51
1994	0.42	0.53	0.55	0.59
1995	0.50	...	...	...

INTERIM DIVIDENDS (Per Share):

Amt.	Decl.	Ex.	Rec.	Pay.
0.22Q	4/7/94	5/16/94	5/20/94	6/10/94
0.22Q	7/21	8/12	8/18	9/8
0.22Q	10/18	11/10	11/17	12/8
0.24Q	1/31/95	2/13/95	2/17/95	3/10/95
0.24Q	4/5	5/15	5/19	6/9

*Indicated div.: $0.96**

CAPITALIZATION (12/31/94):

	($000)	(%)
Minority Interest	15,028	3.2
Common & Surplus	459,219	96.8
Total	474,247	100.0

DIVIDEND ACHIEVER STATUS:
Rank: 184   1984-94 Growth Rate: 9.5%
Total Years of Dividend Growth: 41

RECENT DEVELOPMENTS: For the year ended 12/31/94, DBD posted record net income of $63.5 million, up 31% from $48.4 million the year before. Revenues improved 22% to a record $760.2 million from $623.3 million a year earlier. During the year, the Company reported increases in all product categories and in its international business. For the quarter ended 12/31/94, net income was $17.9 million compared with $15.2 million in the corresponding 1993 period.

PROSPECTS: International markets were responsible for a significant portion of Diebold's positive operating results for the quarter and should continue to be key in earnings and revenues growth. The Asia-Pacific region, China in particular, and Latin American markets are the leaders in these markets. The Company's product backlog was equal to the previous year's demand and should remain strong. The Company has a platform from which to expand into the college and university market with its purchase of Applied Network Technologies, Inc.

BUSINESS

DIEBOLD, INC. is engaged in the automation of self-service transactions, security products, and customer service. Electronic and retail products dispense currency and documents of value, transfer funds, validate checks, authorize credit and perform other point-of-sale functions. Products are used in financial service applications in financial, retail, transportation, government, petroleum, and other industry groups. The Company manufactures electronic and physical security systems. The financial group has traditionally consisted of banks, savings and loan associations and credit unions.

REVENUES

(12/31/94)	($000)	(%)
Products	479,314	63.1
Services	280,857	36.9
Total	760,171	100.0

ANNUAL EARNINGS AND DIVIDENDS PER SHARE

	1994	1993	1992	1991	1990	1989	1988
Earnings Per Share	2.09	1.60	1.37	1.20	0.91	1.22	☑1.06
Dividends Per Share	0.88	0.80	①0.747	0.711	0.667	0.622	0.578
Dividend Payout %	42.1	5.0	54.5	59.3	73.2	50.9	54.6

① Bef acctg chge   ② Before acctg. chg.

ANNUAL FINANCIAL DATA

RECORD OF EARNINGS (IN THOUSANDS):

	1994	1993	1992	1991	1990	1989	1988
Total Revenues	760,171	623,277	543,852	506,217	476,054	468,883	450,571
Costs and Expenses	655,157	540,581	477,549	449,109	431,303	411,369	403,658
Depreciation & Amort	14,240	13,606	12,502	12,808	12,564	11,892	10,334
Operating Profit	90,774	69,090	53,801	44,300	32,187	45,622	36,579
Income Bef Income Taxes	93,978	70,515	54,836	49,166	37,478	53,863	43,870
Income Taxes	30,467	22,141	13,699	13,421	10,367	17,633	12,530
Net Income	63,511	48,374	①41,137	35,745	27,111	36,230	②31,340
Aver. Shs. Outstg	30,330	30,231	20,050	19,893	19,838	19,790	19,764

① Before acctg. change dr$17,932,000.   ② Before acctg. change cr$4,484,000.

BALANCE SHEET (IN THOUSANDS):

	1994	1993	1992	1991	1990	1989	1988
Cash and Cash Equivalents	55,685	71,913	55,970	68,303	85,452	80,440	91,632
Receivables, Net	153,107	129,256	120,691	118,849	106,727	117,280	109,041
Inventories	85,543	74,983	80,750	106,147	96,000	76,757	85,423
Gross Property	152,314	146,400	141,491	133,972	135,336	120,826	117,708
Accumulated Depreciation	87,601	85,740	80,890	75,523	70,723	64,896	58,156
Long-Term Debt	...	...	...	2,000	3,250	4,500	5,000
Net Stockholders' Equity	459,219	427,047	399,674	396,908	378,128	379,532	360,791
Total Assets	661,883	609,019	558,914	535,593	519,932	489,649	454,737
Total Current Assets	326,089	313,326	292,387	321,368	313,314	289,338	298,563
Total Current Liabilities	155,464	138,571	117,612	115,779	116,022	89,991	74,806
Net Working Capital	170,625	174,755	174,775	205,589	197,292	199,347	223,757
Year End Shares Outstg	30,460	30,260	20,081	19,963	19,848	19,805	19,751

STATISTICAL RECORD:

	1994	1993	1992	1991	1990	1989	1988
Operating Profit Margin %	11.9	11.1	9.9	8.8	6.8	9.7	8.1
Book Value Per Share	15.08	14.11	19.90	18.88	19.05	19.16	18.27
Return on Equity %	13.8	11.3	10.3	9.0	7.2	9.5	8.7
Return on Assets %	9.6	7.9	7.4	6.7	5.2	7.4	6.9
Average Yield %	2.2	2.4	3.1	3.7	3.9	3.3	3.2
P/E Ratio	22.4-16.2	25.7-16.3	13.4-10.1	13.1-8.2	15.2-9.8	11.6-8.8	13.4-9.5
Price Range	46¾-33⅞	41⅛-26	27½-20¾	23½-14¾	20⅞-13⅜	21¼-16⅛	21⅜-15⅛

Statistics are as originally reported.

OFFICERS:
R.W. Mahoney, Chmn., Pres. & C.E.O.
G.F. Morris, Exec. V.P. & C.F.O.
C. Francis-Vogelsang, V.P. & Sec.
R.J. Warren, V.P. & Treas.
INCORPORATED: OH, 1876
PRINCIPAL OFFICE: P.O. Box 8230, Canton, OH 44711-8230

TELEPHONE NUMBER: (216) 489-4000
NO. OF EMPLOYEES: 4,731
ANNUAL MEETING: In April
SHAREHOLDERS: 3,400 (approx.)
INSTITUTIONAL HOLDINGS:
No. of Institutions: 167
Shares Held: 16,315,144

REGISTRAR(S): Society National Bank, Cleveland, OH

TRANSFER AGENT(S): Society National Bank, Cleveland, OH

NYS SYMBOL D
Rec. Pr. 36⅜

DOMINION RESOURCES, INC.

YIELD 7.1%
P/E RATIO 12.9

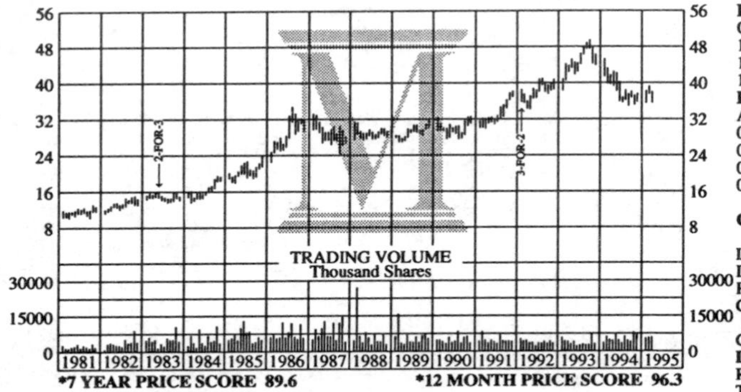

TRADING VOLUME
Thousand Shares
1981 1982 1983 1984 1985 1986 1987 1988 1989 1990 1991 1992 1993 1994 1995

*7 YEAR PRICE SCORE 89.6 *12 MONTH PRICE SCORE 96.3
*NYSE COMPOSITE INDEX=100

INTERIM EARNINGS (Per Share):

Qtr.	Mar.	June	Sept.	Dec.
1992	0.59	0.38	0.92	0.77
1993	0.75	0.63	1.20	0.55
1994	0.84	0.80	0.94	0.23

INTERIM DIVIDENDS (Per Share):

Amt.	Decl.	Ex.	Rec.	Pay.
0.635Q	4/15/94	5/24/94	5/31/94	6/20/94
0.635Q	7/15	8/24	8/30	9/20
0.645Q	10/24	11/25	12/1	12/20
0.645Q	2/17/95	2/24/95	3/2/95	3/20/95

*Indicated div.: $2.58**

CAPITALIZATION (12/31/94):

	($000)	(%)
Long-Term Debt	4,710,600	39.2
Deferred Income Tax	1,902,800	15.8
Preferred Stock	816,100	6.8
Common & Surplus	4,586,100	38.2
Total	12,015,600	100.0
Current Debt	545,100	

DIVIDEND ACHIEVER STATUS:
Rank: 300 1984-94 Growth Rate: 3.9%
Total Years of Dividend Growth: 19

RECENT DEVELOPMENTS: For the quarter ended 12/31/94, net income was $39.3 million compared with $92.0 million in the same period of 1993. Revenues declined 3.0% to $1.00 billion. Results for 1994 reflect a non-recurring charge of $42.0 million associated with an employee-reduction program. For the year ended 12/31/94, net income including the aforementioned charge declined 7.4% to $478.2 million from $516.6 million in 1993. Meanwhile, revenues increased 1.3% to $4.49 billion. Utility earnings were also negatively affected by milder temperatures in 1994.

PROSPECTS: Virginia Power faces potential competition for industrial, commercial and some government customers from cogeneration units that might directly serve those customers. The Virginia State Corporation Commission (VSCC) is investigating the dispute between Dominion Resources and its major subsidiary, Virginia Power. Although the dispute has been resolved internally, the VSCC will examine whether the dispute negatively affected the public's interest.

BUSINESS

DOMINION RESOURCES, INC. is a holding company for Virginia Electric & Power Co., which provides electric services for more than 1.8 million customers in Virginia and northeastern North Carolina. Dominion Capital, a subsidiary, provides investment management services to the holding company and other nonutility subsidiaries. Dominion Lands, Inc. is involved in joint venture real estate development. Dominion Energy has investment or ownership interest in non-utility electric power generation products and is also involved in joint ventures for natural gas and oil exploration.

REVENUES

(12/31/94)	($000)	(%)
Electric utility	4,170,800	92.9
Nonutility	320,300	7.1
Total	4,491,100	100.0

ANNUAL EARNINGS AND DIVIDENDS PER SHARE

	1994	1993	1992	1991	1990	1989	1988
Earnings Per Share	**2.81**	**3.12**	**[1] 2.66**	**2.94**	**2.92**	**2.76**	**3.01**
Dividends Per Share	**2.55**	**2.48**	**2.40**	**[2] 2.313**	**2.233**	**2.153**	**2.073**
Dividend Payout %	**90.7**	**79.5**	**90.2**	**78.7**	**76.5**	**78.0**	**68.8**

[1] Before acctg. chg. [2] 3-for-2 stk split,01/24/92

ANNUAL FINANCIAL DATA

	1994	1993	1992	1991	1990	1989	1988
RECORD OF EARNINGS (IN MILLIONS):							
Total Revenues	4,491.1	4,433.9	3,791.1	3,785.7	3,532.5	3,699.9	3,344.1
Depreciation & Amort	610.7	593.9	560.0	553.2	423.4	468.2	497.7
Maintenance	263.2	279.5	280.6	304.6	281.2	299.3	275.0
Prov for Fed Inc Taxes	171.0	210.2	203.6	210.7	196.1	165.8	124.3
Operating Income	1,038.2	1,127.3	1,029.2	1,095.0	1,050.1	1,039.7	972.2
Net Income	478.2	516.6	[1] 428.9	459.9	445.7	410.7	438.4
Aver. Shs. Outstg. (000)	170,300	165,700	161,100	156,500	152,550	148,800	145,500
[1] Before acctg. change cr$15,600,000.							
BALANCE SHEET (IN MILLIONS):							
Gross Plant	15,415.4	15,009.0	14,416.8	13,580.1	12,845.4	12,282.5	11,441.8
Accumulated Depreciation	5,170.0	4,802.1	4,724.9	4,302.4	3,886.5	3,549.5	3,223.9
Prop, Plant & Equip, Net	10,245.4	10,206.9	9,691.9	9,277.7	8,958.9	8,733.0	8,217.9
Long-term Debt	4,710.6	4,750.5	4,404.1	4,393.3	4,395.6	4,540.6	4,176.6
Net Stockholders' Equity	5,402.2	5,253.9	4,960.5	4,612.9	4,381.7	4,202.9	3,959.9
Total Assets	13,562.2	13,349.5	12,615.1	11,201.4	10,990.9	11,033.5	10,282.3
Year End Shs Outstg (000)	172,405	168,123	163,843	158,851	154,789	150,900	147,150
STATISTICAL RECORD:							
Book Value Per Share	26.60	26.38	25.21	24.41	23.41	22.67	21.91
Op. Inc/Net Pl %	10.1	11.0	10.6	11.8	11.7	11.9	11.8
Dep/Gr. Pl %	3.5	3.4	3.1	3.3	3.3	3.8	4.3
Accum. Dep/Gr. Pl %	33.5	32.0	32.8	31.7	30.3	28.9	28.2
Return on Equity %	9.2	10.3	9.1	10.6	10.9	10.6	12.1
Average Yield %	6.4	5.7	6.4	6.8	7.4	7.3	7.1
P/E Ratio	16.1-12.4	15.9-12.3	15.4-12.8	13.0-10.2	11.2-9.5	11.5-9.7	10.5-9.1
Price Range	45⅜-34⅞	49½-38¼	41-34⅛	38⅛-29⅞	32⅝-27⅝	31⅞-26⅞	31½-27¼

Statistics are as originally reported.

OFFICERS:
T.E. Capps, Chmn. & C.E.O.
T.L. Baucom, Pres. & C.O.O.
L.R. Robertson, S.V.P., C.F.O., Treas. & Sec.

INCORPORATED: VA, Feb., 1983

PRINCIPAL OFFICE: 901 East Byrd St., Richmond, VA 23219-6532

TELEPHONE NUMBER: (804) 775-5700
FAX: (804) 775-5819
NO. OF EMPLOYEES: 12,057
ANNUAL MEETING: In April
SHAREHOLDERS: 235,062
INSTITUTIONAL HOLDINGS:
No. of Institutions: 390
Shares Held: 64,357,373

REGISTRAR(S): Mellon Financial Securities, New York, NY

TRANSFER AGENT(S): Mellon Financial Securities, New York, NY

NYS SYMBOL DNY
Rec. Pr. 35⅜

DONNELLEY (R. R.) & SONS CO.

YIELD 1.8%
P/E RATIO 20.2

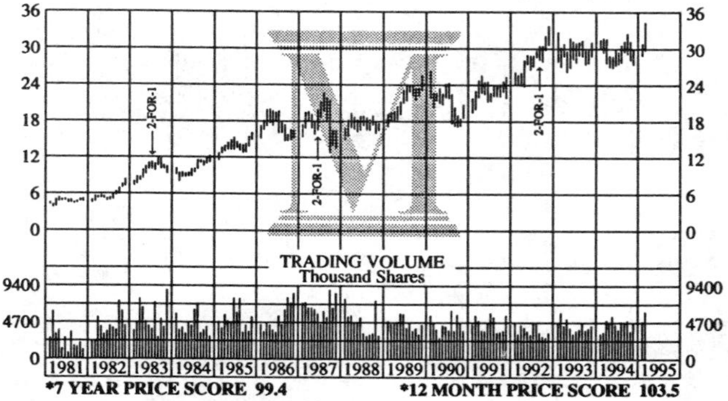

36
30
24
18
12
6
0
2-FOR-1
2-FOR-1
2-FOR-1
TRADING VOLUME
Thousand Shares
9400
4700
0
1981 1982 1983 1984 1985 1986 1987 1988 1989 1990 1991 1992 1993 1994 1995

*7 YEAR PRICE SCORE 99.4 *12 MONTH PRICE SCORE 103.5

*NYSE COMPOSITE INDEX=100

INTERIM EARNINGS (Per Share):

Qtr.	Mar.	June	Sept.	Dec.
1991	0.19	0.28	0.41	0.44
1992	0.23	0.34	0.47	0.47
1993	d0.14	0.34	0.45	0.51
1994	0.28	0.38	0.52	0.57

INTERIM DIVIDENDS (Per Share):

Amt.	Decl.	Ex.	Rec.	Pay.
0.14Q	1/27/94	2/1/94	2/7/94	3/1/94
0.14Q	4/28	5/5	5/11	6/1
0.16Q	7/28	8/8	8/12	9/1
0.16Q	10/27	11/4	11/11	12/1
0.16Q	1/26/95	1/31/95	2/6/95	3/1/95

*Indicated div.: $0.64**

CAPITALIZATION (12/31/94):

	($000)	(%)
Long-Term Debt	1,212,332	34.9
Deferred Income Tax	286,904	8.2
Common & Surplus	1,978,369	56.9
Total	3,477,605	100.0

DIVIDEND ACHIEVER STATUS:
Rank: 193 1984-94 Growth Rate: 9.1%
Total Years of Dividend Growth: 25

RECENT DEVELOPMENTS: For the year ended 12/31/94, net income was $268.6 million compared with $178.9 million in the prior year. Net sales rose 11% to $4.89 billion from $4.39 billion a year ago. The sales growth reflected higher volumes, increased services for new customers, and more new products and services. International sales grew 30% from 1993 levels and now account for 11% of net sales. In 1994, the Company invested about $546.0 million to expand and upgrade its operations.

PROSPECTS: Results will continue to reflect investments over the past few years in technology, product development and a worldwide network to serve local and global customers. Strong growth in international sales is expected for 1995 as a result of new operations in Europe, Asia and Latin America, including a 51% interest in the Chilean-based independent printer Lord Cochrane. Capacity expansions are planned at several existing plants due to major new long-term contracts.

BUSINESS

R.R. DONNELLEY & SONS COMPANY provides printing and related services to publishers of magazines and books, as well as merchandisers, the telephone industry, financial institutions and other firms requiring substantial amounts of printing. The Company is the largest supplier of commercial printing services in the U.S. and produces catalogs and tabloids, magazines, books, directories and financial printing. Services provided to customers are presswork and binding, along with all pre-press operations necessary to create a printing image, and planning for truck, rail and air distribution of the printed product.

BUSINESS LINE ANALYSIS

(12/31/94)	Rev(%)	Inc(%)
Domestic	88.7	99.2
Foreign	11.3	0.8
Total	100.0	100.0

ANNUAL EARNINGS AND DIVIDENDS PER SHARE

	1994	1993	1992	1991	1990	1989	1988
Earnings Per Share	1.75	1.16	1.51	1.32	1.45	1.42	1.32
Dividends Per Share	0.60	0.54	[1] 0.51	0.50	0.48	0.44	0.39
Dividend Payout %	34.3	46.6	33.8	37.9	33.0	30.9	29.5

[1] 2-for-1 stk split,09/01/92

ANNUAL FINANCIAL DATA

	1994	1993	1992	1991	1990	1989	1988
RECORD OF EARNINGS (IN MILLIONS):							
Total Revenues	4,888.8	4,387.8	4,193.1	3,914.8	3,497.9	3,122.3	2,878.4
Costs and Expenses	4,115.9	3,787.4	3,529.4	3,310.5	2,941.9	2,622.5	2,403.5
Depreciation & Amort	313.5	274.8	258.2	241.2	194.3	167.1	161.8
Earnings From Operations	459.4	325.6	405.5	363.1	361.8	332.7	313.1
Earn Bef Income Taxes	395.0	276.6	361.0	320.2	360.2	352.2	317.1
Income Taxes	126.4	97.6	126.4	115.3	134.4	130.3	111.8
Net Income	268.6	109.4	234.7	204.9	225.8	221.9	205.3
Aver. Shs. Outstg. (000)	153,900	154,600	155,400	155,340	155,456	155,674	155,422
BALANCE SHEET (IN MILLIONS):							
Cash and Cash Equivalents	20.6	10.7	12.3	54.6	79.7	52.2	54.9
Receivables, Net	987.5	825.2	791.9	689.4	685.9	526.1	517.4
Inventories	311.2	243.7	198.0	160.4	159.2	159.4	157.8
Gross Property	3,708.8	3,361.3	3,022.9	2,854.1	2,643.1	2,233.6	2,028.5
Accumulated Depreciation	1,852.1	1,686.8	1,490.7	1,307.4	1,158.8	1,023.5	902.7
Long-Term Debt	1,212.3	673.4	522.6	527.5	647.1	62.6	121.0
Net Stockholders' Equity	1,978.4	1,844.0	1,849.0	1,730.4	1,595.6	1,445.8	1,296.4
Total Assets	4,452.1	3,654.0	3,410.2	3,403.8	3,343.1	2,507.3	2,346.3
Total Current Assets	1,353.3	1,109.9	1,021.6	1,003.3	1,011.4	750.9	709.5
Total Current Liabilities	801.9	685.4	611.7	913.6	860.3	780.6	716.6
Net Working Capital	551.5	424.5	409.9	89.7	151.1	d29.7	d7.1
Year End Shs Outstg (000)	153,085	154,158	155,029	155,350	154,930	155,806	155,370
STATISTICAL RECORD:							
Operating Profit Margin %	9.4	7.4	9.7	9.3	10.3	10.7	10.9
Book Value Per Share	7.13	8.76	9.03	8.24	7.31	7.72	6.81
Return on Equity %	13.6	9.7	12.7	11.8	14.2	15.3	15.8
Return on Assets %	6.0	4.9	6.9	6.0	6.8	8.8	8.8
Average Yield %	2.0	1.8	1.8	2.2	2.2	2.1	2.3
P/E Ratio	18.6-15.4	28.2-22.5	22.4-15.7	19.4-14.8	18.2-11.8	18.0-12.1	14.7-11.4
Price Range	32½-26⅞	32¾-26⅛	33¾-23¾	25⅝-19½	26⅜-17⅛	25⅝-17⅛	19⅜-15

Statistics are as originally reported.

OFFICERS:
J.R. Walter, Chmn. & C.E.O.
F.R. Jarc, Exec. V.P. & C.F.O.
R.G. Eidell, Sr. V.P. & Treas.
D.M. Regan, V.P. & Sec.

INCORPORATED: DE, May, 1956

PRINCIPAL OFFICE: 77 West Wacker Drive, Chicago, IL 60601-1696

TELEPHONE NUMBER: (312) 326-8000

FAX: (312) 326-8557

NO. OF EMPLOYEES: 36,500 (approx.)

ANNUAL MEETING: In March

SHAREHOLDERS: 10,900 (approx.)

INSTITUTIONAL HOLDINGS:
No. of Institutions: 436
Shares Held: 113,121,831

REGISTRAR(S): First Chicago Trust Co. of New York, New York, NY 10008

TRANSFER AGENT(S): First Chicago Trust Co. of New York, New York, NY 10008

DOVER CORP.

YIELD 1.6%
P/E RATIO 18.8

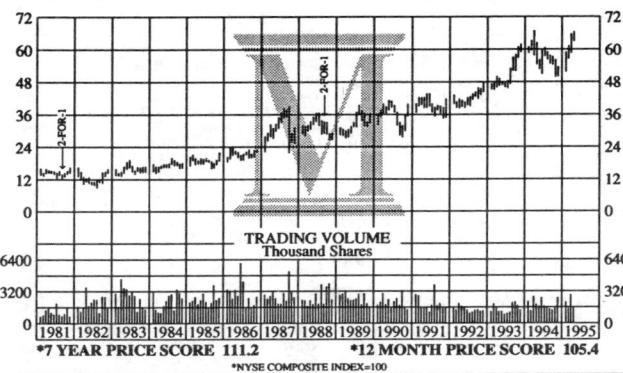

INTERIM EARNINGS (Per Share):

Qtr.	Mar.	June	Sept.	Dec.
1991	0.49	0.58	0.55	0.53
1992	0.51	0.54	0.58	0.60
1993	0.59	0.70	0.74	0.74
1994	0.74	0.92	0.91	0.97

INTERIM DIVIDENDS (Per Share):

Amt.	Decl.	Ex.	Rec.	Pay.
0.23Q	5/6/94	5/23/94	5/27/94	6/15/94
0.26Q	8/4	8/24	8/30	9/15
0.26Q	11/4	11/21	11/28	12/15
0.26Q	2/3/95	2/22/95	2/28/95	3/15/95
0.26Q	5/2	5/22	5/27	6/15

Indicated div.: $1.04

CAPITALIZATION (12/31/94):

	($000)	(%)
Long-Term Debt	253,587	20.3
Deferred Income Tax	2,545	0.2
Common & Surplus	995,859	79.5
Total	1,251,991	100.0

DIVIDEND ACHIEVER STATUS:

Rank: 179   1984-94 Growth Rate: 9.7%
Total Years of Dividend Growth: 39

RECENT DEVELOPMENTS: For the year ended 12/31/94, net income increased 27.9% to $202.4 million compared with $158.3 million a year ago. Sales rose 24.2% to $3.09 billion. Prior-year earnings included a nonrecurring charge of $4.5 million. Four of Dover's five operating segments achieved earnings growth. However, the elevator segment experienced significant declines. Dover completed ten acquisitions for an aggregate investment of $188 million in 1994.

PROSPECTS: Earnings will be enhanced by the ten companies acquired in 1994. Strong backlogs and incoming orders will also have a favorable effect on results. Barring any unforeseen events, DOV will continue to post strong gains. Although the Company did not make any acquisitions in the fourth quarter, aggressive pursuit of suitable acquisitions is anticipated. Volume growth and productivity gains should significantly enhance operating results at Dover Industries.

BUSINESS

DOVER CORP. groups products and services into the following five segments: Dover Resources Inc. includes oilfield operations, domestic oil and gas drilling, Logic Controls and compressor valves for air conditioners and refrigerators. Dover Elevators International involves the manufacture, sale, installation, and servicing of elevators. Dover Technologies include automatic electronic circuitry assembly equipment, component insertion machines, microwave, and R.F. filters. Dover Industries encompasses rotary lifts, food services, and engineered machinery. Dover Diversified includes heat exchangers, bearings, pressure vessels, metals and fabrics, and marine products.

BUSINESS LINE ANALYSIS

(12/31/94)	Rev(%)	Inc(%)
Dover Elevator Intl....	25.7	13.0
Dover Resources	17.0	23.7
Dover Diversified......	15.3	19.0
Dover Industries	22.4	22.9
Dover Technologies ..	19.5	21.5
Total	100.0	100.0

ANNUAL EARNINGS AND DIVIDENDS PER SHARE

	1994	1993	1992	1991	1990	1989	1988
Earnings Per Share	3.54	2.77	2.23	2.15	2.55	2.28	2.22
Dividends Per Share	0.98	0.90	①0.86	0.82	0.76	0.70	②0.62
Dividend Payout %	27.7	32.5	38.6	38.1	29.8	30.7	27.9

① Bef acctg chge ② 2-for-1 stk split, 9/88

ANNUAL FINANCIAL DATA

RECORD OF EARNINGS (IN MILLIONS):

Total Revenues	3,085.3	2,483.9	2,271.6	2,195.8	2,210.3	2,120.4	1,953.8
Costs and Expenses	2,664.1	2,153.1	1,990.9	1,947.1	1,879.5	1,806.1	1,650.2
Depreciation & Amort	95.8	77.0	77.5	85.4	77.5	78.8	73.8
Operating Profit	325.4	253.9	203.2	163.3	253.3	235.5	229.8
Earn Bef Taxes on Income	306.9	245.5	200.3	204.1	244.1	227.0	224.8
Income Taxes	104.5	87.3	71.2	75.9	88.4	83.0	79.0
Net Income	202.4	158.3	①129.1	128.2	155.7	144.0	145.8
Aver. Shs. Outstg. (000)	56,730	57,110	57,988	59,750	61,169	63,250	65,726

① Before acctg. change cr$564,000.

BALANCE SHEET (IN MILLIONS):

Cash and Cash Equivalents	144.9	96.3	101.2	127.4	152.4	175.8	84.5
Receivables, Net	576.6	475.2	389.3	368.0	389.3	389.2	363.8
Inventories	364.6	294.3	250.2	227.3	246.3	236.5	272.4
Gross Property	812.2	714.6	678.1	649.1	636.0	598.5	553.7
Accumulated Depreciation	469.5	431.3	426.9	397.9	367.6	326.4	285.6
Long-Term Debt	253.6	252.1	1.2	6.3	21.0	26.7	27.8
Net Stockholders' Equity	995.9	870.0	804.9	828.4	787.7	746.8	741.1
Total Assets	2,070.6	1,773.7	1,426.1	1,356.6	1,468.4	1,406.4	1,365.6
Total Current Assets	1,133.1	903.6	774.9	756.4	814.7	823.1	738.8
Total Current Liabilities	772.2	595.8	572.3	475.5	608.0	577.3	540.8
Net Working Capital	360.9	307.8	201.6	280.9	206.7	245.8	198.0
Year End Shs Outstg (000)	56,730	57,163	57,085	58,958	59,971	62,243	65,208

STATISTICAL RECORD:

Operating Profit Margin %	10.5	10.2	8.9	7.4	11.5	11.1	11.8
Book Value Per Share	7.42	5.68	7.81	8.96	7.37	7.51	6.69
Return on Equity %	20.3	18.2	16.0	15.5	19.8	19.3	19.7
Return on Assets %	9.8	8.9	9.1	9.5	10.6	10.2	10.7
Average Yield %	1.7	1.7	2.0	2.1	2.2	2.1	2.0
P/E Ratio	18.9-14.1	22.3-16.2	21.4-17.2	20.3-16.0	16.2-10.8	17.3-12.0	16.5-12.0
Price Range	66⅞-49¾	61⅞-45	47⅝-38¼	43¾-34½	41¼-27½	39½-27¼	36⅝-26⅝

Statistics are as originally reported.

OFFICERS:

G.L. Roubos, Chairman
T.L. Reece, Pres. & C.E.O.
J.F. McNiff, V.P.-Fin.
R.G. Kuhbach, V.P., Gen. Coun. & Sec.

INCORPORATED: DE, 1947

PRINCIPAL OFFICE: 280 Park Avenue, New York, NY 10017-1292

TELEPHONE NUMBER: (212) 922-1640

FAX: (212) 922-1656

NO. OF EMPLOYEES: 22,992

ANNUAL MEETING: In April

SHAREHOLDERS: 10,000 (approx.)

INSTITUTIONAL HOLDINGS:
No. of Institutions: 284
Shares Held: 35,829,714

REGISTRAR(S): Harris Trust Co. of N.Y., New York, NY 10005

TRANSFER AGENT(S): Harris Trust Co. of N.Y., New York, NY 10005

NYS SYMBOL DUK
Rec. Pr. 39⅜

DUKE POWER CO.

YIELD 5.0%
P/E RATIO 13.7

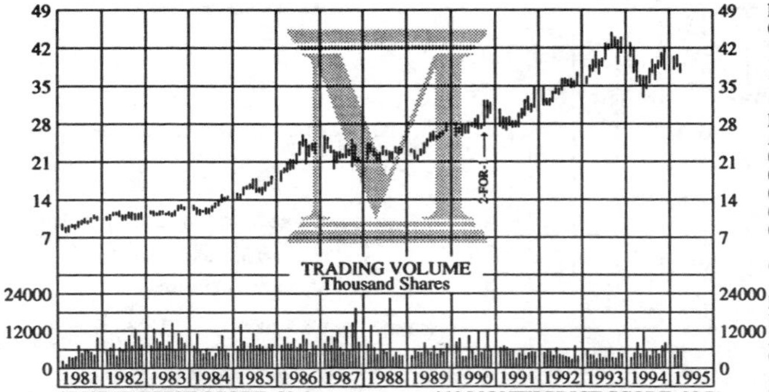

49
42
35
28
21
14
7
2-FOR-1
TRADING VOLUME
Thousand Shares
24000
12000
0
1981 1982 1983 1984 1985 1986 1987 1988 1989 1990 1991 1992 1993 1994 1995

*7 YEAR PRICE SCORE 99.6 *12 MONTH PRICE SCORE 98.7

*NYSE COMPOSITE INDEX=100

INTERIM EARNINGS (Per Share):

Qtr.	Mar.	June	Sept.	Dec.
1991	0.61	0.61	0.96	0.42
1992	0.45	0.36	0.85	0.55
1993	0.63	0.53	1.12	0.52
1994	0.79	0.56	1.13	0.40

INTERIM DIVIDENDS (Per Share):

Amt.	Decl.	Ex.	Rec.	Pay.
0.47Q	1/25/94	2/7/94	2/11/94	3/16/94
0.47Q	4/28	5/9	5/13	6/16
0.49Q	7/25	8/8	8/12	9/16
0.49Q	10/25	11/14	11/18	12/16
0.49Q	1/31/95	2/13/95	2/17/95	3/16/95

*Indicated div.: $1.96**

CAPITALIZATION (12/31/94):

	($000)	(%)
Long-Term Debt	3,567,122	31.0
Deferred Income Tax	2,621,225	22.8
Preferred Stock	779,500	6.8
Common & Surplus	4,532,829	39.4
Total	11,500,676	100.0
Current Debt	93,759	

DIVIDEND ACHIEVER STATUS:
Rank: 284 1984-94 Growth Rate: 9.7%
Total Years of Dividend Growth: 19

RECENT DEVELOPMENTS: For the quarter ended 12/31/94, net income was $93.5 million compared with $120.9 million for the corresponding period of 1993. Revenues were down slightly at $976.4 million from $996.9 million last year. For the twelve months ended 12/31/94, net income was $638.9 million compared with $626.4 million last year. Revenues were relatively flat at $4.28 billion. Electric sales were down 0.7% due to lower residential sales.

PROSPECTS: Operating efficiencies, through the reduction of approximately 1,300 employees and other cost-saving measures, will push earnings growth higher and allow the Company to recoup write-offs taken in 1994. Meanwhile, DUK's non-regulated subsidiaries will allow the Company to earn a higher rate of return on equity. Capital expenditures will increase due to the replacement of steam generators, as well as the construction of a turbine station.

BUSINESS

DUKE POWER provides electricity to 1.7 million people in a 20,000 square-mile service area in the central portion of North Carolina and western portion of South Carolina. DUK's three nuclear generating stations, eight coal-fired stations and 38 hydro-electric stations produced 86 billion kilowatt-hours of electricity in 1994. Duke Power also owns Nantahala Power and Light Co. which serves a five county area in western North Carolina. About 70% of kilowatt-hour sales are derived from North Carolina and 30% from South Carolina. In 1994, nuclear accounted for 60% of generation, coal 38%, hydro and other 2%.

QUARTERLY DATA

(12/31/94) ($000)	Rev	Inc
1st Quarter	1,099,002	173,617
2nd Quarter	1,083,310	128,002
3rd Quarter	1,272,525	243,741
4th Quarter	1,034,076	93,516

ANNUAL EARNINGS AND DIVIDENDS PER SHARE

	1994	1993	1992	1991	1990	1989	1988
Earnings Per Share	**2.88**	**2.80**	**2.21**	**2.60**	**2.40**	**2.57**	**[2] 1.95**
Dividends Per Share	**1.92**	**1.84**	**1.76**	**1.68**	**[1] 1.60**	**1.52**	**1.44**
Dividend Payout %	**66.7**	**65.7**	**79.6**	**64.6**	**66.7**	**59.3**	**73.8**

[1] 2-for-1 stk split, 9/28/90. [2] Before acctg. chg.

ANNUAL FINANCIAL DATA

	1994	1993	1992	1991	1990	1989	1988
RECORD OF EARNINGS (IN MILLIONS):							
Total Revenues	4,488.9	4,281.9	3,961.5	3,817.0	3,681.5	3,639.3	3,627.0
Depreciation & Amort	647.5	664.4	668.5	619.8	405.8	410.9	417.5
Maintenance	...	375.5	403.2	354.7	403.8	348.9	383.3
Income Taxes	397.0	403.0	289.6	293.5	265.7	307.6	272.2
Operating Income	1,179.8	814.1	724.7	706.8	642.8	704.6	629.6
Interest Expense	158.3	241.7	286.1	223.4	172.2	173.5	175.0
Net Income	638.9	626.4	508.1	583.6	538.2	571.6	[1] 448.1
Aver. Shs. Outstg. (000)	204,859	204,859	204,819	203,431	202,570	202,554	202,533
[1] Before acctg. change cr$102,255,000.							
BALANCE SHEET (IN MILLIONS):							
Gross Plant	14,791.5	1,499.7	2,998.9	2,694.2	3,582.0	3,094.7	2,682.5
Accumulated Depreciation	5,225.6	4,837.4	6,071.3	5,638.0	5,167.1	4,771.9	4,323.9
Prop, Plant & Equip, Net	9,565.9	d3,337.7	d3,072.4	d2,943.8	d1,585.1	d1,677.2	d1,641.4
Long-term Debt	3,567.1	3,579.7	3,288.0	3,217.9	3,156.7	2,870.9	2,855.9
Net Stockholders' Equity	5,312.3	5,118.7	4,930.1	4,796.9	4,558.8	4,331.8	4,127.9
Total Assets	12,862.2	d379.9	d1,197.2	d1,359.6	d141.4	d196.6	d231.4
Year End Shs Outstg (000)	204,859	300,000	204,859	204,700	202,584	202,563	202,544
STATISTICAL RECORD:							
Book Value Per Share	22.13	14.46	20.26	19.86	18.84	18.05	17.01
Op. Inc/Net Pl %	12.3	9.1	8.7	8.6	7.6	8.9	8.5
Dep/Gr. Pl %	3.1	32.6	16.4	16.0	11.3	13.3	15.6
Accum. Dep/Gr. Pl %	35.3	322.6	202.4	209.3	144.3	154.2	161.2
Return on Equity %	12.7	12.9	10.9	12.8	12.5	14.0	11.6
Average Yield %	5.1	4.6	5.1	5.4	5.5	6.1	6.3
P/E Ratio	14.9-11.4	16.0-12.6	17.0-14.2	13.5-10.3	13.5-10.6	11.0-8.3	12.6-10.8
Price Range	43-32⅞	44⅞-35⅜	37½-31⅜	35-26¾	32⅜-25½	28¼-21⅜	24½-21⅛

Statistics are as originally reported.

OFFICERS:
W.H. Grigg, Chmn. & C.E.O.
S.C. Griffith, Jr., Vice-Chmn. & Gen. Coun.
R.B. Priory, Pres. & C.O.O.
R.J. Osborne, Sr. V.P. & C.F.O.

INCORPORATED: NC, Jun., 1964

PRINCIPAL OFFICE: 422 S Church St, Charlotte, NC 28242-0001

TELEPHONE NUMBER: (704) 594-0887
FAX: (704) 373-8038
NO. OF EMPLOYEES: 17,052
ANNUAL MEETING: In April
SHAREHOLDERS: 129,637 (common)
INSTITUTIONAL HOLDINGS:
No. of Institutions: 431
Shares Held: 102,540,475

REGISTRAR(S): First Union National Bank of N.C., Charlotte, NC

TRANSFER AGENT(S): At Company's Office

NYS SYMBOL DNB
Rec. Pr. 52¼

DUN & BRADSTREET CORP.

YIELD 5.1%
P/E RATIO 14.1

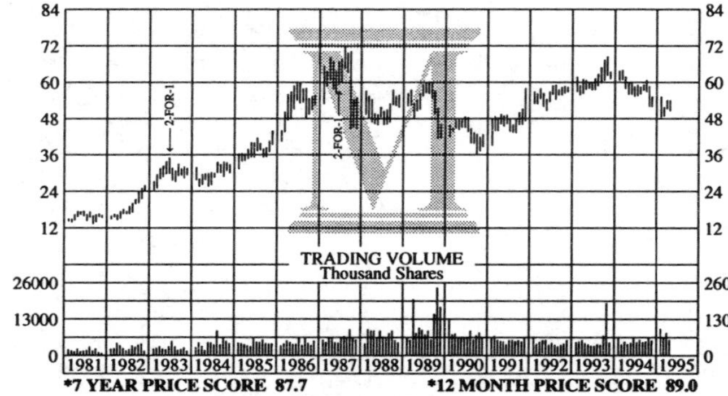

*7 YEAR PRICE SCORE 87.7 *12 MONTH PRICE SCORE 89.0

*NYSE COMPOSITE INDEX=100

INTERIM EARNINGS (Per Share):

Qtr.	Mar.	June	Sept.	Dec.
1991	0.54	0.65	0.80	0.86
1992	0.55	0.72	0.84	0.99
1993	0.59	0.78	0.89	0.15
1994	0.64	0.85	0.98	1.23

INTERIM DIVIDENDS (Per Share):

Amt.	Decl.	Ex.	Rec.	Pay.
0.65Q	4/20/94	5/16/94	5/20/94	6/10/94
0.65Q	7/20	8/15	8/19	9/9
0.65Q	10/19	11/14	11/18	12/9
0.65Q	1/18/95	2/13/95	2/17/95	3/10/95
0.66Q	4/19	5/15	5/19	6/9

Indicated div.: $2.64

CAPITALIZATION (12/31/94):

	($000)	(%)
Common & Surplus	1,318,600	100.0
Total	1,318,600	100.0

DIVIDEND ACHIEVER STATUS:
Rank: 139 1984-94 Growth Rate: 11.0%
Total Years of Dividend Growth: 43

RECENT DEVELOPMENTS: For the quarter ended 12/31/94, net income was $209.5 million compared with $192.9 million a year ago, excluding a restructuring charge of $166.7 million after-tax in the fourth quarter of 1993. Operating revenues rose 6.7% to $1.41 billion from $1.32 billion for the corresponding quarter in 1993. DNB reported operating income of $301.2 million versus $269.2 million a year ago, excluding the restructuring charge.

PROSPECTS: Note: Moody's Investors Service is a wholly-owned subsidiary of The Dun & Bradstreet Corporation. Consequently, no evaluations or projections are made.

BUSINESS

THE DUN & BRADSTREET CORPORATION serves its customers through five business segments: Marketing Information Services, with 1994 revenue (operating income) contribution of 42% (27%), served by IMS International, Nielsen Marketing Research, and Nielsen Media Research. Risk Management and Business Marketing Information Services, 33% (43%), served by D&B Information Services, Moody's Investors Service, and Interactive Data. Software Services, 8% (0%), served by D&B Software, Sales Technologies, and Erisco. Directory Information Services, 9% (21%), served by Reuben H. Donnelley. Other Business Services, 8% (9%), served by Gartner Group, NCH Promotional Services, and Dataquest.

ANNUAL EARNINGS AND DIVIDENDS PER SHARE

	1994	1993	1992	1991	1990	1989	1988
Earnings Per Share	**3.70**	**2.42**	**3.10**	**2.85**	**2.80**	**3.14**	**2.67**
Dividends Per Share	**2.56**	**2.40**	**2.25**	**2.15**	**2.09**	**1.935**	**1.68**
Dividend Payout %	**69.2**	**99.2**	**72.6**	**75.4**	**74.6**	**61.6**	**62.9**

ANNUAL FINANCIAL DATA

	1994	1993	1992	1991	1990	1989	1988
RECORD OF EARNINGS (IN MILLIONS):							
Total Revenues	4,895.7	4,710.4	4,750.7	4,642.8	4,817.7	4,321.8	4,267.4
Costs and Expenses	3,549.1	3,784.2	3,585.9	3,554.3	3,697.8	3,174.1	3,244.6
Depreciation & Amort	421.1	373.7	378.9	350.9	349.0	249.9	219.2
Operating Income	925.5	552.5	785.9	737.6	770.9	897.8	803.5
Inc Bef Prov for Income Taxes	879.2	588.0	795.2	730.6	751.8	914.7	790.7
Income Taxes	249.7	159.3	241.7	222.1	243.6	328.4	291.7
Net Income	629.5	[1] 428.7	553.5	508.5	508.2	586.4	499.0
Aver. Shs. Outstg. (000)	169,946	177,181	178,346	178,556	181,566	186,884	187,093
[1] Before acctg. change dr$390,600,000.							
BALANCE SHEET (IN MILLIONS):							
Cash and Cash Equivalents	362.3	668.6	539.5	310.5	337.7	759.7	1,069.5
Receivables, Net	1,430.3	1,275.3	1,164.2	1,228.7	1,209.3	1,007.9	1,278.7
Inventories	23.7	18.9	18.8	18.7	36.9	56.2	56.6
Gross Property	1,961.5	1,885.8	1,837.7	1,855.6	1,863.2	1,743.6	1,542.3
Accumulated Depreciation	1,043.0	1,024.7	972.9	901.9	828.2	762.8	683.6
Net Stockholders' Equity	1,318.6	1,111.3	2,156.0	2,161.1	2,080.1	2,184.7	2,093.2
Total Assets	5,463.9	5,170.4	4,914.9	4,777.4	4,754.4	5,184.2	5,023.8
Total Current Assets	1,981.0	2,122.4	1,930.4	1,767.4	1,785.5	2,012.6	2,716.7
Total Current Liabilities	2,186.6	2,044.1	1,644.6	1,527.1	1,676.1	1,720.5	1,919.4
Net Working Capital	d205.6	78.3	285.8	240.3	109.4	292.0	797.3
Year End Shs Outstg (000)	169,761	170,282	178,235	178,450	178,622	185,164	187,188
STATISTICAL RECORD:							
Operating Profit Margin %	18.9	11.7	16.5	15.9	16.0	20.8	18.8
Book Value Per Share	7.77	6.52	12.10	12.11	11.65	11.80	11.18
Return on Equity %	47.7	38.6	25.7	23.5	24.4	26.8	23.8
Return on Assets %	11.5	8.3	11.3	10.6	10.7	11.3	9.9
Average Yield %	4.4	3.9	4.1	4.4	4.9	3.8	3.3
P/E Ratio	17.3-14.0	28.3-23.0	19.1-16.3	20.4-13.7	17.4-12.9	19.2-13.1	21.5-17.2
Price Range	64-51⅞	68½-55¾	59⅛-50⅝	58-39⅛	48⅝-36⅛	60¼-41¼	57½-45⅞

Statistics are as originally reported.

OFFICERS:
R.E. Weissman, Chmn. & C.E.O.
E.A. Bescherer, Jr., E.V.P.-Fin. & C.F.O.
E. O'Hanrahan, Asst. V.P. & Sec.
P.C. Danford, V.P. & Treas.

INCORPORATED: DE, Feb., 1973

PRINCIPAL OFFICE: 187 Danbury Road, Wilton, CT 06897

TELEPHONE NUMBER: (203) 834-4200

NO. OF EMPLOYEES: 47,100 (approx.)

ANNUAL MEETING: In April

SHAREHOLDERS: 14,722

INSTITUTIONAL HOLDINGS:
No. of Institutions: 835
Shares Held: 131,067,993

REGISTRAR(S): First Chicago Trust Co. of N.Y., Jersey City, NJ

TRANSFER AGENT(S): First Chicago Trust Co. of N.Y., Jersey City, NJ

DU PONT (E.I.) DE NEMOURS & CO.

YIELD 3.1%
P/E RATIO 16.9

INTERIM EARNINGS (Per Share):

Qtr.	Mar.	June	Sept.	Dec.
1991	0.88	0.81	0.75	d0.36
1992	0.64	0.41	0.63	d0.25
1993	0.73	0.76	d1.01	0.35
1994	0.94	1.16	0.95	0.95

INTERIM DIVIDENDS (Per Share):

Amt.	Decl.	Ex.	Rec.	Pay.
0.44Q	4/27/94	5/9/94	5/13/94	6/11/94
0.47Q	7/27	8/9	8/15	9/12
0.47Q	10/26	11/8	11/15	12/14
0.47Q	1/25/95	2/9/95	2/15/95	3/14/95
0.52Q	4/26	5/9	5/15	6/12

*Indicated div.: $2.08**

CAPITALIZATION (12/31/94):

	($000)	(%)
Long-Term Debt	6,376,000	30.5
Deferred Income Tax	1,494,000	7.2
Minority Interest	197,000	0.9
Preferred Stock..................	237,000	1.1
Common & Surplus	12,585,000	60.3
Total	20,889,000	100.0

TRADING VOLUME
Thousand Shares

DIVIDEND ACHIEVER STATUS:
Rank: 248   1984-94 Growth Rate: 6.5%
Total Years of Dividend Growth: 12

*7 YEAR PRICE SCORE 109.0   ***12 MONTH PRICE SCORE 99.2**

*NYSE COMPOSITE INDEX=100

RECENT DEVELOPMENTS: For the year ended 12/31/94, income before extraordinary items was $2.73 billion compared with $566.0 million in the previous year. Total revenue rose to $40.28 billion from $37.84 billion in the prior year. Sales advanced by 6% to $39.33 billion from $37.10 billion in the year before. Sales in Europe benefited from the continuing economic recovery and increased by 14%. The diversified businesses segment earnings tripled to $676.0 million from $238.0 million.

PROSPECTS: Operating earnings have improved across the board, except for the Petroleum segment, as the restructuring, realigning and elimination efforts of DD are beginning to pay off. Cost reductions have improved margins as sales gain momentum. Additionally, increased demand for automotive products, engineering polymers, nylon, Lycra spandex and nonwovens will improve the bottom line. DD is on track to produce record earnings for 1995.

BUSINESS

DU PONT (E.I.) DE NEMOURS & CO. is the largest chemical company in the United States. The chemicals segment manufactures commodity and specialty products including titanium dioxide, fluorochemicals and polymer intermediates. A diversified mix of specialty fibers is produced to serve end uses such as high-strength composites in aerospace, active sportswear and packaging. Polymers consists of engineering polymers, elastomers and fluoropolymers. Petroleum operations consist of both upstream and downstream activities. Diversified businesses include agricultural products, coal, electronics, imaging systems and medical products.

BUSINESS LINE ANALYSIS

(12/31/94)	Rev(%)	Inc(%)
Chemicals	9.8	12.1
Fibers	16.9	24.4
Polymers....................	16.2	24.4
Petroleum	42.8	25.7
Diversified		
Businesses	14.3	13.4
Total	100.0	100.0

ANNUAL EARNINGS AND DIVIDENDS PER SHARE

	1994	1993	1992	1991	1990	1989	1988
Earnings Per Share	4.00	0.83	① 1.43	2.08	3.40	3.53	3.04
Dividends Per Share	1.82	1.76	② 1.74	1.68	1.62	③ 1.45	1.233
Dividend Payout %	45.5	N.M.	N.M.	80.8	47.6	41.1	40.6

① Before extraord. item & acctg. chg. ② Bef extraord item ③ 3-for-1 stk split, 1/19/90

ANNUAL FINANCIAL DATA

RECORD OF EARNINGS (IN MILLIONS):

Total Revenues	40,259.0	37,841.0	38,352.0	39,523.0	40,559.0	35,991.0	33,342.0
Costs and Expenses	32,484.0	31,621.0	33,210.0	32,876.0	33,007.0	28,514.0	26,887.0
Deprec, Depl & Amort	2,976.0	2,833.0	2,688.0	2,640.0	2,625.0	2,530.0	2,216.0
Operating Profit	6,203.0	4,880.0	4,147.0	5,907.0	6,915.0	6,764.0	6,026.0
Earn Bef Income Taxes	4,382.0	958.0	1,811.0	2,818.0	4,154.0	4,324.0	3,824.0
Income Taxes	1,655.0	392.0	1,415.0	1,415.0	1,844.0	1,844.0	1,634.0
Net Income	2,727.0	① 566.0	② 975.0	1,403.0	2,310.0	2,480.0	2,190.0
Aver. Shs. Outstg. (000)	680,000	677,000	673,000	671,000	676,000	701,000	718,000

① Before extra. item dr$11,000,000. ② Before extra. item dr$69,000,000.

BALANCE SHEET (IN MILLIONS):

Cash and Cash Equivalents	1,109.0	1,194.0	1,674.0	468.0	611.0	692.0	603.0
Receivables, Net	5,771.0	5,656.0	5,808.0	5,546.0	6,204.0	5,298.0	...
Inventories	4,586.0	4,368.0	5,141.0	5,086.0	5,716.0	5,818.0	4,467.0
Gross Property	48,838.0	47,926.0	47,235.0	44,191.0	44,819.0	40,812.0	36,879.0
Accumulated Depreciation	27,718.0	26,503.0	25,353.0	23,581.0	23,717.0	21,936.0	19,658.0
Long-Term Debt	6,376.0	6,531.0	7,193.0	6,396.0	5,583.0	4,080.0	3,158.0
Net Stockholders' Equity	12,822.0	11,230.0	11,765.0	16,739.0	16,418.0	15,799.0	15,580.0
Total Assets	37,509.0	34,479.0	36,596.0	33,722.0	34,959.0	31,986.0	23,272.0
Total Current Assets	11,725.0	11,449.0	12,968.0	11,532.0	13,056.0	12,252.0	5,423.0
Total Current Liabilities	7,565.0	9,439.0	10,226.0	7,493.0	10,023.0	9,348.0	6,696.0
Net Working Capital	4,160.0	2,010.0	2,742.0	4,039.0	3,033.0	2,904.0	d1,273.0
Year End Shs Outstg (000)	681,000	678,000	675,000	671,000	670,000	685,000	718,000

STATISTICAL RECORD:

Operating Profit Margin %	11.9	9.0	6.4	10.1	12.1	13.7	12.7
Book Value Per Share	18.15	16.21	17.08	24.59	24.15	22.72	21.37
Return on Equity %	21.3	5.0	8.3	8.4	14.1	15.7	14.1
Return on Assets %	7.3	1.6	2.7	4.2	6.6	7.8	9.4
Average Yield %	3.3	3.6	3.5	4.1	4.4	4.1	4.4
P/E Ratio	15.6-12.1	64.9-53.6	38.4-30.4	24.0-15.7	12.5-9.2	11.9-8.1	10.2-8.3
Price Range	62⅜-48¼	53⅞-44½	54⅞-43½	50-32¾	42⅜-31⅜	42⅛-28¾	31-25¼

Statistics are as originally reported.

OFFICERS:
E.S. Woolard, Jr., Chmn. & C.E.O.
C.S. Nicandros, Vice Chmn.
J.A. Krol, Vice Chmn.
INCORPORATED: DE
PRINCIPAL OFFICE: 1007 Market Street, Wilmington, DE 19898

TELEPHONE NUMBER: (302) 774-1000
NO. OF EMPLOYEES: 107,000
ANNUAL MEETING: In April
SHAREHOLDERS: 171,207
INSTITUTIONAL HOLDINGS:
No. of Institutions: 727
Shares Held: 261,684,414

REGISTRAR(S): Wilmington Trust Co., Wilmington, DE

TRANSFER AGENT(S): Company Office

EATON VANCE CORP.

YIELD 2.0%
P/E RATIO 10.4

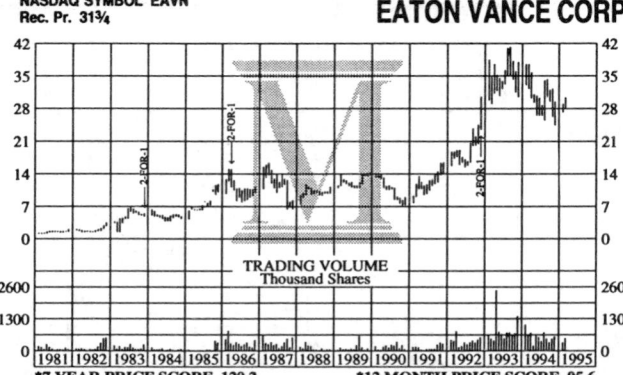

INTERIM EARNINGS (Per Share):

Qtr.	Jan.	Apr.	July	Oct.
1991-92	0.64	0.52	0.78	0.59
1992-93	0.62	0.86	1.19	0.41
1993-94	0.67	0.80	0.65	0.89
1994-95	0.70	...	...	...

INTERIM DIVIDENDS (Per Share):

Amt.	Decl.	Ex.	Rec.	Pay.
0.14Q	1/7/94	1/25/94	1/31/94	2/14/94
0.15Q	4/15	4/25	4/29	5/9
0.15Q	7/6	7/25	7/29	8/8
0.16Q	10/7	10/25	10/31	11/14
0.16Q	1/6/95	1/25/95	1/31/95	2/13/95

Indicated div.: $0.64*

CAPITALIZATION (10/31/94):

	($000)	(%)
Long-Term Debt	60,311	18.9
Deferred Income Tax	89,540	28.1
Minority Interest	3,113	1.0
Common & Surplus	165,608	52.0
Total	318,572	100.0

DIVIDEND ACHIEVER STATUS:
Rank: 18   1984-94 Growth Rate: 19.6%
Total Years of Dividend Growth: 12

*7 YEAR PRICE SCORE 129.2   ***12 MONTH PRICE SCORE 95.6**

*NYSE COMPOSITE INDEX=100

RECENT DEVELOPMENTS: For the quarter ended 1/31/95, net income was $6.4 million compared with $6.4 million, before an accounting change, for the prior-year quarter. Total revenue was $55.0 million, up 3.5% from $53.1 million for the corresponding quarter in 1994. Investment adviser and distribution fees decreased 2.9% to $40.4 million from $41.6 million for the same quarter a year earlier. Bank fee income contributed significantly to revenue growth during the quarter, by increasing 33.4% to $12.1 million from $9.1 million in the 1994 quarter. Income from real estate activities was $856,000 compared with $917,000 in 1994, a decrease of 6.7%. Total expenses grew 4.2% to $42.0 million from $40.3 million the year before. Operating income increased moderately to $13.0 million from $12.8 million a year earlier.

BUSINESS

EATON VANCE CORP. has five main lines of business: (1) management of investment companies, distribution of investment company shares, and investment counseling for individuals and institutions; (2) custodial, trust and banking services, and mutual fund custody, accounting and pricing services through a 77.3% interest in Investors Bank & Trust Company, a state-chartered and FDIC insured bank; (3) real estate investment and consulting through a wholly-owned subsidiary, Northeast Properties, Inc.; (4) the development of precious metal properties through wholly-owned Fulcrum Management, Inc. and MinVen, Inc., and (5) oil and gas activities through wholly-owned Energex Corporation and Marblehead Energy Corporation.

REVENUES

(10/31/94)	($000)	(%)
Investment Advisor Fees	85,769	39.3
Distribution Income	80,069	36.7
Bank Fee Income	42,501	19.5
Bank Net Interest Income	4,887	2.2
Income From Real Estate	3,626	1.7
Other Income	1,154	0.6
Total	218,006	100.0

ANNUAL EARNINGS AND DIVIDENDS PER SHARE

	10/31/94	10/31/93	10/31/92	10/31/91	10/31/90	10/31/89	10/31/88
Earnings Per Share	3.00	3.09	2.49	1.75	1.03	0.99	1.37
Dividends Per Share	0.60	0.49	① 0.36	0.29	0.235	0.205	0.185
Dividend Payout %	20.0	15.9	14.5	16.6	22.9	20.8	13.5

① 2-for-1 stk split, 12/8/92

ANNUAL FINANCIAL DATA

RECORD OF EARNINGS (IN THOUSANDS):

Total Revenues	218,006	189,145	152,979	119,564	94,126	64,395	46,103
Costs and Expenses	① 113,006	① 100,813	89,196	① 74,327	① 52,568	① 38,217	① 21,562
Operating Income	52,206	47,440	35,818	22,721	23,143	16,595	17,641
Income Bef Income Taxes	47,741	47,011	33,133	21,079	16,380	13,531	17,037
Income Taxes	19,255	19,670	13,826	8,361	8,706	6,207	6,634
Net Income	② 28,486	27,341	19,307	12,718	7,674	7,324	10,741
Aver. Shs. Outstg.	9,473	8,848	7,752	7,290	7,500	7,440	7,831

① Incl. Dep. ② Before acctg. change cr$1,300,000.

BALANCE SHEET (IN THOUSANDS):

Cash and Cash Equivalents	34,025	28,655	35,951	49,135	45,923	50,588	10,890
Receivables, Net	3,705	5,930	10,523	6,790	4,094	16,512	1,917
Gross Property	6,728	6,339	5,007	3,821	3,366	4,392	3,025
Long-Term Debt	60,311	73,228	78,358	63,961	50,633	62,907	14,169
Net Stockholders' Equity	165,608	145,300	77,479	59,604	47,932	43,884	37,356
Total Assets	455,506	425,547	330,293	277,795	223,987	241,773	77,395
Total Current Assets	38,963	35,975	47,818	57,208	50,844	67,674	13,222
Total Current Liabilities	131,720	123,927	108,609	104,785	85,500	100,225	7,443
Net Working Capital	d92,757	d87,952	d60,791	d47,577	d34,656	d32,551	5,779
Year End Shares Outstg	9,090	9,134	7,495	7,389	7,291	7,499	7,380

STATISTICAL RECORD:

Return on Equity %	17.2	18.8	24.9	21.3	16.0	16.7	28.8
Return on Assets %	6.3	6.4	5.9	4.6	3.4	3.0	13.9
Average Yield %	1.9	1.4	1.6	2.4	2.2	1.6	1.9
P/E Ratio	12.5-8.2	13.3-9.4	12.2-6.2	9.5-4.5	13.7-7.2	14.3-11.1	8.6-5.5
Price Range	37½-24½	41¼-29	30½-15½	16½-7¾	14-7⅜	14⅛-11	11¾-7½

Statistics are as originally reported.

OFFICERS:
L.T. Clay, Chmn.
M.D. Gardner, Pres. & C.E.O.
W.M. Steul, V.P. & Treas.
T. Otis, V.P. & Sec.

INCORPORATED: MD, May, 1959

PRINCIPAL OFFICE: 24 Federal Street, Boston, MA 02110

TELEPHONE NUMBER: (617) 482-8260

NO. OF EMPLOYEES: 385

ANNUAL MEETING: In January

SHAREHOLDERS: 1,109 (approx.)

INSTITUTIONAL HOLDINGS:
No. of Institutions: 81
Shares Held: 2,633,528

REGISTRAR(S): Bank of Boston, Boston, MA 02102

TRANSFER AGENT(S): Bank of Boston, Boston, MA 02102

EG&G, INC.

YIELD 3.3%
P/E RATIO ...

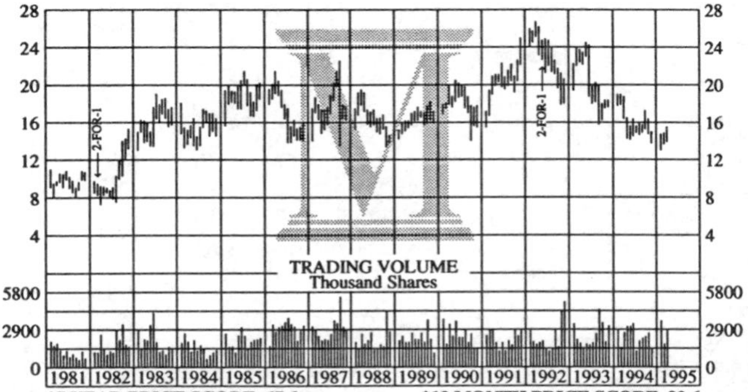

7 YEAR PRICE SCORE 67.6 **12 MONTH PRICE SCORE 92.6**
*NYSE COMPOSITE INDEX=100

INTERIM EARNINGS (Per Share):

Qtr.	Apr.	July	Oct.	Jan.
1993	0.34	0.37	0.27	0.43
1994	0.26	0.30	d1.03	d0.58

INTERIM DIVIDENDS (Per Share):

Amt.	Decl.	Ex.	Rec.	Pay.
0.14Q	5/25/94	7/18/94	7/22/94	8/10/94
0.14Q	7/27	10/17	10/21	11/10
0.14Q	10/26	1/13/95	1/20/95	2/10/95
0.14Q	1/25/95	4/17	4/21	5/10
0.14Q	2/10	2/14	2/8	2/14

Indicated div.: $0.56

CAPITALIZATION (1/1/95):

	($000)	(%)
Long-Term Debt	65,941	12.9
Common & Surplus	445,366	87.1
Total	511,307	100.0

DIVIDEND ACHIEVER STATUS:
Rank: 145   1984-94 Growth Rate: 10.8%
Total Years of Dividend Growth: 21

RECENT DEVELOPMENTS: For the year ended 1/1/95, net loss from continuing operations was $32.1 million compared with income of $54.6 million in the prior year. Year-end results included a combined charge for restructuring and goodwill allowances of $70.7 million. Sales improved to $1.33 billion from $1.32 billion in the year before. EGG's discontinued operations, its Department of Energy related-management and operations, contributed $26.5 million to net income compared with $24.9 million in the prior year.

PROSPECTS: The Company's previous restructuring charges reflect an attempt to streamline operations in the wake of a reduction in Department of Energy-related businesses. In the increasingly competitive environment, revenue growth will be limited and the emphasis will be upon maintaining strong margins. The repositioning, separation, and restructuring costs of the previous year should enable EGG to reach the cost-reduction goals required to strengthen the Company's margins.

BUSINESS

EG&G, INC. provides advanced scientific and technical products and services worldwide. The Instruments segment develops equipment for airport and industrial security and scientific instruments. The Components segment provides mechnical, optical, and electronic devices. Technical services provide vehicle and lubricant testing and support services. Components and subsystems are produced for aviation and aerospace industries. The Defense segment supports the national defense with technical products and with research, management, and field services. The Department of Energy Support segment provides site management, engineering services, precision instrument and components production.

BUSINESS LINE ANALYSIS

(01/01/95)	Rev(%)
Technical Services	46.1
Instruments	20.5
Mechanical	
Components	17.4
Optoelectronics	16.0
Total	100.0

ANNUAL EARNINGS AND DIVIDENDS PER SHARE

	1/1/95	1/2/94	1/3/93	12/29/91	12/31/90	12/31/89	12/31/88
Earnings Per Share	d0.58	1.41	1.56	1.45	1.30	1.20	1.15
Dividends Per Share	0.56	0.52	0.49	0.42	0.38	0.34	0.30
Dividend Payout %	...	36.9	31.4	28.9	29.2	28.3	26.1

ANNUAL FINANCIAL DATA

RECORD OF EARNINGS (IN MILLIONS):

	1/1/95	1/2/94	1/3/93	12/29/91	12/31/90	12/31/89	12/31/88
Total Revenues	1,332.6	2,697.9	1,320.1	2,688.5	2,474.3	1,650.2	1,406.3
Costs and Expenses	1,306.7	2,539.3	1,219.7	2,529.6	2,336.6	1,526.2	1,283.6
Depreciation & Amort	36.8	37.8	36.3	33.7	30.0	25.5	24.6
Income From Operations	d10.9	120.8	123.2	125.2	107.7	98.4	98.0
Income Bef Income Taxes	d17.1	121.9	121.1	120.4	107.2	99.8	97.4
Income Taxes	15.0	42.3	33.3	39.1	33.2	29.9	28.7
Net Income	① d32.1	② 79.6	87.8	81.2	74.0	69.9	68.7
Aver. Shs. Outstg. (000)	55,271	56,504	56,385	55,901	56,989	58,262	59,778

① Before disc. op. cr$26,452,000. ② Before acctg. change dr$20,500,000.

BALANCE SHEET (IN MILLIONS):

Cash and Cash Equivalents	66.4	72.2	69.8	63.0	34.2	28.6	41.9
Receivables, Net	226.3	237.6	261.9	249.7	235.2	237.5	201.8
Inventories	123.3	121.6	114.2	115.7	113.9	117.0	100.9
Gross Property	364.8	327.4	301.9	267.5	230.3	208.5	186.4
Accumulated Depreciation	243.1	221.3	205.8	181.6	159.8	135.4	118.0
Long-Term Debt	65.9	...	...	...	...	8.9	14.8
Net Stockholders' Equity	445.4	477.5	473.6	420.7	369.6	349.0	332.3
Total Assets	793.1	768.8	749.7	697.9	675.2	643.4	539.3
Total Current Assets	481.5	465.0	482.8	455.9	407.6	407.3	364.4
Total Current Liabilities	281.8	369.8	360.6	241.4	257.9	256.2	173.2
Net Working Capital	199.7	95.2	122.2	214.5	149.7	151.2	191.2
Year End Shs Outstg (000)	55,124	56,132	56,813	56,496	56,176	57,994	60,022

STATISTICAL RECORD:

Operating Profit Margin %	...	4.5	9.3	4.7	4.4	6.0	7.0
Book Value Per Share	5.77	5.45	5.80	5.21	3.80	3.88	4.81
Return on Equity %	...	16.7	18.5	19.3	20.0	20.0	20.7
Return on Assets %	...	10.3	11.7	11.6	11.0	10.9	12.7
Average Yield %	3.4	2.8	2.2	2.1	2.2	2.1	1.8
P/E Ratio	...	17.4-11.2	17.1-11.5	17.7-11.0	15.8-10.8	15.2-11.9	17.0-11.6
Price Range	19-13¾	24½-15¾	26¾-17⅞	25-15½	20½-14	18¼-14¼	19½-13⅜

Statistics are as originally reported.

OFFICERS:
J.M. Kucharski, Chmn., Pres. & C.E.O.
T.J. Sauser, Sr. V.P. & C.F.O.
M. Gross, V.P., General Counsel & Clerk
D.T. Heaney, Treas.

INCORPORATED: MA, Nov., 1947

PRINCIPAL OFFICE: 45 William Street, Wellesley, MA 02181

TELEPHONE NUMBER: (617) 237-5100
FAX: (617) 431-4255
NO. OF EMPLOYEES: 32,000 (approx.)
ANNUAL MEETING: In April
SHAREHOLDERS: 15,712 (approx.)
INSTITUTIONAL HOLDINGS:
No. of Institutions: 237
Shares Held: 38,976,772 (adj.)

REGISTRAR(S):

TRANSFER AGENT(S): First National Bank of Boston, Shareholder Services Division, Boston, MA

NYS SYMBOL EMR
Rec. Pr. 70⅜

EMERSON ELECTRIC CO.

YIELD 2.4%
P/E RATIO 21.9

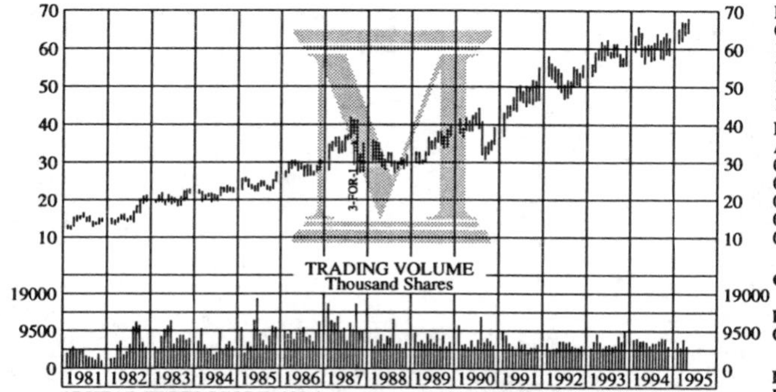

*7 YEAR PRICE SCORE 108.4 *12 MONTH PRICE SCORE 100.7

*NYSE COMPOSITE INDEX=100

INTERIM EARNINGS (Per Share):

Qtr.	Dec.	Mar.	June	Sept.
1991-92	0.68	0.75	0.78	0.75
1992-93	---------- 3.15 ----------			
1993-94	1.31	0.87	0.93	0.41
1994-95	1.01	...	...	...

INTERIM DIVIDENDS (Per Share):

Amt.	Decl.	Ex.	Rec.	Pay.
0.39Q	5/3/94	5/16/94	5/20/94	6/10/94
0.39Q	8/2	8/15	8/19	9/9
0.43Q	11/1	11/21	11/28	12/9
0.43Q	2/7/95	2/13/95	2/20/95	3/10/95
0.43Q	5/2	5/15	5/19	6/9

*Indicated div.: $1.72**

CAPITALIZATION (9/30/94):

	($000)	(%)
Long-Term Debt	279,900	6.1
Common & Surplus	4,341,800	93.9
Total	4,621,700	100.0

DIVIDEND ACHIEVER STATUS:
Rank: 236 1984-94 Growth Rate: 7.3%
Total Years of Dividend Growth: 38

RECENT DEVELOPMENTS: For the quarter ended 12/31/94, net earnings were up 14.3% to $203.4 million from $178.0 million for the prior year. Net sales rose 13.7% to $2.28 billion from $2.01 billion in 1993. All of the geographic areas that EMR serves reported double-digit sales increases for the first quarter, including strengthening European and Japanese markets. The largest sales gains for the quarter were achieved by the heating, ventilating and air conditioning businesses.

PROSPECTS: The Company's profit margins should continue to be high as EMR continues its commitments to cost reduction and productivity improvement. The international market has proved to be a growing sales area and should see continued success as the Company continues to expand and as new products gain acceptance. Improvement in the European economy and stronger consumer and capital goods orders should boost sales in the near term.

BUSINESS

EMERSON ELECTRIC COMPANY is a global manufacturer of a broad range of electrical-electronic products and systems which are sold through independent distributors and to OEMs. EMR produces instruments related to control systems and processing measurements. Commercial and industrial components and systems products include various motor-driven systems such as solid, air and gas control devices. Consumer products offer a variety of tools and accessories primarily for the residential markets, including console humidifiers, electric waste disposers, hot water dispensers, automatic dishwashers and ventilating equipment.

BUSINESS LINE ANALYSIS

(09/30/94)	Rev(%)	Inc(%)
Commercial & Industrial	57.5	44.5
Appliance & Const-Related	42.5	39.7
Corporate & Other Items		15.8
Total	100.0	100.0

ANNUAL EARNINGS AND DIVIDENDS PER SHARE

	9/30/94	9/30/93	9/30/92	9/30/91	9/30/90	9/30/89	9/30/88
Earnings Per Share	3.52	3.15	2.96	2.83	2.75	2.63	2.31
Dividends Per Share	1.60	1.47	1.395	1.335	1.275	1.155	1.03
Dividend Payout %	45.5	46.7	47.1	47.2	46.4	43.9	44.6

ANNUAL FINANCIAL DATA

	9/30/94	9/30/93	9/30/92	9/30/91	9/30/90	9/30/89	9/30/88
RECORD OF EARNINGS (IN MILLIONS):							
Total Revenues	8,607.2	8,173.8	7,706.0	7,427.0	7,573.4	7,071.3	6,651.5
Costs and Expenses	6,868.1	6,555.7	6,219.5	5,981.2	6,160.9	5,767.5	5,427.7
Depreciation & Amort	364.5	340.7	295.2	294.4	269.3	230.8	228.3
Operating Profit	3,054.2	2,884.0	2,651.4	2,585.5	2,571.6	2,408.6	2,218.6
Earnings Bef Income Tax	1,427.8	1,112.0	1,043.9	1,003.1	989.0	954.0	859.8
Income Taxes	523.4	403.9	381.0	371.2	375.8	366.0	331.0
Net Income	[1] 904.4	708.1	662.9	631.9	613.2	588.0	528.8
Aver. Shs. Outstg. (000)	224,232	225,083	224,252	223,589	223,150	223,760	229,246
[1] Before acctg. change dr$115,900,000.							
BALANCE SHEET (IN MILLIONS):							
Cash and Cash Equivalents	113.3	101.9	80.2	102.4	98.3	112.7	108.0
Receivables, Net	1,542.6	1,392.1	1,364.8	1,316.5	1,410.0	1,240.4	1,162.0
Inventories	1,392.2	1,298.3	1,278.2	1,348.6	1,391.6	1,286.0	1,334.6
Gross Property	3,840.7	3,586.6	3,252.2	2,993.8	2,793.5	2,335.3	2,168.2
Accumulated Depreciation	1,893.4	1,706.5	1,557.7	1,410.4	1,257.7	1,137.6	1,046.7
Long-Term Debt	279.9	438.0	448.0	450.2	496.2	418.9	481.4
Net Stockholders' Equity	4,341.8	3,915.1	3,729.8	3,256.9	2,989.9	3,073.4	2,820.1
Total Assets	8,215.0	7,814.5	6,627.0	6,364.4	6,376.4	5,408.0	5,027.0
Total Current Assets	3,338.2	3,074.3	2,977.0	2,988.6	3,138.7	2,850.5	2,763.5
Total Current Liabilities	2,617.3	2,692.6	1,811.9	2,093.8	2,335.9	1,533.2	1,438.0
Net Working Capital	720.9	381.7	1,165.1	894.8	802.8	1,317.3	1,325.5
Year End Shs Outstg (000)	223,586	224,763	224,308	224,069	223,328	222,842	225,378
STATISTICAL RECORD:							
Operating Profit Margin %	16.0	15.6	15.5	15.5	15.1	15.2	15.0
Book Value Per Share	11.09	9.26	11.68	9.83	8.74	10.24	8.80
Return on Equity %	20.8	18.1	17.8	19.4	20.5	19.1	18.8
Return on Assets %	11.0	9.1	10.0	9.9	9.6	10.9	10.5
Average Yield %	2.6	2.6	2.7	2.9	3.4	3.3	3.3
P/E Ratio	18.7-15.9	19.8-16.7	19.6-15.8	19.4-13.0	16.1-11.2	15.2-11.2	15.6-11.8
Price Range	65⅞-56⅛	62⅜-52¾	58-46¾	55-36⅞	44⅜-30¾	39⅞-29½	36-27¼

Statistics are as originally reported.

OFFICERS:
C.F. Knight, Chmn. & C.E.O.
A.E. Suter, Sr. Vice-Chmn. & C.O.O.
J.J. Adorjan, Pres.
W.J. Galvin, Sr. V.P.-Fin. & C.F.O.

INCORPORATED: MO, Sep., 1890

PRINCIPAL OFFICE: 8000 W. Florissant Ave. P.O. Box 4100, St. Louis, MO 63136

TELEPHONE NUMBER: (314) 553-2000
FAX: (314) 553-3527
NO. OF EMPLOYEES: 73,900 (avg.)
ANNUAL MEETING: In February
SHAREHOLDERS: 31,800 (approx.)
INSTITUTIONAL HOLDINGS:
No. of Institutions: 743
Shares Held: 150,276,142

REGISTRAR(S): Boatmen's Trust Co., St.Louis, MO 63101

TRANSFER AGENT(S): Boatmen's Trust Co., St. Louis, MO 63101

NYS SYMBOL EGN
Rec. Pr. 23¼

ENERGEN CORP.

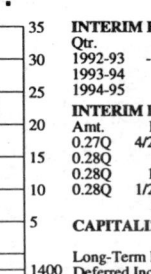

YIELD 4.8%
P/E RATIO 10.5

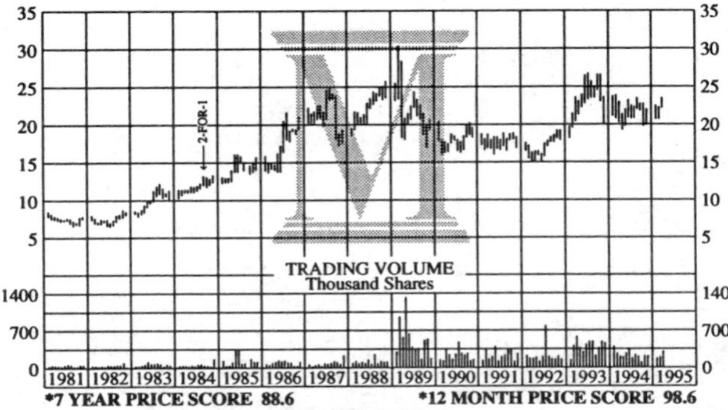

*7 YEAR PRICE SCORE 88.6 *12 MONTH PRICE SCORE 98.6

*NYSE COMPOSITE INDEX=100

INTERIM EARNINGS (Per Share):

Qtr.	Dec.	Mar.	June	Sept.
1992-93		1.77		
1993-94	0.22	2.03	0.36	d0.43
1994-95	0.25	...	...	...

INTERIM DIVIDENDS (Per Share):

Amt.	Decl.	Ex.	Rec.	Pay.
0.27Q	4/27/94	5/9/94	5/13/94	6/1/94
0.28Q	7/27	8/9	8/15	9/1
0.28Q	10/26	11/8	11/15	12/1
0.28Q	1/25/95	2/9/95	2/15/95	3/1/95

*Indicated div.: $1.12**

CAPITALIZATION (9/30/94):

	($000)	(%)
Long-Term Debt	118,302	40.6
Deferred Income Tax	6,296	2.1
Common & Surplus	167,026	57.3
Total	291,624	100.0
Current Debt	16,123	

DIVIDEND ACHIEVER STATUS:
Rank: 258 1984-94 Growth Rate: 6.2%
Total Years of Dividend Growth: 12

RECENT DEVELOPMENTS: For the three months ended 12/31/94, net income was $2.7 million versus $2.3 million for the corresponding 1993 three-month period. The increase of 17.4% was attributed to Alagasco's earning its allowed return for the full three months on an increased level of equity resulting from the prior year's underground storage working gas investment. However, results were partially offset by lower natural gas prices. Revenues declined to $73.5 million from $87.9 million, a drop of 16.4%. For the twelve months ended 12/31/94, net income from current operations was $22.2 million compared with $17.7 million for the like period of 1993. Revenues totaled $362.6 million, a modest increase from the prior year's $360.9 million.

BUSINESS

ENERGEN CORP. is a Birmingham, AL-based diversified energy holding company engaged primarily in natural gas distribution and the production and exploration of oil and gas. The Company was formed in 1978 in connection with the reorganization of its largest subsidiary, Alagasco. Alagasco was formed through the merger of Alabama Gas Company into Birmingham Gas Company.

BUSINESS LINE ANALYSIS

(9/30/94)	Rev(%)	Inc(%)
Natural Gas		
Distribution	91.4	80.4
Oil & Gas Production	5.9	15.3
Other	2.7	4.3
Total	100.0	100.0

ANNUAL EARNINGS AND DIVIDENDS PER SHARE

	9/30/94	9/30/93	9/30/92	9/30/91	9/30/90	9/30/89	9/30/88
Earnings Per Share	2.19	1.77	1.54	1.42	1.15	[1] 1.19	1.67
Dividends Per Share	1.10	1.06	1.02	0.97	0.91	[2] 0.857	0.793
Dividend Payout %	50.2	59.9	66.2	68.3	67.4	72.0	47.4

[1] Before disc. oper. [2] 3-for-2 stk split, 3/1/89

ANNUAL FINANCIAL DATA

	9/30/94	9/30/93	9/30/92	9/30/91	9/30/90	9/30/89	9/30/88
RECORD OF EARNINGS (IN THOUSANDS):							
Total Revenues	377,073	357,116	331,982	325,643	324,860	308,604	363,439
Deprec, Depl & Amort	28,000	25,289	26,274	24,053	23,018	22,427	21,103
Maintenance	9,469	9,235	9,067	8,198	8,371	6,766	8,130
Prov for Fed Inc Taxes	6,611	3,408	382	357	1,288	1,045	2,439
Operating Income	35,908	30,267	22,793	23,453	24,181	19,333	22,087
Interest Expense	11,345	10,605	10,415	9,867	9,753	7,292	7,282
Net Income	23,751	18,081	[1] 15,687	14,112	13,185	[2] 11,121	12,769
Aver. Shs. Outstg.	10,834	10,237	10,168	9,972	9,786	9,321	7,631
[1] Before acctg. change cr$941,000. [2] Before disc. op. dr$2,535,000.							
BALANCE SHEET (IN THOUSANDS):							
Gross Plant	561,561	524,139	486,799	488,052	472,997	434,503	385,811
Accumulated Depreciation	274,379	251,042	232,169	214,513	210,829	187,895	170,190
Prop, Plant & Equip, Net	287,182	273,097	254,630	273,539	262,168	246,608	215,621
Long-term Debt	118,302	85,852	90,609	77,677	82,835	86,188	53,203
Net Stockholders' Equity	167,026	140,313	131,657	123,794	122,325	115,691	91,833
Total Assets	411,314	370,685	342,119	337,516	337,943	303,301	265,968
Year End Shares Outstg	10,918	10,320	10,183	10,105	9,872	9,695	7,989
STATISTICAL RECORD:							
Book Value Per Share	15.30	13.60	12.93	12.25	12.39	11.93	11.49
Op. Inc/Net Pl %	12.5	11.1	9.0	8.6	9.2	7.8	10.2
Dep/Gr. Pl %	5.0	4.8	5.4	4.9	4.9	5.2	5.5
Accum. Dep/Gr. Pl %	48.9	47.9	47.7	44.0	44.6	43.2	44.1
Return on Equity %	14.2	12.9	11.9	11.4	10.8	9.6	13.9
Average Yield %	5.1	4.7	6.0	5.6	5.0	3.6	3.6
P/E Ratio	10.9-8.8	15.1-10.2	12.5-9.7	13.3-11.3	15.2-11.9	25.5-14.3	15.4-11.1
Price Range	23⅞-19¼	26¾-18⅛	19¼-15	18⅞-16	20½-16	30⅜-17	25¾-18½

Statistics are as originally reported.

OFFICERS:
R.J. Lysinger, Chmn. & C.E.O.
W.M. Warren, Jr., Pres. & C.O.O.
G.C. Ketcham, Exec. V.P., C.F.O. & Treas.
D.C. Reynolds, Gen. Couns. & Sec.

INCORPORATED: AL, Jan., 1979

PRINCIPAL OFFICE: 2101 Sixth Avenue North, Birmingham, AL 35203

TELEPHONE NUMBER: (205) 326-2742

FAX: (205) 322-6895

NO. OF EMPLOYEES: 1,488

ANNUAL MEETING: In January

SHAREHOLDERS: 6,118

INSTITUTIONAL HOLDINGS:
No. of Institutions: Not Available
Shares Held: Not Available

REGISTRAR(S): Harris Trust Co. of New York, New York, NY

TRANSFER AGENT(S): Harris Trust Co. of New York, New York, NY

NYS SYMBOL EI
Rec. Pr. 17¾

ENERGYNORTH, INC.

YIELD 6.3%
P/E RATIO 12.2

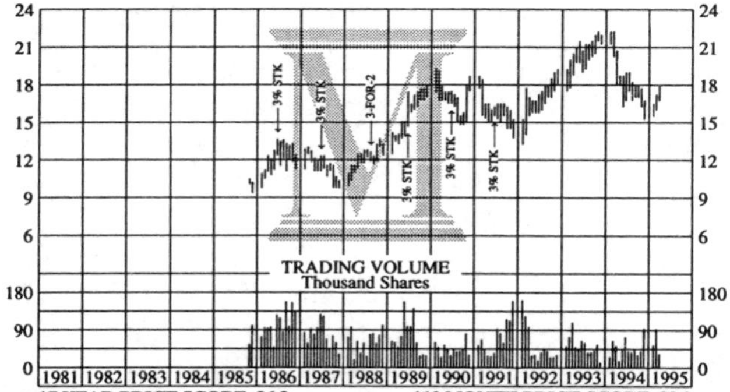

*7 YEAR PRICE SCORE 86.8 *12 MONTH PRICE SCORE 92.0

*NYSE COMPOSITE INDEX=100

INTERIM EARNINGS (Per Share):

Qtr.	Dec.	Mar.	June	Sept.
1993-94	1.04	2.34	d0.63	d1.00
1994-95	0.74	...	...	...

INTERIM DIVIDENDS (Per Share):

Amt.	Decl.	Ex.	Rec.	Pay.
0.27Q	2/2/94	2/23/94	3/1/94	3/15/94
0.27Q	4/21	5/25	6/1	6/15
0.27Q	7/21	8/26	9/1	9/15
0.28Q	10/6	11/25	12/1	12/15
0.28Q	2/1/95	2/23/95	3/1/95	3/15/95

Indicated div.: $1.12

CAPITALIZATION (9/30/94):

	($000)	(%)
Long-Term Debt	32,971	43.1
Cap. Lease Oblig.	530	0.7
Deferred Income Tax	2,151	2.8
Common & Surplus	40,778	53.4
Total	76,430	100.0
Current Debt	2,308	

DIVIDEND ACHIEVER STATUS:
Rank: 246 1984-94 Growth Rate: 6.6%
Total Years of Dividend Growth: 11

RECENT DEVELOPMENTS: For the quarter ended 12/31/94, net income was $2.3 million compared with $3.2 million in the corresponding period of 1993. Operating revenues were $22.5 million, down 13% from $25.9 million a year earlier. Temperatures for the quarter were 15% warmer than the same period in 1993 and approximately 14% warmer than normal. As a result, quarterly earnings were lower because of a 14% decrease in firm utility sendout and volumes transported. ENNI continued to experience customer growth in its utility and propane operations and successfully contained operating expenses. Utility customers rose more than 2% compared with a year earlier, while propane customers grew more than 11%. Retail propane sales volumes increased by more than 2%, resulting mostly from customer growth that was offset by warm weather. EI recently announced its listing on the NYSE.

BUSINESS

ENERGYNORTH, INC. owns all of the common stock of EnergyNorth Natural Gas, Inc. (ENGI), EnergyNorth Propane, Inc. (ENPI), and EnergyNorth Realty, Inc. ENGI is engaged in the purchase, distribution and sale of natural gas for residential, commercial and industrial use in New Hampshire. ENPI is a retailer of liquified petroleum gas and serves customers in central and southern New Hampshire. The service territory of ENGI has a population of approximately 445,000 in 27 communities situated in southern and central New Hampshire, which includes the communities of Nashua, Derry, Manchester, Concord and Laconia. The service area encompasses approximately 911 square miles. ENPI sells propane to residential, commercial and industrial customers in 87 communities primarily located within a 25 mile radius of Nashu, Derry, Manchester, Concord and Tilton.

REVENUES

(9/30/94)	($000)	(%)
Utility Gas Service	88,150	90.8
Propane Gas Sales	8,900	9.2
Total	97,050	100.0

ANNUAL EARNINGS AND DIVIDENDS PER SHARE

	9/30/94	9/30/93	9/30/92	9/30/91	9/30/90	9/30/89	9/30/88
Earnings Per Share	**1.74**	**1.74**	**1.22**	**0.27**	**1.46**	**1.39**	**1.18**
Dividends Per Share	**1.09**	**1.065**	**1.045**	**[1] 1.025**	**[2] 0.981**	**[3] 0.901**	**[4] 0.793**
Dividend Payout %	**61.2**	**85.7**	**85.7**	**N.M.**	**67.3**	**65.0**	**66.7**

[1] 3% stk div,06/25/91 [2] 3% stk div 7/90. [3] 3% stk div, 7/17/89 [4] 3-for-2 stock split, 8/22/88

ANNUAL FINANCIAL DATA

	9/30/94	9/30/93	9/30/92	9/30/91	9/30/90	9/30/89	9/30/88
RECORD OF EARNINGS (IN THOUSANDS):							
Total Revenues	97,050	86,424	80,174	72,839	79,486	72,955	62,044
Depreciation & Amort	4,854	4,555	4,497	4,394	4,216	3,838	3,469
Operating Income	8,739	7,634	7,200	6,040	7,741	7,198	6,297
Interest Expense	3,965	3,765	4,092	4,422	3,911	3,805	3,264
Net Income	5,422	5,368	3,673	738	3,995	3,622	3,031
Aver. Shs. Outstg.	3,120	3,082	3,009	2,777	2,737	2,615	2,553
BALANCE SHEET (IN THOUSANDS):							
Gross Plant	132,524	127,019	132,727	126,695	118,722	107,932	98,287
Accumulated Depreciation	38,521	35,438	37,556	34,121	30,484	27,373	24,722
Prop, Plant & Equip, Net	94,003	91,581	95,171	92,574	88,238	80,559	73,565
Long-term Debt	33,501	35,588	35,687	34,576	36,997	28,122	26,637
Net Stockholders' Equity	40,778	38,054	35,204	31,836	32,673	30,805	27,362
Total Assets	121,019	113,569	113,817	108,890	103,276	93,777	87,368
Year End Shares Outstg	3,142	3,104	3,065	2,846	2,677	2,643	2,496
STATISTICAL RECORD:							
Book Value Per Share	12.98	12.26	11.49	11.10	12.07	11.49	10.74
Op. Inc/Net Pl %	9.3	8.3	7.6	6.5	8.8	8.9	8.6
Dep/Gr. Pl %	3.7	3.6	3.4	3.5	3.6	3.6	3.5
Accum. Dep/Gr. Pl %	29.1	27.9	28.3	26.9	25.7	25.4	25.2
Return on Equity %	13.3	14.1	10.4	2.3	12.4	11.9	11.3
Average Yield %	5.8	5.4	6.4	6.3	5.7	5.9	6.7
P/E Ratio	12.8-8.8	12.8-10.1	15.8-10.9	69.4-50.9	13.3-10.1	12.9-9.0	11.7-8.4
Price Range	22¼-15¼	22¼-17½	19¼-13¼	18¾-13¾	19⅜-14¾	17⅞-12½	13¾-9⅞

Statistics are as originally reported.

OFFICERS:
E.T. Borer, Chmn.
R.R. Giordano, Pres. & C.E.O.
M.J. Mancini, Jr., Sr. V.P. & C.F.O.
R.A. Samuels, Sec.

INCORPORATED: NH, May, 1982

PRINCIPAL OFFICE: 1260 Elm St. P.O. Box 329, Manchester, NH 03105

TELEPHONE NUMBER: (603) 625-4000

FAX: (603) 624-6864

NO. OF EMPLOYEES: 281 (full-time)

ANNUAL MEETING: In February

SHAREHOLDERS: 2,500 (approx.)

INSTITUTIONAL HOLDINGS:
No. of Institutions: 28
Shares Held: 627,999

REGISTRAR(S):

TRANSFER AGENT(S): State Street Bank & Trust Co., Boston, MA 02266

ENGELHARD CORP.

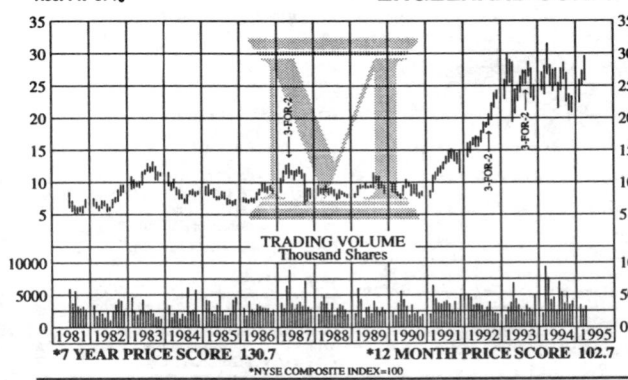

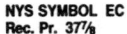

TRADING VOLUME
Thousand Shares

| 1981 | 1982 | 1983 | 1984 | 1985 | 1986 | 1987 | 1988 | 1989 | 1990 | 1991 | 1992 | 1993 | 1994 | 1995 |

*7 YEAR PRICE SCORE 130.7   *12 MONTH PRICE SCORE 102.7
*NYSE COMPOSITE INDEX=100

INTERIM EARNINGS (Per Share):

Qtr.	Mar.	June	Sept.	Dec.
1991	0.21	0.23	0.21	0.23
1992	0.22	0.25	0.24	0.29
1993	0.23	0.29	0.29	d0.64
1994	0.24	0.33	0.31	0.35

INTERIM DIVIDENDS (Per Share):

Amt.	Decl.	Ex.	Rec.	Pay.
0.11Q	3/3/94	3/8/94	3/14/94	3/31/94
0.11Q	6/2	6/8	6/14	6/30
0.12Q	9/1	9/7	9/13	9/30
0.12Q	11/3	12/7	12/13	12/30
0.12Q	3/2/95	3/8/95	3/14/95	3/31/95

Indicated div.: $0.48

CAPITALIZATION (12/31/94):

	($000)	(%)
Long-Term Debt	111,762	15.4
Common & Surplus	614,735	84.6
Total	726,497	100.0

DIVIDEND ACHIEVER STATUS:

Rank: 289   1984-94 Growth Rate: 4.3%
Total Years of Dividend Growth: 13

RECENT DEVELOPMENTS: For the year ended 12/30/94, net income was $118.0 million compared with net income, excluding extraordinary items, of $102.1 million in the previous year. Net sales increased by 11% to $2.39 billion from $2.15 billion in the year before. Increased volume in all core businesses, especially in the automotive and petroleum catalysts and calcined paper pigments, resulted in the boost in net revenue. Higher volume, improved efficiency, and productivity advancements helped to boost operating profit growth.

PROSPECTS: Capital expenditure increases rose by a third over the previous year's levels and should continue throughout the coming fiscal year. Recent acquisitions include a leading North American supplier of proprietary thermal spray coating technology and a petroleum catalyst business in Germany. However, such growth will increase interest expenses due to recent boosts in U.S. interest rates. EC will attempt to offset the increased interest and consolidation expenses by implementing productivity and efficiency improvements.

BUSINESS

ENGELHARD CORP. is a provider of specialty chemical products, engineered materials and precious metals management services. The catalysts and chemicals segment manufactures catalysts, chemical products and process technologies for the petroleum refining, chemical, pharmaceutical, and automotive industries. The pigments and additives segment manufactures coatings and extender pigments for the paper industry and pigments and additives for the paint, coatings, and plastics industries. The engineered materials and precious metals management segment manufactures fabricated metallurgical products and engineered materials and is engaged in precious metals refining, dealing, and management.

BUSINESS LINE ANALYSIS

(12/31/94)	Rev(%)	Inc($000)
United States	65.8	164,700
Foreign	34.2	41,000
Total	100.0	205,700

ANNUAL EARNINGS AND DIVIDENDS PER SHARE

	1994	1993	1992	1991	1990	1989	1988
Earnings Per Share	1.23	0.17	② 1.00	0.87	0.70	d0.77	0.63
Dividends Per Share	0.46	① 0.42	0.329	0.329	0.302	0.249	0.24
Dividend Payout %	37.4	N.M.	37.7	37.8	43.3	...	38.0

① 3-for-2 stk split,09/93 ② Before acctg. chg. ③ 3-for-2 stk. split, 9/92

ANNUAL FINANCIAL DATA

RECORD OF EARNINGS (IN MILLIONS):

	1994	1993	1992	1991	1990	1989	1988
Total Revenues	2,385.8	2,150.9	2,399.7	2,436.4	2,942.2	2,403.0	2,350.7
Costs and Expenses	2,138.1	2,087.3	2,183.3	2,224.3	2,749.9	2,474.0	2,196.9
Deprec, Depl & Amort	69.1	68.2	73.8	77.8	74.4	68.8	56.7
Earnings From Operations	178.6	d4.6	142.6	134.2	117.8	d139.9	97.1
Earn Bef Income Taxes	157.3	d4.7	133.9	117.6	93.7	d126.5	87.2
Income Taxes	39.3	cr21.4	33.7	29.6	23.4	cr49.0	23.4
Net Income	118.0	① 16.7	② 100.1	87.9	70.3	d77.5	63.7
Aver. Shs. Outstg. (000)	96,067	96,792	100,287	101,129	100,580	101,100	100,905

① Before acctg. change dr$16,000,000. ② Before acctg. change dr$89,509,000.

BALANCE SHEET (IN MILLIONS):

	1994	1993	1992	1991	1990	1989	1988
Cash and Cash Equivalents	26.4	25.6	31.3	36.2	46.9	41.0	49.1
Receivables, Net	265.6	230.6	257.3	302.5	315.9	327.1	325.4
Inventories	243.4	216.3	241.4	230.2	249.8	278.7	275.7
Gross Property	① 540.4	1,171.0	1,115.6	1,079.8	1,068.2	1,020.5	1,012.5
Accumulated Depreciation	...	676.6	624.5	569.8	528.1	468.8	405.5
Long-Term Debt	111.8	112.2	113.9	114.5	119.4	220.1	221.3
Net Stockholders' Equity	614.7	531.3	647.2	756.6	709.8	636.9	760.4
Total Assets	1,440.8	1,279.1	1,279.5	1,256.1	1,320.0	1,339.6	1,413.2
Total Current Assets	573.6	516.6	568.7	575.6	618.1	653.0	657.0
Total Current Liabilities	548.7	462.7	366.2	378.2	482.3	475.0	354.6
Net Working Capital	24.9	53.8	202.5	197.5	135.8	178.0	302.4
Year End Shs Outstg (000)	95,098	95,946	98,528	100,879	100,221	100,308	100,616

① Net

STATISTICAL RECORD:

	1994	1993	1992	1991	1990	1989	1988
Operating Profit Margin %	7.5	...	5.9	5.5	4.0	...	4.1
Book Value Per Share	6.46	5.54	6.57	7.50	7.08	6.35	7.56
Return on Equity %	19.2	3.1	15.5	11.6	9.9	...	8.4
Return on Assets %	8.2	1.3	7.8	7.0	5.3	...	4.5
Average Yield %	1.8	1.7	1.3	2.9	3.4	2.6	2.8
P/E Ratio	25.6-17.0	N.M.	24.4-13.9	17.5-8.6	15.0-10.7	...	15.3-11.5
Price Range	31½-20⅞	29⅞-19¾	24⅜-13⅛	15¼-7½	10½-7½	11½-7⅝	9⅝-7¼

Statistics are as originally reported.

OFFICERS:
O.R. Smith, Chmn. & C.E.O.
L.D. LaTorre, Pres. & C.O.O.
R.L. Guyett, Sr. V.P. & C.F.O.

INCORPORATED: DE, Nov., 1938

PRINCIPAL OFFICE: 101 Wood Avenue, Iselin, NJ 08830

TELEPHONE NUMBER: (908) 205-5000

NO. OF EMPLOYEES: 5,800 (approx.)

ANNUAL MEETING: In May

SHAREHOLDERS: 8,772

INSTITUTIONAL HOLDINGS:
No. of Institutions: 172
Shares Held: 22,984,665

REGISTRAR(S): Mellon Securities Trust Co., Ridgefield, NJ

TRANSFER AGENT(S): Mellon Securities Trust Co., Ridgefield, NJ

ENNIS BUSINESS FORMS, INC.

YIELD 4.6%
P/E RATIO 10.3

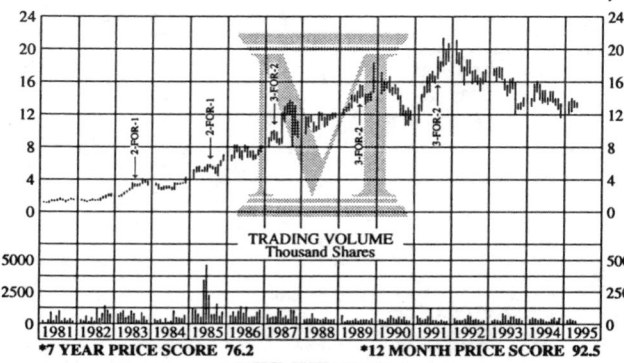

TRADING VOLUME
Thousand Shares

*7 YEAR PRICE SCORE 76.2   *12 MONTH PRICE SCORE 92.5
*NYSE COMPOSITE INDEX=100

INTERIM EARNINGS (Per Share):

Qtr.	May	Aug.	Nov.	Feb.
1991-92	0.25	0.29	0.27	0.34
1992-93	---------------- 1.18 ----------------			
1993-94	0.27	0.27	0.29	0.33
1994-95	0.30	0.30	0.29	0.33

INTERIM DIVIDENDS (Per Share):

Amt.	Decl.	Ex.	Rec.	Pay.
0.14Q	3/28/94	4/11/94	4/15/94	5/2/94
0.145Q	6/16	7/11	7/15	8/1
0.145Q	9/14	10/7	10/14	11/1
0.145Q	12/14	1/9/95	1/16/95	2/1/95
0.145Q	3/31/95	4/7	4/14	5/1

Indicated div.: $0.58

CAPITALIZATION (2/28/95):

	($000)	(%)
Long-Term Debt	360	0.5
Common & Surplus	69,338	99.5
Total	69,698	100.0

DIVIDEND ACHIEVER STATUS:
Rank: 11   1984-94 Growth Rate: 22.6%
Total Years of Dividend Growth: 18

RECENT DEVELOPMENTS: For the year ended 2/28/95, net income was $20.0 million compared with $19.5 million the year before. Sales advanced to $140.1 million from $132.9 million a year ago. Most of the sales increase was from two business forms customers and Connolly Tool, which had a stronger year than in fiscal 1994. Business from smaller customers also improved. Gross margin fell, primarily because of higher raw material costs. Selling, general and administrative expenses totaled $22.9 million, up from $21.5 million in the prior year.

PROSPECTS: EBF will undertake efforts to expand its share of the business-forms industry. However, the industry is in a long-term decline and a reversal in this trend is not anticipated. If Ennis is to achieve significant growth in the future, diversification of its business will be necessary. Healthy cash flows and an extremely small amount of long-term debt will facilitate efforts to expand or acquire new companies. Recent acquisitions have contributed to gains in operating results but substantial contributions to future growth appears unlikely.

BUSINESS

ENNIS BUSINESS FORMS, INC. prints and constructs a broad line of business forms for national distribution. About 92% of the business products manufactured are custom and semi-custom, constructed a variety of sizes, colors, number of parts and quantities on an individual job basis depending upon the customers' specifications. Connolly Tool & Machine Co., a subsidiary, designs and manufacturers tools, dies and special machinery for customers located primarily in the Southwestern part of the U.S. Ennis also offers presentation folders manufactured by its Admore, Inc. subsidiary. The Company operates thirteen manufacturing locations in twelve states.

ANNUAL EARNINGS AND DIVIDENDS PER SHARE

	2/28/95	2/28/94	2/28/93	2/29/92	2/28/91	2/28/90	2/28/89
Earnings Per Share	1.22	1.16	1.18	[1] 1.14	1.12	1.05	0.92
Dividends Per Share	0.575	0.55	0.51	0.47	[2] 0.41	0.32	0.22
Dividend Payout %	47.1	47.4	46.6	43.2	41.2	36.7	30.5

[1] Before disc. oper. & acctg. chg.   [2] 3-for-2 stk split, 7/03/89

ANNUAL FINANCIAL DATA

RECORD OF EARNINGS (IN THOUSANDS):

Total Revenues	140,097	132,945	129,279	131,810	126,164	129,606	128,170
Costs and Expenses	109,468	98,155	92,847	95,264	91,124	94,992	96,339
Depreciation & Amort	3,657	4,107	4,392	4,800	3,694	3,486	3,372
Earnings From Operations	30,629	30,563	31,789	31,402	30,926	30,588	27,856
Earns Fr Cont Opers Bef Inc Taxes	32,041	31,039	32,276	32,303	32,776	32,669	29,287
Income Taxes	12,025	11,582	11,584	11,536	11,676	11,642	10,448
Net Income	20,016	19,457	[1] 20,692	[2] 20,767	21,100	21,027	18,839
Aver. Shs. Outstg.	16,440	16,718	17,558	18,244	18,858	19,910	20,411

[1] Before disc. op. cr$560,000.   [2] Before disc. op. dr$1,051,000.

BALANCE SHEET (IN THOUSANDS):

Cash and Cash Equivalents	10,541	21,577	22,597	25,077	25,513	26,389	16,018
Receivables, Net	18,284	15,106	15,653	16,106	15,496	16,688	16,880
Inventories	10,301	8,760	7,901	7,216	8,081	9,810	11,420
Gross Property	67,924	66,102	64,258	65,482	57,624	54,463	52,092
Accumulated Depreciation	48,403	46,896	43,735	41,811	37,379	34,024	31,586
Long-Term Debt	360	435	505	2,396	3,163	4,172	5,843
Net Stockholders' Equity	69,338	58,897	60,565	66,485	55,830	60,737	52,954
Total Assets	84,991	74,499	75,923	81,244	73,208	79,192	73,826
Total Current Assets	59,265	48,519	48,928	51,035	50,927	55,527	46,797
Total Current Liabilities	12,976	12,548	12,087	9,631	10,203	10,074	10,080
Net Working Capital	46,289	35,971	36,841	41,404	40,724	45,453	36,717
Year End Shares Outstg	16,440	16,437	17,199	18,235	18,300	19,591	19,877

STATISTICAL RECORD:

Operating Profit Margin %	21.9	23.0	24.6	23.8	24.5	23.6	21.7
Book Value Per Share	4.22	3.31	3.28	3.41	3.05	3.10	2.66
Return on Equity %	28.9	33.0	34.2	31.2	37.8	34.6	35.6
Return on Assets %	23.6	26.1	27.3	25.6	28.8	26.6	25.5
Average Yield %	4.1	3.7	2.9	3.2	3.4	2.7	2.9
P/E Ratio	13.2-9.5	15.4-10.3	17.9-12.6	18.8-9.5	15.3-9.5	17.5-11.3	13.5-10.3
Price Range	16½-11⅝	17⅞-12	21⅛-14⅞	21⅜-10⅞	17½-10⅝	18⅜-11⅞	12⅜-9½

Statistics are as originally reported.

OFFICERS:
K.A. McCrady, Chmn. & C.E.O.
C.F. Ray, Pres. & C.O.O.
H. Cathey, V.P.-Fin. & Sec.
V. DiTommaso, Treas.
INCORPORATED: TX, Dec., 1909
PRINCIPAL OFFICE: 107 North Sherman Street, Ennis, TX 75119

TELEPHONE NUMBER: (214) 875-6581
FAX: (214) 875-4915
NO. OF EMPLOYEES: N.A.
ANNUAL MEETING: In June
SHAREHOLDERS: 2,005
INSTITUTIONAL HOLDINGS:
No. of Institutions: 99
Shares Held: 9,090,695

REGISTRAR(S): Society National Bank, Cleveland, OH

TRANSFER AGENT(S): Society National Bank, Cleveland, OH

NYS SYMBOL XON
Rec. Pr. 68½

EXXON CORP.

YIELD 4.4%
P/E RATIO 16.8

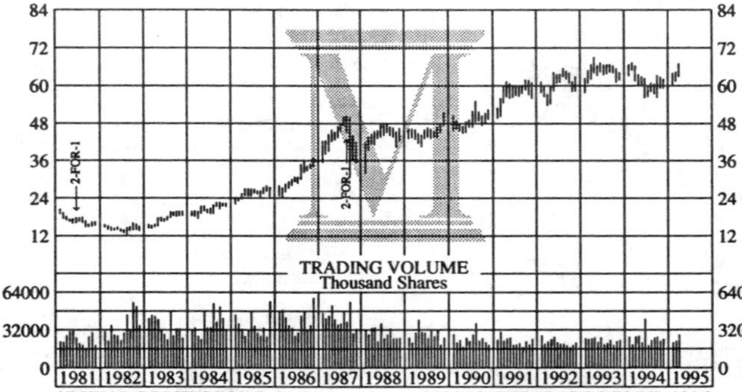

84
72
60
48
36
24
12
2-FOR-1
2-FOR-1
TRADING VOLUME
Thousand Shares
64000
32000
0
1981 1982 1983 1984 1985 1986 1987 1988 1989 1990 1991 1992 1993 1994 1995

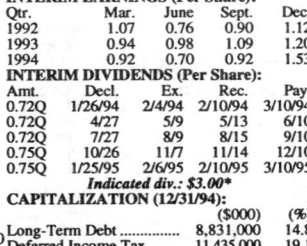

***7 YEAR PRICE SCORE 91.6** ***12 MONTH PRICE SCORE 101.0**

*NYSE COMPOSITE INDEX=100

INTERIM EARNINGS (Per Share):

Qtr.	Mar.	June	Sept.	Dec.
1992	1.07	0.76	0.90	1.12
1993	0.94	0.98	1.09	1.20
1994	0.92	0.70	0.92	1.53

INTERIM DIVIDENDS (Per Share):

Amt.	Decl.	Ex.	Rec.	Pay.
0.72Q	1/26/94	2/4/94	2/10/94	3/10/94
0.72Q	4/27	5/9	5/13	6/10
0.72Q	7/27	8/9	8/15	9/10
0.75Q	10/26	11/7	11/14	12/10
0.75Q	1/25/95	2/6/95	2/10/95	3/10/95

Indicated div.: $3.00*

CAPITALIZATION (12/31/94):

	($000)	(%)
Long-Term Debt	8,831,000	14.8
Deferred Income Tax	11,435,000	19.1
Minority Interest	2,168,000	3.6
Preferred Stock	554,000	0.9
Common & Surplus	36,861,000	61.6
Total	59,849,000	100.0

DIVIDEND ACHIEVER STATUS:
Rank: 269 1984-94 Growth Rate: 5.7%
Total Years of Dividend Growth: 12

RECENT DEVELOPMENTS: For the year ended 12/31/94, net income was $5.10 billion compared with $5.28 billion in 1993. Revenues moved up 2% to $113.41 billion. Results in 1994 included $489.0 million of special credits while 1993 included $676.0 million of such credits. XON reported that liquids production, refinery throughput, and sales of natural gas, pertroleum products, chemicals, coal and copper were all above the 1993 levels. Worldwide liquids production of 1,709 kbd was up from 1,667 kbd in 1993, primarily due to record production from the North Sea.

PROSPECTS: Crude production is on the rise as a result of new developments in the North Sea and Alaska; however, earnings continue to be hampered by the depressed world crude oil market. The possibility of further compensatory and punitive damage awards relating to the grounding of the Exxon Valdez remains a concern. Meanwhile, major expansion efforts are being initiated in the Asia-Pacific region which should provide a foundation for revenue growth.

BUSINESS

EXXON CORP.'S principal business is energy, involving exploration for and production of crude oil and natural gas, manufacturing of petroleum products, transportation and sale of crude oil, natural gas and petroleum products, and exploration for and mining and sale of coal. Exxon Chemical is a major manufacturer and marketer of petrochemicals. Exxon is also engaged in exploration for and mining of minerals in addition to coal. Exxon conducts extensive research programs in support of these businesses. Exxon owns 70% of Imperial Oil.

BUSINESS LINE ANALYSIS

(12/31/94)	Rev(%)	Inc(%)
United States	20.9	30.6
Other Western Hemisphere	15.5	7.3
Eastern Hemisphere	64.5	62.6
Other/Eliminations	-0.9	-0.5
Total	100.0	100.0

ANNUAL EARNINGS AND DIVIDENDS PER SHARE

	1994	1993	1992	1991	1990	1989	1988
Earnings Per Share	**4.07**	**4.21**	**[1] 3.82**	**4.45**	**3.96**	**[1] 2.32**	**3.95**
Dividends Per Share	**2.91**	**2.88**	**[2] 2.83**	**2.68**	**2.47**	**2.30**	**2.15**
Dividend Payout %	**71.5**	**68.4**	**74.1**	**60.2**	**62.4**	**99.1**	**54.4**

[1] Before acctg. chg. [2] Bef acctg chge

ANNUAL FINANCIAL DATA

	1994	1993	1992	1991	1990	1989	1988
RECORD OF EARNINGS (IN MILLIONS):							
Total Revenues	113,904.0	111,211.0	117,106.0	116,492.0	116,940.0	96,285.0	88,563.0
Costs and Expenses	100,079.0	97,344.0	103,744.0	102,173.0	101,643.0	82,207.0	74,175.0
Depreciation & Depletion	5,015.0	4,884.0	5,044.0	4,824.0	5,545.0	5,002.0	4,790.0
Operating Profit	9,476.0	9,631.0	9,126.0	10,409.0	10,709.0	9,948.0	10,577.0
Income Bef Income Taxes	7,804.0	8,052.0	7,287.0	8,518.0	...	...	...
Income Taxes	2,704.0	2,772.0	2,477.0	2,918.0	3,170.0	2,028.0	3,124.0
Net Income	5,100.0	5,280.0	[1] 4,810.0	5,600.0	5,010.0	[2] 2,975.0	5,260.0
Aver. Shs. Outstg. (000)	1,242,000	1,242,000	1,242,000	1,244,000	1,248,000	1,412,000	1,333,000

[1] Before acctg. change dr$40,000,000. [2] Before acctg. change cr$535,000,000.

	1994	1993	1992	1991	1990	1989	1988
BALANCE SHEET (IN MILLIONS):							
Cash and Cash Equivalents	1,775.0	1,652.0	1,515.0	1,587.0	1,379.0	2,016.0	2,409.0
Receivables, Net	8,073.0	6,860.0	8,079.0	8,540.0	9,574.0	7,787.0	6,094.0
Inventories	5,541.0	5,472.0	5,807.0	6,081.0	6,386.0	5,622.0	5,151.0
Gross Property	116,326.0	111,135.0	110,738.0	112,440.0	107,599.0	99,556.0	89,723.0
Accumulated Depreciation	52,901.0	49,173.0	48,939.0	48,576.0	44,911.0	39,131.0	35,664.0
Long-Term Debt	8,831.0	8,506.0	8,637.0	8,582.0	7,687.0	9,275.0	4,689.0
Net Stockholders' Equity	37,415.0	34,792.0	33,776.0	34,927.0	33,055.0	30,244.0	31,767.0
Total Assets	87,862.0	84,145.0	85,030.0	87,560.0	87,707.0	83,219.0	74,293.0
Total Current Assets	16,460.0	14,859.0	16,424.0	17,012.0	18,336.0	16,576.0	14,846.0
Total Current Liabilities	19,493.0	18,590.0	19,663.0	20,854.0	24,025.0	21,984.0	17,479.0
Net Working Capital	d3,033.0	d3,731.0	d3,239.0	d3,842.0	d5,689.0	d5,408.0	d2,633.0
Year End Shs Outstg (000)	1,242,000	1,242,000	1,242,000	1,242,000	1,245,000	1,250,000	1,289,000
STATISTICAL RECORD:							
Operating Profit Margin %	7.7	8.1	7.1	8.2	8.3	9.4	10.8
Book Value Per Share	29.68	27.48	26.57	27.42	25.78	23.39	24.64
Return on Equity %	13.6	15.2	14.2	16.0	15.2	9.8	16.6
Return on Assets %	5.8	6.3	5.7	6.4	5.7	3.6	7.1
Average Yield %	4.7	4.5	4.7	4.8	4.9	5.0	5.4
P/E Ratio	16.6-13.8	16.4-13.7	17.1-14.1	13.9-11.2	13.9-11.3	22.3-17.5	12.1-8.1
Price Range	67⅜-56⅛	69-57¾	65½-53¾	61⅞-49⅝	55⅛-44⅞	51⅝-40½	47¾-32

Statistics are as originally reported.

OFFICERS:
L.R. Raymond, Chmn. & C.E.O.
C.R. Sitter, Pres.
E.A. Robinson, V.P. & Treas.

INCORPORATED: NJ, Aug., 1882

PRINCIPAL OFFICE: 225 E. John W. Carpenter Freeway, Irving, TX 75062-2298

TELEPHONE NUMBER: (214) 444-1000

NO. OF EMPLOYEES: 86,000

ANNUAL MEETING: In April

SHAREHOLDERS: 606,579

INSTITUTIONAL HOLDINGS:
No. of Institutions: 927
Shares Held: 475,150,613

REGISTRAR(S):

TRANSFER AGENT(S):

FAMILY DOLLAR STORES, INC.

YIELD 3.1%
P/E RATIO 11.5

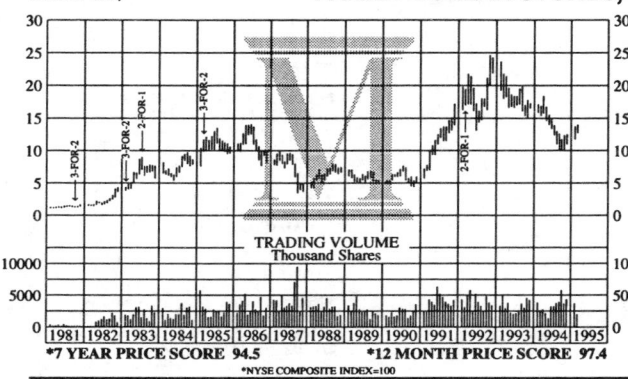

TRADING VOLUME
Thousand Shares

1981 | 1982 | 1983 | 1984 | 1985 | 1986 | 1987 | 1988 | 1989 | 1990 | 1991 | 1992 | 1993 | 1994 | 1995

*7 YEAR PRICE SCORE 94.5   *12 MONTH PRICE SCORE 97.4
*NYSE COMPOSITE INDEX=100

INTERIM EARNINGS (Per Share):

Qtr.	Nov.	Feb.	May	Aug.
1991-92	0.21	0.32	0.27	0.20
1992-93	0.25	0.37	0.31	0.22
1993-94	0.27	0.39	0.31	0.13
1994-95	0.28	…	…	…

INTERIM DIVIDENDS (Per Share):

Amt.	Decl.	Ex.	Rec.	Pay.
0.085Q	1/20/94	3/9/94	3/15/94	4/15/94
0.085Q	5/13	6/9	6/15	7/15
0.085Q	8/16	9/9	9/15	10/14
0.085Q	11/10	12/9	12/15	1/16/95
0.10Q	1/19/95	3/9/95	3/15/95	4/14

Indicated div.: $0.40

CAPITALIZATION (8/31/94):

	($000)	(%)
Deferred Income Tax	17,017	4.4
Common & Surplus	370,172	95.6
Total	387,189	100.0

DIVIDEND ACHIEVER STATUS:
Rank: 23   1984-94 Growth Rate: 18.8%
Total Years of Dividend Growth: 18

RECENT DEVELOPMENTS: For the quarter ended 2/28/95, net income was $17.0 million compared with $22.0 million in the like 1994 quarter. Sales increased to $420.9 million from $398.8 million. Sales in existing stores declined approximately 3.5%. The drop in apparel deparment sales more than offset sales increases in hardlines. The Company's decision to reduce advertising has also adversely affected sales. For the six months ended 2/28/95, net income was $32.6 million, down 11.8% from 1994.

PROSPECTS: Although FDO is in excellent financial shape and has no long-term debt, FDO will focus on improving its declining margins and supporting its price-reduction program by trimming expenditures in areas such as advertising. The elimination of six annual advertising circulars will initially hurt sales, but as customers become more aware of FDO's shift from a promotional-price format to an everyday low-price format, sales should improve.

BUSINESS

FAMILY DOLLAR STORES, INC. operated 2,345 discount stores as of 2/28/95. The stores are located in a contiguous 34-state area ranging as far northwest as Wisconsin, northeast to New Hampshire, southeast to Florida and southwest to Texas. The stores' relatively small size, generally 6,000 to 8,000 square feet, gives FDO flexibility to open them in various markets from small rural towns to large urban centers. The stores are located in strip shopping centers or as freestanding buildings convenient to FDO's low and middle income customer base. The merchandise is sold in a no-frills, low overhead, self-service environment on a cash and carry basis. Most merchandise is priced at $17.99 or less.

QUARTERLY DATA

(08/31/94)	Rev	Inc
1st Quarter	335,092	16,089
2nd Quarter	398,768	22,021
3rd Quarter	349,211	17,570
4th Quarter	345,369	7,419

ANNUAL EARNINGS AND DIVIDENDS PER SHARE

	8/31/94	8/31/93	8/31/92	8/31/91	8/31/90	8/31/89	8/31/88
Earnings Per Share	1.10	1.15	1.00	0.73	0.52	0.39	0.49
Dividends Per Share	0.33	0.29	① 0.25	0.215	0.195	0.175	0.155
Dividend Payout %	30.0	25.2	25.0	29.7	37.5	44.9	31.6

① 2-for-1 stk split, 2/27/92

ANNUAL FINANCIAL DATA

RECORD OF EARNINGS (IN MILLIONS):

	8/31/94	8/31/93	8/31/92	8/31/91	8/31/90	8/31/89	8/31/88
Total Revenues	1,428.4	1,297.4	1,158.7	989.3	874.4	756.9	674.7
Costs and Expenses	1,308.9	1,177.3	1,055.0	912.5	814.1	709.8	620.4
Depreciation & Amort	19.5	17.2	14.7	13.1	12.7	12.0	10.1
Operating Profit	506.3	477.7	424.9	353.2	303.8	258.9	237.2
Income Bef Income Taxes	100.1	102.9	88.9	63.7	47.6	35.1	44.2
Income Taxes	38.2	38.5	33.3	23.5	18.9	13.6	16.8
Net Income	① 62.0	64.4	55.7	40.2	28.7	21.5	27.3
Aver. Shs. Outstg. (000)	56,496	56,250	55,911	55,585	55,482	55,480	56,055

① Before acctg. change cr$1,139,153.

BALANCE SHEET (IN MILLIONS):

Cash and Cash Equivalents	9.9	5.7	1.7	25.0	4.6	0.7	7.0
Receivables, Net	17.6	12.4	12.8	7.1	4.9	2.5	…
Inventories	403.6	379.4	339.0	258.9	239.5	212.4	178.9
Gross Property	263.5	226.0	199.2	173.1	161.1	151.4	134.4
Accumulated Depreciation	111.6	95.9	82.4	69.9	59.0	47.7	36.6
Net Stockholders' Equity	370.2	323.3	271.8	227.3	197.1	179.1	167.3
Total Assets	592.8	537.4	478.0	399.3	355.1	324.0	290.7
Total Current Assets	435.9	402.5	358.7	293.7	251.7	219.0	191.6
Total Current Liabilities	205.6	196.6	188.5	157.5	143.8	131.7	112.7
Net Working Capital	230.2	205.9	170.3	136.2	107.9	87.2	78.9
Year End Shs Outstg (000)	60,039	56,352	56,038	55,760	55,486	55,481	55,478

STATISTICAL RECORD:

Operating Profit Margin %	7.0	7.9	7.7	6.4	5.4	4.6	6.5
Book Value Per Share	6.17	5.74	4.85	4.08	3.55	3.23	3.02
Return on Equity %	16.7	19.9	20.5	17.7	14.6	12.0	16.3
Return on Assets %	10.5	12.0	11.6	10.1	8.1	6.6	9.4
Average Yield %	2.3	1.5	1.3	1.9	3.2	2.9	2.5
P/E Ratio	16.7-9.1	20.5-13.2	24.6-13.1	24.0-8.0	14.7-8.7	18.3-12.5	16.3-8.7
Price Range	18⅜-10	23⅝-15⅛	24⅝-13⅛	17¼-5¾	7⅝-4½	7⅛-4⅞	8-4¼

Statistics are as originally reported.

OFFICERS:
L. Levine, Chmn. & Treas.
J.D. Reier, Pres. & C.O.O.
G.R. Mahoney, Jr., E.V.P., Sec. & Gen. Couns.

INCORPORATED: DE, Nov., 1969

PRINCIPAL OFFICE: 10401 Old Monroe Road, Matthews, NC 28105

TELEPHONE NUMBER: (704) 847-6961

NO. OF EMPLOYEES: 9,000 (full time); 7,500 (part-time).

ANNUAL MEETING: In January

SHAREHOLDERS: 3,200 (approx.)

INSTITUTIONAL HOLDINGS:
No. of Institutions: 173
Shares Held: 31,643,678

REGISTRAR(S): Chemical Bank, New York, NY

TRANSFER AGENT(S): Chemical Bank, New York, NY

FEDERAL REALTY INVESTMENT TRUST

YIELD	7.7%
P/E RATIO	30.3

7 YEAR PRICE SCORE 84.3   **12 MONTH PRICE SCORE 88.2**

*NYSE COMPOSITE INDEX=100

INTERIM EARNINGS (Per Share):

Qtr.	Mar.	June	Sept.	Dec.
1991	0.08	0.08	0.03	0.06
1992	0.08	0.07	0.07	0.08
1993	0.10	0.14	0.16	0.19
1994	0.15	0.17	0.16	0.20

INTERIM DIVIDENDS (Per Share):

Amt.	Decl.	Ex.	Rec.	Pay.
0.39Q	3/3/94	3/21/94	3/25/94	4/15/94
0.39Q	6/7	6/21	6/27	7/15
0.395Q	9/14	9/20	9/26	10/14
0.395Q	11/10	12/27	1/3/95	1/13/95
0.395Q	3/16/95	3/18/95	3/24	4/14

Indicated div.: $1.58

CAPITALIZATION (12/31/94):

	($000)	(%)
Long-Term Debt	178,070	27.0
Cap. Lease Oblig.	132,924	20.2
Minority Interest	2,274	0.4
Common & Surplus	345,155	52.4
Total	658,423	100.0

DIVIDEND ACHIEVER STATUS:
Rank: 267   1984-94 Growth Rate: 5.8%
Total Years of Dividend Growth: 27

RECENT DEVELOPMENTS: For the fiscal year ended 12/31/94, net income was $20.5 million, up 27% from income, before an extraordinary item, of $16.1 million in 1993. Funds from operations, which are defined as income before depreciation and amoritization and extraordinary items less gains on the sale of real estate, moved up 21% to $50.3 million from $41.5 million. Rental income was $128.1 million compared with $105.9 million in the prior year. Expenses increased by 19.5% to $116.9 million from $98.4 million. Rental expenses were $35.8 million or 30.6% of total expenses versus $26.5 million or 26.9% a year earlier. During 1994, FRT purchased four shopping centers totaling 469,000 square feet: Idylwood Plaza in Falls Church, VA; North Lake Commons in Lake Zurich, IL; Garden Shopping Center in Western Springs, IL and Queen Anne Plaza in Nowell, MA.

BUSINESS

FEDERAL REALTY INVESTMENT TRUST is an owner, operator and redeveloper of community and neighborhood shopping centers. The Trust is a self-administered real estate investment trust, founded in 1962, that manages, leases and supervises renovation of its properties. At 12/31/94, FRT owned 53 retail properties containing 11.3 million net rentable square feet. These properties are primarily community and neighborhood centers; however, FRT owns one apartment complex. Properties are located on the east coast between the New York metropolitan area and Richmond, VA.

REVENUES

(12/31/94)	($000)	(%)
Rental	128,133	93.0
Interest	3,933	2.9
Other Property	5,698	4.1
Total	137,764	100.0

ANNUAL EARNINGS AND DIVIDENDS PER SHARE

	1994	1993	1992	1991	1990	1989	1988
Earnings Per Share	0.67	①0.60	②0.30	③0.25	0.35	0.82	0.68
Dividends Per Share	1.565	1.545	1.525	1.49	1.42	1.36	1.23
Dividend Payout %	N.M.	N.M.	N.M.	N.M.	N.M.	N.M.	N.M.

① Before extraord. item ② Before realized gain

ANNUAL FINANCIAL DATA

RECORD OF EARNINGS (IN THOUSANDS):

	1994	1993	1992	1991	1990	1989	1988
Total Revenues	137,764	115,337	100,197	97,652	90,949	82,852	68,108
Costs and Expenses	①54,588	①41,518	33,857	32,618	30,308	28,386	22,918
Depreciation & Amort	...	...	23,033	21,922	19,091	16,174	12,121
Operating Profit	53,375	48,444	43,307	43,112	41,550	38,292	33,069
Net Income	20,466	②16,114	③9,488	④4,385	5,841	11,997	9,274
Aver. Shs. Outstg.	30,679	27,009	22,767	17,304	16,695	14,672	13,684

① Incl. Dep. ② Before extra. item cr$2,016,000. ③ Before extra. item dr$58,000. ④ Before extra. item cr$415,000.

BALANCE SHEET (IN THOUSANDS):

	1994	1993	1992	1991	1990	1989	1988
Cash and Cash Equivalents	3,995	9,635	36,316	43,387	25,064	50,118	15,431
Receivables, Net	31,979	31,442	28,256	24,442	24,919	30,941	27,168
Long-Term Debt	178,070	196,404	216,293	241,469	229,847	231,711	247,460
Capital Lease Obligations	132,924	137,308	125,619	126,393	128,016	128,535	108,870
Net Stockholders' Equity	345,155	284,199	222,878	151,480	129,346	146,114	95,668
Total Assets	753,737	690,943	603,811	563,091	551,319	564,441	475,689
Total Current Assets	55,132	60,576	80,840	82,271	63,216	93,478	51,460
Total Current Liabilities	95,314	70,548	36,396	43,879	63,390	56,281	21,158
Net Working Capital	d40,182	d9,972	44,444	38,392	d174	37,197	30,302
Year End Shares Outstg	31,609	28,018	24,718	19,687	16,716	16,642	13,529

STATISTICAL RECORD:

	1994	1993	1992	1991	1990	1989	1988
Book Value Per Share	10.92	10.14	9.02	7.69	7.74	8.78	7.07
Return on Equity %	5.9	5.7	4.3	2.9	4.5	8.2	9.7
Return on Assets %	2.7	2.3	1.6	0.8	1.1	2.1	2.0
Average Yield %	6.4	5.7	6.9	8.6	8.2	5.8	6.0
P/E Ratio	44.0-29.3	50.4-39.8	84.2-62.5	84.0-54.5	75.9-43.1	78.8-62.9	57.1-48.7
Price Range	29½-19⅝	30¼-23⅞	25¼-18¾	21-13⅝	22-12½	26-20¾	22¼-19

Statistics are as originally reported.

OFFICERS:
S.J. Guttman, Pres. & C.E.O.
M.J. Morrow, Sr., Sr. V.P. & Treas.
C.R. Mack, V.P., Sec. & Gen. Counsel

INCORPORATED: MD, 1962

PRINCIPAL OFFICE: 4800 Hampden Lane, Suite 500, Bethesda, MD 20814

TELEPHONE NUMBER: (301) 652-3360
FAX: (301) 961-9327
NO. OF EMPLOYEES: 204
ANNUAL MEETING: In May
SHAREHOLDERS: 4,549
INSTITUTIONAL HOLDINGS:
No. of Institutions: 124
Shares Held: 13,323,205

REGISTRAR(S):

TRANSFER AGENT(S): American Stock Transfer Co., 40 Wall St., 46th Floor, New York, NY 10005

NASDAQ SYMBOL FITB
Rec. Pr. 52¼

FIFTH THIRD BANCORP

YIELD 2.7%
P/E RATIO 13.8

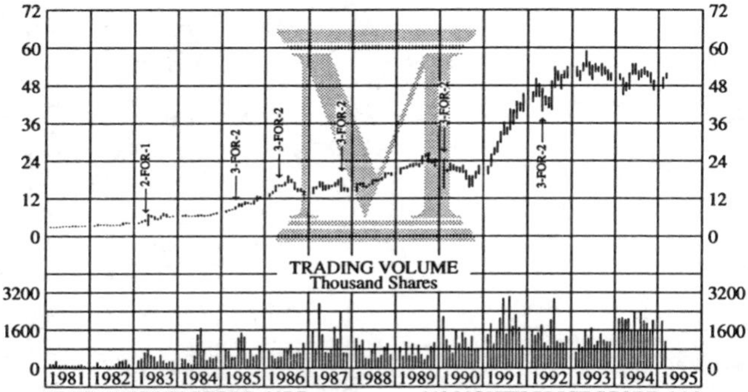

***7 YEAR PRICE SCORE 117.7** ***12 MONTH PRICE SCORE 96.8**

*NYSE COMPOSITE INDEX=100

INTERIM EARNINGS (Per Share):

Qtr.	Mar.	June	Sept.	Dec.
1991	0.52	0.58	0.61	0.62
1992	0.61	0.68	0.72	0.74
1993	0.75	0.80	0.86	0.87
1994	0.89	0.93	0.98	1.00

INTERIM DIVIDENDS (Per Share):

Amt.	Decl.	Ex.	Rec.	Pay.
0.27Q	3/15/94	3/25/94	3/31/94	4/15/94
0.31Q	6/21	6/24	6/30	7/15
0.31Q	9/20	9/26	9/30	10/14
0.31Q	12/20	12/23	12/30	1/13/95
0.35Q	3/21/95	3/27/95	3/31/95	4/14

*Indicated div.: $1.40**

CAPITALIZATION (12/31/94):

	($000)	(%)
Total Deposits	10,630,878	71.7
Total Debt	2,630,931	17.8
Common & Surplus	1,398,774	9.4
Loan Valuation Reserve	155,918	1.1
Total	14,816,501	100.0

DIVIDEND ACHIEVER STATUS:
Rank: 42 1984-94 Growth Rate: 15.7%
Total Years of Dividend Growth: 22

RECENT DEVELOPMENTS: For the year ended 12/31/94, FITB earned $244.5 million compared with $206.2 million earned in 1993. Return on average equity improved to 18.6% from 17.8% while the return on average assets moved up to 1.77% from 1.71%. Net interest income, benefiting from solid commercial loan and lease growth, was $516.8 million, up 9.1% from $473.5 million in 1993. Commercial leases advanced 59% over 1993. Other operating income totaled $255.9 million versus $231.2 million, trust income, service charges on deposit accounts and data processing income advanced 3.4%, 6.5% and 18.0%, respectively. Gains on securities transactions were $393,000, a sharp drop from $6.1 million a year earlier. Operating expenses were $371.5 million, up 5.3% from $352.7 million. FITB announced plans to acquire Falls Financial, Inc., the largest independent thrift in Summit County, OH, with assets of $581 million and 14 banking offices.

BUSINESS

FIFTH THIRD BANCORP is a $15.0 billion bank holding company with its primary subsidiary, the Fifth Third Bank, headquartered in Cincinnati, Ohio, providing full-service banking to individuals as well as to industry and governmental subdivisions. Fifth Third currently has 353 Banking Centers, including 81 seven-day a week locations. The Company offers the Cincinnati retail banking market a variety of services, including the Jeanie® electronic funds transfer system which consists of automated teller machines and telephone banking and features a bill payment service. The service is used by banks and savings and loans in three states. FITB also provides fiduciary services through its Trust Division. The banking services provided to industry and government include demand and time deposit accounts, certificates of deposit, and all types of loans. The Company further serves the requirements of Cincinnati commercial enterprises by offering financial counseling, freight payment, automated payroll programs, cash management, cashiering, and other computer-based services.

ANNUAL EARNINGS AND DIVIDENDS PER SHARE

	1994	1993	1992	1991	1990	1989	1988
Earnings Per Share	**3.80**	**3.28**	**2.75**	**2.33**	**2.05**	**1.86**	**1.75**
Dividends Per Share	**1.16**	**0.99**	**① 0.86**	**0.76**	**② 0.727**	**0.60**	**0.52**
Dividend Payout %	**30.5**	**30.2**	**31.3**	**32.6**	**35.5**	**32.3**	**29.8**

① 3-for-2 stk split, 4/16/92 ② 50% stk div, 1/13/90

ANNUAL FINANCIAL DATA

	1994	1993	1992	1991	1990	1989	1988
RECORD OF EARNINGS (IN MILLIONS):							
Total Interest Income	922.3	812.9	694.5	713.5	696.6	649.8	415.6
Total Interest Expense	405.5	291.0	300.3	381.3	402.9	374.7	226.8
Net Interest Income	516.8	521.9	394.2	332.2	293.6	275.1	188.8
Credit Loss Provision	35.8	44.5	65.3	55.7	39.9	36.5	26.1
Net Income	244.5	196.4	164.1	138.2	120.4	108.3	84.2
Aver. Shs. Outstg. (000)	64,387	59,952	59,632	59,201	58,847	58,263	48,222
BALANCE SHEET (IN MILLIONS):							
Cash & Due From Banks	695.0	580.9	565.9	501.2	564.2	453.4	361.2
Loans & Lse Financing, Net	10,130.5	8,675.9	7,360.1	5,716.3	5,412.0	5,083.9	3,695.4
Total Domestic Deposits	9,617.7	8,458.9	7,461.2	6,672.1	6,383.0	5,780.8	4,090.2
Total Foreign Deposits	1,013.2	169.6	70.7	15.1	2.2	2.8	3.5
Long-term Debt	178.7	282.9	254.1	12.8	13.5	12.6	12.2
Net Stockholders' Equity	1,398.8	1,197.6	1,005.2	879.5	782.7	699.3	508.6
Total Assets	14,957.0	11,966.0	10,213.3	8,826.1	7,955.8	7,143.0	5,245.8
Year End Shs Outstg (000)	64,709	61,402	59,832	59,375	59,081	58,713	49,089
STATISTICAL RECORD:							
Return on Assets %	1.63	1.64	1.61	1.57	1.51	1.52	1.60
Return on Equity %	17.50	16.40	16.30	15.70	15.40	15.50	16.50
Book Value Per Share	21.62	19.50	16.80	14.81	13.25	11.91	10.36
Average Yield %	2.3	1.8	1.8	2.3	3.7	2.6	3.0
P/E Ratio	14.5-11.8	18.0-15.1	19.6-14.5	19.5-8.4	12.0-7.3	14.2-10.6	11.6-8.1
Price Range	55-45	59-49½	54-39¾	45½-19⅝	24⅝-15	26½-19¾	20¼-14⅛

Statistics are as originally reported.

OFFICERS:
G.A. Schaefer, Jr., Pres. & C.E.O.
P.M. Brumm, Sr. V.P. & C.F.O.
M.K. Keating, Sr. V.P., Couns. & Sec.
N.E. Arnold, Treas.

INCORPORATED: OH, 1974

PRINCIPAL OFFICE: Fifth Third Center, Cincinnati, OH 45263

TELEPHONE NUMBER: (513) 579-5300

NO. OF EMPLOYEES: 5,644

ANNUAL MEETING: In March

SHAREHOLDERS: 13,763

INSTITUTIONAL HOLDINGS:
No. of Institutions: 194
Shares Held: 25,343,643

REGISTRAR(S): Fifth Third Bank, Cincinnati, OH 45263

TRANSFER AGENT(S): Fifth Third Bank, Cincinnati, OH 45263

FIRST EMPIRE STATE CORP.

YIELD 1.5%
P/E RATIO 10.0

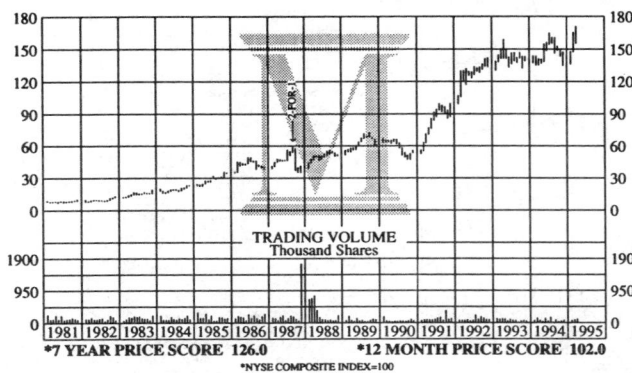

7 YEAR PRICE SCORE 126.0   *12 MONTH PRICE SCORE 102.0*
*NYSE COMPOSITE INDEX=100

INTERIM EARNINGS (Per Share):

Qtr.	Mar.	June	Sept.	Dec.
1991	2.22	2.24	2.37	2.49
1992	3.81	3.82	2.85	2.93
1993	3.31	3.42	3.52	3.62
1994	3.77	3.96	4.09	4.53

INTERIM DIVIDENDS (Per Share):

Amt.	Decl.	Ex.	Rec.	Pay.
0.60Q	10/19/94	11/25/94	12/1/94	12/28/94
0.60Q	10/19	11/25	12/1	12/28
0.60Q	10/19	11/25	12/1	12/28
0.60Q	2/22/95	2/28/95	3/6/95	3/31/95
0.60Q	4/19	5/25	6/1	6/30

*Indicated div.: $2.40**

CAPITALIZATION (12/31/94):

	($000)	(%)
Total Deposits	8,243,073	77.2
Total Debt	1,461,037	13.7
Preferred Stock	40,000	0.4
Common & Surplus	680,996	6.4
Loan Valuation Reserve	243,332	2.3
Total	10,668,438	100.0

DIVIDEND ACHIEVER STATUS:

Rank: 50   1984-94 Growth Rate: 15.4%%
Total Years of Dividend Growth: 14

RECENT DEVELOPMENTS: For the fiscal year ended 12/31/94, net income moved up 15.0% to $117.3 million from $102.0 million in fiscal 1993. The return on average assets and stockholder's equity was 1.17% and 16.64%, respectively compared with 0.98% and 15.61%, respectively a year earlier. Net interest margin was 4.89% versus 4.76%. Net interest income fell slightly to $468.1 million from $470.8 million. Other income advanced to $123.7 million from $110.5 million while other expense increased to $336.9 million from $327.8 million. Both other income and other expense were affected by the disposition of a group of securities, valued at $15.7 million, that were transferred to The M&T Charitable Foundation for future philanthropic gifts. In December 1994, FES acquired Ithaca Bancorp, a $470 million asset bank and seven branch offices from Chemical Bank with $146 million in deposits.

BUSINESS

FIRST EMPIRE STATE CORPORATION is a $10.5 billion bank holding company. Its banking subsidiaries are Manufacturers and Traders Trust Company and The East New York Savings Bank both of which are wholly owned. M&T Bank is a New York-chartered commercial bank with 118 offices throughout Western New York State and New York's Southern Tier, 20 offices in the Hudson Valley of New York State plus offices in New York City, Albany, Syracuse, and Nassau, The Bahamas. East New York, is a New York-chartered savings bank with 18 offices in metropolitan New York City. M&T Bank's subsidiaries include M&T Capital Corporation, a venture capital company, M&T Financial Corporation, an equipment leasing company, M&T Mortgage Corporation, a mortgage banking company, and M&T Discount Brokerage Services, Inc., a discount securities broker.

ANNUAL EARNINGS AND DIVIDENDS PER SHARE

	1994	1993	1992	1991	1990	1989	1988
Earnings Per Share	16.35	13.87	13.41	9.32	7.91	⑪ 7.04	6.02
Dividends Per Share	2.20	1.90	1.60	1.40	1.25	1.10	0.95
Dividend Payout %	13.5	13.7	11.9	15.0	15.8	15.6	15.8

⑪ Before acctg. chg.

ANNUAL FINANCIAL DATA

RECORD OF EARNINGS (IN MILLIONS):

	1994	1993	1992	1991	1990	1989	1988
Total Interest Income	747.3	740.6	756.5	769.0	657.4	576.6	492.5
Total Interest Expense	279.2	269.9	323.6	440.2	426.9	384.4	306.8
Net Interest Income	468.1	470.8	432.9	328.8	230.4	192.2	185.8
Credit Loss Provision	60.5	80.0	85.0	63.4	27.4	15.3	13.9
Net Income	117.3	102.0	97.9	67.2	53.9	⑪ 50.7	44.5
Aver. Shs. Outstg. (000)	6,952	7,091	7,033	6,905	6,818	7,199	7,385

⑪ Before acctg. change dr$9,455,000.

BALANCE SHEET (IN MILLIONS):

	1994	1993	1992	1991	1990	1989	1988
Cash & Due From Banks	377.8	195.8	264.5	269.2	235.8	271.8	253.9
Loans & Lse Financing, Net	7,974.0	7,065.2	6,832.1	5,946.3	5,297.9	4,315.6	3,915.2
Total Domestic Deposits	8,040.5	7,164.2	7,959.3	7,248.1	6,029.4	4,672.2	4,702.7
Total Foreign Deposits	202.6	189.1	117.8	226.2	171.6	198.4	354.7
Long-term Debt	96.2	75.6	75.7	9.5	3.2	13.1	13.5
Net Stockholders' Equity	721.0	724.0	626.8	535.8	437.2	406.3	388.1
Total Assets	10,528.6	10,365.0	9,587.9	9,171.1	7,715.4	6,233.8	5,908.1
Year End Shs Outstg (000)	6,611	6,879	6,840	6,708	6,630	6,836	7,021

STATISTICAL RECORD:

	1994	1993	1992	1991	1990	1989	1988
Return on Assets %	1.11	0.98	1.02	0.73	0.70	0.81	0.75
Return on Equity %	16.30	14.10	15.60	12.50	12.30	12.50	11.50
Book Value Per Share	103.01	99.43	85.79	73.91	65.94	59.44	55.28
Average Yield %	1.5	1.3	1.3	1.8	2.2	1.8	2.0
P/E Ratio	10.1-8.2	11.5-9.4	10.6-7.4	10.7-5.6	8.5-5.9	10.3-7.3	9.3-6.5
Price Range	165-134½	159-130¼	142-99	99¾-52½	67½-47	72½-51⅜	56¼-39

Statistics are as originally reported.

OFFICERS:
R.G. Wilmers, Chmn., Pres. & C.E.O.
J.L. Vardon, Exec. V.P. & C.F.O.
W.C. Rappolt, Exec. V.P. & Treas.

INCORPORATED: NY, Nov., 1969

PRINCIPAL OFFICE: One M&T Plaza 5th Floor P.O. Box 223, Buffalo, NY 14240

TELEPHONE NUMBER: (716) 842-5445

NO. OF EMPLOYEES: 3,792

ANNUAL MEETING: In April

SHAREHOLDERS: 4,505

INSTITUTIONAL HOLDINGS:
No. of Institutions: 104
Shares Held: 3,198,154

REGISTRAR(S): First National Bank of Boston, Shareholder Services Division, Boston, MA

TRANSFER AGENT(S): First National Bank of Boston, Shareholder Services Division, Boston, MA

NASDAQ SYMBOL FHWN
Rec. Pr. 25¾

FIRST HAWAIIAN INC.

YIELD 4.6%
P/E RATIO 11.4

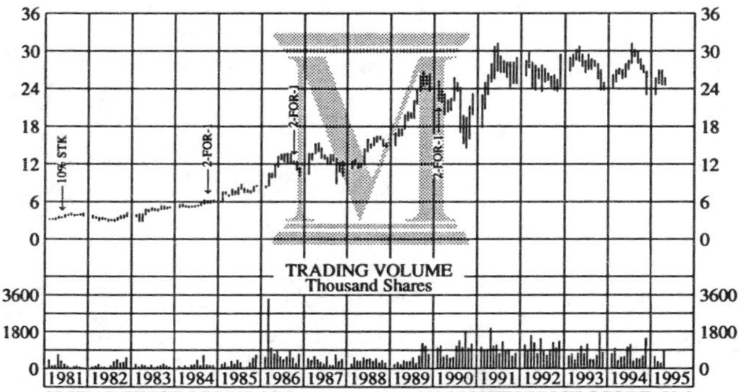

*7 YEAR PRICE SCORE 93.5 *12 MONTH PRICE SCORE 89.2

*NYSE COMPOSITE INDEX=100

INTERIM EARNINGS (Per Share):

Qtr.	Mar.	June	Sept.	Dec.
1991	0.61	0.65	0.63	0.66
1992	0.66	0.69	0.66	0.69
1993	0.56	0.68	0.57	0.60
1994	0.58	0.59	0.61	0.47

INTERIM DIVIDENDS (Per Share):

Amt.	Decl.	Ex.	Rec.	Pay.
0.295Q	2/17/94	2/23/94	3/1/94	3/15/94
0.295Q	5/23	5/25	6/1	6/15
0.295Q	8/18	8/26	9/1	9/15
0.295Q	11/18	11/25	12/1	12/15
0.295Q	2/16/95	2/23/95	3/1/95	3/15/95

*Indicated div.: $1.18**

CAPITALIZATION (12/31/94):

	($000)	(%)
Total Deposits	5,152,213	69.7
Total Debt	1,549,147	21.0
Common & Surplus	627,944	8.5
Loan Valuation Reserve	61,250	0.8
Total	7,390,554	100.0

DIVIDEND ACHIEVER STATUS:
Rank: 86 1984-94 Growth Rate: 13.5%
Total Years of Dividend Growth: 12

RECENT DEVELOPMENTS: For the quarter ended 12/31/94, net income was $15.0 million, down 22.6% from $19.4 million earned in the corresponding 1993 quarter. Current results were affected by FHWN's decision to write off a $5.4 million problem loan related to a commercial office building. Consequently, the allowance for loan losses was raised. Results were also adversely affected by the decreased value of several trust accounts. First Hawaiian acknowledged that some of the investments made in managed trusts accounts may have been done outside of customer guidelines. Losses incurred because of these investments will be covered, though investments in collateralized mortgage obligations were of particular concern. For the year ended 12/31/94, net income totaled $72.5 million compared with $78.2 million, before the cumulative effect of accounting changes, in 1993. Returns on average assets and shareholder's equity were 1.01% and 11.73%, respectively.

BUSINESS

FIRST HAWAIIAN INC. is a $7.5 billion bank holding company whose principal subsidiary, First Hawaiian Bank, was founded in 1858 and is the oldest financial institution on the islands. The bank presently has 59 branches throughout Hawaii, two in Guam, an offshore branch in Grand Cayman, British West Indies and a representative office in Tokyo, Japan. Other major subsidiaries include Pioneer Federal Savings Bank with 19 branches statewide; First Hawaiian Creditcorp, Inc., the state's third-largest financial services loan company with 12 branches statewide and a branch in Guam; and First Hawaiian Leasing, Inc., which is primarily engaged in commercial equipment and vehicle leasing.

LOAN DISTRIBUTION

(12/31/94)	($000)	(%)
Commercial, Fincl & Agric	1,307,145	23.6
Real Est-Construction	320,783	5.8
Real Est-Comml & Resident	2,971,259	53.6
Consumer	467,827	8.5
Lease Financing	230,587	4.2
Foreign	235,964	4.3
Total	5,533,565	100.0

ANNUAL EARNINGS AND DIVIDENDS PER SHARE

	1994	1993	1992	1991	1990	1989	1988
Earnings Per Share	**2.25**	**2.41**	**2.70**	**2.55**	**2.45**	**2.14**	**1.62**
Dividends Per Share	**1.18**	**1.135**	**1.06**	**0.95**	**[1] 0.83**	**0.70**	**0.575**
Dividend Payout %	**52.4**	**56.2**	**39.3**	**37.3**	**33.9**	**32.7**	**35.5**

[1] 2-for-1 stk split, 1/26/90

ANNUAL FINANCIAL DATA

	1994	1993	1992	1991	1990	1989	1988
RECORD OF EARNINGS (IN MILLIONS):							
Total Interest Income	475.8	441.6	486.3	523.6	498.9	431.1	347.7
Total Interest Expense	179.7	163.5	217.7	270.9	283.7	249.7	196.1
Net Interest Income	296.1	278.1	268.6	252.7	215.2	181.5	151.6
Credit Loss Provision	22.9	13.3	12.8	10.3	9.1	9.0	5.8
Net Income	72.5	[1] 78.2	86.9	81.7	71.5	57.4	43.3
Aver. Shs. Outstg. (000)	32,259	32,505	32,225	32,079	29,175	26,909	26,859
[1] Before acctg. change cr$3,650,000.							
BALANCE SHEET (IN MILLIONS):							
Cash & Due From Banks	269.9	436.1	325.7	354.0	324.2	276.8	270.1
Loans & Lse Financing, Net	5,472.3	5,004.6	4,339.6	4,274.2	3,221.9	2,772.6	2,356.1
Total Domestic Deposits	4,752.3	4,968.6	4,901.7	5,146.8	4,487.1	4,174.5	3,587.0
Total Foreign Deposits	399.9	251.6	186.5	189.9	290.4	337.8	186.6
Long-term Debt	219.3	221.8	71.1	61.6	49.9	60.5	60.9
Net Stockholders' Equity	627.9	608.4	562.2	498.3	446.8	281.1	242.1
Total Assets	7,535.1	7,269.1	6,553.4	6,510.6	5,509.4	5,080.1	4,238.6
Year End Shs Outstg (000)	32,026	32,543	32,502	32,079	32,079	26,909	26,909
STATISTICAL RECORD:							
Return on Assets %	0.96	1.08	1.33	1.26	1.30	1.13	1.02
Return on Equity %	11.50	12.90	15.50	16.40	16.00	20.40	17.90
Book Value Per Share	19.61	18.69	17.30	15.53	13.93	10.45	9.00
Average Yield %	4.4	4.2	4.0	3.9	4.1	3.4	4.1
P/E Ratio	13.9-10.2	12.8-9.9	11.0-8.7	12.3-7.0	10.5-5.9	12.5-7.0	10.2-6.9
Price Range	31¼-23	30¾-23¾	29¾-23½	31¼-17¾	25¾-14½	26¾-14⅞	16½-11¼

Statistics are as originally reported.

OFFICERS:
W.A. Dods, Jr., Chmn. & C.E.O.
J.K. Tsui, Vice-Chmn.
H.H. Karr, Exec. V.P. & Treas.

INCORPORATED: DE, Jul., 1974

PRINCIPAL OFFICE: P.O. Box 3200, Honolulu, HI 96847

TELEPHONE NUMBER: (808) 525-7000

NO. OF EMPLOYEES: 3,141

ANNUAL MEETING: In April

SHAREHOLDERS: 5,093

INSTITUTIONAL HOLDINGS:
No. of Institutions: 91
Shares Held: 11,265,449

REGISTRAR(S): First Hawaiian Bank, Honolulu, HI

TRANSFER AGENT(S): First Hawaiian Bank, Honolulu, HI

NASDAQ SYMBOL FNGB
Rec. Pr. 13½

FIRST NORTHERN SAVINGS BANK, S.A.

YIELD 4.1%
P/E RATIO 12.6

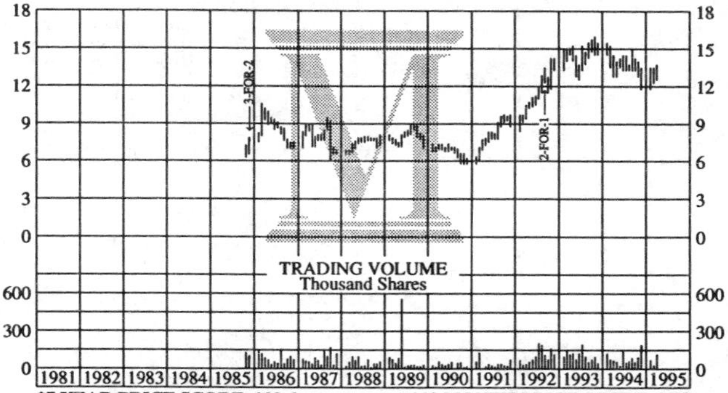

***7 YEAR PRICE SCORE 109.6** ***12 MONTH PRICE SCORE 93.3**

*NYSE COMPOSITE INDEX=100

INTERIM EARNINGS (Per Share):

Qtr.	Mar.	June	Sept.	Dec.
1991	0.26	0.28	0.29	0.25
1992	0.30	0.34	0.35	0.34
1993	0.33	0.33	0.32	0.33
1994	0.28	0.14	0.24	0.25

INTERIM DIVIDENDS (Per Share):

Amt.	Decl.	Ex.	Rec.	Pay.
0.13Q	2/4/94	2/22/94	2/28/94	3/15/94
0.13Q	5/12	5/24	5/31	6/15
0.13Q	8/8	8/25	8/31	9/15
0.13Q	11/8	11/23	11/30	12/15
0.14Q	2/9/95	2/22/95	2/28/95	3/15/95

Indicated div.: $0.56

CAPITALIZATION (12/31/94):

	($000)	(%)
Total Deposits	423,793	78.6
Total Debt	42,900	8.0
Common & Surplus	70,007	13.0
Loan Valuation Reserve	2,400	0.4
Total	539,100	100.0

DIVIDEND ACHIEVER STATUS:

Rank: 10 1984-94 Growth Rate: 22.9%

Total Years of Dividend Growth: 10

RECENT DEVELOPMENTS: For the year ended 12/31/94, net income remained steady at $4.2 million compared with $4.2 million, before accounting changes, for 1993. Interest income was $35.4 million, down 6.2% from $37.8 million a year earlier. Net income was affected by acquisition costs of $465,000, a decrease in the interest rate spread, unrealized losses on loans held for sale of $172,000, and a decrease in the gains on the sale of loans of $530,000. Interest income was pressured by mortgage loans decreasing $2.1 million as a result of interest rate decrease on existing adjustable interest rate mortgage loans in early 1994 and originations of mortgage loans at or below the existing yield on the mortgage portfolio. Provisions for loan losses were reduced by $394,000 due to a lower level of non-performing loans.

BUSINESS

FIRST NORTHERN SAVINGS BANK, S.A. is principally engaged in the business of attracting deposits from the general public, consumer loans, originating first mortgage residential loans and commercial property, as well as loans for land acquisition and construction of one- to four-family residential property. In addition, the Company, through its subsidiaries, Great Northern Financial Services Corporation, Keystone Financial Services, Inc. and Savings Financial Corporation, engages in the sale of credit life and disability insurance and annuities, offers discount brokerage services and owns residential lots, selling and servicing automobile loans.

LOAN DISTRIBUTION

(12/31/94)	($000)	(%)
First Mortgage	388,252	77.1
Consumer	21,756	4.3
Second Mortgage	29,454	5.8
Automobile	53,527	10.6
Education	10,677	2.2
Total	503,666	100.0

ANNUAL EARNINGS AND DIVIDENDS PER SHARE

	1994	1993	1992	1991	1990	1989	1988
Earnings Per Share	**0.91**	**1.31**	**1.33**	**1.07**	**0.95**	**0.78**	**1.00**
Dividends Per Share	**0.52**	**0.48**	[1] **0.40**	**0.36**	**0.34**	**0.32**	**0.30**
Dividend Payout %	**57.1**	**36.6**	**30.1**	**33.6**	**35.8**	**40.8**	**30.0**

[1] 2-for-1 stk split, 9/21/92

ANNUAL FINANCIAL DATA

	1994	1993	1992	1991	1990	1989	1988
RECORD OF EARNINGS (IN THOUSANDS):							
Total Interest Income	35,409	28,744	32,815	33,116	32,405	30,005	27,935
Total Interest Expense	16,854	13,621	17,685	18,669	19,197	18,314	16,652
Net Interest Income	18,555	15,123	15,130	14,447	13,208	11,691	11,283
Credit Loss Provision	145	363	360	394	423	100	14
Income Bef Income Taxes	7,390	7,208	7,052	4,474	3,802	3,028	4,034
Income Taxes	3,192	2,868	2,727	1,823	1,481	1,089	1,586
Net Income	4,198	[1] 4,340	4,325	2,651	2,321	1,938	2,448
Aver. Shs. Outstg.	4,599	3,313	3,253	2,480	2,442	2,468	...
[1] Before acctg. change cr$430,000.							
BALANCE SHEET (IN THOUSANDS):							
Cash & Sec. Etc.	2,644	8,497	23,204	21,286	9,375	6,531	2,039
Investments and Advances	30,882	32,690	26,850	18,346	15,694	20,586	29,152
Loans & Lse Financing, Net	497,061	330,070	321,893	271,498	273,104	253,407	245,435
Long-term Debt	40,000	...	...	...	...	...	...
Net Stockholders' Equity	70,007	53,363	49,539	30,440	28,565	27,054	25,837
Total Assets	546,923	382,648	382,801	318,497	305,470	286,141	282,647
Year End Shares Outstg	4,495	3,232	3,164	2,444	2,422	2,419	2,405
STATISTICAL RECORD:							
Return on Equity %	6.0	8.1	8.7	8.7	8.1	7.2	9.5
Return on Assets %	0.8	1.1	1.1	0.8	0.8	0.7	0.9
Book Value Per Share	15.57	16.51	15.66	12.45	11.79	11.18	10.74
Average Yield %	3.8	3.4	3.5	4.6	5.2	4.0	4.1
P/E Ratio	17.0-12.9	12.2-9.5	10.7-6.3	9.1-5.4	7.8-6.1	11.4-9.0	8.1-6.5
Price Range	15½-11¾	16-12½	14¼-8⅜	9¾-5¾	7⅜-5¾	8⅞-7	8⅛-6½

Statistics are as originally reported.

OFFICERS:
W.E. Klunk, Chmn.
R.D. Pahlow, Vice-Chmn.
M.D. Meeuwsen, Pres. & C.E.O.
R.B. Colberg, V.P. & C.F.O.
T. Carr, V.P. & Sec.

PRINCIPAL OFFICE: 201 North Monroe Avenue, Green Bay, WI 54301

TELEPHONE NUMBER: (414) 437-7101

NO. OF EMPLOYEES: 206

ANNUAL MEETING: In April

SHAREHOLDERS: 2,711

INSTITUTIONAL HOLDINGS:
No. of Institutions: 8
Shares Held: 236,850

REGISTRAR(S): First Trust Co., Milwaukee, Wisc

TRANSFER AGENT(S): First Trust Co., Milwaukee, Wisc

NYS SYMBOL FOA
Rec. Pr. 33⅝

FIRST OF AMERICA BANK CORP.

YIELD	5.0%
P/E RATIO	9.1

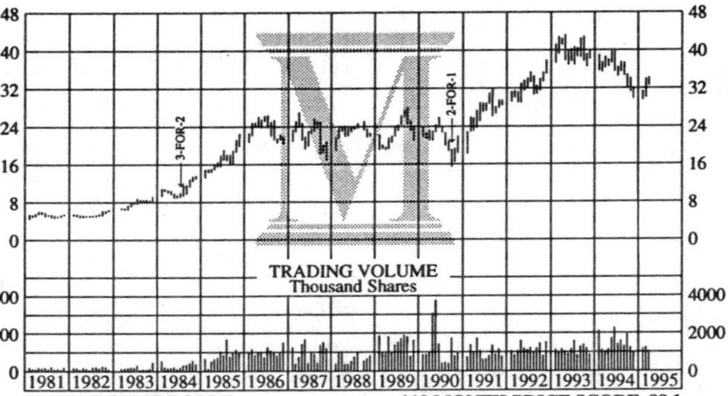

*7 YEAR PRICE SCORE ... *12 MONTH PRICE SCORE 88.1

*NYSE COMPOSITE INDEX=100

INTERIM EARNINGS (Per Share):

Qtr.	Mar.	June	Sept.	Dec.
1991	0.70	0.83	0.89	0.89
1992	0.41	0.45	0.99	0.61
1993	0.99	1.02	1.07	1.13
1994	0.98	0.88	0.96	0.87

INTERIM DIVIDENDS (Per Share):

Amt.	Decl.	Ex.	Rec.	Pay.
0.40Q	2/16/94	4/4/94	4/8/94	4/29/94
0.40Q	5/18	7/1	7/8	7/29
0.42Q	8/17	10/3	10/7	10/28
0.42Q	11/16	1/3/95	1/9/95	1/30/95
0.42Q	2/15/95	4/3	4/7	4/28

*Indicated div.: $1.68**

CAPITALIZATION (12/31/94):

	($000)	(%)
Total Deposits	20,200,266	82.2
Total Debt	2,563,975	10.5
Common & Surplus	1,578,888	6.4
Loan Valuation Reserve	228,115	0.9
Total	24,571,244	100.0

DIVIDEND ACHIEVER STATUS:
Rank: 122 1984-94 Growth Rate: 11.8%
Total Years of Dividend Growth: 11

RECENT DEVELOPMENTS: For the year ended 12/31/94, net income was $220.5 million, down 11% from the $247.4 million for 1993. Results were affected by a lower net interest margin, increased expenses, and additional costs related to acquisitions. Net interest income totaled $938.7 million compared with $902.0 million, an increase of 4%. Net interest margin fell to 4.39% from 4.77% in the prior year. Loans increased 17% over 1993 levels.

PROSPECTS: In December 1994, the Company consolidated seven of its Michigan banks and nine Illinois banks, and streamlined backroom operations of certain businesses. FOA's cost-management program is expected to yield a 5% reduction in operating expenses by the end of the year. The Company's increased presence in the greater Chicago area and entrance into the Florida market should positively favor long-term prospects.

BUSINESS

FIRST OF AMERICA BANK CORPORATION is a $24.6 billion bank holding company serving rural, urban and metropolitan areas in Michigan, Indiana, Illinois and Florida. The Company's primary lines of business are retail consumer banking, retail commercial banking, trust and investment services, and correspondent banking. Non-banking subsidiaries provide mortgage, trust, data processing, discount brokerage, revolving credit and investment advisory services.

LOAN DISTRIBUTION

(12/31/94)	($000)	(%)
Consumer	5,799,025	34.5
Comm, Finl & Agricultural	2,344,969	13.9
Commercial Real Estate	3,423,268	20.3
Residential Real Estate	5,237,400	31.1
Loans Held For Sale	30,196	0.2
Total	16,834,858	100.0

ANNUAL EARNINGS AND DIVIDENDS PER SHARE

	1994	1993	1992	1991	1990	1989	1988
Earnings Per Share	**3.69**	**4.20**	**1 2.86**	**3.32**	**3.26**	**3 2.94**	**3.08**
Dividends Per Share	**1.62**	**1.50**	**1.31**	**1.22**	**2 1.125**	**1.05**	**0.925**
Dividend Payout %	**44.0**	**35.7**	**45.8**	**36.7**	**34.5**	**35.7**	**30.0**

1 Before acctg. chg. 2 2-for-1 stk split, 10/19/90 3 Per primary share

ANNUAL FINANCIAL DATA

	1994	1993	1992	1991	1990	1989	1988
RECORD OF EARNINGS (IN MILLIONS):							
Total Interest Income	1,600.9	1,511.0	1,596.1	1,259.9	1,235.6	1,171.8	793.2
Total Interest Expense	662.1	608.9	721.3	654.2	687.5	651.2	422.2
Net Interest Income	938.7	902.0	874.8	605.7	548.1	520.6	371.0
Credit Loss Provision	86.6	84.7	78.8	45.6	29.4	30.5	21.6
Net Income	220.5	247.4	1 169.5	134.9	131.6	122.9	88.8
Aver. Shs. Outstg. (000)	59,812	57,417	54,842	36,030	35,245	35,470	45,264
1 Before acctg. change dr$21,956,000.							
BALANCE SHEET (IN MILLIONS):							
Cash & Due From Banks	1,060.8	903.5	919.0	884.7	909.9	859.0	639.1
Loans & Lse Financing, Net	16,606.7	14,205.5	13,579.2	11,325.7	9,386.6	8,241.0	6,151.3
Total Domestic Deposits	20,200.3	18,243.7	18,035.6	15,020.8	12,541.2	11,366.4	8,675.4
Long-term Debt	681.2	254.2	254.1	220.7	137.0	124.7	107.8
Net Stockholders' Equity	1,578.9	1,523.4	1,335.5	1,073.6	994.2	947.9	722.8
Total Assets	24,568.7	21,230.5	20,146.8	16,755.0	14,038.6	12,792.7	9,769.4
Year End Shs Outstg (000)	62,849	59,521	57,014	36,022	35,844	35,516	49,672
STATISTICAL RECORD:							
Return on Assets %	0.90	1.17	0.84	0.81	0.94	0.96	0.91
Return on Equity %	14.00	16.20	12.70	12.60	13.20	13.00	12.30
Book Value Per Share	25.12	25.59	22.12	25.21	23.11	21.25	10.58
Average Yield %	4.6	3.8	3.9	4.9	5.5	4.5	4.2
P/E Ratio	10.9-8.1	10.3-8.7	13.2-10.1	9.6-5.5	7.9-4.7	9.5-6.5	16.3-12.3
Price Range	40⅛-29¾	43¼-36½	37⅞-29	31¾-18¼	25⅞-15⅜	28-19⅛	25⅛-19

Statistics are as originally reported.

OFFICERS:
D.R. Smith, Chmn. & C.E.O.
R.F. Chormann, Pres. & C.O.O.
T.W. Lambert, Exec. V.P. & C.F.O.
S.G. Stone, Sr. V.P. & Treas.

INCORPORATED: MI, May, 1971

PRINCIPAL OFFICE: 211 South Rose Street, Kalamazoo, MI 49007

TELEPHONE NUMBER: (616) 376-9000
FAX: (616) 376-7079
NO. OF EMPLOYEES: 13,490
ANNUAL MEETING: In April
SHAREHOLDERS: 30,600
INSTITUTIONAL HOLDINGS:
No. of Institutions: 122
Shares Held: 13,570,212

REGISTRAR(S): Norwest Corporation, Minneapolis, MN

TRANSFER AGENT(S): Norwest Corporation, Minneapolis, MN

NASDAQ SYMBOL FTEN
Rec. Pr. 43½

FIRST TENNESSEE NATIONAL CORP.

YIELD 4.3%
P/E RATIO 9.5

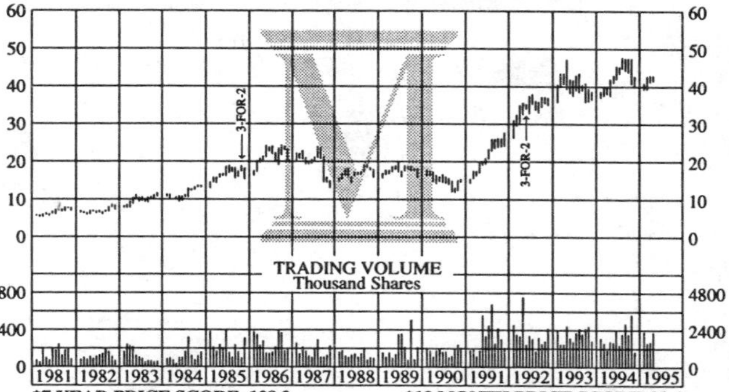

*7 YEAR PRICE SCORE 128.3 *12 MONTH PRICE SCORE 92.4
*NYSE COMPOSITE INDEX=100

INTERIM EARNINGS (Per Share):

Qtr.	Mar.	June	Sept.	Dec.
1991	0.59	0.66	0.70	0.74
1992	0.89	0.93	0.95	0.42
1993	1.07	1.08	1.05	1.06
1994	1.15	1.12	1.14	1.16

INTERIM DIVIDENDS (Per Share):

Amt.	Decl.	Ex.	Rec.	Pay.
0.42Q	4/19/94	6/13/94	6/17/94	7/1/94
0.42Q	7/20	9/12	9/16	10/1
0.47Q	10/19	12/12	12/16	1/1/95
0.47Q	1/17/95	3/13/95	3/17/95	4/1
0.47Q	4/18	6/14	6/16	7/1

Indicated div.: $1.88*

CAPITALIZATION (12/31/94):

	($000)	(%)
Total Deposits	7,688,422	72.3
Total Debt	2,085,218	19.6
Common & Surplus	748,771	7.1
Loan Valuation Reserve	106,989	1.0
Total	10,629,400	100.0

DIVIDEND ACHIEVER STATUS:
Rank: 157 1984-94 Growth Rate: 10.4%
Total Years of Dividend Growth: 17

RECENT DEVELOPMENTS: Net income for the year ended 12/31/94 was $146.3 million, an increase of 38% from the $106.1 million earned in 1993. Earnings were postively affected by a reduced loan loss provision, commercial and consumer loan growth and the expansion of fee-based businesses. Net interest income was $380.6 million versus $363.5 million a year earlier. Results benefited from a 14% increase in commercial loans and a 37% increase in consumer loans. Commercial loans accounted for 42% of total loans while 32% of FTEN's loan portfolio was consumer loans. Noninterest income moved up to $389.2 million from $334.8 million, as income from mortgage banking operations, deposit transactions and cash management, and trust services advanced 38%, 10%, and 10%, respectively. The provision for loan losses was lowered by 53% to $16.7 million. Noninterest expense increased to $545.7 million from $491.9 million in 1993.

BUSINESS

FIRST TENNESSEE NATIONAL CORPORATION is a $10.5 billion bank holding company and is the 58th largest bank holding company in the nation. With principal offices in Memphis, Tennessee, the Company operates 214 banking locations in twenty Tennessee counties and 4 locations in Mississippi. Through its principal subsidiary, First Tennessee National Association and other banking and bank-related subsidiaries, FTEN provides a broad range of financial services including: general banking for consumers and small businesses, corporations, and financial institutions, mortgage banking services; trust, fiduciary and agency services; check clearing; discount brokerage; venture capital; equipment financing and credit life insurance services; investment and financial advisory services; mutual fund sales and check processing software and systems. In terms of assets, FTEN is the largest Tennessee-headquartered bank holding company.

ANNUAL EARNINGS AND DIVIDENDS PER SHARE

	1994	1993	1992	1991	1990	1989	1988
Earnings Per Share	**4.56**	**4.26**	**3.19**	**2.69**	**2.01**	**1.21**	**2.23**
Dividends Per Share	**1.68**	**1.44**	**[1] 1.20**	**1.12**	**1.067**	**0.933**	**0.827**
Dividend Payout %	**36.8**	**33.8**	**37.6**	**41.6**	**53.2**	**76.9**	**37.1**

[1] 3-for-2 stk split, 5/26/92

ANNUAL FINANCIAL DATA

	1994	1993	1992	1991	1990	1989	1988
RECORD OF EARNINGS (IN MILLIONS):							
Total Interest Income	668.7	586.5	599.2	579.7	600.2	582.5	500.5
Total Interest Expense	288.1	239.9	276.3	314.8	357.6	357.3	286.2
Net Interest Income	380.6	346.6	322.9	264.8	242.6	225.2	214.3
Credit Loss Provision	16.7	34.5	43.2	53.6	63.6	63.9	25.4
Net Income	146.3	120.7	89.2	63.8	47.9	28.8	52.3
Aver. Shs. Outstg. (000)	32,114	28,325	27,972	23,669	23,865	23,780	23,516
BALANCE SHEET (IN MILLIONS):							
Cash & Due From Banks	691.1	602.4	496.5	542.8	509.0	558.2	637.1
Loans & Lse Financing, Net	6,240.5	7,683.3	4,425.6	6,079.9	5,854.6	5,631.3	5,602.4
Total Domestic Deposits	7,688.4	7,146.8	6,916.8	6,040.5	5,343.2	4,949.4	4,656.8
Long-term Debt	431.5	448.2	396.8	676.1	327.9	332.9	295.4
Net Stockholders' Equity	748.8	679.0	597.5	437.6	397.8	380.7	372.5
Total Assets	10,522.4	14,244.5	8,925.8	12,375.6	10,231.8	9,771.3	9,148.6
Year End Shs Outstg (000)	31,853	28,326	28,123	23,750	23,565	23,907	23,721
STATISTICAL RECORD:							
Return on Assets %	1.39	0.85	1.00	0.52	0.47	0.29	0.57
Return on Equity %	19.50	17.80	14.90	14.60	12.00	7.60	14.00
Book Value Per Share	23.51	23.97	21.25	18.42	16.88	15.93	15.71
Average Yield %	4.0	3.5	3.7	5.3	7.1	5.3	4.9
P/E Ratio	10.5-8.1	11.1-8.4	11.9-8.2	10.3-5.3	9.0-5.9	16.4-12.9	8.7-6.4
Price Range	47¾-37	47¼-35¾	38-26¼	27⅝-14⅜	18-11⅞	19⅞-15⅝	19⅜-14⅜

Statistics are as originally reported.

OFFICERS:
R. Terry, Chmn.
R. Horn, Pres. & C.E.O.
E.L. Thomas, Sr. V.P. & C.F.O.
T.A. Fehrman, V.P. & Treas.

INCORPORATED: TN, 1968

PRINCIPAL OFFICE: 165 Madison Avenue, Memphis, TN 38103

TELEPHONE NUMBER: (901) 523-4444
FAX: (901) 523-4336
NO. OF EMPLOYEES: 6,468 (approx.)
ANNUAL MEETING: In April
SHAREHOLDERS: 7,893
INSTITUTIONAL HOLDINGS:
No. of Institutions: 151
Shares Held: 13,526,588

REGISTRAR(S):

TRANSFER AGENT(S): Bank of Boston, Boston, MA 02102

NYS SYMBOL FTU
Rec. Pr. 43⅜

FIRST UNION CORP.

YIELD 4.2%
P/E RATIO 8.7

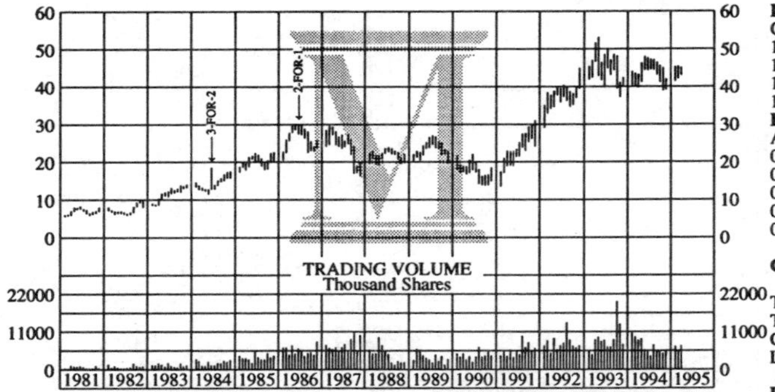

*7 YEAR PRICE SCORE 118.6 *12 MONTH PRICE SCORE 97.5

*NYSE COMPOSITE INDEX=100

INTERIM EARNINGS (Per Share):

Qtr.	Mar.	June	Sept.	Dec.
1991	0.67	0.61	0.61	0.66
1992	0.81	0.90	1.06	0.95
1993	1.17	1.32	1.12	1.12
1994	1.27	1.32	1.35	1.04

INTERIM DIVIDENDS (Per Share):

Amt.	Decl.	Ex.	Rec.	Pay.
0.40Q	2/15/94	2/22/94	2/28/94	3/15/94
0.40Q	4/19	5/24	5/31	6/15
0.46Q	6/21	8/25	8/31	9/15
0.46Q	10/18	11/23	11/30	12/15
0.46Q	2/21/95	2/23/95	3/1/95	3/15/95

Indicated div.: $1.84*

CAPITALIZATION (12/31/94):

	($000)	(%)
Total Deposits	58,958,273	77.3
Total Debt	10,960,857	14.3
Common & Surplus	5,397,517	7.1
Loan Valuation Reserve	978,795	1.3
Total	76,295,442	100.0

DIVIDEND ACHIEVER STATUS:
Rank: 87 1984-94 Growth Rate: 13.4%
Total Years of Dividend Growth: 17

RECENT DEVELOPMENTS: For the year ended 12/31/94, net income before preferred dividends was a record $925.4 million, an increase of 13% from the $817.5 million earned in 1993. Results were attributed to stronger credit quality and accelerated consolidation of acquisitions. Net interest income, benefiting from 15% loan growth, rose to $3.03 billion from $2.77 billion. Commercial loan growth was particularly strong in Florida, North Carolina and Virginia.

PROSPECTS: The Company will acquire Miami-based American Savings and Loan Association in a stock swap valued at $235 million. American has assets of $3.5 billion. FTU will also purchase Coral Gables Fedcorp., a Florida-based bank with 34 offices and $2.5 billion in assets, for approximately $531 million. The Company also entered into an agreement to buy United Financial Corp. of South Carolina for $130.5 million. United has assets of $759 million and 17 branch offices.

BUSINESS

FIRST UNION CORPORATION, as of 12/31/94 had assets of $77.3 billion. FTU operates 1338 full-service banking offices in North Carolina, Florida, Georgia, South Carolina, Tennessee, Maryland and Washington, D.C., as well as 222 non-banking offices in 42 states. FTU also provides mortgage banking, home equity lending, consumer lending, asset-based financing, insurance, export trading and brokerage services. First Union is the ninth-largest banking company in the nation.

LOAN DISTRIBUTION

(12/31/94)	($000)	(%)
Commercial, Finl & Agric	15,907,743	29.1
Real Est-Construc & Other	1,734,095	3.2
Real Estate-Mortgage	5,437,496	9.9
Lease Financing	1,613,763	2.9
Foreign	415,857	0.8
Retail	29,593,128	54.1
Total	54,702,082	100.0

ANNUAL EARNINGS AND DIVIDENDS PER SHARE

	1994	1993	1992	1991	1990	1989	1988
Earnings Per Share	**4.98**	**4.73**	**3.72**	**2.55**	**2.52**	**2.40**	**2.76**
Dividends Per Share	**1.72**	**1.50**	**1.28**	**1.12**	**1.08**	**1.00**	**0.86**
Dividend Payout %	**34.5**	**31.7**	**34.4**	**43.9**	**42.9**	**41.7**	**31.2**

ANNUAL FINANCIAL DATA

	1994	1993	1992	1991	1990	1989	1988
RECORD OF EARNINGS (IN MILLIONS):							
Total Interest Income	5,094.7	4,556.3	3,509.3	4,647.4	3,518.1	2,903.4	2,453.8
Total Interest Expense	2,060.9	1,790.4	1,501.2	2,743.0	2,239.9	1,873.3	1,415.5
Net Interest Income	3,033.7	2,765.9	2,008.2	1,904.4	1,278.2	1,030.0	1,038.3
Credit Loss Provision	100.0	221.8	249.7	648.3	177.7	80.6	61.1
Net Income	925.4	817.5	515.2	318.7	304.3	256.2	296.9
Aver. Shs. Outstg. (000)	172,543	167,692	130,344	112,114	108,046	106,925	107,748
BALANCE SHEET (IN MILLIONS):							
Cash & Due From Banks	3,740.7	3,352.0	2,624.5	2,559.1	2,241.4	2,002.9	2,358.8
Loans & Lse Financing, Net	53,051.0	45,856.0	32,675.5	31,446.5	25,787.0	21,578.6	18,673.2
Total Domestic Deposits	58,958.3	53,742.4	39,389.5	36,597.7	27,680.1	21,498.3	20,033.3
Long-term Debt	3,428.5	3,061.9	2,521.8	2,063.7	1,190.9	871.5	634.1
Net Stockholders' Equity	5,397.5	5,207.6	3,831.7	3,112.5	2,565.6	2,076.1	1,923.5
Total Assets	77,313.5	70,787.0	51,332.4	45,972.1	40,771.9	32,115.0	28,942.2
Year End Shs Outstg (000)	176,034	170,338	136,052	121,065	109,173	107,164	106,966
STATISTICAL RECORD:							
Return on Assets %	1.20	1.15	1.00	0.69	0.75	0.80	1.03
Return on Equity %	17.10	15.70	13.40	10.20	11.90	12.30	15.40
Book Value Per Share	30.66	30.39	27.93	24.62	23.19	19.37	17.98
Average Yield %	4.0	3.3	3.5	5.0	6.0	4.3	4.0
P/E Ratio	9.6-7.8	11.2-7.9	12.1-7.8	12.2-5.3	8.7-5.5	11.3-8.2	8.7-7.0
Price Range	48-39	53⅛-37¼	44⅞-29⅛	31-13½	22-13¾	27-19⅝	23⅞-19¼

Statistics are as originally reported.

OFFICERS:
E.E. Crutchfield, Jr., Chmn. & C.E.O.
J.R. Georgius, Pres.
R.T. Atwood, Exec. V.P. & C.F.O.
K.R. Stanliff, Sr. V.P. & Treas.

INCORPORATED: NC, Dec., 1967

PRINCIPAL OFFICE: One First Union Center, Charlotte, NC 28288-0013

TELEPHONE NUMBER: (704) 374-6565

NO. OF EMPLOYEES: 31,858

ANNUAL MEETING: In April

SHAREHOLDERS: 54,236

INSTITUTIONAL HOLDINGS:
No. of Institutions: 520
Shares Held: 97,316,762

REGISTRAR(S): First Union National Bank of N.C., Charlotte, NC

TRANSFER AGENT(S): First Union National Bank of N.C., Charlotte, NC

NYS SYMBOL FVB
Rec. Pr. 34¾

FIRST VIRGINIA BANKS, INC.

YIELD 3.8%
P/E RATIO 9.9

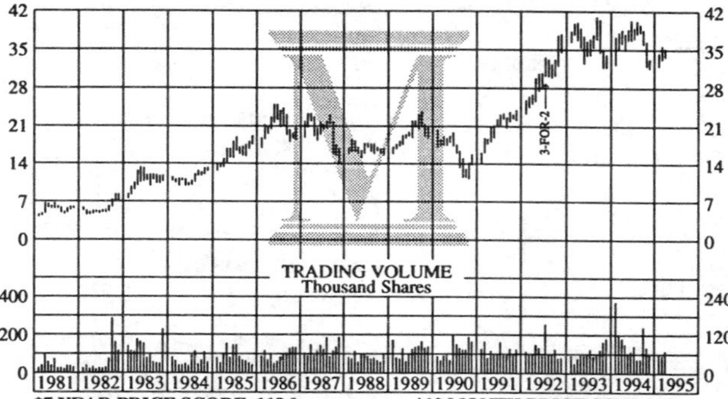

*7 YEAR PRICE SCORE 118.2 *12 MONTH PRICE SCORE 91.2

*NYSE COMPOSITE INDEX=100

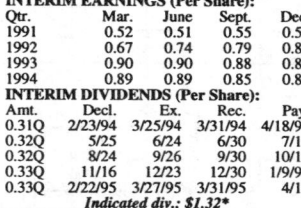

INTERIM EARNINGS (Per Share):

Qtr.	Mar.	June	Sept.	Dec.
1991	0.52	0.51	0.55	0.58
1992	0.67	0.74	0.79	0.82
1993	0.90	0.90	0.88	0.89
1994	0.89	0.89	0.85	0.88

INTERIM DIVIDENDS (Per Share):

Amt.	Decl.	Ex.	Rec.	Pay.
0.31Q	2/23/94	3/25/94	3/31/94	4/18/94
0.32Q	5/25	6/24	6/30	7/18
0.32Q	8/24	9/26	9/30	10/17
0.33Q	11/16	12/23	12/30	1/9/95
0.33Q	2/22/95	3/27/95	3/31/95	4/17

*Indicated div.: $1.32**

CAPITALIZATION (12/31/94):

	($000)	(%)
Total Deposits	6,815,841	85.9
Total Debt	183,223	2.3
Preferred Stock	74,588	0.9
Common & Surplus	806,142	10.2
Loan Valuation Reserve	58,860	0.7
Total	7,938,654	100.0

DIVIDEND ACHIEVER STATUS:
Rank: 189 1984-94 Growth Rate: 9.3%
Total Years of Dividend Growth: 18

RECENT DEVELOPMENTS: For the three months ended 12/31/94, net income was $27.8 million, down 4% from the prior year's $29.0 million. Net interest income was $85.0 million versus $84.0 million in 1993. Other income fell to $20.3 million from $22.1 million. For the year ended 12/31/94, net income was $113.2 million compared with $116.0 million. Net interest income moved up slightly to $342.1 million from $339.8 million.

PROSPECTS: One of the effects of higher interest rates is the competition among banks to secure deposit accounts. FVB's deposit growth was slow throughout 1994 but loans were up 16% from the prior-year end. In December of 1994, FVB completed its acquisition of Farmers National Bancorp, a $709 million asset holding company. Farmers operates three banks in the Annapolis and eastern shore areas of Maryland.

BUSINESS

FIRST VIRGINIA BANKS, INC. with assets of $7.9 billion, provides mortgage banking, consumer finance, insurance, and lease financing services through its subsidiaries. In addition to fourteen banks with 269 banking offices located in Virginia, FVB has five banks with 57 offices in Maryland located in Baltimore and around Washington, D.C., and four banks with 23 offices serving eastern Tennessee. The Company also operates a variety of other financial businesses, including: mortgage servicing; underwriting credit life and disability insurance; an insurance agency; and second mortgage loans.

LOAN DISTRIBUTION

(12/31/94)	($000)	(%)
Consumer	3,728,826	69.7
Real Estate	1,156,801	21.6
Commercial	466,877	8.7
Total	5,352,504	100.0

ANNUAL EARNINGS AND DIVIDENDS PER SHARE

	1994	1993	1992	1991	1990	1989	1988
Earnings Per Share	**3.51**	**3.57**	**3.02**	**2.17**	**2.03**	**2.13**	**1.93**
Dividends Per Share	**1.26**	**1.08**	**[1] 0.963**	**0.893**	**0.84**	**0.787**	**0.733**
Dividend Payout %	**35.9**	**30.3**	**31.9**	**41.2**	**41.3**	**36.9**	**37.9**

[1] 3-for-2 stk split, 7/28/92

ANNUAL FINANCIAL DATA

	1994	1993	1992	1991	1990	1989	1988
RECORD OF EARNINGS (IN MILLIONS):							
Total Interest Income	503.6	504.8	525.3	515.8	501.4	471.6	420.4
Total Interest Expense	161.6	165.0	204.8	260.3	264.9	243.1	211.1
Net Interest Income	342.0	339.8	320.4	255.6	236.6	228.5	209.2
Credit Loss Provision	6.5	6.5	17.4	14.0	13.4	11.0	11.4
Net Income	113.2	116.0	97.5	69.6	65.1	67.4	60.9
Aver. Shs. Outstg. (000)	32,281	32,512	32,252	32,093	32,027	31,583	31,523
BALANCE SHEET (IN MILLIONS):							
Cash and Due From Banks	420.7	326.1	381.4	361.0	291.3	314.1	287.9
Loans & Lse Financing, Net	4,938.3	3,967.2	3,793.0	3,470.6	3,390.5	3,294.8	3,150.8
Total Domestic Deposits	6,815.8	6,136.4	6,013.7	5,350.0	4,715.9	4,426.7	4,223.1
Long-term Debt	3.8	1.0	5.2	11.5	11.8	37.5	38.1
Net Stockholders' Equity	880.7	771.2	607.4	540.1	497.7	454.6	412.2
Total Assets	7,865.4	7,036.9	6,840.5	6,119.3	5,384.1	5,124.0	4,795.8
Year-end Shs Outstg (000)	34,050	32,444	32,185	32,093	32,009	31,563	31,533
STATISTICAL RECORD:							
Return on Assets %	1.44	1.65	1.42	1.14	1.21	1.31	1.27
Return on Equity %	12.90	15.00	16.00	12.90	13.10	14.80	14.80
Book Value Per Share	23.68	21.29	18.85	16.80	15.51	14.37	13.03
Average Yield %	3.5	3.0	3.1	4.7	5.3	4.0	4.3
P/E Ratio	11.5-9.0	11.5-8.9	12.5-7.7	11.1-6.5	10.0-5.5	11.2-7.5	9.7-7.8
Price Range	40⅜-31⅝	41-31¾	37⅞-23⅜	24-14⅛	20⅜-11¼	23¾-15⅞	18⅝-15⅛

Statistics are as originally reported.

OFFICERS:
B.J. Fitzpatrick, Chmn. & C.E.O.
P.H. Geithner, Jr., Pres. & Chief Admin. Off
R.F. Bowman, V.P. & Treas.
T.P. Jennings, V.P., Gen. Couns. & Sec.

INCORPORATED: VA, Oct., 1949

PRINCIPAL OFFICE: One First Virginia Plaza 6400 Arlington Boulevard, Falls Church, VA 22042-2336

TELEPHONE NUMBER: (703) 241-4000
FAX: (703) 241-3090
NO. OF EMPLOYEES: 5,028 (full-time equivalent)
ANNUAL MEETING: In April
SHAREHOLDERS: 19,036
INSTITUTIONAL HOLDINGS:
No. of Institutions: 158
Shares Held: 10,954,153

REGISTRAR(S): Security Trust Company, N.A., Baltimore, MD

TRANSFER AGENT(S): Security Trust Company, N.A., Baltimore, MD

FIRSTAR CORP.

YIELD 4.1%
P/E RATIO 9.2

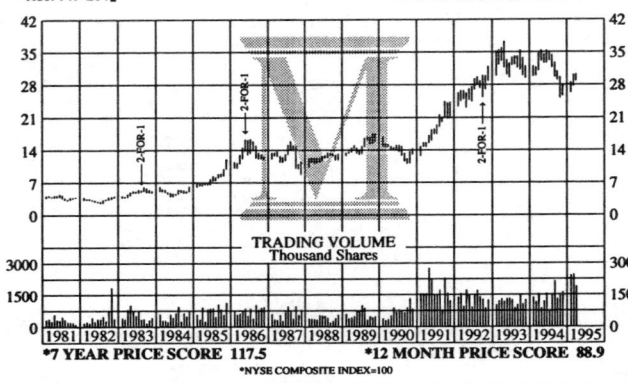

7 YEAR PRICE SCORE 117.5   **12 MONTH PRICE SCORE 88.9**
*NYSE COMPOSITE INDEX=100

INTERIM EARNINGS (Per Share):

Qtr.	Mar.	June	Sept.	Dec.
1991	0.49	0.53	0.55	0.56
1992	0.59	0.65	0.68	0.70
1993	0.78	0.78	0.79	0.80
1994	0.83	0.66	0.87	0.86

INTERIM DIVIDENDS (Per Share):

Amt.	Decl.	Ex.	Rec.	Pay.
0.26Q	1/21/94	1/25/94	1/31/94	2/15/94
0.30Q	4/21	4/26	5/2	5/15
0.30Q	7/22	7/26	8/1	8/15
0.30Q	10/20	10/25	10/31	11/15
0.30Q	1/19/95	1/25/95	1/31/95	2/15/95

Indicated div.: $1.20*

CAPITALIZATION (12/31/94):

	($000)	(%)
Total Deposits	11,235,013	74.9
Total Debt	2,276,544	15.2
Common & Surplus	1,306,528	8.7
Loan Valuation Reserve	172,606	1.2
Total	14,990,691	100.0

DIVIDEND ACHIEVER STATUS:
Rank: 59   1984-94 Growth Rate: 14.7%
Total Years of Dividend Growth: 16

RECENT DEVELOPMENTS: For the year ended 12/31/94, net income rose to $207.7 million compared with $204.3 million in 1993. Average total loans increased 11.1%, paced by an 11.8% rise in commercial loans. Consumer loans rose 10.2%. Net interest revenue was $597.6 million, up 5% from the prior year. Other operating revenue was $335.2 million versus $342.3 million. Trust and investment management fees increased to $117.9 million from $110.2 million.

PROSPECTS: The recently completed acquisition of First Colonial Bankshares will expand the Company's presence in the greater Chicago area nearly three-fold. First Colonial, acquired for $314 million in a stock transaction, has assets of $1.4 billion. In anticipation of the merger with First Colonial, the Company consolidated its four existing Illinois banks into one state-chartered bank. Each branch of First Colonial will also be merged into the new entity, Firstar Bank Illinois.

BUSINESS

FIRSTAR CORPORATION, with $15 billion in assets, is the largest bank holding company headquartered in Wisconsin. FSR has 49 banks with 252 offices in Wisconsin, Iowa, Minnesota, Illinois, Florida and Arizona. Bank subsidiaries provide financial services including issuing and servicing credit cards, engaging in correspondent banking and providing trust and investment services. Nonbank subsidiaries provide retail brokerage services, trust and investment services, title insurance, business insurance, and consumer and credit insurance.

LOAN DISTRIBUTION

(12/31/94)	($000)	(%)
Commercial & Industrial	2,753,251	28.0
Real Estate-Construction	272,266	2.8
Real Estate-Mortgage	2,014,262	20.5
Foreign	32,395	0.3
Other Commercial	905,795	9.2
Consumer	3,850,058	39.2
Total	9,828,027	100.0

ANNUAL EARNINGS AND DIVIDENDS PER SHARE

	1994	1993	1992	1991	1990	1989	1988
Earnings Per Share	3.22	3.15	2.62	2.13	2.05	1.87	2.44
Dividends Per Share	1.16	1.00	① 0.80	0.705	0.635	0.545	0.49
Dividend Payout %	36.0	31.8	30.5	33.0	31.0	29.2	20.1

① 2-for-1 stk split, 10/1/92

ANNUAL FINANCIAL DATA

RECORD OF EARNINGS (IN MILLIONS):

	1994	1993	1992	1991	1990	1989	1988
Total Interest Income	938.0	867.0	898.5	981.7	763.1	727.8	619.8
Total Interest Expense	340.4	298.9	359.4	501.1	427.9	406.4	325.9
Net Interest Income	597.6	568.1	539.2	480.6	335.1	321.4	293.9
Credit Loss Provision	17.1	24.6	44.8	50.3	37.2	43.6	33.6
Net Income	207.7	204.3	166.0	134.3	97.6	87.2	① 109.9
Aver. Shs. Outstg. (000)	64,611	63,747	61,879	60,998	45,578	44,582	42,832

① Before extra. item cr$22,422,000.

BALANCE SHEET (IN MILLIONS):

	1994	1993	1992	1991	1990	1989	1988
Cash & Due From Banks	999.9	1,229.0	1,290.0	1,070.5	966.8	863.6	828.0
Loans & Lse Financing, Net	9,655.4	8,808.9	7,943.0	7,394.0	5,681.1	5,253.7	4,903.3
Total Domestic Deposits	11,235.0	11,163.6	10,884.1	10,063.4	7,494.3	6,810.4	6,220.6
Total Foreign Deposits	...	...	...	...	28.6	24.9	72.9
Long-term Debt	135.1	126.3	157.9	143.8	161.3	165.8	167.4
Net Stockholders' Equity	1,306.5	1,155.9	1,048.4	916.3	659.5	580.1	506.7
Total Assets	15,104.3	13,794.0	13,168.9	12,309.5	9,382.9	8,607.9	7,841.9
Year End Shs Outstg (000)	65,875	64,919	62,640	61,132	46,472	44,634	42,964

STATISTICAL RECORD:

	1994	1993	1992	1991	1990	1989	1988
Return on Assets %	1.38	1.48	1.26	1.09	1.04	1.01	1.40
Return on Equity %	15.90	17.70	15.40	14.70	14.80	15.00	21.70
Book Value Per Share	19.83	17.81	16.73	14.98	14.18	12.98	11.78
Average Yield %	3.8	3.0	2.9	3.8	4.5	3.6	4.1
P/E Ratio	11.0-7.8	11.8-9.3	12.2-8.8	11.4-6.0	8.3-5.4	9.4-6.9	5.6-4.3
Price Range	35⅜-25⅛	37¼-29⅜	31⅞-23⅛	24½-12¾		17-11	17½-12⅞	13½-10⅜

Statistics are as originally reported.

OFFICERS:
R.L. Fitzsimonds, Chmn. & C.E.O.
J.A. Becker, Pres. & C.O.O.
W.H. Risch, Sr. V.P.-Fin. & Treas.

INCORPORATED: WI, 1929

PRINCIPAL OFFICE: 777 East Wisconsin Ave., Milwaukee, WI 53202

TELEPHONE NUMBER: (414) 765-4321
FAX: (414) 765-4349
NO. OF EMPLOYEES: 7,680 (full-time); part-time, 2,196.
ANNUAL MEETING: In April
SHAREHOLDERS: 9,962
INSTITUTIONAL HOLDINGS:
No. of Institutions: 52
Shares Held: 6,882,588

REGISTRAR(S): First Wisconsin Trust Co., Milwaukee, WI

TRANSFER AGENT(S): First Wisconsin Trust Co., Milwaukee, WI

NASDAQ SYMBOL FMER
Rec. Pr. 23¼

FIRSTMERIT CORP.

YIELD 4.3%
P/E RATIO 10.4

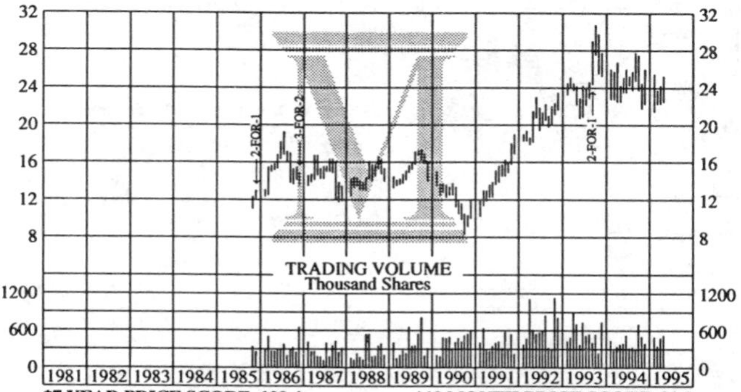

*7 YEAR PRICE SCORE 109.4 *12 MONTH PRICE SCORE 91.8

*NYSE COMPOSITE INDEX=100

INTERIM EARNINGS (Per Share):

Qtr.	Mar.	June	Sept.	Dec.
1991	0.37	0.41	0.41	0.41
1992	0.49	0.48	0.51	0.54
1993	0.52	0.56	0.56	0.54
1994	0.56	0.55	0.55	0.57

INTERIM DIVIDENDS (Per Share):

Amt.	Decl.	Ex.	Rec.	Pay.
0.25Q	8/18/94	8/23/94	8/29/94	09/12/94
0.25Q	11/17	11/21	11/28	12/12
0.25Q	2/16/95	2/21/95	2/27/95	3/13/95

*Indicated div.:$1.00**

CAPITALIZATION (12/31/94):

	($000)	(%)
Common & Surplus	431,538	100.0
Total	431,538	100.0

DIVIDEND ACHIEVER STATUS:
Rank: 202 1984-94 Growth Rate: 8.4%
Total Years of Dividend Growth: 12

RECENT DEVELOPMENTS: For the year ended 12/31/94, net income advanced 8.5% to $60.3 million compared with $55.6 million in the corresponding period of 1993. Interest income rose 4% to $316.8 million versus $304.6 million in the year earlier period. Net income was favorably affected by improved asset quality and increased non-interest income. The return on average assets for FMER equaled 1.31% in 1994 compared with 1.28% in 1993. Net interest income increased 3.1% to $200.9 million from $194.8 million in 1993. The increase resulted from an increase in average earning assets, but was offset slightly by lower yielding assets and interest rate spread. Loan loss reserves were reduced to $33.1 million or 1.04% of loans outstanding due to improved asset quality.

BUSINESS

FIRSTMERIT CORPORATION (formerly First Bancorporation of Ohio) is a multi-bank holding company. Through its subsidiaries it provides a wide range of banking, fiduciary, financial and investment services to corporate, institutional and individual customers throughout northern Ohio and southwestern Florida. In addition to the customary services of accepting funds for deposit and making loans, the Bank provides a wide range of specialized services tailored to specific markets, including personal and corporate trust services, personal financial services, cash management services and international banking. Non-banking subsidiaries provide insurance sales services, reinsurance of credit life and accident and health insurance, and brokerage services.

LOAN DISTRIBUTION

(12/31/94)	($000)	(%)
Comml, Financial & Agri	467,428	14.7
Loans to Individuals	776,757	24.4
Real Estate	1,777,082	55.9
Lease Financing	158,659	5.0
Total	3,179,926	100.0

ANNUAL EARNINGS AND DIVIDENDS PER SHARE

	1994	1993	1992	1991	1990	1989	1988
Earnings Per Share	**2.22**	**2.19**	**2.02**	**1.58**	**(2) 1.39**	**1.60**	**1.56**
Dividends Per Share	**0.985**	**(1) 0.90**	**0.825**	**0.803**	**0.763**	**0.731**	**0.688**
Dividend Payout %	**44.4**	**41.0**	**40.8**	**51.0**	**54.9**	**45.9**	**44.1**

(1) 2-for-1 stk split,09/28/93 (2) Before acctg. chg.

ANNUAL FINANCIAL DATA

	1994	1993	1992	1991	1990	1989	1988
RECORD OF EARNINGS (IN MILLIONS):							
Total Revenues	373.7	332.1	345.7	360.1	364.7	328.7	254.3
Costs and Expenses	287.3	251.3	272.6	305.2	318.7	278.7	212.1
Operating Profit	144.0	133.9	123.4	102.6	90.4	71.5	59.1
Inc Bef Fed Income Taxes	86.4	80.7	73.1	55.0	46.1	50.0	42.1
Income Taxes	26.1	25.5	22.4	15.4	11.2	11.4	8.2
Net Income	60.3	55.2	50.7	39.6	34.9	38.6	(1) 33.9
Aver. Shs. Outstg. (000)	27,152	25,219	25,158	25,110	25,108	24,176	21,742
(1) Before acctg. change cr$1,282,000.							
BALANCE SHEET (IN MILLIONS):							
Cash and Cash Equivalents	226.4	281.0	306.2	272.5	389.4	340.1	305.3
Gross Property	77.3	69.8	67.5	69.8	68.8	64.2	46.9
Net Stockholders' Equity	431.5	391.6	358.3	327.4	307.9	296.5	258.5
Total Assets	4,924.2	3,996.7	3,916.2	3,765.7	3,722.1	3,334.2	3,048.9
Total Current Assets	226.4	281.0	306.2	272.5	389.4	340.1	305.3
Total Current Liabilities	4,492.6	3,605.1	3,557.9	3,438.3	3,414.2	3,037.7	2,790.5
Net Working Capital	d4,266.2	d3,324.1	d3,251.8	d3,165.8	d3,024.8	d2,697.6	d2,485.2
Year End Shs Outstg (000)	27,166	25,249	25,196	25,117	25,108	24,178	21,764
STATISTICAL RECORD:							
Book Value Per Share	15.89	15.51	14.22	13.04	12.26	12.26	11.88
Return on Equity %	14.0	14.1	14.2	12.1	11.3	13.0	13.1
Return on Assets %	1.2	1.4	1.3	1.1	0.9	1.2	1.1
Average Yield %	4.0	3.5	4.0	5.5	6.6	4.8	4.7
P/E Ratio	12.5-9.8	14.0-9.5	11.6-8.8	12.0-6.5	10.8-5.9	10.9-8.3	10.7-7.9
Price Range	27¾-21¾	30¾-20¾	23½-17⅞	19-10¼	15-8¼	17⅜-13¼	16⅝-12⅜

Statistics are as originally reported.

OFFICERS:
H.L. Flood, Chmn.
J.R. Cochran, Pres. & C.E.O.
T.E. Patton, Sr. V.P. & Sec.
G.J. Elek, Sr. V.P. & Treas.

INCORPORATED: OH, Nov., 1981

PRINCIPAL OFFICE: III Cascade Plaza, Akron, OH 44308-1103

TELEPHONE NUMBER: (216) 996-6300

NO. OF EMPLOYEES: 3,300 (approx.)

ANNUAL MEETING: In April

SHAREHOLDERS: 6,828 (approx.)

INSTITUTIONAL HOLDINGS:
No. of Institutions: 70
Shares Held: 2,982,032

REGISTRAR(S): Firstmerit Corp.

TRANSFER AGENT(S): Firstmerit Corp.

FLEETWOOD ENTERPRISES, INC.

YIELD 2.4%
P/E RATIO 12.0

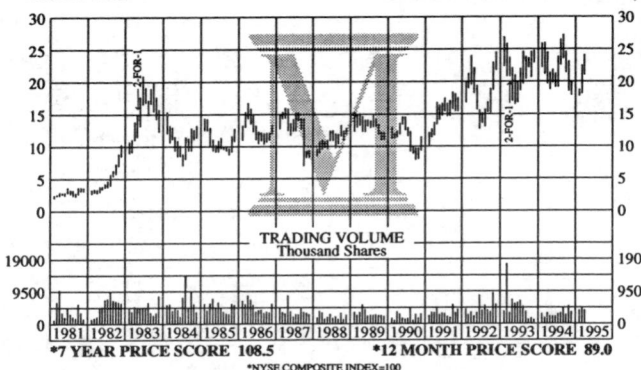

TRADING VOLUME
Thousand Shares

| 1981 | 1982 | 1983 | 1984 | 1985 | 1986 | 1987 | 1988 | 1989 | 1990 | 1991 | 1992 | 1993 | 1994 | 1995 |

*7 YEAR PRICE SCORE 108.5 *12 MONTH PRICE SCORE 89.0
*NYSE COMPOSITE INDEX=100

INTERIM EARNINGS (Per Share):

Qtr.	July	Oct.	Jan.	Apr.
1992-93	-------	1.23	-------	
1993-94	0.33	0.37	0.26	0.50
1994-95	0.63	0.45	0.39	...

INTERIM DIVIDENDS (Per Share):

Amt.	Decl.	Ex.	Rec.	Pay.
0.125Q	3/8/94	3/25/94	4/1/94	5/11/94
0.14Q	6/14	6/27	7/1	8/10
0.14Q	9/13	10/3	10/7	11/9
0.14Q	12/13	12/30	1/6/95	2/8/95
0.14Q	3/14/95	4/3/95	4/7	5/10

Indicated div.: $0.56

CAPITALIZATION (4/24/94):

	($000)	(%)
Minority Interest	d251	0.0
Common & Surplus	546,466	100.0
Total	546,215	100.0

DIVIDEND ACHIEVER STATUS:
Rank: 110   1984-94 Growth Rate: 12.4%
Total Years of Dividend Growth: 12

RECENT DEVELOPMENTS: For the quarter ended 1/29/95, net income increased 50.9% to $18.3 million from $12.1 million in the comparable period of 1993. Revenues were up 20.6% to $661.4 million, compared with $548.6 million the year before. The improvement in earnings was attributed to higher operating income from the manufactured housing segment and higher interest income. A lower tax rate also contributed to the increase. Revenues from housing operations advanced 31.3% to $330.6 million from $251.7 million.

PROSPECTS: Sales growth continues to be driven by strong gains in FLE's manufactured housing and recreational vehicle operations. FLE's manufactured housing group should continue to experience growth as it has further expanded its market share. Revenue growth in the recreational vehicle group is being driven by healthy demand for towable products and motor homes. Despite growth in sales, earnings in FLE's European RV operation continue to lag.

BUSINESS

FLEETWOOD ENTERPRISES is a major producer of recreational vehicles and manufactured homes. FLE's motor homes, travel trailers, folding trailers and slide-in truck campers are used for leisure-time activities, including vacation, sightseeing and fishing trips. The Company offers financing to its Recreational Vehicle (RV) dealers and customers through its wholly-owned subsidiary, Fleetwood Credit Corp., while a supply group produces components for both Fleetwood and other companies. FLE operates manufacturing plants in 18 U.S. states and in Canada and Germany. Products are marketed through independent dealers.

BUSINESS LINE ANALYSIS

(4/24/94)	Rev(%)	Inc(%)
Recreational Vehicles	52.2	37.1
Manufactured Housing	44.4	48.1
Supply Operations	1.5	4.2
Finance Operations	1.9	10.6
Total	100.0	100.0

ANNUAL EARNINGS AND DIVIDENDS PER SHARE

	4/24/94	4/25/93	4/26/92	4/28/91	4/29/90	4/30/89	4/24/88
Earnings Per Share	1.46	1.23	0.88	0.69	1.21	1.53	1.04
Dividends Per Share	0.53	☐ 0.49	0.43	0.40	0.35	0.31	0.28
Dividend Payout %	36.3	49.2	48.9	58.4	28.9	20.3	26.9

☐ 2-for-1 stk split,03/02/93

ANNUAL FINANCIAL DATA

RECORD OF EARNINGS (IN MILLIONS):

Total Revenues	2,369.4	1,941.9	1,589.3	1,400.9	1,549.4	1,618.5	1,406.0
Costs and Expenses	2,246.4	1,842.8	1,519.6	1,351.5	1,459.5	1,504.4	1,331.0
Depreciation	18.6	15.6	15.1	15.1	13.9	12.0	10.3
Operating Income	104.4	83.5	54.7	34.3	76.0	102.1	64.7
Inc Bef Prov for Income Taxes	112.0	91.3	64.1	46.6	86.7	113.7	73.4
Income Taxes	45.9	34.8	23.9	16.2	31.6	43.3	28.1
Net Income	☐ 67.4	56.6	40.2	30.4	55.0	70.5	48.2
Aver. Shs. Outstg. (000)	46,207	45,961	45,648	44,584	45,510	46,106	46,364

☐ Before acctg. change dr$1,500,000.

BALANCE SHEET (IN MILLIONS):

Cash and Cash Equivalents	158.5	158.5	197.1	170.3	155.4	180.5	136.0
Receivables, Net	603.3	525.7	418.4	317.5	370.3	285.2	113.0
Inventories	183.7	154.7	112.3	94.1	106.3	118.2	96.5
Gross Property	345.7	282.9	247.0	230.6	219.9	190.0	160.5
Accumulated Depreciation	124.9	110.5	96.6	86.9	76.5	67.3	57.5
Net Stockholders' Equity	546.5	502.6	468.0	428.1	424.3	400.6	343.9
Total Assets	1,224.1	1,061.9	915.0	764.6	817.5	717.9	514.0
Total Current Assets	945.5	838.9	727.8	581.9	632.0	583.9	360.1
Total Current Liabilities	534.9	438.7	345.3	255.3	315.7	252.3	160.4
Net Working Capital	410.6	400.2	382.5	326.5	316.2	331.5	199.7
Year End Shs Outstg (000)	45,996	45,667	45,606	43,786	44,616	45,816	45,804

STATISTICAL RECORD:

Operating Profit Margin %	4.4	4.3	3.4	2.4	4.9	6.3	4.6
Book Value Per Share	11.88	11.01	10.26	9.78	9.51	8.74	7.51
Return on Equity %	12.3	11.3	8.6	7.1	13.0	17.6	14.0
Return on Assets %	5.5	5.3	4.4	4.0	6.7	9.8	9.4
Average Yield %	2.5	3.2	3.0	3.6	2.7	2.8	2.4
P/E Ratio	18.8-11.5	20.0-10.4	20.9-11.6	21.5-11.6	12.7-9.1	8.7-5.6	15.4-6.7
Price Range	26⅞-16½	24⅝-12¾	18⅜-10¼	14⅝-7⅞	15⅜-11	13⅜-8½	16-7

Statistics are as originally reported.

OFFICERS:
J.C. Crean, Chmn. & C.E.O.
P.M. Bingham, Fin. V.P., C.F.O.
W.H. Lear, V.P., General Counsel & Sec.

INCORPORATED: DE, Sep., 1977; reincorp., CA, 1957

PRINCIPAL OFFICE: 3125 Myers Street, Riverside, CA 92503-5527

TELEPHONE NUMBER: (909) 351-3500

NO. OF EMPLOYEES: 16,000 (approx.)

ANNUAL MEETING: In September

SHAREHOLDERS: 2,000 (approx.)

INSTITUTIONAL HOLDINGS:
No. of Institutions: 163
Shares Held: 14,934,680

REGISTRAR(S): First National Bank of Boston, Boston, MA

TRANSFER AGENT(S): First National Bank of Boston, Boston, MA

NYS SYMBOL FSI
Rec. Pr. 48⅛

FLIGHTSAFETY INTERNATIONAL, INC.

YIELD 1.0%
P/E RATIO 20.5

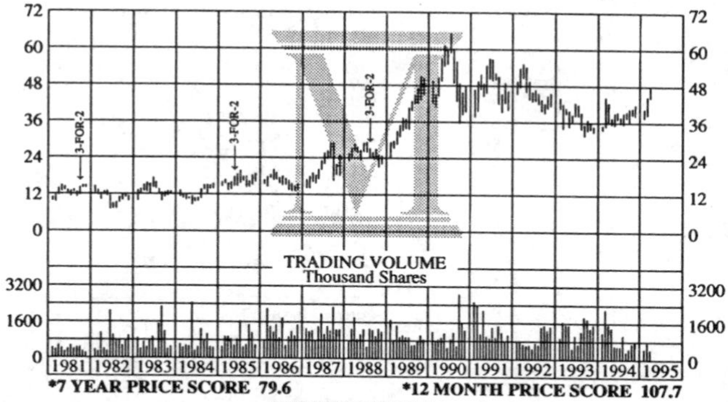

*7 YEAR PRICE SCORE 79.6 *12 MONTH PRICE SCORE 107.7

*NYSE COMPOSITE INDEX=100

INTERIM EARNINGS (Per Share):

Qtr.	Mar.	June	Sept.	Dec.
1991	0.52	0.53	0.48	0.58
1992	0.54	0.58	0.75	0.52
1993	0.50	0.56	0.34	0.61
1994	0.51	0.58	0.51	0.75

INTERIM DIVIDENDS (Per Share):

Amt.	Decl.	Ex.	Rec.	Pay.
0.10Q	3/8/94	4/8/94	4/14/94	5/4/94
0.10Q	6/14	7/8	7/14	8/4
0.12Q	9/13	10/6	10/13	11/3
0.12Q	12/2	1/6/95	1/12/95	2/2/95
0.12Q	3/13/95	4/10	4/17	5/9

Indicated div.: $0.48

CAPITALIZATION (12/31/94):

	($000)	(%)
Long-Term Debt	39,813	5.6
Deferred Income Tax	108,308	15.3
Common & Surplus	560,404	79.1
Total	708,525	100.0

DIVIDEND ACHIEVER STATUS:
Rank: 38 1984-94 Growth Rate: 16.8%
Total Years of Dividend Growth: 18

RECENT DEVELOPMENTS: For the year ended 12/31/94, net income rose 12.1% to $74.5 million from $66.4 million a year ago. Total revenues were $301.3 million, up 1.4% from $297.1 million the year before. Operating income jumped 14.6% to $101.2 million with income from training and product sales contributing 94.6% and 5.4%, respectively. For the quarter ended 12/31/94, net income was $23.5 millon compared with $19.6 million for the year-ago quarter, an increase of 19.7%.

PROSPECTS: In January 1995, FSI signed a joint venture agreement with Xingyun Co. Ltd.'s Yunnan Tobacco Group of the People's Republic of China to establish the Kunming FlightSafety Aviation Training Company, Ltd. in Kunming, China. The company has been awarded a five-year contract from the United States Army as well as a six-year contract from Business Express. Both contracts involve pilot initial and recurrent training. The company is presently offering flight attendant training to airlines.

BUSINESS

FLIGHTSAFETY INTERNATIONAL, INC., offers high-technology training to operators of aircraft, ships, electrical utilities, steam generating and processing plants. Simulators are used that enable trainees to practice and perfect normal and emergency procedures under controlled conditions. FSI's clients include: corporations, commercial airlines, ship operators, military and other government agencies, including 20 aircraft manufacturers. The Company operates 38 learning centers with more than 160 flight simulators in the U.S., Montreal and Toronto, Canada and two locations in France.

REVENUES

(12/31/94)	($000)	(%)
Training Revenue	271,743	90.2
Product Sales	29,556	9.8
Total	301,299	100.0

ANNUAL EARNINGS AND DIVIDENDS PER SHARE

	1994	1993	1992	1991	1990	1989	1988
Earnings Per Share	2.35	2.01	2.39	2.11	[1] 2.48	1.93	1.48
Dividends Per Share	0.42	0.37	0.30	0.25	0.21	0.17	[2] 0.147
Dividend Payout %	17.9	18.4	12.6	11.8	8.5	8.8	9.9

[1] Before acctg. chg. [2] 50% stk. div., 8/88.

ANNUAL FINANCIAL DATA

	1994	1993	1992	1991	1990	1989	1988
RECORD OF EARNINGS (IN THOUSANDS):							
Total Revenues	301,299	297,096	278,435	267,641	283,392	231,297	182,732
Costs and Expenses	147,603	151,575	132,362	131,101	125,409	100,268	79,041
Depreciation & Amort	46,711	44,337	39,951	36,337	30,937	26,548	23,099
Operating Profit	106,985	101,184	106,122	100,203	127,046	104,481	80,592
Income Bef Income Taxes	115,966	109,549	128,015	110,594	119,785	103,691	78,353
Income Taxes	41,491	43,135	45,706	38,152	44,064	38,084	28,339
Net Income	74,475	66,414	82,309	72,442	[1] 75,721	65,607	50,014
Aver. Shs. Outstg.	31,707	33,089	34,410	34,307	34,171	33,991	33,790
[1] Before acctg. change cr$9,011,000.							
BALANCE SHEET (IN THOUSANDS):							
Cash and Cash Equivalents	196,992	181,049	278,676	204,803	158,782	107,601	72,281
Receivables, Net	59,718	48,963	41,358	46,029	37,994	31,624	31,901
Inventories	14,330	14,605	9,858	...	...	...	...
Gross Property	806,651	744,408	680,903	614,099	570,051	493,624	427,703
Accumulated Depreciation	336,590	291,030	247,219	209,527	179,795	152,931	132,765
Long-Term Debt	39,813	41,572	44,630	29,653	35,086	33,760	38,778
Net Stockholders' Equity	560,404	526,433	564,409	490,433	423,234	336,560	273,917
Total Assets	792,929	753,934	814,486	690,594	620,998	524,584	451,397
Total Current Assets	281,376	253,203	338,349	259,825	204,327	145,931	123,170
Total Current Liabilities	79,203	75,078	106,846	75,367	77,590	60,287	49,822
Net Working Capital	202,173	178,125	231,503	184,458	126,737	85,644	73,348
Year End Shares Outstg	31,315	32,008	34,457	34,371	34,245	34,078	33,876
STATISTICAL RECORD:							
Operating Profit Margin %	35.5	34.1	38.1	37.4	44.8	45.2	44.1
Book Value Per Share	17.90	16.45	16.38	14.27	12.36	9.88	8.09
Return on Equity %	13.3	12.6	14.6	14.8	17.9	19.5	18.3
Return on Assets %	9.4	8.8	10.1	10.5	12.2	12.5	11.1
Average Yield %	1.1	1.0	0.6	0.5	0.4	0.5	0.6
P/E Ratio	18.8-14.3	21.9-15.7	23.1-16.3	27.0-17.9	26.3-14.3	26.4-12.5	19.8-14.2
Price Range	44¼-33½	44-31⅝	55¼-39	57-37¾	65¼-35½	51-24⅛	29¼-21

Statistics are as originally reported.

OFFICERS:
A.L. Ueltschi, Chmn. & Pres.
K.W. Motschwiller, V.P. & Treas.

INCORPORATED: NY, Mar., 1951

PRINCIPAL OFFICE: Marine Air Terminal/La Guardia Airport, Flushing, NY 11371-1061

TELEPHONE NUMBER: (718) 565-4100

FAX: (718) 565-4134

NO. OF EMPLOYEES: 2,246 (full-time)

ANNUAL MEETING: In April

SHAREHOLDERS: 10,800 (approx.)

INSTITUTIONAL HOLDINGS:
No. of Institutions: 168
Shares Held: 15,457,470

REGISTRAR(S): Chase Manhattan Bank, N.A., New York, NY 10031

TRANSFER AGENT(S): Chase Manhattan Bank, N.A., New York, NY 10031

NYS SYMBOL FPC
Rec. Pr. 30⅝

FLORIDA PROGRESS CORP.

YIELD 6.6%
P/E RATIO 13.5

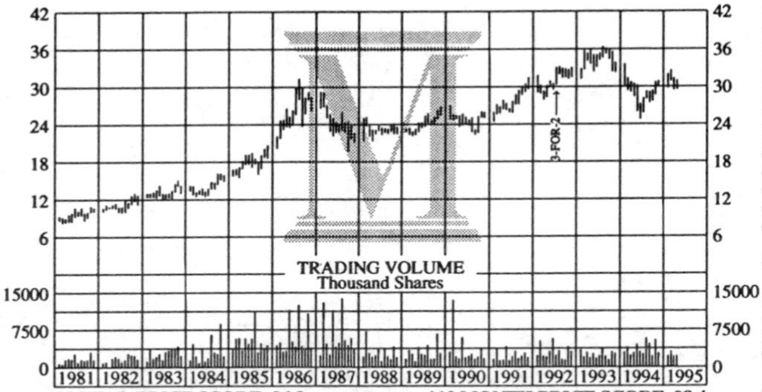

*7 YEAR PRICE SCORE 86.3 *12 MONTH PRICE SCORE 98.4

*NYSE COMPOSITE INDEX=100

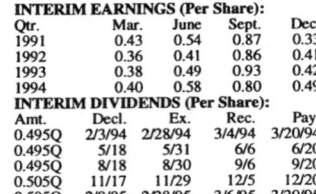

INTERIM EARNINGS (Per Share):

Qtr.	Mar.	June	Sept.	Dec.
1991	0.43	0.54	0.87	0.33
1992	0.36	0.41	0.86	0.41
1993	0.38	0.49	0.93	0.42
1994	0.40	0.58	0.80	0.49

INTERIM DIVIDENDS (Per Share):

Amt.	Decl.	Ex.	Rec.	Pay.
0.495Q	2/3/94	2/28/94	3/4/94	3/20/94
0.495Q	5/18	5/31	6/6	6/20
0.495Q	8/18	8/30	9/6	9/20
0.505Q	11/17	11/29	12/5	12/20
0.505Q	2/9/95	2/28/95	3/6/95	3/20/95

Indicated div.: $2.02*

CAPITALIZATION (12/31/94):

	($000)	(%)
Long-Term Debt	1,859,600	38.4
Deferred Income Tax	854,100	17.6
Preferred Stock	143,500	3.0
Common & Surplus	1,984,400	41.0
Total	4,841,600	100.0
Current Debt	52,900	

DIVIDEND ACHIEVER STATUS:
Rank: 300 1984-94 Growth Rate: 3.9%
Total Years of Dividend Growth: 42

RECENT DEVELOPMENTS: For the quarter ended 12/31/94, net income rose 24% to $46.0 million from $37.2 million in the corresponding 1993 period. Revenues were $682.9 million, up 8%. For the year ended 12/31/94, net income was $212.0 million compared with $195.8 million, before accounting changes, a year earlier. Revenues were up 13% to $2.77 billion. Results were bolstered by the transportation unit.

PROSPECTS: FPC's long-term prospects are positive, due to Florida's resilient economy. Recent restructuring and cost-cutting measures are preparing the Company for increased competition. Competitive pressures are mitigated by FPL's relatively low dependence on industrial sales. Customer growth is expected to continue its strong pace. The Company's diversified operations will provide for higher earnings growth in the future.

BUSINESS

FLORIDA PROGRESS is a diversifed utility holding company whose principal subsidiary is Florida Power Corp. and whose diversified operations include coal mining, real estate, and financial services. Florida Power services over 1.2 million customers in 32 counties along the Gulf Coast through the central ridge sector of Florida. The territory comprises about 20,000 square miles with a population of more than 4.4 million. Electric Fuels Corp. is involved in coal mining, transloading facilities, rail cars, barges and tugs. FPC's other subsidiaries are Talquin Corp., Progress Energy Corp., Progress Technologies Corp., Progress Credit Corp., Inc., and Mid-Continental Life Insurance.

BUSINESS LINE ANALYSIS

(12/31/94)	Rev(%)	Inc(%)
Utility	75.1	88.5
Diversified	24.9	11.5
Total	100.0	100.0

ANNUAL EARNINGS AND DIVIDENDS PER SHARE

	1994	1993	1992	1991	1990	1989	1988
Earnings Per Share	**2.28**	**2.22**	**2.06**	**[2] 2.16**	**[2] 2.33**	**2.45**	**2.35**
Dividends Per Share	**1.99**	**1.95**	**[1] 1.904**	**1.843**	**1.777**	**1.72**	**1.667**
Dividend Payout %	**87.2**	**87.8**	**92.4**	**85.3**	**76.1**	**70.3**	**70.1**

[1] 3-for-2 stk split,07/30/92 [2] Before disc. oper.

ANNUAL FINANCIAL DATA

	1994	1993	1992	1991	1990	1989	1988
RECORD OF EARNINGS (IN MILLIONS):							
Total Revenues	2,771.5	2,449.0	2,095.3	2,074.7	2,010.8	2,129.4	2,002.0
Depreciation	321.7	299.9	268.7	266.3	161.1	195.7	190.4
Maintenance	122.9	136.8	139.7	134.8	126.2	137.6	117.8
Prov for Fed Inc Taxes	109.7	110.4	88.5	91.9	102.4	88.8	63.6
Income From Operations	476.0	442.6	404.8	415.4	434.1	410.2	365.7
Interest Expense	144.8	141.1	134.2	146.1	144.4	131.2	117.3
Net Income	212.0	196.6	175.7	[1] 174.5	[2] 179.8	187.1	179.8
Aver. Shs. Outstg. (000)	93,000	88,300	85,400	80,850	76,950	76,650	76,650
[1] Before disc. op. dr$2,400,000. [2] Before disc. op. dr$15,000,000.							
BALANCE SHEET (IN MILLIONS):							
Gross Plant	6,299.3	6,066.0	5,645.5	5,199.3	4,924.3	4,690.4	4,452.5
Accumulated Depreciation	2,209.2	2,033.0	1,809.9	1,657.7	1,503.9	1,383.4	1,252.4
Prop, Plant & Equip, Net	4,090.1	4,033.0	3,835.6	3,541.6	3,420.4	3,307.0	3,200.1
Long-term Debt	1,859.6	1,866.6	1,656.4	1,581.1	1,326.2	1,126.7	1,050.0
Net Stockholders' Equity	2,127.9	1,969.0	1,953.6	1,818.7	1,657.8	1,605.8	1,550.4
Total Assets	5,718.7	5,638.8	5,333.0	5,024.9	5,045.9	4,634.0	4,303.5
Year End Shs Outstg (000)	95,175	89,260	87,530	82,933	77,551	76,577	76,577
STATISTICAL RECORD:							
Book Value Per Share	20.85	20.40	19.85	19.14	18.37	17.92	17.20
Op. Inc/Net Pl %	11.6	11.0	10.6	11.7	12.7	12.4	11.4
Dep/Gr. Pl %	4.2	4.0	3.7	4.0	3.3	3.6	3.3
Accum. Dep/Gr. Pl %	35.1	33.5	32.1	31.9	30.5	29.5	28.1
Return on Equity %	10.1	10.1	9.4	10.1	11.5	12.4	12.4
Average Yield %	6.8	5.8	6.2	6.6	7.2	7.0	7.2
P/E Ratio	14.7-10.9	16.4-14.1	16.1-13.5	14.6-11.3	11.6-9.6	11.0-9.0	10.7-9.1
Price Range	33⅝-24¾	36⅜-31¼	33¼-27⅞	31½-24⅜	27-22⅜	26⅞-22⅛	25⅛-21⅜

Statistics are as originally reported.

OFFICERS:
Dr. J.B. Critchfield, Chmn. & C.E.O.
J.K. Heinicka, Sr. V.P.-Fin. & C.F.O.
D.R. Kuzma, V.P. & Treas.
K.E. Armstrong, V.P., Gen. Couns. & Sec.

INCORPORATED: FL, Jan., 1982

PRINCIPAL OFFICE: P O Box 33042 One Progress Plaza, St Petersburg, FL 33733

TELEPHONE NUMBER: (813) 824-6400
FAX: (813) 824-6401
NO. OF EMPLOYEES: 7,929
ANNUAL MEETING: In April
SHAREHOLDERS: 58,265
INSTITUTIONAL HOLDINGS:
No. of Institutions: 249
Shares Held: 29,161,777

REGISTRAR(S): Chemical Bank, New York, NY

TRANSFER AGENT(S): Chemical Bank, New York, NY

FLOWERS INDUSTRIES, INC.

YIELD 4.6%
P/E RATIO 25.7

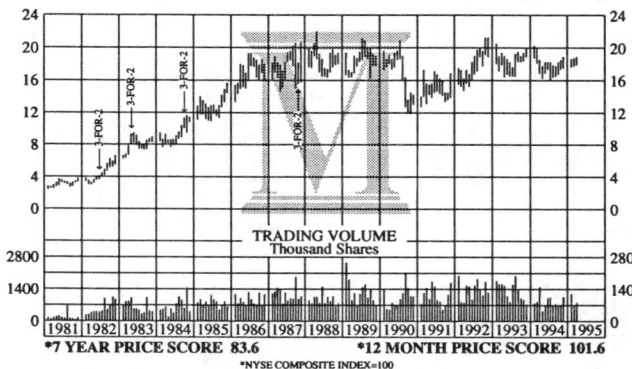

7 YEAR PRICE SCORE 83.6 **12 MONTH PRICE SCORE 101.6**

*NYSE COMPOSITE INDEX=100

INTERIM EARNINGS (Per Share):

Qtr.	Sept.	Dec.	Mar.	June
1991-92	0.11	0.16	0.20	0.44
1992-93	---------------- 1.07 ----------------			
1993-94	0.13	0.22	0.20	0.25
1994-95	0.17	0.28	0.10	0.25

INTERIM DIVIDENDS (Per Share):

Amt.	Decl.	Ex.	Rec.	Pay.
0.195Q	1/21/94	1/31/94	2/4/94	2/18/94
0.1975Q	4/15	4/25	4/29	5/13
0.20Q	8/5	8/15	8/19	9/2
0.2025Q	10/21	10/31	11/4	11/18
0.205Q	1/13/95	1/23/95	1/27/95	2/10/95

*Indicated div.: $0.82**

CAPITALIZATION (7/2/94):

	($000)	(%)
Long-Term Debt	88,986	22.0
Cap. Lease Oblig.	3,900	0.9
Deferred Income Tax	36,296	9.0
Common & Surplus	275,731	68.1
Total	404,913	100.0

DIVIDEND ACHIEVER STATUS:
Rank: 101   1984-94 Growth Rate: 12.9%
Total Years of Dividend Growth: 22

RECENT DEVELOPMENTS: For the 12 weeks ended 12/17/94, net income was a record $10.6 million compared with $8.2 million a year ago. Earnings per share rose 27% to $0.28 from $0.22 a year ago. Net sales increased 15.3% to a record $270.0 million, reflecting volume gains, product mix changes, price increases, and recent acquisitions. For the 24 weeks ended 12/17/94, net income was $16.9 million versus $12.9 million in the prior-year period.

PROSPECTS: The Company's near-term focus will be on improving margins, which have been constrained recently by higher costs and difficult pricing. As part of this strategy, the Company has started to gradually raise prices and eliminate unprofitable volume in capacity-strained areas. In the meantime, bakery products will continue to face competition from private-label brands at grocery stores.

BUSINESS

FLOWERS INDUSTRIES operates in the packaged foods industry, serving primarily the grocery, food service, restaurant and fast-food markets. The Company produces a variety of branded food products, including: fresh and frozen breads, buns, specialty rolls, cakes and snacks, frozen specialty vegetables, batter-dipped and breaded vegetables, and fruits and desserts. Products are distributed primarily in the Southeast, Central and Western United States, and are sold chiefly to restaurants, fast-food chains, wholesalers, institutions, supermarkets and vending companies. Major brands include Beebo, Nature's Own, Stilwell, Cobblestone Mill, Blue Bird, and Sunbeam.

QUARTERLY DATA

(7/2/94)($000)	Rev	Inc
1st Quarter	217,359	4,667
2nd Quarter	234,239	8,193
3rd Quarter	221,659	7,376
4th Quarter	316,525	9,260

ANNUAL EARNINGS AND DIVIDENDS PER SHARE

	7/2/94	7/3/93	6/27/92	6/29/91	6/30/90	7/1/89	7/2/88
Earnings Per Share	0.80	1.07	0.92	0.71	① 0.98	0.85	① 1.18
Dividends Per Share	0.795	0.755	0.715	0.674	0.627	0.55	② 0.47
Dividend Payout %	99.4	70.1	77.7	94.9	64.0	64.7	39.8

① Before extraord. item ② 3-for-2 stk split, 11/87

ANNUAL FINANCIAL DATA

RECORD OF EARNINGS (IN THOUSANDS):

Total Revenues	999,733	972,142	888,722	831,199	843,477	789,291	749,871
Costs and Expenses	914,065	874,972	797,856	750,340	749,960	706,750	654,869
Depreciation & Amort	34,110	33,137	33,438	31,639	29,125	25,727	23,393
Operating Profit	51,558	64,033	57,428	49,220	64,392	56,814	71,609
Income Bef Income Taxes	47,240	60,032	49,236	39,799	55,939	47,497	62,036
Income Taxes	17,744	20,871	17,571	15,754	21,686	17,945	20,560
Net Income	29,496	39,161	31,665	24,045	①34,253	29,552	43,233
Aver. Shs. Outstg.	37,074	37,166	37,326	34,040	34,777	34,848	35,197

① Before extra. item dr$4,955,000.

BALANCE SHEET (IN THOUSANDS):

Cash and Cash Equivalents	19,758	17,162	14,262	11,042	17,424	25,958	23,643
Receivables, Net	93,088	82,267	75,789	68,961	66,786	70,246	68,079
Inventories	59,714	48,856	49,481	41,726	38,112	36,387	35,872
Gross Property	564,102	516,384	482,916	452,405	424,313	413,554	332,238
Accumulated Depreciation	243,846	225,266	205,284	179,344	153,516	146,502	111,722
Long-Term Debt	88,986	35,815	95,397	92,240	91,563	101,825	102,997
Capital Lease Obligations	3,900	700	...	...	...	...	...
Net Stockholders' Equity	275,731	280,154	218,266	206,310	215,766	208,477	198,217
Total Assets	560,852	490,948	462,113	434,905	439,207	448,037	433,575
Total Current Assets	176,085	151,127	142,995	124,421	125,231	136,527	131,241
Total Current Liabilities	121,514	119,604	98,966	86,680	76,970	88,103	79,292
Net Working Capital	54,571	31,523	44,029	37,741	48,261	48,424	51,949
Year End Shares Outstg	37,502	37,699	34,335	33,602	34,425	34,458	34,529

STATISTICAL RECORD:

Operating Profit Margin %	5.2	6.6	6.5	5.9	7.6	7.2	9.5
Book Value Per Share	7.10	7.23	6.20	6.09	6.22	5.82	5.60
Return on Equity %	10.7	14.0	14.5	11.7	15.9	14.2	20.9
Return on Assets %	5.3	8.0	6.9	5.5	7.8	6.6	9.6
Average Yield %	4.4	4.1	4.0	4.5	3.8	2.9	2.4
P/E Ratio	25.3-20.0	19.2-15.3	23.1-16.0	24.3-18.0	21.3-12.1	24.9-19.1	18.6-13.9
Price Range	20¼-16	20½-16⅜	21¼-14¾	17¼-12¾	20⅞-11⅞	21⅛-16¼	22-16⅜

Statistics are as originally reported.

OFFICERS:
A.R. McMullian, Chmn., C.E.O. & mollie H. Varnedoe, III, Pres., & C.O.O.
C.M. Wood, III, Sr. V.P., & C.F.O.
G.A. Campbell, Sec., & Gen. Counsel

INCORPORATED: DE, May, 1968; reincorp., GA, Dec., 1987

PRINCIPAL OFFICE: P.O. Box 1338, Thomasville, GA 31799-1338

TELEPHONE NUMBER: (912) 226-9110

NO. OF EMPLOYEES: 7,900 (approx.)

ANNUAL MEETING: In October

SHAREHOLDERS: 5,329

INSTITUTIONAL HOLDINGS:
No. of Institutions: 114
Shares Held: 13,895,021

REGISTRAR(S): Wachovia Bank of North Carolina, Winston-Salem, NC

TRANSFER AGENT(S): Wachovia Bank of North Carolina, Winston-Salem, NC

FRISCH'S RESTAURANTS, INC.

YIELD 2.7%
P/E RATIO 11.3

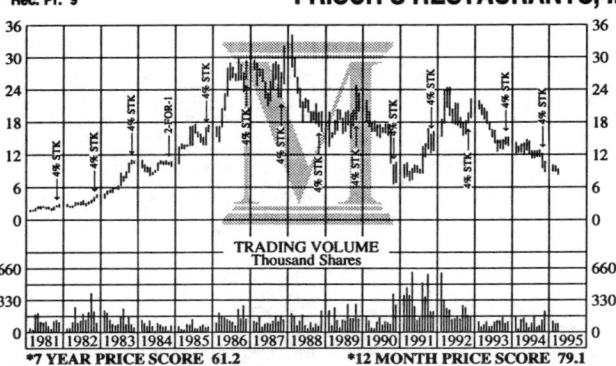

TRADING VOLUME
Thousand Shares

| | 1981 | 1982 | 1983 | 1984 | 1985 | 1986 | 1987 | 1988 | 1989 | 1990 | 1991 | 1992 | 1993 | 1994 | 1995 |

*7 YEAR PRICE SCORE 61.2   ***12 MONTH PRICE SCORE 79.1**
*NYSE COMPOSITE INDEX=100

INTERIM EARNINGS (Per Share):

Qtr.	Sept.	Dec.	Mar.	May
1992-93	----------	0.82	----------	
1993-94	----------	0.77	----------	
1994-95	0.23	0.17	...	...

INTERIM DIVIDENDS (Per Share):

Amt.	Decl.	Ex.	Rec.	Pay.
0.06Q	6/7/94	6/24/94	6/30/94	7/11/94
0.06Q	8/30	9/26	9/30	10/10
4%	11/22	11/28	12/2	12/27
0.06Q	11/22	12/23	12/30	1/10/95
0.06Q	3/14/95	3/27/95	3/31/95	4/10

Indicated div.: $0.24

CAPITALIZATION (5/29/94):

	($000)	(%)
Long-Term Debt	15,264	17.8
Cap. Lease Oblig.	7,022	8.2
Common & Surplus	63,589	74.0
Total	85,875	100.0

DIVIDEND ACHIEVER STATUS:
Rank: 271   1984-94 Growth Rate: 5.5%
Total Years of Dividend Growth: 11

RECENT DEVELOPMENTS: For the twelve weeks ended 3/5/95, the Company had a loss of $752,214 compared with income of $330,854 for the corresponding period of 1994. Total revenue increased to $34.7 million versus $34.1 million a year earlier. The loss was due to lower same store sales and higher operating costs. For the forty weeks ended 3/5/95, net income was $1.8 million, or $0.27 per share, compared with

$3.6 million, or $0.55 per share, in the corresponding period of 1994. Total revenue rose to $124.4 million from $122.8 million a year earlier. Total revenue continued to rise as the result of new Big Boy restaurants opened during the past 12 months. Earnings were pressured by winter storms which swept the Company's market areas for five weekends resulting in higher operating costs.

BUSINESS

FRISCH'S RESTAURANTS, INC. operates and licenses family restaurants with drive-through service under the names Frisch's Big Boy and Kip's Big Boy and operates restaurants under the name Hardee's. These restaurants are located in Ohio, Indiana, Kentucky, Florida, Oklahoma and Texas. Additionally, the Company operates two hotels with restaurants and two specialty restaurants in metropolitan Cincinnati, where it is headquartered. Trademarks which the Company has the right to use include "Frisch's," "Big Boy," "Kip's," "Hardee's," "Quality Hotel," and "Prime'n Wine."

ANNUAL EARNINGS AND DIVIDENDS PER SHARE

	5/29/94	5/30/93	5/31/92	6/2/91	6/3/90	5/28/89	5/29/88
Earnings Per Share	0.77	0.82	0.81	0.50	0.47	0.31	0.52
Dividends Per Share	0.213	①0.205	②0.197	0.189	0.182	0.16	0.155
Dividend Payout %	27.7	25.0	24.3	38.7	51.6	29.8	

Note: 4%stk.div.12/27/94. ① 4% stk div, 11/23/92 ② 4% stk div, 11/22/91

ANNUAL FINANCIAL DATA

RECORD OF EARNINGS (IN THOUSANDS):

Total Revenues	160,066	148,987	138,331	144,501	146,841	147,116	143,740
Costs and Expenses	141,305	130,843	120,622	130,064	132,189	134,122	129,203
Depreciation & Amort	9,289	8,362	8,176	8,004	7,766	7,625	7,542
Operating Profit	9,472	9,782	89,773	93,517	93,339	95,160	82,347
Earn Bef Income Taxes	7,918	8,440	8,143	4,677	5,006	3,319	5,356
Income Taxes	2,842	3,048	2,847	1,431	1,909	1,305	1,949
Net Income	5,076	5,392	5,296	3,247	3,097	①2,015	3,407
Aver. Shs. Outstg.	6,624	6,368	6,564	6,534	6,534	6,534	6,709

① Before acctg. change cr$951,000.

BALANCE SHEET (IN THOUSANDS):

Cash and Cash Equivalents	201	547	2,953	1,680	2,611	2,925	8,075
Receivables, Net	2,404	1,512	1,803	1,986	1,659	1,313	1,255
Inventories	3,572	3,223	3,186	3,238	3,443	3,069	3,297
Gross Property	152,474	142,099	127,541	127,083	121,068	120,056	113,942
Accumulated Depreciation	66,226	63,588	61,396	57,911	54,161	52,905	50,982
Long-Term Debt	15,264	8,482	1,454	6,094	5,382	4,467	6,293
Capital Lease Obligations	7,022	7,400	7,952	8,561	9,165	10,623	10,345
Net Stockholders' Equity	63,589	60,059	56,140	52,038	50,120	48,315	46,490
Total Assets	104,106	97,731	86,625	87,197	84,737	83,590	84,940
Total Current Assets	8,431	7,859	10,306	8,288	9,015	8,631	16,467
Total Current Liabilities	16,201	19,095	16,026	15,555	15,145	14,598	15,093
Net Working Capital	d7,770	d11,236	d5,720	d7,267	d6,130	d5,967	1,374
Year End Shares Outstg	6,619	6,622	6,625	6,283	6,042	6,044	6,527

STATISTICAL RECORD:

Operating Profit Margin %	5.9	6.6	6.9	4.5	4.7	3.6	4.9
Book Value Per Share	9.48	8.80	7.99	7.99	7.98	7.66	6.83
Return on Equity %	8.0	9.0	9.4	6.2	6.2	4.2	7.3
Return on Assets %	4.9	5.5	6.1	3.7	3.7	2.4	4.0
Average Yield %	1.2	1.0	1.6	1.3	0.9	0.6	0.6
P/E Ratio	28.6-16.4	30.0-18.9	20.7-8.9	44.1-13.2	52.6-28.6	N.M	62.0-40.7
Price Range	22⅞-13⅛	25⅜-16	17½-7½	22⅞-6⅞	25¾-14	35⅝-16⅞	33⅜-21⅞

Statistics are as originally reported.

QUARTERLY DATA

(5/30/94)($000)	Rev	Inc
1st Quarter	50,414	2,186
2nd Quarter	38,255	1,098
3rd Quarter	34,085	331
4th Quarter	37,311	1,461

OFFICERS:
J.C. Maier, Chmn.
C.F. Maier, Pres. & C.E.O.
L.J. Ullman, Sr. V.P. & C.F.O.
D.H. Walker, Treas.
A.M. Cohen, Sec.

INCORPORATED: OH, Oct., 1947

PRINCIPAL OFFICE: 2800 Gilbert Avenue, Cincinnati, OH 45206

TELEPHONE NUMBER: (513) 961-2660

FAX: (513) 559-5160

NO. OF EMPLOYEES: 6,300 (approx.)

ANNUAL MEETING: In October

SHAREHOLDERS: 3,200 (approx.)

INSTITUTIONAL HOLDINGS:
No. of Institutions: 26
Shares Held: 2,371,345

REGISTRAR(S):

TRANSFER AGENT(S): Mellon Bank, N.A., Pittsburgh, PA

NYS SYMBOL FRO
Rec. Pr. 20⅜

FRONTIER CORP.

YIELD 4.1%
P/E RATIO 15.3

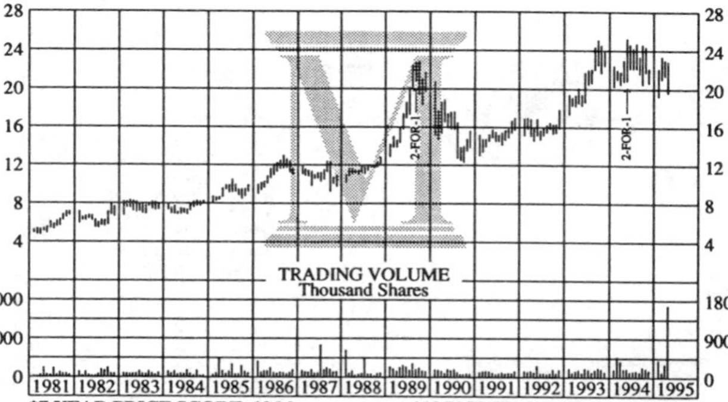

28
24
20
16
12
8
4
2-FOR-1
2-FOR-1
TRADING VOLUME
Thousand Shares
18000
9000
0
1981 1982 1983 1984 1985 1986 1987 1988 1989 1990 1991 1992 1993 1994 1995

***7 YEAR PRICE SCORE 106.0** ***12 MONTH PRICE SCORE 91.7**

*NYSE COMPOSITE INDEX=100

INTERIM EARNINGS (Per Share):

Qtr.	Mar.	June	Sept.	Dec.
1992	0.23	0.24	0.30	0.28
1993	0.27	0.29	0.28	0.37
1994	0.32	0.47	0.35	0.36
1995	0.38	...	...	...

INTERIM DIVIDENDS (Per Share):

Amt.	Decl.	Ex.	Rec.	Pay.
0.2075	4/6/95	4/7/95	4/14/95	5/1/95
rights	...	...	4/24	...

*Indicated div.: $0.83**

CAPITALIZATION (12/31/94):

	($000)	(%)
Long-Term Debt	578,600	38.2
Deferred Income Tax	111,369	7.4
Minority Interest	252	0.0
Preferred Stock	22,777	1.5
Common & Surplus	800,347	52.9
Total	1,513,345	100.0

DIVIDEND ACHIEVER STATUS:
Rank: 307 1984-94 Growth Rate: 3.6%
Total Years of Dividend Growth: 35

RECENT DEVELOPMENTS: For the year ended 12/31/94, income before an accounting change was $109.9 million compared with $82.7 million in 1993. Revenues increased 8.7% to $985.5 million. The long distance business reported a 27.2% increase revenues to $334 million. Revenues for Telephone Operations advanced 2.7% to $609.7 million. Fourth quarter net income was $26.4 million, up 3.1% compared with the same period of 1993. Revenues rose 2.7% to $248.7 million.

PROSPECTS: Rochester Telephone Corp. changed its name to Frontier Corporation and formed a new holding company as part of a major restructuring. As a holding company, FRO will be able to make acquisitions and expand existing lines of business with less restrictive regulatory oversight. Additionally, FRO and New York regulators agreed to a seven-year Open Market Plan that completely opens up Rochester Telephone Corp.'s local network to competition and removes all regulatory earnings oversight.

BUSINESS

FRONTIER CORPORATION (formerly Rochester Telephone Corp.) is the holding company of 34 local exchange telephone companies and seven communications-related subsidiaries. The Telephone Group provides local exchange services to more than 800,000 customers in New York State, Pennsylvania, Michigan, Indiana, Wisconsin, and Illinois. The Telecommunications Group provides competitive services and products throughout the Northeast and Mid-Atlantic region. Rochester Tel Mobile Communications provides cellular and paging services. Rotelcom designs, installs and maintains integrated business communications systems.

BUSINESS LINE ANALYSIS

(12/31/94)	Rev($)	Rev(%)
Local Service	240,687	39.9
Network Access Service	230,938	37.9
Long Distance Network	25,619	4.2
Directory Advertising	118,221	18.0
Total	603,891	100.0

ANNUAL EARNINGS AND DIVIDENDS PER SHARE

	1994	1993	1992	1991	1990	1989	1988
Earnings Per Share	**1.50**	**1.21**	[2] **1.04**	[4] **1.18**	**0.86**	[5] **1.00**	**1.08**
Dividends Per Share	[1] **0.81**	**0.79**	[3] **0.77**	**0.75**	**0.73**	[6] **0.71**	**0.68**
Dividend Payout %	**54.0**	**65.2**	**74.0**	**63.6**	**84.9**	**71.0**	**63.0**

[1] 2-for-1 stk split 5/29/94 [2] Before extraord. item [3] Bef extraord item [4] Before extraod item [5] Before extraord. credit [6] 2-for-1 stk split 09/05/89

ANNUAL FINANCIAL DATA

	1994	1993	1992	1991	1990	1989	1988
RECORD OF EARNINGS (IN MILLIONS):							
Total Revenues	985.5	906.5	804.0	703.2	600.0	562.0	478.7
Costs and Expenses	644.9	596.7	514.9	460.9	404.1	389.2	[1] 316.3
Depreciation	136.5	132.7	121.6	97.1	79.8	65.4	...
Operating Income	223.3	194.9	175.1	145.2	116.1	107.5	100.2
Income Before Taxes	173.8	133.0	112.0	119.3	79.3	76.3	76.9
Income Taxes	63.8	50.2	41.5	46.0	29.6	24.8	26.0
Net Income	102.7	82.7	[2] 70.5	[3] 73.3	49.7	[4] 51.5	50.9
Aver. Shs. Outstg. (000)	72,575	67,454	66,638	64,206	59,348	57,932	45,896

[1] Incl. Dep. [2] Before extra. item dr$1,072,000. [3] Before extra. item cr$3,757,000. [4] Before extra. item cr$20,645,000.

	1994	1993	1992	1991	1990	1989	1988
BALANCE SHEET (IN MILLIONS):							
Cash and Cash Equivalents	326.2	31.6	70.0	45.0	27.9	60.4	9.0
Receivables, Net	168.5	157.3	134.0	119.6	105.0	92.0	75.8
Inventories	8.6	11.2	15.9	18.6	19.3	21.5	19.2
Gross Property	1,759.7	1,748.0	1,755.1	1,651.8	1,315.6	1,124.0	994.3
Accumulated Depreciation	789.8	720.8	715.4	635.0	460.2	367.3	306.3
Long-Term Debt	578.6	492.6	525.6	591.2	363.0	338.1	244.1
Net Stockholders' Equity	823.1	675.1	621.6	587.3	471.7	417.3	356.0
Total Assets	1,761.0	1,510.2	1,513.9	1,475.7	1,179.9	1,052.6	884.7
Total Current Assets	528.5	221.7	241.7	205.8	175.5	192.3	122.6
Total Current Liabilities	201.6	206.4	245.1	185.3	198.4	154.2	151.1
Net Working Capital	326.9	15.4	d3.5	20.5	d23.0	38.1	d28.4
Year End Shs Outstg (000)	73,161	67,936	66,638	66,646	60,684	58,146	45,896
STATISTICAL RECORD:							
Book Value Per Share	10.96	9.60	8.98	8.86	7.77	7.81	7.26
Return on Equity %	13.4	12.3	11.3	12.5	10.5	12.3	14.3
Average Yield %	3.6	3.6	4.7	5.0	4.1	6.2	6.0
P/E Ratio	16.8-13.5	20.8-14.4	17.2-14.1	14.4-11.0	24.1-14.4	22.9-12.9	11.9-9.4
Price Range	25¼-20¼	25⅛-17⅜	18⅞-14	17-13	22⅞-12⅞	12⅞-10⅛	13⅜-9¼

Statistics are as originally reported.

OFFICERS:
R.L. Bittner, Chmn., Pres. & C.E.O.

INCORPORATED: NY, Feb., 1920

PRINCIPAL OFFICE: 180 South Clinton Avenue, Rochester, NY 14646-0700

TELEPHONE NUMBER: (716) 777-1000
FAX: (716) 325-4624
NO. OF EMPLOYEES: 4,240
ANNUAL MEETING: In April
SHAREHOLDERS: 22,674 com.; 995 pfd.
INSTITUTIONAL HOLDINGS:
No. of Institutions: 171
Shares Held: 9,427,991

REGISTRAR(S): Bank of Boston, Boston, MA

TRANSFER AGENT(S): Bank of Boston, Boston, MA

FULLER (H.B.) CO.

YIELD 1.5%
P/E RATIO 16.8

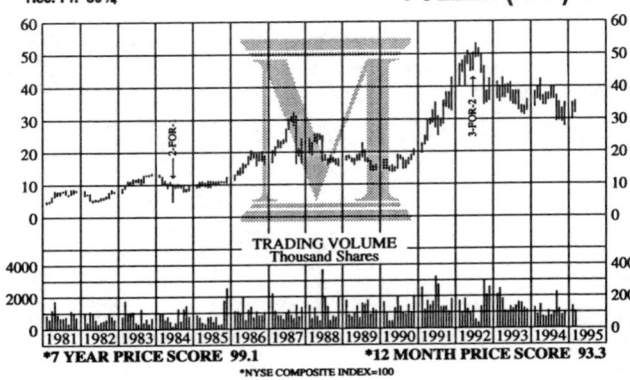

*7 YEAR PRICE SCORE 99.1   ***12 MONTH PRICE SCORE 93.3**
*NYSE COMPOSITE INDEX=100

INTERIM EARNINGS (Per Share):

Qtr.	Feb.	May	Aug.	Nov.
1991-92	0.43	0.73	0.73	0.66
1992-93	0.21	0.63	0.63	0.11
1993-94	0.29	0.66	0.64	0.61
1994-95	0.43	...	...	...

INTERIM DIVIDENDS (Per Share):

Amt.	Decl.	Ex.	Rec.	Pay.
0.14Q	12/2/93	1/20/94	1/26/94	2/10/94
0.145Q	4/21/94	4/26	5/2	5/12
0.145Q	7/21	7/26	8/1	8/11
0.145Q	10/20	10/31	10/31	11/10
0.145Q	12/3/95	1/20/95	1/26/95	2/10/95

Indicated div.: $0.58*

CAPITALIZATION (11/30/94):

	($000)	(%)
Long-Term Debt	130,009	31.1
Deferred Income Tax	7,278	1.7
Minority Interest	6,153	1.5
Preferred Stock	306	0.1
Common & Surplus	274,499	65.6
Total	418,245	100.0

DIVIDEND ACHIEVER STATUS:
Rank: 134   1984-94 Growth Rate: 11.3%
Total Years of Dividend Growth: 27

RECENT DEVELOPMENTS: For the quarter ended 2/28/95, net income, before the cumulative effects of an accounting change, was $6.0 million compared with $4.0 million in the corresponding period of the previous year. FULL's net sales reached a record $295.6 million versus $242.5 million in the prior year, an increase of 22%. Sales in North America advanced by 19% partially as a result of internal growth, but primarily due to an acquisition in the second quarter of the previous year. European operations increased sales by 30% due to acquisition, a more favorable mix of high and low-margined products and beneficial exchange rates. Operations in Latin America and Asia/Pacific regions improved sales by 14% and 41%, respectively. During the period, gross margins did not waver from the previous year's level of approximately 32% despite increases in the costs of raw materials.

BUSINESS

H.B. FULLER COMPANY and its subsidiaries are principally engaged in the manufacture and distribution of industrial adhesives, coatings, sealants, caulks, putties, glazing tapes, mastics and related products in the United States and Canada. The Company also manufactures and distributes cleaners, sanitizers and pesticides for the dairy, food and beverage industries through its Monarch Chemicals Division. The Company's subsidiary, Kativo Chemical Industries, S.A. and its subsidiaries manufacture and distribute paints, adhesives, plastics, printing inks and related chemical products in Central America, Panama, Mexico and South America. LW-Fuller GmbH, the Company's subsidiary in Germany, is a manufacturer of specialty waxes and hot melt compounds for packaging, rubber and electro-technical industries as well as other industrial markets. The Company has 53 plants and technical service centers in 30 U.S. metropolitan areas, and manufacturing and sales operations in 32 countries worldwide.

BUSINESS LINE ANALYSIS

(11/30/94)	Rev(%)	Inc(%)
North America	59.4	57.0
Europe	21.2	15.9
Latin America	15.2	26.7
Other	4.2	0.4
Total	100.0	100.0

ANNUAL EARNINGS AND DIVIDENDS PER SHARE

	11/30/94	11/30/93	11/30/92	11/30/91	11/30/90	11/30/89	11/30/88
Earnings Per Share	2.20	1.55	2.55	2.00	1.53	1.09	1.47
Dividends Per Share	0.575	0.54	① 0.464	0.41	0.397	0.383	0.35
Dividend Payout %	26.1	34.8	18.2	20.5	25.9	35.1	23.9

① 3-for-2 stk split, 6/2/92

ANNUAL FINANCIAL DATA

RECORD OF EARNINGS (IN MILLIONS):

	11/30/94	11/30/93	11/30/92	11/30/91	11/30/90	11/30/89	11/30/88
Total Revenues	1,097.4	975.3	933.7	852.9	792.2	753.4	685.0
Costs and Expenses	998.0	911.8	830.7	764.4	712.7	683.4	619.8
Depreciation & Amort.	33.4	10.0	31.6	28.7	27.6	23.9	18.8
Operating Earnings	66.0	53.5	71.4	59.8	51.9	46.0	46.4
Earn Bef Income Taxes	51.0	40.9	60.9	47.4	37.1	30.3	36.0
Income Taxes	19.8	19.2	24.7	19.2	15.2	13.9	14.4
Net Income	30.9	① 21.7	35.6	27.7	21.1	15.7	21.1
Aver. Shs. Outstg. (000)	14,036	14,018	13,989	13,854	13,799	14,358	14,387

① Before acctg. change dr$11,717,000.

BALANCE SHEET (IN MILLIONS):

	11/30/94	11/30/93	11/30/92	11/30/91	11/30/90	11/30/89	11/30/88
Cash and Cash Equivalents	9.8	17.4	29.1	15.2	14.0	10.4	18.0
Receivables, Net	176.4	139.3	133.9	122.9	110.7	103.0	102.9
Inventories	152.7	123.8	116.2	106.9	106.6	93.5	89.5
Gross Property	513.9	419.6	394.8	351.5	330.2	293.9	255.0
Accumulated Depreciation	218.8	187.1	171.7	144.1	127.8	107.3	93.4
Long-Term Debt	130.0	60.3	53.5	71.8	88.2	101.0	98.5
Net Stockholders' Equity	274.8	249.4	255.0	219.1	197.2	186.5	178.9
Total Assets	742.6	564.5	561.2	508.9	489.6	455.2	434.3
Total Current Assets	361.4	295.9	299.2	259.6	242.3	215.8	218.0
Total Current Liabilities	231.7	175.9	168.4	150.8	146.2	120.1	113.9
Net Working Capital	129.7	119.9	130.8	108.8	96.1	95.6	104.1
Year End Shs Outstg (000)	13,935	13,898	13,825	13,707	13,521	14,033	14,214

STATISTICAL RECORD:

	11/30/94	11/30/93	11/30/92	11/30/91	11/30/90	11/30/89	11/30/88
Operating Profit Margin %	6.0	5.5	7.6	7.0	6.6	6.1	6.8
Book Value Per Share	15.50	16.44	17.08	14.15	12.35	10.71	9.71
Return on Equity %	11.2	8.7	14.0	12.6	10.7	8.4	11.8
Return on Assets %	4.2	3.8	6.3	5.4	4.3	3.4	4.9
Average Yield %	1.6	1.5	1.1	1.3	2.3	2.1	1.7
P/E Ratio	19.2-12.6	27.6-20.2	20.9-13.5	21.4-9.8	13.6-9.0	21.0-12.7	17.6-10.6
Price Range	42¼-27¾	42¾-31¼	53¼-34½	42⅞-19½	20⅞-13¾	22⅞-13⅞	25⅞-15⅝

Statistics are as originally reported.

OFFICERS:
A.L. Andersen, Chmn. & C.E.O.
W. Kissling, Pres. & C.O.O.
J.W. Bolanos, V.P., C.F.O. & Treas.

INCORPORATED: MN, Dec., 1915

PRINCIPAL OFFICE: 2400 Energy Park Dr., Saint Paul, MN 55108-1591

TELEPHONE NUMBER: (612) 645-3401
FAX: (612) 645-6936
NO. OF EMPLOYEES: 6,400 (approx.)
ANNUAL MEETING: In April
SHAREHOLDERS: 5,340 (approx.)
INSTITUTIONAL HOLDINGS:
No. of Institutions: 98
Shares Held: 5,282,421

REGISTRAR(S): Norwest Bank Minnesota, N.A., St. Paul, MN

TRANSFER AGENT(S): Norwest Bank Minnesota, N.A., St. Paul, MN

GALLAGHER (ARTHUR J.) & CO.

YIELD 2.8%
P/E RATIO 16.1

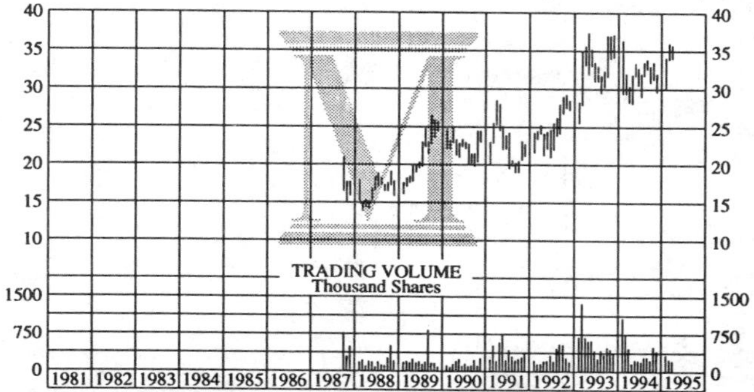

INTERIM EARNINGS (Per Share):

Qtr.	Mar.	June	Sept.	Dec.
1991	0.30	0.12	0.49	0.41
1992	0.21	0.23	0.60	0.53
1993	0.26	0.45	0.74	0.56
1994	0.33	0.29	0.81	0.77

INTERIM DIVIDENDS (Per Share):

Amt.	Decl.	Ex.	Rec.	Pay.
0.22Q	1/20/94	3/25/94	3/31/94	4/15/94
0.22Q	5/10	6/24	6/30	7/15
0.22Q	9/21	9/26	9/30	10/14
0.22Q	11/17	12/23	12/30	1/13/95
0.25Q	1/23/95	3/27/95	3/31/95	4/14

Indicated div.: $1.00

CAPITALIZATION (12/31/94):

	($000)	(%)
Long-Term Debt	3,390	3.4
Common & Surplus	96,731	96.6
Total	100,121	100.0

TRADING VOLUME
Thousand Shares

*7 YEAR PRICE SCORE 106.6   *12 MONTH PRICE SCORE 104.0
*NYSE COMPOSITE INDEX=100

DIVIDEND ACHIEVER STATUS:
Rank: 2   1984-94 Growth Rate: 31.3%
Total Years of Dividend Growth: 10

RECENT DEVELOPMENTS: For the year ended 12/31/94, net income advanced to $34.5 million compared with $26.9 million in the corresponding period of 1993. Revenues were $356.4 million, up 8.2% from $329.3 million a year earlier. Earnings were bolstered by the Company's continued focus on account retention and strong new business development, which produced record earnings despite the continuing soft pricing environment in the commercial insurance area. Cost containment remained a strong strategic focus throughout the year, and the Company's proactive acquisition activity resulted in five new mergers to the Gallagher family of companies. For the three months ended 12/31/94, net income more than doubled to $12.0 million from $5.7 million a year earlier. Revenues rose 9.1% to $94.8 million compared with $86.9 million in 1993.

BUSINESS

ARTHUR J. GALLAGHER & COMPANY, is engaged in providing insurance brokerage, risk management and related services to clients. Risk management involves assisting clients in analyzing risks and determining weather proper protection is best obtained through the purchase of insurance or through retention of all or a portion of those risks and adoption of corporate risk management policies and cost-effective loss control and prevention programs. Risk management services also include claims management, loss-control consulting and property appraisals.

REVENUES

(12/31/94)	($000)	(%)
Commissions	206,820	58.0
Fees	140,063	39.3
Investment Income & Other	9,494	2.7
Total	356,377	100.0

ANNUAL EARNINGS AND DIVIDENDS PER SHARE

	1994	1993	1992	1991	1990	1989	1988
Earnings Per Share	2.17	2.02	1.57	1.31	1.42	1.42	1.41
Dividends Per Share	0.84	0.70	0.64	0.63	0.58	0.51	0.46
Dividend Payout %	38.7	34.7	40.8	48.1	40.8	35.9	32.6

ANNUAL FINANCIAL DATA

RECORD OF EARNINGS (IN THOUSANDS):

	1994	1993	1992	1991	1990	1989	1988
Total Revenues	356,377	317,663	272,725	231,679	198,176	173,206	156,035
Costs and Expenses	301,411	264,570	234,188	202,969	168,914	144,613	129,946
Operating Profit	167,457	156,746	131,602	111,321	99,156	88,516	79,794
Earn Bef Income Taxes	53,238	51,224	36,108	26,458	27,217	26,544	24,025
Income Taxes	18,698	18,953	12,638	7,668	9,526	9,290	7,130
Net Income	34,540	32,271	23,470	18,790	17,691	17,254	16,895
Aver. Shs. Outstg.	15,902	15,989	14,905	14,352	12,439	12,158	12,001

BALANCE SHEET (IN THOUSANDS):

	1994	1993	1992	1991	1990	1989	1988
Cash and Cash Equivalents	108,824	129,649	112,363	116,335	111,533	69,435	84,367
Receivables, Net	179,823	152,529	139,062	122,676	98,086	108,549	90,609
Gross Property	58,930	48,696	40,610	34,119	31,785	25,810	21,673
Accumulated Depreciation	38,918	30,542	24,026	18,811	19,618	15,794	13,310
Long-Term Debt	3,390	24,520	20,000	20,000	20,000	20,000	20,000
Net Stockholders' Equity	96,731	124,001	93,734	88,320	84,473	76,725	70,067
Total Assets	451,110	463,507	401,089	376,336	319,682	293,909	276,620
Total Current Assets	351,072	363,675	273,929	257,392	227,323	194,799	192,108
Total Current Liabilities	341,726	305,572	274,675	255,625	206,237	189,539	179,951
Net Working Capital	9,346	58,103	d746	1,767	21,086	5,260	12,157
Year End Shares Outstg	14,784	15,186	14,130	13,620	11,887	11,487	11,388

STATISTICAL RECORD:

	1994	1993	1992	1991	1990	1989	1988
Book Value Per Share	6.54	8.17	6.63	6.48	7.11	6.68	6.15
Return on Equity %	35.7	26.0	25.0	21.3	20.9	22.5	24.1
Return on Assets %	7.7	7.0	5.9	5.0	5.5	5.9	6.1
Average Yield %	2.6	2.2	2.5	2.7	2.6	2.4	2.8
P/E Ratio	16.8-13.0	18.5-12.6	18.6-13.4	21.8-14.5	17.6-13.9	18.7-11.4	13.6-9.8
Price Range	36⅜-28⅛	37⅜-25½	29¼-21	28½-19	25-19¾	26½-16⅛	19⅛-13⅞

Statistics are as originally reported.

OFFICERS:
R.E. Gallagher, Chmn.
J.P. Gallagher, Vice-Chmn.
J.P. Gallagher, Jr., Pres., C.E.O. & C.O.O.
M.P. Strauch, Treas.
M.J. Cloherty, C.F.O.

PRINCIPAL OFFICE: Two Pierce Place, Itasca, IL 60143-3141

TELEPHONE NUMBER: (708) 773-3800

FAX: (708) 285-4000

NO. OF EMPLOYEES: 3,300 (approx.)

ANNUAL MEETING: In May

SHAREHOLDERS: 600 (approx.)

INSTITUTIONAL HOLDINGS:
No. of Institutions: 54
Shares Held: 5,697,874

REGISTRAR(S): Harris Trust & Savings Bank, Chicago, IL

TRANSFER AGENT(S): Harris Trust & Savings Bank, Chicago, IL

NYS SYMBOL GCI
Rec. Pr. 52⅜

GANNETT CO., INC.

YIELD 2.6%
P/E RATIO 15.7

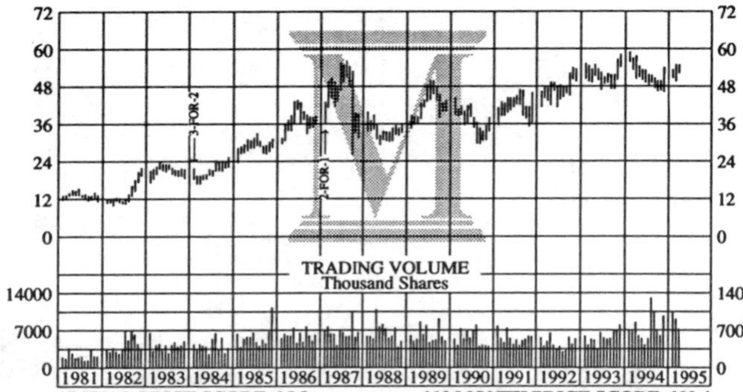

TRADING VOLUME
Thousand Shares

*7 YEAR PRICE SCORE 95.8   *12 MONTH PRICE SCORE 100.4
*NYSE COMPOSITE INDEX=100

INTERIM EARNINGS (Per Share):

Qtr.	Mar.	June	Sept.	Dec.
1993	0.46	0.78	0.61	0.88
1994	0.54	0.90	0.74	1.07
1995	0.62	...	...	...

INTERIM DIVIDENDS (Per Share):

Amt.	Decl.	Ex.	Rec.	Pay.
0.33Q	2/22/94	3/7/94	3/11/94	4/1/94
0.33Q	5/3	6/6	6/10	7/1
0.34Q	8/23	9/12	9/16	10/1
0.34Q	10/25	12/12	12/16	1/3/95
0.34Q	2/21/95	3/6/95	3/10/95	4/1

*Indicated div.: $1.36**

CAPITALIZATION (12/25/94):

	($000)	(%)
Long-Term Debt	767,270	27.8
Deferred Income Tax	164,691	6.0
Common & Surplus	1,822,238	66.2
Total	2,754,199	100.0

DIVIDEND ACHIEVER STATUS:
Rank: 224   1984-94 Growth Rate: 7.6%
Total Years of Dividend Growth: 23

RECENT DEVELOPMENTS: For the year ended 12/25/94, net income increased 17% to $465.4 million compared with $397.8 million the previous year. Revenues were up 5% to $3.82 billion from $3.64 billion in 1993. Newspaper advertising revenues advanced 7.4% to $2.15 billion and circulation revenues were up 1.3% to $849.5 million. Broadcasting revenues increased 2.4% to $406.6 million. In the fourth quarter, television and radio stations experienced the strongest demand for advertising in five years.

PROSPECTS: Broadcasting and newspaper operations are benefiting from strong demand for advertising. Newspaper advertising revenues are being driven by classified ads, particularly employment and automotive. However, the Company's large concentration of newspapers leaves margins vulnerable to newsprint price increases. A strong economy and greater demand for commodities are expected to have an inflationary effect on newsprint prices.

BUSINESS

GANNETT COMPANY, INC. is a diversified news and information company that publishes newspapers, operates broadcasting stations and outdoor advertising businesses, and is engaged in research, marketing, commercial printing, a newswire data service and news programming. The Company has facilities in 41 states, the District of Columbia, Canada, Guam, the U.S., Virgin Islands, London, Paris, Switzerland, Hong Kong and Singapore. Gannett's is the largest U.S. newspaper group, with 82 daily newspapers, including USA Today, 50 non-daily publications and USA Weekend, a weekly newspaper magazine. The Company owns and operates 10 television stations. Gannett Outdoor is the largest outdoor advertising group in North America, with operations in 11 states and Canada.

BUSINESS LINE ANALYSIS

(12/25/94)($000)	Rev(%)	Inc(%)
Newspaper		
Publishing	83.1	90.3
Broadcasting	10.6	15.9
Outdoor Advert	6.3	2.1
Corporate	0.0	-8.3
Total	100.0	100.0

ANNUAL EARNINGS AND DIVIDENDS PER SHARE

	12/25/94	12/26/93	12/27/92	12/29/91	12/30/90	12/31/89	12/25/88
Earnings Per Share	3.23	2.72	2.40	2.00	2.36	2.47	2.26
Dividends Per Share	1.33	1.29	1.25	1.24	1.20	1.08	1.00
Dividend Payout %	41.2	47.4	52.1	62.0	50.8	43.7	44.0

ANNUAL FINANCIAL DATA

RECORD OF EARNINGS (IN MILLIONS):

	12/25/94	12/26/93	12/27/92	12/29/91	12/30/90	12/31/89	12/25/88
Total Revenues	3,824.5	3,641.6	3,469.0	3,382.0	3,441.6	3,518.2	3,314.5
Costs and Expenses	2,802.9	2,717.6	2,653.8	2,623.3	2,568.7	2,571.6	2,449.6
Depreciation & Amort	208.8	209.6	197.9	199.8	194.0	190.1	177.2
Operating Income	812.8	714.4	617.3	558.9	678.8	756.5	687.7
Income Bef Income Taxes	782.1	668.5	574.5	502.7	618.0	647.5	607.5
Income Taxes	316.7	270.7	228.6	201.1	241.0	250.0	243.0
Net Income	465.4	397.8	① 345.7	301.6	377.0	397.5	364.5
Aver. Shs. Outstg. (000)	144,276	146,474	144,148	150,783	160,047	161,253	161,622

① Before acctg. change dr$146,000,000.

BALANCE SHEET (IN MILLIONS):

	12/25/94	12/26/93	12/27/92	12/29/91	12/30/90	12/31/89	12/25/88
Cash and Cash Equivalents	44.3	75.5	73.3	70.7	56.2	55.6	48.7
Receivables, Net	517.4	584.1	454.3	444.6	469.1	485.9	458.8
Inventories	53.0	53.1	48.1	51.4	66.5	61.1	84.2
Gross Property	2,814.5	2,794.6	2,693.3	2,593.5	2,473.0	2,344.3	2,178.4
Accumulated Depreciation	1,386.3	1,316.3	1,218.1	1,108.6	1,000.8	916.9	800.9
Long-Term Debt	767.3	850.7	1,080.8	1,335.4	848.6	922.5	1,134.7
Net Stockholders' Equity	1,822.2	1,907.9	1,580.1	1,539.5	2,063.1	1,995.8	1,786.4
Total Assets	3,707.1	3,823.8	3,609.0	3,684.1	3,826.1	3,782.8	3,792.8
Total Current Assets	650.8	758.0	631.4	636.1	668.7	671.0	665.0
Total Current Liabilities	527.1	455.1	431.6	443.8	500.2	477.8	500.8
Net Working Capital	123.8	302.8	199.9	192.3	168.5	193.2	164.2
Year End Shs Outstg (000)	139,767	146,967	144,402	143,753	158,991	160,971	161,057

STATISTICAL RECORD:

	12/25/94	12/26/93	12/27/92	12/29/91	12/30/90	12/31/89	12/25/88
Operating Profit Margin %	21.3	19.6	17.8	16.5	19.7	21.5	20.7
Book Value Per Share	2.51	2.77	1.49	0.91	3.80	3.23	1.61
Return on Equity %	25.5	20.8	21.9	19.6	18.3	19.9	20.4
Return on Assets %	12.6	10.4	9.6	8.2	9.9	10.5	9.6
Average Yield %	2.5	2.5	2.6	3.0	3.2	2.6	2.9
P/E Ratio	18.3-14.3	21.4-17.2	22.5-17.2	23.5-17.6	18.9-12.5	20.2-14.0	17.6-12.9
Price Range	59-46⅛	58¼-46¾	54-41¼	47-35⅛	44½-29½	49⅞-34½	39⅞-29¼

Statistics are as originally reported.

OFFICERS:
J.J. Curley, Chmn., Pres. & C.E.O.
D.H. McCorkindale, Vice Chmn., C.F.O.
T. Curley, Pres.-USA TODAY

INCORPORATED: NY, Dec., 1923; reincorp., DE, May, 1972

PRINCIPAL OFFICE: 1100 Wilson Boulevard, Arlington, VA 22234

TELEPHONE NUMBER: (703) 284-6000

NO. OF EMPLOYEES: 36,000

ANNUAL MEETING: In May

SHAREHOLDERS: 14,000 approx.

INSTITUTIONAL HOLDINGS:
No. of Institutions: 562
Shares Held: 113,580,631

REGISTRAR(S): Norwest Bank Minnesota, N.A., St. Paul, MN

TRANSFER AGENT(S): Norwest Bank Minnesota, N.A., St. Paul, MN

NYS SYMBOL GEC
Rec. Pr. 50

GEICO CORP.

YIELD 2.2%
P/E RATIO 16.7

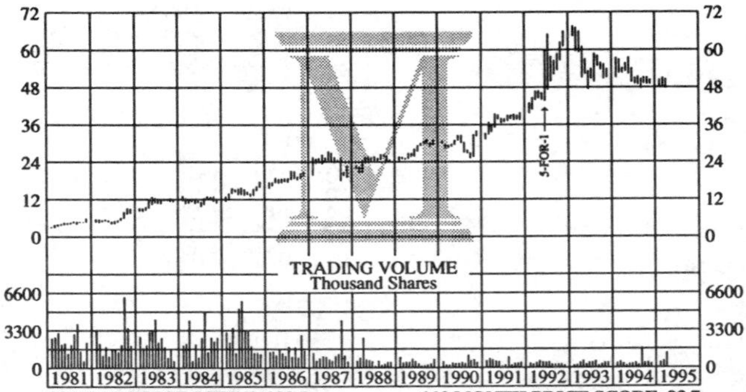

***7 YEAR PRICE SCORE 103.5** ***12 MONTH PRICE SCORE 93.7**

*NYSE COMPOSITE INDEX=100

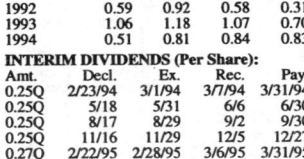

INTERIM EARNINGS (Per Share):

Qtr.	Mar.	June	Sept.	Dec.
1991	0.56	0.70	0.77	0.68
1992	0.59	0.92	0.58	0.31
1993	1.06	1.18	1.07	0.70
1994	0.51	0.81	0.84	0.83

INTERIM DIVIDENDS (Per Share):

Amt.	Decl.	Ex.	Rec.	Pay.
0.25Q	2/23/94	3/1/94	3/7/94	3/31/94
0.25Q	5/18	5/31	6/6	6/30
0.25Q	8/17	8/29	9/2	9/30
0.25Q	11/16	11/29	12/5	12/27
0.27Q	2/22/95	2/28/95	3/6/95	3/31/95

Indicated div.: $1.08

CAPITALIZATION (12/31/94):

	($000)	(%)
Total Debt	391,378	21.3
Common & Surplus	1,445,941	78.7
Total	1,837,319	100.0

DIVIDEND ACHIEVER STATUS:
Rank: 21 1984-94 Growth Rate: 19.0%
Total Years of Dividend Growth: 17

RECENT DEVELOPMENTS: For the year ended 12/31/94, income before accounting changes fell 27.1% to $208.9 million from $286.4 million for the prior year. Net income included after-tax realized investment gains of $9.9 million in 1994 and $81.3 million in 1993. Total revenue increased 2.9% to $2.72 billion from $2.64 billion the year before. Premiums reached $2.48 billion, up 8.4% from $2.28 billion a year earlier. Net investment income was flat at $201.8 million compared with 1993.

PROSPECTS: Policy growth in the primary line of business, voluntary automobile, should continue at a satisfactory rate providing for solid earnings potential. Property/casualty operations continue to benefit from premium growth and modest rate increases. Underwriting results should continue to improve and enhance earnings results. Net investment income is beginning to benefit from a greater proportion of tax-exempt securities in the portfolio. The severity of claims is increasing at a Company predicted level.

BUSINESS

GEICO CORPORATION is primarily an insurance organization whose principal subsidiary, Government Employees Insurance Co., is a property and casualty insurer engaged in writing preferred-risk private passenger automobile insurance and homeowners' insurance. Criterion Life Insurance Company writes structured settlement annuities for its property/casualty affiliates. GEICO Indemnity Co., writes standard-risk private passenger automobile and motorcycle insurance with an emphasis on marketing to military personnel.

REVENUES

(12/31/94)	($000)	(%)
Premiums	2,476,276	91.2
Net Investment Income	201,790	7.4
Realized Gains on Invests	12,898	0.5
Interest	10,347	0.4
Other	14,698	0.5
Total	2,716,009	100.0

ANNUAL EARNINGS AND DIVIDENDS PER SHARE

	1994	1993	1992	1991	1990	1989	1988
Earnings Per Share	2.98	4.01	2.39	2.70	2.73	2.75	2.38
Dividends Per Share	1.00	0.68	[1] 0.60	0.456	0.40	0.36	0.328
Dividend Payout %	33.6	17.0	25.1	16.9	14.7	13.1	13.8

[1] 5-for-1 stk split, 6/4/92

ANNUAL FINANCIAL DATA

	1994	1993	1992	1991	1990	1989	1988
RECORD OF EARNINGS (IN MILLIONS):							
Insurance Premiums	2,476.3	2,283.5	2,084.5	1,888.4	1,692.5	1,621.4	1,556.9
Total Interest Income	10.3	11.5	16.5	20.0	23.6	29.2	31.2
Total Revenues	2,716.0	2,638.3	2,420.0	2,147.0	1,934.9	1,939.4	1,756.9
Losses & Loss Adjust Exps	1,996.5	1,821.8	1,725.0	1,450.1	1,328.5	1,265.2	1,260.7
Income Bef Income Taxes	251.2	378.6	218.0	241.0	222.8	255.4	145.6
Income Taxes	42.4	92.2	45.2	44.6	14.4	42.4	11.2
Net Income	[1] 208.8	[2] 286.4	172.8	196.4	208.4	213.1	189.0
Aver. Shs. Outstg. (000)	69,992	71,417	72,387	72,855	76,397	77,522	79,303
BALANCE SHEET (IN MILLIONS):							
Cash	27.6	18.4	16.1	24.7	35.7	22.7	20.3
Fixed Maturities	3,270.1	3,175.4	2,476.7	2,275.0	1,885.0	1,640.5	1,670.8
Common Stocks	759.8	687.1	724.1	750.4	603.2	691.8	486.6
Total Assets	4,998.1	4,831.4	4,377.6	4,085.8	3,575.9	3,434.4	3,060.6
Benefits and Claims	2,861.0	2,630.8	2,535.4	2,283.1	2,032.6	1,893.1	1,754.6
Net Stockholders' Equity	1,445.9	1,534.6	1,292.5	1,184.3	970.0	898.1	707.4
Year End Shs Outstg (000)	68,291	70,834	71,184	71,047	74,253	75,882	77,200
STATISTICAL RECORD:							
Return on Equity %	14.4	18.7	13.4	16.6	21.5	23.7	26.7
Book Value Per Share	21.17	21.66	18.16	16.67	13.06	11.84	9.16
Average Yield %	1.9	1.2	1.1	1.3	1.4	1.3	1.4
P/E Ratio	19.3-16.0	16.9-11.8	27.6-16.6	14.8-11.6	12.4-9.2	11.4-8.9	15.5-11.9
Price Range	57⅝-47⅝	67⅝-47⅜	66-39⅝	39⅞-31¼	33⅞-25⅛	31¼-24½	26⅜-20¼

[1] Before acctg. change dr$1,051,000. [2] Before acctg. change dr$12,749,000.

Statistics are as originally reported.

OFFICERS:
O.M. Nicely, Pres. & C.E.O.-Ins. Ops.
L.A. Simpson, Pres. & C.E.O.-Cap. Ops.
W.A. Sparks, Jr., Exec. V.P. & C.F.O.

INCORPORATED: DE, Nov., 1978

PRINCIPAL OFFICE: One GEICO Plaza, Washington, DC 20076-0001

TELEPHONE NUMBER: (301) 986-2500

NO. OF EMPLOYEES: 7,453

ANNUAL MEETING: In May

SHAREHOLDERS: 2,998

INSTITUTIONAL HOLDINGS:
No. of Institutions: 141
Shares Held: 60,032,180

REGISTRAR(S): Riggs National Bank of Washington, D.C., 808 17th Street, N.W., Suite 240, Washington, DC 20006-3950
Chemical Bank, New York, NY

TRANSFER AGENT(S): Riggs National Bank of Washington, D.C., 808 17th Street, N.W., Suite 240, Washington, DC 20006-3950
Chemical Bank, New York, NY

GENERAL BINDING CORP.

YIELD 2.4%
P/E RATIO 16.7

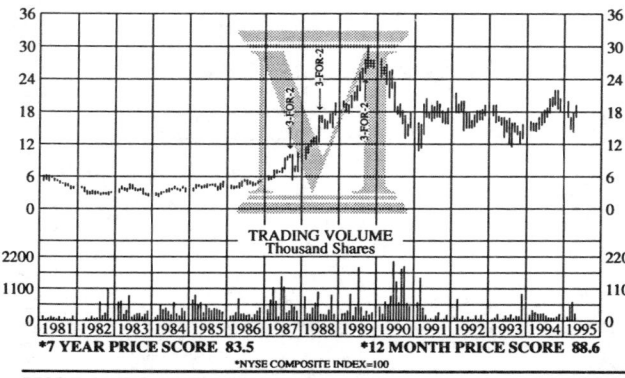

TRADING VOLUME
Thousand Shares

7 YEAR PRICE SCORE 83.5   **12 MONTH PRICE SCORE 88.6**
*NYSE COMPOSITE INDEX=100

INTERIM EARNINGS (Per Share):

Qtr.	Mar.	June	Sept.	Dec.
1992	0.25	0.30	0.26	0.25
1993	0.24	0.26	0.23	0.22
1994	0.28	0.31	0.27	0.14
1995	0.33	...	...	...

INTERIM DIVIDENDS (Per Share):

Amt.	Decl.	Ex.	Rec.	Pay.
0.105Q	11/7/94	11/15/94	11/21/94	12/21/94
0.105Q	11/7	11/15	11/21	12/21
0.105Q	11/7	11/15	11/21	12/21
0.105Q	2/3/95	2/14/95	2/21/95	3/20/95
0.105Q	5/9	5/17	5/23	6/23

Indicated div.: $0.42

CAPITALIZATION (12/31/94):

	($000)	(%)
Long-Term Debt	42,020	22.1
Deferred Income Tax	7,225	3.8
Common & Surplus	141,089	74.1
Total	190,334	100.0

DIVIDEND ACHIEVER STATUS:
Rank: 55   1984-94 Growth Rate: 14.9%
Total Years of Dividend Growth: 19

RECENT DEVELOPMENTS: For the year ended 12/31/94, net income increased 4.7% to $15.7 million, or $1.00 per share, from $15.0 million, or $0.95 per share, in 1993. Earnings included federal income tax benefits of $736,000 and $500,000 in 1994 and 1993, respectively. Net income in 1994 also included $2.5 million in restructuring charges. The charges resulted from the cost of downsizing in selected areas and realigning manufacturing and distribution facilities for improved operational efficiencies. Sales were up 11.8% to $420.4 million, compared with $376.1 million the previous year. Income before taxes rose 5.7% to $25.7 million from $24.3 million. GBND is enthusiastic about the positive acceptance of recently introduced products, and the Company will continue to emphasize research and devlopment as part of its growth strategy.

BUSINESS

GENERAL BINDING CORP. is engaged primarily in the design, manufacture and distribution in the U.S. and abroad binding and laminating systems, paper shredders and other presentation products including machines and related supplies. The Company's products are marketed under the GBC, Velobind, Shredmaster and U.S. RingBinder names. Therm A-Bind Systems binds loose pages, by thermal-activated adhesives, into soft and hard cover books. Plastic Binding punches and binds various printed material into booklets. In addition, it markets a variety of customized metal looseleaf binders, indexes, folders and other items. Laminating Systems seals pages between layers of clear plastic film. Sizes up to thirty-six inches wide and one inch thick can be handled. Photo ID Systems laminates identification cards and coded signature cards into ID cards, and badges. Plastic pouches used are manufactured by the Company. U.S. Ring Binder Corp., a domestic subsidiary of GBC, is a manufacturer of metal loose leaf elements for loose leaf binder manufacturers throughout North America. Standard three ring metals are primarily produced at U.S. Ring's plant in Singapore.

ANNUAL EARNINGS AND DIVIDENDS PER SHARE

	1994	1993	1992	1991	1990	1989	1988
Earnings Per Share	1.00	0.95	1.06	0.80	0.86	1.26	0.93
Dividends Per Share	0.405	0.40	0.37	0.33	0.29	① 0.273	② 0.187
Dividend Payout %	40.5	42.1	34.9	41.3	33.7	21.7	20.1

① 50% stk div, 8/31/89 ② 3-for-2 stk split, 6/6/88

ANNUAL FINANCIAL DATA

RECORD OF EARNINGS (IN THOUSANDS):

Total Revenues	420,449	376,138	368,643	311,199	303,670	283,691	250,626
Costs and Expenses	377,050	336,267	325,893	280,275	272,292	248,436	220,920
Depreciation & Amort	12,081	10,747	10,775	8,239	7,439	6,131	5,878
Operating Profit	35,318	29,124	31,975	24,220	27,535	29,324	24,918
Income Bef Income Taxes	25,700	24,305	27,348	20,255	21,378	28,763	24,457
Income Taxes	9,997	9,311	10,644	7,656	7,723	8,658	9,601
Net Income	15,703	14,994	16,704	12,599	13,655	20,105	14,856
Aver. Shs. Outstg.	15,763	15,777	15,797	15,819	15,889	15,962	16,077

BALANCE SHEET (IN THOUSANDS):

Cash and Cash Equivalents	5,569	4,462	10,769	14,466	22,442	6,151	15,921
Receivables, Net	74,413	63,701	57,262	54,980	48,149	51,046	46,530
Inventories	76,008	65,636	62,095	58,069	52,940	52,974	45,398
Gross Property	130,625	124,599	114,435	108,894	93,402	84,613	75,057
Accumulated Depreciation	65,095	62,504	56,525	51,563	47,104	40,631	36,811
Long-Term Debt	42,020	38,350	32,530	35,530	2,530	4,667	4,558
Capital Lease Obligations	...	214	436	44	264	475	624
Net Stockholders' Equity	141,089	133,531	127,588	119,047	113,620	104,534	92,163
Total Assets	284,276	251,109	239,966	237,773	191,728	173,437	161,227
Total Current Assets	171,152	145,351	141,189	138,871	135,412	120,366	117,980
Total Current Liabilities	84,604	64,760	67,148	71,552	63,641	54,021	56,474
Net Working Capital	86,548	80,591	74,041	67,319	71,771	66,345	61,506
Year End Shares Outstg	13,350	15,761	15,782	15,814	15,862	15,927	15,968

STATISTICAL RECORD:

Operating Profit Margin %	7.4	7.7	8.7	7.3	7.9	10.3	9.5
Book Value Per Share	8.24	6.57	6.16	5.59	7.08	6.47	5.67
Return on Equity %	11.1	11.2	13.1	10.6	12.0	19.2	16.1
Return on Assets %	5.5	6.0	7.0	5.3	7.1	11.6	9.2
Average Yield %	2.2	2.6	2.1	2.1	1.4	1.1	1.3
P/E Ratio	22.0-14.4	20.3-12.1	20.3-13.7	25.6-13.4	32.3-15.1	24.0-14.0	21.3-9.9
Price Range	22-14⅜	19¼-11½	21½-14½	20½-10¾	27¾-13	30¼-17⅝	19⅝-9⅛

Statistics are as originally reported.

OFFICERS:
W.N. Lane, III, Chmn.
R. Grua, Vice-Chmn.
G.C. Reddy, Pres. & C.E.O.
S. Rubin, V.P., Sec. & Gen. Coun.
E.J. McNulty, V.P. & C.F.O.

INCORPORATED: DE, 1947

PRINCIPAL OFFICE: One GBC Plaza, Northbrook, IL 60062

TELEPHONE NUMBER: (708) 272-3700

FAX: (708) 272-1389

NO. OF EMPLOYEES: 3,226

ANNUAL MEETING: In May

SHAREHOLDERS: 828 (com.); 1 (Cl. B.)

INSTITUTIONAL HOLDINGS:
No. of Institutions: 41
Shares Held: 4,518,115

REGISTRAR(S): Harris Trust & Savings Bank, Chicago, IL

TRANSFER AGENT(S): Harris Trust & Savings Bank, Chicago, IL

NYS SYMBOL GE
Rec. Pr. 58⅝

GENERAL ELECTRIC CO.

YIELD 2.8%
P/E RATIO 17.7

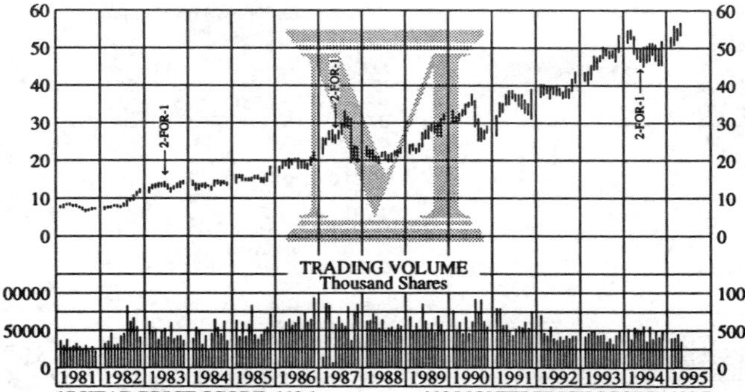

*7 YEAR PRICE SCORE 112.1 *12 MONTH PRICE SCORE 102.7
*NYSE COMPOSITE INDEX=100

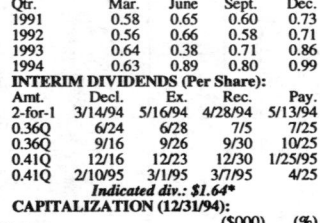

INTERIM EARNINGS (Per Share):

Qtr.	Mar.	June	Sept.	Dec.
1991	0.58	0.65	0.60	0.73
1992	0.56	0.66	0.58	0.71
1993	0.64	0.38	0.71	0.86
1994	0.63	0.89	0.80	0.99

INTERIM DIVIDENDS (Per Share):

Amt.	Decl.	Ex.	Rec.	Pay.
2-for-1	3/14/94	5/16/94	4/28/94	5/13/94
0.36Q	6/24	6/28	7/5	7/25
0.36Q	9/16	9/26	9/30	10/25
0.41Q	12/16	12/23	12/30	1/25/95
0.41Q	2/10/95	3/1/95	3/7/95	4/25

Indicated div.: $1.64*

CAPITALIZATION (12/31/94):

	($000)	(%)
Long-Term Debt	36,979,000	56.7
Minority Interest	1,847,000	2.8
Common & Surplus	26,387,000	40.5
Total	65,213,000	100.0

DIVIDEND ACHIEVER STATUS:
Rank: 137 1984-94 Growth Rate: 11.2%
Total Years of Dividend Growth: 19

RECENT DEVELOPMENTS: For the year ended 12/31/94, income from continuing operations was $5.92 billion compared with $4.18 billion in the previous year. The disposition of Kidder, Peabody resulted in a $1.20 billion charge against net income and was subsequently not included in the continuing operations' results. Revenues from continuing operations increased to $60.11 billion from $55.70 billion in the prior year. GE Capital Services improved its yearly earnings by 33% to $2.09 billion.

PROSPECTS: GE's product and service diversity are the key to its future revenue and earnings growth. The disposition of Kidder, Peabody, the Company's troubled investment bank, has eliminated a much publicized burden on highly profitable GE Capital Management. GE has strengthened its operations overseas by acquisitions and joint ventures, including acquisition agreements in Germany and Japan for GE Capital Management. Continued global expansion represents the Company's commitment to forging new markets.

BUSINESS

GENERAL ELECTRIC COMPANY'S businesses are as follows: Aircraft Engines develops and manufactures engines for commercial aircraft. Broadcasting operations are conducted through NBC. The Industrial segment, through BorgWarner Chemical, has become a leading manufacturer of plastic. Appliances is a leading supplier of kitchen appliances. The Material, Power Systems, Technical Products and Services sectors are providers of medical systems, power generation, motors and transportation systems. Financial services are provided by GE Capital Services.

BUSINESS LINE ANALYSIS

(12/31/94)	Rev(%)	Inc(%)
Aircraft Engines	13.4	13.3
Appliances	14.0	14.0
Broadcasting	8.0	8.0
Industrial	22.1	21.3
Materials & Power	27.3	27.1
Techical Products	10.1	10.0
All other & Corp items	5.1	6.3
Total	100.0	100.0

ANNUAL EARNINGS AND DIVIDENDS PER SHARE

	1994	1993	1992	1991	1990	1989	1988
Earnings Per Share	[1] 3.46	2.59	[1] 2.51	[2] 2.55	2.43	2.18	3.75
Dividends Per Share	1.44	1.26	1.12	1.02	0.94	0.82	0.70
Dividend Payout %	41.6	48.7	44.6	40.0	38.8	37.6	18.7

[1] Before disc. oper. [2] Before acctg. chg.

ANNUAL FINANCIAL DATA

	1994	1993	1992	1991	1990	1989	1988
RECORD OF EARNINGS (IN MILLIONS):							
Total Revenues	60,109.0	60,562.0	57,073.0	60,236.0	58,414.0	54,574.0	50,089.0
Costs and Expenses	29,262.0	28,825.0	27,519.0	31,363.0	31,421.0	29,731.0	28,066.0
Deprec, Depl & Amort	3,207.0	3,261.0	2,818.0	2,832.0	2,508.0	2,256.0	2,266.0
Operating Profit	27,640.0	28,476.0	26,736.0	26,041.0	24,485.0	22,587.0	19,757.0
Earn Bef Income Taxes	8,661.0	6,575.0	6,273.0	6,436.0	6,147.0	5,703.0	4,721.0
Income Taxes	2,746.0	2,151.0	1,968.0	2,001.0	1,844.0	1,764.0	1,335.0
Net Income	[1] 5,915.0	[2] 4,424.0	[3] 4,305.0	[4] 4,435.0	4,303.0	3,939.0	3,386.0
Aver. Shs. Outstg. (000)	1,709,000	1,708,000	1,714,000	1,738,000	1,776,000	1,808,000	1,804,000

[1] Before disc. op. dr$1,189,000,000. [2] Before disc. op. cr$753,000,000; and acctg. chg. dr$862,000,000. [3] Before disc. op. cr$420,000,000. [4] Before acctg. chg. dr$1,799,000,000.

	1994	1993	1992	1991	1990	1989	1988
BALANCE SHEET (IN MILLIONS):							
Cash and Cash Equivalents	33,556.0	103,657.0	65,327.0	47,194.0	44,725.0	33,565.0	26,866.0
Receivables, Net	166,004.0	151,707.0	133,951.0	126,880.0	7,806.0	6,976.0	6,780.0
Inventories	3,880.0	3,824.0	4,574.0	6,398.0	6,707.0	6,655.0	6,486.0
Gross Property	41,670.0	38,179.0	35,655.0	...	...	[1] 15,646.0	[1] 13,611.0
Accumulated Depreciation	18,205.0	16,951.0	15,268.0	15,028.0	13,941.0	...	...
Long-Term Debt	36,979.0	29,014.0	25,376.0	22,682.0	21,043.0	16,110.0	15,082.0
Net Stockholders' Equity	26,387.0	25,824.0	23,459.0	21,683.0	21,680.0	20,890.0	18,466.0
Total Assets	270,841.0	315,454.0	252,264.0	190,007.0	123,312.0	128,344.0	110,865.0
Total Current Assets	203,440.0	259,188.0	203,852.0	180,472.0	59,238.0	47,196.0	40,132.0
Total Current Liabilities	72,854.0	93,594.0	64,086.0	51,261.0	50,102.0	36,702.0	31,378.0
Net Working Capital	130,586.0	165,594.0	139,766.0	129,211.0	9,136.0	10,494.0	8,754.0
Year End Shs Outstg (000)	1,709,000	1,708,000	1,710,000	1,728,000	1,746,000	1,810,000	1,804,000

[1] Net

	1994	1993	1992	1991	1990	1989	1988
STATISTICAL RECORD:							
Operating Profit Margin %	46.0	47.0	46.8	43.2	41.9	41.4	39.4
Book Value Per Share	8.79	9.05	8.16	6.87	7.07	6.67	5.50
Return on Equity %	22.4	17.1	18.4	20.5	19.8	18.9	18.3
Return on Assets %	2.2	1.4	1.7	2.3	3.5	3.1	3.1
Average Yield %	2.9	2.7	2.8	3.1	3.0	3.0	3.2
P/E Ratio	15.9-13.0	20.7-15.6	17.4-14.5	15.3-10.4	15.6-10.3	14.9-10.0	12.8-10.3
Price Range	54⅞-45	53½-40½	43¾-36⅜	39⅛-26½	37¾-25	32⅜-21¾	24-19¼

Statistics are as originally reported.

OFFICERS:
J.F. Welch, Jr., Chmn. & C.E.O.
P. Fresco, Vice-Chmn. & Exec. Off.
D.D. Dammerman, Sr. V.P.-Fin.
B.W. Heineman, Jr., Sr. V.P., Couns. & Sec.

INCORPORATED: NY, Apr., 1892

PRINCIPAL OFFICE: 3135 Easton Turnpike, Fairfield, CT 06431

TELEPHONE NUMBER: (203) 373-2211

NO. OF EMPLOYEES: 221,000 (approx.)

ANNUAL MEETING: In April

SHAREHOLDERS: 460,000 (approx.)

INSTITUTIONAL HOLDINGS:
No. of Institutions: 1,309
Shares Held: 449,398,464

REGISTRAR(S): The Bank of New York, New York, NY

TRANSFER AGENT(S): The Bank of New York, New York, NY

NYS SYMBOL GIS
Rec. Pr. 59⅝

GENERAL MILLS, INC.

YIELD	3.2%
P/E RATIO	27.5

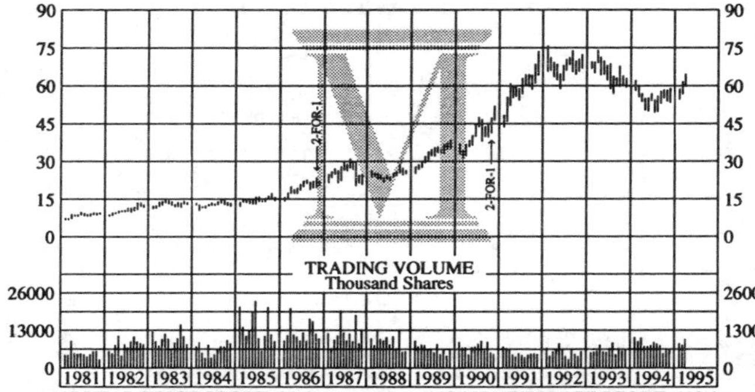

***7 YEAR PRICE SCORE 91.4** ***12 MONTH PRICE SCORE 103.4**

*NYSE COMPOSITE INDEX=100

INTERIM EARNINGS (Per Share):

Qtr.	Aug.	Nov.	Feb.	May
1991-92	0.86	0.77	0.80	0.62
1992-93	----------	---------- 3.10	----------	----------
1993-94	1.04	0.88	0.91	0.12
1994-95	0.95	0.95	0.15	...

INTERIM DIVIDENDS (Per Share):

Amt.	Decl.	Ex.	Rec.	Pay.
0.47Q	2/14/94	4/4/94	4/8/94	5/2/94
0.47Q	6/27	7/1	7/8	8/1
0.47Q	9/19	10/3	10/10	11/1
0.47Q	12/12	1/4/95	1/10/95	2/1/95
0.47Q	2/27/95	4/4	4/10	5/1

Indicated div.: $1.88*

CAPITALIZATION (5/29/94):

	($000)	(%)
Long-Term Debt	1,417,200	49.4
Deferred Income Tax	297,400	10.4
Common & Surplus	1,151,200	40.2
Total	2,865,800	100.0

DIVIDEND ACHIEVER STATUS:
Rank: 87 1984-94 Growth Rate: 13.4%
Total Years of Dividend Growth: 30

RECENT DEVELOPMENTS: For the quarter ended 11/28/93, net income was $140.7 million compared with $138.1 million last year. Sales advanced 4.1% to $2.18 billion. Consumer Foods sales increased 2% to $1.51 billion. Yoplait and Betty Crocker products reported strong profit growth. Big G cereal unit volume decreased 5% due to competitive promotional efforts. North American sales grew 4% at Red Lobster. The Olive Garden's North American operations posted a 14% gain in sales.

PROSPECTS: In the near term, the rate of sales and earnings growth will likely slow; however, the Company should experience significant contributions from Big G Cereals as a result of competitive promotions and new product introductions. Encouraging results from the Company's China Coast units have prompted the Company to open an additional 16 stores in the Midwest, Southwest, and Southeast.

BUSINESS

GENERAL MILLS, INC., is a leading producer of packaged consumer foods and one of North America's largest operators of full-service restaurants. Consumer Foods include Big G cereals, snack products, dessert mixes, side dishes, flour, baking mix, yogurt and frozen seafoods. Brand names include Cheerios, Wheaties and Total cereals; plus Betty Crocker, Bisquick, Yoplait and Gorton's. International Food operations include General Mills Canada Inc. Restaurant operations consist of Red Lobster seafood restaurants and The Olive Garden Italian restaurants.

BUSINESS LINE ANALYSIS

(5/29/94)	Rev(%)	Inc(%)
Consumer Foods	65.2	74.9
Restaurants	34.8	25.1
Total	100.0	100.0

ANNUAL EARNINGS AND DIVIDENDS PER SHARE

	5/29/94	5/30/93	5/31/92	5/26/91	5/27/90	5/28/89	5/29/88
Earnings Per Share	2.95	3.10	[1] 3.05	[1] 2.82	[1] 2.28	[1] [3] 1.93	[1] 1.53
Dividends Per Share	1.88	1.78	1.38	[2] 1.19	1.02	0.87	0.72
Dividend Payout %	63.7	57.4	45.2	42.2	44.8	45.2	47.2

[1] Before disc. oper. [2] 2-for-1 stk split, 11/90 [3] Before acctg. chg.

ANNUAL FINANCIAL DATA

RECORD OF EARNINGS (IN MILLIONS):							
Total Revenues	8,516.9	8,134.6	7,777.8	7,153.2	6,448.3	5,620.6	5,178.8
Costs and Expenses	7,213.7	6,875.8	6,639.5	6,108.1	5,623.1	4,923.3	4,558.3
Depreciation & Amort	303.8	274.2	247.4	218.4	180.1	152.3	140.0
Operating Profit	999.4	984.6	890.9	826.7	645.1	545.0	480.5
Earn Fr Cont Opers Bef Inc Taxes	753.3	844.0	844.5	765.6	612.7	517.5	442.8
Income Taxes	283.6	337.9	338.9	301.4	239.0	202.2	177.4
Net Income	469.9	506.1	[1] 505.6	[2] 464.2	[3] 373.7	[4] 315.3	[5] 265.4
Aver. Shs. Outstg. (000)	159,100	163,100	165,700	164,500	164,400	163,900	174,000

[1] Before disc. op. dr$10,000,000. [2] Before disc. op. cr$8,500,000. [3] Before disc. op. cr$7,700,000. [4] Before disc. op. cr$169,000,000. [5] Before disc. op. cr$17,700,000.

BALANCE SHEET (IN MILLIONS):							
Cash and Cash Equivalents	0.2	100.0	0.5	39.8	70.8	10.6	14.6
Receivables, Net	530.1	429.7	440.6	450.4	370.0	356.1	310.6
Inventories	488.3	439.0	487.2	645.4	537.2	501.1	529.5
Gross Property	4,689.8	4,239.5	3,909.3	3,337.1	2,883.2	2,404.0	2,139.0
Accumulated Depreciation	1,597.2	1,379.9	1,260.7	1,095.8	948.7	815.9	762.6
Long-Term Debt	1,417.2	1,268.3	920.5	879.0	688.5	536.3	361.5
Net Stockholders' Equity	1,151.2	1,218.5	1,370.9	1,113.5	809.7	731.9	648.5
Total Assets	5,198.3	4,650.8	4,305.0	4,053.6	3,432.3	3,019.1	2,777.9
Total Current Assets	1,129.2	1,076.9	1,034.6	1,234.1	1,052.9	972.3	1,091.9
Total Current Liabilities	1,832.1	1,558.8	1,371.7	1,272.4	1,173.2	1,038.4	1,191.4
Net Working Capital	d702.9	d481.9	d337.1	d38.3	d120.3	d66.1	d99.5
Year End Shs Outstg (000)	158,500	160,500	165,500	165,100	163,200	161,200	167,310
STATISTICAL RECORD:							
Operating Profit Margin %	11.7	12.1	11.5	11.6	10.0	9.7	9.3
Book Value Per Share	6.08	6.57	7.79	6.26	4.57	4.19	3.44
Return on Equity %	40.8	41.5	36.9	41.7	46.2	43.1	40.9
Return on Assets %	9.0	10.9	11.7	11.5	10.9	10.4	9.6
Average Yield %	2.9	2.6	2.4	2.9	3.2	3.4	2.8
P/E Ratio	25.1-19.3	24.5-19.0	24.1-14.3	18.4-11.1	17.0-11.1	15.1-11.3	20.3-13.3
Price Range	74⅛-56⅞	75⅞-58¾	73⅝-43½	52-31⅜	38½-25¼	29-21⅝	31⅛-20⅜

Statistics are as originally reported.

OFFICERS:
H.B. Atwater, Jr., Chmn. & C.E.O.
S.W. Sanger, Pres.
S.R. Demeritt, Sr. V.P. & C.E.O.

INCORPORATED: DE, Jun., 1928

PRINCIPAL OFFICE: One General Mills Blvd., Minneapolis, MN 55426

TELEPHONE NUMBER: (612) 540-2311

NO. OF EMPLOYEES: 125,700 (approx.)

ANNUAL MEETING: In September

SHAREHOLDERS: 45,694

INSTITUTIONAL HOLDINGS:
No. of Institutions: 663
Shares Held: 107,951,619

REGISTRAR(S): Harris Trust & Savings Bank, Chicago, IL

TRANSFER AGENT(S): Harris Trust & Savings Bank, Chicago, IL

GENERAL RE CORP.

YIELD 1.5%
P/E RATIO 17.5

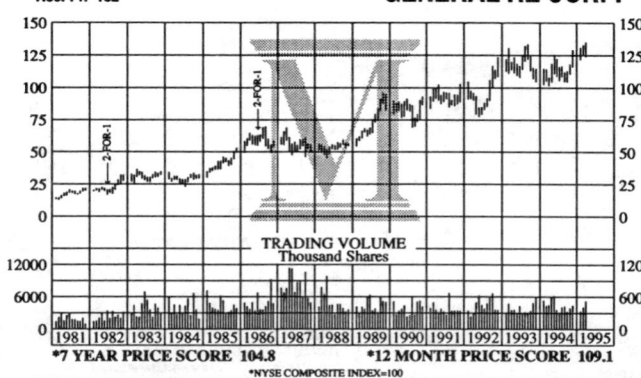

INTERIM EARNINGS (Per Share):

Qtr.	Mar.	June	Sept.	Dec.
1991	1.70	1.82	1.84	2.10
1992	1.68	1.80	1.62	1.76
1993	1.86	2.14	2.03	2.00
1994	1.15	2.12	2.29	2.41

INTERIM DIVIDENDS (Per Share):

Amt.	Decl.	Ex.	Rec.	Pay.
0.48Q	2/9/94	3/17/94	3/23/94	3/31/94
0.48Q	6/8	6/16	6/22	6/30
0.48Q	9/14	9/19	9/23	9/30
0.48Q	12/14	12/16	12/22	12/30
0.49Q	2/8/95	3/17/95	3/23/95	3/31/95

*Indicated div.: $1.96**

CAPITALIZATION (12/31/94):

	($000)	(%)
Total Debt	2,053,000	29.7
Preferred Stock	148,000	2.1
Common & Surplus	4,712,000	68.2
Total	6,913,000	100.0

DIVIDEND ACHIEVER STATUS:
Rank: 162   1984-94 Growth Rate: 10.3%
Total Years of Dividend Growth: 18

RECENT DEVELOPMENTS: For the year ended 12/31/94, net income was $665.3 million compared with income before an accounting change of $696.8 million the year before. Total revenues rose 7.8% to $3.84 billion from $3.56 billion a year ago. The domestic property/casualty operations reported a moderate increase in revenues to $3.15 billion from $3.08 billion in 1993.

PROSPECTS: The domestic and international markets are both enjoying increases in premium volumes. International operations are yielding positive underwriting results and plans for expansion into new geographic areas will provide good opportunities for growth in the future. The financial services segment should continue to benefit from improvements in brokerage operations and increases in fee income from underwriting and investment management operations.

BUSINESS

GENERAL RE CORPORATION is a holding company, the principal subsidiary of which is General Reinsurance Corp., the largest professional property/casualty reinsurer domiciled in the United States. Through the principal subsidiary and several others, GRN provides reinsurance, insurance and related services throughout the United States and in more than thirty other countries. The Company also operates in the securities dervatives markets through General Re Financial Products.

REVENUES

(12/31/94)	($000)	(%)
Premiums Earned	2,788,000	72.7
Net Investment Income	749,000	19.5
Other Revenues	234,000	6.1
Realized Gains on Invests	66,000	1.7
Total	3,837,000	100.0

ANNUAL EARNINGS AND DIVIDENDS PER SHARE

	1994	1993	1992	1991	1990	1989	1988
Earnings Per Share	7.97	8.11	①6.84	7.46	6.89	6.52	5.44
Dividends Per Share	1.92	1.88	1.80	1.68	1.52	1.36	1.20
Dividend Payout %	24.1	23.2	26.3	22.5	22.1	20.9	22.1

① Before acctg. chg.

ANNUAL FINANCIAL DATA

RECORD OF EARNINGS (IN MILLIONS):

	1994	1993	1992	1991	1990	1989	1988
Insurance Premiums	749.0	2,446.0	2,289.0	2,233.0	2,054.0	1,918.0	2,185.0
Total Interest Income	2,788.0	755.0	755.0	752.0	706.0	673.0	570.0
Total Revenues	3,837.0	3,560.0	3,357.0	3,199.0	2,946.0	2,784.0	2,872.0
Claims & Claim Expenses	1,981.0	1,723.0	1,829.0	1,618.0	1,446.0	1,326.0	1,444.0
Income Bef Income Taxes	794.0	885.0	721.0	793.0	738.0	736.0	...
Income Taxes	129.0	188.0	125.0	136.0	124.0	138.0	63.0
Net Income	665.0	①697.0	②596.0	657.0	614.0	599.0	③513.0
Aver. Shs. Outstg. (000)	82,000	85,000	86,000	87,000	88,000	91,000	95,000

① Before acctg. change cr$14,000,000. ② Before acctg. change cr$61,000,000. ③ Before disc. op. dr$33,000,000.

BALANCE SHEET (IN MILLIONS):

	1994	1993	1992	1991	1990	1989	1988
Cash	1,055.0	615.0	157.0	84.0	59.0	27.0	22.0
Fixed Maturities	14,174.0	11,217.0	8,970.0	8,462.0	7,791.0	6,888.0	6,185.0
Equity Securities, At Mkt	2,977.0	2,726.0	2,157.0	1,827.0	1,286.0	1,342.0	1,037.0
Total Assets	29,597.0	18,469.0	13,280.0	12,417.0	11,032.0	10,390.0	9,395.0
Benefits and Claims	15,760.0	9,292.0	7,619.0	7,149.0	6,720.0	6,354.0	6,033.0
Net Stockholders' Equity	4,860.0	4,762.0	4,227.0	3,912.0	3,270.0	3,084.0	2,694.0
Year End Shs Outstg (000)	82,000	84,000	85,000	87,000	87,000	90,000	93,000

STATISTICAL RECORD:

	1994	1993	1992	1991	1990	1989	1988
Return on Equity %	13.7	14.6	14.1	16.8	18.8	19.4	19.0
Book Value Per Share	57.46	54.92	47.98	43.24	35.86	32.60	28.97
Average Yield %	1.2	1.6	1.8	1.8	1.9	1.8	2.3
P/E Ratio	16.2-12.8	16.4-12.9	18.1-11.3	13.8-11.2	13.5-10.0	14.8-8.3	10.9-8.4
Price Range	129⅛-101	133⅜-104	123½-77	102¾-83	93¼-69	96¼-54⅜	59⅜-45½

Statistics are as originally reported.

OFFICERS:
R.E. Ferguson, Chmn., Pres. & C.E.O.
J.C. Etling, Vice-Chmn.
J.P. Brandon, V.P. & C.F.O.
C.F. Barr, V.P., Gen. Couns. & Sec.
E.A. Monrad, V.P., Treas. & Contr.

INCORPORATED: DE, Jun., 1980

PRINCIPAL OFFICE: Financial Centre 695 East Main Street P.O. Box 10351, Stamford, CT 06904-2351

TELEPHONE NUMBER: (203) 328-5000

NO. OF EMPLOYEES: 3,282

ANNUAL MEETING: In May

SHAREHOLDERS: 4,163

INSTITUTIONAL HOLDINGS:
No. of Institutions: 616
Shares Held: 72,479,670

REGISTRAR(S): American Stock Transfer & Trust Co., 40 Wall Street, New York, NY 10005

TRANSFER AGENT(S): American Stock Transfer & Trust Co., 40 Wall Street, New York, NY 10005

GIANT FOOD INC.

YIELD 3.0%
P/E RATIO 15.0

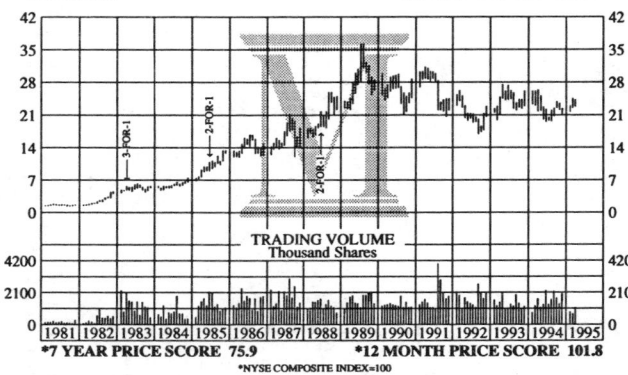

7 YEAR PRICE SCORE 75.9　　**12 MONTH PRICE SCORE 101.8**
*NYSE COMPOSITE INDEX=100

INTERIM EARNINGS (Per Share):

Qtr.	May	Aug.	Nov.	Feb.
1991-92	0.50	0.31	0.24	0.42
1992-93	-------------- 1.37 --------------			
1993-94	0.38	0.24	0.30	0.61
1994-95	0.34	0.25	0.31	0.69

INTERIM DIVIDENDS (Per Share):

Amt.	Decl.	Ex.	Rec.	Pay.
0.175Q	1/21/94	1/31/94	2/4/94	3/4/94
0.18Q	4/28	5/9	5/13	6/3
0.18Q	7/14	8/1	8/5	9/2
0.18Q	10/13	10/31	11/4	12/2
0.18Q	1/12/95	1/30/95	2/3/95	3/3/95

*Indicated div.: $0.72**

CAPITALIZATION (2/26/94):

	($000)	(%)
Long-Term Debt	86,068	8.7
Cap. Lease Oblig.	141,062	14.4
Deferred Income Tax	41,192	4.2
Common & Surplus	713,429	72.7
Total	981,751	100.0

DIVIDEND ACHIEVER STATUS:

Rank: 69　　1984-94 Growth Rate: 14.3%
Total Years of Dividend Growth: 14

RECENT DEVELOPMENTS: For the year ended 2/26/94, earnings before an accounting change increased to $91.3 million, or $1.53 per share, compared with earnings of $81.5 million, or $1.37 per share, for the previous year. Sales rose 2.7% to $3.57 billion from $3.47 billion last year. For the quarter, the series of winter storms that hit GFS's region helped contribute to a sales increase of 4.2%. For stores in operation both years, the increase was 2.1%. Earnings for the quarter

amounted to $36.3 million, or $0.61 per share, compared with $36.7 million, or $0.62 per share, a year ago. The Company opened four food-drug stores during fiscal 1994 and closed two smaller stores, resulting in a net increase of store space of 209,000 square feet. On 4/20/94, GFS opened its first Delaware store. The Company plans to open four food-drug stores during the 1995 fiscal year.

BUSINESS

GIANT FOOD INC. operates a chain of 157 supermarkets selling retail, food and general merchandise in the Delaware, Washington, Maryland and Virginia vicinities. Giant supermarkets are all self-service and offer a full line of nationally advertised groceries, meat, produce, dairy products, seafood, tobacco, flowers and household items. The Company also sells groceries, frozen foods, bakery products and dairy products under its own private label. Unbranded items such as meat and produce are marketed in the Company's supermarkets. Giant operates three freestanding drug stores.

QUARTERLY DATA

(2/26/94)($000)	Rev	Inc
1st Quarter	813,466	26,608
2nd Quarter	795,841	14,604
3rd Quarter	799,056	17,722
4th Quarter	1,159,105	36,297

ANNUAL EARNINGS AND DIVIDENDS PER SHARE

	2/26/94	2/27/93	2/29/92	2/23/91	2/24/90	2/25/89	2/27/88
Earnings Per Share	1.53	1.37	1.47	2.01	1.80	1.63	1.26
Dividends Per Share	0.715	0.695	0.645	0.575	0.50	0.40	① 0.323
Dividend Payout %	45.4	50.7	43.9	28.6	27.8	24.5	26.2

① 3-for-1 stk. split, 3/83 & 2-for-1 stk. split, 6/88 & 6/85.

ANNUAL FINANCIAL DATA

RECORD OF EARNINGS (IN MILLIONS):

Total Revenues	3,567.5	3,472.6	3,489.8	3,349.5	3,248.9	2,987.2	2,721.3
Costs and Expenses	3,301.1	3,224.9	3,238.4	3,063.8	2,991.0	2,759.8	2,528.9
Depreciation & Amort	95.7	94.9	92.0	82.4	71.1	57.0	49.7
Operating Profit	1,064.4	1,021.8	1,034.7	1,047.1	974.1	879.7	787.0
Income Bef Income Taxes	151.8	132.3	142.1	192.1	179.2	159.1	131.7
Income Taxes	60.5	50.8	54.9	73.2	70.8	61.1	56.2
Net Income	① 91.3	81.5	87.2	118.9	108.4	98.0	75.6
Aver. Shs. Outstg. (000)	59,659	59,648	59,447	59,257	60,095	60,166	60,126

① Before acctg. change cr$3,934,000.

BALANCE SHEET (IN MILLIONS):

Cash and Cash Equivalents	228.3	185.2	151.4	168.3	181.9	178.7	147.6
Receivables, Net	37.5	32.7	28.1	26.7	26.1	28.0	26.0
Inventories	217.6	223.9	207.3	211.4	206.6	191.0	183.3
Gross Property	1,420.9	1,329.9	1,281.4	1,126.2	982.7	856.3	763.8
Accumulated Depreciation	599.5	531.2	462.4	395.5	343.0	298.1	261.9
Long-Term Debt	86.1	105.5	113.4	98.4	100.4	101.7	108.0
Capital Lease Obligations	141.1	142.8	142.9	147.0	141.2	131.7	126.8
Net Stockholders' Equity	713.4	663.0	621.0	555.7	493.1	427.7	355.6
Total Assets	1,357.8	1,296.6	1,251.3	1,175.0	1,080.8	982.5	885.0
Total Current Assets	505.5	461.6	404.6	421.7	421.8	404.5	364.8
Total Current Liabilities	341.3	307.1	296.2	296.0	275.4	258.1	239.6
Net Working Capital	164.2	154.5	108.4	125.7	146.4	146.4	125.2
Year End Shs Outstg (000)	59,587	59,690	59,620	58,979	59,757	60,163	60,152

STATISTICAL RECORD:

Operating Profit Margin %	4.8	4.4	4.6	6.1	5.7	5.7	5.2
Book Value Per Share	11.97	11.11	10.42	9.42	8.25	7.11	5.91
Return on Equity %	12.8	12.3	14.0	21.4	22.0	22.9	21.3
Return on Assets %	6.7	6.3	7.0	10.1	10.0	10.0	8.5
Average Yield %	2.9	3.2	2.5	2.3	1.7	1.9	2.0
P/E Ratio	18.0-13.0	19.2-12.3	21.3-14.0	14.9-10.5	20.1-12.3	15.9-9.8	16.8-9.5
Price Range	27½-19⅞	26¼-16⅞	31¼-20⅝	29⅞-21⅛	36¼-22⅛	25⅞-16	21⅛-12

Statistics are as originally reported.

OFFICERS:
I. Cohen, Chmn. & C.E.O.
P.L. Manos, Pres.
D.B. Sykes, Sr. V.P.-Fin., Sec. & Treas.

INCORPORATED: DE, 1935

PRINCIPAL OFFICE: 6300 Sheriff Road, Landover, MD 20785

TELEPHONE NUMBER: (310) 341-4100

NO. OF EMPLOYEES: 24,700 (approx.)

ANNUAL MEETING: In September

SHAREHOLDERS: 38,000 cl. A non-voting com; 1, cl. AC com.; 1, Cl. AL com.

INSTITUTIONAL HOLDINGS:
No. of Institutions: 201
Shares Held: 19,817,207

REGISTRAR(S): American Stock Transfer Co., 40 Wall St., 46th Floor, New York, NY 10005

TRANSFER AGENT(S): American Stock Transfer Co., 40 Wall St., 46th Floor, New York, NY 10005

GILLETTE CO., (THE)

YIELD	1.4%
P/E RATIO	27.3

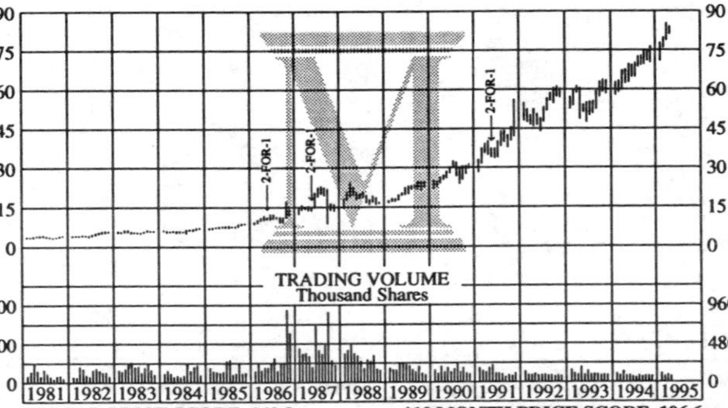

7 YEAR PRICE SCORE 140.8 **12 MONTH PRICE SCORE 106.6**
*NYSE COMPOSITE INDEX=100

INTERIM EARNINGS (Per Share):

Qtr.	Mar.	June	Sept.	Dec.
1991	0.48	0.46	0.48	0.52
1992	0.58	0.55	0.58	0.61
1993	0.64	0.61	0.65	0.02
1994	0.74	0.73	0.77	0.90

INTERIM DIVIDENDS (Per Share):

Amt.	Decl.	Ex.	Rec.	Pay.
0.25Q	7/21/94	7/26/94	8/1/94	9/5/94
0.25Q	10/20	10/26	11/1	12/5
0.25Q	12/16	1/26/95	2/1/95	3/3/95
0.30Q	2/16/95	4/25	5/1	6/5

*Indicated div.: $1.20**

CAPITALIZATION (12/31/94):

	($000)	(%)
Long-Term Debt	715,100	24.3
Deferred Income Tax	186,700	6.4
Minority Interest	17,400	0.6
Preferred Stock	98,200	3.3
Common & Surplus	1,919,100	65.4
Total	2,936,500	100.0

DIVIDEND ACHIEVER STATUS:

Rank: 118	1984-94 Growth Rate: 12.1%
Total Years of Dividend Growth:	17

RECENT DEVELOPMENTS: For the quarter ended 9/30/94, net income increased 18.8% to $172.2 million compared with $145.0 million a year ago. Sales were up 12.2% to $1.50 billion. The improved results were attributable to strong growth in the blade/razor, toiletries and Braun businesses. New product introductions and improved economies in several markets fueled demand for Gillette's products in Europe.

PROSPECTS: Revenues will be enhanced by the introduction of the Sensor Excel Shaving System, featuring an additional rubber strip that provides a closer shave, in the U.S. The product was introduced in Europe during 1993 and received strong customer acceptance. Advertising expenditures in support of Excel are expected to reach $80 million in the 12-month marketing campaign. Separately, management will continue to explore geographic expansion opportunities.

BUSINESS

THE GILLETTE COMPANY is a consumer products firm engaged in the development, manufacture and sale of a wide range of products for personal care. Major lines include blades and razors, toiletries and cosmetics, stationery products, Braun electric shavers and small appliances and Oral-B oral care products. Gillette is the market leader of blades and razors in North America and most other areas of the world. The Company holds a major position in North America in sales of toiletries and writing instruments. Braun markets electric shavers in Germany, Europe, North America and Japan.

BUSINESS LINE ANALYSIS

(12/31/94)	Rev(%)	Inc(%)
Blades & Razors	38.7	68.7
Toiletries &		
Cosmetics	19.2	6.2
Stationary Products	13.3	7.4
Braun Products	22.2	15.7
Oral-B Products	6.6	2.0
Total	100.0	100.0

ANNUAL EARNINGS AND DIVIDENDS PER SHARE

	1994	1993	1992	1991	1990	1989	1988
Earnings Per Share	3.14	1.92	2.32	1.94	1.60	1.35	1.22
Dividends Per Share	0.96	0.81	0.695	① 0.62	0.54	0.48	0.43
Dividend Payout %	30.6	42.2	30.0	30.9	32.8	34.6	35.1

① 2-for-1 stk split,05/23/91

ANNUAL FINANCIAL DATA

RECORD OF EARNINGS (IN MILLIONS):

	1994	1993	1992	1991	1990	1989	1988
Total Revenues	6,070.2	5,410.8	5,162.8	4,683.9	4,344.6	3,818.5	3,581.2
Costs and Expenses	4,628.1	4,367.6	3,984.8	3,629.6	3,394.9	3,005.3	2,826.0
Depreciation & Amort	215.4	218.5	210.9	192.7	177.0	149.1	141.2
Profit From Operations	1,226.7	824.7	967.1	861.6	772.7	664.1	614.0
Income Bef Income Taxes	1,104.1	682.7	829.7	694.1	593.2	473.6	448.6
Income Taxes	405.8	255.8	316.3	266.7	225.3	188.9	180.1
Net Income	698.3	① 426.9	513.4	427.4	367.9	284.7	268.5
Aver. Shs. Outstg. (000)	221,200	220,400	219,500	211,300	194,114	193,444	219,118

① Before acctg. change dr$138,600,000.

BALANCE SHEET (IN MILLIONS):

	1994	1993	1992	1991	1990	1989	1988
Cash and Cash Equivalents	46.1	38.6	39.8	56.7	81.2	136.8	175.0
Receivables, Net	1,647.1	1,226.9	1,186.1	1,083.9	1,015.7	828.5	729.1
Inventories	941.2	874.6	852.4	785.2	758.4	688.2	653.4
Gross Property	2,902.2	2,575.9	2,413.6	2,125.0	1,986.1	1,680.5	1,550.6
Accumulated Depreciation	1,491.2	1,361.4	1,338.2	1,193.6	1,124.5	935.7	867.5
Long-Term Debt	715.1	840.1	554.2	742.2	1,045.7	1,041.0	1,675.2
Net Stockholders' Equity	2,017.3	1,479.0	1,496.4	1,157.1	865.4	670.0	d84.6
Total Assets	5,494.0	5,102.3	4,189.9	3,918.4	3,671.3	3,114.0	2,867.9
Total Current Assets	2,747.4	2,528.0	2,336.2	2,177.8	2,093.5	1,854.5	1,739.7
Total Current Liabilities	1,783.2	1,760.3	1,560.8	1,484.6	1,307.9	1,061.3	965.4
Net Working Capital	964.2	767.7	775.4	693.2	785.6	793.2	774.3
Year End Shs Outstg (000)	221,450	220,890	220,169	219,179	194,436	193,700	193,234

STATISTICAL RECORD:

	1994	1993	1992	1991	1990	1989	1988
Operating Profit Margin %	20.2	15.2	18.7	18.4	17.8	17.4	17.1
Book Value Per Share	9.10	6.70	6.80	5.27	4.45	3.46	N.M.
Return on Equity %	34.6	28.9	34.3	36.9	N.M.	N.M.	. . .
Return on Assets %	12.7	8.4	12.3	10.9	10.0	9.1	9.4
Average Yield %	1.4	1.5	1.3	1.5	2.0	2.3	2.2
P/E Ratio	24.4-18.4	33.2-24.7	26.4-18.9	28.9-14.6	20.4-13.6	18.4-12.2	20.1-12.0
Price Range	76½-57¾	63¾-47⅜	61¼-43⅞	56⅛-28¼	32⅝-21¾	24⅞-16½	24½-14⅝

Statistics are as originally reported.

OFFICERS:
A.M. Zeien, Chmn. & C.E.O.
J.E. Mullaney, Vice-Chmn.-Legal
T.F. Skelly, Sr. V.P.-Fin.
L.B. Swaim, V.P. & Treas.
J.C. Richardson, Sec.

INCORPORATED: DE, Sep., 1917

PRINCIPAL OFFICE: Prudential Tower Bldg., Boston, MA 02199

TELEPHONE NUMBER: (617) 421-7000

NO. OF EMPLOYEES: 32,800 (approx.)

ANNUAL MEETING: In April

SHAREHOLDERS: 30,821

INSTITUTIONAL HOLDINGS:
No. of Institutions: 714
Shares Held: 156,828,983

REGISTRAR(S): First National Bank of Boston, Shareholder Services Division, Boston, MA

TRANSFER AGENT(S): First National Bank of Boston, Shareholder Services Division, Boston, MA

GOLDEN ENTERPRISES, INC.

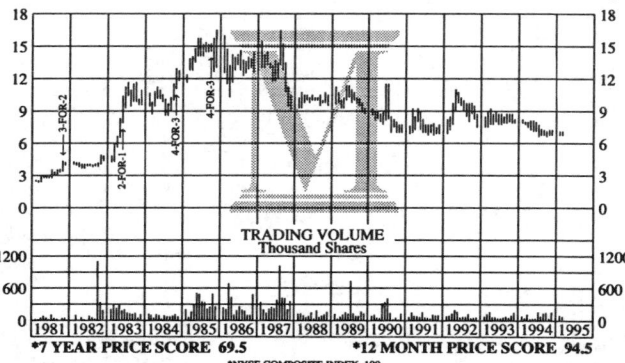

INTERIM EARNINGS (Per Share):

Qtr.	Aug.	Nov.	Feb.	May
1991-92	0.11	0.10	0.10	0.07
1992-93	0.14	0.09	0.08	0.09
1993-94	0.09	0.04	0.01	0.11
1994-95	0.11	0.09	0.10	...

INTERIM DIVIDENDS (Per Share):

Amt.	Decl.	Ex.	Rec.	Pay.
0.1125Q	1/5/94	1/10/94	1/17/94	1/26/94
0.1125Q	3/28	4/5	4/11	4/27
0.1125Q	7/12	7/18	7/22	7/29
0.115Q	9/20	10/3	10/7	10/26
0.115Q	1/4/95	1/9/95	1/16/95	1/25/95

Indicated div.: $0.46*

CAPITALIZATION (5/31/94):

	($000)	(%)
Deferred Income Tax	2,074	4.3
Common & Surplus	45,628	95.7
Total	47,702	100.0

TRADING VOLUME
Thousand Shares

1981 1982 1983 1984 1985 1986 1987 1988 1989 1990 1991 1992 1993 1994 1995

*7 YEAR PRICE SCORE 69.5 *12 MONTH PRICE SCORE 94.5

*NYSE COMPOSITE INDEX=100

DIVIDEND ACHIEVER STATUS:
Rank: 134   1984-94 Growth Rate: 11.3%
Total Years of Dividend Growth: 17

RECENT DEVELOPMENTS: For the quarter ended 2/28/95, income from continuing operations was $1.2 million, or $0.10 per share, compared with $118.9 million, or $0.01 per share, a year earlier. Total revenues advanced 2.2% to $32.6 million from $31.9 million the year before. Income from continuing operations before income taxes was $2.0 million versus $201,683 a year earlier. During the quarter, the Company closed the sale of its fastener division. For the nine months ended 2/28/95, income from continuing operations was $3.7 million, or $0.30 per share, compared with $1.6 million, or $0.13 per share, in the corresponding prior-year period. Total revenues advanced 2.0% to $94.6 million from $92.7 million a year earlier. Income from continuing operations before income taxes was $6.0 million versus $2.5 million a year earlier.

BUSINESS

GOLDEN ENTERPRISES, INC. is a holding concern for two subsidiaries Golden Flake Snack Foods, Inc., a wholly owned subsidiary, manufactures and distributes a variety of food products, such as potato chips, tortilla chips, fried pork skins, cheese curls, corn chips, onion rings, popcorn and peanut butter filled sandwiches. Golden sells its products to commercial establishments in Alabama, Tennessee, Kentucky, Georgia, Florida, Mississippi, Arkansas, Louisiana, North Carolina, South Carolina, and Missouri. Nall & Associates, Inc., a wholly owned subsidiary, represents manufacturers of nuts, bolts and other fasteners. In February 1995, the Company sold its fastener division, Steel City Bolt & Screw, Inc.

BUSINESS LINE ANALYSIS

(5/31/94)	Rev(%)	Inc(%)
Snack Food Products	96.2	96.9
Bolts & Other		
Fasteners	3.8	3.1
Total	100.0	100.0

ANNUAL EARNINGS AND DIVIDENDS PER SHARE

	5/31/94	5/31/93	5/31/92	5/31/91	5/31/90	5/31/89	5/31/88
Earnings Per Share	0.25	0.40	0.38	0.35	0.35	0.42	① 0.52
Dividends Per Share	0.452	0.442	0.405	0.37	② 0.83	0.29	0.25
Dividend Payout %	N.M.	N.M.	N.M.	N.M.	N.M.	69.0	48.1

① Before acctg. chg. ② Inc. $0.50 extra div.

ANNUAL FINANCIAL DATA

RECORD OF EARNINGS (IN THOUSANDS):

Total Revenues	131,876	134,893	132,561	130,424	134,872	127,511	130,086
Costs and Expenses	123,623	122,957	120,693	118,307	122,439	112,778	111,967
Depreciation & Amort.	3,465	3,993	4,330	5,069	5,667	6,467	7,397
Operating Profit	5,427	8,574	8,170	7,692	7,421	9,385	12,343
Income Bef Income Taxes	4,787	7,940	7,531	7,034	6,743	8,231	10,665
Income Taxes	1,714	2,959	2,756	2,633	2,304	2,840	3,927
Net Income	3,073	4,981	4,775	4,401	4,439	5,391	① 6,738
Aver. Shs. Outstg.	12,541	12,594	12,596	12,637	12,707	12,781	12,992

① Before acctg. change cr$1,025,000.

BALANCE SHEET (IN THOUSANDS):

Cash and Cash Equivalents	14,412	16,444	15,882	15,312	11,625	19,198	17,053
Receivables, Net	10,891	9,622	9,274	9,272	9,588	9,879	9,465
Inventories	5,091	5,326	5,246	6,172	5,969	5,908	5,493
Gross Property	72,676	72,771	72,824	71,553	70,880	66,806	66,182
Accumulated Depreciation	52,461	49,884	47,808	44,646	40,070	35,405	32,245
Net Stockholders' Equity	45,628	49,084	50,103	50,614	51,813	58,483	58,010
Total Assets	54,347	58,097	58,902	60,251	61,011	68,528	68,358
Total Current Assets	32,379	33,597	32,641	32,487	29,466	36,696	33,711
Total Current Liabilities	6,167	6,195	5,911	6,923	6,027	6,279	6,819
Net Working Capital	26,212	27,402	26,730	25,564	23,438	30,417	26,892
Year End Shares Outstg	12,496	12,600	12,639	12,668	12,755	12,802	12,895

STATISTICAL RECORD:

Operating Profit Margin %	3.6	5.9	5.7	5.4	5.0	6.5	8.2
Book Value Per Share	3.65	3.90	3.96	4.00	4.06	4.57	4.50
Return on Equity %	6.7	10.1	9.5	8.7	8.6	9.2	11.6
Return on Assets %	5.7	8.6	8.1	7.3	7.3	7.9	9.9
Average Yield %	5.5	4.8	5.1	4.0	8.2	2.9	2.0
P/E Ratio	37.0-30.0	27.5-17.2	24.3-17.8	32.9-20.0	32.5-25.0	25.6-22.0	31.7-17.3
Price Range	9¼-7½	11-6⅞	9¼-6¾	11½-7	11⅜-8¾	10¾-9¼	16½-9

Statistics are as originally reported.

OFFICERS:
S.Y. Bashinsky, Sr., Chmn.
J.S. Stein, Pres. & C.E.O.
J.H. Shannon, V.P. & Sec.

INCORPORATED: DE, Dec., 1967

PRINCIPAL OFFICE: 2101 Magnolia Ave.
South Suite 212, Birmingham, AL 35205

TELEPHONE NUMBER: (205) 326-6101

FAX: (205) 326-6148

NO. OF EMPLOYEES: 1,350 (approx.)

ANNUAL MEETING: In September

SHAREHOLDERS: 1,900 (approx.)

INSTITUTIONAL HOLDINGS:
No. of Institutions: 24
Shares Held: 1,303,444

REGISTRAR(S): AmSouth Bank, N.A.,
Birmingham, AL 35202

TRANSFER AGENT(S): AmSouth Bank, N.A.,
Birmingham, AL 35202

NYS SYMBOL GDW
Rec. Pr. 38¼

GOLDEN WEST FINANCIAL CORP.

YIELD 0.9%
P/E RATIO 10.3

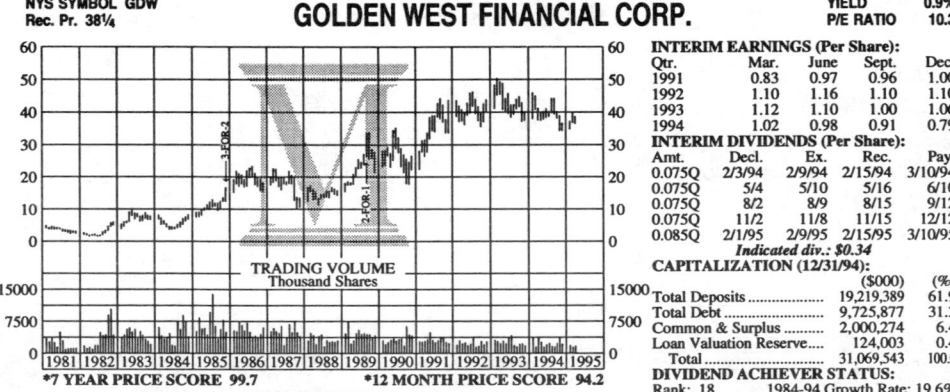

*7 YEAR PRICE SCORE 99.7   ***12 MONTH PRICE SCORE 94.2**

*NYSE COMPOSITE INDEX=100

INTERIM EARNINGS (Per Share):

Qtr.	Mar.	June	Sept.	Dec.
1991	0.83	0.97	0.96	1.00
1992	1.10	1.16	1.10	1.10
1993	1.12	1.10	1.00	1.06
1994	1.02	0.98	0.91	0.79

INTERIM DIVIDENDS (Per Share):

Amt.	Decl.	Ex.	Rec.	Pay.
0.075Q	2/3/94	2/9/94	2/15/94	3/10/94
0.075Q	5/4	5/10	5/16	6/10
0.075Q	8/2	8/9	8/15	9/12
0.075Q	11/2	11/8	11/15	12/12
0.085Q	2/1/95	2/9/95	2/15/95	3/10/95

Indicated div.: $0.34

CAPITALIZATION (12/31/94):

	($000)	(%)
Total Deposits	19,219,389	61.9
Total Debt	9,725,877	31.3
Common & Surplus	2,000,274	6.4
Loan Valuation Reserve	124,003	0.4
Total	31,069,543	100.0

DIVIDEND ACHIEVER STATUS:
Rank: 18   1984-94 Growth Rate: 19.6%
Total Years of Dividend Growth: 11

RECENT DEVELOPMENTS: For the year ended 12/31/94, net income was $230.4 million, down 15.8% from the $273.9 million earned the year before. Net interest income, adversely affected by narrower margins due to higher interest rates, moved down a modest 2% to $721.4 million from $723.8 million. Noninterest income plummeted to $37.5 million from $62.0 million. The Company recorded a $120,000 loss on the sale of securities and mortgage-backed securities compared with income of $22.5 million a year earlier.

PROSPECTS: The Company cites inflation, ongoing business expansion, and charges associated with relocating the operations center as reasons for increased expenses. Rising interest rates have adversely affected GDW's net interest margin by narrowing the gap the Company earns on loans and what it pays on deposits and borrowings. As a result, net interest income has fallen. However, higher interest rates have sparked an interest in adjustable rate mortgages.

BUSINESS

GOLDED WEST FINANCIAL is a savings and loan holding company, which has as its principal asset, World Savings & Loan Association. World Savings is a federally-chartered savings and loan association with operations in California and 7 other states. It operates as a financial intermediary attracting deposits (primarily in the form of savings accounts) and investing funds in loans and securities backed by residential real estate. With a total of 230 branches, World Savings has one of the largest branch networks in the U.S.

LOAN DISTRIBUTION

(12/31/94)	($000)	(%)
1-to-4 Family		
Dwelling	23,217,564	85.0
Over 4-Family		
Dwelling	3,946,446	14.4
Commercial Property	134,189	0.5
Land	1,851	0.0
Savings Accounts	30,460	0.1
Total	27,330,510	100.0

ANNUAL EARNINGS AND DIVIDENDS PER SHARE

	1994	1993	1992	1991	1990	1989	1988
Earnings Per Share	3.71	4.28	4.46	3.76	2.87	2.51	② 2.21
Dividends Per Share	0.30	0.27	0.23	0.19	0.165	① 0.15	0.125
Dividend Payout %	8.1	6.3	5.2	5.1	5.7	6.0	5.7

① 2-for-1 stk split, 9/8/89   ② 2-for1 stock split, payable 09/08/89

ANNUAL FINANCIAL DATA

RECORD OF EARNINGS (IN MILLIONS):

	1994	1993	1992	1991	1990	1989	1988
Total Interest Income	1,876.5	1,870.2	1,984.5	2,214.6	2,098.3	1,906.3	1,383.0
Total Interest Expense	1,155.1	1,137.4	1,267.2	1,582.8	1,601.5	1,485.3	1,006.3
Net Interest Income	721.4	732.8	717.3	631.8	496.8	421.0	376.7
Credit Loss Provision	63.0	65.8	43.2	30.2	13.6	6.7	1.9
Earn Bef Taxes on Income	390.4	457.4	463.7	386.7	282.7	246.2	215.1
Income Taxes	159.9	183.5	180.2	148.1	101.2	88.3	76.8
Net Income	230.4	273.9	283.5	238.6	181.5	157.9	138.3
Aver. Shs. Outstg. (000)	62,129	63,978	63,578	63,442	63,137	62,906	62,781

BALANCE SHEET (IN MILLIONS):

	1994	1993	1992	1991	1990	1989	1988
Cash & Sec. Etc.	242.4	243.2	228.8	245.9	632.7	740.1	728.4
Investments and Advances	3,623.0	4,090.1	3,100.2	3,380.0	3,486.6	3,062.8	3,153.4
Loans & Lse Financing, Net	27,071.3	23,912.6	21,968.7	20,087.4	17,730.4	15,011.0	12,121.0
Long-term Debt	1,221.6	1,220.1	921.7	625.1	426.2	113.7	113.5
Net Stockholders' Equity	2,000.3	2,065.6	1,727.4	1,449.1	1,220.4	1,046.3	896.4
Total Assets	31,683.7	28,829.3	25,890.9	24,297.8	22,562.1	19,520.6	16,721.0
Year End Shs Outstg (000)	58,590	63,929	63,925	63,499	63,330	63,002	62,821

STATISTICAL RECORD:

	1994	1993	1992	1991	1990	1989	1988
Return on Equity %	11.5	13.3	16.4	16.5	14.9	15.1	15.4
Return on Assets %	0.7	1.0	1.1	1.0	0.8	0.8	0.8
Book Value Per Share	34.14	32.31	27.02	22.82	19.27	16.61	14.27
Average Yield %	0.7	0.6	0.6	0.6	0.6	0.6	0.9
P/E Ratio	12.4-9.2	11.8-8.7	10.4-8.0	11.8-5.9	12.3-6.1	13.4-6.1	7.9-5.1
Price Range	46-34¼	50⅜-37⅛	46¼-35½	44¼-22¼	35¼-17⅝	33¾-15⅜	17⅜-11¼

Statistics are as originally reported.

OFFICERS:
M.O. Sandler, Chmn. & C.E.O.
H.M. Sandler, Chmn. & C.E.O.
R.W. Kettell, Pres.
R.C. Rowe, V.P. & Sec.
INCORPORATED: DE, May, 1959
PRINCIPAL OFFICE: 1901 Harrison Street, Oakland, CA 94612

TELEPHONE NUMBER: (510) 446-3420
FAX: (510) 446-4259
NO. OF EMPLOYEES: 3,635
ANNUAL MEETING: In April
SHAREHOLDERS: 1,860
INSTITUTIONAL HOLDINGS:
No. of Institutions: 232
Shares Held: 39,256,786

REGISTRAR(S): First Interstate, San Francisco, CA

TRANSFER AGENT(S): First Interstate, San Francisco, CA

GORMAN-RUPP CO.

YIELD 3.4%
P/E RATIO 13.3

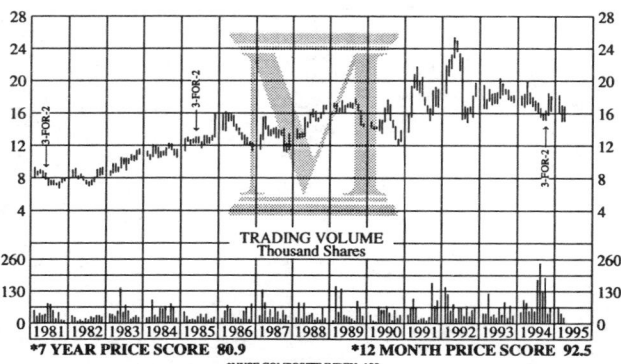

TRADING VOLUME
Thousand Shares

1981 | 1982 | 1983 | 1984 | 1985 | 1986 | 1987 | 1988 | 1989 | 1990 | 1991 | 1992 | 1993 | 1994 | 1995

*7 YEAR PRICE SCORE 80.9   *12 MONTH PRICE SCORE 92.5

*NYSE COMPOSITE INDEX=100

INTERIM EARNINGS (Per Share):

Qtr.	Mar.	June	Sept.	Dec.
1992	0.25	0.26	0.21	0.21
1993	0.26	0.26	0.29	0.21
1994	0.35	0.30	0.27	0.17
1995	0.29	...	...	...

INTERIM DIVIDENDS (Per Share):

Amt.	Decl.	Ex.	Rec.	Pay.
0.18Q	4/21/94	5/4/94	5/10/94	6/10/94
0.18Q	7/21	8/4	8/10	9/9
3-for-2	8/25	10/28	9/29	10/27
0.13Q	10/27	11/4	11/10	12/9
0.13Q	1/19/95	2/6/95	2/10/95	3/10/95

Indicated div.: $0.52

CAPITALIZATION (12/31/94):

	($000)	(%)
Long-Term Debt	4,715	7.1
Common & Surplus	61,608	92.9
Total	66,323	100.0

DIVIDEND ACHIEVER STATUS:
Rank: 295   1984-94 Growth Rate: 4.0%
Total Years of Dividend Growth: 22

RECENT DEVELOPMENTS: For the year ended 12/31/94, net income was $9.3 million compared with $8.8 million, an increase of 6% for the corresponding period of 1993. Net sales advanced to $137.5 million versus $131.5 million a year earlier. The increase in net sales was principally the result of increased business in the waste and fresh water business, and to a lesser degree, increases in unit pricing. Cost of products sold as a percentage of net sales was 74% in 1994, compared to 75.1% in 1993. Continued efforts to improve manufacturing efficiencies and cost containment procedures coupled with increased utilization of the manufacturing facilities at the Company's largest division resulted in improved cost of products sold for the comparative periods. SG&A was 15.5% of net sales versus 14.8% in 1993. The rise was associated with the design and implementation of an upgraded information management systems.

BUSINESS

GORMAN-RUPP CO. designs, manufactures and sells pumps and related equipment for use in construction, industrial, pertroleum, agricultural, water and wastewater, original equipment, fire, military and other liquid-handling applications. Its product line is composed of pump models ranging in rated capacity from less than one gallon per minute up to 200,000 gallons per minute. The types of pumps which the Company produces include self priming centrifugal, standard centrifugal, magnetic drive centrifugal, rotary gear, diaphragm, bellows and oscillating. The pumps have drives that range from 1/35 horsepower electric motors up to much larger electric motors or internal combustion engines. The Company's larger pumps are sold principally for use in the construction, industrial, sewage and waste handling fields; for pumping refined petroleum products, including the ground refueling of aircraft; for agricultural applications; and for fire fighting. Many of the Company's smallest pumps are sold to customers for incorporation into such products as X-ray processing equipment, gas air conditioning equipment, office copy machines, chemical feeding, instrumention and ice cube making machinery; photographic processing and soft-drink dispensing equipment; laser cooling applications; graphic arts equipment; and floor cleaning equipment.

ANNUAL EARNINGS AND DIVIDENDS PER SHARE

	1994	1993	1992	1991	1990	1989	1988
Earnings Per Share	1.09	1.02	① 0.92	0.89	0.79	0.76	0.68
Dividends Per Share	③ 0.49	0.48	② 0.46	0.44	0.43	0.39	0.38
Dividend Payout %	35.5	46.8	49.2	49.8	51.0	54.2	51.5

① Before acctg. chg. ② 3-for-2 stk split, 7/13/92 ③ 3-for-2 stk split, 10/27/94

ANNUAL FINANCIAL DATA

RECORD OF EARNINGS (IN THOUSANDS):

	1994	1993	1992	1991	1990	1989	1988
Total Revenues	138,019	132,124	126,540	124,100	120,422	114,965	84,386
Costs and Expenses	118,533	113,992	109,856	107,873	104,483	99,833	70,943
Depreciation & Amort	4,534	4,274	4,025	3,874	3,709	3,723	2,604
Operating Profit	36,274	33,288	31,496	30,530	29,309	28,375	23,944
Income Bef Income Taxes	14,952	13,858	12,659	12,353	12,230	11,409	10,839
Income Taxes	5,625	5,063	4,693	4,664	4,888	4,638	4,221
Net Income	9,327	8,795	① 7,966	7,689	7,342	6,771	6,618
Aver. Shs. Outstg.	8,580	8,588	8,594	8,594	8,594	8,594	8,655

① Before acctg. change dr$11,886,000.

BALANCE SHEET (IN THOUSANDS):

	1994	1993	1992	1991	1990	1989	1988
Cash and Cash Equivalents	3,062	2,782	3,402	3,043	3,643	3,002	3,575
Receivables, Net	28,060	29,370	24,432	24,800	22,745	20,804	18,852
Inventories	30,814	25,614	23,991	27,893	25,647	26,070	22,062
Gross Property	76,663	70,726	62,670	60,672	54,723	50,097	45,612
Accumulated Depreciation	35,784	33,891	31,863	29,834	28,589	25,618	22,817
Long-Term Debt	4,715	4,274	668	6,238	2,437	2,187	1,151
Net Stockholders' Equity	61,608	56,911	52,759	61,256	57,310	53,711	50,476
Total Assets	109,744	101,448	88,971	88,045	80,040	76,660	70,244
Total Current Assets	62,714	58,488	52,689	56,556	52,928	50,893	45,667
Total Current Liabilities	16,391	14,382	12,380	14,471	14,805	15,871	14,789
Net Working Capital	46,323	44,106	40,309	42,085	38,123	35,022	30,878
Year End Shares Outstg	8,580	8,580	8,595	8,595	8,595	8,595	8,595

STATISTICAL RECORD:

	1994	1993	1992	1991	1990	1989	1988
Operating Profit Margin %	10.8	10.5	10.0	10.0	10.2	9.9	12.8
Book Value Per Share	7.18	6.63	6.14	7.13	6.67	6.25	5.83
Return on Equity %	15.1	15.5	15.1	12.6	12.8	12.6	13.1
Return on Assets %	8.5	8.7	9.0	8.7	9.2	8.8	9.4
Average Yield %	2.8	2.6	2.3	2.5	2.9	2.7	2.6
P/E Ratio	18.3-13.9	19.8-16.2	27.4-16.0	24.4-15.3	20.7-14.1	22.4-18.1	22.4-16.9
Price Range	20-15⅛	20⅜-16⅝	25⅜-14⅞	21¾-13⅝	17⅝-12	17¾-14⅜	17-12⅞

Statistics are as originally reported.

OFFICERS:
J.C. Gorman, Chmn. & C.E.O.
J.A. Walter, Pres. & C.O.O.
K.E. Dudley, Treas.
R.E. Kirkendall, Sec. & Asst. Treas.

INCORPORATED: OH, Apr., 1934

PRINCIPAL OFFICE: 305 Bowman Street, Mansfield, OH 44903

TELEPHONE NUMBER: (419) 755-1011

FAX: (419) 755-1233

NO. OF EMPLOYEES: 993

ANNUAL MEETING: In April

SHAREHOLDERS: 1,306

INSTITUTIONAL HOLDINGS:
No. of Institutions: 40
Shares Held: 1,922,549

REGISTRAR(S): National City Bank, Cleveland, OH 44114

TRANSFER AGENT(S): National City Bank, Cleveland, OH 44114

ASE SYMBOL GWW
Rec. Pr. 59½

GRAINGER (W.W.), INC.

YIELD 1.3%
P/E RATIO 23.8

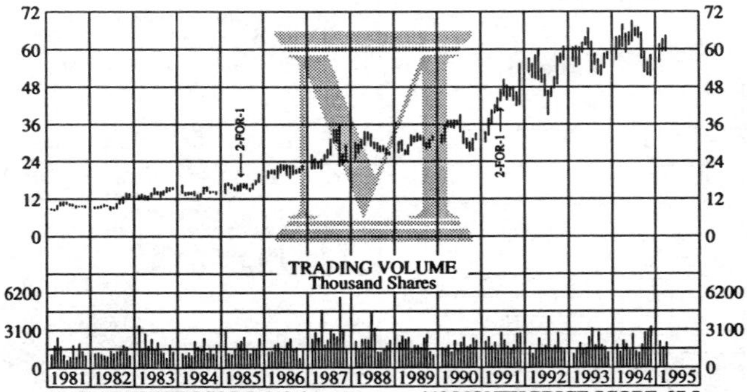

*7 YEAR PRICE SCORE 112.6 *12 MONTH PRICE SCORE 97.5

*NYSE COMPOSITE INDEX=100

INTERIM EARNINGS (Per Share):

Qtr.	Mar.	June	Sept.	Dec.
1991	0.52	0.62	0.58	0.65
1992	0.53	0.67	0.70	0.68
1993	0.65	0.68	0.75	0.80
1994	0.81	0.83	0.84	0.02

INTERIM DIVIDENDS (Per Share):

Amt.	Decl.	Ex.	Rec.	Pay.
0.18Q	1/26/94	2/1/94	2/7/94	3/1/94
0.20Q	4/27	5/3	5/9	6/1
0.20Q	8/3	8/9	8/15	9/1
0.20Q	10/26	11/1	11/7	12/1
0.20Q	1/25/95	1/31/95	2/6/95	3/1/95

Indicated div.: $0.80

CAPITALIZATION (12/31/94):

	($000)	(%)
Long-Term Debt	1,023	0.1
Deferred Income Tax	15,177	1.4
Common & Surplus	1,032,805	98.5
Total	1,049,005	100.0

DIVIDEND ACHIEVER STATUS:
Rank: 179 1984-94 Growth Rate: 9.7%
Total Years of Dividend Growth: 23

RECENT DEVELOPMENTS: For the quarter ended 12/31/94, net earnings totaled $967,000 compared with $40.9 million for the corresponding quarter in 1993. The 1994 quarter's earnings included an after-tax restructuring charge of $48.4 million related to the Company's previously-announced integration of its business units and its administrative support functions. Net sales for the quarter rose 16% to $768.9 million from $663.0 million for the same period a year earlier.

PROSPECTS: Sales volumes are benefiting from management's market initiatives and growth in the U.S. economy. Margins are being pressured by reduced selling prices in certain product lines and cost increases. Price reductions in portable heating and air conditioning, controls, air treatment, other HVAC products, and lighting have been implemented as GWW focuses on gaining market share. Efforts to improve branch data-processing will continue through 1995.

BUSINESS

W.W. GRAINGER, INC., is a nationwide distributor of equipment, components, and supplies to the commercial, industrial, contractor and institutional markets. Products include motors, fans, blowers, pumps, compressors, air and power tools, heating and air conditioning equipments, as well as other items offered in its Wholesale Net Price Catalog which features more than 53,000 products. Grainger serves its more than one million customers from regional distribution facilities in Chicago, IL, Kansas City, MO, Los Angeles, CA, and Greenville County, SC through a nationwide network of 337 branches in 50 states. Other Business Units includes Allied Safety Inc., Ball Industries, Bossert Industrial Supply, Inc., Grainger Sanitary Supplies and Equipment, Lab Safety Supply, and Parts Co. of America.

QUARTERLY DATA

(12/31/94)($000)	Rev	Inc
1st Quarter	706,369	41,538
2nd Quarter	768,554	42,324
3rd Quarter	779,300	43,045
4th Quarter	768,853	967

ANNUAL EARNINGS AND DIVIDENDS PER SHARE

	1994	1993	1992	1991	1990	1989	1988
Earnings Per Share	2.50	2.88	2.58	2.37	2.31	2.20	1.96
Dividends Per Share	0.78	0.705	0.65	[1] 0.61	0.565	0.50	0.43
Dividend Payout %	31.2	24.5	25.2	25.7	24.4	22.8	21.9

[1] 2-for-1 stk. split, 6/10/91

ANNUAL FINANCIAL DATA

	1994	1993	1992	1991	1990	1989	1988
RECORD OF EARNINGS (IN MILLIONS):							
Total Revenues	3,023.1	2,628.4	2,364.4	2,077.2	1,935.2	1,727.5	1,535.5
Costs and Expenses	2,724.9	2,317.1	2,086.9	1,837.4	1,689.6	1,502.8	1,329.1
Depreciation & Amort	66.7	59.2	49.1	35.6	41.9	33.6	28.5
Operating Earnings	231.5	252.2	228.4	204.2	203.7	191.1	177.8
Earn Bef Income Taxes	228.8	250.0	227.2	209.4	208.5	196.5	179.7
Income Taxes	100.9	100.8	90.0	81.7	81.7	76.9	70.9
Net Income	127.9	[1] 149.3	137.2	127.7	126.8	119.6	108.8
Aver. Shs. Outstg. (000)	51,227	51,911	53,257	54,001	54,905	54,520	55,574
[1] Before acctg. change dr$820,000.							
BALANCE SHEET (IN MILLIONS):							
Cash and Cash Equivalents	15.3	2.6	44.8	141.0	147.5	81.4	79.2
Receivables, Net	414.2	344.3	305.4	262.7	257.3	255.4	206.5
Inventories	520.0	466.2	432.2	443.3	416.7	412.4	329.9
Gross Property	810.2	716.8	626.7	553.0	520.8	481.5	465.4
Accumulated Depreciation	341.1	307.4	274.0	241.4	209.2	179.2	156.8
Long-Term Debt	1.0	6.2	6.9	11.3	14.5	2.8	16.5
Net Stockholders' Equity	1,032.8	941.9	931.2	860.4	817.1	733.6	635.5
Total Assets	1,534.8	1,376.7	1,310.5	1,216.6	1,162.4	1,065.2	936.2
Total Current Assets	963.6	823.9	794.3	854.3	828.6	755.2	619.6
Total Current Liabilities	451.7	381.4	315.5	280.2	268.5	261.6	236.9
Net Working Capital	512.0	442.5	478.8	574.0	560.0	493.6	382.7
Year End Shs Outstg (000)	50,750	50,685	52,376	52,913	54,108	54,498	42,344
STATISTICAL RECORD:							
Operating Profit Margin %	7.7	9.6	9.7	9.8	10.5	11.1	11.6
Book Value Per Share	18.65	18.58	17.78	16.26	15.10	13.46	15.01
Return on Equity %	12.4	15.8	14.7	14.8	15.5	16.3	17.1
Return on Assets %	8.3	10.8	10.5	10.5	10.9	11.2	11.6
Average Yield %	1.3	1.2	1.3	1.4	1.7	1.7	1.5
P/E Ratio	27.7-20.6	23.2-17.9	23.6-15.1	23.4-12.8	17.0-11.8	15.1-12.0	17.2-12.6
Price Range	69⅛-51½	66¾-51⅝	61-39	55½-30¼	39¼-27¼	33⅛-26¼	33¾-24⅝

Statistics are as originally reported.

OFFICERS:
D.W. Grainger, Chmn.
R.L. Keyser, Pres. & C.E.O.
J.M. Baisley, Sr. V.P., Gen. Couns. & Sec.
P.J. Wallace, V.P.-Fin. Svcs.

INCORPORATED: IL, Dec., 1928

PRINCIPAL OFFICE: 5500 W. Howard St., Skokie, IL 60077-2699

TELEPHONE NUMBER: (708) 982-9000

FAX: (708) 982-3489

NO. OF EMPLOYEES: 11,343

ANNUAL MEETING: In April

SHAREHOLDERS: 2,200 (approx.)

INSTITUTIONAL HOLDINGS:
No. of Institutions: 349
Shares Held: 32,338,204

REGISTRAR(S): First National Bank of Boston, Shareholder Services Division, Boston, MA

TRANSFER AGENT(S): First National Bank of Boston, Shareholder Services Division, Boston, MA

NYS SYMBOL GLK
Rec. Pr. 56⅝

GREAT LAKES CHEMICAL CORP.

YIELD 0.7%
P/E RATIO 14.4

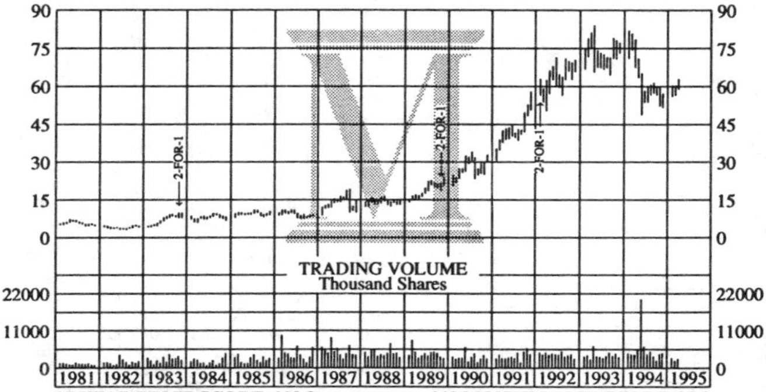

*7 YEAR PRICE SCORE 108.8 *12 MONTH PRICE SCORE 98.3

*NYSE COMPOSITE INDEX=100

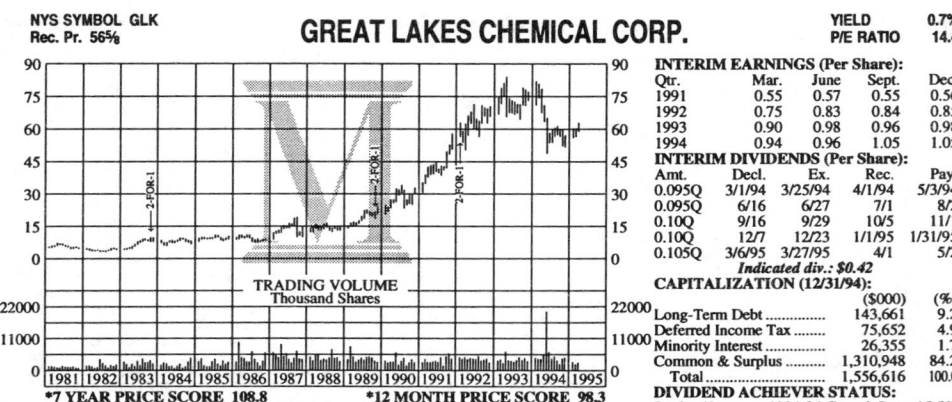

INTERIM EARNINGS (Per Share):

Qtr.	Mar.	June	Sept.	Dec.
1991	0.55	0.57	0.55	0.56
1992	0.75	0.83	0.84	0.85
1993	0.90	0.98	0.96	0.98
1994	0.94	0.96	1.05	1.05

INTERIM DIVIDENDS (Per Share):

Amt.	Decl.	Ex.	Rec.	Pay.
0.095Q	3/1/94	3/25/94	4/1/94	5/3/94
0.095Q	6/16	6/27	7/1	8/2
0.10Q	9/16	9/29	10/5	11/1
0.10Q	12/7	12/23	1/1/95	1/31/95
0.105Q	3/6/95	3/27/95	4/1	5/2

Indicated div.: $0.42

CAPITALIZATION (12/31/94):

	($000)	(%)
Long-Term Debt	143,661	9.2
Deferred Income Tax	75,652	4.9
Minority Interest	26,355	1.7
Common & Surplus	1,310,948	84.2
Total	1,556,616	100.0

DIVIDEND ACHIEVER STATUS:
Rank: 49 1984-94 Growth Rate: 15.5%
Total Years of Dividend Growth: 21

RECENT DEVELOPMENTS: For the year ended 12/31/94, net income rose to $278.7 million from $272.8 million in the previous year. Total revenues increased 15% to $2.11 billion versus $1.83 billion in the prior year. Net sales improved 15% to $2.07 billion from $1.79 billion a year earlier. The Company overcame the unexpected market adjustments of the first six months and saw compound volumes revert back to historical levels.

PROSPECTS: Recently, GLK implemented organizational changes including the restructuring of its global operations. Most of the Company's businesses are reporting improved sales growth. Capacity expansions should enable GLK to meet the rising demand for its value-added, bromine-based products. Necessary capital improvements and the rising costs of key raw materials will push prices higher, which should improve the divisions revenues.

BUSINESS

GREAT LAKES CHEMICAL Corp. is the world's leading producer of bromine, brominated specialty chemicals, and furfural derivatives. The Company has more than 50 sales, production, and distribution facilities in the U.S., Europe, and Japan. Through subsidiaries and affiliates, GLK is a leader in global specialty chemical markets. The Company has an 87.8% interest in Octel Associates.

BUSINESS LINE ANALYSIS

(12/31/94)	Rev(%)	Inc(%)
United States	45.4	32.1
Foreign	54.6	67.9
Total	100.0	100.0

ANNUAL EARNINGS AND DIVIDENDS PER SHARE

	1994	1993	1992	1991	1990	1989	1988
Earnings Per Share	**4.00**	**3.82**	**3.27**	**2.23**	**2.01**	**1.76**	**1.49**
Dividends Per Share	**0.38**	**0.34**	**[1] 0.30**	**0.26**	**0.22**	**[2] 0.19**	**0.175**
Dividend Payout %	**9.5**	**8.9**	**9.2**	**11.7**	**11.0**	**10.8**	**11.5**

[1] 2-for-1 stk split, 1/31/92 [2] 2-for-1 stk split, 10/31/89.

ANNUAL FINANCIAL DATA

	1994	1993	1992	1991	1990	1989	1988
RECORD OF EARNINGS (IN MILLIONS):							
Total Revenues	2,065.0	1,792.0	1,496.5	1,307.6	1,066.3	792.3	557.8
Costs and Expenses	1,553.7	1,304.8	1,075.0	948.0	752.6	591.5	436.6
Depreciation & Depletion	72.7	62.5	58.4	49.8	43.3	36.9	28.6
Operating Profit	438.7	424.8	363.0	309.9	270.5	163.9	92.6
Income Before Taxes	402.7	383.4	332.7	225.5	209.4	167.9	143.5
Income Taxes	124.0	110.6	100.0	68.0	68.6	45.0	40.2
Net Income	278.7	272.8	232.7	157.5	140.8	122.9	103.3
Aver. Shs. Outstg. (000)	69,659	71,329	71,164	70,700	70,287	69,885	69,659
BALANCE SHEET (IN MILLIONS):							
Cash and Cash Equivalents	144.7	179.7	140.8	81.0	60.6	30.4	12.2
Receivables, Net	493.6	383.1	340.9	294.6	301.5	229.6	102.3
Inventories	316.6	275.1	258.0	240.3	223.5	165.8	90.1
Gross Property	1,038.1	830.8	738.1	693.4	611.8	487.0	409.1
Accumulated Depreciation	432.2	362.8	308.2	287.8	248.1	211.1	174.7
Long-Term Debt	143.7	61.0	45.6	139.8	75.7	113.7	19.3
Net Stockholders' Equity	1,310.9	1,256.6	1,052.9	900.3	744.2	590.9	482.2
Total Assets	2,111.5	1,900.9	1,732.0	1,649.1	1,406.3	1,097.4	663.8
Total Current Assets	979.7	856.9	773.2	640.9	608.2	447.1	222.9
Total Current Liabilities	427.9	367.7	431.1	302.9	307.1	210.4	122.6
Net Working Capital	551.7	489.2	342.2	338.0	301.1	236.6	100.2
Year End Shs Outstg (000)	67,297	71,275	71,410	70,924	70,443	70,099	69,654
STATISTICAL RECORD:							
Operating Profit Margin %	21.2	23.7	24.3	23.7	25.4	20.7	16.6
Book Value Per Share	13.37	12.84	10.55	9.47	7.64	6.11	6.18
Return on Equity %	21.3	21.7	22.1	17.5	18.9	20.8	21.4
Return on Assets %	13.2	14.4	13.4	9.5	10.0	11.2	15.6
Average Yield %	0.6	0.5	0.5	0.6	0.8	1.0	1.2
P/E Ratio	20.5-12.2	22.0-16.9	21.8-15.4	26.0-13.6	17.0-10.2	13.6-8.0	11.1-8.2
Price Range	82-48¾	84-64½	71⅞-50¼	58-30⅜	34-20⅜	24-14⅛	16½-12⅛

Statistics are as originally reported.

OFFICERS:
R.B. McDonald, Pres. & C.E.O.
R.T. Jeffares, Exec. V.P. & C.F.O.
R.R. Ferguson, V.P. & Treas.
M.P. McClanahan, Corp. Sec.

INCORPORATED: MI, 1933; reincorp., DE, Sep., 1970

PRINCIPAL OFFICE: One Great Lakes Boulevard, West Lafayette, IN 47906-0200

TELEPHONE NUMBER: (317) 497-6100

NO. OF EMPLOYEES: 7,900 (approx.)

ANNUAL MEETING: In May

SHAREHOLDERS: 4,900 (approx.)

INSTITUTIONAL HOLDINGS:
No. of Institutions: 396
Shares Held: 57,320,135

REGISTRAR(S): Harris Trust Co. of N.Y., New York, NY 10005

TRANSFER AGENT(S): Harris Trust Co. of N.Y., New York, NY 10005

NYS SYMBOL GMP
Rec. Pr. 25¾

GREEN MOUNTAIN POWER CORP.

YIELD 8.2%
P/E RATIO 11.1

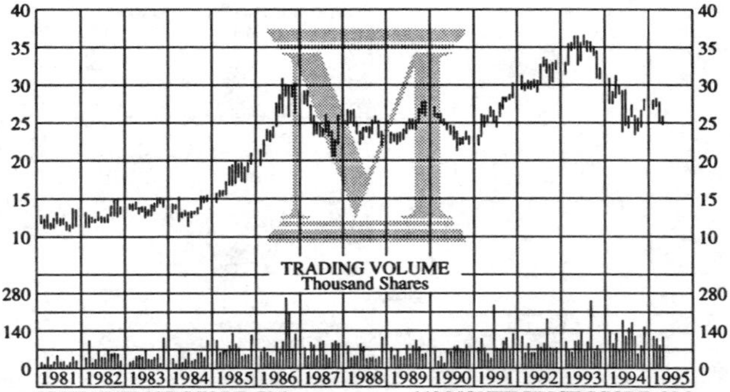

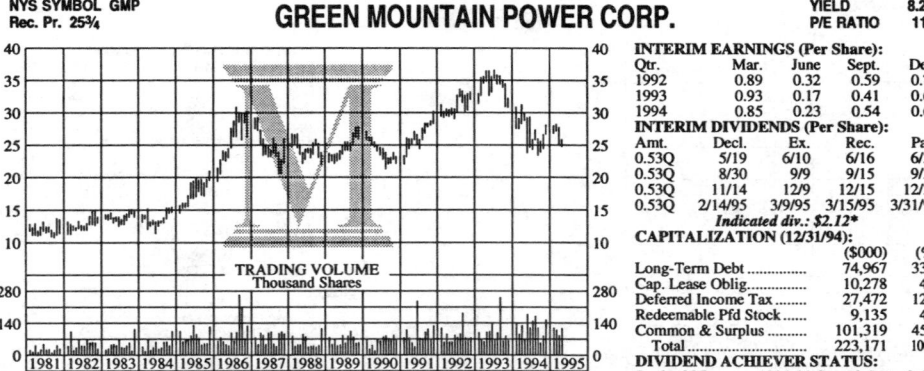

*7 YEAR PRICE SCORE 79.1 *12 MONTH PRICE SCORE 93.3

*NYSE COMPOSITE INDEX=100

INTERIM EARNINGS (Per Share):

Qtr.	Mar.	June	Sept.	Dec.
1992	0.89	0.32	0.59	0.74
1993	0.93	0.17	0.41	0.69
1994	0.85	0.23	0.54	0.62

INTERIM DIVIDENDS (Per Share):

Amt.	Decl.	Ex.	Rec.	Pay.
0.53Q	5/19	6/10	6/16	6/30
0.53Q	8/30	9/9	9/15	9/30
0.53Q	11/14	12/9	12/15	12/30
0.53Q	2/14/95	3/9/95	3/15/95	3/31/95

*Indicated div.: $2.12**

CAPITALIZATION (12/31/94):

	($000)	(%)
Long-Term Debt	74,967	33.6
Cap. Lease Oblig.	10,278	4.6
Deferred Income Tax	27,472	12.3
Redeemable Pfd Stock	9,135	4.1
Common & Surplus	101,319	45.4
Total	223,171	100.0

DIVIDEND ACHIEVER STATUS:
Rank: 325 1984-94 Growth Rate: 2.4%
Total Years of Dividend Growth: 20

RECENT DEVELOPMENTS: For the year ended 12/31/94, net income was $11.0 million compared with $10.6 million in 1993. Revenues increased slightly to $148.2 million. The modest increases over 1993's results reflect an adverse ruling by the Vermont Supreme Court and the effects of warm winter weather during the fourth quarter. Total electricity sales were up 1.9% and the number of customers served grew by 1.3%. Fourth quarter net income was $3.1 million, down 6.1% from $3.3 million in the corresponding 1993 period.

PROSPECTS: GMP will increase its rates by 9.25%, effective 6/15/95. The new rates will provide an additional $12.5 million in annual revenues, most of which will pay for higher power supply costs. GMP is heavily dependent on purchased power, which will require ongoing rate relief in an increasingly uncertain regulatory environment. Timely rate treatment will be very important for GMP. Consequently, GMP's competitive position is weakened.

BUSINESS

GREEN MOUNTAIN POWER is an electric utility serving 79,100 retail customers in Vermont. GMP also sells electricity at wholesale to other utilities, three of which receive almost all of their power requirements from the Company. GMP's service territory cuts across central Vermont in a 25-mile wide strip from Lake Champlain to the Connecticut River, and also includes three non-contiguous population centers in southern Vermont. GMP has a whole or partial ownership interest in generational facilities that supply 40% of its total capacity of 417 megawatts. The balance of the generating capacity and 60% of the energy GMP distributes is purchased from other utilities. GMP holds a 30% interest in Vermont Electric Power, which owns nearly all of the transmission network that services Vermont.

QUARTERLY DATA

(12/31/94) ($000)	Rev	Inc
1st Quarter	40,611	4,040
2nd Quarter	33,603	1,237
3rd Quarter	36,684	2,653
4th Quarter	37,299	3,072

ANNUAL EARNINGS AND DIVIDENDS PER SHARE

	1994	1993	1992	1991	1990	1989	1988
Earnings Per Share	**2.23**	**2.20**	**2.54**	**2.45**	**2.29**	**2.36**	**2.41**
Dividends Per Share	**2.12**	**2.11**	**2.08**	**2.04**	**2.00**	**1.95**	**1.89**
Dividend Payout %	**95.0**	**95.9**	**81.9**	**83.3**	**87.3**	**82.6**	**78.4**

ANNUAL FINANCIAL DATA

	1994	1993	1992	1991	1990	1989	1988
RECORD OF EARNINGS (IN THOUSANDS):							
Total Revenues	148,197	147,253	145,240	143,555	147,633	144,028	128,613
Depreciation & Amort	10,683	8,572	8,065	7,046	6,754	5,907	5,440
Maintenance	4,465	4,352	4,692	4,340	4,377	4,822	5,514
Prov for Fed Inc Taxes	5,395	6,249	6,915	6,022	4,970	5,048	4,357
Operating Income	14,517	14,826	16,412	14,514	13,708	12,175	11,101
Interest Expense	7,196	6,828	6,819	6,972	6,865	5,479	4,579
Net Income	11,002	10,631	11,852	10,456	8,966	9,028	9,246
Aver. Shs. Outstg.	4,588	4,457	4,345	3,919	3,729	3,697	3,688
BALANCE SHEET (IN THOUSANDS):							
Gross Plant	256,562	246,968	233,828	219,880	208,220	183,479	164,155
Accumulated Depreciation	69,246	64,226	58,516	58,970	54,486	50,152	44,932
Prop, Plant & Equip, Net	187,316	182,742	175,312	160,910	153,734	133,327	119,223
Long-term Debt	85,245	90,829	79,594	68,897	73,423	56,992	41,558
Net Stockholders' Equity	110,454	106,534	102,220	97,280	82,029	72,833	71,592
Total Assets	294,611	283,085	257,218	229,216	214,940	189,072	170,157
Year End Shares Outstg	4,662	4,520	4,414	4,292	3,768	3,697	3,694
STATISTICAL RECORD:							
Book Value Per Share	21.08	20.72	20.08	20.38	19.09	18.79	18.39
Op. Inc/Net Pl %	7.8	8.1	9.4	9.0	8.9	9.1	9.3
Dep/Gr. Pl %	4.2	3.5	3.4	3.2	3.2	3.2	3.3
Accum. Dep/Gr. Pl %	27.0	26.0	25.0	26.8	26.2	27.3	27.4
Return on Equity %	10.9	10.9	12.8	12.0	12.5	13.0	13.6
Average Yield %	7.8	6.3	6.6	7.8	8.3	7.8	7.8
P/E Ratio	14.0-10.5	16.6-14.0	13.2-11.4	12.3-9.0	11.8-9.3	11.8-9.4	11.1-9.1
Price Range	31¼-23⅜	36⅝-30¾	33⅝-29	30¼-22	27⅛-21¼	27⅞-22⅛	26¾-22

Statistics are as originally reported.

OFFICERS:
D.G. Hyde, Pres. & C.E.O.
E.M. Norse, V.P., C.F.O. & Treas.

INCORPORATED: VT, Apr., 1893

PRINCIPAL OFFICE: 25 Green Mountain Drive, South Burlington, VT 05403

TELEPHONE NUMBER: (802) 864-5731
FAX: (802) 865-9129
NO. OF EMPLOYEES: 388
ANNUAL MEETING: In May
SHAREHOLDERS: 6,852 Com.; 6 Pfd.
INSTITUTIONAL HOLDINGS:
No. of Institutions: 39
Shares Held: 808,518

REGISTRAR(S): Manufacturers Hanover Trust Co., New York, NY

TRANSFER AGENT(S): Manufacturers Hanover Trust Co., New York, NY

NYS SYMBOL GTE
Rec. Pr. 33¼

GTE CORP.

YIELD 5.7%
P/E RATIO 13.0

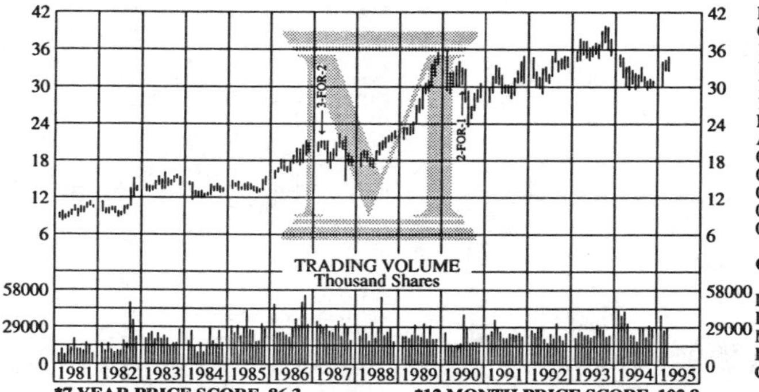

***7 YEAR PRICE SCORE 86.3** ***12 MONTH PRICE SCORE 102.8**

*NYSE COMPOSITE INDEX=100

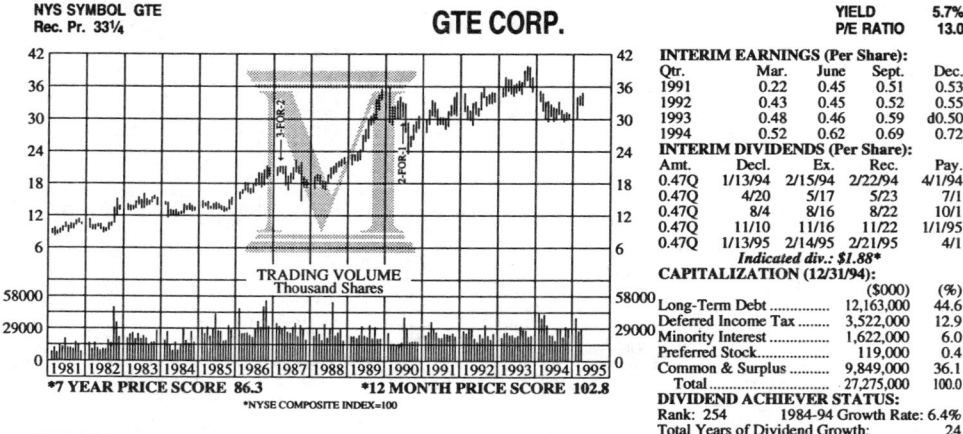

INTERIM EARNINGS (Per Share):

Qtr.	Mar.	June	Sept.	Dec.
1991	0.22	0.45	0.51	0.53
1992	0.43	0.45	0.52	0.55
1993	0.48	0.46	0.59	d0.50
1994	0.52	0.62	0.69	0.72

INTERIM DIVIDENDS (Per Share):

Amt.	Decl.	Ex.	Rec.	Pay.
0.47Q	1/13/94	2/15/94	2/22/94	4/1/94
0.47Q	4/20	5/17	5/23	7/1
0.47Q	8/4	8/16	8/22	10/1
0.47Q	11/10	11/16	11/22	1/1/95
0.47Q	1/13/95	2/14/95	2/21/95	4/1

Indicated div.: $1.88*

CAPITALIZATION (12/31/94):

	($000)	(%)
Long-Term Debt	12,163,000	44.6
Deferred Income Tax	3,522,000	12.9
Minority Interest	1,622,000	6.0
Preferred Stock	119,000	0.4
Common & Surplus	9,849,000	36.1
Total	27,275,000	100.0

DIVIDEND ACHIEVER STATUS:
Rank: 254 1984-94 Growth Rate: 6.4%
Total Years of Dividend Growth: 24

RECENT DEVELOPMENTS: Net income for the year ended 12/31/94 was $2.45 billion compared with $990.0 million, including after-tax charges totaling $1.29 billion and gains of $91 million, in 1993. The results for 1994 included after-tax gains of $162 million on the sale of telephone properties. Revenues edged up 1.0% to $19.94 billion. Telephone Operations reported strong increases in unit volumes, partially offset by lower more competitive pricing.

PROSPECTS: Prospects for continued growth are favorable. Results should benefit from increases in the number of access lines in service, rapid cellular growth and GTE's restructuring efforts. However, competitive-pricing pressures continue to be a factor. GTE will purchase the remaining 10% of Contel Cellular Inc. Class A common stock that it does not already own. Regulatory approval is required.

BUSINESS

GTE CORPORATION has three major business segments: telephone operations, telecommunications products and services, and electrical products. GTE has other subsidiaries engaged in financing, insurance, leasing and other activities offering financial and related services primarily to GTE operating companies. In March, 1991, GTE and Contel Corporation merged operations. With the merger, GTE is now the largest U.S.-based local exchange telephone company and the second-largest cellular-telephone operator in the United States.

REVENUES

(12/31/94)	($000)	(%)
Telephone Opers	15,905,000	79.7
Telecomm Products & Svces	4,039,000	20.3
Total	19,944,000	100.0

ANNUAL EARNINGS AND DIVIDENDS PER SHARE

	1994	1993	1992	1991	1990	1989	1988
Earnings Per Share	2.55	1.03	①②1.95	①1.69	2.26	2.08	1.79
Dividends Per Share	1.88	1.835	1.73	1.61	③1.49	1.37	1.28
Dividend Payout %	73.7	N.M.	88.7	95.3	65.9	65.9	71.5

① Before disc. oper. ② Before extraord. item ③ 2-for-1 stk split, 6/22/90

ANNUAL FINANCIAL DATA

	1994	1993	1992	1991	1990	1989	1988
RECORD OF EARNINGS (IN MILLIONS):							
Total Revenues	19,944.0	19,748.0	19,984.0	19,621.0	18,374.0	17,424.4	16,459.9
Costs and Expenses	11,460.0	13,560.0	12,479.0	12,625.0	12,169.0	11,613.8	10,849.2
Depreciation & Amort	3,432.0	3,419.0	3,289.0	3,254.0	2,753.0	2,621.3	2,559.1
Operating Income	4,846.0	2,565.0	4,216.0	3,742.0	3,452.0	3,189.2	3,051.6
Income Bef Income Taxes	3,983.0	1,558.0	2,754.0	2,191.0	2,230.0	2,064.1	1,841.0
Income Taxes	1,532.0	568.0	967.0	662.0	689.0	646.8	616.3
Net Income	2,451.0	900.0	①1,787.0	②1,529.0	1,541.0	1,417.3	1,224.7
Aver. Shs. Outstg. (000)	958,000	945,000	905,000	882,000	664,000	659,298	657,178

① Before disc. op. dr$48,000,000. ② Before disc. op. cr$51,000,000.

	1994	1993	1992	1991	1990	1989	1988
BALANCE SHEET (IN MILLIONS):							
Cash and Cash Equivalents	323.0	322.0	354.0	517.0	431.0	395.8	307.0
Receivables, Net	4,343.0	4,164.0	3,676.0	3,869.0	3,652.0	3,499.0	3,159.9
Inventories	676.0	659.0	814.0	910.0	1,376.0	1,416.1	1,263.9
Gross Property	48,545.0	47,259.0	47,429.0	45,612.0	38,796.0	36,661.7	34,681.6
Accumulated Depreciation	19,217.0	18,539.0	17,609.0	16,289.0	14,264.0	12,961.4	11,694.8
Long-Term Debt	12,163.0	13,019.0	14,182.0	16,049.0	11,974.0	10,909.4	9,704.7
Net Stockholders' Equity	9,968.0	11,037.0	11,564.0	12,862.0	10,699.0	10,078.6	8,933.3
Total Assets	42,500.0	41,575.0	42,144.0	42,437.0	33,769.0	31,987.1	31,103.9
Total Current Assets	5,634.0	5,948.0	6,296.0	7,566.0	5,874.0	5,597.3	5,611.9
Total Current Liabilities	8,221.0	7,933.0	7,511.0	7,226.0	5,711.0	5,703.2	5,870.1
Net Working Capital	d2,587.0	d1,985.0	d1,215.0	340.0	163.0	d105.9	d258.2
Year End Shs Outstg (000)	965,000	951,762	939,530	888,900	669,392	660,602	652,578
STATISTICAL RECORD:							
Book Value Per Share	7.98	9.11	9.70	11.27	13.59	13.87	12.01
Return on Equity %	24.9	9.1	15.7	12.1	14.7	14.5	14.2
Average Yield %	5.8	5.0	5.4	5.2	5.0	4.8	6.4
P/E Ratio	13.8-11.6	38.7-33.1	18.3-14.8	20.7-16.3	15.9-10.4	17.1-10.3	12.8-9.4
Price Range	35¼-29½	39⅞-34⅛	35¾-28⅞	35-27½	36-23½	35⅝-21½	23-16⅞

Statistics are as originally reported.

OFFICERS:
C.R. Lee, Chmn., C.E.O. & C.O.O.
J. Murphy, V.P. & Treas.
M. Drost, Corporate Sec.

INCORPORATED: NY, Feb., 1935

PRINCIPAL OFFICE: One Stamford Forum, Stamford, CT 06904

TELEPHONE NUMBER: (203) 965-2000
FAX: (203) 965-2520
NO. OF EMPLOYEES: 117,000 (approx.)
ANNUAL MEETING: In April
SHAREHOLDERS: 567,000
INSTITUTIONAL HOLDINGS:
No. of Institutions: 993
Shares Held: 412,870,375

REGISTRAR(S): GTE Shareholder Services Inc.(T/A), North Quincy, MA 02171
State Street Bank & Trust Co., Boston, MA 02266

TRANSFER AGENT(S): GTE Shareholder Services Inc.(T/A), North Quincy, MA 02171
State Street Bank & Trust Co., Boston, MA 02266

NYS SYMBOL HRD
Rec. Pr. 26¾

HANNAFORD BROS. CO.

YIELD 1.6%
P/E RATIO 21.6

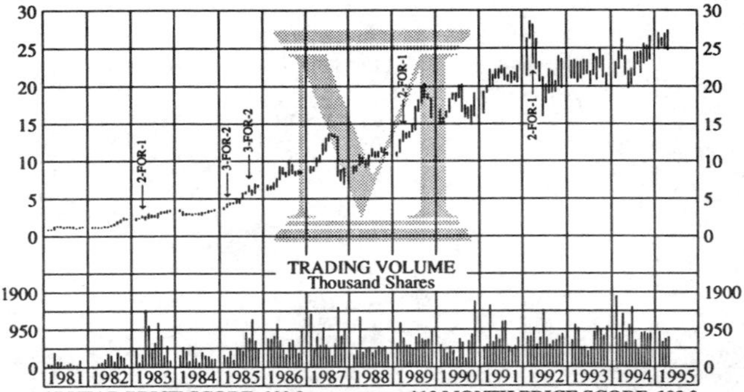

30
25
20
15
10
5
0
2-FOR-1
3-FOR-2
3-FOR-2
2-FOR-1
2-FOR-1
TRADING VOLUME
Thousand Shares
1900
950
0
1981 1982 1983 1984 1985 1986 1987 1988 1989 1990 1991 1992 1993 1994 1995

***7 YEAR PRICE SCORE 102.2** ***12 MONTH PRICE SCORE 102.0**

*NYSE COMPOSITE INDEX=100

INTERIM EARNINGS (Per Share):

Qtr.	Mar.	June	Sept.	Dec.
1991	0.20	0.30	0.31	0.27
1992	----------	1.21	----------	
1993	0.24	0.35	0.39	0.35
1994	0.27	0.37	0.46	0.10

INTERIM DIVIDENDS (Per Share):

Amt.	Decl.	Ex.	Rec.	Pay.
0.095Q	2/8/94	3/7/94	3/11/94	3/24/94
0.095Q	5/19	6/6	6/10	6/23
0.095Q	8/11	9/2	9/9	9/22
0.095Q	10/19	12/5	12/9	12/22
0.105Q	2/7/95	3/6/95	3/10/95	3/23/95

*Indicated div.: $0.42**

CAPITALIZATION (12/31/94):

	($000)	(%)
Long-Term Debt	153,687	22.0
Cap. Lease Oblig.	69,552	9.9
Deferred Income Tax	21,886	3.1
Common & Surplus	454,475	65.0
Total	699,600	100.0

DIVIDEND ACHIEVER STATUS:
Rank: 61 1984-94 Growth Rate: 14.6%
Total Years of Dividend Growth: 23

RECENT DEVELOPMENTS: For the year ended 12/31/94, net income was $62.3 million compared with $54.6 million in the prior-year period. Prior-year's results were before an accounting credit of $2.1 million. Total revenues, including the acquisition of Wilson's Supermarkets, advanced 11.5% to $2.29 billion. Excluding sales figures from Wilson's, HRD's sales increased 5.8%. Same-store sales increased 1.6%.

PROSPECTS: The acquisition of Wilson's Supermarkets will enable the Company to diversify geographically, primarily in the Southeast, and establish a strong store base for future acquisitions. Meanwhile, HRD has adopted a strong competitive pricing and merchandising platform in response to increased competition from wholesale clubs. This program coupled with expense control measures should aid earnings growth.

BUSINESS

HANNAFORD BROTHERS COMPANY is involved in the retail food and drug business through supermarkets, drug stores and supermarket/drug combination stores. It operates 95 supermarkets throughout Maine and in parts of New York, New Hampshire, Massachusetts and Vermont under the names Shop 'n Save, Alexander's, Martin's and Sun Foods. In addition, the Company operates 45 separate pharmacies within its supermarkets or combination stores. In July 1994, the Company acquired 20 supermarkets in North and South Carolina from Wilson's Supermarkets based in Wilmington, NC. Wholesale sales are made to 19 independent customers in which Hannaford has no ownership interest. The Sobey Family of Nova Scotia owns 25.6% of HRD.

QUARTERLY DATA

(12/31/94)($000)	Rev	Inc
1st Quarter	519,078	11,059
2nd Quarter	538,216	15,409
3rd Quarter	622,554	19,102
4th Quarter	611,907	16,718

ANNUAL EARNINGS AND DIVIDENDS PER SHARE

	12/31/94	1/1/94	1/2/93	12/28/91	12/29/90	12/31/89	12/31/88
Earnings Per Share	**1.50**	**1.33**	**1.21**	**1.08**	**1.06**	[2] **0.95**	**0.77**
Dividends Per Share	**0.38**	**0.34**	**0.30**	[1] **0.26**	**0.22**	[3] **0.18**	**0.16**
Dividend Payout %	**20.0**	**25.6**	**24.1**	**24.1**	**20.7**	**18.8**	**20.8**

[1] 2-for-1 stk split,03/11/92 [2] Before acctg. chg. [3] 2-for-1 stk split, 2/89

ANNUAL FINANCIAL DATA

RECORD OF EARNINGS (IN MILLIONS):							
Total Revenues	2,291.8	2,054.9	2,066.0	2,008.0	1,687.6	1,520.6	1,261.7
Costs and Expenses	[1] 2,166.0	1,887.0	1,908.7	1,863.9	1,569.4	1,420.0	1,181.5
Depreciation & Amort	...	56.4	54.9	50.7	35.5	28.1	23.8
Operating Profit	125.7	111.5	102.4	93.4	82.7	358.0	337.9
Earn Bef Income Taxes	104.3	92.2	81.7	72.6	69.7	62.4	48.7
Income Taxes	42.1	37.6	32.5	29.3	27.5	25.0	18.8
Net Income	62.3	[2] 54.6	49.2	43.4	42.2	[3] 37.4	28.9
Aver. Shs. Outstg. (000)	41,544	41,049	40,520	39,939	39,435	38,869	37,512

[1] Incl. Dep. [2] Before acctg. change cr$2,100,000. [3] Before acctg. change cr$1,874,000.

BALANCE SHEET (IN MILLIONS):							
Cash and Cash Equivalents	41.0	97.4	99.8	33.2	[1] 0.0	6.7	3.7
Receivables, Net	29.3	31.6	30.7	23.7	19.8	13.4	13.7
Inventories	132.4	129.9	124.9	150.0	148.9	112.2	92.6
Gross Property	814.3	696.5	656.3	600.9	524.9	408.2	330.5
Accumulated Depreciation	251.5	208.8	190.6	158.2	116.9	94.6	78.7
Long-Term Debt	153.7	156.7	171.6	165.3	159.5	94.3	77.0
Capital Lease Obligations	69.6	58.8	54.9	49.3	49.0	29.8	23.2
Net Stockholders' Equity	454.5	398.6	348.6	300.6	258.8	216.8	169.9
Total Assets	885.1	803.3	777.8	710.9	632.7	472.0	389.2
Total Current Assets	208.9	263.6	259.3	211.0	173.1	134.9	112.3
Total Current Liabilities	158.6	136.8	144.9	137.5	115.3	95.7	83.4
Net Working Capital	50.2	126.8	114.4	73.5	57.9	39.2	28.9
Year End Shs Outstg (000)	41,779	41,211	40,776	40,148	39,629	39,063	37,740

[1] Equal to $49,000.

STATISTICAL RECORD:							
Operating Profit Margin %	5.5	5.4	5.0	4.7	4.9	4.8	4.5
Book Value Per Share	8.25	8.48	7.31	6.08	5.23	4.96	4.10
Return on Equity %	13.7	13.8	14.2	14.6	16.5	17.5	17.3
Return on Assets %	7.0	6.8	6.3	6.1	6.7	7.9	7.4
Average Yield %	1.6	1.7	1.5	1.3	1.2	1.2	1.6
P/E Ratio	17.8-13.2	18.8-15.0	23.7-13.2	21.1-15.2	19.2-14.0	21.4-11.2	15.4-10.9
Price Range	26⅝-19¾	25-20	28⅝-16	22¾-16⅜	20⅜-14⅞	20⅜-10⅝	11⅞-8⅜

Statistics are as originally reported.

OFFICERS:
J.L. Moody, Jr., Chmn.
H.G. Farrington, Pres. & C.E.O.
N.E. Brackett, Sr. V.P. & C.F.O.

INCORPORATED: ME, Dec., 1902

PRINCIPAL OFFICE: 145 Pleasant Hill Rd., Scarborough, ME 04074

TELEPHONE NUMBER: (207) 883-2911

FAX: (207) 885-3165

NO. OF EMPLOYEES: 1,972

ANNUAL MEETING: In May

SHAREHOLDERS: 5,934

INSTITUTIONAL HOLDINGS:
No. of Institutions: 95
Shares Held: 14,529,628

REGISTRAR(S): Continental Stock Transfer & Trust Co., New York, NY

TRANSFER AGENT(S): Continental Stock Transfer & Trust Co., New York, NY

HARCOURT GENERAL, INC.

YIELD 1.5%
P/E RATIO 29.6

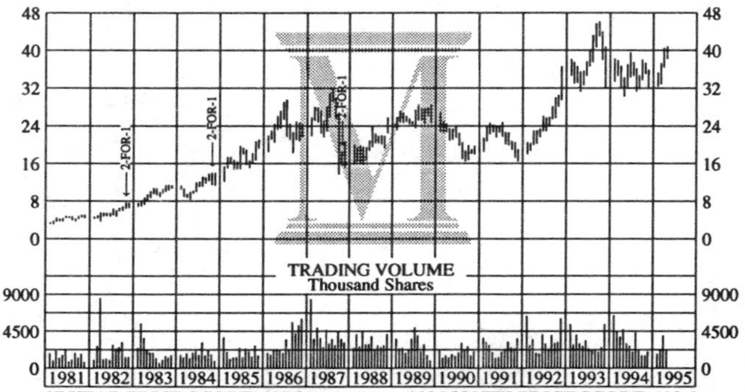

TRADING VOLUME
Thousand Shares

*7 YEAR PRICE SCORE 107.8   *12 MONTH PRICE SCORE 103.6

*NYSE COMPOSITE INDEX=100

INTERIM EARNINGS (Per Share):

Qtr.	Jan.	Apr.	July	Oct.
1991-92	0.34	d0.04	0.89	0.25
1992-93	0.40	0.07	1.34	0.39
1993-94	0.25	0.14	0.57	0.54
1994-95	0.15	...	...	...

INTERIM DIVIDENDS (Per Share):

Amt.	Decl.	Ex.	Rec.	Pay.
0.15Q	3/11/94	4/7/94	4/13/94	4/29/94
0.15Q	6/16	7/11	7/15	7/29
0.16Q	9/16	10/11	10/17	10/31
0.16Q	12/15	1/6/95	1/12/95	1/31/95
0.16Q	3/10/95	4/17	4/22	4/28

Indicated div.: $0.64*

CAPITALIZATION (10/31/94):

	($000)	(%)
Long-Term Debt	905,298	42.1
Deferred Income Tax	196,664	9.1
Preferred Stock	1,453	0.1
Common & Surplus	1,045,902	48.7
Total	2,149,317	100.0

DIVIDEND ACHIEVER STATUS:
Rank: 85   1984-94 Growth Rate: 13.6%
Total Years of Dividend Growth: 27

RECENT DEVELOPMENTS: For the quarter ended 1/31/95, earnings from continuing operations were $11.8 million compared with $5.9 million a year earlier. Revenues rose 2% to $720.7 million. The Company attributed the improvement to an increase in operating earnings from specialty retailing and higher investment income, partially offset by a larger loss from publishing operations and lower earnings from the Company's professional services business.

PROSPECTS: Operating results will benefit from robust elementary and secondary textbook adoptions, in which states purchase textbooks for their entire school system, in 1995. Demand has been particularly strong for elementary reading and math programs, science and language arts in the secondary market, and scientific and medical books and journals in the domestic and international markets. Meanwhile, the Specialty Retailing segment is reporting improved results.

BUSINESS

HARCOURT GENERAL, INC. (formerly General Cinema) has core businesses in publishing and specialty retailing. It also has a professional services segment consisting of the Drake Beam Morin outplacement operations. Speciality Retailing includes Neiman Marcus (65%-owned) which manages Neiman Marcus, Bergdorf Goodman, Contempo Casuals and NM Direct mail order businesses. Publishing consists primarily of Harcourt Brace & Co., a publisher in the educational, scientific, technical, medical, legal and trade fields. Professional services provides human resources consulting services to corporations worldwide. In October 1994, the Company completed the sale of its insurance business.

REVENUES

(10/31/94)	($000)	(%)
Publishing	919	29.2
Specialty Retail	2,093	66.3
Professional Services	142	4.5
Total	3,154	100.0

ANNUAL EARNINGS AND DIVIDENDS PER SHARE

	10/31/94	10/31/93	10/31/92	10/31/91	10/31/90	10/31/89	10/31/88
Earnings Per Share	1.22	2.08	① 1.44	d3.88	1.51	② 1.43	② 1.12
Dividends Per Share	0.61	0.57	0.53	0.49	0.45	0.41	0.37
Dividend Payout %	50.0	27.4	36.8	...	29.8	28.7	33.0

① Before extraord. item & acctg. chg. ② Before disc. oper.

ANNUAL FINANCIAL DATA

RECORD OF EARNINGS (IN MILLIONS):

Total Revenues	54.3	3,655.7	3,716.9	3,587.8	2,149.5	1,913.8	2,323.8
Costs and Expenses	2,820.2	3,172.2	3,302.2	3,412.4	2,033.2	1,762.8	2,064.9
Depreciation & Amort	163.1	169.3	173.6	315.2	62.5	58.6	85.4
Operating Earnings	224.4	314.3	241.1	d139.8	53.7	92.4	173.6
Earn Bef Income Taxes	152.4	262.1	187.0	d359.7	175.9	180.1	132.9
Income Taxes	54.9	96.6	72.9	cr69.9	61.4	71.0	46.7
Net Income	① 97.5	② 165.5	⑤ 114.1	d293.1	111.3	④ 105.9	⑥ 82.9
Aver. Shs. Outstg. (000)	79,809	79,600	79,139	78,876	73,823	73,842	73,557

① Before disc. op. cr$80,012,000. ② Before disc. op. cr$5,843,000. ③ Before extra. item cr$419,557,000. ④ Before disc. op. cr$865,935,000. ⑤ Before disc. op. cr$4,855,000.

BALANCE SHEET (IN MILLIONS):

Cash and Cash Equivalents	819.7	466.9	430.7	1,619.0	1,634.4	1,687.8	22.9
Receivables, Net	669.1	513.4	399.3	318.2	199.5	190.7	207.3
Inventories	466.2	470.5	411.1	417.6	276.9	251.2	258.6
Gross Property	824.7	796.4	1,507.4	1,413.1	794.2	697.1	956.6
Accumulated Depreciation	303.0	279.8	655.9	584.3	218.5	168.3	332.9
Long-Term Debt	905.3	923.6	902.3	625.7	731.8	677.6	816.9
Net Stockholders' Equity	1,047.4	1,051.6	924.4	472.8	1,629.0	1,548.9	605.0
Total Assets	3,242.4	5,976.8	5,287.1	6,208.3	3,068.4	3,403.6	1,897.5
Total Current Assets	2,021.0	1,503.9	1,294.0	2,553.2	2,196.9	2,208.1	570.9
Total Current Liabilities	875.0	791.9	745.6	2,554.1	580.6	1,081.7	344.4
Net Working Capital	1,146.0	712.0	548.3	d0.8	1,616.2	1,126.5	226.5
Year End Shs Outstg (000)	77,887	77,307	76,292	75,160	69,589	69,325	68,626

STATISTICAL RECORD:

Operating Profit Margin %	413.2	8.6	6.5	...	2.5	4.8	7.5
Book Value Per Share	8.00	8.40	6.64	0.54	20.71	19.76	6.93
Return on Equity %	9.3	15.7	12.3	...	6.8	6.8	13.7
Return on Assets %	3.0	2.8	2.2	...	3.6	3.1	4.4
Average Yield %	1.7	1.5	1.9	2.4	2.1	1.6	1.8
P/E Ratio	32.4-24.8	22.2-15.0	25.4-12.5	...	17.9-10.9	19.9-16.2	23.0-14.1
Price Range	39½-30¼	46⅛-31¼	36⅝-18	24¾-16½	27-16½	28½-23⅛	25¾-15¾

Statistics are as originally reported.

OFFICERS:
R.A. Smith, Chmn.
R.J. Tarr, Jr., Pres., C.E.O. & C.O.O.
J.R. Cook, Sr. V.P. & C.F.O.
E.P. Geller, Sr. V.P., Gen. Counsel & Sec.
P.F. Gibbons, V.P., Treas. & V.P.-Taxation

INCORPORATED: DE, 1950

PRINCIPAL OFFICE: 27 Boylston St., Chestnut Hill, MA 02167

TELEPHONE NUMBER: (617) 232-8200

NO. OF EMPLOYEES: 15,430

ANNUAL MEETING: In March

SHAREHOLDERS: 12,803 common; 691r. A pfd.

INSTITUTIONAL HOLDINGS:
No. of Institutions: 375
Shares Held: 43,034,607

REGISTRAR(S): First National Bank of Boston, Boston, MA

TRANSFER AGENT(S): First National Bank of Boston, Boston, MA

NYS SYMBOL JH
Rec. Pr. 23¼

HARLAND (JOHN H.) CO.

YIELD 4.4%
P/E RATIO 13.8

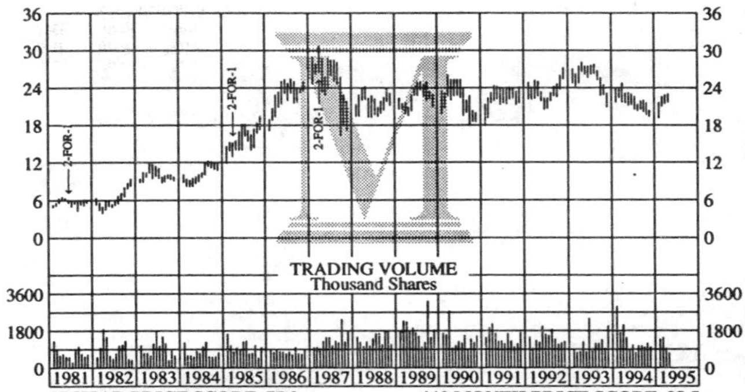

***7 YEAR PRICE SCORE 77.9** ***12 MONTH PRICE SCORE 98.5**

*NYSE COMPOSITE INDEX=100

INTERIM EARNINGS (Per Share):

Qtr.	Mar.	June	Sept.	Dec.
1991	0.42	0.41	0.37	0.13
1992	0.41	0.40	0.39	0.39
1993	0.39	0.42	0.42	0.39
1994	0.43	0.42	0.43	0.40

INTERIM DIVIDENDS (Per Share):

Amt.	Decl.	Ex.	Rec.	Pay.
0.245Q	4/3/94	5/13/94	5/19/94	6/2/94
0.245Q	7/22	8/12	8/18	9/1
0.245Q	10/28	11/10	11/17	12/1
0.255Q	1/27/95	2/10/95	2/16/95	3/2/95
0.255Q	4/28	5/12	5/18	6/1

Indicated div.: $1.02*

CAPITALIZATION (12/31/94):

	($000)	(%)
Long-Term Debt	115,226	35.6
Deferred Income Tax	4,806	1.5
Common & Surplus	203,414	62.9
Total	323,446	100.0

DIVIDEND ACHIEVER STATUS:
Rank: 45 1984-94 Growth Rate: 15.6%
Total Years of Dividend Growth: 42

RECENT DEVELOPMENTS: For the year ended 12/31/94, net income was $51.2 million compared with $52.5 million in 1993. Sales were $521.3 million, up slightly from $519.5 million in the previous year. The Financial Services and Data Services Groups performed particularly well. During the year, JH formed its Information Services Group, which contains Marketing Profiles, Inc. and FormAtion Technologies, Inc., both acquired in 1994.

PROSPECTS: JH has installed an aggessive acquisition strategy to cope with the fiercely competitive check-printing market. Two new business units, Information Services and Direct Marketing, were formed in 1994. Revenues for The Check Store have been better than expected. JH plans to capitalize on opportunities in the direct check market by increasing marketing expenditures for this segment. Meanwhile, the Company reports that the Financial Services and Data Services Groups are turning in strong operating performances.

BUSINESS

JOHN H. HARLAND is a financial stationer primarily involved in the printing of checks and related items. Principal products consist of MICR encoded checks, deposit tickets and related forms for financial institutions and their customers. Financial institutions include commercial banks, savings & loan associations, brokerage firms and insurance companies. The Company offers a number of different styles of pocket checks, including checks incorporating multi-colored background scenes, three-to-the page personal checks, three-to-the page business checks, voucher checks, window checks and carbonized payroll checks. Harland operates 52 printing plants nationwide and in Puerto Rico. The direct mail subsidiary, The Check Store, began operations in March of 1993.

BUSINESS LINE ANALYSIS

(12/31/94)	Rev(%)	Inc($000)
Financial Services	83.2	98,364
Data Services	11.2	7,863
Information Services	5.0	42
Corporate & Other	0.6	(14,257)
Total	100.0	92,012

ANNUAL EARNINGS AND DIVIDENDS PER SHARE

	1994	1993	1992	1991	1990	1989	1988
Earnings Per Share	**1.68**	**1.62**	**1.59**	**[1] 1.33**	**1.52**	**1.54**	**1.41**
Dividends Per Share	**0.98**	**0.94**	**0.90**	**0.86**	**0.78**	**0.68**	**0.58**
Dividend Payout %	**58.3**	**58.0**	**56.6**	**64.2**	**51.3**	**44.2**	**41.1**

[1] Before acctg. chg.

ANNUAL FINANCIAL DATA

	1994	1993	1992	1991	1990	1989	1988
RECORD OF EARNINGS (IN THOUSANDS):							
Total Revenues	521,266	519,486	444,980	378,659	371,346	344,734	333,315
Costs and Expenses	417,664	423,477	356,777	281,507	265,321	240,432	239,881
Depreciation & Amort	41,539	35,102	29,662	22,684	20,871	18,042	16,380
Income From Operations	92,012	87,307	83,530	74,468	85,154	86,260	77,054
Income Bef Income Taxes	85,126	85,674	88,267	79,702	90,577	91,778	81,260
Income Taxes	33,886	33,152	31,629	29,882	33,410	33,727	27,936
Net Income	51,240	52,522	56,638	[1] 49,820	57,167	58,052	53,323
Aver. Shs. Outstg.	30,517	32,460	35,689	37,469	37,604	37,797	37,934
[1] Before acctg. change dr$2,385,000.							
BALANCE SHEET (IN THOUSANDS):							
Cash and Cash Equivalents	15,299	28,124	19,283	71,423	44,584	78,856	57,776
Receivables, Net	65,874	70,354	56,700	47,956	59,326	53,816	52,472
Inventories	25,428	26,000	27,121	24,234	23,877	21,809	19,536
Gross Property	335,668	305,042	278,283	251,693	264,653	234,162	211,150
Accumulated Depreciation	173,867	152,656	130,554	111,566	109,940	90,721	77,716
Long-Term Debt	115,226	111,542	12,622	11,661	12,649	11,276	11,232
Net Stockholders' Equity	203,414	183,674	256,222	292,263	295,686	272,595	244,367
Total Assets	414,373	356,451	339,880	351,554	356,639	321,081	295,364
Total Current Assets	117,223	134,895	110,659	150,389	138,009	162,777	137,770
Total Current Liabilities	79,320	43,979	59,466	35,053	28,401	24,016	29,664
Net Working Capital	37,903	90,916	51,193	115,336	109,608	138,761	108,106
Year End Shares Outstg	30,439	30,486	34,049	36,570	37,355	37,572	37,682
STATISTICAL RECORD:							
Operating Profit Margin %	17.7	16.8	18.8	19.7	22.9	25.0	23.1
Book Value Per Share	3.34	4.25	6.42	7.99	7.92	7.26	6.48
Return on Equity %	25.2	28.6	22.1	17.0	19.3	21.3	21.8
Return on Assets %	12.4	14.7	16.7	14.2	16.0	18.1	18.1
Average Yield %	4.4	3.8	3.8	4.1	3.5	3.1	2.7
P/E Ratio	14.7-11.5	17.4-12.9	17.1-12.9	18.3-13.4	17.2-11.8	16.2-12.7	17.2-13.7
Price Range	24¾-19⅜	28⅛-20⅞	27¼-20½	24⅜-17⅞	26⅛-17⅞	25-19½	24¼-19¼

Statistics are as originally reported.

OFFICERS:
R.R. Woodson, Chmn. & C.E.O.
W.M. Dollar, V.P., C.F.O. & Treas.
V.P. Weyand, V.P. & Sec.

INCORPORATED: GA, Jun., 1923

PRINCIPAL OFFICE: 2939 Miller Road, Decatur, GA 30035

TELEPHONE NUMBER: (404) 981-9460
FAX: (404) 593-5619
NO. OF EMPLOYEES: 7,300 (approx.)
ANNUAL MEETING: In April
SHAREHOLDERS: 7,782
INSTITUTIONAL HOLDINGS:
No. of Institutions: 261
Shares Held: 18,513,035

REGISTRAR(S): Trust Company Bank, Atlanta, GA

TRANSFER AGENT(S): Trust Company Bank, Atlanta, GA

HARTFORD STEAM BOILER INSPECTION & INSURANCE CO.

YIELD 4.9%
P/E RATIO 17.0

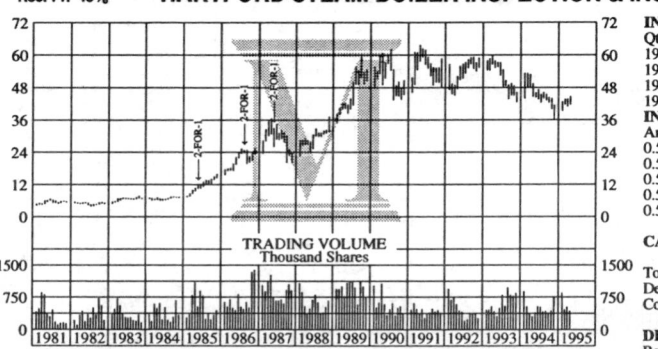

*7 YEAR PRICE SCORE 73.8   *12 MONTH PRICE SCORE 93.8

*NYSE COMPOSITE INDEX=100

INTERIM EARNINGS (Per Share):

Qtr.	Mar.	June	Sept.	Dec.
1992	0.85	0.89	0.13	0.83
1993	0.86	0.26	d1.09	0.60
1994	0.58	0.70	0.60	0.66
1995	0.69	...	...	...

INTERIM DIVIDENDS (Per Share):

Amt.	Decl.	Ex.	Rec.	Pay.
0.53Q	3/28/94	4/4/94	4/8/94	4/28/94
0.53Q	6/27	7/1	7/8	7/28
0.55Q	9/26	10/3	10/10	10/27
0.55Q	11/28	1/4/95	1/10/95	1/26/95
0.55Q	3/27/95	4/4	4/10	4/27

Indicated div.: $2.20*

CAPITALIZATION (12/31/94):

	($000)	(%)
Total Debt	79,300	21.1
Deferred Income Tax	d4,600	-1.1
Common & Surplus	299,500	80.0
Total	374,200	100.0

DIVIDEND ACHIEVER STATUS:
Rank: 21   1984-94 Growth Rate: 19.0%
Total Years of Dividend Growth: 29

RECENT DEVELOPMENTS: For the year ended 12/31/94, net income was $51.9 million compared with income, before an accounting change, of $13.1 million the year before. Insurance premiums declined 3.6% to $336.6 million. Net engineering services revenues were relatively flat at $213.9 million. Investment income fell 15.6% to $26.2 million. On 12/30/94, HSB acquired General Reinsurance Corp.'s 50.0% interest in Engineering Insurance Group, the joint partnership of the Company and General Reinsurance.

PROSPECTS: Insurance operations are benefiting from underwriting changes which are producing lower loss ratios. Engineering services operations should continue to grow moderately and produce more consistent profitability in the future. Results for investment operations are expected to improve due to increases in current returns. HSB is focusing on increasing the penetration of its services in the commercial market, as well as expanding the global market for its special risks insurance business.

BUSINESS

HARTFORD STEAM BOILER INSPECTION & INS. CO. offers engineering services and property insurance that help protect people, property and the environment. The core business is boiler and machinery and all risk property insurance for commercial and industrial facilities. Other areas include environmental services, property insurance and products and services for the international market. Subsidiaries include The Boiler Inspection and Insurance Co. of Canada, Radian Corp., and Engineering Insurance Group.

REVENUES

(12/31/94)	($000)	(%)
Insurance Premiums ..	336,600	55.8
Net Engineering Services	232,100	38.5
Net Investment Income..................	26,200	4.3
Realized Investment Gains......................	8,700	1.4
Total	603,600	100.0

ANNUAL EARNINGS AND DIVIDENDS PER SHARE

	1994	1993	1992	1991	1990	1989	1988
Earnings Per Share	2.54	0.63	①2.71	3.53	3.80	3.78	3.46
Dividends Per Share	2.14	2.12	②2.03	1.85	1.70	1.50	1.15
Dividend Payout %	84.3	N.M.	74.9	52.4	44.7	39.7	33.2

① Before acctg. chg. ② Bef acctg chge

ANNUAL FINANCIAL DATA

RECORD OF EARNINGS (IN THOUSANDS):

	1994	1993	1992	1991	1990	1989	1988
Insurance Premiums	336,600	349,200	350,100	323,303	298,600	286,792	291,794
Total Interest Income	26,200	29,300	36,500	41,449	42,403	41,679	35,773
Total Revenues	603,600	636,100	682,100	630,433	562,373	500,977	458,742
Claims & Adjustment	143,200	199,100	177,700	141,510	111,206	95,606	102,263
Income Before Taxes	73,600	16,900	73,400	101,036	110,489	109,645	96,001
Income Taxes	21,700	3,800	17,100	27,168	31,741	32,074	25,342
Net Income	51,900	①13,100	②56,300	73,868	78,748	77,571	70,659
Aver. Shs. Outstg.	20,500	20,700	20,800	20,950	20,741	20,520	20,409

① Before acctg. change dr$3,600,000. ② Before acctg. change dr$15,100,000.

BALANCE SHEET (IN THOUSANDS):

	1994	1993	1992	1991	1990	1989	1988
Cash	12,100	7,300	8,700	5,985	11,644	5,572	5,183
Fixed Maturities	198,900	154,900	151,600	154,613	194,172	190,261	231,248
Eq Secur, At Fair Value	204,900	290,000	309,900	332,769	251,499	302,163	224,904
Total Assets	905,700	877,900	888,000	888,542	827,317	794,510	730,143
Benefits and Claims	400,700	383,700	305,200	272,118	268,793	283,689	301,421
Net Stockholders' Equity	299,500	324,700	374,300	409,321	355,251	335,472	266,476
Year End Shares Outstg	20,400	20,500	20,700	21,018	20,833	20,599	20,442

STATISTICAL RECORD:

	1994	1993	1992	1991	1990	1989	1988
Return on Equity %	17.3	4.0	15.0	18.0	22.2	23.1	26.5
Book Value Per Share	14.68	15.84	18.08	19.47	17.05	16.29	13.04
Average Yield %	4.8	4.1	3.9	3.4	3.2	3.2	3.8
P/E Ratio	21.0-14.1	95.0-67.7	21.9-16.7	18.1-13.1	16.3-11.4	15.7-9.2	10.8-6.5
Price Range	53⅜-35⅞	59⅞-42⅝	59¼-45⅛	63¾-46⅛	62⅛-43½	59¼-34¾	37¼-22½

Statistics are as originally reported.

OFFICERS:
G.W. Kreh, Pres.
R.K. Price, Sr. V.P. & Corp. Sec.

INCORPORATED: CT, 1866

PRINCIPAL OFFICE: One State Street P.O. Box 5024, Hartford, CT 06102-5024

TELEPHONE NUMBER: (203) 722-5727
FAX: (203) 722-5710
NO. OF EMPLOYEES: 4,000 (approx.)
ANNUAL MEETING: In April
SHAREHOLDERS: 5,782
INSTITUTIONAL HOLDINGS:
No. of Institutions: 193
Shares Held: 11,338,776

REGISTRAR(S): First National Bank of Boston,, Boston, MA

TRANSFER AGENT(S): First National Bank of Boston,, Boston, MA

ASE SYMBOL HAS
Rec. Pr. 32⅛

HASBRO, INC.

YIELD 1.0%
P/E RATIO 15.8

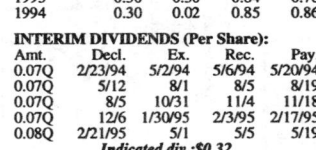

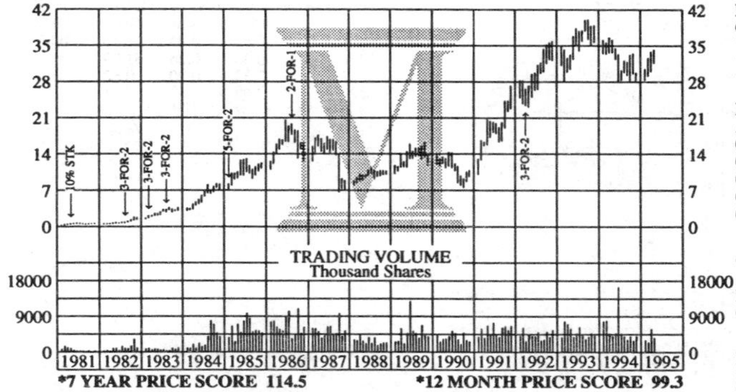

INTERIM EARNINGS (Per Share):

Qtr.	Mar.	June	Sept.	Dec.
1992	0.26	0.26	0.75	0.73
1993	0.30	0.30	0.84	0.78
1994	0.30	0.02	0.85	0.86

INTERIM DIVIDENDS (Per Share):

Amt.	Decl.	Ex.	Rec.	Pay.
0.07Q	2/23/94	5/2/94	5/6/94	5/20/94
0.07Q	5/12	8/1	8/5	8/19
0.07Q	8/5	10/31	11/4	11/18
0.07Q	12/6	1/30/95	2/3/95	2/17/95
0.08Q	2/21/95	5/1	5/5	5/19

Indicated div.:$0.32

CAPITALIZATION (12/31/94):

	($000)	(%)
Long-Term Debt	150,000	9.7
Common & Surplus	1,395,417	90.3
Total	1,545,417	100.0

DIVIDEND ACHIEVER STATUS:
Rank: 9   1984-94 Growth Rate: 23.0%
Total Years of Dividend Growth: 13

RECENT DEVELOPMENTS: For the year ended 12/25/94, net income before an accounting adjustment declined 10% to $179.3 million compared with $200.0 million in the previous year. Revenues fell 2.8% to $2.67 billion. The 1994 results included restructuring charges of $12.5 million in 1994 and $15.5 million in 1993. In late November, Hasbro acquired the games division of John Waddington PLC. This acquisition provides HAS with the worldwide rights to the board game Clue and returns the international rights for Monopoly.

PROSPECTS: Restructuring of the Hasbro Toy Group, adjustment of plant capacities to match manufacturing needs, consolidation of certain international operations and the formation of the Hasbro Games group will enhance the Company's operating efficiency. International operations should continue to make significant contributions to earnings growth. However, Barney and Jurassic Park product sales are expected to decline. Customer buying patterns are shifting toward the second half of the year.

BUSINESS

HASBRO INC. is the world's largest toy manufacturer, offering a diverse line of toys, board and card games, dolls, preschool toys, boys' and girls' action toys as well as infant care products. In 1984, HAS acquired Milton Bradley Co. Hasbro's extensive portfolio was further strengthened and expanded with the 1991 acquisition of Tonka Corp., which in addition to the well-known Tonka products also included Parker Bros. and Kenner. The Company's products now include Milton Bradley games and puzzles, Parker Bros. games, G.I. Joe, Fashion Plates, Fantastic Flowers, Playskool, Tonka trucks and the Kenner products including Easy Bake Oven and Play-Doh.

QUARTERLY DATA

(12/31/94)	Rev($000)	Inc($000)
1st Quarter	489,133	22,435
2nd Quarter	444,324	1,634
3rd Quarter	796,222	77,151
4th Quarter	940,583	75,813
TOTAL	2,670,262	175,033

ANNUAL EARNINGS AND DIVIDENDS PER SHARE

	12/31/94	12/26/93	12/27/92	12/29/91	12/30/90	12/31/89	12/25/88
Earnings Per Share	2.01	2.22	2.01	0.94	1.03	1.04	0.83
Dividends Per Share	0.27	0.23	0.19	0.153	0.127	0.10	0.075
Dividend Payout %	13.4	10.4	9.5	16.3	12.3	9.6	9.1

ANNUAL FINANCIAL DATA

RECORD OF EARNINGS (IN MILLIONS):

	12/31/94	12/26/93	12/27/92	12/29/91	12/30/90	12/31/89	12/25/88
Total Revenues	2,670.3	2,747.2	2,541.1	2,141.1	1,520.0	1,409.7	1,357.9
Costs and Expenses	[1] 2,337.7	2,360.6	2,183.0	1,874.4	1,339.2	1,196.7	1,152.9
Depreciation & Amort	...	100.6	62.1	81.9	39.7	42.9	51.0
Operating Profit	295.7	351.2	324.5	237.4	160.3	170.1	154.1
Earn Bef Income Taxes	291.6	325.2	292.2	145.6	152.4	156.8	131.4
Income Taxes	112.3	125.2	113.2	63.9	63.3	64.6	59.0
Net Income	[2] 179.3	200.0	[3] 179.0	81.7	89.2	92.2	72.4
Aver. Shs. Outstg. (000)	89,331	90,031	89,086	86,983	87,119	88,779	79,548

[1] Incl. Dep. [2] Before acctg. change dr$4,282,000. [3] Before acctg. change cr$214,000.

BALANCE SHEET (IN MILLIONS):

	12/31/94	12/26/93	12/27/92	12/29/91	12/30/90	12/31/89	12/25/88
Cash and Cash Equivalents	137.0	186.3	126.0	120.6	289.3	278.2	231.8
Receivables, Net	717.9	720.4	638.3	551.4	353.0	324.4	337.1
Inventories	244.4	250.1	217.9	208.4	137.4	142.7	116.3
Gross Property	472.2	413.0	363.1	325.0	252.8	236.8	226.2
Accumulated Depreciation	163.4	133.2	111.8	99.9	83.6	67.0	61.2
Long-Term Debt	150.0	200.5	206.2	380.3	56.9	57.6	126.6
Net Stockholders' Equity	1,395.4	1,276.7	1,105.6	955.3	867.8	802.3	703.2
Total Assets	2,378.4	2,293.0	2,082.8	1,950.1	1,284.8	1,246.5	1,111.9
Total Current Assets	1,252.5	1,301.1	1,116.9	1,025.2	861.6	806.9	736.0
Total Current Liabilities	763.7	748.3	701.3	593.8	357.6	384.1	272.5
Net Working Capital	488.7	552.8	415.6	431.4	504.0	422.8	463.5
Year End Shs Outstg (000)	87,528	87,795	87,176	86,184	84,744	88,067	79,280

STATISTICAL RECORD:

	12/31/94	12/26/93	12/27/92	12/29/91	12/30/90	12/31/89	12/25/88
Operating Profit Margin %	11.1	12.8	12.8	11.1	10.5	12.1	11.3
Book Value Per Share	7.08	7.01	4.76	3.52	7.46	6.21	6.30
Return on Equity %	12.9	15.7	16.2	8.5	10.3	11.5	10.3
Return on Assets %	7.5	8.7	8.6	4.2	6.9	7.4	6.5
Average Yield %	0.8	0.7	0.6	0.8	1.2	0.8	0.8
P/E Ratio	18.2-13.9	18.1-12.7	17.8-11.5	29.0-10.8	14.1-7.4	15.6-9.7	13.7-9.6
Price Range	36⅝-27⅞	40⅛-28⅛	35⅞-23⅛	27¼-10⅛	14⅜-7½	16¼-10⅛	11⅜-8

Statistics are as originally reported.

OFFICERS:
A.G. Hassenfeld, Chmn. & C.E.O.
J.T. O'Neill, Exec. V.P. & C.F.O.
D.M. Robbins, S.V.P., Gen. Coun. & Sec.

INCORPORATED: RI, Jan., 1926

PRINCIPAL OFFICE: 1027 Newport Ave. P O Box 1059, Pawtucket, RI 02861

TELEPHONE NUMBER: (401) 431-8697
FAX: (401) 431-8400
NO. OF EMPLOYEES: 12,500
ANNUAL MEETING: In May
SHAREHOLDERS: 5,000 (approx.)
INSTITUTIONAL HOLDINGS:
No. of Institutions: 370
Shares Held: 62,302,985

REGISTRAR(S): First National Bank of Boston, Shareholder Services Division, Boston, MA

TRANSFER AGENT(S): First National Bank of Boston, Shareholder Services Division, Boston, MA

NASDAQ SYMBOL HAVT
Rec. Pr. 10⅝

HAVERTY FURNITURE COS., INC.

YIELD 2.8%
P/E RATIO 9.7

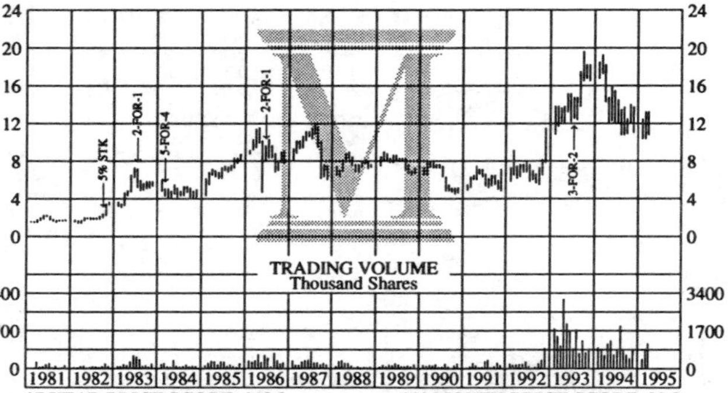

*7 YEAR PRICE SCORE 113.3 *12 MONTH PRICE SCORE 90.8

*NYSE COMPOSITE INDEX=100

INTERIM EARNINGS (Per Share):

Qtr.	Mar.	June	Sept.	Dec.
1991	0.07	0.03	0.05	0.11
1992	0.09	0.01	0.13	0.29
1993	0.21	0.14	0.21	0.35
1994	0.24	0.18	0.26	0.42

INTERIM DIVIDENDS (Per Share):

Amt.	Decl.	Ex.	Rec.	Pay.
0.0675Q	2/8/94	2/14/94	2/18/94	2/28/94
0.0675Q	5/6	5/10	5/16	5/25
0.07Q	8/5	8/9	8/15	8/25
0.07Q	11/4	11/7	11/14	11/25
0.075Q	2/7/95	2/13/95	2/17/95	2/27/95

Indicated div.: $0.30

CAPITALIZATION (12/31/94):

	($000)	(%)
Long-Term Debt	87,164	39.7
Deferred Income Tax	1,347	0.6
Common & Surplus	131,055	59.7
Total	219,566	100.0

DIVIDEND ACHIEVER STATUS:
Rank: 216 1984-94 Growth Rate: 7.9%
Total Years of Dividend Growth: 20

RECENT DEVELOPMENTS: For the year ended 12/31/94, net income was $12.5 million compared with $9.7 million a year earlier. Net sales increased 14.6% to $370.1 million from $322.9 million the year before. Comparable-store sales increased 10.0%. As a percentage of sales, gross profit increased to 47.4% from 47.2% a year earlier. Selling, general and administrative expenses were 41.7% of sales compared with 42.3% a year earlier. For the quarter ended 12/31/94, net income was $4.8 million versus $3.9 million the year before. Net sales increased 11.7% to $102.8 million from $92.1 million in the prior-year period. Comparable-store sales increased 7.5%. Results were aided by lower operating costs and improved account collection practices. As a percentage of sales, gross profit increased to 48.3% from 47.5% a year earlier. Selling, general and administrative expenses were 39.6% of sales versus 40.2% a year earlier.

BUSINESS

HAVERTY FURNITURE COMPANIES, INC. currently operates 90 retail furnishings stores in eleven states throughout the Southeast and Southwest, including four stores dedicated to the Thomasville line and 23 stores that feature Thomasville galley displays. The Company targets middle and upper-middle income families as its chief market. The Company has maintained a continual program of store relocation, modernization of older units, and upgrading of its merchandising. The relocation program, principally a shift to suburban areas, has been completed. To complement these retail units and provide delivery of merchandise to customers, the Company operates a warehouse in each city in which it is located.

QUARTERLY DATA

(12/31/94)($000)	Rev	Inc
1st Quarter	88,016	2,726
2nd Quarter	84,747	2,060
3rd Quarter	94,529	2,947
4th Quarter	102,840	4,805

ANNUAL EARNINGS AND DIVIDENDS PER SHARE

	1994	1993	1992	1991	1990	1989	1988
Earnings Per Share	**1.10**	**0.91**	**0.53**	**0.27**	**0.75**	**0.90**	**0.88**
Dividends Per Share	**0.275**	[1] **0.265**	**0.257**	**0.253**	**0.247**	**0.24**	**0.235**
Dividend Payout %	**25.0**	**29.1**	**48.7**	**95.0**	**32.7**	**26.7**	**26.7**

[1] 3-for-2 stk split,07/01/93

ANNUAL FINANCIAL DATA

	1994	1993	1992	1991	1990	1989	1988
RECORD OF EARNINGS (IN THOUSANDS):							
Total Revenues	381,796	333,359	292,511	257,956	260,799	242,974	239,968
Costs and Expenses	[1] 349,179	300,024	268,882	238,741	235,472	219,270	217,080
Depreciation & Amort	...	6,875	6,069	5,479	5,232	4,934	4,590
Operating Profit	32,617	26,460	17,560	13,736	20,095	18,770	18,298
Income Bef Income Taxes	20,279	15,650	7,188	3,555	8,795	10,903	10,905
Income Taxes	7,741	5,934	2,656	1,315	2,364	3,110	3,251
Net Income	12,538	9,716	4,532	2,240	6,431	7,793	7,654
Aver. Shs. Outstg.	11,425	10,733	8,571	8,492	8,552	8,670	8,726
[1] Incl. Dep.							
BALANCE SHEET (IN THOUSANDS):							
Cash and Cash Equivalents	1,925	614	1,189	1,741	1,481	2,938	4,069
Receivables, Net	163,801	138,823	112,502	92,931	97,682	78,748	78,280
Inventories	64,582	54,739	50,573	49,483	50,443	44,616	40,159
Gross Property	129,418	112,374	102,320	95,567	88,715	90,943	85,930
Accumulated Depreciation	49,220	44,935	41,024	37,668	33,234	29,861	25,660
Long-Term Debt	87,164	94,197	79,630	74,406	80,149	77,229	74,505
Capital Lease Obligations	...	...	...	...	...	6,163	6,573
Net Stockholders' Equity	131,055	120,418	83,567	80,804	80,969	76,960	72,469
Total Assets	315,103	264,353	229,184	208,653	208,862	191,097	186,882
Total Current Assets	232,994	195,174	165,637	148,345	150,905	127,440	123,484
Total Current Liabilities	93,299	47,441	62,170	49,155	43,264	26,077	28,779
Net Working Capital	139,695	147,733	103,467	99,190	107,641	101,363	94,705
Year End Shares Outstg	11,494	11,372	5,084	8,467	8,515	8,576	8,720
STATISTICAL RECORD:							
Operating Profit Margin %	8.5	7.9	6.0	5.3	7.7	7.7	7.6
Book Value Per Share	11.40	10.59	16.44	9.54	9.51	8.97	8.31
Return on Equity %	9.6	8.1	5.4	2.8	7.9	10.1	10.6
Return on Assets %	4.0	3.7	2.0	1.1	3.1	4.1	4.1
Average Yield %	1.8	2.2	3.0	4.1	4.0	3.1	3.1
P/E Ratio	17.5-9.8	21.6-12.0	21.7-10.4	27.8-18.1	10.7-6.0	10.0-7.2	10.2-7.2
Price Range	19¼-10¾	19⅝-10⅞	11½-5½	7½-4⅞	8-4½	9-6½	9-6⅜

Statistics are as originally reported.

OFFICERS:
R. Haverty, Chmn.
J.E. Slater, Jr., Pres. & C.E.O.
D.L. Fink, Sr. V.P. & C.F.O.
H.G. Wells, Jr., V.P. & Treas.

INCORPORATED: MD, Sep., 1929

PRINCIPAL OFFICE: 866 W. Peachtree St., N.W., Atlanta, GA 30308-1123

TELEPHONE NUMBER: (404) 881-1911

NO. OF EMPLOYEES: 2,590

ANNUAL MEETING: In April

SHAREHOLDERS: 2,700 com.; 500, cl. A com. (approx.)

INSTITUTIONAL HOLDINGS:
No. of Institutions: 76
Shares Held: 5,844,823

REGISTRAR(S): Wachovia Bank of North Carolina, N.A., P.O. Box 3001, Winston-Salem, NC 27102

TRANSFER AGENT(S): Wachovia Bank of North Carolina, N.A., P.O. Box 3001, Winston-Salem, NC 27102

NYS SYMBOL HE
Rec. Pr. 34⅞

HAWAIIAN ELECTRIC INDUSTRIES, INC.

YIELD 6.8%
P/E RATIO 17.0

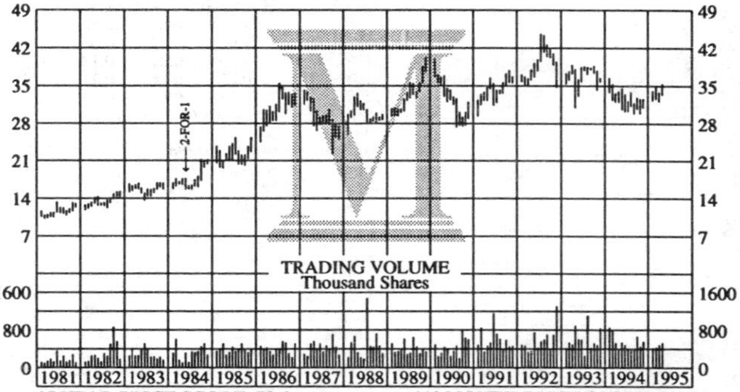

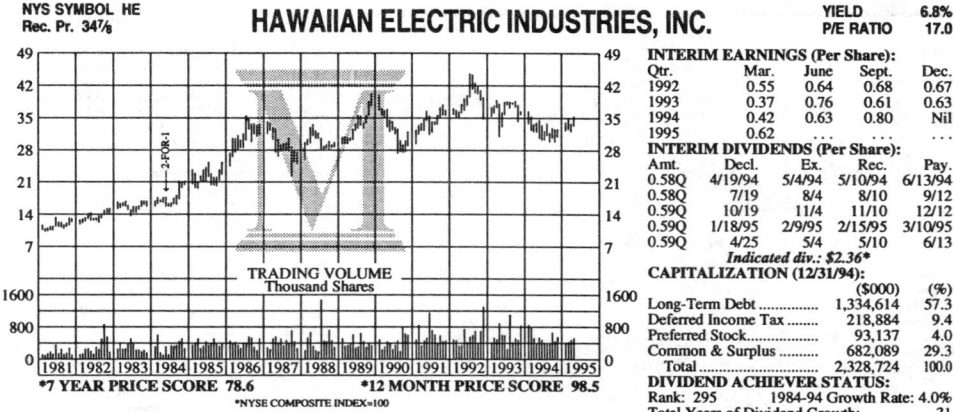

*7 YEAR PRICE SCORE 78.6 *12 MONTH PRICE SCORE 98.5

*NYSE COMPOSITE INDEX=100

INTERIM EARNINGS (Per Share):

Qtr.	Mar.	June	Sept.	Dec.
1992	0.55	0.64	0.68	0.67
1993	0.37	0.76	0.61	0.63
1994	0.42	0.63	0.80	Nil
1995	0.62	...	...	...

INTERIM DIVIDENDS (Per Share):

Amt.	Decl.	Ex.	Rec.	Pay.
0.58Q	4/19/94	5/4/94	5/10/94	6/13/94
0.58Q	7/19	8/4	8/10	9/12
0.59Q	10/19	11/4	11/10	12/12
0.59Q	1/18/95	2/9/95	2/15/95	3/10/95
0.59Q	4/25	5/4	5/10	6/13

*Indicated div.: $2.36**

CAPITALIZATION (12/31/94):

	($000)	(%)
Long-Term Debt	1,334,614	57.3
Deferred Income Tax	218,884	9.4
Preferred Stock	93,137	4.0
Common & Surplus	682,089	29.3
Total	2,328,724	100.0

DIVIDEND ACHIEVER STATUS:
Rank: 295 1984-94 Growth Rate: 4.0%
Total Years of Dividend Growth: 31

RECENT DEVELOPMENTS: For the quarter ended 12/31/94, net income was up 21% to $20.9 million compared with income of $17.3 million from continuing operations in 1993. Revenues were $319.8 million up from $281.7 million in 1993. For the year ended 12/31/94, net income from continuing operations was $73.0 million versus income of $61.7 million a year earlier. Revenues were $1.19 billion, up 4%. The improved performance reflects the gradual recovery of Hawaii's economy and improving trends for the Company.

PROSPECTS: The Hawaii Public Utilities Commission authorized HE to increase rates on two of the five islands it serves, primarily to help pay for system improvements and offset the rising costs of serving customers. The gradual recovery of Hawaii's economy should bolster demand for electricity and add to earnings. American Savings Bank's results were lower because of higher interest rates, which resulted in narrower margins, while loan loss reserves were increased to combat a weaker economy.

BUSINESS

HAWAIIAN ELECTRIC INDUSTRIES, INC. is a Hawaii-based electric utility holding company with subsidiaries in energy, banking, maritime freight transportation and real estate development. The three utilities supply electricity to about 95% of Hawaii's population. Diversified manufacturing and a large tourist business are the major factors in the local economy. Non-utility companies include: American Savings Bank, HEI Investment Corporation, Hawaiian Tug and Barge Corporation, Malama Pacific Corporation and Hawaiian Electric Renewable Systems, Inc.

BUSINESS LINE ANALYSIS

(12/31/94)	Rev(%)	Inc(%)
Electric Utility	76.9	78.5
Savings Bank	18.1	24.4
Other	5.0	-2.9
Total	100.0	100.0

ANNUAL EARNINGS AND DIVIDENDS PER SHARE

	1994	1993	1992	1991	1990	1989	1988
Earnings Per Share	1.85	2.38	[1] 2.54	2.40	2.02	3.06	2.90
Dividends Per Share	2.33	2.29	2.25	2.21	2.17	2.07	1.95
Dividend Payout %	N.M.	96.2	88.6	92.1	N.M.	67.6	67.2

[1] Before disc. oper.

ANNUAL FINANCIAL DATA

	1994	1993	1992	1991	1990	1989	1988
RECORD OF EARNINGS (IN MILLIONS):							
Total Revenues	1,188.5	1,142.2	1,031.4	1,083.8	1,010.8	884.1	732.7
Depreciation & Amort	72.3	64.3	61.9	61.9	54.7	48.5	39.5
Operating Income	174.1	157.6	136.2	131.2	116.3	131.9	117.1
Interest Expense	45.0	46.2	40.4	43.6	41.2	38.1	34.3
Net Income	73.0	[1] 61.7	[2] 61.7	54.8	43.6	64.1	55.0
Aver. Shs. Outstg. (000)	28,137	25,938	24,275	22,882	21,559	20,960	18,984
[1] Before disc. op. dr$13,025,000. [2] Before disc. op. dr$73,297,000.							
BALANCE SHEET (IN MILLIONS):							
Gross Plant	2,425.3	2,221.2	2,002.9	1,857.7	1,707.2	1,574.1	1,425.1
Accumulated Depreciation	747.5	678.2	615.1	572.9	517.6	467.5	422.5
Prop, Plant & Equip, Net	1,677.8	1,543.0	1,387.8	1,284.8	1,189.7	1,106.6	1,002.6
Long-term Debt	1,334.6	987.5	776.6	798.6	683.5	698.3	643.8
Net Stockholders' Equity	775.2	738.1	633.0	668.4	599.0	583.0	514.3
Total Assets	6,274.3	5,220.3	4,911.2	4,924.1	4,688.8	3,130.3	2,683.2
Year End Shs Outstg (000)	28,655	27,675	24,762	23,867	21,918	21,266	20,681
STATISTICAL RECORD:							
Book Value Per Share	22.22	21.44	20.06	21.89	20.33	19.93	18.23
Op. Inc/Net Pl %	10.4	10.2	9.8	10.2	9.8	11.9	11.7
Accum. Dep/Gr. Pl %	30.8	30.5	30.7	30.8	30.3	29.7	29.6
Return on Equity %	10.0	8.9	10.6	8.9	8.0	12.1	11.2
Average Yield %	7.0	6.6	5.7	6.6	6.5	5.9	6.6
P/E Ratio	14.0-11.5	16.3-13.0	17.6-13.7	15.8-12.2	19.8-13.5	13.2-9.6	11.6-8.9
Price Range	36½-29⅞	38⅞-31	44⅝-34¾	37⅞-29⅜	40-27¼	40¼-29⅜	33⅝-25⅞

Statistics are as originally reported.

OFFICERS:
R.F. Clarke, Pres. & C.E.O.
R.F. Mougeot, Financial V.P. & C.F.O.
C.H. Lau, Treas.

INCORPORATED: HI, Jul., 1981

PRINCIPAL OFFICE: 900 Richards Street, Honolulu, HI 96813

TELEPHONE NUMBER: (808) 543-5662
FAX: (808) 543-7966
NO. OF EMPLOYEES: 3,386
ANNUAL MEETING: In April
SHAREHOLDERS: 23,867
INSTITUTIONAL HOLDINGS:
No. of Institutions: 140
Shares Held: 9,390,291

REGISTRAR(S):

TRANSFER AGENT(S): First Chicago Trust Co. of New York, New York, NY 10008

NYS SYMBOL HNZ
Rec. Pr. 43⅝

HEINZ (H.J.) CO.

YIELD 3.3%
P/E RATIO 19.9

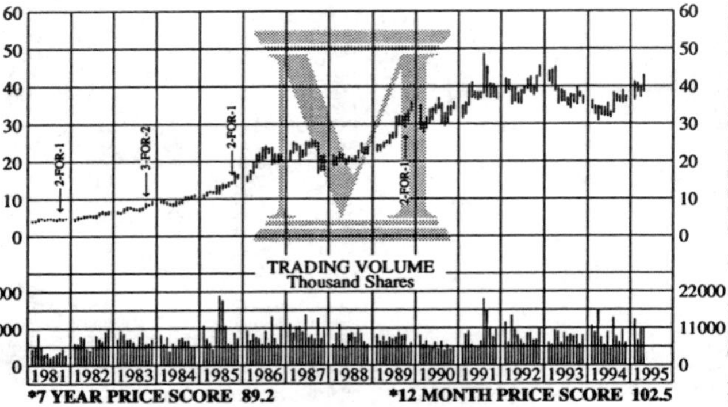

*7 YEAR PRICE SCORE 89.2 *12 MONTH PRICE SCORE 102.5

*NYSE COMPOSITE INDEX=100

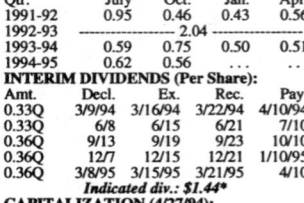

INTERIM EARNINGS (Per Share):

Qtr.	July	Oct.	Jan.	Apr.
1991-92	0.95	0.46	0.43	0.56
1992-93		2.04		
1993-94	0.59	0.75	0.50	0.51
1994-95	0.62	0.56	...	...

INTERIM DIVIDENDS (Per Share):

Amt.	Decl.	Ex.	Rec.	Pay.
0.33Q	3/9/94	3/16/94	3/22/94	4/10/94
0.33Q	6/8	6/15	6/21	7/10
0.36Q	9/13	9/19	9/23	10/10
0.36Q	12/7	12/15	12/21	1/10/95
0.36Q	3/8/95	3/15/95	3/21/95	4/10

*Indicated div.: $1.44**

CAPITALIZATION (4/27/94):

	($000)	(%)
Long-Term Debt	1,727,002	40.0
Deferred Income Tax	248,630	5.8
Preferred Stock	398	0.0
Common & Surplus	2,338,153	54.2
Total	4,314,183	100.0

DIVIDEND ACHIEVER STATUS:
Rank: 73 1984-94 Growth Rate: 14.1%
Total Years of Dividend Growth: 31

RECENT DEVELOPMENTS: In February 1995, HNZ agreed to acquire the U.S. and Canadian pet food businesses of Quaker Oats Company for $725 million. For the quarter ended 10/26/94, net income was $139.6 million compared with $193.1 million a year earlier. Sales advanced 9% to $1.98 billion, resulting from volume gains of 4% and acquisitions. Volume gains were posted in many of the Company's core retail product lines, including certain foodservice products.

PROSPECTS: The acquisition of Quaker Oats' pet food division is expected to double the revenues and profits of HNZ's pet food division, and complement HNZ's existing strength in canned cat food. Meanwhile, Heinz is continuing efforts to streamline its operations and improve productivity in order to compete more effectively with private-label manufacturers. Over the longer term, HNZ will focus on expanding its international baby food business.

BUSINESS

H.J. HEINZ COMPANY packs and sells canned foods, including: ketchup, soups, baby and junior foods, beans, canned prepared meals, pickles, vinegar, and other specialties, under the Heinz label and trademark '57 Varieties'. Under the StarKist label it produces tuna products; cat food under the 9-Lives label; and frozen potato and onion products under Ore-Ida. Weight Watchers prepares diet foods and operates weight control meetings. Overseas, Heinz has factories in England, Holland, Belgium, Italy, Australia, Venezuela, Ireland, Denmark, Portugal, Korea and Japan. Foreign operations produced 43% of revenues and 52% of operating income in the year ended 4/27/94.

QUARTERLY DATA

(4/27/94)($000)	Rev	Inc
1st Quarter	1,583,312	152,719
2nd Quarter	1,807,729	193,125
3rd Quarter	1,710,209	128,567
4th Quarter	1,945,488	129,073

ANNUAL EARNINGS AND DIVIDENDS PER SHARE

	4/27/94	4/28/93	4/29/92	5/1/91	5/2/90	5/3/89	4/27/88
Earnings Per Share	2.35	① 2.04	2.40	2.13	1.90	1.67	1.46
Dividends Per Share	1.35	1.23	0.99	0.87	0.75	0.645	0.56
Dividend Payout %	57.4	60.3	41.3	41.0	39.5	38.6	38.5

① Before acctg. chg.

ANNUAL FINANCIAL DATA

	4/27/94	4/28/93	4/29/92	5/1/91	5/2/90	5/3/89	4/27/88
RECORD OF EARNINGS (IN MILLIONS):							
Total Revenues	7,046.7	7,103.4	6,581.9	6,647.1	6,085.7	5,800.9	5,244.2
Costs and Expenses	5,718.6	6,007.6	5,263.6	5,413.9	4,995.2	4,849.3	4,422.9
Depreciation & Amort	259.8	234.9	211.8	196.1	168.5	148.1	133.3
Operating Income	1,068.3	860.9	1,106.5	1,037.1	921.9	803.5	688.0
Income Bef Income Taxes	922.4	715.8	984.3	903.0	811.4	724.9	622.6
Income Taxes	319.4	185.8	346.1	335.0	307.0	284.7	236.6
Net Income	602.9	① 529.9	638.3	568.0	504.5	440.2	386.0
Aver. Shs. Outstg. (000)	256,812	259,788	266,339	266,629	266,078	263,568	265,412
① Before acctg. change dr$133,630,000.							
BALANCE SHEET (IN MILLIONS):							
Cash and Cash Equivalents	142.4	224.3	273.1	314.0	241.1	237.7	252.8
Receivables, Net	812.5	978.9	830.8	678.1	640.8	507.5	491.9
Inventories	1,145.7	1,185.4	1,034.9	967.9	993.6	902.7	797.1
Gross Property	3,442.9	3,328.4	2,979.8	2,764.5	2,495.5	2,184.1	2,025.7
Accumulated Depreciation	1,275.2	1,166.1	1,067.7	1,041.7	927.8	818.1	771.8
Long-Term Debt	1,727.0	1,009.4	178.4	716.9	875.2	693.5	524.4
Net Stockholders' Equity	2,338.6	2,321.0	2,367.4	2,274.9	1,886.9	1,777.2	1,593.9
Total Assets	6,381.1	6,821.3	5,931.9	4,935.4	4,487.5	4,001.8	3,605.1
Total Current Assets	2,291.5	2,623.4	2,280.3	2,119.8	2,013.7	1,775.2	1,664.4
Total Current Liabilities	1,692.4	2,866.3	2,844.0	1,429.7	1,280.0	1,115.9	1,074.7
Net Working Capital	599.2	d242.9	d563.7	690.1	733.7	659.3	589.7
Year End Shs Outstg (000)	249,041	254,365	254,057	259,435	253,518	256,962	255,236
STATISTICAL RECORD:							
Operating Profit Margin %	15.2	12.1	16.8	15.6	15.1	13.9	13.1
Book Value Per Share	4.00	3.73	4.67	5.88	4.89	4.56	4.35
Return on Equity %	25.8	22.8	27.0	25.0	26.7	24.8	24.2
Return on Assets %	9.4	7.8	10.8	11.5	11.2	11.0	10.7
Average Yield %	3.4	2.8	2.5	2.7	2.6	2.9	2.6
P/E Ratio	19.3-14.5	22.3-17.2	20.3-13.1	17.4-12.9	18.9-11.8	15.0-11.2	17.7-11.5
Price Range	45¼-34⅛	45½-35⅛	48⅝-31½	37-27½	35⅞-22½	25-18¾	25⅞-16¾

Statistics are as originally reported.

OFFICERS:
A.J. O'Reilly, Chmn., Pres. & C.E.O.
J.J. Bogdanovich, Vice-Chmn.
D.R. Williams, Sr. V.P. & C.F.O.
P.F. Renne, V.P. & Treas.

INCORPORATED: PA, Jul., 1900

PRINCIPAL OFFICE: 600 Grant St., Pittsburgh, PA 15219

TELEPHONE NUMBER: (412) 456-5700

NO. OF EMPLOYEES: 35,700 (approx.)

ANNUAL MEETING: In September

SHAREHOLDERS: 61,655 (approx.)

INSTITUTIONAL HOLDINGS:
No. of Institutions: 624
Shares Held: 143,160,878

REGISTRAR(S): Mellon Bank, N.A., Pittsburgh, PA

TRANSFER AGENT(S): Mellon Bank, N.A., Pittsburgh, PA

HELMERICH & PAYNE, INC.

YIELD 1.7%
P/E RATIO 40.9

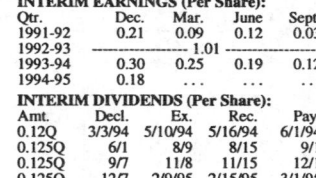

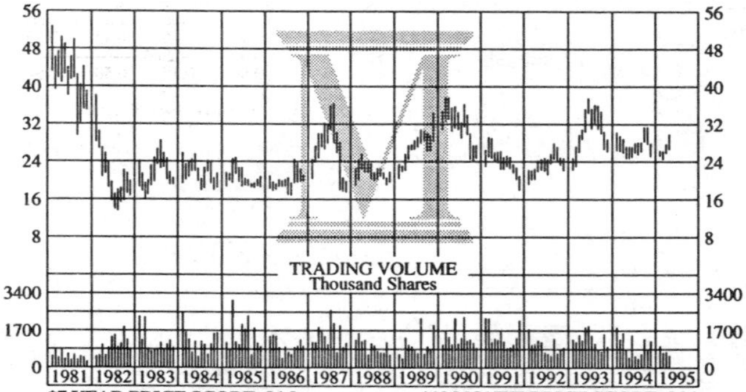

INTERIM EARNINGS (Per Share):

Qtr.	Dec.	Mar.	June	Sept.
1991-92	0.21	0.09	0.12	0.03
1992-93	------- 1.01 -------			
1993-94	0.30	0.25	0.19	0.12
1994-95	0.18	...	...	...

INTERIM DIVIDENDS (Per Share):

Amt.	Decl.	Ex.	Rec.	Pay.
0.12Q	3/3/94	5/10/94	5/16/94	6/1/94
0.125Q	6/1	8/9	8/15	9/1
0.125Q	9/7	11/8	11/15	12/1
0.125Q	12/7	2/9/95	2/15/95	3/1/95
0.125Q	3/1/95	5/9	5/15	6/1

Indicated div.: $0.50

CAPITALIZATION (9/30/94):

	($000)	(%)
Deferred Income Tax	44,462	7.8
Common & Surplus	524,334	92.2
Total	568,796	100.0

DIVIDEND ACHIEVER STATUS:
Rank: 306   1984-94 Growth Rate: 3.7%
Total Years of Dividend Growth: 18

*7 YEAR PRICE SCORE 84.3   *12 MONTH PRICE SCORE 96.1
*NYSE COMPOSITE INDEX=100

RECENT DEVELOPMENTS: For the quarter ended 12/31/94, net income was $4.4 million compared with income of $7.3 million, before an accounting change, in the corresponding 1993 period. Revenues slipped 3% to $79.9 million, primarily due to sharply lower natural gas prices. The Exploration and Production Division reported a pre-tax loss of $538,000 compared with pre-tax income of $5.1 million in the first quarter of 1993. Along with the lower natural gas prices, production volumes fell to 78.2 Mmc/d from 84.1 Mmc/d in the comparable 1993 period.

PROSPECTS: The combination of lower oil and natural gas prices, curtailed natural gas production, and increased exploration expenses have dampened earnings. However, recent acquisitions will boost production and provide long-term growth. Operations in Venezuela and Colombia will continue to show favorable growth rates and should directly contribute to earnings for the contract drilling group. Favorable market conditions will spur growth in the real estate segment while improved margins and volumes should benefit the chemicals unit.

BUSINESS

HELMERICH & PAYNE, INC. is a diversified, energy-oriented company engaged primarily in exploration for and production of crude oil and natural gas and in contract drilling of oil and gas wells for the petroleum industry. The Company also manufactures and distributes odorants for use in the gas transmission and distribution industry and engages as well in the ownership, development, and operation of commercial real estate. On 9/30/94, proven reserves totaled 6.7 million barrels of crude oil and 290.7 billion cubic feet of natural gas. 1994 revenues were derived: contract drilling, 56.1%; oil and gas, 33.7%; chemicals, 5.7%; real estate, 2.4%; and other, 2.1%.

ANNUAL EARNINGS AND DIVIDENDS PER SHARE

	9/30/94	9/30/93	9/30/92	9/30/91	9/30/90	9/30/89	9/30/88
Earnings Per Share	0.86	1.01	0.45	0.88	1.97	0.94	0.83
Dividends Per Share	0.49	0.48	0.47	0.46	0.445	0.425	0.405
Dividend Payout %	57.0	47.5	N.M.	52.3	22.6	45.2	48.8

ANNUAL FINANCIAL DATA

RECORD OF EARNINGS (IN THOUSANDS):

	9/30/94	9/30/93	9/30/92	9/30/91	9/30/90	9/30/89	9/30/88
Total Revenues	329,001	315,097	239,700	213,946	238,544	171,169	160,565
Costs and Expenses	248,249	223,243	167,255	138,160	129,273	91,234	85,521
Deprec, Depl & Amort	50,068	48,609	47,738	40,345	41,550	41,651	37,642
Operating Profit	41,053	50,138	27,921	41,508	73,485	40,614	38,801
Inc Bef Fed Income Taxes	30,299	42,320	24,075	35,061	70,381	32,400	31,119
Income Taxes	10,232	17,368	8,641	12,280	22,194	9,812	6,286
Net Income	24,971	24,550	10,849	21,241	47,562	22,700	20,150
Aver. Shs. Outstg.	24,416	24,307	24,210	24,182	24,178	24,167	24,167

BALANCE SHEET (IN THOUSANDS):

Cash and Cash Equivalents	38,444	70,765	50,714	70,054	134,481	121,067	116,916
Receivables, Net	59,897	56,305	42,819	37,532	37,755	31,323	29,485
Inventories	20,995	5,783	17,611	16,697	10,559	8,786	7,748
Gross Property	943,102	873,322	848,793	783,416	703,381	694,410	650,372
Accumulated Depreciation	542,451	514,524	484,197	446,894	420,689	401,932	369,424
Long-Term Debt	...	3,600	8,339	5,693	5,648	49,087	70,715
Net Stockholders' Equity	524,334	508,927	493,286	491,133	479,485	443,396	430,804
Total Assets	624,827	599,072	585,504	575,168	582,927	591,229	576,473
Total Current Assets	122,939	138,636	133,128	142,175	200,661	168,308	161,799
Total Current Liabilities	46,701	46,414	35,881	33,963	53,920	53,949	26,524
Net Working Capital	76,238	92,222	97,247	108,212	146,741	114,359	135,275
Year End Shares Outstg	24,710	24,637	24,577	24,487	24,485	24,173	24,166

STATISTICAL RECORD:

Operating Profit Margin %	9.3	13.7	10.3	16.6	28.4	22.4	23.3
Book Value Per Share	21.22	20.66	20.07	20.06	19.58	18.34	17.83
Return on Equity %	4.8	4.8	2.2	4.3	9.9	5.1	4.7
Return on Assets %	4.0	4.1	1.9	3.7	8.2	3.8	3.5
Average Yield %	1.7	1.6	2.0	1.9	1.4	1.5	1.8
P/E Ratio	36.5-28.8	37.1-22.0	61.9-42.5	33.2-20.5	19.2-12.2	36.7-21.7	31.0-22.9
Price Range	31⅜-24¾	37½-22¼	27⅞-19⅛	29¼-18	37¾-24	34½-20⅜	25¾-19

Statistics are as originally reported.

NYS SYMBOL HSY
Rec. Pr. 52¼

HERSHEY FOODS CORP.

YIELD 2.5%
P/E RATIO 24.6

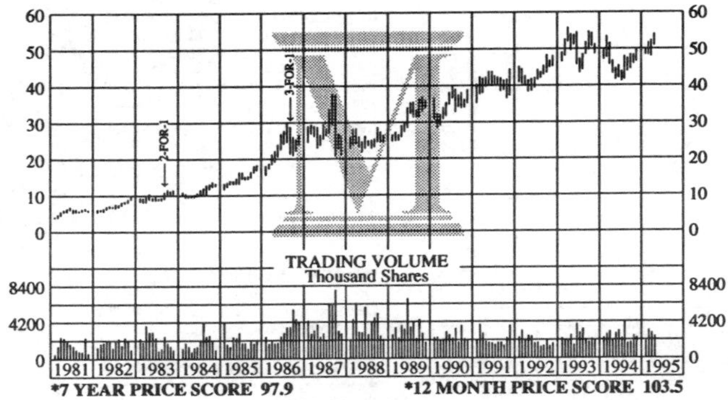

*7 YEAR PRICE SCORE 97.9 *12 MONTH PRICE SCORE 103.5

*NYSE COMPOSITE INDEX=100

INTERIM EARNINGS (Per Share):

Qtr.	Mar.	June	Sept.	Dec.
1991	0.54	0.35	0.71	0.83
1992	0.65	0.39	0.74	0.91
1993	1.16	0.29	0.82	1.04
1994	0.61	0.29	0.93	0.29

INTERIM DIVIDENDS (Per Share):

Amt.	Decl.	Ex.	Rec.	Pay.
0.30Q	4/25/94	5/17/94	5/23/94	6/15/94
0.325Q	8/2	8/22	8/26	9/15
0.325Q	11/1	11/15	11/21	12/15
0.325Q	2/7/95	2/17/95	2/24/95	3/15/95
0.325Q	4/24	5/17	5/23	6/15

*Indicated div.: $1.30**

CAPITALIZATION (12/31/94):

	($000)	(%)
Long-Term Debt	92,046	5.1
Deferred Income Tax	193,377	10.7
Common & Surplus	1,517,742	84.2
Total	1,803,165	100.0

DIVIDEND ACHIEVER STATUS:
Rank: 124 1984-94 Growth Rate: 11.7%
Total Years of Dividend Growth: 21

RECENT DEVELOPMENTS: For the year ended 12/31/94, net income was $184.2 milion compared with $297.2 million, before the cumulative effect of an accounting change, in the previous year. However, 1994 results include an after-tax restructuring charge of $80.2 million, or $0.92 per share. Revenues rose 3% to a record $3.61 billion. The sales growth was attributable to new confectionery products, international acquisitions, and pasta price increases.

PROSPECTS: Several overseas acquisitions should continue to contribute to sales growth at Hershey International. HSY's ongoing program to modernize and expand production capacity will help reduce production costs and improve margins, while line extensions and new product introductions should continue to boost future earnings growth. Meanwhile, the higher costs of durum wheat have been passed along to the consumer in the form of higher pasta prices.

BUSINESS

HERSHEY FOODS CORP. produces a broad line of chocolate, confectionery and pasta products, including chocolate bars, breakfast cocoa, baking and chocolate syrup. Principal U.S. brands include Hershey's, Reese's, Peter Paul and Ludens. Canadian operations include these brands plus Oh Henry, Life Savers and Planters. Hershey Pasta Group produces eight regional brands led by San Giorgio, Ronzoni and American Beauty. Hershey International Manufactures and exports chocolate and confectionery products. In August 1988, HSY acquired Cadbury Schweppes' U.S. confectionary business, Peter Paul/Cadbury. In February 1990, HSY acquired Ronzoni Foods Corp.

BUSINESS LINE ANALYSIS

(12/31/94)	Rev(%)	Inc($000)
Domestic	86.6	446,585
International	13.4	(78,090)
Total	100.0	368,495•

ANNUAL EARNINGS AND DIVIDENDS PER SHARE

	1994	1993	1992	1991	1990	1989	1988
Earnings Per Share	**2.12**	**3.31**	**2.69**	**2.43**	**2.39**	**1.90**	**[1] 1.60**
Dividends Per Share	**1.25**	**1.14**	**1.03**	**0.94**	**0.84**	**0.74**	**0.66**
Dividend Payout %	**59.0**	**34.4**	**38.3**	**38.7**	**35.1**	**38.9**	**39.8**

[1] Before disc. oper.

ANNUAL FINANCIAL DATA

	1994	1993	1992	1991	1990	1989	1988
RECORD OF EARNINGS (IN MILLIONS):							
Total Revenues	3,606.3	3,488.2	3,219.8	2,899.2	2,715.6	2,421.0	2,168.0
Costs and Expenses	3,108.7	2,837.3	2,694.5	2,423.5	2,255.6	2,044.9	1,850.1
Depreciation & Amort	129.0	113.1	97.1	85.4	73.9	65.7	51.9
Income Before Interest	368.5	537.9	428.2	390.3	386.1	310.3	266.1
Income Bef Income Taxes	333.1	510.9	401.0	363.5	361.5	289.9	236.1
Income Taxes	148.9	213.6	158.4	143.9	145.6	118.9	91.6
Net Income	184.2	[1] 297.2	242.6	219.5	215.9	171.1	[2] 144.5
Aver. Shs. Outstg. (000)	87,019	89,757	90,186	90,186	90,186	90,186	90,186
[1] Before acctg. change dr$103,908,000. [2] Before disc. op. cr$69,443,000.							
BALANCE SHEET (IN MILLIONS):							
Cash and Cash Equivalents	26.7	16.0	203.2	71.1	26.6	52.5	70.1
Receivables, Net	437.6	380.5	220.1	159.8	143.0	121.9	166.8
Inventories	445.7	453.4	457.2	436.9	379.1	309.8	308.8
Gross Property	2,123.5	2,041.8	1,797.4	1,581.3	1,323.6	1,150.3	1,018.9
Accumulated Depreciation	655.1	580.9	501.4	435.6	371.5	320.4	282.9
Long-Term Debt	92.0	165.8	174.3	282.9	273.4	216.1	233.0
Net Stockholders' Equity	1,517.7	1,495.4	1,554.7	1,431.1	1,243.5	1,117.1	1,005.9
Total Assets	2,891.0	2,855.1	2,672.9	2,341.8	2,078.8	1,814.1	1,764.7
Total Current Assets	948.7	889.0	940.0	744.5	661.8	567.6	619.1
Total Current Liabilities	796.2	813.8	736.9	470.7	341.2	285.7	345.4
Net Working Capital	152.4	75.2	203.0	273.7	320.6	281.8	273.7
Year End Shs Outstg (000)	86,735	87,613	90,186	90,186	90,186	90,186	90,186
STATISTICAL RECORD:							
Operating Profit Margin %	10.2	15.4	13.3	13.5	14.2	12.8	12.3
Book Value Per Share	12.27	11.66	12.81	11.19	9.16	8.25	7.04
Return on Equity %	12.1	19.9	15.6	15.3	17.4	15.3	14.4
Return on Assets %	6.4	10.4	9.1	9.4	10.4	9.4	8.2
Average Yield %	2.6	2.3	2.4	2.4	2.5	2.4	2.6
P/E Ratio	25.2-19.4	16.9-13.1	18.0-14.2	18.3-14.5	16.6-11.8	19.4-13.0	17.9-13.7
Price Range	53½-41⅛	55⅞-43½	48⅜-38¼	44½-35⅛	39⅝-28¼	36⅞-24¾	28⅝-21⅞

Statistics are as originally reported.

OFFICERS:
K.L. Wolfe, Chmn. & C.E.O.
J.P. Viviano, Pres. & C.O.O.
W.F. Christ, Sr. V.P. & C.F.O.
T.C. Fitzgerald, V.P. & Treas.

INCORPORATED: DE, Oct., 1927

PRINCIPAL OFFICE: 100 Crystal A Drive, Hershey, PA 17033

TELEPHONE NUMBER: (717) 534-4001
FAX: (717) 534-6724
NO. OF EMPLOYEES: 14,000 full-time (approx.); 1,600 part-time (approx.)
ANNUAL MEETING: In April
SHAREHOLDERS: 34,327
INSTITUTIONAL HOLDINGS:
No. of Institutions: 421
Shares Held: 25,064,705

REGISTRAR(S): Chemical Bank, New York, NY

TRANSFER AGENT(S): Chemical Bank, New York, NY

NYS SYMBOL HB
Rec. Pr. 29¾

HILLENBRAND INDUSTRIES, INC.

YIELD 2.0%
P/E RATIO 23.6

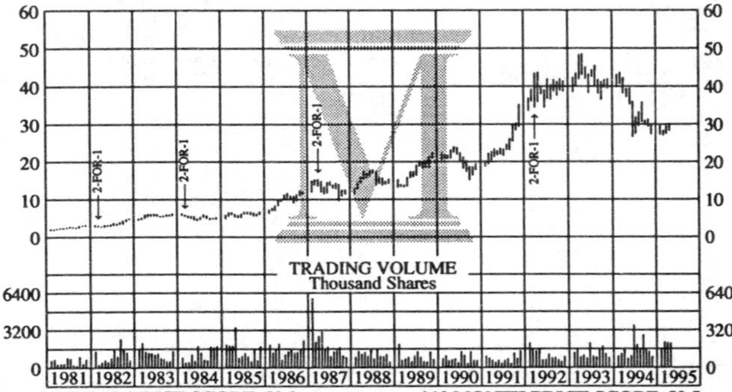
2-FOR-1
2-FOR-1
2-FOR-1
2-FOR-1
TRADING VOLUME
Thousand Shares
1981 1982 1983 1984 1985 1986 1987 1988 1989 1990 1991 1992 1993 1994 1995

*7 YEAR PRICE SCORE 89.9 *12 MONTH PRICE SCORE 89.5

*NYSE COMPOSITE INDEX=100

INTERIM EARNINGS (Per Share):

Qtr.	Feb.	May	Aug.	Nov.
1991-92	0.37	0.41	0.35	0.34
1992-93	0.47	0.52	0.41	0.47
1993-94	0.53	0.46	d0.30	0.57

INTERIM DIVIDENDS (Per Share):

Amt.	Decl.	Ex.	Rec.	Pay.
0.1425Q	4/5/94	4/18/94	4/22/94	5/27/94
0.1425Q	7/5	7/18	7/22	8/26
0.1425Q	10/4	10/17	10/21	11/25
0.15Q	1/25/95	2/6/95	2/10/95	2/24/95
0.15Q	4/11	4/17	4/21	5/26

Indicated div.:$0.60

CAPITALIZATION (12/3/94):

	($000)	(%)
Long-Term Debt	208,729	22.7
Deferred Income Tax	19,470	2.1
Common & Surplus	693,491	75.2
Total	921,690	100.0

DIVIDEND ACHIEVER STATUS:
Rank: 41 1984-94 Growth Rate: 16.2%
Total Years of Dividend Growth: 24

RECENT DEVELOPMENTS: For the year ended 12/3/94, income from continuing operations declined 32.5% to $89.5 million from $221.5 million the year before. The decline in earnings resulted from a third quarter settlement of a patent infringement suit that resulted in an unusual charge of $84.8 million pre-tax. Net revenues were $1.58 billion, up 8.9% from $1.45 billion a year earlier. The funeral services segment reported revenues of $652.9 million and operating profit of $122.9 million.

PROSPECTS: Most of the Company's businesses are delivering impressive results. Batesville Casket's expanded product line, improved operating efficiences and cost controls are yielding stronger earnings. Increases in revenues at Forethought, Inc. are resulting from increased insurance in force and investment income. Strong sales in the health care business are expected to continue.

BUSINESS

HILLENBRAND INDUSTRIES, INC. is the parent company of six wholly owned and separately managed operating companies. The companies are organized into Industrial and Insurance groups and serve four diversified market segments. The Industrial Group consists of: Hill-Rom Co., Inc., the leading producer of electric hospital beds, patient room furniture and handling equipment. SSI Medical Services Inc., provides rental therapy units. BLOCK Medical Inc., is a provider of home infusion therapy products. Medeco Security Locks, Inc., is a producer of high-security mechanical locks, and Batesville Casket Co., is the leading producer of burial caskets. Forecorp, Inc., the insurance company, provides pre-need funeral planning services.

QUARTERLY DATA

(12/03/94) ($000)	Rev	Inc
1st Quarter	377,406	37,691
2nd Quarter	382,705	32,758
3rd Quarter	377,815	(21,540)
4th Quarter	439,108	40,553
TOTAL	1,577,034	89,462

ANNUAL EARNINGS AND DIVIDENDS PER SHARE

	12/3/94	11/27/93	11/30/92	11/30/91	12/1/90	12/2/89	12/3/88
Earnings Per Share	**1.26**	**1.86**	**1.47**	**1.22**	**1.03**	**1.01**	**0.93**
Dividends Per Share	**0.57**	**0.45**	**0.35**	**0.29**	**0.275**	**0.25**	**0.20**
Dividend Payout %	**45.2**	**24.2**	**23.8**	**23.7**	**10.7**	**24.8**	**21.5**

ANNUAL FINANCIAL DATA

RECORD OF EARNINGS (IN MILLIONS):							
Total Revenues	1,577.0	1,447.9	1,429.8	1,198.9	1,106.6	1,138.3	884.3
Costs and Expenses	1,235.7	1,100.9	1,125.1	946.1	875.1	916.9	680.0
Depreciation & Amort	97.5	112.7	115.3	95.0	94.0	81.0	68.8
Operating Profit	159.0	234.3	189.4	157.8	137.4	140.5	135.4
Inc Fr Cont Opers Bef Income Taxes	144.8	221.5	171.3	145.7	126.3	127.3	120.4
Income Taxes	55.3	89.1	65.8	56.5	50.7	52.3	50.7
Net Income	89.5	[1] 132.5	[2] 105.5	89.2	75.7	75.0	69.7
Aver. Shs. Outstg. (000)	71,278	71,407	71,915	72,885	73,971	74,376	75,116

[1] Before disc. op. cr$13,332,000. [2] Before acctg. change cr$10,747,000.

BALANCE SHEET (IN MILLIONS):							
Cash and Cash Equivalents	120.4	210.2	150.0	54.9	86.8	49.0	28.2
Receivables, Net	299.6	253.8	248.9	198.0	185.8	181.8	185.1
Inventories	104.2	90.9	111.6	111.1	109.6	103.6	84.8
Gross Property	836.2	787.2	784.1	703.4	660.3	612.4	525.1
Accumulated Depreciation	477.6	460.4	477.0	406.0	346.8	274.1	213.9
Long-Term Debt	208.7	107.9	185.1	103.6	108.1	113.4	117.9
Net Stockholders' Equity	693.5	639.9	547.7	490.8	436.5	405.1	353.3
Total Assets	2,693.8	2,270.7	1,935.2	1,532.2	1,267.7	1,009.8	734.7
Total Current Assets	546.1	574.0	533.4	383.5	400.1	342.3	306.0
Total Current Liabilities	238.9	290.0	254.4	226.8	183.9	150.2	154.1
Net Working Capital	307.3	284.0	279.0	156.6	216.2	192.1	151.9
Year End Shs Outstg (000)	80,324	71,263	71,580	72,659	73,221	74,226	74,592
STATISTICAL RECORD:							
Operating Profit Margin %	10.1	16.2	13.2	13.2	12.4	12.3	15.3
Book Value Per Share	6.29	7.04	5.37	4.26	4.59	4.14	3.58
Return on Equity %	12.9	20.7	19.3	18.2	17.3	18.5	19.7
Return on Assets %	3.3	5.8	5.5	5.8	6.0	7.4	9.5
Average Yield %	1.6	1.1	0.9	1.1	1.4	1.4	1.4
P/E Ratio	34.6-21.1	26.1-19.6	29.7-22.8	28.9-15.4	23.5-14.8	22.4-13.1	19.2-12.2
Price Range	43⅝-26⅝	48⅝-36½	43⅝-33½	35¼-18¾	24-15⅛	22⅝-13¼	17⅞-11⅜

Statistics are as originally reported.

OFFICERS:
D.A. Hillenbrand, Chmn.
W. Hillenbrand, Pres. & C.E.O.
T.E. Brewer, Sr. V.P., C.F.O. & Treas.
M.R. Lindenmeyer, V.P., Gen. Coun. & Sec.

INCORPORATED: IN, Aug., 1969

PRINCIPAL OFFICE: 1069 State Route 46e, Batesville, IN 47006-9166

TELEPHONE NUMBER: (812) 934-7000

NO. OF EMPLOYEES: 10,000 (approx.)

ANNUAL MEETING: In April

SHAREHOLDERS: 29,000 (approx.)

INSTITUTIONAL HOLDINGS:
No. of Institutions: 185
Shares Held: 24,576,959

REGISTRAR(S): Harris Trust & Savings Bank, Chicago, IL

TRANSFER AGENT(S): Harris Trust & Savings Bank, Chicago, IL

HOME BENEFICIAL CORP.

YIELD 4.1%
P/E RATIO 10.0

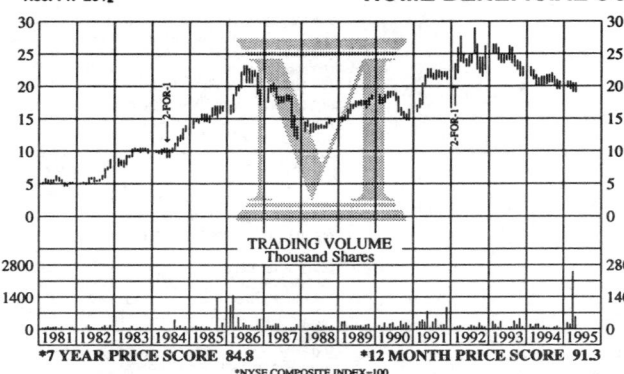

30
25
20
15
10
5
0
2-FOR-1
2-FOR-1
TRADING VOLUME
Thousand Shares
2800
1400
0
1981|1982|1983|1984|1985|1986|1987|1988|1989|1990|1991|1992|1993|1994|1995
*7 YEAR PRICE SCORE 84.8   *12 MONTH PRICE SCORE 91.3
*NYSE COMPOSITE INDEX=100

INTERIM EARNINGS (Per Share):

Qtr.	Mar.	June	Sept.	Dec.
1992	0.58	0.64	0.63	0.65
1993	0.61	0.66	0.52	0.56
1994	0.52	0.48	0.51	0.53
1995	0.54	...	...	...

INTERIM DIVIDENDS (Per Share):

Amt.	Decl.	Ex.	Rec.	Pay.
0.20Q	4/19/94	5/16/94	5/20/94	6/10/94
0.20Q	7/19	8/15	8/19	9/9
0.20Q	10/18	11/14	11/18	12/9
0.20Q	1/17/95	2/13/95	2/20/95	3/10/95
0.21Q	5/19	5/15	5/19	6/9

Indicated div.: *$0.84*

CAPITALIZATION (12/31/94):

	($000)	(%)
Common & Surplus	466,770	100.0
Total	466,770	100.0

DIVIDEND ACHIEVER STATUS:
Rank: 238   1984-94 Growth Rate: 7.2%
Total Years of Dividend Growth: 31

RECENT DEVELOPMENTS: For the year ended 12/31/94, net income was $36.2 million, or $2.04 per share, compared with $42.6 million, or $2.35 per share, a year earlier. The decline in net income was due to realized investment gains in the Company's securities portfolio during 1993. Total revenues decreased 5.8% to $200.9 million. Premiums declined slightly to $116.1 million from $116.4 million the year before. Net investment income declined 12.4% to $84.9 million from $96.9 million a year earlier. Total assets of $1.29 billion, along with total investments under management, reached an all-time high. At 12/31/94, net life insurance in force increased 2.4% to $10.22 billion. At 12/31/94, approximately 76% of the Company's mortgages were on residential or commercial properties located in Virginia.

BUSINESS

HOME BENEFICIAL CORPORATION is a holding company located in the state of Virginia with one principal operating subsidiary, Home Beneficial Life Insurance Company (the Life Company), which is engaged in the life and accident and health insurance business. The Life Company sells group life insurance and substantially all the forms of ordinary insurance, including universal life, whole life, term and annuities, together with accidental death and disability riders. In addition, the Life Company participates in several group life insurance programs as a reinsurer and also assumes reinsurance on a facultative (individual risk) basis from two other life insurance companies. The Life Company's business is concentrated in six Mid-Atlantic states and the District of Columbia and its policies are marketed through its own sales force of approximately 1,150 full time personnel.

REVENUES

(12/31/94)	($000)	(%)
Premiums	116,071	57.8
Net Investment	84,859	42.2
Total	200,930	100.0

ANNUAL EARNINGS AND DIVIDENDS PER SHARE

	1994	1993	1992	1991	1990	1989	1988
Earnings Per Share	2.04	2.35	①2.50	2.51	①3.29	2.13	1.98
Dividends Per Share	0.795	0.775	②0.76	0.69	0.645	0.59	0.555
Dividend Payout %	39.0	33.0	30.4	27.5	19.6	27.8	28.1

① Before acctg. chg. ② 2-for-1 stk split, 1/3/92

ANNUAL FINANCIAL DATA

RECORD OF EARNINGS (IN MILLIONS):

	1994	1993	1992	1991	1990	1989	1988
Insurance Premiums	116.1	116.4	117.9	103.5	102.2	99.6	103.9
Total Interest Income	84.9	96.9	93.6	93.9	136.8	87.9	83.9
Total Revenues	200.9	213.2	211.5	197.4	239.1	187.4	187.8
Benefits & Claims	91.1	94.6	88.4	76.1	77.7	75.4	78.7
Income Taxes	19.4	21.3	22.3	23.5	45.6	21.9	19.5
Net Income	36.2	42.6	①46.5	47.4	66.6	44.3	42.5
Aver. Shs. Outstg. (000)	17,757	18,126	18,600	18,869	20,274	20,838	21,520

① Before acctg. change dr$29,444,884. ② Equal to d$29,000.

BALANCE SHEET (IN MILLIONS):

Cash	1.7	6.0	3.3	2.6	1.3	2.3	1.7
Fixed Maturities	692.0	705.7	561.7	459.9	428.5	420.4	414.7
Equity Securities, At Mkt	24.2	27.3	28.6	28.4	23.3	25.9	23.3
Policy Loans	53.4	52.7	52.1	50.8	48.1	46.5	45.5
Mtge Loans on Real Estate	338.5	316.4	382.5	489.3	518.4	494.9	423.5
Total Assets	1,288.8	1,280.2	1,248.4	1,205.3	1,159.8	1,110.8	1,069.4
Benefits and Claims	762.6	747.3	727.2	712.9	696.7	679.3	641.5
Net Stockholders' Equity	466.8	473.3	460.4	456.9	430.1	403.4	396.8
Year End Shs Outstg (000)	17,564	17,939	18,527	18,716	19,103	20,693	21,486

STATISTICAL RECORD:

Book Value Per Share	26.58	26.38	24.85	24.41	22.52	19.49	18.47
Return on Equity %	7.8	9.0	10.1	10.4	15.5	11.0	10.7
Return on Assets %	2.8	3.3	3.7	3.9	5.7	4.0	4.0
Average Yield %	3.7	3.2	3.0	3.6	3.8	3.5	4.0
P/E Ratio	11.3-9.6	11.3-9.1	11.6-8.4	9.1-6.4	5.9-4.5	8.8-6.8	7.6-6.5
Price Range	23-19½	26½-21½	29-21	22¾-16	19¼-14¾	18¾-14½	15-12¾

Statistics are as originally reported.

OFFICERS:
R.W. Wiltshire, Sr., Chmn.
R.W. Wiltshire, Jr., Pres. & C.E.O.
J.M. Wiltshire, Jr., V.P., Sec. & Couns.
W.V. Collins, V.P. & Sec.
D.M. Westerhouse, Jr., Treas.

INCORPORATED: VA, Mar., 1970

PRINCIPAL OFFICE: 3901 West Broad Street
P.O. Box 27572, Richmond, VA 23261

TELEPHONE NUMBER: (804) 358-8431

NO. OF EMPLOYEES: 1,150 (approx.)

ANNUAL MEETING: In April

SHAREHOLDERS: 2,000 (approx.)

INSTITUTIONAL HOLDINGS:
No. of Institutions: 58
Shares Held: 6,045,176

REGISTRAR(S): Jefferson National Bank, Charlottesville, VA 23241

TRANSFER AGENT(S):

NYS SYMBOL HON
Rec. Pr. 38¾

HONEYWELL, INC.

YIELD 2.6%
P/E RATIO 21.6

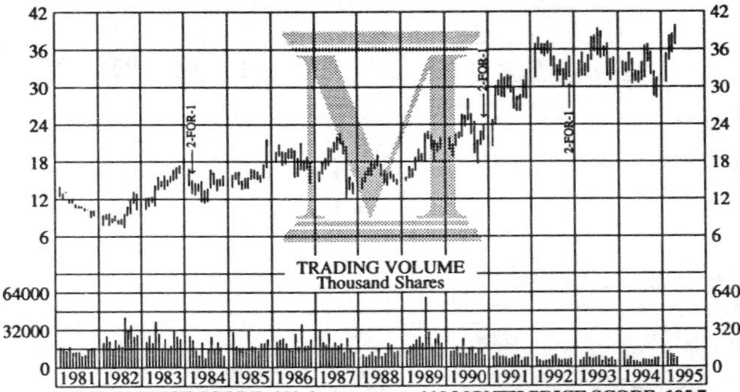

*7 YEAR PRICE SCORE 100.6 *12 MONTH PRICE SCORE 105.7

*NYSE COMPOSITE INDEX=100

INTERIM EARNINGS (Per Share):

Qtr.	Mar.	June	Sept.	Dec.
1991	0.50	0.55	0.56	0.73
1992	0.82	0.58	1.25	0.23
1993	0.42	0.53	0.60	0.85

INTERIM DIVIDENDS (Per Share):

Amt.	Decl.	Ex.	Rec.	Pay.
0.24Q	4/19/94	5/23/94	5/27/94	6/13/94
0.24Q	7/19	8/22	8/26	9/12
0.25Q	11/14	11/18	11/25	12/12
0.25Q	2/21/95	2/27/95	3/3/95	3/20/95
0.25Q	4/18	5/22	5/26	6/12

*Indicated div.: $1.00**

CAPITALIZATION (12/31/94):

	($000)	(%)
Long-Term Debt	501,500	20.9
Deferred Income Tax	39,800	1.7
Common & Surplus	1,854,700	77.4
Total	2,396,000	100.0

DIVIDEND ACHIEVER STATUS:
Rank: 234 1984-94 Growth Rate: 7.4%
Total Years of Dividend Growth: 19

RECENT DEVELOPMENTS: For the year ended 12/31/94, net income was $278.9 million, down 13% from $322.2 million in the previous year. Sales advanced to $6.06 billion from $5.96 billion in the prior year. Operating profit, excluding special charges, in the home and building control and the industrial control divisions increased by 9.3% and 11.2%, respectively. However, the gains could not offset the disappointing performance of the space and aviation division which saw operating profits fall by 35% from the prior year.

PROSPECTS: Further interest rate increases should not affect the Industrial unit sales as manufacturers seek to improve efficiency and should increase new plant orders to the division. Despite the soft aviation market, HON has been awarded a contract by Tupolev, an aircraft designer in the Commonwealth of Independent States, to develop avionics for commercial aircraft. The Tupolev contract follows HON's contract to develop cockpit display systems for Boeing's 737-700 jet.

BUSINESS

HONEYWELL, INC. is engaged in the design, development, manufacture, marketing and service of systems and products in three industry segments. Home and Buildings include automation, energy management, environmental controls and fire and security systems for commercial and residential systems. Industrial provides customers with products and digital systems for industrial process and manufacturing automation. Space and Aviation provides controls and guidance systems for commercial and military aircraft, space and satellite applications.

BUSINESS LINE ANALYSIS

(12/31/94)	Rev(%)	Inc(%)
United States	63.8	65.6
Europe	24.4	26.5
Other areas	11.8	7.9
Total	100.0	100.0

ANNUAL EARNINGS AND DIVIDENDS PER SHARE

	1994	1993	1992	1991	1990	1989	1988
Earnings Per Share	2.15	2.40	[1] [2] 2.88	2.35	[4] 2.45	[4] 3.23	d5.11
Dividends Per Share	0.97	0.907	[3] 0.841	0.769	[5] 0.703	0.566	0.525
Dividend Payout %	45.1	37.9	29.2	32.7	28.7	17.5	...

[1] Before extraord. item & acctg. chg. [2] Before acctg. chg. [3] 2-for-1 stk split,12/21/92 [4] Before disc. oper. [5] 2-for-1 stk split,12/26/90

ANNUAL FINANCIAL DATA

	1994	1993	1992	1991	1990	1989	1988
RECORD OF EARNINGS (IN MILLIONS):							
Total Revenues	6,057.0	5,963.0	6,222.6	6,192.9	6,309.1	6,058.6	7,148.3
Costs and Expenses	5,287.5	5,147.8	5,412.0	5,350.7	5,475.3	5,417.7	6,741.9
Depreciation & Amort	287.4	284.9	292.7	286.0	283.0	247.8	283.1
Operating Profit	801.1	867.7	830.5	856.9	830.4	758.2	446.7
Income Bef Income Taxes	369.7	478.5	634.7	509.4	516.4	675.9	d200.9
Income Taxes	90.8	156.3	234.8	178.3	144.6	125.6	234.0
Net Income	278.9	322.2	[1] 399.9	331.1	[2] 371.8	[3] 550.3	d434.9
Aver. Shs. Outstg. (000)	129,400	134,200	138,500	140,900	151,800	170,400	170,400

[1] Before extra. item dr$8,600,000. [2] Before disc. op. cr$10,100,000. [3] Before disc. op. cr$53,800,000.

	1994	1993	1992	1991	1990	1989	1988
BALANCE SHEET (IN MILLIONS):							
Cash and Cash Equivalents	274.8	256.1	346.2	508.2	367.9	254.1	180.4
Receivables, Net	1,614.4	1,534.0	1,534.0	1,286.4	1,242.0	1,475.0	1,448.7
Inventories	760.2	760.1	827.6	904.3	972.3	1,071.6	1,134.5
Gross Property	2,716.8	2,549.4	2,497.9	2,446.6	2,315.8	2,280.9	2,540.4
Accumulated Depreciation	1,617.3	1,487.4	1,384.4	1,300.4	1,165.5	1,092.0	1,181.7
Long-Term Debt	501.5	504.0	512.1	639.8	616.3	692.5	800.7
Net Stockholders' Equity	1,854.7	1,773.0	1,790.4	1,850.8	1,696.9	1,918.2	1,731.3
Total Assets	4,984.4	4,661.9	4,870.1	4,806.7	4,746.2	5,258.2	5,089.1
Total Current Assets	2,649.4	2,550.2	2,707.8	2,698.9	2,582.2	2,800.7	2,763.6
Total Current Liabilities	2,071.8	1,856.1	1,969.2	2,095.0	2,175.1	2,415.8	2,394.0
Net Working Capital	577.6	694.1	738.6	603.9	407.1	384.9	369.6
Year End Shs Outstg (000)	127,255	131,560	136,680	139,656	141,562	159,996	172,512
STATISTICAL RECORD:							
Operating Profit Margin %	8.0	8.9	8.3	9.0	8.7	6.5	1.7
Book Value Per Share	10.13	9.76	9.04	9.44	7.90	8.23	6.58
Return on Equity %	15.0	18.2	22.3	17.9	21.9	28.7	...
Return on Assets %	5.6	6.9	8.2	6.9	7.8	10.5	...
Average Yield %	3.0	2.6	2.5	2.9	3.1	3.0	3.2
P/E Ratio	17.2-13.1	16.4-12.9	13.2-10.5	13.9-8.7	11.5-7.2	7.1-4.6	...
Price Range	36⅞-28¼	39⅜-31	38-30¼	32¾-20½	28⅛-17⅝	23-14⅞	19⅛-13⅝

Statistics are as originally reported.

OFFICERS:
M.R. Bonsignore, Chmn. & C.E.O.
D.L. Moore, Pres. & C.O.O.
W.L. Trubeck, Sr. V.P. & C.F.O.

INCORPORATED: DE, Oct., 1927

PRINCIPAL OFFICE: Honeywell Plaza, Minneapolis, MN 55408-1792

TELEPHONE NUMBER: (612) 951-1000
FAX: (612) 870-3875
NO. OF EMPLOYEES: 50,800 (approx.)
ANNUAL MEETING: In April
SHAREHOLDERS: 32,025
INSTITUTIONAL HOLDINGS:
No. of Institutions: 484
Shares Held: 89,086,537

REGISTRAR(S): Chemical Bank, New York, NY

TRANSFER AGENT(S): Chemical Bank, New York, NY

HORMEL FOODS CORP.

YIELD	2.2%
P/E RATIO	15.1

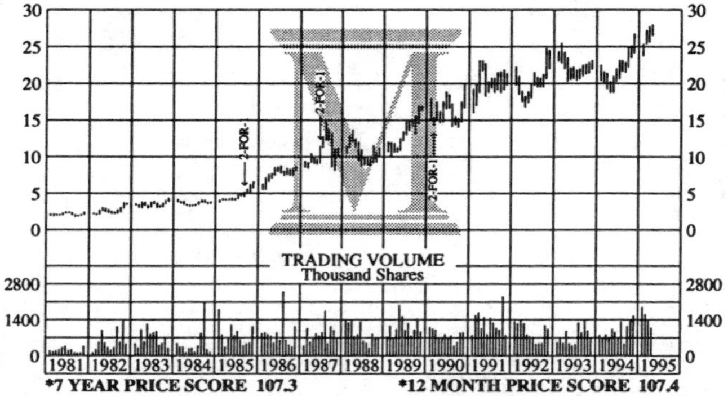

TRADING VOLUME
Thousand Shares

| 1981 | 1982 | 1983 | 1984 | 1985 | 1986 | 1987 | 1988 | 1989 | 1990 | 1991 | 1992 | 1993 | 1994 | 1995 |

*7 YEAR PRICE SCORE 107.3   *12 MONTH PRICE SCORE 107.4
*NYSE COMPOSITE INDEX=100

INTERIM EARNINGS (Per Share):

Qtr.	Jan.	Apr.	July	Oct.
1991-92	0.22	0.26	0.21	0.55
1992-93	0.25	0.28	0.25	0.57
1993-94	0.27	0.30	0.26	0.71
1994-95	0.46	...	...	...

INTERIM DIVIDENDS (Per Share):

Amt.	Decl.	Ex.	Rec.	Pay.
0.125Q	3/28/94	4/18/94	4/23/94	5/15/94
0.125Q	5/24	7/22	7/28	8/15
0.125Q	9/26	10/17	10/22	11/15
0.145Q	11/21	1/13/95	1/21/95	2/15/95
0.145Q	3/27/95	4/17	4/22	5/15

Indicated div.: $0.58*

CAPITALIZATION (10/29/94):

	($000)	(%)
Long-Term Debt	10,300	1.5
Common & Surplus	661,089	98.5
Total	671,389	100.0

DIVIDEND ACHIEVER STATUS:
Rank: 64   1984-94 Growth Rate: 14.4%
Total Years of Dividend Growth: 27

RECENT DEVELOPMENTS: For the quarter ended 1/28/95, net income was a record $35.5 million compared with $20.6 million a year ago. Net sales increased 2.0% to $730.7 million. During the quarter, the Company benefited from ample supplies of raw materials and a 6.7% increase in tonnage growth due to strong customer acceptance of newly introduced products. Results were also aided by increased sales of Cure 81 ham, Black Label bacon, Hormel microwave bacon, and Light & Lean 97 franks.

PROSPECTS: In the near term, pork prices are expected to rise to more normal levels, which will cause the Company's earnings growth to moderately decrease. However, HRL will continue to introduce new products and further extend current lines in an effort to offset the slower growth rate in earnings. Additionally, the Company is investing in new technology and equipment in its pork slaughtering and processing areas in order to boost operational efficiencies.

BUSINESS

HORMEL FOODS CORPORATION and its subsidiaries produce and market thousands of processed, packaged food products. The principal products of the Company are meat and meat products, hams, sausages, wieners, sliced bacon, luncheon meats, stews, chilies, hash and meat spreads. The products are sold fresh, frozen, cured, smoked, cooked or canned. The majority of products are sold under the Hormel name. Other tradenames include Spam, Wranglers, Light & Lean, Frank'N Stuff, Farm Fresh, Dinty Moore, Black Label, Top Shelf and Mary Kitchen, By George, Kids Kitchen and Old Smokehouse. Through two wholly-owned subsidiaries, the Company is a producer and marketer of whole and processed turkey products and grain-fed, farm-raised catfish.

QUARTERLY DATA
(10/30/94)($000)

	Rev	Inc
1st Quarter	716,169	(109,250)
2nd Quarter	767,018	20,661
3rd Quarter	741,144	18,168
4th Quarter	840,462	43,662

ANNUAL EARNINGS AND DIVIDENDS PER SHARE

	10/29/94	10/30/93	10/31/92	10/26/91	10/28/90	10/28/89	10/29/88
Earnings Per Share	1.54	1.31	1.24	1.13	1.01	0.91	0.79
Dividends Per Share	0.50	0.44	0.36	0.30	0.26	0.22	0.18
Dividend Payout %	32.5	33.6	29.0	26.5	25.7	24.2	22.9

ANNUAL FINANCIAL DATA

RECORD OF EARNINGS (IN MILLIONS):

Total Revenues	3,064.8	2,854.0	2,813.7	2,836.2	2,681.2	2,340.5	2,292.8
Costs and Expenses	2,841.1	2,666.5	2,628.2	2,666.2	2,525.6	2,193.8	2,158.5
Depreciation & Amort	36.6	32.2	39.0	36.3	35.6	36.9	35.5
Operating Income	187.1	155.3	146.5	133.7	120.0	109.8	98.8
Earn Bef Income Taxes	191.1	161.1	151.1	137.9	121.4	110.8	95.4
Income Taxes	73.1	60.4	55.9	51.5	44.2	40.7	35.2
Net Income	118.0	① 100.8	95.2	86.4	77.1	70.1	60.2

① Before acctg. change dr$127,529,000.

BALANCE SHEET (IN MILLIONS):

Cash and Cash Equivalents	260.0	172.4	225.5	172.1	102.4	78.3	68.9
Receivables, Net	242.6	230.9	189.8	192.5	194.4	169.5	158.6
Inventories	199.2	208.1	185.9	176.4	184.3	165.0	143.0
Gross Property	637.2	585.3	543.9	533.8	514.0	511.9	512.9
Accumulated Depreciation	366.3	340.3	327.5	302.0	278.9	267.5	249.9
Long-Term Debt	10.3	5.7	7.6	22.8	24.5	19.2	20.4
Net Stockholders' Equity	661.1	570.9	644.3	583.4	513.8	470.9	418.7
Total Assets	1,196.7	1,093.6	913.0	856.8	799.4	727.4	706.5
Total Current Assets	708.2	619.9	609.1	546.4	486.9	417.0	376.0
Total Current Liabilities	264.9	227.1	207.9	200.3	193.1	188.0	219.5
Net Working Capital	443.3	392.8	401.2	346.2	293.8	229.0	156.5
Year End Shs Outstg (000)	76,852	76,672	76,627	76,641	76,664	76,652	76,652

STATISTICAL RECORD:

Operating Profit Margin %	6.1	5.4	5.2	4.7	4.5	4.7	4.3
Book Value Per Share	7.57	6.50	7.88	7.02	6.08	5.57	4.87
Return on Equity %	17.8	17.7	14.8	14.8	15.0	14.9	14.4
Return on Assets %	9.9	9.2	10.4	10.1	9.6	9.6	8.5
Average Yield %	2.2	1.9	1.7	1.5	...	1.6	1.6
P/E Ratio	17.4-12.2	19.5-15.5	20.0-13.5	20.5-14.2	19.6-13.9	18.7-11.1	17.6-11.2
Price Range	26¾-18¾	25½-20¼	24¾-16¾	23⅛-16	19¾-14	17-10⅛	13¾-8¾

Statistics are as originally reported.

OFFICERS:
R.L. Knowlton, Chmn.
J.W. Johnson, Pres. & C.E.O.
D.J. Hodapp, Exec. V.P. & C.F.O.

INCORPORATED: DE, Sep., 1928

PRINCIPAL OFFICE: 1 Hormel Place, Austin, MN 55912-3680

TELEPHONE NUMBER: (507) 437-5611
NO. OF EMPLOYEES: 9,500 (approx.)
ANNUAL MEETING: In January
SHAREHOLDERS: 7,186 (approx.)
INSTITUTIONAL HOLDINGS:
No. of Institutions: 126
Shares Held: 18,611,949

REGISTRAR(S): Norwest Bank Minnesota, N.A., South St. Paul, MN

TRANSFER AGENT(S): Norwest Bank Minnesota, N.A., South St. Paul, MN

NYS SYMBOL HTN
Rec. Pr. 49⅛

HOUGHTON MIFFLIN CO.

YIELD 1.8%
P/E RATIO 12.9

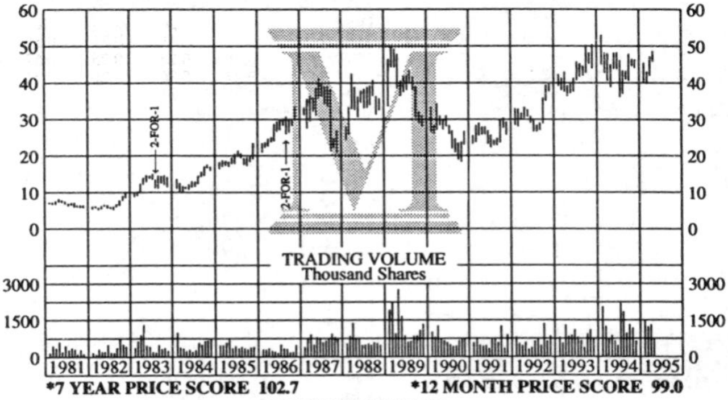

*7 YEAR PRICE SCORE 102.7 *12 MONTH PRICE SCORE 99.0

*NYSE COMPOSITE INDEX=100

INTERIM EARNINGS (Per Share):

Qtr.	Mar.	June	Sept.	Dec.
1991	d1.09	0.87	2.36	d0.39
1992	d0.98	0.82	2.46	d0.92
1993	d1.08	0.32	3.00	0.02
1994	0.23	0.63	3.45	d0.51

INTERIM DIVIDENDS (Per Share):

Amt.	Decl.	Ex.	Rec.	Pay.
0.215Q	4/27/94	5/5/94	5/11/94	5/25/94
0.215Q	7/27	8/4	8/10	8/24
0.225Q	10/26	11/3	11/9	11/23
0.225Q	1/25/95	2/2/95	2/8/95	2/22/95
0.225Q	4/26	5/4	5/10	5/24

*Indicated div.: $0.90**

CAPITALIZATION (12/31/94):

	($000)	(%)
Long-Term Debt	99,445	28.9
Common & Surplus	244,473	71.1
Total	343,918	100.0

DIVIDEND ACHIEVER STATUS:
Rank: 243 1984-94 Growth Rate: 6.8%
Total Years of Dividend Growth: 12

RECENT DEVELOPMENTS: For the year ended 12/31/94, income before an extraordinary item was $52.4 million compared with $31.4 million in the corresponding period of 1993. The 1994 results include a gain of $1.65 per share, relating to the first-quarter 1994 spin-off of the Company's Software Division, and special charges of $0.29 per share from the completion of restructuring efforts begun in 1991. Meanwhile, sales rose 4% to $483.1 million from $463.0 million the year before.

PROSPECTS: Operating results are expected to benefit from several large-state, including California, elementary and secondary textbook adoptions, in which states make bulk-purchases for entire school systems. In addition, earnings will be enhanced by cost-reduction efforts and productivity gains. However, profits will be partially offset by increased interest expenses. The higher interest expenses are anticipated as a result of sharp increases in long-term debt and rising interest rates.

BUSINESS

HOUGHTON MIFFLIN CO. has four principal subsidiaries: The Riverside Publishing Co., a publisher of educational materials; Houghton Mifflin Canada Limited, a purveyor of educational materials; and Ticknor & Fields, Inc., a trade book imprint. HMR, Inc. manages the Company's investment in real estate, marketable securities, and other short-term cash equivalent investments. HTN's principal business is publishing and its operations are classified into two industry segments: textbooks and other educational materials and services for the school and college markets; and general publishing, including fiction, nonfiction, children's books, dictionary and reference materials. In 1992, HTN acquired the test-publishing assets of the Assessment Division of DLM, Inc.

BUSINESS LINE ANALYSIS

(12/31/94)	Rev(%)	Inc(%)
Textbooks & Other	80.2	90.2
General Publishing	19.8	9.8
Total	100.0	100.0

ANNUAL EARNINGS AND DIVIDENDS PER SHARE

	1994	1993	1992	1991	1990	1989	1988
Earnings Per Share	3.79	2.27	[1] 1.35	1.75	1.27	1.62	1.70
Dividends Per Share	0.87	0.83	[2] 0.79	0.75	0.71	0.67	0.63
Dividend Payout %	23.0	36.6	58.5	42.9	55.9	41.4	37.1

[1] Before acctg. chg. [2] Bef acctg chge

ANNUAL FINANCIAL DATA

	1994	1993	1992	1991	1990	1989	1988
RECORD OF EARNINGS (IN THOUSANDS):							
Total Revenues	483,076	462,969	454,706	466,801	421,600	404,359	368,289
Costs and Expenses	[1] 429,612	372,238	368,116	383,230	353,125	331,810	295,479
Depreciation & Amort	...	39,361	42,280	39,419	34,227	32,546	32,163
Operating Income	53,464	51,370	44,310	44,152	34,248	40,003	40,647
Inc Bef Taxes on Income	85,140	49,023	28,444	40,446	31,257	37,007	38,872
Income Taxes	32,710	17,650	9,373	15,369	13,222	13,997	14,771
Net Income	51,191	30,371	4,414	25,077	18,035	23,010	24,101
Aver. Shs. Outstg.	13,822	13,823	14,029	14,314	14,255	14,214	14,160
[1] Incl. Dep.							
BALANCE SHEET (IN THOUSANDS):							
Cash and Cash Equivalents	47,193	85,349	68,635	92,804	77,434	37,335	22,622
Receivables, Net	139,097	104,489	86,867	90,972	83,633	87,247	75,277
Inventories	61,661	64,001	61,547	67,781	74,234	70,682	65,565
Gross Property	116,809	103,161	114,663	113,637	150,985	143,497	91,271
Accumulated Depreciation	47,921	36,991	40,619	36,451	74,005	70,298	25,959
Long-Term Debt	99,445	26,438	52,608	52,975	52,985	28,973	2,262
Net Stockholders' Equity	244,473	224,082	199,839	223,181	209,504	199,850	185,233
Total Assets	497,266	398,221	371,421	381,780	366,496	321,176	261,967
Total Current Assets	250,101	267,849	233,771	268,362	250,903	210,316	175,600
Total Current Liabilities	104,710	111,270	83,934	92,083	92,617	81,880	66,681
Net Working Capital	145,391	156,579	149,837	176,279	158,286	128,436	108,919
Year End Shares Outstg	14,430	14,526	14,411	14,281	14,259	14,235	14,177
STATISTICAL RECORD:							
Operating Profit Margin %	11.1	11.1	9.7	9.5	8.1	9.9	11.0
Book Value Per Share	8.32	14.07	12.34	14.91	13.90	12.82	12.65
Return on Equity %	21.4	14.0	9.5	11.2	8.6	11.5	13.0
Return on Assets %	10.5	7.9	5.1	6.6	4.9	7.2	9.2
Average Yield %	2.0	1.9	2.4	2.9	2.7	1.7	1.9
P/E Ratio	14.0-9.5	22.2-16.0	29.5-19.7	17.4-12.7	27.1-14.5	31.0-17.4	25.0-14.3
Price Range	53-36⅛	50⅜-36⅜	39⅞-26⅝	30⅜-22¼	34⅜-18⅜	50¼-28⅛	42½-24⅜

Statistics are as originally reported.

OFFICERS:
N.F. Darehshori, Chmn., Pres. & C.E.O.
S.O. Jaeger, Exec. V.P., C.F.O. & Treas.
P.D. Weaver, Sr. V.P., Clerk, Sec. & Gen. Coun.

INCORPORATED: MA, May, 1908

PRINCIPAL OFFICE: 222 Berkeley Street, Boston, MA 02116-3764

TELEPHONE NUMBER: (617) 351-5000
FAX: (617) 573-4914
NO. OF EMPLOYEES: 2,023 (approx.)
ANNUAL MEETING: In April
SHAREHOLDERS: 4,512 (approx.)
INSTITUTIONAL HOLDINGS:
No. of Institutions: 202
Shares Held: 10,551,618

REGISTRAR(S): Bank of Boston, Boston, MA

TRANSFER AGENT(S): Bank of Boston, Boston, MA

NYS SYMBOL HI
Rec. Pr. 46⅝

HOUSEHOLD INTERNATIONAL, INC.

YIELD 2.7%
P/E RATIO 13.2

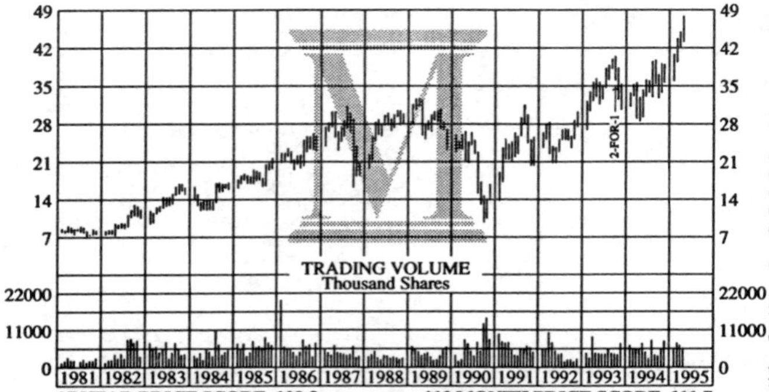

*7 YEAR PRICE SCORE 109.3 *12 MONTH PRICE SCORE 111.7

*NYSE COMPOSITE INDEX=100

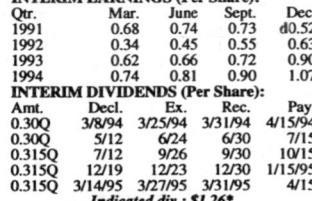

INTERIM EARNINGS (Per Share):

Qtr.	Mar.	June	Sept.	Dec.
1991	0.68	0.74	0.73	d0.52
1992	0.34	0.45	0.55	0.63
1993	0.62	0.66	0.72	0.90
1994	0.74	0.81	0.90	1.07

INTERIM DIVIDENDS (Per Share):

Amt.	Decl.	Ex.	Rec.	Pay.
0.30Q	3/8/94	3/25/94	3/31/94	4/15/94
0.30Q	5/12	6/24	6/30	7/15
0.315Q	7/12	9/26	9/30	10/15
0.315Q	12/19	12/23	12/30	1/15/95
0.315Q	3/14/95	3/27/95	3/31/95	4/15

*Indicated div.: $1.26**

CAPITALIZATION (12/31/94):

	($000)	(%)
Long-Term Debt	10,274,100	80.3
Preferred Stock..................	322,600	2.5
Common & Surplus	2,200,400	17.2
Total	12,797,100	100.0

DIVIDEND ACHIEVER STATUS:
Rank: 307 1984-94 Growth Rate: 3.6%
Total Years of Dividend Growth: 42

RECENT DEVELOPMENTS: For the year ended 12/31/94, net income totaled $367.6 million compared with $298.7 million a year earlier, an increase of 23.1%. The finance and banking segment earnings were $316.5 million, 24.8% higher than 1993 earnings of $253.5 million resulting from higher profits from the credit card businesses, domestic Household Finance Corp. and the United Kingdom. Net income for the individual life insurance segment was $51.1 million, a 13.0% increase over 1993.

PROSPECTS: The bank card portfolio continues to be the driving force behind earnings. The finance and banking unit continues to benefit from solid operations in the United Kingdom. The Company discontinued its domestic traditional first mortgage origination business, further integrated its Canadian business into its domestic operations and reduced staff, primarily in its consumer banking and related support operations. Improved productivity and higher credit card-related fee income bode well for future results.

BUSINESS

HOUSEHOLD INTERNATIONAL INC., with over 85% of its receivables in the U.S., is a major provider of consumer finance, banking services, consumer life insurance and investment products. Its subsidiaries include: Household Finance Corp., the nation's oldest and largest consumer finance company; Household Credit Services, the 5th-largest issuer of VISA and MasterCards; Household Retail Services, the second-largest private-label credit card issuer; Household Bank, f.s.b., the 12th-largest thrift and the 4th-largest mortgage servicer in the country; and Alexander Hamilton Life Insurance Co., which ranks in the top 3% of North American life insurance companies in terms of assets.

BUSINESS LINE ANALYSIS

(12/31/94)	Rev(%)	Inc(%)
Finance & Banking....	87.2	84.9
Individual Life Insurance	12.8	15.1
Total	100.0	100.0

ANNUAL EARNINGS AND DIVIDENDS PER SHARE

	1994	1993	1992	1991	1990	1989	1988
Earnings Per Share	3.52	2.91	1.97	1.58	(2) (3) 3.03	(2) 2.94	(2) 2.49
Dividends Per Share	1.22	(1) 1.17	1.138	1.108	1.08	1.07	1.017
Dividend Payout %	34.7	40.2	57.9	70.3	35.7	36.5	40.9

(1) 2-for-1 stk split,10/18/93 (2) Before disc. oper. (3) Primary shares

ANNUAL FINANCIAL DATA

	1994	1993	1992	1991	1990	1989	1988
RECORD OF EARNINGS (IN MILLIONS):							
Total Revenues	4,603.3	4,454.5	4,180.6	4,593.9	4,319.7	3,490.1	2,637.4
Costs and Expenses	4,075.0	4,003.8	3,902.6	5,585.9	3,971.0	3,157.1	2,345.1
Operating Profit	528.3	450.7	278.0	d992.0	348.7	333.0	292.3
Income Bef Income Taxes	528.3	450.7	278.0	199.8	348.7	333.0	292.3
Income Taxes	160.7	152.0	87.1	50.0	113.4	114.6	108.6
Net Income	367.6	298.7	190.9	149.8	235.3	(1) 218.4	(2) 183.7
Aver. Shs. Outstg. (000)	97,200	94,800	86,000	83,000	71,000	70,800	69,400
(1) Before disc. op. cr$21,100,000. (2) Before disc. op. cr$63,000,000.							
BALANCE SHEET (IN MILLIONS):							
Cash and Cash Equivalents	541.2	317.4	255.8	227.9	226.1	228.8	182.3
Receivables, Net	20,778.3	19,563.0	18,960.6	18,987.1	21,802.6	20,016.7	16,123.2
Gross Property	512.0	434.3	397.4	423.8	347.9	319.8	212.7
Long-Term Debt	10,274.1	9,113.8	9,014.4	9,594.5	9,561.3	7,915.9	6,560.3
Net Stockholders' Equity	2,523.0	2,417.6	1,881.6	1,829.3	1,612.9	1,343.7	1,251.0
Total Assets	34,338.4	32,961.5	31,128.4	29,982.3	29,454.7	26,162.7	21,032.4
Total Current Assets	21,319.5	19,880.4	19,216.4	19,215.0	22,028.7	20,245.5	16,305.5
Total Current Liabilities	12,811.1	13,158.2	13,283.6	12,112.0	12,618.8	11,926.6	9,592.7
Net Working Capital	8,508.4	6,722.2	5,932.8	7,103.0	9,409.9	8,318.9	6,712.8
Year End Shs Outstg (000)	96,603	94,448	82,876	79,553	71,596	70,614	69,887
STATISTICAL RECORD:							
Book Value Per Share	22.78	22.00	18.65	19.17	18.77	16.91	16.79
Return on Equity %	14.6	12.4	10.1	8.2	14.6	16.3	14.7
Return on Assets %	1.1	0.9	0.6	0.5	0.8	0.8	0.9
Average Yield %	3.6	3.5	4.5	4.9	5.9	3.8	4.0
P/E Ratio	11.3-8.1	13.9-9.3	15.4-10.5	19.9-8.7	8.8-3.2	11.2-7.9	12.2-7.9
Price Range	39¾-28½	40½-27	30¼-20¾	31½-13¾	26⅝-9¾	32¾-23¼	30½-19¾

Statistics are as originally reported.

OFFICERS:
D.C. Clark, Chmn.
W.F. Aldinger, Pres. & C.E.O.
E.D. Ancona, V.P. & Treas.

INCORPORATED: DE, Feb., 1981

PRINCIPAL OFFICE: 2700 Sanders Road, Prospect Heights, IL 60070-2799

TELEPHONE NUMBER: (708) 564-5000

NO. OF EMPLOYEES:

ANNUAL MEETING: In May

SHAREHOLDERS: 14,212

INSTITUTIONAL HOLDINGS:
No. of Institutions: 440
Shares Held: 68,907,911

REGISTRAR(S): Harris Trust & Savings Bank, Chicago, IL

TRANSFER AGENT(S): Harris Trust & Savings Bank, Chicago, IL

HUBBELL, INC.

YIELD 3.2%
P/E RATIO 16.2

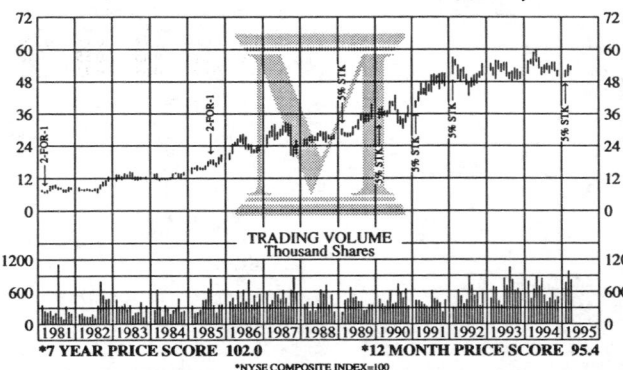

7 YEAR PRICE SCORE 102.0 **12 MONTH PRICE SCORE 95.4**
*NYSE COMPOSITE INDEX=100

INTERIM EARNINGS (Per Share):

Qtr.	Mar.	June	Sept.	Dec.
1991	0.71	0.75	0.69	0.72
1992	0.74	0.77	0.72	0.74
1993	0.76	0.79	0.74	d0.19
1994	0.77	0.83	0.86	0.86

INTERIM DIVIDENDS (Per Share):

Amt.	Decl.	Ex.	Rec.	Pay.
0.43Q	6/15/94	6/21/94	6/27/94	7/11/94
0.43Q	9/8	9/13	9/19	10/11
0.43Q	12/14	12/19	12/26	1/11/95
5%	12/14	1/9/95	1/13/95	2/3
0.43Q	3/14/95	3/21	3/27	4/11

*Indicated div.: $1.72**

CAPITALIZATION (12/31/94):

	($000)	(%)
Long-Term Debt	2,700	0.4
Deferred Income Tax	12,924	2.1
Common & Surplus	608,996	97.5
Total	624,620	100.0

DIVIDEND ACHIEVER STATUS:
Rank: 118   1984-94 Growth Rate: 12.1%
Total Years of Dividend Growth: 34

RECENT DEVELOPMENTS: For the quarter ended 12/31/94, net income was $28.5 million compared with a net loss of $6.1 million for the same period in 1993. Net sales for the quarter rose more than 30% to a record $277.2 million from $211.7 million in the prior year. For the year ended 12/31/94, net income increased more than 60% to a record $106.5 million from $66.3 million in 1993. Net sales also achieved a record level, rising 22% to $1.01 billion from $832.4 million in 1993.

PROSPECTS: The stable growth of HUB's Distribution group should continue to drive sales and earnings. The Company's High Voltage group is also experiencing growth, boosted by the April 1994 acquisition of A.B. Chance Industries Inc. HUB's Industrial Controls subsidiary continues to drive Specialty Products revenues. This trend should continue through new markets opened by product line expansions. Plant expansions in Connecticut, North Carolina, Puerto Rico and Mexico remain on schedule.

BUSINESS

HUBBELL, INCORPORATED specializes in the engineering, manufacture and sale of electrical and electronic products for the commercial, industrial, utility and telecommunications markets. These products may be classified into three segments: products with low-voltage applications, products with high-voltage applications and those not directly related to the electrical business. A global operation, the Company manufactures products in Hong Kong, the United Kingdom, Mexico, Singapore, Puerto Rico, Canada and the United States.

QUARTERLY DATA

(12/31/94)	Rev	Inc
First Quarter	207,044	24,328
Second Quarter	261,935	26,459
Third Quarter............	267,545	27,289
Fourth Quarter..........	277,176	28,457

ANNUAL EARNINGS AND DIVIDENDS PER SHARE

	1994	1993	1992	1991	1990	1989	1988
Earnings Per Share	3.05	2.10	①2.97	2.87	2.74	2.52	2.25
Dividends Per Share	1.68	1.62	②1.561	③1.43	1.352	④1.06	0.872
Dividend Payout %	55.1	77.1	52.6	49.8	49.3	42.1	38.7

Note: 5% stk. div., 2/3/95. ① Before acctg. chg. ② 5% stk. div., 1/6/92 ③ 5% stk. div., 1/7/91 ④ 5% stk. div., 2/89

ANNUAL FINANCIAL DATA

RECORD OF EARNINGS (IN MILLIONS):

Total Revenues	1,013.7	832.4	786.1	756.1	719.5	668.8	614.2
Costs and Expenses	839.1	732.1	641.3	615.4	590.6	547.2	501.9
Depreciation & Amort	34.0	30.1	26.8	22.2	17.7	16.6	15.0
Operating Income	140.6	70.2	117.9	118.5	111.1	105.0	97.4
Income Bef Income Taxes	145.9	81.5	130.7	129.4	124.7	116.7	106.4
Income Taxes	39.4	15.2	36.6	38.8	38.6	37.4	35.1
Net Income	106.5	66.3	①94.1	90.6	86.0	79.4	71.3
Aver. Shs. Outstg. (000)	33,291	31,620	31,643	31,570	31,414	31,478	31,735

① Before acctg. change dr$16,506,000.

BALANCE SHEET (IN MILLIONS):

Cash and Cash Equivalents	38.9	44.2	28.3	91.6	103.3	101.1	66.9
Receivables, Net	143.9	110.0	115.6	93.7	91.9	83.8	71.1
Inventories	224.1	181.7	177.9	140.8	141.3	128.0	124.4
Gross Property	406.1	336.7	315.6	292.3	264.3	227.2	209.0
Accumulated Depreciation	204.1	182.0	162.2	144.6	132.5	119.2	106.6
Long-Term Debt	2.7	2.7	2.7	8.1	8.1	8.1	8.1
Net Stockholders' Equity	609.0	557.7	541.3	518.9	468.7	427.8	392.5
Total Assets	1,041.6	874.3	806.7	685.3	624.7	576.3	523.5
Total Current Assets	444.9	362.1	329.9	343.7	354.2	341.0	278.8
Total Current Liabilities	332.1	230.2	200.5	110.8	105.1	101.5	88.3
Net Working Capital	112.8	131.9	129.4	232.9	249.0	239.6	190.4
Year End Shs Outstg (000)	32,952	31,259	31,185	31,153	29,531	29,526	31,247

STATISTICAL RECORD:

Operating Profit Margin %	13.9	8.4	15.0	15.7	15.4	15.7	15.9
Book Value Per Share	14.19	15.71	15.44	15.55	15.39	14.17	12.24
Return on Equity %	17.5	11.9	17.4	17.5	18.4	18.6	18.2
Return on Assets %	10.2	7.6	11.7	13.2	13.8	13.8	13.6
Average Yield %	3.1	3.1	3.1	3.2	3.7	3.2	3.3
P/E Ratio	18.7-15.6	28.1-24.2	20.2-15.1	17.9-13.3	15.7-11.1	15.8-10.9	13.1-10.6
Price Range	59⅞-50	56⅛-48⅜	57⅛-42¾	51⅜-38¼	43-30⅜	39¾-27⅜	29½-23⅞

Statistics are as originally reported.

OFFICERS:
G.J. Ratcliffe, Chmn., Pres. & C.E.O.
J.H. Biggart, Jr., Treas.
R.W. Davies, Gen. Couns. & Sec.

INCORPORATED: CT, May, 1905

PRINCIPAL OFFICE: 584 Derby Milford Rd., Orange, CT 06477-4024

TELEPHONE NUMBER: (203) 799-4100
FAX: (203) 799-4333
NO. OF EMPLOYEES: 7,405
ANNUAL MEETING: In May
SHAREHOLDERS: 1,327 (Cl. A com.); 5,354 (Cl. B.)
INSTITUTIONAL HOLDINGS:
No. of Institutions: 226
Shares Held: 15,550,544 Cl. B

REGISTRAR(S): Manufacturers Hanover Trust Co., New York, NY

TRANSFER AGENT(S): Manufacturers Hanover Trust Co., New York, NY

HUNT MANUFACTURING CO.

YIELD 2.6%
P/E RATIO 13.2

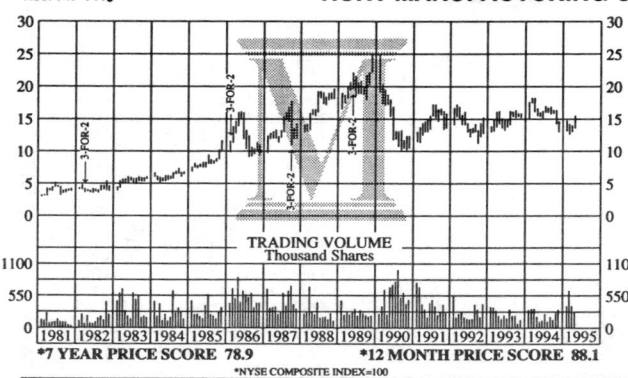

TRADING VOLUME Thousand Shares														

*7 YEAR PRICE SCORE 78.9   *12 MONTH PRICE SCORE 88.1
*NYSE COMPOSITE INDEX=100

INTERIM EARNINGS (Per Share):

Qtr.	Feb.	May	Aug.	Nov.
1991-92	0.14	0.20	0.24	0.25
1992-93	0.16	0.22	0.24	0.31
1993-94	0.19	0.25	0.27	0.36
1994-95	0.21	...	...	...

INTERIM DIVIDENDS (Per Share):

Amt.	Decl.	Ex.	Rec.	Pay.
0.09Q	4/14/94	4/19/94	4/25/94	5/3/94
0.09Q	6/8	6/14	6/20	7/28
0.09Q	10/27	11/1	11/7	11/15
0.095Q	12/15	12/21	12/28	1/5/95
0.095Q	2/17/95	3/22/95	3/28/95	4/5

Indicated div.: $0.38

CAPITALIZATION (11/27/94):

	($000)	(%)
Long-Term Debt	3,559	2.6
Deferred Income Tax	4,331	3.2
Common & Surplus	129,234	94.2
Total	137,124	100.0

DIVIDEND ACHIEVER STATUS:
Rank: 148   1984-94 Growth Rate: 10.7%
Total Years of Dividend Growth: 27

RECENT DEVELOPMENTS: For the year ended 11/27/94, the Company reported income of $17.2 million, before an accounting change, compared with $14.9 million in the previous year. Net sales rose 13% to a record $288.2 million. Both of the Company's business segments reported sales growth of 13% compared with the year before. The office products sales increase was led by higher sales of office furniture, up 17%; desktop accessories and supplies, up 13%; and mechanical and electromechanical products, up 10%.

PROSPECTS: Record sales are driving earnings higher. Office product revenues should continue to reflect improving sales of desktop accessories and supplies, mechanical and electromechanical products, and office furniture. Sales of Schwan-STABILO highlighter markers and BOSTON brand office products are on the rise. Office furniture sales are benefiting from strong sales of BEVIS brand furniture products. The Art/Craft segment is performing well due to increased presentation graphics sales.

BUSINESS

HUNT MANUFACTURING CO. is a producer and distributor of office and art/craft products. It manufactures more than 10,000 items and distributes them to more than 60 countries. Office products include pencil sharpeners, paper punches, paper shredders, letter openers, air cleaners, and staplers; metal office files, racks, machine stands, fax and printer cabinets, and cash boxes; furniture for computers and the home/office; covers for printers; budget office furniture, and data product accessories. Art/craft products include Speedball dip pens, paints, inks, calligraphy kits, screen and block printing products, and Seal and Ademco-Seal mounting and laminating materials.

BUSINESS LINE ANALYSIS

(11/27/94)	Rev (%)	Inc (%)
Office Products	55.6	36.5
Art/Craft Products	44.4	63.5
Total	100.0	100.0

ANNUAL EARNINGS AND DIVIDENDS PER SHARE

	11/27/94	11/28/93	11/29/92	12/1/91	12/2/90	12/3/89	11/27/88
Earnings Per Share	1.07	0.93	0.83	0.60	0.75	1.17	1.01
Dividends Per Share	0.36	0.35	0.34	0.32	0.31	① 0.267	0.227
Dividend Payout %	33.6	37.6	41.0	53.3	41.3	22.8	22.5

① 3-for-2 stk split, 5/89

ANNUAL FINANCIAL DATA

RECORD OF EARNINGS (IN THOUSANDS):

Total Revenues	288,203	256,150	234,929	228,622	220,099	203,444	178,755
Costs and Expenses	252,798	223,925	204,477	202,090	192,909	169,077	146,706
Depreciation & Amort	8,039	7,664	7,558	7,467	6,866	5,560	5,769
Income From Operations	27,366	24,561	22,894	19,065	20,324	28,807	26,280
Income Bef Income Taxes	27,081	24,038	21,609	17,118	18,737	29,430	25,939
Income Taxes	9,884	9,110	8,307	7,532	6,726	10,626	9,772
Net Income	① 17,197	14,928	13,302	9,586	12,011	18,804	16,167
Aver. Shs. Outstg.	16,102	16,107	16,104	16,080	16,083	16,080	16,059

① Before acctg. change cr$795,000.

BALANCE SHEET (IN THOUSANDS):

Cash and Cash Equivalents	13,807	10,778	6,013	8,738	7,532	15,839	17,424
Receivables, Net	46,441	39,472	39,565	39,278	36,485	34,176	30,302
Inventories	33,550	27,960	25,007	28,250	30,233	26,406	17,573
Gross Property	95,892	88,950	81,840	78,756	76,926	60,356	53,334
Accumulated Depreciation	46,163	42,333	39,185	35,074	30,788	26,764	22,718
Long-Term Debt	3,559	3,003	6,160	17,271	26,498	9,674	10,790
Net Stockholders' Equity	129,234	116,267	107,456	102,384	99,539	90,029	75,660
Total Assets	173,385	156,317	144,170	151,824	154,361	127,947	112,970
Total Current Assets	95,318	80,842	72,302	77,181	74,880	76,839	65,557
Total Current Liabilities	30,715	33,714	26,850	29,531	24,391	23,741	22,366
Net Working Capital	64,603	47,128	45,452	47,650	50,489	53,098	43,191
Year End Shares Outstg	16,100	16,107	16,082	16,095	16,054	16,106	16,077

STATISTICAL RECORD:

Operating Profit Margin %	9.5	9.6	9.7	8.3	9.2	14.2	14.7
Book Value Per Share	6.41	5.54	4.95	4.50	4.19	4.57	3.73
Return on Equity %	13.3	12.8	12.4	9.4	12.1	20.9	21.4
Return on Assets %	9.9	9.5	9.2	6.3	7.8	14.7	14.3
Average Yield %	2.3	2.4	2.4	2.2	1.8	1.3	1.4
P/E Ratio	17.1-12.1	17.6-14.0	20.8-13.6	28.8-19.0	33.2-13.7	21.2-14.1	19.4-12.9
Price Range	18¼-13	16⅜-13	17¼-11¼	17¼-11⅜	24⅞-10¼	24¾-16½	19⅝-13

Statistics are as originally reported.

OFFICERS:
R.J. Naples, Chmn.
R.B. Fritsch, Pres., C.E.O. & C.O.O.
W.E. Chandler, Sr. V.P.-C.F.O. & Sec.

INCORPORATED: PA, Nov., 1962

PRINCIPAL OFFICE: One Commerce Square 2005 Market Street, Philadelphia, PA 19103-7085

TELEPHONE NUMBER: (215) 656-0300
FAX: (215) 656-3700
NO. OF EMPLOYEES: 2,200 (approx.)
ANNUAL MEETING: In April
SHAREHOLDERS: 1,000 (approx.)
INSTITUTIONAL HOLDINGS:
No. of Institutions: 72
Shares Held: 6,949,170

REGISTRAR(S): Mellon Bank (East) N.A., Philadelphia, PA

TRANSFER AGENT(S): Mellon Bank (East), N.A., Philadelphia, PA

NASDAQ SYMBOL HBAN
Rec. Pr. 18

HUNTINGTON BANCSHARES, INC.

YIELD 4.4%
P/E RATIO 9.6

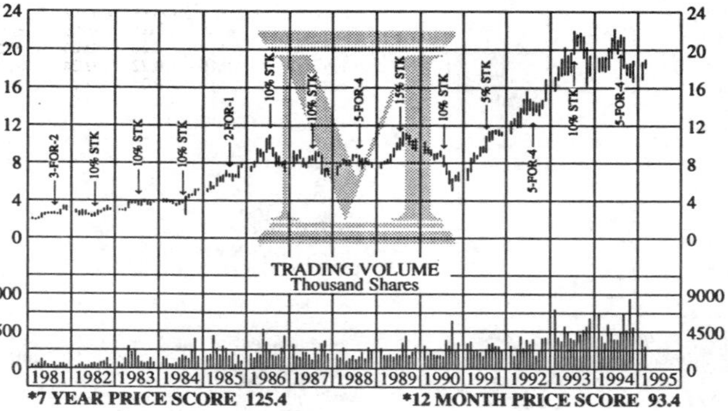

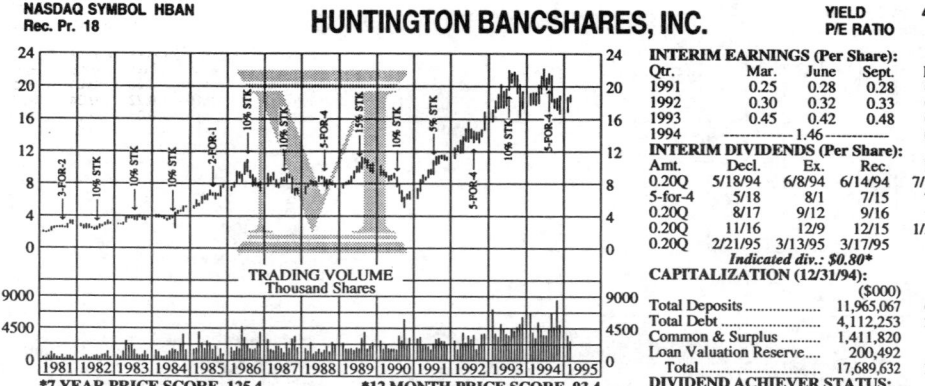

*7 YEAR PRICE SCORE 125.4 *12 MONTH PRICE SCORE 93.4

*NYSE COMPOSITE INDEX=100

INTERIM EARNINGS (Per Share):

Qtr.	Mar.	June	Sept.	Dec.
1991	0.25	0.28	0.28	0.30
1992	0.30	0.32	0.33	0.36
1993	0.45	0.42	0.48	0.49
1994	------------ 1.46 ------------			0.41

INTERIM DIVIDENDS (Per Share):

Amt.	Decl.	Ex.	Rec.	Pay.
0.20Q	5/18/94	6/8/94	6/14/94	7/1/94
5-for-4	5/18	8/1	7/15	7/29
0.20Q	8/17	9/12	9/16	10/3
0.20Q	11/16	12/9	12/15	1/3/95
0.20Q	2/21/95	3/13/95	3/17/95	4/3

*Indicated div.: $0.80**

CAPITALIZATION (12/31/94):

	($000)	(%)
Total Deposits	11,965,067	67.6
Total Debt	4,112,253	23.3
Common & Surplus	1,411,820	8.0
Loan Valuation Reserve	200,492	1.1
Total	17,689,632	100.0

DIVIDEND ACHIEVER STATUS:
Rank: 120 1984-94 Growth Rate: 12.0%
Total Years of Dividend Growth: 28

RECENT DEVELOPMENTS: Net income for the year ended 12/31/94 was $242.6 million, up a modest 2.4% from $236.9 million in 1993. Net interest income fell by 5% to $756.1 million. The decrease was attributed to lower levels of earning assets and the interest rate environment. Noninterest income was $235.4 million, down 23% from the prior year's $305.8 million. Mortgage banking income declined significantly due to slower origination activity. The 81% reduction in the provision for loan losses illustrates improved credit quality. Nonperforming assets fell to $96.4 million or 0.78% of total loans and other real estate. Noninterest expense was $609.7 million versus $658.9 million a year earlier. HBAN acquired FirstFed Northern Kentucky Bancorp, Inc., a $261 million bank holding company based in Covington, KY. The acquisitions of Security National Corp. and Reliance Bank of Florida are pending.

BUSINESS

HUNTINGTON BANCSHARES INCORPORATED is a $17.77 billion regional bank holding company headquartered in Columbus, Ohio. The Company's banking subsidiaries operate 344 offices in Ohio, Florida, Illinois, Indiana, Kentucky, Michigan, Pennsylvania and West Virginia. In addition, the Company's mortgage, trust, investment banking and automobile finance subsidiaries manage 84 offices in the eight states mentioned as well as Connecticut, Delaware, Maryland, Massachusetts, New Jersey, North Carolina, Rhode Island and Virginia. International banking services are maintained through the headquarters office in Columbus, Ohio and through an additional branch located in the Cayman Islands.

LOAN DISTRIBUTION

(12/31/94)	($000)	(%)
Commercial	3,610,892	29.4
Tax-Free	58,006	0.5
Real Estate-Construction	304,769	2.5
Real Estate-Commercial	1,378,398	11.2
Real Estate-Residential	1,624,367	13.2
Consumer	4,641,946	37.9
Direct Lease Financing	646,058	5.3
Total	12,264,436	100.0

ANNUAL EARNINGS AND DIVIDENDS PER SHARE

	1994	1993	1992	1991	1990	1989	1988
Earnings Per Share	**1.87**	**1.85**	**1.31**	**1.10**	**0.80**	**1.06**	**0.98**
Dividends Per Share	**[2] 0.68**	**[1] 0.568**	**[2] 0.528**	**[3] 0.494**	**[4] 0.429**	**[5] 0.37**	**0.332**
Dividend Payout %	**36.4**	**43.3**	**40.3**	**44.9**	**53.6**	**34.9**	**33.9**

[1] 10% stk div,07/12/93 [2] 5-for-4 stk split, 7/29/94 & 8/03/92 [3] 5% stk div, 7/9/91 [4] 10% stk div, 7/31/90 [5] 15% stk div, 7/31/89

ANNUAL FINANCIAL DATA

	1994	1993	1992	1991	1990	1989	1988
RECORD OF EARNINGS (IN MILLIONS):							
Total Interest Income	1,219.7	1,236.3	1,022.8	1,035.7	1,102.3	1,020.1	774.4
Total Interest Expense	463.7	440.1	412.6	558.1	678.4	631.2	446.9
Net Interest Income	756.1	796.2	610.2	477.5	423.9	389.0	327.6
Credit Loss Provision	15.3	79.3	75.7	56.7	71.0	39.9	26.3
Net Income	242.6	236.9	139.0	117.0	85.2	108.0	87.6
Aver. Shs. Outstg. (000)	129,724	128,314	105,999	84,655	93,188	89,276	75,574
BALANCE SHEET (IN MILLIONS):							
Cash & Due From Banks	885.3	704.0	599.9	634.7	718.7	866.4	829.4
US Treas & Fed Agencies	317.7	94.5	2,825.0	2,174.9	2,024.8	2,344.0	1,076.2
States & Political Subdiviss	153.6	232.7	222.7	293.6	340.1	406.5	356.6
Loans & Lse Financing, Net	12,063.9	10,742.1	8,043.8	7,558.6	7,552.2	7,032.0	5,815.3
Total Domestic Deposits	11,558.1	11,681.1	9,668.6	9,435.3	9,087.8	8,570.3	7,035.5
Total Foreign Deposits	407.0	363.6	284.1	75.4	27.1	19.3	71.1
Long-term Debt	1,214.1	762.3	269.6	136.7	141.4	152.6	152.6
Net Stockholders' Equity	1,411.8	1,324.6	941.4	853.0	785.5	720.7	570.4
Total Assets	17,770.6	17,618.7	13,894.9	12,332.6	11,808.8	11,679.8	9,506.0
Year End Shs Outstg (000)	130,215	129,761	106,124	84,533	93,002	81,341	76,111
STATISTICAL RECORD:							
Return on Assets %	1.37	1.34	1.00	0.95	0.72	0.92	0.92
Return on Equity %	17.20	17.90	14.80	13.70	10.80	15.00	15.40
Book Value Per Share	10.84	10.21	8.87	10.09	8.45	8.86	7.49
Average Yield %	3.5	3.0	3.8	5.6	5.6	3.9	4.3
P/E Ratio	11.9-8.9	11.9-8.5	12.9-8.5	8.4-4.4	11.3-5.4	9.4-6.2	7.6-5.8
Price Range	22¼-16⅝	22-15⅝	16⅞-11⅛	11⅝-6⅛	10⅜-5	11⅜-7½	8⅞-6¾

Statistics are as originally reported.

OFFICERS:
F. Wobst, Chmn. & C.E.O.
Z. Sofia, Pres., C.O.O. & Treas.
G.R. Williams, Exec. V.P. & C.F.O.

INCORPORATED: MD, Apr., 1966

PRINCIPAL OFFICE: Huntington Center 41 South High Street, Columbus, OH 43287

TELEPHONE NUMBER: (614) 480-8300

NO. OF EMPLOYEES: 8,152

ANNUAL MEETING: In April

SHAREHOLDERS: 30,943

INSTITUTIONAL HOLDINGS:
No. of Institutions: 158
Shares Held: 26,816,196

REGISTRAR(S):

TRANSFER AGENT(S): Huntington National Bank, Stock Transfer Department, Columbus, OH 43287

NYS SYMBOL ITW
Rec. Pr. 48

ILLINOIS TOOL WORKS, INC.

YIELD 1.3%
P/E RATIO 19.6

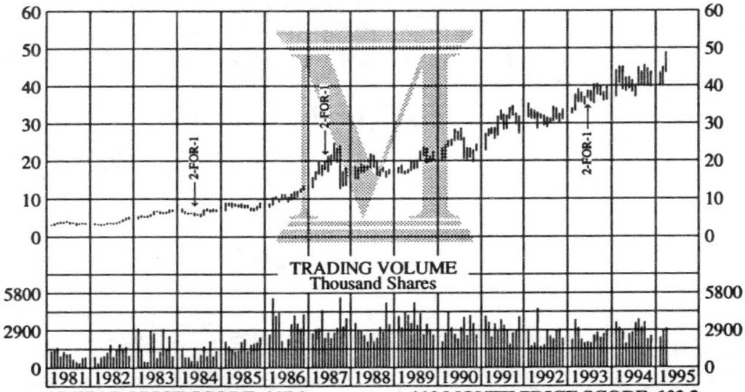

TRADING VOLUME
Thousand Shares
2-FOR-1
2-FOR-1
2-FOR-1
1981 1982 1983 1984 1985 1986 1987 1988 1989 1990 1991 1992 1993 1994 1995

*7 YEAR PRICE SCORE 117.1 *12 MONTH PRICE SCORE 102.3

*NYSE COMPOSITE INDEX=100

INTERIM EARNINGS (Per Share):

Qtr.	Mar.	June	Sept.	Dec.
1991	0.38	0.43	0.41	0.42
1992	0.36	0.46	0.44	0.46
1993	0.38	0.49	0.45	0.52
1994	0.45	0.62	0.63	0.75

INTERIM DIVIDENDS (Per Share):

Amt.	Decl.	Ex.	Rec.	Pay.
0.13Q	2/18/94	5/2/94	5/6/94	6/1/94
0.13Q	5/6	8/1	8/5	9/1
0.15Q	8/5	9/26	9/30	10/25
0.15Q	10/21	12/23	12/30	1/25/95
0.15Q	2/17/95	3/27/95	3/31/95	4/25

Indicated div.: $0.60*

CAPITALIZATION (12/31/94):

	($000)	(%)
Long-Term Debt	272,987	14.5
Deferred Income Tax	69,516	3.7
Common & Surplus	1,541,521	81.8
Total	1,884,024	100.0

DIVIDEND ACHIEVER STATUS:
Rank: 90 1984-94 Growth Rate: 13.2%
Total Years of Dividend Growth: 32

RECENT DEVELOPMENTS: For the year ended 12/31/94, net income increased 34.5% to $277.8 million from $206.6 million in 1993. Revenues advanced 9.6% to $3.46 billion. ITW reported a 29.4% improvement in operating income to $498.8 million from $385.6 million a year earlier. Operating income in the Engineered Components segment increased 32.8% as sales climbed 21.2%. The Industrial Systems and Consumables segment's earnings rose 33.9% while revenues grew 13.1% over the prior-year period.

PROSPECTS: The Engineered Components segment remains the principal contributor to sales and earnings growth as its worldwide automotive and construction businesses continue to improve. Revenue growth in the Industrial Systems and Consumables segment is being fueled by ITW's worldwide industrial packaging group and finishing systems businesses, along with the international consumer packaging group. Earnings growth is being driven by the domestic industrial packaging and worldwide finishing systems businesses.

BUSINESS

ILLINOIS TOOL WORKS INC. manufactures engineered components, industrial systems and consumables, and specialty mechanical and chemical products through two business segments. Engineered Components produces short lead-time plastic and metal components and small assemblies, industrial fluids and adhesives, plastic and metal fasteners and fastening tools and equipment. The Industrial Systems and Consumables segment manufactures longer lead-time systems and related consumables for packaging, finishing, furniture, inspection and quality assurance applications. The Company serves the appliance, automotive and truck, electronics, agricultural and telecommunications markets with more than 250 operations in 33 countries.

QUARTERLY DATA

(12/31/94)($000)	Rev	Inc
1st Quarter	771,439	50,915
2nd Quarter	881,042	70,727
3rd Quarter	870,911	71,399
4th Quarter	937,923	84,742

ANNUAL EARNINGS AND DIVIDENDS PER SHARE

	1994	1993	1992	1991	1990	1989	1988
Earnings Per Share	**2.45**	**1.83**	**1.72**	**1.63**	**1.67**	**1.53**	**1.33**
Dividends Per Share	**0.54**	**[1] 0.49**	**0.45**	**0.40**	**0.33**	**0.27**	**0.22**
Dividend Payout %	**22.0**	**26.8**	**26.2**	**24.6**	**19.7**	**17.6**	**16.5**

[1] 2-for-1 stk split,06/21/93

ANNUAL FINANCIAL DATA

	1994	1993	1992	1991	1990	1989	1988
RECORD OF EARNINGS (IN MILLIONS):							
Total Revenues	3,461.3	3,159.2	2,811.6	2,639.7	2,544.2	2,172.7	1,929.8
Costs and Expenses	2,940.2	2,751.7	2,323.9	2,201.4	2,097.3	1,784.9	1,582.1
Depreciation & Amort	132.1	131.7	125.3	115.4	102.1	84.7	75.1
Operating Income	498.8	385.6	362.4	322.9	344.7	303.2	272.7
Income Bef Income Taxes	450.3	335.9	309.8	287.8	299.9	269.0	232.8
Income Taxes	172.5	129.3	117.7	107.2	117.5	105.2	92.8
Net Income	277.8	206.6	192.1	180.6	182.4	163.8	140.0
Aver. Shs. Outstg. (000)	113,387	112,979	111,746	111,178	108,872	107,028	105,350
BALANCE SHEET (IN MILLIONS):							
Cash and Cash Equivalents	76.9	35.4	31.2	93.1	46.8	30.9	26.7
Receivables, Net	685.4	602.0	525.3	515.7	507.3	403.6	334.1
Inventories	439.5	403.9	400.6	427.2	468.0	365.2	315.6
Gross Property	1,400.8	1,205.9	1,073.3	1,014.6	916.9	768.2	661.3
Accumulated Depreciation	759.6	622.1	549.2	488.9	433.3	354.7	318.5
Long-Term Debt	273.0	375.6	252.0	307.1	430.6	334.4	225.9
Net Stockholders' Equity	1,541.5	1,258.7	1,339.7	1,212.1	1,091.8	871.1	744.7
Total Assets	2,580.5	2,336.9	2,204.2	2,257.1	2,150.3	1,688.0	1,380.2
Total Current Assets	1,262.9	1,093.6	1,004.8	1,088.0	1,143.5	824.2	713.6
Total Current Liabilities	628.4	546.1	512.7	646.0	528.4	383.8	321.4
Net Working Capital	634.5	547.5	492.1	442.0	615.1	440.4	392.3
Year End Shs Outstg (000)	114,358	113,150	112,013	111,436	109,609	107,332	105,588
STATISTICAL RECORD:							
Operating Profit Margin %	14.4	12.2	12.9	12.2	13.5	14.0	14.1
Book Value Per Share	8.86	6.79	7.64	7.73	7.27	5.42	5.31
Return on Equity %	18.0	16.4	14.3	14.9	16.7	18.8	18.8
Return on Assets %	10.8	8.8	8.7	8.0	8.5	9.7	10.1
Average Yield %	1.3	1.3	1.4	1.4	1.4	1.3	1.2
P/E Ratio	18.6-15.1	22.1-17.8	20.6-16.6	21.3-14.0	17.2-11.8	15.5-10.8	16.4-11.4
Price Range	45½-37	40½-32½	35⅜-28½	34¾-22⅞	28¾-19⅝	23¾-16½	21⅞-15⅛

Statistics are as originally reported.

OFFICERS:
J.D. Nichols, Chmn. & C.E.O.
W.J. Farrell, Pres.
S.S. Hudnut, Sr. V.P., Gen. Coun. & Sec.
M.J. Robinson, V.P. & Treas.

INCORPORATED: DE, Jun., 1961

PRINCIPAL OFFICE: 3600 West Lake Ave., Glenview, IL 60025-5811

TELEPHONE NUMBER: (708) 724-7500
FAX: (708) 657-4261
NO. OF EMPLOYEES: 19,500
ANNUAL MEETING: In May
SHAREHOLDERS: 3,700 (approx.)
INSTITUTIONAL HOLDINGS:
No. of Institutions: 494
Shares Held: 83,324,124

REGISTRAR(S): Continental Bank, N.A., Chicago, IL 60697

TRANSFER AGENT(S): Continental Bank, N.A., Chicago, IL 60697

INDIANA ENERGY, INC.

YIELD 5.9%
P/E RATIO 13.3

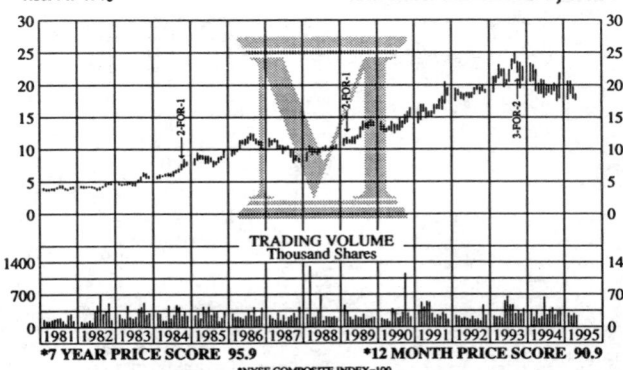

INTERIM EARNINGS (Per Share):

Qtr.	Dec.	Mar.	June	Sept.
1991-92	0.53	0.73	d0.05	d0.06
1992-93	-------	1.62	-------	
1993-94	0.67	0.96	0.11	d0.21
1994-95	0.48	...	...	

INTERIM DIVIDENDS (Per Share):

Amt.	Decl.	Ex.	Rec.	Pay.
0.255Q	4/29/94	5/9/94	5/13/94	6/1/94
0.265Q	7/29	8/9	8/15	9/1
0.265Q	10/28	11/8	11/15	12/1
0.265Q	1/9/95	2/9/95	2/15/95	3/1/95
0.265Q	4/28	5/9	5/15	6/1

Indicated div.: $1.06*

CAPITALIZATION (9/30/94):

	($000)	(%)
Long-Term Debt	158,766	31.6
Deferred Income Tax	72,920	14.5
Common & Surplus	271,245	53.9
Total	502,931	100.0

DIVIDEND ACHIEVER STATUS:
Rank: 266   1984-94 Growth Rate: 5.9%
Total Years of Dividend Growth: 19

TRADING VOLUME Thousand Shares

1981 1982 1983 1984 1985 1986 1987 1988 1989 1990 1991 1992 1993 1994 1995

*7 YEAR PRICE SCORE 95.9   *12 MONTH PRICE SCORE 90.9
*NYSE COMPOSITE INDEX=100

RECENT DEVELOPMENTS: For the quarter ended 12/31/94, net income was $10.9 million compared with $15.2 million in 1993. Revenues fell 26% to $113.1 million. The decline in earnings is attributable to weather that was 26% warmer than last year and 25% warmer than normal. Warmer weather was offset somewhat by reductions in operating expenses. For the year ended 12/31/94, net income was up slightly to $30.1 million compared with $29.1 million in 1993.

PROSPECTS: Indiana Gas's prospects for continued growth look bright. Increasing gas conversions by residential customers, as well as commercial and industrial customers' increasing usage will help push earnings higher. Higher economic activity in IEI's service area, which continues to outperform most of the country, will help spark revenue growth. Higher margins should be achieved through cost-control measures instituted last year, which should provide an earnings stimulus.

BUSINESS

INDIANA ENERGY, INC., is a gas distribution and related-services holding company. IEI's principal subsidiary, Indiana Gas Company, provides gas utility service to more than 442,000 customers in north central, central, and southern portions of Indiana. Terre Haute Gas Corp. and Richmond Gas Corp. were acquired in July 1990. Both companies are public utilities providing local distribution of natural gas in the state of Indiana. While the Companies technically still exist as separate corporate entities, their business operations were merged with those of Indiana Gas in 1991. IEI Investments is a wholly-owned subsidiary formed to group the operations and financing of non-regulated buinesses. IEI has a wholly-owned subsidiary, IGC Energy.

ANNUAL EARNINGS AND DIVIDENDS PER SHARE

	9/30/94	9/30/93	9/30/92	9/30/91	9/30/90	9/30/89	9/30/88
Earnings Per Share	1.53	1.62	1.16	1.11	1.27	1.28	1.22
Dividends Per Share	1.04	①1.00	0.967	0.927	0.88	②0.827	0.753
Dividend Payout %	68.0	61.7	83.3	83.2	69.5	64.6	61.7

① 3-for-2 stk split,10/04/93 ② 2-for-1 stock split, 2/2/89

ANNUAL FINANCIAL DATA

RECORD OF EARNINGS (IN THOUSANDS):

Total Revenues	475,297	713,049	805,357	672,502	572,491	344,676	322,890
Depreciation & Amort	29,404	26,806	25,136	23,568	22,243	20,682	19,177
Prov for Fed Inc Taxes	...	16,823	14,821	12,672	12,357	12,785	11,489
Interest Expense	16,037	16,820	14,624	15,041	12,539	11,663	10,940
Net Income	34,441	34,578	23,969	23,051	21,749	21,157	20,091
Aver. Shs. Outstg.	22,554	21,376	20,706	20,667	17,204	16,515	16,488

BALANCE SHEET (IN THOUSANDS):

Gross Plant	824,839	773,174	725,312	667,252	597,850	517,687	485,445
Accumulated Depreciation	291,823	267,629	248,677	226,088	206,537	180,973	165,801
Prop, Plant & Equip, Net	533,016	505,545	476,635	441,170	391,313	336,714	319,644
Long-term Debt	158,766	164,901	150,311	161,135	102,946	121,330	114,642
Net Stockholders' Equity	271,245	258,647	232,310	226,026	221,261	159,919	152,029
Total Assets	666,813	631,280	627,719	556,008	544,238	398,872	388,061
Year End Shares Outstg	22,557	22,460	20,769	20,672	20,584	16,515	16,514

STATISTICAL RECORD:

Book Value Per Share	12.02	11.52	10.22	9.97	8.66	8.47	7.99
Dep/Gr. Pl %	3.5	3.5	3.5	3.5	3.7	4.0	4.0
Accum. Dep/Gr. Pl %	35.4	34.6	34.3	33.9	34.5	35.0	34.2
Return on Equity %	12.7	13.4	10.3	10.2	9.8	13.2	13.2
Average Yield %	5.1	4.6	5.2	5.4	6.1	6.6	8.0
P/E Ratio	15.3-11.4	15.4-11.7	17.2-15.1	18.5-12.6	13.0-9.8	11.4-8.2	8.8-6.7
Price Range	23⅜-17½	24⅞-18⅞	20-17½	20½-14	16½-12½	14⅝-10½	10¾-8⅛

Statistics are as originally reported.

QUARTERLY DATA

(09/30/94)($000)	Rev	Inc
1st Quarter	151,892	18,894
2nd Quarter	195,672	24,630
3rd Quarter	77,827	5,551
4th Quarter	49,906	(1,232)

OFFICERS:
D.M. Amundson, Chmn.
L.A. Ferger, Pres. & C.E.O.
N.C. Ellerbrook, V.P., Treas. & C.F.O.

INCORPORATED: IN, Oct., 1985

PRINCIPAL OFFICE: 1630 North Meridian Street, Indianapolis, IN 46202-1496

TELEPHONE NUMBER: (317) 926-3351
NO. OF EMPLOYEES: 1,129 (full-time); 25 (part-time)
ANNUAL MEETING: In January
SHAREHOLDERS: 11,369
INSTITUTIONAL HOLDINGS:
No. of Institutions: 104
Shares Held: 4,613,907

REGISTRAR(S): Continental Bank, N.A., Chicago, IL 60697

TRANSFER AGENT(S): Continental Bank, N.A., Chicago, IL 60697

NYS SYMBOL IFF
Rec. Pr. 50⅝

INTERNATIONAL FLAVORS & FRAGRANCES

YIELD 2.4%
P/E RATIO 24.9

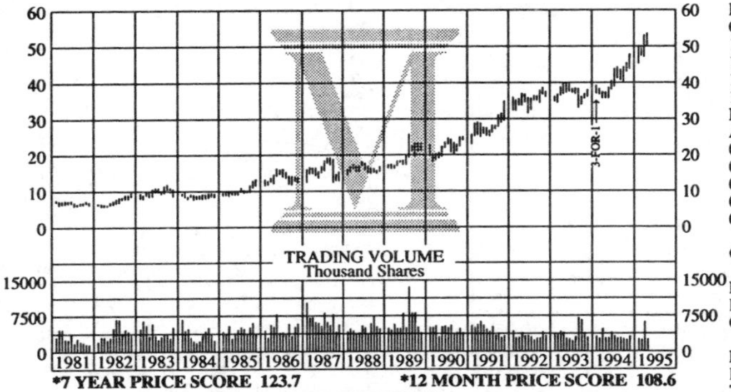

60
50
40
30
20
10
0
3-FOR-1
TRADING VOLUME
Thousand Shares
15000
7500
0
1981 1982 1983 1984 1985 1986 1987 1988 1989 1990 1991 1992 1993 1994 1995

*7 YEAR PRICE SCORE 123.7 *12 MONTH PRICE SCORE 108.6

*NYSE COMPOSITE INDEX=100

INTERIM EARNINGS (Per Share):

Qtr.	Mar.	June	Sept.	Dec.
1991	0.41	0.43	0.37	0.26
1992	0.44	0.48	0.43	0.19
1993	0.49	0.53	0.43	0.32
1994	0.53	0.58	0.53	0.39

INTERIM DIVIDENDS (Per Share):

Amt.	Decl.	Ex.	Rec.	Pay.
0.27Q	2/8/94	3/16/94	3/22/94	4/8/94
0.27Q	5/12	6/16	6/22	7/8
0.27Q	9/13	9/21	9/27	10/10
0.31Q	12/13	12/21	12/28	1/10/95
0.31Q	2/14/95	3/21/95	3/27/95	4/11

Indicated div.: $1.24*

CAPITALIZATION (12/31/94):

	($000)	(%)
Long-Term Debt	14,342	1.4
Deferred Income Tax	14,350	1.4
Common & Surplus	1,008,079	97.2
Total	1,036,771	100.0

DIVIDEND ACHIEVER STATUS:
Rank: 126 1984-94 Growth Rate: 11.6%
Total Years of Dividend Growth: 33

RECENT DEVELOPMENTS: For the year ended 12/31/94, net income rose 11.6% to $226.0 million from $202.5 million for the prior year. Net sales were $1.32 billion compared with $1.19 billion a year ago, an increase of 10.7%. Operating profit was $348.6 million, up 13.9% from $306.0 million the year before. For the quarter ended 12/31/94, net income jumped 21.3% to $43.3 million from $35.7 million for the year-earlier quarter. Net sales were $304.8 million versus $259.6 million in the 1993 quarter.

PROSPECTS: The Company continues to experience growth trends in both flavor and fragrance sales. Flavor sales are benefiting from the trend toward healthier diets and lifestyles. Flavor systems designed to replenish the taste deficiencies resulting from the removal of unwanted components such as sodium, fat, calories and sugar are making significant contributions to sales growth. Expansion and acquisition efforts will be facilitated by a strong balance sheet, with a very low level of long-term debt, and improving cash flows from operating activities.

BUSINESS

INTERNATIONAL FLAVORS & FRAGRANCES supplies compounds that enhance the aroma or taste of other manufacturers' products. It is one of the largest companies in its field producing and marketing on an international basis. Fragrance products are sold to makers of perfumes and cosmetics, hair and other personal care products, soaps and detergents, household and other cleaning products and area fresheners. Approximately 60% of total sales come from fragrances and aroma chemicals. The remainder came from the sale of flavors, principally to the food and beverage industries for use in such consumer products as soft drinks, snacks, dairy, meat and other processed foods, pharmaceuticals, and animal foods. The United States accounted for 32% of sales.

BUSINESS LINE ANALYSIS

(12/31/94)	Rev(%)	Inc(%)
United States	32.6	29.7
Western Europe	40.8	46.9
Other Foreign	26.6	23.4
Total	100.0	100.0

ANNUAL EARNINGS AND DIVIDENDS PER SHARE

	1994	1993	1992	1991	1990	1989	1988
Earnings Per Share	**2.03**	**1.78**	**[2] 1.53**	**1.47**	**1.37**	**1.22**	**1.13**
Dividends Per Share	**1.08**	**[1] 1.00**	**0.907**	**0.80**	**0.72**	**0.64**	**0.533**
Dividend Payout %	**53.2**	**56.2**	**59.3**	**54.4**	**52.6**	**52.6**	**47.1**

[1] Adj for 3-for-1 stk split, 01/20/94 [2] Before acctg. chg.

ANNUAL FINANCIAL DATA

	1994	1993	1992	1991	1990	1989	1988
RECORD OF EARNINGS (IN MILLIONS):							
Total Revenues	1,315.2	1,188.6	1,126.4	1,017.0	962.8	869.5	839.5
Costs and Expenses	930.3	847.6	828.8	733.4	695.3	631.1	605.8
Depreciation	36.4	35.1	34.0	29.4	28.2	24.3	22.7
Operating Profit	430.0	381.3	354.8	316.4	296.7	266.3	260.7
Inc Bef Taxes on Income	360.4	323.8	281.5	269.5	252.1	223.1	209.3
Income Taxes	134.3	121.3	104.8	100.8	95.4	84.5	80.6
Net Income	226.0	202.5	[1] 176.7	168.7	156.7	138.6	128.7
Aver. Shs. Outstg. (000)	111,527	113,925	115,454	114,642	114,366	113,979	113,643
[1] Before acctg. change dr$6,089,000.							
BALANCE SHEET (IN MILLIONS):							
Cash and Cash Equivalents	373.0	435.4	649.1	686.0	624.0	289.0	235.6
Receivables, Net	249.2	221.6	196.7	187.2	178.3	166.7	153.8
Inventories	362.1	302.9	297.7	290.3	278.5	254.1	241.6
Gross Property	736.9	610.6	553.8	563.1	516.6	445.1	414.3
Accumulated Depreciation	331.2	287.2	267.5	273.5	249.8	208.6	186.1
Net Stockholders' Equity	1,008.1	891.9	977.1	960.1	898.2	764.9	695.4
Total Assets	1,471.0	1,349.3	1,486.8	1,493.4	1,377.2	969.6	882.3
Total Current Assets	1,035.7	1,003.1	1,184.3	1,193.8	1,100.7	723.9	646.1
Total Current Liabilities	259.7	226.6	194.7	180.8	157.9	140.2	126.5
Net Working Capital	776.0	776.5	989.6	1,013.0	942.7	583.7	519.6
Year End Shs Outstg (000)	111,464	112,060	115,263	114,498	114,504	114,204	113,754
STATISTICAL RECORD:							
Operating Profit Margin %	26.5	25.7	23.4	25.0	24.9	24.6	25.1
Book Value Per Share	9.04	7.96	8.48	8.38	7.84	6.70	6.11
Return on Equity %	22.4	22.7	18.1	17.6	17.4	18.1	18.5
Return on Assets %	15.4	15.0	11.9	11.3	11.4	14.3	14.6
Average Yield %	2.6	2.7	2.6	2.8	3.3	3.0	3.3
P/E Ratio	23.6-17.5	22.4-18.5	25.3-20.6	23.8-15.6	18.2-13.3	21.3-13.2	16.0-12.7
Price Range	47⅞-35⅝	39⅞-33	38¾-31½	35-22⅞	25-18¼	25⅞-16⅛	18⅛-14⅜

Statistics are as originally reported.

OFFICERS:
E.P. Grisanti, Chmn. & Pres.
T.H. Hoppel, V.P., Fin. & Treas.
S.A. Block, V.P.-Law & Sec.

INCORPORATED: NY, Dec., 1909

PRINCIPAL OFFICE: 521 West 57th Street, New York, NY 10019-2960

TELEPHONE NUMBER: (212) 765-5500

NO. OF EMPLOYEES: 4,573

ANNUAL MEETING: In May

SHAREHOLDERS: 5,289

INSTITUTIONAL HOLDINGS:
No. of Institutions: 523
Shares Held: 65,204,129

REGISTRAR(S): The Bank of New York, New York, NY

TRANSFER AGENT(S): The Bank of New York, New York, NY

INTERPUBLIC GROUP OF COS., INC.

YIELD 1.5%
P/E RATIO 23.7

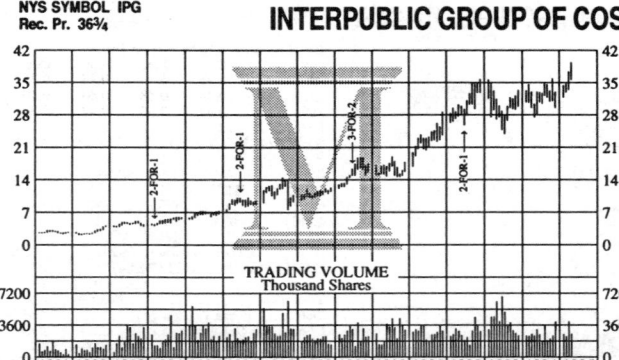

TRADING VOLUME
Thousand Shares

*7 YEAR PRICE SCORE 116.6   *12 MONTH PRICE SCORE 104.2

*NYSE COMPOSITE INDEX=100

INTERIM EARNINGS (Per Share):

Qtr.	Mar.	June	Sept.	Dec.
1992	0.13	0.58	0.17	0.62
1993	0.15	0.65	0.20	0.67
1994	0.17	0.72	0.23	0.40
1995	0.20	...	...	...

INTERIM DIVIDENDS (Per Share):

Amt.	Decl.	Ex.	Rec.	Pay.
0.125Q	2/14/94	2/18/94	2/25/94	3/15/94
0.14Q	5/17	5/23	5/27	6/15
0.14Q	7/19	8/24	8/30	9/15
0.14Q	10/20	11/22	11/29	12/15
0.14Q	2/16/95	2/21/95	2/27/95	3/15/95

*Indicated div.: $0.56**

CAPITALIZATION (12/31/94):

	($000)	(%)
Long-Term Debt	241,803	26.7
Minority Interest	12,485	1.4
Common & Surplus	649,427	71.9
Total	903,715	100.0

DIVIDEND ACHIEVER STATUS:
Rank: 104   1984-94 Growth Rate: 12.7%
Total Years of Dividend Growth: 13

RECENT DEVELOPMENTS: For the year ended 12/31/94, net income before an accounting adjustment declined 8% to $115.2 million compared with $125.3 million the previous year. Revenues were up 10.6% to $1.98 billion from $1.79 billion. Earnings included a restructuring charge of $25.7 million. If the restructuring charge had not been incurred, earnings would have advanced 12% to $141.0 million. U.S. operating revenues rose 23.1% to $720.3 million from $585.1 million in the prior-year.

PROSPECTS: A strong domestic economy, improving conditions in Europe and new business gains will propel revenue growth. In addition, margins will be enhanced by efforts to control expenses. The Company has formed a strategic alliance with two of CKS Group's operating units, CKS Pictures and CKS Interactive. This alliance will allow IPG to explore new marketing options on the information superhighway, which include infomercials, home shopping, CD-ROM, and on-line services.

BUSINESS

INTERPUBLIC GROUP OF COMPANIES, INC. is a large organization of advertising agencies. The agencies owned include: McCann-Erickson Worldwide, Lintas, Worldwide, Dailey & Associates and The Lowe Group. The Company also offers advertising agency services through association arrangements with local agencies in various parts of the world. Other activities conducted by IPG within the area of marketing communications include market research, sales promotion, product development, direct marketing, telemarketing, and other related services. Interpublic employs more than 17,000 people in over 90 countries.

BUSINESS LINE ANALYSIS

(12/31/94)	Rev(%)	Inc(%)
United States	37.2	37.7
Europe	37.6	24.1
Far East	14.0	18.6
Latin America	8.0	17.5
Other International	3.2	2.1
Total	100.0	100.0

ANNUAL EARNINGS AND DIVIDENDS PER SHARE

	1994	1993	1992	1991	1990	1989	1988
Earnings Per Share	1.53	1.67	[1] 1.50	1.30	1.19	1.05	0.90
Dividends Per Share	0.545	0.49	[2] 0.45	0.41	0.37	[3] 0.322	0.257
Dividend Payout %	35.6	29.3	30.0	31.5	31.1	30.6	28.3

[1] Before acctg. chg. [2] 2-for-1 stk split, 6/16/92 [3] 3-for-2 stk split, 6/89

ANNUAL FINANCIAL DATA

RECORD OF EARNINGS (IN MILLIONS)

	1994	1993	1992	1991	1990	1989	1988
Total Revenues	1,984.3	1,793.9	1,856.0	1,677.5	1,368.2	1,256.9	1,191.9
Costs and Expenses	1,705.0	1,493.1	1,576.0	1,421.8	1,172.1	1,081.9	1,034.3
Depreciation & Amort	45.6	42.5	39.6	36.9	27.6	22.3	19.1
Operating Profit	282.4	258.2	240.4	218.8	168.4	152.6	138.5
Inc Bef Prov for Income Taxes	200.8	231.8	207.2	185.3	149.5	137.6	128.3
Income Taxes	86.3	99.8	91.3	87.7	72.5	68.1	67.8
Net Income	[1] 115.2	[2] 125.3	[3] 111.9	94.6	80.1	70.6	60.1
Aver. Shs. Outstg. (000)	75,570	75,216	74,975	72,860	67,349	67,334	66,214

[1] Before acctg. change dr$21,780,000. [2] Before acctg. change dr$512,000. [3] Before acctg. change dr$24,640,000.

BALANCE SHEET (IN MILLIONS)

Cash and Cash Equivalents	441.6	322.4	290.7	276.4	216.4	123.0	180.0
Receivables, Net	2,177.6	1,625.9	1,572.3	1,705.6	1,656.0	1,225.3	1,092.9
Gross Property	460.9	387.7	342.2	333.1	305.5	225.8	195.3
Accumulated Depreciation	212.8	171.0	161.7	146.3	126.7	93.8	83.2
Long-Term Debt	241.8	226.1	200.2	170.5	144.5	36.5	42.6
Net Stockholders' Equity	649.4	564.0	511.2	586.8	509.7	367.6	332.9
Total Assets	3,793.4	2,869.8	2,623.3	2,784.3	2,584.1	1,740.7	1,600.0
Total Current Assets	2,675.3	2,003.2	1,914.8	2,031.6	1,914.8	1,372.8	1,296.8
Total Current Liabilities	2,595.2	1,836.0	1,690.2	1,853.6	1,769.3	1,210.5	1,116.8
Net Working Capital	80.1	167.2	224.5	178.0	145.5	162.4	180.1
Year End Shs Outstg (000)	77,704	74,801	75,063	75,427	73,477	69,138	69,892

STATISTICAL RECORD:

Operating Profit Margin %	11.8	14.4	13.0	13.0	12.3	12.1	11.6
Book Value Per Share	0.62	0.97	1.50	1.80	1.77	3.54	3.30
Return on Equity %	17.7	22.2	21.9	16.1	15.7	19.2	18.1
Return on Assets %	3.0	4.4	4.3	3.4	3.1	4.1	3.8
Average Yield %	1.7	1.6	1.5	1.8	2.2	2.1	2.3
P/E Ratio	23.4-18.0	21.3-14.3	23.8-17.2	22.0-13.0	16.0-12.3	18.1-11.5	13.6-10.6
Price Range	35⅞-27½	35⅝-23⅞	35¾-25¾	28⅝-16⅞	19-14⅝	19-12⅛	12⅜-9⅝

Statistics are as originally reported.

OFFICERS:
P.H. Geier, Jr., Chmn., Pres. & C.E.O.
E.P. Beard, E.V.P.-Fin. & Oper. & C.F.O.
C. Rudge, Sr. V.P., Gen. Couns. & Sec.

INCORPORATED: DE, Sep., 1930

PRINCIPAL OFFICE: 1271 Ave. of the Americas, New York, NY 10020

TELEPHONE NUMBER: (212) 399-8000
FAX: (212) 399-8130
NO. OF EMPLOYEES: 18,100
ANNUAL MEETING: In May
SHAREHOLDERS: 5,773
INSTITUTIONAL HOLDINGS:
No. of Institutions: 423
Shares Held: 62,749,995

REGISTRAR(S): First Chicago Trust Company of NY, New York, NY

TRANSFER AGENT(S): First Chicago Trust Company of NY, New York, NY

NYS SYMBOL JP
Rec. Pr. 53⅛

JEFFERSON-PILOT CORP.

YIELD 3.6%
P/E RATIO 11.0

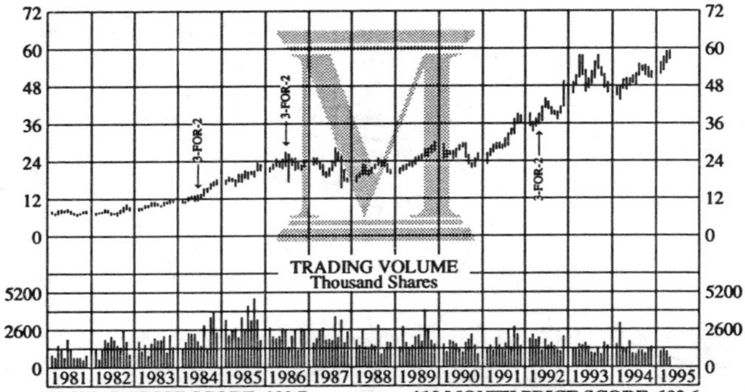

3-FOR-2
3-FOR-2
3-FOR-2
TRADING VOLUME
Thousand Shares
1981 1982 1983 1984 1985 1986 1987 1988 1989 1990 1991 1992 1993 1994 1995

*7 YEAR PRICE SCORE 120.7 *12 MONTH PRICE SCORE 102.6

*NYSE COMPOSITE INDEX=100

INTERIM EARNINGS (Per Share):

Qtr.	Mar.	June	Sept.	Dec.
1992	0.96	0.94	0.96	1.12
1993	0.99	1.04	1.04	1.30
1994	1.11	1.20	1.21	1.33
1995	1.07	...	...	...

INTERIM DIVIDENDS (Per Share):

Amt.	Decl.	Ex.	Rec.	Pay.
0.43Q	8/3/94	8/15/94	8/19/94	9/2/94
0.43Q	11/7	11/14	11/18	12/2
0.43Q	11/7	2/6/95	2/10/95	3/3/95
0.48Q	2/13/95	5/8	5/13	6/2
0.48Q	5/5	8/16	8/18	9/1

*Indicated div.: $1.92**

CAPITALIZATION (12/31/94):

	($000)	(%)
Total Debt	296,188	13.8
Deferred Income Tax	122,253	5.7
Common & Surplus	1,732,543	80.5
Total	2,150,984	100.0

DIVIDEND ACHIEVER STATUS:
Rank: 130 1984-94 Growth Rate: 11.4%
Total Years of Dividend Growth: 27

RECENT DEVELOPMENTS: For the year ended 12/31/94, income from continuing operations was $229.9 million, up 9.7% from $209.6 million a year earlier. Total revenues climbed 6.4% to $1.27 billion. Life and annuity premiums were $399.1 million compared with $386.6 million a year ago. Accident and health premiums more than doubled to $13.8 million from $6.4 million a year ago. For the quarter ended 12/31/94, income from continuing operations rose 3.2% to $64.3 million from $62.3 million for the prior-year quarter. Total revenues increased 5.9% to $334.6 million.

PROSPECTS: The Company has completed the sale of its title insurance operations and has announced an agreement, subject to regulatory approval, to sell its property-casualty operations. The market's favorable reception to the Company's new strategies and products should continue to provide for solid growth in the life insurance and annuity businesses. Profits continue to rise for both the individual and group insurance operations. The acquisiton of WCSC-TV in Charleston, SC is contributing to the communication segment's good performance.

BUSINESS

JEFFERSON-PILOT CORPORATION is the parent of Jefferson-Pilot Life Insurance Company, which offers both group and individual life insurance, health insurance, annuity and pension products. Other subsidiaries provide fire and casualty insurance, title insurance and mutual fund sales and management services. Jefferson-Pilot Communications Co. provides information and entertainment services through three network television and thirteen radio stations. Contributions to revenues (and operating income) in 1994 were as follows: life and accident and health insurance, 85% (88%); communications, 14% (12%) and other, 0.8% (0.2%).

REVENUES

(12/31/94)	($000)	(%)
Life, Accident, & Health	1,025,672	80.8
Communications	172,501	13.6
Other	70,637	5.6
Total	1,268,810	100.0

ANNUAL EARNINGS AND DIVIDENDS PER SHARE

	1994	1993	1992	1991	1990	1989	1988
Earnings Per Share	**4.73**	**4.36**	**3.99**	**3.43**	**2.94**	**2.43**	**1.72**
Dividends Per Share	**1.68**	**1.51**	**1.30**	**1 1.093**	**0.987**	**0.893**	**0.84**
Dividend Payout %	**35.5**	**34.6**	**32.6**	**31.9**	**33.6**	**36.7**	**48.8**

1 3-for-2 stk split,04/15/92

ANNUAL FINANCIAL DATA

	1994	1993	1992	1991	1990	1989	1988
RECORD OF EARNINGS (IN MILLIONS):							
Insurance Premiums	655.3	669.8	658.4	658.3	661.3	659.2	781.1
Total Interest Income	375.2	369.6	360.9	352.8	342.1	333.5	313.8
Total Revenues	1,268.8	1,246.6	1,202.3	1,173.5	1,162.6	1,140.2	1,223.5
Ins Policyholder Bens	627.9	629.8	511.7	527.4	548.6	572.6	637.1
Inc Bef Income Taxes & Acctg Chang	347.6	322.0	285.6	244.8	221.6	197.9	138.8
Income Taxes	117.7	102.8	82.4	69.1	64.0	60.2	42.5
Net Income	1 229.9	2 219.3	203.2	175.7	157.6	137.7	101.2
Aver. Shs. Outstg. (000)	48,462	50,252	50,952	51,319	53,636	56,589	58,602
1 Before disc. op. cr$9,341,000. 2 Before acctg. change dr$24,109,000.							
BALANCE SHEET (IN MILLIONS):							
Fixed Maturities	3,546.9	3,221.9	2,773.8	2,571.7	2,327.4	2,229.7	2,033.4
Common Stocks	718.0	833.4	837.9	784.0	610.0	780.0	544.2
Policy Loans	206.4	214.6	220.7	227.9	231.8	236.7	247.9
Mtge Loans on Real Estate	680.6	583.6	561.0	541.2	535.7	506.1	498.8
Total Assets	6,140.3	5,640.6	5,235.8	4,925.2	4,454.9	4,529.6	4,174.1
Benefits and Claims	3,544.7	3,373.7	3,123.7	2,957.2	2,776.9	2,639.8	2,471.1
Net Stockholders' Equity	1,732.5	1,733.1	1,686.8	1,563.0	1,353.0	1,474.7	1,336.0
Year End Shs Outstg (000)	48,451	49,464	50,439	51,292	51,785	56,054	57,822
STATISTICAL RECORD:							
Book Value Per Share	35.76	35.04	33.44	30.47	26.13	26.31	23.11
Return on Equity %	13.3	12.7	12.0	11.2	11.7	9.3	7.6
Return on Assets %	3.7	3.9	3.9	3.6	3.5	3.0	2.4
Average Yield %	3.4	2.9	3.1	3.5	3.8	3.6	4.0
P/E Ratio	11.7-9.2	13.3-10.4	12.4-8.4	11.4-6.7	10.2-7.4	12.5-8.2	15.0-10.3
Price Range	55⅛-43⅜	57⅞-45½	49½-33⅜	39⅛-22⅞	29⅞-21⅝	30⅜-19⅞	25-17⅛

Statistics are as originally reported.

OFFICERS:
R.H. Spilman, Chmn.
D.A. Stonecipher, Pres. & C.E.O.
D.R. Glass, Sr. V.P., C.F.O. & Treas.

INCORPORATED: NC, Jan., 1968

PRINCIPAL OFFICE: 100 North Greene Street, Greensboro, NC 27401

TELEPHONE NUMBER: (919) 691-3441
NO. OF EMPLOYEES: 3,600 (approx.)
ANNUAL MEETING: In May
SHAREHOLDERS: 10,671
INSTITUTIONAL HOLDINGS:
No. of Institutions: 324
Shares Held: 19,895,797

REGISTRAR(S): First Union National Bank of N.C., Charlotte, NC

TRANSFER AGENT(S): First Union National Bank of N.C., Charlotte, NC

NYS SYMBOL JCI
Rec. Pr. 54⅞

JOHNSON CONTROLS, INC.

YIELD 2.8%
P/E RATIO 14.1

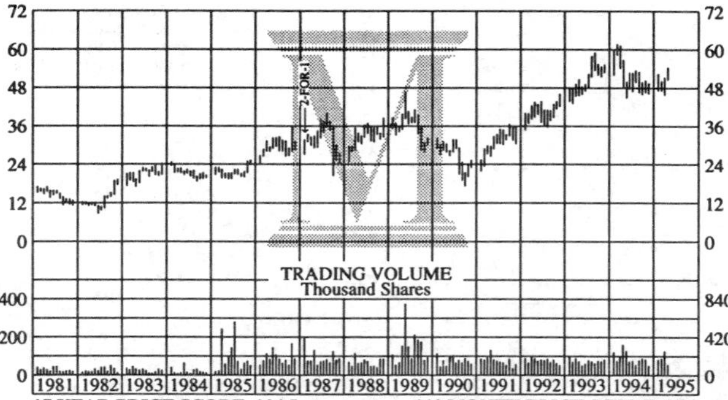

72
60
48
36
24
12
0
2-FOR-1
TRADING VOLUME
Thousand Shares
8400
4200
0
1981 1982 1983 1984 1985 1986 1987 1988 1989 1990 1991 1992 1993 1994 1995

*7 YEAR PRICE SCORE 104.5 *12 MONTH PRICE SCORE 96.9

*NYSE COMPOSITE INDEX=100

INTERIM EARNINGS (Per Share):

Qtr.	Dec.	Mar.	June	Sept.
1991-92	0.66	0.36	0.86	0.98
1992-93	---------------- 0.17 ----------------			
1993-94	0.87	0.56	1.06	1.31
1994-95	0.95	...	...	...

INTERIM DIVIDENDS (Per Share):

Amt.	Decl.	Ex.	Rec.	Pay.
0.36Q	5/25/94	5/27/94	6/3/94	6/30/94
0.36Q	7/27	9/2	9/9	9/30
rights	...	...	11/30	...
0.39Q	11/16	12/5	12/9	1/3/95
0.39Q	1/25/95	2/27/95	3/3/95	3/31

*Indicated div.: $1.56**

CAPITALIZATION (9/30/94):

	($000)	(%)
Long-Term Debt	635,400	33.9
Cap. Lease Oblig.	34,900	1.9
Preferred Stock	164,100	8.8
Common & Surplus	1,038,700	55.4
Total	1,873,100	100.0

DIVIDEND ACHIEVER STATUS:

Rank: 275 1984-94 Growth Rate: 5.4%

Total Years of Dividend Growth: 19

RECENT DEVELOPMENTS: For the quarter ended 3/31/95, net income rose to $32.3 million from $25.5 million a year earlier. Net sales improved by 22% to $2.05 billion. The automotive seating division in the U.S. and Europe benefited from new production contracts and existing agreements that increased production levels. JCI supplied 100% of the seats for the Ford Escort to be produced in the United Kingdom, Germany and Spain. The controls segment boosted its operating earnings as businesses attempted to control costs by replacing antiquated systems with newer more efficient ones.

PROSPECTS: Interest rate hikes have begun to place pressure on automobile sales which may slow production. Such a situation may limit JCI's sales growth, but should not adversely affect earnings in the near term. The specter of lower production levels in the automotive unit should be offset by the Company's controls unit as demand for retrofit systems remains high. The economic recovery in Europe will benefit JCI, especially its plastic machinery unit. The assimilation of businesses that were acquired in the previous year should not place significant pressure on earnings.

BUSINESS

JOHNSON CONTROLS, INC. is a market leader in facility services and control systems, automotive seating systems, plastic packaging and automotive batteries. The Controls segment, which contributed 33% of 1994 sales (26%, operating income), installs and services control systems for temperature and lighting control and services mechanical equipment. The Automotive division, 42% (39%), offers complete seating systems and components. Plastics, 14% (20%), produces containers for household use as well as injection molding tools and plastic components for the auto industry. The Battery segment, 11% (15%), supplies automotive and specialty batteries.

BUSINESS LINE ANALYSIS

(09/30/94)	Rev(%)	Inc(%)
Automotive	41.8	39.4
Controls	32.9	25.9
Plastics	14.5	19.7
Battery	10.8	15.0
Total	100.0	100.0

ANNUAL EARNINGS AND DIVIDENDS PER SHARE

	9/30/94	9/30/93	9/30/92	9/30/91	9/30/90	9/30/89	9/30/88
Earnings Per Share	**3.80**	**[1] 3.17**	**2.86**	**2.19**	**2.13**	**2.55**	**2.83**
Dividends Per Share	**1.44**	**1.36**	**1.28**	**1.24**	**1.20**	**1.16**	**1.10**
Dividend Payout %	**37.9**	**43.0**	**44.8**	**56.6**	**56.3**	**45.5**	**38.9**

[1] Before acctg. chg.

ANNUAL FINANCIAL DATA

	9/30/94	9/30/93	9/30/92	9/30/91	9/30/90	9/30/89	9/30/88
RECORD OF EARNINGS (IN MILLIONS):							
Total Revenues	6,870.5	6,181.7	5,156.5	4,559.0	4,504.0	3,683.6	3,099.6
Costs and Expenses	6,274.9	5,645.1	4,659.9	4,133.3	4,094.6	3,334.9	2,773.7
Depreciation & Amort	230.4	238.3	231.1	196.9	181.4	143.7	115.6
Operating Income	365.2	298.3	265.5	228.8	228.0	205.0	210.3
Income Bef Income Taxes	326.4	250.7	227.7	176.0	172.8	178.9	186.5
Income Taxes	140.3	112.8	104.7	80.9	80.4	81.4	83.0
Net Income	165.2	[1] 137.9	123.0	95.1	92.4	97.5	103.5
Aver. Shs. Outstg. (000)	41,000	40,800	40,100	39,600	39,400	37,100	36,600
[1] Before acctg. change dr$122,000,000.							
BALANCE SHEET (IN MILLIONS):							
Cash and Cash Equivalents	132.6	87.7	96.2	91.7	54.3	27.0	20.0
Receivables, Net	1,067.0	912.1	899.4	780.9	765.6	667.8	592.9
Inventories	304.7	281.3	316.0	287.4	319.0	270.4	256.8
Gross Property	2,669.2	2,367.0	2,125.9	1,791.7	1,654.1	1,375.3	1,194.3
Accumulated Depreciation	1,335.8	1,153.4	968.6	805.9	675.3	537.1	434.3
Long-Term Debt	635.4	500.4	503.3	490.6	483.0	445.1	342.1
Net Stockholders' Equity	1,202.8	1,079.0	1,194.2	1,064.0	1,035.5	977.9	852.5
Total Assets	3,806.9	3,230.8	3,179.5	2,841.0	2,798.8	2,415.0	2,013.3
Total Current Assets	1,778.5	1,532.0	1,524.3	1,376.1	1,290.6	1,100.8	958.5
Total Current Liabilities	1,516.4	1,284.9	1,245.2	1,105.3	1,099.4	837.9	695.7
Net Working Capital	262.1	247.1	279.1	270.8	191.2	262.9	262.8
Year End Shs Outstg (000)	40,748	38,800	40,100	39,600	39,400	39,400	36,400
STATISTICAL RECORD:							
Operating Profit Margin %	5.3	4.8	5.1	5.0	5.1	5.6	6.8
Book Value Per Share	13.37	15.19	17.44	16.33	15.37	14.91	18.25
Return on Equity %	13.7	12.8	10.3	8.9	8.9	10.0	12.1
Return on Assets %	4.3	4.3	3.9	3.3	3.3	4.0	5.1
Average Yield %	2.7	2.7	3.2	4.2	4.9	3.1	3.5
P/E Ratio	16.3-11.8	N.M	16.1-12.1	16.7-10.0	15.1-8.0	18.3-10.9	13.6-8.7
Price Range	61¾-44⅞	59⅛-43	46⅛-34⅝	36⅝-21⅞	32¼-17⅛	46¾-27⅞	38½-24¾

Statistics are as originally reported.

OFFICERS:
J.H. Keyes, Chmn. & C.E.O.
S.A. Roell, V.P. & C.F.O.
J.P. Kennedy, V.P., Sec. & General Counsel

INCORPORATED: WI, Jul., 1900

PRINCIPAL OFFICE: 5757 N. Green Bay Ave. P.O. Box 591, Milwaukee, WI 53201

TELEPHONE NUMBER: (414) 228-1200

NO. OF EMPLOYEES: 54,800

ANNUAL MEETING: In January

SHAREHOLDERS: 33,381

INSTITUTIONAL HOLDINGS:
No. of Institutions: 389
Shares Held: 25,617,705

REGISTRAR(S): First Wisconsin Trust Co., Milwaukee, WI

TRANSFER AGENT(S): First Wisconsin Trust Co., Milwaukee, WI

JOHNSON & JOHNSON

YIELD 2.0%
P/E RATIO 20.3

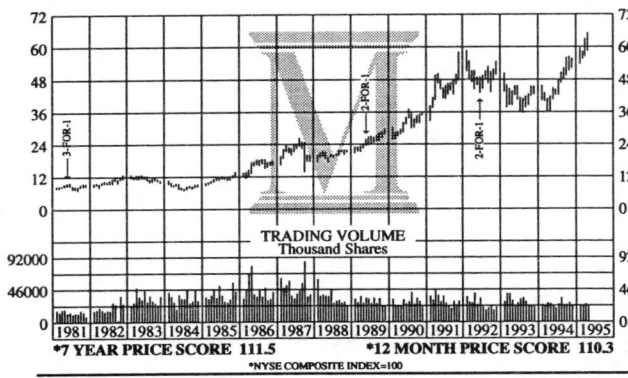

INTERIM EARNINGS (Per Share):

Qtr.	Mar.	June	Sept.	Dec.
1993	0.77	0.75	0.70	0.52
1994	0.85	0.86	0.82	0.59
1995	1.02	...	...	...

INTERIM DIVIDENDS (Per Share):

Amt.	Decl.	Ex.	Rec.	Pay.
0.29Q	4/28/94	5/11/94	5/17/94	6/7/94
0.29Q	7/18	8/10	8/16	9/6
0.29Q	10/17	11/8	11/15	12/6
0.29Q	1/3/95	2/8/95	2/14/95	3/7/95
0.33Q	4/27	5/10	5/16	6/6

Indicated div.: $1.32*

CAPITALIZATION (1/1/95):

	($000)	(%)
Long-Term Debt	2,199,000	23.6
Common & Surplus	7,122,000	76.4
Total	9,321,000	100.0

TRADING VOLUME
Thousand Shares

| 1981 | 1982 | 1983 | 1984 | 1985 | 1986 | 1987 | 1988 | 1989 | 1990 | 1991 | 1992 | 1993 | 1994 | 1995 |

*7 YEAR PRICE SCORE 111.5 ***12 MONTH PRICE SCORE 110.3**

*NYSE COMPOSITE INDEX=100

DIVIDEND ACHIEVER STATUS:
Rank: 64   1984-94 Growth Rate: 14.4%
Total Years of Dividend Growth: 32

RECENT DEVELOPMENTS: For the year ended 1/1/95, net income increased 12.3% to $2.01 billion from $1.79 billion a year earlier. This is the first time the Company's earnings have exceeded $2 billion. Sales rose 11.3% to $15.73 billion. The improved results reflect the success of new products, cost-efficiency gains and strategic acquisitions. All geographic areas around the world generated sales growth. The Pharmaceutical, Professional and Consumer businesses each made positive contributions to operating results.

PROSPECTS: Operating results will continue to reflect the Company's well-diversified product positions in the steadily growing health and personal-care market. Strong demand for new products should enable the Pharmaceutical business to increase earnings at a rate higher than the industry average. These new products include Risperdal, an anti-psychotic drug, and Propulsid, a gastrointestinal drug. However, pharmaceutical margins will be affected by pricing pressures.

BUSINESS

JOHNSON & JOHNSON is engaged in the manufacture and sale of a broad range of products in the health care and other fields. The Consumer segment, 33% of 1994 sales and (15% of operating profit) consists of toiletries and hygienic products. The Professional segment, 34% (29%), includes ligatures and sutures, mechanical wound closure products, diagnostic products, dental products, medical equipment and devices, surgical dressings, surgical apparel and accessories, surgical instruments and related items. The Pharmaceutical segment, 33% (56%), consists of prescription drugs including contraceptives and therapeutics, antifungal, and dermatological products.

BUSINESS LINE ANALYSIS

(1/1/95)	Rev(%)	Inc(%)
Consumer	33.4	15.0
Pharmaceutical	32.8	56.5
Professional	33.8	28.5
Total	100.0	100.0

ANNUAL EARNINGS AND DIVIDENDS PER SHARE

	1/1/95	1/2/94	1/3/93	12/29/91	12/30/90	12/31/89	1/1/89
Earnings Per Share	3.12	2.74	①2.46	2.20	1.72	1.63	1.43
Dividends Per Share	1.13	1.01	0.89	0.77	0.655	0.56	0.48
Dividend Payout %	36.2	36.9	36.2	35.1	38.2	34.5	33.6

① Before acctg. chg.

ANNUAL FINANCIAL DATA

RECORD OF EARNINGS (IN MILLIONS):

Total Revenues	15,734.0	14,138.0	13,753.0	12,447.0	11,232.0	9,757.0	9,000.0
Costs and Expenses	12,203.0	11,127.0	10,916.0	9,790.0	8,870.0	7,682.0	7,205.0
Depreciation & Amort.	724.0	617.0	560.0	493.0	474.0	414.0	391.0
Operating Profit	4,085.0	3,576.0	3,404.0	3,144.0	2,826.0	2,380.0	2,078.0
Earn Bef Prov for Taxes on Inc	2,681.0	2,332.0	2,207.0	2,038.0	1,623.0	1,514.0	1,396.0
Income Taxes	675.0	545.0	582.0	577.0	480.0	432.0	422.0
Net Income	2,006.0	1,787.0	①1,625.0	1,461.0	1,143.0	1,082.0	974.0
Aver. Shs. Outstg. (000)	643,000	652,000	660,000	662,000	666,000	666,000	681,000

① Before acctg. change dr$595,000,000.

BALANCE SHEET (IN MILLIONS):

Cash and Cash Equivalents	704.0	476.0	878.0	792.0	931.0	583.0	660.0
Receivables, Net	3,183.0	2,506.0	2,182.0	2,001.0	1,751.0	1,516.0	1,318.0
Inventories	2,161.0	1,717.0	1,742.0	1,702.0	1,543.0	1,353.0	1,273.0
Gross Property	7,655.0	6,783.0	6,303.0	5,691.0	5,098.0	4,517.0	3,969.0
Accumulated Depreciation	2,745.0	2,377.0	2,188.0	2,024.0	1,851.0	1,671.0	1,476.0
Long-Term Debt	2,199.0	1,493.0	1,365.0	1,301.0	1,316.0	1,170.0	1,166.0
Net Stockholders' Equity	7,122.0	5,568.0	5,171.0	5,626.0	4,900.0	4,148.0	3,503.0
Total Assets	15,668.0	12,242.0	11,884.0	10,513.0	9,506.0	7,919.0	7,119.0
Total Current Assets	6,680.0	5,217.0	5,423.0	4,933.0	4,664.0	3,776.0	3,503.0
Total Current Liabilities	4,266.0	3,212.0	3,427.0	2,689.0	2,623.0	1,927.0	1,868.0
Net Working Capital	2,414.0	2,005.0	1,996.0	2,244.0	2,041.0	1,849.0	1,635.0
Year End Shs Outstg (000)	643,000	643,000	655,000	666,000	666,000	666,000	666,000

STATISTICAL RECORD:

Operating Profit Margin %	17.8	16.9	16.6	17.4	16.8	17.0	15.6
Book Value Per Share	7.34	7.22	6.80	7.34	6.30	5.17	4.35
Return on Equity %	28.2	32.1	31.4	26.0	23.3	26.1	27.8
Return on Assets %	12.8	14.6	13.7	13.9	12.0	13.7	13.7
Average Yield %	2.4	2.3	1.7	1.7	2.1	2.2	2.4
P/E Ratio	18.1-11.5	18.4-13.0	23.9-17.5	26.5-15.0	21.6-14.9	18.3-12.7	15.4-12.2
Price Range	56½-36	50⅜-35⅝	58¾-43	58⅛-32¾	37⅛-25⅜	29¾-20¾	22-17⅜

Statistics are as originally reported.

OFFICERS:
R.S. Larsen, Chmn. & C.E.O.
R.E. Campbell, Vice-Chmn.
R.N. Wilson, Vice-Chmn.
J.H. Heisen, Treas.

INCORPORATED: NJ, Nov., 1887

PRINCIPAL OFFICE: One Johnson & Johnson Plaza, New Brunswick, NJ 08933

TELEPHONE NUMBER: (908) 524-0400
FAX: (908) 214-0332
NO. OF EMPLOYEES: 81,500
ANNUAL MEETING: In April
SHAREHOLDERS: 104,700
INSTITUTIONAL HOLDINGS:
No. of Institutions: 1,332
Shares Held: 392,359,883

REGISTRAR(S): First Chicago Trust Co. of New York, New York, NY 10008

TRANSFER AGENT(S): First Chicago Trust Co. of New York, New York, NY 10008

K MART CORP.

YIELD 3.6%
P/E RATIO 22.9

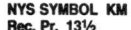

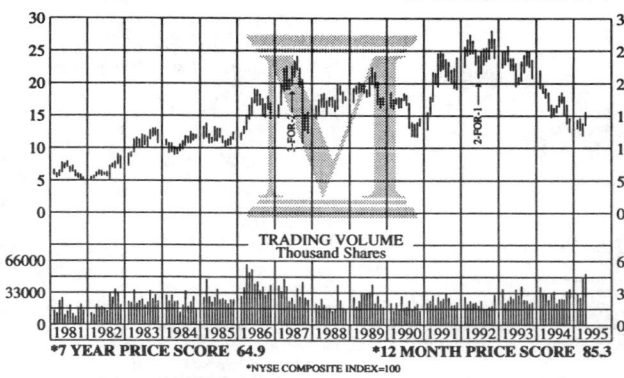

TRADING VOLUME
Thousand Shares

| 1981 | 1982 | 1983 | 1984 | 1985 | 1986 | 1987 | 1988 | 1989 | 1990 | 1991 | 1992 | 1993 | 1994 | 1995 |

*7 YEAR PRICE SCORE 64.9   *12 MONTH PRICE SCORE 85.3

*NYSE COMPOSITE INDEX=100

INTERIM EARNINGS (Per Share):

Qtr.	Apr.	July	Oct.	Jan.
1991-92	0.27	0.40	0.25	1.06
1992-93		2.06		
1993-94	d0.02	0.22	0.20	d1.26
1994-95	0.04	0.20	0.08	0.27

INTERIM DIVIDENDS (Per Share):

Amt.	Decl.	Ex.	Rec.	Pay.
0.24Q	3/15/94	5/6/94	5/12/94	6/13/94
0.24Q	7/19	8/5	8/11	9/12
0.24Q	10/18	11/4	11/10	12/12
0.24Q	1/17/95	2/3/95	2/9/95	3/13/95
0.12Q	4/25	5/5	5/11	6/12

*Indicated div.: $0.48**

CAPITALIZATION (1/26/94):

	($000)	(%)
Long-Term Debt	2,227,000	22.2
Cap. Lease Oblig.	1,720,000	17.1
Preferred Stock	1,143,000	11.4
Common & Surplus	4,950,000	49.3
Total	10,040,000	100.0

DIVIDEND ACHIEVER STATUS:
Rank: 193   1984-94 Growth Rate: 9.1%
Total Years of Dividend Growth: 30

RECENT DEVELOPMENTS: For the year ended 1/25/95, KM reported income from continuing operations of $260 million versus a loss of $347 million a year earlier. Sales declined 7.3% to $34.03 billion. Comparisons were made with restated prior-year figures. Gross margin declined to 23.6% of sales from 25.0% a year earlier, due to increased promotional activity and increased sales of lower-margined merchandise. Selling, general and administrative expenses increased to 22.6% of sales from 22.4% a year earlier.

PROSPECTS: Despite having completed the initial public offering of shares in OfficeMax and The Sports Authority, which will help its financial flexibility, Kmart's sales and earnings growth will continue to be adversely affected by increased competition and poor margin growth. Additionally, continued inventory-management problems and flat clothing sales will further hamper Kmart's sales and earnings comparisons. KM has promised to cut costs substantially; however, KM's market share has been declining steadily.

BUSINESS

K MART CORP. is one of the world's largest mass merchandise retailers, operating nearly 4,000 retail outlets in the United States, the Czech Republic, Slovakia, Canada and Puerto Rico. The Company's businesses include: Kmart discount stores; Super Kmart Centers, which feature grocery items, in addition to general merchandise; Builders Square, which manages do-it-yourself home improvement retail stores; and Borders Group, which consists of Borders Bookstores and Waldenbooks. The Company also has interests of approximately 25% in OfficeMax and 30% in The Sports Authority, both of which were offered to the public in November 1994.

QUARTERLY DATA

(1/26/94) ($000)	Rev	Inc
1st Quarter	7,415	23
2nd Quarter	8,539	102
3rd Quarter	8,183	94
4th Quarter	10,420	(1,193)

ANNUAL EARNINGS AND DIVIDENDS PER SHARE

	1/26/94	1/27/93	1/29/92	1/30/91	1/31/90	1/25/89	1/27/88
Earnings Per Share	d0.73	2.06	2.02	1.89	0.81	2.00	1.70
Dividends Per Share	0.96	0.95	0.875	0.85	0.78	0.64	①0.56
Dividend Payout %	N.M.	44.2	43.4	45.0	96.9	32.0	32.9

① 3-for-2 stk split, 6/87

ANNUAL FINANCIAL DATA

RECORD OF EARNINGS (IN MILLIONS):

Total Revenues	34,447.0	38,019.0	34,859.0	32,339.0	29,793.0	27,583.0	25,886.0
Costs and Expenses	33,927.0	35,581.0	32,678.0	30,376.0	28,566.0	25,661.0	24,076.0
Depreciation & Amort	703.0	685.0	589.0	531.0	461.0	437.0	401.0
Operating Profit	1,165.0	1,753.0	1,592.0	1,432.0	1,406.0	1,485.0	1,409.0
Income Bef Income Taxes	d550.0	1,426.0	1,301.0	1,146.0	515.0	1,244.0	1,171.0
Income Taxes	cr222.0	485.0	442.0	390.0	192.0	441.0	479.0
Net Income	d974.0	941.0	859.0	756.0	323.0	803.0	692.0
Aver. Shs. Outstg. (000)	457,000	458,000	426,000	400,000	401,000	401,000	407,000

BALANCE SHEET (IN MILLIONS):

Cash and Cash Equivalents	449.0	611.0	565.0	278.0	353.0	948.0	449.0
Inventories	7,252.0	8,752.0	7,546.0	6,891.0	6,933.0	5,671.0	5,571.0
Gross Property	10,862.0	11,029.0	9,559.0	8,339.0	7,507.0	7,034.0	6,537.0
Accumulated Depreciation	4,976.0	4,624.0	4,294.0	3,978.0	3,657.0	3,138.0	2,793.0
Long-Term Debt	2,227.0	3,237.0	...	...	...	...	...
Capital Lease Obligations	1,720.0	1,698.0	1,638.0	1,598.0	1,549.0	1,588.0	1,557.0
Net Stockholders' Equity	6,093.0	7,536.0	6,891.0	5,384.0	4,972.0	5,009.0	4,409.0
Total Assets	17,504.0	18,931.0	15,999.0	13,899.0	13,145.0	12,126.0	11,106.0
Total Current Assets	9,847.0	10,509.0	8,990.0	7,896.0	7,984.0	7,146.0	6,373.0
Total Current Liabilities	5,724.0	5,495.0	4,308.0	4,377.0	4,299.0	3,492.0	3,370.0
Net Working Capital	4,123.0	5,014.0	4,682.0	3,519.0	3,685.0	3,654.0	3,003.0
Year End Shs Outstg (000)	409,000	407,000	404,000	400,000	399,000	399,000	399,000

STATISTICAL RECORD:

Operating Profit Margin %	...	4.6	4.6	4.4	2.6	5.4	5.4
Book Value Per Share	10.40	13.15	12.63	13.46	12.46	12.55	11.05
Return on Equity %	...	12.5	12.5	14.0	6.5	16.0	15.7
Return on Assets %	...	5.0	5.4	5.4	2.5	6.6	6.2
Average Yield %	4.2	3.7	4.7	5.6	4.0	3.7	3.2
P/E Ratio	...	13.7-10.1	12.3-6.3	9.9-6.2	28.0-20.3	9.9-7.3	14.2-6.3
Price Range	25¾-19½	28⅛-20⅞	24¾-12¾	18⅝-11⅝	22⅜-16¼	19⅞-14½	24⅛-10¾

Statistics are as originally reported.

OFFICERS:
A.N. Palizzi, Pres., E.V.P. & Gen. Coun.
T.F. Murasky, Exec. V.P. & C.F.O.
J.P. Churilla, V.P. & Treas.
N.W. LaDuke, V.P. & Sec.
INCORPORATED: MI, Mar., 1916
PRINCIPAL OFFICE: 3100 West Big Beaver Rd., Troy, MI 48084

TELEPHONE NUMBER: (810) 643-1000
NO. OF EMPLOYEES: 300,000 (approx.)
ANNUAL MEETING: In May
SHAREHOLDERS: 85,920
INSTITUTIONAL HOLDINGS:
No. of Institutions: 697
Shares Held: 286,407,363

REGISTRAR(S): NBD Bank, N.A., Securities Transfer Services, Detroit, MI 02266

TRANSFER AGENT(S): NBD Bank, N.A., Securities Transfer Services, Detroit, MI 02266

NYS SYMBOL K
Rec. Pr. 62⅝

KELLOGG CO.

YIELD 2.3%
P/E RATIO 19.9

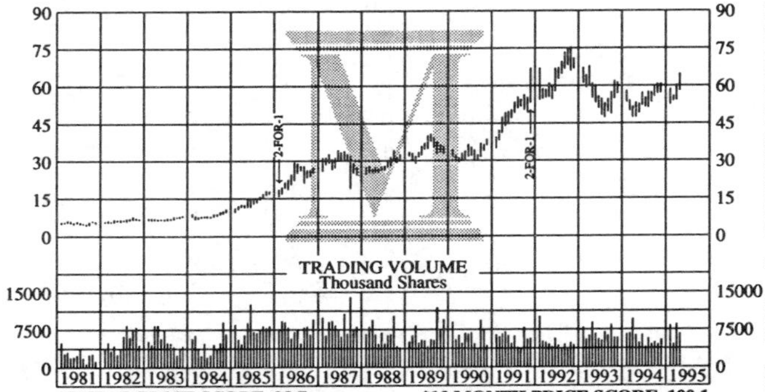

*7 YEAR PRICE SCORE 98.7 *12 MONTH PRICE SCORE 100.1

*NYSE COMPOSITE INDEX=100

INTERIM EARNINGS (Per Share):

Qtr.	Mar.	June	Sept.	Dec.
1991	0.68	0.63	0.71	0.49
1992	0.82	0.70	0.86	0.54
1993	0.76	0.62	0.90	0.66
1994	0.81	0.68	0.96	0.70

INTERIM DIVIDENDS (Per Share):

Amt.	Decl.	Ex.	Rec.	Pay.
0.34Q	5/11/94	5/25/94	6/1/94	6/15/94
0.36Q	7/22	8/26	9/1	9/15
0.36Q	11/9	11/25	12/1	12/15
0.36Q	2/8/95	2/23/95	3/1/95	3/15/95
0.36Q	4/21	5/25	6/1	6/15

*Indicated div.: $1.44**

CAPITALIZATION (12/31/94):

	($000)	(%)
Long-Term Debt	719,200	26.4
Deferred Income Tax	198,100	7.3
Common & Surplus	1,807,500	66.3
Total	2,724,800	100.0

DIVIDEND ACHIEVER STATUS:
Rank: 104 1984-94 Growth Rate: 12.7%
Total Years of Dividend Growth: 38

RECENT DEVELOPMENTS: In February 1995, K announced a program to improve productivity and streamline its cereal production operations, which will result in annual savings of approximately $12 million to $15 million. For the year ended 12/31/94, net income, excluding one-time events, was $705.4 million compared with $680.7 million a year ago. Net sales advanced 4.2% to $6.56 billion. As a percentage of sales, selling and administrative expenses increased to 37.3% from 35.5% a year ago.

PROSPECTS: As a result of increased competition, K will continue to aggressively advertise and reduce price-promotion spending for its established brands such as Corn Flakes, Raisin Bran and Frosted Flakes. These measures, coupled with continued development of new products, brand-building marketing programs, and cost containment initiatives, should allow the Company to keep U.S. cereal volumes steady. Over the long term, K will look to capitalize on expanding its presence in international markets.

BUSINESS

KELLOGG CO. is the world's leading producer of ready-to-eat-cereal products. It also manufactures a wide variety of food products in the United States and abroad, including frozen pies, toaster pastries, frozen waffles, cereal bars, snack items and other convenience foods. Brand names include: Kellogg's, Mrs. Smith' s, and Eggo. Products are manufactured in 18 countries and distributed in 150 countries, including many in Asia, Australia, Europe, Africa and Latin America. Contributions to sales (and earnings) in 1994 were: Kellogg USA, 59% (61%); Kellogg Europe, 25% (24%); and other areas, 16% (15%).

BUSINESS LINE ANALYSIS

(12/31/94)	Rev(%)	Inc(%)
United States	58.5	60.9
Europe	25.0	24.0
Other Areas	16.5	15.1
Total	100.0	100.0

ANNUAL EARNINGS AND DIVIDENDS PER SHARE

	1994	1993	1992	1991	1990	1989	1988
Earnings Per Share	**3.15**	**2.94**	**2.86**	**2.51**	**2.08**	**3 1.73**	**1.95**
Dividends Per Share	**1.40**	**1.32**	**1 1.20**	**2 1.075**	**0.96**	**0.86**	**0.76**
Dividend Payout %	**44.4**	**44.9**	**42.0**	**42.8**	**46.2**	**49.7**	**39.0**

1 Bef acctg chge 2 2-for-1 stk split,12/17/91 3 Before acctg. chg.

ANNUAL FINANCIAL DATA

	1994	1993	1992	1991	1990	1989	1988
RECORD OF EARNINGS (IN MILLIONS):							
Total Revenues	6,562.0	6,295.4	6,190.6	5,801.2	5,176.3	4,634.5	4,368.2
Costs and Expenses	5,143.3	4,961.3	4,896.3	4,535.9	4,095.2	3,751.6	3,415.0
Depreciation	256.1	265.2	231.5	222.8	200.2	167.6	139.7
Operating Profit	1,162.6	1,068.9	1,062.8	2,972.5	2,499.7	2,220.7	2,134.8
Earn Bef Income Taxes	1,130.0	1,034.1	1,070.4	984.2	814.7	667.0	774.7
Income Taxes	424.6	353.4	387.6	378.2	311.9	244.9	294.3
Net Income	705.4	680.7	1 682.8	606.0	502.8	2 422.1	480.4
Aver. Shs. Outstg. (000)	224,200	231,500	238,900	241,200	241,600	244,200	246,376
1 Before acctg. change dr$251,600,000. 2 Before acctg. change cr$48,100,000.							
BALANCE SHEET (IN MILLIONS):							
Cash and Cash Equivalents	266.3	98.1	126.3	178.0	100.5	80.3	185.0
Receivables, Net	643.9	622.3	585.3	483.5	500.6	355.2	404.6
Inventories	396.3	403.1	416.4	401.1	359.7	394.0	362.2
Gross Property	4,600.5	4,272.5	3,993.7	3,889.7	3,672.0	3,302.4	2,916.4
Accumulated Depreciation	1,707.7	1,504.1	1,331.0	1,243.2	1,076.6	896.1	784.5
Long-Term Debt	719.2	521.6	314.9	15.2	295.6	371.4	272.1
Net Stockholders' Equity	1,807.5	1,713.4	1,945.2	2,159.8	1,901.8	1,634.4	1,483.2
Total Assets	4,467.3	4,237.1	4,015.0	3,925.8	3,749.4	3,390.4	3,297.9
Total Current Assets	1,433.5	1,245.1	1,236.6	1,173.0	1,041.4	906.1	1,063.2
Total Current Liabilities	1,185.2	1,214.6	1,071.0	1,324.4	1,109.6	1,037.2	1,183.5
Net Working Capital	248.3	30.5	165.6	d151.4	d68.2	d131.1	d120.3
Year End Shs Outstg (000)	221,701	227,920	237,319	240,463	241,317	243,752	245,856
STATISTICAL RECORD:							
Operating Profit Margin %	17.7	17.0	17.2	18.0	17.0	15.4	18.6
Book Value Per Share	8.13	7.26	7.97	8.77	7.62	6.56	5.82
Return on Equity %	39.0	39.7	35.1	28.1	26.4	25.8	32.4
Return on Assets %	15.8	16.1	17.0	15.4	13.4	12.4	14.6
Average Yield %	2.6	2.3	1.8	2.1	2.8	2.5	2.6
P/E Ratio	19.3-15.0	23.1-16.1	41.6-30.0	26.7-13.9	18.6-14.1	23.6-16.7	17.6-12.6
Price Range	60¾-47⅜	67⅞-47¼	75⅜-54⅜	67-35	38¾-29⅜	40⅞-28⅞	34¼-24½

Statistics are as originally reported.

OFFICERS:
A.G. Langbo, Chmn. & C.E.O.
C.W. Elliot, Exec. V.P. & C.F.O.
R.M. Clark, Sr. V.P., Gen. Coun. & Sec.
C.E. French, V.P.-Fin. & Treas.

INCORPORATED: DE, Dec., 1922

PRINCIPAL OFFICE: One Kellogg Square, Battle Creek, MI 49016-3599

TELEPHONE NUMBER: (616) 961-2000

NO. OF EMPLOYEES: 15,657 (approx.)

ANNUAL MEETING: In April

SHAREHOLDERS: 29,721 (approx.)

INSTITUTIONAL HOLDINGS:
No. of Institutions: 528
Shares Held: 165,785,280

REGISTRAR(S): Harris Trust & Savings Bank, Chicago, IL

TRANSFER AGENT(S): Harris Trust & Savings Bank, Chicago, IL

KELLY SERVICES, INC.

YIELD 2.4%
P/E RATIO 18.5

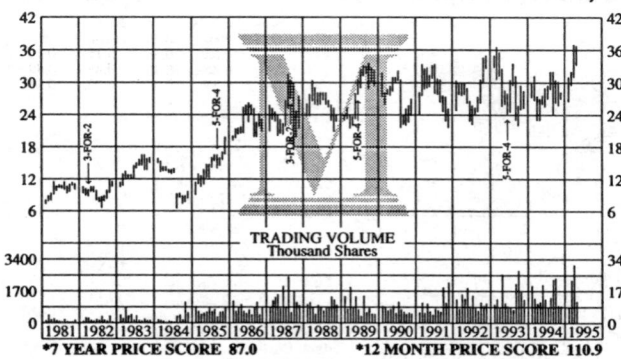

INTERIM EARNINGS (Per Share):

Qtr.	Mar.	June	Sept.	Dec.
1992	0.17	0.22	0.30	0.34
1993	0.18	0.27	0.37	0.36
1994	0.24	0.38	0.51	0.48

INTERIM DIVIDENDS (Per Share):

Amt.	Decl.	Ex.	Rec.	Pay.
0.16Q	2/16/94	2/22/94	2/28/94	3/14/94
0.18Q	5/18	5/24	5/31	6/14
0.18Q	8/17	8/23	8/29	9/12
0.18Q	11/16	11/21	11/28	12/12
0.18Q	2/15/95	2/21/95	2/27/95	3/13/95

Indicated div.: $0.72

CAPITALIZATION (1/1/95):

	($000)	(%)
Common & Surplus	431,516	100.0
Total	431,516	100.0

DIVIDEND ACHIEVER STATUS:

Rank: 82   1984-94 Growth Rate: 13.7%
Total Years of Dividend Growth: 23

RECENT DEVELOPMENTS: For the year ended 1/1/95, net income jumped 37.0% to $61.1 million from $44.6 million a year earlier. Sales of services reached $2.36 billion, up 20.9% from $1.95 billion the year before. Improved sales and earnings resulted from a robust economy in the United States, recovery and strong sales in several countries served by the International Division, new businesses and new services. Earnings from operations were $91.7 million compared with $63.9 million in the prior year, an increase of 43.6%. For the quarter ended 1/1/95, net income was $18.1 million, a gain of 32.8% over $13.6 million for the corresponding quarter in 1994. Sales of services rose 25.2% to $631.4 million from $504.3 million in the 1993 quarter. Earnings from operations were $27.3 million, up 35.9% from $20.1 million for the year-earlier quarter.

BUSINESS

KELLY SERVICES, INC. is a service organization that provides temporary help in the areas of office clerical, marketing, technical, industrial, nursing and home health care and other business services to a diversified group of customers. KELLY OFFICE SERVICES: provides guaranteed temporary office help to accomodate customers' needs caused by absences due to vacations and illness, for planned programs and for unexpected or short-term work volume increases. KELLY MARKETING: offers coordinated marketing support services everything from market surveys to direct selling. KELLY LIGHT INDUSTRIAL: supplies semi-skilled light industrial services for a variety of needs. KELLY TECHNICAL: puts a wide range of technical and scientific assistance at the disposal of business when and where it is needed. KELLY ASSISTED LIVING: provides a wide range of paraprofessional nursing services for in-the-home care.

QUARTERLY DATA

(01/01/95)($000)	Rev	Inc
1st Quarter	530,191	9,233
2nd Quarter	570,813	14,420
3rd Quarter	630,196	19,289
4th Quarter	631,361	18,115

ANNUAL EARNINGS AND DIVIDENDS PER SHARE

	1/1/95	1/2/94	1/3/93	12/29/91	12/31/90	12/31/89	1/1/89
Earnings Per Share	1.61	1.18	1.04	1.02	1.90	1.89	1.60
Dividends Per Share	0.70	0.632	① 0.584	0.576	0.528	② 0.462	0.384
Dividend Payout %	43.5	53.6	56.2	56.3	27.8	24.4	23.9

① 5-for-4 stk split, 6/93 ② 5-for-4 stk split, 6/89 ① 3-for-2 stk split, 9/87

ANNUAL FINANCIAL DATA

RECORD OF EARNINGS (IN MILLIONS):

	1/1/95	1/2/94	1/3/93	12/29/91	12/31/90	12/31/89	1/1/89
Total Revenues	2,362.6	1,954.5	1,722.5	1,437.9	1,470.5	1,377.5	1,269.4
Costs and Expenses	2,253.5	1,874.0	1,647.5	1,367.8	1,348.7	1,256.6	1,162.7
Depreciation	17.3	16.6	14.0	9.8	8.8	7.9	7.4
Operating Profit	91.7	63.9	350.1	322.2	372.0	360.2	325.1
Earn Bef Income Taxes	98.5	70.9	61.0	60.2	113.0	112.9	99.4
Income Taxes	37.4	26.3	21.8	21.6	41.8	42.1	39.0
Net Income	61.1	44.6	39.2	38.6	71.2	70.8	60.3
Aver. Shs. Outstg. (000)	37,956	37,728	37,668	37,616	37,586	37,548	37,510

BALANCE SHEET (IN MILLIONS):

Cash and Cash Equivalents	191.9	181.0	184.3	227.5	217.4	189.3	147.2
Receivables, Net	307.5	248.2	209.0	170.8	163.5	154.4	135.5
Gross Property	124.9	112.1	107.3	80.7	62.6	58.0	55.3
Accumulated Depreciation	54.7	43.8	37.9	29.2	24.8	24.0	24.5
Net Stockholders' Equity	431.5	386.2	367.3	355.0	337.8	283.7	229.9
Total Assets	642.1	542.1	496.1	479.4	443.8	394.3	326.4
Total Current Assets	526.4	447.1	408.6	411.5	393.2	353.9	292.2
Total Current Liabilities	210.6	155.9	128.8	124.4	106.0	110.6	96.5
Net Working Capital	315.8	291.2	279.8	287.0	287.2	243.4	195.7
Year End Shs Outstg (000)	37,963	37,755	37,706	37,624	37,603	37,570	37,520

STATISTICAL RECORD:

Operating Profit Margin %	3.9	3.3	3.5	4.2	7.7	8.2	7.8
Book Value Per Share	10.17	9.52	9.26	9.43	8.98	7.55	6.13
Return on Equity %	14.1	11.5	10.7	10.9	21.1	25.0	26.2
Return on Assets %	9.5	8.2	7.9	8.1	16.0	18.0	18.5
Average Yield %	2.5	2.2	2.0	2.1	2.0	1.7	1.5
P/E Ratio	19.9-14.3	31.0-18.6	33.7-21.4	32.7-21.2	17.0-11.4	17.8-11.4	18.9-12.9
Price Range	32-23	36⅝-22	35-22¼	33⅜-21⅝	32¼-21⅝	33⅝-21½	30⅜-20¾

Statistics are as originally reported.

OFFICERS:
W.R. Kelly, Chmn.
T.E. Adderley, Pres. & C.E.O.
R.F. Stoner, Sr. V.P., C.F.O., Treas. & Contr.

INCORPORATED: DE, Aug., 1952

PRINCIPAL OFFICE: 999 W. Big Beaver Rd., Troy, MI 48084

TELEPHONE NUMBER: (810) 362-4444

NO. OF EMPLOYEES: 4,300 Perm.; 630,000 Temp.

ANNUAL MEETING: In May

SHAREHOLDERS: 1,323 Cl. A.; 320 Cl. B.

INSTITUTIONAL HOLDINGS:
No. of Institutions: 156
Shares Held: 15,130,589

REGISTRAR(S): NBD Bank, N.A., Securities Transfer Services, Detroit, MI 02266

TRANSFER AGENT(S): NBD Bank, N.A., Securities Transfer Services, Detroit, MI 02266

NASDAQ SYMBOL KTCO
Rec. Pr. 20¼

KENAN TRANSPORT CO.

YIELD 1.2%
P/E RATIO 13.2

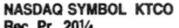

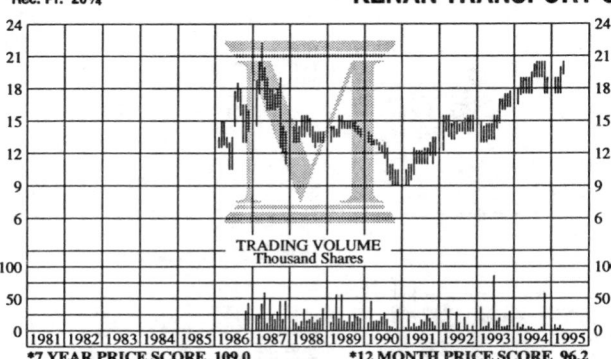

24
21
18
15
12
9
6
TRADING VOLUME
Thousand Shares
100
50
0
1981 1982 1983 1984 1985 1986 1987 1988 1989 1990 1991 1992 1993 1994 1995

*7 YEAR PRICE SCORE 109.0 *12 MONTH PRICE SCORE 96.2

*NYSE COMPOSITE INDEX=100

INTERIM EARNINGS (Per Share):

Qtr.	Mar.	June	Sept.	Dec.
1991	0.27	0.20	0.26	0.36
1992	0.35	0.27	0.28	0.39
1993	0.39	0.31	0.32	0.43
1994	0.43	0.33	0.34	0.45

INTERIM DIVIDENDS (Per Share):

Amt.	Decl.	Ex.	Rec.	Pay.
0.06Q	3/15/94	3/25/94	3/31/94	4/15/94
0.0625Q	6/15	6/24	6/30	7/15
0.0625Q	9/15	9/26	9/30	10/15
0.0625Q	12/15	12/23	12/30	1/16/95
0.0625Q	3/15/95	3/27/95	3/31/95	4/14

Indicated div.: $0.25

CAPITALIZATION (12/31/94):

	($000)	(%)
Deferred Income Tax	7,975	16.7
Common & Surplus	39,771	83.3
Total	47,746	100.0

DIVIDEND ACHIEVER STATUS:
Rank: 262 1984-94 Growth Rate: 6.1%
Total Years of Dividend Growth: 11

RECENT DEVELOPMENTS: For the year ended 12/31/94, income before an extraordinary item was $3.7 million compared with net income of $3.4 million in 1993. Revenues advanced 3.6% to $59.1 million from $57.1 million a year earlier. As a result of Federal preemption of state regulation of trucking rates, routes and entry, the Company wrote off $823,000 in recorded values of intrastate operating rights as an extraordinay item in the third quarter of 1994. Net income for the fourth quarter ended 12/31/94 was $1.1 million, up 6% from $1.0 million in the corresponding period of 1993. Revenues were $15.2 million compared with $15.0 million a year earlier. For the quarter ended 9/30/94, income before an extraordinary item was $801,000 compared with $755,000 a year ago. Revenue was flat at $14.2 million. Revenue growth during the quarter was adversely affected by reduced availability of driver candidates in some labor markets.

BUSINESS

KENAN TRANSPORT COMPANY is a tank truck carrier serving the petroleum, propane gas and chemical industries in the southeastern United States. KTCO conducts bulk trucking operations intrastate in Virginia, North Carolina, South Carolina, Georgia, and Florida and interstate among these five states and points throughout the United States. It is ranked among the fifteen largest tank truck carriers in the country. KTCO transports a wide variety of products including gasoline to service stations; petroleum products to wholesalers and industrial plants; propane gas to agricultural, rural and industrial consumers and liquid and dry bulk chemicals to manufacturers. Each of the products transported requires specialized trailers and experienced personnel with special skills necessary for safe and efficient handling of these varied bulk materials.

QUARTERLY DATA

(12/31/94)($000)	Rev	Inc
1st Quarter	15,550	1,020
2nd Quarter	14,088	774
3rd Quarter	14,229	801
4th Quarter	15,233	1,087

ANNUAL EARNINGS AND DIVIDENDS PER SHARE

	1994	1993	1992	1991	1990	1989	1988
Earnings Per Share	**1.55**	**1.45**	**1.29**	**1.08**	**0.64**	**1.07**	**[1] 1.24**
Dividends Per Share	**0.245**	**0.235**	**0.225**	**0.215**	**0.205**	**0.19**	**0.175**
Dividend Payout %	**15.8**	**16.6**	**17.4**	**19.9**	**32.0**	**17.8**	**14.1**

[1] Before acctg. chg.

ANNUAL FINANCIAL DATA

	1994	1993	1992	1991	1990	1989	1988
RECORD OF EARNINGS (IN THOUSANDS):							
Total Revenues	59,100	57,063	53,750	49,175	48,392	46,271	47,585
Operating Expenses	48,000	46,710	44,307	40,659	41,762	37,894	38,599
Depreciation	5,313	4,932	4,741	4,722	4,469	4,377	4,197
Operating Income	5,787	5,421	4,702	3,794	2,161	4,000	4,789
Inc Bef Prov for Income Taxes	6,121	5,778	5,086	4,296	2,527	4,178	4,859
Income Taxes	2,439	2,343	2,032	1,743	1,021	1,668	1,937
Net Income	[1] 3,682	3,435	3,054	2,553	1,506	2,510	[2] 2,922
Aver. Shs. Outstg.	2,377	2,368	2,359	2,355	2,355	2,355	2,351
[1] Before extra. item dr$823,000. [2] Before acctg. change cr$1,500,000.							
BALANCE SHEET (IN THOUSANDS):							
Cash and Cash Equivalents	13,759	11,996	10,816	9,147	7,499	4,436	3,099
Receivables, Net	5,909	5,856	4,157	3,622	3,524	3,520	3,781
Gross Property	59,274	55,661	52,330	49,381	46,763	45,676	44,673
Accumulated Depreciation	24,259	22,914	22,753	21,481	19,699	17,384	17,517
Prop, Plant & Equip, Net	35,015	32,747	29,577	27,900	27,064	28,292	27,156
Net Stockholders' Equity	39,771	37,363	34,348	31,767	29,727	28,710	26,614
Total Assets	57,625	54,727	48,568	44,640	42,215	40,182	38,042
Total Current Assets	22,139	20,831	17,884	15,711	14,145	10,866	9,850
Total Current Liabilities	9,879	10,065	8,840	7,333	6,765	5,134	5,621
Net Working Capital	12,260	10,766	9,044	8,378	7,380	5,732	4,229
Year End Shares Outstg	2,378	2,370	2,360	2,355	2,355	2,355	2,352
STATISTICAL RECORD:							
Operating Profit Margin %	9.8	9.5	8.7	7.7	4.5	8.6	10.1
Book Value Per Share	16.72	15.76	14.55	13.49	12.62	12.19	10.92
Return on Equity %	9.3	9.2	8.9	8.0	5.1	8.7	11.0
Return on Assets %	6.4	6.3	6.3	5.7	3.6	6.2	7.7
Average Yield %	1.3	1.5	1.6	1.9	1.8	1.3	1.3
P/E Ratio	13.2-10.6	12.2-9.0	12.0-9.5	12.5-8.3	21.9-14.1	14.5-12.1	12.5-10.1
Price Range	20½-16½	17¾-13	15½-12¼	13½-9	14-9	15½-13	15½-12½

Statistics are as originally reported.

OFFICERS:
F.H. Kenan, Chmn. & C.E.O.
L.P. Shaffer, Pres. & C.O.O.
W.L. Boone, V.P.-Fin. & Sec.

INCORPORATED: NC, 1949

PRINCIPAL OFFICE: University Square-West, 143 W. Franklin St. P.O. Box 2729, Chapel Hill, NC 27516-3910

TELEPHONE NUMBER: (919) 967-8221

FAX: (919) 967-1546

NO. OF EMPLOYEES: 720

ANNUAL MEETING: In May

SHAREHOLDERS: 643 common

INSTITUTIONAL HOLDINGS:
No. of Institutions: 22
Shares Held: 694,332

REGISTRAR(S):

TRANSFER AGENT(S): First Union National Bank of N.C., Charlotte, NC

NYS SYMBOL KEY
Rec. Pr. 28

KEYCORP

YIELD 5.1%
P/E RATIO 8.0

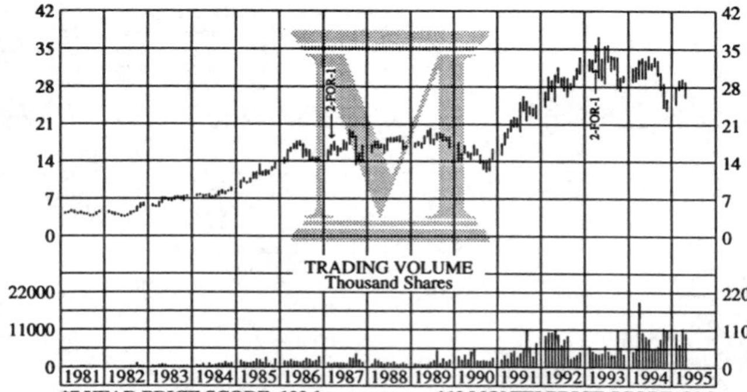

***7 YEAR PRICE SCORE 102.1** ***12 MONTH PRICE SCORE 91.0**

*NYSE COMPOSITE INDEX=100

INTERIM EARNINGS (Per Share):

Qtr.	Mar.	June	Sept.	Dec.
1991	0.61	0.64	0.66	0.53
1992	0.36	0.74	0.69	0.72
1993	0.79	0.82	0.83	0.49
1994	0.85	0.89	0.97	0.79

INTERIM DIVIDENDS (Per Share):

Amt.	Decl.	Ex.	Rec.	Pay.
0.32Q	5/19/94	5/24/94	5/31/94	6/15/94
0.32Q	7/20	8/25	8/31	9/15
0.32Q	11/17	11/25	12/1	12/15
0.36Q	1/19/95	2/22/95	2/28/95	3/15/95

Indicated div.: $1.44*

CAPITALIZATION (12/31/94):

	($000)	(%)
Total Deposits	48,564,237	73.1
Total Debt	12,346,522	18.6
Preferred Stock	160,000	0.2
Common & Surplus	4,538,450	6.8
Loan Valuation Reserve	830,298	1.3
Total	66,439,507	100.0

DIVIDEND ACHIEVER STATUS:
Rank: 124 1984-94 Growth Rate: 11.7%
Total Years of Dividend Growth: 29

RECENT DEVELOPMENTS: For the twelve months ended 12/31/94, net income advanced 20.2% to $853.5 million from $709.9 million for 1993. Net interest income totaled $2.69 billion, relatively flat compared with the $2.68 billion recorded for 1993. Noninterest income fell 11.9% to $882.6 million from $1.00 billion. Mortgage banking income plummeted to $88 million from $127.9 million, a drop of 31%. Special asset management fees tumbled 62% to $17.3 million while trust income moved down 10%.

PROSPECTS: In line with the trend of several banks across the country to reduce mortgage operations because of the fluctuation in income, KEY announced it will sell the $25 billion mortgage-servicing portfolio of KeyCorp Mortgage, Inc. to NationsBank for approximately $500 million. KEY will exit the wholesale and correspondent-mortgage production business and significantly reduce its secondary market activity. KEY has also decided to acquire Omnibancorp, a Denver, Colorado-based $500 million asset bank.

BUSINESS

KEYCORP, with assets over $66.8 billion, is a multi-regional bank. Banking offices serve individual consumers, small-to-medium sized businesses, and municipalities in eight states: Alaska, Maine, Oregon, Washington State, New York (upstate New York and Long Island, exclusive of New York City), Wyoming, Idaho, and Utah. Non-bank services include trust, leasing, discount brokerage, finance, investment management, credit life reinsurance, mortgage banking, and data processing.

LOAN DISTRIBUTION

(12/31/94)	($000)	(%)
Commercial, Finan & Agri	10,190,582	22.0
Real Estate-Construction	1,287,195	2.8
Real Estate-Resident Mtge	13,567,077	29.4
Real Estate-Comm Mortgage	6,774,860	14.7
Consumer	10,183,798	22.0
Student Loans Held	1,816,524	3.9
Lease Finance & Foreign	2,404,608	5.2
Total	46,224,644	100.0

ANNUAL EARNINGS AND DIVIDENDS PER SHARE

	1994	1993	1992	1991	1990	1989	1988
Earnings Per Share	**3.45**	**2.93**	**2.51**	**2.45**	**[2] 2.32**	**0.05**	**2.10**
Dividends Per Share	**1.28**	**1.19**	**[1] 0.98**	**0.92**	**0.88**	**0.80**	**0.68**
Dividend Payout %	**37.1**	**40.6**	**39.0**	**37.6**	**38.0**	**N.M.**	**32.5**

[1] 2-for-1 stk split,03/23/93 [2] Before acctg. chg.

ANNUAL FINANCIAL DATA

	1994	1993	1992	1991	1990	1989	1988
RECORD OF EARNINGS (IN MILLIONS):							
Total Interest Income	4,490.1	1,871.3	1,904.3	1,384.1	1,486.9	987.3	825.5
Total Interest Expense	1,796.8	672.3	773.0	697.3	862.6	561.3	465.5
Net Interest Income	2,693.2	1,199.0	1,131.3	686.8	624.3	426.0	360.0
Credit Loss Provision	125.2	72.2	147.4	79.8	94.7	51.6	24.9
Net Income	853.5	347.2	301.2	163.0	[1] 155.2	110.0	100.1
Aver. Shs. Outstg. (000)	243,067	118,323	117,349	66,569	66,893	46,672	46,814
[1] Before acctg. change cr$2,714,000.							
BALANCE SHEET (IN MILLIONS):							
Cash & Due From Banks	3,511.4	1,375.6	1,345.1	850.3	999.5	783.2	745.7
Loans & Lse Financing, Net	45,394.3	17,417.0	15,699.0	9,417.4	9,895.1	6,719.9	6,175.4
Total Domestic Deposits	45,139.1	17,866.2	17,542.8	11,377.8	11,933.2	7,741.1	7,415.2
Total Foreign Deposits	3,425.1	2,014.5	1,115.2	157.3	184.9	683.4	260.5
Long-term Debt	3,569.8	952.7	886.1	177.1	183.2	122.2	182.5
Net Stockholders' Equity	4,698.5	2,038.6	1,868.1	1,116.7	1,005.2	746.2	689.5
Total Assets	66,798.1	27,007.3	24,978.3	15,404.5	15,110.2	10,903.3	10,009.6
Year End Shs Outstg (000)	240,362	117,377	116,726	66,057	65,537	43,496	44,356
STATISTICAL RECORD:							
Return on Assets %	1.28	1.29	1.21	1.06	1.03	1.01	1.00
Return on Equity %	18.20	17.00	16.10	14.60	15.40	14.70	14.50
Book Value Per Share	18.88	17.37	15.49	16.90	15.34	16.58	14.98
Average Yield %	4.5	3.7	3.4	4.4	5.9	4.4	4.0
P/E Ratio	9.8-6.8	12.7-9.3	13.3-9.7	10.7-6.2	7.6-5.2	8.7-7.1	9.0-7.4
Price Range	33¾-23⅝	37¼-27¼	33½-24¼	26¼-15¼	17⅝-12	20¼-16½	18⅞-15½

Statistics are as originally reported.

OFFICERS:
V.J. Riley, Jr., Chmn. & C.E.O.
R.W. Gillespie, Pres. & C.O.O.
J.W. Wert, Sr. Exec. V.P. & C.F.O.
L. Irving, Exec. V.P. & Treas.

INCORPORATED: OH, 1958

PRINCIPAL OFFICE: 127 Public Square, Cleveland, OH 44114-1306

TELEPHONE NUMBER: (216) 689-3000

NO. OF EMPLOYEES: 29,211

ANNUAL MEETING: In May

SHAREHOLDERS: 52,974

INSTITUTIONAL HOLDINGS:
No. of Institutions: 552
Shares Held: 117,247,860

REGISTRAR(S): Society National Bank, Cleveland, OH

TRANSFER AGENT(S): Society National Bank, Cleveland, OH

KEYSTONE INTERNATIONAL, INC.

YIELD 3.3%
P/E RATIO 23.7

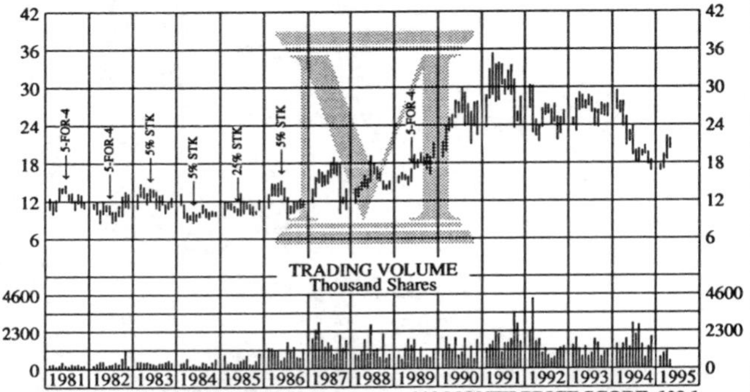

TRADING VOLUME
Thousand Shares

| | 1981 | 1982 | 1983 | 1984 | 1985 | 1986 | 1987 | 1988 | 1989 | 1990 | 1991 | 1992 | 1993 | 1994 | 1995 |

*7 YEAR PRICE SCORE 70.3   ***12 MONTH PRICE SCORE 100.1**
*NYSE COMPOSITE INDEX=100

INTERIM EARNINGS (Per Share):

Qtr.	Mar.	June	Sept.	Dec.
1991	0.27	0.34	0.27	d0.22
1992	0.27	0.34	0.34	0.27
1993	0.28	0.30	0.27	0.27
1994	0.21	0.26	0.21	0.26

INTERIM DIVIDENDS (Per Share):

Amt.	Decl.	Ex.	Rec.	Pay.
0.185Q	3/16/94	4/28/94	5/5/94	5/18/94
0.185Q	6/15	7/28	8/3	8/17
0.185Q	9/21	10/27	11/2	11/16
0.185Q	12/14	1/26/95	2/1/95	2/15/95
0.185Q	3/15/95	4/27	5/3	5/17

Indicated div.: $0.74*

CAPITALIZATION (12/31/94):

	($000)	(%)
Long-Term Debt	60,455	17.1
Deferred Income Tax	6,575	1.9
Common & Surplus	286,399	81.0
Total	353,429	100.0

DIVIDEND ACHIEVER STATUS:
Rank: 170   1984-94 Growth Rate: 9.9%
Total Years of Dividend Growth: 23

RECENT DEVELOPMENTS: For the year ended 12/31/94, net income declined by 20% to $33.0 million from $41.0 million in the previous year. Net sales rose 3.7% to $535.1 million. The higher sales were partially offset by a plant closure and the related costs, which totalled $4.7 million. Net income during the fourth quarter fell by 4% to $9.1 million versus $9.5 million in the equivalent period of the year before. Net sales rose 10.2% to $144.4 million.

PROSPECTS: Recent company-wide restructuring efforts should cut operating costs through the relocation of several plants to Mexico. Approximately 250 employees will be laid off from the Indiana facility from all levels of operations, engineering, administrative and production, with the majority of the positions moving to other locations. The plant closure is expected to reduce administrative and manufacturing costs and more efficiently serve customers' needs.

BUSINESS

KEYSTONE INTERNATIONAL INC. primarily designs, manufactures and markets, on a worldwide basis, valves and other specialized industrial products that control the flow of liquids, gas and solid materials, including food and beverage, water and sewage, petroleum production and refining, natural gas, chemical, pulp and paper and power. Keystone is one of the leading manufacturers of specialty valves in the world. In 1994, revenues were derived from the following geographic areas: United States, 43%; Europe, the Middle East and Africa, 27%; Asia-Pacific, 23%; and North and South America except U.S., 7%.

ANNUAL EARNINGS AND DIVIDENDS PER SHARE

	1994	1993	1992	1991	1990	1989	1988
Earnings Per Share	0.94	1.12	1.22	① 0.66	1.31	② 1.10	0.96
Dividends Per Share	0.735	0.71	0.67	0.63	0.59	③ 0.532	0.44
Dividend Payout %	78.2	63.4	54.9	95.5	45.0	48.4	45.8

① Before acctg. chg. ② Before disc. oper. ③ 5-for-4 stk split, 5/25/89

ANNUAL FINANCIAL DATA

RECORD OF EARNINGS (IN THOUSANDS):

	1994	1993	1992	1991	1990	1989	1988
Total Revenues	535,099	516,140	528,372	520,496	446,232	375,709	346,010
Costs and Expenses	452,489	420,940	425,292	443,740	343,696	287,676	270,952
Depreciation & Amort	25,608	24,537	22,749	22,492	18,965	16,930	12,796
Operating Profit	61,374	70,663	80,331	76,636	83,571	71,103	62,262
Inc Bef Income Taxes & Acctg Chg	52,337	62,121	69,854	43,107	72,089	59,713	51,080
Income Taxes	19,365	22,985	27,313	20,273	28,064	22,953	19,206
Net Income	32,972	41,015	42,541	17,906	44,025	① 36,760	31,874
Aver. Shs. Outstg.	35,250	35,085	34,902	34,676	33,654	33,515	33,301

① Before disc. op. dr$558,000.

BALANCE SHEET (IN THOUSANDS):

	1994	1993	1992	1991	1990	1989	1988
Cash and Cash Equivalents	18,688	19,873	29,390	12,467	32,335	29,695	30,699
Receivables, Net	131,532	119,750	105,304	117,056	101,883	85,053	73,202
Inventories	157,807	134,608	138,034	156,027	130,621	116,225	113,325
Gross Property	302,727	274,890	257,009	255,032	204,630	169,407	155,823
Accumulated Depreciation	154,164	140,037	133,035	123,411	95,896	80,261	72,263
Long-Term Debt	60,455	62,300	14,312	58,365	48,221	51,465	69,762
Net Stockholders' Equity	286,399	270,632	252,609	239,373	231,312	198,831	180,537
Total Assets	496,270	456,500	438,099	458,752	417,441	365,856	339,697
Total Current Assets	312,652	279,744	277,533	290,217	269,849	234,092	220,546
Total Current Liabilities	126,968	107,917	156,931	147,049	120,452	103,277	79,099
Net Working Capital	185,684	171,827	120,602	143,168	149,397	130,815	141,447
Year End Shares Outstg	35,306	35,142	34,927	34,658	33,586	33,500	33,313

STATISTICAL RECORD:

	1994	1993	1992	1991	1990	1989	1988
Operating Profit Margin %	10.7	13.7	15.2	10.4	18.7	18.9	18.0
Book Value Per Share	8.11	7.70	7.23	6.91	6.89	5.94	5.42
Return on Equity %	11.5	14.5	16.8	9.5	19.0	18.5	17.7
Return on Assets %	6.6	8.6	9.7	5.0	10.5	10.0	9.4
Average Yield %	3.2	2.7	2.6	2.1	2.4	3.0	2.9
P/E Ratio	31.4-17.8	26.0-20.5	24.9-17.5	53.6-35.6	22.7-14.4	19.3-13.2	20.1-12.1
Price Range	29½-16¾	29⅛-23	30⅜-21⅜	35⅜-23½	29¾-18⅞	21¼-14½	19¼-11⅝

Statistics are as originally reported.

OFFICERS:
R.A. LeBlanc, Chmn. & C.E.O.
M.D. Clark, Pres. & C.O.O.
M.E. Baldwin, V.P. & C.F.O.

INCORPORATED: TX, 1947

PRINCIPAL OFFICE: 9600 West Gulf Bank Drive, Houston, TX 77040

TELEPHONE NUMBER: (713) 466-1176

FAX: (713) 466-6328

NO. OF EMPLOYEES: 4,200 (approx.)

ANNUAL MEETING: In May

SHAREHOLDERS: 3,538 (approx.)

INSTITUTIONAL HOLDINGS:
No. of Institutions: 160
Shares Held: 20,717,999

REGISTRAR(S): NationsBank of Texas, NA, Houston, TX

TRANSFER AGENT(S): NationsBank of Texas, NA, Houston, TX

KIMBALL INTERNATIONAL, INC.

YIELD		3.3%
P/E RATIO		14.4

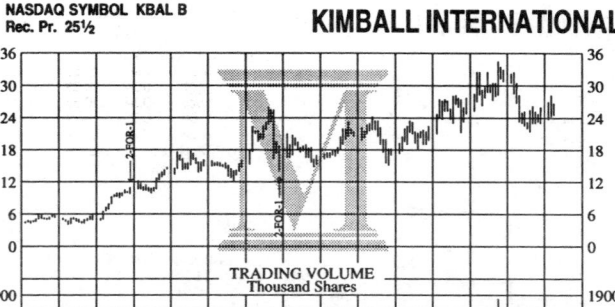

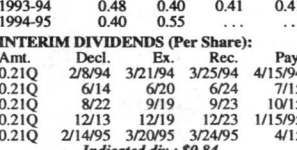

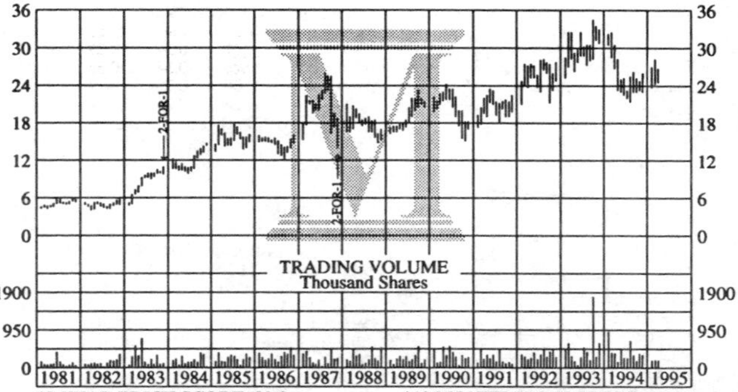

TRADING VOLUME
Thousand Shares

*7 YEAR PRICE SCORE 89.8   *12 MONTH PRICE SCORE 102.5
*NYSE COMPOSITE INDEX=100

INTERIM EARNINGS (Per Share):

Qtr.	Sept.	Dec.	Mar.	June
1991-92	0.43	0.39	0.42	0.59
1992-93	0.34	0.23	0.43	0.45
1993-94	0.48	0.40	0.41	0.41
1994-95	0.40	0.55	...	...

INTERIM DIVIDENDS (Per Share):

Amt.	Decl.	Ex.	Rec.	Pay.
0.21Q	2/8/94	3/21/94	3/25/94	4/15/94
0.21Q	6/14	6/20	6/24	7/15
0.21Q	8/22	9/19	9/23	10/15
0.21Q	12/13	12/19	12/23	1/15/95
0.21Q	2/14/95	3/20/95	3/24/95	4/15

Indicated div.: $0.84

CAPITALIZATION (6/30/94):

	($000)	(%)
Long-Term Debt	811	0.2
Common & Surplus	350,952	99.8
Total	351,763	100.0

DIVIDEND ACHIEVER STATUS:
Rank: 89   1984-94 Growth Rate: 13.3%
Total Years of Dividend Growth: 11

RECENT DEVELOPMENTS: For the quarter ended 12/31/94, net income increased 38.7% to $11.7 million from $8.4 million in the corresponding period of 1993. Net sales for the quarter were $230.1 million, up 11.8% compared with $205.8 million the previous year. The Company's gross profit climbed 14.9% to $65.0 million as the cost of sales declined to 71.7% of sales from 72.5%. Operating income rose 36.1% to $18.3 million. KBAL's strong performance was driven by expanded market share and improved capacity utilization. Improvement in the Furniture and Cabinet segment was led by volume gains in office systems, select seating lines and wood office casegoods. Growth in the Electronic Contract Assemblies segment resulted from strong demand in automotive, telecommunications and computer markets. KBAL's metal office furniture operation is experiencing manufacturing difficulties.

BUSINESS

KIMBALL INTERNATIONAL, INC. has three business segments which are as follows: (1) Furniture and Cabinet sales include office, lodging and home furniture; television and stereo cabinets; pianos and piano cases, keys and actions; and other miscellaneous products; (2) Electronic Contract Assemblies includes the sale of electronic and electomechanical products (electronic assemblies) manufactured on a contract basis to customers specifications; (3) Processed Wood Products and Other includes the sale of lumber, lumber banded particleboard, dimension lumber, plywood, veneer and other sales. Other sales include plastic components, carbide cutting tools and related services on cutting tools, fleet and automotive services and other miscellaneous products and services.

BUSINESS LINE ANALYSIS

(6/30/94)	Rev(%)	Inc(%)
Furniture & Cabinets.	66.7	62.7
Elect Contract Assemblies	24.8	23.8
Procees Wood Prod & Other.................	8.5	13.5
Total	100.0	100.0

ANNUAL EARNINGS AND DIVIDENDS PER SHARE

	6/30/94	6/30/93	6/30/92	6/30/91	6/30/90	6/30/89	6/30/88
Earnings Per Share	1.70	1.45	1.83	1.42	2.05	1.62	1.68
Dividends Per Share	0.84	0.80	0.72	0.68	0.60	0.52	⓵ 0.44
Dividend Payout %	49.4	55.1	39.3	47.9	29.0	32.1	26.2

⓵ 2-for-1 stk split, 12/87

ANNUAL FINANCIAL DATA

RECORD OF EARNINGS (IN THOUSANDS):

	6/30/94	6/30/93	6/30/92	6/30/91	6/30/90	6/30/89	6/30/88
Total Revenues	822,484	722,400	617,301	555,263	612,956	595,005	529,840
Costs and Expenses	736,551	648,495	542,879	490,833	524,053	518,646	455,635
Depreciation & Amort	28,726	27,328	25,282	23,643	22,987	21,835	19,032
Operating Income	57,207	46,577	49,140	40,787	65,916	54,525	55,173
Inc Bef Taxes on Income	59,419	53,322	60,714	49,133	71,053	56,359	58,817
Income Taxes	23,250	22,739	22,086	19,116	27,578	22,060	23,197
Net Income	36,169	30,583	38,628	30,017	43,475	34,299	35,620
Aver. Shs. Outstg.	21,165	21,199	21,151	21,165	21,195	21,200	21,234

BALANCE SHEET (IN THOUSANDS):

Cash and Cash Equivalents	91,946	107,222	117,728	120,119	99,839	41,940	40,536
Receivables, Net	96,118	87,623	75,796	57,259	63,903	69,720	61,485
Inventories	81,083	84,666	72,912	57,906	61,443	72,106	76,526
Gross Property	376,270	336,819	316,282	292,338	277,753	264,524	229,934
Accumulated Depreciation	205,027	184,458	173,978	156,581	136,987	120,840	104,831
Long-Term Debt	811	2,017	3,157	4,392	6,873	8,933	11,297
Net Stockholders' Equity	350,952	333,341	321,137	294,463	279,351	246,975	224,718
Total Assets	471,413	452,705	422,023	382,685	377,983	337,746	320,364
Total Current Assets	288,238	295,458	275,507	242,726	233,856	191,004	191,685
Total Current Liabilities	102,164	100,070	80,769	65,262	72,371	64,364	69,260
Net Working Capital	186,074	195,388	194,738	177,464	161,485	126,640	122,425
Yr End Class A & B Shs Outstg	21,162	21,174	21,232	21,145	21,195	21,190	21,200

STATISTICAL RECORD:

Operating Profit Margin %	7.0	6.4	8.0	7.3	10.8	9.2	10.4
Book Value Per Share	16.58	15.74	15.13	13.93	13.18	11.66	10.60
Return on Equity %	10.3	9.2	12.0	10.2	15.6	13.9	15.9
Return on Assets %	7.7	6.8	9.2	7.8	11.5	10.2	11.1
Average Yield %	3.1	2.7	2.9	3.3	3.0	2.6	2.5
P/E Ratio	19.0-12.5	24.0-17.5	15.5-11.5	16.5-12.1	11.8-7.4	14.4-10.0	12.5-8.8
Price Range	32½-21⅜	34½-25¼	28¼-21	23½-17¼	24¼-15⅛	23¼-16¼	21-14¾

Statistics are as originally reported.

OFFICERS:
T.L. Habig, Chmn.
D.A. Habig, Pres. & C.E.O.
J.C. Thyen, Sr. E.V.P., Chief Fin. & Admin. Off. & Treas.

INCORPORATED: IN, 1939

PRINCIPAL OFFICE: 1600 Royal St., Jasper, IN 47549-1001

TELEPHONE NUMBER: (812) 482-1600

NO. OF EMPLOYEES: 8,463

ANNUAL MEETING: In October

SHAREHOLDERS: 661 cl. A com.; 2,559 cl. B com.

INSTITUTIONAL HOLDINGS:
No. of Institutions: 82
Shares Held: 5,387,805

REGISTRAR(S): Mellon Securities Trust Co., New York, NY

TRANSFER AGENT(S): Mellon Securities Trust Company, New York, NY

NYS SYMBOL KMB
Rec. Pr. 57

KIMBERLY-CLARK CORP.

YIELD 3.2%
P/E RATIO 17.1

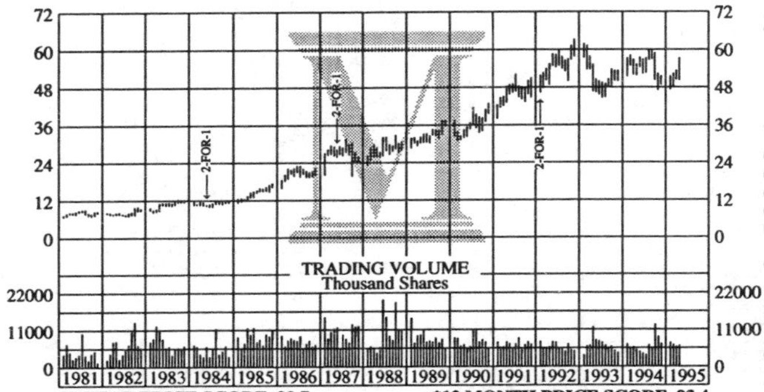

*7 YEAR PRICE SCORE 99.7 *12 MONTH PRICE SCORE 93.4

*NYSE COMPOSITE INDEX=100

INTERIM EARNINGS (Per Share):

Qtr.	Mar.	June	Sept.	Dec.
1991	0.75	0.76	0.79	0.87
1992	0.82	0.84	0.84	d0.35
1993	0.78	0.83	0.69	0.88
1994	0.85	0.94	0.88	0.66

INTERIM DIVIDENDS (Per Share):

Amt.	Decl.	Ex.	Rec.	Pay.
0.44Q	4/21/94	6/6/94	6/10/94	7/5/94
0.44Q	7/27	9/2	9/9	10/4
0.44Q	11/17	12/5	12/9	1/3/95
0.45Q	2/17/95	3/6/95	3/10/95	4/4
0.45Q	4/20	6/6	6/9	7/5

Indicated div.: $1.80*

CAPITALIZATION (12/31/94):

	($000)	(%)
Long-Term Debt	929,500	22.0
Deferred Income Tax	612,800	14.5
Minority Interest	80,100	1.9
Common & Surplus	2,595,800	61.6
Total	4,218,200	100.0

DIVIDEND ACHIEVER STATUS:
Rank: 110 1984-94 Growth Rate: 12.4%
Total Years of Dividend Growth: 21

RECENT DEVELOPMENTS: For the year ended 12/31/94, net income increased 4.7% to $535.1 million from $510.9 million in 1993. Earnings for 1994 included a charge of $39.2 million to cover translation losses resulting from the devaluation of the Mexican peso. Revenues were up 5.6% to $7.36 billion, compared with $6.97 billion the previous year. The sales increase was attributed to higher volumes of Consumer products in Europe, Asia and North America.

PROSPECTS: The Company continues to focus on the global expansion of its consumer products business. KMB is experiencing worldwide volume growth in its Huggies, Kleenex bathroom tissue, and Kotex feminine-care products. The Company continues to face stiff competition in its diapers business. The generation of short-term earnings growth will be a challenge due to the timing of price increases on tissue products and the ongoing impact of the weaker Mexican peso.

BUSINESS

KIMBERLY-CLARK CORP. manufactures household, personal care and health care products, as well as newsprint and premium business, correspondence and specialty papers. The Class I segment, constituting 79% of 1994 sales (76%, operating income), includes tissue products; infant, child, feminine and incontinence care products; industrial and commercial wipers; health care products; and related products. Brand names include Kleenex, Huggies, Kotex and Depend. Class II, 15% (20%), includes newsprint, printing papers, premium papers, premium business and correspondence papers, tobacco industry papers and products, technical papers, and related products. Class III, 6% (3%), includes airline services, commercial air transportation and other products and services.

BUSINESS LINE ANALYSIS

(12/31/94)	Rev(%)	Inc($000)
United States	71.3	817,200
Canada	7.9	25,000
Europe	13.8	(59,400)
Asia & Latin America	7.0	80,400
Total	100.0	863,200

ANNUAL EARNINGS AND DIVIDENDS PER SHARE

	1994	1993	1992	1991	1990	1989	1988
Earnings Per Share	**3.33**	**3.18**	**[1] 2.15**	**3.18**	**2.70**	**2.63**	**2.36**
Dividends Per Share	**1.75**	**1.70**	**[2] 1.64**	**1.45**	**1.345**	**1.175**	**0.78**
Dividend Payout %	**52.6**	**53.5**	**76.3**	**45.6**	**49.8**	**44.7**	**33.1**

[1] Before acctg. chges [2] 2-for-1 stk split, 1/3/92

ANNUAL FINANCIAL DATA

	1994	1993	1992	1991	1990	1989	1988
RECORD OF EARNINGS (IN MILLIONS):							
Total Revenues	7,364.2	6,972.9	7,091.1	6,776.9	6,407.3	5,733.6	5,393.5
Costs and Expenses	6,215.5	5,883.5	6,259.0	5,769.6	5,413.4	4,849.3	4,565.3
Depreciation	329.6	295.9	289.0	265.5	240.3	210.9	187.6
Operating Profit	819.1	793.5	543.1	741.8	753.6	673.4	640.6
Income Bef Income Taxes	740.6	713.0	461.9	684.3	660.8	630.8	583.9
Income Taxes	276.4	284.4	186.3	236.1	277.2	242.4	229.8
Net Income	535.1	510.9	[1] 345.0	508.3	432.1	423.8	378.6
Aver. Shs. Outstg. (000)	160,900	160,900	160,400	160,000	160,000	161,200	160,800
[1] Before acctg. change dr$210,000,000.							
BALANCE SHEET (IN MILLIONS):							
Cash and Cash Equivalents	23.8	34.8	41.1	42.8	60.2	164.3	84.1
Receivables, Net	937.3	832.4	856.9	691.1	623.1	624.8	584.9
Inventories	804.2	775.9	719.7	935.0	668.0	615.5	859.9
Gross Property	6,604.0	6,372.8	5,974.1	5,591.8	5,188.0	4,753.6	4,154.3
Accumulated Depreciation	2,404.6	2,330.0	2,199.3	1,981.6	1,801.7	1,712.7	1,579.0
Long-Term Debt	929.5	933.1	994.6	874.7	728.5	745.1	743.3
Net Stockholders' Equity	2,595.8	2,457.2	2,191.1	2,519.7	2,259.7	2,085.8	1,865.6
Total Assets	6,715.7	6,380.7	6,029.1	5,899.4	5,283.9	4,923.0	4,561.0
Total Current Assets	1,809.9	1,675.2	1,682.6	1,723.8	1,397.1	1,443.2	1,528.9
Total Current Liabilities	2,058.8	1,908.5	1,822.8	1,126.7	1,056.3	969.9	868.5
Net Working Capital	d248.9	d233.3	d140.2	597.1	340.8	473.3	660.4
Year End Shs Outstg (000)	160,200	160,900	160,759	160,077	159,834	161,400	161,200
STATISTICAL RECORD:							
Operating Profit Margin %	11.1	11.4	7.7	10.9	11.8	11.7	11.9
Book Value Per Share	16.20	15.27	13.63	15.74	14.14	12.92	11.57
Return on Equity %	20.6	20.8	15.7	20.2	19.1	20.3	20.3
Return on Assets %	8.0	8.0	5.7	8.6	8.2	8.6	8.3
Average Yield %	3.3	3.2	3.0	3.2	3.7	3.5	2.8
P/E Ratio	18.0-14.1	19.5-14.0	29.4-21.5	16.4-11.9	15.9-11.4	14.4-10.9	13.9-9.8
Price Range	60-47	62-44 5/8	63 1/4-46 1/4	52 1/4-38	42 7/8-30 3/4	37 3/4-28 3/4	32 7/8-23 1/8

Statistics are as originally reported.

OFFICERS:
W.R. Sanders, Chmn. & C.E.O.
J.W. Donehower, Sr. V.P. & C.F.O.
W.A. Gamron, V.P. & Treas.
D.M. Crook, V.P. & Sec.

INCORPORATED: DE, Jun., 1928

PRINCIPAL OFFICE: P.O. Box 619100, Dallas, TX 75261-9100

TELEPHONE NUMBER: (214) 830-1200
FAX: (214) 830-1490
NO. OF EMPLOYEES: 42,707
ANNUAL MEETING: In April
SHAREHOLDERS: 25,637
INSTITUTIONAL HOLDINGS:
No. of Institutions: 600
Shares Held: 107,841,629

REGISTRAR(S): First National Bank of Boston, Shareholder Services Division, Boston, MA

TRANSFER AGENT(S): First National Bank of Boston, Shareholder Services Division, Boston, MA

KU ENERGY CORP.

YIELD 6.1%
P/E RATIO 13.6

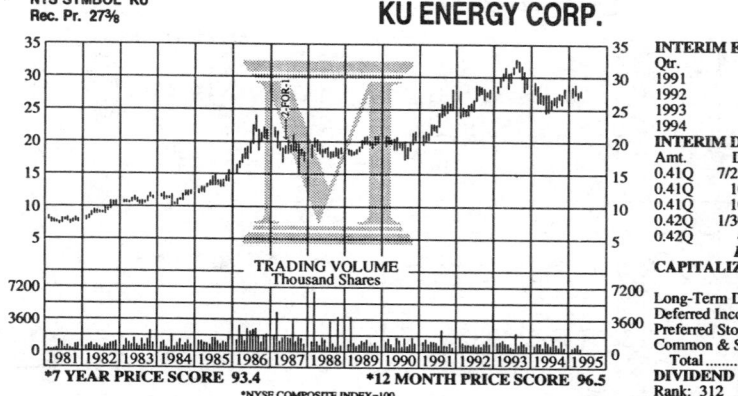

*7 YEAR PRICE SCORE 93.4   *12 MONTH PRICE SCORE 96.5
*NYSE COMPOSITE INDEX=100

INTERIM EARNINGS (Per Share):

Qtr.	Mar.	June	Sept.	Dec.
1991	0.62	0.46	0.64	0.41
1992	0.58	0.42	0.59	0.37
1993	0.63	0.44	0.64	0.40
1994	0.66	0.38	0.60	0.37

INTERIM DIVIDENDS (Per Share):

Amt.	Decl.	Ex.	Rec.	Pay.
0.41Q	7/25/94	8/19/94	8/25/94	9/15/94
0.41Q	10/24	11/17	11/23	12/15
0.41Q	10/24	11/17	11/23	12/15
0.42Q	1/30/95	2/17/95	2/24/95	3/15/95
0.42Q	4/25	5/19	5/25	6/15

Indicated div.: $1.68

CAPITALIZATION (12/31/94):

	($000)	(%)
Long-Term Debt	496,012	35.3
Deferred Income Tax	253,741	18.1
Preferred Stock	40,000	2.8
Common & Surplus	616,092	43.8
Total	1,405,845	100.0

DIVIDEND ACHIEVER STATUS:

Rank: 312   1984-94 Growth Rate: 3.3%
Total Years of Dividend Growth: 13

RECENT DEVELOPMENTS: For the quarter ended 12/31/94, net income was down 8.7% to $13.9 million from $15.3 million in the comparable 1993 period. Revenues rose 5.1% to $159.6 million compared with $151.8 million a year earlier. The fourth quarter was affected by warmer than normal temperatures, which led to a 7% decline in residential sales. For the year ended 12/31/94, net income fell 5.1% to $75.9 million, while revenues climbed 4.9% to $636.6 million.

PROSPECTS: Further growth in the Company's service area and a return to more favorable weather conditions should stimulate sales. KU's strategy is to diversify into nonregulated investments, which will enable the Company to earn a higher rate of return on equity. The investments will be centered around independent power projects and equipment leases to other utilities. KU is contesting an environmental surcharge to comply with the Clean Air Act.

BUSINESS

KU ENERGY CORP. is a holding company for Kentucky Utilities, which furnishes electricity to about 437,000 customers, 77 Kentucky counties and in five counties in south-western Virginia. Among the principal industries in the territory served are coal mining, automotive and related industries, agriculture, primary metals processing, crude oil production, pipeline transportation, and the manufacture of electrical and other machinery, and of paper and paper products. Virtually all of KU's electric generation is coal-fired.

ANNUAL EARNINGS AND DIVIDENDS PER SHARE

	1994	1993	1992	1991	1990	1989	1988
Earnings Per Share	2.01	2.11	1.96	2.13	☐ 1.97	☐ 2.02	1.94
Dividends Per Share	1.64	1.60	1.56	1.50	1.46	1.40	1.34
Dividend Payout %	81.6	75.8	79.6	70.4	74.1	69.3	69.1
☐ Before acctg. chg.							

ANNUAL FINANCIAL DATA

RECORD OF EARNINGS (IN MILLIONS):

Total Revenues	636.6	606.6	576.3	587.7	553.8	531.9	559.8
Depreciation	65.4	60.8	58.9	58.3	56.2	54.8	51.7
Maintenance	66.1	59.5	61.3	58.6	52.6	48.1	47.8
Prov for Fed Inc Taxes	43.9	47.8	41.0	45.8	42.3	45.1	48.4
Net Operating Income	99.7	104.5	105.3	109.5	102.2	107.1	106.5
Interest Expense	34.1	32.7	40.9	38.1	37.3	36.6	36.6
Net Income	75.9	80.0	74.2	80.6	80.1	☐ 82.3	79.3
Aver. Shs. Outstg. (000)	37,818	37,818	37,818	37,818	37,818	37,818	37,818
☐ Before acctg. change cr$11,470,000.							

BALANCE SHEET (IN MILLIONS):

Gross Plant	2,343.3	2,163.5	1,992.6	1,917.1	1,595.3	1,557.2	1,525.6
Accumulated Depreciation	933.4	880.0	823.5	771.0	718.7	670.7	620.1
Prop, Plant & Equip, Net	1,409.9	1,283.6	1,169.1	1,146.0	876.6	886.5	905.5
Long-term Debt	496.0	442.0	444.0	408.2	409.0	396.9	397.4
Net Stockholders' Equity	656.1	642.5	623.3	608.2	586.5	598.1	565.8
Total Assets	1,669.3	1,609.6	1,473.7	1,425.7	1,162.1	1,133.4	1,108.0
Year End Shs Outstg (000)	37,818	37,818	37,818	37,818	37,818	37,818	37,818

STATISTICAL RECORD:

Book Value Per Share	16.29	15.93	15.42	15.02	14.45	13.94	13.01
Op. Inc/Net Pl %	7.1	8.1	9.0	9.6	11.7	12.1	11.8
Accum. Dep/Gr. Pl %	39.8	40.7	41.3	40.2	45.1	43.1	40.6
Return on Equity %	11.6	12.4	11.9	13.3	13.7	14.5	14.9
Average Yield %	6.1	5.3	5.9	6.3	7.5	7.2	7.0
P/E Ratio	14.6-12.2	15.5-13.1	14.7-12.1	13.2-9.2	11.0-8.8	10.3-8.8	10.6-9.0
Price Range	29¼-24½	32¾-27⅝	28¾-23¾	28⅛-19½	21⅝-17¼	20⅞-17⅝	20⅝-17½

Statistics are as originally reported.

REVENUES

(12/31/94)	($000)	(%)
Residential	213,574	32.5
Commercial	142,207	21.7
Industrial	120,043	18.3
Mine Power	36,498	5.6
Public Authorities	49,869	7.6
Other Electric Utilities	89,665	13.7
Miscellaneous & Other	4,157	0.6
Total	656,013	100.0

OFFICERS:
J.T. Newton, Chmn.
M.R. Whitley, Pres.
W.N. English, Treas.

INCORPORATED: KY

PRINCIPAL OFFICE: One Quality Street, Lexington, KY 40507

TELEPHONE NUMBER: (606) 255-2100
FAX: (606) 288-1125
NO. OF EMPLOYEES: 307
ANNUAL MEETING: In April
SHAREHOLDERS: 23,798 common; 1,872 preferred
INSTITUTIONAL HOLDINGS:
No. of Institutions: 130
Shares Held: 8,320,120

REGISTRAR(S): Harris Trust & Savings Bank, Chicago, IL

TRANSFER AGENT(S): Illinois Stock Transfer Co., Chicago, IL 60606
Harris Trust & Savings Bank, Chicago, IL

NYS SYMBOL LZB
Rec. Pr. 27

LA-Z-BOY CHAIR CO.

YIELD	2.5%
P/E RATIO	13.7

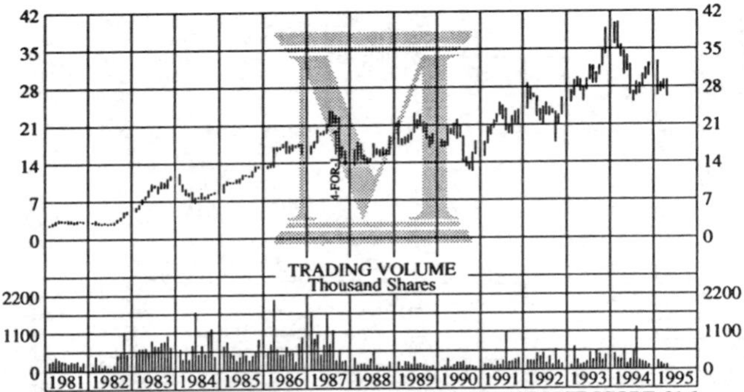

***7 YEAR PRICE SCORE 103.0** ***12 MONTH PRICE SCORE 91.6**

*NYSE COMPOSITE INDEX=100

INTERIM EARNINGS (Per Share):

Qtr.	July	Oct.	Jan.	Apr.
1991-92	0.16	0.47	0.28	0.48
1992-93	0.15	0.36	0.35	0.64
1993-94	0.22	0.57	0.44	0.67
1994-95	0.23	0.67	0.40	...

INTERIM DIVIDENDS (Per Share):

Amt.	Decl.	Ex.	Rec.	Pay.
0.17Q	1/11/94	2/7/94	2/11/94	3/10/94
0.17Q	5/3	5/11	5/17	6/10
0.17Q	7/26	8/11	8/17	9/9
0.17Q	10/10	11/10	11/17	12/9
0.17Q	1/9/95	2/7/95	2/13/95	3/10/95

Indicated div.: $0.68*

CAPITALIZATION (4/30/94):

	($000)	(%)
Long-Term Debt	52,495	15.0
Deferred Income Tax	6,949	2.0
Common & Surplus	290,911	83.0
Total	350,355	100.0

DIVIDEND ACHIEVER STATUS:
Rank: 209 1984-94 Growth Rate: 8.2%
Total Years of Dividend Growth: 13

RECENT DEVELOPMENTS: For the thirteen weeks ended 1/28/95, net income decreased 9.6% to $7.2 million from $8.0 million in the comparable period the year before. Sales were up 9.4% to $210.8 million, compared with $192.6 million last year. All five operating divisions reported higher sales, with particular strength at LZB's Hammary unit. Earnings were negatively affected by the cumulative impact of higher health-care costs, unfavorable Canadian exchange rates and taxes, and raw material cost increases.

PROSPECTS: Incoming sales orders and backlogs remain solid. Higher costs and sales associated with the Company's new television advertising campaign will continue to affect results. The new consumer advertising program is part of a long-term effort to further expand LZB's market share and reposition the Company as a complete furniture resource. Recognizing the need to expand its presentation, LZB has doubled the size of its High Point Home Furnishings Market showroom presentation.

BUSINESS

LA-Z-BOY CHAIR COMPANY is the nation's leading manufacturer of upholstered seating, and the third largest manufacturer of residential furniture overall. La-Z-Boy controls a majority share of the marketplace for upholstered recliners. La-Z-Boy sleep sofas, swivel rockers, modular seating units, and stationary sofas and loveseats are some of the Company's other popular products. The Company has become a complete source of furniture for family rooms, living rooms, bedrooms and dining rooms. The Company is also a volume supplier of seating and quality wood furniture to the contract market which includes offices, hotels, hospitals, and clinics. LZB operates 24 manufacturing plants in the U.S. and Canada and licenses its products abroad.

QUARTERLY DATA

(4/30/94)($000)	Rev	Inc
1st Quarter	162,096	3,974
2nd Quarter	209,044	10,415
3rd Quarter	192,648	7,988
4th Quarter	241,110	12,340

ANNUAL EARNINGS AND DIVIDENDS PER SHARE

	4/30/94	4/24/93	4/25/92	4/27/91	4/28/90	4/29/89	4/30/88
Earnings Per Share	**1.90**	**1.50**	**1.39**	**1.30**	**1.58**	**1.54**	**[1] 1.45**
Dividends Per Share	**0.68**	**0.62**	**0.57**	**0.56**	**0.52**	**0.44**	**0.40**
Dividend Payout %	**35.8**	**41.3**	**41.0**	**43.1**	**32.9**	**29.0**	**27.6**

[1] Before extraord. item

ANNUAL FINANCIAL DATA

RECORD OF EARNINGS (IN THOUSANDS):							
Total Revenues	804,898	684,122	619,471	608,032	592,273	553,187	486,793
Costs and Expenses	730,576	623,229	561,103	550,702	528,261	491,106	429,220
Depreciation & Amort	14,014	14,061	14,840	14,039	13,735	13,607	14,203
Operating Profit	60,308	46,832	43,528	43,291	50,277	48,474	43,370
Income Bef Income Taxes	58,155	45,299	39,905	38,370	45,535	43,974	42,024
Income Taxes	23,438	18,015	14,805	15,009	17,282	16,508	15,543
Net Income	[1] 34,717	27,284	25,100	23,361	28,253	27,466	26,481
Aver. Shs. Outstg.	18,268	18,172	18,064	17,941	17,868	17,886	18,285
[1] Before acctg. change cr$3,352,000.							
BALANCE SHEET (IN THOUSANDS):							
Cash and Cash Equivalents	25,926	28,808	21,737	12,960	6,720	18,159	13,207
Receivables, Net	198,275	184,258	168,264	156,953	155,955	143,141	130,584
Inventories	67,236	60,487	57,808	60,407	69,568	65,641	66,822
Gross Property	204,456	191,169	185,789	173,888	158,683	146,409	139,340
Accumulated Depreciation	110,179	100,762	92,349	78,380	69,542	66,564	55,180
Long-Term Debt	52,495	55,370	55,912	62,187	69,066	70,641	76,215
Net Stockholders' Equity	290,911	263,386	246,359	229,217	214,585	194,293	178,765
Total Assets	430,253	401,064	376,722	363,085	361,856	349,007	336,592
Total Current Assets	295,585	278,976	253,579	238,222	240,411	235,822	219,438
Total Current Liabilities	71,463	77,451	69,148	65,233	70,119	76,875	72,374
Net Working Capital	224,122	201,525	184,431	172,989	170,292	158,947	147,064
Year End Shares Outstg	18,287	18,195	18,135	17,979	17,905	17,078	18,024
STATISTICAL RECORD:							
Operating Profit Margin %	7.5	6.8	7.0	7.1	8.5	8.8	8.9
Book Value Per Share	14.77	13.29	12.32	11.43	10.61	9.88	8.46
Return on Equity %	11.9	10.4	10.2	10.2	13.2	14.1	14.8
Return on Assets %	8.1	6.8	6.7	6.4	7.8	7.9	7.9
Average Yield %	2.1	2.6	2.8	3.3	2.6	2.7	2.2
P/E Ratio	20.5-13.2	19.2-11.8	18.1-10.9	16.9-9.5	14.7-10.7	12.3-8.8	16.3-9.0
Price Range	38⅞-25⅛	28¾-17¾	25⅛-15⅛	22-12⅜	23¼-16⅞	19-13½	23⅝-13

Statistics are as originally reported.

OFFICERS:
C.T. Knabusch, Chmn. & Pres.
E.J. Shoemaker, Vice-Chmn. & Exec. V.P.-Engineering
G.M. Hardy, Sec. & Treas.

INCORPORATED: MI, May, 1941

PRINCIPAL OFFICE: 1284 N. Telegraph Rd., Monroe, MI 48161-3390

TELEPHONE NUMBER: (313) 242-1444
FAX: (313) 457-2005
NO. OF EMPLOYEES: 9,370
ANNUAL MEETING: In July
SHAREHOLDERS: 12,615
INSTITUTIONAL HOLDINGS:
No. of Institutions: 55
Shares Held: 3,723,285

REGISTRAR(S):

TRANSFER AGENT(S):

NYS SYMBOL LEE
Rec. Pr. 36¼

LEE ENTERPRISES, INC.

YIELD 2.4%
P/E RATIO 15.6

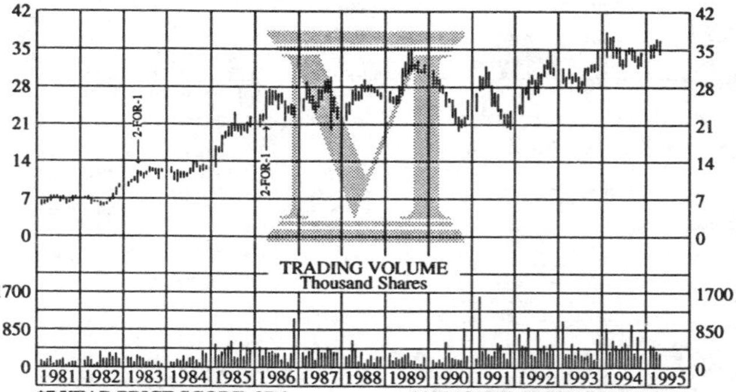

*7 YEAR PRICE SCORE 97.4 *12 MONTH PRICE SCORE 99.1

*NYSE COMPOSITE INDEX=100

INTERIM EARNINGS (Per Share):

Qtr.	Dec.	Mar.	June	Sept.
1991-92	0.42	0.27	0.50	0.46
1992-93	0.49	0.28	0.51	0.49
1993-94	0.57	0.41	0.61	0.58
1994-95	0.73	...	...	...

INTERIM DIVIDENDS (Per Share):

Amt.	Decl.	Ex.	Rec.	Pay.
0.21Q	4/25/94	5/25/94	6/1/94	7/1/94
0.21Q	7/22	8/26	9/1	9/30
0.22Q	11/17	12/5	12/9	1/2/95
0.22Q	2/3/95	2/23/95	3/1/95	4/3
0.22Q	4/13	5/25	6/1	7/3

Indicated div.: $0.88

CAPITALIZATION (9/30/94):

	($000)	(%)
Long-Term Debt	98,641	29.0
Common & Surplus	241,930	71.0
Total	340,571	100.0

DIVIDEND ACHIEVER STATUS:
Rank: 138 1984-94 Growth Rate: 11.1%
Total Years of Dividend Growth: 34

RECENT DEVELOPMENTS: For the quarter ended 12/31/94, net income increased 26.3% to $16.8 million compared with $13.3 million a year ago. Revenues were up 10.8% to $113.1 million from $102.1 million. Operating results were fueled by gains in advertising revenues, reflecting higher average rates and increased advertising inches. Classified advertising was driven by employment and private party ads, which more than offset soft automotive and real estate segments. However, increased newsprint prices were incurred.

PROSPECTS: Demand for classified advertising will continue to fuel revenue growth in the newspaper division. However, these gains will be partially offset by rising newsprint prices. The broadcasting group is also generating higher national, regional and local advertising revenues. In addition, management efforts to improve local viewership have been successful. The Company will continue to benefit from a steady stream of cash flow, which provides significant operational and financial flexibility.

BUSINESS

LEE ENTERPRISES is a diversified media company in the business information and entertainment industry. It publishes daily newspapers in Illinois, Iowa, Minnesota, Montana, Nebraska, North and South Dakota, Oregon, and Wisconsin; operates television stations in Hawaii, Arizona, Nebraska, Oregon and West Virginia; participates in cable television services in Iowa and Wisconsin; and serves the graphic arts industry through NAPP Systems Inc., a producer of photosensitive polymer printing plates for newspapers. Lee and its subsidiaries purchase newprint, its core raw material, from U.S. and Canadian producers. The Company owns and operates 8 television stations, and publishes 19 daily newspapers and 38 specialty publications.

REVENUES

(9/30/94)	($000)	(%)
Newspapers	241,032	61.5
Broadcasting	90,000	22.9
Media Products & Services	61,357	15.6
Total	392,389	100.0

ANNUAL EARNINGS AND DIVIDENDS PER SHARE

	9/30/94	9/30/93	9/30/92	9/30/91	9/30/90	9/30/89	9/30/88
Earnings Per Share	**2.17**	**1.76**	**1.65**	**1.35**	**1.82**	**1.74**	**1.63**
Dividends Per Share	**1.06**	**0.80**	**0.77**	**0.76**	**0.72**	**0.68**	**0.64**
Dividend Payout %	**48.8**	**45.4**	**46.7**	**56.3**	**39.6**	**39.1**	**39.3**

ANNUAL FINANCIAL DATA

RECORD OF EARNINGS (IN THOUSANDS):							
Total Revenues	392,389	363,358	355,630	339,548	274,473	250,013	234,749
Costs and Expenses	283,578	266,992	258,889	251,933	200,574	187,256	171,017
Depreciation & Amort	23,469	24,776	23,726	23,868	17,336	13,981	12,641
Operating Income	95,477	81,139	81,303	70,459	69,567	68,226	68,879
Inc Bef Taxes on Income	84,885	67,930	66,006	53,244	60,631	62,833	61,536
Income Taxes	34,031	26,694	27,514	21,743	17,137	19,786	20,615
Net Income	50,854	41,236	38,492	31,501	43,494	43,047	40,921
Aver. Shs. Outstg.	23,425	23,460	23,341	23,292	23,928	24,794	25,082
BALANCE SHEET (IN THOUSANDS):							
Cash and Cash Equivalents	57,643	62,572	48,071	18,324	16,105	20,506	29,689
Receivables, Net	48,339	45,421	45,638	41,835	50,824	34,195	30,728
Inventories	13,147	11,177	12,489	13,934	11,955	3,552	2,934
Gross Property	220,614	204,413	197,652	196,369	188,365	140,796	119,105
Accumulated Depreciation	138,450	129,057	120,854	112,189	101,255	78,765	72,462
Long-Term Debt	98,641	127,466	153,174	166,074	177,743	76,327	73,840
Net Stockholders' Equity	241,930	223,482	203,812	183,035	173,343	176,382	167,196
Total Assets	474,701	482,317	474,830	459,269	465,777	328,800	307,837
Total Current Assets	135,707	135,122	125,925	94,457	91,057	69,652	74,035
Total Current Liabilities	99,730	91,708	85,991	76,925	85,280	50,774	41,811
Net Working Capital	35,977	43,414	39,934	17,532	5,777	18,878	32,224
Year End Shares Outstg	22,760	23,100	23,128	23,070	23,247	24,198	24,717
STATISTICAL RECORD:							
Operating Profit Margin %	24.3	22.3	22.9	20.8	25.3	27.3	29.3
Return on Equity %	21.0	18.5	18.9	17.2	25.1	24.4	24.5
Return on Assets %	10.7	8.5	8.1	6.9	9.3	13.1	13.3
Average Yield %	3.0	2.6	2.7	2.9	2.8	2.3	2.5
P/E Ratio	17.6-14.5	19.9-15.3	21.1-13.9	23.6-14.9	17.1-10.9	20.0-14.2	18.0-13.3
Price Range	38¼-31½	35-27	34⅞-23	31⅞-20⅛	31⅛-19¾	34¾-24¾	29⅜-21¾

Statistics are as originally reported.

OFFICERS:
L.G. Schermer, Chmn.
R.D. Gottlieb, Pres. & C.E.O.
L.L. Bloom, V.P. & Treas.
C.D. Waterman, III, Sec.

INCORPORATED: DE, Sep., 1950

PRINCIPAL OFFICE: 215 N. Main Street, Davenport, IA 52801

TELEPHONE NUMBER: (319) 383-2100

NO. OF EMPLOYEES: 4,700 (approx.)

ANNUAL MEETING: In January

SHAREHOLDERS: 5,118 com.; 3,026 class B.

INSTITUTIONAL HOLDINGS:
No. of Institutions: 100
Shares Held: 8,668,720

REGISTRAR(S): First Chicago Trust Co. of New York, New York, NY 10008

TRANSFER AGENT(S): First Chicago Trust Co. of New York, New York, NY 10008

LEGG MASON, INC.

YIELD 1.8%
P/E RATIO 16.8

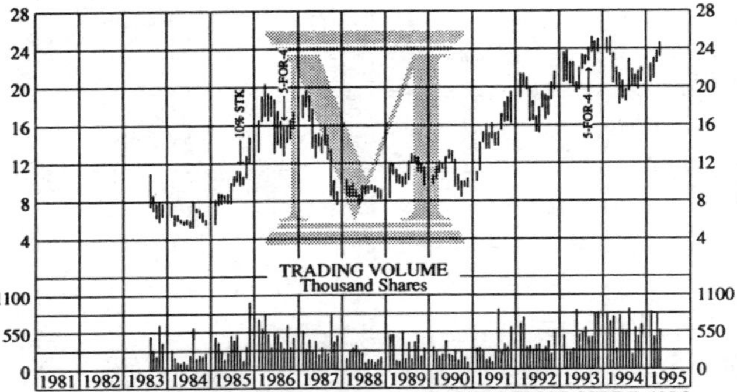

INTERIM EARNINGS (Per Share):

Qtr.	June	Sept.	Dec.	Mar.
1991-92	0.37	0.41	0.50	0.58
1992-93	0.74	0.61	0.59	0.66
1993-94	0.68	0.94	0.81	0.55
1994-95	0.32	0.25	0.33	...

INTERIM DIVIDENDS (Per Share):

Amt.	Decl.	Ex.	Rec.	Pay.
0.10Q	4/15/94	6/10/94	6/16/94	7/11/94
0.11Q	7/28	9/16	9/22	10/17
0.11Q	10/18	12/9	12/15	1/9/95
0.11Q	1/19/95	3/10/95	3/16/95	4/10
0.11Q	4/20	6/13	6/15	7/10

Indicated div.: $0.44

CAPITALIZATION (3/31/94):

	($000)	(%)
Common & Surplus	211,686	100.0
Total	211,686	100.0

*7 YEAR PRICE SCORE 108.6   ***12 MONTH PRICE SCORE 105.3**

*NYSE COMPOSITE INDEX=100

DIVIDEND ACHIEVER STATUS:
Rank: 73   1984-94 Growth Rate: 14.1%
Total Years of Dividend Growth: 11

RECENT DEVELOPMENTS: For the three months ended 12/31/94, the Company earned $4.1 million, 58% less than the $9.9 million earned in the corresponding 1993 period. LM cited reduced investment banking, and securities and brokerage revenues as primary reasons for results. Investment banking revenues totaled $8.5 million, a sharp decline from $23.3 million a year earlier. Principal transaction revenues fell 22% to $15.3 million and commission revenue dropped 15.4% to $30.0 million. Investment advisory and related fee revenue grew 26% to $21.2 million.

PROSPECTS: The Company acquired Batterymarch Financial Management in a transaction valued at $120 million. Batterymarch is a Boston, MA-based company with assets under management totaling approximately $5 billion. This acquisition bodes well for earnings and should propel investment advisory and related fee revenue further. Activity in corporate and municipal finance has been significantly reduced and securities and brokerage transactions have also slowed considerably due to increased interest rates.

BUSINESS

LEGG MASON, INC. is a holding company that provides securities brokerage, investment advisory, corporate and public finance, and mortgage banking services to individuals, institutions, corporations and municipalities. The Company serves brokerage clients through 88 offices. As investment advisors, the Company manages more than $17.3 billion in assets for private accounts and mutual funds. Its mortgage-banking subsidiaries have direct and master servicing responsibility for $12 billion of commercial mortgages.

REVENUES

(3/31/94)	($000)	(%)
Commissions	141,375	35.6
Principal Transactions	53,949	13.6
Invest Advis & Rltd Fees........................	65,583	16.5
	79	
Invest banking	283	19.9
Interest........................	29,990	7.5
Other..........................	27,354	6.9
Total	397,534	100.0

ANNUAL EARNINGS AND DIVIDENDS PER SHARE

	3/31/94	3/31/93	3/31/92	3/31/91	3/31/90	3/31/89	3/31/88
Earnings Per Share	2.98	2.61	1.86	1.22	②1.10	0.56	0.70
Dividends Per Share	①0.34	0.296	0.264	0.232	0.20	0.18	0.164
Dividend Payout %	11.4	11.3	14.2	19.1	18.1	32.1	23.3

① 5-for-4 stk split,09/27/93 ② Per primary share

ANNUAL FINANCIAL DATA

RECORD OF EARNINGS (IN THOUSANDS):

	3/31/94	3/31/93	3/31/92	3/31/91	3/31/90	3/31/89	3/31/88
Principal Transactions	53,949	55,000	53,191	61,808	56,527	50,249	46,432
Commissions	141,375	117,305	112,556	91,233	99,954	79,841	92,008
Total Revenues	397,534	336,347	292,356	242,723	243,676	213,447	215,571
Compensation & Benefits	228,998	193,857	164,595	132,277	132,639	114,512	122,506
Interest Expense	15,396	11,629	13,433	14,198	17,095	18,521	11,454
Sell, Gen. & Admin. Exp.	284,659	243,055	212,171	178,901	179,654	160,759	163,680
Earn Bef Income Taxes	59,214	48,983	35,015	21,222	19,532	9,633	12,728
Income Taxes	23,166	18,780	13,898	8,309	7,687	3,628	5,152
Net Income	36,048	30,203	21,117	12,913	11,845	6,005	7,576
Aver. Shs. Outstg. (000)	12,110	11,574	11,386	10,626	10,719	10,685	10,765

BALANCE SHEET (IN THOUSANDS):

Cash & Marketable Secs.	294,915	209,318	221,837	161,605	33,740	74,513	108,221
Customer Receivables	250,237	208,273	164,960	176,350	269,800	210,322	186,749
Rec Fr Brokers & Dealers	5,074	8,296	5,533	3,949	10,078	13,104	16,160
Securities Inventory	57,617	109,097	94,648	64,562	53,316	42,415	64,053
Total Assets	811,488	640,454	579,883	496,266	432,556	419,202	444,097
Payable to Customers	298,943	267,316	236,979	241,383	201,919	188,497	180,830
Long-Term Debt	102,487	34,597	35,020	35,120	35,120	35,545	36,369
Net Stockholders' Equity	211,686	176,928	147,957	126,363	116,080	107,794	104,057
Year End Shares Outstg	11,735	8,999	11,062	10,379	10,310	10,424	10,461

STATISTICAL RECORD:

Return on Assets %	4.4	4.7	3.6	2.6	2.7	1.4	1.7
Return on Equity %	17.0	17.1	14.3	10.2	10.2	5.6	7.3
Book Value Per Share	18.04	19.66	13.38	12.17	11.26	10.34	9.95
Average Yield %	1.5	1.6	1.8	2.1	1.9	2.0	1.2
P/E Ratio	8.5-6.5	8.3-5.8	10.5-5.5	11.0-6.9	11.8-7.5	18.3-13.6	28.0-10.9
Price Range	25¼-19⅜	21⅝-15¼	19½-10⅛	13⅜-8⅜	13-8¼	10¼-7⅝	19⅝-7⅝

Statistics are as originally reported.

OFFICERS:
R.A. Mason, Chmn., Pres. & C.E.O.
C.A. Bacigalupo, Sr. V.P. & Sec.
T.C. Scheve, V.P. & Treas.

PRINCIPAL OFFICE: 111 South Calvert Street, P.O. Box 1476, Baltimore, MD 21203-1476

TELEPHONE NUMBER: (410) 539-0000
NO. OF EMPLOYEES: 2,652
ANNUAL MEETING: In July
SHAREHOLDERS: 1,366
INSTITUTIONAL HOLDINGS:
No. of Institutions: Not Available
Shares Held: Not Available

REGISTRAR(S): Security Trust Company
Baltimore, MD

TRANSFER AGENT(S): Security Trust Company Baltimore, MD

LEGGETT & PLATT, INC.

YIELD 1.8%
P/E RATIO 14.3

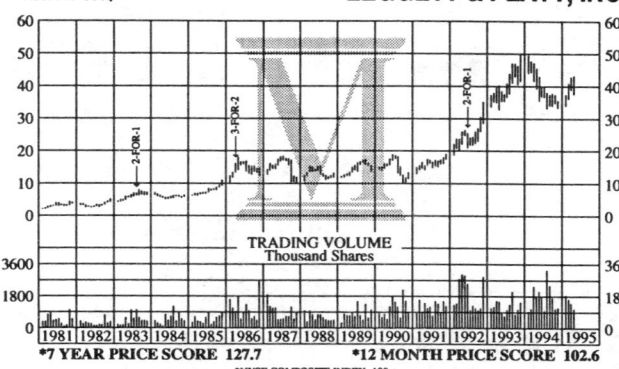

TRADING VOLUME
Thousand Shares

| | 1981 | 1982 | 1983 | 1984 | 1985 | 1986 | 1987 | 1988 | 1989 | 1990 | 1991 | 1992 | 1993 | 1994 | 1995 |

*7 YEAR PRICE SCORE 127.7   *12 MONTH PRICE SCORE 102.6
*NYSE COMPOSITE INDEX=100

INTERIM EARNINGS (Per Share):

Qtr.	Mar.	June	Sept.	Dec.
1991	0.22	0.28	0.34	0.28
1992	0.38	0.39	0.46	0.41
1993	0.48	0.51	0.54	0.56
1994	0.63	0.68	0.73	0.74

INTERIM DIVIDENDS (Per Share):

Amt.	Decl.	Ex.	Rec.	Pay.
0.15Q	2/9/94	2/18/94	2/25/94	3/15/94
0.15Q	5/12	5/23	5/27	6/15
0.16Q	8/10	8/22	8/26	9/15
0.16Q	11/9	11/18	11/25	1/2/95
0.18Q	2/8/95	2/17/95	2/24/95	3/15

Indicated div.: $0.72

CAPITALIZATION (12/31/94):

	($000)	(%)
Long-Term Debt	204,900	23.5
Deferred Income Tax	42,200	4.8
Common & Surplus	625,200	71.7
Total	872,300	100.0

DIVIDEND ACHIEVER STATUS:

Rank: 51   1984-94 Growth Rate: 15.2%
Total Years of Dividend Growth: 25

RECENT DEVELOPMENTS: For the year ended 12/31/94, net income increased 34.3% to $115.4 million from $85.9 million in 1993. Sales for the year were up 21.7% to $1.86 billion, compared with $1.53 billion the previous year. Pretax earnings climbed 34.4% to $189.5 million from $141.0 million. LEG's gross margin was 23.1% of sales, up from 22.9% the prior year. Margin improvement was the result of stronger market conditions in the aluminum and foam industries and gains in overall manufacturing efficiencies.

PROSPECTS: Improvement in the furnishings industry and the diversified markets served by LEG is likely to continue as modest economic growth continues. The extent of future growth will depend on how the continued rise in interest rates affects consumer demand for furnishings and durable goods. Acquisitions completed in 1994 have expanded LEG's annual sales base by approximately $200 million and have provided the Company with excellent opportunities for further profit growth.

BUSINESS

LEGGETT & PLATT INC., is engaged primarily in the manufacture and distribution of components used by companies that manufacture furniture and bedding for homes, offices and institutions. Also in the furnishings area, the Company produces and sells some finished products for the furnishings industry. These finished products include sleep-related finished furniture and carpet cushioning materials. In addition, a group of diversified products made principally from steel, steel wire, aluminum, plastics, textile fibers and woven and non-woven fabrics is sold in many different markets unrelated to the home furnishings industry. LEG's international division is involved primarily in the sale of machinery and equipment designed to manufacture the Company's Mira-Coil innersprings.

BUSINESS LINE ANALYSIS

(12/31/94)	Rev(%)	Inc(%)
Furnishings Products	75.2	73.7
Diversified	24.8	26.3
Total	100.0	100.0

ANNUAL EARNINGS AND DIVIDENDS PER SHARE

	1994	1993	1992	1991	1990	1989	1988
Earnings Per Share	2.78	2.09	1.64	1.11	0.84	1.33	1.11
Dividends Per Share	0.62	0.54	☐ 0.45	0.425	0.41	0.355	0.31
Dividend Payout %	22.3	25.8	27.4	38.3	48.8	26.7	27.9

☐ 2-for-1 stk split, 6/16/92

ANNUAL FINANCIAL DATA

RECORD OF EARNINGS (IN MILLIONS):

	1994	1993	1992	1991	1990	1989	1988
Total Revenues	1,858.1	1,526.7	1,170.5	1,081.8	1,088.6	991.6	809.9
Costs and Expenses	1,599.2	1,324.8	1,023.5	967.3	986.9	874.7	719.0
Depreciation & Amort	56.9	45.3	38.2	36.4	34.4	28.4	23.9
Operating Profit	202.0	156.6	108.8	78.1	87.7	88.5	67.0
Earn Bef Income Taxes	189.5	141.0	99.8	63.9	50.6	75.7	60.0
Income Taxes	74.1	55.1	37.3	24.5	21.2	29.8	22.3
Net Income	115.4	85.9	62.5	39.4	29.4	45.9	37.7
Aver. Shs. Outstg. (000)	41,600	41,100	38,052	35,450	35,218	34,698	34,172

BALANCE SHEET (IN MILLIONS):

Cash and Cash Equivalents	2.7	0.4	4.0	5.3	3.3	2.9	7.0
Receivables, Net	254.3	204.7	156.8	140.8	146.2	136.5	114.8
Inventories	255.5	209.1	161.1	157.3	172.0	144.2	122.4
Gross Property	699.5	571.2	438.5	418.1	380.0	350.1	295.5
Accumulated Depreciation	303.5	258.1	207.8	184.0	155.2	140.9	119.3
Long-Term Debt	204.9	165.8	101.5	179.4	212.8	147.5	106.8
Net Stockholders' Equity	625.2	515.6	425.2	332.6	302.6	281.6	245.4
Total Assets	1,119.9	901.9	678.0	656.1	726.2	608.3	513.0
Total Current Assets	544.7	435.6	340.2	321.7	342.4	292.8	250.5
Total Current Liabilities	232.9	166.2	118.6	110.6	128.0	112.7	103.1
Net Working Capital	311.8	269.4	221.6	211.1	214.5	180.1	147.3
Year End Shs Outstg (000)	41,597	40,318	38,165	35,299	34,921	34,472	34,046

STATISTICAL RECORD:

Operating Profit Margin %	10.9	10.3	9.3	7.2	6.2	8.9	8.3
Book Value Per Share	11.60	9.84	9.59	7.75	7.13	7.41	6.60
Return on Equity %	18.5	16.7	14.7	11.8	9.7	16.3	15.4
Return on Assets %	10.3	9.5	9.2	6.0	4.1	7.5	7.4
Average Yield %	1.5	1.3	1.7	2.6	2.8	2.4	2.4
P/E Ratio	17.8-12.0	24.0-15.7	21.5-11.4	17.2-11.7	22.6-11.9	13.2-8.9	14.0-9.7
Price Range	49½-33¼	50⅛-32¾	35¼-18¾	19⅛-13	19-10	17½-11⅞	15½-10¾

Statistics are as originally reported.

OFFICERS:
H.M. Cornell, Jr., Chmn. & C.E.O.
F.E. Wright, Pres. & C.O.O.

INCORPORATED: MO, 1901

PRINCIPAL OFFICE: No. 1 -- Leggett Rd., Carthage, MO 64836

TELEPHONE NUMBER: (417) 358-8131
FAX: (417) 358-6045
NO. OF EMPLOYEES: 16,000 (approx.)
ANNUAL MEETING: In May
SHAREHOLDERS: 8,087
INSTITUTIONAL HOLDINGS:
No. of Institutions: 143
Shares Held: 10,751,487

REGISTRAR(S): Mellon Securities Trust Co., New York, NY

TRANSFER AGENT(S): Mellon Securities Trust Company, New York, NY

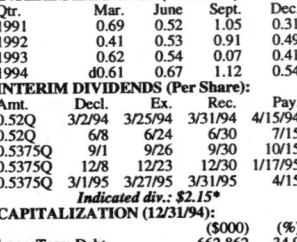

NYS SYMBOL LGE
Rec. Pr. 38⅝

LG&E ENERGY CORP.

YIELD 5.6%
P/E RATIO 24.3

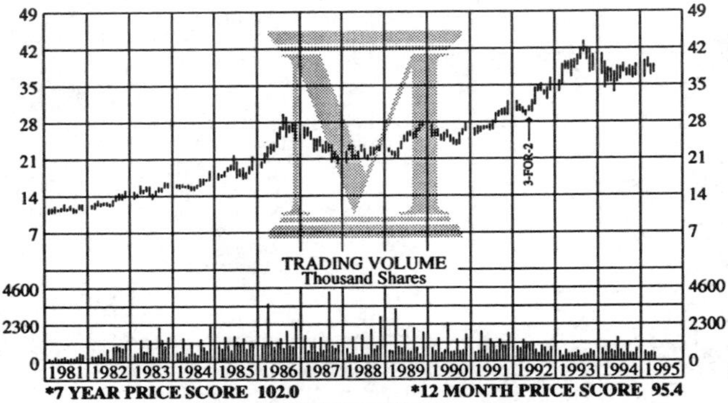

49
42
35
28
21
14
7
3-FOR-2
TRADING VOLUME
Thousand Shares
4600
2300
0
1981 1982 1983 1984 1985 1986 1987 1988 1989 1990 1991 1992 1993 1994 1995

*7 YEAR PRICE SCORE 102.0 *12 MONTH PRICE SCORE 95.4

*NYSE COMPOSITE INDEX=100

INTERIM EARNINGS (Per Share):

Qtr.	Mar.	June	Sept.	Dec.
1991	0.69	0.52	1.05	0.31
1992	0.41	0.53	0.91	0.49
1993	0.62	0.54	0.07	0.41
1994	d0.61	0.67	1.12	0.54

INTERIM DIVIDENDS (Per Share):

Amt.	Decl.	Ex.	Rec.	Pay.
0.52Q	3/2/94	3/25/94	3/31/94	4/15/94
0.52Q	6/8	6/24	6/30	7/15
0.5375Q	9/1	9/26	9/30	10/15
0.5375Q	12/8	12/23	12/30	1/17/95
0.5375Q	3/1/95	3/27/95	3/31/95	4/15

Indicated div.: $2.15*

CAPITALIZATION (12/31/94):

	($000)	(%)
Long-Term Debt	662,862	34.9
Deferred Income Tax	358,607	18.9
Preferred Stock	116,716	6.1
Common & Surplus	762,515	40.1
Total	1,900,700	100.0

DIVIDEND ACHIEVER STATUS:
Rank: 320 1984-94 Growth Rate: 2.8%
Total Years of Dividend Growth: 40

RECENT DEVELOPMENTS: For the quarter ended 12/31/94, net income was $19.2 million compared with $15.0 million in the corresponding 1993 period. Revenues were $190.3 million, down 20.8%. For the year ended 12/31/94, income, from continuing operations, was $56.8 million versus $80.8 million in 1993. Revenues were $829.7 million, down 7.8%. The decrease in revenues was due primarily to abnormally warm weather in the fourth quarter and diminished construction activities within non-utility operations.

PROSPECTS: Non-utility earnings are being driven higher by the start-up of Roanoke Valley I and Rensselaer, two independent power projects, and the operation of two wind projects. The Company is well-positioned to ward off increased competition through a low-risk service territory, clean coal-fired generating capacity, and a competitive rate structure, which will enable it to sign long-term contracts with customers. LGE is not likely to need additional plant generating capacity until the end of the decade.

BUSINESS

LG & E ENERGY CORP. is a diversified energy-services holding corporation. LG&E Energy Services, a wholly-owned subsidiary, will oversee non-utility electric power project development domestically and internationally. LG&E Power Inc., LGE's independent power subsidiary, develops, designs, engineers, builds, finances, operates and maintains power plants. Louisville Gas and Electric Company supplies electricity and natural gas to an estimated 594,000 people in Louisville and surrounding territory in Kentucky.

BUSINESS LINE ANALYSIS

(12/31/94)	Rev(%)	Inc(%)
Electric	67.4	84.8
Gas	24.1	8.6
Non-Utility	8.5	6.6
Total	100.0	100.0

ANNUAL EARNINGS AND DIVIDENDS PER SHARE

	1994	1993	1992	1991	1990	1989	1988
Earnings Per Share	1.72	2.47	2.34	2.57	[2] 2.30	2.13	2.47
Dividends Per Share	2.097	2.027	[1] 1.965	1.907	1.863	1.823	1.783
Dividend Payout %	21.9	82.2	84.0	74.1	81.0	85.5	72.3

[1] 3-for-2 stk split, 5/18/92 [2] Before extraord. item

ANNUAL FINANCIAL DATA

	1994	1993	1992	1991	1990	1989	1988
RECORD OF EARNINGS (IN MILLIONS):							
Total Revenues	829.7	900.0	834.7	715.0	699.0	676.9	659.7
Depreciation & Amort	84.2	82.7	79.7	76.7	55.6	55.3	50.7
Maintenance	...	...	...	49.6	48.5	52.0	52.5
Net Operating Income	140.3	193.0	182.1	137.4	137.0	127.6	129.8
Interest Expense	58.0	48.2	51.2	52.7	53.7	51.1	...
Net Income	[1] 56.8	[2] 80.8	75.6	83.0	[3] 73.2	66.6	75.6
Aver. Shs. Outstg. (000)	32,991	32,689	32,307	32,256	31,857	31,271	30,615

[1] Before disc. op. cr$51,805,000; and acctg. chg dr$3,369,000. [2] Before disc. op. cr$7,435,000. [3] Before disc. op. cr$18,236,000.

	1994	1993	1992	1991	1990	1989	1988
BALANCE SHEET (IN MILLIONS):							
Gross Plant	2,537.9	2,464.1	2,373.5	2,285.5	2,215.2	2,277.4	2,109.6
Accumulated Depreciation	881.9	823.1	754.4	693.2	631.4	582.8	507.7
Prop, Plant & Equip, Net	1,656.0	1,641.0	1,619.1	1,592.2	1,583.7	1,694.6	1,602.0
Long-term Debt	662.9	662.9	686.1	686.5	687.4	613.3	560.1
Net Stockholders' Equity	879.2	846.4	802.0	791.5	766.0	719.9	696.0
Total Assets	2,217.5	2,284.8	2,160.6	2,054.2	2,001.4	1,905.3	1,763.1
Year End Shs Outstg (000)	33,016	32,956	32,328	32,284	32,106	31,532	30,908
STATISTICAL RECORD:							
Book Value Per Share	23.10	22.14	21.20	20.89	20.22	19.12	18.70
Op. Inc/Net Pl %	8.5	11.8	11.2	8.6	8.7	7.5	8.1
Dep/Gr. Pl %	3.3	3.2	3.4	3.4	2.5	2.4	2.4
Accum. Dep/Gr. Pl %	34.7	33.4	31.8	30.3	28.5	25.6	24.1
Return on Equity %	6.5	9.5	9.4	10.5	9.6	9.3	10.9
Average Yield %	5.6	5.3	6.0	6.6	7.2	7.4	8.1
P/E Ratio	23.8-19.5	17.6-13.7	15.5-12.4	12.5-9.9	12.2-10.2	13.1-10.0	9.6-8.1
Price Range	41-33⅝	43⅜-33¾	36⅜-29⅛	32-25⅜	28-23½	27⅞-21⅜	23¾-20⅛

Statistics are as originally reported.

OFFICERS:
R.W. Hale, Chmn., Pres. & C.E.O.
J.R. McCall, Exec. V.P., General Couns. & Corp. Sec.
C.A. Markel, III, V.P.-Fin. & Treas.

INCORPORATED: KY, Nov., 1989

PRINCIPAL OFFICE: 220 W Main St P.O. Box 32030, Louisville, KY 40232

TELEPHONE NUMBER: (502) 627-2000

NO. OF EMPLOYEES: 2,971

ANNUAL MEETING: In May

SHAREHOLDERS: 31,711

INSTITUTIONAL HOLDINGS:
No. of Institutions: 155
Shares Held: 8,704,915

REGISTRAR(S):

TRANSFER AGENT(S): At Company's Office
Continental Stock Transfer & Trust Co., New York, NY

NYS SYMBOL LLY
Rec. Pr. 76½

LILLY (ELI) & CO.

YIELD 3.4%
P/E RATIO 17.5

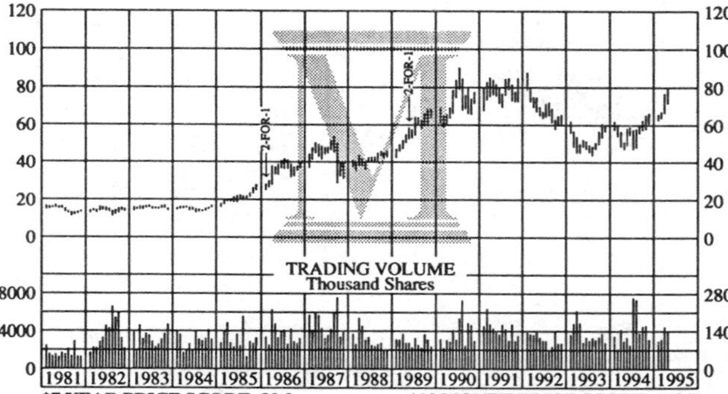

120
100
80
60
40
20
0
2-FOR-1
2-FOR-1
TRADING VOLUME
Thousand Shares
28000
14000
0
1981 1982 1983 1984 1985 1986 1987 1988 1989 1990 1991 1992 1993 1994 1995

*7 YEAR PRICE SCORE 82.0 *12 MONTH PRICE SCORE 113.7

*NYSE COMPOSITE INDEX=100

INTERIM EARNINGS (Per Share):

Qtr.	Mar.	June	Sept.	Dec.
1991	1.35	1.08	1.01	1.06
1992	1.51	1.16	d0.91	Nil
1993	1.28	1.18	1.00	d1.77
1994	1.14	1.20	1.10	0.93

INTERIM DIVIDENDS (Per Share):

Amt.	Decl.	Ex.	Rec.	Pay.
0.625Q	4/18/94	5/9/94	5/13/94	6/10/94
0.625Q	7/18	8/9	8/15	9/12
0.625Q	10/17	11/8	11/15	12/12
0.645Q	12/19/95	2/9/95	2/15/95	3/10/95
0.645Q	4/17	5/9	5/15	6/12

*Indicated div.: $2.58**

CAPITALIZATION (12/31/94):

	($000)	(%)
Long-Term Debt	2,125,800	28.4
Common & Surplus	5,355,600	71.6
Total	7,481,400	100.0

DIVIDEND ACHIEVER STATUS:
Rank: 90 1984-94 Growth Rate: 13.2%
Total Years of Dividend Growth: 27

RECENT DEVELOPMENTS: For the year ended 12/31/94, net income from continuing operations increased to $1.19 billion compared with $464.8 million in the previous year. Sales advanced 9.9% to $5.71 billion. Comparisons were made with restated 1993 results. Revenues received a boost from the September acquisition of Sphinx Pharmaceuticals Corporation. In late November, the Company completed the acquisition of PCS Health Systems, a pharmacy-management company.

PROSPECTS: The substantial burden Lilly has undertaken to acquire PCS Health Systems will cause debt and interest charges to increase significantly. Initially these charges will exceed the operating earnings contributed by PCS by a wide margin. However, this acquisition has enhanced LLY's competitive position in managed-care markets. PCS will help the Company defend Prozac, an anti-depressant, and Axid, an ulcer treatment, against competition that is certain to intensify.

BUSINESS

LILLY (ELI) & CO. is a global research-based corporation that develops, manufactures, and markets pharmaceuticals, including Ceclor, Keflex®, Kefzol®, Iorabid, Nebcin®, Tazidime®, and Vancocin HCI. Medical devices and diagnostics include intravenous fluid-delivery and control systems, implantable cardiac pacemakers and defibrillators, external cardiac defibrillators and monitors, coronary angioplasty catheter systems, peripheral and coronary atherectomy catheter systems, patient vital signs measurement and monitoring systems, and diagnostic products that include test incorporating monclonal antibodies. Central-nervous-system agents include Prozac and Darvon®. Other major groups are diabetic-care products which include Humulin and Iletin® and animal health products, that includes Rumensin®, Micotil, Tylan and Coban.

REVENUES

(12/31/94)	($000)	(%)
Anti-Infectives	1,634,400	28.6
Central Nervous System	1,835,600	32.2
Gastrointestinal	487,400	8.5
Diabetic Care	774,400	13.6
Animal Health	463,600	8.1
All Other	516,200	9.0
Total	5,711,600	100.0

ANNUAL EARNINGS AND DIVIDENDS PER SHARE

	1994	1993	1992	1991	1990	1989	1988
Earnings Per Share	**4.10**	**1.67**	**[1] 2.81**	**4.50**	**3.90**	**3.20**	**2.67**
Dividends Per Share	**2.50**	**2.42**	**2.20**	**2.00**	**1.64**	**[2] 1.35**	**1.15**
Dividend Payout %	**61.0**	**44.9**	**78.3**	**44.4**	**42.1**	**42.2**	**43.2**

[1] Before acctg. chg. [2] 2-for-1 stk split, 4/28/89

ANNUAL FINANCIAL DATA

	1994	1993	1992	1991	1990	1989	1988
RECORD OF EARNINGS (IN MILLIONS):							
Total Revenues	5,711.6	6,452.4	6,167.3	5,725.7	5,191.6	4,175.6	4,069.7
Costs and Expenses	3,608.9	5,401.5	4,643.7	3,657.9	3,404.7	2,781.5	2,818.9
Depreciation & Amort	432.2	398.3	368.1	299.5	247.5	229.3	204.0
Operating Profit	2,633.6	2,779.9	2,646.1	1,768.3	1,539.4	1,164.8	1,587.6
Inc Bef Income Taxes & Acctg Chges	1,698.6	701.9	1,182.3	1,879.2	1,599.0	1,329.9	1,115.8
Income Taxes	513.5	210.8	354.7	564.5	471.7	390.4	354.8
Net Income	[1] 1,185.1	[2] 491.1	[3] 827.6	1,314.7	1,127.3	939.5	761.0
Aver. Shs. Outstg. (000)	289,189	294,289	294,478	294,224	289,993	294,507	287,374

[1] Before disc. op. cr$101,000,000. [2] Before acctg. change dr$10,900,000. [3] Before acctg. change dr$118,900,000.

	1994	1993	1992	1991	1990	1989	1988
BALANCE SHEET (IN MILLIONS):							
Cash and Cash Equivalents	746.7	987.1	728.3	782.4	750.8	652.0	761.5
Receivables, Net	2,079.6	1,284.1	1,051.1	1,126.0	878.7	845.8	761.7
Inventories	968.9	1,103.0	938.4	796.9	673.0	599.5	674.3
Gross Property	7,026.4	6,566.5	6,148.1	5,568.6	4,515.8	3,478.4	3,047.2
Accumulated Depreciation	2,614.9	2,366.3	2,076.0	1,786.1	1,579.1	1,363.8	1,240.6
Long-Term Debt	2,125.8	835.2	582.3	395.5	277.0	269.5	387.7
Net Stockholders' Equity	5,355.6	4,568.8	4,892.1	4,966.1	3,467.5	3,757.1	3,225.3
Total Assets	14,507.4	9,623.6	8,672.8	8,298.6	7,142.8	5,848.0	5,262.7
Total Current Assets	3,962.3	3,697.1	3,006.0	2,939.3	2,501.3	2,274.4	2,414.7
Total Current Liabilities	5,669.5	2,928.0	2,398.6	2,272.0	2,817.6	1,328.8	1,288.8
Net Working Capital	d1,707.2	769.1	607.4	667.3	d316.3	945.6	1,125.9
Year End Shs Outstg (000)	291,936	292,748	292,686	292,623	267,138	278,816	274,242
STATISTICAL RECORD:							
Operating Profit Margin %	29.2	10.1	18.7	30.9	29.7	27.9	25.7
Book Value Per Share	3.23	14.22	15.14	15.52	11.22	11.85	10.27
Return on Equity %	22.1	10.7	16.9	26.5	32.5	25.0	23.6
Return on Assets %	8.2	5.1	9.5	15.8	15.8	16.1	14.5
Average Yield %	4.4	4.6	3.0	2.6	2.2	2.4	2.8
P/E Ratio	16.2-11.5	37.1-26.1	31.2-20.6	18.9-15.0	23.2-15.1	21.4-13.2	17.2-13.2
Price Range	66¼-47⅛	62-43⅝	87¾-57¾	85⅛-67½	90⅜-58¾	68½-42⅜	45⅞-35⅜

Statistics are as originally reported.

OFFICERS:
R.L. Tobias, Chmn. & C.E.O.

INCORPORATED: IN, Jan., 1901

PRINCIPAL OFFICE: Lilly Corporate Center Drop Code 1112, Indianapolis, IN 46285

TELEPHONE NUMBER: (317) 276-2000
FAX: (317) 276-3492
NO. OF EMPLOYEES: 24,900 approx.
ANNUAL MEETING: In April
SHAREHOLDERS: 55,900
INSTITUTIONAL HOLDINGS:
No. of Institutions: 681
Shares Held: 177,956,581

REGISTRAR(S): At Company's Office

TRANSFER AGENT(S): At Company's Office

LINCOLN NATIONAL CORP.

YIELD 4.2%
P/E RATIO 12.1

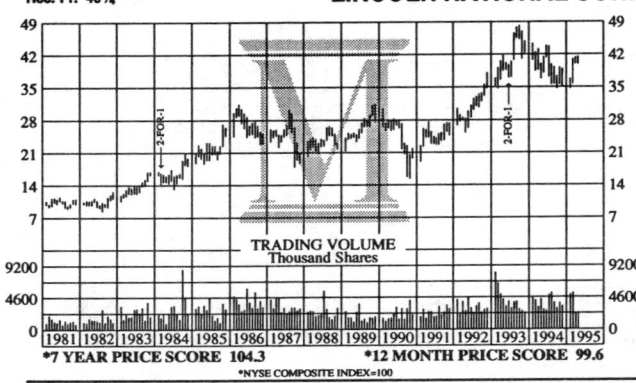

TRADING VOLUME
Thousand Shares

*7 YEAR PRICE SCORE 104.3   *12 MONTH PRICE SCORE 99.6
*NYSE COMPOSITE INDEX=100

INTERIM EARNINGS (Per Share):

Qtr.	Mar.	June	Sept.	Dec.
1991	0.45	0.88	0.81	0.18
1992	1.10	0.75	1.23	0.83
1993	0.71	1.23	1.82	0.31
1994	1.46	0.45	0.56	0.90

INTERIM DIVIDENDS (Per Share):

Amt.	Decl.	Ex.	Rec.	Pay.
0.41Q	3/10/94	4/4/94	4/8/94	5/1/94
0.41Q	5/12	7/1	7/8	8/1
0.41Q	8/11	10/3	10/10	11/1
0.43Q	11/10	1/4/95	1/10/95	2/1/95
0.43Q	3/9/95	4/4	4/10	5/1

*Indicated div.: $1.72**

CAPITALIZATION (12/31/94):

	($000)	(%)
Total Debt	694,917	18.6
Preferred Stock	311,333	8.3
Common & Surplus	2,730,727	73.1
Total	3,736,977	100.0

DIVIDEND ACHIEVER STATUS:

Rank: 241   1984-94 Growth Rate: 6.9%
Total Years of Dividend Growth: 11

RECENT DEVELOPMENTS: In January 1995, LNC (UK) completed the acquisition of Liberty Life Assurance Company Limited. For the year ended 12/31/94, net income was $349.9 million compared with income before an accounting change of $415.3 million the year before. Total revenue fell 15.8% to $6.98 billion from $8.29 billion for the prior year. Income from operations totaled $389.8 million, up 13.5% from $343.5 million a year ago. Net premiums written for the property/casualty segment declined 5.8% to $1.66 billion.

PROSPECTS: The acquisition of Delaware Management Holdings Inc. is expected to close in the second quarter of fiscal 1995. The Company continues to expand its presence in Britain's life and pension marketplace. Earnings for the life insurance segment are improving due to contributions from LNC's British subsidiary. The property/casualty segment is benefiting from significant increases in operating income. LNC should continue to record strong growth in assets under management.

BUSINESS

LINCOLN NATIONAL CORPORA-TION, a multi-line holding company, is one of the nation's largest diversified financial services companies. Subsidiaries provide, on a national basis, individual life insurance, employee benefits and property-casualty insurance. Through its subsidiaries, Lincoln National writes more individual life insurance than any other publicly-held group.

BUSINESS LINE ANALYSIS

(12/31/94)	Rev(%)	Inc(%)
Property-Casualty	28.2	47.1
Life Insur & Annuities	37.4	28.4
Life-Health Reinsurance	28.7	27.3
Employee Life-Health Ben	4.5	6.1
Other Operations	1.2	-8.9
Total	100.0	100.0

ANNUAL EARNINGS AND DIVIDENDS PER SHARE

	1994	1993	1992	1991	1990	1989	1988
Earnings Per Share	3.37	4.06	3.91	2.30	2.14	②3.03	2.06
Dividends Per Share	1.64	①1.52	1.46	1.36	1.30	1.24	1.18
Dividend Payout %	48.7	37.4	37.4	59.1	60.6	40.9	57.3

① 2-for-1 stk split,06/28/93   ② Per primary share

ANNUAL FINANCIAL DATA

RECORD OF EARNINGS (IN MILLIONS):

Insurance Premiums	4,444.1	5,356.8	5,298.9	6,730.2	6,328.6	5,961.2	5,714.7
Total Interest Income	2,011.4	2,146.5	1,987.3	1,799.3	1,653.4	1,580.2	1,439.5
Total Revenues	6,984.4	8,289.8	8,034.1	9,169.0	8,489.6	8,081.1	7,312.3
Bens & Settlement Exps	4,849.2	5,628.3	5,700.4	6,886.8	6,358.1	5,939.8	5,370.4
Inc Bef Fed Income Taxes	376.3	587.8	424.7	198.8	200.1	330.3	180.1
Income Taxes	26.4	172.5	61.8	cr9.6	8.7	61.5	cr5.3
Net Income	349.9	①415.3	362.9	208.4	191.5	268.9	146.7
Aver. Shs. Outstg. (000)	103,863	102,307	92,977	90,659	86,086	83,900	84,000

① Before acctg. change dr$96,431,000.

BALANCE SHEET (IN MILLIONS):

Fixed Matur, At Amortized Costs	21,644.2	23,964.3	18,352.3	16,037.3	14,211.3	13,076.7	10,462.9
Eq Secur, At Mkt Value	1,038.6	1,080.3	923.4	1,025.5	833.7	868.3	570.4
Policy Loans	553.3	595.1	563.5	530.3	485.4	456.8	480.3
Mtge Loans on Real Estate	2,853.1	3,301.0	3,135.1	3,144.6	3,230.1	3,053.8	2,845.1
Total Assets	49,330.1	48,380.4	39,671.7	34,094.8	27,597.3	25,070.1	20,964.3
Benefits and Claims	29,048.9	28,383.0	24,954.3	22,122.4	18,989.4	17,071.9	14,680.7
Net Stockholders' Equity	3,042.1	4,072.3	2,951.2	2,776.5	2,393.7	2,391.8	2,244.3
Year End Shs Outstg (000)	94,478	94,183	84,142	92,548	88,001	84,076	83,112

STATISTICAL RECORD:

Book Value Per Share	28.90	39.93	31.37	26.63	25.45	26.08	24.60
Return on Equity %	11.5	10.2	12.3	7.5	8.0	11.2	6.5
Return on Assets %	0.7	0.9	0.9	0.6	0.7	1.1	0.7
Average Yield %	4.2	3.7	4.6	5.8	5.7	4.7	5.0
P/E Ratio	13.2-10.3	11.9-8.6	9.8-6.5	12.0-8.3	14.3-7.2	10.4-7.1	13.0-9.8
Price Range	44⅜-34⅝	48¼-34¾	38⅛-25¼	27⅝-19	30⅝-15⅜	31½-21⅜	26¾-20⅛

Statistics are as originally reported.

OFFICERS:
I.M. Rolland, Chmn. & C.E.O.
R.A. Anker, Pres. & C.O.O.
R.C. Vaughan, Exec. V.P. & C.F.O.
M.A. Roesler, Treas.
C.S. Womack, Sec.

INCORPORATED: IN, Jan., 1968

PRINCIPAL OFFICE: 200 East Berry Street, Fort Wayne, IN 46802-2706

TELEPHONE NUMBER: (219) 455-2000

NO. OF EMPLOYEES: 8,995

ANNUAL MEETING: In May

SHAREHOLDERS: 13,730

INSTITUTIONAL HOLDINGS:
No. of Institutions: 230
Shares Held: 27,881,800

REGISTRAR(S): First National Bank of Boston, Boston, MA

TRANSFER AGENT(S): First National Bank of Boston, Boston, MA

LIQUI-BOX CORP.

YIELD 1.2%
P/E RATIO 16.6

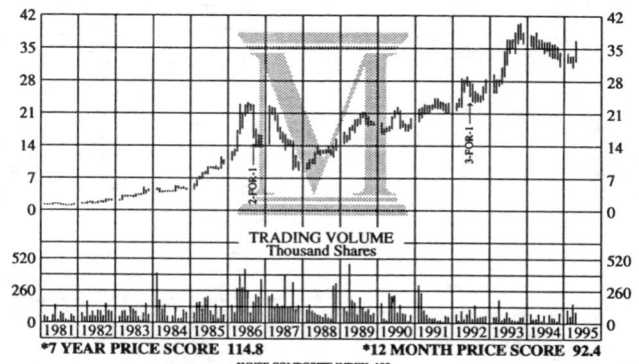

*7 YEAR PRICE SCORE 114.8   *12 MONTH PRICE SCORE 92.4
*NYSE COMPOSITE INDEX=100

INTERIM EARNINGS (Per Share):

Qtr.	Apr.	July	Oct.	Dec.
1993-94	0.40	0.62	0.58	0.40
1994-95	0.46	0.66	0.61	0.33
1995-96	0.37	...	...	...

INTERIM DIVIDENDS (Per Share):

Amt.	Decl.	Ex.	Rec.	Pay.
0.10Q	3/15/94	3/25/94	4/1/94	4/15/94
0.10Q	6/15	6/27	7/1	7/15
0.10Q	9/15	9/26	10/1	10/15
0.10Q	12/12	12/23	1/1/95	1/15/95
0.10Q	3/15/95	3/27/95	4/1	4/15

Indicated Div.: $0.40

CAPITALIZATION (12/31/94):

	($000)	(%)
Deferred Income Tax	830	1.1
Common & Surplus	73,683	98.9
Total	74,513	100.0

DIVIDEND ACHIEVER STATUS:
Rank: 42   1984-94 Growth Rate: 15.7%
Total Years of Dividend Growth: 16

RECENT DEVELOPMENTS: For the twelve months ended 12/31/94, net income increased 3.0% to $13.3 million from $12.9 million in 1993. Net sales for the year advanced 13.6% to $147.8 million, compared with $130.1 million the previous year. Gross profit remained essentially flat at $45.8 million due to an increase in the cost of sales as a percentage of sales to 69.0% from 65.0%. Higher sales were attributed to increased domestic unit shipments and stronger sales by the

Company's European subsidiary. Increased selling prices on most of LIQB's products helped to offset the dramatic increase in the cost of plastic resin, the Company's prime raw material. For the three months ended 12/31/94, net income declined 18.7% to $2.1 million from $2.6 million in the corresponding 1993 period. Revenues were up 10.2% to $31.3 million from $28.4 million.

BUSINESS

LIQUI-BOX CORPORATION designs and manufactures environmentally friendly bag-in-box packaging, blow molded containers and bulk liquid dispensing systems for the beverage, wine, dairy, processed foods, specialty chemicals and bottled water industries. The Company markets its products in more than 45 countries. The Company operates 14 plants in the United States and two in Europe.

QUARTERLY DATA

(12/31/94) ($000)	Rev	Inc
1st Quarter................	33,857	3,007
2nd Quarter...............	40,340	4,258
3rd Quarter	42,301	3,962
4th Quarter................	31,274	2,100

ANNUAL EARNINGS AND DIVIDENDS PER SHARE

	12/31/94	1/1/94	1/2/93	1/4/92	12/29/90	12/30/89	12/31/88
Earnings Per Share	2.06	2.00	1.73	1.48	1.46	1.23	1.18
Dividends Per Share	0.40	0.38	0.346	0.333	0.317	0.267	0.22
Dividend Payout %	19.4	19.0	20.0	22.5	21.7	21.7	18.6

ANNUAL FINANCIAL DATA

RECORD OF EARNINGS (IN THOUSANDS):

Total Revenues	147,772	130,081	116,117	107,790	113,130	102,760	90,365
Costs and Expenses	118,947	102,066	89,661	83,468	88,480	83,071	73,239
Depreciation & Amort	6,466	6,067	6,983	7,087	7,005	5,244	4,253
Operating Income	22,359	21,948	19,473	17,235	17,645	14,445	12,873
Income Bef Income Taxes	22,246	21,594	18,848	16,421	16,386	14,111	13,078
Income Taxes	8,919	8,657	7,598	6,790	6,510	5,460	4,909
Net Income	13,327	12,937	11,250	9,631	9,876	8,651	8,169
Aver. Shs. Outstg.	6,475	6,484	6,495	6,512	6,769	7,025	6,927

BALANCE SHEET (IN THOUSANDS):

Cash and Cash Equivalents	4,341	6,376	9,710	4,171	5,208	2,298	2,784
Receivables, Net	16,274	14,224	10,672	9,617	9,349	9,285	8,060
Inventories	24,417	19,805	14,121	12,005	9,740	8,975	9,053
Gross Property	79,683	75,648	67,334	68,655	65,081	61,750	50,151
Accumulated Depreciation	52,467	48,138	43,518	40,868	34,991	29,227	25,000
Long-Term Debt	...	...	...	511	10,068	3,421	1,781
Capital Lease Obligations	...	55	105	155	336	463	650
Net Stockholders' Equity	73,683	65,210	55,972	47,740	42,130	42,305	33,204
Total Assets	89,185	86,072	68,974	63,512	64,223	64,161	46,511
Total Current Assets	47,848	44,341	37,088	27,189	25,283	21,538	20,454
Total Current Liabilities	14,672	19,452	10,384	12,104	7,568	14,318	6,938
Net Working Capital	33,176	24,889	26,704	15,085	17,715	7,220	13,516
Year End Shares Outstg	6,268	6,360	6,383	6,407	6,509	6,987	6,771

STATISTICAL RECORD:

Operating Profit Margin %	15.1	16.9	16.8	16.0	15.6	14.1	14.2
Book Value Per Share	10.04	8.54	7.56	6.21	5.19	4.74	4.90
Return on Equity %	18.1	19.8	20.1	20.2	23.4	20.4	24.6
Return on Assets %	14.9	15.0	16.3	15.2	15.4	13.5	17.6
Average Yield %	1.1	1.2	1.4	1.5	1.6	1.5	1.8
P/E Ratio	18.7-15.2	20.3-12.8	16.8-12.5	16.5-12.9	15.3-11.3	17.4-11.8	13.1-7.5
Price Range	38½-31¼	40½-25½	29-21⅝	24⅜-19⅛	22⅜-16½	21⅜-14½	15½-8⅞

Statistics are as originally reported.

OFFICERS:
S.B. Davis, Chmn., Pres., C.E.O. & Treas.
R.S. Hamilton, Vice-Chmn.
P.J. Linn, Sr. V.P. & Sec.

INCORPORATED: OH, Jan., 1962

PRINCIPAL OFFICE: 6950 Worthington
Galena Rd, Worthington, OH 43085

TELEPHONE NUMBER: (614) 888-9280

FAX: (614) 888-0982

NO. OF EMPLOYEES: 818 (approx.)

ANNUAL MEETING: In April

SHAREHOLDERS: 868

INSTITUTIONAL HOLDINGS:
No. of Institutions: 39
Shares Held: 461,191

REGISTRAR(S):

TRANSFER AGENT(S): Huntington National Bank, Stock Transfer Department, Columbus, OH 43287

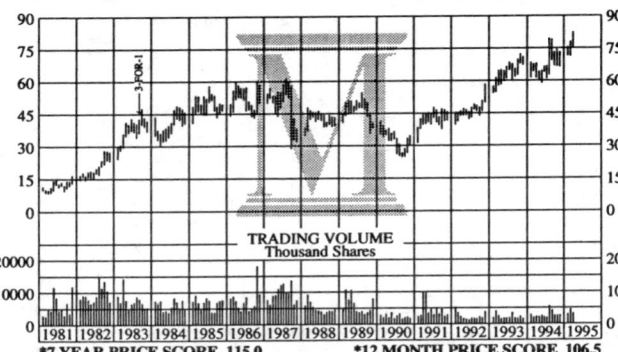

LOCKHEED CORP.

YIELD 2.8%
P/E RATIO 11.6

INTERIM EARNINGS (Per Share):

Qtr.	Mar.	June	Sept.	Dec.
1992	1.06	1.24	1.40	1.95
1993	1.22	1.50	1.85	2.13
1994	1.45	1.64	1.76	2.15

INTERIM DIVIDENDS (Per Share):

Amt.	Decl.	Ex.	Rec.	Pay.
0.53Q	2/7/94	2/14/94	2/21/94	3/7/94
0.57Q	5/10	5/17	5/23	6/6
0.57Q	8/1	8/16	8/22	9/6
0.57Q	10/3	11/15	11/21	12/5
0.57Q	2/6/95	2/13/95	2/20/95	3/6/95

Indicated div.: $2.28*

CAPITALIZATION (12/25/94):

	($000)	(%)
Long-Term Debt	2,232,000	38.3
Cap. Lease Oblig.	16,000	0.3
Common & Surplus	3,571,000	61.4
Total	5,819,000	100.0

DIVIDEND ACHIEVER STATUS:
Rank: 33 1984-94 Growth Rate: 17.4%
Total Years of Dividend Growth: 10

TRADING VOLUME
Thousand Shares

*7 YEAR PRICE SCORE 115.0   *12 MONTH PRICE SCORE 106.5
*NYSE COMPOSITE INDEX=100

RECENT DEVELOPMENTS: For the year ended 12/25/94, net income was $445 million compared with $422 million a year ago. Sales advanced slightly to $13.13 billion from $13.07 billion a year ago. Results were aided by strong performances on core defense and NASA contracts, along with a significant improvement in commercial electronics operations. Margins were flat at 6.5% of sales. The percentage of nondefense business was 36% in 1994, of which 16% was to foreign governments. At 12/25/94, backlog was $25.6 billion.

PROSPECTS: Lockheed's merger agreement with Martin Marietta was cleared by the Federal Trade Commission in January. Meanwhile, Lockheed Fort Worth Co. will play an important role in LK's long-term strategy with the continued building of the F-16 and development of the F-22 advanced tactical fighter program. Additionally, the Lockheed C-130J passed its critical design review and was selected by the U.K. Royal Air Force as a replacement aircraft.

BUSINESS

LOCKHEED is a major aerospace defense contractor. Missiles and Space Systems is a leading provider of spacecraft, space instruments, and technology. It is the prime contractor for Milstar, a military communications satellite network, and works on NASA's Space Station, Freedom. The group also produces the Trident II fleet ballistic missile. Aeronautical Systems is involved in the design and production of cargo aircraft and tactical fighters. Major projects include the F-117A fighter and the C-130 transport. Technology Services serves NASA, other federal agencies, commercial markets and state and local governments. Electronics Systems serves military and industrial markets.

REVENUES

(12/25/94)	($mill)	(%)
Aeronautical Sys	6,573	50.1
Missiles & Space Sys	3,608	27.5
Electronic Sys	1,650	12.6
Technology Services	1,299	9.8
Total	13,130	100.0

ANNUAL EARNINGS AND DIVIDENDS PER SHARE

	12/25/94	12/26/93	12/27/92	12/29/91	12/31/90	12/31/89	12/25/88
Earnings Per Share	7.00	6.70	5.65	4.86	5.30	①0.10	7.34
Dividends Per Share	2.24	2.12	2.09	1.95	1.80	1.75	1.55
Dividend Payout %	32.0	31.6	37.0	40.1	34.0	N.M.	21.0

① Before disc. oper.

ANNUAL FINANCIAL DATA

RECORD OF EARNINGS (IN MILLIONS):

Total Revenues	13,130.0	13,071.0	10,100.0	9,809.0	9,958.0	9,891.0	10,590.0
Costs and Expenses	11,790.0	11,729.0	9,101.0	8,894.0	9,029.0	9,470.0	9,533.0
Depreciation & Amort	485.0	498.0	355.0	339.0	368.0	368.0	375.0
Total Program Profits	855.0	844.0	644.0	576.0	561.0	53.0	682.0
Earn Bef Income Taxes	695.0	676.0	549.0	474.0	430.0	d40.0	580.0
Income Taxes	250.0	254.0	201.0	166.0	95.0	cr46.0	138.0
Net Income	445.0	422.0	①348.0	308.0	335.0	②6.0	③442.0
Aver. Shs. Outstg. (000)	64,000	63,000	62,000	63,000	63,000	63,000	60,000

① Before acctg. change dr$631,000,000. ② Before disc. op. dr$4,000,000. ③ Before disc. op. cr$182,000,000.

BALANCE SHEET (IN MILLIONS):

Cash and Cash Equivalents	452.0	147.0	294.0	266.0	372.0	86.0	269.0
Receivables, Net	123.0	1,644.0	1,590.0	1,590.0	1,880.0	1,786.0	1,816.0
Inventories	1,631.0	1,699.0	1,178.0	1,352.0	1,187.0	1,266.0	1,067.0
Gross Property	4,346.0	4,591.0	4,448.0	4,192.0	4,064.0	4,053.0	3,765.0
Accumulated Depreciation	2,540.0	2,641.0	2,566.0	2,353.0	2,205.0	2,150.0	1,907.0
Long-Term Debt	2,232.0	2,547.0	1,328.0	1,401.0	1,929.0	1,835.0	693.0
Net Stockholders' Equity	3,571.0	3,257.0	2,904.0	3,407.0	3,253.0	3,042.0	2,476.0
Total Assets	7,381.0	8,961.0	6,754.0	6,617.0	6,860.0	6,792.0	6,643.0
Total Current Assets	2,410.0	3,840.0	3,226.0	3,350.0	3,578.0	3,398.0	3,292.0
Total Current Liabilities	2,730.0	2,533.0	2,581.0	2,713.0	2,622.0	2,895.0	3,474.0
Net Working Capital	d320.0	1,307.0	645.0	637.0	956.0	503.0	d182.0
Year End Shs Outstg (000)	63,000	63,000	61,000	63,000	63,000	63,000	59,000

STATISTICAL RECORD:

Operating Profit Margin %	6.5	6.5	6.4	5.9	5.6	0.5	6.4
Book Value Per Share	23.62	16.67	34.25	40.73	38.02	34.08	26.88
Return on Equity %	12.5	13.0	12.0	9.0	10.3	0.2	17.9
Return on Assets %	6.0	4.7	5.2	4.7	4.9	0.1	6.7
Average Yield %	3.2	3.3	4.3	4.9	5.4	3.9	3.7
P/E Ratio	11.4-8.4	10.8-8.1	10.3-7.0	9.8-6.4	7.8-4.7	N.M	6.5-4.7
Price Range	79½-58¾	72⅝-54¼	58⅜-39⅞	47¾-31¼	41½-24¾	54¾-35¾	48-34¾

Statistics are as originally reported.

OFFICERS:
D.M. Tellep, Chmn. & C.E.O.
V.N. Marafino, Vice-Chmn. & C.F.O.
C.R. Marshall, V.P., Sec. & Gen. Couns.

INCORPORATED: CA, Jun., 1932; reincorp., DE, 1986

PRINCIPAL OFFICE: 4500 Park Granada Blvd., Calabasas, CA 91399

TELEPHONE NUMBER: (818) 876-2000

NO. OF EMPLOYEES: 82,500 (approx.)

ANNUAL MEETING: In May

SHAREHOLDERS: 11,000 (approx.)

INSTITUTIONAL HOLDINGS:
No. of Institutions: 230
Shares Held: 37,998,122

REGISTRAR(S): First Interstate Bank
Calabasas, CA

TRANSFER AGENT(S): First Interstate Bank
Calabasas, CA

NYS SYMBOL LOR
Rec. Pr. 47⅞

LORAL CORP.

YIELD 1.3%
P/E RATIO 14.7

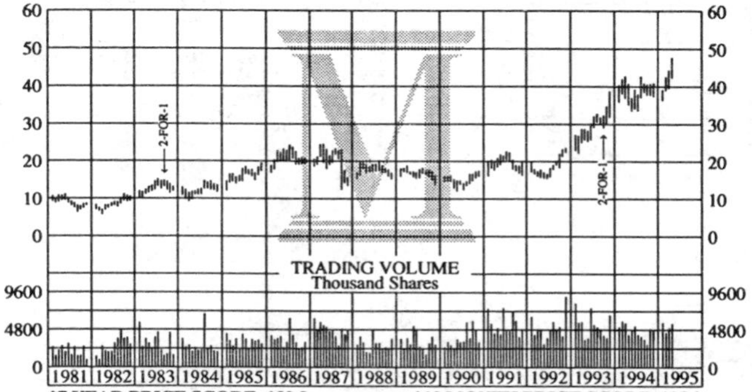

60
50
40
30
20
10
0
2-FOR-1
2-FOR-1
TRADING VOLUME
Thousand Shares
9600
4800
0
1981 1982 1983 1984 1985 1986 1987 1988 1989 1990 1991 1992 1993 1994 1995

*7 YEAR PRICE SCORE 139.8 *12 MONTH PRICE SCORE 105.0

*NYSE COMPOSITE INDEX=100

INTERIM EARNINGS (Per Share):

Qtr.	June	Sept.	Dec.	Mar.
1991-92	0.42	0.47	0.48	0.64
1992-93	0.43	0.53	0.58	0.76
1993-94	0.49	0.56	0.68	1.00
1994-95	0.65	0.78	0.83	...

INTERIM DIVIDENDS (Per Share):

Amt.	Decl.	Ex.	Rec.	Pay.
0.14Q	3/9/94	5/23/94	5/27/94	6/15/94
0.15Q	7/26	8/22	8/26	9/15
0.15Q	9/23	11/23	11/30	12/15
0.15Q	12/13	2/23/95	2/28/95	3/15/95
0.15Q	3/13/95	5/22	5/26	6/15

Indicated div.: $0.60

CAPITALIZATION (3/31/94):

	($000)	(%)
Long-Term Debt	1,624,061	54.0
Common & Surplus	1,381,306	46.0
Total	3,005,367	100.0

DIVIDEND ACHIEVER STATUS:
Rank: 179 1984-94 Growth Rate: 9.7%
Total Years of Dividend Growth: 18

RECENT DEVELOPMENTS: For the quarter ended 12/31/94, net income increased 24.8% to $71.0 million. Sales advanced 48% to $1.33 billion. Results for 1994 included figures for Federal Systems, which was acquired on 1/1/94. During the quarter, LOR booked an initial $95 million of a $515 million contract from the U.S. Army for the enginnering and manufacturing development of LOR's Patriot Advanced Capability missile. Loral also booked $87 million for its Army Tactical Missile System.

PROSPECTS: Increasing margins and continuing operating improvements should lead to a favorable increase in near-term earnings and bookings. LOR will continue to seek new contracts for its systems integration area, and pursue new market opportunities in telecommunications and information systems that leverage its expertise in CI, satellites, and commercial space. Specifically, LOR's PAC-3 missile program with the U.S. Army has the potential to become a $2 billion program over the long term.

BUSINESS

LORAL CORPORATION designs and manufactures defense electronics. LOR's principal business areas are: electronic combat (self-protection); command, control, communications and intelligence (CI); training and simulation; tactical weapons systems and guidance; reconnaissance and surveillance; and space systems. In fiscal 1994, U.S. Government agencies accounted for 64% of sales, and foreign governments accounted for 14%. In October 1990, Loral acquired Ford Aerospace Corporation, a leading defense electronics and space systems company, for approximately $150 million. In August 1992, Loral acquired Loral Vought Systems from LTV Corp. for $261.3 million.

QUARTERLY DATA

(3/31/94)($000)	Rev	Inc
1st Quarter	849,451	40,351
2nd Quarter	836,633	46,717
3rd Quarter	902,003	56,945
4th Quarter	1,420,646	84,255

ANNUAL EARNINGS AND DIVIDENDS PER SHARE

	3/31/94	3/31/93	3/31/92	3/31/91	3/31/90	3/31/89	3/31/88
Earnings Per Share	2.72	[2] [3] 2.06	2.00	1.78	[4] 1.54	[4] 1.21	1.51
Dividends Per Share	[1] 0.53	0.49	0.46	0.42	0.37	0.33	0.31
Dividend Payout %	19.5	23.8	23.0	23.6	24.0	27.3	20.5

[1] 2-for-1 stk split,10/8/93 [2] Before extraord. item [3] Before acctg. chg. [4] Before disc. oper.

ANNUAL FINANCIAL DATA

	3/31/94	3/31/93	3/31/92	3/31/91	3/31/90	3/31/89	3/31/88
RECORD OF EARNINGS (IN MILLIONS):							
Total Revenues	4,008.7	3,335.4	2,881.8	2,126.8	1,274.3	1,187.0	1,440.8
Costs and Expenses	3,429.2	2,885.1	2,461.0	1,811.2	1,046.9	988.0	1,186.9
Depreciation & Amort	178.2	154.0	128.6	100.1	78.7	66.2	73.1
Operating Income	401.4	296.3	292.2	215.5	148.7	132.8	180.7
Inc Fr Contin Oper Bef Income Taxes	362.4	255.5	241.0	165.8	123.1	94.9	121.9
Income Taxes	135.3	94.6	89.2	61.3	45.5	34.6	47.5
Net Income	228.3	[1] 159.1	121.8	90.4	[2] 77.5	[3] 60.3	[4] 74.3

[1] Before extra. item dr$17,776,000. [2] Before disc. op. cr$707,000. [3] Before disc. op. cr$27,326,000. [4] Before disc. op. cr$24,956,000.

	3/31/94	3/31/93	3/31/92	3/31/91	3/31/90	3/31/89	3/31/88
BALANCE SHEET (IN MILLIONS):							
Cash and Cash Equivalents	238.5	116.9	191.1	75.1	105.0	87.5	27.4
Receivables, Net	2,429.1	883.5	673.6	715.6	359.7	246.6	293.5
Inventories	d1,554.0	324.7	320.8	365.1	270.0	226.7	297.8
Gross Property	1,927.0	1,271.5	1,098.3	980.8	714.2	524.9	581.5
Accumulated Depreciation	620.6	489.8	408.5	321.5	256.3	199.5	159.2
Long-Term Debt	1,624.1	490.8	561.7	783.7	419.1	423.2	583.6
Net Stockholders' Equity	1,381.3	1,187.9	997.3	672.0	584.5	517.9	438.3
Total Assets	5,176.2	3,228.1	2,658.6	2,532.2	1,535.2	1,461.5	1,414.8
Total Current Assets	1,844.6	1,365.2	1,204.4	1,177.5	748.8	898.2	631.3
Total Current Liabilities	1,290.2	754.7	608.2	719.8	436.2	435.4	326.0
Net Working Capital	554.4	610.5	596.1	457.7	312.6	462.8	305.4
Year End Shs Outstg (000)	83,337	82,532	63,778	51,882	51,208	51,030	50,640
STATISTICAL RECORD:							
Operating Profit Margin %	10.0	8.9	10.1	10.1	11.7	11.2	12.5
Book Value Per Share	0.46	7.88	11.16	7.25	6.10	6.09	2.26
Return on Equity %	16.5	13.4	12.2	13.4	13.3	11.6	17.0
Return on Assets %	4.4	4.9	4.6	3.6	5.1	4.1	5.3
Average Yield %	1.7	2.5	2.4	3.5	1.8	1.9	1.2
P/E Ratio	14.2-8.2	11.5-7.5	11.4-8.1	9.9-6.8	12.3-8.9	16.8-12.7	24.6-12.5
Price Range	38¾-22¼	23¾-15⅜	22¾-16⅛	17½-12⅛	19-13¾	20¼-15¼	24⅝-12½

Statistics are as originally reported.

OFFICERS:
B.L. Schwartz, Chmn. & C.E.O.
F.C. Lanza, Pres. & C.O.O.
M.P. DeBlasio, Sr. V.P.-Fin.
M.B. Targoff, Sr. V.P. & Sec.
N.C. Moren, V.P. & Treas.

INCORPORATED: NY, Feb., 1948

PRINCIPAL OFFICE: 600 Third Avenue, New York, NY 10016

TELEPHONE NUMBER: (212) 697-1105

FAX: (212) 682-4553

NO. OF EMPLOYEES: 32,600 (approx.)

ANNUAL MEETING: In July

SHAREHOLDERS: 4,500 (approx.)

INSTITUTIONAL HOLDINGS:
No. of Institutions: 219
Shares Held: 20,779,499

REGISTRAR(S): First Interstate Bank of California, Los Angeles, CA

TRANSFER AGENT(S): First Interstate Bank of California, Los Angeles, CA

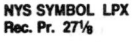

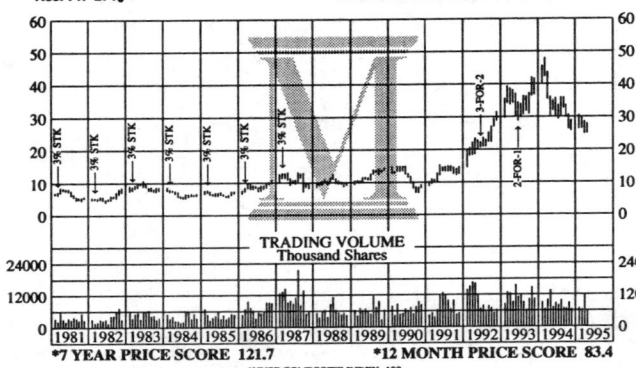

NYS SYMBOL LPX
Rec. Pr. 27⅛

LOUISIANA-PACIFIC CORP.

YIELD 2.1%
P/E RATIO 12.9

TRADING VOLUME
Thousand Shares

7 YEAR PRICE SCORE 121.7   *12 MONTH PRICE SCORE 83.4*
NYSE COMPOSITE INDEX=100

INTERIM EARNINGS (Per Share):

Qtr.	Mar.	June	Sept.	Dec.
1992	0.34	0.41	0.52	0.38
1993	0.80	0.60	0.38	0.54
1994	0.77	0.75	0.86	0.77
1995	0.50	...	...	...

INTERIM DIVIDENDS (Per Share):

Amt.	Decl.	Ex.	Rec.	Pay.
0.125Q	5/3/94	5/12/94	5/18/94	6/1/94
0.125Q	7/25	8/9	8/15	8/31
0.125Q	10/31	11/10	11/17	12/1
0.125Q	1/30/95	2/8/95	2/14/95	3/1/95
0.14Q	5/1	5/12	5/18	6/1

Indicated div.: $0.56*

CAPITALIZATION (12/31/94):

	($000)	(%)
Long-Term Debt	209,800	9.0
Deferred Income Tax	269,800	11.6
Common & Surplus	1,849,400	79.4
Total	2,329,000	100.0

DIVIDEND ACHIEVER STATUS:
Rank: 229   1984-94 Growth Rate: 7.5%
Total Years of Dividend Growth: 18

RECENT DEVELOPMENTS: For the year ended 12/31/94, net income increased 36.4% to $346.9 million from $254.4 million, before a $10.4 million accounting charge, in 1993. Net sales were up 21.0% to $3.04 billion, compared with $2.51 billion a year earlier. Sales of structural panel products advanced 20.2% to $1.21 billion. Lumber sales grew 6.3% to $866.9 million, compared with $815.9 million. Pulp sales jumped to $219.4 million from $85.4 million. Pulp operations reported a profit compared with a loss last year.

PROSPECTS: LPX is benefiting from the dramatic turnaround in the pulp market and continued strength in panel product operations. The Company's pulp business has returned to profitability due to stronger demand and improved pricing for market pulp. Operating results are also benefiting from increases in both demand and pricing for structural panel products, particularly oriented strand board. Results for LPX's lumber operations are being hurt by weak demand and increased costs.

BUSINESS

LOUISIANA-PACIFIC, spun-off from Georgia-Pacific in 1973, is a major forest products firm which manufactures lumber, pulp, structural and other panel products. LPX's business is divided into two segments: building products and pulp. Panel products include Inner-Seal oriented strand board, industrial particleboard, medium-density fiberboard and hardboard. LPX owns or has long-term rights on more than 2.0 million acres of timberlands and operates 129 facilities in 27 states and three provinces in Canada and Mexico. In June 1988, LPX completed the spin-off of Fibreboard Corp.

BUSINESS LINE ANALYSIS

(12/31/94)	Rev(%)	Inc($000)
Building Products	92.8	636,000
Pulp	7.2	(5,000)
Total	100.0	631,000

ANNUAL EARNINGS AND DIVIDENDS PER SHARE

	1994	1993	1992	1991	1990	1989	1988
Earnings Per Share	3.15	2.32	1.63	0.51	1.23	2.52	③ 1.77
Dividends Per Share	0.485	① 0.43	② 0.39	0.36	0.347	0.327	0.297
Dividend Payout %	15.4	18.5	23.9	70.6	28.2	13.0	16.8

① 2-for-1 stk split,06/09/93 ② 3-for-2 stock split, 6/8/92 ③ Before disc. oper. & extraord. item

ANNUAL FINANCIAL DATA

RECORD OF EARNINGS (IN MILLIONS):

	1994	1993	1992	1991	1990	1989	1988
Total Revenues	3,039.5	2,511.3	2,184.7	1,702.1	1,793.3	2,009.5	1,799.4
Costs and Expenses	2,337.1	1,945.7	1,765.8	1,481.2	1,535.5	1,595.4	1,471.1
Depreciation & Amort	143.8	133.0	121.4	114.6	152.3	141.8	145.1
Operating Profit	612.1	482.8	339.1	141.5	183.7	335.9	258.6
Income Before Taxes	559.6	427.6	283.1	87.4	137.0	291.9	214.1
Income Taxes	209.8	173.2	106.2	31.5	45.9	99.3	78.9
Net Income	346.9	① 254.4	176.9	55.9	91.1	192.6	299.6
Aver. Shs. Outstg. (000)	110,140	109,670	108,500	107,980	111,060	114,600	114,630

① Before acctg. change dr$10,400,000.

BALANCE SHEET (IN MILLIONS):

	1994	1993	1992	1991	1990	1989	1988
Cash and Cash Equivalents	315.9	261.6	228.1	190.8	209.1	352.8	256.4
Receivables, Net	157.4	110.9	113.0	79.7	71.2	94.1	86.6
Inventories	213.8	234.7	192.3	184.3	220.8	203.3	189.1
Gross Property	2,358.2	2,112.8	1,944.7	1,868.9	1,773.7	1,511.0	1,337.1
Accumulated Depreciation	1,085.0	966.9	874.4	802.8	736.9	684.0	619.3
Long-Term Debt	209.8	288.6	386.3	492.7	588.7	529.5	369.6
Net Stockholders' Equity	1,849.4	1,571.4	1,361.0	1,203.6	1,166.7	1,176.5	1,137.1
Total Assets	2,716.2	2,466.3	2,206.0	2,107.1	2,104.1	2,031.7	1,796.4
Total Current Assets	694.4	614.1	539.1	461.4	509.1	653.6	536.3
Total Current Liabilities	344.8	317.2	295.5	259.5	195.5	180.0	162.8
Net Working Capital	349.6	296.9	243.6	201.9	313.6	473.6	373.5
Year End Shs Outstg (000)	111,992	110,181	109,218	107,734	107,610	114,034	111,826

STATISTICAL RECORD:

	1994	1993	1992	1991	1990	1989	1988
Operating Profit Margin %	18.4	17.2	13.6	6.2	8.1	15.1	12.3
Book Value Per Share	16.51	14.26	12.46	11.17	10.84	10.32	10.17
Return on Equity %	18.8	16.2	13.0	4.6	7.8	16.4	26.3
Return on Assets %	12.8	10.3	8.0	2.7	4.3	9.5	16.7
Average Yield %	1.3	1.2	1.7	3.0	3.2	2.7	2.8
P/E Ratio	15.2-8.2	18.2-12.4	19.3-9.0	29.6-17.1	18.4-8.2	8.6-5.6	10.6-7.2
Price Range	48-25¾	42⅛-28¾	31½-14⅝	15⅜-8⅞	15⅛-6¾	14½-9⅜	12½-8½

Statistics are as originally reported.

OFFICERS:
H.A. Merlo, Chmn. & Pres.
W.L. Hebert, Treas. & C.F.O.
A.C. Kirchhof, Jr., Gen. Couns. & Sec.

INCORPORATED: DE, Jul., 1972

PRINCIPAL OFFICE: 111 S.W. 5th Avenue, Portland, OR 97204

TELEPHONE NUMBER: (503) 221-0800
FAX: (503) 796-0204
NO. OF EMPLOYEES: 13,000 (approx.)
ANNUAL MEETING: In May
SHAREHOLDERS: 25,600 (approx.)
INSTITUTIONAL HOLDINGS:
No. of Institutions: 364
Shares Held: 61,665,664

REGISTRAR(S): First Chicago Trust Co. of New York, New York, NY 10008

TRANSFER AGENT(S): First Chicago Trust Co. of New York, New York, NY 10008

NYS SYMBOL LOW
Rec. Pr. 28¼

LOWE'S COS., INC.

YIELD 0.6%
P/E RATIO 19.5

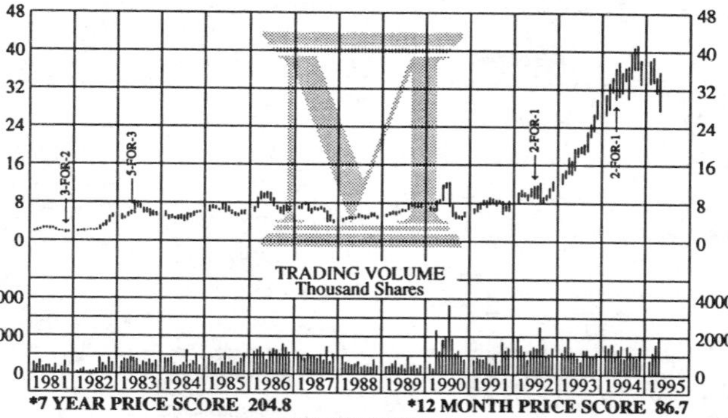

*7 YEAR PRICE SCORE 204.8 *12 MONTH PRICE SCORE 86.7

*NYSE COMPOSITE INDEX=100

INTERIM EARNINGS (Per Share):

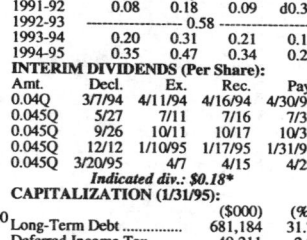

Qtr.	Apr.	July	Oct.	Jan.
1991-92	0.08	0.18	0.09	d0.30
1992-93		0.58		
1993-94	0.20	0.31	0.21	0.18
1994-95	0.35	0.47	0.34	0.29

INTERIM DIVIDENDS (Per Share):

Amt.	Decl.	Ex.	Rec.	Pay.
0.04Q	3/7/94	4/11/94	4/16/94	4/30/94
0.045Q	5/27	7/11	7/16	7/31
0.045Q	9/26	10/11	10/17	10/31
0.045Q	12/12	1/10/95	1/17/95	1/31/95
0.045Q	3/20/95	4/7	4/15	4/29

*Indicated div.: $0.18**

CAPITALIZATION (1/31/95):

	($000)	(%)
Long-Term Debt	681,184	31.7
Deferred Income Tax	49,211	2.3
Common & Surplus	1,419,890	66.0
Total	2,150,285	100.0

DIVIDEND ACHIEVER STATUS:
Rank: 219 1984-94 Growth Rate: 7.8%
Total Years of Dividend Growth: 17

RECENT DEVELOPMENTS: For the year ended 1/31/95, net income was $223.6 million compared with $131.8 million a year ago. Net sales advanced 35% to $6.11 billion. Gross margin increased to 24.8% of sales from 23.8% a year ago due to favorable changes in the product mix. SG&A expenses decreased to 15.4% of sales from 15.8% a year ago. Lowe's opened 50 stores (26 new and 24 relocated) during the year. For the quarter ended 1/31/95, net income and net sales were $46.3 million and $1.49 billion, respecitvely.

PROSPECTS: The Company is experiencing significant sales and earnings growth as a result of its conversion into a large store format. Lowe's will continue to emphasize its Everyday Competitive Pricing program and a wider product selection, while relying less on promotional advertising. The program should also continue to help increase sales volumes and margin dollars, while reducing expenses as a percentage of sales. Meanwhile, LOW will face stiff competition as it increases its presence in the Midwest.

BUSINESS

LOWE'S COMPANIES, INC. is a specialty retailer that combines the merchandise, sales and service of a home improvement center, a building materials supplier and a consumer-durables retailer to serve the do-it-yourself home improvement and construction markets. As of 1/31/95, 336 retail stores were in operation in 20 states, located principally in the South Atlantic and South Central regions of the U.S. Contributions to sales were: 16%, Structural Lumber; 21%, Building Commodities & Millwork; 18%, Home Decorating; 11%, Kitchen, Bathroom & Laundry; 6%, Heating Cooling & Water System; 5%, Home Entertainment; 11%, Yard, Patio & Garden; 6%, Tools; and 6%, Special Order.

ANNUAL EARNINGS AND DIVIDENDS PER SHARE

	1/31/95	1/31/94	1/31/93	1/31/92	1/31/91	1/31/90	1/31/89
Earnings Per Share	**1.44**	**0.89**	**0.58**	**0.05**	**0.48**	**0.50**	**0.46**
Dividends Per Share	**0.21**	**0.17**	**[1] 0.16**	**0.067**	**0.065**	**0.06**	**0.056**
Dividend Payout %	**14.6**	**19.1**	**27.6**	**N.M.**	**27.2**	**23.9**	**24.6**

Note: 2-for-1stk.split,3/31/94. [1] 2-for-1 stk split, 6/29/92

ANNUAL FINANCIAL DATA

	1/31/95	1/31/94	1/31/93	1/31/92	1/31/91	1/31/90	1/31/89
RECORD OF EARNINGS (IN MILLIONS):							
Total Revenues	6,110.5	4,538.0	3,846.4	3,056.2	2,833.1	2,650.5	2,516.9
Costs and Expenses	5,629.5	4,240.9	3,635.1	2,976.1	2,664.0	2,476.4	2,349.1
Depreciation & Amort	112.9	82.1	69.8	58.3	51.4	46.1	41.2
Operating Profit	371.4	216.6	141.5	93.2	117.7	128.0	126.6
Pre-tax Earnings	343.5	198.3	125.9	5.0	100.3	108.8	105.6
Income Taxes	120.0	66.5	41.2	cr1.5	29.2	33.9	36.4
Net Income	223.6	131.8	84.7	6.5	71.1	74.9	69.2
Aver. Shs. Outstg. (000)	154,926	147,398	146,152	146,052	148,856	149,112	150,992
BALANCE SHEET (IN MILLIONS):							
Cash and Cash Equivalents	268.5	108.5	54.8	30.8	50.1	55.6	60.3
Receivables, Net	127.3	65.6	61.8	122.2	96.4	123.1	128.4
Inventories	1,132.3	853.7	594.2	602.8	460.8	407.7	379.4
Gross Property	1,742.2	1,317.0	1,067.9	869.8	776.5	706.2	641.6
Accumulated Depreciation	344.4	296.8	280.7	256.8	235.1	198.4	161.7
Long-Term Debt	519.2	531.8	279.5	98.2	159.2	167.9	190.1
Capital Lease Obligations	162.0	60.6	34.1	15.5	...	...	...
Net Stockholders' Equity	1,419.9	873.7	733.2	668.6	682.7	645.6	586.9
Total Assets	3,105.2	2,201.6	1,608.9	1,441.2	1,203.1	1,147.4	1,085.8
Total Current Assets	1,557.2	1,083.9	745.6	770.1	616.5	595.9	577.6
Total Current Liabilities	945.9	681.2	499.6	589.0	337.7	307.9	285.7
Net Working Capital	611.3	402.7	245.9	181.1	278.8	288.1	291.8
Year End Shs Outstg (000)	159,527	147,887	145,946	145,760	145,840	149,020	148,556
STATISTICAL RECORD:							
Operating Profit Margin %	6.1	4.8	3.7	0.7	4.2	4.8	5.0
Book Value Per Share	8.90	5.91	5.02	4.59	4.68	4.33	3.95
Return on Equity %	15.7	15.1	11.6	1.0	10.4	11.6	11.8
Return on Assets %	7.2	6.0	5.3	0.5	5.9	6.5	6.4
Average Yield %	0.6	0.8	1.5	1.8	1.5	1.8	2.2
P/E Ratio	28.7-19.3	33.7-13.6	22.0-13.8	N.M	25.8-9.6	16.0-10.5	13.5-9.1
Price Range	41⅜-27¾	30-12⅛	12¾-8	9¼-5¾	12⅜-4⅝	8-5¼	6⅛-4⅛

Statistics are as originally reported.

OFFICERS:
R.L. Strickland, Chmn.
L.G. Herring, Pres. & C.E.O.
H.B. Underwood, II, Sr. V.P., C.F.O. & Treas.

INCORPORATED: NC, Aug., 1952

PRINCIPAL OFFICE: State Highway 268 East, North Wilkesboro, NC 28659

TELEPHONE NUMBER: (910) 651-4000

FAX: (910) 651-4766

NO. OF EMPLOYEES: 28,843

ANNUAL MEETING: In May

SHAREHOLDERS: 7,446

INSTITUTIONAL HOLDINGS:
No. of Institutions: 201
Shares Held: 19,537,149

REGISTRAR(S): Wachovia Bank & Trust Co., N.A., Winston-Salem, NC 27102

TRANSFER AGENT(S): Wachovia Bank & Trust Co., N.A., Winston-Salem, NC 27102

NYS SYMBOL LUB
Rec. Pr. 19⅛

LUBY'S CAFETERIAS, INC.

YIELD 3.5%
P/E RATIO 12.7

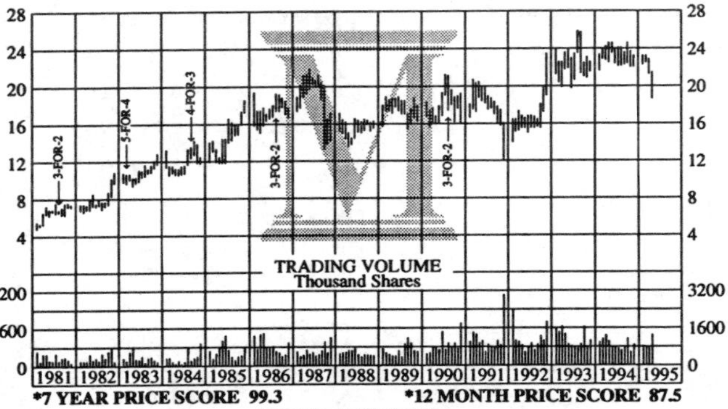

*7 YEAR PRICE SCORE 99.3 *12 MONTH PRICE SCORE 87.5

*NYSE COMPOSITE INDEX=100

INTERIM EARNINGS (Per Share):

Qtr.	Nov.	Feb.	May	Aug.
1991-92	0.24	0.26	0.33	0.36
1992-93	0.29	0.29	0.36	0.37
1993-94	0.25	0.40	0.40	0.40
1994-95	0.35	0.36	...	...

INTERIM DIVIDENDS (Per Share):

Amt.	Decl.	Ex.	Rec.	Pay.
0.15Q	4/12/94	6/6/94	6/10/94	6/27/94
0.165Q	7/20	9/2	9/9	9/26
0.165Q	10/10	12/12	12/16	1/3/95
0.165Q	1/13/95	3/6/95	3/10/95	3/27
0.165Q	3/27	6/6	6/9	6/26

*Indicated div.: $0.66**

CAPITALIZATION (8/31/94):

	($000)	(%)
Common & Surplus	213,526	100.0
Total	213,526	100.0

DIVIDEND ACHIEVER STATUS:
Rank: 134 1984-94 Growth Rate: 11.3%
Total Years of Dividend Growth: 21

RECENT DEVELOPMENTS: For the quarter ended 11/30/94, net income was $8.7 million compared with $8.6 million, before an accounting change, for the corresponding quarter in 1993. Sales climbed 7.7% to $101.4 million from $94.2 million for the year-earlier quarter. For the year ended 8/31/94, income before an accounting change was $37.8 million compared with $35.5 million the year before, an increase of 6.3%. Sales were $390.7 million, up 6.2% from $367.8 million a year earlier.

PROSPECTS: In September 1994, LUB purchased 2.3 million shares of its common stock for approximately $51 million. LUB will continue to develop and expand its marketing capabilities and benefit from the positive customer count and sales trend. LUB should stand strong against competition from other restaurant franchises. LUB's current operating structure should continue contributing to improved operating margins. LUB plans to open 14 cafeterias and relocate one unit in Beaumont, Texas during fiscal 1995.

BUSINESS

LUBY'S CAFETERIAS owns and operates one of the nation's largest cafeteria chains in the Southwest and Florida. As of 11/30/94, Luby's operated 180 cafeterias in eleven states comprised of four in New Mexico, eleven in Arizona, three in Arkansas, five in Florida, two in Kansas, one in Louisiana, two in Missouri, nine in Oklahoma, six in Tennessee and 126 in Texas. The cafeterias are typically located convenient to shopping and business developments, as well as to residential areas. They cater primarily to shoppers, store and office personnel at lunch and to families at dinner. Generally from 10,000 to 11,000 square feet in area, a cafeteria can typically accommodate 300 customers.

QUARTERLY DATA

(8/31/94) ($000)	Rev	Inc
1st Quarter	94,166	10,168
2nd Quarter	93,719	8,581
3rd Quarter	101,060	10,386
4th Quarter	101,747	10,200

ANNUAL EARNINGS AND DIVIDENDS PER SHARE

	8/31/94	8/31/93	8/31/92	8/31/91	8/31/90	8/31/89	8/31/88
Earnings Per Share	1.45	1.31	1.19	1.18	1.17	1.08	1.01
Dividends Per Share	0.615	0.555	0.51	0.47	[1] 0.435	0.387	0.343
Dividend Payout %	42.4	42.4	42.9	39.8	37.2	35.8	34.1

[1] 3-for-2 stk split, 8/3/90

ANNUAL FINANCIAL DATA

RECORD OF EARNINGS (IN THOUSANDS):							
Total Revenues	390,692	367,757	346,359	328,236	311,325	283,252	254,301
Costs and Expenses	315,942	297,700	282,708	267,985	253,000	230,937	206,548
Depreciation & Amort	15,700	15,415	14,453	12,994	11,385	9,921	8,636
Income From Operations	59,050	54,642	49,198	47,257	46,940	42,394	39,117
Income Bef Income Taxes	60,435	56,216	50,517	48,848	48,512	44,377	41,247
Income Taxes	22,663	20,687	17,924	16,502	16,412	14,895	13,738
Net Income	[1] 37,772	35,529	32,593	32,346	32,100	29,482	27,509
Aver. Shs. Outstg.	25,982	27,195	27,344	27,392	27,365	27,352	27,350
[1] Before acctg. change cr$1,563,000.							
BALANCE SHEET (IN THOUSANDS):							
Cash and Cash Equivalents	10,909	34,305	12,294	14,200	12,327	15,266	20,177
Receivables, Net	275	602	241	190	157	251	468
Inventories	3,851	3,426	3,642	4,267	3,732	4,574	3,427
Gross Property	374,026	348,187	330,250	304,373	269,240	231,209	196,265
Accumulated Depreciation	116,194	103,401	89,705	77,565	65,288	55,720	46,895
Long-Term Debt	...	...	1,384	1,851	2,328	2,832	3,515
Net Stockholders' Equity	213,526	238,948	217,251	202,782	182,968	162,635	143,697
Total Assets	289,668	302,099	276,319	260,704	235,344	210,102	184,534
Total Current Assets	18,134	43,818	20,897	21,225	18,447	21,949	25,928
Total Current Liabilities	56,362	43,324	38,865	40,400	32,546	28,562	23,022
Net Working Capital	d38,228	494	d17,968	d19,175	d14,099	d6,613	2,906
Year End Shares Outstg	25,118	27,227	27,134	27,398	27,374	27,359	27,350
STATISTICAL RECORD:							
Operating Profit Margin %	15.1	14.9	14.2	14.4	15.1	15.0	15.4
Book Value Per Share	8.50	8.78	8.01	7.40	6.68	5.94	5.25
Return on Equity %	17.7	14.9	15.0	16.0	17.5	18.1	19.1
Return on Assets %	13.0	11.8	11.8	12.4	13.6	14.0	14.9
Average Yield %	2.7	2.4	2.7	2.9	2.4	2.3	2.2
P/E Ratio	17.0-14.9	19.8-15.1	19.7-11.8	17.6-10.2	18.2-13.4	17.5-14.2	17.0-13.4
Price Range	24⅝-21⅝	25⅞-19¾	23½-14	20¾-12	21¼-15⅝	18⅞-15⅜	17⅛-13½

Statistics are as originally reported.

OFFICERS:
J.B. Lahourcade, Chmn.
R. Erben, Pres. & C.E.O.
J.E. Curtis, Jr., Sr. V.P., C.F.O. & Treas.

INCORPORATED: TX, 1959; reincorp., DE, Dec., 1991

PRINCIPAL OFFICE: 2211 Northeast Loop 410 P.O. Box 33069, San Antonio, TX 78265-3069

TELEPHONE NUMBER: (210) 654-9000

NO. OF EMPLOYEES: 10,100 (approx.)

ANNUAL MEETING: In January

SHAREHOLDERS: 4,218 (approx.)

INSTITUTIONAL HOLDINGS:
No. of Institutions: 142
Shares Held: 10,780,993

REGISTRAR(S): AmeriTrust Texas, N.A., Dallas, TX 75270

TRANSFER AGENT(S): AmeriTrust Texas, N.A., Dallas, TX 75270

ASE SYMBOL MNS
Rec. Pr. 14¼

MACNEAL-SCHWENDLER CORP.

YIELD 4.5%
P/E RATIO ...

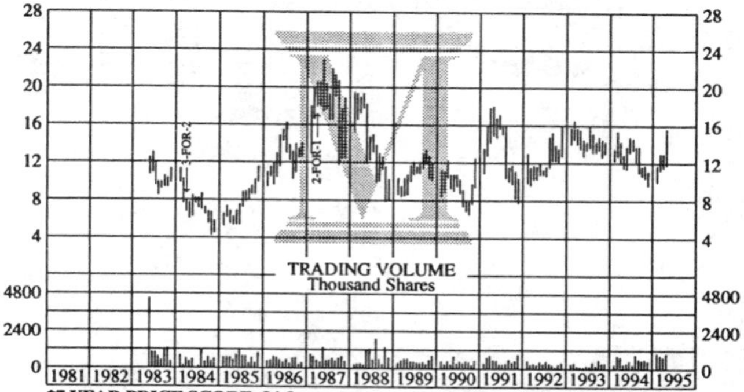

28
24
20
16
12
8
4
4800
2400
0
2-FOR-1
2-FOR-1
TRADING VOLUME
Thousand Shares
1981 1982 1983 1984 1985 1986 1987 1988 1989 1990 1991 1992 1993 1994 1995

*7 YEAR PRICE SCORE 84.3 *12 MONTH PRICE SCORE 100.1

*NYSE COMPOSITE INDEX=100

INTERIM EARNINGS (Per Share):

Qtr.	Apr.	July	Oct.	Dec.
1992-93		1.03		
1993-94	0.27	0.27	0.22	0.19
1994-95	0.20	0.22	d3.16	0.47
1995-96	0.23	...	...	...

INTERIM DIVIDENDS (Per Share):

Amt.	Decl.	Ex.	Rec.	Pay.
0.16Q	3/18/94	5/16/94	5/20/94	6/1/94
0.16Q	6/13	8/15	8/19	9/7
0.16Q	9/15	11/14	11/18	12/7
0.16Q	12/9	2/13/95	2/17/95	3/1/95
0.16Q	3/16/95	5/15	5/19	6/7

Indicated div.: $0.64

CAPITALIZATION (1/31/95):

	($000)	(%)
Deferred Income Tax	6,810	35.5
Common & Surplus	12,375	64.5
Total	19,185	100.0

DIVIDEND ACHIEVER STATUS:
Rank: 6 1984-94 Growth Rate: 24.9%
Total Years of Dividend Growth: 11

RECENT DEVELOPMENTS: For the year ended 1/31/95, the Company reported a net loss of $30.4 million compared with net income of $11.4 million in the prior year. Results for 1994 included a one-time charge of $41.7 million related to the August 1994 acquisition of PDA Engineering. However, revenue jumped 26.5% to $100.7 million from $79.6 million the year before, benefiting from strong demand for the Company's software that analyzes the performance of new products on computer before they are built. For the quarter ended 1/31/95, net income more than doubled to $6.3 million from $2.5 million in the year-earlier quarter. Revenue soared 63.7% to $32.2 million from $19.7 million in the corresponding 1994 quarter. Income from operations was $5.6 million, up 54.0% from $3.6 million the year before.

BUSINESS

MACNEAL SCHWENDLER CORP. is a provider of finite element modeling and analysis products to the computer-aided engineering (CAE) market. The Company also is a leading provider of other products for the CAE market, including pre- and post-processing geometric modeling products. The Company's five major product lines are MSC/NASTRAN, MSC/PATRAN, MSC/ARIES, MSC/EMAS and MSC/DYTRAN. These products are used by engineers and designers to model structures and assemblies and then analyze prior to manufacture their strength, dynamic response and heat transfer characteristics as well as electromagnetic reactions. The Company's products are marketed worldwide through offices in the United States, Europe and the Far East.

QUARTERLY DATA

(1/31/95)($000)	Rev	Inc
1st Quarter	19,755	2,705
2nd Quarter	21,102	2,932
3rd Quarter	27,655	d42,331
4th Quarter	32,174	6,312

ANNUAL EARNINGS AND DIVIDENDS PER SHARE

	1/31/95	1/31/94	1/31/93	1/31/92	1/31/91	1/31/90	1/31/89
Earnings Per Share	**d2.27**	**0.86**	**1.03**	**d0.12**	**0.94**	**0.82**	**0.73**
Dividends Per Share	**0.64**	**0.60**	**0.46**	**0.38**	**0.31**	**0.26**	**0.175**
Dividend Payout %	**...**	**69.8**	**44.7**	**...**	**33.0**	**31.7**	**24.0**

ANNUAL FINANCIAL DATA

	1/31/95	1/31/94	1/31/93	1/31/92	1/31/91	1/31/90	1/31/89
RECORD OF EARNINGS (IN THOUSANDS):							
Total Revenues	100,686	79,574	65,474	55,826	56,611	45,016	39,873
Costs and Expenses	127,687	57,426	42,686	49,047	33,866	28,702	24,646
Depreciation & Amort	5,576	5,363	4,758	7,491	6,154	3,277	2,254
Operating Income	d27,732	16,785	18,030	d712	16,591	13,037	12,973
Income Bef Income Taxes	d29,082	16,948	18,708	d699	16,984	14,897	13,576
Income Taxes	1,300	5,508	6,548	761	5,775	5,065	4,722
Net Income	d30,382	11,440	12,160	d1,460	11,209	9,832	8,854
Aver. Shs. Outstg.	13,386	13,368	11,843	11,852	11,926	12,019	12,186
BALANCE SHEET (IN THOUSANDS):							
Cash and Cash Equivalents	14,019	27,890	19,873	12,833	10,300	11,376	18,394
Receivables, Net	33,822	16,463	13,999	12,647	17,865	13,482	10,129
Gross Property	24,347	26,819	21,488	24,015	21,586	17,031	12,869
Accumulated Depreciation	14,075	16,834	10,233	10,860	9,630	6,712	4,558
Net Stockholders' Equity	12,375	51,519	47,601	40,268	48,377	43,221	38,161
Total Assets	118,751	78,504	68,860	58,689	68,421	59,627	50,455
Total Current Assets	58,398	48,955	39,135	27,997	31,075	27,826	30,174
Total Current Liabilities	42,990	20,227	21,259	12,761	13,035	10,682	8,837
Net Working Capital	15,408	28,728	17,876	15,236	18,040	17,144	21,337
Year End Shares Outstg	13,380	13,376	11,858	11,774	11,846	11,993	12,024
STATISTICAL RECORD:							
Operating Profit Margin %	...	21.1	27.5	...	29.3	29.0	32.5
Book Value Per Share	N.M.	2.49	2.57	2.01	2.06	1.93	2.25
Return on Equity %	...	22.2	25.5	...	23.2	22.7	23.2
Return on Assets %	...	14.6	17.7	...	16.4	16.5	17.5
Average Yield %	5.1	4.1	...	3.6	4.0	2.9	1.9
P/E Ratio	...	19.2-14.7	15.4-9.3	...	13.3-6.9	16.3-10.2	26.7-10.8
Price Range	15⅜-9⅝	16½-12⅝	15⅞-9⅝	18-7¾	12½-6½	13⅜-8⅜	19½-7⅞

Statistics are as originally reported.

OFFICERS:
R.H. MacNeal, Chmn. & C.E.O.
T.C. Curry, Pres. & C.O.O.
L.A. Greco, C.F.O. & Sec.

INCORPORATED: CA, 1963; reincorp., DE, Sep., 1994

PRINCIPAL OFFICE: 815 Colorado Blvd., Los Angeles, CA 90041

TELEPHONE NUMBER: (213) 258-9111

FAX: (213) 259-3838

NO. OF EMPLOYEES: 411

ANNUAL MEETING: In June

SHAREHOLDERS: 408

INSTITUTIONAL HOLDINGS:
No. of Institutions: 71
Shares Held: 8,251,056

REGISTRAR(S): Chemical Trust Company of California, Los Angeles, CA

TRANSFER AGENT(S): Chemical Trust Company of California, Los Angeles, CA

MADISON GAS & ELECTRIC CO.

YIELD 6.1%
P/E RATIO 13.5

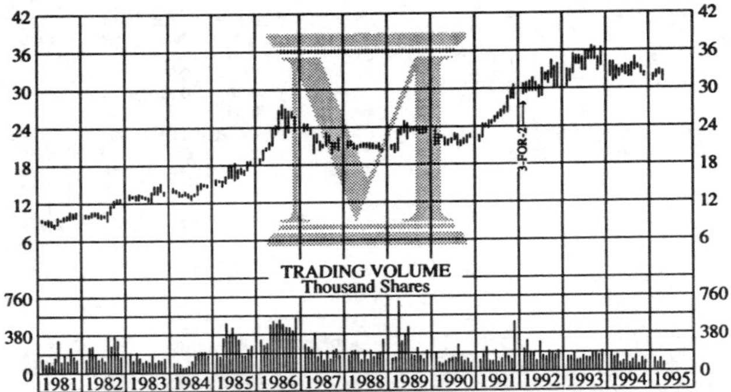

*7 YEAR PRICE SCORE 98.2   *12 MONTH PRICE SCORE 93.4
*NYSE COMPOSITE INDEX=100

TRADING VOLUME
Thousand Shares

INTERIM EARNINGS (Per Share):

Qtr.	Mar.	June	Sept.	Dec.
1991	0.65	0.23	0.78	0.62
1992	0.60	0.31	0.57	0.69
1993	0.75	0.36	0.58	0.57
1994	0.88	0.25	0.59	0.57

INTERIM DIVIDENDS (Per Share):

Amt.	Decl.	Ex.	Rec.	Pay.
0.465Q	2/18/94	2/23/94	3/1/94	3/15/94
0.465Q	5/20	5/25	6/1	6/15
0.47Q	8/12	8/26	9/1	9/15
0.47Q	11/18	11/25	12/1	12/15
0.47Q	2/17/95	2/23/95	3/1/95	3/15/95

*Indicated div.: $1.88**

CAPITALIZATION (12/31/94):

	($000)	(%)
Long-Term Debt	130,800	33.1
Deferred Income Tax	69,593	17.6
Redeemable Pfd Stock	5,100	1.3
Common & Surplus	189,489	48.0
Total	394,982	100.0

Current Debt.................. 29,230

DIVIDEND ACHIEVER STATUS:
Rank: 322   1984-94 Growth Rate: 2.7%
Total Years of Dividend Growth: 19

RECENT DEVELOPMENTS: For the quarter ended 12/31/94, net income was $6.2 million versus $6.2 milllion for the same period a year earlier. Operating revenues dropped 11% to $60.3 million compared with $67.4 million in the corresponding period of 1993. For the year ended 12/31/94, the Company reported the highest annual earnings in its history, with net income advancing 1.4% to $25.0 million, or $2.29 per share, compared with $24.7 million, or $2.26 per share, a year earlier. Operating revenues remained relatively flat at $245.0 million. Earnings were led higher through aggressive business planning and cost-saving measures. Operating expenses were held to 1993 levels, and interest costs were reduced 4% from the year earlier period. Nonregulated business activities also contributed to the Company's record earnings.

BUSINESS

MADISON GAS & ELECTRIC COMPANY is a public utility engaged in the generation and transmission of electric energy and its distribution in Madison, WI and its environs, (250 sq. miles) and in the purchase, transportation and distribution of natural gas in Madison and its immediate surrounding territory (1,300 sq. miles). At 12/31/94, MDSN supplied electric service to more than 118,000 customers, which are located in the cities of Fitchburg, Madison, Middleton, Monona and in adjacent areas. On 12/31/94, MDSN supplied gas service to nearly 100,000 customers in the counties of Columbia, Crawford, Dane, Iowa, Juneau, Monroe and Vernon.

BUSINESS LINE ANALYSIS

(12/31/94)	Rev(%)	Inc(%)
Electric	61.1	76.2
Gas	38.9	23.8
Total	100.0	100.0

ANNUAL EARNINGS AND DIVIDENDS PER SHARE

	1994	1993	1992	1991	1990	1989	1988
Earnings Per Share	2.29	2.26	2.18	2.28	2.04	1.95	1.99
Dividends Per Share	1.87	1.84	① 1.79	1.747	1.72	1.68	1.633
Dividend Payout %	81.7	81.4	82.1	76.6	84.3	86.3	82.2

① 3-for-2 stk split, 1/22/92

ANNUAL FINANCIAL DATA

RECORD OF EARNINGS (IN THOUSANDS):

	1994	1993	1992	1991	1990	1989	1988
Total Revenues	244,972	244,133	228,002	232,200	220,568	217,588	214,323
Depreciation & Amort	22,383	21,791	21,427	21,025	22,098	19,878	18,231
Maintenance	12,416	13,029	12,544	13,170	11,538	12,588	10,954
Prov for Fed Inc Taxes	...	12,389	11,253	13,010	10,972	7,718	9,053
Net Oper Income	34,062	34,230	35,062	36,374	34,798	33,606	31,331
Interest Expense	11,122	11,624	13,436	12,684	14,198	14,553	12,457
Net Income	25,011	24,675	23,807	24,880	22,029	20,596	20,538
Aver. Shs. Outstg.	10,704	10,704	10,697	10,696	10,530	10,290	10,032

BALANCE SHEET (IN THOUSANDS):

Gross Plant	695,177	671,497	651,397	638,456	623,160	604,943	578,336
Accumulated Depreciation	323,511	302,904	284,248	265,278	245,427	279,515	261,315
Prop, Plant & Equip, Net	371,666	368,593	367,149	373,178	377,733	325,428	317,021
Long-term Debt	130,800	120,396	122,363	124,859	135,813	140,842	141,806
Net Stockholders' Equity	194,589	190,395	185,967	182,013	176,168	167,153	159,362
Total Assets	487,759	465,364	460,143	455,065	450,334	407,325	388,449
Year End Shares Outstg	10,720	10,720	10,697	10,697	10,680	10,415	10,188

STATISTICAL RECORD:

Book Value Per Share	17.68	17.26	16.86	16.47	15.93	15.45	15.01
Op. Inc/Net Pl %	9.2	9.3	9.5	9.7	9.2	10.3	9.9
Dep/Gr. Pl %	3.2	3.2	3.3	3.3	3.5	3.3	3.2
Accum. Dep/Gr. Pl %	46.5	45.1	43.6	41.5	39.4	46.2	45.2
Return on Equity %	13.2	13.3	13.2	14.1	12.9	12.8	13.4
Average Yield %	5.7	5.5	5.7	6.7	7.7	7.5	7.8
P/E Ratio	15.3-13.5	16.3-13.4	15.8-13.1	13.4-9.4	11.6-10.2	12.8-10.2	11.0-10.1
Price Range	35-31	36¾-30¼	34½-28½	30⅝-21½	23⅝-20⅞	25-19⅞	21⅞-20

Statistics are as originally reported.

OFFICERS:
D.C. Mebane, Chmn., Pres. & C.E.O.
J.T. Krzos, V.P.-Fin.
G.J. Wolter, V.P.-Admin. & Sec.
T.A. Hanson, Treas.
INCORPORATED: WI, Apr., 1896
PRINCIPAL OFFICE: 133 S. Blair Street P.O. Box 1231, Madison, WI 53701-1231

TELEPHONE NUMBER: (608) 252-7923
FAX: (608) 252-7098
NO. OF EMPLOYEES: 683
ANNUAL MEETING: In May
SHAREHOLDERS: 16,238
INSTITUTIONAL HOLDINGS:
No. of Institutions: 56
Shares Held: 1,181,977

REGISTRAR(S): Harris Trust & Savings Bank, Chicago, IL

TRANSFER AGENT(S): Harris Trust & Savings Bank, Chicago, IL

NASDAQ SYMBOL MTWN
Rec. Pr. 31¼

MARK TWAIN BANCSHARES, INC.

YIELD 3.5%
P/E RATIO 12.1

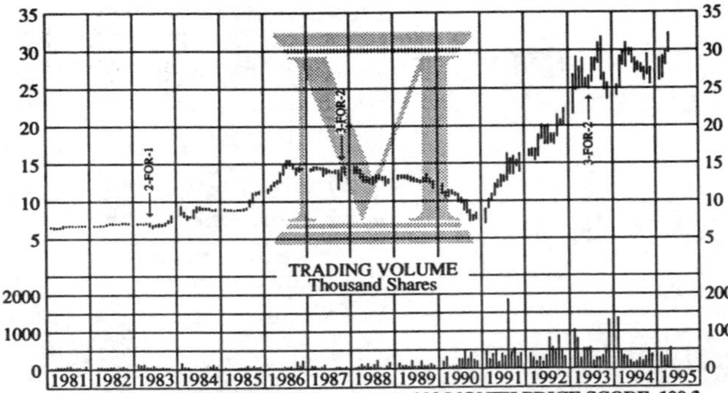

*7 YEAR PRICE SCORE 129.9 *12 MONTH PRICE SCORE 100.3

*NYSE COMPOSITE INDEX=100

INTERIM EARNINGS (Per Share):

Qtr.	Mar.	June	Sept.	Dec.
1991	0.34	0.37	0.39	0.44
1992	0.45	0.49	0.51	0.53
1993	0.55	0.57	0.57	0.59
1994	0.62	0.63	0.65	0.69

INTERIM DIVIDENDS (Per Share):

Amt.	Decl.	Ex.	Rec.	Pay.
0.24Q	4/7/94	4/18/94	4/22/94	5/13/94
0.24Q	7/5	7/18	7/22	8/12
0.24Q	10/5	10/17	10/21	11/14
0.27Q	1/4/95	1/23/95	1/27/95	2/10/95
0.27Q	4/4	4/17	4/21	5/12

*Indicated div.: $1.08**

CAPITALIZATION (12/31/94):

	($000)	(%)
Total Deposits	2,272,057	84.0
Total Debt	168,507	6.2
Common & Surplus	234,049	8.7
Loan Valuation Reserve	28,894	1.1
Total	2,703,507	100.0

DIVIDEND ACHIEVER STATUS:
Rank: 143 1984-94 Growth Rate: 10.9%
Total Years of Dividend Growth: 24

RECENT DEVELOPMENTS: Net income reached a record $41 million for the year ended 12/31/94, an increase of 16.7% from the $35.1 million earned in 1993. Results benefited from solid loan growth, a strong net interest margin and improved credit quality. The Company also posted a record low efficiency ratio of 56.23%. Net interest income rose 11% to $124.0 million from $111.7 million. Other income; however, declined 19.3% to $35.5 million from $44.0 million. The provision for loan losses was lowered to $5.5 million from $6.3 million. Loan outstandings increased 8.38% in year-over-year comparisons. During 1994, MTWN acquired St. Louis-based Century Bank, a $99 million asset bank with two locations. Also acquired was Kansas City-based United Kansas Bank, an $87 million asset bank also operating two locations.

BUSINESS

MARK TWAIN BANCSHARES, INC. owns or controls substantially all of the capital stock of three banks: Mark Twain Bank, which operates eighteen separate locations in the metropolitan St. Louis area; Mark Twain Kansas City Bank, which operates five separate locations in the metropolitan Kansas City area; and Mark Twain Illinois Bank, which operates four locations on the Illinois side of the St. Louis metropolitan area. In 1993, MTWN acquired First National Bank of Shawnee, Kansas, which operates three locations on the Kansas side of the Kansas City metropolitan area. Mark Twain Properties, Inc. owns, holds under lease or manages property by present banking centers. Mark Twain Community Development Corp. provides services and housing opportunities for low-and moderate-income persons. Tarquad Corp. acts as a trustee of deeds of trust for MTWN's subsidiaries. Mark Twain Asset Recovery, Inc. purchases certain assets acquired by subsidiary banks in collection of loans.

ANNUAL EARNINGS AND DIVIDENDS PER SHARE

	1994	1993	1992	1991	1990	1989	1988
Earnings Per Share	**2.54**	**2.28**	**1.98**	**1.55**	**1.35**	**1.37**	**1.27**
Dividends Per Share	**0.96**	[1] **0.807**	**0.68**	**0.613**	**0.587**	**0.52**	**0.453**
Dividend Payout %	**37.8**	**35.4**	**34.3**	**39.5**	**43.6**	**37.9**	**35.6**

[1] Adj for 3-for-2 stk split, 6/22/93

ANNUAL FINANCIAL DATA

	1994	1993	1992	1991	1990	1989	1988
RECORD OF EARNINGS (IN MILLIONS):							
Total Interest Income	194.6	164.2	165.9	189.2	192.7	184.9	165.5
Total Interest Expense	70.6	59.3	73.7	106.0	116.9	112.3	95.6
Net Interest Income	124.0	105.0	92.1	83.2	75.7	72.5	69.9
Credit Loss Provision	5.5	5.9	8.2	14.1	7.4	4.5	4.1
Net Income	41.0	33.1	27.0	19.6	16.1	16.2	14.3
Aver. Shs. Outstg. (000)	16,103	14,494	13,653	12,649	12,047	11,683	11,236
BALANCE SHEET (IN MILLIONS):							
Cash & Due From Banks	139.9	100.8	105.5	102.4	101.2	113.5	116.7
Loans & Lse Financing, Net	1,831.3	1,580.1	1,417.0	1,451.3	1,484.2	1,363.7	1,293.2
Total Domestic Deposits	2,272.1	2,033.9	1,891.4	1,844.4	1,857.3	1,668.8	1,636.2
Long-term Debt	20.4	22.4	26.3	27.4	32.2	33.1	34.0
Net Stockholders' Equity	234.0	201.0	167.4	148.8	116.6	109.5	99.4
Total Assets	2,688.7	2,408.0	2,213.1	2,170.4	2,127.7	1,949.2	1,834.7
Year End Shs Outstg (000)	15,977	14,594	13,496	13,434	11,688	11,424	11,385
STATISTICAL RECORD:							
Return on Assets %	1.52	1.37	1.22	0.90	0.76	0.83	0.78
Return on Equity %	17.50	16.40	16.10	13.20	13.80	14.80	14.40
Book Value Per Share	14.65	13.78	12.40	11.08	9.98	9.34	8.48
Average Yield %	3.5	3.0	3.6	5.2	6.0	4.1	3.4
P/E Ratio	12.2-9.4	13.9-9.4	11.3-7.8	10.5-4.5	9.2-5.4	9.9-8.5	11.5-9.4
Price Range	31-24	31¾-21½	22⅜-15⅜	16⅜-7	12⅜-7¼	13⅝-11⅝	14⅝-12

Statistics are as originally reported.

OFFICERS:
A.J. Siteman, Chmn.
J.P. Dubinsky, Pres. & C.E.O.
K. Miller, Sr. V.P. & C.F.O.
R.W. Holle, Treas.

INCORPORATED: MO, Apr., 1967

PRINCIPAL OFFICE: 8820 Ladue Road, St. Louis, MO 63124

TELEPHONE NUMBER: (314) 727-1000

FAX: (314) 889-0784

NO. OF EMPLOYEES: 1,014

ANNUAL MEETING: In April

SHAREHOLDERS: 2,400 (approx.)

INSTITUTIONAL HOLDINGS:
No. of Institutions: 56
Shares Held: 3,461,155

REGISTRAR(S): Society National Bank, Cleveland, OH

TRANSFER AGENT(S): Society National Bank, Cleveland, OH

NYS SYMBOL MMC
Rec. Pr. 78

MARSH & MCLENNAN COS., INC.

YIELD 3.7%
P/E RATIO 15.0

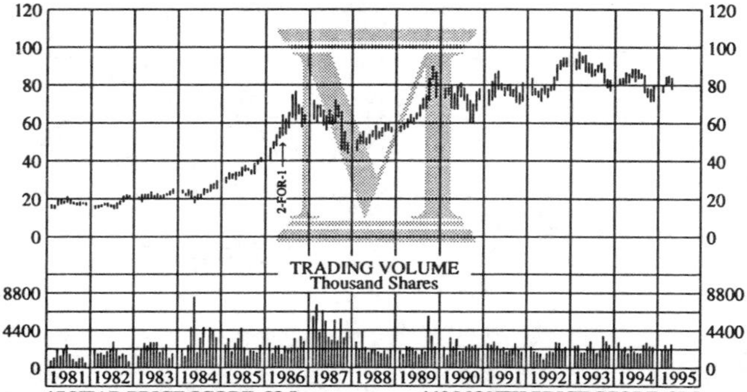

120
100
80
60
40
20
0
2-FOR-1
TRADING VOLUME
Thousand Shares
8800
4400
0
1981 1982 1983 1984 1985 1986 1987 1988 1989 1990 1991 1992 1993 1994 1995

*7 YEAR PRICE SCORE 88.5 *12 MONTH PRICE SCORE 95.5

*NYSE COMPOSITE INDEX=100

INTERIM EARNINGS (Per Share):

Qtr.	Mar.	June	Sept.	Dec.
1991	1.31	1.10	1.02	0.75
1992	1.40	1.11	0.96	0.74
1993	1.46	1.18	1.04	0.84
1994	1.77	1.30	1.14	0.98

INTERIM DIVIDENDS (Per Share):

Amt.	Decl.	Ex.	Rec.	Pay.
0.675Q	3/15/94	4/5/94	4/11/94	5/16/94
0.725Q	5/15	7/5	7/11	8/15
0.725Q	9/20	10/4	10/11	11/15
0.725Q	11/15	1/5/95	1/11/95	2/15/95
0.725Q	3/16/95	4/5	4/11	5/15

*Indicated div.: $2.90**

CAPITALIZATION (12/31/94):

	($000)	(%)
Long-Term Debt	409,400	21.9
Common & Surplus	1,460,600	78.1
Total	1,870,000	100.0

DIVIDEND ACHIEVER STATUS:
Rank: 184 1984-94 Growth Rate: 9.5%
Total Years of Dividend Growth: 33

RECENT DEVELOPMENTS: For the quarter ended 12/31/94, income before an accounting change jumped 14.9% to $382.0 million from $332.4 million a year earlier. Total revenue was $3.44 million compared with $3.16 million the year before, an increase of 8.6%. Revenues from insurance services, consulting, and investment management grew 5.4%, 9.2% and 18.8%, respectively. Compensation and benefits expense totaled $1.74 billion versus $1.64 billion for the prior year.

PROSPECTS: Results for MMC's consulting services indicate good growth potential with strong demand in the global practices of general management and compensation consulting. The investment management segment is protected by strong growth in the level of assets under management on which management fees are earned. Insurance broking revenues should continue to increase as new business is developed in Continental Europe. Reinsurance broking revenue is relatively flat reflecting lower demand in the London market.

BUSINESS

MARSH & MCLENNAN COMPANIES, INC. is engaged in the worldwide business of providing retail and wholesale insurance services, principally as a broker or consultant for insurers, insurance underwriters and other brokers. Marsh & McLennan Inc., the major subsidiary, is the largest insurance broker in the world. Other subsidiaries render advisory services in the area of employee benefits and compensation consulting, management consulting, economic consulting, environmental consulting and investment management services.

REVENUES

(12/31/94)	($000)	(%)
Insurance Services	1,886,500	54.9
Consulting	933,100	27.2
Investment Management	615,400	17.9
Total	3,435,000	100.0

ANNUAL EARNINGS AND DIVIDENDS PER SHARE

	1994	1993	1992	1991	1990	1989	1988
Earnings Per Share	5.19	4.52	4.21	4.18	4.15	4.10	4.09
Dividends Per Share	2.80	2.70	[1] 2.65	2.60	2.55	2.50	2.425
Dividend Payout %	54.0	59.7	62.9	62.2	61.4	61.0	59.3

[1] Bef acctg chge

ANNUAL FINANCIAL DATA

	1994	1993	1992	1991	1990	1989	1988
RECORD OF EARNINGS (IN MILLIONS):							
Total Revenues	3,435.0	3,163.4	2,937.0	2,779.2	2,723.0	2,427.7	2,272.4
Costs and Expenses	2,764.7	2,570.6	2,396.0	2,281.1	2,195.7	1,918.2	1,757.0
Operating Income	670.3	592.8	541.0	498.1	527.3	509.5	515.4
Income Bef Income Taxes	631.5	558.6	519.3	526.8	528.8	517.3	516.4
Income Taxes	249.5	226.2	215.5	221.3	224.7	222.4	220.1
Net Income	[1] 382.0	332.4	[2] 303.8	305.5	304.1	294.9	296.3
Aver. Shs. Outstg. (000)	73,600	73,500	72,200	73,100	73,300	71,900	72,400

[1] Before acctg. change dr$10,500,000. [2] Before acctg. change dr$40,100,000.

	1994	1993	1992	1991	1990	1989	1988
BALANCE SHEET (IN MILLIONS):							
Cash and Cash Equivalents	294.9	332.0	371.1	349.0	304.6	293.0	252.2
Receivables, Net	955.0	853.0	827.0	690.0	748.2	618.1	535.6
Gross Property	1,314.8	1,226.9	1,196.7	1,177.4	1,139.2	1,018.5	912.4
Accumulated Depreciation	574.5	538.8	488.9	443.4	379.8	337.1	292.9
Long-Term Debt	409.4	409.8	411.2	318.0	319.9	319.4	266.2
Net Stockholders' Equity	1,460.6	1,365.3	1,102.9	1,035.0	1,085.3	873.0	755.1
Total Assets	3,830.6	3,546.6	3,088.4	2,382.2	2,411.2	2,035.2	1,830.0
Total Current Assets	1,446.0	1,312.4	1,260.4	1,039.0	1,052.8	911.1	787.8
Total Current Liabilities	1,392.3	1,178.7	1,016.5	736.0	732.6	624.9	626.4
Net Working Capital	53.7	133.7	243.9	303.0	320.2	286.2	161.4
Year End Shs Outstg (000)	73,200	73,932	73,275	71,841	73,521	72,426	71,515
STATISTICAL RECORD:							
Book Value Per Share	19.95	18.47	15.05	14.41	14.76	12.05	10.56
Return on Equity %	26.2	24.3	27.5	29.5	28.0	33.8	39.2
Return on Assets %	10.0	9.4	9.8	12.8	12.6	14.5	16.2
Average Yield %	3.5	3.1	3.2	3.3	3.6	3.5	4.6
P/E Ratio	17.1-13.7	21.6-17.0	22.4-16.9	20.9-16.5	19.5-14.4	21.9-13.4	14.6-11.1
Price Range	88¾-71¼	97⅝-77	94½-71¼	87¼-69⅛	81-59¾	89¾-55⅛	59¾-45¼

Statistics are as originally reported.

OFFICERS:
A. Smith, Chmn.
P.L. Wroughton, Vice-Chmn.
F.J. Borelli, Sr. V.P. & C.F.O.
G.F. Van Gundy, General Counsel & Sec.

INCORPORATED: DE, Mar., 1969

PRINCIPAL OFFICE: 1166 Avenue of the Americas, New York, NY 10036

TELEPHONE NUMBER: (212) 345-5000
FAX: (212) 345-5669
NO. OF EMPLOYEES: 26,100
ANNUAL MEETING: In May
SHAREHOLDERS: 10,439
INSTITUTIONAL HOLDINGS:
No. of Institutions: 451
Shares Held: 47,791,200

REGISTRAR(S): Harris Trust Co. of N.Y., New York, NY 10005

TRANSFER AGENT(S): Harris Trust Co. of N.Y., New York, NY 10005

NASDAQ SYMBOL MRIS
Rec. Pr. 19⅞

MARSHALL & ILSLEY CORP.

YIELD 3.1%
P/E RATIO 19.9

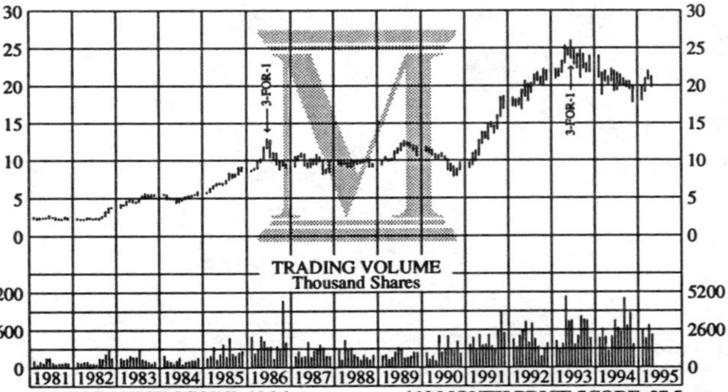

30
25
20
15
10
5
0
3-FOR-1
3-FOR-1
TRADING VOLUME
Thousand Shares
5200
2600
0
1981 1982 1983 1984 1985 1986 1987 1988 1989 1990 1991 1992 1993 1994 1995

*7 YEAR PRICE SCORE 106.4 *12 MONTH PRICE SCORE 97.5

*NYSE COMPOSITE INDEX=100

INTERIM EARNINGS (Per Share):

Qtr.	Mar.	June	Sept.	Dec.
1991	0.39	0.35	0.39	0.37
1992	0.41	0.43	0.42	0.46
1993	0.46	0.47	0.46	0.49
1994	0.44	d0.39	0.45	0.45

INTERIM DIVIDENDS (Per Share):

Amt.	Decl.	Ex.	Rec.	Pay.
0.15Q	8/23/94	8/26/94	8/31/94	9/14/94
0.15Q	10/13	11/23	11/30	12/14
0.15Q	10/13	11/23	11/30	12/14
0.15Q	2/16/95	2/23/95	2/28/95	3/14/95
0.165Q	4/25	5/24	5/31	6/14

Indicated div.: $0.66*

CAPITALIZATION (12/31/94):

	($000)	(%)
Total Deposits	9,499,080	76.1
Total Debt	1,764,919	14.2
Preferred Stock	349	0.0
Common & Surplus	1,060,947	8.5
Loan Valuation Reserve	153,961	1.2
Total	12,479,256	100.0

DIVIDEND ACHIEVER STATUS:
Rank: 176 1984-94 Growth Rate: 9.8%%
Total Years of Dividend Growth: 21

RECENT DEVELOPMENTS: MRIS earned $94.4 million before extraordinary items for the year ended 12/31/94, a 44.9% decrease from the $171.4 million earned in 1993. Results for 1994 were affected by a $75.2 million restructuring charge, associated with the acquisition of Valley Bancorporation, taken in the second quarter. At year end, assets totaled $12.61 billion versus $12.49 billion in 1993, while deposits fell to $9.50 billion from $10.17 billion. Net loans rose a modest 1.8% to $8.64 billion. Net interest income was $491.2 million versus $480.3 million. Other income declined to $361.5 million from $371.9 million as a loss of $5.8 million was recorded on securities transactions compared with a gain of $8.3 million a year earlier. The provision for loan losses was raised to $24.9 million from the prior year's $18.0 million.

BUSINESS

MARSHALL & ILSLEY CORP. is a $12.6 billion multibank holding company headquartered in Milwaukee, Wisconsin. M&I Marshall and Ilsley Bank is the Corporation's lead bank. The Corporation has 34 affiliated banks serving the state from 225 banking offices and one bank in Phoenix, Arizona with 12 offices. In addition, the holding company has a leasing company with fourteen offices, an investment management company, two mortgage banking companies, an insurance subsidiary, a venture capital company, a data services company with six offices, and trust companies in Wisconsin, Arizona, and Florida.

LOAN DISTRIBUTION

(12/31/94)	($000)	(%)
Comm, Finl & Agricultural	2,644,928	30.1
Indus Dev Rev Bonds	31,796	0.4
Residential Mortgage	2,240,287	25.5
Commercial Mortgage	2,062,022	23.4
Personal	1,178,453	13.4
Lease Financing	256,690	2.9
Construction	378,316	4.3
Total	8,792,492	100.0

ANNUAL EARNINGS AND DIVIDENDS PER SHARE

	1994	1993	1992	1991	1990	1989	1988
Earnings Per Share	**0.95**	**1.87**	**[2] 1.73**	**1.50**	**1.08**	**1.28**	**1.16**
Dividends Per Share	**0.59**	**[1] 0.543**	**[3] 0.48**	**0.43**	**0.39**	**0.35**	**0.31**
Dividend Payout %	**62.1**	**29.0**	**27.8**	**28.7**	**36.0**	**27.3**	**26.7**

[1] 3-for-1 stk split,06/01/93 [2] Before acctg. chg. [3] Bef acctg chge

ANNUAL FINANCIAL DATA

	1994	1993	1992	1991	1990	1989	1988
RECORD OF EARNINGS (IN MILLIONS):							
Total Interest Income	817.3	487.5	532.1	607.9	641.8	612.0	525.0
Total Interest Expense	326.1	178.4	224.3	318.9	366.4	358.4	294.6
Net Interest Income	491.2	309.2	307.8	289.0	275.4	253.5	230.4
Credit Loss Provision	24.9	9.1	15.2	20.6	39.8	12.3	8.3
Net Income	[1] 94.4	125.5	[2] 116.6	99.3	71.3	85.4	76.2
Aver. Shs. Outstg. (000)	99,420	67,047	67,523	66,162	65,943	66,797	66,170

[1] Before extra. item cr$11,542,000. [2] Before acctg. change dr$7,387,000.

	1994	1993	1992	1991	1990	1989	1988
BALANCE SHEET (IN MILLIONS):							
Cash & Due From Banks	685.9	479.5	491.8	551.9	614.5	516.5	515.6
Loans & Lse Financing, Net	8,638.5	5,277.9	4,792.8	4,699.6	4,699.1	4,567.7	4,021.7
Total Domestic Deposits	9,499.1	6,195.9	6,212.1	6,133.1	5,979.6	5,585.3	5,211.1
Long-term Debt	653.8	202.8	130.2	182.3	178.4	148.9	177.0
Net Stockholders' Equity	1,061.3	750.4	760.6	675.0	599.2	564.2	497.7
Total Assets	12,612.9	7,970.2	7,850.3	7,627.8	7,460.1	7,150.8	6,774.9
Year End Shs Outstg (000)	92,529	66,425	64,356	63,491	62,610	63,744	63,219
STATISTICAL RECORD:							
Return on Assets %	0.75	1.57	1.49	1.30	0.96	1.19	1.12
Return on Equity %	8.90	16.70	15.30	14.70	11.90	15.10	15.30
Book Value Per Share	11.47	11.29	11.82	10.63	9.57	8.85	7.87
Average Yield %	2.8	3.4	2.5	3.1	4.0	3.2	3.2
P/E Ratio	25.3-18.7	13.9-11.2	12.9-9.8	12.4-5.9	11.0-7.2	9.9-7.3	8.7-7.9
Price Range	24-17¾	26-20⅞	22¼-16⅞	18⅝-8⅞	11⅞-7¾	12⅝-9⅜	10⅛-9⅛

Statistics are as originally reported.

OFFICERS:
J.B. Wigdale, Chmn. & C.E.O.
D.J. Kuester, Pres.
G.H. Gunnlaugsson, Exec. V.P. & C.F.O.
M.A. Hatfield, Sr. V.P., Sec. & Treas.

INCORPORATED: WI, Feb., 1959

PRINCIPAL OFFICE: 770 North Water Street, Milwaukee, WI 53202

TELEPHONE NUMBER: (800) 342-2265

NO. OF EMPLOYEES: 9,250 (approx.)

ANNUAL MEETING: In April

SHAREHOLDERS: 18,882

INSTITUTIONAL HOLDINGS:
No. of Institutions: 127
Shares Held: 23,616,807

REGISTRAR(S): The Bank of New York, New York, NY

TRANSFER AGENT(S): The Bank of New York, New York, NY

MARTIN MARIETTA CORP.

YIELD 1.9%
P/E RATIO 8.4

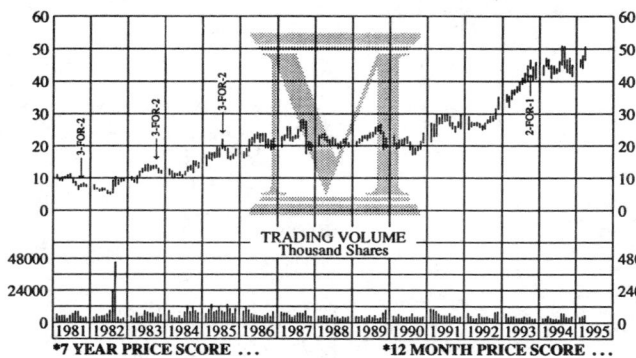

INTERIM EARNINGS (Per Share):

Qtr.	Mar.	June	Sept.	Dec.
1991	0.72	0.99	1.00	0.45
1992	0.76	1.03	1.02	0.81
1993	0.81	1.14	1.21	1.08
1994	1.77	1.54	1.39	1.30

INTERIM DIVIDENDS (Per Share):

Amt.	Decl.	Ex.	Rec.	Pay.
0.225Q	4/28/94	5/25/94	6/1/94	6/30/94
0.24Q	7/28	8/26	9/1	9/30
0.24Q	10/27	11/25	12/1	12/30
0.24Q	1/26/95	2/22/95	2/28/95	3/14/95

Indicated div.: $0.96*

CAPITALIZATION (12/31/94):

	($000)	(%)
Long-Term Debt	1,346,000	28.5
Preferred Stock	1,000,000	21.2
Common & Surplus	2,371,000	50.3
Total	4,717,000	100.0

TRADING VOLUME
Thousand Shares

1981 1982 1983 1984 1985 1986 1987 1988 1989 1990 1991 1992 1993 1994 1995

7 YEAR PRICE SCORE ...   **12 MONTH PRICE SCORE ...**

*NYSE COMPOSITE INDEX=100

DIVIDEND ACHIEVER STATUS:
Rank: 224   1984-94 Growth Rate: 7.6%
Total Years of Dividend Growth: 23

RECENT DEVELOPMENTS: For the year ended 12/31/94, income before accounting changes was $635.6 million versus $450.3 million in 1993. Net sales advanced 4.6% to $9.87 billion. The Space Group posted a 2% rise in sales to $3.49 billion, and its operating income increased 36% to $338.4 million. Electronics Group sales fell 2% to $3.87 billion, while its operating profit rose 16% to $385.7 million. The Information Group recorded sales of $1.52 billion, up 26% from 1993. Operating profit was $126.2 million.

PROSPECTS: Martin Marietta's merger agreement with Lockheed Corporation was cleared by the Federal Trade Commission in January. The merger will create a very focused aerospace company with increased financial flexibilty. Meanwhile, the Company will continue to benefit from consolidation efficiencies associated with its previous acquisitions of GE Aerospace and the former General Dynamics Space Systems business.

BUSINESS

MARTIN MARIETTA CORP. is a major aerospace and information technology company operating in the following business segments: Electronics produces high-performance electronic systems for undersea, shipboard, land-based and airborne applications. Space Group consists of space launch vehicles, spacecraft, space and ground-based strategic systems and the Space Shuttle external tank. Information provides simulation and automated test systems and image processing for government and commercial applications. Services provides technical and management services. Materials, consists of aggregate operations and magnesia specialties. Energy and Other includes research for the Dept. of Energy and real estate activities.

QUARTERLY DATA

(12/31/94)($000,000)	Rev	Inc
1st Quarter	2,034	184
2nd Quarter	2,491	163
3rd Quarter	2,563	149
4th Quarter	2,786	140

ANNUAL EARNINGS AND DIVIDENDS PER SHARE

	1994	1993	1992	1991	1990	1989	1988
Earnings Per Share	6.00	4.25	② 3.61	3.15	3.26	2.91	⑧ 3.01
Dividends Per Share	0.93	① 1.00	0.76	0.75	0.693	0.612	0.55
Dividend Payout %	15.5	23.5	11.0	11.9	10.7	10.5	9.0

① 2-for-1 stk split, 10/1/93 ② 2-for-1 stock split,10/01/93 ⑧ Before extraord. item

ANNUAL FINANCIAL DATA

RECORD OF EARNINGS (IN MILLIONS):

	1994	1993	1992	1991	1990	1989	1988
Total Revenues	9,874.0	9,436.0	5,954.0	6,075.0	6,126.0	5,796.0	5,727.0
Costs and Expenses	8,558.0	8,298.0	5,179.0	5,313.0	5,467.0	5,125.0	5,132.0
Deprec, Depl & Amort	338.0	350.0	226.0	225.0	216.0	207.0	199.0
Earnings From Operations	978.0	788.0	549.0	537.0	442.0	465.0	397.0
Earn Bef Taxes on Inc & Acctg Chge	1,072.0	725.0	512.0	421.0	435.0	429.0	475.0
Income Taxes	436.0	275.0	167.0	108.0	108.0	122.0	155.0
Net Income	636.0	① 450.0	345.0	313.0	328.0	307.0	② 320.0
Aver. Shs. Outstg. (000)	96,000	95,000	96,000	99,000	101,000	106,000	106,000

① Before acctg. change dr$429,000,000. ② Before extra. item cr$39,000,000.

BALANCE SHEET (IN MILLIONS):

	1994	1993	1992	1991	1990	1989	1988
Cash and Cash Equivalents	358.0	373.0	240.0	171.0	87.0	68.0	77.0
Receivables, Net	1,709.0	1,674.0	851.0	860.0	809.0	779.0	737.0
Inventories	603.0	359.0	301.0	539.0	457.0	539.0	444.0
Gross Property	3,830.0	3,805.0	3,144.0	3,049.0	2,843.0	2,626.0	2,502.0
Accumulated Depreciation	2,181.0	2,112.0	1,887.0	1,734.0	1,502.0	1,325.0	1,204.0
Long-Term Debt	1,346.0	1,479.0	475.0	596.0	463.0	478.0	484.0
Net Stockholders' Equity	3,371.0	2,877.0	1,945.0	1,805.0	1,541.0	1,355.0	1,201.0
Total Assets	8,538.0	7,745.0	3,599.0	3,896.0	3,611.0	3,505.0	3,322.0
Total Current Assets	2,760.0	2,448.0	1,434.0	1,616.0	1,400.0	1,440.0	1,294.0
Total Current Liabilities	1,811.0	1,810.0	587.0	948.0	993.0	926.0	909.0
Net Working Capital	949.0	638.0	847.0	668.0	407.0	514.0	385.0
Year End Shs Outstg (000)	96,000	96,000	94,000	99,000	98,000	102,000	106,000

STATISTICAL RECORD:

	1994	1993	1992	1991	1990	1989	1988
Operating Profit Margin %	9.9	8.4	9.2	8.8	7.2	8.0	6.9
Book Value Per Share	35.1	30.06	20.69	18.23	15.72	13.28	11.33
Return on Equity %	18.9	15.6	17.7	17.3	21.3	22.7	26.6
Return on Assets %	7.4	5.8	9.6	8.0	9.1	8.8	9.6
Average Yield %	2.3	2.2	2.5	2.9	3.4	2.7	2.5
P/E Ratio	8.5-6.8	5.8-4.0	4.9-3.5	4.8-3.4	7.4-5.3	9.2-6.5	8.0-6.4
Price Range	51 - 40⅞	46⅝ - 32	35¼ - 25	30¼ - 21¼	24⅛ - 17⅛	26¾ - 18⅞	24⅛ - 19⅛

Statistics are as originally reported.

OFFICERS:
N.R. Augustine, Chmn. & C.E.O.
A.T. Young, Pres. & C.O.O.
M.C. Bennett, Sr. V.P. & C.F.O.
J.L. McGregor, Treasurer
K.T. Sheehan, Secretary
INCORPORATED: MD, Oct., 1961
PRINCIPAL OFFICE: 6801 Rockledge Drive, Bethesda, MD 20817

TELEPHONE NUMBER: (301) 897-6000
FAX: (301) 897-6083
NO. OF EMPLOYEES: 2,409
ANNUAL MEETING: In April
SHAREHOLDERS: 10,952
INSTITUTIONAL HOLDINGS:
No. of Institutions: 366
Shares Held: 33,171,676

REGISTRAR(S): First Chicago Trust Co. of New York, New York, NY 10008
Maryland National Bank, Baltimore, MD 21201

TRANSFER AGENT(S): First Chicago Trust Co. of New York, New York, NY 10008
Maryland National Bank, Baltimore, MD 21201

MASCO CORP.

YIELD 2.6%
P/E RATIO 22.0

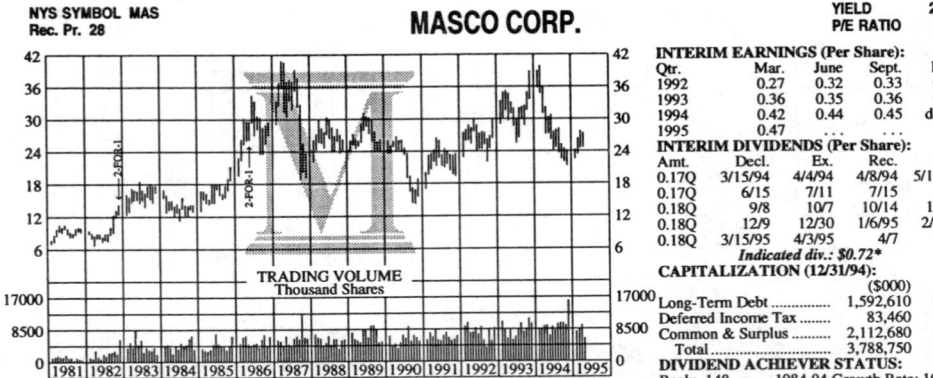

*7 YEAR PRICE SCORE 80.6   *12 MONTH PRICE SCORE 96.8
*NYSE COMPOSITE INDEX=100

INTERIM EARNINGS (Per Share):

Qtr.	Mar.	June	Sept.	Dec.
1992	0.27	0.32	0.33	0.29
1993	0.36	0.35	0.36	0.38
1994	0.42	0.44	0.45	d0.09
1995	0.47	...	...	...

INTERIM DIVIDENDS (Per Share):

Amt.	Decl.	Ex.	Rec.	Pay.
0.17Q	3/15/94	4/4/94	4/8/94	5/10/94
0.17Q	6/15	7/11	7/15	8/8
0.18Q	9/8	10/7	10/14	11/14
0.18Q	12/9	12/30	1/6/95	2/6/95
0.18Q	3/15/95	4/3/95	4/7	5/8

Indicated div.: $0.72*

CAPITALIZATION (12/31/94):

	($000)	(%)
Long-Term Debt	1,592,610	42.0
Deferred Income Tax	83,460	2.2
Common & Surplus	2,112,680	55.8
Total	3,788,750	100.0

DIVIDEND ACHIEVER STATUS:
Rank: 148   1984-94 Growth Rate: 10.7%
Total Years of Dividend Growth: 36

RECENT DEVELOPMENTS: Net income for the year ended 12/31/94, including a net non-recurring charge of $79.3 million, decreased 12.4% to $193.7 million from $221.1 million in 1993. Sales for the twelve months were up 15.0% to $4.47 billion, compared with $3.89 billion the prior year. Operating profit reached a record $510 million, up 26% from 1993. Including companies acquired in 1994, sales of building and home improvement products and sales of home furnishings products both advanced 15.0%.

PROSPECTS: Operating profit margins in both of the Company's major business segments are benefiting from increased sales and the positive effects of profit improvement programs. Restructuring activities at MascoTech have recently put a strain on earnings. MascoTech is divesting non-core businesses in order to focus on its core transportation-related business. The expanding economy should serve to somewhat offset the adverse effect of rising interest rates on housing starts.

BUSINESS

MASCO CORP. manufactures building, home improvement and home furnishings products. Masco's building and home improvement segment, includes faucets, plumbing fittings, kitchen and bathroom cabinets, bathtubs and whirlpools, builders' hardware, venting and ventilating equipment, insulucts and water pumps. Home furnishings and other specialty products, include high-quality furniture and other home furnishings products, giftware, and recreational accessories. Brand-names include Delta, Delex, Peerless, Artistic and Epic faucets; Merillat kitchen and bathroom cabinets; Weiser and Baldwin locks, Brass-Craft and Plumb Shop plumbing fittings; Thermador and Waste King appliances.

BUSINESS LINE ANALYSIS

(12/31/94)	Rev(%)	Inc(%)
Building & Home		
Improvement	56.5	85.0
Home Furnishings		
Products	43.5	15.0
Total	100.0	100.0

ANNUAL EARNINGS AND DIVIDENDS PER SHARE

	1994	1993	1992	1991	1990	1989	1988
Earnings Per Share	1.22	1.45	1.21	0.30	0.91	1.42	2.10
Dividends Per Share	0.69	0.65	0.61	0.57	0.54	0.50	0.44
Dividend Payout %	56.6	44.8	50.4	N.M.	59.3	35.2	21.0

ANNUAL FINANCIAL DATA

RECORD OF EARNINGS (IN MILLIONS):

	1994	1993	1992	1991	1990	1989	1988
Total Revenues	4,468.0	3,886.0	3,525.0	3,141.0	3,209.0	3,150.5	2,438.6
Costs and Expenses	3,837.8	3,366.2	3,052.0	2,790.0	2,752.7	2,656.5	1,967.8
Depreciation & Amort	120.6	116.0	114.5	102.7	93.5	89.1	74.6
Operating Profit	509.6	403.8	358.5	248.3	362.8	405.0	396.2
Income Bef Income Taxes	322.6	362.6	304.8	97.6	235.9	327.1	421.4
Income Taxes	128.9	141.5	121.7	52.7	97.1	106.2	133.1
Net Income	193.7	221.1	183.1	44.9	138.8	220.9	288.3
Aver. Shs. Outstg. (000)	158,800	152,700	151,700	149,900	152,600	155,600	137,500

BALANCE SHEET (IN MILLIONS):

	1994	1993	1992	1991	1990	1989	1988
Cash and Cash Equivalents	71.1	124.9	54.3	70.3	68.9	113.1	143.1
Receivables, Net	745.2	610.1	547.8	497.0	480.5	512.9	372.0
Inventories	948.8	824.1	781.7	738.9	753.4	712.3	550.9
Gross Property	1,917.9	1,683.4	1,554.0	1,460.2	1,375.0	1,252.6	920.8
Accumulated Depreciation	686.1	588.2	523.5	460.1	404.9	372.0	268.7
Long-Term Debt	1,592.6	1,418.3	1,487.1	1,369.3	1,334.3	1,153.2	999.2
Net Stockholders' Equity	2,112.7	1,998.4	1,886.9	1,798.9	1,774.0	1,858.4	1,546.1
Total Assets	4,575.0	4,315.8	4,233.5	4,024.6	4,024.6	3,878.8	3,201.8
Total Current Assets	1,891.4	1,643.8	1,465.5	1,375.9	1,365.2	1,393.3	1,137.9
Total Current Liabilities	601.3	490.4	491.5	260.5	326.5	299.7	152.2
Net Working Capital	1,290.2	1,153.4	974.0	1,115.4	1,038.7	1,093.5	985.7
Year End Shs Outstg (000)	156,990	152,850	152,470	151,010	147,760	155,620	136,810

STATISTICAL RECORD:

	1994	1993	1992	1991	1990	1989	1988
Operating Profit Margin %	11.4	10.4	10.2	7.9	11.3	12.9	16.2
Book Value Per Share	8.96	9.12	8.26	7.73	7.67	7.91	7.11
Return on Equity %	9.2	11.1	9.7	2.5	7.8	11.9	18.6
Return on Assets %	4.2	5.1	4.3	1.1	3.4	5.7	9.0
Average Yield %	2.3	2.0	2.3	2.6	2.6	1.8	1.7
P/E Ratio	32.7-17.4	26.8-17.6	24.8-18.2	88.3-56.7	29.4-15.7	21.9-16.7	14.5-10.5
Price Range	39⅞-21¼	38⅞-25½	30-22	26½-17	26¾-14¼	31⅛-23¾	30⅜-22

Statistics are as originally reported.

OFFICERS:
R.A. Manoogian, Chmn. & C.E.O.
W.B. Lyon, Pres. & C.O.O.
R.G. Mosteller, Sr. V.P.-Fin.
E.A. Gargaro, Jr., V.P. & Sec.
INCORPORATED: MI, Dec., 1929; reincorp., DE, 1968
PRINCIPAL OFFICE: 21001 Van Born Rd., Taylor, MI 48180

TELEPHONE NUMBER: (313) 274-7400
FAX: (313) 563-5975
NO. OF EMPLOYEES: 51,300 (approx.)
ANNUAL MEETING: In May
SHAREHOLDERS: 6,680 (approx.)
INSTITUTIONAL HOLDINGS:
No. of Institutions: 389
Shares Held: 100,346,917

REGISTRAR(S): NBD Bank, N.A., Securities Transfer Services, Detroit, MI 02266

TRANSFER AGENT(S): NBD Bank, N.A., Securities Transfer Services, Detroit, MI 02266

NYS SYMBOL MA
Rec. Pr. 38¼

MAY DEPARTMENT STORES CO. (THE)

YIELD 3.0%
P/E RATIO 12.8

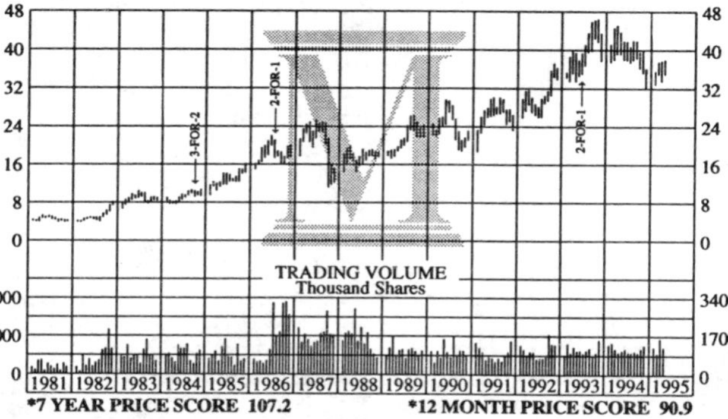

48
40
32
24
16
8
0
3-FOR-2
2-FOR-1
2-FOR-1
TRADING VOLUME
Thousand Shares
34000
17000
0
1981 1982 1983 1984 1985 1986 1987 1988 1989 1990 1991 1992 1993 1994 1995

*7 YEAR PRICE SCORE 107.2 *12 MONTH PRICE SCORE 90.9

*NYSE COMPOSITE INDEX=100

INTERIM EARNINGS (Per Share):

Qtr.	Apr.	July	Oct.	Jan.
1992-93		2.35		
1993-94	0.37	0.45	0.51	1.44
1994-95	0.43	0.50	0.54	1.51

INTERIM DIVIDENDS (Per Share):

Amt.	Decl.	Ex.	Rec.	Pay.
0.26Q	11/1/94	11/25/94	12/1/94	12/15/94
0.26Q	11/1	11/25	12/1	12/15
0.26Q	2/1/95	2/23/95	3/1/95	3/15/95
0.285Q	2/21	5/25	6/1	6/15
0.285Q	5/19	8/30	9/1	9/15

*Indicated div.: $1.14**

CAPITALIZATION (1/28/95):

	($000)	(%)
Long-Term Debt	2,802,000	38.0
Cap. Lease Oblig.	73,000	1.0
Deferred Income Tax	359,000	4.9
Common & Surplus	4,135,000	56.1
Total	7,369,000	100.0

DIVIDEND ACHIEVER STATUS:
Rank: 168 1984-94 Growth Rate: 10.0%
Total Years of Dividend Growth: 19

RECENT DEVELOPMENTS: For the year ended 1/28/95, net income was $782 million compared with $711 million a year earlier. Total sales increased 8.1% to $11.88 billion. The Department stores posted a 9.7% increase in operating income to $1.40 billion on an 8.2% rise in sales to $9.76 billion. Payless ShoeSource recorded a 2.7% decline in operating income to $219 million, although sales jumped 7.6% to $2.12 billion. Gross margin increased slightly to 31.5% of revenues from 31.4% a year ago.

PROSPECTS: The Company has significantly improved its buying processes and the quality and pricing of its private-label programs, which should provide an opportunity for long-term sales and earnings growth; however, any strong growth trends in the near-term will depend on the movement of interest rates and their effect on consumers' demand. A five-year $4.6 billion capital spending plan should boost the department store division to more than 400 stores and the Payless division to nearly 4,800 stores.

BUSINESS

THE MAY DEPARTMENT STORES COMPANY operates 4,749 stores, consisting of 314 department stores and 4,435 Payless ShoeSource stores. The Department store segment operates 8 chains: Lord & Taylor, Foley's, Hecht's, Robinsons-May, Famous-Barr, Kaufmann's, Filene's and Meier & Frank. Payless ShoeSource, the nation's largest chain of self-service family shoe stores, operates in 49 states, Puerto Rico and the District of Columbia. Thalhimers was acquired for $317 million in 1990, and was consolidated with the Hecht's division in January 1992.

BUSINESS LINE ANALYSIS

(1/28/95)	Rev(%)	Inc(%)
Department Stores	82.2	85.0
Payless ShoeSource	17.8	15.0
Total	100.0	100.0

ANNUAL EARNINGS AND DIVIDENDS PER SHARE

	1/28/95	1/29/94	1/30/93	2/1/92	2/2/91	2/3/90	1/28/89
Earnings Per Share	3.06	2.77	2.35	2.01	1.94	[2] 1.82	[3] 1.71
Dividends Per Share	1.01	0.898	[1] 0.825	0.805	0.77	0.692	0.622
Dividend Payout %	33.0	32.4	35.1	40.0	39.1	38.0	36.4

[1] 2-for-1 stk split,06/15/93 [2] Before disc. oper. [3] Earnings before discontin oper.

ANNUAL FINANCIAL DATA

	1/28/95	1/29/94	1/30/93	2/1/92	2/2/91	2/3/90	1/28/89
RECORD OF EARNINGS (IN MILLIONS):							
Total Revenues	12,223.0	11,529.0	11,150.0	10,615.0	10,066.0	9,602.0	11,742.0
Costs and Expenses	10,319.0	9,758.0	9,552.0	9,184.0	8,730.0	8,301.0	10,402.0
Depreciation & Amort	374.0	348.0	341.0	319.0	294.0	269.0	330.0
Operating Profit	3,849.0	3,619.0	3,459.0	3,276.0	3,088.0	3,021.0	3,289.0
Earn Bef Income Taxes	1,296.0	1,178.0	791.0	796.0	762.0	799.0	781.0
Income Taxes	514.0	467.0	188.0	281.0	262.0	284.0	278.0
Net Income	782.0	711.0	603.0	515.0	500.0	[1] 515.0	[2] 503.0
Aver. Shs. Outstg. (000)	249,000	250,000	249,000	248,000	249,000	267,000	294,000

[1] Before disc. op. dr$17,000,000. [2] Before disc. op. cr$31,000,000.

	1/28/95	1/29/94	1/30/93	2/1/92	2/2/91	2/3/90	1/28/89
BALANCE SHEET (IN MILLIONS):							
Cash and Cash Equivalents	55.0	46.0	172.0	207.0	80.0	92.0	124.0
Receivables, Net	2,436.0	2,394.0	2,367.0	2,404.0	2,494.0	2,274.0	2,160.0
Inventories	2,207.0	2,020.0	1,791.0	1,741.0	1,628.0	1,491.0	1,788.0
Gross Property	5,794.0	5,047.0	4,731.0	4,540.0	4,180.0	3,736.0	4,421.0
Accumulated Depreciation	1,928.0	1,636.0	1,573.0	1,389.0	1,195.0	1,070.0	1,315.0
Long-Term Debt	2,802.0	2,739.0	2,782.0	3,918.0	3,565.0	3,003.0	2,483.0
Capital Lease Obligations	73.0	83.0	97.0	...	...	...	...
Net Stockholders' Equity	4,135.0	3,639.0	3,181.0	2,781.0	2,467.0	2,319.0	3,050.0
Total Assets	9,472.0	8,800.0	8,545.0	8,728.0	8,295.0	7,802.0	8,144.0
Total Current Assets	4,910.0	4,679.0	4,654.0	4,574.0	4,377.0	4,053.0	4,168.0
Total Current Liabilities	1,895.0	1,771.0	1,975.0	1,522.0	1,742.0	1,994.0	2,074.0
Net Working Capital	3,015.0	2,908.0	2,679.0	3,052.0	2,635.0	2,059.0	2,094.0
Year End Shs Outstg (000)	248,000	248,000	248,000	247,000	246,000	249,000	298,000
STATISTICAL RECORD:							
Operating Profit Margin %	12.5	12.3	11.3	10.5	10.4	10.7	8.6
Book Value Per Share	14.25	12.18	10.26	8.63	7.44	7.04	8.13
Return on Equity %	18.9	19.5	19.0	18.5	20.3	22.2	16.5
Return on Assets %	8.3	8.1	7.1	5.9	6.0	6.6	6.2
Average Yield %	2.6	2.2	2.6	3.3	3.2	3.2	3.6
P/E Ratio	14.7-10.5	16.8-12.1	15.9-11.0	15.0-9.3	15.3-9.7	14.0-9.2	11.7-8.4
Price Range	45⅛-32¼	46½-33½	37¼-25⅞	30¼-18¾	29⅝-18⅞	26⅜-17⅜	20-14⅜

Statistics are as originally reported.

OFFICERS:
D.C. Farrell, Chmn. & C.E.O.
J.T. Loeb, Pres. & C.F.O.
J.R. Kniffen, Sr. V.P. & Treas.
R.A. Brickson, V.P., Sec. & Sr. Couns.

INCORPORATED: NY, Jun., 1910

PRINCIPAL OFFICE: 611 Olive Street, St. Louis, MO 63101-1799

TELEPHONE NUMBER: (314) 342-6300

NO. OF EMPLOYEES: 113,000 (approx)

ANNUAL MEETING: In May

SHAREHOLDERS: 46,000 (approx.)

INSTITUTIONAL HOLDINGS:
No. of Institutions: 616
Shares Held: 177,932,351

REGISTRAR(S): Boatmen's Trust Co., St.Louis, MO 63101

TRANSFER AGENT(S): Boatmen's Trust Co., St. Louis, MO 63101

NYS SYMBOL MCD
Rec. Pr. 36⅜

MCDONALD'S CORP.

YIELD 0.7%
P/E RATIO 18.2

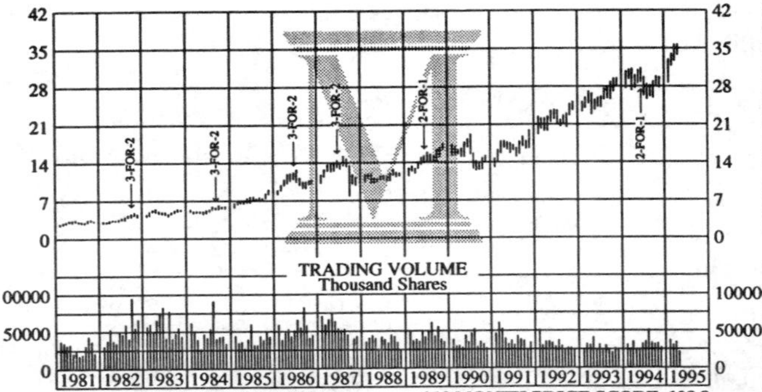

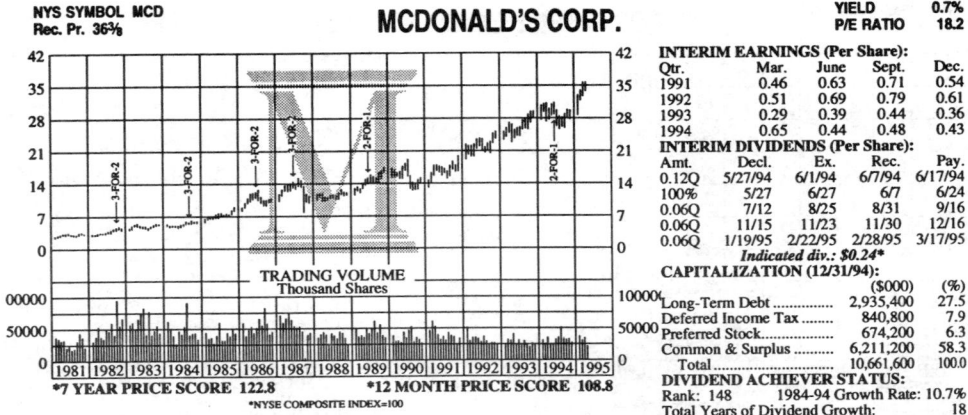

*7 YEAR PRICE SCORE 122.8 *12 MONTH PRICE SCORE 108.8

*NYSE COMPOSITE INDEX=100

INTERIM EARNINGS (Per Share):

Qtr.	Mar.	June	Sept.	Dec.
1991	0.46	0.63	0.71	0.54
1992	0.51	0.69	0.79	0.61
1993	0.29	0.39	0.44	0.36
1994	0.65	0.44	0.48	0.43

INTERIM DIVIDENDS (Per Share):

Amt.	Decl.	Ex.	Rec.	Pay.
0.12Q	5/27/94	6/1/94	6/7/94	6/17/94
100%	5/27	6/27	6/7	6/24
0.06Q	7/12	8/25	8/31	9/16
0.06Q	11/15	11/23	11/30	12/16
0.06Q	1/19/95	2/22/95	2/28/95	3/17/95

*Indicated div.: $0.24**

CAPITALIZATION (12/31/94):

	($000)	(%)
Long-Term Debt	2,935,400	27.5
Deferred Income Tax	840,800	7.9
Preferred Stock	674,200	6.3
Common & Surplus	6,211,200	58.3
Total	10,661,600	100.0

DIVIDEND ACHIEVER STATUS:
Rank: 148 1984-94 Growth Rate: 10.7%
Total Years of Dividend Growth: 18

RECENT DEVELOPMENTS: For the year ended 12/31/94, net income jumped 13.1% to $1.22 billion from $1.08 billion a year earlier. Total revenues were $8.32 billion compared with $7.41 billion the year before, an increase of 12.3%. Sales by Company-operated restaurants rose 12.3% to $5.79 billion from $5.16 billion for the prior year. Revenues from franchised restaurants were $2.53 billion, up 12.3% from $2.25 billion in 1993. Operating income grew 13.0% to $2.24 billion from $2.00 billion a year ago.

PROSPECTS: Driven primarily by expansion and value, MCD's global foodservice business should continue to demonstrate excellent growth. Both U.S. and international operations are delivering good sales and strong operating margins. MCD plans to improve profitability by reducing average development costs on a worldwide basis through global sourcing, standardization, and new restaurant and equipment designs. MCD plans to open 1,200 to 1,500 new restaurants annually over the next several years.

BUSINESS

MCDONALD'S CORP. develops, licenses, leases and services a worldwide system of restaurants. Units serve a standardized menu of moderately priced food consisting of hamburgers, cheeseburgers, chicken sandwiches, salads, desserts and beverages. As of 12/31/94, there were 10,458 units operated by franchisees, 3,083 units operated by the Company, and 1,664 units operated by affiliates. There are 15,000 MCD restaurants in 79 countries. Independent operators normally lease on a 20-year basis with rental derived as a percentage of sales.

REVENUES

(12/31/94)	($000)	(%)
Sales by Co. restaurants	5,792,600	69.6
Revs from franchised rest	2,528,200	30.4
Total	8,320,800	100.0

ANNUAL EARNINGS AND DIVIDENDS PER SHARE

	1994	1993	1992	1991	1990	1989	1988
Earnings Per Share	**1.68**	**1.46**	**1.30**	**1.18**	**1.10**	**0.98**	**0.86**
Dividends Per Share	**[1] 0.23**	**0.21**	**0.20**	**0.18**	**0.17**	**[2] 0.15**	**0.14**
Dividend Payout %	**13.7**	**14.4**	**15.4**	**15.3**	**15.5**	**15.3**	**16.3**

[1] 2-for-1 stk split, 6/94 [2] 2-for-1 stk split, 6/89

ANNUAL FINANCIAL DATA

	1994	1993	1992	1991	1990	1989	1988
RECORD OF EARNINGS (IN MILLIONS):							
Total Revenues	8,320.8	7,408.1	7,133.3	6,695.0	6,639.6	6,142.0	5,566.3
Costs and Expenses	5,451.0	4,917.7	4,780.8	4,616.1	4,645.7	4,319.0	3,958.5
Depreciation & Amort	628.6	568.4	554.9	514.2	493.3	364.0	324.0
Operating Profit	2,241.2	1,984.0	1,861.6	1,678.5	1,595.9	2,350.0	2,099.2
Inc Bef Prov for Income Taxes	1,886.6	1,675.7	1,448.1	1,299.4	1,246.3	1,157.0	1,046.5
Income Taxes	662.2	593.2	489.5	439.8	444.0	430.0	400.6
Net Income	1,224.4	1,082.5	958.6	859.6	802.3	727.0	645.9
Aver. Shs. Outstg. (000)	701,800	711,800	726,400	716,200	718,000	742,000	753,836
BALANCE SHEET (IN MILLIONS):							
Cash and Cash Equivalents	179.9	185.8	436.5	220.2	142.8	137.0	184.4
Receivables, Net	379.3	314.6	279.6	274.4	255.0	234.0	204.0
Inventories	50.5	43.5	43.5	42.6	42.9	46.0	48.5
Gross Property	15,184.6	13,459.0	12,658.0	12,368.0	11,535.5	9,874.0	8,647.8
Accumulated Depreciation	3,856.2	3,377.6	3,060.6	2,809.5	2,488.4	2,116.0	1,847.5
Long-Term Debt	2,935.4	3,489.4	3,176.4	4,267.4	4,428.7	3,901.0	3,111.1
Net Stockholders' Equity	6,885.4	6,274.1	5,892.4	4,835.1	4,182.3	3,550.0	3,412.8
Total Assets	13,591.9	12,035.2	11,681.2	11,349.1	10,667.5	9,175.0	8,158.7
Total Current Assets	740.7	662.8	864.7	646.0	549.0	495.0	516.4
Total Current Liabilities	2,451.3	1,102.0	1,544.6	1,287.9	1,198.7	1,017.0	1,003.6
Net Working Capital	d1,710.6	d439.2	d679.9	d641.9	d649.7	d522.0	d487.2
Year End Shs Outstg (000)	693,700	707,400	727,200	717,400	718,200	724,000	750,952
STATISTICAL RECORD:							
Operating Profit Margin %	26.9	26.8	26.1	25.1	24.0	23.8	23.1
Book Value Per Share	8.26	7.32	6.63	5.81	5.01	4.18	4.13
Return on Equity %	17.8	17.3	16.3	17.8	19.2	20.5	18.9
Return on Assets %	9.0	9.0	8.2	7.6	7.5	7.9	7.9
Average Yield %	0.8	0.8	0.9	1.1	1.1	1.0	1.2
P/E Ratio	18.7-15.3	20.4-15.7	19.4-14.7	17.0-11.2	17.5-11.4	17.9-11.8	14.9-12.0
Price Range	31⅜-25⅝	29⅝-22¾	25¼-19⅛	20-13⅛	19¼-12½	17½-11½	12¾-10¼

Statistics are as originally reported.

OFFICERS:
F.L. Turner, Senior Chmn.
M.R. Quinlan, Chmn. & C.E.O.
J.M. Greenberg, Vice-Chmn. & C.F.O.
E.H. Rensi, Pres. & C.E.O.

INCORPORATED: DE, Mar., 1965

PRINCIPAL OFFICE: McDonald's Plaza, Oak Brook, IL 60521

TELEPHONE NUMBER: (708) 575-3000
FAX: (708) 575-5004
NO. OF EMPLOYEES: 183,000 (approx.)
ANNUAL MEETING: In May
SHAREHOLDERS: 537,000 com. (approx.)
INSTITUTIONAL HOLDINGS:
No. of Institutions: 795
Shares Held: 228,370,557

REGISTRAR(S): First Chicago Trust Co. of New York, New York, NY 10008

TRANSFER AGENT(S): First Chicago Trust Co. of New York, New York, NY 10008

NYS SYMBOL MHP
Rec. Pr. 74

MCGRAW-HILL COS., INC. (THE)

YIELD 3.2%
P/E RATIO 18.1

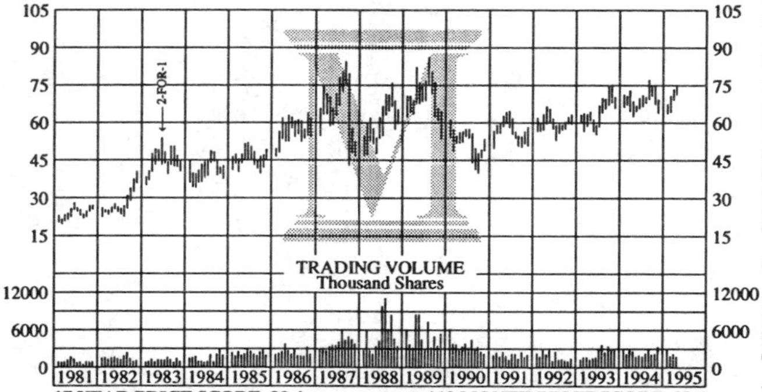

105
90
75
60
45
30
15
2-FOR-1
TRADING VOLUME
Thousand Shares
12000
6000
0
1981 1982 1983 1984 1985 1986 1987 1988 1989 1990 1991 1992 1993 1994 1995

*7 YEAR PRICE SCORE 92.4 *12 MONTH PRICE SCORE 98.6

*NYSE COMPOSITE INDEX=100

INTERIM EARNINGS (Per Share):

Qtr.	Mar.	June	Sept.	Dec.
1992	0.25	0.75	1.22	0.91
1993	0.31	0.88	d1.87	0.91
1994	0.30	0.97	1.82	1.01
1995	0.28	...	...	...

INTERIM DIVIDENDS (Per Share):

Amt.	Decl.	Ex.	Rec.	Pay.
0.58Q	4/27/94	5/20/94	5/26/94	6/10/94
0.58Q	7/27	8/22	8/26	9/12
0.58Q	10/19	11/21	11/28	12/12
0.60Q	1/25/95	2/17/95	2/24/95	3/10/95
0.60Q	4/26	5/22	5/26	6/12

*Indicated div.: $2.40**

CAPITALIZATION (12/31/94):

	($000)	(%)
Long-Term Debt	657,517	38.7
Deferred Income Tax	129,750	7.6
Preferred Stock	15	0.0
Common & Surplus	913,037	53.7
Total	1,700,319	100.0

DIVIDEND ACHIEVER STATUS:
Rank: 248 1984-94 Growth Rate: 6.5%
Total Years of Dividend Growth: 21

RECENT DEVELOPMENTS: For the year ended 12/31/94, net income was $203.1 million compared with $11.4 million in 1993. However, 1993 results include $160.8 million of non-recurring charges. Revenues rose 26% to $2.76 billion. Of the increase, $459.0 million is attributable to revenue from the School Publishing Company. MHP acquired its partner's 50% interest in the school publishing venture on 10/4/93 and now owns 100%. During 1994, profit margins improved in all three business segments.

PROSPECTS: Higher revenues and stronger profits are being attained by each business unit. With the recent integration of the School Publishing Company, MHP is expecting strong results from its school publishing business. The Company has reported that first quarter 1995 results may be negatively affected by increased investments to fuel a strong 1995 adoption cycle in school publishing. MHP is pursuing alliances in the emerging markets of the Asia-Pacific Region.

BUSINESS

THE MCGRAW-HILL COS., INC., a multimedia publishing and information services company, serves worldwide markets in education,. business, industry, professions and government. It provides information in print through books, magazines and newsletters; on-line over electronic networks; over the air by television, satellite and FM sideband; and on software, videotape, facsimile and compact disks. McGraw-Hill produces information in many frequencies instantly, daily, weekly, monthly, annually to meet growing and changing customer requirements in a global marketplace.

BUSINESS LINE ANALYSIS

(12/31/94)	Rev(%)	Inc($000)
Info & Media Services	30.9	108,343
Educat & Pro Publishing	42.1	125,765
Financial Services	27.0	217,212
Total	100.0	451,320

ANNUAL EARNINGS AND DIVIDENDS PER SHARE

	1994	1993	1992	1991	1990	1989	1988
Earnings Per Share	**4.10**	**0.23**	**[1] 3.13**	**3.03**	**3.53**	**[1] 0.82**	**3.83**
Dividends Per Share	**2.32**	**2.28**	**2.24**	**2.20**	**2.16**	**2.05**	**1.84**
Dividend Payout %	**56.6**	**N.M.**	**71.6**	**72.6**	**61.2**	**N.M.**	**48.0**

[1] Before acctg. chg.

ANNUAL FINANCIAL DATA

	1994	1993	1992	1991	1990	1989	1988
RECORD OF EARNINGS (IN MILLIONS):							
Total Revenues	2,760.9	2,195.5	2,050.5	1,943.0	1,938.6	1,789.0	1,818.0
Costs and Expenses	2,155.2	1,992.9	1,692.1	1,601.3	1,546.7	1,689.8	1,627.0
Depreciation & Amort	230.0	139.6	74.3	72.1	66.8	45.9	66.2
Operating Profit	375.7	292.7	284.1	269.6	325.2	273.3	274.3
Inc Bef Taxes on Income	345.4	66.3	267.3	258.3	302.6	86.6	379.6
Income Taxes	142.3	54.8	114.1	110.3	130.1	46.8	194.1
Net Income	203.1	11.4	[1] 153.2	148.0	172.5	[2] 39.8	185.5
Aver. Shs. Outstg. (000)	49,499	49,189	48,889	48,821	48,819	48,725	48,475
[1] Before acctg. change dr$124,587,000. [2] Before acctg. change cr$8,000,000.							
BALANCE SHEET (IN MILLIONS):							
Cash and Cash Equivalents	8.1	48.0	13.2	16.6	20.6	34.6	24.5
Receivables, Net	781.0	731.1	617.6	624.2	655.3	498.1	489.2
Inventories	213.3	215.2	188.5	192.1	188.0	166.5	309.8
Gross Property	788.7	753.5	669.6	646.1	620.5	533.2	518.0
Accumulated Depreciation	442.9	408.1	384.9	357.5	328.9	299.7	274.4
Long-Term Debt	657.5	757.6	358.7	437.3	507.6	377.6	1.9
Net Stockholders' Equity	913.1	823.0	908.8	999.0	954.3	880.2	922.8
Total Assets	3,008.5	3,084.2	2,508.1	2,525.2	2,533.6	2,208.2	1,758.4
Total Current Assets	1,124.1	1,131.8	911.0	942.3	961.1	839.7	883.7
Total Current Liabilities	1,008.0	1,068.9	840.7	818.7	844.7	792.5	726.3
Net Working Capital	116.1	62.9	70.3	123.6	116.4	47.2	157.5
Year End Shs Outstg (000)	49,672	49,414	49,134	49,049	48,932	44,014	48,531
STATISTICAL RECORD:							
Operating Profit Margin %	13.6	2.9	13.9	13.9	16.8	3.0	6.9
Book Value Per Share	18.4	16.7	18.5	20.4	19.5	20.0	19.0
Return on Equity %	22.2	1.4	16.9	14.8	18.1	4.5	20.1
Return on Assets %	6.8	0.4	6.1	5.9	6.8	1.8	10.5
Average Yield %	3.3	3.5	3.7	3.8	4.3	2.9	3.0
P/E Ratio	18.8-15.2	N.M	21.2-16.9	21.4-16.4	17.3-11.3	N.M	19.8-12.2
Price Range	77¼-62½	75¼-55¼	66½-53	64¾-49¾	61⅛-39⅞	86⅛-53½	76-46¾

Statistics are as originally reported.

OFFICERS:
J.L. Dionne, Chmn. & C.E.O.
H. McGraw, III, Pres. & C.O.O.
R.J. Bahash, Exec. V.P. & C.F.O.
R.N. Landes, Exec. V.P., Sec. & Couns.

INCORPORATED: NY, Dec., 1925

PRINCIPAL OFFICE: 1221 Avenue of the Americas, New York, NY 10020

TELEPHONE NUMBER: (212) 512-2000
FAX: (212) 512-3514
NO. OF EMPLOYEES: 15,339
ANNUAL MEETING: In April
SHAREHOLDERS: 5,606
INSTITUTIONAL HOLDINGS:
No. of Institutions: 372
Shares Held: 31,767,072

REGISTRAR(S): Chemical Bank, New York, NY

TRANSFER AGENT(S): Chemical Bank, New York, NY

NYS SYMBOL MDT
Rec. Pr. 73½

MEDTRONIC, INC.

YIELD 0.6%
P/E RATIO 30.8

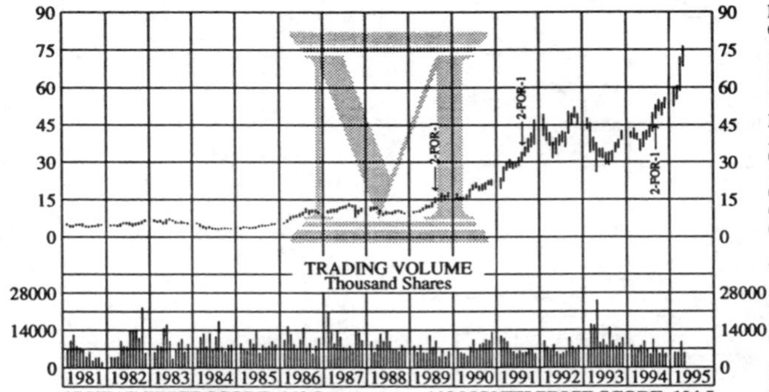

*7 YEAR PRICE SCORE 142.5 *12 MONTH PRICE SCORE 124.5
*NYSE COMPOSITE INDEX=100

INTERIM EARNINGS (Per Share):

Qtr.	July	Oct.	Jan.	Apr.
1991-92	0.31	0.33	0.33	0.40
1992-93	0.39	0.51	0.40	0.49
1993-94	0.46	0.49	0.50	0.59
1994-95	0.57	0.61	0.62	...

INTERIM DIVIDENDS (Per Share):

Amt.	Decl.	Ex.	Rec.	Pay.
0.205Q	6/22/94	7/1/94	7/8/94	7/29/94
100%	8/31	9/30	9/15	9/29
0.1025Q	9/22	10/7	10/14	10/28
0.1025Q	12/1	12/30	1/6/95	1/27/95
0.1025Q	3/8/95	4/3/95	4/7	4/30

Indicated div.: $0.41*

CAPITALIZATION (4/30/94):

	($000)	(%)
Long-Term Debt	20,232	1.8
Deferred Income Tax	15,915	1.5
Common & Surplus	1,053,492	96.7
Total	1,089,639	100.0

DIVIDEND ACHIEVER STATUS:
Rank: 53 1984-94 Growth Rate: 15.0%
Total Years of Dividend Growth: 17

RECENT DEVELOPMENTS: For the quarter ended 1/27/95, net income increased 24.5% to $71.4 million compared with $56.9 million in the previous year. Sales were up 23.6% to $413.7 million from $334.6 million in the corresponding period of 1993. The improved results reflect the impact of new product introductions in markets around the world. Pacemaker volume and revenue growth was driven by the new Thera product line and the Model 9790 pacemaker programmer.

PROSPECTS: New product introductions are favorably affecting operating results in all major world markets. European, Canadian and Japanese revenues are particularly strong due primarily to physician acceptance of MDT's latest pacing technologies, the Jewel PCD devices for tachycardia (abnormally fast heartbeats) and Thera for bradycardia (abnormally slow heartbeats). Separately, the Company maintains a strong balance sheet that features a very low level of long-term debt.

BUSINESS

MEDTRONIC, INC. is a medical technology company serving the worldwide marketplace with technically sophisticated products and services designed to improve cardiovascular and neurological health. The Company is a major provider of prosthetic heart valves, membrane oxygenators, therapeutic catheters, vascular graphs, nerve and muscle stimulation devices, drug delivery systems and other products. The Company's activities are grouped in five medical categories: bradycardia pacing, tachyarrhythmia management, cardiovascular surgery, vascular therapy and neurological stimulation. Most of its products are physcian prescribed therapeutic devices.

BUSINESS LINE ANALYSIS

(4/30/94)	Rev(%)	Inc(%)
United States	61.3	63.5
Europe	25.7	16.1
Other International	13.0	20.4
Total	100.0	100.0

ANNUAL EARNINGS AND DIVIDENDS PER SHARE

	4/30/94	4/30/93	4/30/92	4/30/91	4/30/90	4/30/89	4/30/88
Earnings Per Share	**2.03**	**[1] 1.78**	**1.36**	**1.13**	**1.01**	**0.92**	**0.79**
Dividends Per Share	**0.31**	**0.26**	**[2] 0.23**	**0.19**	**[3] 0.17**	**0.14**	**0.12**
Dividend Payout %	**15.3**	**14.6**	**16.9**	**16.8**	**16.8**	**15.2**	**15.2**

Note: 100%stk.div.9/29/94. [1] Before acctg. chg. [2] 2-for-1 stk split,08/30/91 [3] 2-for-1 stock split, 8/89.

ANNUAL FINANCIAL DATA

	4/30/94	4/30/93	4/30/92	4/30/91	4/30/90	4/30/89	4/30/88
RECORD OF EARNINGS (IN MILLIONS):							
Total Revenues	1,390.9	1,328.2	1,176.9	1,021.4	836.6	741.7	653.3
Costs and Expenses	979.7	1,033.1	871.5	768.5	632.2	567.4	494.2
Depreciation & Amort	78.6	69.6	59.4	46.5	39.4	44.6	29.0
Operating Profit	489.0	410.1	355.2	295.9	244.3	195.6	183.2
Earn Bef Income Taxes	346.8	313.5	242.9	196.2	159.9	150.4	131.1
Income Taxes	114.4	101.9	81.4	62.9	51.2	52.9	44.6
Net Income	232.4	[1] 211.6	161.5	133.4	108.7	97.4	86.5
Aver. Shs. Outstg. (000)	114,808	118,832	119,212	118,580	108,028	106,748	109,516
[1] Before acctg. change dr$14,356,000.							
BALANCE SHEET (IN MILLIONS):							
Cash and Cash Equivalents	181.4	156.0	110.4	113.0	51.6	51.3	78.5
Receivables, Net	340.9	350.0	332.9	300.0	253.1	211.1	202.6
Inventories	213.3	189.1	173.2	139.4	128.0	119.6	107.3
Gross Property	609.9	550.5	497.6	426.0	360.4	307.2	264.3
Accumulated Depreciation	308.2	267.7	240.8	208.8	182.3	155.9	136.0
Long-Term Debt	20.2	10.9	8.6	7.9	8.0	7.8	9.1
Net Stockholders' Equity	1,053.5	841.5	796.5	683.2	541.0	473.6	395.9
Total Assets	1,623.3	1,286.5	1,163.5	1,024.1	856.5	759.6	640.8
Total Current Assets	845.9	774.7	695.9	612.1	478.8	421.2	420.8
Total Current Liabilities	439.4	348.1	308.6	292.0	260.4	231.6	188.8
Net Working Capital	406.4	426.6	387.3	320.1	218.3	189.6	232.1
Year End Shs Outstg (000)	116,258	115,640	118,862	119,064	108,440	107,120	106,560
STATISTICAL RECORD:							
Operating Profit Margin %	23.9	20.9	20.9	20.2	19.7	17.5	19.9
Book Value Per Share	5.90	6.07	5.56	4.56	3.67	3.03	3.20
Return on Equity %	22.1	25.1	20.3	19.5	20.1	20.6	21.9
Return on Assets %	14.3	16.4	13.9	13.0	12.7	12.8	13.5
Average Yield %	0.8	0.6	0.7	1.0	1.2	1.4	1.1
P/E Ratio	23.5-12.7	29.4-17.8	34.8-14.2	20.4-13.1	17.6-9.5	13.7-9.4	17.2-10.1
Price Range	47¾-25⅞	52¼-31⅝	47⅛-19¼	23-14¾	17¾-9⅝	12½-8⅝	13⅝-8

Statistics are as originally reported.

OFFICERS:
W.R. Wallin, Chmn.
W.W. George, Pres. & C.E.O.
R.L. Ryan, Sr. V.P. & C.F.O.
R.E. Lund, Sr. V.P., Gen. Counsel & Sec.

INCORPORATED: MN, 1957

PRINCIPAL OFFICE: 7000 Central Avenue N.E., Minneapolis, MN 55432-3576

TELEPHONE NUMBER: (612) 574-4000
FAX: (612) 574-4879
NO. OF EMPLOYEES: 9,856
ANNUAL MEETING: In August
SHAREHOLDERS: 12,276
INSTITUTIONAL HOLDINGS:
No. of Institutions: 449
Shares Held: 40,014,705

REGISTRAR(S): Norwest Trust Company, New York, NY
Chase Manhattan Bank, N.A., New York, NY 10031

TRANSFER AGENT(S): Norwest Trust Company, New York, NY
Chase Manhattan Bank, N.A., New York, NY 10031

MERCANTILE BANKSHARES CORP.

| | | | YIELD | 3.8% |
| | | | P/E RATIO | 11.1 |

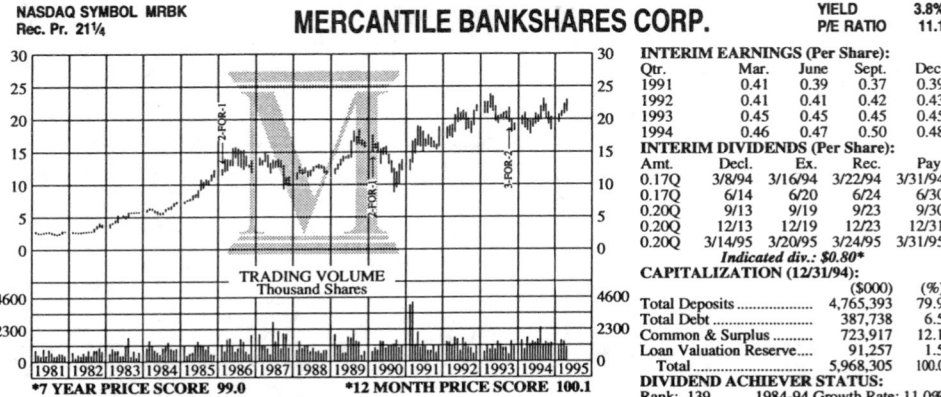

INTERIM EARNINGS (Per Share):

Qtr.	Mar.	June	Sept.	Dec.
1991	0.41	0.39	0.37	0.39
1992	0.41	0.41	0.42	0.43
1993	0.45	0.45	0.45	0.45
1994	0.46	0.47	0.50	0.48

INTERIM DIVIDENDS (Per Share):

Amt.	Decl.	Ex.	Rec.	Pay.
0.17Q	3/8/94	3/16/94	3/22/94	3/31/94
0.17Q	6/14	6/20	6/24	6/30
0.20Q	9/13	9/19	9/23	9/30
0.20Q	12/13	12/19	12/23	12/31
0.20Q	3/14/95	3/20/95	3/24/95	3/31/95

Indicated div.: $0.80*

CAPITALIZATION (12/31/94):

	($000)	(%)
Total Deposits	4,765,393	79.9
Total Debt	387,738	6.5
Common & Surplus	723,917	12.1
Loan Valuation Reserve	91,257	1.5
Total	5,968,305	100.0

DIVIDEND ACHIEVER STATUS:
Rank: 139   1984-94 Growth Rate: 11.0%
Total Years of Dividend Growth: 18

TRADING VOLUME
Thousand Shares

7 YEAR PRICE SCORE 99.0   **12 MONTH PRICE SCORE 100.1**
*NYSE COMPOSITE INDEX=100

RECENT DEVELOPMENTS: For the year ended 12/31/94, net income climbed 8.4% to $90.4 million from $83.5 million a year earlier. Total interest income was $403.4 million, up 4.5% from $385.9 million the year before. The provision for loan losses totaled $7.1 million compared with $13.0 million in the prior year, a decrease of 45.6%. Total assets at year-end were $5.94 billion. Total non-performing assets fell 50.6% to $43.8 million from $88.7 million a year earlier.

Deposits increased moderately to $4.77 billion from $4.74 billion in the comparable 1993 period. Return on average assets was 1.52% versus 1.48% in 1993. For the quarter ended 12/31/94, net income rose 6.5% to $22.9 million from $21.5 million in the corresponding 1993 quarter. Total interest income was $107.4 million, a gain of 10.9% over $96.8 million in the 1993 quarter.

BUSINESS

MERCANTILE BANKSHARES CORPORATION is a bank holding company that owns substantially all of the outstanding shares of capital stock of twenty banks, the Affiliated Banks. The Affiliated Banks are engaged in a general commerical and retail banking business with normal banking services, including acceptance of demand, savings and time deposits and the making of various types of loans. Mercantile-Safe Deposit and Trust Company offers a full range of personal trust services, investment management services and (for corporate and institutional customers) investment advisory, financial and pension and profit sharing services. The Company also owns all of the outstanding shares of Mercantile Mortgage Corporation, a mortgage banking company, MBC Agency, Inc., an insurance agency and MBC Realty, Inc., which owns and operates various properties used by Mercantile-Safe Deposit and Trust Company.

ANNUAL EARNINGS AND DIVIDENDS PER SHARE

	1994	1993	1992	1991	1990	1989	1988
Earnings Per Share	1.88	1.80	☐ 1.67	1.56	1.55	1.40	1.39
Dividends Per Share	0.74	0.64	0.58	0.57	0.543	☐ 0.483	0.416
Dividend Payout %	39.4	35.6	34.7	36.5	35.0	30.2	29.9

☐ 3-for-2 stock split,10/01/93 ☐ 2-for-1 stock split, 12/31/89.

ANNUAL FINANCIAL DATA

RECORD OF EARNINGS (IN MILLIONS):

Total Interest Income	403.4	370.8	394.6	436.2	431.0	374.4	308.3
Total Interest Expense	140.4	133.2	166.1	227.6	230.9	194.1	154.9
Net Interest Income	263.0	237.6	228.5	208.6	200.1	180.3	153.4
Credit Loss Provision	7.1	12.6	45.3	20.9	15.0	9.2	8.7
Net Income	90.4	82.4	76.3	70.6	68.9	62.0	53.4
Aver. Shs. Outstg. (000)	48,166	45,901	47,827	45,182	44,470	38,770	38,505

BALANCE SHEET (IN MILLIONS):

Cash & Due From Banks	257.0	161.5	212.9	201.0	237.6	217.7	211.8
Loans & Lse Financing, Net	3,846.8	3,487.6	3,401.2	3,309.0	3,258.3	2,851.1	2,582.2
Total Domestic Deposits	4,765.4	4,524.0	4,517.2	4,273.9	3,988.1	3,367.4	3,011.1
Long-term Debt	31.5	32.4	15.1	16.6	17.3	23.1	28.9
Net Stockholders' Equity	723.9	654.9	598.1	542.1	486.6	402.3	353.3
Total Assets	5,938.2	5,554.0	5,459.6	5,182.9	4,885.6	4,018.0	3,642.5
Year End Shs Outstg (000)	48,114	45,997	45,777	45,374	44,572	39,027	38,568

STATISTICAL RECORD:

Return on Assets %	1.52	1.48	1.40	1.36	1.41	1.54	1.47
Return on Equity %	12.50	12.60	12.80	13.00	14.20	15.40	15.10
Book Value Per Share	15.05	14.24	13.07	11.95	10.92	10.31	9.16
Average Yield %	3.6	3.1	3.0	3.7	4.1	3.2	3.5
P/E Ratio	12.3-9.4	13.3-10.0	13.2-10.2	12.2-7.8	11.4-5.7	11.5-7.3	9.4-7.8
Price Range	23⅛-17¾	23⅞-18	22⅛-17	19-12⅛	17⅝-8⅞	18⅜-11⅝	13⅛-10⅞

Statistics are as originally reported.

LOAN DISTRIBUTION

(12/31/94)	($000)	(%)
Commercial	1,311,064	33.6
Mortgage	1,804,621	46.2
Construction	311,806	8.0
Consumer	477,694	12.2
Total	3,905,185	100.0

OFFICERS:
H.F. Baldwin, Chmn. & C.E.O.
D.W. Dodge, Vice-Chmn.
E.K. Dunn, Jr., Pres.
K.A. Bourne, Jr., Exec. V.P. & Treas.
J.A. O'Connor, Jr., Sr. V.P. & Sec.

INCORPORATED: MD, May, 1969

PRINCIPAL OFFICE: Two Hopkins Plaza
P.O. Box 1477, Baltimore, MD 21203

TELEPHONE NUMBER: (410) 237-5900

NO. OF EMPLOYEES: 2,845

ANNUAL MEETING: In April

SHAREHOLDERS: 8,538

INSTITUTIONAL HOLDINGS:
No. of Institutions: 117
Shares Held: 12,972,248

REGISTRAR(S):

TRANSFER AGENT(S): Mercantile Safe &
Deposit Trust Co., Baltimore, MD 21203

NYS SYMBOL MRK
Rec. Pr. 44¼

MERCK & CO., INC.

YIELD 2.7%
P/E RATIO 18.6

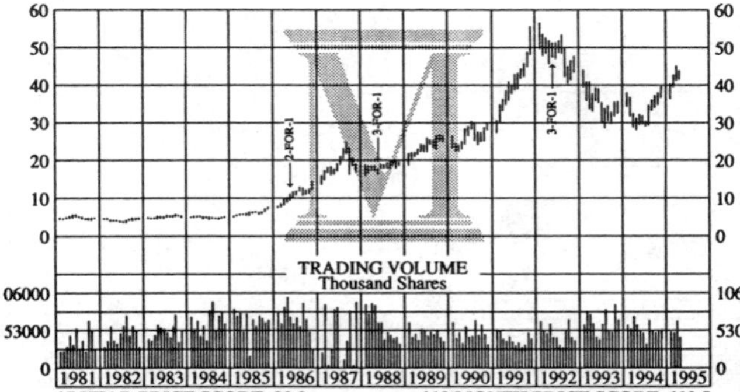

*7 YEAR PRICE SCORE 90.2 *12 MONTH PRICE SCORE 112.5

*NYSE COMPOSITE INDEX=100

INTERIM EARNINGS (Per Share):

Qtr.	Mar.	June	Sept.	Dec.
1991	0.42	0.48	0.48	0.46
1992	0.48	0.56	0.55	0.53
1993	0.54	0.15	0.62	0.56
1994	0.54	0.61	0.62	0.61

INTERIM DIVIDENDS (Per Share):

Amt.	Decl.	Ex.	Rec.	Pay.
0.28Q	2/22/94	3/2/94	3/8/94	4/1/94
0.28Q	5/24	6/2	6/8	7/1
0.30Q	7/26	9/2	9/9	10/1
0.30Q	11/22	12/2	12/8	1/2/95
0.30Q	2/28/95	3/3/95	3/9/95	4/3

Indicated div.: $1.20

CAPITALIZATION (12/31/94):

	($000)	(%)
Long-Term Debt	1,145,900	8.5
Minority Interest	1,208,800	9.0
Common & Surplus	11,139,000	82.5
Total	13,493,700	100.0

DIVIDEND ACHIEVER STATUS:
Rank: 13 1984-94 Growth Rate: 21.2%
Total Years of Dividend Growth: 11

RECENT DEVELOPMENTS: For the year ended 12/31/94, net income increased 38.4% to $3.00 billion compared with $2.17 billion a year earlier. Sales rose 42.6% to $14.97 billion from $10.50 billion. Prior-year results included a restructuring charge of $521 million. Sales gains were attributable to the Company's newer products and the continued growth of the Merck-Medco Managed Care Division. Merck has entered definitive agreements to sell two divisions unrelated to the core human and animal-health businesses.

PROSPECTS: Operating results will be enhanced by the ongoing realization of synergies between Merck and the Medco Managed Care Division, which was acquired in late 1993. The number of patients participating in disease management programs, for patients with chronic diseases, is rising. MRK continues to focus on cost-containment and productivity initiatives. Approximately $350 million in costs will be eliminated by the end of 1996. Pricing pressures will continue to affect pharmaceutical margins.

BUSINESS

MERCK & CO., INC. is engaged in the business of discovering, developing, producing, and marketing products and services for the maintenance or restoration of health. Merck's human and animal health products include therapeutic and preventive agents for the treatment of human disorders. Human and animal health products also include poultry-breeding stock, agricultural chemicals, antihypertensive and cardiovascular products. Animal health/agricultural products include anthelmintics and antiparasitics for the control of parasites. The Merck-Medco U.S. Managed Care Division markets medicines to managed-care organizations and Medco's pharmaceutical-care services to health benefit sponsors in the United States.

QUARTERLY DATA

(12/31/94)	Rev	Inc
1st Quarter	3,514,300	675,200
2nd Quarter	3,792,000	764,100
3rd Quarter	3,792,000	784,800
4th Quarter	3,871,500	773,000

ANNUAL EARNINGS AND DIVIDENDS PER SHARE

	1994	1993	1992	1991	1990	1989	1988
Earnings Per Share	2.38	1.87	[1] 2.12	1.83	1.52	1.26	1.02
Dividends Per Share	1.14	1.03	[2] 0.92	0.77	0.637	0.547	[3] 0.426
Dividend Payout %	47.9	55.1	43.4	42.1	41.9	43.4	41.9

[1] Before acctg. chg. [2] 3-for-1 stk split, 5/26/92 [3] 3-for-1 stk. split, 5/88.

ANNUAL FINANCIAL DATA

	1994	1993	1992	1991	1990	1989	1988
RECORD OF EARNINGS (IN MILLIONS):							
Total Revenues	14,969.8	10,498.2	9,662.5	8,602.7	7,671.5	6,550.5	5,939.5
Costs and Expenses	9,689.2	6,972.8	5,867.4	5,239.0	4,766.1	4,092.5	3,867.8
Depreciation & Amort	681.6	386.5	303.6	254.0	254.0	221.7	204.9
Operating Profit	5,829.6	5,086.7	4,603.1	4,097.5	3,505.4	2,986.8	2,535.6
Income Before Taxes	4,415.2	3,102.7	3,563.6	3,166.7	2,698.8	2,283.0	1,871.0
Income Taxes	1,418.2	936.5	1,117.0	1,045.0	917.6	787.6	664.2
Net Income	2,997.0	2,166.2	[1] 2,446.6	2,121.7	1,781.2	1,495.4	1,206.8
Aver. Shs. Outstg. (000)	1,257,200	1,156,500	1,153,500	1,159,900	1,172,100	1,188,300	1,186,800
[1] Before acctg. change dr$462,400,000.							
BALANCE SHEET (IN MILLIONS):							
Cash and Cash Equivalents	2,269.7	1,542.3	1,093.5	1,411.8	1,197.3	1,143.5	1,550.0
Receivables, Net	2,351.5	2,094.3	1,736.9	1,545.5	1,345.8	1,265.6	1,022.8
Inventories	1,660.9	1,641.7	1,182.6	991.3	892.6	779.7	657.7
Gross Property	7,672.9	7,172.8	6,530.9	5,606.8	4,630.5	3,993.9	3,590.5
Accumulated Depreciation	2,376.6	2,278.2	2,259.8	2,102.3	1,908.8	1,701.4	1,519.8
Long-Term Debt	1,145.9	1,120.8	495.7	493.7	124.1	117.8	142.8
Net Stockholders' Equity	11,139.0	10,021.7	5,002.9	4,916.2	3,834.4	3,520.6	2,855.8
Total Assets	21,856.6	19,927.5	11,086.0	9,498.5	8,029.8	6,756.7	6,127.5
Total Current Assets	6,921.7	5,734.6	4,399.7	4,310.8	3,766.3	3,409.8	3,389.3
Total Current Liabilities	5,448.6	5,895.7	3,617.3	2,814.3	2,827.1	1,907.3	1,909.0
Net Working Capital	1,473.1	d161.1	782.4	1,496.5	939.2	1,502.5	1,480.3
Year End Shs Outstg (000)	1,247,826	1,253,935	1,144,698	1,159,529	1,160,974	1,186,224	1,190,220
STATISTICAL RECORD:							
Operating Profit Margin %	30.7	29.9	36.1	36.1	34.6	34.1	31.4
Book Value Per Share	3.15	2.69	4.24	4.24	3.30	2.97	2.40
Return on Equity %	26.9	21.6	48.9	43.2	46.5	42.5	42.3
Return on Assets %	13.7	10.9	22.1	22.3	22.2	22.1	19.7
Average Yield %	3.4	2.8	1.9	1.9	2.4	2.4	2.4
P/E Ratio	16.6-11.8	23.6-15.3	26.7-19.1	30.4-15.0	20.0-14.7	21.3-14.9	19.5-15.7
Price Range	39½-28⅛	44⅛-28⅝	56⅝-40½	55⅝-27⅜	30⅜-22⅜	26⅞-18¾	19⅞-16

Statistics are as originally reported.

OFFICERS:
R.V. Gilmartin, Chmn., Pres. & C.E.O.

INCORPORATED: NJ, Jun., 1927

PRINCIPAL OFFICE: One Merck Drive P.O. Box 100, Whitehouse Station, NJ 08889-0100

TELEPHONE NUMBER: (908) 423-1000

NO. OF EMPLOYEES: 47,500

ANNUAL MEETING: In April

SHAREHOLDERS: 244,700

INSTITUTIONAL HOLDINGS:
No. of Institutions: 1,003
Shares Held: 216,134,848

REGISTRAR(S): Norwest Bank, South St. Paul, MN

TRANSFER AGENT(S): Norwest Bank, South St. Paul, MN

MIDDLESEX WATER CO.

YIELD 6.8%
P/E RATIO 15.4

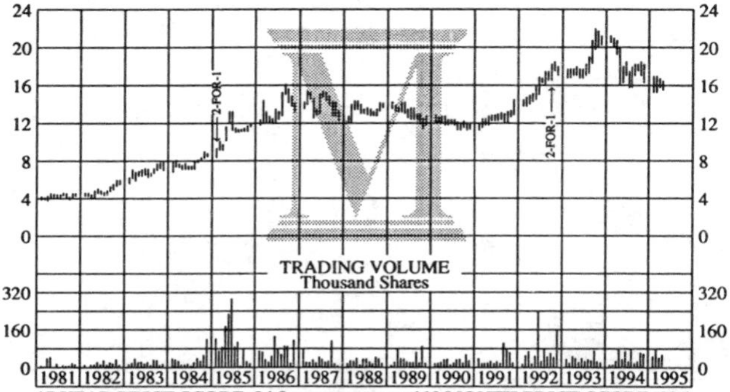

7 YEAR PRICE SCORE 94.3 **12 MONTH PRICE SCORE 90.1**
*NYSE COMPOSITE INDEX=100

INTERIM EARNINGS (Per Share):

Qtr.	Mar.	June	Sept.	Dec.
1991	0.16	0.31	0.47	0.21
1992	0.24	0.32	0.35	0.30
1993	0.27	0.34	0.46	0.26
1994	0.29	0.37	0.39	0.28

INTERIM DIVIDENDS (Per Share):

Amt.	Decl.	Ex.	Rec.	Pay.
0.2625Q	4/29/94	5/10/94	5/16/94	6/1/94
0.2625Q	7/26	8/9	8/15	9/1
0.27Q	10/27	11/8	11/15	12/1
0.27Q	1/30/95	2/9/95	2/15/95	3/1/95
0.27Q	5/1	5/9	5/15	6/1

*Indicated div.: $1.08**

CAPITALIZATION (12/31/94):

	($000)	(%)
Long-Term Debt	49,500	45.3
Deferred Income Tax	12,219	11.2
Preferred Stock	2,790	2.5
Common & Surplus	44,851	41.0
Total	109,361	100.0

DIVIDEND ACHIEVER STATUS:
Rank: 295   1984-94 Growth Rate: 4.0%
Total Years of Dividend Growth: 22

RECENT DEVELOPMENTS: For the year ended 12/31/94, net income remained unchanged at $5.5 million versus $5.4 million in the previous year. Operating revenues increased slightly to $36.1 million from $35.5 million in the year before. Lower taxes and interest charges and higher earnings from the Company's Tidewater operations were primary factors in the 2% improvement of net income. Total operating expenses remained relatively stable at $27.6 million, up only 1% from $27.3 million in 1993. The modest increase in operating revenues was attributed to a decrease in consumption across all classes of customers. In the absence of a rate hike, the only increases in revenue are likely to reflect inflationary trends in the overall economy.

BUSINESS

MIDDLESEX WATER COMPANY is engaged in the business of supplying water for domestic, commercial, industrial, and fire protection purposes. Located approximately 30 miles southwest of New York City, the Company supplies water on a retail basis, to a population of 210,000 in South Plainfield, Metuchen, Carteret, Woodbridge, Edison, portions of Clark and, on a wholesale basis, to the Township of Edison and the Borough of Highland Park, Old Bridge Municipal Utilites Authority Borough of Sayreville and, under special contract, to East Brunswick.

REVENUES

(12/31/94)	($000)	(%)
Residential	14,306	39.6
Commercial	4,282	11.9
Industrial	6,598	18.3
Fire Protection	4,352	12.0
Contract Sales	6,322	17.5
Other	262	.7
Total	36,122	100.0

ANNUAL EARNINGS AND DIVIDENDS PER SHARE

	1994	1993	1992	1991	1990	1989	1988
Earnings Per Share	1.33	1.33	1.20	1.14	0.96	0.91	1.14
Dividends Per Share	1.057	1.012	① 0.97	0.945	0.925	0.898	0.868
Dividend Payout %	79.5	76.1	80.8	82.9	96.4	98.6	76.0

① 2-for-1 stk split, 10/2/92

ANNUAL FINANCIAL DATA

RECORD OF EARNINGS (IN THOUSANDS):

	1994	1993	1992	1991	1990	1989	1988
Total Revenues	36,122	35,479	30,861	29,853	26,417	23,499	24,034
Depreciation	2,650	2,376	1,961	1,834	1,592	1,398	1,317
Maintenance	1,550	1,460	1,389	1,295	1,380	1,501	1,418
Prov for Fed Inc Taxes	2,766	3,072	2,351	2,377	1,426	1,415	1,781
Operating Income	8,565	8,225	7,248	7,056	6,013	5,315	5,820
Interest Expense	3,044	3,014	3,267	3,156	2,828	2,998	2,509
Net Income	5,495	5,480	4,462	4,105	3,467	2,987	3,626
Aver. Shs. Outstg.	4,003	3,924	3,568	3,477	3,439	3,090	3,031

BALANCE SHEET (IN THOUSANDS):

	1994	1993	1992	1991	1990	1989	1988
Gross Plant	130,812	125,223	118,525	101,697	99,214	93,218	84,034
Accumulated Depreciation	21,669	19,677	17,796	16,075	14,804	13,675	12,777
Prop, Plant & Equip, Net	109,143	105,547	100,729	85,621	84,411	79,543	71,257
Long-term Debt	49,500	24,500	38,800	45,350	39,350	39,350	39,350
Net Stockholders' Equity	47,641	46,790	44,057	35,608	34,580	34,197	30,078
Total Assets	132,413	125,676	113,843	100,014	93,093	92,058	88,827
Year End Shares Outstg	4,031	3,979	3,891	3,503	3,456	3,423	3,046

STATISTICAL RECORD:

	1994	1993	1992	1991	1990	1989	1988
Book Value Per Share	11.13	10.77	10.29	9.44	9.25	9.21	8.98
Op. Inc/Net PI %	7.8	7.8	7.2	8.2	7.1	6.7	8.2
Dep/Gr. PI %	2.0	1.9	1.7	1.8	1.6	1.5	1.6
Accum. Dep/Gr. PI %	16.6	15.7	15.0	15.8	14.9	14.7	15.2
Return on Equity %	11.5	11.7	10.1	11.5	10.0	8.7	12.1
Average Yield %	5.7	5.2	6.0	7.3	7.7	7.0	6.6
P/E Ratio	16.0-11.8	16.5-12.6	15.4-11.5	12.8-9.9	13.4-11.7	15.7-12.5	12.6-10.5
Price Range	21¼-15¾	22-16¾	18½-13¾	14½-11¼	12⅞-11¼	14¼-11⅜	14⅜-12

Statistics are as originally reported.

OFFICERS:
J.R. Tompkins, Chmn. & Pres.
E.C. Gere, Sr. V.P. & C.F.O.
M.F. Reynolds, V.P., Sec. & Treas.

INCORPORATED: NJ, 1897

PRINCIPAL OFFICE: 1500 Ronson Road, Iselin, NJ 08830-3020

TELEPHONE NUMBER: (908) 634-1500
FAX: (908) 750-5981
NO. OF EMPLOYEES: 137
ANNUAL MEETING: In May
SHAREHOLDERS: 2,244
INSTITUTIONAL HOLDINGS:
No. of Institutions: 24
Shares Held: 742,716

REGISTRAR(S):

TRANSFER AGENT(S): Registrar & Transfer Co., Cranford, NJ 07016

MILLIPORE CORP.

YIELD 1.0%
P/E RATIO 28.3

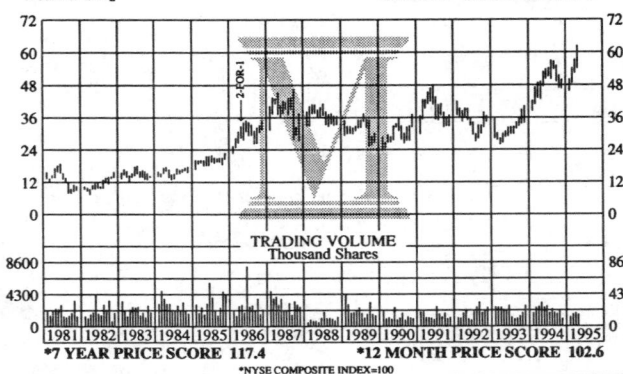

INTERIM EARNINGS (Per Share):

Qtr.	Mar.	June	Sept.	Dec.
1991	0.55	0.56	0.40	0.66
1992	0.30	0.17	0.46	0.24
1993	0.03	0.46	0.38	0.50
1994	0.54	0.62	0.61	0.40

INTERIM DIVIDENDS (Per Share):

Amt.	Decl.	Ex.	Rec.	Pay.
0.14Q	2/10/94	3/21/94	3/25/94	4/22/94
0.15Q	6/9	6/20	6/24	7/22
0.15Q	9/15	10/7	10/14	10/21
0.15Q	12/8	12/23	12/30	1/27/95
0.15Q	2/9/95	3/20/95	3/24/95	4/21

Indicated div.: $0.60*

TRADING VOLUME
Thousand Shares

7 YEAR PRICE SCORE 117.4   *12 MONTH PRICE SCORE 102.6*
*NYSE COMPOSITE INDEX=100

CAPITALIZATION (12/31/94):

	($000)	(%)
Long-Term Debt	100,231	31.2
Common & Surplus	221,277	68.8
Total	321,508	100.0

DIVIDEND ACHIEVER STATUS:

Rank: 148   1984-94 Growth Rate: 10.7%
Total Years of Dividend Growth: 24

RECENT DEVELOPMENTS: For the year ended 12/31/94, income from continuing operations advanced by 22% to $59.6 million from $49.0 million in the year before. MIL increased net sales to $497.3 million, a 12% gain versus $445.4 million in the prior year. The Asia/Pacific region posted an increase of 21% over the previous year, far outpacing the growth of 8% and 7% in the Americas and Europe, respectively. The growth resulted from the boom in sales in the electronics/industrial market.

PROSPECTS: Sales will benefit from demand for new products which include sample handling devices, gas purification products, filter cartridges, DNA sequencing kits and a family of information management systems. Significant opportunity for growth lies in the expanding Asia/Pacific region. MIL's decision to leave the chromatography and non-membrane businesses bodes well for earnings growth as demand heats up for membrane products utilized in the research, environmental, pharmaceutical and biotechnology markets.

BUSINESS

MILLIPORE CORP. manufactures and sells products which are used for the analysis and purification of fluids as well as the analysis, synthesis and sequencing of nucleic acids and peptides. The principal separation and synthesis technologies utilized by the Company are based on membrane filter products. These technologies and products are used in a wide range of industries including the pharmaceutical, biotechnology, microelectronics, environmental, chemical and food and beverage industries.

BUSINESS LINE ANALYSIS

(12/31/94)	Rev(%)	Inc(%)
Americas	36.4	52.7
Europe	31.1	23.2
Pacific	32.5	24.1
Total	100.0	100.0

ANNUAL EARNINGS AND DIVIDENDS PER SHARE

	1994	1993	1992	1991	1990	1989	1988
Earnings Per Share	2.18	1.75	☐ 1.17	2.17	1.00	1.90	1.96
Dividends Per Share	0.58	0.54	☐ 0.50	0.46	0.42	0.38	0.34
Dividend Payout %	26.6	30.9	42.7	21.2	42.0	20.0	17.4

☐ Before acctg. chg. ☐ Bef discont opers

ANNUAL FINANCIAL DATA

RECORD OF EARNINGS (IN THOUSANDS):

	1994	1993	1992	1991	1990	1989	1988
Total Revenues	497,252	445,366	777,001	747,979	703,162	657,515	621,893
Costs and Expenses	378,989	350,399	681,304	633,657	635,821	564,232	522,568
Depreciation & Amort	27,604	23,775	33,993	29,181	28,741	24,757	23,504
Operating Income	90,659	71,192	61,704	85,141	38,600	68,526	75,821
Income Bef Income Taxes	76,915	63,223	51,485	77,915	35,416	67,363	72,728
Income Taxes	17,306	14,225	11,584	17,531	7,615	14,483	18,180
Net Income	☐ 59,609	☐ 48,998	☐ 39,901	60,384	27,801	52,880	54,548
Aver. Shs. Outstg.	27,363	27,951	28,242	27,857	27,870	27,886	27,892

☐ Before disc. op. dr$3,400,000. ☐ Before disc. op. dr$10,851,000; and extra. item dr$3,544,000. ☐ Before acctg. change dr$6,718,000.

BALANCE SHEET (IN THOUSANDS):

Cash and Cash Equivalents	30,236	40,642	70,451	76,261	55,239	57,447	36,211
Receivables, Net	152,008	99,655	182,370	199,782	191,763	168,172	166,717
Inventories	71,209	65,187	161,794	149,205	150,023	137,068	136,019
Gross Property	352,561	357,966	471,441	443,967	404,078	333,361	298,614
Accumulated Depreciation	165,036	163,071	210,377	188,499	168,416	144,120	136,026
Long-Term Debt	100,231	102,047	103,240	102,452	103,347	104,048	104,978
Net Stockholders' Equity	221,277	461,154	452,835	478,160	434,853	406,948	365,547
Total Assets	527,563	702,604	786,957	783,706	734,339	650,621	576,149
Total Current Assets	258,804	356,961	429,965	441,728	411,823	376,469	346,853
Total Current Liabilities	158,155	120,287	206,512	191,017	187,132	130,362	97,576
Net Working Capital	100,649	236,674	223,453	250,711	224,691	246,107	249,277
Year End Shares Outstg	23,133	28,003	27,974	27,956	27,849	27,860	27,919

STATISTICAL RECORD:

Operating Profit Margin %	18.2	16.0	7.9	11.4	5.5	10.4	12.2
Book Value Per Share	9.34	16.37	15.22	16.28	14.72	13.44	12.03
Return on Equity %	26.9	10.6	8.8	12.6	6.4	13.0	14.9
Return on Assets %	11.3	7.0	5.1	7.7	3.8	8.1	9.5
Average Yield %	1.2	1.6	1.4	1.2	1.4	1.2	0.9
P/E Ratio	26.1-17.6	23.0-14.8	35.9-23.2	22.1-13.7	37.3-24.3	19.7-13.3	21.0-16.6
Price Range	57-38⅜	40¼-25⅞	42-27⅛	47⅞-29¾	37¼-24¼	37⅜-25¼	41⅛-32⅝

Statistics are as originally reported.

OFFICERS:
J.A. Gilmartin, Chmn., Pres. & C.E.O.
M.P. Carroll, V.P., C.F.O. & Treas.

INCORPORATED: MA, May, 1954

PRINCIPAL OFFICE: 80 Ashby Road, Bedford, MA 01730-2271

TELEPHONE NUMBER: (617) 275-9200
FAX: (617) 275-5550
NO. OF EMPLOYEES: 3,117
ANNUAL MEETING: In April
SHAREHOLDERS: 5,602 (approx.)
INSTITUTIONAL HOLDINGS:
No. of Institutions: 246
Shares Held: 21,623,422

REGISTRAR(S): First National Bank of Boston, Shareholder Services Division, Boston, MA

TRANSFER AGENT(S): First National Bank of Boston, Shareholder Services Division, Boston, MA

MINE SAFETY APPLIANCES CO.

YIELD 2.4%
P/E RATIO 17.4

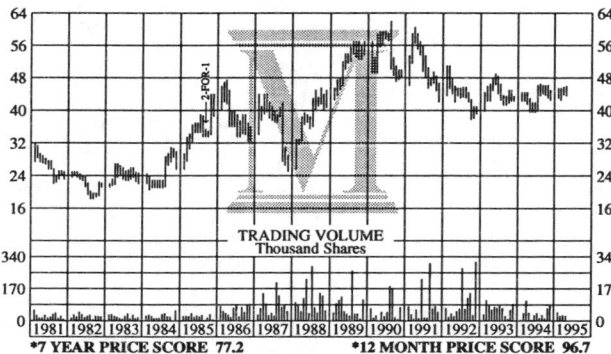

*7 YEAR PRICE SCORE 77.2   *12 MONTH PRICE SCORE 96.7

*NYSE COMPOSITE INDEX=100

INTERIM EARNINGS (Per Share):

Qtr.	Mar.	June	Sept.	Dec.
1991	0.88	0.78	0.72	0.54
1992	0.71	0.98	0.58	0.40
1993	0.41	0.48	0.24	0.60
1994	0.43	0.57	0.78	0.80

INTERIM DIVIDENDS (Per Share):

Amt.	Decl.	Ex.	Rec.	Pay.
0.23Q	6/20/94	8/8/94	8/12/94	9/10/94
0.25Q	10/31	11/14	11/18	12/10
0.25Q	10/31	11/14	11/18	12/10
0.25Q	1/17/95	2/13/95	2/17/95	3/10/95
0.27Q	4/26	5/8	5/12	6/10

*Indicated div.: $1.08**

CAPITALIZATION (12/31/94):

	($000)	(%)
Long-Term Debt	16,564	5.6
Deferred Income Tax	14,424	4.8
Preferred Stock.................	3,569	1.2
Common & Surplus	262,406	88.4
Total	296,963	100.0

DIVIDEND ACHIEVER STATUS:
Rank: 197   1984-94 Growth Rate: 8.9%
Total Years of Dividend Growth: 24

RECENT DEVELOPMENTS: For the year ended 12/31/94, net income increased 45.2% to $15.3 million compared with $10.6 million a year earlier. Sales advanced 7.1% to $459.6 million from $429.2 million in 1993. Operating results included charges related to facilities consolidation and restructuring of $3.1 million. Sales growth was enhanced by the inclusion of HAZCO Services Inc., which was acquired in the second half of 1993. HAZCO equipment rentals to the hazardous materials/environmental market have increased significantly since the acquisition. Earnings growth reflected moderate increases in shipments to the U.S. military, rising sales of instruments and specialty chemicals, stabilized economic conditions in Europe, growth in several overseas markets, and cost reductions achieved through restructuring. In March, MNES announced plans to restructure the Mines Safety Products Division.

BUSINESS

MINE SAFETY APPLIANCES CO.'s primary business is the manufacture and sale of products designed to safeguard the safety and health of workers throughout the world. Principal products include respiratory protective equipment that is air-purifying, air-supplied and self-contained in design. MSA also produces instruments that monitor and analyze workplace environments and control industrial processes. Personal protective products include head, eye and face, body and hearing protectors. For the mining industry, MSA provides mine lighting, rockdusting equipment, firefighting foam and foam application equipment. MSA health-related products include emergency care items, hospital filters and instruments and heart pacemaker power cells. MSA also manufactures specialized high-efficiency space filters with applications ranging from safeguarding clean rooms to the protection of sophisticated electronic equipment. Many of these products have wide application for workers in industries that include manufacturing, public utilities, chemicals, petroleum, construction, transportation, municipal fire departments, the military and hazardous materials clean-up.

ANNUAL EARNINGS AND DIVIDENDS PER SHARE

	1994	1993	1992	1991	1990	1989	1988
Earnings Per Share	2.58	1.73	① ② 2.67	2.92	4.50	4.19	3.67
Dividends Per Share	0.94	0.92	0.89	0.88	0.82	0.73	0.60
Dividend Payout %	36.4	53.2	33.3	30.1	18.2	17.4	16.4

① Before acctg. chg. ② Before disc. oper.

ANNUAL FINANCIAL DATA

RECORD OF EARNINGS (IN THOUSANDS):

	1994	1993	1992	1991	1990	1989	1988
Total Revenues	465,070	435,105	512,121	510,347	482,918	427,044	406,264
Costs and Expenses	414,525	394,656	460,437	452,905	410,232	360,700	343,109
Depreciation	18,527	17,294	16,831	17,927	14,991	13,758	15,255
Operating Profit	35,104	22,932	37,553	39,515	57,695	52,586	47,900
Income Bef Income Taxes	25,826	18,241	27,810	34,956	51,115	45,147	40,997
Income Taxes	10,497	7,686	11,107	16,305	21,911	17,640	16,766
Net Income	15,329	10,555	② 16,703	18,651	29,204	27,507	24,231
Aver. Shs. Outstg.	5,921	6,069	6,225	6,353	6,471	6,545	6,592

② Before disc. op. dr$5,067,000.

BALANCE SHEET (IN THOUSANDS):

Cash and Cash Equivalents	54,420	46,434	55,409	54,636	68,575	44,507	40,187
Receivables, Net	88,698	81,897	75,779	83,962	86,315	77,397	76,872
Inventories	76,966	81,454	87,784	100,452	88,933	87,830	77,242
Gross Property	322,109	306,691	305,908	314,221	307,583	270,263	261,571
Accumulated Depreciation	170,153	153,162	149,763	141,673	130,142	111,535	108,387
Long-Term Debt	16,564	27,476	28,868	23,009	24,606	22,544	19,040
Net Stockholders' Equity	265,975	259,744	263,194	279,176	279,511	249,269	234,729
Total Assets	417,051	407,884	407,772	436,350	443,151	387,106	360,914
Total Current Assets	237,316	224,609	232,412	254,225	258,225	221,270	204,245
Total Current Liabilities	70,822	60,410	55,125	68,770	70,525	57,633	54,093
Net Working Capital	166,494	164,199	177,287	185,455	187,700	163,637	150,152
Year End Shares Outstg	5,816	6,012	6,079	6,276	6,397	6,507	6,588

STATISTICAL RECORD:

Operating Profit Margin %	6.9	5.3	6.8	7.7	11.9	12.3	11.8
Book Value Per Share	45.12	42.61	42.71	43.91	43.14	37.76	35.09
Return on Equity %	5.8	4.1	6.3	6.7	10.4	11.0	10.3
Return on Assets %	3.7	2.6	4.1	4.3	6.6	7.1	6.7
Average Yield %	2.2	2.1	2.0	1.7	1.5	1.5	1.7
P/E Ratio	18.0-15.3	28.3-23.0	19.1-14.1	20.7-14.4	13.8-10.4	13.6-10.1	12.4-6.9
Price Range	46½-39½	49-39¾	51-37¾	60½-42	62-47	57-42½	45½-25½

Statistics are as originally reported.

OFFICERS:
J.T. Ryan, III, Chmn., Pres. & C.E.O.
J.E. Herald, V.P.-Fin. & C.F.O.
D.L. Zeitler, Treas.
D.H. Cuozzo, Sec.

INCORPORATED: PA, Jan., 1917

PRINCIPAL OFFICE: 121 Gamma Dr., RIDC Industrial Park O'Hara Township, Pittsburgh, PA 15238

TELEPHONE NUMBER: (412) 967-3000

FAX: (412) 967-3452

NO. OF EMPLOYEES: 4,500 (approx.)

ANNUAL MEETING: In April

SHAREHOLDERS: 450 (approx.)

INSTITUTIONAL HOLDINGS:
No. of Institutions: 49
Shares Held: 3,094,312

REGISTRAR(S):

TRANSFER AGENT(S): Mellon Bank, N.A., Pittsburgh, PA

NYS SYMBOL MMM
Rec. Pr. 60

MINNESOTA MINING & MANUFACTURING CO.

YIELD 3.1%
P/E RATIO 20.0

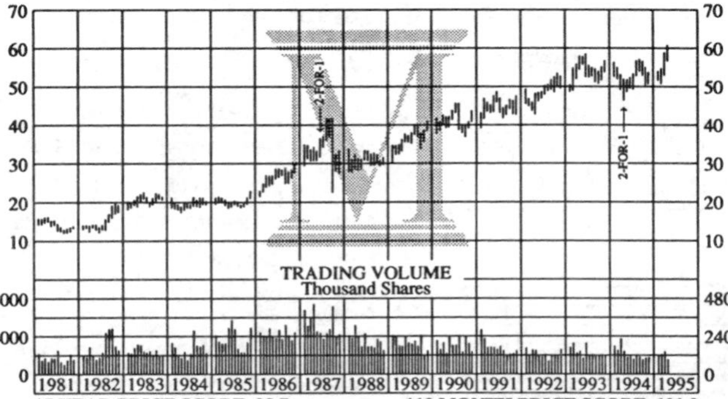

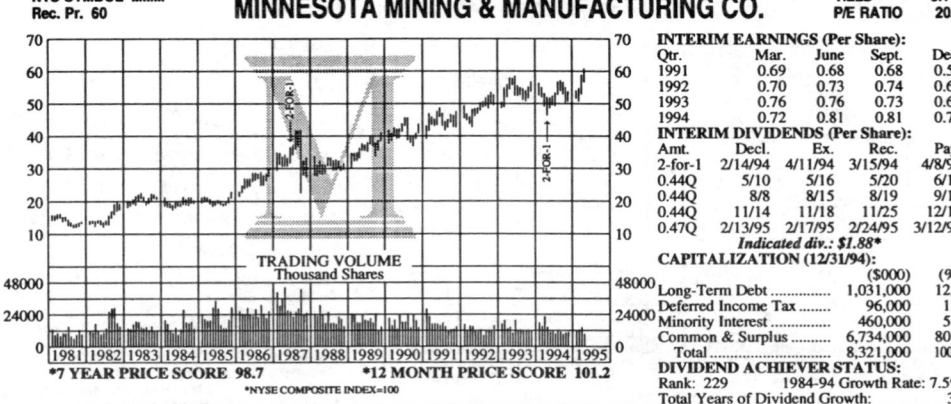

*7 YEAR PRICE SCORE 98.7 *12 MONTH PRICE SCORE 101.2

*NYSE COMPOSITE INDEX=100

INTERIM EARNINGS (Per Share):

Qtr.	Mar.	June	Sept.	Dec.
1991	0.69	0.68	0.68	0.59
1992	0.70	0.73	0.74	0.66
1993	0.76	0.76	0.73	0.66
1994	0.72	0.81	0.81	0.79

INTERIM DIVIDENDS (Per Share):

Amt.	Decl.	Ex.	Rec.	Pay.
2-for-1	2/14/94	4/11/94	3/15/94	4/8/94
0.44Q	5/10	5/16	5/20	6/12
0.44Q	8/8	8/15	8/19	9/12
0.44Q	11/14	11/18	11/25	12/12
0.47Q	2/13/95	2/17/95	2/24/95	3/12/95

*Indicated div.: $1.88**

CAPITALIZATION (12/31/94):

	($000)	(%)
Long-Term Debt	1,031,000	12.4
Deferred Income Tax	96,000	1.2
Minority Interest	460,000	5.5
Common & Surplus	6,734,000	80.9
Total	8,321,000	100.0

DIVIDEND ACHIEVER STATUS:
Rank: 229 1984-94 Growth Rate: 7.5%
Total Years of Dividend Growth: 36

RECENT DEVELOPMENTS: Net income for the quarter ended 12/31/94 increased 16% to $332 million from $286 million for the same quarter in 1993. Net sales for the period rose 11% to $3.86 billion from $3.48 billion in the 1993 fourth quarter. The record results were boosted by a 7% increase in U.S. sales volume and an 11% increase in international sales volume. MMM reported gains in all three of its business sectors, as the Company's focus remained on innovative products and strong service.

PROSPECTS: The Company will continue striving to foster growth through a focus on new product introduction, continuous productivity improvement, enhanced customer satisfaction, and aggressive expansion into foreign markets. MMM continues to experience strong volume gains in Latin America and other Asian countries due to healthy economic conditions. Europe, the Company's largest market outside of the U.S., continues to show signs of strenthening as sales and volume gains continue to improve with the economy.

BUSINESS

MINNESOTA MINING & MANUFACTURING (3M) is a worldwide producer of a diverse variety of industrial and consumer products. The Company operates three business sectors. Industrial and Consumer produces adhesive tapes, abrasives, specialty chemicals, roofing granules, decorative products and products for the aerospace, automotive and industrial markets. Products also include Scotch tape and Post-It notes. Information, Imaging and Electronic products include films, videocassettes, computer disks, electrical tapes, laser imagers and fiber optics. Life Sciences, provides medical products, pharmaceuticals, dental and disposable products, and traffic and personal safety products.

BUSINESS LINE ANALYSIS

(12/31/94)	Rev(%)	Inc(%)
Industrial & Consumer	39.0	44.4
Inform, Imaging & Electr	30.8	13.0
Life Sciences	30.2	42.6
Total	100.0	100.0

ANNUAL EARNINGS AND DIVIDENDS PER SHARE

	1994	1993	1992	1991	1990	1989	1988
Earnings Per Share	3.13	2.91	[1] 2.83	2.63	2.96	2.80	5.09
Dividends Per Share	1.76	1.66	1.60	1.56	1.46	1.30	1.06
Dividend Payout %	56.2	57.1	56.6	59.3	49.4	46.4	20.8

[1] Before acctg. chg.

ANNUAL FINANCIAL DATA

	1994	1993	1992	1991	1990	1989	1988
RECORD OF EARNINGS (IN MILLIONS):							
Total Revenues	15,079.0	14,020.0	13,883.0	13,340.0	13,021.0	11,990.0	10,581.0
Costs and Expenses	11,727.0	10,988.0	10,687.0	10,412.0	9,981.0	9,079.0	8,697.0
Depreciation & Amort	1,101.0	1,076.0	1,087.0	969.0	849.0	761.0	1.0
Operating Income	2,251.0	1,956.0	1,994.0	1,959.0	2,191.0	2,150.0	1,883.0
Income Bef Income Taxes	2,154.0	2,002.0	1,947.0	1,877.0	2,135.0	2,099.0	1,882.0
Income Taxes	771.0	707.0	687.0	691.0	798.0	825.0	728.0
Net Income	1,322.0	1,263.0	[1] 1,236.0	1,154.0	1,308.0	1,244.0	1,154.0
Aver. Shs. Outstg. (000)	423,000	434,000	438,000	440,000	442,000	444,000	454,000
[1] Before acctg. change dr$3,000,000.							
BALANCE SHEET (IN MILLIONS):							
Cash and Cash Equivalents	491.0	656.0	722.0	502.0	591.0	887.0	897.0
Receivables, Net	3,160.0	2,903.0	2,394.0	2,362.0	2,367.0	2,075.0	1,727.0
Inventories	2,763.0	2,401.0	2,315.0	2,292.0	2,355.0	2,120.0	1,831.0
Gross Property	12,403.0	11,488.0	10,828.0	10,080.0	9,383.0	7,938.0	6,665.0
Accumulated Depreciation	7,349.0	6,658.0	6,036.0	5,414.0	4,994.0	4,231.0	3,592.0
Long-Term Debt	1,031.0	796.0	687.0	764.0	760.0	885.0	406.0
Net Stockholders' Equity	6,734.0	6,512.0	6,599.0	6,293.0	6,110.0	5,378.0	5,514.0
Total Assets	13,496.0	12,197.0	11,955.0	11,083.0	11,079.0	9,776.0	8,922.0
Total Current Assets	6,928.0	6,363.0	6,209.0	5,585.0	5,729.0	5,382.0	4,741.0
Total Current Liabilities	3,605.0	3,282.0	3,241.0	3,236.0	3,339.0	2,721.0	2,371.0
Net Working Capital	3,323.0	3,081.0	2,968.0	2,349.0	2,390.0	2,661.0	2,370.0
Year End Shs Outstg (000)	420,000	430,000	438,000	438,000	440,000	446,000	448,000
STATISTICAL RECORD:							
Operating Profit Margin %	14.9	14.0	14.4	14.7	16.8	17.9	17.8
Book Value Per Share	16.03	15.14	15.07	14.37	13.89	12.06	12.31
Return on Equity %	19.6	19.4	18.7	18.3	21.4	23.1	20.9
Return on Assets %	9.8	10.4	10.3	10.4	11.8	12.7	12.9
Average Yield %	3.4	3.1	3.3	3.6	3.5	3.7	3.5
P/E Ratio	18.3-14.8	20.1-16.7	19.0-15.2	18.5-14.9	15.5-12.5	14.6-10.8	13.3-10.9
Price Range	57⅛-46⅜	58½-48⅝	53½-42¾	48¾-39⅛	45¾-36⅞	41-30⅛	33¾-27⅝

Statistics are as originally reported.

OFFICERS:
L.D. DeSimone, Chmn. & C.E.O.
G. Agostini, Sr. V.P.-Fin.

INCORPORATED: MN, Jul., 1902; reincorp., DE, Jun., 1902

PRINCIPAL OFFICE: 3M Center, St Paul, MN 55144

TELEPHONE NUMBER: (612) 733-1110

NO. OF EMPLOYEES: 85,166

ANNUAL MEETING: In May

SHAREHOLDERS: 125,339

INSTITUTIONAL HOLDINGS:
No. of Institutions: 896
Shares Held: 143,773,247

REGISTRAR(S): Norwest Bank Minnesota, N.A., St. Paul, MN

TRANSFER AGENT(S): Norwest Bank Minnesota, N.A., St. Paul, MN

MINNESOTA POWER & LIGHT CO.

YIELD 7.8%
P/E RATIO 15.1

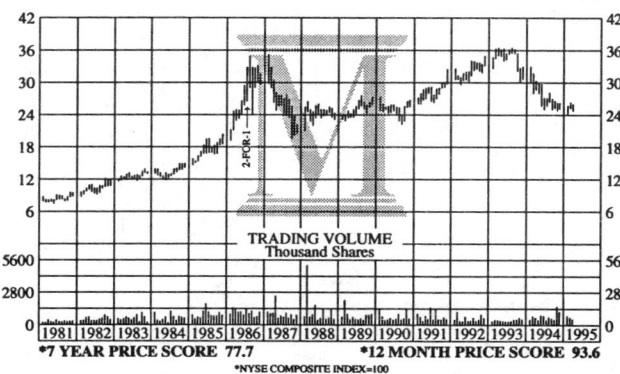

*7 YEAR PRICE SCORE 77.7   ***12 MONTH PRICE SCORE 93.6**
*NYSE COMPOSITE INDEX=100

INTERIM EARNINGS (Per Share):

Qtr.	Mar.	June	Sept.	Dec.
1992	0.54	0.65	0.46	0.66
1993	0.62	0.45	0.59	0.49
1994	0.30	0.44	0.51	0.81

INTERIM DIVIDENDS (Per Share):

Amt.	Decl.	Ex.	Rec.	Pay.
0.505Q	7/27/94	8/9/94	8/15/94	9/1/94
0.505Q	7/27	8/9	8/15	9/1
0.505Q	10/26	11/8	11/15	12/1
0.505Q	10/26	11/8	11/15	12/1
0.51Q	1/25/95	2/9/95	2/15/95	3/1/95

Indicated div.: $2.04*

CAPITALIZATION (12/31/94):

	($000)	(%)
Long-Term Debt	601,317	42.8
Deferred Income Tax	192,441	13.7
Preferred Stock	48,547	3.5
Common & Surplus	561,687	40.0
Total	1,403,992	100.0
Current Debt	12,814	

DIVIDEND ACHIEVER STATUS:
Rank: 284   1984-94 Growth Rate: 4.7%
Total Years of Dividend Growth: 24

RECENT DEVELOPMENTS: For the quarter ended 12/31/94, net income was $23.8 million compared with $14.4 million in the corresponding 1993 period. Revenues were $179.1 million, up 18%. For the year ended 12/31/94, net income was $61.3 million versus $62.6 million a year earlier. Revenues were $637.8 million, up 8% from $589.6 million in 1993. Revenues were higher due in part to a 4% increase in kilowatt-hour sales.

PROSPECTS: MPL and ADESA Corp. have signed a letter of intent to merge. Under the agreement ADESA will become an 80% owned subsidiary of the Company, with ADESA shareholders receiving $17 a share. Earnings could rise sharply as MPL's customers, steel, taconite, paper, and wood-products producers, are expected to run at full capacity until 1996. Near-term dividend growth could be strained due to a high dividend payout ratio.

BUSINESS

MINNESOTA POWER & LIGHT is primarily engaged in the generation, purchase, transmission, distribution and sale of electric energy within a service area of 26,000 square miles located in 16 counties in central and northeastern Minnesota. Electric service in northern Wisconsin is provided by its subsidiary, Superior Water, Light & Power Co., which also sells water and natural gas. Non-electric businesses include BNI Coal, Ltd., which mines and sells lignite coal; Lake Superior Paper Industries, a joint-venture mill that makes super-calendered paper; water and waste-water treatment utilities in Florida and the Carolinas.

REVENUES

(12/31/94)	($000)	(%)
Electric Utility Opers	453,182	71.1
Water Utility Operations	91,224	14.3
Investment & Corporate	93,376	14.6
Total	637,782	100.0

ANNUAL EARNINGS AND DIVIDENDS PER SHARE

	1994	1993	1992	1991	1990	1989	1988
Earnings Per Share	2.06	2.20	①2.31	2.46	2.37	2.90	2.35
Dividends Per Share	2.02	1.98	②1.94	1.90	1.86	1.78	1.72
Dividend Payout %	98.1	90.0	84.0	77.2	78.5	61.4	73.0

① Before extraord. item ② Bef extraord item

ANNUAL FINANCIAL DATA

RECORD OF EARNINGS (IN MILLIONS):

Total Revenues	637.8	505.5	489.4	484.1	477.5	463.9	460.5
Depreciation	50.2	43.5	39.1	37.2	35.7	36.6	40.2
Maintenance	...	26.7	24.8	26.1	26.8	29.0	26.1
Income Taxes	21.5	20.8	19.5	12.2	16.3	14.1	19.6
Operating Income	82.8	77.5	76.9	69.3	72.6	72.2	73.3
Interest Expense	52.1	87.1	95.0	100.3	93.2	89.8	84.2
Net Income	61.3	62.6	①68.5	75.5	74.6	88.9	72.9
Aver. Shs. Outstg. (000)	28,239	26,987	29,442	30,362	29,600	29,044	28,915

① Before extra. item cr$4,831,000.

BALANCE SHEET (IN MILLIONS):

Gross Plant	1,080.4	1,601.7	1,553.4	1,489.3	1,414.5	1,424.3	1,350.3
Accumulated Depreciation	582.1	535.9	505.1	473.4	437.3	425.2	406.4
Prop, Plant & Equip, Net	1,080.4	1,065.9	1,048.2	1,015.9	977.2	999.2	943.9
Long-term Debt	601.3	596.1	542.0	534.0	520.3	517.1	509.0
Net Stockholders' Equity	610.2	611.2	538.0	524.7	578.9	566.6	548.6
Total Assets	1,881.8	1,858.8	1,679.1	1,642.1	1,619.5	1,553.7	1,483.8
Year End Shs Outstg (000)	31,247	31,207	29,453	29,475	31,932	29,105	28,946

STATISTICAL RECORD:

Book Value Per Share	17.98	18.03	16.58	16.02	16.36	17.46	16.86
Op. Inc/Net Pl %	7.7	7.3	7.3	6.8	7.4	7.2	7.8
Dep/Gr. Pl %	3.4	2.7	2.5	2.5	2.5	2.6	3.0
Accum. Dep/Gr. Pl %	40.3	33.5	32.5	31.8	30.9	29.8	30.1
Return on Equity %	10.4	10.6	13.2	15.1	13.5	16.6	14.1
Average Yield %	7.0	6.0	6.0	6.5	7.5	7.0	7.2
P/E Ratio	16.0-12.0	16.6-13.6	14.2-12.0	13.2-10.6	11.6-9.4	9.5-7.9	11.3-8.9
Price Range	33-24¾	36½-30	35-29⅝	32½-26	27⅜-22¼	27⅝-22⅞	26½-21

Statistics are as originally reported.

OFFICERS:
A.J. Sandbulte, Chmn., Pres. & C.E.O.
D.G. Gartzke, Sr. V.P.-Fin. & C.F.O.
J.K. Vizanko, Corp. Treas.
P.R. Halverson, Gen. Couns. & Corp. Sec.

INCORPORATED: MN, 1906

PRINCIPAL OFFICE: 30 West Superior Street, Duluth, MN 55802-2093

TELEPHONE NUMBER: (218) 722-2641
FAX: (218) 723-3996
NO. OF EMPLOYEES: 2,500
ANNUAL MEETING: In May
SHAREHOLDERS: 26,882 (common); 2,671 preferred
INSTITUTIONAL HOLDINGS:
No. of Institutions: 127
Shares Held: 4,561,397

REGISTRAR(S): First Bank - Duluth, Duluth, MN

TRANSFER AGENT(S): At Company's Office

MOBILE GAS SERVICE CORP.

YIELD 5.2%
P/E RATIO 11.2

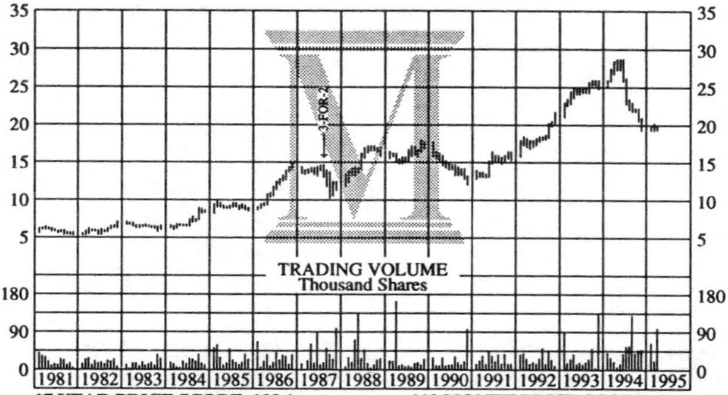

TRADING VOLUME
Thousand Shares

| 1981 | 1982 | 1983 | 1984 | 1985 | 1986 | 1987 | 1988 | 1989 | 1990 | 1991 | 1992 | 1993 | 1994 | 1995 |

*7 YEAR PRICE SCORE 103.1   *12 MONTH PRICE SCORE 82.6

*NYSE COMPOSITE INDEX=100

INTERIM EARNINGS (Per Share):

Qtr.	Dec.	Mar.	June	Sept.
1991-92	0.49	1.07	0.34	0.06
1992-93	0.52	1.07	0.25	d0.05
1993-94	0.57	1.18	0.12	d0.09

INTERIM DIVIDENDS (Per Share):

Amt.	Decl.	Ex.	Rec.	Pay.
0.25Q	3/4/94	3/14/94	3/18/94	4/1/94
0.26Q	6/3	6/13	6/17	7/1
0.26Q	9/2	9/19	9/23	10/1
0.26Q	12/2	12/13	12/19	1/1/95
0.26Q	3/3/95	3/13/95	3/17/95	4/1

Indicated div.: $1.04*

CAPITALIZATION (9/30/94):

	($000)	(%)
Long-Term Debt	59,047	53.4
Deferred Income Tax	7,274	6.6
Common & Surplus	44,251	40.0
Total	110,572	100.0
Current Debt	1,369	

DIVIDEND ACHIEVER STATUS:
Rank: 281   1984-94 Growth Rate: 5.2%
Total Years of Dividend Growth: 17

RECENT DEVELOPMENTS: For the quarter ended 12/31/94, net income fell by more than 50% to $740,000 from $1.6 million in the equivalent period of last year. Total operating revenues declined by 20% to $13.8 million from $17.2 million in the same period of the year before. The unseasonably warmer weather during the quarter resulted in a 29% decrease in volume. Commencement of operations at Bay Gas Storage Co. Ltd. on 9/12/94 lessened the Company's dependency upon outside suppliers for peak demand periods, which had previously affected net income. However, MBLE incurred significantly higher interest and depreciation expenses in association with the Bay Gas investment, which adversely affected this period's results.

BUSINESS

MOBILE GAS SERVICE CORP. is a natural gas utility is engaged principally in the distribution of natural gas to customers in southwest Alabama. The Company serves nearly 100,000 residential, commercial and industrial customers. Gas sales to these customers are categorized as utility operations which are regulated by the Alabama Public Service Commission. Nonutility operations include the delivery of of gas for industrial customers, appliance sales activities, and contract and consulting work for utilities and industrial customers.

REVENUES

(9/30/94)	($000)	(%)
Residential Sales	40,535	67.0
Commercial Sales	9,076	15.0
Industrial-Firm	767	1.3
Industrial-Interruptible	3,554	5.9
Transportation	5,881	9.7
Other	657	1.1
Total	60,470	100.0

ANNUAL EARNINGS AND DIVIDENDS PER SHARE

	9/30/94	9/30/93	9/30/92	9/30/91	9/30/90	9/30/89	9/30/88
Earnings Per Share	1.78	1.79	1.96	1.48	1.01	1.22	1.42
Dividends Per Share	1.02	0.96	0.90	0.86	0.82	0.78	0.74
Dividend Payout %	57.3	53.6	45.9	58.1	81.2	63.9	52.1

ANNUAL FINANCIAL DATA

RECORD OF EARNINGS (IN THOUSANDS):

Total Revenues	63,294	56,817	53,622	50,742	49,050	46,094	58,119
Depreciation & Amort	4,207	3,645	3,029	2,862	2,643	2,377	2,218
Maintenance	1,490	1,249	1,664	1,127	1,077	965	1,075
Prov for Fed Inc Taxes	2,796	2,752	2,074	1,375	953	991	1,618
Interest Expense	3,416	2,909	2,008	2,116	2,123	1,987	1,081
Net Income	4,893	4,920	5,368	4,052	2,765	3,316	3,866
Aver. Shs. Outstg.	2,752	2,733	2,726	2,718	2,709	2,702	2,694

BALANCE SHEET (IN THOUSANDS):

Gross Plant	137,746	110,345	86,414	75,733	72,094	65,172	58,100
Accumulated Depreciation	28,657	26,532	24,233	22,194	20,087	17,979	16,692
Prop, Plant & Equip, Net	109,089	83,813	62,181	53,539	52,007	47,193	41,408
Long-term Debt	59,047	60,416	26,833	14,765	16,205	17,145	9,485
Net Stockholders' Equity	44,251	33,431	31,021	28,004	26,197	25,561	24,263
Total Assets	134,529	116,839	80,531	67,281	62,871	58,750	51,211
Year End Shares Outstg	3,202	2,736	2,729	2,721	2,712	2,705	2,697

STATISTICAL RECORD:

Book Value Per Share	13.82	12.00	11.15	10.07	9.44	9.23	8.77
Dep/Gr. Pl %	2.9	3.1	3.5	3.8	3.7	3.6	3.8
Accum. Dep/Gr. Pl %	20.8	24.0	28.0	29.3	27.9	27.6	28.7
Return on Equity %	11.1	14.7	17.3	14.5	10.6	13.0	15.9
Average Yield %	4.3	4.1	4.8	5.9	5.5	4.8	5.1
P/E Ratio	16.2-10.8	14.5-11.7	11.1-8.6	11.1-8.6	17.6-11.9	14.8-12.1	12.1-8.3
Price Range	28¾-19¼	26-21	21¾-15¾	16½-12¾	17¾-12	18-14¾	17¼-11¾

Statistics are as originally reported.

OFFICERS:
W.J. Hearin, Chmn.
W.L. Hovell, Pres. & C.E.O.
C.P. Huffman, C.F.O., Treasurer & Ass't. Sec.
G.E. Downing, Jr., Sec. & Gen. Couns.

INCORPORATED: AL, May, 1933

PRINCIPAL OFFICE: 2828 Dauphin Street, Mobile, AL 36606

TELEPHONE NUMBER: (205) 476-2720
FAX: (205) 478-5817
NO. OF EMPLOYEES: 260
ANNUAL MEETING: In January
SHAREHOLDERS: 1,628 (shareholders of record)
INSTITUTIONAL HOLDINGS:
No. of Institutions: 18
Shares Held: 315,997

REGISTRAR(S): AmSouth Bank, N.A., Birmingham, AL 35202

TRANSFER AGENT(S): AmSouth Bank, N.A., Birmingham, AL 35202

NYS SYMBOL MTC
Rec. Pr. 82⅛

MONSANTO CO.

YIELD 3.4%
P/E RATIO 15.4

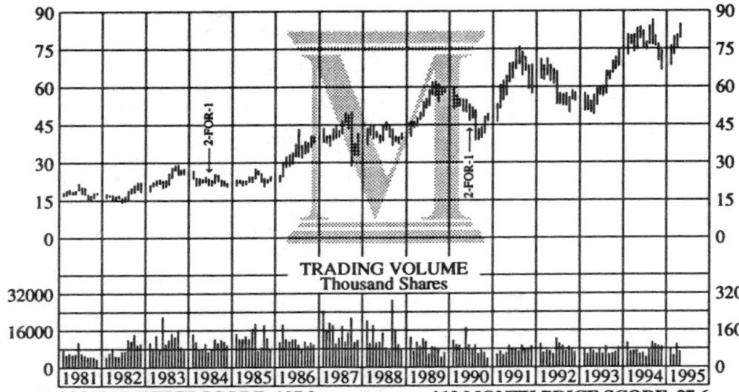

7 YEAR PRICE SCORE 107.9   **12 MONTH PRICE SCORE 97.6**
*NYSE COMPOSITE INDEX=100

INTERIM EARNINGS (Per Share):

Qtr.	Mar.	June	Sept.	Dec.
1992	1.17	0.78	0.39	d3.35
1993	1.17	1.66	0.78	0.49
1994	1.63	2.19	0.99	0.51

INTERIM DIVIDENDS (Per Share):

Amt.	Decl.	Ex.	Rec.	Pay.
0.63Q	7/22	8/8	8/12	9/12
0.63Q	10/28	11/4	11/10	12/12
0.63Q	1/27/95	2/6/95	2/10/95	3/10/95
0.69Q	4/28	5/8	5/12	6/12

*Indicated div.: $2.76**

CAPITALIZATION (12/31/94):

	($000)	(%)
Long-Term Debt	1,405,000	31.8
Deferred Income Tax	65,000	1.5
Common & Surplus	2,948,000	66.7
Total	4,418,000	100.0

DIVIDEND ACHIEVER STATUS:

Rank: 209   1984-94 Growth Rate: 8.2%
Total Years of Dividend Growth: 22

RECENT DEVELOPMENTS: For the year ended 12/31/94, net income was $622.0 million compared with $494.0 million in the year before. Net sales rose by 5% to $8.27 billion from $7.90 billion in the prior year. MTC's chemical division benefited from the improved economy worldwide and reduced costs. The only operating division to post lower year-over-year results was the NutraSweet Company.

PROSPECTS: The Agricultural Group continues to report strong sales of Posilac bovine somatotropin (BST) and Roundup; however, higher raw material costs have cut into margins. The Chemical group is improving results due to the continued strength of the North American automotive, housing, and home furnishings markets coupled with the start of an economic recovery in Western Europe.

BUSINESS

MONSANTO COMPANY is one of the largest chemical companies in the U.S. Products include herbicides, detergents, phosphates, fibers, plastics, resins, rubber, specialty chemicals, control valves, pharmaceuticals, and aspartame. In 1994, sales were derived as follows: agricultural products, 28%; chemicals, 47%; NutraSweet,17%; and Searle, the pharmaceutical division, 8%. Some of the Company's trade names include Lasso and Roundup, herbicides; Saflex, a plastic interlayer; Cytotec, an ulcer preventive drug, Calan, a calcium channel blocker and Equal, Nutrasweet, Simplesse, and Simple Pleasures.

QUARTERLY DATA

(12/31/94)($000)	Rev	Inc
1st Quarter	2,001,000	194,000
2nd Quarter	2,269,000	258,000
3rd Quarter	1,912,000	116,000
4th Quarter	2,090,000	54,000

ANNUAL EARNINGS AND DIVIDENDS PER SHARE

	1994	1993	1992	1991	1990	1989	1988
Earnings Per Share	5.32	4.10	①d1.01	2.33	③4.23	5.02	4.14
Dividends Per Share	2.47	2.30	②2.20	2.045	④1.91	1.65	1.48
Dividend Payout %	46.4	56.1	...	87.8	45.2	32.9	36.0

① Before disc. oper. & acctg. chg. ② Bef discont opers ③ Before extraord. item ④ 2-for-1 stk split, 6/90

ANNUAL FINANCIAL DATA

RECORD OF EARNINGS (IN MILLIONS):

	1994	1993	1992	1991	1990	1989	1988
Total Revenues	8,272.0	7,902.0	7,763.0	8,864.0	8,995.0	8,681.0	8,293.0
Costs and Expenses	7,268.0	7,011.0	7,468.0	8,055.0	7,851.0	7,377.0	7,107.0
Depreciation & Amort	561.0	572.0	765.0	751.0	739.0	690.0	703.0
Operating Income	923.0	810.0	58.0	570.0	909.0	1,078.0	955.0
Income Bef Income Taxes	895.0	729.0	d174.0	442.0	809.0	1,015.0	893.0
Income Taxes	273.0	235.0	cr48.0	146.0	263.0	336.0	302.0
Net Income	622.0	494.0	①d126.0	296.0	546.0	679.0	591.0
Aver. Shs. Outstg. (000)	112,000	120,000	123,000	127,000	129,000	135,000	143,000

① Before disc. op. cr$578,000,000; and acctg chg dr$540,000,000.

BALANCE SHEET (IN MILLIONS):

	1994	1993	1992	1991	1990	1989	1988
Cash and Cash Equivalents	507.0	273.0	729.0	189.0	204.0	253.0	221.0
Receivables, Net	1,851.0	1,787.0	1,800.0	1,843.0	1,669.0	1,503.0	1,422.0
Inventories	1,212.0	1,224.0	1,156.0	1,349.0	1,270.0	1,197.0	1,170.0
Gross Property	7,555.0	7,382.0	7,602.0	7,902.0	7,620.0	6,937.0	6,926.0
Accumulated Depreciation	4,738.0	4,580.0	4,597.0	4,540.0	4,128.0	3,764.0	3,780.0
Long-Term Debt	1,405.0	1,502.0	1,423.0	1,877.0	1,652.0	1,471.0	1,408.0
Net Stockholders' Equity	2,948.0	2,855.0	3,005.0	3,654.0	4,089.0	3,941.0	3,800.0
Total Assets	8,891.0	8,640.0	9,085.0	9,227.0	9,236.0	8,604.0	8,461.0
Total Current Assets	3,883.0	3,672.0	4,060.0	3,711.0	3,513.0	3,248.0	3,097.0
Total Current Liabilities	2,435.0	2,295.0	2,548.0	2,175.0	2,190.0	1,922.0	1,980.0
Net Working Capital	1,448.0	1,377.0	1,512.0	1,536.0	1,323.0	1,326.0	1,117.0
Year End Shs Outstg (000)	112,000	116,000	120,000	123,000	126,000	132,000	138,000

STATISTICAL RECORD:

	1994	1993	1992	1991	1990	1989	1988
Operating Profit Margin %	11.2	10.3	0.7	6.4	10.1	12.4	11.5
Book Value Per Share	16.20	14.36	16.16	19.22	21.14	17.11	14.57
Return on Equity %	21.1	17.3	...	8.1	13.4	17.2	15.6
Return on Assets %	7.0	5.7	...	3.2	5.9	7.9	7.0
Average Yield %	3.2	3.7	3.6	3.4	3.9	3.2	3.6
P/E Ratio	16.3-12.5	18.3-11.9	...	32.6-19.7	14.2-9.2	12.4-8.0	11.2-8.9
Price Range	86½-66½	75-48⅞	71¼-49¾		76-46	60⅛-38¾	62⅛-40¼	46¼-36¾

Statistics are as originally reported.

OFFICERS:
R.J. Mahoney, Chmn. & C.E.O.
N.L. Reding, Vice-Chmn.
R.B. Shapiro, Pres. & C.O.O.
F.A. Stroble, Sr. V.P. & C.F.O.

INCORPORATED: DE, Apr., 1933

PRINCIPAL OFFICE: 800 N. Lindbergh Blvd., St. Louis, MO 63167

TELEPHONE NUMBER: (314) 694-1000

FAX: (314) 694-8421

NO. OF EMPLOYEES: 30,019

ANNUAL MEETING: In April

SHAREHOLDERS: 56,601

INSTITUTIONAL HOLDINGS:
No. of Institutions: 625
Shares Held: 86,833,782

REGISTRAR(S): First National Bank of Boston, Shareholder Services Division, Boston, MA

TRANSFER AGENT(S): First National Bank of Boston, Shareholder Services Division, Boston, MA

MORGAN (J. P.) & CO. INC.

YIELD 4.6%
P/E RATIO 11.7

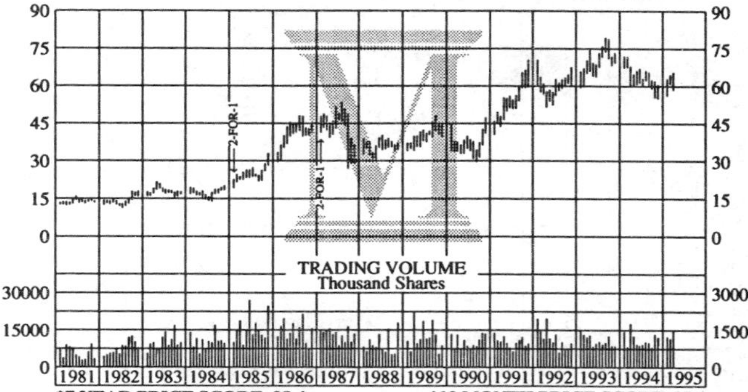

7 YEAR PRICE SCORE 98.4 **12 MONTH PRICE SCORE 97.4**
*NYSE COMPOSITE INDEX=100

INTERIM EARNINGS (Per Share):

Qtr.	Mar.	June	Sept.	Dec.
1993	2.16	2.12	2.30	1.92
1994	1.69	1.73	1.63	0.96
1995	1.27	...	...	...

INTERIM DIVIDENDS (Per Share):

Amt.	Decl.	Ex.	Rec.	Pay.
0.68Q	3/9/94	3/15/94	3/21/94	4/15/94
0.68Q	6/1	6/14	6/20	7/15
0.68Q	9/14	9/20	9/26	10/14
0.75Q	12/14	12/20	12/27	1/13/95
0.75Q	3/8/95	3/14/95	3/20/95	4/14

*Indicated div.: $3.00**

CAPITALIZATION (12/31/94):

	($000)	(%)
Total Deposits	43,085,000	29.3
Total Debt	93,384,000	63.4
Preferred Stock	494,000	0.3
Common & Surplus	9,074,000	6.2
Loan Valuation Reserve	1,131,000	0.8
Total	147,168,000	100.0

DIVIDEND ACHIEVER STATUS:
Rank: 153   1984-94 Growth Rate: 10.5%
Total Years of Dividend Growth: 18

RECENT DEVELOPMENTS: For the year ended 12/31/94, net income was $1.22 billion versus $1.72 billion, before an accounting change, in 1993. Net interest revenue increased to $1.98 billion from $1.77 billion. Noninterest income, suffering from lower underwriting activity, fell 21% to $3.54 billion. Trading revenue was slashed to $1.02 billion from $2.06 billion a year earlier.

PROSPECTS: JPM has implemented a major cost-cutting program to counter the effects interest rates are having on revenue and earnings growth in certain business lines. JPM has not disclosed which areas are slated for cutbacks nor the number of staff positions to be eliminated. The investment management and operational services units continue to show solid income growth.

BUSINESS

J.P. MORGAN & COMPANY INC., a $154.9 billion global financial firm, provides a wide range of financial services to corporations, governments, financial institutions, institutional investors, financially sophisticated individuals, private firms, and non-profit organizations. Activities include providing corporate finance advice and executing financing transactions; underwriting, trading, and investing in securities, providing trust, agency, and operational services; and serving as an investment advisor and manager. The Company's principal subsidiary is Morgan Guaranty Trust Company of New York.

LOAN DISTRIBUTION

(12/31/94)	($000)	(%)
Commercial & Industrial	11,498,000	52.1
Financial Institution	5,596,000	25.3
Collateral by Real Estate	694,000	3.2
Foreign Governments	846,000	3.8
Other	3,446,000	15.6
Total	22,080,000	100.0

ANNUAL EARNINGS AND DIVIDENDS PER SHARE

	1994	1993	1992	1991	1990	1989	1988
Earnings Per Share	6.02	8.48	6.92	①5.63	②3.99	d7.04	5.38
Dividends Per Share	2.72	2.40	2.18	1.98	1.82	1.66	1.50
Dividend Payout %	45.2	28.3	38.5	35.2	45.6	...	27.9

① Before extraord. item ② Before acctg. chg.

ANNUAL FINANCIAL DATA

RECORD OF EARNINGS (IN MILLIONS):

Total Interest Income	8,379.0	7,442.0	7,281.0	7,786.0	8,430.0	8,657.0	6,283.0
Total Interest Expense	6,398.0	5,670.0	5,573.0	6,302.0	7,272.0	7,513.0	4,513.0
Net Interest Income	1,981.0	1,772.0	1,708.0	1,484.0	1,158.0	1,144.0	1,770.0
Credit Loss Provision	...	...	55.0	40.0	50.0	2,045.0	200.0
Net Income	1,215.0	1,586.0	1,382.0	①1,114.0	②775.0	d1,275.0	1,002.0

① Before extra. item cr$32,000,000. ② Before acctg. change cr$230,000,000.

BALANCE SHEET (IN MILLIONS):

Cash and Due From Banks	2,210.0	1,008.0	1,149.0	1,555.0	2,200.0	1,951.0	2,561.0
Loans & Lse Financing, Net	20,949.0	23,223.0	25,180.0	26,378.0	25,712.0	26,030.0	26,842.0
Total Domestic Deposits	5,519.0	7,082.0	5,804.0	6,756.0	9,111.0	8,827.0	12,622.0
Total Foreign Deposits	37,566.0	33,320.0	26,715.0	30,220.0	28,446.0	30,331.0	29,847.0
Long-term Debt	6,802.0	5,276.0	5,443.0	5,395.0	4,723.0	4,690.0	4,052.0
Net Stockholders' Equity	9,568.0	9,859.0	7,066.0	6,068.0	5,189.0	4,495.0	5,778.0
Total Assets	154,917.0	133,888.0	102,941.0	103,468.0	93,103.0	88,964.0	83,923.0
Year End Shs Outstg (000)	188,000	193,000	192,000	190,000	186,000	184,000	181,000

STATISTICAL RECORD:

Return on Assets %	0.78	1.29	1.34	1.08	0.83	...	1.19
Return on Equity %	12.70	17.50	19.60	18.40	14.90	...	17.30
Book Value Per Share	48.27	48.52	34.23	29.34	25.24	21.74	30.57
Average Yield %	4.3	3.5	3.6	3.6	4.7	4.0	4.2
P/E Ratio	12.0-9.2	9.4-7.0	10.2-7.4	12.5-7.2	11.8-7.4	...	7.5-5.7
Price Range	72-55⅛	79⅜-59⅜	70½-51½	70½-40½	47¼-29⅝	48⅛-34	40¼-30¾

Statistics are as originally reported.

OFFICERS:
D.A. Warner, III, Chmn., Pres. & C.E.O.
R.G. Mendoza, Vice-Chmn.
K.F. Viermetz, Vice-Chmn.
R.B. Wagner, Vice-Chmn.
J.T. Flynn, C.F.O.
INCORPORATED: DE, Dec., 1968
PRINCIPAL OFFICE: 60 Wall Street, New York, NY 10260-0060

TELEPHONE NUMBER: (212) 483-2323
NO. OF EMPLOYEES: 17,055
ANNUAL MEETING: In May
SHAREHOLDERS: 29,596
INSTITUTIONAL HOLDINGS:
No. of Institutions: 825
Shares Held: 125,975,190

REGISTRAR(S): First Chicago Trust Co. of New York, New York, NY 10008

TRANSFER AGENT(S): First Chicago Trust Co. of New York, New York, NY 10008

MYERS INDUSTRIES INC.

YIELD 1.1%
P/E RATIO 12.4

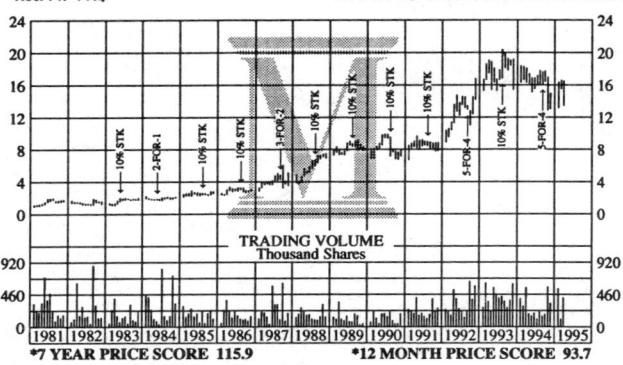

TRADING VOLUME
Thousand Shares

*7 YEAR PRICE SCORE 115.9   *12 MONTH PRICE SCORE 93.7
*NYSE COMPOSITE INDEX=100

INTERIM EARNINGS (Per Share):

Qtr.	Mar.	June	Sept.	Dec.
1992	0.23	0.35	0.24	0.36
1993	0.23	0.30	0.21	0.31
1994	0.23	0.34	0.25	0.35
1995	0.25	...	...	...

INTERIM DIVIDENDS (Per Share):

Amt.	Decl.	Ex.	Rec.	Pay.
5-for-4	7/29/94	9/1/94	8/9/94	8/31/94
0.04Q	7/29	9/6	9/12	10/3
0.04Q	7/29	9/6	9/12	10/3
0.04Q	10/27	12/5	12/9	1/3/95
0.04Q	1/18/95	3/6/95	3/10/95	4/3

Indicated div.: $0.16*

CAPITALIZATION (12/31/94):

	($000)	(%)
Long-Term Debt	4,155	3.0
Deferred Income Tax	2,870	2.1
Common & Surplus	130,909	94.9
Total	137,933	100.0

DIVIDEND ACHIEVER STATUS:
Rank: 153   1984-94 Growth Rate: 10.5%
Total Years of Dividend Growth: 18

RECENT DEVELOPMENTS: For the year ended 12/31/94, net income advanced by 16% to $17.8 million from $15.4 million in the year before. Both operational segments contributed to the record net sales level of $274.1 million, up by 12% from $245.1 million in the previous year. The manufacturing segment benefited from established product lines and the introduction of new products, and increased its sales by 11%. The global economic recovery and specifically strong equipment sales elevated sales in the distribution segment by 14% year-over-year. The higher volumes, which drove the revenue increases and required the increased purchase of raw materials, pushed MYE's cost of goods sold and operating expenses up by 12% and 9%, respectively. The higher costs were the result of the rising prices of resins and rubber.

BUSINESS

MYERS INDUSTRIES, INC. is a diversified manufacturer of reusable plastic storage systems and other polymer and metal products for domestic and international markets, and a specialized nationwide distributor of tools, equipment and supplies for the tire servicing and transportation industries. The Company's manufacturing plants are located in Ohio, Kentucky, North Carolina and Missouri. The Company has 42 aftermarket distribution centers in the United States.

BUSINESS LINE ANALYSIS

(12/31/94)	Rev(%)	Inc(%)
Aftermarket Repair		
Prods..........	42.7	31.8
Polymer & Metal		
Products.................	57.3	68.2
Total	100.0	100.0

ANNUAL EARNINGS AND DIVIDENDS PER SHARE

	1994	1993	1992	1991	1990	1989	1988
Earnings Per Share	1.17	1.05	0.94	0.76	0.78	0.70	0.74
Dividends Per Share	① 0.148	② 0.133	③ 0.12	④ 0.108	⑤ 0.098	⑥ 0.089	0.081
Dividend Payout %	8.4	4.5	12.9	14.2	12.7	12.8	13.9

① 5-for-4 stk split, 8/31/94 ② 10% stk div,08/09/93 ③ 5-for-4 stk split,09/01/92 ④ 10% stk div,08/12/91 ⑤ 10% stk split, 8/31/90 ⑥ 10% stock div, 9/01/89.

ANNUAL FINANCIAL DATA

RECORD OF EARNINGS (IN THOUSANDS):

	1994	1993	1992	1991	1990	1989	1988
Total Revenues	274,054	245,136	229,255	195,581	202,104	194,772	183,811
Costs and Expenses	234,566	211,519	200,154	170,322	175,933	169,832	161,752
Depreciation	8,821	7,077	5,922	5,677	5,399	5,031	4,569
Operating Income	30,666	26,540	23,179	19,583	20,772	19,909	17,489
Income Bef Income Taxes	30,046	25,449	21,837	17,844	17,992	16,216	13,865
Income Taxes	12,215	10,054	8,727	7,308	7,234	6,595	5,797
Net Income	17,831	15,395	13,110	10,536	10,758	9,621	8,068
Aver. Shs. Outstg.	15,300	14,725	14,063	12,602	12,565	12,525	12,482

BALANCE SHEET (IN THOUSANDS):

	1994	1993	1992	1991	1990	1989	1988
Cash and Cash Equivalents	1,795	1,662	3,416	3,156	2,515	2,472	1,633
Receivables, Net	51,227	40,405	38,310	30,605	30,702	30,084	29,127
Inventories	39,382	34,942	30,877	25,132	27,778	26,000	25,239
Gross Property	116,557	105,307	91,976	76,378	70,296	61,046	55,410
Accumulated Depreciation	55,179	47,613	41,313	37,041	31,597	27,033	22,651
Long-Term Debt	4,155	10,655	24,917	14,560	25,362	29,834	38,433
Net Stockholders' Equity	130,909	115,287	83,883	72,454	63,194	53,293	44,767
Total Assets	172,027	152,386	142,081	113,030	116,373	111,104	109,669
Total Current Assets	94,725	78,922	74,892	60,723	63,311	61,479	58,853
Total Current Liabilities	34,094	24,381	31,686	25,346	26,346	26,398	24,796
Net Working Capital	60,631	54,542	43,207	35,377	36,965	35,082	34,057
Year End Shares Outstg	15,300	15,279	14,093	13,876	13,836	13,802	13,745

STATISTICAL RECORD:

	1994	1993	1992	1991	1990	1989	1988
Operating Profit Margin %	11.2	10.8	10.1	10.0	10.3	10.2	9.5
Book Value Per Share	7.74	6.69	4.98	4.45	3.72	2.95	2.24
Return on Equity %	13.6	13.4	15.6	14.5	17.0	18.1	18.0
Return on Assets %	10.4	10.1	9.2	9.3	9.2	8.7	7.4
Average Yield %	0.9	0.7	0.9	1.3	1.2	1.1	1.4
P/E Ratio	15.7-11.0	19.4-14.6	18.0-9.5	12.8-8.7	12.7-8.7	13.3-10.4	12.7-6.3
Price Range	18⅜-12⅞	20⅜-15¼	16⅞-8⅞	9¾-6⅝	9⅞-6¾	9¼-7¼	7½-3¾

Statistics are as originally reported.

OFFICERS:
S.E. Myers, Pres. & C.E.O.
M.I. Wiskind, Sr. V.P. & Sec.
G.J. Stodnick, V.P.-Fin. & C.F.O.

INCORPORATED: OH, Jan., 1955

PRINCIPAL OFFICE: 1293 South Main Street, Akron, OH 44301

TELEPHONE NUMBER: (216) 253-5592

FAX: (216) 253-6568

NO. OF EMPLOYEES: 1,663

ANNUAL MEETING: In April

SHAREHOLDERS: 1,800 (approx.)

INSTITUTIONAL HOLDINGS:
No. of Institutions: 43
Shares Held: 2,867,520

REGISTRAR(S): National City Bank, Cleveland, OH 44114

TRANSFER AGENT(S): National City Bank, Cleveland, OH 44114

NACCO INDUSTRIES INC.

YIELD 1.2%
P/E RATIO 11.0

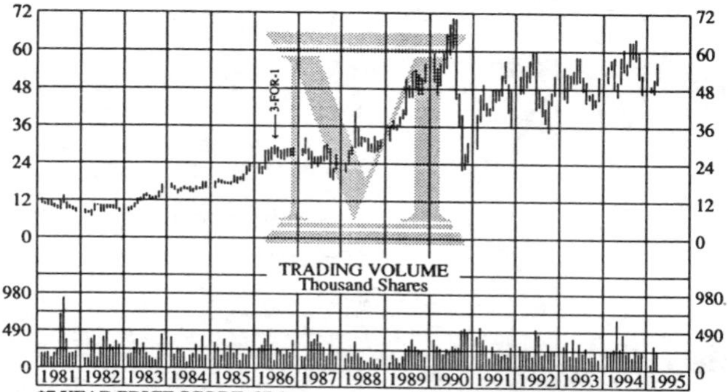

TRADING VOLUME
Thousand Shares

| | 1981 | 1982 | 1983 | 1984 | 1985 | 1986 | 1987 | 1988 | 1989 | 1990 | 1991 | 1992 | 1993 | 1994 | 1995 |

*7 YEAR PRICE SCORE 97.1 ***12 MONTH PRICE SCORE 90.9**
*NYSE COMPOSITE INDEX=100

INTERIM EARNINGS (Per Share):

Qtr.	Mar.	June	Sept.	Dec.
1991	0.20	0.53	0.44	1.14
1992	0.12	0.16	1.08	1.35
1993	Nil	d0.02	0.23	1.09
1994	0.31	1.03	1.23	2.49

INTERIM DIVIDENDS (Per Share):

Amt.	Decl.	Ex.	Rec.	Pay.
0.165Q	2/9/94	2/23/94	3/1/94	3/15/94
0.17Q	5/11	5/25	6/1	6/15
0.17Q	8/10	8/26	9/1	9/15
0.17Q	11/9	11/25	12/1	12/15
0.17Q	2/8/95	2/23/95	3/1/95	3/15/95

Indicated div.: $0.68

CAPITALIZATION (12/31/94):

	($000)	(%)
Long-Term Debt	773,552	70.7
Minority Interest	40,542	3.7
Common & Surplus	279,391	25.6
Total	1,093,485	100.0

DIVIDEND ACHIEVER STATUS:
Rank: 224   1984-94 Growth Rate: 7.6%
Total Years of Dividend Growth: 11

RECENT DEVELOPMENTS: For the year ended 12/31/94, net income surged to $45.3 million compared with $11.6 million in 1993. Revenues advanced 20.4% to $1.86 billion. North American Coal's earnings rose 20.7% to $21.0 million due primarily to increased royalty income. However, this gain was partially offset by higher general and administrative expenses that resulted from consolidation activities. Hamilton Beach/Proctor-Silex's revenues rose 5.9% to $377.5 million and its earnings more than doubled to $25.3 million.

PROSPECTS: The NACCO Materials Handling Group will continue to benefit from strong demand for lift-trucks in the United States, as well as improving European and Asian markets. Hamilton Beach/Proctor-Silex earnings will reflect improved factory and distribution center operations. However, increased interest rates could have a dampening effect on the U.S. economy. Recent efforts to reduce long-term debt will mitigate the negative effect of rising interest rates.

BUSINESS

NACCO INDUSTRIES, INC. is a holding company with four operating subsidiaries; NACCO Materials Handling Group, The North American Coal Corp., Hamilton Beach/Proctor-Silex, Inc., and the Kitchen Collection, Inc. NACCO Materials Handling Group is a world leader in the design and manufacture of forklift trucks, marketed under the Hyster and Yale brand names. North American Coal mines and markets lignite coal primarily, as fuel for power generation by electric utilities. Hamilton Beach/Proctor-Silex is a leading manufacturer of small electric appliances. The Kitchen Collection is a national specialty retailer of kitchenware and small electric appliances.

BUSINESS LINE ANALYSIS

(12/31/94)	Rev(%)	Inc(%)
NAACO Materials Handling	63.0	45.4
Hamilton Beach/Proctor-Si ...	20.2	17.5
North American Coal	13.4	33.5
Kitchen Collection	3.4	3.7
Bellaire	- - -	(0.1)
Total	100.0	100.0

ANNUAL EARNINGS AND DIVIDENDS PER SHARE

	1994	1993	1992	1991	1990	1989	1988
Earnings Per Share	5.06	1.30	① 2.71	2.31	3.49	6.08	5.08
Dividends Per Share	0.675	0.655	0.635	0.615	0.595	0.575	0.55
Dividend Payout %	13.3	50.4	23.4	26.6	17.0	18.9	21.7

① Before extraord. item

ANNUAL FINANCIAL DATA

RECORD OF EARNINGS (IN MILLIONS):

	1994	1993	1992	1991	1990	1989	1988
Total Revenues	1,864.9	1,549.4	1,481.5	1,369.2	1,385.0	1,187.6	616.5
Costs and Expenses	1,716.1	1,442.2	1,295.3	1,189.9	1,193.3	992.7	523.7
Deprec, Depl & Amort	80.2	78.1	67.9	66.5	64.3	52.3	32.2
Operating Profit	135.1	93.4	118.3	112.7	127.4	142.6	60.6
Income Bef Income Taxes	78.5	24.7	43.5	30.0	50.0	92.3	60.3
Income Taxes	30.7	13.5	19.4	9.5	19.1	38.3	15.3
Net Income	① 45.3	② 11.6	③ 24.1	20.5	30.9	53.9	45.0
Aver. Shs. Outstg. (000)	8,948	8,938	8,891	8,878	8,877	8,874	8,850

① Before extra. item dr$3,218,000. ② Before extra. item dr$3,292,000. ③ Before extra. item dr$110,000,000.

BALANCE SHEET (IN MILLIONS):

	1994	1993	1992	1991	1990	1989	1988
Cash and Cash Equivalents	19.5	29.1	33.8	52.3	100.8	172.0	95.0
Receivables, Net	236.2	200.1	181.2	201.0	215.5	180.0	94.8
Inventories	299.0	238.2	235.5	225.1	259.1	252.6	118.4
Gross Property	825.1	782.2	745.1	674.8	627.1	549.0	433.8
Accumulated Depreciation	339.8	286.0	248.0	211.5	170.8	131.9	121.2
Long-Term Debt	773.6	855.6	959.8	746.2	825.5	596.6	54.7
Net Stockholders' Equity	279.4	235.6	239.6	350.3	352.9	300.8	246.0
Total Assets	1,694.3	1,642.5	1,664.3	1,608.5	1,722.0	1,680.2	837.0
Total Current Assets	586.6	504.8	495.9	531.6	657.6	701.7	357.3
Total Current Liabilities	481.4	397.5	330.6	373.7	408.5	462.4	226.7
Net Working Capital	105.2	107.3	165.3	157.9	249.1	239.2	130.6
Year End Shs Outstg (000)	9,952	8,036	8,935	8,882	8,878	8,876	8,870

STATISTICAL RECORD:

	1994	1993	1992	1991	1990	1989	1988
Operating Profit Margin %	7.2	6.0	8.0	8.2	9.2	12.0	9.8
Book Value Per Share	31.21	29.38	26.82	39.44	39.65	33.80	27.64
Return on Equity %	16.2	4.9	10.1	5.9	8.8	17.9	18.3
Return on Assets %	2.7	0.7	1.4	1.3	1.8	3.2	5.4
Average Yield %	1.2	1.3	1.3	1.4	1.3	1.3	1.8
P/E Ratio	12.6-9.0	44.8-32.3	22.1-12.6	24.6-12.6	20.2-6.3	9.2-5.1	8.0-4.2
Price Range	64-45¾	58¼-42	60-34¼	56⅞-29	70½-22	56-31¼	40¾-21¼

Statistics are as originally reported.

OFFICERS:
A.M. Rankin, Jr., Chmn., Pres. & C.E.O.
F.B. O'Brien, Sr. V.P. - & C.F.O.
C.A. Bittenbender, V.P., Gen. Counsel & Sec.

INCORPORATED: DE, 1986

PRINCIPAL OFFICE: 5875 Landerbrook Drive, Mayfield Heights, OH 44124-4017

TELEPHONE NUMBER: (216) 449-9600
NO. OF EMPLOYEES: 10,780 (approx.)
ANNUAL MEETING: In May
SHAREHOLDERS: 900 Cl. A com. (approx.); 600 Cl. B com. (approx.)
INSTITUTIONAL HOLDINGS:
No. of Institutions: 99
Shares Held: 5,037,554

REGISTRAR(S): Society National Bank, Cleveland, OH

TRANSFER AGENT(S): Society National Bank, Cleveland, OH

NASH-FINCH CO.

YIELD 4.4%
P/E RATIO 11.4

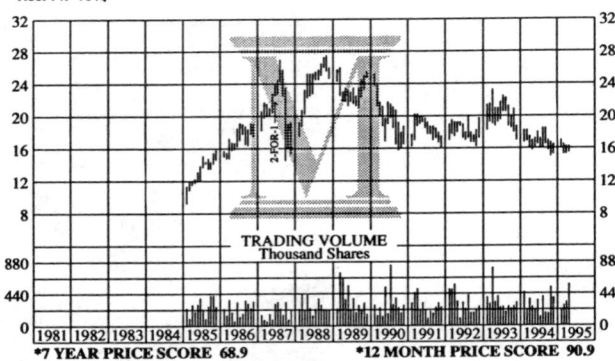

INTERIM EARNINGS (Per Share):

Qtr.	Mar.	June	Sept.	Dec.
1993	---------------- 1.85 ----------------			
1993	0.23	0.46	0.27	0.50
1994	0.24	0.48	0.37	0.33

INTERIM DIVIDENDS (Per Share):

Amt.	Decl.	Ex.	Rec.	Pay.
0.18Q	5/11/94	5/23/94	5/27/94	6/10/94
0.18Q	8/16	8/22	8/26	9/9
0.18Q	11/15	11/18	11/25	12/9
0.01E	11/15	11/18	11/25	12/9
0.18Q	2/14/95	2/17/95	2/24/95	3/10/95

*Indicated div.: $0.72**

CAPITALIZATION (12/31/94):

	($000)	(%)
Long-Term Debt	85,289	28.2
Cap. Lease Oblig.	10,671	3.5
Common & Surplus	206,269	68.3
Total	302,229	100.0

TRADING VOLUME
Thousand Shares

*7 YEAR PRICE SCORE 68.9   ***12 MONTH PRICE SCORE 90.9**

*NYSE COMPOSITE INDEX=100

DIVIDEND ACHIEVER STATUS:
Rank: 293   1984-94 Growth Rate: 4.1%
Total Years of Dividend Growth: 25

RECENT DEVELOPMENTS: For the year ended 12/31/94, net earnings declined slightly to $15.5 million from $15.9 million in the previous year. Total sales and revenues edged a bit higher to $2.83 billion from $2.72 billion in the year before. A glut of quality products in the Company's West Coast produce operations forced prices lower and adversely affected that division's earnings. Additionally, higher LIFO charges, interest expenses and health care claim costs drove expenses upward and pressured margins, thereby decreasing earnings. For the quarter ended 12/31/94, net earnings fell by 32% to $3.6 million from $5.4 million in the equivalent period of the previous year. Total sales and revnues advanced to $656.5 million from $634.7 million in the prior-year quarter.

BUSINESS

NASH-FINCH COMPANY is one of the largest food wholesalers in the country, supplying products to approximately 700 affiliated and independent supermarkets and some 5,000 other independent retailers and military bases in 31 states. The Company also owns and operates approximately 120 supermarkets, warehouse stores and mass merchandise stores in 15 states and produce marketing subsidiaries in California.

BUSINESS LINE ANALYSIS

(12/31/94)	Rev(%)	Inc(%)
Wholesale Distrib	65.7	71.2
Retail Distrib	32.8	25.5
Produce Mktg & Oth.	1.5	3.3
Total	100.0	100.0

ANNUAL EARNINGS AND DIVIDENDS PER SHARE

	12/31/94	1/1/94	1/2/93	12/28/91	12/29/90	12/30/89	12/31/88
Earnings Per Share	1.42	1.46	1.85	1.75	1.64	1.21	1.67
Dividends Per Share	0.73	0.72	0.71	0.70	0.69	0.67	0.65
Dividend Payout %	51.4	49.3	38.4	40.0	42.1	55.4	38.9

ANNUAL FINANCIAL DATA

RECORD OF EARNINGS (IN MILLIONS):

	12/31/94	1/1/94	1/2/93	12/28/91	12/29/90	12/30/89	12/31/88
Total Revenues	2,832.0	2,723.5	2,515.4	2,343.3	2,374.9	2,223.8	2,097.8
Costs and Expenses	2,763.0	2,657.6	2,446.5	2,277.4	2,311.7	2,171.2	2,037.7
Depreciation & Amort	31.8	29.1	27.0	26.1	25.6	23.2	20.2
Operating Profit	37.2	36.8	41.9	39.8	37.6	29.4	40.0
Earn Bef Income Taxes	25.8	26.7	32.6	30.8	29.0	21.2	29.0
Income Taxes	10.3	10.8	12.5	11.7	11.1	8.0	10.9
Net Income	15.5	15.9	20.1	19.1	17.8	13.2	18.2
Aver. Shs. Outstg. (000)	10,873	10,872	10,872	10,871	10,870	10,868	10,881

BALANCE SHEET (IN MILLIONS):

Cash and Cash Equivalents	1.1	0.9	0.8	0.6	0.6	12.8	0.7
Receivables, Net	101.2	100.0	194.6	134.3	110.6	97.8	116.7
Inventories	198.6	186.6	205.0	167.1	172.8	145.1	155.6
Gross Property	391.9	382.6	359.6	323.1	295.7	262.1	246.3
Accumulated Depreciation	205.0	196.4	184.3	159.3	138.7	117.2	102.1
Long-Term Debt	85.3	89.8	92.1	80.4	71.8	75.0	63.0
Capital Lease Obligations	10.7	8.1	2.0	2.1	2.5	2.9	3.2
Net Stockholders' Equity	206.3	199.3	191.2	178.8	167.4	157.0	151.0
Total Assets	531.6	521.7	610.9	496.8	471.5	429.7	446.6
Total Current Assets	309.5	294.9	407.1	307.0	289.4	261.2	278.3
Total Current Liabilities	220.1	215.0	213.7	155.0	158.0	128.2	153.1
Net Working Capital	89.5	79.9	193.4	152.0	131.4	133.0	125.2
Year End Shs Outstg (000)	10,875	10,873	10,872	10,871	10,871	10,869	10,865

STATISTICAL RECORD:

Operating Profit Margin %	1.3	1.4	1.7	1.7	1.6	1.3	1.9
Book Value Per Share	18.25	17.45	17.59	16.45	15.40	14.45	13.87
Return on Equity %	7.5	8.0	10.5	10.7	10.7	8.4	12.0
Return on Assets %	2.9	3.0	3.3	3.8	3.8	3.1	4.1
Average Yield %	4.4	3.6	3.9	3.8	3.4	2.9	2.9
P/E Ratio	13.0-10.6	15.9-11.6	10.7-8.8	11.6-9.2	15.4-9.6	21.5-17.4	16.5-10.5
Price Range	18½-15	23¼-17	19⅞-16¼	20¼-16⅛	25¼-15¾	26-21	27½-17½

Statistics are as originally reported.

OFFICERS:
A.N. Flaten, Pres. & C.E.O.
R.F. Nash, V.P. & Treas.
N.R. Soland, V.P., Sec. & Gen. Couns.

INCORPORATED: DE, 1921

PRINCIPAL OFFICE: 7600 France Avenue South P.O. Box 355, Minneapolis, MN 55440-0355

TELEPHONE NUMBER: (612) 832-0534

NO. OF EMPLOYEES: 6,200 (full-time); 6,300 (part-time)

ANNUAL MEETING: In May

SHAREHOLDERS: 2,074

INSTITUTIONAL HOLDINGS:
No. of Institutions: 51
Shares Held: 3,578,825

REGISTRAR(S): Norwest Bank Minnesota, N.A., St. Paul, MN

TRANSFER AGENT(S): Norwest Bank Minnesota, N.A., St. Paul, MN

NYS SYMBOL NFG
Rec. Pr. 29

NATIONAL FUEL GAS COMPANY

YIELD 5.4%
P/E RATIO 13.4

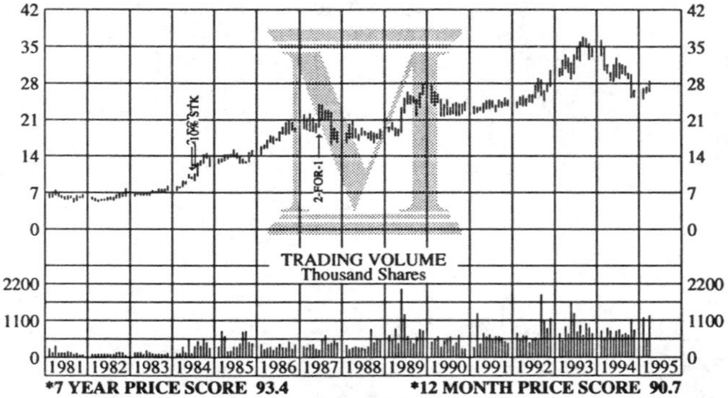

*7 YEAR PRICE SCORE 93.4 *12 MONTH PRICE SCORE 90.7

*NYSE COMPOSITE INDEX=100

INTERIM EARNINGS (Per Share):

Qtr.	Dec.	Mar.	June	Sept.
1991-92	0.87	1.29	0.06	d0.28
1992-93		2.15		
1993-94	0.76	1.18	0.26	0.03
1994-95	0.69	...	...	...

INTERIM DIVIDENDS (Per Share):

Amt.	Decl.	Ex.	Rec.	Pay.
0.385Q	3/16/94	3/25/94	3/31/94	4/15/94
0.395Q	6/9	6/24	6/30	7/15
0.395Q	9/16	9/26	9/30	10/15
0.395Q	12/7	12/23	12/31	1/15/95
0.395Q	3/15/95	3/27/95	3/31/95	4/15

*Indicated div.: $1.58**

CAPITALIZATION (9/30/94):

	($000)	(%)
Long-Term Debt	462,500	30.2
Deferred Income Tax	287,617	18.8
Common & Surplus	780,288	51.0
Total	1,530,405	100.0
Current Debt	208,500	

DIVIDEND ACHIEVER STATUS:
Rank: 262 1984-94 Growth Rate: 6.1%
Total Years of Dividend Growth: 23

RECENT DEVELOPMENTS: For the quarter ended 12/31/94, net income was $25.9 million compared with $27.8 million, before an accounting change, in the corresponding 1993 period. Operating revenues declined 12% to $271.5 million from $310.1 million in the same period a year earlier, due to warmer winter weather and falling gas prices. The Company's nonregulated operations reported earnings growth, which was offset by a decline in regulated operations.

PROSPECTS: It will be difficult for NFG to match 1994's results in 1995. Allowed returns on pipeline equity have decreased as a result of allegedly lower risks now associated with that business. The Company anticipates a lower return on equity for the rates expected to become effective late in fiscal 1995. The Utility segment's allowed return on equity for New York has been reduced to 10.7% from 12.0%.

BUSINESS

NATIONAL FUEL GAS COMPANY is the public utility holding company of National Fuel Gas Supply, National Fuel Gas Distribution Corp., Seneca Resources, Penn-York Energy Corp., Empire Exploration, Inc., Utility Constructors, Inc. and National Fuel Resources Inc. These operations are involved in all phases of the natural gas industry; marketing, exploration, production, purchasing, gathering, transmission, storage, sale at wholesale, and distribution, together with by-product operations. Seneca Resources Corp. also markets timber and coal. Other subsidiaries included Highland Land & Minerals Inc., a sawmill operation, Data-Track, Inc., a collection service and Enerop Corporation.

ANNUAL EARNINGS AND DIVIDENDS PER SHARE

	9/30/94	9/30/93	9/30/92	9/30/91	9/30/90	9/30/89	9/30/88
Earnings Per Share	**2.23**	**2.15**	**1.94**	**1.63**	**1.83**	**1.93**	**1.65**
Dividends Per Share	**1.56**	**1.52**	**1.48**	**1.44**	**1.38**	**1.30**	**1.23**
Dividend Payout %	**68.2**	**70.7**	**76.3**	**88.3**	**75.4**	**67.4**	**74.5**

ANNUAL FINANCIAL DATA

	9/30/94	9/30/93	9/30/92	9/30/91	9/30/90	9/30/89	9/30/88
RECORD OF EARNINGS (IN MILLIONS):							
Total Revenues	1,141.3	1,020.4	919.8	865.1	892.0	855.8	768.9
Maintenance	31.0	24.3	22.4	20.5	18.7	20.1	21.1
Prov for Fed Inc Taxes	47.8	41.0	35.2	23.3	27.5	25.8	18.7
Operating Income	125.9	122.3	113.6	98.4	102.3	98.0	79.1
Interest Expense	47.1	51.9	59.0	61.3	57.8	51.6	41.3
Net Income	[1] 82.4	75.2	60.3	49.0	52.0	52.4	42.6
Aver. Shs. Outstg. (000)	37,046	34,939	31,153	29,996	28,404	27,191	25,885
[1] Before acctg. change cr$3,237,000.							
BALANCE SHEET (IN MILLIONS):							
Gross Plant	2,166.3	2,039.4	1,918.4	1,772.5	1,625.3	1,472.6	1,353.2
Accumulated Depreciation	623.5	561.4	502.0	458.8	418.9	385.1	350.7
Prop, Plant & Equip, Net	1,542.7	1,478.0	1,416.4	1,313.8	1,206.4	1,087.5	1,002.4
Long-term Debt	462.5	478.4	479.5	442.1	397.4	383.9	297.2
Net Stockholders' Equity	780.3	736.2	632.3	542.1	484.0	464.2	406.1
Total Assets	1,981.7	1,801.5	1,760.8	1,560.8	1,436.7	1,311.6	1,176.9
Year End Shs Outstg (000)	37,278	36,661	33,856	30,927	28,532	28,245	25,936
STATISTICAL RECORD:							
Book Value Per Share	20.93	20.08	18.68	17.53	16.96	16.44	15.66
Op. Inc/Net Pl %	8.2	8.3	8.0	7.5	8.5	9.0	7.9
Dep/Gr. Pl %	3.5	3.4	2.9	2.9	2.7	3.0	3.2
Accum. Dep/Gr. Pl %	28.8	27.5	26.2	25.9	25.8	26.2	25.9
Return on Equity %	10.6	10.2	9.5	9.0	10.7	11.3	10.5
Average Yield %	4.9	4.6	5.5	6.1	5.6	5.7	6.6
P/E Ratio	16.3-11.3	17.2-13.4	15.7-12.0	15.5-13.6	15.1-11.8	14.4-9.3	12.6-10.0
Price Range	36¼-25¼	36⅞-28¾	30½-23¼	25¼-22⅛	27⅝-21⅝	27⅞-17⅞	20¾-16½

Statistics are as originally reported.

QUARTERLY DATA

(9/30/94)($000)	Rev	Inc
1st Quarter	310,131	38,745
2nd Quarter	473,722	54,686
3rd Quarter	216,281	19,782
4th Quarter	141,190	12,690

OFFICERS:
B.J. Kennedy, Chmn., Pres. & C.E.O.
J.P. Pawlowski, Treas.
R.M. DiValerio, Sec.

INCORPORATED: NJ, Dec., 1902

PRINCIPAL OFFICE: 30 Rockefeller Plaza, New York, NY 10112

TELEPHONE NUMBER: (212) 541-7533

FAX: (212) 541-7841

NO. OF EMPLOYEES: 3,148

ANNUAL MEETING: In February

SHAREHOLDERS: 22,465

INSTITUTIONAL HOLDINGS:
No. of Institutions: 153
Shares Held: 11,132,670

REGISTRAR(S): Chemical Bank, New York, NY

TRANSFER AGENT(S): Chemical Bank, New York, NY

NASDAQ SYMBOL NPBC
Rec. Pr. 24½

NATIONAL PENN BANCSHARES, INC.

YIELD 3.4%
P/E RATIO 12.0

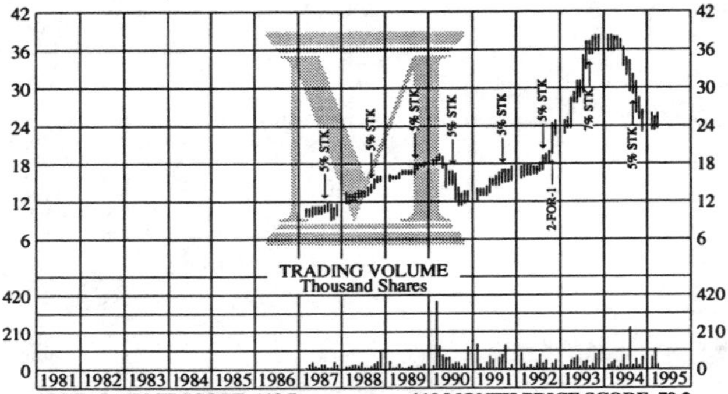

*7 YEAR PRICE SCORE 118.7 *12 MONTH PRICE SCORE 79.2

*NYSE COMPOSITE INDEX=100

INTERIM EARNINGS (Per Share):

Qtr.	Mar.	June	Sept.	Dec.
1991	0.38	0.35	0.38	0.36
1992	0.40	0.39	0.41	0.44
1993	0.50	0.44	0.50	0.46
1994	---------------- 1.94 ----------------			

INTERIM DIVIDENDS (Per Share):

Amt.	Decl.	Ex.	Rec.	Pay.
0.20Q	6/22/94	7/25/94	7/29/94	8/17/94
5%	6/22	9/26	9/30	10/31
0.20Q	9/28	10/25	10/31	11/17
0.21Q	12/28	1/25/95	1/31/95	2/17/95
0.21Q	3/22/95	4/24	4/28	5/17

Indicated div.: $0.84

CAPITALIZATION (12/31/94):

	($000)	(%)
Total Deposits	864,640	75.5
Total Debt	176,018	15.4
Common & Surplus	84,871	7.4
Loan Valuation Reserve	19,310	1.7
Total	1,144,839	100.0

DIVIDEND ACHIEVER STATUS:
Rank: 24 1984-94 Growth Rate: 18.7%
Total Years of Dividend Growth: 11

RECENT DEVELOPMENTS: For the year ended 12/31/94, net income improved to $14.6 million from $13.3 million in the year before. NPBC's total interest income rose to $84.3 million from $71.3 million in the year prior, but a 21% increase in total interest expense to $28.8 million from $23.8 million in the year before eroded some of the Company's gains. For the three months ended 12/31/94, net income advanced by 14% to $3.9 million from $3.2 million in the equivalent period of 1994. Total interest income was $22.7 million compared with $18.3 million in the prior-year quarter. The strong gain in interest income did not translate into an equally strong bottom line due to a 44% boost in NPBC's total interest expense of $8.6 million. NPBC's net income on average equity remained stable at 17.3% versus 17.4% in the previous year.

BUSINESS

NATIONAL PENN BANCSHARES, INC. is a bank holding company. Through its banking subsidairy, National Penn Bank, National Penn operates 30 offices in Berks, Bucks, Chester, Lehigh, Montgomery and Philadelphia counties. In addition, National Penn has two wholly-owned non-bank subsidiaries engaged in activities related to the business of banking.

LOAN DISTRIBUTION

(12/31/94)	($000)	(%)
Commerical & Industrial	79,726	9.6
Loans Purch & Carry Secur	778	0.1
Loans to Financial Instit	821	0.1
Real Estate	732,898	88.2
Individual	16,400	2.0
Total	830,623	100.0

ANNUAL EARNINGS AND DIVIDENDS PER SHARE

	1994	1993	1992	1991	1990	1989	1988
Earnings Per Share	**1.94**	**1.87**	**1.61**	**1.45**	**1.34**	**1.24**	**1.15**
Dividends Per Share	**[1] 0.73**	**[2] 0.60**	**[3] 0.50**	**[4] 0.45**	**[5] 0.41**	**[6] 0.37**	**[7] 0.30**
Dividend Payout %	**37.7**	**34.7**	**33.0**	**33.2**	**32.6**	**31.6**	**29.6**

[1] 5% stk div,10/31/94 [2] 7% stk div,09/24/93 [3] 5% stk div,08/25/92 [4] 5% stk div,09/30/91 [5] 5% stk div, 10/16/90 [6] 5% stock dividend, 10/16/89. [7] 5% stk. div., 10/88

ANNUAL FINANCIAL DATA

	1994	1993	1992	1991	1990	1989	1988
RECORD OF EARNINGS (IN MILLIONS):							
Total Interest Income	84.3	71.3	69.1	71.7	61.4	57.8	46.2
Total Interest Expense	28.8	23.8	26.7	36.4	32.9	31.7	23.3
Net Interest Income	55.4	47.4	42.4	35.3	28.4	26.1	22.9
Credit Loss Provision	3.2	5.1	6.2	4.8	1.8	1.3	1.8
Net Income	14.6	[1] 12.8	11.3	10.1	9.3	8.6	[2] 7.9
Aver. Shs. Outstg. (000)	7,165	7,121	7,035	6,954	6,931	6,918	6,862

[1] Before acctg. change cr$500,000. [2] Before acctg. change dr$215,000.

	1994	1993	1992	1991	1990	1989	1988
BALANCE SHEET (IN MILLIONS):							
Cash & Due From Banks	33.2	23.3	17.2	24.3	23.4	20.8	19.6
Loans & Lse Financing, Net	811.3	719.9	591.5	520.3	506.0	390.3	328.7
Total Domestic Deposits	864.6	748.2	631.2	616.6	600.4	482.3	411.3
Long-term Debt	77.8	51.1	41.1	25.1	6.7	3.0	3.0
Net Stockholders' Equity	84.9	82.2	70.7	61.6	54.6	48.6	42.0
Total Assets	1,137.2	933.7	775.9	739.5	726.5	572.7	493.9
Year End Shs Outstg (000)	7,135	7,192	7,068	6,953	6,944	6,610	6,257
STATISTICAL RECORD:							
Return on Assets %	1.29	1.37	1.46	1.37	1.28	1.50	1.59
Return on Equity %	17.30	15.60	16.00	16.40	17.00	17.70	18.70
Book Value Per Share	11.90	11.43	10.00	8.86	7.87	7.34	6.71
Average Yield %	2.5	2.1	2.6	3.2	2.8	2.3	2.3
P/E Ratio	18.8-11.3	21.3-12.6	15.5-9.7	11.7-8.0	14.0-8.0	14.0-11.7	13.4-9.7
Price Range	38⅜-23	38⅜-22¾	24⅞-15⅝	17⅝-12⅛	19⅝-11¼	18¼-15¼	16⅛-11⅝

Statistics are as originally reported.

OFFICERS:
L.T. Jilk, Jr., Pres. & C.E.O.
G.L. Rhoads, Treas.
S.L. Spayd, Sec.

INCORPORATED: PA, Jan., 1982

PRINCIPAL OFFICE: P.O. Box 547, Boyertown, PA 19512-0547

TELEPHONE NUMBER: (610) 369-6291
FAX: (610) 369-6349
NO. OF EMPLOYEES: 559
ANNUAL MEETING: In April
SHAREHOLDERS: 2,787
INSTITUTIONAL HOLDINGS:
No. of Institutions: 7
Shares Held: 61,047

REGISTRAR(S): Mellon Securities Trust Co., Pittsburgh, PA

TRANSFER AGENT(S): Mellon Securities Trust Co., Pittsburgh, PA

NYS SYMBOL NSI
Rec. Pr. 28⅛

NATIONAL SERVICE INDUSTRIES, INC.

YIELD 4.0%
P/E RATIO 16.2

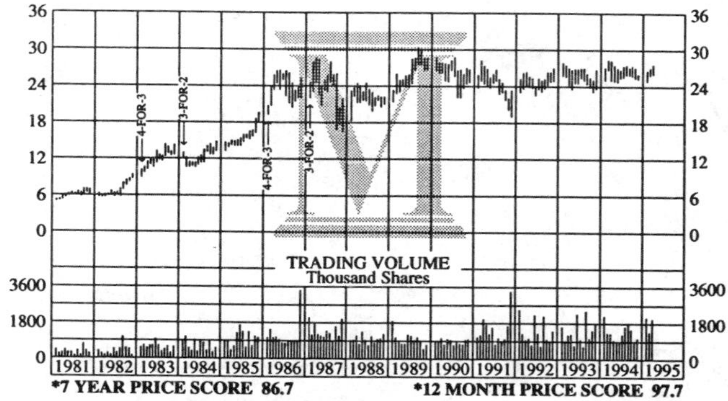

36
30
24
18
12
6
0
4-FOR-3
3-FOR-2
4-FOR-3
3-FOR-2
TRADING VOLUME
Thousand Shares
3600
1800
0
1981 1982 1983 1984 1985 1986 1987 1988 1989 1990 1991 1992 1993 1994 1995

*7 YEAR PRICE SCORE 86.7 *12 MONTH PRICE SCORE 97.7

*NYSE COMPOSITE INDEX=100

INTERIM EARNINGS (Per Share):

Qtr.	Nov.	Feb.	May	Mar.
1991-92	0.36	0.32	0.40	0.42
1992-93	0.38	0.30	0.41	0.43
1993-94	0.39	0.33	0.46	0.49
1994-95	0.43	0.36	...	...

INTERIM DIVIDENDS (Per Share):

Amt.	Decl.	Ex.	Rec.	Pay.
0.27Q	3/16/94	3/22/94	3/28/94	4/8/94
0.27Q	6/15	6/21	6/27	7/7
0.27Q	9/21	9/23	9/29	10/14
0.28Q	12/21	12/23	12/30	1/10/95
0.28Q	3/15/95	3/21/95	3/27/95	4/5

*Indicated div.: $1.12**

CAPITALIZATION (8/31/94):

	($000)	(%)
Long-Term Debt	26,863	3.2
Deferred Income Tax	78,814	9.5
Common & Surplus	727,385	87.3
Total	833,062	100.0

DIVIDEND ACHIEVER STATUS:
Rank: 186 1984-94 Growth Rate: 9.4%
Total Years of Dividend Growth: 33

RECENT DEVELOPMENTS: For the quarter ended 11/30/94, net income was $21.1 million, up 10.1% from $19.2 million for the comparable quarter in 1993. Total revenues rose 4.6% to $481.0 million from $459.9 million for the year-earlier quarter. Net sales of products were $344.9 million compared with $325.2 million a year ago, an increase of 6.0%. Service revenues increased moderately to $136.1 million from $134.7 million in the 1993 quarter. Operating profit rose 15.1% to 6.7% of revenues.

PROSPECTS: NSI completed the sale of its marketing services division and anticipates a $30 million drop in 1995 sales with a negligible effect on operating income. The textile rental business should continue to post marginally higher sales despite soft market conditions. Results from the chemical sector are improving due to sales gains in the U.S. and operating efficiencies in the European and Canadian operations.

BUSINESS

NATIONAL SERVICE INDUSTRIES INC., is a diversified manufacturing and service company with operations in six separate divisions. The lighting equipment division manufactures a wide variety of lighting equipment for commercial, industrial, institutional, and residential use. The textile rental division rents textile items to restaurants and lodging, hospitals, clinics, nursing homes and industrial concerns. The chemical division manufactures a broad line of specialty chemicals for industrial and commercial maintenance, sanitation and housekeeping. Other divisions include marketing services, envelope, and insulation services.

BUSINESS LINE ANALYSIS

(08/31/94)	Rev(%)	Inc(%)
Lighting Equipment	40.6	35.0
Textile Rental	28.9	34.1
Chemical	17.7	24.7
Other	12.8	6.2
Total	100.0	100.0

ANNUAL EARNINGS AND DIVIDENDS PER SHARE

	8/31/94	8/31/93	8/31/92	8/31/91	8/31/90	8/31/89	8/31/88
Earnings Per Share	**1.67**	**1.52**	**1.50**	**0.65**	**2.02**	**1.92**	**1.75**
Dividends Per Share	**1.08**	**1.04**	**1.00**	**0.96**	**0.92**	**0.84**	**0.76**
Dividend Payout %	**64.7**	**68.4**	**66.7**	**N.M.**	**45.5**	**43.8**	**43.4**

ANNUAL FINANCIAL DATA

	8/31/94	8/31/93	8/31/92	8/31/91	8/31/90	8/31/89	8/31/88
RECORD OF EARNINGS (IN MILLIONS):							
Total Revenues	1,881.9	1,804.8	1,633.8	1,601.7	1,647.8	1,539.5	1,414.2
Costs and Expenses	1,678.3	1,608.7	1,455.9	1,501.9	1,448.8	1,359.7	1,252.1
Depreciation & Amort	60.5	62.1	53.8	50.2	42.8	36.3	31.0
Operating Profit	143.0	134.0	124.1	113.1	156.2	143.6	131.0
Inc Bef Prov for Income Taxes	132.2	119.5	116.9	48.6	155.7	148.0	133.2
Income Taxes	49.5	44.4	42.8	16.4	56.0	53.3	47.1
Net Income	82.7	75.1	74.1	32.2	99.7	94.7	86.1
Aver. Shs. Outstg. (000)	49,547	49,556	49,539	49,540	49,389	49,255	49,258
BALANCE SHEET (IN MILLIONS):							
Cash and Cash Equivalents	61.2	20.6	109.6	87.6	125.2	129.0	134.0
Receivables, Net	256.1	250.0	204.0	199.0	202.2	193.7	181.9
Inventories	178.6	171.5	151.7	165.0	178.1	173.5	163.8
Gross Property	726.6	724.0	679.5	649.3	581.0	510.2	451.2
Accumulated Depreciation	378.3	358.9	339.2	307.0	280.1	249.4	222.8
Long-Term Debt	26.9	28.4	28.4	31.4	27.5	20.8	21.4
Net Stockholders' Equity	727.4	704.0	683.0	660.6	675.4	612.7	558.2
Total Assets	1,106.8	1,087.5	1,042.4	1,012.0	962.1	887.8	825.3
Total Current Assets	608.3	556.9	567.5	549.3	576.5	570.1	552.4
Total Current Liabilities	250.8	243.7	209.8	197.7	142.4	133.6	126.0
Net Working Capital	357.5	313.2	357.8	351.6	434.1	436.5	426.4
Year End Shs Outstg (000)	49,240	49,561	49,538	49,602	49,604	49,255	49,255
STATISTICAL RECORD:							
Operating Profit Margin %	7.6	7.4	7.6	3.1	9.5	9.3	9.3
Book Value Per Share	14.78	14.19	13.79	13.32	13.61	12.44	11.33
Return on Equity %	11.4	10.7	10.9	4.9	14.8	15.5	15.4
Return on Assets %	7.5	6.9	7.1	3.2	10.4	10.7	10.4
Average Yield %	4.1	4.1	4.0	4.1	3.6	3.2	3.6
P/E Ratio	17.0-14.8	18.3-15.2	18.0-15.0	43.5-29.2	14.2-11.0	15.8-11.1	14.0-10.4
Price Range	28⅜-24¾	27⅞-23⅛	27-22½	28¼-19	28¾-22⅛	30⅜-21⅜	24½-18¼

Statistics are as originally reported.

OFFICERS:
D.R. Riddle, Chmn. & C.E.O.
D.W. Hubble, Pres. & C.O.O.
J.R. Hipps, Sr. V.P.-Fin.
K.W. Murphy, Sec. & Asst. Couns.

INCORPORATED: DE, Aug., 1928

PRINCIPAL OFFICE: 1420 Peachtree Street, N.E., Atlanta, GA 30309-3002

TELEPHONE NUMBER: (404) 853-1000

FAX: (404) 883-1015

NO. OF EMPLOYEES: 22,000 (approx.)

ANNUAL MEETING: In January

SHAREHOLDERS: 7,034

INSTITUTIONAL HOLDINGS:
No. of Institutions: 205
Shares Held: 28,258,088

REGISTRAR(S): Wachovia Bank & Trust Co., N.A., Winston-Salem, NC 27102

TRANSFER AGENT(S): Wachovia Bank & Trust Co., N.A., Winston-Salem, NC 27102

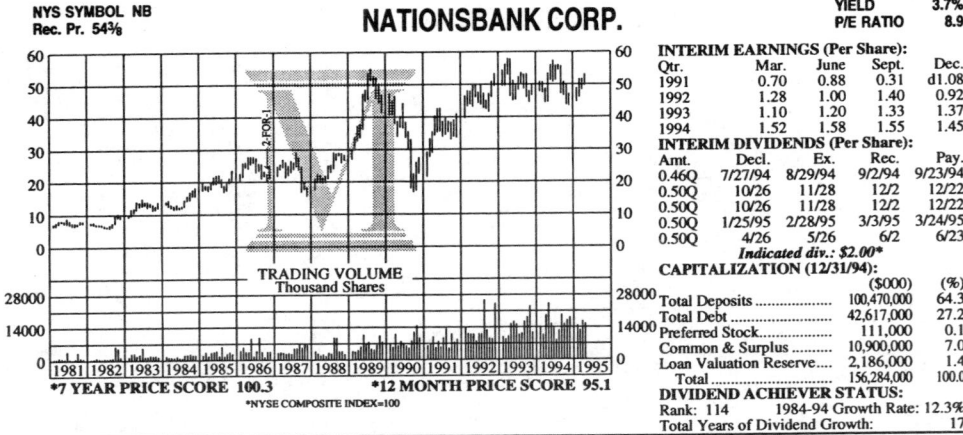

NATIONSBANK CORP.

YIELD 3.7%
P/E RATIO 8.9

INTERIM EARNINGS (Per Share):

Qtr.	Mar.	June	Sept.	Dec.
1991	0.70	0.88	0.31	d1.08
1992	1.28	1.00	1.40	0.92
1993	1.10	1.20	1.33	1.37
1994	1.52	1.58	1.55	1.45

INTERIM DIVIDENDS (Per Share):

Amt.	Decl.	Ex.	Rec.	Pay.
0.46Q	7/27/94	8/29/94	9/2/94	9/23/94
0.50Q	10/26	11/28	12/2	12/22
0.50Q	10/26	11/28	12/2	12/22
0.50Q	1/25/95	2/28/95	3/3/95	3/24/95
0.50Q	4/26	5/26	6/2	6/23

*Indicated div.: $2.00**

CAPITALIZATION (12/31/94):

	($000)	(%)
Total Deposits	100,470,000	64.3
Total Debt	42,617,000	27.2
Preferred Stock	111,000	0.1
Common & Surplus	10,900,000	7.0
Loan Valuation Reserve	2,186,000	1.4
Total	156,284,000	100.0

DIVIDEND ACHIEVER STATUS:
Rank: 114   1984-94 Growth Rate: 12.3%
Total Years of Dividend Growth: 17

TRADING VOLUME
Thousand Shares

*7 YEAR PRICE SCORE 100.3   *12 MONTH PRICE SCORE 95.1
*NYSE COMPOSITE INDEX=100

RECENT DEVELOPMENTS: For the year ended 12/31/94, income was $1.69 billion, up 30% from the $1.30 billion earned in 1993. NB cited loan growth and increased fee income as principal reasons for record results. Net interest income increased to $5.31 billion from $4.72 billion, the 12.5% hike was attributed to an 18% rise in average consumer loans and a 9% rise in commercial loans. The provision for credit losses was lowered to $310 million from $430 million.

PROSPECTS: As part of the Company's focus to grow fee income, NationsBank is expanding the size of its mortgage business. KeyCorp Mortgage Inc. agreed to sell its $25 billion mortgage-servicing portfolio and related servicing assets to NB for $500 million. The Company also announced plans to buy $10 billion in mortgage-servicing rights from Source One Mortgage Services Corp. This acquisition will make NB's servicing portfolio the 11th largest in the nation.

BUSINESS

NATIONSBANK CORP. (formerly NCNB Corp.) is the nation's third largest banking company with total assets of $170 billion and 1,929 banking centers in nine states and the District of Columbia. It was created by the December 31, 1991 combination of NCNB Corp. and C&S/Sovran Corp. The Company provides diversified financial services, including general, international and merchant banking, consumer and commercial finance, leasing, factoring, and trust services.

LOAN DISTRIBUTION

(12/31/94)	($000)	(%)
Commercial	55,135,000	55.0
Residential Mortgage	17,311,000	17.1
Home Equity	2,644,000	3.0
Bank Card	4,756,000	4.1
Other Consumer	18,209,000	18.0
Foreign	1,984,000	2.0
Factored Accts Receivable	1,004,000	1.0
Total	101,043,000	100.2

ANNUAL EARNINGS AND DIVIDENDS PER SHARE

	1994	1993	1992	1991	1990	1989	1988
Earnings Per Share	6.12	5.00	4.60	0.76	3.40	4.62	2.90
Dividends Per Share	1.88	1.64	1.51	1.48	1.42	1.10	0.94
Dividend Payout %	30.7	32.8	32.8	N.M.	41.8	23.8	32.4

ANNUAL FINANCIAL DATA

RECORD OF EARNINGS (IN MILLIONS):

Total Interest Income	10,574.0	8,221.0	7,824.0	9,502.0	5,802.0	5,414.0	2,514.0
Total Interest Expense	5,318.0	3,570.0	3,682.0	5,599.0	3,912.0	3,589.0	1,567.0
Net Interest Income	5,256.0	4,651.0	4,142.0	3,903.0	1,890.0	1,825.0	947.0
Credit Loss Provision	310.0	430.0	715.0	1,582.0	505.0	239.0	122.0
Net Income	1,690.0	①1,301.0	1,145.0	202.0	366.0	447.0	252.0
Aver. Shs. Outstg. (000)	274,656,000	258,000	243,748,000	226,000	102,000	92,000	85,000
① Before acctg. change cr$200,000,000.							

BALANCE SHEET (IN MILLIONS):

Loans & Lse Financing, Net	101,185.0	89,838.0	71,260.0	67,503.0	36,436.0	33,944.0	18,677.0
Total Domestic Deposits	87,867.0	87,079.0	80,690.0	86,715.0	48,496.0	46,427.0	19,814.0
Total Foreign Deposits	12,603.0	4,034.0	2,037.0	1,360.0	1,726.0	2,149.0	857.0
Long-term Debt	8,488.0	8,352.0	3,066.0	2,876.0	1,697.0	1,465.0	493.0
Net Stockholders' Equity	11,011.0	9,979.0	7,814.0	6,518.0	3,208.0	2,962.0	1,943.0
Total Assets	169,604.0	157,686.0	118,059.0	110,319.0	65,283.0	66,192.0	29,849.0
Year End Shs Outstg (000)	276,452,000	271,000	252,990,000	231,000	103,000	101,000	86,000

STATISTICAL RECORD:

Return on Assets %	1.00	0.83	0.97	0.18	0.56	0.68	0.84
Return on Equity %	15.30	13.00	14.70	3.10	11.40	15.10	13.00
Book Value Per Share	39.70	36.39	30.80	27.97	28.72	26.85	22.53
Average Yield %	3.7	3.2	3.2	4.6	4.4	2.7	4.0
P/E Ratio	9.4-7.1	11.6-8.9	11.6-8.6	56.3-28.3	13.9-5.0	11.9-5.8	10.0-6.0
Price Range	57⅜-43⅜	58-44½	53⅜-39⅝	42¾-21½	47¼-16⅞		55-27 29⅛-17½

Statistics are as originally reported.

OFFICERS:
H.L. McColl, Jr., Chmn. & C.E.O.
J.H. Hance, Vice-Chmn. & C.F.O.
K.D. Lewis, Pres.
INCORPORATED: NC, Jul., 1968
PRINCIPAL OFFICE: NationsBank Corporate Center, Charlotte, NC 28255

TELEPHONE NUMBER: (704) 386-5000
NO. OF EMPLOYEES: 61,484
ANNUAL MEETING: In April
SHAREHOLDERS: 105,774
INSTITUTIONAL HOLDINGS:
No. of Institutions: 643
Shares Held: 149,763,972

REGISTRAR(S):

TRANSFER AGENT(S): Chemical Bank, New York, NY

NYS SYMBOL NBD
Rec. Pr. 30½

NBD BANCORP, INC.

YIELD 4.3%
P/E RATIO 8.6

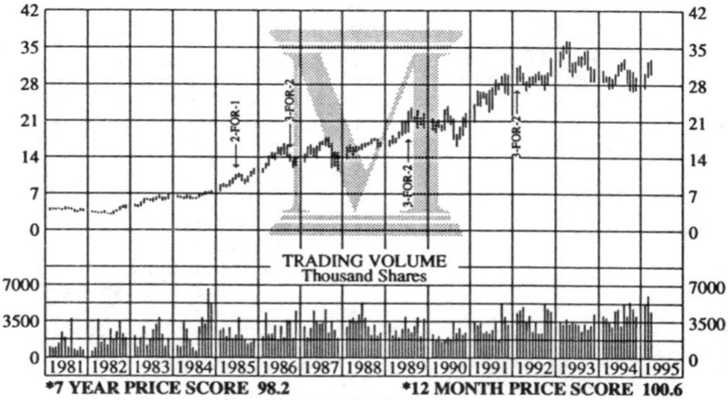

*7 YEAR PRICE SCORE 98.2 *12 MONTH PRICE SCORE 100.6

*NYSE COMPOSITE INDEX=100

INTERIM EARNINGS (Per Share):

Qtr.	Mar.	June	Sept.	Dec.
1992	0.62	0.56	0.23	0.70
1993	0.71	0.76	0.77	0.74
1994	0.77	0.84	0.93	0.91
1995	0.88	...	...	...

INTERIM DIVIDENDS (Per Share):

Amt.	Decl.	Ex.	Rec.	Pay.
0.30Q	3/21/94	4/13/94	4/19/94	5/10/94
0.30Q	6/20	7/14	7/20	8/10
0.30Q	9/19	10/14	10/20	11/10
0.33Q	12/19	1/13/95	1/20/95	2/10/95
0.33Q	3/20/95	4/12	4/19	5/10

*Indicated div.: $1.32**

CAPITALIZATION (12/31/94):

	($000)	(%)
Total Deposits	33,229,441	71.3
Total Debt	9,624,320	20.7
Common & Surplus	3,291,543	7.1
Loan Valuation Reserve	435,051	0.9
Total	46,580,355	100.0

DIVIDEND ACHIEVER STATUS:
Rank: 90 1984-94 Growth Rate: 13.2%
Total Years of Dividend Growth: 28

RECENT DEVELOPMENTS: For the year ended 12/31/94, income before an extraordinary item and accounting method adjustments was $547.3 million versus $481.8 million in 1993. Net interest income was $1.62 billion, a modest gain of 4%. The provision for loan losses was slashed 56.5% to $52.0 million. Noninterest expense was down to $1.30 billion from $1.32 billion. For the quarter ended 12/31/94, net income advanced 19% from the prior-year quarter to $141.5 million. Net interest income was $422.3 million, up 10%.

PROSPECTS: NBD completed its acquisition of Amerifed Financial Corp, a Joliet, IL-based company with assets of $910 million and ten branch offices. Amerifed will significantly boost the Company's presence in southwest Chicago. The transaction is valued at $148 million. NBD also announced plans to purchase Deerbank Corp. in a transaction worth approximately $120 million. Deerbank has $766 million in assets and 15 offices in Lake McHenry and Cook Counties, IL.

BUSINESS

NBD BANCORP, INC. is a regional bank holding company with assets of $47.1 billion. It operates banks in Michigan, Illinois, Indiana, Ohio and Florida markets and bank-related subsidiaries that provide commercial finance, mortgage banking, insurance, trust services, leasing, consumer credit processing and securities trading services to corporate, retail and trust customers across the country and throughout the world. The Company maintains 52 offices in Chicago; 23 offices in Columbus and Dayton, Ohio; 233 offices in Indiana and offices in Venice, Sarasota, North Palm Beach, Boca Raton, Fort Myers and Naples, Florida. Its principal subsidiary, NBD Bank, N.A., is the 18th-largest bank in the country.

LOAN DISTRIBUTION

(12/31/94)	($000)	(%)
Commercial	15,525,645	53.1
Real Estate-Construction	817,452	3.0
Real Estate-Mortgage	3,351,840	11.4
Consumer	7,667,907	26.2
Lease Financing	363,200	1.2
Foreign	1,473,449	5.0
Mortgages Held For Sale	30,171	0.1
Total	29,229,664	100.0

ANNUAL EARNINGS AND DIVIDENDS PER SHARE

	1994	1993	1992	1991	1990	1989	1988
Earnings Per Share	3.45	2.98	1 2.11	2.49	2.50	2.39	2.14
Dividends Per Share	1.17	1.08	2 1.02	0.933	0.893	3 0.751	0.605
Dividend Payout %	33.9	36.2	48.3	37.5	35.7	31.4	28.3

1 Before acctg. chg. 2 3-for-2 stk split, 1/7/92 3 3-for-2 stk. split, 6/89

ANNUAL FINANCIAL DATA

	1994	1993	1992	1991	1990	1989	1988
RECORD OF EARNINGS (IN MILLIONS):							
Total Interest Income	2,915.4	2,622.8	2,843.8	2,386.9	2,408.4	2,281.9	1,935.3
Total Interest Expense	1,290.6	1,064.7	1,334.0	1,378.9	1,516.6	1,447.2	1,178.1
Net Interest Income	1,624.8	1,558.1	1,509.8	1,008.0	891.8	834.7	757.1
Credit Loss Provision	52.0	119.7	228.5	95.8	65.8	55.1	46.0
Net Income	1 547.3	2 481.8	3 338.0	293.0	274.8	258.8	227.2
Aver. Shs. Outstg. (000)	158,808	161,253	160,716	117,598	109,892	108,178	105,984

1 Before acctg. change dr$15,615,000. 2 Before acctg. change cr$3,950,000. 3 Before acctg. change dr$37,885,000.

	1994	1993	1992	1991	1990	1989	1988
BALANCE SHEET (IN MILLIONS):							
Cash and Due From Banks	2,587.0	2,405.7	2,549.3	1,507.3	1,417.1	1,668.8	1,913.4
Loans & Lse Financing, Net	28,794.6	25,127.8	24,725.9	17,457.4	16,061.2	15,117.2	14,444.6
Total Domestic Deposits	27,426.2	27,755.1	29,187.6	20,624.3	19,851.8	18,362.4	17,932.5
Total Foreign Deposits	5,803.2	2,066.0	1,813.1	1,568.4	1,394.2	1,443.7	1,562.3
Long-term Debt	2,504.3	1,434.9	975.4	450.0	222.6	265.0	390.5
Net Stockholders' Equity	3,291.5	3,248.6	2,940.9	2,089.5	1,860.3	1,673.8	1,503.5
Total Assets	47,111.1	40,775.9	40,937.2	29,513.5	26,746.6	25,771.3	24,176.2
Year End Shs Outstg (000)	155,909	160,715	160,386	115,917	109,425	107,948	106,968
STATISTICAL RECORD:							
Return on Assets %	1.16	1.18	0.83	0.99	1.03	1.00	0.94
Return on Equity %	16.60	14.80	11.50	14.00	14.80	15.50	15.10
Book Value Per Share	21.11	20.21	18.34	18.03	17.00	15.51	14.06
Average Yield %	3.9	3.3	3.4	3.7	4.5	3.8	3.9
P/E Ratio	9.6-7.8	12.2-9.6	15.7-12.7	12.1-8.3	9.6-6.5	9.9-6.7	8.3-6.4
Price Range	33-26¾	36⅜-28⅝	33⅛-26¾	30⅛-20¾	23⅞-16⅛	23⅝-16⅛	17¾-13⅝

Statistics are as originally reported.

OFFICERS:
V.G. Istock, Chmn. & C.E.O.
T.H. Jeffs, II, Pres. & C.O.O.
P.S. Jones, Exec. V.P., C.F.O. & Treas.
D.T. Lis, Sr. V.P. & Sec.

INCORPORATED: DE, Jul., 1972

PRINCIPAL OFFICE: 611 Woodward Ave., Detroit, MI 48226

TELEPHONE NUMBER: (313) 225-1000

NO. OF EMPLOYEES: 17,836 (approx.)

ANNUAL MEETING: In May

SHAREHOLDERS: 26,000 (approx.)

INSTITUTIONAL HOLDINGS:
No. of Institutions: 347
Shares Held: 71,939,912

REGISTRAR(S): NBD Bank, N.A., Securities Transfer Services, Detroit, MI 02266

TRANSFER AGENT(S): NBD Bank, N.A., Securities Transfer Services, Detroit, MI 02266

NEW PLAN REALTY TRUST

YIELD 6.5%
P/E RATIO 18.4

TRADING VOLUME
Thousand Shares

*7 YEAR PRICE SCORE 89.2   ***12 MONTH PRICE SCORE 95.5**
NYSE COMPOSITE INDEX=100

INTERIM EARNINGS (Per Share):

Qtr.	Oct.	Jan.	Apr.	July
1991-92	0.26	0.20	0.23	0.39
1992-93	0.22	0.22	0.23	0.22
1993-94	0.25	00.2600	0.27	0.28
1994-95	0.29	0.30	...	...

INTERIM DIVIDENDS (Per Share):

Amt.	Decl.	Ex.	Rec.	Pay.
0.33Q	2/25/94	3/11/94	3/16/94	4/6/94
0.3325Q	5/26	6/9	6/15	7/6
0.335Q	8/29	9/9	9/15	10/4
0.3375Q	12/14	12/27	1/3/95	1/17/95
0.34Q	3/7/95	3/10/95	3/16	4/4

Indicated div.: $1.36

CAPITALIZATION (7/31/94):

	($000)	(%)
Long-Term Debt	28,060	4.7
Common & Surplus	565,493	95.3
Total	593,553	100.0

DIVIDEND ACHIEVER STATUS:

Rank: 202   1984-94 Growth Rate: 8.4%
Total Years of Dividend Growth: 13

RECENT DEVELOPMENTS: For the quarter ended 1/31/95, net income was $15.8 million compared with $12.9 million in the equivalent period of 1994. Total revenues climbed 29% to $32.1 million from $24.9 million in the prior-year quarter. The drastic 31% improvement in rental income and related revenues offset a slight decline in interest and dividend income. For the six months ended 1/31/95, net income advanced to $31.1 million from $25.0 million in the same period of 1994, an increase of 24%. Rental income and related revenues rose to $60.4 million from $43.9 million in the prior-year period, and buoyed the 33% increase in total revenues to $62.0 million. NPR operates 130 commercial or residential properties in 19 states. The Company's active acquisition program has garnered more than $500.0 million in properties over the previous three years.

BUSINESS

NEW PLAN REALTY TRUST is the nation's largest real estate investment trust. The trust owns 130 properties in 19 states, including traditional shopping centers, factory outlet centers, garden apartment properties and other real estate. The trust has been publicly-owned since 1962 and has been a real estate investment trust since 1972.

REVENUES

(7/31/94)	($000)	(%)
Rental Inc & Rel Rev	96,384	95.5
Int & Div Inc	4,570	4.5
Total	100,955	100.0

ANNUAL EARNINGS AND DIVIDENDS PER SHARE

	7/31/94	7/31/93	7/31/92	7/31/91	7/31/90	7/31/89	7/31/88
Earnings Per Share	1.06	0.89	1.08	1.05	1.01	0.95	0.88
Dividends Per Share	1.325	1.285	1.23	1.15	1.07	0.99	0.91
Dividend Payout %	N.M.	N.M.	N.M.	N.M.	N.M.	N.M.	N.M.

ANNUAL FINANCIAL DATA

	7/31/94	7/31/93	7/31/92	7/31/91	7/31/90	7/31/89	7/31/88
RECORD OF EARNINGS (IN THOUSANDS):							
Total Revenues	100,955	76,309	64,692	57,383	54,123	43,541	37,320
Costs and Expenses	35,572	23,826	17,690	15,944	16,691	13,357	11,764
Operating Income	54,041	44,909	41,951	37,234	33,870	27,019	22,988
Net Income	52,317	43,229	49,446	39,878	35,047	27,111	23,450
Aver. Shs. Outstg.	49,502	48,838	45,971	38,138	34,844	28,620	26,734
BALANCE SHEET (IN THOUSANDS):							
Cash and Cash Equivalents	9,409	150,301	219,322	281,863	141,495	170,844	90,016
Receivables, Net	30,828	29,955	38,565	24,450	18,295	11,890	5,803
Long-Term Debt	28,060	23,321	17,494	18,643	22,713	22,746	22,523
Net Stockholders' Equity	565,493	500,571	506,339	437,206	279,490	274,199	161,866
Total Assets	616,993	534,248	530,827	461,913	307,678	301,282	187,320
Total Current Assets	42,665	181,720	258,909	307,120	160,723	183,300	96,589
Total Current Liabilities	9,774	1,548	1,442	1,274	1,305	1,248	1,120
Net Working Capital	32,891	180,173	257,467	305,846	159,418	182,051	95,468
Year End Shares Outstg	52,594	48,957	48,385	44,491	35,151	34,713	26,847
STATISTICAL RECORD:							
Return on Equity %	9.3	8.6	9.8	9.1	12.5	9.9	14.5
Return on Assets %	8.5	8.1	9.3	8.6	11.4	9.0	12.5
Book Value Per Share	10.75	10.22	10.46	9.83	7.95	7.90	6.03
Average Yield %	6.1	5.4	5.4	5.7	6.6	5.8	6.1
P/E Ratio	23.1-17.7	29.6-24.2	24.2-18.2	23.3-15.4	18.4-13.6	19.7-16.1	19.0-15.1
Price Range	24½-18¾	26⅜-21½	26⅛-19⅝	24½-16⅛	18⅝-13¾	18¾-15¼	16¾-13¼

Statistics are as originally reported.

OFFICERS:
W. Newman, Chmn. & C.E.O.
A. Laubich, Pres. & C.O.O.
W. Kirshenbaum, V.P. & Treas.
S.F. Siegel, Sec. & General Counsel
M.I. Brown, C.F.O. & Contr.

PRINCIPAL OFFICE: 1120 Avenue Of The Americas, New York, NY 10036

TELEPHONE NUMBER: (212) 869-3000

NO. OF EMPLOYEES: 318

ANNUAL MEETING: In December

SHAREHOLDERS: 11,895

INSTITUTIONAL HOLDINGS:
No. of Institutions: 119
Shares Held: 8,037,643

REGISTRAR(S): First National Bank of Boston, Boston, MA

TRANSFER AGENT(S): First National Bank of Boston, Boston, MA

NASDAQ SYMBOL NDSN
Rec. Pr. 55⅝

NORDSON CORP.

YIELD 1.2%
P/E RATIO 22.1

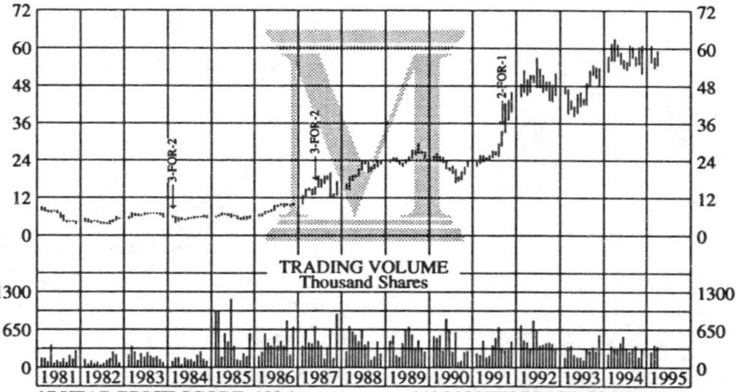

TRADING VOLUME
Thousand Shares

*7 YEAR PRICE SCORE 128.1   *12 MONTH PRICE SCORE 95.0
*NYSE COMPOSITE INDEX=100

INTERIM EARNINGS (Per Share):

Qtr.	Jan.	May	July	Oct.
1992-93	0.35	0.46	0.63	0.69
1993-94	0.41	0.56	0.69	0.79
1994-95	0.48	...	...	...

INTERIM DIVIDENDS (Per Share):

Amt.	Decl.	Ex.	Rec.	Pay.
0.14Q	2/16/94	2/28/94	3/4/94	3/29/94
0.14Q	5/18	5/27	6/3	6/28
0.14Q	8/17	8/29	9/2	9/27
0.16Q	11/16	11/28	12/2	1/3/95
0.16Q	2/15/95	2/27/95	3/3/95	3/28

Indicated div.: $0.64

CAPITALIZATION (10/30/94):

	($000)	(%)
Long-Term Debt	15,212	6.6
Cap. Lease Oblig.	4,042	1.7
Common & Surplus	212,424	91.7
Total	231,678	100.0

DIVIDEND ACHIEVER STATUS:
Rank: 145   1984-94 Growth Rate: 10.8%
Total Years of Dividend Growth: 13

RECENT DEVELOPMENTS: For the quarter ended 1/29/95, net income was $8.9 million, or $0.48 per share, compared with $7.8 million, or $0.41 per share, in the same period of 1993. Sales leaped 17.9% to $123.5 million, up from $104.7 million in the year-earlier quarter. Revenue gains for the quarter consisted of a 13% increase in sales volume, with the balance attributable to favorable currency effects. Combined reve-

nues from North America and Pacific South operations rose more than 20% over the prior period, while revenues from European operations were up 8% in local currencies. Shipments to customers in Japan were slightly below prior-year levels, primarily due to persistent sluggish economic conditions. Gross margins, as a percentage of sales, were 57.8%, compared with 60.4%, due to changes in product sales mix.

BUSINESS

NORDSON CORPORATION develops, manufactures and markets worldwide industrial application equipment, along with the software and application technologies that enhance its use. The Company's customers produce consumer and industrial products by processes in which the use of adhesives, sealants, coatings and other technology-oriented materials are utilized. In the packaging and product assembly business, Nordson designs, engineers and manufactures equipment to melt, pump, transfer and apply a variety of adhesives, sealants, caulking and other materials. These compounds are used in the manufacture and sealing of packages, and in numerous industrial production and processing applications. In the powder and liquid finishing businesses, Nordson designs, engineers and manufactures coating equipment ranging from relatively simple manual systems to sophisticated, programmable, automatic systems.

BUSINESS LINE ANALYSIS

(10/31/94)	Rev(%)	Inc(%)
North America	44.6	77.1
Europe	33.1	14.1
Japan	14.7	6.2
Pacific & Latin America	7.6	2.6
Total	100.0	100.0

ANNUAL EARNINGS AND DIVIDENDS PER SHARE

	10/30/94	10/31/93	11/1/92	11/3/91	10/28/90	10/29/89	10/30/88
Earnings Per Share	2.45	2.13	2.03	1.77	1.53	1.77	1.56
Dividends Per Share	0.56	0.48	0.44	① 0.40	0.36	0.32	0.28
Dividend Payout %	22.9	22.5	21.7	22.6	23.6	18.1	18.0

① Adj for 2-for-1 stk split, 9/25/91

ANNUAL FINANCIAL DATA

RECORD OF EARNINGS (IN THOUSANDS):

Total Revenues	506,692	461,557	425,618	387,962	344,904	282,098	245,028
Costs and Expenses	413,870	377,076	341,645	314,952	282,027	220,877	188,935
Depreciation & Amort	18,418	17,107	16,679	14,747	13,076	8,427	6,875
Operating Profit	74,404	67,374	67,294	58,263	49,801	52,794	49,218
Income Bef Income Taxes	70,858	62,248	60,767	51,960	44,802	51,787	48,559
Income Taxes	24,204	21,473	21,230	18,173	15,456	17,600	16,976
Net Income	46,654	① 40,775	39,537	33,787	29,346	34,187	31,583
Aver. Shs. Outstg.	19,067	19,184	19,471	19,093	19,266	19,386	20,340

① Before acctg. change dr$4,784,000.

BALANCE SHEET (IN THOUSANDS):

Cash and Cash Equivalents	11,064	23,363	13,009	10,481	8,837	5,753	16,065
Receivables, Net	140,648	129,103	127,308	102,801	95,019	79,092	60,194
Inventories	93,615	84,661	87,674	78,471	68,027	68,662	41,794
Gross Property	167,611	146,939	139,102	124,881	118,042	100,001	66,875
Accumulated Depreciation	78,956	68,250	61,730	50,441	44,353	35,783	26,741
Long-Term Debt	15,212	17,667	22,075	22,172	22,261	17,742	11,019
Capital Lease Obligations	4,042	4,422	4,748	3,359	3,240	2,396	2,230
Net Stockholders' Equity	212,424	196,405	177,720	152,714	130,374	106,918	89,109
Total Assets	380,944	357,970	346,297	296,930	269,523	235,551	162,912
Total Current Assets	250,307	241,672	231,836	193,915	173,924	156,168	119,837
Total Current Liabilities	123,311	116,281	126,698	106,911	107,831	102,334	55,797
Net Working Capital	126,996	125,391	105,138	87,004	66,093	53,834	64,040
Year End Shares Outstg	18,399	18,726	18,752	18,754	18,794	18,810	19,176

STATISTICAL RECORD:

Operating Profit Margin %	14.7	14.6	15.8	15.0	14.4	18.7	20.1
Book Value Per Share	9.92	9.03	7.79	6.87	5.99	4.98	4.56
Return on Equity %	22.0	20.8	22.2	22.1	22.5	32.0	35.4
Return on Assets %	12.2	11.4	11.4	11.4	10.9	14.5	19.4
Average Yield %	1.0	1.0	0.9	1.2	1.7	1.2	1.4
P/E Ratio	25.7-21.2	25.7-18.0	28.1-21.2	26.0-12.5	17.3-11.1	16.7-12.4	15.5-9.3
Price Range	63-52	54¾-38¼	57-43	46-22⅛	26¼-16⅞	29½-22	24⅛-14½

Statistics are as originally reported.

OFFICERS:
E.T. Nord, Chmn.
W.P. Madar, Pres. & C.E.O.
N.D. Pellecchia, V.P.-Fin. & Treas.
W.D. Ginn, Sec.

INCORPORATED: OH, 1954

PRINCIPAL OFFICE: 28601 Clemens Road, Westlake, OH 44145

TELEPHONE NUMBER: (216) 892-1580

FAX: (216) 892-9507

NO. OF EMPLOYEES: 3,034 (approx.)

ANNUAL MEETING: In March

SHAREHOLDERS: 3,281 (approx.)

INSTITUTIONAL HOLDINGS:
No. of Institutions: 117
Shares Held: 4,762,150

REGISTRAR(S): Society National Bank, Cleveland, OH

TRANSFER AGENT(S): Society National Bank, Cleveland, OH

NORDSTROM, INC.

YIELD	1.3%
P/E RATIO	15.7

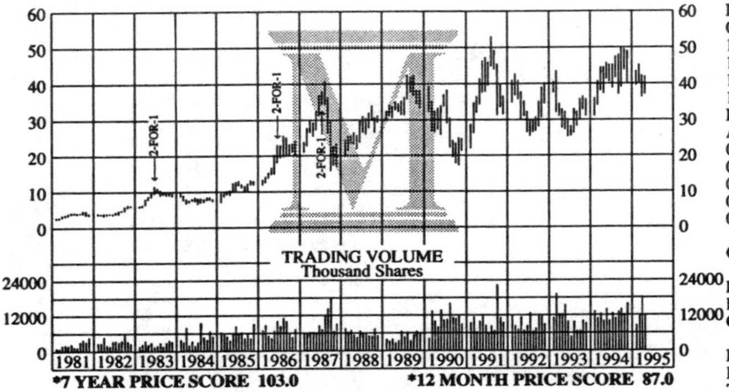

TRADING VOLUME
Thousand Shares

1981 1982 1983 1984 1985 1986 1987 1988 1989 1990 1991 1992 1993 1994 1995

7 YEAR PRICE SCORE 103.0   **12 MONTH PRICE SCORE 87.0**
*NYSE COMPOSITE INDEX=100

INTERIM EARNINGS (Per Share):

Qtr.	Apr.	July	Oct.	Jan.
1991-92	0.31	0.61	0.24	0.50
1992-93	---------------- 1.67 ----------------			
1993-94	0.14	0.52	0.31	0.74
1994-95	0.39	0.77	0.46	0.85

INTERIM DIVIDENDS (Per Share):

Amt.	Decl.	Ex.	Rec.	Pay.
0.10Q	11/15/94	11/23/94	11/30/94	12/15/94
0.10Q	11/15	11/23	11/30	12/15
0.10Q	11/15	11/23	11/30	12/15
0.125Q	2/21/95	2/27/95	3/3/95	3/15/95
0.125Q	5/17	5/24	5/31	6/15

Indicated div.: $0.50

CAPITALIZATION (1/31/95):

	($000)	(%)
Long-Term Debt	297,943	17.5
Deferred Income Tax	64,586	3.8
Common & Surplus	1,343,800	78.7
Total	1,706,329	100.0

DIVIDEND ACHIEVER STATUS:
Rank: 64   1984-94 Growth Rate: 14.4%
Total Years of Dividend Growth: 21

RECENT DEVELOPMENTS: For the year ended 1/31/95, net income was $203.0 million, up 44.5% from $140.4 million a year earlier. Net sales advanced 8.5% to $3.89 billion from $3.59 billion in the prior year. Comparable store sales increased 4.4%. Selling, general and administrative expenses increased to 26.3% of sales from 26.2% a year earlier. Gross margin increased to 33.3% of sales from 31.2% a year earlier. Results were aided by better inventory management and

improvement in the women's apparel category. For the quarter ended 1/31/95, net income was $69.9 million compared with $61.0 million the year before. Net sales increased 7.5% to $1.19 billion from $1.11 billion in the prior-year period. Comparable store sales rose 1.5%. Gross margin increased to 33.1% of sales from 32.2% a year earlier. Selling, general and administrative expenses increased to 24.7% of sales from 24.2% a year earlier.

BUSINESS

NORDSTROM, INC. operates 76 large specialty stores in Washington, Oregon, California, Utah, Alaska, Virginia, New Jersey, Illinois, Maryland and Minnesota, selling a wide selection of apparel, shoes and accessories for women, men and children. The Company also operates sixteen clearance stores under the name "Nordstrom Rack," which serve as outlets for clearance merchandise from the Company's large specialty stores. Racks also purchase merchandise directly from manufacturers. The Racks are located in Washington, Oregon, California, Utah, Virginia and Maryland. The Company also operates four smaller specialty stores under the name "Place Two" in Washington, one clearance store in Arizona under the name "Last Chance" and leased shoe departments in 11 department stores in Hawaii.

QUARTERLY DATA
(1/31/95)($000)

	Rev	Inc
1st Quarter..................	762,062	31,973
2nd Quarter.................	1,079,501	63,023
3rd Quarter	861,968	38,079
4th Quarter..................	1,190,947	69,883

ANNUAL EARNINGS AND DIVIDENDS PER SHARE

	1/31/95	1/31/94	1/31/93	1/31/92	1/31/91	1/31/90	1/31/89
Earnings Per Share	2.47	1.71	1.67	1.66	1.42	1.41	1.51
Dividends Per Share	0.385	0.34	0.32	0.31	0.30	0.28	0.22
Dividend Payout %	15.6	45.2	19.2	18.7	21.1	19.9	14.6

ANNUAL FINANCIAL DATA

RECORD OF EARNINGS (IN MILLIONS):

	1/31/95	1/31/94	1/31/93	1/31/92	1/31/91	1/31/90	1/31/89
Total Revenues	3,894.5	3,589.9	3,422.0	3,179.8	2,893.9	2,671.1	2,327.9
Costs and Expenses	3,512.1	3,306.4	3,138.4	2,904.9	2,662.4	2,427.7	2,086.2
Depreciation & Amort	110.8	103.5	102.8	96.0	85.6	70.9	60.6
Operating Profit	1,294.9	1,120.6	1,082.9	1,010.4	893.7	841.7	764.1
Earn Bef Income Taxes	335.6	230.9	221.1	217.2	178.3	179.4	198.4
Income Taxes	132.6	90.5	85.5	81.4	62.5	64.5	75.1
Net Income	203.0	140.4	136.6	135.8	115.8	114.9	123.3
Aver. Shs. Outstg. (000)	82,144	82,003	81,893	81,780	81,675	81,528	...

BALANCE SHEET (IN MILLIONS):

Cash and Cash Equivalents	32.5	91.2	29.1	14.7	24.7	33.1	16.1
Receivables, Net	675.9	586.4	603.2	608.2	575.5	536.3	481.6
Inventories	627.9	585.6	536.7	506.6	448.3	420.0	403.8
Gross Property	1,730.9	1,499.6	1,385.1	1,327.2	1,184.9	994.3	837.6
Accumulated Depreciation	746.7	654.0	560.9	470.8	378.7	302.4	243.6
Long-Term Debt	297.9	336.4	440.6	502.2	457.7	418.5	346.5
Net Stockholders' Equity	1,343.8	1,166.5	1,052.0	939.2	826.4	733.3	639.9
Total Assets	2,396.8	2,177.5	2,053.2	2,041.9	1,902.6	1,707.4	1,511.7
Total Current Assets	1,397.7	1,314.9	1,219.8	1,177.6	1,090.4	1,011.1	914.9
Total Current Liabilities	690.5	627.5	511.2	553.9	551.8	489.9	448.2
Net Working Capital	707.3	687.4	708.6	623.7	538.5	521.3	466.8
Year End Shs Outstg (000)	82,244	82,059	81,975	81,844	81,738	81,585	81,465

STATISTICAL RECORD:

Operating Profit Margin %	7.0	5.0	5.3	5.6	5.0	6.5	7.8
Book Value Per Share	16.34	14.22	12.83	11.48	10.11	8.99	7.86
Return on Equity %	15.1	12.0	13.0	14.5	14.0	15.7	19.3
Return on Assets %	8.5	6.4	6.7	6.7	6.1	6.7	8.2
Average Yield %	1.0	1.1	1.0	0.8	1.1	0.8	0.8
P/E Ratio	20.1-12.6	25.4-14.8	25.6-15.3	31.9-13.3	27.6-12.1	30.1-21.1	22.5-13.1
Price Range	49¾-31	43½-25¼	42¾-25½		53-22	39¼-17¼	42½-29¾	34-19¾

Statistics are as originally reported.

OFFICERS:
B.A. Nordstrom, Co-Chmn.
J.N. Nordstrom, Co-Chmn.
J.F. Nordstrom, Co.-Chmn.
J.A. McMillan, Co.-Chmn.
R.A. Johnson, Co-Pres.
J.J. Whitacre, Co-Pres.
INCORPORATED: WA, 1946
PRINCIPAL OFFICE: 1501 Fifth Avenue, Seattle, WA 98101-1603

TELEPHONE NUMBER: (206) 628-2111
FAX: (206) 628-1707
NO. OF EMPLOYEES: 33,000 (approx.)
ANNUAL MEETING: In May
SHAREHOLDERS: 71,500 (approx.)
INSTITUTIONAL HOLDINGS:
No. of Institutions: 425
Shares Held: 42,819,065

REGISTRAR(S): First Interstate Bank of California, Los Angeles, CA

TRANSFER AGENT(S): First Interstate Bank of California, Los Angeles, CA

NYS SYMBOL NCG
Rec. Pr. 22¼

NORTH CAROLINA NATURAL GAS CORP.

YIELD 5.5%
P/E RATIO 13.2

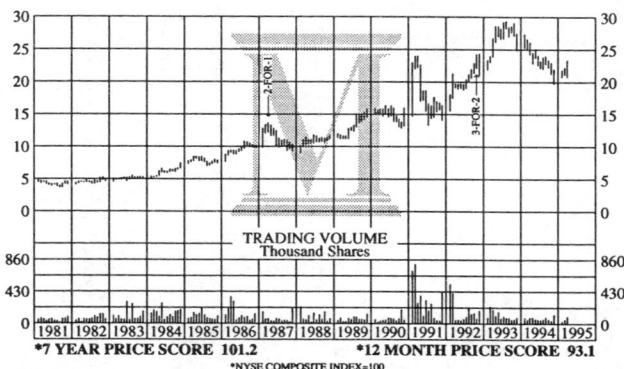

7 YEAR PRICE SCORE 101.2　　**12 MONTH PRICE SCORE 93.1**
*NYSE COMPOSITE INDEX=100

INTERIM EARNINGS (Per Share):

Qtr.	Dec.	Mar.	June	Sept.
1992-93	---------------- 1.84 ----------------		
1993-94	0.59	1.15	0.02	Nil
1994-95	0.52	...	...	...

INTERIM DIVIDENDS (Per Share):

Amt.	Decl.	Ex.	Rec.	Pay.
0.29Q	1/11/94	2/23/94	3/1/94	3/15/94
0.29Q	5/11	5/25	6/1	6/15
0.29Q	8/3	8/26	9/1	9/15
0.29Q	11/10	11/25	12/1	12/15
0.305Q	1/10/95	2/23/95	3/1/95	3/15/95

*Indicated div.: $1.22**

CAPITALIZATION (9/30/94):

	($000)	(%)
Long-Term Debt	37,000	25.5
Deferred Income Tax	21,401	14.8
Common & Surplus	86,399	59.7
Total	144,800	100.0
Current Debt................	11,282	

DIVIDEND ACHIEVER STATUS:
Rank: 224　　1984-94 Growth Rate: 7.6%
Total Years of Dividend Growth: 16

RECENT DEVELOPMENTS: For the quarter ended 12/31/94, net income declined to $3.3 million from $3.7 million in the equivalent period of 1994. The Company's operating revenues were $34.4 million compared with $42.1 million in the same period of the previous year, a decrease of 18%. The decline in operating revenues was tempered by a sharp increase in NCG's gross margin, which rose by almost six percentage points to 41.9% from 36.0% in the corresponding period of the year before. Additionally, operating expenses and taxes actually declined year-over-year and helped to push profit margin higher to 11.9% from 10.5% in the same period of 1993. Operations, maintenance and depreciation expenses all rose slightly and partially offset actual declines in general and income tax expenses.

BUSINESS

NORTH CAROLINA NATURAL GAS CORP. is engaged in the transmission and distribution of natural gas through approximately 1,006 miles of transmission pipeline and approximately 2,490 miles of distribution mains. Natural gas is sold under regulated rates to approximately 135,500 residential, commercial, industrial and municipal customers in 63 cities and towns and four municipal gas distribution systems in eastern and southcentral North Carolina. The Company purchases and transports natural gas under long-term contracts with Transcontinental Gas Pipe Line Corporation, Columbia Gas Transmission Corporation and several major oil and gas producers. A small volume of gas is purchased from NCNG Exploration Corporation, a subsidiary of the Company. The Company also serves propane gas to approximately 8,200 customers and sells gas appliances and home insulation services to gas customers and new home builders.

QUARTERLY DATA

(9/30/94)($000)	Rev	Inc
1st Quarter................	42,082	3,693
2nd Quarter...............	62,615	7,301
3rd Quarter	29,523	127
4th Quarter................	26,117	28

ANNUAL EARNINGS AND DIVIDENDS PER SHARE

	9/30/94	9/30/93	9/30/92	9/30/91	9/30/90	9/30/89	9/30/88
Earnings Per Share	1.76	1.84	1.79	1.31	1.40	1.53	1.35
Dividends Per Share	1.16	1.08	③ 1.00	0.933	0.893	0.80	0.733
Dividend Payout %	65.9	58.7	55.9	71.4	63.8	52.4	54.2

③ 3-for-2 stk split, 11/2/92

ANNUAL FINANCIAL DATA

RECORD OF EARNINGS (IN THOUSANDS):

Total Revenues	160,337	173,145	150,510	126,601	128,539	143,186	136,216
Depreciation	7,373	6,891	6,125	5,360	4,853	4,578	4,291
Maintenance	2,739	2,873	3,184	2,915	2,131	2,036	1,878
Prov for Fed Inc Taxes	4,995	4,942	3,990	3,274	2,557	3,819	3,430
Operating Income	14,403	15,092	14,231	10,951	10,343	11,309	10,307
Interest Expense	4,055	4,424	5,011	5,227	4,716	4,261	3,965
Net Income	11,150	10,977	9,697	7,014	7,441	8,058	7,085
Aver. Shs. Outstg.	6,331	5,981	5,414	5,362	5,311	5,279	5,247

BALANCE SHEET (IN THOUSANDS):

Gross Plant	243,877	224,946	210,761	187,879	167,361	152,143	140,719
Accumulated Depreciation	79,034	72,403	66,348	60,673	55,717	51,383	47,161
Prop, Plant & Equip, Net	164,843	152,543	144,412	127,205	111,644	100,760	93,559
Long-term Debt	37,000	39,000	45,088	23,452	27,741	30,030	32,319
Net Stockholders' Equity	86,399	80,944	57,413	51,967	49,106	45,696	41,407
Total Assets	205,087	194,178	186,550	151,714	138,472	123,356	115,564
Year End Shares Outstg	6,367	6,301	5,448	5,388	5,337	5,296	5,265

STATISTICAL RECORD:

Book Value Per Share	13.57	12.85	10.54	9.65	9.20	8.63	7.86
Op. Inc/Net Pl %	8.7	9.9	9.9	8.6	9.3	11.2	11.0
Dep/Gr. Pl %	3.0	3.1	2.9	2.9	2.9	3.0	3.0
Accum. Dep/Gr. Pl %	32.4	32.2	31.5	32.3	33.3	33.8	33.5
Return on Equity %	12.9	13.6	16.9	13.5	15.2	17.6	17.1
Average Yield %	4.9	4.2	5.0	5.0	6.1	5.9	7.0
P/E Ratio	15.6-11.2	16.0-11.9	13.6-8.7	18.3-10.2	11.7-9.2	10.4-7.3	8.8-6.7
Price Range	27⅜-19¾	29⅜-21⅞	24⅜-15½	24-13⅜	16⅜-12⅞	15⅞-11⅛	11⅞-9

Statistics are as originally reported.

OFFICERS:
C.B. Wells, Chmn., Pres. & C.E.O.
G.A. Teele, Sr. V.P. & C.F.O.
C.C. Dew, V.P. & Treas.
S.T. Sowers, Sec.

INCORPORATED: DE, Oct., 1955

PRINCIPAL OFFICE: 150 Rowan Street
P.O.Box 909, Fayetteville, NC 28302

TELEPHONE NUMBER: (910) 483-0315

FAX: (910) 483-0336

NO. OF EMPLOYEES: 536 approx.

ANNUAL MEETING: In January

SHAREHOLDERS: 5,250

INSTITUTIONAL HOLDINGS:
No. of Institutions: 40
Shares Held: 721,095

REGISTRAR(S):

TRANSFER AGENT(S): Wachovia Bank of North Carolina, N.A., P.O. Box 3001, Winston-Salem, NC 27102

NYS SYMBOL NSP
Rec. Pr. 44⅛

NORTHERN STATES POWER CO.

YIELD 6.0%
P/E RATIO 12.5

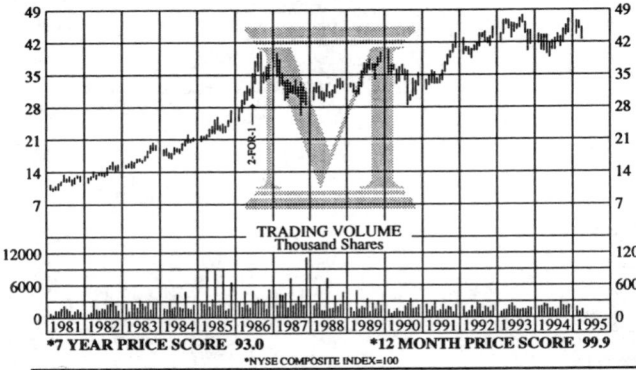

49				49
42				42
35				35
28				28
21				21
14				14
7				7

TRADING VOLUME
Thousand Shares

12000		12000
6000		6000
0		0

| 1981 | 1982 | 1983 | 1984 | 1985 | 1986 | 1987 | 1988 | 1989 | 1990 | 1991 | 1992 | 1993 | 1994 | 1995 |

*7 YEAR PRICE SCORE 93.0   *12 MONTH PRICE SCORE 99.9
*NYSE COMPOSITE INDEX=100

INTERIM EARNINGS (Per Share):

Qtr.	Mar.	June	Sept.	Dec.
1991	0.82	0.32	1.36	0.52
1992	0.63	0.43	0.83	0.42
1993	0.81	0.50	0.84	0.75
1994	0.94	0.74	1.09	0.68

INTERIM DIVIDENDS (Per Share):

Amt.	Decl.	Ex.	Rec.	Pay.
0.66Q	8/25/94	9/27/94	10/3/94	10/20/94
0.66Q	12/15	12/30	1/6/95	1/20/95
0.66Q	3/27/95	4/3/95	4/7	4/20

Indicated div.: $2.64*

CAPITALIZATION (12/31/94):

	($000)	(%)
Long-Term Debt	1,463,354	31.7
Deferred Income Tax	1,022,708	22.1
Preferred Stock	240,469	5.2
Common & Surplus	1,896,967	41.0
Total	4,623,498	100.0
Current Debt	396,145	

DIVIDEND ACHIEVER STATUS:

Rank: 278   1984-94 Growth Rate: 5.3%
Total Years of Dividend Growth: 19

RECENT DEVELOPMENTS: For the quarter ended 12/31/94, net income was $49.8 million versus $53.7 million in the corresponding quarter of 1993. Revenues were $609.8 million compared with $616.0 million a year earlier. For the year ended 12/31/94, net income advanced 15% to $243.5 million versus $211.7 million in the prior-year quarter. Revenues were $2.49 billion, up 3% from $2.40 billion in 1993.

PROSPECTS: NSP's non-regulated subsidiary, NRG Energy, Inc., is providing a boost to earnings through its investments in Saale Energie GmbH, a German corporation that provides electricity, a joint venture coal-fired power plant in Australia, and other international investments. Furthermore, NSP acquired a 50% interest for $15 million in Sunnyside Cogeneration Associates and STS HydroPower Limited, both are independent power producers.

BUSINESS

NORTHERN STATES POWER CO., an operating holding company, provides electric energy to customers in parts of Minnesota, Wisconsin, North and South Dakota, and Michigan's Upper Peninsula. NSP generates, transmits and distributes electric power to 1.3 million customers and distributes gas to more than 393,461 people in its 49,000 square mile service area. The Company also supplies telephone service in the Minot, North Dakota, area. Of total kwh sales, 23.4% is residential sales, 58.9% is commercial and industrial sales and 17.7% is other. Gas sales in thousands of mcf for 1994 were: residential 45.2%, commercial and industrial 54.5% and 0.3% miscellaneous.

REVENUES

(12/31/94)	($000)	(%)
Electric	2,066,644	83.1
Gas	419,903	16.9
Total	2,486,547	100.0

ANNUAL EARNINGS AND DIVIDENDS PER SHARE

	1994	1993	1992	1991	1990	1989	1988
Earnings Per Share	3.45	3.02	①2.31	②3.02	②2.79	3.24	3.11
Dividends Per Share	2.61	2.55	2.47	2.37	2.27	2.17	2.07
Dividend Payout %	75.7	84.4	N.M.	78.5	81.4	67.0	66.6

① Before acctg. chg. ② Before disc. oper.

ANNUAL FINANCIAL DATA

RECORD OF EARNINGS (IN MILLIONS):

Total Revenues	2,486.5	2,404.0	2,159.5	2,201.2	2,064.5	1,989.7	2,006.5
Depreciation & Amort	304.6	286.9	242.9	215.6	215.6	209.9	208.6
Maintenance	170.1	161.4	180.6	182.5	172.0	151.1	172.3
Prov for Fed Inc Taxes	129.2	128.3	90.7	117.3	114.4	108.5	117.1
Operating Income	308.3	303.9	256.0	305.5	288.8	306.7	303.2
Interest Expense	107.2	108.1	116.1	114.2	108.6	106.0	102.7
Net Income	243.5	211.7	206.4	①207.0	②193.0	222.0	214.8
Aver. Shs. Outstg. (000)	66,845	65,211	62,641	62,566	62,541	62,541	62,541

① Before disc. op. cr$17,035,000. ② Before disc. op. cr$2,516,000.

BALANCE SHEET (IN MILLIONS):

Gross Plant	8,109.2	7,775.9	7,349.5	6,979.0	6,703.0	6,475.7	6,210.5
Accumulated Depreciation	3,835.5	3,561.8	3,223.8	2,982.0	2,748.5	2,579.5	2,351.7
Prop, Plant & Equip, Net	4,273.7	4,214.1	4,125.7	3,997.0	3,954.6	3,896.2	3,858.8
Long-term Debt	1,463.4	1,291.9	1,299.9	1,233.9	1,239.5	1,262.7	1,275.7
Net Stockholders' Equity	2,137.4	2,067.9	1,897.6	1,877.3	1,827.6	1,786.5	1,777.3
Total Assets	5,954.5	5,587.7	4,977.8	4,752.6	4,834.8	4,621.7	4,548.3
Year End Shs Outstg (000)	66,922	66,880	62,598	62,541	62,541	62,541	62,541

STATISTICAL RECORD:

Book Value Per Share	27.14	26.26	25.91	25.21	24.43	23.77	22.82
Op. Inc/Net Pl %	7.2	7.2	6.2	7.6	7.3	7.9	7.9
Dep/Gr. Pl %	3.4	3.4	3.2	3.3	3.2	3.2	3.4
Accum. Dep/Gr. Pl %	47.3	45.8	43.9	42.7	41.0	39.8	37.9
Return on Equity %	11.4	10.2	8.5	11.0	10.6	12.4	12.1
Average Yield %	6.1	5.8	5.9	6.3	6.6	6.2	6.5
P/E Ratio	13.6-11.2	15.9-13.3	19.6-16.7	14.6-10.5	14.5-10.2	12.3-9.3	11.0-9.4
Price Range	47-38⅜	47⅛-40⅛	45⅜-38½	44-31¾	40½-28⅜	40-30¼	34¼-29¼

Statistics are as originally reported.

OFFICERS:
J.J. Howard, Chmn. & C.E.O.
E. Theisen, Pres. & C.O.O.
H.M. Winston, V.P., Sec. & Gen. Couns.
E.J. McIntyre, V.P. & C.F.O.

INCORPORATED: MN, Jun., 1909

PRINCIPAL OFFICE: 414 Nicollet Mall, Minneapolis, MN 55401

TELEPHONE NUMBER: (612) 330-5500

NO. OF EMPLOYEES: 8,231

ANNUAL MEETING: In April

SHAREHOLDERS: 72,525

INSTITUTIONAL HOLDINGS:
No. of Institutions: 281
Shares Held: 18,367,414

REGISTRAR(S): Norwest Bank Minnesota, N.A., Minneapolis, MN

TRANSFER AGENT(S): At Company's Office

NORTHWEST NATURAL GAS CO.

YIELD 5.7%
P/E RATIO 12.7

TRADING VOLUME Thousand Shares

| 1981|1982|1983|1984|1985|1986|1987|1988|1989|1990|1991|1992|1993|1994|1995 |

*7 YEAR PRICE SCORE 91.2   ***12 MONTH PRICE SCORE 96.0**

*NYSE COMPOSITE INDEX=100

INTERIM EARNINGS (Per Share):

Qtr.	Mar.	June	Sept.	Dec.
1991	1.48	0.37	d0.34	d0.50
1992	1.06	d0.33	d0.71	1.08
1993	1.82	0.15	d0.40	1.05
1994	1.37	0.13	d0.34	1.29

INTERIM DIVIDENDS (Per Share):

Amt.	Decl.	Ex.	Rec.	Pay.
0.44Q	4/7/94	4/25/94	4/29/94	5/16/94
0.44Q	7/14	7/25	7/29	8/15
0.44Q	10/11	10/25	10/31	11/15
0.44Q	1/5/95	1/25/95	1/31/95	2/15/95
0.44Q	4/18	4/24	4/28	5/15

Indicated div.: $1.76*

CAPITALIZATION (12/31/94):

	($000)	(%)
Long-Term Debt	291,076	39.7
Deferred Income Tax	125,963	17.2
Preferred Stock	42,202	5.7
Common & Surplus	274,408	37.4
Total	733,649	100.0
Current Debt	1,000	

DIVIDEND ACHIEVER STATUS:
Rank: 323   1984-94 Growth Rate: 2.6%
Total Years of Dividend Growth: 38

RECENT DEVELOPMENTS: For the quarter ended 12/31/94, net income jumped 23% to $18.0 million compared with $14.7 million in the corresponding period of 1993. Operating revenues were $124.7 million, up 3.3% from $120.8 million a year earlier. Higher earnings were a result of cooler weather, continuing customer growth, and productivity improvements. The Company's customer base grew by 19,211 customers or 5.2%, due to new construction and con-versions from other fuels. For the year ended 12/31/94, net income dropped to $35.5 million from $37.6 million a year earlier. Operating revenues advanced 3% to $368.3 million compared with $358.7 million in 1993. Earnings were pres-sured by effects of warm weather in the first and second quarters. Weather was 10% warmer than in 1993 and 7% warmer than average. The Company plans to offer 1.1 mil-lion shares of stock in the first quarter of 1995.

BUSINESS

NORTHWEST NATURAL GAS CO. is principally engaged in the distribu-tion of natural gas to customers in western Oregon and southwestern Washington, including the Portland metropolitan area. NWNG has four subsidiaries: Oregon Natural Gas Development Corporation, NNG Financial Corporation, NNG Energy Systems Inc. and Pacific Square Cor-poration. Oregon Natural is engaged in natural gas exploration, develop-ment and production, and through Westar Marketing Company, a part-nership between Oregon Natural and a subsidiary of Questar Pipeline Corpo-ration, in the purchase, marketing and arranging for transportation of natural gas in Oregon and other western states. Energy Systems, through its wholly-owned subsidiary, Agrico Cogeneration Corporation, owns a 25 megawatt cogeneration plant near Fresno, California. The Financial Corp. holds financial investments as a limited partner in four solar electric generating systems, four windmill projects and a hydroelectric project, all located in California, and in a low-income housing project in Portland. Pacific Square is engaged in real estate management, principally in connection with two office buildings in Portland and other Company-owned properties adjacent to those buildings.

ANNUAL EARNINGS AND DIVIDENDS PER SHARE

	1994	1993	1992	1991	1990	1989	1988
Earnings Per Share	2.44	2.61	1.11	1.01	2.43	2.37	2.00
Dividends Per Share	1.76	1.75	1.72	1.69	1.65	1.61	1.57
Dividend Payout %	72.1	67.0	N.M.	N.M.	67.9	67.9	78.5

ANNUAL FINANCIAL DATA

RECORD OF EARNINGS (IN THOUSANDS):

Total Revenues	368,261	358,717	274,366	295,938	296,281	260,924	277,564
Deprec, Depl & Amort	38,058	39,683	33,035	33,623	27,967	...	...
Income From Operations	72,271	83,917	49,726	41,883	68,225	45,991	39,893
Interest Expense	24,919	25,107	26,733	26,591	24,333	18,770	16,350
Net Income	35,461	37,647	15,775	14,377	30,724	28,420	23,720
Aver. Shs. Outstg.	13,295	13,074	11,909	11,698	11,522	10,799	10,553

BALANCE SHEET (IN THOUSANDS):

Gross Plant	908,238	840,030	779,274	722,069	668,664	623,114	567,489
Accumulated Depreciation	279,112	255,282	233,385	207,165	183,404	163,678	147,923
Prop, Plant & Equip, Net	629,126	584,748	545,889	514,904	485,260	459,436	419,566
Long-term Debt	291,076	272,931	253,766	252,995	215,230	220,503	182,290
Net Stockholders' Equity	316,610	302,239	296,522	247,297	251,573	240,283	215,691
Total Assets	889,304	849,036	731,834	731,494	687,835	611,386	559,351
Year End Shares Outstg	13,419	13,177	12,973	11,785	11,604	11,430	10,641

STATISTICAL RECORD:

Book Value Per Share	20.45	19.62	18.62	18.35	18.91	18.06	16.88
Op. Inc/Net Pl %	11.5	14.4	9.1	8.1	14.1	10.0	9.5
Dep/Gr. Pl %	4.2	4.7	4.2	4.7	4.2	3.7	4.1
Accum. Dep/Gr. Pl %	30.7	30.4	29.9	28.7	27.4	26.3	26.1
Return on Equity %	11.8	13.2	5.9	6.6	13.9	13.6	13.0
Average Yield %	5.4	5.2	5.8	5.8	6.9	7.1	7.7
P/E Ratio	15.0-11.6	14.8-10.9	30.6-23.2	33.2-24.5	11.1-8.6	11.3-7.9	10.9-9.6
Price Range	36½-28¼	38¾-28½	34-25¾	33½-24¾	26⅞-20⅞	26⅞-18¾	21¾-19⅛

Statistics are as originally reported.

OFFICERS:
R.L. Ridgley, Pres. & C.E.O.
B.R. DeBolt, Sr. V.P.-Fin. & C.F.O.
D.J. Wilson, Treas. & Contr.
C.J. Rue, Sec. & Asst. Treas.

INCORPORATED: OR, Jan., 1910

PRINCIPAL OFFICE: 220 N.W. Second Ave., Portland, OR 97209

TELEPHONE NUMBER: (503) 226-4211

NO. OF EMPLOYEES: 1,293

ANNUAL MEETING: In May

SHAREHOLDERS: 13,181

INSTITUTIONAL HOLDINGS:
No. of Institutions: 97
Shares Held: 3,524,994

REGISTRAR(S): United States National Bank of Oregon, Portland, OR 97204

TRANSFER AGENT(S): At Company's Office

NORTHWESTERN PUBLIC SERVICE CO.

YIELD 6.2%
P/E RATIO 13.8

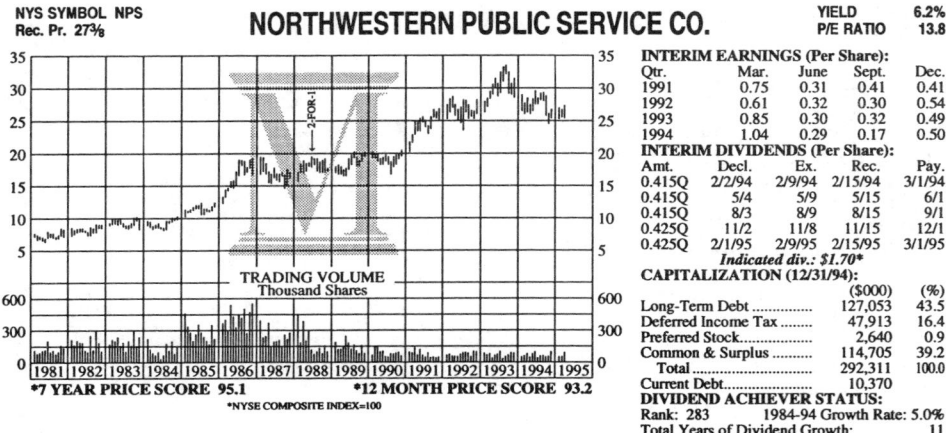

7 YEAR PRICE SCORE 95.1   **12 MONTH PRICE SCORE 93.2**
*NYSE COMPOSITE INDEX=100

INTERIM EARNINGS (Per Share):

Qtr.	Mar.	June	Sept.	Dec.
1991	0.75	0.31	0.41	0.41
1992	0.61	0.32	0.30	0.54
1993	0.85	0.30	0.32	0.49
1994	1.04	0.29	0.17	0.50

INTERIM DIVIDENDS (Per Share):

Amt.	Decl.	Ex.	Rec.	Pay.
0.415Q	2/2/94	2/9/94	2/15/94	3/1/94
0.415Q	5/4	5/9	5/15	6/1
0.415Q	8/3	8/9	8/15	9/1
0.425Q	11/2	11/8	11/15	12/1
0.425Q	2/1/95	2/9/95	2/15/95	3/1/95

*Indicated div.: $1.70**

CAPITALIZATION (12/31/94):

	($000)	(%)
Long-Term Debt	127,053	43.5
Deferred Income Tax	47,913	16.4
Preferred Stock	2,640	0.9
Common & Surplus	114,705	39.2
Total	292,311	100.0

Current Debt 10,370

DIVIDEND ACHIEVER STATUS:
Rank: 283   1984-94 Growth Rate: 5.0%
Total Years of Dividend Growth: 11

RECENT DEVELOPMENTS: For the year ended 12/31/94, net income was $15.4 million compared with net income of $15.2 million in the previous year. Total revenues climbed to $157.3 million from $153.3 million in 1994. Gains in the electric and manufacturing operations of 4% and 22%, respectively, offset a 4% decline in sales from the Company's gas division. Warmer weather conditions, particularly in the fourth quarter, and the absence of a rate hike like the one that benefited last year's earnings pushed the gas division's sales lower year-over-year. Increased electrical usage in residential and commercial sectors increased retail kwh sales by approximately 6%. Retails sales gains were partially offset by a 5% decline in wholesale kwh sales to other utilities in the power pool.

BUSINESS

NORTHWESTERN PUBLIC SERVICE COMPANY is an electric and gas utility engaged in generating, transmitting, distributing and selling electric energy in eastern South Dakota, where it furnishes electric service to 54,863 customers in more than 100 communities and adjacent rural areas. The Company also purchases, distributes, sells, and transports natural gas to 74,892 customers in four communities in Nebraska and 56 communities in eastern South Dakota.

BUSINESS LINE ANALYSIS

(12/31/94)	Rev(%)	Inc(%)
Electric	46.5	84.5
Gas	39.5	8.4
Other	14.0	7.1
Total	100.0	100.0

ANNUAL EARNINGS AND DIVIDENDS PER SHARE

	1994	1993	1992	1991	1990	1989	1988
Earnings Per Share	2.00	1.96	1.77	1.88	2.23	2.04	1.72
Dividends Per Share	1.67	1.63	1.59	1.535	1.475	1.415	①1.351
Dividend Payout %	83.5	83.2	89.8	81.6	66.1	69.4	78.6

① 2-for-1 stock split, 6/88.

ANNUAL FINANCIAL DATA

RECORD OF EARNINGS (IN THOUSANDS):

	1994	1993	1992	1991	1990	1989	1988
Total Revenues	157,266	153,257	119,197	122,900	114,150	115,961	115,518
Depreciation	12,439	11,559	11,062	10,506	10,986	9,979	9,742
Maintenance	6,170	6,368	5,889	5,836	5,217	5,540	5,486
Total Operating Income	30,369	20,306	19,574	20,775	19,755	19,198	19,823
Interest Expense	9,670	8,945	8,105	7,244	6,804	6,886	6,981
Net Income	15,440	15,190	13,721	14,815	17,506	16,123	13,876
Aver. Shs. Outstg.	7,677	7,677	7,677	7,677	7,677	7,677	7,677

BALANCE SHEET (IN THOUSANDS):

Gross Plant	389,926	369,106	351,818	335,104	316,083	303,238	293,619
Accumulated Depreciation	139,381	130,610	122,085	113,205	107,117	99,186	92,076
Prop, Plant & Equip, Net	250,545	238,496	229,733	221,899	208,966	204,052	201,543
Long-term Debt	127,053	126,600	106,422	92,003	78,236	79,469	80,702
Net Stockholders' Equity	117,345	112,337	109,781	111,369	108,903	103,301	98,719
Total Assets	359,066	342,387	313,452	297,759	283,074	272,261	264,809
Year End Shares Outstg	7,667	7,677	7,677	7,677	7,677	7,677	7,677

STATISTICAL RECORD:

Book Value Per Share	14.96	14.29	13.95	13.78	13.43	12.68	12.05
Op. Inc/Net Pl %	12.1	8.5	8.5	9.4	9.5	9.4	9.8
Dep/Gr. Pl %	3.2	3.1	3.1	3.1	3.2	3.3	3.3
Accum. Dep/Gr. Pl %	35.7	35.4	34.7	33.8	33.9	32.7	31.4
Return on Equity %	13.2	13.5	12.5	13.7	16.6	16.1	14.6
Average Yield %	6.2	5.5	6.1	6.5	7.9	7.7	7.7
P/E Ratio	14.8-12.3	17.1-13.4	16.2-13.3	14.3-10.8	9.2-7.5	9.9-8.1	11.3-9.1
Price Range	29⅝-24½	33½-26¼	28¾-23½	26⅞-20¼	20½-16¾	20¼-16½	19½-15⅝

Statistics are as originally reported.

OFFICERS:
R.A. Wilkens, Chmn.
M.D. Lewis, Pres. & C.E.O.
A.D. Dietrich, V.P.-Legal & Corp. Sec.
R.R. Hylland, V.P.-Fin. & Corp. Devel.

INCORPORATED: DE, Nov., 1923

PRINCIPAL OFFICE: 33 Third St. SE P.O. Box 1318, Huron, SD 57350-1318

TELEPHONE NUMBER: (605) 352-8411

NO. OF EMPLOYEES: 473

ANNUAL MEETING: In May

SHAREHOLDERS: 8,231

INSTITUTIONAL HOLDINGS:
No. of Institutions: 29
Shares Held: 1,232,939

REGISTRAR(S): Norwest Bank Minnesota, N.A., South St. Paul, MN

TRANSFER AGENT(S): Norwest Bank Minnesota, N.A., South St. Paul, MN

NYS SYMBOL NUE
Rec. Pr. 48½

NUCOR CORP.

YIELD 0.6%
P/E RATIO 18.7

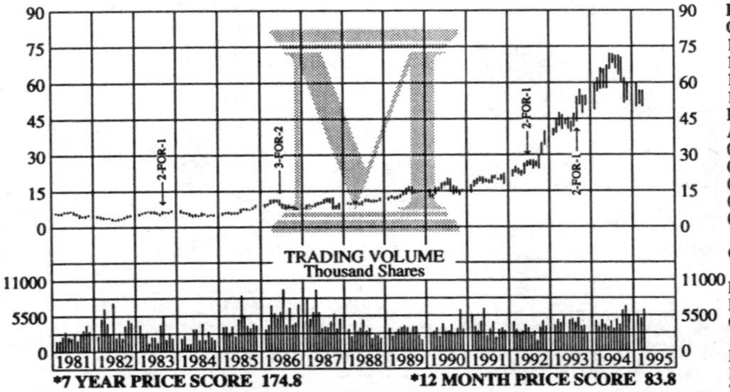

*7 YEAR PRICE SCORE 174.8 *12 MONTH PRICE SCORE 83.8

*NYSE COMPOSITE INDEX=100

INTERIM EARNINGS (Per Share):

Qtr.	Mar.	June	Sept.	Dec.
1991	0.16	0.16	0.18	0.26
1992	0.19	0.20	0.24	0.29
1993	0.25	0.35	0.40	0.42
1994	0.40	0.57	0.74	0.89

INTERIM DIVIDENDS (Per Share):

Amt.	Decl.	Ex.	Rec.	Pay.
0.045Q	3/11/94	3/25/94	3/31/94	5/12/94
0.045Q	6/16	6/24	6/30	8/11
0.045Q	9/14	9/26	9/30	11/11
0.045Q	12/19	12/23	12/30	2/10/95
0.07Q	3/2/95	3/27/95	3/31/95	5/12

Indicated div.: $0.28*

CAPITALIZATION (12/31/94):

	($000)	(%)
Long-Term Debt	173,000	11.7
Minority Interest	175,985	12.0
Common & Surplus	1,122,609	76.3
Total	1,471,594	100.0

DIVIDEND ACHIEVER STATUS:
Rank: 79 1984-94 Growth Rate: 13.9%
Total Years of Dividend Growth: 22

RECENT DEVELOPMENTS: For the twelve months ended 12/31/94, net income increased 83.5% to $226.6 million from $123.5 million in 1993. Sales for the year advanced 32.0% to $2.98 billion, compared with $2.25 billion the previous year. Steel production in 1994 totaled 7.0 million tons compared with 5.7 million tons in 1993. Steel sales to outside customers grew 21.1% to 6.0 million tons from 4.9 million tons. Steel joist production rose 16.8% to 487,000 tons.

PROSPECTS: The start-up process continues at NUE's new facility in Trinidad to produce 320,000 tons-per-year of iron carbide. The iron carbide will replace a portion of the scrap used at NUE's sheet steel mills. The Company has announced plans to build a new 40,000 tons-per-year steel fastener facility in Conway, Arkansas. NUE has formed a joint venture with rival U.S. Steel to explore a new steelmaking process by which steel would made directly from iron carbide.

BUSINESS

NUCOR CORP. is engaged in the manufacture of steel and steel products. The Nucor Steel Division produces merchant bar and structural steel products, and is a major supplier of steel angles. The Vulcraft Division is the nation's largest producer of steel joists and joist girders for building construction. Nucor Grinding Balls produces steel grinding balls in Utah for the mining industry. Other products include steel deck, steel fasteners and steel bearings. In 1994, production of the Nucor Steel Division was 7.0 million tons while total steel joist production reached 487,000 tons.

QUARTERLY DATA

(12/31/94)($000)	Rev	Inc
1st Quarter	649,701	34,880
2nd Quarter	740,102	49,680
3rd Quarter	786,425	64,524
4th Quarter	799,369	77,549

ANNUAL EARNINGS AND DIVIDENDS PER SHARE

	1994	1993	1992	1991	1990	1989	1988
Earnings Per Share	**2.60**	**1.42**	**0.92**	**0.75**	**0.88**	**0.68**	**[3] 0.84**
Dividends Per Share	**0.175**	**[1] 0.155**	**[2] 0.138**	**0.127**	**0.118**	**0.108**	**0.097**
Dividend Payout %	**6.7**	**10.9**	**15.0**	**17.0**	**13.4**	**15.9**	**7.6**

[1] 2-for-1 stk split,09/20/93 [2] 2-for-1 stk split, 6/22/92 [3] Before disc. oper.

ANNUAL FINANCIAL DATA

	1994	1993	1992	1991	1990	1989	1988
RECORD OF EARNINGS (IN MILLIONS):							
Total Revenues	2,975.6	2,253.7	1,619.2	1,465.5	1,481.6	1,269.0	1,061.4
Costs and Expenses	2,447.5	1,931.2	1,396.4	1,276.2	1,278.6	1,095.7	895.0
Depreciation	157.7	122.3	97.8	93.6	85.0	76.6	56.3
Operating Profit	483.8	287.9	201.9	162.7	188.5	163.8	172.2
Earn Bef Fed Inc Taxes	356.9	187.1	117.3	95.8	111.2	85.6	107.6
Income Taxes	130.3	63.6	38.1	31.1	36.2	27.8	36.7
Net Income	226.6	123.5	79.2	64.7	75.1	57.8	[1] 70.9
Aver. Shs. Outstg. (000)	87,166	86,909	86,584	86,240	85,764	85,372	84,896
[1] Before disc. op. cr$38,559,000.							
BALANCE SHEET (IN MILLIONS):							
Cash and Cash Equivalents	101.9	27.3	25.5	38.3	51.6	32.6	26.4
Receivables, Net	258.1	202.2	132.1	109.5	126.7	107.0	97.4
Inventories	243.0	215.0	206.4	186.1	136.6	139.5	123.2
Gross Property	1,977.6	1,821.0	1,574.1	1,261.5	1,086.4	1,048.0	942.3
Accumulated Depreciation	614.4	460.0	448.3	414.2	363.1	294.2	240.4
Long-Term Debt	173.0	352.3	246.8	72.8	28.8	156.0	113.2
Net Stockholders' Equity	1,122.6	902.2	784.2	711.6	652.8	584.4	532.3
Total Assets	2,001.9	1,829.3	1,490.4	1,181.6	1,038.4	1,033.8	949.7
Total Current Assets	638.7	468.2	364.6	334.3	315.1	280.0	247.8
Total Current Liabilities	382.5	350.5	272.0	229.2	225.6	193.6	216.1
Net Working Capital	256.2	117.7	92.6	105.1	89.5	86.5	31.7
Year End Shs Outstg (000)	87,333	87,073	86,737	86,418	85,951	85,600	85,152
STATISTICAL RECORD:							
Operating Profit Margin %	12.4	8.9	7.7	6.5	8.0	7.6	10.4
Book Value Per Share	12.85	10.36	9.04	8.23	7.59	6.83	6.25
Return on Equity %	20.2	13.7	10.1	9.1	11.5	9.9	13.3
Return on Assets %	11.3	6.8	5.3	5.5	7.2	5.6	7.5
Average Yield %	0.3	0.3	0.5	0.7	0.7	0.8	0.9
P/E Ratio	27.7-18.8	40.3-26.8	43.5-22.8	29.8-19.0	23.3-13.8	24.8-16.5	14.6-10.9
Price Range	72-48¾	57¼-38	40-21	22⅜-14¼	20½-12⅛	16⅞-11¼	12¼-9⅛

Statistics are as originally reported.

OFFICERS:
F.K. Iverson, Chmn. & C.E.O.
J.D. Correnti, Pres. & C.O.O.
S. Siegel, Vice-Chmn., C.F.O., Treas. & Sec.

INCORPORATED: MI, Jan., 1940; reincorp., DE, Mar., 1958

PRINCIPAL OFFICE: 2100 Rexford Road, Charlotte, NC 28211

TELEPHONE NUMBER: (704) 366-7000

FAX: (704) 362-4208

NO. OF EMPLOYEES: 5,900

ANNUAL MEETING: In May

SHAREHOLDERS: 38,000

INSTITUTIONAL HOLDINGS:
No. of Institutions: 237
Shares Held: 14,996,550

REGISTRAR(S):

TRANSFER AGENT(S): First Union National Bank of N.C., Charlotte, NC

NYNEX CORP.

YIELD 5.9%
P/E RATIO 19.4

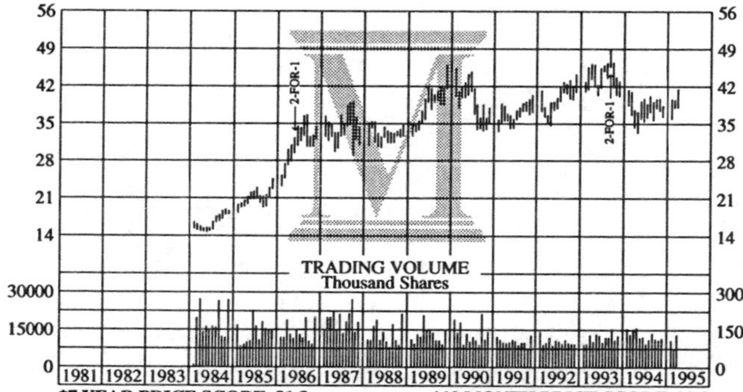

TRADING VOLUME
Thousand Shares

*7 YEAR PRICE SCORE 81.8   *12 MONTH PRICE SCORE 99.8

*NYSE COMPOSITE INDEX=100

INTERIM EARNINGS (Per Share):

Qtr.	Mar.	June	Sept.	Dec.
1991	0.67	0.72	0.72	d0.62
1992	0.83	0.81	0.77	0.79
1993	0.80	0.83	0.72	d3.00
1994	0.70	0.18	0.72	0.47

INTERIM DIVIDENDS (Per Share):

Amt.	Decl.	Ex.	Rec.	Pay.
0.59Q	3/17/94	3/25/94	3/31/94	5/1/94
0.59Q	6/16	6/24	6/30	8/1
0.59Q	9/22	9/26	9/30	11/1
0.59Q	12/15	12/23	12/30	2/1/95
0.59Q	3/16/95	3/27/95	3/31/95	5/1

Indicated div.: $2.36

CAPITALIZATION (12/31/94):

	($000)	(%)
Long-Term Debt	7,784,500	38.9
Deferred Income Tax	3,669,100	18.3
Common & Surplus	8,581,400	42.8
Total	20,035,000	100.0

DIVIDEND ACHIEVER STATUS:

Rank: 222   1984-94 Growth Rate: 7.7%
Total Years of Dividend Growth: 10

RECENT DEVELOPMENTS: For the year ended 12/31/94, net income was $792.6 million compared with a loss of $272.4 million, including a $1.51 billion charge, in 1993. Revenues fell slightly to $13.31 billion. Results for 1994 reflect after-tax charges of $452.8 million related to employee reductions. Revenues were negatively affected by more than $300 million in NYPUC-ordered revenue reductions.

PROSPECTS: NYNEX will combine its domestic cellular properties with those of Bell Atlantic, creating a new nationwide cellular company. The combination is expected to be completed in the second quarter of 1995. NYNEX's lucrative service region in combination with new regulations designed to promote competition will invite other telecommunication providers to chip away at NYNEX's market share.

BUSINESS

NYNEX CORPORATION is one of seven regional holding companies divested by AT & T. It is the parent corporation of New York Telephone Company and New England Telephone & Telegraph Company, both of which are engaged in the furnishing of exchange telecommunication and exchange access service in the states of New York, Maine, Massachusetts, New Hampshire, Rhode Island, Vermont and a small portion of Connecticut. NYNEX's other subsidiaries include: NYNEX Mobile (Cellular), NYNEX Information Resources (Publishing), NYNEX Credit, NYNEX Capital Funding, and NYNEX Properties (Finance and Real Estate), AGS Computers, BIS Group LTD, NYNEX Business Information Systems and NYNEX Computer Service Company.

REVENUES

(12/31/94)	($000)	(%)
Local Service	6,605,400	49.6
Long Distance	1,081,200	8.1
Network Access	3,447,000	25.9
Other	2,173,300	16.4
Total	13,306,600	100.0

ANNUAL EARNINGS AND DIVIDENDS PER SHARE

	1994	1993	1992	1991	1990	1989	1988
Earnings Per Share	1.89	d0.66	3.20	1.49	2.39	2.05	3.32
Dividends Per Share	2.36	① 2.35	2.31	2.28	2.255	2.14	1.99
Dividend Payout %	N.M.	...	72.2	N.M.	94.4	N.M.	60.0

① 2-for-1 stk split,09/16/93

ANNUAL FINANCIAL DATA

RECORD OF EARNINGS (IN MILLIONS):

	1994	1993	1992	1991	1990	1989	1988
Total Revenues	13,306.6	13,407.8	13,155.0	13,228.8	13,585.3	13,210.6	12,660.8
Costs and Expenses	9,903.0	11,579.4	9,164.1	10,345.5	10,324.0	10,130.1	9,256.8
Depreciation & Amort	2,640.6	2,534.0	2,518.0	2,397.5	2,337.3	2,316.9	2,154.4
Operating Income	1,756.2	333.3	2,527.5	1,608.4	2,015.3	1,756.7	2,237.9
Earn Bef Inc Taxes & Cumulat	1,096.3	d445.1	1,881.6	792.9	1,317.7	1,073.5	1,688.2
Income Taxes	303.7	cr172.7	570.4	192.1	368.3	265.9	373.2
Net Income	792.6	② d272.4	1,311.2	600.8	949.4	807.6	1,315.0
Aver. Shs. Outstg. (000)	418,800	412,700	409,800	403,000	397,400	394,000	396,600

② Before acctg. change dr$121,700,000.

BALANCE SHEET (IN MILLIONS):

	1994	1993	1992	1991	1990	1989	1988
Cash and Cash Equivalents	137.5	157.8	88.9	158.0	121.7	155.0	125.7
Receivables, Net	2,532.5	2,439.1	2,382.2	2,490.0	2,642.1	2,498.5	2,510.4
Inventories	173.3	169.2	186.5	237.9	436.7	401.4	386.4
Gross Property	35,467.1	33,969.4	33,078.4	31,653.6	30,515.4	30,274.2	28,751.3
Accumulated Depreciation	14,843.7	13,719.4	13,105.2	11,738.7	10,786.5	10,809.7	9,462.8
Long-Term Debt	7,784.5	6,937.8	7,018.2	6,833.1	6,945.4	6,465.0	6,241.3
Net Stockholders' Equity	8,581.4	8,415.5	9,723.7	9,119.9	9,148.8	9,369.1	9,419.5
Total Assets	30,068.0	29,458.4	27,713.9	27,502.6	26,650.7	25,909.0	25,362.1
Total Current Assets	3,798.0	3,921.7	3,524.3	3,818.1	3,913.4	3,668.6	3,630.2
Total Current Liabilities	5,850.5	6,806.7	4,794.5	5,400.2	5,491.6	4,550.2	4,147.5
Net Working Capital	d2,052.5	d2,885.0	d1,270.2	d1,582.1	d1,578.2	d881.6	d517.3
Year End Shs Outstg (000)	423,597	414,885	413,648	407,448	400,248	394,090	393,890

STATISTICAL RECORD:

	1994	1993	1992	1991	1990	1989	1988
Book Value Per Share	20.26	20.28	23.51	22.38	22.86	23.77	23.91
Return on Equity %	9.2	...	13.5	6.6	10.4	8.6	14.0
Average Yield %	6.3	5.3	5.9	6.2	5.7	5.4	6.0
P/E Ratio	21.9-17.6	...	13.8-10.8	27.1-22.5	19.0-14.1	22.4-15.9	10.7-9.2
Price Range	41⅜-33¼	48⅞-40⅛	44¼-34⅝	40⅜-33½	45½-33⅝	46-32⅝	35½-30½

Statistics are as originally reported.

OFFICERS:
W.C. Ferguson, Chmn.
F.V. Salerno, Vice-Chmn.-Fin. & Bus. Dev.
I.G. Seidenberg, Pres. & C.E.O.
R.F. Burke, Exec. V.P.-Law & Sec.
A.Z. Senter, Exec. V.P. & C.F.O.
C.P. Turner, V.P. & Treas.

INCORPORATED: DE, Oct., 1983
PRINCIPAL OFFICE: 1095 Avenue of the Americas, New York, NY 10036

TELEPHONE NUMBER: (212) 395-2121

NO. OF EMPLOYEES: 65,400 (approx.)

ANNUAL MEETING: In May

SHAREHOLDERS: 936,468

INSTITUTIONAL HOLDINGS:
No. of Institutions: 574
Shares Held: 74,582,874

REGISTRAR(S):

TRANSFER AGENT(S):

OHIO CASUALTY CORP.

YIELD 5.0%
P/E RATIO 11.4

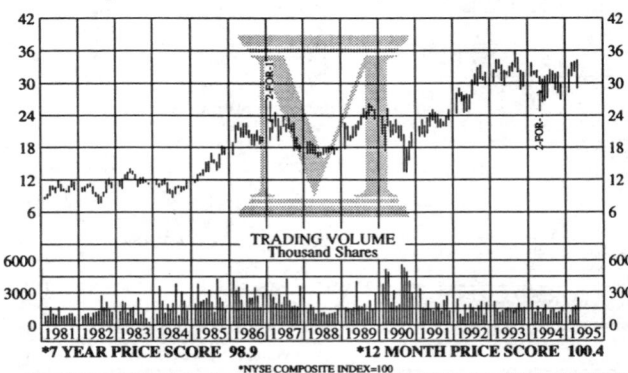

*7 YEAR PRICE SCORE 98.9   ***12 MONTH PRICE SCORE 100.4**
*NYSE COMPOSITE INDEX=100

INTERIM EARNINGS (Per Share):

Qtr.	Mar.	June	Sept.	Dec.
1991	1.00	1.50	2.08	1.44
1992	1.33	1.35	1.02	1.79
1993	0.55	0.87	0.51	0.50
1994	0.26	1.12	0.94	0.36

INTERIM DIVIDENDS (Per Share):

Amt.	Decl.	Ex.	Rec.	Pay.
2-for-1	2/17/94	4/25/94	4/1/94	4/22/94
0.365Q	5/19	5/25	6/1	6/10
0.365Q	8/18	8/26	9/1	9/10
0.365Q	11/16	11/25	12/1	12/10
0.38Q	2/16/95	2/23/95	3/1/95	3/10/95

Indicated div.: $1.52*

CAPITALIZATION (12/31/94):

	($000)	(%)
Total Debt	70,000	7.6
Common & Surplus	850,790	92.4
Total	920,790	100.0

DIVIDEND ACHIEVER STATUS:
Rank: 213   1984-94 Growth Rate: 8.1%
Total Years of Dividend Growth: 49

RECENT DEVELOPMENTS: For the year ended 12/31/94, net income climbed 2.0% to $88.7 million from $87.0 million the year before. Net written premiums for the property and casualty segment were flat at $1.3 billion. Realized capital gains, after tax, amounted to $15.1 million compared with $30.5 million a year earlier. Operating income rose 30.3% to $73.6 million from $56.5 million in the prior year. Consolidated net investment income was $213.8 million, down 2.6% from $219.4 million in 1993. The combined ratio was 103.8% in 1994 versus 110.3% in 1993. For the quarter ended 12/31/94, net income dropped 73.7% to $4.7 million from $17.8 million for the corresponding quarter in 1993. The decline in net income reflected after-tax realized capital losses of $2.1 million compared with $4.3 million in capital gains for the 1993 quarter. Premium income for the property and casualty segment slipped 0.8% to $302.6 million, while premium income for life insurance operations rose 47.9% to $7.1 million.

BUSINESS

OHIO CASUALTY CORPORATION operates primarily as a holding company and is principally engaged, through its direct and indirect subsidiaries, in the business of property and casualty insurance, life insurance and insurance premium finance. The Corporation conducts its property and casualty insurance business through The Ohio Casualty Insurance and its three property and casualty insurance subsidiaries: West American Insurance Company; Ohio Security Insurance Company; and American Fire and Casualty Company. This group of companies presently underwrites most forms of property and casualty insurance. The Corporation conducts its life insurance business through The Ohio Life Insurance Company, and its insurance premium finance business through Ocasco Budget, Inc. Ohio Life and Ocasco are direct subsidiaries of Ohio Casualty Insurance Company.

BUSINESS LINE ANALYSIS

(12/31/94)	Rev(%)	Inc(%)
Property & Casualty ..	96.4	96.5
Life Insurance............	3.3	6.4
Premium Finance & Other......................	0.3	(2.9)
Total	100.0	100.0

ANNUAL EARNINGS AND DIVIDENDS PER SHARE

	1994	1993	1992	1991	1990	1989	1988
Earnings Per Share	2.69	3.14	① 3.47	6.02	4.38	4.74	6.53
Dividends Per Share	1.46	1.42	② 1.344	1.24	1.16	1.04	0.94
Dividend Payout %	54.3	58.8	49.6	41.2	53.0	43.9	28.8

① Before acctg. chg. ② Bef acctg chge

ANNUAL FINANCIAL DATA

RECORD OF EARNINGS (IN MILLIONS):

	1994	1993	1992	1991	1990	1989	1988
Insurance Premiums	1,321.6	1,400.6	1,538.4	1,488.6	1,455.9	1,381.2	1,384.6
Total Interest Income	213.8	219.4	221.0	218.1	204.1	216.4	191.5
Total Revenues	1,558.7	1,669.8	1,812.1	1,714.2	1,637.5	1,577.1	1,576.1
Losses & Bens for Policyholders	828.8	919.8	992.6	914.4	909.0	821.3	785.1
Income Bef Income Taxes	116.9	96.2	117.7	124.3	83.3	116.4	165.9
Income Taxes	19.6	9.2	20.7	16.4	cr0.8	14.9	23.8
Net Income	① 97.2	87.0	② 97.1	107.9	84.1	101.5	128.0
Aver. Shs. Outstg. (000)	36,033	18,008	17,976	17,924	19,218	21,429	21,778

① Before acctg. change dr$319,000. ② Before acctg. change cr$1,471,000.

BALANCE SHEET (IN MILLIONS):

	1994	1993	1992	1991	1990	1989	1988
Cash	15.1	14.3	20.0	14.3	9.4	3.1	13.9
Fixed Maturities	2,510.0	2,629.2	2,664.7	2,411.9	1,960.4	1,996.9	1,758.9
Equity Securities, At Mkt	520.0	492.2	438.2	423.0	354.6	432.4	376.3
Total Assets	3,739.0	3,816.8	3,760.7	3,531.3	3,252.9	3,145.7	2,922.0
Benefits and Claims	2,542.3	2,617.9	2,552.4	2,443.9	2,322.3	2,159.9	1,966.5
Net Stockholders' Equity	850.8	862.3	825.2	774.5	651.2	775.0	718.5
Year End Shs Outstg (000)	35,999	18,015	17,994	17,944	17,899	20,983	21,573

STATISTICAL RECORD:

	1994	1993	1992	1991	1990	1989	1988
Return on Equity %	11.4	10.1	11.8	13.9	12.9	13.1	17.8
Book Value Per Share	23.63	47.87	45.86	43.16	36.38	36.94	33.30
Average Yield %	4.8	4.4	4.7	5.5	6.0	4.7	5.3
P/E Ratio	12.5-9.8	11.5-9.2	9.6-7.0	4.2-3.3	5.8-3.1	5.5-3.7	2.9-2.5
Price Range	33¾-26½	36-28⅞	33⅜-24⅜	25⅛-20	25⅜-13⅜	26¼-17¾	19⅛-16⅛

Statistics are as originally reported.

OFFICERS:
J.L. Marcum, Chmn.
L.N. Patch, Pres. & C.E.O.
H.L. Sloneker, III, V.P. & Sec.
B.S. Porter, C.F.O. & Treas.

INCORPORATED: OH, Aug., 1969

PRINCIPAL OFFICE: 136 North Third Street, Hamilton, OH 45025

TELEPHONE NUMBER: (513) 867-3000
FAX: (513) 867-3215
NO. OF EMPLOYEES: 4,000
ANNUAL MEETING: In April
SHAREHOLDERS: 6,100
INSTITUTIONAL HOLDINGS:
No. of Institutions: 136
Shares Held: 19,518,716

REGISTRAR(S): Mellon Bank, N.A., Pittsburgh, PA

TRANSFER AGENT(S): Mellon Bank, N.A., Pittsburgh, PA

OLD KENT FINANCIAL CORP.

YIELD 4.0%
P/E RATIO 8.7

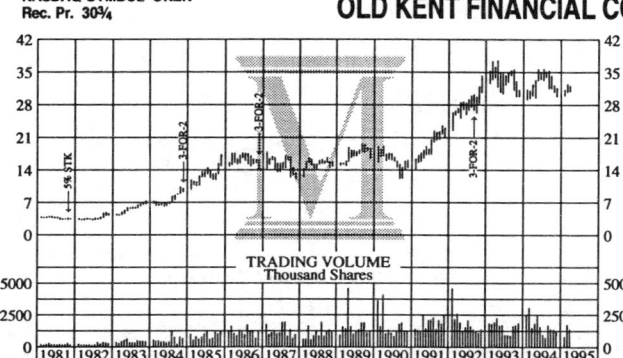

INTERIM EARNINGS (Per Share):

Qtr.	Mar.	June	Sept.	Dec.
1991	0.56	0.58	0.59	0.59
1992	0.61	0.71	0.71	0.72
1993	0.74	0.82	0.83	0.75
1994	0.79	0.87	0.87	1.02

INTERIM DIVIDENDS (Per Share):

Amt.	Decl.	Ex.	Rec.	Pay.
0.31Q	10/17/94	11/8/94	11/15/94	12/15/94
0.31Q	10/17	11/8	11/15	12/15
0.31Q	10/17	11/8	11/15	12/15
0.31Q	1/16/95	2/9/95	2/15/95	3/15/95
0.31Q	4/18	5/9	5/15	6/15

Indicated div.: $1.24*

CAPITALIZATION (12/31/94):

	($000)	(%)
Long-Term Debt	1,119	0.1
Common & Surplus	859,496	99.9
Total	860,615	100.0

TRADING VOLUME
Thousand Shares

*7 YEAR PRICE SCORE 114.5   ***12 MONTH PRICE SCORE 93.2**

*NYSE COMPOSITE INDEX=100

DIVIDEND ACHIEVER STATUS:
Rank: 108   1984-94 Growth Rate: 12.6%
Total Years of Dividend Growth: 14

RECENT DEVELOPMENTS: On February 1, 1995, OKEN completed its acquisition of First National Bank Corp., a $531 million asset bank that operates 15 offices in Macomb County, MI. Macomb County is located in the northeastern suburban area of Detroit. For the year ended 12/31/94, net income was $136.1 million compared with $127.9 million for 1993, an increase of 6.4%. Higher income was attributed to loan growth, stronger credit quality and acquisitions. During 1994, the Company acquired Princeton Financial Corp., a mortgage company based in Orlando, FL and Edgemark Financial Corp., a Chicago-based banking company. At year end, loans outstanding were up 29.5% to $6.50 billion from $5.02 billion. Assets increased by 11% to $10.9 billion as deposits rose 12.4% to $8.96 billion. The return on average assets was 1.33%, down from 1.38%, and return on average total equity was 16.04%, down from 16.65% a year earlier.

BUSINESS

OLD KENT FINANCIAL CORPORATION, with assets of $10.9 billion, is a bank holding company headquartered in Grand Rapids, Michigan. The Company's affiliated banks operate 181 full-service offices in Michigan and 26 in Illinois. OKEN provides a full range of banking and fiduciary services. Old Kent Bank and Trust is the largest subsidiary and lead bank.

LOAN DISTRIBUTION

(12/31/94)	($000)	(%)
Commercial	1,608,483	24.7
Real Estate-		
Commercial	1,185,535	18.2
Real Estate-		
Construction	194,517	3.0
Real Estate-		
Residential	1,077,652	16.6
Real Estate-		
Consumer Home....	543,992	8.4
Consumer	1,674,839	25.8
Other-Cred Card &		
Lease.....................	213,014	3.3
Total	6,498,032	100.8

ANNUAL EARNINGS AND DIVIDENDS PER SHARE

	1994	1993	1992	1991	1990	1989	1988
Earnings Per Share	3.35	3.14	① 2.75	2.31	2.19	2.15	1.97
Dividends Per Share	1.18	1.07	② 0.903	0.787	0.723	0.637	0.583
Dividend Payout %	35.2	34.1	32.8	34.0	33.0	29.6	29.7

① Primary ② 3-for-2 stk split, 9/16/92

ANNUAL FINANCIAL DATA

RECORD OF EARNINGS (IN MILLIONS):

	1994	1993	1992	1991	1990	1989	1988
Total Revenues	874.8	806.8	815.2	862.5	870.3	863.1	725.8
Costs and Expenses	669.9	613.3	651.3	729.1	747.1	745.1	622.1
Operating Profit	204.9	193.6	164.0	133.4	123.2	118.0	103.7
Income Bef Income Taxes	204.9	193.6	164.0	133.4	123.2	118.0	103.7
Income Taxes	68.8	65.7	52.9	40.4	35.7	32.6	26.5
Net Income	136.1	127.9	111.1	93.0	87.5	85.4	77.1
Aver. Shs. Outstg. (000)	40,629	40,748	40,357	40,245	39,647	37,875	36,989

BALANCE SHEET (IN MILLIONS):

Cash and Cash Equivalents	4,108.0	4,578.4	3,566.2	3,495.6	2,648.7	2,818.4	2,906.5
Gross Property	156.9	133.9	117.1	112.4	114.3	102.1	99.1
Long-Term Debt	1.1	1.2	16.2	74.7	80.9	87.6	93.4
Net Stockholders' Equity	859.5	812.8	726.3	672.6	607.6	600.1	540.8
Total Assets	10,946.4	9,855.7	8,698.6	8,826.1	8,205.0	8,127.2	7,854.1
Total Current Assets	4,108.0	4,578.4	3,566.2	3,495.6	2,648.7	2,818.4	2,906.5
Total Current Liabilities	9,955.7	8,929.4	7,880.7	8,009.4	7,442.3	7,343.6	7,128.5
Net Working Capital	d5,847.7	d4,351.1	d4,314.5	d4,513.8	d4,793.5	d4,525.2	d4,222.0
Year End Shs Outstg (000)	40,541	40,539	40,442	40,156	39,920	38,156	37,142

STATISTICAL RECORD:

Book Value Per Share	21.20	20.05	17.96	16.75	15.22	15.08	13.76
Return on Equity %	15.8	15.7	15.3	13.8	14.4	14.2	14.3
Return on Assets %	1.2	1.3	1.3	1.1	1.1	1.1	1.0
Average Yield %	3.6	3.2	3.2	4.2	4.6	3.7	4.0
P/E Ratio	10.7-8.7	11.9-9.5	12.5-8.2	10.2-6.2	8.8-5.5	9.2-6.9	8.5-6.3
Price Range	35¾-29⅛	37½-29¾	34¼-22½	23⅝-14¼	19¼-12⅛	19¾-14⅞	16¾-12⅜

Statistics are as originally reported.

OFFICERS:
J. C. Canepa, C.E.O. & Chmn.
D. J. Wagner, President
B. P. Sherwood, III, Vice-Chmn. & Treas.
R. W. Wroten, Exec. V.P. & C.F.O.

INCORPORATED: DE, Oct., 1971

PRINCIPAL OFFICE: One Vandenberg Center, Grand Rapids, MI 49503

TELEPHONE NUMBER: (616) 771-5000

NO. OF EMPLOYEES: 4,745

ANNUAL MEETING: In April

SHAREHOLDERS: 12,700 (approx.)

INSTITUTIONAL HOLDINGS:
No. of Institutions: 133
Shares Held: 14,353,358

REGISTRAR(S):

TRANSFER AGENT(S): At Company's Office

NYS SYMBOL ORI
Rec. Pr. 25⅝

OLD REPUBLIC INTERNATIONAL CORP.

YIELD 1.9%
P/E RATIO 13.4

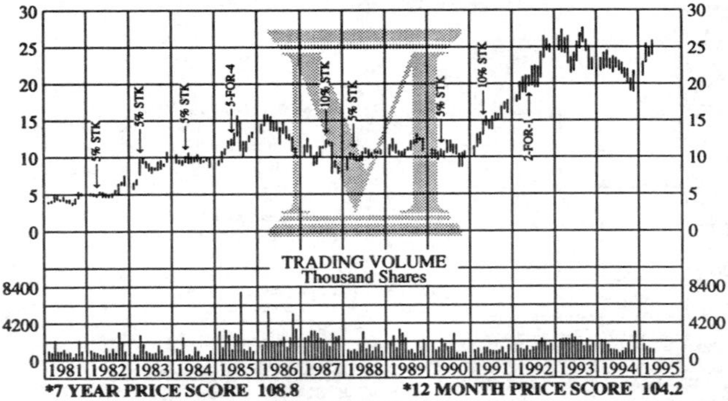

30
25
20
15
10
5
0
5% STK
5% STK
5% STK
5-FOR-4
10% STK
5% STK
5% STK
10% STK
2-FOR-1
TRADING VOLUME
Thousand Shares
8400
4200
0
1981 1982 1983 1984 1985 1986 1987 1988 1989 1990 1991 1992 1993 1994 1995

***7 YEAR PRICE SCORE 108.8** ***12 MONTH PRICE SCORE 104.2**

*NYSE COMPOSITE INDEX=100

INTERIM EARNINGS (Per Share):

Qtr.	Mar.	June	Sept.	Dec.
1992	0.62	0.76	1.05	0.66
1993	0.53	0.73	0.70	0.86
1994	0.57	0.61	0.64	0.62

INTERIM DIVIDENDS (Per Share):

Amt.	Decl.	Ex.	Rec.	Pay.
0.11Q	2/25/94	3/7/94	3/11/94	3/21/94
0.12Q	5/20	6/6	6/10	6/20
0.12Q	8/18	9/2	9/9	9/19
0.12Q	12/1	12/5	12/9	12/19
0.12Q	2/28/95	3/6/95	3/10/95	3/20/95

Indicated div.: $0.48*

CAPITALIZATION (12/31/94):

	($000)	(%)
Total Debt	314,700	17.5
Preferred Stock	75,400	4.2
Common & Surplus	1,408,900	78.3
Total	1,799,000	100.0

DIVIDEND ACHIEVER STATUS:
Rank: 248 1984-94 Growth Rate: 6.5%
Total Years of Dividend Growth: 13

RECENT DEVELOPMENTS: For the year ended 12/31/94, net income was $151.0 million, down 9.3% from $166.4 million, before accounting charges, the year before. Total revenues slipped 3.3% to $1.68 billion from $1.74 billion for the prior year. Net premiums and fees were relatively flat at $1.42 billion compared with 1993. Net investment income climbed 3.1% to $227.5 million reflecting a larger asset base fueled by positive operating cash flow and rising interest rates. Results included realized investment gains of $7.7 million compared with $40.2 million in 1993.

PROSPECTS: The title insurance industry is not expected to show any significant recovery until well into 1995 at the earliest. Accordingly, operations in this business will be geared toward aggressive expense reductions. The Company will continue to concentrate on improving results in the General Insurance Group through selected market expansion and continued underwriting selectivity. Prospects are favorable for the short term and long term.

BUSINESS

OLD REPUBLIC INTERNATIONAL CORP. is a multiple lines insurance holding company. Its subsidiaries market, underwrite, and manage a wide range of specialty and general insurance programs in the property & liability, title, mortgage guaranty insurance and life & disability. The Company primarily serves the insurance and related needs of major financial services and industrial corporations, with an emphasis on coal and energy services, construction and forest products, transportation and housing industries.

BUSINESS LINE ANALYSIS

(12/31/94)	($000)	(%)
General Insurance Group	1,051,400	63.0
Title Isurance Group	404,700	24.3
Mortgage Guaranty Group	158,300	9.5
Life Insurance Group	55,700	3.4
Other	9,000	0.6
Total	1,671,200	100.0

ANNUAL EARNINGS AND DIVIDENDS PER SHARE

	1994	1993	1992	1991	1990	1989	1988
Earnings Per Share	2.44	2.83	3.09	2.48	2.02	1.93	[5] 0.87
Dividends Per Share	0.47	0.43	[1] 0.392	[2] 0.363	[3] 0.339	[4] 0.316	[6] 0.301
Dividend Payout %	19.3	15.5	12.7	14.7	16.8	16.4	34.7

[1] 2-for-1 stk split, 5/1/92 [2] 10% stk div, 4/2/91 [3] Adj for 5% stk div, 5/15/90 [4] Adj for 5% stk div, 3/10/89 [5] Before realized gains [6] Adj for 5% stk div, 5/06/88

ANNUAL FINANCIAL DATA

	1994	1993	1992	1991	1990	1989	1988
RECORD OF EARNINGS (IN MILLIONS):							
Insurance Premiums	1,282.9	1,246.0	1,103.5	972.0	886.4	812.5	804.7
Total Interest Income	227.5	220.7	221.5	219.3	206.6	198.3	173.2
Total Revenues	1,678.8	1,736.1	1,616.9	1,374.3	1,242.4	1,181.8	1,101.9
Income Bef Income Taxes	225.9	243.3	250.7	175.2	132.8	119.4	33.5
Income Taxes	73.3	77.9	74.9	45.3	29.0	21.2	cr11.6
Net Income	151.0	[1] 166.4	174.7	131.0	104.6	98.9	50.9
Aver. Shs. Outstg. (000)	57,208	57,078	54,517	52,408	51,206	50,481	48,475

[1] Before acctg. change cr$8,600,000.

	1994	1993	1992	1991	1990	1989	1988
BALANCE SHEET (IN MILLIONS):							
Cash	31.1	43.9	42.4	...	20.9	27.2	36.1
Fixed Maturities	3,347.5	3,152.2	2,846.3	2,518.6	2,210.1	2,008.1	1,736.0
Equity Securities (at Mkt)	263.8	191.9	125.9	51.4	40.1	11.5	29.1
Total Assets	6,262.1	6,180.8	4,217.6	3,817.2	3,327.7	3,122.8	3,057.8
Benefits and Claims	4,184.2	4,097.8	2,403.5	2,285.3	2,143.1	2,023.5	1,919.4
Net Stockholders' Equity	1,484.3	1,334.8	1,165.5	962.3	789.1	696.2	591.8
Year End Shs Outstg (000)	51,536	51,871	50,693	46,896	46,221	44,406	41,978
STATISTICAL RECORD:							
Book Value Per Share	27.34	24.23	21.40	18.80	16.54	14.93	13.29
Return on Equity %	10.3	12.6	15.2	13.9	13.5	14.7	8.9
Return on Assets %	2.4	2.7	4.1	3.4	3.1	3.2	1.7
Average Yield %	2.2	1.8	1.8	2.6	3.2	2.7	3.1
P/E Ratio	9.6-7.4	9.8-7.6	8.6-5.7	7.2-4.0	6.1-4.3	6.8-5.3	12.4-9.1
Price Range	24½-18⅞	27⅝-21½	26½-17½	17⅞-10	12¼-8⅝	13⅛-10⅛	11¼-8¼

Statistics are as originally reported.

OFFICERS:
A.C. Zucaro, Chmn., Pres. & C.E.O.
P.D. Adams, Sr. V.P., C.F.O. & Treas.
S. LeRoy, III, Sr. V.P., Sec. & Gen. Couns.

INCORPORATED: DE, 1969

PRINCIPAL OFFICE: 307 North Michigan Avenue, Chicago, IL 60601

TELEPHONE NUMBER: (312) 346-8100
NO. OF EMPLOYEES: 5,400 (approx.)
ANNUAL MEETING: In May
SHAREHOLDERS: 3,799
INSTITUTIONAL HOLDINGS:
No. of Institutions: 164
Shares Held: 37,462,569

REGISTRAR(S):

TRANSFER AGENT(S):

NYS SYMBOL ORU
Rec. Pr. 31¾

ORANGE & ROCKLAND UTILITIES, INC.

YIELD 8.1%
P/E RATIO 12.7

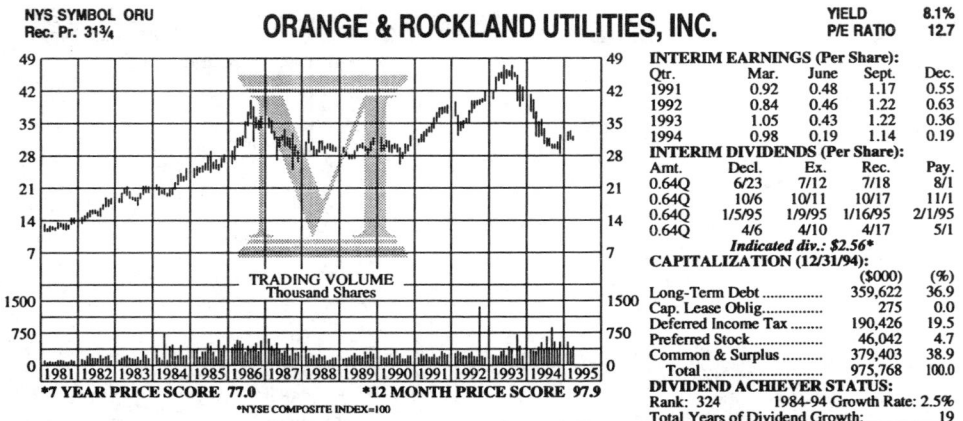

*7 YEAR PRICE SCORE 77.0 *NYSE COMPOSITE INDEX=100 ***12 MONTH PRICE SCORE 97.9**

INTERIM EARNINGS (Per Share):

Qtr.	Mar.	June	Sept.	Dec.
1991	0.92	0.48	1.17	0.55
1992	0.84	0.46	1.22	0.63
1993	1.05	0.43	1.22	0.36
1994	0.98	0.19	1.14	0.19

INTERIM DIVIDENDS (Per Share):

Amt.	Decl.	Ex.	Rec.	Pay.
0.64Q	6/23	7/12	7/18	8/1
0.64Q	10/6	10/11	10/17	11/1
0.64Q	1/5/95	1/9/95	1/16/95	2/1/95
0.64Q	4/6	4/10	4/17	5/1

Indicated div.: $2.56*

CAPITALIZATION (12/31/94):

	($000)	(%)
Long-Term Debt	359,622	36.9
Cap. Lease Oblig.	275	0.0
Deferred Income Tax	190,426	19.5
Preferred Stock	46,042	4.7
Common & Surplus	379,403	38.9
Total	975,768	100.0

DIVIDEND ACHIEVER STATUS:
Rank: 324   1984-94 Growth Rate: 2.5%
Total Years of Dividend Growth: 19

RECENT DEVELOPMENTS: For the year ended 12/31/94, net income declined 17% to $37.2 million from $44.8 million in 1993. Meanwhile, revenues increased 5% to $1.02 billion. The decline in earnings was partially attributed to the expenses associated with the continuing investigation and litigation involving misappropriation of ORU funds. For the quarter ended 12/31/94, net income plunged 42% to $3.4 million as revenues moved up 1.6% to $258.7 million.

PROSPECTS: Results will be negatively affected by the adverse effects of the regulatory actions resulting from the aforementioned investigation and the provision to refund to customers those funds, with interest, found to have been improperly spent. Moreover, regulators cut the allowed return on common equity and denied ORU the opportunity for rate adjustments in the third and fourth year of an four-year gas rate agreement.

BUSINESS

ORANGE & ROCKLAND UTILI-TIES, INC. is an investor-owned utility serving 257,000 electric customers and 109,500 natural gas customers in a 1,350 square-mile territory in southeastern New York as well as in adjacent sections of northern New Jersey and northeastern Pennsylvania. ORU has two wholly-owned utility subsidiaries - Rockland Electric Company and Pike County Light and Power Company. The Company also has three wholly-owned non-utility subsidiaries - Clove Development Corporation, a real estate operation, O & R Energy Development, Inc., a gas and oil exploration company and O & R Development Inc., an industrial and corporate development company.

REVENUES

(12/31/94)	($000)	(%)
Electric	472,393	46.5
Gas	157,168	15.5
Electric Sales to Other Utilities	6,636	0.7
Diversified Activities	380,705	37.3
Total	1,016,902	100.0

ANNUAL EARNINGS AND DIVIDENDS PER SHARE

	1994	1993	1992	1991	1990	1989	1988
Earnings Per Share	2.50	3.06	3.15	3.12	⊡2.99	3.14	3.18
Dividends Per Share	2.54	2.49	2.43	2.37	2.32	2.28	2.24
Dividend Payout %	N.M.	81.4	77.1	76.0	77.6	72.6	70.4

⊡ Before extraord. item

ANNUAL FINANCIAL DATA

RECORD OF EARNINGS (IN MILLIONS):

	1994	1993	1992	1991	1990	1989	1988
Total Revenues	1,016.9	971.4	844.2	732.0	559.2	536.2	486.7
Depreciation & Amort.	35.9	34.5	34.5	32.1	24.2	27.8	26.9
Maintenance	44.0	42.9	42.5	40.3	36.7	32.1	32.6
Income Taxes	24.5	25.9	22.2	19.7	15.4	20.2	25.2
Income From Operations	75.9	82.5	79.2	77.3	74.4	75.3	74.6
Interest Expense	33.4	34.1	35.4	34.1	33.4	31.2	28.8
Net Income	37.2	44.8	45.8	44.9	⊡42.6	44.1	44.2
Aver. Shs. Outstg. (000)	13,594	13,532	13,438	13,238	13,040	12,840	12,659

⊡ Before extra. item cr$7,205,000.

BALANCE SHEET (IN MILLIONS):

	1994	1993	1992	1991	1990	1989	1988
Gross Plant	1,289.5	1,239.3	1,197.2	1,151.6	1,091.4	1,037.3	992.7
Accumulated Depreciation	412.6	385.3	360.4	336.8	311.7	300.6	285.0
Prop., Plant & Equip, Net	876.9	854.0	836.8	814.8	779.7	736.7	707.7
Long-term Debt	359.9	381.1	381.5	378.6	373.8	292.7	290.4
Net Stockholders' Equity	425.4	423.5	417.2	401.2	386.0	369.7	354.5
Total Assets	1,313.0	1,281.0	1,135.2	1,087.8	1,036.9	978.3	922.2
Year End Shs Outstg (000)	13,653	13,532	13,531	13,328	13,132	12,932	12,728

STATISTICAL RECORD:

	1994	1993	1992	1991	1990	1989	1988
Book Value Per Share	27.79	27.79	27.22	26.33	25.46	24.17	23.23
Op. Inc/Net Pl %	8.7	9.7	9.5	9.5	9.5	10.2	10.5
Dep/Gr. Pl %	2.8	2.8	2.9	2.8	2.2	2.7	2.7
Accum. Dep/Gr. Pl %	32.0	31.1	30.1	29.2	28.6	29.0	28.7
Return on Equity %	8.8	10.7	11.1	11.4	11.3	12.4	13.0
Average Yield %	7.3	5.8	6.5	6.8	7.9	7.7	7.3
P/E Ratio	16.5-11.4	15.5-12.6	13.3-10.3	12.5-9.9	10.8-8.7	10.2-8.7	10.5-8.8
Price Range	41¼-28⅜	47½-38⅝	41⅞-32⅜	39-30⅞	32⅜-26⅛	32-27¼	33½-27⅞

Statistics are as originally reported.

OFFICERS:
D.L. Peoples, C.E.O. & Vice-Chmn.
V.J. Blanchet, Jr., Pres. & C.O.O.
V.A. Roque, V.P., Gen. Counsel & Sec.
R.J. McBennett, Treasurer

INCORPORATED: NY, May, 1926

PRINCIPAL OFFICE: One Blue Hill Plaza, Pearl River, NY 10965

TELEPHONE NUMBER: (914) 352-6000
FAX: (914) 577-2730
NO. OF EMPLOYEES: 1,700
ANNUAL MEETING: In April
SHAREHOLDERS: 24,328 common; 570, pfd.; 1,038, pref.
INSTITUTIONAL HOLDINGS:
No. of Institutions: 75
Shares Held: 1,622,794

REGISTRAR(S): Chemical Bank, New York, NY

TRANSFER AGENT(S): Chemical Bank, New York, NY

SYMBOL OSH A
Rec. Pr. 20

OSHAWA GROUP LTD.

YIELD 2.6%
P/E RATIO 20.8

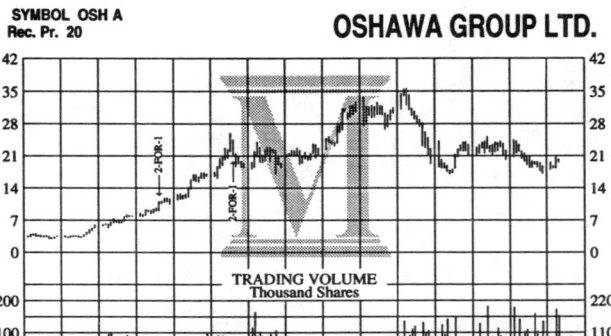

TRADING VOLUME
Thousand Shares

| 1981 | 1982 | 1983 | 1984 | 1985 | 1986 | 1987 | 1988 | 1989 | 1990 | 1991 | 1992 | 1993 | 1994 | 1995 |

*7 YEAR PRICE SCORE ...   *12 MONTH PRICE SCORE 104.4
*NYSE COMPOSITE INDEX=100

INTERIM EARNINGS (Per Share):

Qtr.	Apr.	Aug.	Nov.	Jan.
1990-91	0.29	0.66	0.43	0.41
1991-92	0.35	0.29	0.10	0.22
1992-93	0.16	0.42	0.23	0.33
1993-94	0.21	0.48	0.25	0.41
1994-95	---------------- 1.41 ----------------

INTERIM DIVIDENDS (Per Share):

Amt.	Decl.	Ex.	Rec.	Pay.
0.125Q	3/25/94	5/10/94	5/16/94	6/10/94
0.125Q	6/6	8/10	8/16	9/10
0.125Q	10/6	11/10	11/16	12/10
0.125Q	2/3/95	2/10/95	2/16/95	3/10/95
0.13Q	3/31	5/10	5/16	6/10

Indicated div.:$0.52

CAPITALIZATION (1/25/95):

	($000)	(%)
Long-Term Debt	123,500	29.7
Deferred Income Tax	39,900	9.6
Common & Surplus	252,100	60.7
Total	415,500	100.0

DIVIDEND ACHIEVER STATUS:
Rank: 189   1984-94 Growth Rate: 9.3%
Total Years of Dividend Growth: 16

RECENT DEVELOPMENTS: For the year ended 1/28/95, net earnings were $53.2 million compared with $50.2 million in the year before. Total revenues advanced to a record level of $6.07 billion from $5.73 billion in the previous year. Revenues in the food service division advanced by 12% to $5.64 billion from $5.29 billion in the prior year. Despite an increase in cigarette volume, cigarette revenues fell in the wake of higher federal and provincial tobacco taxes. Whole-sale and retail food sales rose by 3% to $5.18 billion from $5.02 billion in the previous year due to strong sales at OSH's "IGA" and other food markets franchises. Sales at the Company's Pharma Plus Drugmarts, Ltd. declined to $413.8 million from $417.7 million in the equivalent period of the year before. Additionally, margins were strained due to the emergence of mass merchants that offered low dispensing fees and discounted prices.

BUSINESS

OSHAWA GROUP LTD. is a Canadian company operating in nine provinces. The Company services 645 "IGA" food stores as well as 794 additional independent grocers trading under the names "Knechtel," "Food Town," "Bonichoix" and others. Oshawa manages 110 corporate stores including 45 "IGA," 37 "Food City" and 16 "Price Chopper" supermarkets. Through its foodservice operation, the Company wholesales to restaurants, hotels and institutions such as hospitals, schools and company cafeterias. Oshawa also has 146 pharmacies operating in Ontario and Manitoba under the name "Pharma Plus." Other divisions include produce packaging and wholesaling facilities, public cold storage warehouses, a dairy, a uniform rental company and revenue-producing real estate. Oshawa's Class A shares are listed on both the Toronto Stock Exchange and the Montreal Exchange.

BUSINESS LINE ANALYSIS

(1/25/95)	Rev(%)	Inc(%)
Food	92.9	84.5
Drug Stores & Pharmacies	6.8	4.6
Real Estate	0.3	10.9
Total	100.0	100.0

ANNUAL EARNINGS AND DIVIDENDS PER SHARE

	1/28/95	1/22/94	1/23/93	1/25/92	1/26/91	1/27/90	1/28/89
Earnings Per Share	1.41	1.35	1.14	0.96	① 1.95	2.11	1.78
Dividends Per Share	0.495	0.475	0.46	0.455	0.43	0.39	0.35
Dividend Payout %	35.1	35.2	40.4	47.4	22.1	18.5	19.7

ANNUAL FINANCIAL DATA

RECORD OF EARNINGS (IN MILLIONS):

Sales and Other Revenue	6,069.8	5,727.8	5,011.4	4,613.8	4,598.8	4,948.2	4,274.5
Costs and Expenses	5,921.1	5,590.2	4,904.1	4,531.9	4,456.7	4,793.2	4,144.4
Depreciation & Amort	58.3	53.1	43.3	38.2	33.8	35.5	29.0
Operating Income	90.4	84.5	64.0	38.6	102.0	107.0	94.6
Earn Bef Income Taxes	82.6	77.9	64.2	54.5	112.7	114.0	99.4
Income Taxes	29.4	27.7	22.4	19.4	42.4	44.4	42.5
Net Income	53.2	50.2	41.8	35.1	① 70.3	69.6	56.9
Aver. Shs. Outstg. (000)	37,761	37,235	36,800	36,499	36,029	32,915	32,037

① Before disc. op. dr$9,948,000.

BALANCE SHEET (IN MILLIONS):

Cash & Short-term Invests	54.6	35.1	5.2	94.8	112.4	37.7	3.1
Receivables, Net	260.0	260.0	237.0	198.2	198.1	161.5	136.6
Inventories	331.1	318.1	313.4	285.5	286.5	365.8	324.8
Gross Property	801.1	760.3	712.3	564.9	536.8	530.3	452.0
Accumulated Depreciation	330.5	286.4	245.8	214.7	190.2	186.8	161.0
Long-Term Debt	123.5	124.2	23.7	23.2	25.3	30.5	38.2
Net Stockholders' Equity	751.0	707.3	664.9	633.2	607.0	552.9	389.6
Total Assets	1,313.7	1,259.7	1,158.1	1,006.4	994.0	953.8	795.2
Total Current Assets	662.5	627.3	566.1	588.2	605.7	579.2	479.4
Total Current Liabilities	376.6	371.1	411.0	290.8	303.2	348.8	345.8
Net Working Capital	285.9	256.2	155.1	297.4	302.5	230.4	133.6
Year End Shs Outstg (000)	36,824	36,825	36,301	36,618	36,346	35,844	32,114

STATISTICAL RECORD:

Operating Profit Margin %	1.5	1.5	1.3	0.8	2.2	2.2	2.2
Book Value Per Share	20.13	17.07	16.47	17.29	16.70	15.42	12.13
Return on Equity %	7.1	7.1	6.3	5.5	11.6	12.6	14.6
Return on Assets %	4.0	4.0	3.6	3.5	7.1	7.3	7.2
Average Yield %	2.5	2.1	2.2	1.6	1.4	1.4	1.6
P/E Ratio	17.2-12.1	18.7-14.9	21.2-14.9	37.1-21.7	17.4-13.7	15.5-10.5	13.3-10.7
Price Range	24¼ - 17⅛	25¼ - 20⅛	24⅛ - 17	35⅝-20⅞	33⅞-26¾	32¾-22¼	23⅝-19⅛

Statistics are as originally reported.

OFFICERS:
A.P. Graham, Chmn. & C.E.O.
J.A. Wolfe, Pres. & C.O.O.
R.E. Boyd, Exec. V.P.-Fin. & C.F.O.
L. Eisen, Treas.
H.J. Wolfe, Sec.

PRINCIPAL OFFICE: 302 The East Mall, Etobicoke, Ontario, Canada M9B 6B8

TELEPHONE NUMBER: (416) 236-1971
FAX: (416) 236-2071
NO. OF EMPLOYEES: 17,479
ANNUAL MEETING: In June
SHAREHOLDERS:
INSTITUTIONAL HOLDINGS:
No. of Institutions: Not Available
Shares Held: Not Available

REGISTRAR(S): Montreal Trust Co., Montreal, Vancouver, Calgary, Regina, Winnipeg, Toronto, Canada

TRANSFER AGENT(S): Montreal Trust Co., Montreal, Vancouver, Calgary, Regina, Winnipeg, Toronto, Canada

OTTER TAIL POWER CO.

YIELD 5.5%
P/E RATIO 13.6

7 YEAR PRICE SCORE 95.4   **12 MONTH PRICE SCORE 99.8**
*NYSE COMPOSITE INDEX=100

INTERIM EARNINGS (Per Share):

Qtr.	Mar.	June	Sept.	Dec.
1991	0.80	0.44	0.43	0.47
1992	0.75	0.53	0.36	0.53
1993	0.77	0.46	0.45	0.54
1994	0.78	0.43	0.48	0.65

INTERIM DIVIDENDS (Per Share):

Amt.	Decl.	Ex.	Rec.	Pay.
0.43Q	4/12/94	5/9/94	5/13/94	6/10/94
0.43Q	7/18	8/9	8/15	9/10
0.43Q	10/18	11/8	11/15	12/10
0.44Q	1/30/95	2/9/95	2/15/95	3/10/95
0.44Q	4/10	5/9	5/15	6/10

*Indicated div.: $1.76**

CAPITALIZATION (12/31/94):

	($000)	(%)
Long-Term Debt	162,196	32.8
Deferred Income Tax	117,082	23.7
Preferred Stock	38,831	7.8
Common & Surplus	176,648	35.7
Total	494,757	100.0
Current Debt	11,639	

DIVIDEND ACHIEVER STATUS:
Rank: 320   1984-94 Growth Rate: 2.8%
Total Years of Dividend Growth: 19

RECENT DEVELOPMENTS: For the quarter ended 12/31/94, net income was $7.8 million up 6.5% from $6.7 million for the corresponding period of 1993. Operating revenues were $74.0 million versus $67.4 million a year earlier. Earnings were boosted by the Electric and Health Services segments reporting higher revenues. The Electric segments' revenues rose 6.7% to $51.3 million and the Health Service segments' revenues rose 59% to $10.9 million. For the year ended 12/31/94, net income increased 4% to $28.5 million, or $2.34 per share, from $27.4 million, or $2.23 per share, for the comparable period a year earlier. Operating revenues were up 3.4% to $198.8 million compared with $192.3 million in 1993. Operating revenues for OTTR's Diversified Operations and Health Service segments were up 5.6% and 42.1%, respectively.

BUSINESS

OTTER TAIL POWER COMPANY is an operating electric utility engaged in the production, transmission and distribution and sale of electric energy in western Minnesota, eastern North Dakota and northeastern South Dakota. OTTR, through its subsidiaries, is also engaged in telephone, health services, and other nonutility operations. The aggregate population of OTTR's retail service area is approximately 230,000. The territory served by OTTR is predominately agricultural, including part of the Red River Valley. Quadrant Co. operates a municipal building facility. Mid-States Development, Inc. owns six nonutility businesses in such industries as manufacturing (fabricated metal parts and agricultural equipment), radio broadcasting, and utility contracting for overhead and underground systems. North Central Utilities, Inc. owns RD Communications, Inc., an independent telephone company.

ANNUAL EARNINGS AND DIVIDENDS PER SHARE

	1994	1993	1992	1991	1990	1989	1988
Earnings Per Share	2.34	2.22	2.17	2.15	1.99	1.94	1.92
Dividends Per Share	1.72	1.68	1.64	1.60	1.56	1.52	① 1.48
Dividend Payout %	73.5	75.7	75.6	74.4	78.4	78.4	77.1

① 100% stk. div., 6/88.

ANNUAL FINANCIAL DATA

RECORD OF EARNINGS (IN THOUSANDS):

	1994	1993	1992	1991	1990	1989	1988
Total Revenues	287,523	265,227	209,538	179,660	172,541	172,840	178,221
Depreciation & Amort	25,899	25,348	21,115	17,816	17,431	17,849	18,944
Maintenance	13,725	12,914	10,927	11,866	10,760	10,638	9,622
Prov for Fed Inc Taxes	15,931	14,331	14,024	14,328	13,850	12,948	17,361
Operating Income	40,513	39,655	38,362	36,121	34,072	34,561	35,853
Interest Expense	13,687	13,825	13,165	11,462	9,965	10,337	10,371
Net Income	28,475	27,369	26,538	26,096	24,852	25,266	25,317
Aver. Shs. Outstg.	11,180	11,180	11,185	11,196	11,455	11,917	11,968
BALANCE SHEET (IN THOUSANDS):							
Gross Plant	745,143	722,249	691,567	654,835	638,274	616,298	605,593
Accumulated Depreciation	287,902	270,385	252,663	236,506	225,539	212,004	198,183
Prop, Plant & Equip, Net	457,241	451,864	438,904	418,329	412,735	404,294	407,410
Long-term Debt	162,196	166,563	159,295	146,103	134,929	118,959	121,815
Net Stockholders' Equity	215,479	209,277	203,342	188,091	183,452	193,454	193,564
Total Assets	578,972	563,905	530,456	487,663	474,356	467,233	482,570
Year End Shares Outstg	11,180	11,180	11,180	11,185	11,223	11,795	11,968
STATISTICAL RECORD:							
Book Value Per Share	15.80	15.25	14.71	14.25	13.74	13.83	13.55
Op. Inc/Net Pl %	8.9	8.8	8.7	8.6	8.3	8.5	8.8
Dep/Gr. Pl %	2.8	2.8	2.7	2.7	2.7	2.9	3.1
Accum. Dep/Gr. Pl %	38.6	37.4	36.5	36.1	35.3	34.4	32.7
Return on Equity %	14.4	14.3	14.3	14.9	14.6	14.1	14.3
Average Yield %	5.4	4.7	4.9	5.6	6.4	7.0	7.3
P/E Ratio	14.9-12.6	18.5-13.7	16.7-14.1	15.1-11.5	13.4-11.1	12.6-9.7	11.6-9.5
Price Range	34¾-29½	41¼-30⅝	36¼-30½	32½-24¾	26¾-22	24⅜-18¾	22¼-18¼

Statistics are as originally reported.

OFFICERS:
J.C. MacFarlane, Chmn., Pres. & C.E.O.
D.R. Emmen, Sr. V.P.-Fin., Treas. & C.F.O.
J.D. Myster, V.P.-Gov. & Legal & Corp. Sec.

INCORPORATED: MN, Jul., 1907

PRINCIPAL OFFICE: 215 South Cascade St.
Box 496, Fergus Falls, MN 56538-0496

TELEPHONE NUMBER: (218) 739-8200
FAX: (218) 739-8218
NO. OF EMPLOYEES: 794 (Electric Company)
ANNUAL MEETING: In April
SHAREHOLDERS: 13,634 common; 880 pfd.
INSTITUTIONAL HOLDINGS:
No. of Institutions: 61
Shares Held: 1,095,738

REGISTRAR(S): Community First National Bank, Fergus Falls, MN

TRANSFER AGENT(S): Shareholder Services, Fergus Falls, MN 56537
Norwest Bank Minnesota, N.A., St. Paul, MN

NYS SYMBOL PLL
Rec. Pr. 22⅝

PALL CORP.

YIELD 1.9%
P/E RATIO 24.6

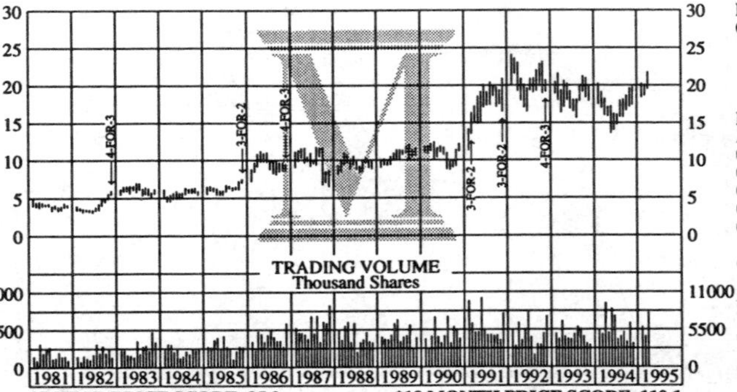

4-FOR-3
3-FOR-2
4-FOR-3
3-FOR-2
3-FOR-2
4-FOR-3
TRADING VOLUME
Thousand Shares
1981 1982 1983 1984 1985 1986 1987 1988 1989 1990 1991 1992 1993 1994 1995

*7 YEAR PRICE SCORE 95.2 *12 MONTH PRICE SCORE 110.1

*NYSE COMPOSITE INDEX=100

INTERIM EARNINGS (Per Share):

Qtr.	Oct.	Jan.	Apr.	July
1991-92	0.07	0.17	0.23	0.32
1992-93	0.09	0.03	0.22	0.34
1993-94	0.10	0.19	0.24	0.33
1994-95	0.12	0.23	...	...

INTERIM DIVIDENDS (Per Share):

Amt.	Decl.	Ex.	Rec.	Pay.
0.0925Q	4/18/94	4/28/94	5/4/94	5/16/94
0.0925Q	7/11	7/18	7/22	8/5
0.0925Q	10/3	10/7	10/14	10/28
0.105Q	1/9/95	1/13/95	1/20/95	2/3/95
0.105Q	4/18	4/24	4/28	5/12

Indicated div.: $0.42*

CAPITALIZATION (7/30/94):

	($000)	(%)
Long-Term Debt	54,097	8.0
Deferred Income Tax	31,450	4.7
Common & Surplus	587,206	87.3
Total	672,753	100.0

DIVIDEND ACHIEVER STATUS:
Rank: 24 1984-94 Growth Rate: 18.7%
Total Years of Dividend Growth: 14

RECENT DEVELOPMENTS: For the three months ended 1/29/94, net income jumped to $22.0 million from $3.3 million, including a pretax charge of $26.7 million for restructuring, in the prior-year period. Sales improved slightly to $169.7 million from $167.5 million. Foreign currency exchange rates reduced sales by $2.3 million. A 9% reduction in Military Aerospace sales was offset by sales growth of 10% in the Industrial Hydraulics Division, while overall Aeropower sales remained flat.

PROSPECTS: Pall's earnings, of which a sizeable amount are derived outside the United States, continue to be affected by the sluggish European economy. However, orders are increasing in many of Pall's business segments in the U.S. The Company's entry into the high end of the industrial separations market is exposing PLL to industrial markets with a sales potential approaching that of its traditional filtration products.

BUSINESS

PALL CORPORATION is a leading supplier of fine filters primarily produced by the Company using its proprietary filter media, and other fluid clarification equipment for the removal of solid, liquid and gaseous contaminants from a variety of liquids and gases. The Company serves its diversified customer base through integrated businesses in the U.S. and Europe. Sales (operating profit) in the Western Hemisphere accounted for 43% (50%) of the total, with Europe and the Pacific Basin accounting for 40% (42%) and 17% (8%), respectively.

BUSINESS LINE ANALYSIS

(07/30/94)	Rev(%)	Inc(%)
Health Care	50.2	64.6
Aeropower	25.6	20.4
Fluid Processing	24.2	15.0
Total	100.0	100.0

ANNUAL EARNINGS AND DIVIDENDS PER SHARE

	7/30/94	7/31/93	8/1/92	8/3/91	7/28/90	7/29/89	7/30/88
Earnings Per Share	**0.86**	**0.68**	**[1] 0.77**	**0.69**	**0.57**	**0.50**	**0.52**
Dividends Per Share	**0.37**	**0.32**	**[2] 0.27**	**0.22**	**0.187**	**0.16**	**0.134**
Dividend Payout %	**43.0**	**43.1**	**35.1**	**31.8**	**32.6**	**31.8**	**25.8**

[1] Before acctg. chg. [2] 3-for-2 stk split, 12/30/91

ANNUAL FINANCIAL DATA

	7/30/94	7/31/93	8/1/92	8/3/91	7/28/90	7/29/89	7/30/88
RECORD OF EARNINGS (IN THOUSANDS):							
Total Revenues	706,122	691,935	690,464	663,094	575,582	505,888	435,482
Costs and Expenses	527,088	543,785	519,223	499,643	429,515	375,936	327,450
Depreciation	36,804	35,188	34,360	31,854	26,803	24,673	21,895
Operating Profit	187,209	179,708	175,358	161,873	143,253	125,442	102,939
Earn Bef Income Taxes	135,098	104,279	126,201	115,825	97,403	84,069	84,862
Income Taxes	36,176	25,967	35,968	35,904	31,168	26,388	27,458
Net Income	98,922	78,312	[1] 90,233	79,921	66,235	57,681	57,404
Aver. Shs. Outstg.	115,678	115,856	116,928	116,193	115,735	114,873	111,095
[1] Before acctg. change cr$2,475,000.							
BALANCE SHEET (IN THOUSANDS):							
Cash and Cash Equivalents	89,024	107,052	101,329	59,069	81,401	128,743	91,636
Receivables, Net	224,337	216,662	220,074	168,306	173,669	155,262	131,891
Inventories	138,382	127,525	144,947	140,923	142,931	130,035	101,354
Gross Property	620,629	544,002	561,104	489,449	454,704	366,767	306,732
Accumulated Depreciation	223,012	186,382	195,041	157,616	135,735	110,943	89,339
Long-Term Debt	54,097	24,540	59,003	51,605	56,343	40,419	39,508
Net Stockholders' Equity	587,206	542,878	545,595	487,998	441,439	373,692	321,353
Total Assets	959,579	902,273	912,876	774,459	786,364	707,274	570,444
Total Current Assets	470,425	470,288	482,724	385,065	414,721	433,339	339,260
Total Current Liabilities	256,839	277,760	259,391	202,753	261,306	268,928	185,540
Net Working Capital	213,586	192,528	223,333	182,312	153,415	164,411	153,720
Year End Shares Outstg	115,319	116,063	86,708	116,811	115,915	115,639	111,452
STATISTICAL RECORD:							
Operating Profit Margin %	20.1	16.3	19.8	19.8	20.7	20.8	19.8
Book Value Per Share	5.09	4.68	6.29	4.18	3.81	3.23	2.88
Return on Equity %	16.8	14.4	16.5	16.4	15.0	15.4	17.9
Return on Assets %	10.3	8.7	9.9	10.3	8.4	8.2	10.1
Average Yield %	2.2	1.7	1.3	1.4	1.8	1.5	1.4
P/E Ratio	23.5-15.8	31.8-23.0	31.3-21.4	30.3-16.3	21.9-15.4	24.3-18.0	21.2-15.4
Price Range	20¼-13⅝	21⅝-15⅝	24⅛-16½	20⅞-11¼	12½-8¾	12⅛-9	11-8

Statistics are as originally reported.

OFFICERS:
E. Krasnoff, Chmn. & C.E.O.
J. Hayward-Surry, Pres., Treas. & C.F.O.
P. Schwartzman, Sec.

INCORPORATED: NY, Jul., 1946

PRINCIPAL OFFICE: 2200 Northern Blvd., East Hills, NY 11548

TELEPHONE NUMBER: (516) 484-5400
FAX: (516) 484-5228
NO. OF EMPLOYEES: 6,200 (approx.)
ANNUAL MEETING: In November
SHAREHOLDERS: 7,200 (approx.)
INSTITUTIONAL HOLDINGS:
No. of Institutions: 346
Shares Held: 75,821,839 (adj.)

REGISTRAR(S): Wachovia Bank & Trust Co., N.A., Winston-Salem, NC 27102

TRANSFER AGENT(S): Wachovia Bank & Trust Co., N.A., Winston-Salem, NC 27102

PENTAIR, INC.

YIELD 1.8%
P/E RATIO 17.9

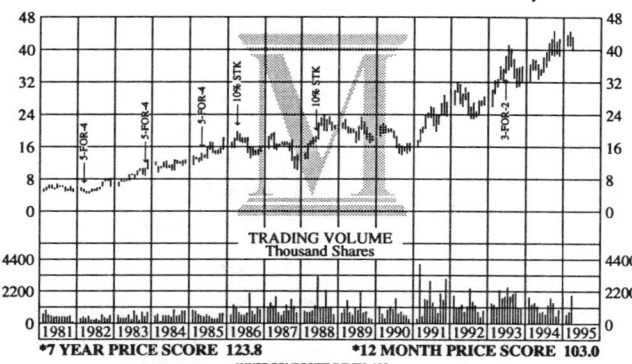

*7 YEAR PRICE SCORE 123.8 *12 MONTH PRICE SCORE 103.0
*NYSE COMPOSITE INDEX=100

INTERIM EARNINGS (Per Share):

Qtr.	Mar.	June	Sept.	Dec.
1992	0.39	0.36	0.59	0.80
1993	0.45	0.46	0.66	0.69
1994	0.53	0.57	0.64	0.80

INTERIM DIVIDENDS (Per Share):

Amt.	Decl.	Ex.	Rec.	Pay.
0.18Q	4/8/94	4/18/94	4/22/94	5/13/94
0.18Q	7/8	7/18	7/22	8/12
0.18Q	10/7	10/17	10/21	11/11
0.20Q	1/18/95	1/24/95	1/30/95	2/13/95
0.20Q	4/19	4/25	5/1	5/15

*Indicated div.: $0.80**

CAPITALIZATION (12/31/94):

	($000)	(%)
Long-Term Debt	408,503	43.9
Deferred Income Tax	22,706	2.4
Preferred Stock	68,444	7.3
Common & Surplus	431,974	46.4
Total	931,627	100.0

DIVIDEND ACHIEVER STATUS:
Rank: 214   1984-94 Growth Rate: 8.0%
Total Years of Dividend Growth: 18

RECENT DEVELOPMENTS: For the year ended 12/31/94, net income increased 15.0% to $53.6 million from $46.6 million for the comparable period of 1993. Net sales were $1.65 billion, up 24.2% from $1.34 billion the previous year. Results for 1994 included the first full year of sales from the newly acquired Schroff business. Total operating expenses rose 24.7% to $1.53 billion and increased slightly as a percentage of sales. PNTA's equity in joint venture income was

$1.8 million compared with a loss of $1.9 million the year before. Earnings of the general industrial equipment group were boosted by 80% due to strong durable goods and sporting ammunition markets. Specialty products group earnings climbed 15% as a result of continued growth of sales through home center distribution channels. Paper group earnings fell 52% due to overcapacity and higher raw material costs.

BUSINESS

PENTAIR INC. is comprised of 11 businesses that manufacture woodworking equipment, electric-power tools, sporting ammunition, electrical enclosures, automotive service equipment, industrial lubrication systems, material dispensing equipment, pumps and paper. Paper manufacturing is the largest business segment. Niagara of Wisconsin Paper Corporation, Niagara, Wisconsin, makes coated papers for magazines, catalogs and commercial printing. Miami Paper Corporation, West Carrollton, Ohio offers book papers as well as printing and specialty grades. Flambeau Paper Corp., Par Falls, Wisconsin, produces business and commercial printing papers. Industrial manufacturing is an expanding segment of the Company. Porter-Cable Corporation, Jackson, Tennessee, makes portable power tools for professional and industrial markets. Delta International Machinery Corporation, Pittsburgh, Pennsylvania, produces woodworking machinery for construction trades and industry. Delta has a plant in Tupelo, Mississippi, and subsidiaries in Guelph, Ontario and in Brazil.

ANNUAL EARNINGS AND DIVIDENDS PER SHARE

	1994	1993	1992	1991	1990	1989	1988
Earnings Per Share	2.62	2.26	② 2.15	2.20	1.69	1.99	2.47
Dividends Per Share	0.72	① 0.68	③ 0.653	0.613	0.587	0.533	④ 0.445
Dividend Payout %	22.5	30.4	30.4	27.9	34.8	26.8	18.0

① 3-for-2 stk split,06/14/93 ② Before acctg. chg. ③ Bef acctg chge ④ 10% stk. div., 6/88.

ANNUAL FINANCIAL DATA

RECORD OF EARNINGS (IN MILLIONS):

	1994	1993	1992	1991	1990	1989	1988
Total Revenues	1,649.2	1,328.2	1,238.7	1,169.1	1,175.9	1,163.6	823.3
Costs and Expenses	1,467.6	1,177.9	1,098.5	1,034.4	1,056.3	1,042.5	718.7
Depreciation & Amort	64.1	50.1	47.9	47.2	43.8	40.4	27.4
Operating Income	119.2	98.2	94.0	95.1	80.6	87.1	78.7
Income Bef Income Taxes	89.1	77.4	72.7	74.1	57.4	62.4	68.3
Income Taxes	35.5	30.8	29.9	33.0	24.4	26.0	28.5
Net Income	53.6	46.6	① 42.8	41.1	33.0	36.4	39.8
Aver. Shs. Outstg. (000)	18,422	17,891	17,891	15,936	15,779	16,070	16,212	14,954
① Before acctg. change dr$41,625,000.							

BALANCE SHEET (IN MILLIONS):

	1994	1993	1992	1991	1990	1989	1988
Cash and Cash Equivalents	32.7	10.3	8.4	6.1	8.8	8.7	9.9
Receivables, Net	282.9	222.0	201.1	198.6	184.4	178.5	177.6
Inventories	243.7	198.8	182.9	158.6	155.4	166.7	181.1
Gross Property	764.4	621.6	551.9	491.1	457.8	448.3	373.9
Accumulated Depreciation	353.4	305.8	262.1	232.8	194.2	165.6	130.0
Long-Term Debt	408.5	238.9	211.5	198.4	224.7	251.1	252.1
Net Stockholders' Equity	500.4	440.2	457.5	470.6	437.6	372.8	349.3
Total Assets	1,281.5	958.8	869.4	790.6	768.9	781.4	744.7
Total Current Assets	569.2	438.8	398.6	372.6	356.6	360.2	374.9
Total Current Liabilities	285.7	218.5	209.5	185.2	172.2	167.7	167.4
Net Working Capital	283.5	220.3	189.2	187.4	184.4	192.5	207.5
Year End Shs Outstg (000)	18,248	18,135	10,548	15,685	15,551	16,223	16,046

STATISTICAL RECORD:

	1994	1993	1992	1991	1990	1989	1988
Operating Profit Margin %	7.2	7.4	7.6	8.1	6.9	7.5	9.6
Book Value Per Share	14.30	15.54	23.31	16.30	14.12	12.81	11.58
Return on Equity %	10.7	10.6	9.4	8.7	7.5	9.8	11.4
Return on Assets %	4.2	4.9	4.9	5.2	4.3	4.7	5.4
Average Yield %	1.9	2.0	2.4	2.7	3.3	2.6	2.4
P/E Ratio	17.1-12.3	18.3-11.5	14.9-10.6	13.1-7.2	12.9-8.3	11.7-8.5	9.7-5.2
Price Range	44¾-32¼	41¼-26	32-22⅞	28⅞-15⅞	21⅞-14	23⅜-17	23⅞-12⅞

Statistics are as originally reported.

OFFICERS:
W.H. Buxton, Chmn., Pres. & C.E.O.
D.D. Harrison, Sr. V.P. & C.F.O.
R.T. Rueb, V.P. & Treas.

INCORPORATED: MN, Aug., 1966

PRINCIPAL OFFICE: 1500 County Road B2
West, St. Paul, MN 55113-3105

TELEPHONE NUMBER: (612) 636-7920

FAX: (612) 639-5251

NO. OF EMPLOYEES: 9,700 (approx.)

ANNUAL MEETING: In April

SHAREHOLDERS: 3,285

INSTITUTIONAL HOLDINGS:
No. of Institutions: 161
Shares Held: 11,108,496

REGISTRAR(S): Norwest Bank Minnesota, N.A., St. Paul, MN

TRANSFER AGENT(S): Norwest Bank Minnesota, N.A., St. Paul, MN

NYS SYMBOL PGL
Rec. Pr. 25⅜

PEOPLES ENERGY CORP.

YIELD 7.1%
P/E RATIO 14.7

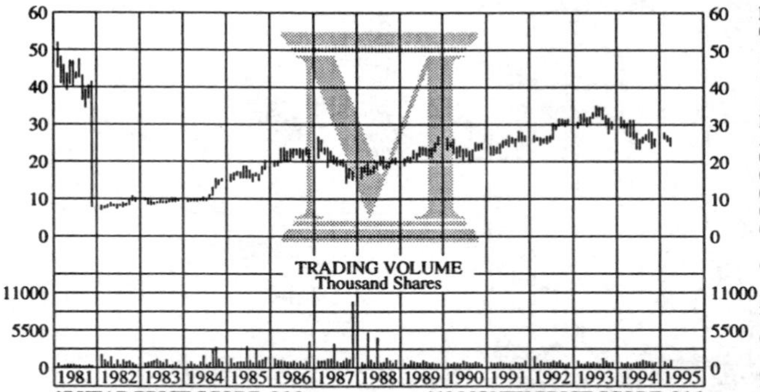

60
50
40
30
20
10
0
TRADING VOLUME
Thousand Shares
11000
5500
0
1981
1982
1983
1984
1985
1986
1987
1988
1989
1990
1991
1992
1993
1994
1995

*7 YEAR PRICE SCORE 86.3 *12 MONTH PRICE SCORE 94.1

*NYSE COMPOSITE INDEX=100

INTERIM EARNINGS (Per Share):

Qtr.	Dec.	Mar.	June	Sept.
1991-92	0.94	1.29	0.30	d0.43
1992-93	-------	2.11	-------	
1993-94	1.12	1.39	0.07	d0.45
1994-95	0.72	...	...	...

INTERIM DIVIDENDS (Per Share):

Amt.	Decl.	Ex.	Rec.	Pay.
0.45Q	2/2/94	3/14/94	3/18/94	4/15/94
0.45Q	5/4	6/13	6/17	7/15
0.45Q	8/3	9/13	9/19	10/14
0.45Q	12/7	12/13	12/19	1/13/95
0.45Q	2/1/95	3/13/95	3/17/95	4/14

Indicated div.: $1.80*

CAPITALIZATION (9/30/94):

	($000)	(%)
Long-Term Debt	626,075	41.8
Deferred Income Tax	229,825	15.4
Common & Surplus	641,378	42.8
Total	1,497,278	100.0
Current Debt	4,900	

DIVIDEND ACHIEVER STATUS:
Rank: 271 1984-94 Growth Rate: 5.5%
Total Years of Dividend Growth: 11

RECENT DEVELOPMENTS: For the twelve months ended 12/31/94, net income was $60.5 million compared with $81.3 million in the equivalent 1993 period. Revenues fell 4% to $1.21 billion. For the three months ended 12/31/94, net income was $25.1 million versus $39.0 million a year earlier. Revenues dropped 19% to $307.1 million. The results were negatively affected due to last fall's mild weather and increased operating expenses.

PROSPECTS: Earnings are being pressured by a significant increase in operation and maintenance expenses. Increased rates are critical for PGL's earnings growth. Meanwhile, earnings will be negatively affected by expenses related to uncollectible accounts and customer conservation efforts. The Company has formed a partnership to develop unregulated, on-site fueling services for natural gas powered fleet vehicles in the Chicago area.

BUSINESS

PEOPLES ENERGY CORP. is the holding company of two natural gas utilites that are engaged in the distribution of natural gas. Peoples Gas Light and Coke Co. distributes natural and synthetic gas to about 850,000 customers in Chicago. Another subsidiary, North Shore Gas Company, is engaged in the sale of gas at retail to 124,000 customers in Northeastern Illinois. A new subsidiary, Peoples District Energy Corp. joined with a partner to offer energy for heating and cooling Chicago buildings. In 1981, PGL spun-off its gas transmission contract drilling, oil and gas exploration and coal mining operations.

REVENUES

(09/30/94)	($000)	(%)
Residential	951,037	74.3
Commercial	160,912	12.6
Industrial	41,979	3.3
Transportation	110,128	8.6
Other	15,432	1.2
Total	1,279,488	100.0

ANNUAL EARNINGS AND DIVIDENDS PER SHARE

	9/30/94	9/30/93	9/30/92	9/30/91	9/30/90	9/30/89	9/30/88
Earnings Per Share	**2.13**	**2.11**	**2.06**	**2.05**	**2.07**	**[1] 2.39**	**2.31**
Dividends Per Share	**1.795**	**1.775**	**1.75**	**1.705**	**1.645**	**1.58**	**1.50**
Dividend Payout %	**84.3**	**84.1**	**85.0**	**83.2**	**79.2**	**66.1**	**64.9**

[1] Before acctg. chg.

ANNUAL FINANCIAL DATA

	9/30/94	9/30/93	9/30/92	9/30/91	9/30/90	9/30/89	9/30/88
RECORD OF EARNINGS (IN MILLIONS):							
Total Revenues	1,279.5	1,258.9	1,096.8	1,103.7	1,165.2	1,188.0	1,116.8
Depreciation	64.7	60.8	57.3	55.4	54.8	49.8	46.8
Maintenance	37.9	35.7	36.8	36.7	34.1	33.7	33.2
Prov for Fed Inc Taxes	32.1	37.6	33.6	35.0	37.3	41.4	46.8
Operating Income	101.8	113.0	107.3	105.0	102.1	103.0	105.5
Interest Expense	48.1	45.2	46.5	48.2	45.8	42.6	43.9
Net Income	74.4	73.4	70.4	67.0	67.5	[1] 78.0	75.3
Aver. Shs. Outstg. (000)	34,854	34,809	34,151	32,741	32,672	32,596	32,549
[1] Before acctg. change cr$9,663,000.							
BALANCE SHEET (IN MILLIONS):							
Gross Plant	2,019.4	1,951.0	1,843.6	1,746.9	1,667.8	1,593.0	1,472.2
Accumulated Depreciation	677.4	633.0	600.0	565.6	533.8	508.0	472.2
Prop, Plant & Equip, Net	1,341.9	1,318.0	1,243.6	1,181.2	1,134.0	1,085.1	1,000.0
Long-term Debt	626.1	528.1	489.6	493.0	502.2	452.8	459.8
Net Stockholders' Equity	641.4	628.5	629.1	571.9	563.9	554.1	521.1
Total Assets	1,809.3	1,765.9	1,615.8	1,541.4	1,534.2	1,470.6	1,407.9
Year End Shs Outstg (000)	34,868	34,823	34,774	32,762	32,701	32,614	32,569
STATISTICAL RECORD:							
Book Value Per Share	18.39	18.05	17.72	16.95	16.61	16.20	15.09
Op. Inc/Net Pl %	7.6	8.6	8.6	8.9	9.0	9.5	10.5
Dep/Gr. Pl %	3.2	3.1	3.1	3.2	3.3	3.1	3.2
Accum. Dep/Gr. Pl %	33.5	32.4	32.5	32.4	32.0	31.9	32.1
Return on Equity %	11.6	11.7	11.4	12.1	12.4	14.8	15.3
Average Yield %	6.5	5.7	6.3	6.8	7.1	6.9	8.1
P/E Ratio	15.1-11.0	16.6-13.0	15.4-11.8	13.8-10.6	12.8-9.7	11.2-7.9	9.3-6.7
Price Range	32⅛-23⅜	35-27½	31⅝-24⅜	28¼-21¾	26½-20	26¾-18⅞	21½-15⅜

Statistics are as originally reported.

OFFICERS:
R.E. Terry, Chmn. & C.E.O.
J.B. Hasch, Pres. & C.O.O.
E.P. Cassidy, Sec. & Treas.

INCORPORATED: IL, 1967

PRINCIPAL OFFICE: 122 South Michigan Avenue, Chicago, IL 60603-9942

TELEPHONE NUMBER: (312) 431-4000
FAX: (312) 431-4082
NO. OF EMPLOYEES: 3,278 approx.
ANNUAL MEETING: In February
SHAREHOLDERS: 28,922
INSTITUTIONAL HOLDINGS:
No. of Institutions: 186
Shares Held: 14,658,613

REGISTRAR(S): Harris Trust & Savings Bank, Chicago, IL

TRANSFER AGENT(S): Harris Trust & Savings Bank, Chicago, IL

NYS SYMBOL PBY
Rec. Pr. 28½

PEP BOYS-MANNY, MOE & JACK

YIELD 0.7%
P/E RATIO 21.6

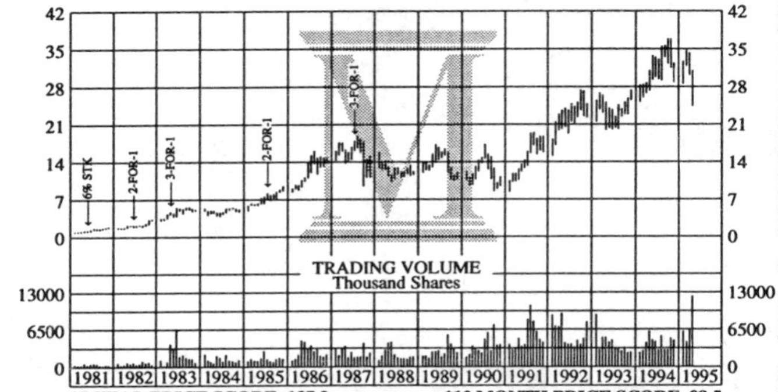

*7 YEAR PRICE SCORE 137.9 *12 MONTH PRICE SCORE 88.5

*NYSE COMPOSITE INDEX=100

INTERIM EARNINGS (Per Share):

Qtr.	Apr.	July	Oct.	Jan.
1991-92	0.13	0.20	0.19	0.17
1992-93		0.90		
1993-94	0.22	0.31	0.28	0.25
1994-95	0.29	0.39	0.34	0.30

INTERIM DIVIDENDS (Per Share):

Amt.	Decl.	Ex.	Rec.	Pay.
0.0425Q	3/30/94	4/5/94	4/11/94	4/25/94
0.0425Q	6/9	7/5	7/11	7/25
0.0425Q	9/8	10/3	10/10	10/24
0.0425Q	11/30	1/3/95	1/9/95	1/23/95
0.0475Q	3/31/95	4/4	4/10	4/24

Indicated div.: $0.19*

CAPITALIZATION (1/28/95):

	($000)	(%)
Long-Term Debt	294,537	32.2
Deferred Income Tax	34,528	3.8
Common & Surplus	586,253	64.0
Total	915,318	100.0

DIVIDEND ACHIEVER STATUS:
Rank: 126 1984-94 Growth Rate: 11.6%
Total Years of Dividend Growth: 17

RECENT DEVELOPMENTS: For the year ended 1/28/95, income, before a charge of $4.3 million for an accounting change, was $80.0 million compared with $65.5 million a year earlier. Total revenues advanced 13% to $1.41 billion. Comparable store sales increased 5%. During the year, the Company opened 50 automotive supercenters and one PARTS USA store. For the quarter ended 1/28/95, net income increased 18% to $18.3 million from $15.5 million a year earlier. Total revenues advanced 13% to $335.7 million.

PROSPECTS: Near-term earnings will continue to benefit from an ongoing cost-control program. PBY will continue its superstore expansion program, with plans to open approximately 50 supercenters in 1995. PBY also opted to increase the number of PARTS USA stores to be opened in 1995 to 25 from 10 due to the favorable sales and merchandise margins that its first PARTS USA store is generating. PBY is also initiating its first expansion outside of the continental U.S., with eight superstores in Puerto Rico in 1995.

BUSINESS

PEP BOYS operates a chain of specialty retail stores that sell a full range of brand name and private label automotive parts and accessories at discount prices. Most Pep Boys stores contain service centers for automobile maintenance and service, as well as for installation of automotive parts and accessories sold by PBY. As of 1/28/95, PBY operated 435 stores, including both full-service and satellite stores. The stores are located in 32 states mostly in the middle Atlantic, west Southwest and Southeast regions of U.S. PBY operates about 23,000 gross square feet per store.

REVENUES

(1/28/95)	($000)	(%)
Merchandise Sales	1,211,536	86.1
Service Revenue	195,449	13.9
Total	1,406,985	100.0

ANNUAL EARNINGS AND DIVIDENDS PER SHARE

	1/28/95	1/29/94	1/30/93	2/1/92	2/2/91	2/3/90	1/28/89
Earnings Per Share	**[1] 1.32**	**1.06**	**0.90**	**0.69**	**0.67**	**0.63**	**[1] 0.68**
Dividends Per Share	**0.17**	**0.165**	**0.147**	**0.125**	**0.115**	**0.105**	**0.09**
Dividend Payout %	**12.9**	**13.9**	**16.3**	**18.1**	**17.2**	**16.7**	**13.2**

[1] Before acctg. chg. [2] 3-for-1 stk split, 7/87

ANNUAL FINANCIAL DATA

	1/28/95	1/29/94	1/30/93	2/1/92	2/2/91	2/3/90	1/28/89
RECORD OF EARNINGS (IN MILLIONS):							
Total Revenues	1,407.0	1,241.1	1,155.6	1,001.5	884.7	798.7	656.0
Costs and Expenses	1,280.5	1,081.4	1,016.1	884.4	779.4	706.7	573.0
Depreciation & Amort	43.3	39.1	36.7	33.4	27.8	22.9	17.0
Operating Profit	148.9	120.6	102.8	83.7	77.4	69.1	65.9
Earn Bef Income Taxes	126.5	104.5	85.6	60.5	58.8	55.1	60.2
Income Taxes	46.5	39.0	31.0	21.6	21.2	20.1	22.5
Net Income	[1] 80.0	65.5	54.6	38.9	37.5	35.1	[2] 37.7
Aver. Shs. Outstg. (000)	61,502	61,891	60,636	56,494	56,109	55,890	55,431
[1] Before acctg change $4,300,000. [2] Before acctg. change cr$4,688,000.							
BALANCE SHEET (IN MILLIONS):							
Cash and Cash Equivalents	11.7	12.1	11.6	14.4	15.1	14.3	20.0
Receivables, Net	3.8	10.6	10.2	2.1	2.5	1.7	2.6
Inventories	366.8	305.9	295.2	230.9	234.7	163.8	117.2
Gross Property	1,105.0	923.2	796.9	728.4	665.8	566.4	488.6
Accumulated Depreciation	243.1	199.7	168.0	139.8	108.8	85.8	72.4
Long-Term Debt	380.8	253.0	209.3	279.3	285.9	227.6	187.0
Net Stockholders' Equity	586.3	547.8	509.8	378.5	344.6	311.8	275.7
Total Assets	1,291.0	1,078.5	967.8	856.9	819.4	676.0	581.8
Total Current Assets	411.3	341.7	327.1	258.8	259.9	186.9	146.5
Total Current Liabilities	289.5	249.2	222.5	176.9	168.1	116.8	101.3
Net Working Capital	121.9	92.5	104.6	81.9	91.8	70.2	45.2
Year End Shs Outstg (000)	61,501	60,112	60,669	55,774	55,606	55,436	54,603
STATISTICAL RECORD:							
Operating Profit Margin %	10.6	9.7	8.9	8.4	8.8	8.6	10.0
Book Value Per Share	9.53	9.11	8.40	6.79	6.20	5.62	5.05
Return on Equity %	13.4	12.0	10.7	10.3	10.9	11.2	13.7
Return on Assets %	5.9	6.1	5.6	4.5	4.6	5.2	6.5
Average Yield %	0.5	0.6	0.7	0.9	0.9	0.8	0.7
P/E Ratio	27.9-20	25.8-18.8	30.4-16.8	28.3-12.1	25.7-12.7	27.4-16.7	23.3-15.3
Price Range	36⅞ - 26	27⅜-19⅞	27⅜-15⅛	19½-8⅜	17¼-8½	17¼-10½	15⅞-10⅜

Statistics are as originally reported.

OFFICERS:
M.G. Leibovitz, Chmn., C.E.O. & Pres.
M.J. Holden, Sr. V.P., C.F.O. & Treas.
F.A. Stampone, Sr. V.P., Chief Admin. Off. & Sec.

INCORPORATED: PA, Jan., 1925

PRINCIPAL OFFICE: 3111 West Allegheny Avenue, Philadelphia, PA 19132

TELEPHONE NUMBER: (215) 229-9000

FAX: (215) 227-4067

NO. OF EMPLOYEES: 14,895

ANNUAL MEETING: In May

SHAREHOLDERS: 3,682

INSTITUTIONAL HOLDINGS:
No. of Institutions: 251
Shares Held: 36,023,234

REGISTRAR(S): American Stock Transfer & Trust Co., 40 Wall Street, New York, NY 10005

TRANSFER AGENT(S): American Stock Transfer & Trust Co., 40 Wall Street, New York, NY 10005

NYS SYMBOL PEP
Rec. Pr. 41¼

PEPSICO INC.

YIELD 1.7%
P/E RATIO 18.6

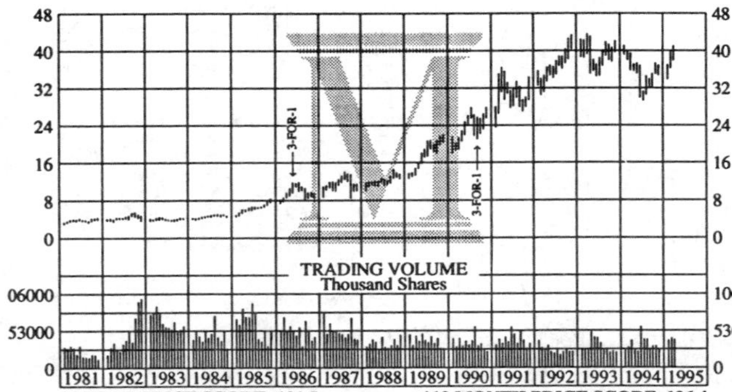

*7 YEAR PRICE SCORE 101.5 *12 MONTH PRICE SCORE 106.4

*NYSE COMPOSITE INDEX=100

INTERIM EARNINGS (Per Share):

Qtr.	Mar.	June	Sept.	Dec.
1992	0.30	0.48	0.53	0.32
1993	0.32	0.53	0.56	0.55
1994	0.35	0.55	0.68	0.64

INTERIM DIVIDENDS (Per Share):

Amt.	Decl.	Ex.	Rec.	Pay.
0.16Q	2/24/94	3/7/94	3/11/94	3/31/94
0.18Q	5/4	6/6	6/10	6/30
0.18Q	7/28	9/2	9/9	9/30
0.18Q	11/17	12/5	12/9	1/1/95
0.18Q	2/23/95	3/6/95	3/10/95	3/31

*Indicated div.: $0.72**

CAPITALIZATION (12/31/94):

	($000)	(%)
Long-Term Debt	8,840,500	50.0
Deferred Income Tax	1,972,900	11.2
Common & Surplus	6,856,100	38.8
Total	17,669,500	100.0

DIVIDEND ACHIEVER STATUS:
Rank: 79 1984-94 Growth Rate: 13.9%
Total Years of Dividend Growth: 23

RECENT DEVELOPMENTS: For the 53 weeks ended 12/31/94, PEP reported that income, before accounting changes, rose 12% to $1.78 billion from $1.59 billion in 1993. Net sales rose 14% to $28.47 billion. Pepsi-Cola and Frito-Lay each reported record volumes and profits. However, restaurant earnings were offset somewhat by soft profits at Pizza Hut. For the year, Pizza Hut earnings fell 21% to $294.8 million from $372.1 million a year earlier.

PROSPECTS: Near-term earnings will be affected by reduced contributions from the Restaurant segment. In particular, Pizza Hut is experiencing lower customer traffic and higher promotional costs, which have resulted in a significant drop in same store sales. Meanwhile, the Snack Food segment will continue to post strong volume gains. In the domestic beverage market, contributions from Mountain Dew and the new line of Lipton products should boost sales and earnings.

BUSINESS

PEPSICO INC. operates on a worldwide basis within three distinct business segments: soft drinks, snackfoods and restaurants. The Beverages segment, which accounted for 34% of sales in 1994 (37% of operating profit), manufactures concentrates, and markets Pepsi-Cola, Diet Pepsi, Mountain Dew, Slice and allied brands worldwide, and 7-up internationally. This segment also operates soft drink bottling businesses principally in the United States. Snack Foods, 29% (41%), manufactures and markets snack chips through Frito-Lay Inc. Well-known brands include: Doritos, Ruffles and Lays. The Restaurant segment, 37% (22%), consists of Pizza Hut, Taco Bell and Kentucky Fried Chicken.

ANNUAL EARNINGS AND DIVIDENDS PER SHARE

	12/31/94	12/25/93	12/26/92	12/28/91	12/29/90	12/30/89	12/31/88
Earnings Per Share	[1] 2.22	1.96	[1] 1.61	1.35	[2] 1.37	1.13	0.97
Dividends Per Share	0.68	0.58	0.50	0.44	0.367	0.31	0.25
Dividend Payout %	30.6	29.6	31.1	32.6	26.8	27.1	26.2

[1] Bef. acct. chg. of $0.04 per share, 1994; and $1.15 per share, 1992. [2] Bef. disc. op. of $13.7 mill.

ANNUAL FINANCIAL DATA

	12/31/94	12/25/93	12/26/92	12/28/91	12/29/90	12/30/89	12/31/88
RECORD OF EARNINGS (IN MILLIONS):							
Total Revenues	28,472.4	25,020.7	21,970.0	19,607.9	17,802.7	15,242.4	13,007.0
Costs and Expenses	24,959.0	21,810.5	19,332.9	17,276.3	15,558.0	13,309.1	11,017.7
Depreciation & Amort	1,576.5	1,444.2	1,214.9	1,034.5	884.0	772.0	629.3
Operating Profit	3,201.2	2,906.5	2,371.2	2,122.9	2,055.6	1,782.9	1,360.0
Income Bef Income Taxes	2,664.4	2,422.5	1,898.8	1,670.3	1,667.4	1,350.5	1,137.6
Income Taxes	880.4	834.6	597.1	590.1	576.8	449.1	375.4
Net Income	[1] 1,784.0	1,587.9	[2] 1,301.7	1,080.2	[3] 1,090.6	901.4	762.2
Aver. Shs. Outstg. (000)	803,600	810,100	806,700	802,500	798,700	795,900	790,500

[1] Before acctg. change dr$32 mill. [2] Before acctg. change dr$927.4 mill. [3] Before disc. op. dr$13,7 mill.

	12/31/94	12/25/93	12/26/92	12/28/91	12/29/90	12/30/89	12/31/88
BALANCE SHEET (IN MILLIONS):							
Cash and Cash Equivalents	1,488.1	1,856.2	2,058.4	2,036.0	1,815.7	1,533.9	1,617.8
Receivables, Net	2,050.9	1,883.4	1,588.5	1,481.7	1,414.7	1,239.7	979.3
Inventories	970.0	924.7	768.8	661.5	585.8	546.1	442.4
Gross Property	16,130.1	14,250.0	12,095.2	10,501.7	8,977.7	7,818.4	6,658.4
Accumulated Depreciation	6,247.3	5,394.4	4,653.2	3,907.0	3,266.8	2,688.2	2,195.9
Long-Term Debt	8,840.5	7,442.6	7,964.8	7,806.2	5,600.1	5,777.1	2,356.6
Net Stockholders' Equity	6,856.1	6,338.7	5,355.7	5,545.4	4,904.2	3,891.1	3,161.0
Total Assets	24,792.0	23,705.8	20,951.2	18,775.1	17,143.4	15,126.7	11,135.3
Total Current Assets	5,072.2	5,164.1	4,842.3	4,566.1	4,081.4	3,550.8	3,264.7
Total Current Liabilities	5,270.4	6,574.9	4,324.4	3,722.1	4,770.5	3,691.8	3,873.6
Net Working Capital	d198.2	d1,410.8	517.9	844.0	d689.1	d141.0	d608.9
Year End Shs Outstg (000)	789,900	798,800	798,800	789,101	788,389	791,057	863,100
STATISTICAL RECORD:							
Operating Profit Margin %	11.2	11.6	10.8	10.8	11.5	11.7	10.5
Return on Equity %	26.0	25.1	24.3	19.5	22.2	23.2	24.1
Return on Assets %	7.2	6.7	6.2	5.8	6.4	6.0	6.8
Average Yield %	1.9	1.5	1.4	1.5	1.6	1.8	2.0
P/E Ratio	18.5-13.2	22.3-17.6	26.9-18.9	27.0-17.4	20.3-13.1	19.5-11.2	14.9-10.3
Price Range	41⅛-29¼	43⅝-34½	43⅜-30½	36½-23½	27⅞-18	22-12⅝	14½-10

Statistics are as originally reported.

OFFICERS:
W. Calloway, Chmn. & C.E.O.
R.G. Dettmer, Exec. V.P. & C.F.O.
R.C. Barnes, Sr. V.P. & Treas.
E.V. Lahey, Jr., Sr. V.P., Gen. Coun. & Sec.

INCORPORATED: NC, Dec., 1986

PRINCIPAL OFFICE: 700 Anderson Hill Rd., Purchase, NY 10577-1444

TELEPHONE NUMBER: (914) 253-2000

FAX: (914) 253-2070

NO. OF EMPLOYEES: 471,000

ANNUAL MEETING: In May

SHAREHOLDERS: 147,500

INSTITUTIONAL HOLDINGS:
No. of Institutions: 1,243
Shares Held: 461,667,420

REGISTRAR(S): Bank of Boston, Boston, MA

TRANSFER AGENT(S): Bank of Boston, Boston, MA

NYS SYMBOL PFE
Rec. Pr. 86⅝

PFIZER INC.

YIELD 1.2%
P/E RATIO 19.9

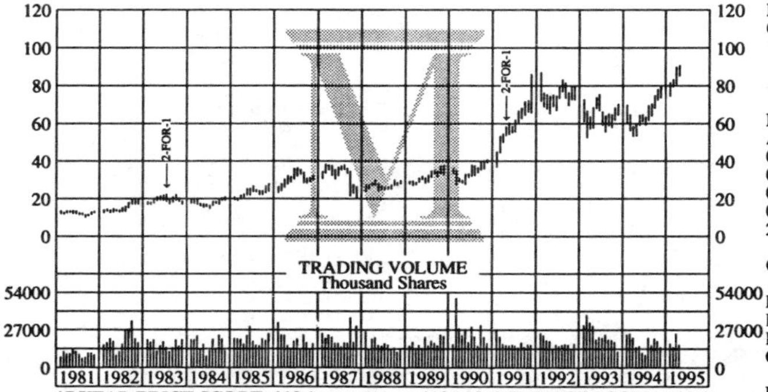

*7 YEAR PRICE SCORE 113.1 *12 MONTH PRICE SCORE 112.4

*NYSE COMPOSITE INDEX=100

INTERIM EARNINGS (Per Share):

Qtr.	Mar.	June	Sept.	Dec.
1992	0.88	0.66	0.88	0.83
1993	1.01	0.79	d0.65	0.90
1994	1.18	0.84	1.09	1.08
1995	1.35	...	...	...

INTERIM DIVIDENDS (Per Share):

Amt.	Decl.	Ex.	Rec.	Pay.
0.47Q	10/27/94	11/4/94	11/11/94	12/15/94
0.47Q	10/27	11/4	11/11	12/15
0.52Q	1/26/95	2/6/95	2/10/95	3/16/95
0.52Q	4/27	5/8	5/12	6/15
2-for-1	4/27	7/3	6/1	6/30

Indicated div.: $1.04*

CAPITALIZATION (12/31/94):

	($000)	(%)
Long-Term Debt	604,200	11.7
Deferred Income Tax	211,700	4.1
Minority Interest	38,800	0.7
Common & Surplus	4,323,900	83.5
Total	5,178,600	100.0

DIVIDEND ACHIEVER STATUS:
Rank: 139 1984-94 Growth Rate: 11.0%
Total Years of Dividend Growth: 27

RECENT DEVELOPMENTS: For the year ended 12/31/94, net income nearly doubled to $1.30 billion compared with $657.5 million the previous year. Sales were up 10.7% to $8.28 billion. Prior-year results included a pretax charge of $752 million. Worldwide sales of six pharmaceuticals introduced in the 1990's advanced a combined 44% to more than $2.70 billion. All business segments except Food Science generated sales gains.

PROSPECTS: Products introduced in the 1990s continue to fuel sales growth. However, sales gains will be contingent on volume as pricing pressures persist in the pharmaceutical industry. In January, Pfizer completed the acquisition of SimthKline Beecham Animal Health for $1.45 billion. The acquisition has more than doubled the size of the animal-health segment with a broader range of products and expanded geographic reach.

BUSINESS

PFIZER INC. is a research-based, diversified health care company with global operations. Health care products, which contributed 84% of 1994 sales (95%, operating profit), consists of pharmaceutical products and medical devices. Animal Health, 7% (2%), includes animal health products. Food Science, 4% (1%), consist of bulk antibiotics, food grade chemicals, vitamins, industrial chemicals and specialty products. Consumer Health Care products, 5% (2%), include proprietary health items such as Visine, Ben-Gay, Plax, and Unisom. U.S. sales represented 53% of total sales; Europe 22%; Asia 15%; Canada/Latin America 8%; and Africa/Middle East 2%.

ANNUAL EARNINGS AND DIVIDENDS PER SHARE

	1994	1993	1992	1991	1990	1989	1988
Earnings Per Share	**4.19**	**2.05**	**[1] 3.25**	**2.13**	**2.39**	**2.02**	**2.35**
Dividends Per Share	**1.88**	**1.68**	**1.48**	**[2] 1.32**	**1.20**	**1.10**	**1.00**
Dividend Payout %	**44.9**	**82.0**	**45.5**	**62.0**	**50.3**	**54.5**	**42.6**

Note: 2-for-1stk.split,6/30/95. [1] Before acctg. chg. [2] 2-for-1 stk split, 4/1/91

ANNUAL FINANCIAL DATA

	1994	1993	1992	1991	1990	1989	1988
RECORD OF EARNINGS (IN MILLIONS):							
Total Revenues	8,281.3	7,477.7	7,230.2	6,950.0	6,406.0	5,671.5	5,385.4
Costs and Expenses	6,016.8	6,306.2	5,412.4	5,752.4	5,127.4	4,496.2	4,179.0
Depreciation & Amort	292.0	258.2	263.9	244.1	224.8	207.1	194.5
Operating Profit	3,111.9	2,639.7	2,306.6	953.5	1,053.8	968.2	1,011.9
Inc Bef Taxes on Income	1,861.5	851.4	1,534.8	943.7	1,103.3	916.5	1,103.8
Income Taxes	558.5	191.3	438.6	218.4	297.9	231.3	309.4
Net Income	1,298.4	657.5	[1] 1,093.5	722.1	801.2	681.1	791.3
Aver. Shs. Outstg. (000)	310,215	320,400	336,500	339,343	337,152	339,392	338,800
[1] Before acctg. change dr$282,600,000.							
BALANCE SHEET (IN MILLIONS):							
Cash and Cash Equivalents	2,018.6	1,176.5	1,703.7	1,548.1	1,068.2	1,057.7	807.5
Receivables, Net	2,026.3	1,925.6	2,020.6	1,756.5	1,962.1	2,064.9	2,015.6
Inventories	1,264.9	1,093.5	1,067.8	1,171.5	1,142.6	1,080.5	1,089.4
Gross Property	4,992.9	4,300.7	3,816.4	4,007.5	3,616.3	3,252.5	3,153.6
Accumulated Depreciation	1,919.7	1,668.2	1,511.3	1,626.5	1,506.5	1,468.4	1,498.5
Long-Term Debt	604.2	570.5	571.3	396.6	193.3	190.6	226.9
Net Stockholders' Equity	4,323.9	3,865.5	4,718.6	5,026.3	5,092.0	4,535.8	4,301.1
Total Assets	11,098.5	9,330.9	9,590.1	9,634.6	9,052.0	8,324.8	7,637.6
Total Current Assets	5,788.4	4,733.2	5,384.8	4,808.2	4,435.9	4,504.8	4,094.8
Total Current Liabilities	4,825.9	3,443.6	3,217.4	3,420.5	3,116.9	2,911.6	2,344.3
Net Working Capital	962.5	1,289.6	2,167.4	1,387.7	1,319.0	1,593.2	1,750.5
Year End Shs Outstg (000)	314,226	320,922	325,141	329,647	330,244	330,626	330,792
STATISTICAL RECORD:							
Operating Profit Margin %	23.8	12.2	21.5	13.7	16.5	17.1	18.8
Book Value Per Share	12.72	11.32	13.38	14.08	13.91	12.42	11.73
Return on Equity %	30.0	17.0	23.2	14.4	15.7	15.0	18.4
Return on Assets %	11.7	7.0	11.4	7.5	8.9	8.2	10.4
Average Yield %	2.8	2.6	1.9	2.1	3.5	3.4	3.7
P/E Ratio	18.9-12.7	36.9-25.6	26.8-20.0	40.4-17.3	17.2-11.4	18.8-13.4	12.8-10.1
Price Range	79⅜-53⅛	75⅝-52½	87-65⅛	86⅛-36¾	40⅞-27¼	37⅞-27	30⅛-23¾

Statistics are as originally reported.

OFFICERS:
W.C. Steere, Jr., Chmn. & C.E.O.
H.A. McKinnell, Ph.D., Exec. V.P. & C.F.O.
D.L. Shedlarz, V.P.-Finance
A.G. Levin, Treas.

INCORPORATED: DE, 1942

PRINCIPAL OFFICE: 235 East 42nd Street, New York, NY 10017-5755

TELEPHONE NUMBER: (212) 573-2323

FAX: (212) 573-2641

NO. OF EMPLOYEES: 40,800 (approx.)

ANNUAL MEETING: In April

SHAREHOLDERS: 59,749 (approx.)

INSTITUTIONAL HOLDINGS:
No. of Institutions: 1,131
Shares Held: 212,851,200

REGISTRAR(S): Mellon Securities Trust Co., New York, NY

TRANSFER AGENT(S): At Company's Office

NYS SYMBOL MO
Rec. Pr. 71¼

PHILIP MORRIS COS., INC.

YIELD 4.6%
P/E RATIO 16.0

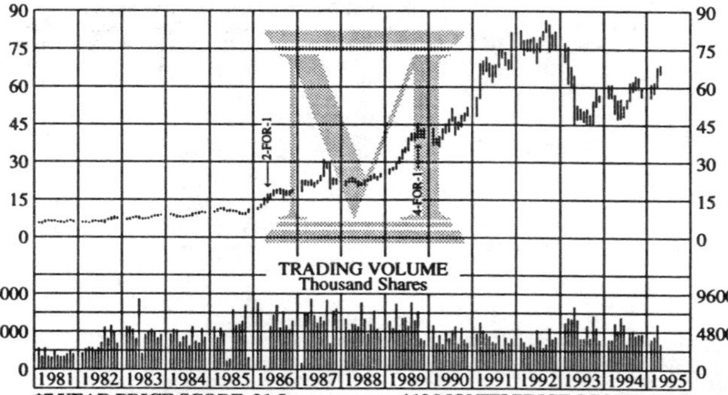

2-FOR-1
4-FOR-1
TRADING VOLUME
Thousand Shares
1981 1982 1983 1984 1985 1986 1987 1988 1989 1990 1991 1992 1993 1994 1995

*7 YEAR PRICE SCORE 91.5 *12 MONTH PRICE SCORE 105.7

*NYSE COMPOSITE INDEX=100

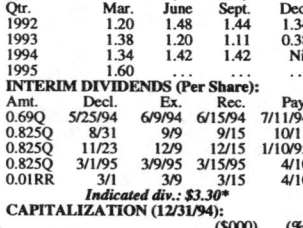

INTERIM EARNINGS (Per Share):

Qtr.	Mar.	June	Sept.	Dec.
1992	1.20	1.48	1.44	1.34
1993	1.38	1.20	1.11	0.38
1994	1.34	1.42	1.42	Nil
1995	1.60	...	...	...

INTERIM DIVIDENDS (Per Share):

Amt.	Decl.	Ex.	Rec.	Pay.
0.69Q	5/25/94	6/9/94	6/15/94	7/11/94
0.825Q	8/31	9/9	9/15	10/11
0.825Q	11/23	12/9	12/15	1/10/95
0.825Q	3/1/95	3/9/95	3/15/95	4/10
0.01RR	3/1	3/9	3/15	4/10

*Indicated div.: $3.30**

CAPITALIZATION (12/31/94):

	($000)	(%)
Long-Term Debt	14,975,000	48.1
Deferred Income Tax	3,395,000	10.9
Common & Surplus	12,786,000	41.0
Total	31,156,000	100.0

DIVIDEND ACHIEVER STATUS:
Rank: 12 1984-94 Growth Rate: 21.4%
Total Years of Dividend Growth: 26

RECENT DEVELOPMENTS: For the quarter ended 3/31/95, net earnings improved to $1.34 billion from $1.71 billion in the corresponding period of last year. The Company's operating revenues were $16.52 billion versus $15.10 billion in the prior-year quarter, an increase of 7%. Because volume rose steadily throughout Europe and the Asia/Pacific Rim regions, the tobacco segment increased its operating income by 20%.

PROSPECTS: Despite the success of a new pricing strategy and marketing and promotional campaigns for the domestic tobacco segment, MO will continue to face volatile and competitive market conditions, while international tobacco results should benefit from higher cigarette volumes as a result of several acquisitions. Miller's new ice-brewed products are performing well and should continue to boost sales and volumes.

BUSINESS

PHILIP MORRIS COS., INC. is one of the world's largest consumer products company with major operations in tobacco, food, and beer. Tobacco (59% of 1994 operating profit) operates through Philip Morris U.S.A. and Philip Morris International Inc. Food (35%) consists of the Kraft General Foods Group which operates seven divisions domestically and internationally. Miller Brewing Co. (4%) produces Miller/Miller Lite, Lowenbrau and Miller Genuine Draft beers. MO also has interests in financial services and real estate (2%). In May 1993, Kraft General Foods acquired Freia Marabou a.s., a Norwegian confectionary and snack food company.

ANNUAL EARNINGS AND DIVIDENDS PER SHARE

	1994	1993	1992	1991	1990	1989	1988
Earnings Per Share	**5.45**	**4.06**	**5.45**	**[1] 4.24**	**3.83**	**3.18**	**[1] 2.21**
Dividends Per Share	**2.855**	**2.60**	**2.225**	**1.815**	**1.461**	**[2] 1.188**	**0.956**
Dividend Payout %	**52.4**	**64.0**	**40.8**	**42.8**	**38.1**	**37.4**	**10.8**

[1] Before acctg. chg. [2] 4-for-1 stk split, 10/10/89

ANNUAL FINANCIAL DATA

	1994	1993	1992	1991	1990	1989	1988
RECORD OF EARNINGS (IN MILLIONS):							
Total Revenues	65,125.0	60,901.0	59,131.0	56,458.0	51,169.0	44,759.0	31,742.0
Costs and Expenses	55,072.0	52,745.0	48,551.0	47,337.0	42,775.0	37,585.0	27,220.0
Depreciation & Amort	1,722.0	1,619.0	1,542.0	1,497.0	1,367.0	1,194.0	0.8
Operating Income	9,449.0	7,587.0	10,059.0	8,622.0	7,946.0	6,789.0	4,397.0
Earn Bef Income Taxes	8,216.0	6,196.0	8,608.0	6,971.0	6,311.0	5,058.0	3,727.0
Income Taxes	3,491.0	2,628.0	3,669.0	3,044.0	2,771.0	2,112.0	1,663.0
Net Income	4,725.0	[1] 3,568.0	4,939.0	[2] 3,927.0	3,540.0	2,946.0	[3] 2,064.0
Aver. Shs. Outstg. (000)	867,289,000	878,121	906,178	925,123	925,191	926,521	932,000

[1] Before acctg. change dr$477,000,000. [2] Before acctg. change dr$921,000,000. [3] Before acctg. change cr$273,000,000.

	1994	1993	1992	1991	1990	1989	1988
BALANCE SHEET (IN MILLIONS):							
Cash and Cash Equivalents	184.0	182.0	1,021.0	126.0	146.0	118.0	168.0
Receivables, Net	4,382.0	3,982.0	4,147.0	4,121.0	4,101.0	2,956.0	2,222.0
Inventories	7,987.0	7,358.0	7,785.0	7,445.0	7,153.0	5,751.0	5,384.0
Gross Property	18,254.0	16,930.0	16,512.0	15,281.0	14,281.0	12,357.0	11,932.0
Accumulated Depreciation	7,083.0	6,467.0	5,982.0	5,335.0	4,677.0	3,900.0	3,284.0
Long-Term Debt	14,975.0	15,221.0	14,583.0	14,213.0	16,121.0	14,861.0	17,122.0
Net Stockholders' Equity	12,786.0	11,627.0	12,563.0	12,512.0	11,947.0	9,571.0	7,679.0
Total Assets	52,649.0	51,205.0	50,014.0	47,384.0	46,569.0	38,528.0	36,960.0
Total Current Assets	13,908.0	12,808.0	13,906.0	12,594.0	12,367.0	9,380.0	8,151.0
Total Current Liabilities	13,569.0	14,468.0	14,021.0	12,642.0	12,084.0	9,266.0	8,233.0
Net Working Capital	339.0	d1,660.0	d115.0	d48.0	283.0	114.0	d82.0
Year End Shs Outstg (000)	852,859,000	877,091	892,757	919,851	926,219	928,530	924,000
STATISTICAL RECORD:							
Operating Profit Margin %	14.5	12.5	17.0	15.3	15.5	15.2	13.9
Return on Equity %	37.0	30.7	39.3	31.4	29.6	30.8	26.9
Return on Assets %	9.0	7.0	9.9	8.3	7.6	7.6	5.6
Average Yield %	5.1	4.2	2.9	2.8	3.3	3.4	4.2
P/E Ratio	11.8-8.7	19.1-11.1	15.9-12.8	19.3-11.4	13.6-9.4	14.4-7.9	11.5-9.1
Price Range	64½-47¼	77⅝-45	86⅝-69½	81¾-48¼	52-36	45¾-25	25½-20⅛

Statistics are as originally reported.

OFFICERS:
G.C. Bible, Chmn. & C.E.O.
H.G. Storr, Exec. V.P. & C.F.O.
G.R. Lewis, V.P. & Treas.

INCORPORATED: VA, Mar., 1985

PRINCIPAL OFFICE: 120 Park Avenue, New York, NY 10017

TELEPHONE NUMBER: (212) 880-5000

NO. OF EMPLOYEES: 165,000 (approx.)

ANNUAL MEETING: In April

SHAREHOLDERS: 154,300 (approx.)

INSTITUTIONAL HOLDINGS:
No. of Institutions: 1,426
Shares Held: 484,135,408

REGISTRAR(S): First Chicago Trust Co. of New York, New York, NY 10008

TRANSFER AGENT(S): First Chicago Trust Co. of New York, New York, NY 10008

NYS SYMBOL PNY
Rec. Pr. 20¼

PIEDMONT NATURAL GAS CO., INC.

YIELD 5.4%
P/E RATIO 10.1

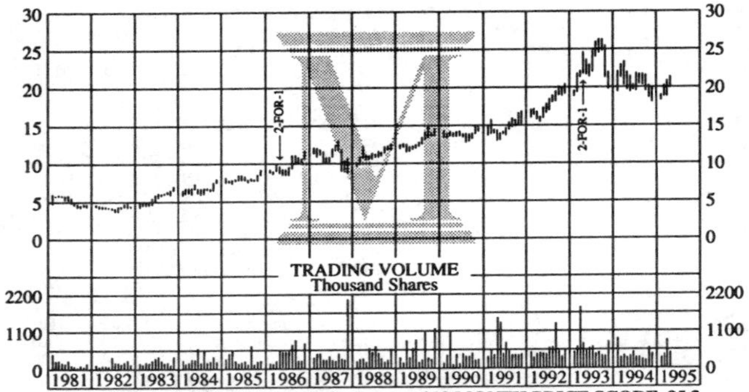

*7 YEAR PRICE SCORE 99.9 *12 MONTH PRICE SCORE 95.3

*NYSE COMPOSITE INDEX=100

INTERIM EARNINGS (Per Share):

Qtr.	Jan.	Apr.	July	Oct.
1991-92	0.99	0.79	d0.15	d0.21
1992-93	1.06	0.87	d0.20	d0.28
1993-94	1.06	0.87	d0.27	d0.30
1994-95	1.13	...	...	...

INTERIM DIVIDENDS (Per Share):

Amt.	Decl.	Ex.	Rec.	Pay.
0.26Q	2/25/94	3/21/94	3/25/94	4/15/94
0.26Q	6/10	6/20	6/25	7/15
0.26Q	8/26	9/19	9/23	10/14
0.26Q	12/2	12/16	12/22	1/13/95
0.275Q	2/27/95	3/27/95	3/31/95	4/14

*Indicated div.: $1.10**

CAPITALIZATION (10/31/94):

	($000)	(%)
Long-Term Debt	313,000	44.9
Deferred Income Tax	82,213	11.8
Common & Surplus	301,992	43.3
Total	697,205	100.0
Current Debt	5,000	

DIVIDEND ACHIEVER STATUS:

Rank: 245 1984-94 Growth Rate: 6.7%

Total Years of Dividend Growth: 15

RECENT DEVELOPMENTS: For the quarter ended 1/31/95, net income jumped 9% to $30.2 million compared with $27.7 million in the corresponding quarter of 1994. Revenues decreased 13.1% to $202.5 million from $233.1 million a year earlier. Revenues were affected by temperatures being warmer than last year and a 7% drop in gas delivered for the quarter. For the twelve months ended 1/31/95, net income dropped 0.2% to $38.0 million.

PROSPECTS: The Company should start to feel the full effects of the $24.3 million rate increase granted on 11/1/94. The weather-normalization clause in PHY's service area has protected it from the effects of weather that was warmer-than-normal over the recent months. However, the propane distribution business has been adversely affected by the weather. Near-term the Company will offer 1.5 million shares to pay for capital projects.

BUSINESS

PIEDMONT NATURAL GAS CO., INC. is engaged in the purchase, distribution and sale of natural gas to residential, commercial and industrial customers in North Carolina, South Carolina and Tennessee. Non-utility subsidiaries and divisions are involved in the exploration, development, marketing and transportation of natural gas, oil, and propane. PNY's utility operations are subject to regulation by the North Carolina Utilities Commission, the Tennessee Public Service Commission and the Public Service Commisssion of South Carolina. PNY also owns Tennessee Natural Resources, Inc., and its subsidiaries. In 1994, revenues were derived: 41.1% residential, 28.8% commercial, 28.8% industrial, 0.7% public housing and 0.6% other. PNY serves 46,900 propane customers in a three-state area.

ANNUAL EARNINGS AND DIVIDENDS PER SHARE

	10/31/94	10/31/93	10/31/92	10/31/91	10/31/90	10/31/89	10/31/88
Earnings Per Share	**1.35**	**1.45**	**1.39**	**0.88**	**1.22**	**1.21**	**1.18**
Dividends Per Share	**1.025**	**[1] 0.965**	**0.91**	**0.87**	**0.83**	**0.785**	**0.72**
Dividend Payout %	**75.9**	**66.6**	**65.2**	**98.3**	**68.0**	**64.9**	**60.8**

[1] 2-for-1 stk split,04/01/93

ANNUAL FINANCIAL DATA

	10/31/94	10/31/93	10/31/92	10/31/91	10/31/90	10/31/89	10/31/88
RECORD OF EARNINGS (IN MILLIONS):							
Total Revenues	575.4	552.8	459.9	411.5	403.8	420.8	399.0
Depreciation & Amort	28.5	25.2	23.1	20.9	18.5	14.9	13.1
Maintenance	15.5	15.0	13.3	13.1	11.6	10.1	8.9
Income Taxes	19.6	21.6	19.1	9.8	12.8	12.9	11.6
Operating Income	55.9	56.6	53.4	40.1	43.9	41.2	34.8
Interest Expense	24.5	21.9	21.5	22.5	21.6	19.4	15.1
Net Income	35.5	37.5	35.3	20.6	25.7	24.9	22.4
Aver. Shs. Outstg. (000)	26,346	25,960	25,345	23,282	21,130	20,528	18,948
BALANCE SHEET (IN MILLIONS):							
Gross Plant	1,003.4	900.3	818.2	744.3	677.8	609.7	549.2
Accumulated Depreciation	243.3	222.4	202.7	185.0	169.9	157.3	146.0
Prop, Plant & Equip, Net	760.1	677.9	615.5	559.3	507.9	452.3	403.1
Long-term Debt	313.0	278.0	231.3	220.5	173.7	186.3	141.9
Net Stockholders' Equity	302.0	285.0	264.9	238.7	196.2	181.4	167.8
Total Assets	887.8	796.5	724.0	665.9	617.1	560.3	512.3
Year End Shs Outstg (000)	26,577	26,152	25,796	24,728	21,433	20,783	20,335
STATISTICAL RECORD:							
Book Value Per Share	11.36	10.90	10.27	9.65	9.15	8.73	8.25
Op. Inc/Net Pl %	7.4	8.3	8.7	7.2	8.7	9.1	8.6
Dep/Gr. Pl %	2.4	2.5	2.5	2.4	2.3	2.4	2.4
Accum. Dep/Gr. Pl %	24.2	24.7	24.8	24.9	25.1	25.8	26.6
Return on Equity %	11.8	13.2	13.3	8.6	13.1	13.7	13.4
Average Yield %	5.0	4.3	5.1	5.8	6.0	6.0	6.5
P/E Ratio	17.3-13.3	18.2-13.0	14.7-11.2	19.2-14.8	12.2-10.5	12.3-9.5	10.7-8.2
Price Range	23⅜-18	26⅜-18⅞	20½-15½	16⅞-13	14⅞-12¾	14⅞-11½	12⅝-9⅝

Statistics are as originally reported.

OFFICERS:
J.H. Maxheim, Chmn., Pres. & C.E.O.
E. C. Hinson, Sr. V.P.-Fin. & C.F.O.
M. C. Ruegsegger, Secretary

INCORPORATED: NY, May, 1950

PRINCIPAL OFFICE: 1915 Rexford Road, Charlotte, NC 28211

TELEPHONE NUMBER: (704) 364-3120

FAX: (704) 365-3849

NO. OF EMPLOYEES: 1,968

ANNUAL MEETING: In February

SHAREHOLDERS: 12,467

INSTITUTIONAL HOLDINGS:
No. of Institutions: 110
Shares Held: 5,791,434

REGISTRAR(S): Wachovia Bank & Trust Co., N.A., Winston-Salem, NC 27102

TRANSFER AGENT(S): Wachovia Bank & Trust Co., N.A., Winston-Salem, NC 27102

NYS SYMBOL PBI
Rec. Pr. 36¾

PITNEY BOWES, INC.

YIELD 3.3%
P/E RATIO 16.6

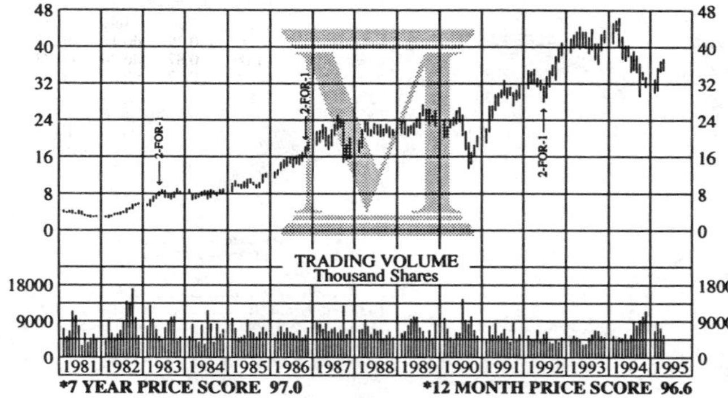

***7 YEAR PRICE SCORE 97.0** ***12 MONTH PRICE SCORE 96.6**

*NYSE COMPOSITE INDEX=100

INTERIM EARNINGS (Per Share):

Qtr.	Mar.	June	Sept.	Dec.
1991	0.43	0.43	0.44	0.51
1992	0.42	0.46	0.48	0.60
1993	0.52	0.55	0.43	0.72
1994	0.51	0.55	0.54	0.61

INTERIM DIVIDENDS (Per Share):

Amt.	Decl.	Ex.	Rec.	Pay.
0.26Q	4/11/94	5/23/94	5/27/94	6/12/94
0.26Q	7/11	8/22	8/26	9/12
0.26Q	11/14	11/18	11/25	12/12
0.30Q	2/13/95	2/17/95	2/24/95	3/12/95
0.30Q	4/10	5/22	5/26	6/12

Indicated div.: $1.20*

CAPITALIZATION (12/31/94):

	($000)	(%)
Long-Term Debt	779,217	26.2
Deferred Income Tax	453,438	15.2
Preferred Stock	2,838	0.1
Common & Surplus	1,742,231	58.5
Total	2,977,724	100.0

DIVIDEND ACHIEVER STATUS:

Rank: 55 1984-94 Growth Rate: 14.9%
Total Years of Dividend Growth: 11

RECENT DEVELOPMENTS: For the year ended 12/31/94, PBI reported income from continuing operations was $348.4 million versus $305.7 million in the previous year. Total revenues rose by 9% to $3.27 billion from $3.00 billion in the year before. Discontinued operations during the year included Dictaphone Corp. and Monarch Marking Systems, Inc., which contributed a combined $45.2 million to net income.

PROSPECTS: The technological progression of Pitney Bowes' businesses will require a workforce reduction of 2,000 employees around the world over this year, and the hiring of 850 better skilled employees. In addition, German operations will be reorganized to focus solely on the mailing business, the U.K. cost structure will be reduced and the business of financing non-Pitney Bowes products outside the U.S. will continue to be phased out.

BUSINESS

PITNEY BOWES, INC. is a multinational manufacturing and marketing company that provides mailing, shipping, copying, facsimile and retail systems; business supplies and services; and product financing. Products and services include postage meters; mailing machines; scales; folding and inserting machines; manifest shipping systems; copiers and copier supplies; facsimile equipment and supplies; mailroom and reprographics facilities management; and leasing services. The business equipment and services segment accounted for 79% of 1994 sales (65% of operating profits) and financial services, 21% (35%).

ANNUAL EARNINGS AND DIVIDENDS PER SHARE

	1994	1993	1992	1991	1990	1989	1988
Earnings Per Share	2.21	2.22	[1] [2] 1.96	[1] 1.80	[1] 1.30	[1] [2] 1.13	1.50
Dividends Per Share	1.04	0.90	[3] 0.78	0.68	0.60	0.52	0.46
Dividend Payout %	47.1	40.5	39.4	37.8	46.2	45.8	30.8

[1] Before disc. oper. [2] Before acctg. chg. [3] 2-for-1 stk split, 6/3/92

ANNUAL FINANCIAL DATA

	1994	1993	1992	1991	1990	1989	1988
RECORD OF EARNINGS (IN MILLIONS):							
Total Revenues	3,270.6	3,542.9	3,434.1	3,332.5	3,195.6	2,875.7	2,649.9
Costs and Expenses	2,272.0	2,529.1	2,472.8	2,389.0	2,308.0	2,081.3	1,958.9
Depreciation & Amort	268.3	263.0	250.8	238.1	220.6	194.5	166.2
Operating Profit	808.9	849.7	812.1	819.3	776.3	687.1	604.3
Income Bef Income Taxes	566.5	574.8	495.4	461.6	327.6	261.1	364.2
Income Taxes	218.1	221.6	183.2	173.7	121.0	80.9	127.2
Net Income	[1] 348.4	353.2	[2] 312.2	[3] 287.9	[4] 206.6	[5] 180.1	[6] 237.0
Aver. Shs. Outstg. (000)	157,729	159,369	159,235	159,955	159,250	158,646	158,000

[1] Before disc. op. cr$45,161,000; and acctg. chg dr$119,532,000. [2] Before disc. op. cr$2,700,000; and acctg. chg dr$214,631,000. [3] Before disc. op. cr$7,440,000. [4] Before disc. op. cr$6,646,000. [5] Before disc. op. cr$6,609,000; and acctg. chg cr$66,048,000. [6] Before disc. op. cr$6,315,000.

	1994	1993	1992	1991	1990	1989	1988
BALANCE SHEET (IN MILLIONS):							
Cash and Cash Equivalents	75.7	55.8	73.1	118.5	79.9	61.1	45.7
Receivables, Net	1,472.4	1,406.8	1,362.4	1,387.8	1,280.4	1,156.6	1,061.3
Inventories	430.6	394.7	344.4	342.1	381.4	440.2	372.6
Gross Property	2,741.4	2,612.0	2,446.8	2,416.8	2,286.2	2,057.9	1,816.6
Accumulated Depreciation	1,454.7	1,400.0	1,277.6	1,205.9	1,092.4	927.5	798.8
Long-Term Debt	779.2	847.3	1,015.4	1,058.8	1,099.4	1,369.3	1,059.2
Net Stockholders' Equity	1,745.1	1,871.6	1,652.9	1,800.7	1,589.4	1,428.3	1,269.2
Total Assets	7,399.7	6,793.8	6,498.8	6,380.6	6,060.5	5,611.1	4,788.4
Total Current Assets	2,083.7	1,936.7	1,838.7	1,935.5	1,799.1	1,698.6	1,519.3
Total Current Liabilities	3,978.5	3,273.4	3,096.5	2,995.4	2,888.9	2,270.9	1,853.1
Net Working Capital	d1,894.7	d1,336.6	d1,257.8	d1,059.9	d1,089.8	d572.3	d333.8
Year End Shs Outstg (000)	151,276	158,174	157,175	158,764	157,377	156,730	156,250
STATISTICAL RECORD:							
Operating Profit Margin %	22.3	21.2	20.7	21.2	20.9	20.9	19.8
Book Value Per Share	10.05	10.35	9.59	10.34	9.06	8.11	7.62
Return on Equity %	20.0	18.9	18.9	16.0	13.0	12.6	18.7
Return on Assets %	4.7	5.2	4.8	4.5	3.4	3.2	5.0
Average Yield %	2.8	2.2	2.3	2.6	3.0	2.2	2.3
P/E Ratio	21.0-13.2	20.0-16.3	20.9-14.3	18.2-10.6	20.6-10.4	24.2-18.1	15.8-11.3
Price Range	46⅜-29¼	44½-36¼	41-28	32¾-19	26¾-13½	27⅜-20½	23¾-16⅞

Statistics are as originally reported.

OFFICERS:
G.B. Harvey, Chmn., Pres. & C.E.O.
C.F. Adimando, V.P.-Fin. & Admn., & Treas.

INCORPORATED: DE, Apr., 1920

PRINCIPAL OFFICE: 1 Elmcroft Rd., Stamford, CT 06926-0700

TELEPHONE NUMBER: (203) 356-5000

NO. OF EMPLOYEES: 32,792

ANNUAL MEETING: In May

SHAREHOLDERS: 31,226

INSTITUTIONAL HOLDINGS:
No. of Institutions: 635
Shares Held: 120,202,047

REGISTRAR(S): Chemical Banking Corp., New York, NY

TRANSFER AGENT(S): Chemical Banking Corp., New York, NY

POTLATCH CORP.

YIELD 3.7%
P/E RATIO 18.6

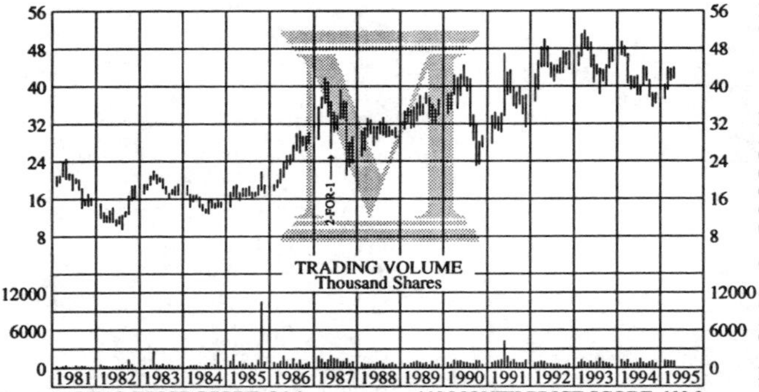

7 YEAR PRICE SCORE 86.4   **12 MONTH PRICE SCORE 100.0**
*NYSE COMPOSITE INDEX=100

INTERIM EARNINGS (Per Share):

Qtr.	Mar.	June	Sept.	Dec.
1992	0.55	1.19	0.61	0.36
1993	0.76	0.09	d0.07	0.53
1994	0.18	0.21	0.37	0.92
1995	0.81	...	...	...

INTERIM DIVIDENDS (Per Share):

Amt.	Decl.	Ex.	Rec.	Pay.
0.39Q	2/24/94	5/12/94	5/18/94	6/6/94
0.39Q	7/28	8/11	8/17	9/6
0.40Q	9/16	11/9	11/16	12/5
0.40Q	1/26/95	2/8/95	2/14/95	3/6/95
0.40Q	3/3	5/10	5/16	6/5

*Indicated div.: $1.60***

CAPITALIZATION (12/31/94):

	($000)	(%)
Long-Term Debt	633,473	37.1
Deferred Income Tax	151,082	8.9
Common & Surplus	920,207	54.0
Total	1,704,762	100.0

DIVIDEND ACHIEVER STATUS:
Rank: 236   1984-94 Growth Rate: 7.3%
Total Years of Dividend Growth: 11

RECENT DEVELOPMENTS: For the year ended 12/31/94, net income increased 27.8% to $49.0 million from $38.3 million, before an accounting charge of $31.7 million, in 1993. Net sales advanced 7.5% to $1.47 billion, compared with $1.37 billion the previous year. Operating income for the wood products group remained flat at $160.3 million as sales grew 9.7% to $552.7 million. These strong results were attributed to higher oriented strand board sales realizations.

PROSPECTS: PCH's pulp-based businesses will benefit further from improving market conditions. However, higher pulp costs and competitive conditions for tissue products are negatively affecting results in the consumer products division. The Northwest paper division is experiencing strong demand for its coated papers. This division's earnings are benefiting from an improved product mix, which is helping to offset higher pulp costs.

BUSINESS

POTLATCH CORP. is an integrated forest products company with 1.5 million acres of timberland in Arkansas, Idaho and Minnesota, supplying about 80% of the Company's total fiber needs. PCH's manufacturing facilities convert wood fiber into two main lines of products: wood items (lumber, plywood, oriented strand board, particleboard and wood specialties) and bleached fiber products (bleached kraft pulp, paperboard and packaging, printing papers and consumer tissue). Contributions to sales (operating income) in 1994 were: wood products, 38% (109%); printing papers, 27% (27%); and other pulp-based products, 35% (d36%). Exports accounted for approximately 8% of sales.

ANNUAL EARNINGS AND DIVIDENDS PER SHARE

	1994	1993	1992	1991	1990	1989	1988
Earnings Per Share	1.68	1.32	2.71	1.92	3.41	4.79	4.04
Dividends Per Share	1.57	1.515	1.425	1.34	1.23	1.08	0.95
Dividend Payout %	93.5	N.M.	52.6	69.8	36.1	22.5	23.5

ANNUAL FINANCIAL DATA

RECORD OF EARNINGS (IN MILLIONS):

	1994	1993	1992	1991	1990	1989	1988
Total Revenues	1,471.3	1,368.9	1,326.6	1,237.0	1,252.9	1,227.6	1,084.1
Costs and Expenses	1,204.3	1,148.2	1,090.3	1,020.9	991.3	923.3	817.9
Depreciation & Amort	138.3	123.5	107.2	96.9	86.2	77.3	72.4
Earnings From Operations	128.7	97.1	129.2	119.2	175.5	227.0	193.8
Earn Bef Taxes on Income	76.0	65.0	124.6	85.2	152.3	208.6	175.6
Income Taxes	27.0	26.7	45.7	29.4	53.7	71.8	63.3
Net Income	49.0	☐ 38.3	78.9	55.8	98.6	136.7	112.4
Aver. Shs. Outstg. (000)	29,217	29,184	29,110	29,012	28,935	28,513	26,884

☐ Before acctg. change dr$31,704,000.

BALANCE SHEET (IN MILLIONS):

	1994	1993	1992	1991	1990	1989	1988
Cash and Cash Equivalents	55.8	8.3	13.4	22.0	1.7	221.1	84.6
Receivables, Net	137.4	118.6	115.0	100.7	96.6	117.3	103.3
Inventories	152.2	155.6	151.6	147.7	148.9	132.9	123.1
Gross Property	2,687.7	2,618.2	2,424.7	2,292.0	2,047.6	1,759.1	1,646.6
Accumulated Depreciation	1,018.5	926.0	825.3	765.8	693.4	642.9	596.0
Long-Term Debt	633.5	707.1	634.2	563.0	391.9	458.5	367.5
Net Stockholders' Equity	920.2	919.7	955.6	914.8	896.1	829.5	722.0
Total Assets	2,081.2	2,066.8	1,998.8	1,891.8	1,707.8	1,686.0	1,417.7
Total Current Assets	371.3	308.3	324.0	310.4	292.4	516.2	344.9
Total Current Liabilities	228.6	179.1	183.7	196.0	205.7	190.5	145.9
Net Working Capital	142.7	129.1	140.3	114.5	86.7	325.7	199.1
Year End Shs Outstg (000)	29,224	29,199	29,144	29,033	28,972	28,859	26,908

STATISTICAL RECORD:

	1994	1993	1992	1991	1990	1989	1988
Operating Profit Margin %	8.7	7.1	9.7	9.6	14.0	18.5	17.9
Book Value Per Share	31.49	31.50	32.79	31.51	30.93	28.74	24.98
Return on Equity %	5.3	4.2	8.3	6.1	11.0	16.5	15.6
Return on Assets %	2.4	1.9	3.9	2.9	5.8	8.1	7.9
Average Yield %	3.7	3.4	3.3	3.6	3.6	3.1	3.3
P/E Ratio	29.5-21.1	39.6-29.2	18.5-13.6	24.5-14.5	13.0-6.7	8.1-6.4	8.3-6.2
Price Range	49½-35½	51⅞-38¼	50-36¾	47-27¾	44½-23	38⅝-30¾	33⅜-25

Statistics are as originally reported.

OFFICERS:
J.M. Richards, Chmn. & C.E.O.
L.P. Siegel, Pres.
G.E. Pfautsch, Sr. V.P.-Fin.
S.T. Powell, V.P.-Fin. Services & Sec.

INCORPORATED: ME, 1931; reincorp., DE, Aug., 1931

PRINCIPAL OFFICE: One Maritime Plaza, San Francisco, CA 94111

TELEPHONE NUMBER: (415) 576-8800

NO. OF EMPLOYEES: 6,700 (approx.)

ANNUAL MEETING: In May

SHAREHOLDERS: 3,600 (approx.)

INSTITUTIONAL HOLDINGS:
No. of Institutions: 251
Shares Held: 14,738,917

REGISTRAR(S): Harris Trust & Savings Bank, Chicago, IL

TRANSFER AGENT(S): Harris Trust & Savings Bank, Chicago, IL

NYS SYMBOL POM
Rec. Pr. 19½

POTOMAC ELECTRIC POWER CO.

YIELD 8.5%
P/E RATIO 10.9

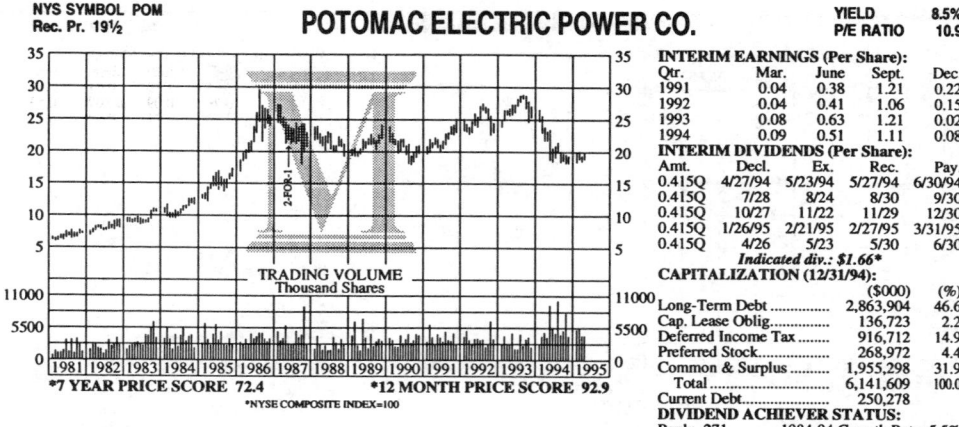

*7 YEAR PRICE SCORE 72.4　　***12 MONTH PRICE SCORE 92.9**
*NYSE COMPOSITE INDEX=100

INTERIM EARNINGS (Per Share):

Qtr.	Mar.	June	Sept.	Dec.
1991	0.04	0.38	1.21	0.22
1992	0.04	0.41	1.06	0.15
1993	0.08	0.63	1.21	0.02
1994	0.09	0.51	1.11	0.08

INTERIM DIVIDENDS (Per Share):

Amt.	Decl.	Ex.	Rec.	Pay.
0.415Q	4/27/94	5/23/94	5/27/94	6/30/94
0.415Q	7/28	8/24	8/30	9/30
0.415Q	10/27	11/22	11/29	12/30
0.415Q	1/26/95	2/21/95	2/27/95	3/31/95
0.415Q	4/26	5/23	5/30	6/30

Indicated div.: $1.66*

CAPITALIZATION (12/31/94):

	($000)	(%)
Long-Term Debt	2,863,904	46.6
Cap. Lease Oblig.	136,723	2.2
Deferred Income Tax	916,712	14.9
Preferred Stock	268,972	4.4
Common & Surplus	1,955,298	31.9
Total	6,141,609	100.0
Current Debt	250,278	

DIVIDEND ACHIEVER STATUS:
Rank: 271　　1984-94 Growth Rate: 5.5%
Total Years of Dividend Growth: 18

RECENT DEVELOPMENTS: For the year ended 12/31/94, net income declined 6.0% to $227.2 million from $241.6 million in 1993. Meanwhile, revenues increased 5.7% to $1.82 billion. The decrease in earnings reflected the effect on electricity sales of mild weather during the 1994 summer cooling season. Total kilowatthour sales in 1994 were down 0.6%. Earnings for Potomac Capital Investment Corp. were $19.1 million versus $25.1 million in 1993.

PROSPECTS: Potomac Electric benefits from a stable service territory and competitive electric rates. POM's small industrial base bodes well in an environment of increasing deregulation. POM filed an application with regulators requesting an increase of $60 million in annual base rate revenue. POM's nonutility subsidiary continues to be negatively affected by low rental income from its equipment leasing portfolio.

BUSINESS

POTOMAC ELECTRIC POWER CO. (PEPCO) furnishes electricity to the District of Columbia and adjoining sections of Maryland and Virginia, a 640-square mile area. PEPCO also sells electricity wholesale to the Southern Maryland Electric Cooperative, Inc. PEPCO's service area has a stable government workforce and a growing number of high technology and private sector businesses. In 1994, sources of revenue were: 47% commercial, 29% residential, 14% federal government, 3% local government, 6% wholesale and 1% other. System fuel mix is 74% coal, 13% oil and gas, and 13% purchased capacity.

ANNUAL EARNINGS AND DIVIDENDS PER SHARE

	1994	1993	1992	1991	1990	1989	1988
Earnings Per Share	1.79	1.95	1.66	1.87	1.62	2.16	2.14
Dividends Per Share	1.66	1.64	①1.60	1.56	1.52	1.46	1.38
Dividend Payout %	92.7	84.1	96.4	83.4	93.8	67.6	64.5
① Bef acctg chge							

ANNUAL FINANCIAL DATA

RECORD OF EARNINGS (IN MILLIONS):

Total Revenues	1,823.1	1,725.2	1,601.6	1,552.1	1,411.7	1,394.9	1,349.8
Depreciation & Amort	180.0	163.6	149.8	134.3	123.8	119.8	120.8
Maintenance	92.6	93.7	90.8	90.4	90.6	93.3	92.9
Prov for Fed Inc Taxes	119.9	114.0	75.3	82.7	74.1	89.2	92.8
Operating Income	324.5	324.7	279.5	290.2	256.1	274.5	273.0
Interest Expense	129.6	131.6	124.4	119.1	109.6	100.2	92.2
Net Income	227.2	241.6	①200.8	210.2	170.2	214.6	211.1
Aver. Shs. Outstg. (000)	118,006	115,640	112,390	105,911	98,621	95,203	94,450
① Before acctg. change cr$16,022,000.							

BALANCE SHEET (IN MILLIONS):

Gross Plant	5,938.0	5,665.1	5,367.6	5,048.1	4,659.3	4,270.7	3,945.7
Accumulated Depreciation	1,639.8	1,534.0	1,436.4	1,341.3	1,261.3	1,173.2	1,088.7
Prop, Plant & Equip, Net	4,298.3	4,131.1	3,931.3	3,706.9	3,398.0	3,097.5	2,857.0
Long-term Debt	3,000.6	2,617.3	2,467.6	2,483.0	2,117.5	1,638.9	1,531.0
Net Stockholders' Equity	2,224.3	2,227.7	2,096.9	1,942.1	1,611.1	1,519.5	1,392.1
Total Assets	6,965.8	6,665.5	6,142.3	5,853.8	5,239.7	4,642.7	4,146.5
Year End Shs Outstg (000)	118,248	117,798	114,296	111,106	99,715	97,910	94,453

STATISTICAL RECORD:

Book Value Per Share	16.54	16.60	15.95	15.45	14.39	14.23	13.22
Op. Inc/Net Pl %	7.5	7.9	7.1	7.8	7.5	8.9	9.6
Dep/Gr. Pl %	3.0	2.9	2.8	2.7	2.7	2.8	3.1
Accum. Dep/Gr. Pl %	27.6	27.1	26.8	26.6	27.1	27.5	27.6
Return on Equity %	10.9	11.6	10.3	11.4	10.9	14.6	15.9
Average Yield %	7.4	6.2	6.4	7.0	7.2	6.7	6.4
P/E Ratio	14.9-10.2	14.8-12.2	16.6-13.6	13.4-10.5	14.8-11.1	11.2-8.9	11.2-9.0
Price Range	26⅝-18¼	28⅞-23⅞	27½-22⅝	25⅛-19⅝	24-18	24¼-19¼	24-19¼
Statistics are as originally reported.							

OFFICERS:
E.F. Mitchell, Chmn. & C.E.O.
H.L. Davis, Vice-Chmn. & C.F.O.
J.M. Derrick, Jr., Pres. & C.O.O.
D.R. Wraase, Sr. V.P.-Fin. & Acctg.
INCORPORATED: DC, Dec., 1896
PRINCIPAL OFFICE: 1900 Pennsylvania Avenue Northwest, Washington, DC 20068

TELEPHONE NUMBER: (202) 872-2000
FAX: (202) 331-6874
NO. OF EMPLOYEES: 4,863
ANNUAL MEETING: In April
SHAREHOLDERS: 98,892
INSTITUTIONAL HOLDINGS:
No. of Institutions: 245
Shares Held: 21,415,920

REGISTRAR(S): Bank of New York, New York, NY

TRANSFER AGENT(S): Bank of New York, New York, NY

PP&L RESOURCES, INC.

YIELD 9.2%
P/E RATIO 9.3

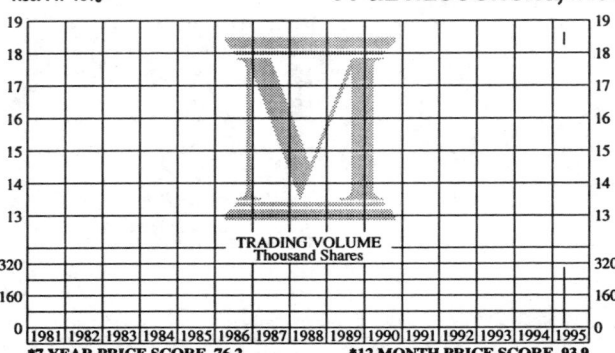

7 YEAR PRICE SCORE 76.2 **12 MONTH PRICE SCORE 93.9**
*NYSE COMPOSITE INDEX=100

INTERIM EARNINGS (Per Share):

Qtr.	Mar.	June	Sept.	Dec.
1991	0.65	0.41	0.46	0.49
1992	0.68	0.39	0.41	0.53
1993	0.70	0.40	0.49	0.48
1994	0.70	0.31	0.46	...

INTERIM DIVIDENDS (Per Share):

Amt.	Decl.	Ex.	Rec.	Pay.
0.4175Q	5/25/94	6/6/94	6/10/94	7/1/94
0.4175Q	8/24	9/2	9/9	10/1
0.4175Q	11/23	12/5	12/9	1/1/95
0.4175Q	2/22/95	3/6/95	3/10/95	4/1
0.4175Q	5/24	6/6	6/9	7/1

Indicated div.: $1.67

CAPITALIZATION (12/31/94):

	($000)	(%)
Long-Term Debt	2,940,750	35.5
Cap. Lease Oblig.	151,083	1.8
Deferred Income Tax	2,276,925	27.5
Preferred Stock	466,375	5.6
Common & Surplus	2,454,468	29.6
Total	8,289,601	100.0
Current Debt	147,889	

DIVIDEND ACHIEVER STATUS:
Rank: 316 1984-94 Growth Rate: 3.1%
Total Years of Dividend Growth: 18

RECENT DEVELOPMENTS: For the year ended 12/31/93, net income was $348.1 million versus $346.7 million last year. Revenues were down slightly to $2.73 billion. The earnings increased due to increasing economic activity in Pennsylvania and the effects of hot weather on sales. Net income for the fourth quarter was $80.7 million, including a $17.1 million charge related to complaints against the Company's Energy Cost Rate, down 11.3%. over the past four years.

PROSPECTS: Construction expenditures will be higher over the next five years, but will not include any base-load plant construction. However, such spending requirements are manageable and approximately 90% of this program should be funded internally. PPL will reduce the number of employees to 7500 from 7780 by 1996. Prospects for continued sound financial performance are good.

BUSINESS

PP&L RESOURCES, INC., formerly Pennsylvania Power & Light, derives almost all of its revenues from electric service. It serves a 10,000 sq. mile territory in 29 counties in central eastern Pennsylvania. The area has a high percentage of open land as well as 116 communities with populations of over 5,000, the largest of which are Allentown, Bethlehem, Harrisburg, Hazelton, Lancaster, Scranton, Williamsport and Wilkes-Barre.

ELECTRIC REVENUES

(12/31/94)	($000)	(%)
Residential	931,427	34.2
Commercial	755,352	27.7
Industrial	526,175	19.3
Other Energy Sales	93,422	3.4
Sales to Other Utilities	300,261	11.0
Other	117,026	4.4
Total	2,723,663	100.0

ANNUAL EARNINGS AND DIVIDENDS PER SHARE

	1994	1993	1992	1991	1990	1989	1988
Earnings Per Share	1.41	2.07	2.02	2.01	1.98	2.03	1.87
Dividends Per Share	1.665	1.637	① 1.587	1.535	1.475	1.418	1.37
Dividend Payout %	N.M.	79.1	78.6	76.7	74.7	70.0	73.5

① 2-for-1 stk split, 5/12/92

ANNUAL FINANCIAL DATA

RECORD OF EARNINGS (IN MILLIONS):

	1994	1993	1992	1991	1990	1989	1988
Total Revenues	2,725.1	2,727.0	2,744.1	2,559.7	2,388.7	2,356.4	2,213.9
Depreciation & Amort	317.3	289.1	270.0	246.2	234.3	222.5	234.3
Maintenance	180.0	193.2	201.3	206.9	223.5	234.1	224.4
Income Taxes	218.2	235.2	228.3	217.4	196.3	227.2	191.2
Operating Income	501.2	562.8	573.4	582.3	590.4	618.9	605.1
Interest Expense	226.3	232.6	245.5	245.4	258.0	275.9	283.7
Net Income	244.3	348.1	346.7	348.4	343.9	353.4	332.0
Aver. Shs. Outstg. (000)	153,458	151,904	151,676	151,382	150,924	150,628	150,142

BALANCE SHEET (IN MILLIONS):

Gross Plant	9,809.6	9,550.4	9,219.2	8,934.0	8,749.0	8,553.1	8,374.9
Accumulated Depreciation	2,615.1	2,404.9	2,199.7	2,004.4	1,854.8	1,686.4	1,533.4
Prop, Plant & Equip, Net	7,194.5	7,145.6	7,019.5	6,929.6	6,894.2	6,866.6	6,841.6
Long-term Debt	3,091.8	2,788.3	2,784.9	2,767.3	2,648.4	2,878.1	2,898.4
Net Stockholders' Equity	2,920.8	2,932.2	2,916.2	2,894.0	2,836.8	2,780.7	2,719.5
Total Assets	9,371.7	9,454.1	8,191.8	7,934.6	7,735.4	7,599.0	7,524.6
Year End Shs Outstg (000)	155,482	152,132	151,885	151,655	151,298	150,846	150,496

STATISTICAL RECORD:

Book Value Per Share	15.79	15.95	15.58	15.15	14.68	14.18	13.62
Op. Inc/Net Pl %	7.0	7.9	8.2	8.4	8.6	9.0	8.8
Dep/Gr. Pl %	3.2	3.0	2.9	2.7	2.5	2.3	2.2
Accum. Dep/Gr. Pl %	26.7	25.2	23.9	22.4	21.2	19.7	18.3
Return on Equity %	8.4	11.9	11.9	12.0	12.1	12.7	12.2
Average Yield %	7.3	5.7	6.1	6.5	7.1	7.3	7.7
P/E Ratio	19.3-13.2	15.0-12.6	14.0-11.8	13.1-10.4	11.3-9.9	10.6-8.4	10.2-8.9
Price Range	27¼-18⅝	31-26⅛	28¼-23⅞	26⅜-20⅞	22¼-19½	21½-17⅛	19-16⅝

Statistics are as originally reported.

OFFICERS:
W.F. Hecht, Chmn., Pres. & C.E.O.
R.J. Grey, V.P., Gen. Couns. & Sec.
J.R. Biggar, V.P.-Fin.
J.P. Kierzkowski, V.P. & Treas.
INCORPORATED: PA, Jun., 1920
PRINCIPAL OFFICE: Two North Ninth Street, Allentown, PA 18101-1179

TELEPHONE NUMBER: (215) 774-5151
FAX: (215) 774-4198
NO. OF EMPLOYEES: 7,489
ANNUAL MEETING: In April
SHAREHOLDERS: 132,632 (common)
INSTITUTIONAL HOLDINGS:
No. of Institutions: 243
Shares Held: 40,569,940

REGISTRAR(S): First Chicago Trust Co. of New York, New York, NY 10008
At Company's Office

TRANSFER AGENT(S): First Chicago Trust Co. of New York, New York, NY 10008
At Company's Office

NYS SYMBOL PPG
Rec. Pr. 38¾

PPG INDUSTRIES, INC.

YIELD 3.0%
P/E RATIO 15.9

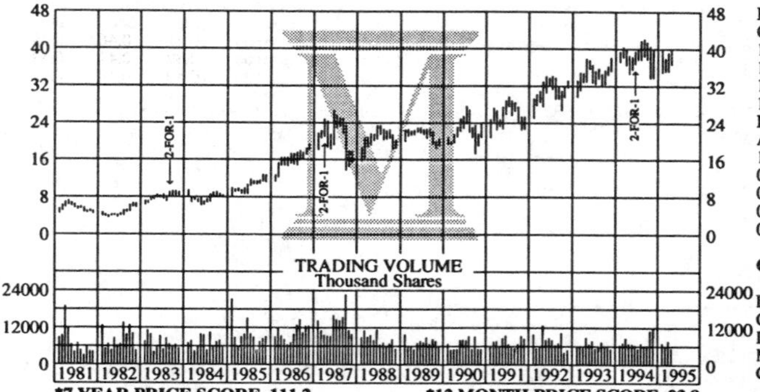

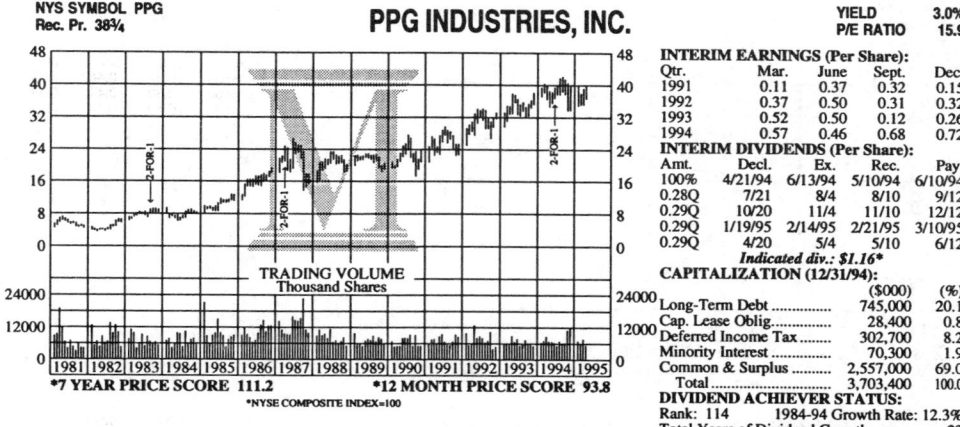

***7 YEAR PRICE SCORE 111.2** ***12 MONTH PRICE SCORE 93.8**

*NYSE COMPOSITE INDEX=100

INTERIM EARNINGS (Per Share):

Qtr.	Mar.	June	Sept.	Dec.
1991	0.11	0.37	0.32	0.15
1992	0.37	0.50	0.31	0.32
1993	0.52	0.50	0.12	0.26
1994	0.57	0.46	0.68	0.72

INTERIM DIVIDENDS (Per Share):

Amt.	Decl.	Ex.	Rec.	Pay.
100%	4/21/94	6/13/94	5/10/94	6/10/94
0.28Q	7/21	8/4	8/10	9/12
0.29Q	10/20	11/4	11/10	12/12
0.29Q	1/19/95	2/14/95	2/21/95	3/10/95
0.29Q	4/20	5/4	5/10	6/12

Indicated div.: $1.16*

CAPITALIZATION (12/31/94):

	($000)	(%)
Long-Term Debt	745,000	20.1
Cap. Lease Oblig.	28,400	0.8
Deferred Income Tax	302,700	8.2
Minority Interest	70,300	1.9
Common & Surplus	2,557,000	69.0
Total	3,703,400	100.0

DIVIDEND ACHIEVER STATUS:
Rank: 114 1984-94 Growth Rate: 12.3%
Total Years of Dividend Growth: 23

RECENT DEVELOPMENTS: For the year ended 12/31/94, net income was $514.6 million versus income, before an accounting change, of $295.0 million in 1993. Current and prior year results included after-tax charges of $51.9 million and $94.2 million, respectively. Sales were $6.33 billion compared with $5.75 billion in the previous year. Chemicals sales and earnings benefited from economic recovery worldwide and a long awaited recovery of chemical prices.

PROSPECTS: Despite concerns in the automobile sector that increasing interest rates may temper retail sales, PPG is well positioned to increase shipments and market share to international and domestic automobile manufacturers. Original equipment glass, coatings, and resins sales should all benefit from increased production. Additionally, the continuing economic recovery in North America and Europe should edge commodity chemical prices slightly higher.

BUSINESS

PPG INDUSTRIES, INC. is a leading supplier of products for manufacturing, building, processing and numerous other industries. This diversified global manufacturer makes flat glass and fabricated glass products, continuous-strand fiberglass, original and refinish coatings, and industrial and specialty chemicals. PPG operates 73 major manufacturing facilities in countries including Canada, France, Italy, Mexico, Spain, Taiwan, the U.K., the U.S. and Germany. In 1994 coatings and resins contributed 41% of total sales (and 52% of operating earnings); glass, 38% (33%); chemicals, 21% (24%); and other 0% (8%).

ANNUAL EARNINGS AND DIVIDENDS PER SHARE

	1994	1993	1992	1991	1990	1989	1988
Earnings Per Share	2.43	1.39	1.51	[1] 0.95	2.22	2.09	4.26
Dividends Per Share	1.12	1.04	0.94	0.86	0.82	0.74	1.33
Dividend Payout %	46.1	74.8	62.5	90.5	37.0	35.4	31.2

[1] Before acctg. chg.

ANNUAL FINANCIAL DATA

	1994	1993	1992	1991	1990	1989	1988
RECORD OF EARNINGS (IN MILLIONS):							
Total Revenues	6,331.2	5,753.9	5,813.9	5,672.6	6,021.4	5,734.1	5,616.7
Costs and Expenses	5,002.6	4,706.2	4,777.6	4,755.0	4,793.5	4,605.5	4,444.3
Depreciation & Amort	335.2	350.2	373.2	351.2	323.5	292.3	292.6
Operating Profit	1,229.2	917.8	887.8	786.8	1,122.3	1,068.9	1,125.3
Income Bef Income Taxes	855.7	544.1	541.8	353.5	778.7	756.7	788.3
Income Taxes	325.2	236.2	218.4	146.7	292.1	283.5	311.4
Net Income	514.6	[1] 295.0	319.4	[2] 201.4	474.8	465.2	467.6
Aver. Shs. Outstg. (000)	211,900	212,600	212,200	212,400	214,400	222,600	219,600
[1] Before acctg. change dr$272,800,000. [2] Before acctg. change cr$74,800,000.							
BALANCE SHEET (IN MILLIONS):							
Cash and Cash Equivalents	62.1	111.9	61.4	37.6	59.3	64.6	103.4
Receivables, Net	1,346.3	1,144.1	1,073.3	1,057.9	1,069.3	1,107.9	1,010.0
Inventories	686.4	683.3	742.3	875.3	945.1	753.7	683.1
Gross Property	6,162.7	6,041.9	6,157.7	6,212.4	5,995.0	5,447.5	5,005.6
Accumulated Depreciation	3,420.4	3,254.6	3,186.2	3,029.2	2,739.9	2,440.7	2,247.9
Long-Term Debt	745.0	743.9	837.6	1,124.2	1,148.6	1,139.0	838.0
Capital Lease Obligations	28.4	30.1	34.7	39.0	37.6	38.5	38.9
Net Stockholders' Equity	2,557.0	2,473.1	2,698.9	2,654.5	2,546.5	2,282.3	2,243.4
Total Assets	5,893.9	5,651.5	5,661.7	6,056.2	6,108.2	5,645.4	5,154.1
Total Current Assets	2,168.2	2,025.9	1,950.8	2,173.3	2,216.9	2,056.3	1,899.0
Total Current Liabilities	1,424.5	1,281.0	1,253.0	1,340.5	1,470.5	1,337.7	1,264.5
Net Working Capital	743.7	744.9	697.8	832.8	746.4	718.6	634.5
Year End Shs Outstg (000)	206,988	213,682	212,270	212,340	212,082	217,612	219,120
STATISTICAL RECORD:							
Operating Profit Margin %	16.0	12.5	11.8	10.0	15.0	14.6	16.0
Book Value Per Share	12.35	11.57	12.71	12.50	12.01	10.49	10.24
Return on Equity %	20.1	11.9	11.8	7.6	18.6	20.4	20.8
Return on Assets %	8.7	5.2	5.6	3.3	7.8	8.2	9.1
Average Yield %	3.0	3.1	3.2	3.4	3.7	3.6	6.8
P/E Ratio	17.3-13.9	27.4-21.4	22.8-16.6	31.3-21.8	12.5-7.8	11.0-8.9	11.0-7.3
Price Range	42⅛-33¾	38⅛-29¾	34¼-25	29¾-20¾	27⅝-17¼	23-18½	23½-15⅝

Statistics are as originally reported.

OFFICERS:
J.E. Dempsey, Chmn. & C.E.O.
J. Maaghul, Pres.-PPG Asia/Pacific
W.H. Hernandez, Sr. V.P.-Fin.
H.K. Linge, Treas.

INCORPORATED: PA, Nov., 1883; reincorp., PA, Nov., 1920

PRINCIPAL OFFICE: One PPG Place 9 West, Pittsburgh, PA 15272

TELEPHONE NUMBER: (412) 434-3131

NO. OF EMPLOYEES: 30,800 (avg.)

ANNUAL MEETING: In April

SHAREHOLDERS: 33,352

INSTITUTIONAL HOLDINGS:
No. of Institutions: 628
Shares Held: 112,040,575

REGISTRAR(S): Chemical Bank, New York, NY

TRANSFER AGENT(S): Chemical Bank, New York, NY

PRATT & LAMBERT UNITED, INC.

YIELD 2.7%
P/E RATIO 23.7

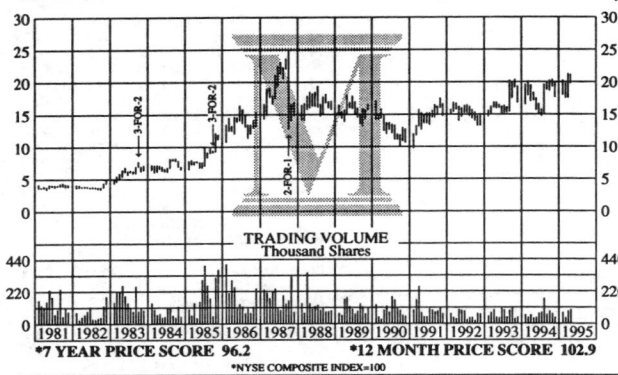

TRADING VOLUME
Thousand Shares

*7 YEAR PRICE SCORE 96.2   ***12 MONTH PRICE SCORE 102.9**
*NYSE COMPOSITE INDEX=100

INTERIM EARNINGS (Per Share):

Qtr.	Mar.	June	Sept.	Dec.
1992	0.07	0.40	0.35	0.10
1993	0.08	0.44	0.40	0.18
1994	0.05	0.47	0.48	d0.16
1995	0.14	...	...	...

INTERIM DIVIDENDS (Per Share):

Amt.	Decl.	Ex.	Rec.	Pay.
0.15Q	6/2/94	6/7/94	6/13/94	7/1/94
0.15Q	9/1	9/6	9/12	10/3
0.15Q	12/1		12/12	1/3/95
0.15Q	2/24/95	3/14/95	3/20/95	4/3
0.15Q	5/4	6/8	6/12	7/3

Indicated div.: $0.60

CAPITALIZATION (12/31/94):

	($000)	(%)
Long-Term Debt	71,103	32.6
Deferred Income Tax	6,845	3.1
Common & Surplus	140,396	64.3
Total	218,344	100.0

DIVIDEND ACHIEVER STATUS:

Rank: 241   1984-94 Growth Rate: 6.9%
Total Years of Dividend Growth: 16

RECENT DEVELOPMENTS: For the year ended 12/31/94, net income declined 11.2% to $5.5 million compared with $6.2 million in the previous year. Sales advanced 36% to $328.9 million from $241.8 million the year before. The improved sales were primarily attributable to the August 1994 acquisition of United Coatings, Inc., a producer of paint for the private label market. PLU purchased United Coatings, which generates over $175 million in annual revenues, for approximately $17 million in cash and the assumption of United Coatings' debt. However, the acquisition also resulted in higher cost of sales; selling, general and administrative expenses; and interest expenses. Sales of Pratt & Lambert branded products increased moderately. Demand for specialty chemicals remained strong reflecting consumer acceptance of the Company's industrial coatings and construction adhesives.

BUSINESS

PRATT & LAMBERT, INC. operates in one dominant industry segment which consists of the development, production and sale of architectural finishes and chemical specialties, comprised of industrial coatings and adhesives. Architectural finishes include paints and allied products which are distributed largely through independent dealers for application by consumers, contractors and maintenance users. Specialty products consist of coatings and adhesives marketed through specialized intermediaries for construction, remodeling and do-it-yourself applications.

QUARTERLY DATA

(12/31/94)($000)	Rev	Inc
1st Quarter	57,360	279
2nd Quarter	68,664	2,681
3rd Quarter	102,633	4,234
4th Quarter	100,234	(1,677)

ANNUAL EARNINGS AND DIVIDENDS PER SHARE

	1994	1993	1992	1991	1990	1989	1988
Earnings Per Share	0.71	1.10	0.92	0.85	0.98	1.06	1.18
Dividends Per Share	0.60	0.57	0.56	0.53	0.52	0.46	0.44
Dividend Payout %	84.5	51.8	60.9	62.4	53.1	43.4	37.3

ANNUAL FINANCIAL DATA

RECORD OF EARNINGS (IN THOUSANDS):

	1994	1993	1992	1991	1990	1989	1988
Total Revenues	328,901	241,761	235,628	238,953	243,098	245,536	232,939
Costs and Expenses	310,703	225,861	220,637	224,049	226,739	228,154	216,099
Depreciation	5,783	4,735	4,669	4,602	4,257	3,956	3,449
Income From Operations	12,415	11,165	10,322	10,302	12,102	13,426	13,391
Inc Bef Taxes on Income	9,812	10,206	8,823	7,947	9,321	10,557	11,923
Income Taxes	4,295	3,995	3,660	3,191	3,702	4,112	4,680
Net Income	5,517	6,211	5,163	4,756	5,619	6,445	7,243
Aver. Shs. Outstg.	7,782	5,553	5,534	5,520	5,687	6,005	6,010

BALANCE SHEET (IN THOUSANDS):

Cash and Cash Equivalents	3,370	2,443	4,349	2,381	2,176	2,015	2,020
Receivables, Net	63,174	39,950	36,000	36,367	35,396	36,254	34,578
Inventories	62,326	38,401	32,897	41,592	38,625	38,329	38,222
Gross Property	104,379	78,679	72,053	67,232	64,751	61,450	57,263
Accumulated Depreciation	58,021	43,872	38,926	35,720	33,057	29,729	26,545
Long-Term Debt	71,103	20,069	21,363	21,363	21,427	22,236	19,182
Net Stockholders' Equity	140,396	59,774	57,331	55,866	53,937	55,223	56,336
Total Assets	291,543	128,278	118,744	124,032	119,939	119,632	116,497
Total Current Assets	138,329	86,623	78,724	85,835	80,782	80,654	78,799
Total Current Liabilities	73,199	43,893	36,624	43,296	40,288	39,075	37,466
Net Working Capital	65,130	42,730	42,100	42,539	40,494	41,579	41,333
Year End Shares Outstg	10,607	5,585	5,539	5,531	5,519	5,833	6,120

STATISTICAL RECORD:

Operating Profit Margin %	3.8	4.6	4.4	4.3	5.0	5.5	5.7
Book Value Per Share	4.24	10.66	10.35	10.10	9.77	9.47	9.21
Return on Equity %	3.9	10.4	9.0	8.5	10.4	11.7	12.9
Return on Assets %	1.9	4.8	4.3	3.8	4.7	5.4	6.2
Average Yield %	3.4	3.3	3.7	3.9	3.8	2.9	2.6
P/E Ratio	28.7-20.8	18.5-13.3	18.3-14.4	20.6-11.5	17.5-10.3	17.0-12.5	16.4-11.9
Price Range	20⅜-14¾	20⅜-14⅝	16⅞-13¼	17½-9¾	17⅛-10⅛	18-13¼	19⅜-14

Statistics are as originally reported.

OFFICERS:
R.D. Stevens, Jr., Chmn.
J.J. Castiglia, Pres. & C.E.O.
J.R. Boldt, V.P.-Fin., C.F.O. & Sec.
J.M. Culligan, Treas.

INCORPORATED: NY, Mar., 1885

PRINCIPAL OFFICE: 75 Tonawanda Street, Buffalo, NY 14207

TELEPHONE NUMBER: (716) 873-6000

NO. OF EMPLOYEES: 2,039

ANNUAL MEETING: In May

SHAREHOLDERS: 1,985 (approx.)

INSTITUTIONAL HOLDINGS:
No. of Institutions: 50
Shares Held: 4,626,163

REGISTRAR(S): Mellon Securities Trust Co., New York, NY

TRANSFER AGENT(S): Mellon Securities Trust Company, New York, NY

PREMIER INDUSTRIAL CORP.

YIELD 1.8%
P/E RATIO 19.9

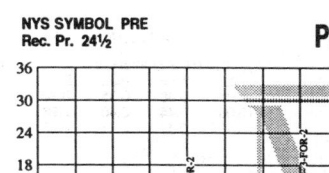

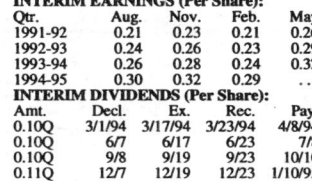

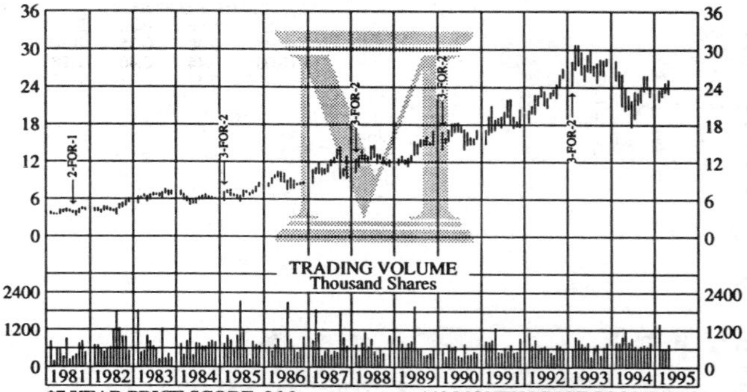

TRADING VOLUME
Thousand Shares

| | 1981 | 1982 | 1983 | 1984 | 1985 | 1986 | 1987 | 1988 | 1989 | 1990 | 1991 | 1992 | 1993 | 1994 | 1995 |

*7 YEAR PRICE SCORE 96.2   *12 MONTH PRICE SCORE 99.5
*NYSE COMPOSITE INDEX=100

INTERIM EARNINGS (Per Share):

Qtr.	Aug.	Nov.	Feb.	May
1991-92	0.21	0.23	0.21	0.26
1992-93	0.24	0.26	0.23	0.29
1993-94	0.26	0.28	0.24	0.32
1994-95	0.30	0.32	0.29	...

INTERIM DIVIDENDS (Per Share):

Amt.	Decl.	Ex.	Rec.	Pay.
0.10Q	3/1/94	3/17/94	3/23/94	4/8/94
0.10Q	6/7	6/17	6/23	7/8
0.10Q	9/8	9/19	9/23	10/10
0.11Q	12/7	12/19	12/23	1/10/95
0.11Q	3/7/95	3/17/95	3/23/95	4/10

Indicated div.: $0.44

CAPITALIZATION (5/31/94):

	($000)	(%)
Long-Term Debt	6,500	1.5
Deferred Income Tax	16,133	3.6
Common & Surplus	423,199	94.9
Total	445,832	100.0

DIVIDEND ACHIEVER STATUS:

Rank: 42   1984-94 Growth Rate: 15.7%
Total Years of Dividend Growth: 20

RECENT DEVELOPMENTS: For the quarter ended 2/28/95, net earnings improved 18.4% to a record $24.5 million from $20.7 million for the corresponding quarter in 1994. Revenues were up 11.7% to a record $199.8 million compared with $178.8 million a year earlier. For the nine months ended 2/28/95, net earnings increased 15.4% to a record $77.1 million from $66.8 million in 1994. Revenues rose 11.0% to a record $601.4 million from a record $541.9 million in 1994.

PROSPECTS: High customer demand continues to fuel operating performance as the Company has achieved its 34th year of record earnings in 36 years as a public company. PRE is likely to take advantage of an expanding market in Europe where previous recessionary constraints have hindered sales. To gain from European expansion, the Company has begun marketing electronics in France and Germany.

BUSINESS

PREMIER INDUSTRIAL CORPORATION is a broad-line distributor of electronic components used in the production and maintenance of equipment, a supplier of maintenance products for industrial, commercial and institutional applications, and a manufacturer of high-performance firefighting accessories. PRE's business is broken down into two categories: Electronics Distribution supplies communications, research, and maintenance and repair applications; General Products manufacturers equipment, vehicle and building maintenance products. At 5/31/94, sales and (operating profit) were derived: Electronics Distribution, 72.2% (73.4%); and General Products, 27.8% (26.6%).

ANNUAL EARNINGS AND DIVIDENDS PER SHARE

	5/31/94	5/31/93	5/31/92	5/31/91	5/31/90	5/31/89	5/31/88
Earnings Per Share	1.10	1.02	0.91	0.86	0.86	0.75	0.65
Dividends Per Share	0.40	① 0.36	0.307	0.273	② 0.267	0.18	③ 0.13
Dividend Payout %	36.4	35.3	33.6	31.5	31.0	23.5	19.9

① 3-for-2 stk split, 01/11/93 ② 3-for-2 stk split, 1/10/90 ③ 50% stk split, 1/88

ANNUAL FINANCIAL DATA

RECORD OF EARNINGS (IN THOUSANDS):

Total Revenues	743,309	695,012	646,087	641,122	629,255	602,341	535,936
Costs and Expenses	587,247	548,586	513,018	521,376	509,652	490,137	432,130
Depreciation & Amort	7,963	7,845	7,873	7,368	6,738	7,169	5,712
Operating Profit	148,099	138,581	125,196	112,378	112,865	105,035	98,094
Earn Bef Income Taxes	147,795	138,229	124,753	111,766	112,495	104,787	97,938
Income Taxes	53,549	50,005	45,918	37,048	37,780	35,083	33,909
Net Income	94,246	88,224	78,835	74,718	74,715	69,704	64,029
Aver. Shs. Outstg.	85,995	86,868	86,569	86,413	87,149	92,501	98,222

BALANCE SHEET (IN THOUSANDS):

Cash and Cash Equivalents	129,588	144,583	107,477	77,990	48,767	33,230	130,188
Receivables, Net	107,911	102,888	95,470	90,392	90,869	85,961	78,309
Inventories	155,261	131,484	128,292	104,984	106,743	89,276	79,008
Gross Property	120,391	111,668	103,467	100,240	95,793	85,480	74,446
Accumulated Depreciation	67,807	63,673	58,453	52,327	46,587	43,896	39,073
Long-Term Debt	6,500	6,500	6,500	6,500	6,500	6,503	6,561
Net Stockholders' Equity	423,199	398,459	344,947	292,078	251,319	212,434	289,026
Total Assets	493,748	466,060	407,417	348,666	320,807	277,833	354,817
Total Current Assets	402,937	384,307	336,518	277,587	250,220	214,625	292,700
Total Current Liabilities	47,916	48,218	44,284	38,599	51,049	45,626	42,519
Net Working Capital	355,021	336,089	292,234	238,988	199,171	168,999	250,181
Year End Shares Outstg	84,946	85,887	86,293	86,118	86,564	87,402	98,388

STATISTICAL RECORD:

Operating Profit Margin %	19.9	19.9	19.4	17.5	17.9	17.4	18.3
Book Value Per Share	4.98	4.64	4.00	3.39	2.90	2.43	2.94
Return on Equity %	22.3	22.1	22.9	25.6	29.7	32.8	22.2
Return on Assets %	19.1	18.9	19.3	21.4	23.3	25.1	18.0
Average Yield %	1.5	1.6	1.7	1.7	1.9	1.4	1.1
P/E Ratio	28.0-22.0	26.5-18.0	24.3-16.3	21.1-16.1	19.8-13.1	19.7-13.8	22.3-13.1
Price Range	30¼-24¼	27-18⅜	22½-14⅞	18⅜-14	17-11¼	14¼-10⅜	14½-8½

Statistics are as originally reported.

OFFICERS:
M.L. Mandel, Chmn.
B.W. Johnson, Pres.
S.D. Neidus, V.P. & Treas.
H.P. Frank, V.P. & Sec.

INCORPORATED: OH, Jun., 1946

PRINCIPAL OFFICE: 4500 Euclid Ave., Cleveland, OH 44103

TELEPHONE NUMBER: (216) 391-8300

NO. OF EMPLOYEES: 4,300 (approx.)

ANNUAL MEETING: In October

SHAREHOLDERS: 8,100 (approx.)

INSTITUTIONAL HOLDINGS:
No. of Institutions: 137
Shares Held: 15,230,312

REGISTRAR(S): National City Bank, Cleveland, OH

TRANSFER AGENT(S): National City Bank, Cleveland, OH

NYS SYMBOL PG
Rec. Pr. 71⅝

PROCTER & GAMBLE CO.

YIELD 2.0%
P/E RATIO 21.1

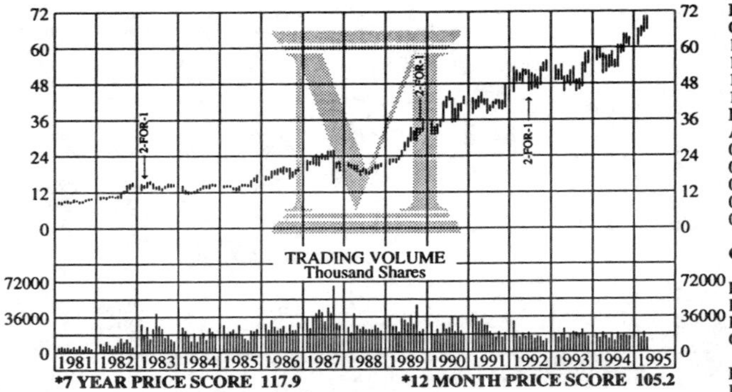

*7 YEAR PRICE SCORE 117.9 *12 MONTH PRICE SCORE 105.2
*NYSE COMPOSITE INDEX=100

INTERIM EARNINGS (Per Share):

Qtr.	Sept.	Dec.	Mar.	June
1991-92	0.76	0.74	0.67	0.46
1992-93	0.57	0.81	0.70	d1.83
1993-94	0.95	0.92	0.66	0.56
1994-95	1.12	1.06	...	...

INTERIM DIVIDENDS (Per Share):

Amt.	Decl.	Ex.	Rec.	Pay.
0.31Q	4/12/94	4/18/94	4/22/94	5/16/94
0.35Q	7/12	7/18	7/22	8/15
0.35Q	10/11	10/17	10/21	11/15
0.35Q	1/10/95	1/13/95	1/20/95	2/15/95
0.35Q	4/11	4/17	4/21	5/15

*Indicated div.: $1.40**

CAPITALIZATION (6/30/94):

	($000)	(%)
Long-Term Debt	4,980,000	35.2
Deferred Income Tax	347,000	2.4
Preferred Stock	1,942,000	13.7
Common & Surplus	6,890,000	48.7
Total	14,159,000	100.0

DIVIDEND ACHIEVER STATUS:
Rank: 219 1984-94 Growth Rate: 7.8%
Total Years of Dividend Growth: 41

RECENT DEVELOPMENTS: For the quarter ended 12/31/94, net income was $750.0 million compared with $653.0 million for the year-ago quarter, an increase of 14.9%. Net sales increased 8.7% to $8.47 billion from $7.79 billion in the 1993 quarter. Operating income was $1.19 billion, up 16.3% from $1.02 billion for the prior-year quarter. Net earnings in the U.S. increased 7.0% for the quarter, on 6.0% sales growth.

PROSPECTS: The Company announced that it will take an estimated $50.0 million after-tax charge to earnings in the 1995 third quarter for costs associated with the earthquake in Japan. The Company's decision to lower prices on most of its products that have lost market share to competitors, primarily in the soap, hard-surface cleaner, food and diaper categories, is helping to increase earnings. PG is aggressively pursuing opportunities in developing nations.

BUSINESS

PROCTER & GAMBLE CO. manufactures and markets laundry, cleaning and personal-care products, pharmaceuticals, foods and beverages, and business and industrial products. Leading brands are: Cheer, Spic & Span and Tide cleansing compounds; Crisco shortenings, Crest toothpastes, Ivory soaps, and Prell and Head and Shoulders shampoos. Other products include Vick's cough and cold remedies, Charmin toilet tissue, Pampers diapers, Oil of Olay skin products, Old Spice deodorants and fragrances, Folger's coffee and Hawaiian Punch fruit drinks. In the fiscal year ending 6/30/94, 53% of sales originated overseas. Citrus Hill was discontinued in 1992.

REVENUES

(6/30/94)	($000)	(%)
Laundry & Cleaning	9,762	32.1
Personal Care	16,640	54.7
Food & Beverage	3,290	10.8
Pulp & Chemicals	750	2.4
Total	30,442	100.0

ANNUAL EARNINGS AND DIVIDENDS PER SHARE

	6/30/94	6/30/93	6/30/92	6/30/91	6/30/90	6/30/89	6/30/88
Earnings Per Share	3.09	[1] 0.25	2.62	2.46	2.25	1.78	1.49
Dividends Per Share	1.32	1.17	[2] 1.075	1.00	[3] 0.925	0.825	0.70
Dividend Payout %	42.7	N.M.	41.0	40.7	41.2	67.4	47.0

[1] Before acctg. chg. [2] 2-for-1 stk split,06/15/92 [3] 2-for-1 stk split, 11/89

ANNUAL FINANCIAL DATA

	6/30/94	6/30/93	6/30/92	6/30/91	6/30/90	6/30/89	6/30/88
RECORD OF EARNINGS (IN MILLIONS):							
Total Revenues	30,296.0	30,433.0	29,890.0	27,406.0	24,642.0	21,689.0	19,491.0
Costs and Expenses	25,582.0	28,837.0	25,444.0	23,368.0	20,920.0	18,592.0	16,843.0
Deprec, Depl & Amort	1,134.0	1,140.0	1,051.0	956.0	859.0	767.0	697.0
Operating Profit	3,580.0	456.0	3,395.0	3,082.0	2,863.0	2,330.0	1,951.0
Earn Bef Income Taxes	3,346.0	349.0	2,885.0	2,687.0	2,421.0	1,939.0	1,630.0
Income Taxes	1,135.0	80.0	1,013.0	914.0	819.0	733.0	610.0
Net Income	2,211.0	[1] 269.0	1,872.0	1,773.0	1,602.0	1,206.0	1,020.0
Aver. Shs. Outstg. (000)	683,000	680,000	677,000	690,000	692,000	669,000	677,000
[1] Before acctg. change dr$925,000,000.							
BALANCE SHEET (IN MILLIONS):							
Cash and Cash Equivalents	2,656.0	2,628.0	1,776.0	1,384.0	1,407.0	1,587.0	1,065.0
Receivables, Net	3,831.0	3,851.0	3,699.0	3,024.0	2,647.0	2,090.0	1,759.0
Inventories	2,877.0	2,903.0	3,311.0	3,190.0	2,865.0	2,337.0	2,292.0
Gross Property	15,896.0	14,877.0	15,184.0	13,034.0	11,789.0	10,546.0	10,170.0
Accumulated Depreciation	5,872.0	5,392.0	5,488.0	4,761.0	4,353.0	3,753.0	3,392.0
Long-Term Debt	4,980.0	5,174.0	5,223.0	4,111.0	3,588.0	3,698.0	2,462.0
Net Stockholders' Equity	8,832.0	7,441.0	9,071.0	7,736.0	7,518.0	6,215.0	6,337.0
Total Assets	25,535.0	24,935.0	24,025.0	20,468.0	18,487.0	16,351.0	14,820.0
Total Current Assets	9,988.0	9,975.0	9,366.0	8,435.0	7,644.0	6,578.0	5,593.0
Total Current Liabilities	8,040.0	8,287.0	7,642.0	6,733.0	5,417.0	4,656.0	4,224.0
Net Working Capital	1,948.0	1,688.0	1,724.0	1,702.0	2,227.0	1,922.0	1,369.0
Year End Shs Outstg (000)	684,000	682,000	679,000	676,000	693,000	648,000	677,000
STATISTICAL RECORD:							
Operating Profit Margin %	11.8	1.5	11.4	11.2	11.6	10.7	10.0
Book Value Per Share	4.58	2.51	4.75	4.23	5.66	4.49	6.49
Return on Equity %	25.0	3.6	20.6	22.9	21.3	19.4	16.1
Return on Assets %	8.7	1.1	7.8	8.7	8.7	7.4	6.9
Average Yield %	2.3	2.2	2.1	2.3	2.4	4.3	3.5
P/E Ratio	20.9-16.6	N.M	21.3-17.2	19.4-15.4	20.3-13.7	19.8-11.9	14.8-11.9
Price Range	64⅝-51¼	58⅞-45¼	55¾-45⅛	47¾-38	45⅝-30⅞	35¼-21⅛	22-17¾

Statistics are as originally reported.

OFFICERS:
J.E. Pepper, Chmn. & C.E.O.
D.I. Jager, Pres. & C.O.O.
E.G. Nelson, Sr. V.P. & C.F.O.
C.C. Daley, Jr., V.P. & Treas.

INCORPORATED: OH, May, 1905

PRINCIPAL OFFICE: One Procter & Gamble Plaza, Cincinnati, OH 45202

TELEPHONE NUMBER: (513) 983-1100

NO. OF EMPLOYEES: 96,500 (approx.)

ANNUAL MEETING: In October

SHAREHOLDERS: 198,078 (of record)

INSTITUTIONAL HOLDINGS:
No. of Institutions: 1,147
Shares Held: 331,260,305

REGISTRAR(S): PNC Bank, Ohio, N.A., Cincinnati, OH 45202

TRANSFER AGENT(S): At Company's Office

PROGRESSIVE CORP.

YIELD 0.6%
P/E RATIO 10.7

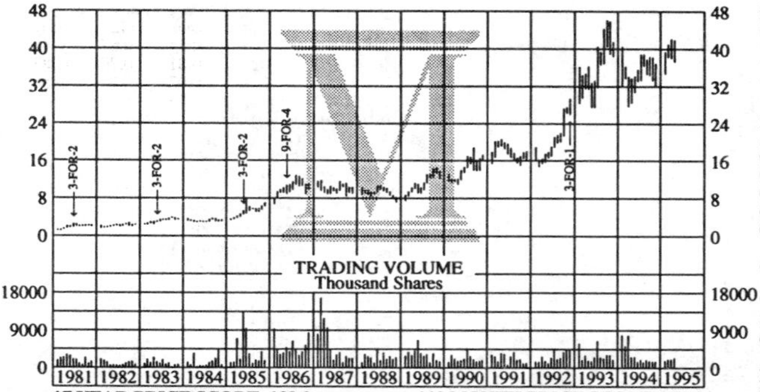

*7 YEAR PRICE SCORE 139.2   ***12 MONTH PRICE SCORE 102.9**
NYSE COMPOSITE INDEX=100

INTERIM EARNINGS (Per Share):

Qtr.	Mar.	June	Sept.	Dec.
1991	0.34	0.13	0.13	d0.25
1992	0.31	0.60	0.70	0.50
1993	0.71	1.11	1.10	0.68
1994	0.62	0.79	0.85	1.34

INTERIM DIVIDENDS (Per Share):

Amt.	Decl.	Ex.	Rec.	Pay.
0.055Q	8/5/94	9/2/94	9/9/94	9/30/94
0.055Q	10/21	12/5	12/9	12/31
0.055Q	10/21	12/5	12/9	12/31
0.055Q	2/10/95	3/6/95	3/10/95	3/31/95
0.055Q	5/1	6/6	6/9	6/30

Indicated div.: $0.22

CAPITALIZATION (12/31/94):

	($000)	(%)
Total Debt	675,600	37.0
Preferred Stock	85,800	4.7
Common & Surplus	1,066,100	58.3
Total	1,827,500	100.0

DIVIDEND ACHIEVER STATUS:

Rank: 3   1984-94 Growth Rate: 29.5%
Total Years of Dividend Growth: 25

RECENT DEVELOPMENTS: For the year ended 12/31/94, net income was $274.3 million compared with $267.3 million the year before, a modest increase of 2.6%. Total revenues jumped 23.6% to $2.42 billion from $1.95 billion. Net premiums written were $2.46 billion, up 35.1% from $1.82 billion in the previous year. Investment income before taxes, including net realized gains on security sales, was $182.3 million compared with $242.4 million in 1993.

PROSPECTS: The Company's core divisions, which write insurance for private passenger automobiles and small commercial and recreational vehicles, account for 95% of total year-to-date net premiums written. During fiscal 1994, net premiums written for the diversified divisions fell, while net premiums written for the core divisions rose. However, the service portion of the diversified division is reporting solid results.

BUSINESS

PROGRESSIVE CORP. is an insurance holding company that writes specialty property-casualty and credit-related insurance. Personal insurance lines include nonstandard automobile, recreational vehicle and mobile home coverage. Nonstandard automobile programs provide insurance for private passenger auto risks that are rejected or cancelled by other companies. Recreational vehicle programs provide insurance for motor homes, travel trailers, recreational vans and motorcycles. Mobile home programs offer insurance for factory-built housing. Commercial insurance lines include both nonstandard and standard vehicle coverages for commercial and industrial activities. Credit-related insurance lines provide collateral protection. P.B. Lewis holds about 14% of PGR stock.

ANNUAL EARNINGS AND DIVIDENDS PER SHARE

	1994	1993	1992	1991	1990	1989	1988
Earnings Per Share	3.59	3.59	① 2.09	0.41	1.28	0.98	1.29
Dividends Per Share	0.21	0.20	② 0.19	0.173	0.16	0.147	0.133
Dividend Payout %	5.9	5.6	9.1	42.6	12.5	15.0	10.4

① Before acctg. chg.   ② 3-for-1 stk split,12/09/92

ANNUAL FINANCIAL DATA

RECORD OF EARNINGS (IN MILLIONS):

Insurance Premiums	2,191.1	1,668.7	1,426.1	1,286.9	1,191.2	1,196.5	1,215.4
Total Interest Income	158.5	134.5	139.0	144.8	139.7	168.1	...
Total Revenues	2,415.3	1,954.8	1,738.9	1,493.1	1,376.2	1,392.7	1,227.3
Losses & Loss Adj Exps	1,397.3	1,028.0	930.9	858.0	762.9	799.3	752.0
Income Bef Income Taxes	379.8	373.1	178.7	32.9	88.1	86.1	132.0
Income Taxes	105.5	105.8	39.1	...	cr5.3	8.1	23.9
Gain on Sale Of Securities	...	...	...	...	...	...	117.4
Net Income	274.3	267.3	① 139.6	32.9	93.4	78.0	108.1
Aver. Shs. Outstg. (000)	74,000	71,800	62,300	66,600	72,900	79,800	80,700

① Before acctg. change cr$14,200,000.

BALANCE SHEET (IN MILLIONS):

Cash	13.4	8.7	22.9	19.2	18.7	21.7	17.7
Fixed Maturities	2,424.6	2,101.7	1,687.5	1,466.9	1,190.5	1,091.1	...
Eq Secur- Available for Sale, At Mkt	476.3	453.9	398.6	349.4	184.4	243.3	...
Total Assets	4,675.1	4,011.3	3,440.9	2,979.1	2,694.5	2,646.8	2,307.1
Benefits and Claims	2,518.4	2,180.7	1,941.1	1,440.7	1,336.4	1,298.1	1,223.0
Net Stockholders' Equity	1,151.9	997.9	629.0	465.7	408.5	435.2	417.2
Year End Shs Outstg (000)	71,200	72,100	67,100	63,300	69,300	76,200	80,700

STATISTICAL RECORD:

Return on Equity %	23.8	26.8	22.2	7.1	22.9	17.9	25.9
Book Value Per Share	14.97	12.62	7.94	5.83	5.89	5.71	5.17
Average Yield %	0.6	0.5	0.9	1.0	1.1	1.3	1.5
P/E Ratio	11.3-7.7	12.8-7.7	14.1-7.1	50.3-36.6	14.6-8.6	14.8-7.7	8.3-5.6
Price Range	40½-27¾	46½-27½	29⅜-14¾	20⅝-15	18¾-11	14½-7½	10¾-7¼

Statistics are as originally reported.

BUSINESS LINE ANALYSIS

(12/31/94)	Rev(%)	Inc(%)
Insurance Operations.	90.7	56.7
Services Operations...	1.7	2.3
Investment Income	7.5	41.0
Total	100.0	100.0

OFFICERS:
P.B. Lewis, Chmn., Pres. & C.E.O.
C.B. Chokel, Treas.
D.M. Schneider, Sec.

INCORPORATED: OH, Feb., 1965

PRINCIPAL OFFICE: 6000 Parkland Boulevard, Mayfield Heights, OH 44124

TELEPHONE NUMBER: (216) 464-8000

NO. OF EMPLOYEES: 7,544

ANNUAL MEETING: In April

SHAREHOLDERS: 4,911

INSTITUTIONAL HOLDINGS:
No. of Institutions: 218
Shares Held: 46,259,516

REGISTRAR(S): National City Bank, Cleveland, OH 44114

TRANSFER AGENT(S): National City Bank, Cleveland, OH 44114

NYS SYMBOL PVN
Rec. Pr. 34½

PROVIDIAN CORPORATION

YIELD 2.6%
P/E RATIO 11.5

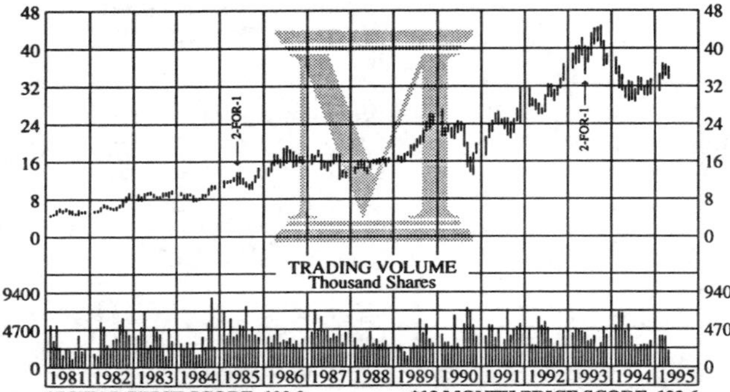

*7 YEAR PRICE SCORE 100.0 *12 MONTH PRICE SCORE 102.6

*NYSE COMPOSITE INDEX=100

INTERIM EARNINGS (Per Share):

Qtr.	Mar.	June	Sept.	Dec.
1991	1.21	1.39	1.36	1.37
1992	1.27	1.51	1.73	1.76
1993	0.64	0.89	0.71	0.88
1994	0.62	0.82	0.87	0.70

INTERIM DIVIDENDS (Per Share):

Amt.	Decl.	Ex.	Rec.	Pay.
0.20Q	11/8/94	11/25/94	12/1/94	12/15/94
0.20Q	11/8	11/25	12/1	12/15
0.20Q	11/8	11/25	12/1	12/15
0.225Q	12/7	2/23/95	3/1/95	3/15/95
0.225Q	5/5/95	5/25	6/1	6/15

Indicated div.: $0.90

CAPITALIZATION (12/31/94):

	($000)	(%)
Total Debt	694,250	22.6
Deferred Income Tax	149,831	4.9
Preferred Stock	100,000	3.3
Common & Surplus	2,121,862	69.2
Total	3,065,943	100.0

DIVIDEND ACHIEVER STATUS:
Rank: 214 1984-94 Growth Rate: 8.0%
Total Years of Dividend Growth: 25

RECENT DEVELOPMENTS: For the year ended 12/31/94, net income declined 6.8% to $300.9 million from $322.7 million for the prior year. Realized investment losses, net of tax, were $72.6 million compared with $19.4 million the year before. Total revenues were $2.96 billion compared with $2.88 billion a year earlier, a modest increase of 2.8%. For the quarter ended 12/31/94, net income was $69.1 million, down 24.5% from $91.5 million for the year-ago quarter.

PROSPECTS: Agency Group earnings are down primarily due to lower interest spreads, lower partnership earnings and severance costs. Providian Direct Insurance, formerly Direct Response Group, should continue to report solid results reflecting continual focus on profit-improvement initiatives. Providian Bancorp is reporting outstanding results reflecting increased fee-based income, growth in total managed loans and lower overall credit losses.

BUSINESS

PROVIDIAN CORPORATION (formerly Capital Holding Corp.) is a consumer-oriented insurance company. The business segments follow: Agency Group markets a full range of life and health insurance products through home service representatives. Providian Direct Insurance markets life and health insurance products through National Liberty Corp., media, direct mail, telephone and third-party programs. Providian Bancorp consists of First Deposit Corp. and its subsidiaries which offer consumer lending and desposit products nationwide. Accumulation and Investment Group is responsible for the management of investment products.

REVENUES

(12/31/94)	($000)	(%)
Premiums	1,141	38.6
Investment income	1,612	54.5
Consumer loan servicing	207	7.0
Realized invest income	(100)	(3.4)
Other income	100	3.3
Total	2,959	100.0

ANNUAL EARNINGS AND DIVIDENDS PER SHARE

	1994	1993	1992	1991	1990	1989	1988
Earnings Per Share	**3.02**	**3.12**	**3.14**	**2.67**	**[1] 1.70**	**[1] 2.93**	**4.00**
Dividends Per Share	**0.80**	**[2] 0.73**	**0.66**	**0.60**	**0.54**	**0.50**	**0.47**
Dividend Payout %	**26.5**	**23.4**	**21.0**	**22.5**	**31.9**	**17.1**	**23.5**

[1] Before acctg. chg. [2] 2-for-1 stk. split, 4/93.

ANNUAL FINANCIAL DATA

	1994	1993	1992	1991	1990	1989	1988
RECORD OF EARNINGS (IN MILLIONS):							
Insurance Premiums	1,141.2	1,167.7	1,190.0	1,056.0	1,171.5	1,026.9	982.4
Total Interest Income	1,818.6	1,634.3	1,593.8	1,589.9	1,400.9	1,292.8	1,018.9
Total Revenues	2,959.1	2,879.0	2,853.3	2,670.7	2,577.3	2,500.1	2,045.9
Benefits & Claims	832.5	846.6	865.9	788.1	736.2	731.3	652.4
Income Before Income Tax	440.5	487.1	452.0	345.9	224.7	384.5	259.2
Income Taxes	135.9	164.4	129.5	95.7	58.5	108.8	69.3
Net Income	300.9	322.7	322.5	250.2	166.2	219.7	189.9
Aver. Shs. Outstg. (000)	99,319	101,132	100,532	90,700	91,820	90,594	91,272
BALANCE SHEET (IN MILLIONS):							
Fixed Maturities	9,744.4	10,622.5	8,996.3	8,102.6	7,360.2	6,640.9	6,002.8
Policy Loans	390.6	351.5	315.4	300.8	243.4	219.7	193.2
Mortgage	5,199.9	4,195.9	4,340.6	4,350.4	3,774.9	2,989.3	2,390.3
Total Assets	23,613.4	22,929.0	20,588.3	18,873.0	16,668.5	14,970.0	12,963.3
Benefits and Claims	16,514.0	15,500.5	13,928.8	12,877.5	11,965.2	10,486.2	8,931.7
Net Stockholders' Equity	2,221.9	2,492.9	2,185.9	1,930.9	1,552.5	1,516.3	1,257.5
Year End Shs Outstg (000)	97,536	101,426	94,802	92,706	89,566	92,284	89,790
STATISTICAL RECORD:							
Book Value Per Share	21.75	23.59	20.55	17.86	15.66	14.81	12.89
Return on Equity %	13.5	12.9	14.8	13.0	10.7	14.5	15.1
Return on Assets %	1.3	1.4	1.6	1.3	1.0	1.5	1.5
Average Yield %	2.4	2.3	4.2	4.9	5.4	4.8	6.2
P/E Ratio	12.6-9.5	14.4-11.1	11.7-8.3	12.0-6.5	16.0-7.7	8.9-5.3	8.5-6.7
Price Range	38⅛-28⅝	44⅞-34½	36¾-26	31⅞-17¼	27⅛-13⅛	26⅛-15⅝	17-13⅜

Statistics are as originally reported.

OFFICERS:
I.W. Bailey, II, Chmn. & C.E.O.
S.J. Mehta, Pres. & C.O.O.
R.L. Walker, Sr. V.P. & C.F.O.
E.J. Robinson, V.P. & Treas.

INCORPORATED: DE, Mar., 1969

PRINCIPAL OFFICE: 400 West Market Street P.O. Box 32830, Louisville, KY 40232

TELEPHONE NUMBER: (502) 560-2000

NO. OF EMPLOYEES: 9,360 (approx.)

ANNUAL MEETING: In May

SHAREHOLDERS: 17,200 (approx.)

INSTITUTIONAL HOLDINGS:
No. of Institutions: 412
Shares Held: 71,349,365 223

REGISTRAR(S): First Chicago Trust Co. of NY, Jersey City, NJ

TRANSFER AGENT(S): First Chicago Trust Co. of NY, Jersey City, NJ

NYS SYMBOL PGS
Rec. Pr. 15⅛

PUBLIC SERVICE COMPANY OF NORTH CAROLINA, INC.

YIELD 5.6%
P/E RATIO 11.6

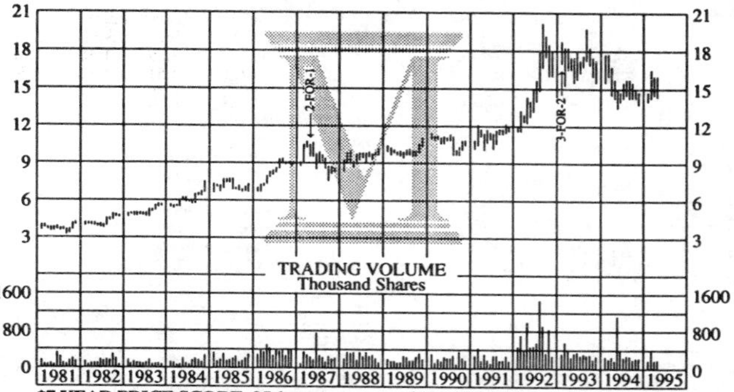

21
18
15
12
9
6
3
2-FOR-1
3-FOR-2
TRADING VOLUME
Thousand Shares
1600
800
0
1981 1982 1983 1984 1985 1986 1987 1988 1989 1990 1991 1992 1993 1994 1995

*7 YEAR PRICE SCORE 95.1 *12 MONTH PRICE SCORE 97.4

*NYSE COMPOSITE INDEX=100

INTERIM EARNINGS (Per Share):

Qtr.	Dec.	Mar.	June	Sept.
1991-92	0.33	0.99	0.05	d0.28
1992-93	0.28	0.94	Nil	d0.32
1993-94	0.31	1.04	0.10	d0.20
1994-95	0.36	...	...	...

INTERIM DIVIDENDS (Per Share):

Amt.	Decl.	Ex.	Rec.	Pay.
0.205Q	5/3/94	6/6/94	6/10/94	7/1/94
0.205Q	7/28	9/2	9/9	10/1
0.205Q	11/3	12/5	12/9	1/1/95
0.205Q	1/27/95	3/6/95	3/10/95	4/1
0.2125Q	4/20	6/6	6/9	7/1

Indicated div.: $0.85*

CAPITALIZATION (9/30/94):

	($000)	(%)
Long-Term Debt	113,680	34.7
Deferred Income Tax	53,550	16.3
Common & Surplus	160,555	49.0
Total	327,785	100.0
Current Debt	28,240	

DIVIDEND ACHIEVER STATUS:
Rank: 307 1984-94 Growth Rate: 3.6%
Total Years of Dividend Growth: 26

RECENT DEVELOPMENTS: For the quarter ended 12/31/94, net income advanced 32.8% to $6.7 million, or $0.36 per share, compared with $5.0 million, or $0.31 per share, in the corresponding period of 1993. Operating revenues were $66.8 million, down 6.4% from $71.4 million a year earlier. Net margin for the quarter increased 12% to $30.9 million. Operating income was $9.8 milllion, up 25% from $7.8 million in 1993. Earnings were boosted through an 8% reduction in operating and maintenance expense and a decrease in interest expense, due to lower debt levels. For the twelve months ended 12/31/94, net income leaped 46% to $21.6 million, or $1.23 per share, compared with $14.8 million, or $0.93 per share, in the year-earlier period. Operating revenue dropped 2% to $269.1 million versus $274.5 million in 1993.

BUSINESS

PUBLIC SERVICE COMPANY OF NORTH CAROLINA, INC. is engaged primarily in the business of distributing natural gas to over 268,000 customers at regulated rates in 87 cities, towns and villages in North Carolina. The Company's 26-county service area has a population in excess of 2.5 million and includes the Raleigh-Durham area, with the Research Triangle Park, sections of the Piedmont and western parts of the State. Industrial activities in the service area are diverse, including the manufacture of textiles, chemicals, ceramics and clay products, glass, automotive products, minerals, pharmaceuticals, plastics, fabricated metals, electronic equipment, furniture, as well as the processing of tobacco and food. The Company, through its subsidiaries, participates in oil and gas exploration and development activities and sells propane at retail in and around its natural gas service area. In connection with its gas distribution business, the Company promotes, sells and installs both new and replacement cooking, water heating, laundry and space heating gas appliances.

ANNUAL EARNINGS AND DIVIDENDS PER SHARE

	9/30/94	9/30/93	9/30/92	9/30/91	9/30/90	9/30/89	9/30/88
Earnings Per Share	1.17	0.90	1.09	0.70	0.84	0.93	1.03
Dividends Per Share	0.805	0.775	[1] 0.747	0.733	0.723	0.693	0.667
Dividend Payout %	68.8	86.1	68.5	N.M.	86.1	74.3	64.5

[1] 3-for-2 stk split,01/05/93

ANNUAL FINANCIAL DATA

	9/30/94	9/30/93	9/30/92	9/30/91	9/30/90	9/30/89	9/30/88
RECORD OF EARNINGS (IN THOUSANDS):							
Total Revenues	273,705	279,989	240,403	193,239	201,940	213,712	200,717
Depreciation	17,638	16,652	15,687	13,792	12,335	11,180	8,781
Maintenance	4,645	4,868	5,216	4,333	4,365	3,894	3,479
Prov for Fed Inc Taxes	8,031	5,917	8,072	4,756	5,277	5,938	6,497
Operating Income	28,656	28,376	30,647	24,159	23,240	22,919	21,684
Interest Expense	13,249	13,891	13,510	13,454	13,037	10,083	7,888
Net Income	19,976	14,219	16,750	10,590	12,305	13,310	14,382
Aver. Shs. Outstg.	17,012	15,812	15,373	14,928	14,502	14,099	13,725
BALANCE SHEET (IN THOUSANDS):							
Gross Plant	520,567	491,366	455,024	427,970	389,329	358,264	316,566
Accumulated Depreciation	153,416	144,121	134,722	123,186	111,581	102,094	93,199
Prop, Plant & Equip, Net	367,152	347,245	320,302	304,784	277,748	256,170	223,367
Long-term Debt	113,680	124,518	130,056	104,094	108,511	85,436	89,360
Net Stockholders' Equity	160,555	123,662	115,069	106,118	102,592	97,046	90,945
Total Assets	427,939	399,226	380,541	352,125	317,822	290,722	257,260
Year End Shares Outstg	18,212	15,992	10,368	15,081	14,651	14,243	13,851
STATISTICAL RECORD:							
Book Value Per Share	8.82	7.73	11.10	6.92	6.87	6.66	6.34
Op. Inc/Net Pl %	7.8	8.2	9.6	7.9	8.4	8.9	9.7
Dep/Gr. Pl %	2.9	2.9	2.9	2.9	2.8	2.8	2.8
Accum. Dep/Gr. Pl %	29.5	29.3	29.6	28.8	28.7	28.5	29.4
Return on Equity %	12.4	11.5	14.6	10.1	12.2	14.0	16.4
Average Yield %	5.2	4.4	4.7	6.6	6.9	6.8	7.2
P/E Ratio	15.2-11.5	21.9-16.9	18.6-10.8	17.3-14.5	13.5-11.5	12.0-10.1	9.8-8.1
Price Range	17¾-13½	19¾-15¼	20⅛-11⅝	12⅛-10⅛	11⅜-9⅝	11⅛-9⅜	10⅛-8⅜

Statistics are as originally reported.

OFFICERS:
C.E. Zeigler, Jr., Chmn., Pres. & C.E.O.
R.D. Voigt, Sr. V.P.-Fin. & Treas.
J.P. Douglas, V.P.-Regulatory Counsel & Corporate Sec.

INCORPORATED: NC, Sep., 1938

PRINCIPAL OFFICE: 400 Cox Road P.O. Box 1398, Gastonia, NC 28053-1398

TELEPHONE NUMBER: (704) 864-6731

NO. OF EMPLOYEES: 1,130 (full-time)

ANNUAL MEETING: In January

SHAREHOLDERS: 11,700 (approx.)

INSTITUTIONAL HOLDINGS:
No. of Institutions: 49
Shares Held: 2,640,381

REGISTRAR(S): First Union National Bank of N.C., Charlotte, NC

TRANSFER AGENT(S): First Union National Bank of N.C., Charlotte, NC

QUAKER CHEMICAL CORP.

YIELD 4.1%
P/E RATIO 16.3

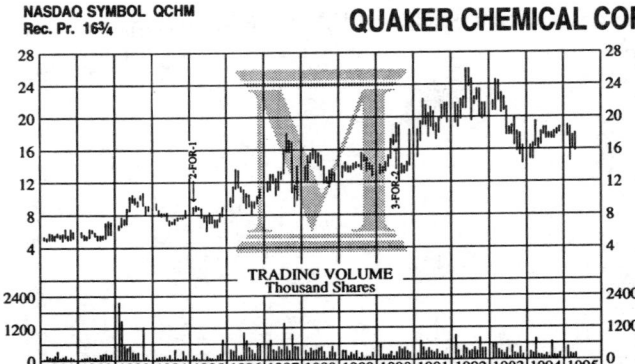

TRADING VOLUME
Thousand Shares

*7 YEAR PRICE SCORE 84.1   *12 MONTH PRICE SCORE 90.6
*NYSE COMPOSITE INDEX=100

INTERIM EARNINGS (Per Share):

Qtr.	Mar.	June	Sept.	Dec.
1991	0.35	0.36	0.30	0.19
1992	0.41	0.37	0.35	0.20
1993	0.30	d0.05	0.08	d0.52
1994	0.24	0.24	0.26	0.29

INTERIM DIVIDENDS (Per Share):

Amt.	Decl.	Ex.	Rec.	Pay.
0.155Q	3/10/94	4/11/94	4/15/94	4/30/94
0.155Q	7/1	7/11	7/15	7/30
0.155Q	9/14	10/7	10/14	10/30
0.17Q	12/14	1/9/95	1/13/95	1/30/95
0.17Q	4/4/95	4/7	4/13	4/30

Indicated div.: $0.68

CAPITALIZATION (12/31/94):

	($000)	(%)
Long-Term Debt	12,207	10.9
Deferred Income Tax	3,081	2.8
Minority Interest	2,603	2.3
Common & Surplus	93,677	84.0
Total	111,568	100.0

DIVIDEND ACHIEVER STATUS:
Rank: 157   1984-94 Growth Rate: 10.4%
Total Years of Dividend Growth: 23

RECENT DEVELOPMENTS: For the quarter ended 12/31/94, net income was $2.6 million compared with a loss of $4.8 million in the same period of 1993. Revenues were $52.1 million versus $46.9 million in the year-earlier period. Operating results improved notably when compared with 1993 primarily due to increased customer production levels, benefits associated with the Company's 1993 repositioning program, and a lower effective tax rate in 1994. However, improvement in the quarter was partially offset by raw material cost inflation, and investment costs related to the enhancement of marketing capabilities and infrastructure in the Asia Pacific and South American regions. For the year ended 12/31/94, net income was $9.4 million versus a loss of $1.8 million a year earlier. Revenues were $194.7 million, down slightly from 1993.

BUSINESS

QUAKER CHEMICAL CORPORATION develops, produces and markets a wide range of high performance products and services used in industrial, institutional and manufacturing to protect, make more efficient and extend the life of manufacturing equipment. Certain resin products are used in industrial, institutional and marine markets for specialty deckings and floorings. For the steel industry, the Company produces lubricants for the hot and cold reduction of flat-rolled steel, aluminum and other metals; cleaners for processing steel, metal parts and industrial maintenance; and additives to prolong life of rolling solutions. For the pulp and paper industry, the Company makes agents to improve absorbency; agents to increase the utilization of recycled fibers; dispersants to prevent the build-up of scale in manufacturing systems; drainage acids and cleaners for use on wires, felts and for cleaning paper machines. For the metals industry, the Company produces machinery and grinding coolants for producing all types of metal parts; corrosion preventatives.

ANNUAL EARNINGS AND DIVIDENDS PER SHARE

	1994	1993	1992	1991	1990	1989	1988
Earnings Per Share	1.03	d0.19	① 1.33	① 1.20	1.51	1.35	1.21
Dividends Per Share	0.62	0.60	0.56	0.52	0.497	0.40	0.36
Dividend Payout %	60.2	...	42.1	43.3	32.9	29.7	29.7

① Before acctg. chg.

ANNUAL FINANCIAL DATA

RECORD OF EARNINGS (IN THOUSANDS):

	1994	1993	1992	1991	1990	1989	1988
Total Revenues	196,929	196,425	214,970	194,150	205,155	184,874	170,196
Costs and Expenses	173,912	190,945	189,011	172,016	177,656	161,767	② 152,836
Depreciation & Amort	7,250	7,566	7,812	6,742	5,945	4,785	...
Income From Operations	15,767	d2,086	18,147	15,392	21,554	18,322	17,360
Income Before Taxes	14,921	d2,177	...	...	...	...	...
Income Taxes	5,916	234	6,947	6,098	8,474	6,807	7,208
Net Income	9,402	d1,758	12,098	③ 10,790	14,106	12,840	11,731

① Incl. Dep. ② Before acctg. change dr$5,675,000.

BALANCE SHEET (IN THOUSANDS):

	1994	1993	1992	1991	1990	1989	1988
Cash and Cash Equivalents	11,345	20,293	24,508	23,808	26,371	22,562	20,474
Receivables, Net	45,314	39,965	37,970	35,064	36,268	33,292	30,014
Inventories	17,837	17,547	17,736	17,135	18,694	16,626	15,742
Gross Property	105,649	106,066	97,698	89,004	83,697	68,993	62,026
Accumulated Depreciation	53,955	50,525	45,519	40,343	37,382	32,454	29,205
Long-Term Debt	12,207	16,095	18,604	5,219	5,453	5,665	5,000
Net Stockholders' Equity	93,677	91,383	101,642	98,898	99,113	90,440	82,884
Total Assets	170,172	170,985	166,613	155,593	152,408	131,430	121,125
Total Current Assets	83,400	84,387	85,567	82,725	84,833	75,427	69,326
Total Current Liabilities	43,427	42,642	28,126	36,592	40,342	27,848	26,924
Net Working Capital	39,973	41,745	57,441	46,133	44,491	47,579	42,402
Year End Shares Outstg	8,819	9,242	9,188	9,028	8,921	9,473	9,669

STATISTICAL RECORD:

	1994	1993	1992	1991	1990	1989	1988
Operating Profit Margin %	8.0	...	8.4	7.9	10.5	9.9	10.2
Book Value Per Share	9.23	8.32	10.03	10.05	10.14	8.64	7.66
Return on Equity %	10.0	...	11.9	10.9	14.2	14.2	14.2
Return on Assets %	5.5	...	7.3	6.9	9.3	9.8	9.7
Average Yield %	3.6	3.1	2.5	2.8	3.2	2.8	2.6
P/E Ratio	18.9-14.3	...	19.5-14.1	18.5-12.5	12.7-7.9	11.6-9.3	13.3-9.4
Price Range	19½-14¾	24⅝-14¼	26-18¾	22¼-15	19¼-12	15⅝-12½	16⅛-11⅜

Statistics are as originally reported.

OFFICERS:
P.A. Benoliel, Chmn.
S.W. Lubsen, Pres. & C.E.O.
K.H. Spaeth, V.P. & Corp. Sec.
R.J. Fagan, Corp. Contr. & Acting Treas.

INCORPORATED: PA, 1930

PRINCIPAL OFFICE: Elm & Lee Streets, Conshohocken, PA 19428

TELEPHONE NUMBER: (215) 832-4000
FAX: (215) 832-4494
NO. OF EMPLOYEES: 955
ANNUAL MEETING: In May
SHAREHOLDERS: 1,041
INSTITUTIONAL HOLDINGS:
No. of Institutions: 50
Shares Held: 3,798,569

REGISTRAR(S): American Stock Transfer & Trust Co., 40 Wall Street, New York, NY 10005

TRANSFER AGENT(S): American Stock Transfer & Trust Co., 40 Wall Street, New York, NY 10005

QUAKER OATS CO.

YIELD 3.3%
P/E RATIO 13.6

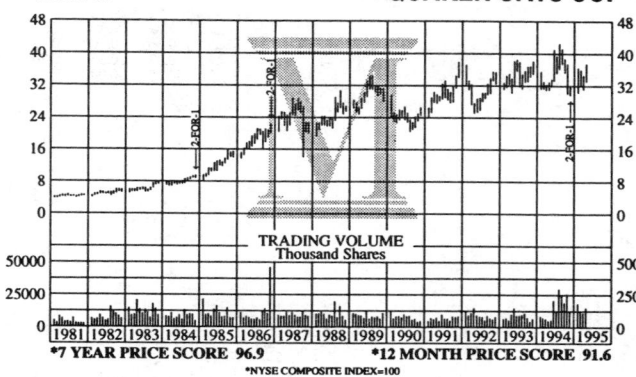

TRADING VOLUME
Thousand Shares

| | 1981 | 1982 | 1983 | 1984 | 1985 | 1986 | 1987 | 1988 | 1989 | 1990 | 1991 | 1992 | 1993 | 1994 | 1995 |

*7 YEAR PRICE SCORE 96.9   *12 MONTH PRICE SCORE 91.6

*NYSE COMPOSITE INDEX=100

INTERIM EARNINGS (Per Share):

Qtr.	Sept.	Dec.	Mar.	June
1991-92	0.54	0.58	0.75	1.38
1992-93	0.84	0.80	1.08	1.30
1993-94	1.31	0.63	1.08	0.34
1994-95	0.90	0.25	...	...

INTERIM DIVIDENDS (Per Share):

Amt.	Decl.	Ex.	Rec.	Pay.
0.53Q	5/11/94	6/13/94	6/17/94	7/15/94
0.57Q	9/14	9/15	9/21	10/14
2-for-1	9/14	9/14	11/9	12/5
0.285Q	11/9	12/12	12/16	1/13/95
0.285Q	3/8/95	3/13/95	3/17/95	4/17

*Indicated div.: $1.14***

CAPITALIZATION (6/30/94):

	($000)	(%)
Long-Term Debt	759,500	54.9
Deferred Income Tax	82,200	5.9
Preferred Stock	96,100	7.0
Common & Surplus	445,800	32.2
Total	1,383,600	100.0

DIVIDEND ACHIEVER STATUS:
Rank: 69   1984-94 Growth Rate: 14.3%
Total Years of Dividend Growth: 28

RECENT DEVELOPMENTS: For the quarter ended 12/31/94, net income was $34.4 million compared with $42.8 million a year earlier. Net sales advanced 11.4% to $1.51 billion. The decline in earnings was attributable to financing and other costs related to the acquisition of Snapple and higher marketing expenditures, especially for Gatorade and cereals. U.S. and Canadian Grocery Products posted a 13.9% decline in operating income.

PROSPECTS: In February 1995, OAT announced an agreement to sell its European pet foods business to Dalgety PLC for $700 million, and its U.S. and Canadian pet foods business to H.J. Heinz for $725 million. The European and North American pet foods businesses accounted for approximately 22% of the Company's fiscal 1994 sales. In conjunction with these divestitures, the Company will restructure its existing businesses.

BUSINESS

QUAKER OATS COMPANY is a major international producer of foods, beverages and pet foods. U.S. & Canadian Grocery products accounted for 71% of sales (80% of operating income) in the year ended 6/30/94. The Company produces ready-to-eat cereals, hot cereals, grain-based snacks, fresh breakfast products, beverages, rice, pasta, pet food and institutional and food service products. Brandname products include: Quaker cereals, Gatorade thirst quencher and Aunt Jemima breakfast products. International Grocery products, which accounted for 29% of sales (20% of operating income) produce and market food and pet food products in Europe, Latin America and the Pacific region.

BUSINESS LINE ANALYSIS

(6/30/94)	Rev(%)	Inc(%)
United States	67.6	80.4
Canada	3.8	(0.2)
Europe	19.6	3.3
Latin America & Pacific	9.0	16.5
Total	100.0	100.0

ANNUAL EARNINGS AND DIVIDENDS PER SHARE

	6/30/94	6/30/93	6/30/92	6/30/91	6/30/90	6/30/89	6/30/88
Earnings Per Share	3.36	①3.93	3.25	②3.05	②2.93	2.56	3.20
Dividends Per Share	1.08	0.985	0.885	0.80	0.72	0.625	0.525
Dividend Payout %	32.1	25.1	54.5	52.5	49.1	48.8	32.8

Note: 2-for-1stk.split,12/5/94. ① Before acctg. chg. ② Before disc. oper.

ANNUAL FINANCIAL DATA

RECORD OF EARNINGS (IN MILLIONS):

Total Revenues	5,955.0	5,730.6	5,576.4	5,491.2	5,030.6	5,724.2	5,329.8
Costs and Expenses	5,289.2	4,980.9	4,874.8	4,783.2	4,367.5	5,049.4	4,690.2
Depreciation & Amort	171.2	156.9	155.9	177.7	162.5	135.5	121.9
Operating Profit	603.2	592.8	545.7	530.3	500.6	539.3	517.7
Income Bef Income Taxes	378.7	467.6	421.5	411.5	382.4	328.7	413.6
Income Taxes	147.2	180.8	173.9	175.7	153.5	125.7	157.9
Net Income	231.5	①286.8	247.6	②235.8	③228.9	203.0	255.7
Aver. Shs. Outstg. (000)	67,618	71,974	74,881	75,904	76,537	79,307	79,835

① Before acctg. change dr$115,500,000. ② Before disc. op. dr$30,000,000. ③ Before disc. op. dr$59,900,000.

BALANCE SHEET (IN MILLIONS):

Cash and Cash Equivalents	140.4	61.0	95.2	30.2	18.3	23.7	91.2
Receivables, Net	509.4	478.9	575.3	691.1	629.9	872.1	826.0
Inventories	385.5	354.0	435.3	422.3	473.9	589.4	539.8
Gross Property	2,125.9	2,059.2	2,066.1	1,914.6	1,745.6	1,725.2	1,628.6
Accumulated Depreciation	911.7	831.0	792.8	681.9	591.5	633.3	600.2
Long-Term Debt	759.5	632.6	688.7	701.2	740.3	766.8	299.1
Net Stockholders' Equity	541.9	648.4	940.5	1,000.3	1,117.5	1,237.1	1,251.1
Total Assets	3,043.2	2,815.9	3,039.9	3,016.1	3,326.1	3,221.9	2,974.6
Total Current Assets	1,253.6	1,067.6	1,256.2	1,258.1	1,481.3	1,598.2	1,490.3
Total Current Liabilities	1,259.1	1,105.1	1,054.6	926.9	1,138.5	902.4	1,072.8
Net Working Capital	d5.5	d37.5	201.6	331.2	342.8	695.8	417.5
Year End Shs Outstg (000)	66,804	69,456	73,403	76,329	75,587	78,767	79,396

STATISTICAL RECORD:

Operating Profit Margin %	8.3	10.3	9.8	9.7	10.0	9.4	9.7
Book Value Per Share	8.11	9.33	12.81	13.11	14.78	15.71	15.76
Return on Equity %	42.7	44.2	26.3	23.6	20.5	16.4	20.4
Return on Assets %	7.6	10.2	8.1	7.8	6.9	6.3	8.6
Average Yield %	1.5	1.4	2.8	2.6	2.9	2.1	2.1
P/E Ratio	25.3-18.4	19.6-15.4	22.9-15.5	24.8-15.5	20.3-14.0	26.9-19.4	19.2-12.0
Price Range	85-61⅞	77-60⅜	74⅜-50¼	75¼-47¾	59½-41	68⅞-49⅝	61½-38½

Statistics are as originally reported.

OFFICERS:
W.D. Smithburg, Chmn. & C.E.O.
P.A. Marineau, Pres. & C.O.O.
L.C. McKinney, Sr. V.P.-Law, Corp. Affairs & Corp. Sec.

INCORPORATED: NJ, Sep., 1901

PRINCIPAL OFFICE: Quaker Tower 321 North Clark St., Chicago, IL 60610-4714

TELEPHONE NUMBER: (312) 222-7111

NO. OF EMPLOYEES: 20,000

ANNUAL MEETING: In November

SHAREHOLDERS: 28,197

INSTITUTIONAL HOLDINGS:
No. of Institutions: 521
Shares Held: 66,955,886

REGISTRAR(S): Harris Trust & Savings Bank, Chicago, IL

TRANSFER AGENT(S): Harris Trust & Savings Bank, Chicago, IL

QUESTAR CORPORATION

YIELD 3.8%
P/E RATIO 24.8

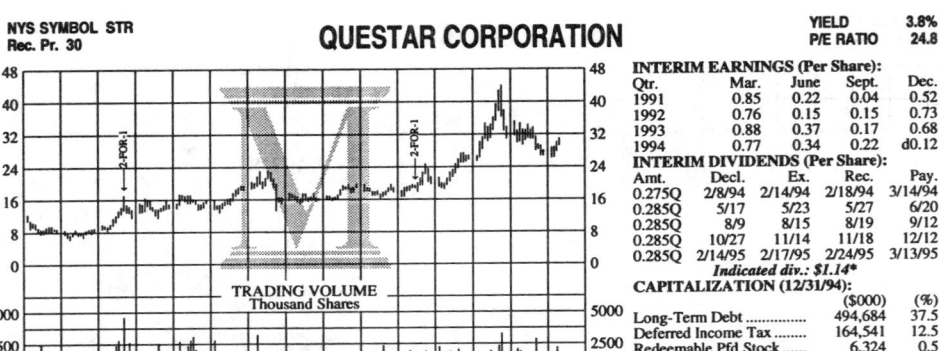

*7 YEAR PRICE SCORE 105.7   *12 MONTH PRICE SCORE 93.9

*NYSE COMPOSITE INDEX=100

INTERIM EARNINGS (Per Share):

Qtr.	Mar.	June	Sept.	Dec.
1991	0.85	0.22	0.04	0.52
1992	0.76	0.15	0.15	0.73
1993	0.88	0.37	0.17	0.68
1994	0.77	0.34	0.22	d0.12

INTERIM DIVIDENDS (Per Share):

Amt.	Decl.	Ex.	Rec.	Pay.
0.275Q	2/8/94	2/14/94	2/18/94	3/14/94
0.285Q	5/17	5/23	5/27	6/20
0.285Q	8/9	8/15	8/19	9/12
0.285Q	10/27	11/14	11/18	12/12
0.285Q	2/14/95	2/17/95	2/24/95	3/13/95

*Indicated div.: $1.14**

CAPITALIZATION (12/31/94):

	($000)	(%)
Long-Term Debt	494,684	37.5
Deferred Income Tax	164,541	12.5
Redeemable Pfd Stock	6,324	0.5
Common & Surplus	653,589	49.5
Total	1,319,138	100.0

Current Debt....................... 94,900

DIVIDEND ACHIEVER STATUS:
Rank: 289   1984-94 Growth Rate: 4.3%
Total Years of Dividend Growth: 15

RECENT DEVELOPMENTS: For the year ended 12/31/94, income from continuing operations was $49.4 million compared with $84.5 million in 1993. However, 1994 results reflect the writedown of the Company's investment in Nextel Communications. This amounted to $38.1 million, or $0.95 per share, after income taxes. Revenues moved up approximately 2% to $670.3 million. Exploration and Production's earnings improved 20% to $59.3 million.

PROSPECTS: Reserves for Questar's exploration and production segment have increased significantly due to acquisitions. During 1994 the exploration and production segment completed several acqusitions that bode well for long-term earnings. The Company's financial results will benefit from a full year of production from these new wells. Meanwhile, the customer base of the gas-distribution subsidiary, Mountain Fuel Supply Co., continues to expand.

BUSINESS

QUESTAR CORPORATION is a diversified energy company that, through its affiliates, conducts oil and gas exploration and production, interstate natural gas transmission, and retail gas distribution. Celsius Energy Company conducts oil and gas exploration activities primarily in the Rocky Mountain region. Questar Pipeline Co. operates a 2,400 mile system in Colorado, Wyoming and Utah. The utility operations transport gas to market areas in southwestern Wyoming and northern and central Utah through two major pipeline systems. Other operations include Questar Service Corp., which conducts microwave communications and data processing; and Questar Development Corp.

BUSINESS LINE ANALYSIS

(12/31/94)	Rev(%)	Inc(%)
Explor & Production .	49.5	38.3
Natl Gas		
Transmission	17.2	34.2
Natl Gas Distribution	56.4	25.4
Other Operations	4.4	2.1
Intercompany		
Transactions	(27.5)	0.0
Total	100.0	100.0

ANNUAL EARNINGS AND DIVIDENDS PER SHARE

	1994	1993	1992	1991	1990	1989	1988
Earnings Per Share	1.21	2.10	[1] 1.79	1.63	1.45	1.28	0.64
Dividends Per Share	1.13	1.09	1.04	[2] 1.01	0.97	0.945	0.94
Dividend Payout %	93.4	51.9	58.1	62.0	66.7	74.1	N.M.

[1] Before acctg. chg.   [2] 2-for-1 stk split,06/18/91

ANNUAL FINANCIAL DATA

RECORD OF EARNINGS (IN MILLIONS):

	1994	1993	1992	1991	1990	1989	1988
Total Revenues	670.3	660.4	604.8	632.3	536.3	509.4	486.0
Depreciation & Amort	97.6	91.2	77.2	67.9	63.3	60.0	...
Prov for Fed Inc Taxes	7.2	28.8	29.3	34.3	30.1	27.1	...
Operating Income	154.7	148.3	133.9	129.7	116.0	105.3	64.3
Interest Expense	39.8	44.0	35.8	36.1	35.6	32.2	29.6
Net Income	87.5	81.7	[1] 71.3	64.0	57.5	50.8	25.9
Aver. Shs. Outstg. (000)	40,292	39,995	39,492	38,715	38,898	38,928	38,466

[1] Before acctg. change cr$9,303,000.

BALANCE SHEET (IN MILLIONS):

	1994	1993	1992	1991	1990	1989	1988
Gross Plant	2,263.2	2,024.4	1,898.2	1,749.5	1,637.3	1,546.0	1,479.4
Accumulated Depreciation	955.5	871.7	800.5	728.9	675.9	651.9	610.2
Prop, Plant & Equip, Net	1,307.6	1,152.7	1,097.7	1,020.6	961.3	894.1	869.2
Long-term Debt	494.7	371.7	364.6	354.4	328.2	275.6	249.3
Net Stockholders' Equity	659.9	609.5	562.5	511.9	471.6	468.2	464.8
Total Assets	1,585.6	1,417.7	1,323.7	1,219.6	1,151.0	1,075.0	1,026.1
Year End Shs Outstg (000)	40,429	40,169	39,795	39,277	38,515	39,512	37,976

STATISTICAL RECORD:

	1994	1993	1992	1991	1990	1989	1988
Book Value Per Share	16.17	14.99	13.55	12.49	11.76	11.54	11.88
Op. Inc/Net Pl %	11.8	12.9	12.2	12.7	12.1	11.8	7.4
Dep/Gr. Pl %	4.1	4.3	4.1	3.9	3.9	3.9	4.3
Accum. Dep/Gr. Pl %	42.2	43.1	42.2	41.7	41.3	42.2	41.2
Return on Equity %	13.4	13.6	12.9	12.8	12.5	10.8	5.6
Average Yield %	3.7	3.1	4.5	4.9	5.4	5.3	5.7
P/E Ratio	29.1-22.0	21.0-12.1	15.4-10.3	15.2-10.2	13.7-11.3	15.5-12.3	27.9-23.4
Price Range	35¼-26⅝	44-25⅜	27½-18½	24¾-16⅝	19⅞-16⅜	19⅞-15¾	17⅞-15

Statistics are as originally reported.

OFFICERS:
R.D. Cash, Chmn., Pres. & C.E.O.
W.F. Edwards, Sr. V.P. & C.F.O.
C.C. Holbrook, V.P. & Corp. Sec.

INCORPORATED: UT, Oct., 1984

PRINCIPAL OFFICE: 180 East First South
P.O. Box 45433, Salt Lake City, UT 84145-0433

TELEPHONE NUMBER: (801) 534-5000

NO. OF EMPLOYEES: 2,624 (Co. and affiliates)

ANNUAL MEETING: In May

SHAREHOLDERS: 11,545

INSTITUTIONAL HOLDINGS:
No. of Institutions: 230
Shares Held: 31,521,125

REGISTRAR(S): Mellon Bank, N.A., Pittsburgh, PA

TRANSFER AGENT(S): At Company's Office
First Chicago Trust Co. of New York, Jersey City, NJ

NYS SYMBOL RTN
Rec. Pr. 74¼

RAYTHEON COMPANY

YIELD 2.0%
P/E RATIO 16.4

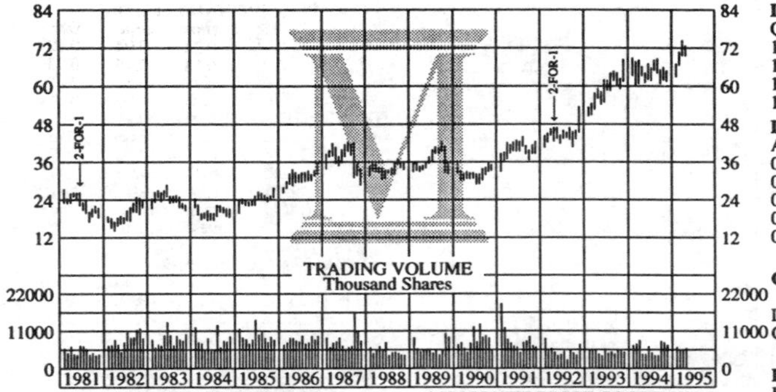

***7 YEAR PRICE SCORE 118.9** ***12 MONTH PRICE SCORE 102.8**

*NYSE COMPOSITE INDEX=100

INTERIM EARNINGS (Per Share):

Qtr.	Mar.	June	Sept.	Dec.
1991	1.02	1.15	1.12	1.19
1992	1.07	1.23	1.16	1.26
1993	1.16	1.32	1.26	1.37
1994	0.05	1.43	1.45	1.61

INTERIM DIVIDENDS (Per Share):

Amt.	Decl.	Ex.	Rec.	Pay.
0.35Q	3/23/94	4/5/94	4/11/94	5/2/94
0.375Q	5/25	7/5	7/11	8/1
0.375Q	9/29	10/3	10/10	10/31
0.375Q	12/20	1/3/95	1/9/95	1/30/95
0.375Q	3/22/95	4/4	4/10	5/1

Indicated div.: $1.50

CAPITALIZATION (12/31/94):

	($000)	(%)
Long-Term Debt	24,522	0.6
Common & Surplus	3,928,168	99.4
Total	3,952,690	100.0

DIVIDEND ACHIEVER STATUS:
Rank: 224 1984-94 Growth Rate: 7.6%
Total Years of Dividend Growth: 10

RECENT DEVELOPMENTS: For the year ended 12/31/94, net income was $596.9 million, including an after-tax restructuring charge of $162.3 million, versus $693.0 million a year earlier. Revenues increased 8.8% to a record $10.01 billion. The Appliance Group posted record income of $84 million, aided by strong customer acceptance of new products. The Electronics segment posted a 15.9% decline in income to $683 million, while sales fell 15.1% to $4.07 billion.

PROSPECTS: Raytheon has implemented a two-year restructuring program designed to help maintain its competitive position in a shrinking defense market and improve productivity in its commercial businesses. As part of this program, all defense-related business units will be consolidated into the Raytheon Electric Systems division. Meanwhile, several new product introductions in the appliance business have been well received.

BUSINESS

RAYTHEON COMPANY has operations in electronics, aviation, energy and appliances. Electronics (41% of 1994 sales) designs, engineers, manufactures and services electronic devices, equipment and systems for commercial and governmental customers. Aircraft Products (17%) produces commuter, business and military aircraft, and also engages in contractor support for the military and other aerospace projects. Engineering & Construction (28%) includes geophysical exploration, design, engineering and construction of refineries, petrochemical facilities and electrical generating plants. Major Appliances (14%) includes Amana and Caloric companies and Speed Queen laundry equipment.

ANNUAL EARNINGS AND DIVIDENDS PER SHARE

	1994	1993	1992	1991	1990	1989	1988
Earnings Per Share	**4.51**	**5.11**	**4.72**	**4.48**	**4.27**	**4.01**	**3.68**
Dividends Per Share	**1.45**	**1.40**	**[1] 1.30**	**1.20**	**1.175**	**1.075**	**1.00**
Dividend Payout %	**32.2**	**27.4**	**27.5**	**26.8**	**27.5**	**26.8**	**27.2**

[1] 2-for-1 stk split, 4/3/92

ANNUAL FINANCIAL DATA

	1994	1993	1992	1991	1990	1989	1988
RECORD OF EARNINGS (IN MILLIONS):							
Total Revenues	10,012.9	9,201.2	9,058.2	9,274.2	9,267.7	8,796.1	8,192.1
Costs and Expenses	8,909.5	8,003.3	7,862.5	8,146.4	8,165.3	7,768.8	7,292.1
Depreciation	274.7	277.9	302.1	306.1	303.5	281.6	259.0
Operating Income	828.6	919.9	893.6	821.7	798.9	745.6	641.0
Income Bef Income Taxes	899.9	1,047.3	956.0	872.7	836.9	757.7	705.5
Income Taxes	303.1	354.4	320.9	281.0	279.6	228.8	216.0
Net Income	596.9	693.0	635.1	591.8	557.3	528.8	489.6
Aver. Shs. Outstg. (000)	132,368	135,583	134,504	132,230	130,666	132,054	133,242
BALANCE SHEET (IN MILLIONS):							
Cash and Cash Equivalents	202.2	190.2	88.8	138.0	137.6	99.3	108.1
Receivables, Net	3,093.2	2,751.9	2,523.3	2,496.4	2,361.5	2,058.5	1,842.4
Inventories	1,499.5	1,500.4	1,051.1	1,014.6	1,016.0	852.0	726.3
Gross Property	3,691.0	3,590.3	3,478.2	3,599.4	3,484.9	3,177.1	2,917.0
Accumulated Depreciation	2,330.2	2,168.2	2,058.1	2,082.8	1,952.8	1,720.8	1,561.8
Long-Term Debt	24.5	24.4	25.3	39.3	46.4	46.0	41.3
Net Stockholders' Equity	3,928.2	4,297.9	3,843.2	3,323.4	2,846.5	2,426.1	2,121.0
Total Assets	7,395.4	7,257.7	6,015.1	6,087.1	6,119.4	5,338.3	4,739.5
Total Current Assets	4,985.5	4,609.2	3,775.8	3,747.6	3,603.5	3,104.5	2,844.3
Total Current Liabilities	3,283.1	2,909.8	2,136.8	2,716.1	3,145.6	2,822.0	2,577.2
Net Working Capital	1,702.4	1,699.5	1,639.0	1,031.5	457.8	282.4	267.1
Year End Shs Outstg (000)	123,322	135,214	135,660	133,440	130,710	131,240	132,746
STATISTICAL RECORD:							
Operating Profit Margin %	8.3	10.0	9.9	8.9	8.6	8.5	7.8
Book Value Per Share	31.85	31.79	28.33	24.91	21.78	18.49	15.98
Return on Equity %	15.2	16.1	16.5	17.8	19.6	21.8	23.1
Return on Assets %	8.1	9.5	10.6	9.7	9.1	9.9	10.3
Average Yield %	2.2	2.4	2.8	3.1	3.6	2.9	3.0
P/E Ratio	15.3-13.4	13.4-9.9	11.3-8.6	9.8-7.3	8.3-6.8	10.6-8.1	10.1-8.3
Price Range	68⅞-60½	68½-50½	53½-40⅝	44⅛-32⅞	35⅝-28⅞	42½-32⅜	37-30½

Statistics are as originally reported.

OFFICERS:
D.J. Picard, Chmn. & C.E.O.
M.E. Bleck, Pres.
H. Deitcher, Sr. V.P. & Treas.

INCORPORATED: DE, May, 1928

PRINCIPAL OFFICE: 141 Spring Street, Lexington, MA 02173

TELEPHONE NUMBER: (617) 862-6600

FAX: (617) 860-2172

NO. OF EMPLOYEES: 60,200

ANNUAL MEETING: In May

SHAREHOLDERS: 21,978

INSTITUTIONAL HOLDINGS:
No. of Institutions: 775
Shares Held: 92,593,298

REGISTRAR(S): State Street Bank and Trust Co., Boston, MA

TRANSFER AGENT(S): State Street Bank and Trust Co., Boston, MA

NASDAQ SYMBOL RGBK
Rec. Pr. 36¾

REGIONS FINANCIAL CORP.

YIELD 3.6%
P/E RATIO 10.8

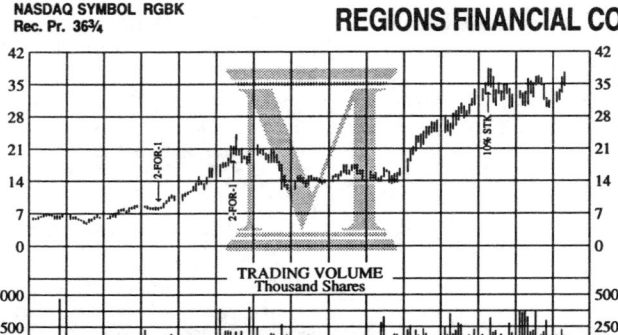

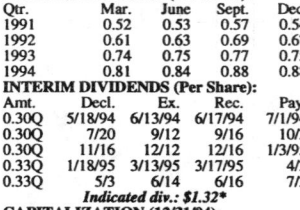

TRADING VOLUME
Thousand Shares

| | 1981 | 1982 | 1983 | 1984 | 1985 | 1986 | 1987 | 1988 | 1989 | 1990 | 1991 | 1992 | 1993 | 1994 | 1995 |

*7 YEAR PRICE SCORE 115.8   *12 MONTH PRICE SCORE 99.3

*NYSE COMPOSITE INDEX=100

INTERIM EARNINGS (Per Share):

Qtr.	Mar.	June	Sept.	Dec.
1991	0.52	0.53	0.57	0.54
1992	0.61	0.63	0.69	0.67
1993	0.74	0.75	0.77	0.75
1994	0.81	0.84	0.88	0.88

INTERIM DIVIDENDS (Per Share):

Amt.	Decl.	Ex.	Rec.	Pay.
0.30Q	5/18/94	6/13/94	6/17/94	7/1/94
0.30Q	7/20	9/12	9/16	10/3
0.30Q	11/16	12/12	12/16	1/3/95
0.33Q	1/18/95	3/13/95	3/17/95	4/3
0.33Q	5/3	6/14	6/16	7/3

*Indicated div.: $1.32**

CAPITALIZATION (12/31/94):

	($000)	(%)
Total Deposits	10,093,135	79.1
Total Debt	1,530,779	12.0
Common & Surplus	1,013,870	8.0
Loan Valuation Reserve	116,988	0.9
Total	12,754,772	100.0

DIVIDEND ACHIEVER STATUS:
Rank: 196   1984-94 Growth Rate: 9.0%
Total Years of Dividend Growth: 23

RECENT DEVELOPMENTS: For the fiscal year ended 12/31/94, net income was a record $145.9 million, an increase of 30% from the $112.0 million earned in 1993. During 1994, the Company completed 9 acquisitions, establishing a market presence in Rome, GA; Baton Rouge, Houma, Monroe, New Roads and Shreveport, LA; Panama City, FL; and Atmore, Brewton and Fayette, AL. Total assets grew 23% from 1993 to $12.8 billion as deposits increased to $10.09 billion from $8.77 billion. Net loans soared 32% to $9.02 billion from $6.83 billion the year before. RGBK reported a return on average total assets of 1.29%, down from 1.40% a year earlier. The return on average stockholder's equity fell to 15.97% from 16.14%. Net income for the quarter ended 12/31/94 was $37.2 million, up 33% from the prior-year quarter's $28.1 million.

BUSINESS

REGIONS FINANCIAL CORP., formerly First Alabama Bancshares, Inc., is a $12.8 billion bank holding company. The Company operates 270 full-service banking offices in Alabama, Tennessee, Florida, Louisiana and Georgia. RGBK offers commercial banking services and trust services in several locations. First Alabama Bank, the Company's principal banking subsidiary, operates 166 full-service banking offices throughout Alabama. Regions Bank of Florida, the Company's Florida banking affiliate, operates 15 full-service banking offices in northwest Florida. Supplementing the Company's banking operations are a mortgage banking company, credit-life insurance related companies and a registered broker/dealer firm. The Company also has real estate loan origination offices in Georgia, Tennessee, Mississippi and South Carolina.

LOANS DISTRIBUTION

(12/31/94)	($000)	(%)
Commercial	1,871,311	20.7
Real Estate-Construction	341,431	3.8
Real Estate-Mortgage	4,546,178	50.3
Consumer	2,278,547	25.2
Total	9,043,467	100.0

ANNUAL EARNINGS AND DIVIDENDS PER SHARE

	1994	1993	1992	1991	1990	1989	1988
Earnings Per Share	3.40	3.01	2.60	2.16	1.91	1.73	1.61
Dividends Per Share	1.16	0.984	① 0.90	0.864	0.818	0.755	0.718
Dividend Payout %	34.1	32.7	34.6	39.9	42.9	43.7	44.6

① 10% stk div,03/01/93

ANNUAL FINANCIAL DATA

RECORD OF EARNINGS (IN MILLIONS):

	1994	1993	1992	1991	1990	1989	1988
Total Interest Income	785.8	555.7	536.7	556.8	519.8	496.4	404.6
Total Interest Expense	350.1	213.6	224.1	292.0	297.6	292.7	219.9
Net Interest Income	435.6	342.1	312.7	264.8	222.1	203.7	184.7
Credit Loss Provision	19.0	21.5	27.1	24.0	24.2	15.8	10.8
Net Income	145.9	112.0	95.0	78.3	68.9	62.6	58.2
Aver. Shs. Outstg. (000)	42,906	37,205	36,532	36,191	36,097	36,331	36,281

BALANCE SHEET (IN MILLIONS):

	1994	1993	1992	1991	1990	1989	1988
Cash & Due From Banks	551.1	462.0	496.5	327.8	323.4	351.7	293.8
U.S. Treas & Fed Agcy Securs	903.4	963.4	1,440.6	1,347.8	1,246.9	929.2	996.9
Obligs Of States & Political Subdivs	253.1	223.7	170.3	170.5	173.1	171.8	175.8
Loans & Lse Financing, Net	8,900.8	6,732.5	5,061.3	4,220.2	4,047.3	3,514.9	3,134.8
Total Domestic Deposits	10,093.1	8,770.7	6,701.1	5,917.0	5,353.2	4,744.4	4,331.7
Long-term Debt	519.2	462.9	137.0	18.8	19.7	45.3	20.6
Net Stockholders' Equity	1,013.9	851.0	656.7	573.0	524.1	489.4	455.6
Total Assets	12,839.3	10,476.3	7,881.0	6,745.1	6,344.4	5,549.6	5,173.6
Year End Shs Outstg (000)	45,008	41,049	37,272	36,352	36,048	36,299	37,348

STATISTICAL RECORD:

	1994	1993	1992	1991	1990	1989	1988
Return on Assets %	1.14	1.07	1.21	1.16	1.09	1.13	1.13
Return on Equity %	14.40	13.20	14.50	13.70	13.10	12.80	12.80
Book Value Per Share	22.53	20.73	17.62	15.76	14.54	13.48	12.20
Average Yield %	3.5	2.9	3.1	4.0	5.4	4.8	5.2
P/E Ratio	10.8-8.8	12.7-9.8	13.0-9.1	12.6-7.3	8.8-6.9	10.2-7.9	9.5-7.5
Price Range	36¼-29¾	38⅜-29⅝	33⅞-23¾	27⅛-15⅞	16⅞-13¼	17⅝-13¾	15¼-12⅛

Statistics are as originally reported.

OFFICERS:
J.S. Mackin, Chmn. & C.E.O.
R.D. Horsley, Vice-Chmn. & Exec. Fin. Off.
S.E. Upchurch, Gen. Counsel & Sec.

INCORPORATED: DE, Jun., 1970

PRINCIPAL OFFICE: 417 North 20th St. P.O. Box 10247, Birmingham, AL 35202-0247

TELEPHONE NUMBER: (205) 326-7100

FAX: (205) 240-2840

NO. OF EMPLOYEES: 5,439

ANNUAL MEETING: In April

SHAREHOLDERS: 23,622

INSTITUTIONAL HOLDINGS:
No. of Institutions: 184
Shares Held: 14,527,176

REGISTRAR(S): First Alabama Bank, Montgomery, AL 36103

TRANSFER AGENT(S): First Alabama Bank, Montgomery, AL 36103

NYS SYMBOL RLR
Rec. Pr. 35⅜

RELIASTAR FINANCIAL CORP.

YIELD 2.8%
P/E RATIO 10.7

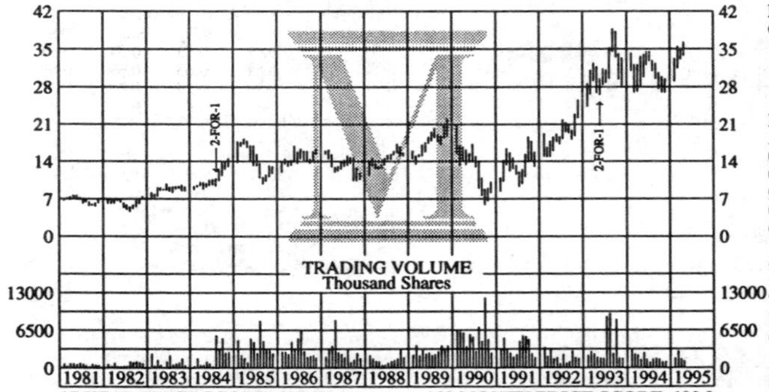

*7 YEAR PRICE SCORE 127.1 *12 MONTH PRICE SCORE 102.9

*NYSE COMPOSITE INDEX=100

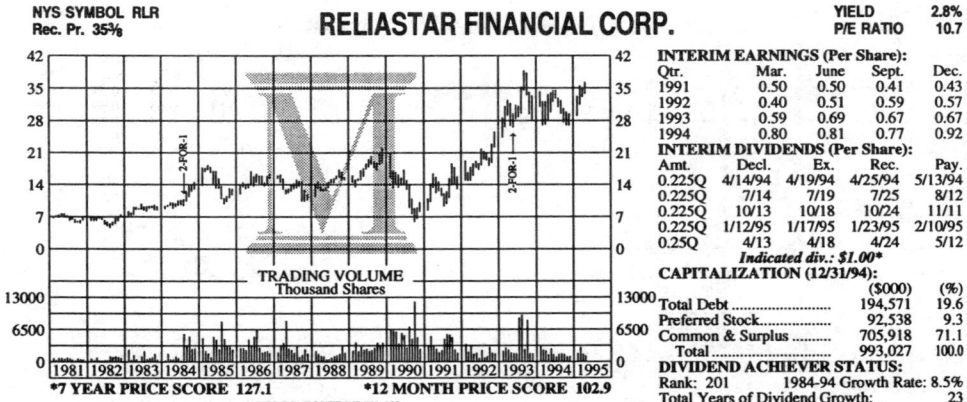

INTERIM EARNINGS (Per Share):

Qtr.	Mar.	June	Sept.	Dec.
1991	0.50	0.50	0.41	0.43
1992	0.40	0.51	0.59	0.57
1993	0.59	0.69	0.67	0.67
1994	0.80	0.81	0.77	0.92

INTERIM DIVIDENDS (Per Share):

Amt.	Decl.	Ex.	Rec.	Pay.
0.225Q	4/14/94	4/19/94	4/25/94	5/13/94
0.225Q	7/14	7/19	7/25	8/12
0.225Q	10/13	10/18	10/24	11/11
0.225Q	1/12/95	1/17/95	1/23/95	2/10/95
0.25Q	4/13	4/18	4/24	5/12

*Indicated div.: $1.00**

CAPITALIZATION (12/31/94):

	($000)	(%)
Total Debt	194,571	19.6
Preferred Stock	92,538	9.3
Common & Surplus	705,918	71.1
Total	993,027	100.0

DIVIDEND ACHIEVER STATUS:
Rank: 201 1984-94 Growth Rate: 8.5%
Total Years of Dividend Growth: 23

RECENT DEVELOPMENTS: For the year ended 12/31/94, income from continuing operations increased 30.6% to $107.7 million compared with $82.5 million the previous year. Revenues advanced 5.4% to $1.57 billion from $1.49 billion in 1993. Premium revenues rose 10.2% to $726.9 million from $659.6 million. However, net investment income fell 2.6% to $618.3 million from $635.0 million. The Individual Insurance segment benefited from improved interest margins, which were the result of lower crediting rates and increased levels of invested assets. These actions increased pretax income in this segment by approximately $21.5 million. Credit ratings are reset annually at the beginning of the calendar year and are guaranteed for one year on most of the business. In early 1994, the Company reduced credit rates on most in force life insurance and annuity contracts. The Life and Health Reinsurance results improved due to increased earned premiums with about the same overall loss ratio.

BUSINESS

RELIASTAR FINANCIAL CORP., formerly The NWNL Companies, is a Minneapolis-based holding company that provides financial securing through individual life insurance and annuities, employee benefits, retirement plans, life and health reinsurance, and mutual funds. The Company's major businesses are the individual life insurance, employee benefits, life and health reinsurance, and retirement plan operations of Northwestern National Life, Minneapolis; the annuity operations of Northern Life, Seattle; the individual insurance operations of North Atlantic Life, Jericho, NY; the individual insurance operations of Bankers Security Life, Uniondale, NY; the individual insurance operations of United Services Life, Arlington, VA; the mutual fund operations of Northstar Investment Management Corporation, Greenwich, CT; and the residential mortgage banking operations of Washington Square Mortgage Company, West Des Moines, IA.

ANNUAL EARNINGS AND DIVIDENDS PER SHARE

	1994	1993	1992	1991	1990	1989	1988
Earnings Per Share	3.30	2.63	② 2.07	③ 1.72	③ 2.45	2.07	④ 2.01
Dividends Per Share	0.875	① 0.785	0.73	0.69	0.645	0.59	0.54
Dividend Payout %	26.5	29.9	35.3	40.2	26.3	28.5	26.9

① 2-for-1 stk split,05/24/93 ② Before extraord. item ③ Before disc. oper. ④ Before realized invest gains

ANNUAL FINANCIAL DATA

	1994	1993	1992	1991	1990	1989	1988
RECORD OF EARNINGS (IN MILLIONS):							
Insurance Premiums	726.9	659.6	589.9	548.0	535.9	583.4	1,806.5
Total Interest Income	618.3	635.0	606.7	616.1	651.2	660.8	420.4
Total Revenues	1,570.8	1,490.4	1,378.0	1,339.8	1,331.7	1,393.2	2,270.6
Benefits to Policyholders	1,025.3	1,006.3	950.1	928.8	922.4	958.7	682.3
Income Bef Income Taxes	166.6	128.6	89.6	70.8	69.2	86.3	65.7
Income Taxes	58.9	46.1	29.0	23.1	7.4	27.9	20.4
Net Income	① 107.7	65.3	59.3	② 47.2	③ 61.2	53.5	33.0
Aver. Shs. Outstg. (000)	30,122	28,151	24,800	24,092	25,010	25,814	21,912

① Before disc. op. dr$2,600,000. ② Before disc. op. dr$350,000. ③ Before disc. op. dr$11,585,000.

	1994	1993	1992	1991	1990	1989	1988
BALANCE SHEET (IN MILLIONS):							
Cash	20.3	34.0	37.6	29.6	32.7	20.9	18.7
Fixed Maturities	5,781.0	5,359.4	4,662.9	3,954.0	3,606.9	3,450.5	2,119.9
Equity Securities	43.7	44.9	30.3	45.3	28.7	32.1	68.0
Policy Loans	306.8	257.4	217.9	179.0	140.7	117.5	169.1
Mtge Loans on Real Estate	1,570.3	1,781.1	1,859.8	2,010.7	2,340.9	2,510.9	1,623.5
Total Assets	10,366.8	9,912.9	9,014.4	8,770.3	8,473.7	8,270.7	7,593.9
Benefits and Claims	8,174.3	7,809.9	7,251.6	7,099.2	6,879.0	6,602.3	4,292.4
Net Stockholders' Equity	798.5	800.6	679.8	594.1	513.4	500.1	409.1
Year End Shs Outstg (000)	29,788	29,446	26,910	24,528	24,528	25,848	21,816
STATISTICAL RECORD:							
Book Value Per Share	23.70	24.04	21.80	20.42	20.93	19.35	18.75
Return on Equity %	13.5	10.3	8.9	8.0	11.9	10.7	8.1
Return on Assets %	1.0	0.8	0.7	0.5	0.7	0.7	0.4
Average Yield %	2.8	3.7	3.6	5.1	4.8	3.3	3.8
P/E Ratio	10.5-8.2	14.7-9.3	12.4-7.2	10.9-4.9	8.6-2.4	10.7-6.5	8.6-5.7
Price Range	34½-27	38¾-24⅜	25⅝-14⅞	18⅝-8⅜	21-5⅞	22⅛-13½	17¼-11⅜

Statistics are as originally reported.

OFFICERS:
J.G. Turner, Chmn. & C.E.O.
J.H. Flittie, Pres. & C.O.O.
R.N. Sanner, Sr. V.P., Sec. & Gen. Counsel
R.C. Salipante, Sr. V.P. & C.F.O.

INCORPORATED: MN, Jan., 1989

PRINCIPAL OFFICE: 20 Washington Avenue South, Minneapolis, MN 55401

TELEPHONE NUMBER: (612) 372-5432
FAX: (612) 342-3966
NO. OF EMPLOYEES: 2,596
ANNUAL MEETING: In May
SHAREHOLDERS: 30,905 common; 684 preferred
INSTITUTIONAL HOLDINGS:
No. of Institutions: Not Available
Shares Held: Not Available

REGISTRAR(S): Norwest Bank Minnesota, South St. Paul, MN

TRANSFER AGENT(S): Norwest Bank Minnesota, South St. Paul, MN

REPUBLIC NEW YORK CORPORATION

YIELD 2.9%
P/E RATIO 8.4

*7 YEAR PRICE SCORE 97.0 ***12 MONTH PRICE SCORE 99.9**

*NYSE COMPOSITE INDEX=100

TRADING VOLUME
Thousand Shares

INTERIM EARNINGS (Per Share):

Qtr.	Mar.	June	Sept.	Dec.
1991	0.97	0.99	0.99	1.00
1992	1.04	1.08	1.16	1.14
1993	1.18	1.30	1.34	1.38
1994	1.38	1.35	1.55	1.51

INTERIM DIVIDENDS (Per Share):

Amt.	Decl.	Ex.	Rec.	Pay.
0.33Q	4/20/94	6/9/94	6/15/94	7/1/94
0.33Q	7/20	9/9	9/15	10/1
0.33Q	10/20	12/9	12/15	1/1/95
0.36Q	1/18/95	3/9/95	3/15/95	4/1
0.36Q	4/19	6/13	6/15	7/1

Indicated div.: $1.44

CAPITALIZATION (12/31/94):

	($000)	(%)
Total Deposits	22,726,002	60.2
Total Debt	12,044,085	31.9
Preferred Stock	672,500	1.8
Common & Surplus	1,966,888	5.2
Loan Valuation Reserve	319,220	0.9
Total	37,728,695	100.0

DIVIDEND ACHIEVER STATUS:
Rank: 264   1984-94 Growth Rate: 6.0%
Total Years of Dividend Growth: 19

RECENT DEVELOPMENTS: RNB reported net income of $340.0 million for the year ended 12/31/94, an increase of 12.4% from the prior year. Net interest income was $846.5 million, up 9% from $775.9 million in 1993. The increase was attributed to higher earning asset levels. Other operating income, hurt by a 65% drop in trading account profits and commissions to $27.4 million, was $386.4 million compared with $395.5 million a year earlier.

PROSPECTS: Republic New York Securities Corp., a wholly-owned subsidiary, formed a futures division and has been licensed to trade in futures and options on futures in non-financial commodities, including energy, agricultural, and non-precious metals. RNB agreed to acquire a branch in Brazil from Banco Exterior de Espana S.A. The Company has opened an office in Copenhagen to market institutional banking services in Scandinavian countries.

BUSINESS

REPUBLIC NEW YORK CORPORATION is a bank holding company whose principal subsidiaries are Republic National Bank of New York and The Manhattan Savings Bank. The Company provides a variety of commercial banking services, with primary emphasis on international banking. With assets of $41.1 billion, Republic New York is one of the largest bank holding companies in the nation. RNB owns 49% of Safra Republic Holdings, a European international private banking group.

LOAN DISTRIBUTION

(12/31/94)	($000)	(%)
Real Estate-		
Residential	1,245,500	13.9
Real Estate-		
Commercial	1,813,878	20.2
Banks, Brokers &		
Others	642,029	7.2
Commercial &		
Industrial	2,242,124	25.0
Individuals	106,195	1.2
All Other	11,810	0.1
Foreign	2,899,063	32.4
Total	8,960,599	100.0

ANNUAL EARNINGS AND DIVIDENDS PER SHARE

	1994	1993	1992	1991	1990	1989	1988
Earnings Per Share	5.79	5.20	4.42	3.95	3.62	0.03	3.34
Dividends Per Share	1.26	1.06	1.00	① 0.92	0.873	0.84	0.793
Dividend Payout %	21.7	20.4	22.6	23.3	24.1	N.M.	23.8

① 3-for-2 stk split, 10/22/91

ANNUAL FINANCIAL DATA

RECORD OF EARNINGS (IN MILLIONS):

	1994	1993	1992	1991	1990	1989	1988
Total Interest Income	2,173.3	1,932.9	2,038.6	2,263.9	2,501.6	2,347.5	1,927.5
Total Interest Expense	1,326.9	1,157.1	1,318.2	1,682.7	2,044.2	1,990.6	1,499.3
Net Interest Income	846.5	775.9	720.4	581.2	457.3	356.9	428.2
Credit Loss Provision	19.0	85.0	120.0	62.0	40.0	209.0	41.5
Net Income	340.0	301.2	258.9	227.4	201.2	24.0	169.7
Aver. Shs. Outstg. (000)	52,736	52,466	52,204	51,852	49,726	45,223	44,942

BALANCE SHEET (IN MILLIONS):

	1994	1993	1992	1991	1990	1989	1988
Cash & Due From Banks	867.2	636.6	490.7	412.0	424.9	397.9	375.3
Loans & Lse Financing, Net	8,594.3	9,196.7	7,766.4	8,341.5	8,768.2	6,292.9	5,544.0
Total Domestic Deposits	10,236.2	10,152.3	10,401.2	9,925.1	10,532.2	8,291.4	8,434.9
Total Foreign Deposits	12,489.8	12,648.9	10,701.0	10,457.8	9,454.6	8,233.4	7,911.4
Long-term Debt	4,987.1	4,854.8	4,633.4	3,120.4	2,416.2	2,521.3	2,272.4
Net Stockholders' Equity	2,639.4	2,747.2	2,263.4	1,997.6	1,683.0	1,372.0	1,426.3
Total Assets	41,067.9	39,493.5	37,146.4	31,220.8	29,597.0	25,467.0	24,519.0
Year End Shs Outstg (000)	52,621	52,703	52,190	52,045	51,608	45,332	45,060

STATISTICAL RECORD:

	1994	1993	1992	1991	1990	1989	1988
Return on Assets %	0.83	0.76	0.70	0.73	0.68	0.09	0.69
Return on Equity %	12.90	11.00	11.40	11.40	12.00	1.70	11.90
Book Value Per Share	37.38	41.57	32.71	29.60	26.61	23.44	24.79
Average Yield %	2.7	2.2	2.3	2.3	2.9	2.7	2.7
P/E Ratio	9.0-7.2	10.3-8.5	10.9-8.6	12.0-7.9	9.6-6.9	N.M	9.6-7.9
Price Range	52¼-41⅞	53¾-44⅜	48¼-38	47¼-31⅜	34⅞-24⅞	34⅜-28⅜	32⅛-26⅜

Statistics are as originally reported.

OFFICERS:
W.H. Weiner, Chmn. & C.E.O.
E. Ginsburg, Vice-Chmn. & Gen. Coun.
J.C. Keil, Exec. V.P. & Treas.

INCORPORATED: MD, Sep., 1973

PRINCIPAL OFFICE: 452 Fifth Avenue, New York, NY 10018

TELEPHONE NUMBER: (212) 525-5000

NO. OF EMPLOYEES: 5,500 (approx.)

ANNUAL MEETING: In May

SHAREHOLDERS: 3,027

INSTITUTIONAL HOLDINGS:
No. of Institutions: 187
Shares Held: 26,225,702

REGISTRAR(S): Chemical Bank, New York, NY

TRANSFER AGENT(S): Chemical Bank, New York, NY

NYS SYMBOL RLI
Rec. Pr. 20¼ (adj.)

RLI CORP.

YIELD 3.2%
P/E RATIO ...

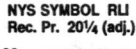

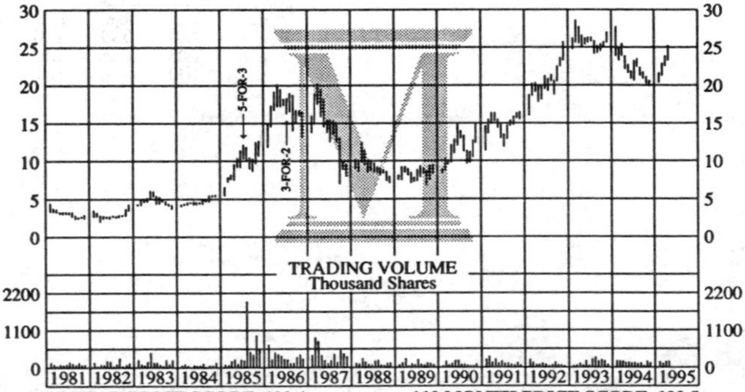
30
25
20
15
10
5
0
5-FOR-3
3-FOR-2
TRADING VOLUME
Thousand Shares
2200
1100
0
1981
1982
1983
1984
1985
1986
1987
1988
1989
1990
1991
1992
1993
1994
1995

*7 YEAR PRICE SCORE 109.4 *12 MONTH PRICE SCORE 102.5

*NYSE COMPOSITE INDEX=100

INTERIM EARNINGS (Per Share):

Qtr.	Mar.	June	Sept.	Dec.
1991	0.36	0.42	0.44	0.56
1992	0.42	0.46	0.46	0.50
1993	0.41	0.53	0.26	0.74
1994	d2.02	0.61	0.07	0.60

INTERIM DIVIDENDS (Per Share):

Amt.	Decl.	Ex.	Rec.	Pay.
0.15Q	8/11/94	9/26/94	9/30/94	10/15/94
0.15Q	12/9	12/23	12/31	1/13/95
0.15Q	3/10/95	3/27/95	3/31/95	4/14
5-for-4	5/11	6/22	6/15	6/21
0.1625Q	5/12	6/28	6/30	7/14

Indicated div.: $0.65*

CAPITALIZATION (12/31/94):

	($000)	(%)
Total Debt	52,255	28.7
Common & Surplus	129,597	71.3
Total	181,852	100.0

DIVIDEND ACHIEVER STATUS:

Rank: 153 1984-94 Growth Rate: 10.5%

Total Years of Dividend Growth: 18

RECENT DEVELOPMENTS: For the year ended 12/31/94, net loss amounted to $5.0 million compared with income of $14.1 million, before an accounting adjustment, a year earlier. Gross sales (premiums written, Protech sales, net investment income and realized investment gain or loss) increased 12.1% to $312.1 million from $278.5 million in 1993. The increase was attributable to significant growth in premiums written and net investment income. However, these gains were partially offset by realized investment losses incurred in the fourth quarter. The losses were taken to recoup taxes that were paid in previous years. Operating results were adversely affected by the Northride, California, earthquake in January of 1994. This catastrophe resulted in losses, expenses and the reduction of revenues due to reinstatement of reinsurance coverages. Aftertax earnings were reduced by $25 million or $4.19 per share.

BUSINESS

RLI CORP. is a holding company, which, through its subsidiaries, underwrites specialty property and casualty insurance, administers extended service programs, markets computers and automated practice management software to the ophthalmic industry, distributes contact and other lenses, provides licensing services for agents and brokers and writes miscellaneous surety bonds. The RLI Insurance Group is composed primarily of two main insurance companies. RLI Insurance Company, the principal subsidiary, writes multiple lines of insurance on an admitted basis in all 50 states, the District of Columbia and Puerto Rico. Mt. Hawley Insurance Company, a subsidiary of RLI Insurance Company, writes multiple lines of insurance on an admitted basis in Delaware and surplus lines insurance in the remaining 49 states, District of Columbia, Puerto Rico, the Virgin Islands and Guam. RLI Professional Technologies distributes contact lenses and administers approximately 6,900 individual ophthalmic practitioners' extended service programs that entitle enrolled patients to receive certain goods and services.

ANNUAL EARNINGS AND DIVIDENDS PER SHARE

	1994	1993	1992	1991	1990	1989	1988
Earnings Per Share	**d0.67**	**1.94**	**1.83**	**1.78**	**1.64**	**1.14**	**0.97**
Dividends Per Share	**0.46**	**0.42**	**0.39**	**0.36**	**0.33**	**0.30**	**0.27**
Dividend Payout %	**...**	**21.9**	**21.4**	**20.3**	**20.0**	**26.6**	**28.1**

Adj. for 5-for-4 stk split, 6/21/95.

ANNUAL FINANCIAL DATA

	1994	1993	1992	1991	1990	1989	1988
RECORD OF EARNINGS (IN THOUSANDS):							
Insurance Premiums	140,184	125,989	103,177	76,763	72,610	70,389	85,701
Total Interest Income	20,133	16,857	13,483	12,742	11,065	9,558	7,811
Total Revenues	171,902	155,125	129,757	102,343	92,221	88,995	103,135
Losses & Settlement Exps	101,642	79,737	62,187	46,493	37,688	39,436	49,898
Earn Bef Income Taxes	d11,922	18,149	21,226	22,706	14,729	9,886	9,193
Income Taxes	cr6,921	4,017	5,019	5,906	3,108	1,376	1,425
Net Income	d5,001	[1] 14,132	16,207	16,800	11,621	8,200	7,254
Aver. Shs. Outstg.	7,473	7,286	3,409	7,074	7,074	7,189	7,475
[1] Before acctg. change cr$1,665,000.							
BALANCE SHEET (IN THOUSANDS):							
Cash	8,534	9,247	4,394	7,964	3,038	9,467	2,801
Fixed Maturities	260,135	242,052	172,831	146,182	141,081	108,723	107,220
Eq Secur, At Mkt Value	104,067	116,529	75,934	63,323	39,914	35,870	25,048
Total Assets	752,301	668,921	529,660	303,553	266,787	243,895	228,384
Benefits and Claims	514,784	416,799	358,786	157,789	142,823	129,120	126,973
Net Stockholders' Equity	129,597	139,299	117,393	92,816	77,205	70,276	64,026
Year End Shares Outstg	7,536	7,398	7,201	7,074	7,074	7,074	7,475
STATISTICAL RECORD:							
Return on Equity %	...	10.1	13.8	18.1	15.1	11.7	11.3
Book Value Per Share	17.20	18.83	16.30	13.12	10.91	9.93	8.57
Average Yield %	2.4	2.0	2.3	3.2	3.5	4.6	3.4
P/E Ratio	...	11.8-9.9	11.3-7.0	7.4-5.1	7.2-4.1	6.7-4.8	10.3-5.9
Price Range	22¼-15⅞	22⅞-19¼	20⅝-12¾	13¼-9⅛	11⅞-6¾	7⅝-5½	10-5¾

Statistics are as originally reported.

OFFICERS:
G.D. Stephens, Pres. & C.E.O.
J.E. Dondanville, V.P. & C.F.O.
T. Kreuger, Treas.
K.J. Hensey, Corp. Sec.

INCORPORATED: DE, May, 1984

PRINCIPAL OFFICE: 9025 N. Lindbergh Drive, Peoria, IL 61615

TELEPHONE NUMBER: (309) 692-1000

FAX: (309) 692-1068

NO. OF EMPLOYEES: 426

ANNUAL MEETING: In May

SHAREHOLDERS: 745

INSTITUTIONAL HOLDINGS:
No. of Institutions: 52
Shares Held: 3,175,355 (adj.)

REGISTRAR(S): Norwest Bank Minnesota, N.A., South St. Paul, MN

TRANSFER AGENT(S): Norwest Bank Minnesota, N.A., South St. Paul, MN

ROCKWELL INTERNATIONAL CORP.

YIELD 2.4%
P/E RATIO 15.0

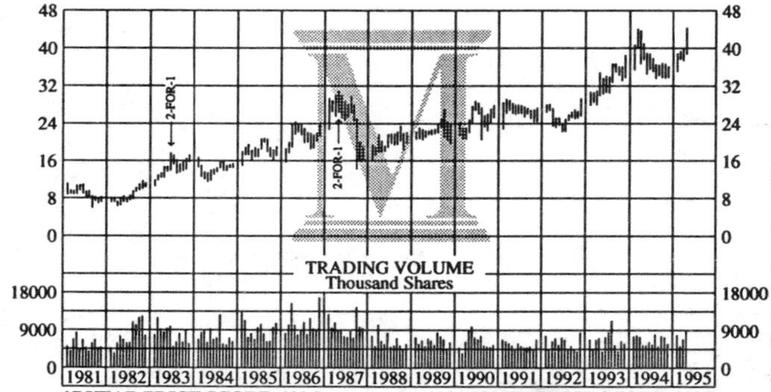

TRADING VOLUME
Thousand Shares

*7 YEAR PRICE SCORE 109.2 *12 MONTH PRICE SCORE 103.0
*NYSE COMPOSITE INDEX=100

INTERIM EARNINGS (Per Share):

Qtr.	Dec.	Mar.	June	Sept.
1991-92	0.54	0.45	0.55	0.62
1992-93	0.58	0.63	0.66	0.68
1993-94	0.68	0.70	0.74	0.75
1994-95	0.76	...	...	...

INTERIM DIVIDENDS (Per Share):

Amt.	Decl.	Ex.	Rec.	Pay.
0.25Q	5/4/94	5/10/94	5/16/94	6/6/94
0.27Q	7/6	8/9	8/15	9/6
0.27Q	11/2	11/7	11/14	12/5
0.27Q	2/1/95	2/7/95	2/13/95	3/6/95
0.27Q	5/3	5/9	5/15	6/5

*Indicated div.: $1.08**

CAPITALIZATION (9/30/94):

	($000)	(%)
Long-Term Debt	831,000	19.9
Preferred Stock	1,400	0.0
Common & Surplus	3,354,200	80.1
Total	4,186,600	100.0

DIVIDEND ACHIEVER STATUS:
Rank: 216   1984-94 Growth Rate: 7.9%
Total Years of Dividend Growth: 18

RECENT DEVELOPMENTS: For the quarter ended 12/31/94, net income increased 10.2% to $164.7 million. Sales advanced 2.9% to $2.62 billion. The Electronics segment posted a 4.3% decline in income to $161.6 million, as a 76% rise in Automation's earnings was offset by lower earnings in Avionics and Telecommunications. Automotive's earnings rose 39% to $48.9 million, aided by continuing strong North American truck sales.

PROSPECTS: At the end of January 1995, Rockwell completed its acquisition of Reliance Electric Co., a move that is expected to boost ROK's leadership in the global automation markets. Meanwhile, the Automotive segment should continue to benefit from increased sales of heavy and light trucks. The Electronics segment is expected to enjoy increased sales and earnings from its telecommunications products.

BUSINESS

ROCKWELL INTERNATIONAL CORP. is a multi-industry company applying advanced technology to products in the electronics, aerospace, automotive and graphics industries. Aerospace, which contributed 24% to fiscal 1994 sales (30% of operating income), is a leader in spacecraft and rocket propulsion systems, and a designer and producer of military and commercial aircraft. Electronics, 45% (56%), includes industrial automation controls, avionics, telecommunications and defense electronics products and systems. Automotive, 25% (11%), manufactures components for trucks, buses, trailers, heavy-duty, off-highway vehicles, and passenger cars. Graphics, 6% (3%), manufactures high-speed printing presses and related graphic arts equipment. Government contracts accounted for 35% of sales in 1994.

ANNUAL EARNINGS AND DIVIDENDS PER SHARE

	9/30/94	9/30/93	9/30/92	9/30/91	9/30/90	9/30/89	9/30/88
Earnings Per Share	2.87	2.55	① 2.16	2.57	2.56	2.87	3.04
Dividends Per Share	1.04	0.98	0.92	0.875	0.82	0.765	0.72
Dividend Payout %	36.2	38.4	42.6	34.1	32.0	26.7	23.7

① Before acctg. chg.

ANNUAL FINANCIAL DATA

RECORD OF EARNINGS (IN MILLIONS):

Total Revenues	11,204.7	10,920.9	11,027.1	12,359.2	12,462.5	12,797.4	12,098.6
Costs and Expenses	9,592.9	9,421.8	9,583.2	10,599.2	10,765.9	10,962.5	10,450.3
Depreciation & Amort	493.9	490.9	558.1	601.4	500.3	496.5	493.9
Operating Profit	1,117.9	1,008.2	885.8	1,430.1	1,196.3	1,338.4	1,154.4
Income Bef Income Taxes	1,021.3	904.1	778.4	1,023.5	1,052.0	1,205.7	1,053.0
Income Taxes	387.2	342.2	295.4	423.0	427.7	470.8	241.1
Net Income	634.1	561.9	① 483.0	600.5	624.3	734.9	811.9
Aver. Shs. Outstg. (000)	220,500	219,800	223,600	233,700	244,100	255,605	266,605

① Before acctg. change dr$1,519,000,000.

BALANCE SHEET (IN MILLIONS):

Cash and Cash Equivalents	628.3	772.8	602.6	503.8	411.2	332.4	899.7
Receivables, Net	2,267.2	2,209.1	2,316.9	2,486.4	2,425.7	2,137.2	2,209.0
Inventories	1,532.8	1,430.8	1,445.9	1,387.1	1,619.6	1,574.1	1,526.7
Gross Property	6,160.4	6,018.1	5,988.7	5,887.7	6,006.1	5,575.0	5,527.0
Accumulated Depreciation	3,777.0	3,692.3	3,613.9	3,426.5	3,337.9	2,980.8	2,886.6
Long-Term Debt	831.0	1,028.2	1,035.4	740.3	552.9	552.1	745.3
Net Stockholders' Equity	3,355.6	2,956.0	2,778.0	4,223.7	4,185.9	3,977.6	3,693.0
Total Assets	9,860.8	9,885.1	9,731.0	9,375.5	9,738.1	8,938.8	9,208.5
Total Current Assets	4,927.8	4,946.4	4,889.0	4,823.1	4,775.3	4,366.8	4,924.8
Total Current Liabilities	3,019.8	2,990.9	3,112.2	3,322.0	3,843.4	3,482.2	3,795.9
Net Working Capital	1,908.0	1,955.5	1,776.8	1,501.1	931.9	884.6	1,128.9
Year End Shs Outstg (000)	218,600	221,000	220,300	228,200	238,900	249,800	261,100

STATISTICAL RECORD:

Operating Profit Margin %	10.0	9.2	8.0	9.4	9.6	10.5	9.5
Book Value Per Share	11.79	9.71	8.83	14.46	12.61	11.53	10.10
Return on Equity %	18.9	19.0	17.4	14.2	14.9	18.5	22.0
Return on Assets %	6.4	5.7	5.0	6.4	6.4	8.2	8.8
Average Yield %	2.7	3.0	3.6	3.4	3.3	3.3	3.6
P/E Ratio	15.4-11.7	15.1-10.9	13.6-10.3	11.4-8.9	11.2-8.0	9.5-6.9	7.7-5.3
Price Range	44⅛-33½	38½-27⅝	29⅜-22¼	29¼-22¾	28¾-20½	27⅛-19¾	23½-16⅛

Statistics are as originally reported.

OFFICERS:
D.R. Beall, Chmn. & C.E.O.
K.M. Black, Exec. V.P. & C.O.O.
D.H. Davis, Jr, Exec. V.P. & C.O.O.
W.M. Barnes, Sr. V.P.-Fin. & Plan., & C.F.O.

INCORPORATED: DE, Dec., 1928

PRINCIPAL OFFICE: 2201 Seal Beach Boulevard, Seal Beach, CA 90740-8250

TELEPHONE NUMBER: (310) 797-3311

NO. OF EMPLOYEES: 71,891

ANNUAL MEETING: In February

SHAREHOLDERS: 74,660 common; 57,750, class A common

INSTITUTIONAL HOLDINGS:
No. of Institutions: 572
Shares Held: 77,043,489

REGISTRAR(S): Mellon Bank, N.A., Pittsburgh, PA

TRANSFER AGENT(S): Mellon Bank, N.A., Pittsburgh, PA

ROHM & HAAS CO.

YIELD 2.4%
P/E RATIO 16.0

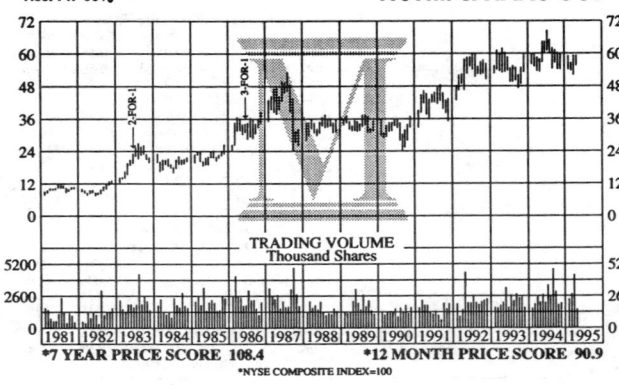

INTERIM EARNINGS (Per Share):

Qtr.	Mar.	June	Sept.	Dec.
1991	0.62	0.79	0.59	0.45
1992	0.89	1.15	0.75	d0.15
1993	0.84	0.90	d0.34	0.35
1994	0.96	1.37	0.78	0.68

INTERIM DIVIDENDS (Per Share):

Amt.	Decl.	Ex.	Rec.	Pay.
0.35Q	5/2/94	5/9/94	5/13/94	6/1/94
0.37Q	7/25	8/1	8/5	9/1
0.37Q	10/13	10/31	11/4	12/1
0.37Q	2/3/95	2/13/95	2/17/95	3/1/95
0.37Q	5/1	5/8	5/12	6/1

Indicated div.: $1.48

CAPITALIZATION (12/31/94):

	($000)	(%)
Long-Term Debt	629,000	26.2
Deferred Income Tax	92,000	3.8
Minority Interest	61,000	2.5
Preferred Stock.................	134,000	5.6
Common & Surplus	1,486,000	61.9
Total	2,402,000	100.0

DIVIDEND ACHIEVER STATUS:
Rank: 193   1984-94 Growth Rate: 9.1%
Total Years of Dividend Growth: 17

TRADING VOLUME
Thousand Shares

1981 1982 1983 1984 1985 1986 1987 1988 1989 1990 1991 1992 1993 1994 1995

*7 YEAR PRICE SCORE 108.4   *12 MONTH PRICE SCORE 90.9

*NYSE COMPOSITE INDEX=100

RECENT DEVELOPMENTS: For the year ended 12/31/94, earnings were $264.0 million compared with $126.0 million, including unusual charges of $74.0 million, in the year before. Sales improved by 8% to $3.53. billion. An initially strong sales growth rate in 1994 for the North American region was tempered as the year progressed. The strength of the chemicals industry worldwide and internal efforts to control costs directly benefited the bottom line.

PROSPECTS: Earnings are benefiting from increased volumes, improved manufacturing operations, and effective cost controls. A stronger European economy has helped as well. However, rising costs for key feedstocks such as propylene, methanol, acetone, ammonia and styrene may depress margins. To compensate for this, the Company will have to raise its own selling prices for certain products.

BUSINESS

ROHM & HAAS CO. is a multinational producer of specialty polymers and biologically active compounds. Products range from basic petrochemicals such as propylene, acetone and styrene to differentiated specialty products. It has developed acrylic plastics, a field which it pioneered with its development of Plexiglas (used in outdoor signs, industrial lighting, skylights, and boat windshields). Other products include polymers, resins and monomers which are geared toward a wide variety of industrial applications. The Company also manufactures agricultural and industrial chemicals. In 1994 polymers, resins and monomers accounted for 47% of total sales; plastics, 18%; performance chemicals, 23%; and agricultural chemicals, 12%.

ANNUAL EARNINGS AND DIVIDENDS PER SHARE

	1994	1993	1992	1991	1990	1989	1988
Earnings Per Share	3.79	1.74	2.53	2.45	3.10	2.65	3.46
Dividends Per Share	1.44	1.36	① 1.28	1.24	1.22	1.16	1.02
Dividend Payout %	38.0	78.2	50.6	50.6	39.4	43.8	29.5
① Bef acctg chge							

ANNUAL FINANCIAL DATA

RECORD OF EARNINGS (IN MILLIONS):

	1994	1993	1992	1991	1990	1989	1988
Total Revenues	3,534.0	3,269.0	3,063.0	2,763.0	2,824.0	2,661.0	2,535.0
Costs and Expenses	2,828.0	2,743.0	2,559.0	2,331.0	2,367.0	2,246.0	2,055.0
Depreciation	231.0	226.0	203.0	183.0	159.0	150.0	128.0
Operating Profit	676.0	505.0	500.0	432.0	476.0	440.0	508.0
Earn Bef Income Taxes	407.0	194.0	261.0	240.0	313.0	251.0	346.0
Income Taxes	143.0	68.0	87.0	77.0	106.0	75.0	116.0
Net Income	264.0	① 126.0	② 174.0	163.0	207.0	176.0	230.0
Aver. Shs. Outstg. (000)	67,707	67,619	66,396	64,103	66,218	66,593	66,561
① Before acctg. change dr$19,000,000. ② Before acctg. change dr$179,000,000.							

BALANCE SHEET (IN MILLIONS):

Cash and Cash Equivalents	127.0	35.0	91.0	208.0	65.0	150.0	223.0
Receivables, Net	679.0	604.0	549.0	473.0	458.0	420.0	394.0
Inventories	487.0	394.0	437.0	343.0	386.0	347.0	340.0
Gross Property	3,969.0	3,696.0	3,470.0	3,015.0	2,770.0	2,396.0	2,062.0
Accumulated Depreciation	2,009.0	1,827.0	1,702.0	1,545.0	1,380.0	1,248.0	1,127.0
Long-Term Debt	629.0	690.0	699.0	718.0	598.0	359.0	288.0
Net Stockholders' Equity	1,620.0	1,441.0	1,428.0	1,231.0	1,233.0	1,311.0	1,207.0
Total Assets	3,861.0	3,524.0	3,445.0	2,897.0	2,702.0	2,455.0	2,242.0
Total Current Assets	1,440.0	1,200.0	1,257.0	1,141.0	1,009.0	1,011.0	1,032.0
Total Current Liabilities	932.0	701.0	713.0	535.0	585.0	577.0	547.0
Net Working Capital	508.0	499.0	544.0	606.0	424.0	434.0	485.0
Year End Shs Outstg (000)	67,692	67,645	67,564	64,156	63,981	66,618	66,541

STATISTICAL RECORD:

Operating Profit Margin %	13.4	9.2	9.8	9.0	10.6	10.0	13.9
Book Value Per Share	21.95	19.29	19.12	19.19	19.27	19.68	18.14
Return on Equity %	16.3	8.7	12.2	13.2	16.8	13.4	19.1
Return on Assets %	6.8	3.6	5.1	5.6	7.7	7.2	10.3
Average Yield %	2.4	2.5	2.5	3.1	4.0	3.4	3.1
P/E Ratio	18.1-14.1	35.6-27.2	23.6-16.9	19.8-13.4	11.9-7.8	14.2-11.7	10.8-8.1
Price Range	68½-53¼	62-47¼	59⅝-42¾	48½-32¾	37-24¼	37½-31	37½-28

Statistics are as originally reported.

OFFICERS:
J.L. Wilson, Chmn. & C.E.O.
J.P. Mulroney, Pres. & C.O.O.
F.W. Shaffer, V.P. & C.F.O.
A.F. Smith, Treas.

INCORPORATED: DE, Apr., 1917

PRINCIPAL OFFICE: 100 Independence Mall West, Philadelphia, PA 19106-2399

TELEPHONE NUMBER: (215) 592-3000

NO. OF EMPLOYEES: 12,000 (approx.)

ANNUAL MEETING: In May

SHAREHOLDERS: 4,889

INSTITUTIONAL HOLDINGS:
No. of Institutions: 393
Shares Held: 48,363,915

REGISTRAR(S): Wachovia Bank of North Carolina, N.A., North Carolina, NC

TRANSFER AGENT(S): Wachovia Bank of North Carolina, N.A., North Carolina, NC

RPM, INC.

YIELD 2.8%
P/E RATIO 19.9

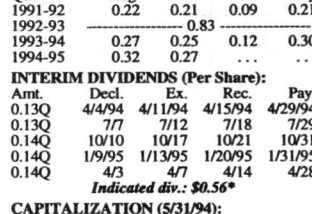

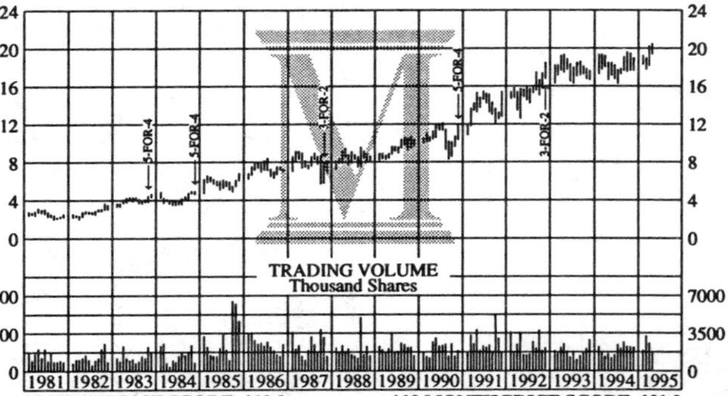

INTERIM EARNINGS (Per Share):

Qtr.	Aug.	Nov.	Feb.	May
1991-92	0.22	0.21	0.09	0.21
1992-93		0.83		
1993-94	0.27	0.25	0.12	0.30
1994-95	0.32	0.27	...	...

INTERIM DIVIDENDS (Per Share):

Amt.	Decl.	Ex.	Rec.	Pay.
0.13Q	4/4/94	4/11/94	4/15/94	4/29/94
0.13Q	7/7	7/12	7/18	7/29
0.14Q	10/10	10/17	10/21	10/31
0.14Q	1/9/95	1/13/95	1/20/95	1/31/95
0.14Q	4/3	4/7	4/14	4/28

Indicated div.: $0.56*

CAPITALIZATION (5/31/94):

	($000)	(%)
Long-Term Debt	233,039	42.6
Common & Surplus	314,476	57.4
Total	547,515	100.0

DIVIDEND ACHIEVER STATUS:
Rank: 103   1984-94 Growth Rate: 12.8%
Total Years of Dividend Growth: 21

RECENT DEVELOPMENTS: For the quarter ended 11/30/94, net income jumped 10% to $15.3 million compared with $13.9 million for the corresponding quarter a year earlier. Earnings per share totaled $0.27 per share, an 8% increase over the prior-year quarter's of $0.25. Sales for the quarter were a record $253.2 million, a 25% increase over the prior-year's sales of $202.2 million. Sales growth was significantly affected by the June 1994 acquisition of Rust-Oleum Corpo-

ration, but did not help the bottom line due to related acquisition costs and the normal seasonality of the business. Earnings for the quarter came from the Company's core operations. For the six months ended 11/30/94, net income totaled $33.7 million, a 15% gain over the prior year's $29.2 million. Sales for the period were $506.7 million, up 23% from $411.6 million in the same period a year earlier.

BUSINESS

RPM, INC. is a widely-diversified manufacturer of protective coatings, marketing products to more than 110 countries and operating 39 plants in the United States, Belgium, Canada and Luxembourg. The Company participates in five broad market categories worldwide: (1) industrial waterproofing and general maintenance; (2) industrial corrosion-control; (3) specialty chemicals; (4) consumer do-it-yourself (D-I-Y); and (5) consumer hobby and leisure. More than 60% of the Company's sales are derived from the three industrial market sectors, with the remainder in consumer products. The vast majority of RPM's specialty coatings, both consumer and industrial, protect existing goods or structures and are generally not affected by cyclical movements in the economy.

QUARTERLY DATA

(5/31/94)($000)	Rev	Inc
1st Quarter	209,347	15,262
2nd Quarter	202,243	13,933
3rd Quarter	186,562	6,565
4th Quarter	217,446	16,880

ANNUAL EARNINGS AND DIVIDENDS PER SHARE

	5/31/94	5/31/93	5/31/92	5/31/91	5/31/90	5/31/89	5/31/88
Earnings Per Share	0.93	0.83	0.73	0.69	0.65	0.57	0.51
Dividends Per Share	0.53	① 0.49	0.423	② 0.373	0.339	0.307	0.267
Dividend Payout %	57.0	59.0	57.7	54.4	51.6	53.2	52.6

① 3-for-2 stk split,12/07/92 ② 5-for-4 stk split, 12/7/90

ANNUAL FINANCIAL DATA

RECORD OF EARNINGS (IN THOUSANDS):

Total Revenues	815,598	625,680	552,092	500,258	444,824	376,117	341,966
Costs and Expenses	688,172	546,118	460,942	427,431	378,198	318,884	289,542
Depreciation & Amort	25,905	21	19,422	14,400	12,199	10,144	9,588
Operating Profit	101,521	79,541	71,729	58,427	54,427	47,089	42,835
Income Bef Income Taxes	88,094	66,100	57,280	51,681	45,006	39,128	35,295
Income Taxes	35,454	26,724	22,769	19,849	17,228	14,790	13,955
Net Income	52,640	39,376	34,466	31,849	27,710	24,243	21,368
Aver. Shs. Outstg.	56,717	47,589	47,112	46,541	43,392	42,283	42,243

BALANCE SHEET (IN THOUSANDS):

Cash and Cash Equivalents	25,399	24,750	27,324	18,604	2,522	6,048	6,449
Receivables, Net	162,256	127,155	116,455	93,838	90,787	68,321	60,636
Inventories	130,487	115,482	110,916	85,741	87,399	71,645	62,933
Gross Property	263,194	221,652	202,065	134,597	129,735	107,126	93,907
Accumulated Depreciation	112,160	87,433	75,779	52,059	48,158	41,008	33,365
Long-Term Debt	233,039	220,942	238,882	114,479	145,170	76,946	75,401
Net Stockholders' Equity	314,476	239,079	221,782	206,281	161,032	147,045	136,436
Total Assets	660,838	584,609	558,936	401,221	375,301	286,185	260,784
Total Current Assets	334,530	280,673	263,032	205,392	185,618	150,127	133,307
Total Current Liabilities	107,536	117,929	90,059	75,680	63,210	56,836	44,398
Net Working Capital	226,994	162,744	172,973	129,712	122,408	93,291	88,909
Year End Shares Outstg	56,751	47,322	47,177	46,562	43,318	42,167	42,041

STATISTICAL RECORD:

Operating Profit Margin %	12.4	12.7	13.0	11.7	12.2	12.5	12.5
Book Value Per Share	3.13	2.12	1.69	2.44	1.41	2.08	1.97
Return on Equity %	16.7	16.5	15.5	15.4	17.2	16.5	15.7
Return on Assets %	8.0	6.7	6.2	7.9	7.4	8.5	8.2
Average Yield %	3.0	3.2	3.2	3.7	3.6	3.6	3.6
P/E Ratio	20.8-17.5	22.3-15.2	21.2-14.9	17.6-12.0	16.3-12.7	16.9-12.7	17.9-11.3
Price Range	19⅜-16¼	18½-12⅝	15½-10⅞	12⅛-8¼	10⅝-8¼	9⅝-7¼	9⅛-5¾

Statistics are as originally reported.

OFFICERS:
T.C. Sullivan, Chmn. & C.E.O.
J.A. Karman, Pres. & C.O.O.
F.C. Sullivan, V.P. & C.F.O.
R.E. Klar, V.P. & Treas.

INCORPORATED: OH, May, 1947

PRINCIPAL OFFICE: 2628 Pearl Road, Medina, OH 44258

TELEPHONE NUMBER: (216) 273-5090

FAX: (216) 225-8743

NO. OF EMPLOYEES: 4,500 approx.

ANNUAL MEETING: In October

SHAREHOLDERS: 25,000 approx.

INSTITUTIONAL HOLDINGS:
No. of Institutions: 183
Shares Held: 21,165,744

REGISTRAR(S): Society National Bank, Cleveland, OH

TRANSFER AGENT(S): Society National Bank, Cleveland, OH

NYS SYMBOL RBD
Rec. Pr. 30¾

RUBBERMAID, INC.

YIELD 1.6%
P/E RATIO 21.4

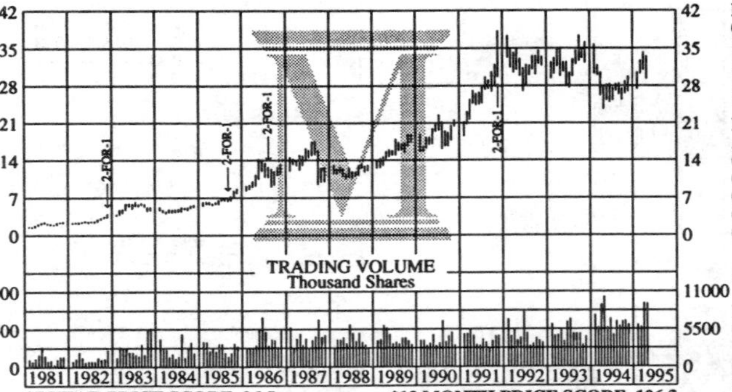

*7 YEAR PRICE SCORE 96.5 *12 MONTH PRICE SCORE 106.3

*NYSE COMPOSITE INDEX=100

INTERIM EARNINGS (Per Share):

Qtr.	Mar.	June	Sept.	Dec.
1992	0.16	0.27	0.33	0.28
1993	0.31	0.32	0.37	0.32
1994	0.32	0.35	0.41	0.34
1995	0.34	...	...	...

INTERIM DIVIDENDS (Per Share):

Amt.	Decl.	Ex.	Rec.	Pay.
0.1125Q	4/26/94	5/9/94	5/13/94	6/1/94
0.1125Q	6/28	8/8	8/12	9/1
0.125Q	10/25	11/4	11/11	12/1
0.125Q	1/12/95	2/6/95	2/10/95	3/1/95
0.125Q	4/25	5/8	5/12	6/1

*Indicated div.: $0.50**

CAPITALIZATION (12/31/94):

	($000)	(%)
Long-Term Debt	11,576	0.9
Common & Surplus	1,285,826	99.1
Total	1,297,402	100.0

DIVIDEND ACHIEVER STATUS:
Rank: 38 1984-94 Growth Rate: 16.8%
Total Years of Dividend Growth: 40

RECENT DEVELOPMENTS: For the twelve months ended 12/31/94, net income increased 7.9% to $228.1 million from $211.4 million in 1993. Net sales for the year were $2.17 billion, an increase of 10.7% over the prior-year amount of $1.96 billion. The strong earnings performance was primarily attributed to volume and productivity improvements, which were partially offset by lower margins resulting from higher plastic resin costs.

PROSPECTS: The integration of several recent acquisitions and the consolidation of Rubbermaid Japan will continue to spur sales and earnings growth. RBD has made progress in improving productivity and controlling expenses, although rising resin costs have somewhat dampened the positive effect of these efforts. The Company is now focused on growth initiatives including the globalization of all of RBD's operating businesses.

BUSINESS

RUBBERMAID, INC. operates in a single line of business, the manufacture and sale of plastic and rubber products for the consumer and institutional markets. The Housewares Products Division manufactures sinkware, home organizers and food storage products. Seasonal products such as outdoor casual furniture, insulated products, and home horticulture are assimilated under the Specialty Products division. The Little Tikes Co. manufactures pre-school toys and furniture. Commercial Products Division designs and manufactures goods for the institutional and industrial markets. The Office Products group develops a wide range of office accessory products.

BUSINESS LINE ANALYSIS

(12/31/94)	Rev(%)	Inc(%)
United States	87.9	92.8
Foreign	12.1	7.2
Total	100.0	100.0

ANNUAL EARNINGS AND DIVIDENDS PER SHARE

	1994	1993	1992	1991	1990	1989	1988
Earnings Per Share	**1.42**	**1.32**	**[1] 1.04**	**1.02**	**0.90**	**0.79**	**0.67**
Dividends Per Share	**0.463**	**0.405**	**0.352**	**[2] 0.31**	**0.27**	**0.23**	**0.19**
Dividend Payout %	**32.6**	**30.7**	**33.8**	**30.4**	**30.0**	**29.1**	**28.1**

[1] Before acctg. chg. [2] 2-for-1 stk split,12/02/91

ANNUAL FINANCIAL DATA

	1994	1993	1992	1991	1990	1989	1988
RECORD OF EARNINGS (IN MILLIONS):							
Total Revenues	2,169.4	1,960.2	1,805.3	1,667.3	1,534.0	1,343.9	1,193.5
Costs and Expenses	1,719.8	1,529.3	1,464.7	1,347.8	1,245.8	1,078.5	975.1
Depreciation & Amort	93.7	85.4	73.8	62.7	55.3	62.7	47.4
Operating Profit	355.9	345.5	294.3	256.8	232.8	202.6	171.0
Earn Bef Income Taxes	367.2	341.9	266.8	262.6	231.3	190.6	159.5
Income Taxes	139.0	130.5	99.9	99.9	87.7	74.1	60.3
Net Income	228.1	211.4	[1] 166.9	162.7	143.5	116.4	99.3
Aver. Shs. Outstg. (000)	160,894	160,318	160,207	160,126	159,688	147,324	147,080
[1] Before acctg. change dr$2,831,000.							
BALANCE SHEET (IN MILLIONS):							
Cash and Cash Equivalents	210.3	260.3	122.5	153.3	77.5	97.2	33.7
Receivables, Net	471.4	322.3	295.0	277.0	302.3	238.4	212.1
Inventories	295.2	303.4	271.9	225.2	216.7	176.5	159.0
Gross Property	1,163.2	1,081.1	960.2	855.5	746.9	670.0	594.0
Accumulated Depreciation	555.6	508.9	443.1	394.1	341.3	303.6	257.8
Long-Term Debt	11.6	19.4	20.3	27.8	39.2	50.3	39.0
Net Stockholders' Equity	1,285.8	1,130.5	987.6	885.7	768.2	598.4	511.4
Total Assets	1,768.2	1,579.4	1,326.6	1,244.5	1,114.2	915.4	781.7
Total Current Assets	985.7	896.0	699.7	664.0	602.6	515.7	407.5
Total Current Liabilities	295.6	259.3	223.2	245.5	235.3	202.4	186.0
Net Working Capital	690.1	636.7	476.4	418.5	367.3	313.2	221.5
Year End Shs Outstg (000)	160,801	160,357	160,239	160,189	159,985	147,328	147,124
STATISTICAL RECORD:							
Operating Profit Margin %	16.4	17.6	14.8	15.4	15.2	15.1	14.3
Book Value Per Share	8.00	7.05	6.16	5.53	4.80	4.06	3.48
Return on Equity %	17.7	18.7	16.9	18.4	18.7	19.5	19.4
Return on Assets %	12.9	13.4	12.6	13.1	12.9	12.7	12.7
Average Yield %	1.6	1.2	1.1	1.1	1.4	1.5	1.6
P/E Ratio	25.2-16.6	28.3-20.9	35.9-26.0	37.5-18.1	25.0-17.2	23.9-15.8	20.1-15.7
Price Range	35¾-23⅝	37⅜-27⅝	37⅜-27	38¼-18½	22½-15½	18⅞-12½	13½-10½

Statistics are as originally reported.

OFFICERS:
W.R. Schmitt, Chmn. & C.E.O.
C.A. Carroll, Pres. & C.O.O.
J.A. Morgan, Sr. V.P., Gen. Couns. & Sec.
G.C. Weigand, Sr. V.P. & C.F.O.

INCORPORATED: OH, Apr., 1920

PRINCIPAL OFFICE: 1147 Akron Rd., Wooster, OH 44691-6000

TELEPHONE NUMBER: (216) 264-6464

FAX: (216) 287-2864

NO. OF EMPLOYEES: 12,939 (avg.)

ANNUAL MEETING: In April

SHAREHOLDERS: 30,889

INSTITUTIONAL HOLDINGS:
No. of Institutions: 489
Shares Held: 74,477,785

REGISTRAR(S): Society National Bank, Cleveland, OH

TRANSFER AGENT(S): Society National Bank, Cleveland, OH

SAFECO CORP.

YIELD 3.7%
P/E RATIO 11.4

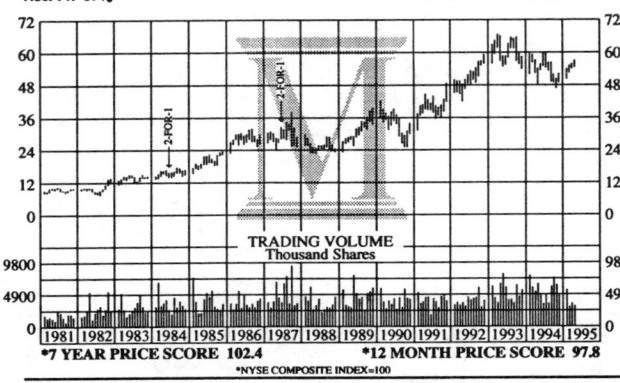

INTERIM EARNINGS (Per Share):

Qtr.	Mar.	June	Sept.	Dec.
1991	0.88	0.82	1.09	1.35
1992	1.35	0.67	1.28	1.66
1993	1.15	2.06	1.49	2.07
1994	0.89	1.43	1.15	1.52

INTERIM DIVIDENDS (Per Share):

Amt.	Decl.	Ex.	Rec.	Pay.
0.49Q	5/4/94	7/1/94	7/8/94	7/25/94
0.49Q	8/3	10/3	10/7	10/24
0.49Q	11/3	12/30	1/6/95	1/23/95
0.49Q	2/1/95	4/3/95	4/7	4/24
0.53Q	5/3	7/5	7/7	7/24

Indicated div.: $2.12

CAPITALIZATION (12/31/94):

	($000)	(%)
Total Debt	982,909	25.6
Deferred Income Tax	35,860	0.9
Common & Surplus	2,829,479	73.5
Total	3,848,248	100.0

DIVIDEND ACHIEVER STATUS:
Rank: 157   1984-94 Growth Rate: 10.4%
Total Years of Dividend Growth: 19

TRADING VOLUME
Thousand Shares

*7 YEAR PRICE SCORE 102.4   *12 MONTH PRICE SCORE 97.8
*NYSE COMPOSITE INDEX=100

RECENT DEVELOPMENTS: For the year ended 12/31/94, net income was $314.4 million compared with $425.9 million the year before, a decrease of 26.2%. Total revenues reached $3.73 billion, a gain of 5.3% over $3.54 billion a year earlier. Realized gains from investments were $25.9 million versus $118.9 million in the previous year. Insurance companies' income fell 16.7% to $206.1 million from $247.5 million in 1993. However, the personal auto line continued strong in 1994 producing an underwriting profit of $42.9 million for the year. Significant increases in earnings from the pension and annuity lines as a result of rising interest rates offset a slight decline in group insurance earnings. For the quarter ended 12/31/94, net income declined 26.5% to $95.8 million from $130.3 million in the corresponding quarter in 1993. Total revenues were $917.6 million, up 3.1% from $889.6 million in the prior-year quarter. The 1994 fourth quarter included a $3.7 million underwriting loss.

BUSINESS

SAFECO CORPORATION is one of the 25 largest diversified financial corporations, with more than 100 offices across the United States and Canada. Its insurance operations include property, casualty, life, health and surety. The Property and Casualty group underwrites personal and commercial lines of insurance covering automobiles, homes, business and related insurance risks. The Surety segment provides bonding services. The Life and Health group provides individual and group coverage, including medical/dental plans, IRA products, Keogh tax-favored universal life, traditional life insurance products and annuities.

REVENUES

(12/31/94)	($000)	(%)
Insurance	2,330,202	65.9
Real Estate	107,315	3.0
Finance	53,851	1.5
Asset Management	15,055	0.4
Net Investment Income	991,610	28.0
Realized Investment Gain	39,040	1.1
Total	3,537,073	100.0

ANNUAL EARNINGS AND DIVIDENDS PER SHARE

	1994	1993	1992	1991	1990	1989	1988
Earnings Per Share	4.99	6.77	4.96	4.14	4.41	4.75	3.59
Dividends Per Share	1.88	1.72	1.56	1.42	1.28	1.14	1.02
Dividend Payout %	37.1	25.4	31.5	34.3	29.0	24.0	28.4

ANNUAL FINANCIAL DATA

RECORD OF EARNINGS (IN MILLIONS):

	1994	1993	1992	1991	1990	1989	1988
Insurance Premiums	2,330.2	2,235.7	2,083.0	1,969.4	1,976.2	1,850.2	2,079.6
Total Interest Income	991.6	951.8	903.0	846.8	764.8	670.0	537.0
Total Revenues	3,537.1	3,516.7	3,294.7	3,148.3	3,043.5	2,807.6	2,872.9
Income Bef Income Taxes	389.7	576.9	403.3	317.3	304.0	375.4	...
Income Taxes	75.4	151.0	92.0	57.7	25.6	75.1	41.8
Gain on Sale Of Securities	...	...	...	35.1	10.7	52.8	36.1
Net Income	314.4	①425.9	311.3	259.6	278.4	300.2	268.6
Aver. Shs. Outstg. (000)	63,207	62,879	62,792	62,739	63,119	63,192	65,450

① Before acctg. change cr$2,877,000.

BALANCE SHEET (IN MILLIONS):

	1994	1993	1992	1991	1990	1989	1988
Cash	63.5	67.8	73.1	60.3	41.4	37.3	28.4
Mktable Eq Secur, At Market Value	855.1	910.3	919.2	864.1	724.5	772.5	674.6
Policy Loans	53.3	50.5	50.5	45.4	41.1	37.9	34.1
Mortgage Loans	419.0	402.1	391.1	369.4	349.0	273.2	239.9
Total Assets	15,901.7	14,807.3	13,391.1	11,907.2	10,552.9	9,278.7	7,732.1
Benefits and Claims	11,276.6	10,328.7	9,366.5	8,217.6	7,185.7	6,028.4	4,856.9
Net Stockholders' Equity	2,829.5	2,774.4	2,448.1	2,221.1	1,975.7	1,850.7	1,570.4
Year End Shs Outstg (000)	62,952	62,932	62,815	62,748	62,722	63,232	63,137

STATISTICAL RECORD:

	1994	1993	1992	1991	1990	1989	1988
Book Value Per Share	44.95	44.09	38.97	35.40	31.50	29.27	24.87
Return on Equity %	11.1	15.4	12.7	11.7	14.1	16.2	17.1
Return on Assets %	2.0	2.9	2.3	2.2	2.6	3.2	3.5
Average Yield %	3.5	2.9	3.1	3.6	3.6	3.6	3.9
P/E Ratio	12.0-9.4	9.9-8.0	12.0-8.5	11.8-7.5	9.6-5.7	8.4-4.9	7.3-5.5
Price Range	59¾-46¾	66¾-53⅞	59⅜-42	48¾-31¼	42⅜-25⅛	39¾-23⅛	30-22¾

Statistics are as originally reported.

OFFICERS:
R.H. Eigsti, Chmn., C.E.O. & Pres.
B.A. Dickey, Exec. V.P. & C.F.O.
R.A. Pierson, Sr. V.P., Contr. & Sec.

INCORPORATED: WA, Jul., 1929

PRINCIPAL OFFICE: SAFECO Plaza, Seattle, WA 98185

TELEPHONE NUMBER: (206) 545-5000
FAX: (206) 543-5363
NO. OF EMPLOYEES: 7,300 (approx.)
ANNUAL MEETING: In May
SHAREHOLDERS: 4,700 (approx.)
INSTITUTIONAL HOLDINGS:
No. of Institutions: 414
Shares Held: 46,182,281

REGISTRAR(S):

TRANSFER AGENT(S): First Chicago Trust Co. of New York, Jersey City, NJ

NYS SYMBOL SAJ
Rec. Pr. 28⅜

ST. JOSEPH LIGHT & POWER CO.

YIELD 6.5%
P/E RATIO 10.1

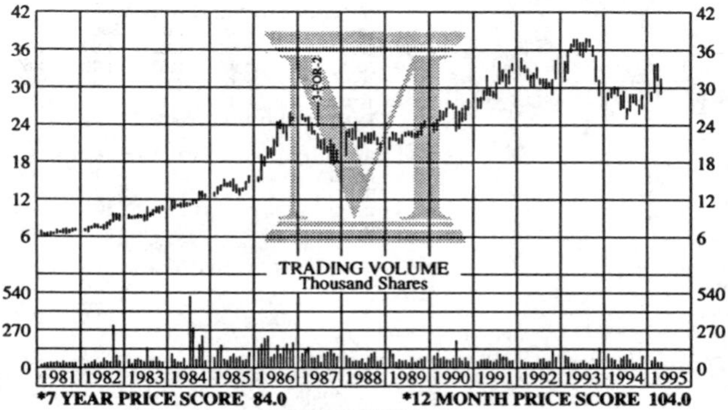

***7 YEAR PRICE SCORE 84.0** ***12 MONTH PRICE SCORE 104.0**

*NYSE COMPOSITE INDEX=100

INTERIM EARNINGS (Per Share):

Qtr.	Mar.	June	Sept.	Dec.
1991	0.61	0.45	0.98	0.40
1992	0.35	0.49	0.84	0.55
1993	0.62	0.45	0.83	0.08
1994	0.50	1.12	0.86	0.33

INTERIM DIVIDENDS (Per Share):

Amt.	Decl.	Ex.	Rec.	Pay.
0.45Q	3/16/94	4/28/94	5/3/94	5/18/94
0.45Q	7/20	7/28	8/3	8/18
0.45Q	9/21	10/28	11/3	11/18
0.46Q	1/18/95	1/30/95	2/3/95	2/17/95
0.46Q	3/15	4/27	5/3	5/18

Indicated div.: $1.84*

CAPITALIZATION (12/31/94):

	($000)	(%)
Long-Term Debt	53,100	32.1
Cap. Lease Oblig.	2,527	1.5
Deferred Income Tax	32,509	19.6
Common & Surplus	77,592	46.8
Total	165,728	100.0
Current Debt	15,403	

DIVIDEND ACHIEVER STATUS:
Rank: 278 1984-94 Growth Rate: 5.3%
Total Years of Dividend Growth: 14

RECENT DEVELOPMENTS: For the year ended 12/31/94, net income was $11.1 million compared with $7.9 million in the corresponding period in 1993. Revenues advanced 3% to $90.8 million versus $88.5 million a year earlier. Operating income increased 27% to $15.5 million compared with $12.2 million in the comparable period of 1993. Earnings were affected by a $5.9 milllion one-time charge to eliminate a regulatory liability established in 1993.

PROSPECTS: Revenues are being affected by the loss of two major industrial customers, which is being offset by growth in retail electric sales and other sales. The rebound in the Company's service area coupled with the rising growth in customers will provide the opportunity to increase revenue growth. Furthermore, the recently awarded $2.15 million annual rate increase will help strengthen earnings growth.

BUSINESS

ST. JOSEPH LIGHT & POWER COMPANY is engaged primarily in the generation, transmission and distribution of electric energy to customers in its ten-county service territory in northwest Missouri. It supplies this service in St. Joseph and 53 other incorporated communities and the intervening rural territory. The service area contains 3,300 square miles. Natural gas for residential, commercial and industrial purposes is provided to customers in Maryville, a town of nearly 10,000, and 14 other smaller communities in northwest Missouri.

BUSINESS LINE ANALYSIS

(12/31/94)	Rev(%)	Inc(%)
Electric	86.9	97.5
Other	13.1	2.5
Total	100.0	100.0

ANNUAL EARNINGS AND DIVIDENDS PER SHARE

	1994	1993	1992	1991	1990	1989	1988
Earnings Per Share	**2.81**	**1.98**	**2.23**	**2.44**	**2.48**	**2.45**	**2.34**
Dividends Per Share	**1.80**	**1.76**	**1.72**	**1.66**	**1.60**	**1.52**	**1.40**
Dividend Payout %	**64.1**	**88.9**	**77.1**	**68.0**	**64.5**	**62.0**	**59.8**

ANNUAL FINANCIAL DATA

	1994	1993	1992	1991	1990	1989	1988
RECORD OF EARNINGS (IN THOUSANDS):							
Total Revenues	90,782	88,539	82,555	89,580	79,752	79,082	76,858
Depreciation	9,834	9,514	9,134	8,735	8,307	7,783	7,361
Maintenance	8,262	8,186	8,170	8,319	8,342	7,807	7,708
Prov for Fed Inc Taxes	5,211	cr1,562	4,358	5,205	5,394	5,426	5,058
Operating Income	15,538	12,248	13,405	14,692	14,201	14,620	14,855
Interest Expense	4,460	4,457	4,681	4,856	4,133	4,409	4,756
Net Income	11,066	7,922	8,958	9,790	10,215	10,678	10,712
Aver. Shs. Outstg.	3,942	4,008	4,019	4,019	4,126	4,351	4,585
BALANCE SHEET (IN THOUSANDS):							
Gross Plant	283,707	276,444	267,153	257,030	245,929	235,021	221,680
Accumulated Depreciation	135,415	131,107	123,729	115,341	106,735	99,293	91,066
Prop, Plant & Equip, Net	148,292	145,337	143,424	141,689	139,194	135,728	130,614
Long-term Debt	55,627	55,642	53,779	53,038	41,261	45,295	48,205
Net Stockholders' Equity	77,592	76,462	75,458	73,819	70,995	72,631	74,129
Total Assets	199,699	180,985	178,743	170,893	165,223	162,743	165,624
Year End Shares Outstg	3,908	4,009	4,005	4,019	4,030	4,241	4,490
STATISTICAL RECORD:							
Book Value Per Share	19.85	19.07	18.84	18.37	17.62	17.13	16.51
Op. Inc/Net Pl %	10.5	8.4	9.3	10.4	10.2	10.8	11.4
Dep/Gr. Pl %	3.5	3.4	3.4	3.4	3.4	3.3	3.3
Accum. Dep/Gr. Pl %	47.7	47.4	46.3	44.9	43.4	42.2	41.1
Return on Equity %	14.3	10.4	11.9	13.3	14.4	14.7	14.5
Average Yield %	6.5	5.3	5.4	5.5	6.3	6.8	6.4
P/E Ratio	10.8-8.9	19.1-14.5	15.6-12.9	14.0-10.9	11.4-9.2	10.1-8.2	10.5-8.1
Price Range	30¼-25	37⅞-28¾	34¾-28⅞	34¼-26⅝	28¼-22¾	24⅝-20	24½-19

Statistics are as originally reported.

OFFICERS:
T.F. Steinbecker, Pres. & C.E.O.
L.J. Stoll, V.P.-Finance, Treas. & Asst. Sec.
G.L. Myers, Gen. Counsel & Sec.

INCORPORATED: MO, Nov., 1895

PRINCIPAL OFFICE: 520 Francis Street P.O. Box 998, St. Joseph, MO 64502-0998

TELEPHONE NUMBER: (816) 233-8888

NO. OF EMPLOYEES: 354 (Approx.)

ANNUAL MEETING: In May

SHAREHOLDERS: 5,452

INSTITUTIONAL HOLDINGS:
No. of Institutions: 48
Shares Held: 948,406

REGISTRAR(S): Harris Trust & Savings Bank, Chicago, IL
Chemical Bank, New York, NY

TRANSFER AGENT(S): Harris Trust & Savings Bank, Chicago, IL
Chemical Bank, New York, NY

SAN DIEGO GAS & ELECTRIC CO.

YIELD 7.3%
P/E RATIO 18.4

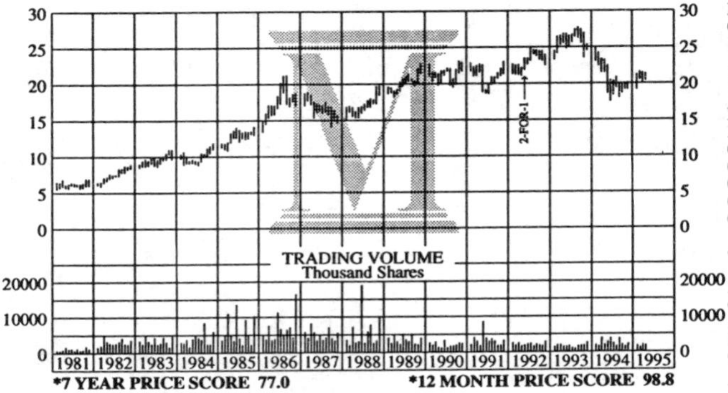

TRADING VOLUME
Thousand Shares

| 1981 | 1982 | 1983 | 1984 | 1985 | 1986 | 1987 | 1988 | 1989 | 1990 | 1991 | 1992 | 1993 | 1994 | 1995 |

*7 YEAR PRICE SCORE 77.0   *12 MONTH PRICE SCORE 98.8

*NYSE COMPOSITE INDEX=100

INTERIM EARNINGS (Per Share):

Qtr.	Mar.	June	Sept.	Dec.
1991	0.45	0.46	0.45	0.40
1992	0.46	0.34	0.46	0.51
1993	0.49	0.36	0.49	0.47
1994	0.50	d0.30	0.50	0.47

INTERIM DIVIDENDS (Per Share):

Amt.	Decl.	Ex.	Rec.	Pay.
0.38Q	3/1/94	3/4/94	3/10/94	4/15/94
0.38Q	5/23	6/6	6/10	7/15
0.38Q	8/22	9/2	9/10	10/15
0.38Q	11/28	12/5	12/10	1/15/95
0.39Q	2/27/95	3/6/95	3/10/95	4/15

Indicated div.: $1.56*

CAPITALIZATION (12/31/94):

	($000)	(%)
Long-Term Debt	1,236,662	34.7
Cap. Lease Oblig.	103,575	2.9
Deferred Income Tax	632,841	17.8
Preferred Stock	118,493	3.3
Common & Surplus	1,474,430	41.3
Total	3,566,001	100.0

DIVIDEND ACHIEVER STATUS:
Rank: 293   1984-94 Growth Rate: 4.1%
Total Years of Dividend Growth: 18

RECENT DEVELOPMENTS: For the year ended 12/31/94, net income was $143.5 million versus $218.7 million in 1993. Revenues were relatively flat at $1.98 billion. The decline in earnings was attributable to a one-time writedown of $80.0 million. For the quarter ended 12/31/94, net income was $57.1 million, up 1% from $56.8 million in the corresponding quarter of 1993. Revenues were down slightly to $523.2 million.

PROSPECTS: SDO will benefit from two recently received rate increases. The California Public Utilities Commission awarded a return on equity of 12.05% from 10.85%, which will increase revenues by $35.7 million. In addition, a performance based program was instituted, which could boost revenues by $48.5 million. The Company's environmental systems subsidiary continues to negatively influence earnings and could possible incur further writedowns.

BUSINESS

SAN DIEGO GAS & ELECTRIC CO. distributes electricity and gas in San Diego County and the southwestern section of Orange County. The Company services a population of about 2.7 million and an electric and gas customer base of 1,129,000 and 690,000 customers, respectively. Major economic factors in the area are education, tourism, manufacturing, and a large concentration of Navy facilities. More than 90% of the Company's revenues come from electric and natural gas sales. The remainder comes from Wahlco Environmental Systems, a subsidiary that markets air pollution controls world wide. SDO also has two other active subsidiaries, Pacific Diversified Capital, an independently-operated holding company, and Califia Company.

BUSINESS LINE ANALYSIS

(12/31/94)	Rev(%)	Inc(%)
Electric	76.2	79.4
Gas	17.5	15.6
Diversified		
Operations	6.3	5.0
Total	100.0	100.0

ANNUAL EARNINGS AND DIVIDENDS PER SHARE

	1994	1993	1992	1991	1990	1989	1988
Earnings Per Share	1.17	1.81	1.77	1.76	1.76	1.58	1.59
Dividends Per Share	1.51	1.47	① 1.43	1.375	1.35	1.338	1.287
Dividend Payout %	N.M.	81.2	80.8	77.9	76.7	84.9	81.0

① 2-for-1 stk split, 5/28/92

ANNUAL FINANCIAL DATA

RECORD OF EARNINGS (IN MILLIONS):

Total Revenues	1,982.0	1,980.1	1,870.9	1,789.0	1,771.9	2,082.5	2,076.1
Deprec & Decommising	265.2	250.6	213.7	195.4	185.9	177.1	172.8
Maintenance	70.8	81.8	73.0	68.1	62.9	67.6	66.5
Income Taxes	150.1	148.5	149.3	130.6	146.4	141.8	118.4
Operating Income	321.9	293.7	296.3	315.5	301.1	280.0	272.2
Interest Expense	105.3	101.3	106.3	106.3	108.7	101.5	102.1
Net Income	143.5	218.7	210.7	208.1	207.8	187.1	189.4
Aver. Shs. Outstg. (000)	116,484	116,049	113,806	111,988	111,842	111,790	111,750

BALANCE SHEET (IN MILLIONS):

Gross Plant	5,329.2	5,134.3	4,818.9	4,823.2	4,594.3	4,383.8	4,159.2
Accumulated Depreciation	2,180.1	2,016.6	1,840.2	1,791.4	1,606.4	1,433.8	1,221.0
Prop, Plant & Equip, Net	3,149.1	3,117.6	2,978.7	3,031.8	2,987.8	2,950.0	2,938.2
Long-term Debt	1,340.2	1,411.9	1,495.7	1,164.2	1,167.1	1,112.7	1,179.5
Net Stockholders' Equity	1,592.9	1,634.7	1,579.8	1,497.2	1,445.8	1,403.1	1,379.9
Total Assets	4,855.8	4,907.9	4,398.5	3,747.6	3,656.6	3,546.5	3,532.7
Year End Shs Outstg (000)	116,537	116,515	115,034	112,496	111,898	111,844	111,796

STATISTICAL RECORD:

Book Value Per Share	12.65	12.55	12.11	11.55	11.22	10.86	10.65
Op. Inc/Net PI %	10.2	9.4	9.9	10.4	10.1	9.5	9.3
Dep/Gr. PI %	5.0	4.9	4.4	4.1	4.0	4.0	4.2
Accum. Dep/Gr. PI %	40.9	39.3	38.2	37.1	35.0	32.7	29.4
Return on Equity %	9.2	13.6	13.9	14.4	14.9	13.9	14.4
Average Yield %	7.2	5.8	6.2	6.6	6.3	6.5	7.4
P/E Ratio	21.4-15.0	15.3-12.8	14.1-11.9	13.1-10.6	13.1-11.1	14.5-11.6	12.4-9.4
Price Range	25-17½	27¾-23¼	25-21⅛	23⅛-18⅝	23⅛-19½	22⅞-18¼	19¾-15

Statistics are as originally reported.

OFFICERS:
T.A. Page, Chmn. & C.E.O.
S.L. Baum, Exec. Vice Pres.
M.K. Malquist, V.P.-Fin. & Treas.

INCORPORATED: CA, Apr., 1905

PRINCIPAL OFFICE: 101 Ash Street, San Diego, CA 92112

TELEPHONE NUMBER: (619) 696-2000
NO. OF EMPLOYEES: 3,998
ANNUAL MEETING: In April
SHAREHOLDERS: 70,356
INSTITUTIONAL HOLDINGS:
No. of Institutions: 152
Shares Held: 19,970,151

REGISTRAR(S): First Interstate Bank of California, Los Angeles, CA

TRANSFER AGENT(S): First Interstate Bank of California, Los Angeles, CA

SARA LEE CORP.

YIELD 2.6%
P/E RATIO 51.0

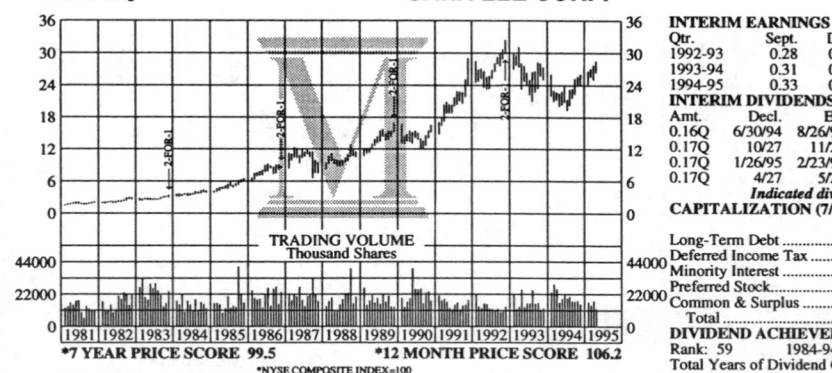

TRADING VOLUME
Thousand Shares

*7 YEAR PRICE SCORE 99.5   *12 MONTH PRICE SCORE 106.2
*NYSE COMPOSITE INDEX=100

INTERIM EARNINGS (Per Share):

Qtr.	Sept.	Dec.	Mar.	June
1992-93	0.28	0.44	0.30	0.38
1993-94	0.31	0.48	0.30	d0.65
1994-95	0.33	0.51	0.33	...

INTERIM DIVIDENDS (Per Share):

Amt.	Decl.	Ex.	Rec.	Pay.
0.16Q	6/30/94	8/26/94	9/1/94	10/1/94
0.17Q	10/27	11/25	12/1	1/1/95
0.17Q	1/26/95	2/23/95	3/1/95	4/1
0.17Q	4/27	5/25	6/1	7/1

*Indicated div.: $0.68**

CAPITALIZATION (7/2/94):

	($000)	(%)
Long-Term Debt	1,496,000	25.1
Deferred Income Tax	290,000	4.9
Minority Interest	520,000	8.7
Preferred Stock	331,000	5.5
Common & Surplus	3,326,000	55.8
Total	5,963,000	100.0

DIVIDEND ACHIEVER STATUS:
Rank: 59   1984-94 Growth Rate: 14.7%
Total Years of Dividend Growth: 18

RECENT DEVELOPMENTS: For the quarter ended 12/31/94, income before an accounting change was $252 million compared with $236 million a year earlier. Net sales increased 15.9% to $4.65 billion. Packaged Meats and Bakery posted a 12.2% increase in operating income on a 14.9% increase in sales. Coffee and Grocery experienced a 29.8% rise in operating income. Personal Products recorded sales and earnings increases of 12.2% and 11.2%, respectively.

PROSPECTS: The restructuring of Sara Lee's hosiery business will continue to be supported by increased sales of higher-margin products. Meanwhile, an expanded collection of Champion T-shirts, combined with the national roll-out of Hanes boxer brief, should contribute to favorable near-term sales and earnings comparisons. Strong growth of SLE's international direct-selling business should boost sales of personal products and insecticides.

BUSINESS

SARA LEE CORP. is a global brand-name foods and consumer products company. Packaged Foods manufactures and markets brand-name food products which includes Hillshire Farm packaged meats, and Sara Lee baked goods in North America, Europe and Australia. This segment, which comprises two lines of business: Packaged Meats and Bakery, and Coffee and Grocery, accounted for 49% of sales (44% of operating income) in fiscal 1994. Packaged Consumer Products, 51% (56%), includes brand-name products such as Hanes, L'eggs, Champion, Kiwi and Playtex. The segment comprises two lines of business: Personal Products and Household and Personal Care.

BUSINESS LINE ANALYSIS

(7/2/94)	Rev(%)	Inc($000)
Packaged Meats & Bakery	35.2	50.3
Coffee & Grocery	13.4	43.4
Personal Products	41.5	(11.2)
Household & Personal Care	9.9	17.5
Total	100.0	100.0

ANNUAL EARNINGS AND DIVIDENDS PER SHARE

	7/2/94	7/3/93	6/27/92	6/29/91	6/30/90	7/1/89	7/2/88
Earnings Per Share	0.44	1.40	1.54	1.08	0.96	0.88	0.71
Dividends Per Share	0.64	0.58	① 0.62	0.47	0.42	0.36	0.30
Dividend Payout %	N.M.	41.4	40.3	43.7	44.0	41.1	42.4

① Incl. $0.12 special div.

ANNUAL FINANCIAL DATA

RECORD OF EARNINGS (IN MILLIONS):

	7/2/94	7/3/93	6/27/92	6/29/91	6/30/90	7/1/89	7/2/88
Total Revenues	15,536.0	14,580.0	13,243.0	12,381.5	11,605.9	11,717.7	10,423.8
Costs and Expenses	13,702.0	12,894.0	11,725.0	11,037.5	10,395.6	10,696.7	9,563.3
Depreciation & Amort	568.0	522.0	472.0	393.8	351.4	279.9	250.9
Operating Profit	5,836.0	5,541.0	4,937.0	4,309.4	3,851.3	3,677.2	3,327.1
Income Bef Income Taxes	389.0	1,082.0	1,174.0	829.5	713.4	639.5	513.3
Income Taxes	155.0	378.0	413.0	294.5	243.1	229.0	188.3
Net Income	① 234.0	704.0	761.0	535.0	470.3	410.5	325.1
Aver. Shs. Outstg. (000)	480,000	485,000	476,000	464,324	460,088	453,580	446,680

① Before acctg. change dr$35,000,000.

BALANCE SHEET (IN MILLIONS):

Cash and Cash Equivalents	189.0	325.0	198.0	124.9	169.4	117.5	178.6
Receivables, Net	1,472.0	1,171.0	1,180.0	946.0	922.2	813.7	717.5
Inventories	2,567.0	2,280.0	2,160.0	1,706.9	1,653.7	1,452.0	1,127.5
Gross Property	5,237.0	4,842.0	4,409.0	3,948.3	3,611.4	2,887.2	2,484.6
Accumulated Depreciation	2,337.0	1,964.0	1,836.0	1,559.2	1,407.2	1,114.2	1,067.9
Long-Term Debt	1,496.0	1,164.0	1,389.0	1,399.1	1,523.9	1,488.2	...
Net Stockholders' Equity	3,657.0	3,908.0	3,733.0	2,894.7	2,629.5	2,097.4	1,800.1
Total Assets	11,665.0	10,862.0	9,989.0	8,122.0	7,636.4	6,522.7	5,012.1
Total Current Assets	4,469.0	3,976.0	3,695.0	2,919.9	2,868.3	2,499.7	2,088.9
Total Current Liabilities	4,919.0	4,269.0	3,300.0	2,526.7	2,482.7	2,275.4	1,806.2
Net Working Capital	d450.0	d293.0	395.0	393.2	385.5	224.3	282.7
Year End Shs Outstg (000)	480,765	485,378	479,725	465,368	460,678	454,669	444,234

STATISTICAL RECORD:

Operating Profit Margin %	8.1	8.0	7.9	7.7	7.4	6.3	5.8
Return on Equity %	7.0	19.7	22.4	20.9	20.5	21.4	20.6
Return on Assets %	2.0	6.5	7.6	6.6	6.2	6.3	6.5
Average Yield %	2.8	2.2	2.2	2.1	2.9	2.6	2.8
P/E Ratio	59.1-44.0	22.2-15.0	21.1-15.2	27.0-13.8	17.4-12.6	19.2-12.2	18.1-11.6
Price Range	26-19⅜	31⅛-21	32½-23⅜	29⅛-14⅞	16¾-12⅛	16⅞-10¾	12⅞-8¼

Statistics are as originally reported.

OFFICERS:
J.H. Bryan, Chmn. & C.E.O.
M.E. Murphy, Vice Chmn., C.F.O. & C.A.O.
J. Langford Kelly, Sr. V.P., Sec. & Gen. Counsel
M.M. Culhane, V.P.-Fin. & Treas.
INCORPORATED: MD, Sep., 1941
PRINCIPAL OFFICE: Three First National Plaza, Chicago, IL 60602-4260

TELEPHONE NUMBER: (312) 726-2600

NO. OF EMPLOYEES: 145,900 (approx.)

ANNUAL MEETING: In October

SHAREHOLDERS: 96,470

INSTITUTIONAL HOLDINGS:
No. of Institutions: 646
Shares Held: 226,300,526

REGISTRAR(S): At Company's Office

TRANSFER AGENT(S): At Company's Office

NYS SYMBOL SBC
Rec. Pr. 44¾

SBC COMMUNICATIONS, INC.

YIELD 3.7%
P/E RATIO 16.0

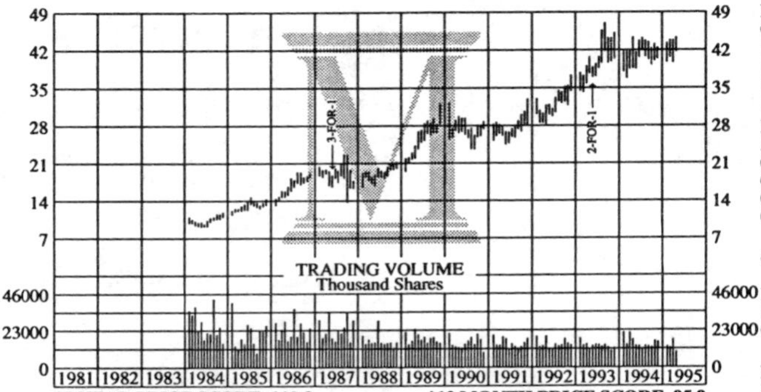

49
42
35
28
21
14
7
3-FOR-1
2-FOR-1
TRADING VOLUME
Thousand Shares
46000
23000
0
1981 1982 1983 1984 1985 1986 1987 1988 1989 1990 1991 1992 1993 1994 1995

***7 YEAR PRICE SCORE 110.3** ***12 MONTH PRICE SCORE 95.9**

*NYSE COMPOSITE INDEX=100

INTERIM EARNINGS (Per Share):

Qtr.	Mar.	June	Sept.	Dec.
1992	0.44	0.50	0.64	0.59
1993	0.50	0.56	0.69	0.64
1994	0.59	0.64	0.80	0.71
1995	0.65	...	...	...

INTERIM DIVIDENDS (Per Share):

Amt.	Decl.	Ex.	Rec.	Pay.
0.395Q	6/24/94	7/1/94	7/10/94	8/1/94
0.395Q	9/30	10/4	10/11	11/1
0.395Q	12/16	1/4/95	1/10/95	2/1/95
0.4125Q	3/31/95	4/4	4/10	5/1

Indicated div.: $1.65*

CAPITALIZATION (12/31/94):

	($000)	(%)
Long-Term Debt	5,848,300	34.6
Deferred Income Tax	2,689,500	15.9
Common & Surplus	8,355,600	49.5
Total	16,893,400	100.0

DIVIDEND ACHIEVER STATUS:
Rank: 202 1984-94 Growth Rate: 8.4%
Total Years of Dividend Growth: 10

RECENT DEVELOPMENTS: For the year ended 12/31/94, net income was $1.65 billion compared with $1.44 billion, before extraordinary charges and accounting adjustments, in 1993. Revenues rose 8.7% to $11.62 billion. SBC added 467,000 access lines and 636,000 cellular customers in 1994. Telephone results benefited from the introduction of new services. Yellow Pages classified advertising revenues grew 7.4%.

PROSPECTS: Growth prospects are positive. New services being introduced by the Telephone Company are being well received. Long-term growth will benefit from SBC's continued expansion into international ventures. SBC acquired a 10% ownership of SFR, France's second national cellular company. SBC was also selected as a partner in a consortium that will design, build and operate a second nationwide cellular network in South Korea.

BUSINESS

SBC COMMUNICATIONS, INC. (formerly Southwestern Bell) is one of seven regional holding companies divested by AT&T. SBC owns 10.2% of the assets of the former AT&T. SBC's subsidiary, Southwestern Bell Telephone Co., is engaged in furnishing communications services in Arkansas, Kansas, Missouri, Oklahoma, and Texas. Other subsidiaries are Southwestern Bell Mobile Systems, Southwestern Bell Telecom, Inc., Southwestern Bell Publications, Inc., Metromedia Paging Services and Gulf Printing Co. Revenue breakdown in 1994 was: local service, 50%; access charges, 25%; long-distance, 8%; directory advertising, 8%; and other, 9%.

ANNUAL EARNINGS AND DIVIDENDS PER SHARE

	1994	1993	1992	1991	1990	1989	1988
Earnings Per Share	**2.74**	**2.39**	**2.17**	**[2] 1.92**	**1.84**	**1.82**	**1.77**
Dividends Per Share	**1.56**	**[1] 1.498**	**1.45**	**1.41**	**1.36**	**1.285**	**1.22**
Dividend Payout %	**56.9**	**62.7**	**66.8**	**73.2**	**74.1**	**70.6**	**69.1**

[1] 2-for-1 stk split,05/26/93 [2] Before extraord. item

ANNUAL FINANCIAL DATA

	1994	1993	1992	1991	1990	1989	1988
RECORD OF EARNINGS (IN MILLIONS):							
Total Revenues	15,392.6	14,353.0	13,574.9	12,799.3	12,808.4	12,439.8	12,150.7
Costs and Expenses	6,790.4	6,303.7	5,975.8	5,433.3	5,369.9	4,825.3	4,651.1
Depreciation & Amort	2,037.8	2,007.0	1,842.2	1,765.0	1,691.1	1,891.4	1,844.5
Operating Income	2,790.3	2,379.6	2,197.4	2,133.6	2,051.9	2,013.1	1,957.1
Income Bef Income Taxes	2,433.8	2,060.2	1,869.7	1,644.2	1,541.0	1,479.5	1,410.1
Income Taxes	785.1	625.0	568.0	487.7	439.6	386.7	350.0
Net Income	1,648.7	[1] 1,435.2	1,301.7	[2] 1,156.5	1,101.4	1,092.8	1,060.1
Aver. Shs. Outstg. (000)	601,400	599,800	600,200	600,300	600,800	601,200	601,000

[1] Before extra. item dr$153,200,000. [2] Before extra. item dr$80,700,000.

	1994	1993	1992	1991	1990	1989	1988
BALANCE SHEET (IN MILLIONS):							
Cash and Cash Equivalents	364.6	618.4	505.2	327.5	250.2	263.3	206.8
Receivables, Net	2,385.3	2,252.2	2,016.1	1,872.4	1,819.1	1,783.3	1,557.0
Inventories	141.8	148.9	130.1	86.5	94.4	127.6	176.9
Gross Property	29,256.4	28,170.6	26,978.4	25,755.4	24,670.3	24,528.5	23,650.8
Accumulated Depreciation	11,939.8	11,079.1	10,079.0	9,245.1	8,348.0	8,450.6	7,347.1
Long-Term Debt	5,848.3	5,459.4	5,716.1	5,675.4	5,483.1	5,455.7	5,039.2
Net Stockholders' Equity	8,355.6	7,608.6	9,304.3	8,859.2	8,581.2	8,366.5	8,504.2
Total Assets	26,005.3	24,307.5	23,810.0	23,179.4	22,195.5	21,160.5	20,985.1
Total Current Assets	3,493.3	3,619.8	3,203.1	2,723.9	2,686.0	2,493.8	2,330.4
Total Current Liabilities	5,190.8	4,488.5	4,132.4	4,094.2	3,605.0	2,818.5	3,008.0
Net Working Capital	d1,697.5	d868.7	d929.3	d1,370.3	d919.0	d324.7	d677.6
Year End Shs Outstg (000)	609,082	600,234	599,747	600,316	599,739	601,166	600,828
STATISTICAL RECORD:							
Book Value Per Share	9.37	10.76	13.31	12.49	12.25	11.84	12.02
Return on Equity %	19.7	18.9	14.0	13.1	12.8	13.1	12.5
Average Yield %	3.8	4.0	4.4	4.9	4.9	5.0	6.4
P/E Ratio	16.2-13.4	17.2-14.3	17.2-13.1	17.1-12.7	17.6-12.8	17.7-10.7	12.1-9.3
Price Range	44⅜-36¾	41-34¼	37⅜-28⅜	33-24½	32⅜-23⅝	32¼-19½	21⅜-16½

Statistics are as originally reported.

OFFICERS:
E.E. Whitacre, Jr., Chmn. & C.E.O.
D.E. Kiernan, Sr. V.P., Treas. & C.F.O.
J. Sahm, Secretary
S. Fox, Investor Contact

INCORPORATED: DE, 1983

PRINCIPAL OFFICE: P.O. Box 2933, San Antonio, TX

TELEPHONE NUMBER: (210) 821-4105

NO. OF EMPLOYEES: 58,750

ANNUAL MEETING: In April

SHAREHOLDERS: 963,355

INSTITUTIONAL HOLDINGS:
No. of Institutions: 979
Shares Held: 220,260,414

REGISTRAR(S): Bank of New York, New York, NY

TRANSFER AGENT(S): Bank of New York, New York, NY

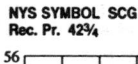

NYS SYMBOL SCG
Rec. Pr. 42¾

SCANA CORP.

YIELD 3.4%
P/E RATIO 13.4

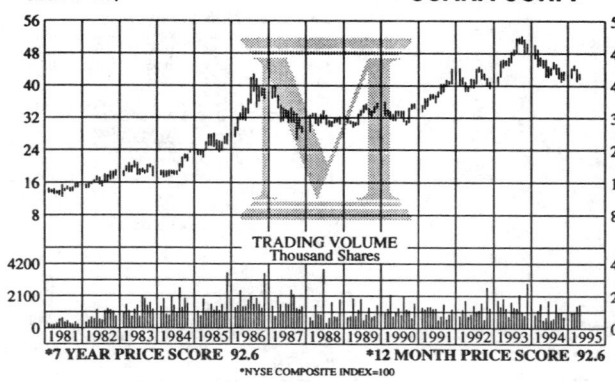

56
48
40
32
24
16
8
TRADING VOLUME
Thousand Shares
4200
2100
0
1981 1982 1983 1984 1985 1986 1987 1988 1989 1990 1991 1992 1993 1994 1995

*7 YEAR PRICE SCORE 92.6 *12 MONTH PRICE SCORE 92.6

*NYSE COMPOSITE INDEX=100

INTERIM EARNINGS (Per Share):

Qtr.	Mar.	June	Sept.	Dec.
1991	0.94	0.60	1.25	0.58
1992	0.83	0.41	0.96	0.64
1993	1.02	0.61	1.41	0.68
1994	1.07	0.62	1.04	0.46

INTERIM DIVIDENDS (Per Share):

Amt.	Decl.	Ex.	Rec.	Pay.
0.705Q	8/24/94	9/2/94	9/9/94	10/1/94
0.705Q	10/18	12/5	12/9	1/1/95
0.72Q	2/14/95	3/6/95	3/10/95	4/1
2-for-1	4/27	5/26	5/11	5/25
0.36Q	4/27	6/6	6/9	7/1

*Indicated div.: $1.44**

CAPITALIZATION (12/31/94):

	($000)	(%)
Long-Term Debt	1,537,624	41.5
Deferred Income Tax	680,375	18.4
Preferred Stock	75,555	2.0
Common & Surplus	1,410,438	38.1
Total	3,703,992	100.0
Current Debt	223,500	

DIVIDEND ACHIEVER STATUS:

Rank: 315 1984-94 Growth Rate: 3.2%

Total Years of Dividend Growth: 43

RECENT DEVELOPMENTS: For the quarter ended 12/31/94, net income dropped 30% to $22.2 million compared with $31.5 million in the corresponding period of 1993. Revenues increased to $317.4 million versus $302.5 million a year earlier. Results were affected by SCANA Petroleum Resources losses' widening. Otherwise, higher gas margins and lower maintenance expenses more than offset higher fixed expenses and a lower electric margin.

PROSPECTS: Industrial and commercial electric sales are leading the Company's earnings growth higher, reflecting a stronger economy. The Public Service Commission (PSC) awarded an increase in the gas cost component of SCG's firm gas rates from $0.471 to $0.51058 per therm. In addition, the State Consumer Advocate unseccessfully attempted to lower the Company's ROE since the weather normalization adjustment was left in place.

BUSINESS

SCANA CORP. is a holding company for South Carolina Electric & Gas (SCE&G) which provides electricity (73.8% of revenues) and natural gas (25.9%) in central and southern South Carolina. SCANA has 11 other direct subsidiaries and 1 indirect subsidiary. Natural gas pipeline operations fall under South Carolina Pipeline Corp., another subsidiary of SCANA Corp. SCG's natural gas service area covers more than 80% of South Carolina. Electric generating capacity is over 3,800 megawatts with the fuel mix comprised of 68% coal, 21% nuclear, and 11% hydro and other. Other subsidiaries (0.3%) are engaged in oil and natural gas production, propane operations, real estate, digital telecommunications services, power plant operations maintenance and natural gas marketing.

ANNUAL EARNINGS AND DIVIDENDS PER SHARE

	1994	1993	1992	1991	1990	1989	1988
Earnings Per Share	**3.19**	**3.72**	**2.84**	**3.37**	**4.44**	**3.04**	**3.00**
Dividends Per Share	**2.82**	**2.725**	**2.665**	**2.595**	**2.505**	**2.445**	**2.38**
Dividend Payout %	**88.4**	**73.3**	**93.8**	**77.0**	**56.4**	**80.4**	**79.3**

Note: 2-for-1stk.split,5/25/95.

ANNUAL FINANCIAL DATA

	1994	1993	1992	1991	1990	1989	1988
RECORD OF EARNINGS (IN MILLIONS):							
Total Revenues	1,322.1	1,264.2	1,138.4	1,147.8	1,133.2	1,123.3	1,083.3
Depreciation & Amort	210.9	158.0	126.7	102.7	97.1	102.3	97.4
Maintenance	63.7	67.7	65.4	61.6	67.5	69.3	54.1
Prov for Fed Inc Taxes	94.5	90.0	60.9	77.6	77.4	65.5	69.0
Operating Income	259.6	245.3	209.8	222.4	226.0	213.2	204.7
Interest Expense	108.4	101.2	97.6	91.5	92.3	90.4	80.1
Net Income	151.2	168.0	117.6	135.9	181.6	122.6	120.7
Aver. Shs. Outstg. (000)	47,381	45,203	41,475	40,361	40,882	40,296	40,296
BALANCE SHEET (IN MILLIONS):							
Gross Plant	4,627.0	4,263.8	4,003.2	3,788.9	3,586.9	3,400.4	3,257.7
Accumulated Depreciation	1,333.4	1,259.7	1,192.9	1,124.3	1,037.1	956.1	873.1
Prop, Plant & Equip, Net	3,293.7	3,004.1	2,810.3	2,664.7	2,549.8	2,444.3	2,384.6
Long-term Debt	1,537.6	1,424.4	1,204.8	1,122.4	938.9	1,004.0	885.7
Net Stockholders' Equity	1,486.0	1,411.9	1,244.1	1,116.9	1,094.4	1,012.3	999.0
Total Assets	4,393.1	4,040.5	3,557.7	3,305.9	3,144.9	2,984.5	2,887.3
Year End Shs Outstg (000)	48,018	46,619	43,911	40,784	40,882	40,296	40,296
STATISTICAL RECORD:							
Book Value Per Share	29.37	28.59	26.46	25.23	24.56	22.79	22.23
Op. Inc/Net Pl %	7.9	8.2	7.5	8.3	8.9	8.7	8.6
Dep/Gr. Pl %	2.6	2.6	2.7	2.7	2.7	3.0	3.0
Accum. Dep/Gr. Pl %	28.8	29.5	29.8	29.7	28.9	28.1	26.8
Return on Equity %	10.5	12.4	9.9	12.9	17.6	13.0	13.1
Average Yield %	6.3	5.9	6.4	6.7	7.6	7.5	7.6
P/E Ratio	15.7-12.9	14.0-10.8	15.8-13.6	13.1-9.9	8.1-6.8	11.8-9.7	11.3-9.5
Price Range	50⅛-41	52¼-40⅛	44¾-38⅝	44¼-33½	35⅞-30¼	35¾-29⅝	33¾-28½

Statistics are as originally reported.

OFFICERS:
L.M. Gressette, Jr., Chmn., Pres. & C.E.O.
W.B. Timmerman, Exec. V.P.- Contr. & C.F.O.
K.B. Marsh, V.P.-Fin., Treas. & Sec.

INCORPORATED: SC, Oct., 1984

PRINCIPAL OFFICE: Palmetto Center 1426 Main Street, Columbia, SC 29201

TELEPHONE NUMBER: (803) 748-3000

NO. OF EMPLOYEES: 4,575

ANNUAL MEETING: In April

SHAREHOLDERS: 39,516

INSTITUTIONAL HOLDINGS:
No. of Institutions: 227
Shares Held: 20,638,160

REGISTRAR(S): Company Office

TRANSFER AGENT(S): Company Office

NYS SYMBOL SVM
Rec. Pr. 25⅛

SERVICEMASTER L.P.

YIELD 3.8%
P/E RATIO 13.9

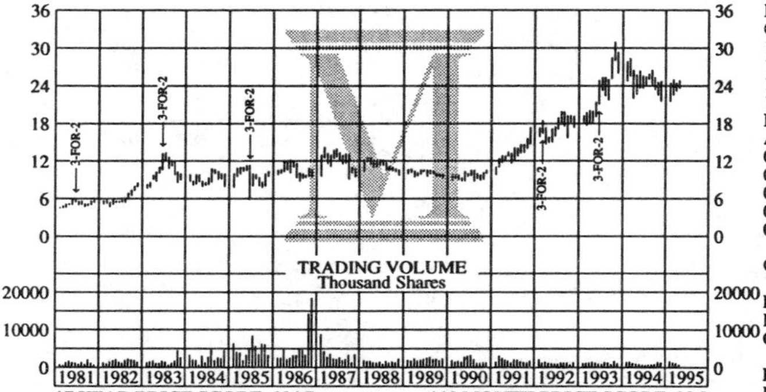

***7 YEAR PRICE SCORE 124.7** ***12 MONTH PRICE SCORE 93.8**

*NYSE COMPOSITE INDEX=100

INTERIM EARNINGS (Per Share):

Qtr.	Mar.	June	Sept.	Dec.
1992	0.16	0.79	0.33	0.32
1993	0.28	0.81	0.41	0.40
1994	0.32	0.52	0.49	0.48
1995	0.37	...	...	...

INTERIM DIVIDENDS (Per Share):

Amt.	Decl.	Ex.	Rec.	Pay.
0.23Q	4/29/94	7/11/94	7/15/94	7/31/94
0.23Q	10/10	10/14	10/20	10/31
0.23Q	12/12	1/9/95	1/13/95	1/31/95
0.24Q	3/17/95	4/7	4/14	4/30
0.24Q	5/5	7/12	7/14	7/31

*Indicated div.: $0.96**

CAPITALIZATION (12/31/94):

	($000)	(%)
Long-Term Debt	386,511	46.6
Minority Interest	135,272	16.3
Common & Surplus	307,266	37.1
Total	829,049	100.0

DIVIDEND ACHIEVER STATUS:
Rank: 229 1984-94 Growth Rate: 7.5%
Total Years of Dividend Growth: 24

RECENT DEVELOPMENTS: Net income for the year ended 12/31/94, rose 20.9% to $139.9 million from $115.7 million a year earlier. Results for 1993 are before a gain on the issuance of subsidiary shares totaling $30.2 million. Operating revenues were $2.99 billion compared with $2.76 billion the year before, an increase of 8.2%. For the quarter ended 12/31/94, net income was $36.8 million, up 18.8% from $31.0 million in the corresponding 1993 quarter.

PROSPECTS: The consumer services segment is benefiting from quality service delivery, innovative marketing and strong management and cost controls. The diversified health services segment continues to achieve excellent growth in revenue and profits. Profits for management services declined slightly; however, the education market is providing for strong growth opportunities that should benefit results for this segment.

BUSINESS

SERVICEMASTER LIMITED PARTNERSHIP, the parent for The ServiceMaster Company, Terminix, TruGreen-ChemLawn, Merry Maids, and American Home Shield, consists of two major segments. ServiceMaster Management Services provides facility management services for more than 2,000 healthcare, education, industrial and commercial customers. These services include: housekeeping, maintenance, food service, laundry and linen care, grounds and landscaping. ServiceMaster Consumer Services includes 5 market-leading companies operating a network of more than 5,700 company-owned and independent franchises worldwide. Services include carpet and upholstery cleaning, janitorial, termite and pest control services, lawn care, maid service, radon testing and warranty plans.

BUSINESS LINE ANALYSIS

(12/31/94)	Rev(%)	Inc(%)
Management Services	61.1	30.8
Consumer Services	34.9	58.3
Intl & New Bus & Parent	4.0	10.9
Total	100.0	100.0

ANNUAL EARNINGS AND DIVIDENDS PER SHARE

	1994	1993	1992	1991	1990	1989	1988
Earnings Per Share	**1.81**	**1.90**	**1.61**	**1.19**	**1.17**	**0.93**	**0.90**
Dividends Per Share	**0.92**	**[1] 0.89**	**[2] 0.867**	**0.845**	**0.822**	**0.782**	**0.747**
Dividend Payout %	**50.8**	**46.8**	**53.7**	**71.2**	**70.6**	**83.8**	**83.2**

[1] 3-for-2 stk split, 06/23/93 [2] 3-for-2 stk split, 2/3/92

ANNUAL FINANCIAL DATA

	1994	1993	1992	1991	1990	1989	1988
RECORD OF EARNINGS (IN MILLIONS):							
Total Revenues	2,985.2	2,758.9	2,488.9	2,109.9	1,825.8	1,609.3	1,531.3
Costs and Expenses	2,717.0	2,535.9	2,380.1	1,950.3	1,700.1	1,492.9	1,424.1
Depreciation & Amort	54.2	50.0	46.3	38.2	29.9	23.6	21.7
Operating Income	214.0	173.0	62.4	121.4	95.8	92.8	85.5
Income Bef Income Taxes	142.6	148.1	130.8	87.4	85.4	68.8	67.4
Income Taxes	2.8	2.1	1.2	1.4	2.3	0.7	...
Net Income	139.9	145.9	[1] 129.6	86.0	83.1	68.0	64.6
Aver. Shs. Outstg. (000)	77,438	76,846	75,688	72,557	71,206	72,957	71,858
[1] Before acctg. change dr$7,500,000.							
BALANCE SHEET (IN MILLIONS):							
Cash and Cash Equivalents	34.4	32.7	41.6	43.1	68.5	73.3	76.4
Receivables, Net	211.7	173.3	140.9	115.4	114.6	105.9	91.1
Inventories	36.1	37.9	36.3	26.3	23.4	19.3	18.8
Gross Property	260.2	226.5	204.5	158.3	151.6	111.7	96.0
Accumulated Depreciation	131.7	110.7	93.2	75.2	62.5	54.9	44.6
Long-Term Debt	386.5	384.5	426.9	334.7	341.8	389.2	280.0
Net Stockholders' Equity	307.3	289.2	209.7	122.0	96.0	39.1	51.4
Total Assets	1,230.8	1,122.5	1,000.1	843.7	796.9	593.7	498.5
Total Current Assets	331.0	291.3	254.4	217.5	237.3	231.3	202.2
Total Current Liabilities	304.4	239.6	203.7	157.5	158.0	138.1	81.2
Net Working Capital	26.7	51.7	50.8	60.1	79.2	93.2	121.0
Year End Shs Outstg (000)	76,022	76,426	75,774	72,717	71,982	68,265	70,212
STATISTICAL RECORD:							
Operating Profit Margin %	7.2	6.3	2.5	5.8	5.2	5.8	5.6
Return on Equity %	45.5	50.5	61.8	70.5	86.5	N.M.	N.M.
Return on Assets %	11.4	13.0	13.0	10.2	10.4	11.5	13.0
Average Yield %	3.7	3.7	5.0	6.2	8.5	7.8	6.7
P/E Ratio	15.7-11.9	16.3-9.3	12.3-9.1	14.6-8.2	9.0-7.5	11.6-9.9	14.0-10.8
Price Range	28⅜-21½	31-17⅝	19⅞-14⅝	17⅜-9¾	10½-8¾	10¾-9¼	12⅝-9¾

Statistics are as originally reported.

OFFICERS:
C.W. Pollard, Chmn.
C.H. Cantu, Pres. & C.E.O. E.J. Mrozek, Sr. V.P. & C.F.O.
S.D. Krause, V.P. & Corp. Sec.

INCORPORATED: DE, Oct., 1986

PRINCIPAL OFFICE: One ServiceMaster Way, Downers Grove, IL 60515

TELEPHONE NUMBER: (708) 271-1300

NO. OF EMPLOYEES: 34,000

ANNUAL MEETING: In April

SHAREHOLDERS: 65,000 (approx.)

INSTITUTIONAL HOLDINGS:
No. of Institutions: 139
Shares Held: 10,448,416

REGISTRAR(S): Harris Trust & Savings Bank, Chicago, IL

TRANSFER AGENT(S): Harris Trust & Savings Bank, Chicago, IL

NYS SYMBOL SHW
Rec. Pr. 36½

SHERWIN-WILLIAMS CO.

YIELD 1.8%
P/E RATIO 16.9

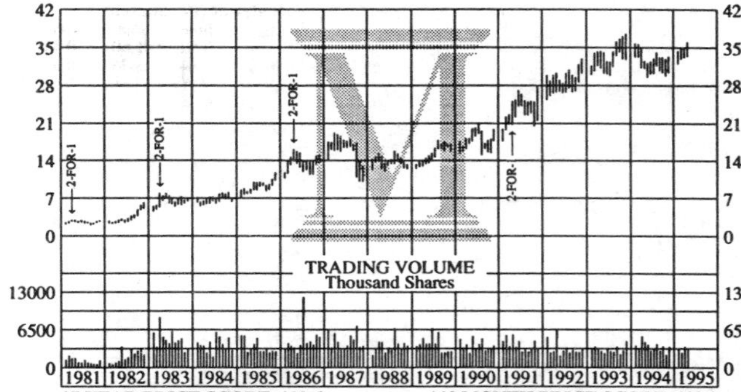

*7 YEAR PRICE SCORE 110.6 *12 MONTH PRICE SCORE 100.2

*NYSE COMPOSITE INDEX=100

INTERIM EARNINGS (Per Share):

Qtr.	Mar.	June	Sept.	Dec.
1991	0.09	0.54	0.57	0.26
1992	0.13	0.60	0.63	0.26
1993	0.15	0.68	0.72	0.30
1994	0.17	0.80	0.83	0.36

INTERIM DIVIDENDS (Per Share):

Amt.	Decl.	Ex.	Rec.	Pay.
0.14Q	4/27/94	5/23/94	5/27/94	6/10/94
0.14Q	7/20	8/22	8/26	9/9
0.14Q	10/19	11/14	11/18	12/2
0.16Q	2/15/95	2/21/95	2/27/95	3/13/95
0.16Q	4/26	5/22	5/26	6/9

*Indicated div.: $0.64**

CAPITALIZATION (12/31/94):

	($000)	(%)
Long-Term Debt	20,465	1.9
Common & Surplus	1,053,344	98.1
Total	1,073,809	100.0

DIVIDEND ACHIEVER STATUS:
Rank: 130 1984-94 Growth Rate: 11.4%
Total Years of Dividend Growth: 15

RECENT DEVELOPMENTS: For the twelve months ended 12/31/94, net income increased 12.9% to $186.6 million from $165.2 million in 1993. Revenues for the year were up 5.1% to $3.10 billion, compared with $2.95 billion the previous year. Operating profit in the Paint Stores segment climbed 20.3% to $140.6 million on a sales increase of 8.5% to $1.99 billion. Comparable-store sales grew 7.8%. The Coatings segment's operating income increased by 3.4% despite a slight decline in sales to $1.10 billion.

PROSPECTS: Sales in the Coatings segment are falling behind as major customers continue adjusting their inventories. However, improved manufacturing and distribution efficiencies and stable raw material costs are offsetting the effect of lower sales in the Consumer Brands division. Profitability in the Paint Stores segment continues to improve due to a more favorable product mix and market share gains. SHW is confident that it can offset future increases in raw material costs with selected price increases.

BUSINESS

SHERWIN-WILLIAMS is engaged in the manufacture and distribution of coatings and related products. SHW sells Sherwin-Williams labeled architectural coatings, industrial maintenance products, industrial finishes, and other associated products and tools through 2,030 company-operated paint and wallcovering stores in 48 states and Canada. Other products include paint, wallcoverings, floorcoverings, window treatments and spray equipment. SHW also manufactures and sells coatings such as Dutch Boy, Martin-Senour, Kem-Tone, Dupli-Color, and Krylon, plus private label brands to independent dealers, mass merchandisers, and home improvement centers.

BUSINESS LINE ANALYSIS

(12/31/94)	Rev(%)	Inc(%)
Paint Stores	64.1	40.3
Coatings	35.5	57.4
Other	0.4	2.3
Total	100.0	100.0

ANNUAL EARNINGS AND DIVIDENDS PER SHARE

	1994	1993	1992	1991	1990	1989	1988
Earnings Per Share	**2.15**	**1.85**	**① 1.63**	**1.45**	**1.41**	**1.26**	**1.15**
Dividends Per Share	**0.56**	**0.50**	**0.44**	**② 0.42**	**0.38**	**0.35**	**0.32**
Dividend Payout %	**26.0**	**27.0**	**27.0**	**29.0**	**27.0**	**27.8**	**27.8**

① Before acctg. chg. ② 2-for-1 stk split, 4/1/91

ANNUAL FINANCIAL DATA

	1994	1993	1992	1991	1990	1989	1988
RECORD OF EARNINGS (IN MILLIONS):							
Total Revenues	3,100.1	2,949.3	2,747.8	2,541.4	2,266.7	2,123.5	1,950.5
Costs and Expenses	① 2,791.1	2,609.4	2,437.8	2,278.3	2,039.1	1,918.8	1,778.6
Depreciation & Amort	...	68.8	66.3	47.9	44.5	42.0	36.9
Operating Profit	1,327.4	1,252.3	1,158.4	1,041.1	928.8	848.4	763.6
Income Bef Income Taxes	298.5	264.4	226.0	198.8	187.3	170.2	163.0
Income Taxes	111.9	99.1	81.4	70.6	64.6	61.3	62.0
Net Income	186.6	165.2	② 144.6	128.2	122.7	108.9	101.1
Aver. Shs. Outstg. (000)	86,862	89,436	88,905	88,182	87,056	86,326	87,830
① Incl. Dep. ② Before acctg. change dr$81,771,000.							
BALANCE SHEET (IN MILLIONS):							
Cash and Cash Equivalents	251.4	269.8	167.7	100.8	99.0	202.1	154.2
Receivables, Net	384.9	297.5	277.3	246.5	229.9	205.7	195.7
Inventories	459.2	428.9	407.8	421.8	373.3	326.5	323.0
Gross Property	892.6	838.8	786.9	734.9	687.9	646.7	599.5
Accumulated Depreciation	483.4	444.7	399.0	357.8	314.5	287.9	266.9
Long-Term Debt	20.5	37.9	60.1	71.8	138.0	105.0	129.6
Net Stockholders' Equity	1,053.3	1,033.2	905.8	868.0	763.7	667.6	601.3
Total Assets	1,962.0	1,914.7	1,729.9	1,611.9	1,504.4	1,375.0	1,258.7
Total Current Assets	1,188.6	1,151.1	988.2	887.1	824.3	845.9	766.1
Total Current Liabilities	597.0	567.5	505.8	488.4	432.2	433.3	378.0
Net Working Capital	591.6	583.6	482.3	398.7	392.1	412.5	388.1
Year End Shs Outstg (000)	84,826	88,506	88,381	87,643	86,739	86,254	86,082
STATISTICAL RECORD:							
Operating Profit Margin %	10.0	9.2	8.9	8.5	8.1	7.7	6.9
Book Value Per Share	12.42	11.67	10.25	9.90	8.80	7.74	6.98
Return on Equity %	17.7	16.0	16.0	14.8	16.1	16.3	16.8
Return on Assets %	9.5	8.6	8.4	8.0	8.2	7.9	8.0
Average Yield %	1.7	1.5	1.5	1.9	2.1	2.3	2.3
P/E Ratio	16.6-13.7	20.3-16.1	20.2-15.6	19.1-12.2	15.0-10.7	14.2-9.9	13.8-10.4
Price Range	35¾-29½	37½-29⅞	32⅞-25⅜	27¾-17⅝	21⅛-15⅛	17⅞-12½	15⅞-12

Statistics are as originally reported.

OFFICERS:
J.G. Breen, Chmn. & C.E.O.
T.A. Commes, Pres. & C.O.O.
L.J. Pitorak, Sr. V.P.-Fin., C.F.O. & Treas.
L.E. Stellato, V.P., General Counsel & Sec.

INCORPORATED: OH, Jul., 1884

PRINCIPAL OFFICE: 101 Prospect Ave. N.W., Cleveland, OH 44115-1075

TELEPHONE NUMBER: (216) 566-2000
FAX: (216) 566-3310
NO. OF EMPLOYEES: 17,900 (approx.)
ANNUAL MEETING: In April
SHAREHOLDERS: 12,312
INSTITUTIONAL HOLDINGS:
No. of Institutions: 359
Shares Held: 55,214,201

REGISTRAR(S): Society National Bank, Cleveland, OH

TRANSFER AGENT(S): Society National Bank, Cleveland, OH

SIGMA-ALDRICH CORP.

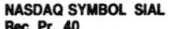

YIELD 0.9%
P/E RATIO 18.1

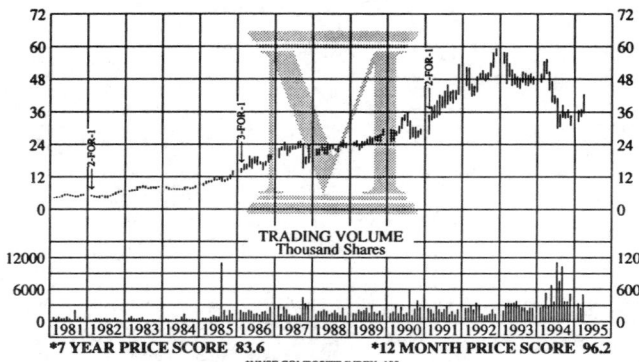

TRADING VOLUME
Thousand Shares

*7 YEAR PRICE SCORE 83.6   ***12 MONTH PRICE SCORE 96.2**

*NYSE COMPOSITE INDEX=100

INTERIM EARNINGS (Per Share):

Qtr.	Mar.	June	Sept.	Dec.
1991	0.41	0.40	0.40	0.39
1992	0.48	0.48	0.50	0.46
1993	0.54	0.54	0.54	0.53
1994	0.60	0.54	0.54	0.53

INTERIM DIVIDENDS (Per Share):

Amt.	Decl.	Ex.	Rec.	Pay.
0.0825Q	2/15/94	2/23/94	3/1/94	3/15/94
0.0825Q	5/3	5/25	6/1	6/15
0.0825Q	7/20	8/26	9/1	9/15
0.09Q	11/8	12/9	12/15	1/3/95
0.09Q	2/21/95	2/23/95	3/1/95	3/15

Indicated div.: $0.36

CAPITALIZATION (12/31/94):

	($000)	(%)
Long-Term Debt	14,478	2.0
Common & Surplus	699,505	98.0
Total	713,983	100.0

DIVIDEND ACHIEVER STATUS:
Rank: 58   1984-94 Growth Rate: 14.8%
Total Years of Dividend Growth: 13

RECENT DEVELOPMENTS: For the year ended 12/31/94, net income was $110.3 million compared with $107.2 million, before an accounting change, the year before, an increase of 3.0%. Net sales totaled $851.2 million, up 15.1% from $739.4 million a year earlier. Net sales for the chemical products division rose 11.9% to $686.3 million from $613.1 million in the previous year. The metal products division reported net sales of $164.9 million, 30.5% higher than

$126.4 million in 1993. Gross profit as a percentage of sales was 52.4% versus 83.6% in the prior year. The backlog of firm orders of chemical products was $14.7 million while B-Line Systems, Inc. had a backlog of orders amounting to $5.2 million. For the quarter ended 12/31/94, net income was flat at $26.6 million compared with the 1993 quarter. Net sales were $212.9 million, up 15.2% from $184.8 million in the prior-year quarter.

BUSINESS

SIGMA-ALDRICH CORP. is in two lines of business. The Company and its subsidiary, Fluka Chemie AG, develop, manufacture and distribute approximately 76,000 biochemicals, organic and inorganic chemicals, diagnostic reagents and related products. These are used primarily in research and development, in the diagnosis of disease, and as specialty chemicals for manufacturing purposes. B-Line Systems, Inc., a subsidiary, manufactures and sells metal components for strut, cable tray, pipe support and telecommunications systems. These components are used in routing electrical and mechanical services in industrial installations and supporting telecommunications applications.

BUSINESS LINE ANALYSIS

(12/31/94)	Rev(%)	Inc(%)
Chemical...................	80.6	86.4
Metal..........................	19.4	13.6
Total	100.0	100.0

ANNUAL EARNINGS AND DIVIDENDS PER SHARE

	1994	1993	1992	1991	1990	1989	1988
Earnings Per Share	2.21	2.15	1.92	1.60	1.44	1.29	1.14
Dividends Per Share	0.33	0.29	0.25	[1] 0.22	0.20	0.18	0.16
Dividend Payout %	14.9	13.5	13.0	13.8	13.9	13.9	14.0

[1] 2-for-1 stk split, 1/3/91

ANNUAL FINANCIAL DATA

RECORD OF EARNINGS (IN THOUSANDS):

Total Revenues	851,190	739,435	654,406	589,371	529,103	441,099	375,282
Costs and Expenses	644,226	541,313	478,231	438,667	394,719	324,800	274,185
Depreciation & Amort	36,655	32,505	28,863	26,826	24,356	16,427	12,575
Operating Profit	446,080	402,796	355,758	311,401	273,007	226,019	196,303
Income Bef Income Taxes	170,309	165,617	147,312	123,878	110,028	99,872	88,522
Income Taxes	59,969	58,463	51,854	44,085	38,780	35,914	32,045
Net Income	110,340	[1]107,154	95,458	79,793	71,248	63,958	56,477
Aver. Shs. Outstg.	49,829	49,802	49,770	49,716	49,618	49,472	49,324

[1] Before acctg. change dr$10,806,000.

BALANCE SHEET (IN THOUSANDS):

Cash and Cash Equivalents	9,745	10,252	44,932	28,119	6,578	9,675	5,722
Receivables, Net	134,893	113,439	91,927	83,737	79,386	64,812	49,206
Inventories	330,333	305,487	261,738	261,738	232,981	194,994	166,348
Gross Property	506,719	425,536	329,402	311,579	290,725	247,530	174,276
Accumulated Depreciation	204,030	168,214	141,099	119,888	98,353	71,099	54,758
Long-Term Debt	14,478	17,266	18,737	69,275	70,804	61,465	15,694
Net Stockholders' Equity	699,505	591,140	511,777	440,953	368,468	298,851	243,906
Total Assets	851,973	753,431	615,790	596,513	546,190	472,424	359,671
Total Current Assets	502,345	450,807	415,776	391,013	340,606	284,046	233,426
Total Current Liabilities	105,037	111,357	66,159	70,906	92,868	98,626	88,155
Net Working Capital	397,308	339,450	349,617	320,107	247,738	185,420	145,271
Year End Shares Outstg	49,832	49,805	49,776	49,746	49,658	49,538	49,356

STATISTICAL RECORD:

Operating Profit Margin %	20.0	22.4	22.5	21.0	20.8	22.6	23.6
Book Value Per Share	14.04	11.87	10.28	8.86	7.42	6.03	4.94
Return on Equity %	15.8	18.1	18.7	18.1	19.3	21.4	23.2
Return on Assets %	13.0	14.2	15.5	13.4	13.0	13.5	15.7
Average Yield %	0.8	0.6	0.5	0.5	0.5	0.7	0.7
P/E Ratio	25.0-13.6	27.0-20.7	30.9-21.7	33.4-17.3	24.9-17.4	23.1-17.0	22.3-17.3
Price Range	55¼-30	58-44½	59¼-41¾	53½-27¾	35⅞-25	29¾-21⅞	25⅝-19⅞

Statistics are as originally reported.

OFFICERS:
C.T. Cori, Chmn. & C.E.O.
D.R. Harvey, Pres. & C.O.O.
T.M. Tallarico, V.P. & Sec.
P.A. Gleich, V.P. & Treas.

INCORPORATED: DE, Jul., 1975

PRINCIPAL OFFICE: 3050 Spruce St., St. Louis, MO 63103

TELEPHONE NUMBER: (314) 771-5765

NO. OF EMPLOYEES: 5,534

ANNUAL MEETING: In May

SHAREHOLDERS: 2,574

INSTITUTIONAL HOLDINGS:
No. of Institutions: 348
Shares Held: 30,641,436

REGISTRAR(S): Boatmen's Trust Co., St.Louis, MO 63101

TRANSFER AGENT(S): Boatmen's Trust Co., St. Louis, MO 63101

ASE SYMBOL SJW
Rec. Pr. 32⅞

SJW CORP.

YIELD 6.6%
P/E RATIO 10.8

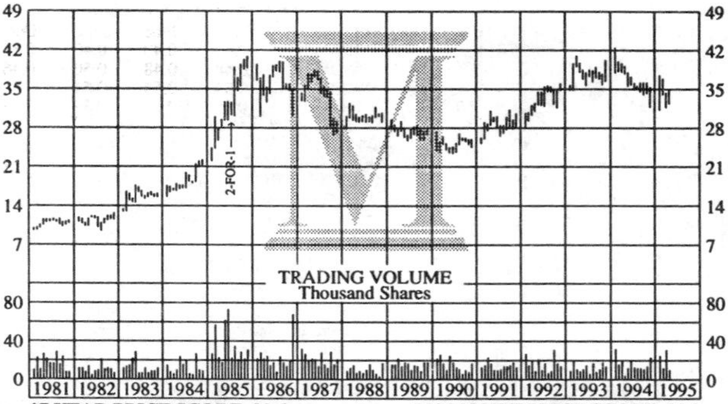

TRADING VOLUME
Thousand Shares
2-FOR-1
1981 1982 1983 1984 1985 1986 1987 1988 1989 1990 1991 1992 1993 1994 1995

*7 YEAR PRICE SCORE 92.6 *12 MONTH PRICE SCORE 90.0
*NYSE COMPOSITE INDEX=100

INTERIM EARNINGS (Per Share):

Qtr.	Mar.	June	Sept.	Dec.
1991	d0.16	0.43	0.64	2.07
1992	0.49	1.28	1.36	0.47
1993	0.43	0.74	1.45	1.01
1994	0.25	0.97	1.21	0.62

INTERIM DIVIDENDS (Per Share):

Amt.	Decl.	Ex.	Rec.	Pay.
0.54Q	1/26/95	1/31/95	2/6/95	3/1/95
0.54Q	4/21	4/25	5/1	6/1

Indicated div.: $2.16

CAPITALIZATION (12/31/94):

	($000)	(%)
Long-Term Debt	62,500	34.4
Deferred Income Tax	15,278	8.4
Common & Surplus	104,098	57.2
Total	181,876	100.0
Current Debt	6,300	

DIVIDEND ACHIEVER STATUS:
Rank: 284 1984-94 Growth Rate: 4.7%
Total Years of Dividend Growth: 28

RECENT DEVELOPMENTS: For the year ended 12/31/94, net income fell 16% to $9.9 million from $11.8 million in the previous year. Revenues increased 4.6% to $99.4 million from $95.0 million in 1993. Earnings per common share for the year ended 12/31/94 were $3.05 compared with $3.64 per common share for 1993. For the quarter ended 12/31/94, net income decreased 39% to $2.0 million from $3.3 million in the corresponding period of 1993. Revenues were down 3.2% to $21.8 million from $22.6 million a year earlier. Earnings per common share for the quarter were $0.62 compared with $1.02 for the fourth quarter of 1993.

BUSINESS

SJW CORP. is a holding company with three wholly-owned subsidiaries, San Jose Water Company, SJW Land Company and Western Precision, Inc. The Company's primary business is the production, storage, purification, distribution and retail sales of water. San Jose Water Company provides water service to a population of approximately 913,000 in an area comprising about 134 square miles in the metropolitan San Jose, California area. Western Precision, Inc. holds a 9.7% interest in California Water Service Company and also operates a precision parts manufacturing facility located in Sunnyvale, California and Austin, Texas. Utilization of rates, service and other matters affecting business are subject to regulation by the Public Utilities Commission of the state of California.

QUARTERLY DATA

(12/31/94)($000)	Rev	Inc
1st Quarter	18,991	824
2nd Quarter	26,715	3,137
3rd Quarter	31,888	3,923
4th Quarter	21,828	2,018

ANNUAL EARNINGS AND DIVIDENDS PER SHARE

	1994	1993	1992	1991	1990	1989	1988
Earnings Per Share	**3.05**	**3.64**	**3.60**	**2.98**	**3.00**	**1.50**	**2.50**
Dividends Per Share	**2.10**	**2.04**	[1] **2.13**	**1.92**	**1.86**	**1.82**	**1.76**
Dividend Payout %	**68.9**	**56.0**	**59.2**	**64.4**	**62.0**	**N.M.**	**70.4**

[1] Incl. special div. of $0.15.

ANNUAL FINANCIAL DATA

	1994	1993	1992	1991	1990	1989	1988
RECORD OF EARNINGS (IN THOUSANDS):							
Total Revenues	99,422	95,045	89,109	76,281	70,458	56,044	62,627
Depreciation	7,292	6,823	6,153	5,773	5,249	5,019	4,797
Maintenance	6,289	5,417	4,397	3,778	3,963	3,098	3,151
Prov for Fed Inc Taxes	6,387	8,071	7,619	6,123	5,660	3,057	4,818
Operating Income	13,767	14,960	14,123	12,152	11,587	6,774	10,038
Interest Expense	5,082	4,489	4,002	3,865	3,504	2,467	3,794
Net Income	9,902	11,767	10,227	8,448	8,539	4,307	7,190
Aver. Shs. Outstg.	3,251	3,237	2,838	2,838	2,838	2,831	2,819
BALANCE SHEET (IN THOUSANDS):							
Gross Plant	308,515	293,683	272,999	255,325	244,068	233,010	222,288
Accumulated Depreciation	95,083	90,030	84,158	78,675	73,405	69,118	64,548
Prop, Plant & Equip, Net	213,432	203,653	188,841	176,650	170,663	163,892	157,740
Long-term Debt	62,500	64,000	58,503	41,248	35,193	38,138	42,583
Net Stockholders' Equity	104,098	103,130	96,155	77,374	74,374	72,444	73,019
Total Assets	262,530	256,851	230,198	197,095	188,313	185,905	187,856
Year End Shares Outstg	2,251	3,251	3,256	2,838	2,838	2,838	2,825
STATISTICAL RECORD:							
Book Value Per Share	45.21	31.14	29.07	27.27	26.21	25.08	25.39
Op. Inc/Net Pl %	6.5	7.3	7.5	6.9	6.8	4.1	6.4
Dep/Gr. Pl %	2.4	2.3	2.3	2.3	2.2	2.2	2.2
Accum. Dep/Gr. Pl %	30.8	30.7	30.8	30.8	30.1	29.7	29.0
Return on Equity %	9.5	11.4	10.6	10.9	11.5	6.0	9.9
Average Yield %	5.7	5.4	6.6	6.8	7.3	6.6	5.8
P/E Ratio	13.9-10.4	11.3-9.5	10.0-7.8	10.5-8.4	9.1-7.8	19.7-17.1	13.0-11.1
Price Range	42½-31¾	41-34¾	36-28¼	31¼-25⅛	27⅜-23⅜	29½-25⅝	32½-27¾

Statistics are as originally reported.

OFFICERS:
J.W. Weinhardt, Pres. & C.E.O.
W.R. Roth, V.P.-Fin.
B.Y. Nilsen, Sec.

INCORPORATED: CA, Apr., 1985

PRINCIPAL OFFICE: 374 West Santa Clara St., San Jose, CA 95196

TELEPHONE NUMBER: (408) 279-7822

FAX: (408) 279-7934

NO. OF EMPLOYEES: 282 (approx.)

ANNUAL MEETING: In April

SHAREHOLDERS: 1,565 (approx.)

INSTITUTIONAL HOLDINGS:
No. of Institutions: 22
Shares Held: 344,031

REGISTRAR(S): First National Bank of Boston, Shareholder Services Division, Boston, MA

TRANSFER AGENT(S): First National Bank of Boston, Shareholder Services Division, Boston, MA

SMUCKER (J.M.) CO.

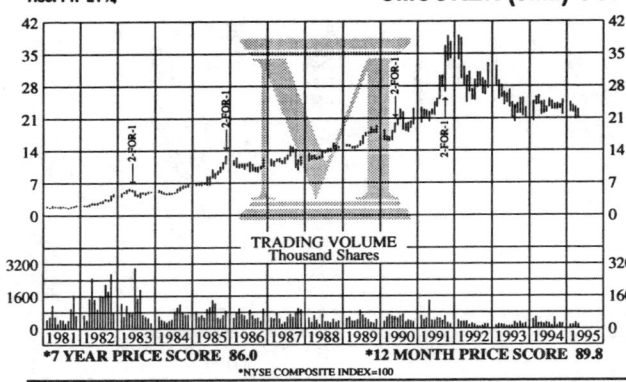

TRADING VOLUME
Thousand Shares

1981	1982	1983	1984	1985	1986	1987	1988	1989	1990	1991	1992	1993	1994	1995

*7 YEAR PRICE SCORE 86.0   *12 MONTH PRICE SCORE 89.8

*NYSE COMPOSITE INDEX=100

INTERIM EARNINGS (Per Share):

Qtr.	July	Oct.	Jan.	Apr.
1991-92	0.30	0.32	0.23	0.31
1992-93	----------------- 1.27 -----------------			
1993-94	0.31	0.35	0.26	0.13
1994-95	0.32	0.42	0.30	...

INTERIM DIVIDENDS (Per Share):

Amt.	Decl.	Ex.	Rec.	Pay.
0.125Q	4/15/94	5/12/94	5/18/94	6/1/94
0.125Q	7/20	8/12	8/18	9/1
0.125Q	10/28	11/10	11/17	12/1
0.125Q	1/20/95	2/9/95	2/15/95	3/1/95
0.13Q	4/18	5/12	5/18	6/1

*Indicated div.: $0.52**

CAPITALIZATION (4/30/94):

	($000)	(%)
Long-Term Debt	48,558	17.0
Deferred Income Tax	2,469	0.9
Common & Surplus	234,402	82.1
Total	285,429	100.0

DIVIDEND ACHIEVER STATUS:
Rank: 45   1984-94 Growth Rate: 15.6%
Total Years of Dividend Growth: 19

RECENT DEVELOPMENTS: For the quarter ended 1/31/95, net income was $8.7 million compared with $7.4 million a year earlier. Net sales advanced 36.1% to $157.3 million, with most of the increase attributable to contributions from Mrs. Smith's pie business, which was acquired in March 1994. The Consumer business experienced a slight increase in sales due to continued growth in the dessert toppings category. Fruit spread grocery market sales declined during the quarter.

PROSPECTS: The Company's recent acquisitions, such as Mrs. Smith's pie business, will complement the Company's existing businesses well. Mrs. Smith's contributed significantly to earnings over the past three reporting periods; however, the level of contribution will be minimal through mid-1995 due to the seasonal nature of its business. Meanwhile, the international area will continue to improve, but will be affected by economic conditions abroad.

BUSINESS

THE J.M. SMUCKER COMPANY manufactures and markets a wide variety of jams, jellies, preserves and marmalades. The Company also produces ice cream toppings, spreads, pancake syrups, ketchup, mustard, fruit butter, puree, syrups, low sugar items, and juices. Well recognized brand names include: Smucker's, Dickinson's, Magic Shell and Goober Jelly. The Company also provides industrial fruit products such as baker and dairy fillings. Products are sold primarily through brokers to various grocery accounts, plus food service distributors and chains. SJM's distribution outside of the U.S. is principally in Canada and the U.K., although products are exported to other countries.

ANNUAL EARNINGS AND DIVIDENDS PER SHARE

	4/30/94	4/30/93	4/30/92	4/30/91	4/30/90	4/30/89	4/30/88
Earnings Per Share	1.05	[1] 1.27	1.16	1.07	1.03	0.94	0.78
Dividends Per Share	0.49	0.45	0.39	[2] 0.32	0.25	0.21	0.173
Dividend Payout %	46.7	35.4	37.9	29.8	24.4	22.4	22.1

[1] Before acctg. chg.   [2] 2-for-1 stk split, 5/30/90

ANNUAL FINANCIAL DATA

RECORD OF EARNINGS (IN THOUSANDS):

Total Revenues	511,525	491,309	483,472	454,976	422,357	366,855	314,245
Costs and Expenses	445,365	418,519	416,213	391,660	362,906	314,455	268,655
Depreciation & Amort	15,378	13,052	12,808	11,771	10,452	9,679	8,018
Operating Income	50,782	59,738	54,451	51,545	48,999	42,721	37,572
Income Bef Income Taxes	52,723	61,470	56,083	52,581	49,944	44,582	38,592
Income Taxes	22,225	24,071	21,965	20,837	19,767	17,027	15,722
Net Income	30,498	[1] 37,399	34,118	31,744	30,177	27,555	22,870

[1] Before acctg. change dr$4,454,000.

BALANCE SHEET (IN THOUSANDS):

Cash and Cash Equivalents	14,059	50,445	36,268	24,513	18,402	36,652	27,111
Receivables, Net	47,828	40,354	41,565	42,328	35,591	29,640	24,799
Inventories	103,236	71,863	77,777	66,531	61,495	47,180	47,000
Gross Property	218,784	166,904	150,879	136,722	122,168	102,484	88,036
Accumulated Depreciation	81,278	70,578	62,556	53,813	46,750	40,570	34,053
Long-Term Debt	48,558	...	...	215	4,267	4,954	3,081
Net Stockholders' Equity	234,402	220,694	212,215	190,223	167,125	144,536	125,322
Total Assets	378,641	294,811	277,768	252,429	224,840	198,457	170,025
Total Current Assets	171,685	168,399	161,571	141,036	119,947	118,129	101,847
Total Current Liabilities	83,195	56,543	53,560	50,029	45,742	41,856	35,624
Net Working Capital	88,490	111,856	108,011	91,007	74,205	76,273	66,223
Year End Shares Outstg	29,110	29,199	29,538	29,535	29,540	29,428	29,452

STATISTICAL RECORD:

Operating Profit Margin %	9.9	12.2	11.3	11.3	11.6	11.6	12.0
Book Value Per Share	5.99	6.76	6.47	5.68	4.86	4.44	3.86
Return on Equity %	13.0	17.0	16.1	16.7	18.1	19.1	18.2
Return on Assets %	8.1	12.7	12.3	12.6	13.4	13.9	13.5
Average Yield %	1.7	1.4	1.3	1.6	1.5	1.5	1.4
P/E Ratio	30.8-19.3	30.7-19.3	33.5-17.2	21.6-15.0	18.9-14.0	16.6-12.4	19.2-12.5
Price Range	32⅜-20¼	39-24½	38⅞-20	23⅛-16	19½-14⅜	15⅝-11⅝	15-9¾

Statistics are as originally reported.

BUSINESS LINE ANALYSIS

(4/30/94)	Rev(%)	Inc($000)
United States	88.7	81,013
Foreign	11.3	(1,216)
Total	100.0	79,797

OFFICERS:
T. Smucker, Chmn.
R.K. Smucker, Pres.
P.P. Yuschak, Treas.
S.J. Ellcessor, Sec. & Gen. Couns.

INCORPORATED: OH, Sep., 1921

PRINCIPAL OFFICE: One Strawberry Lane, Orrville, OH 44667-0280

TELEPHONE NUMBER: (216) 682-3000

NO. OF EMPLOYEES: 2,600 (approx.)

ANNUAL MEETING: In August

SHAREHOLDERS: 7,159 cl. A; 5,308 cl. B.

INSTITUTIONAL HOLDINGS:
No. of Institutions: 102
Shares Held: 6,866,401

REGISTRAR(S): National City Bank, Cleveland, OH 44114

TRANSFER AGENT(S): National City Bank, Cleveland, OH 44114

SONOCO PRODUCTS CO.

YIELD 2.4%
P/E RATIO 17.6

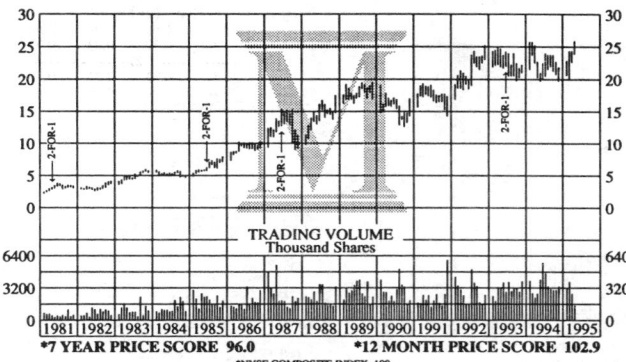

TRADING VOLUME
Thousand Shares

*7 YEAR PRICE SCORE 96.0 *12 MONTH PRICE SCORE 102.9
*NYSE COMPOSITE INDEX=100

INTERIM EARNINGS (Per Share):

Qtr.	Mar.	June	Sept.	Dec.
1992	0.26	0.33	0.32	0.03
1993	0.31	0.36	0.33	0.35
1994	0.30	0.36	0.35	0.39

INTERIM DIVIDENDS (Per Share):

Amt.	Decl.	Ex.	Rec.	Pay.
0.14Q	7/20/94	8/15/94	8/19/94	9/9/94
0.14Q	10/20	11/14	11/18	12/9
0.14Q	2/1/95	2/13/95	2/17/95	3/10/95
5%	4/19	5/15	5/19	6/9
0.15Q	4/19	5/15	5/19	6/9

Indicated div.:$0.60*

CAPITALIZATION (12/31/94):

	($000)	(%)
Long-Term Debt	487,959	36.9
Preferred Stock	172,500	13.1
Common & Surplus	659,718	50.0
Total	1,320,177	100.0

DIVIDEND ACHIEVER STATUS:
Rank: 90   1984-94 Growth Rate: 13.2%
Total Years of Dividend Growth: 11

RECENT DEVELOPMENTS: For the year ended 12/31/94, net income rose 9.3% to $129.8 million from $118.8 million, including an unusual charge of $5.8 million, in 1993. Sales grew 18.1% to $2.30 billion from $1.95 billion the previous year. During the first half of 1994, SON experienced only modest growth as higher raw material costs were offsetting volume and productivity gains. In response to higher material costs, SON raised prices in its paper and converting operations.

PROSPECTS: SON's earnings are benefiting from improved volumes and prices for its products. SON's management has set a goal to grow 10% to 15% compounded annually, which means doubling sales to about $5 billion and achieving profits in the range of $250 million to $300 million by the year 2000. The Company purchased M. Harland & Son of England and bought the remaining 50% ownership in its CMB/Sonoco Composites joint venture. SON's common stock began trading on the New York Stock Exchange on 3/9/95.

BUSINESS

SONOCO PRODUCTS CO. is a major packaging manufacturer serving a wide variety of consumer and industrial markets with containers and carriers made from paper, plastic, metal and wood. Sonoco has 250 operations in 24 countries. The Converted Products Segment manufactures fibre and plastic tubes, cores and cones used primarily as industrial carriers; composite canisters used to package a variety of products including frozen concentrates, snack foods; caulking cartridges used for packaging adhesives and sealants; fibre drums, plastic drums, intermediate bulk containers used for packaging a wide variety of products for bulk packaging; protective packaging products like solid fibre partitions, edgeboard and Sonopost corner posts. The Paper Segment consists of 21 U.S. cylinder board machines, one Fourdrinier paper machine and Paper Stock Dealers, Inc., a recovered paper collection and processing subsidiary. The Miscellaneous Segment includes High Density Film Products, producers of plastic sacks for the grocery and retail industries, agricultural mulch film and other products. Also included is Baker Reels, a national manufacturer of nailed wood and metal reels for the wire and cable industries.

ANNUAL EARNINGS AND DIVIDENDS PER SHARE

	1994	1993	1992	1991	1990	1989	1988
Earnings Per Share	1.40	1.35	[2] 0.94	1.10	0.58	1.18	1.10
Dividends Per Share	0.555	[1] 0.53	[3] 0.49	0.46	0.45	0.405	0.32
Dividend Payout %	39.6	39.3	52.4	41.8	77.6	34.3	29.1

Note: 5%stk.div.6/9/95. [1] 2-for-1 stk split,06/11/93 [2] Before acctg. chg. [3] Bef acctg chge

ANNUAL FINANCIAL DATA

RECORD OF EARNINGS (IN MILLIONS):

	1994	1993	1992	1991	1990	1989	1988
Total Revenues	2,300.1	1,947.2	1,838.0	1,697.1	1,669.1	1,655.8	1,599.8
Costs and Expenses	1,942.9	1,639.2	1,557.8	1,452.0	1,409.1	1,401.0	1,343.3
Deprec, Depl & Amort	112.8	95.7	83.3	76.6	72.2	67.3	69.1
Operating Profit	244.4	212.2	197.0	168.5	187.9	187.5	187.4
Inc Fr Opers Bef Income Taxes	210.9	192.9	131.0	155.7	87.0	158.1	162.2
Income Taxes	82.5	75.2	51.8	63.6	43.9	60.9	67.0
Net Income	129.8	118.8	[1] 81.3	94.8	50.4	103.6	96.3
Aver. Shs. Outstg. (000)	87,090	87,316	86,732	86,304	87,109	87,794	87,632

[1] Before acctg. change dr$37,892,000.

BALANCE SHEET (IN MILLIONS):

	1994	1993	1992	1991	1990	1989	1988
Cash and Cash Equivalents	28.4	25.9	38.1	28.6	39.9	25.7	20.4
Receivables, Net	304.7	270.4	238.6	198.8	201.6	164.8	164.3
Inventories	207.7	186.1	159.6	156.0	157.1	151.6	163.7
Gross Property	1,411.5	1,315.7	1,135.0	1,052.1	986.1	856.7	877.6
Accumulated Depreciation	648.4	578.5	521.0	471.3	423.5	362.4	344.1
Long-Term Debt	488.0	455.3	241.0	227.5	279.1	226.2	275.5
Net Stockholders' Equity	832.2	788.4	561.9	562.3	512.8	511.6	454.5
Total Assets	1,835.1	1,707.1	1,246.5	1,135.9	1,113.6	995.1	977.5
Total Current Assets	570.7	513.1	464.9	420.7	431.7	376.2	377.8
Total Current Liabilities	348.6	303.2	312.5	256.9	247.6	183.1	189.8
Net Working Capital	222.1	209.9	152.5	163.9	184.1	193.0	188.1
Year End Shs Outstg (000)	86,908	87,447	87,144	86,490	86,100	87,453	87,722

STATISTICAL RECORD:

	1994	1993	1992	1991	1990	1989	1988
Operating Profit Margin %	10.6	10.9	10.7	9.9	11.3	11.3	11.7
Book Value Per Share	3.46	3.16	5.77	5.80	5.30	5.03	4.66
Return on Equity %	15.6	15.1	14.5	16.9	9.8	20.2	21.2
Return on Assets %	7.1	7.0	6.5	8.3	4.5	10.4	9.8
Average Yield %	2.4	2.4	2.3	2.7	2.8	2.3	2.3
P/E Ratio	18.4-14.1	18.4-14.6	26.9-18.0	17.6-13.0	33.0-21.8	16.5-13.8	15.9-8.9
Price Range	25¾-19¾	24⅞-19¾	25¼-16⅞	19⅜-14¼	19⅛-12⅝	19½-16¼	17½-9¾

Statistics are as originally reported.

OFFICERS:
C.W. Coker, Chmn. & C.E.O.
F.T. Hill, Jr., V.P.-Fin.
C.J. Hupfer, Treas.
J.L. Coker, Sec.
INCORPORATED: SC, May, 1899
PRINCIPAL OFFICE: North Second Street,
Hartsville, SC 29550

TELEPHONE NUMBER: (803) 383-7000
FAX: (803) 339-6078
NO. OF EMPLOYEES: 17,200 (approx.)
ANNUAL MEETING: In April
SHAREHOLDERS: 34,000 (approx.)
INSTITUTIONAL HOLDINGS:
No. of Institutions: 141
Shares Held: 12,683,860

REGISTRAR(S):

TRANSFER AGENT(S): Wachovia Bank & Trust Co., N.A., Winston-Salem, NC

NYS SYMBOL SCW
Rec. Pr. 17½

SOUTHERN CALIFORNIA WATER CO.

YIELD 6.9%
P/E RATIO 12.2

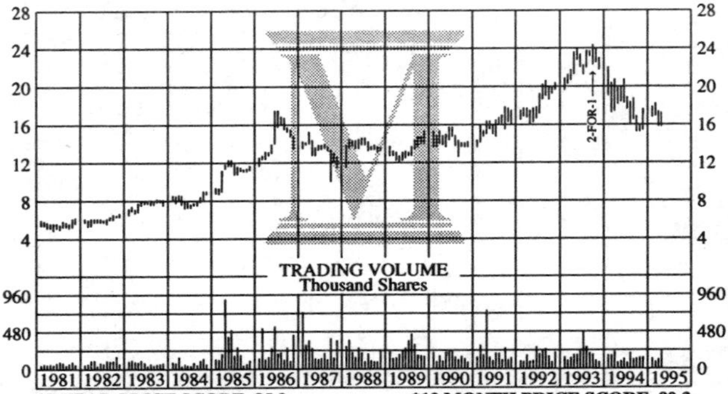

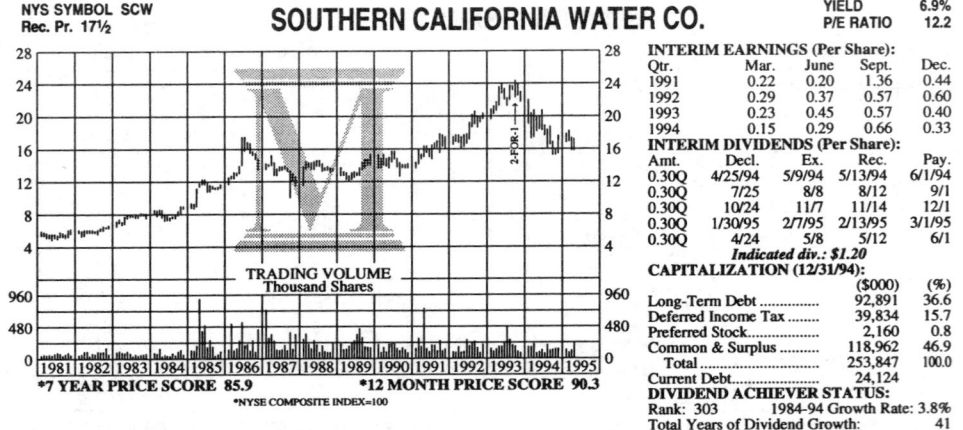

*7 YEAR PRICE SCORE 85.9 *12 MONTH PRICE SCORE 90.3

*NYSE COMPOSITE INDEX=100

INTERIM EARNINGS (Per Share):

Qtr.	Mar.	June	Sept.	Dec.
1991	0.22	0.20	1.36	0.44
1992	0.29	0.37	0.57	0.60
1993	0.23	0.45	0.57	0.40
1994	0.15	0.29	0.66	0.33

INTERIM DIVIDENDS (Per Share):

Amt.	Decl.	Ex.	Rec.	Pay.
0.30Q	4/25/94	5/9/94	5/13/94	6/1/94
0.30Q	7/25	8/8	8/12	9/1
0.30Q	10/24	11/7	11/14	12/1
0.30Q	1/30/95	2/7/95	2/13/95	3/1/95
0.30Q	4/24	5/8	5/12	6/1

Indicated div.: $1.20

CAPITALIZATION (12/31/94):

	($000)	(%)
Long-Term Debt	92,891	36.6
Deferred Income Tax	39,834	15.7
Preferred Stock	2,160	0.8
Common & Surplus	118,962	46.9
Total	253,847	100.0
Current Debt	24,124	

DIVIDEND ACHIEVER STATUS:
Rank: 303 1984-94 Growth Rate: 3.8%
Total Years of Dividend Growth: 41

RECENT DEVELOPMENTS: For the year ended 12/31/94, net income decreased 5.7% to $11.3 million from $12.0 million in 1993. Revenues advanced 13.1% to $122.7 million. The increase in revenues was attributable to general rate increases necessary to recover previously unrecovered supply costs, which does not increase earnings due to regulatory balancing account mechanisms. Total operating expenses increased 17.3% in 1994.

PROSPECTS: Earnings are being negatively affected by lower returns on common equity authorized by regulators and delays in obtaining rate relief to recover operating expenses. SCW filed for rate increases in six of its water operating districts and anticipates filing in its electric district. However, significant rate relief from these filings is not anticipated until early 1996. Earnings for 1995 are not expected to match levels recorded in 1991, 1992 and 1993.

BUSINESS

SOUTHERN CALIFORNIA WATER CO. is engaged principally in the purchase, distribution and sale of water. The Company also distributes electricity in one community. The Company provides service in 17 separate rate-making districts, 16 of which are water districts and one an electric district, located in 75 communities in ten counties throughout the state of California. The Company serves approximately 237,000 water customers and approximately 20,000 electric customers.

REVENUES

(12/31/94)	($000)	(%)
Water	112,087	91.4
Electric	10,588	8.6
Total	122,675	100.0

ANNUAL EARNINGS AND DIVIDENDS PER SHARE

	1994	1993	1992	1991	1990	1989	1988
Earnings Per Share	**1.43**	**1.66**	**1.82**	**2.34**	**1.40**	**1.38**	**0.97**
Dividends Per Share	**1.20**	**1 1.1875**	**1.15**	**1.10**	**1.07**	**1.035**	**1.01**
Dividend Payout %	**83.9**	**71.5**	**63.4**	**47.0**	**76.2**	**75.0**	**N.M.**

1 2-for-1 stk split,10/06/93

ANNUAL FINANCIAL DATA

	1994	1993	1992	1991	1990	1989	1988
RECORD OF EARNINGS (IN THOUSANDS):							
Total Revenues	122,675	108,506	100,660	90,660	90,398	85,564	80,175
Depreciation	8,049	7,398	6,526	6,027	5,173	4,689	4,403
Maintenance	6,916	6,450	5,091	5,147	4,982	4,610	5,006
Prov for Fed Inc Taxes	8,865	5,491	7,791	5,340	6,034	4,233	3,902
Operating Income	18,930	20,050	19,098	16,825	14,733	14,814	12,191
Interest Expense	7,828	8,378	7,890	7,583	6,421	7,673	6,230
Net Income	11,338	12,026	12,142	15,363	8,907	8,730	6,127
Aver. Shs. Outstg.	7,842	7,186	6,628	6,518	6,272	6,242	6,218
BALANCE SHEET (IN THOUSANDS):							
Gross Plant	407,558	379,798	355,399	330,514	299,925	275,399	275,043
Accumulated Depreciation	92,679	84,808	77,874	71,956	64,212	60,934	60,380
Prop, Plant & Equip, Net	314,879	294,990	277,525	258,558	235,713	214,465	214,663
Long-term Debt	92,891	84,286	84,195	82,634	67,246	67,767	73,532
Net Stockholders' Equity	118,922	116,463	88,229	83,162	71,141	68,602	68,074
Total Assets	383,627	358,533	312,491	293,444	268,028	254,346	237,450
Year End Shs Outstg	7,845	7,805	6,643	6,607	6,272	6,258	6,230
STATISTICAL RECORD:							
Book Value Per Share	15.16	14.92	13.28	12.59	11.34	10.96	10.61
Op. Inc/Net Pl %	6.0	6.8	6.9	6.5	6.3	6.9	5.7
Dep/Gr. Pl %	2.0	1.9	1.8	1.8	1.7	1.7	1.6
Accum. Dep/Gr. Pl %	22.7	22.3	21.9	21.8	21.4	22.1	22.0
Return on Equity %	9.4	10.2	13.5	18.1	12.2	12.4	9.1
Average Yield %	6.4	9.4	6.3	7.0	7.5	7.5	7.7
P/E Ratio	15.4-10.7	14.7-11.8	11.3-8.8	7.6-5.8	11.3-9.0	11.1-8.8	15.1-11.9
Price Range	22-15¼	24⅜-19⅝	20⅝-16	17⅞-13⅝	15¾-12⅝	15⅜-12⅛	14⅝-11½

Statistics are as originally reported.

OFFICERS:
W.V. Caveney, Chmn.
F.E. Wicks, Pres. & C.E.O.
J.B. Gallagher, V.P.-Fin., C.F.O. & Sec.

INCORPORATED: CA, Dec., 1929

PRINCIPAL OFFICE: 630 East Foothill Boulevard, San Dimas, CA 91773

TELEPHONE NUMBER: (909) 394-3600
FAX: (909) 394-0711
NO. OF EMPLOYEES: 467
ANNUAL MEETING: In April
SHAREHOLDERS: 5,670
INSTITUTIONAL HOLDINGS:
No. of Institutions: 41
Shares Held: 810,284

REGISTRAR(S):

TRANSFER AGENT(S): First Interstate Bank of California, Los Angeles, CA

NYS SYMBOL SIG
Rec. Pr. 30⅞

SOUTHERN INDIANA GAS & ELECTRIC CO.

YIELD 5.5%
P/E RATIO 12.2

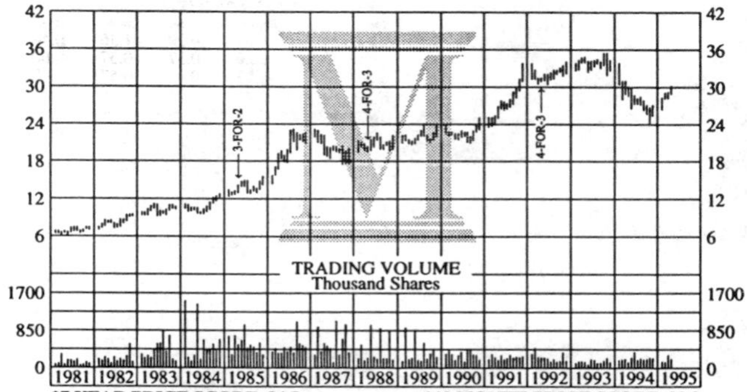

*7 YEAR PRICE SCORE 84.7 *12 MONTH PRICE SCORE 99.9

*NYSE COMPOSITE INDEX=100

INTERIM EARNINGS (Per Share):

Qtr.	Mar.	June	Sept.	Dec.
1991	0.86	0.48	0.82	0.22
1992	0.70	0.64	0.71	0.21
1993	0.79	0.57	0.93	0.17
1994	0.92	0.49	0.88	0.25

INTERIM DIVIDENDS (Per Share):

Amt.	Decl.	Ex.	Rec.	Pay.
0.4125Q	10/21/94	11/14/94	11/18/94	12/20/94
0.4125Q	10/21	11/14	11/18	12/20
0.4125Q	10/21	11/14	11/18	12/20
0.4225Q	1/17/95	2/6/95	2/10/95	3/20/95
0.4225Q	4/18	5/15	5/19	6/20

Indicated div.: $1.69*

CAPITALIZATION (12/31/94):

	($000)	(%)
Long-Term Debt	273,617	37.2
Deferred Income Tax	145,278	19.8
Preferred Stock	19,605	2.7
Common & Surplus	296,576	40.3
Total	735,076	100.0
Current Debt	64,737	

DIVIDEND ACHIEVER STATUS:
Rank: 267 1984-94 Growth Rate: 5.8%
Total Years of Dividend Growth: 35

RECENT DEVELOPMENTS: For the quarter ended 12/31/94, net income was $4.2 million compared with $2.9 million in the corresponding period of 1993. Revenues were $73.8 million, down 4%. Electric revenues increased 1%, but were offset by gas revenues declining 3%. For the year ended 12/31/94, net income advanced 3.6% to $41.0 million compared with $39.6 million a year earlier. Revenues were $330.0 million versus $329.5 million in 1993.

PROSPECTS: SIG is expecting a decision on its December 1993 petition for $12.4 million or 5.7% in higher retail rates in the second quarter. The retail rate increase is necessary to cover the financing costs related to the scrubber for the Cully coal-fired units and demand-side management outlays. The Company is restructuring to separate regulated and nonregulated businesses and seeking approval to form a holding company that will be the parent company of SIG.

BUSINESS

SOUTHERN INDIANA GAS & ELECTRIC CO. is an operating public utility engaged in the generation, transmission, distribution and sale of electricity, and the purchase of natural gas and its transportation, distribution, and sale in a service area which covers ten counties in Southwestern Indiana. Siegeco's electric business services approximately 118,163 customers in Evansville and 74 cities, towns, communities and adjacent areas. Additionally, wholesale electric service is supplied to another nine communities. The Company's gas business services approximately 100,398 customers in the Evansville area and 63 cities, towns and nearby communities and their environs.

REVENUES

(12/31/94)	($000)	(%)
Electric	260,936	79.1
Gas	69,099	20.9
Total	330,035	100.0

ANNUAL EARNINGS AND DIVIDENDS PER SHARE

	1994	1993	1992	1991	1990	1989	1988
Earnings Per Share	**2.53**	**2.45**	**2.26**	**2.37**	**2.27**	**2.11**	**2.22**
Dividends Per Share	**1.65**	**1.61**	[1] **1.56**	**1.50**	**1.425**	**1.35**	[2] **1.275**
Dividend Payout %	**65.2**	**65.7**	**69.0**	**63.3**	**62.9**	**64.1**	**57.4**

[1] 33.3% stk div, 4/20/92 [2] 4-for-3 stk split, 3/11/88

ANNUAL FINANCIAL DATA

	1994	1993	1992	1991	1990	1989	1988
RECORD OF EARNINGS (IN MILLIONS):							
Total Revenues	330.0	328.5	305.9	322.6	322.5	311.5	312.8
Depreciation & Amort	37.7	36.9	36.2	36.8	34.5	33.5	32.7
Maintenance	30.4	26.7	21.9	27.1	29.3	26.6	22.5
Operating Income	52.4	51.6	50.9	53.2	51.9	51.6	56.2
Interest Expense	19.0	18.5	18.2	19.2	18.9	20.8	20.0
Net Income	41.0	39.7	36.8	38.5	37.7	36.2	38.2
Aver. Shs. Outstg. (000)	15,755	15,705	15,705	15,705	16,092	16,584	16,550
BALANCE SHEET (IN MILLIONS):							
Gross Plant	1,134.9	1,059.2	988.7	942.9	911.3	858.4	834.5
Accumulated Depreciation	456.9	423.7	391.5	358.9	327.9	302.5	276.6
Prop, Plant & Equip, Net	677.9	635.5	597.1	584.0	583.4	555.9	557.9
Long-term Debt	273.6	274.0	212.0	235.7	255.5	218.6	228.6
Net Stockholders' Equity	316.2	301.8	288.6	278.1	264.5	270.6	258.1
Total Assets	917.2	860.0	761.3	747.4	738.8	721.1	698.9
Year End Shs Outstg (000)	15,755	15,705	15,705	15,705	15,705	16,584	16,584
STATISTICAL RECORD:							
Book Value Per Share	18.82	17.97	17.12	16.46	15.59	15.13	14.37
Op. Inc/Net Pl %	7.7	8.1	8.5	9.1	8.9	9.3	10.1
Dep/Gr. Pl %	3.3	3.5	3.7	3.9	3.8	3.9	3.9
Accum. Dep/Gr. Pl %	40.3	40.0	39.6	38.1	36.0	35.2	33.1
Return on Equity %	13.3	13.5	13.1	13.8	14.3	13.4	14.8
Average Yield %	5.7	4.8	4.8	5.2	6.2	6.0	6.1
P/E Ratio	13.4-9.5	14.5-13.0	15.1-13.4	14.3-9.9	11.1-9.2	11.4-9.8	10.2-8.7
Price Range	33⅞-24	35½-31⅞	34⅛-30⅜	33⅞-23½	25-20⅞	24⅛-20⅝	22⅝-19⅜

Statistics are as originally reported.

OFFICERS:
R.G. Reherman, Chmn., Pres. & C.E.O.
A.E. Goebel, Sr. V.P., C.F.O., Sec. & Treas.

INCORPORATED: IN, Jun., 1912

PRINCIPAL OFFICE: 20 Northwest Fourth Street, Evansville, IN 47741-0001

TELEPHONE NUMBER: (812) 464-4554
FAX: (812) 464-4554
NO. OF EMPLOYEES: 962 (Consol.)
ANNUAL MEETING: In March
SHAREHOLDERS: 9,350 common
INSTITUTIONAL HOLDINGS:
No. of Institutions: 95
Shares Held: 3,835,528

REGISTRAR(S): Continental Stock Transfer & Trust Co., New York, NY
The National City Bank of Evansville, Evansville, IN 47705

TRANSFER AGENT(S): Continental Stock Transfer & Trust Co., New York, NY
The National City Bank of Evansville, Evansville, IN 47705

SOUTHERN NATIONAL CORP.

YIELD 3.6%
P/E RATIO 9.3

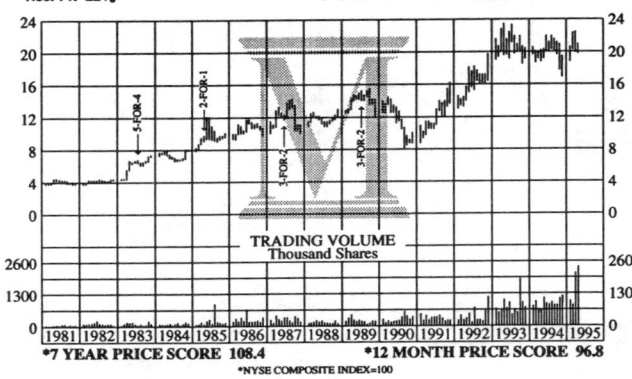

TRADING VOLUME
Thousand Shares

*7 YEAR PRICE SCORE 108.4   *12 MONTH PRICE SCORE 96.8
*NYSE COMPOSITE INDEX=100

INTERIM EARNINGS (Per Share):

Qtr.	Mar.	June	Sept.	Dec.
1991	0.30	0.32	0.36	0.38
1992	0.41	0.43	0.50	0.49
1993	0.65	0.54	0.54	0.54
1994	0.57	0.59	0.61	0.62

INTERIM DIVIDENDS (Per Share):

Amt.	Decl.	Ex.	Rec.	Pay.
0.17Q	4/6/94	4/11/94	4/15/94	5/1/94
0.20Q	7/5	7/11	7/15	8/1
0.20Q	10/5	10/7	10/14	11/1
0.20Q	1/3/95	1/9/95	1/13/95	2/1/95
0.20Q	3/10	4/10	4/17	5/1

*Indicated div.: $0.80**

CAPITALIZATION (12/31/94):

	($000)	(%)
Total Deposits	6,165,080	71.3
Total Debt	1,851,995	21.4
Preferred Stock	3,850	0.0
Common & Surplus	628,494	7.3
Total	8,649,419	100.0

DIVIDEND ACHIEVER STATUS:
Rank: 163   1984-94 Growth Rate: 10.2%
Total Years of Dividend Growth: 23

RECENT DEVELOPMENTS: On March 1, 1995, the Company completed its merger with BB&T Financial Corp. For the year ended 12/31/94, net income was $109.6 million compared with a net loss of $19.0 million in 1993. Comparisons are made with restated 1993 results. Net interest income, benefiting from a 4.5% increase in interest and fees on loans and leases, totaled $322.7 million versus $310.5 million for 1993. Noninterest income was $83.0 million, down 5.3% from $87.7 million. Noninterest expense was reduced by 31.2% to $231.4 million.

PROSPECTS: The Company completed its merger with BB&T Financial Corp., forming the nation's 36th-largest banking company with assets of approximately $20 billion. The new company will be headquartered in Winston-Salem, NC. The lead bank will carry the name Branch Banking and Trust Company. In November 1994, SNB acquired Prime Rate Premium Finance Corp., a Florence, SC-based company. Prime Rate is one of the largest premium finance businesses in the Southeast.

BUSINESS

SOUTHERN NATIONAL CORPORATION, with $8.7 billion in assets, is one of the largest bank holding companies in North Carolina and South Carolina. Its principal subsidiaries form a network of banking and thrift offices in 117 cities and communities. Subsidiaries offer a wide range of personal and commercial banking and related financial services. Insurance services are offered through Unified Investors Life Insurance Co. Other subsidiaries include Southern National Leasing Corp., and two savings and loans. During 1994, SNB acquired The First Savings Bank, Regency Bancshares, Inc., Home Federal Savings Bank and Prime Rate Premium Finance Corp.

LOAN DISTRIBUTION

(12/31/94)	($000)	(%)
Comm, Financial & Agric	1,301,504	25.0
Real Estate-Construction	121,561	2.4
Real Estate-Mortgage	3,055,865	58.7
Consumer	701,862	13.5
Loans Held For Sale	21,968	0.4
Total	5,202,760	100.0

ANNUAL EARNINGS AND DIVIDENDS PER SHARE

	1994	1993	1992	1991	1990	1989	1988
Earnings Per Share	2.38	2.28	1.84	1.36	1.01	1.19	1.13
Dividends Per Share	0.74	0.64	0.50	0.46	0.42	[1] 0.387	0.36
Dividend Payout %	31.1	28.1	27.2	33.8	41.6	32.5	31.9

[1] 3-for-2 stk split, 6/30/89

ANNUAL FINANCIAL DATA

RECORD OF EARNINGS (IN MILLIONS):

	1994	1993	1992	1991	1990	1989	1988
Total Interest Income	578.4	547.3	338.6	323.3	323.4	279.9	222.5
Total Interest Expense	255.7	236.8	145.1	171.9	191.4	170.6	125.3
Net Interest Income	322.7	310.5	193.4	151.4	132.1	109.3	97.3
Credit Loss Provision	7.2	31.4	14.8	18.8	21.3	9.3	6.9
Net Income	109.6	[1] 8.2	50.1	30.8	22.9	23.8	21.6
Aver. Shs. Outstg. (000)	43,829	42,331	24,801	22,669	22,674	20,027	19,043

[1] Before acctg. change dr$27,217,000.

BALANCE SHEET (IN MILLIONS):

	1994	1993	1992	1991	1990	1989	1988
Cash & Due Fr Depoy Institutions	264.7	283.9	205.7	169.4	162.8	225.4	170.6
US Government Securities	...	...	...	543.3	524.1	639.9	516.4
States & Political Subdiviss	...	...	...	50.9	62.0	71.5	73.8
Loans & Lse Financing, Net	5,364.3	4,768.8	2,785.3	2,357.3	2,169.0	1,862.3	1,711.6
Total Domestic Deposits	6,165.1	6,394.9	3,790.7	3,221.0	2,772.5	2,427.8	2,212.1
Long-term Debt	197.5	479.7	33.2	24.2	29.4	35.3	35.8
Net Stockholders' Equity	632.3	564.9	377.2	235.3	214.8	170.6	147.8
Total Assets	8,756.1	8,274.5	4,598.4	4,741.0	4,108.5	3,642.6	3,200.6
Year End Shs Outstg (000)	44,159	31,845	25,228	22,669	22,662	20,085	19,043

STATISTICAL RECORD:

	1994	1993	1992	1991	1990	1989	1988
Return on Assets %	1.25	0.10	1.09	0.65	0.56	0.65	0.67
Return on Equity %	17.30	1.50	13.30	13.10	10.60	13.90	14.60
Book Value Per Share	14.23	17.62	14.80	10.38	9.48	8.49	7.76
Average Yield %	3.8	3.0	3.1	3.7	3.7	2.8	3.0
P/E Ratio	9.2-7.1	N.M	10.7-7.1	11.9-6.4	14.4-7.9	13.0-10.1	11.5-9.6
Price Range	22-16⅞	23½-18½	19¾-13	16¼-8¾	14½-8	15½-12	13-10⅞

Statistics are as originally reported.

OFFICERS:
J.A. Allison, Chmn. of Exec. Comm. & C.E.O.
S.E. Reed, C.F.O.
INCORPORATED: NC, 1968
PRINCIPAL OFFICE: 500 North Chestnut Street, Lumberton, NC 28358

TELEPHONE NUMBER: (919) 671-2000
NO. OF EMPLOYEES: 3,609 (approx.)
ANNUAL MEETING: In April
SHAREHOLDERS:
INSTITUTIONAL HOLDINGS:
No. of Institutions: 62
Shares Held: 3,568,117

REGISTRAR(S): Southern National Bank of NC

TRANSFER AGENT(S): Southern National Bank of NC

NASDAQ SYMBOL SOTR
Rec. Pr. 22⅜

SOUTHTRUST CORP.

YIELD 3.6%
P/E RATIO 10.1

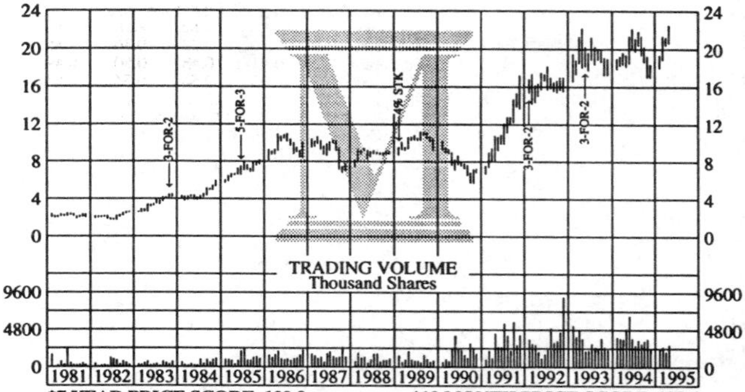

24
20
16
12
8
4
0
3-FOR-2
5-FOR-3
4% STK
3-FOR-2
3-FOR-2
TRADING VOLUME
Thousand Shares
9600
4800
0
1981
1982
1983
1984
1985
1986
1987
1988
1989
1990
1991
1992
1993
1994
1995

***7 YEAR PRICE SCORE 120.3** ***12 MONTH PRICE SCORE 100.6**

*NYSE COMPOSITE INDEX=100

INTERIM EARNINGS (Per Share):

Qtr.	Mar.	June	Sept.	Dec.
1992	0.39	0.41	0.42	0.44
1993	0.46	0.48	0.50	0.50
1994	0.51	0.53	0.55	0.56
1995	0.57	...	...	...

INTERIM DIVIDENDS (Per Share):

Amt.	Decl.	Ex.	Rec.	Pay.
0.17Q	4/20/94	5/23/94	5/27/94	7/1/94
0.17Q	7/20	8/22	8/26	10/1
0.17Q	10/19	11/18	11/25	1/2/95
0.20Q	1/18/95	2/17/95	2/24/95	4/1
0.20Q	4/19	5/22	5/26	7/1

Indicated div.: $0.80*

CAPITALIZATION (12/31/94):

	($000)	(%)
Total Deposits	12,801,239	72.8
Total Debt	3,468,728	19.7
Common & Surplus	1,135,268	6.5
Loan Valuation Reserve	171,692	1.0
Total	17,576,927	100.0

DIVIDEND ACHIEVER STATUS:

Rank: 126 1984-94 Growth Rate: 11.6%

Total Years of Dividend Growth: 25

RECENT DEVELOPMENTS: For the year ended 12/31/94, net income was $173.0 million, up 14.9% from the $150.5 million earned the year before. Total assets grew 20% from 1993 to $17.63 billion while deposits increased by 11% to $12.80 billion. Loans, net of unearned income, jumped 28% to $12.12 billion. Net interest income was $607.5 million compared with $529.8 million a year earlier. Noninterest income moved up to $184.8 million from $174.7 million; growth was led by a 12.5% increase in service charges on deposit accounts. However, the 17.8% decline in mortgage origination and servicing fees partially offset results. The provision for loan losses was unchanged from the prior year at $45.0 million. Noninterest expense increased 11.7% to $486.0 million from $435.0 million in 1993. For the quarter ended 12/31/94, net income was $45.4 million versus $39.4 million in the comparable 1993 period.

BUSINESS

SOUTHTRUST CORPORATION, a multibank holding company with headquarters in Birmingham, Alabama, owns 39 banks and more than 400 offices in Alabama, Florida, Georgia, North Carolina, South Carolina and Tennessee. Consolidated total assets of $17.6 billion rank the Company as one of the major bank holding companies in the Southeast. The banks serve their customers from 396 offices located throughout the six-state area. The lead bank of the Company is the $4.8 billion SouthTrust Bank of Alabama in Birmingham. Bank-related subsidiaries include SouthTrust Securities, Inc., an investment subsidiary; SouthTrust Mortgage Insurance Agency; SouthTrust Data Services, a bank data-processing company; SouthTrust Insurance Agency Inc.; SouthTrust Life Insurance Company, a credit-life insurance company; SouthTrust Leasing, Inc., SouthTrust Estate and Trust Company of Florida; and SouthTrust Estate and Trust Company of Georgia.

ANNUAL EARNINGS AND DIVIDENDS PER SHARE

	1994	1993	1992	1991	1990	1989	1988
Earnings Per Share	**2.15**	**1.94**	**1.66**	**1.42**	**1.14**	**1.21**	**1.14**
Dividends Per Share	**0.66**	**①0.577**	**②0.51**	**0.475**	**0.453**	**0.414**	**0.369**
Dividend Payout %	**30.7**	**29.7**	**30.7**	**33.4**	**39.7**	**34.1**	**32.4**

① 3-for-2 stk split,05/20/93 ② 3-for-2 stk split, 1/27/92

ANNUAL FINANCIAL DATA

	1994	1993	1992	1991	1990	1989	1988
RECORD OF EARNINGS (IN MILLIONS):							
Total Interest Income	1,108.6	927.6	832.2	827.2	780.4	688.0	560.8
Total Interest Expense	501.1	397.7	382.9	474.5	498.3	450.1	345.3
Net Interest Income	607.5	529.8	449.3	352.8	282.1	237.8	215.5
Credit Loss Provision	45.0	45.0	43.3	38.0	44.6	21.2	19.1
Net Income	173.0	150.5	114.2	90.0	69.7	72.8	67.6
Aver. Shs. Outstg. (000)	80,628	77,772	68,948	63,255	61,148	60,077	59,333
BALANCE SHEET (IN MILLIONS):							
Cash and Due From Banks	650.4	607.8	540.5	431.2	403.9	375.1	333.3
Loans & Lse Financing, Net	11,950.2	9,313.1	7,442.8	5,884.6	5,460.6	4,630.8	4,024.8
Total Domestic Deposits	10,761.5	9,732.5	8,484.5	7,171.6	6,175.4	5,125.5	4,269.6
Long-term Debt	640.7	470.0	258.2	140.2	148.8	144.8	147.0
Net Stockholders' Equity	1,135.3	1,051.8	860.4	662.0	549.6	507.1	445.8
Total Assets	17,632.1	14,708.0	12,714.4	10,158.1	9,005.9	7,763.2	6,645.3
Year End Shs Outstg (000)	81,426	79,401	74,477	65,836	61,167	61,013	59,522
STATISTICAL RECORD:							
Return on Assets %	0.98	1.02	0.90	0.89	0.77	0.94	1.02
Return on Equity %	15.20	14.30	13.30	13.60	12.70	14.40	15.20
Book Value Per Share	13.94	13.25	11.55	10.06	8.98	8.31	7.49
Average Yield %	3.4	3.0	3.2	4.0	5.6	4.1	4.4
P/E Ratio	10.3-7.9	11.4-8.6	10.9-8.5	12.1-4.7	9.1-5.0	9.3-7.2	8.3-6.5
Price Range	22⅛-17	22⅛-16⅝	18⅛-14⅛	17¼-6⅝	10⅜-5¾	11¼-8¾	9½-7⅜

Statistics are as originally reported.

OFFICERS:
W.D. Malone, Jr., Chmn. & C.E.O.
R.W. Gilbert, Jr., Pres. & C.O.O.
A.D. Barnard, Sec., Treas. & Contr. & Contr.

INCORPORATED: DE, 1968

PRINCIPAL OFFICE: 420 North 20th Street, Birmingham, AL 35203

TELEPHONE NUMBER: (205) 254-5509

FAX: (205) 254-5404

NO. OF EMPLOYEES: 7,000 (approx.)

ANNUAL MEETING: In April

SHAREHOLDERS: 10,632 (approx.)

INSTITUTIONAL HOLDINGS:
No. of Institutions: 195
Shares Held: 32,819,882

REGISTRAR(S):

TRANSFER AGENT(S): Mellon Securities Trust Company, New York, NY

NYS SYMBOL STH
Rec. Pr. 30

STANHOME, INC.

YIELD 3.5%
P/E RATIO 13.3

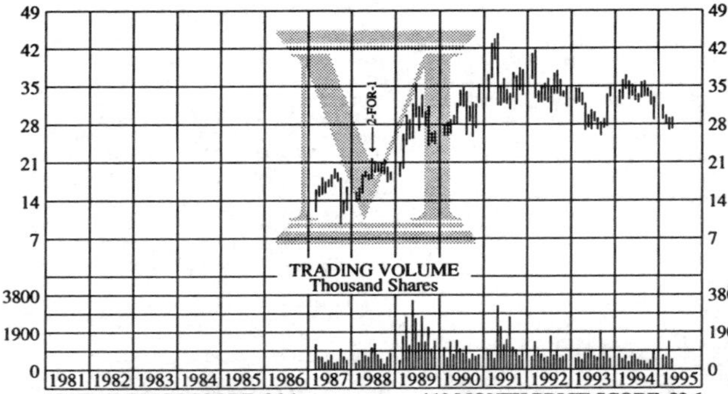
49
42
35
28
21
14
7
2-FOR-1
TRADING VOLUME
Thousand Shares
3800
1900
0
1981 1982 1983 1984 1985 1986 1987 1988 1989 1990 1991 1992 1993 1994 1995

***7 YEAR PRICE SCORE 86.4** ***12 MONTH PRICE SCORE 83.6**

*NYSE COMPOSITE INDEX=100

INTERIM EARNINGS (Per Share):

Qtr.	Mar.	June	Sept.	Dec.
1991	0.34	0.47	0.58	0.83
1992	0.41	0.57	0.58	0.76
1993	0.31	d0.06	0.60	0.83
1994	0.41	0.59	0.67	0.58

INTERIM DIVIDENDS (Per Share):

Amt.	Decl.	Ex.	Rec.	Pay.
0.25Q	3/2/94	3/10/94	3/16/94	4/1/94
0.25Q	5/31	6/9	6/15	7/1
0.265Q	9/7	9/15	9/21	10/1
0.265Q	12/7	12/13	12/19	1/1/95
0.265Q	3/1/95	3/9/95	3/15/95	4/1

Indicated div.: $1.06*

CAPITALIZATION (12/31/94):

	($000)	(%)
Common & Surplus	269,396	100.0
Total	269,396	100.0

DIVIDEND ACHIEVER STATUS:
Rank: 82 1984-94 Growth Rate: 13.7%
Total Years of Dividend Growth: 11

RECENT DEVELOPMENTS: For the year ended 12/31/94, net income increased 33% to $44.1 million compared with $33.1 million the previous year. Sales were up 5.3% to $790.2 million from $750.7 million. The prior-year results included a restructuring charge of $17.0 million. The improved operating results were driven by the Enesco Worldwide Giftware Group. Hamilton Direct Response Group also contributed to the sales and earnings growth.

PROSPECTS: Operating results will benefit from several acquisitions made in the United States and Europe during 1994. These acquisitions have broadened the Company's product lines and expanded its presence in the consumer products market. The Enesco Worldwide Giftware Group continues to benefit from strong demand for the Precious Moments and Cherished Teddies collectible product lines.

BUSINESS

STANHOME INC. is a worldwide marketer of consumer products. The Company's key product segments include designed giftware and collectibles sold to retailers; collectible dolls, plates and figurines sold through direct response; and home care, personal care and giftware items sold through direct selling. The Enesco Giftware Group is a leader in designed giftware including licensed lines and collectibles. The group encompasses the businesses of Enesco Corp., Tomorrow-Today Corp, Sports Impressions, Inc., Hamilton Gifts Ltd., and Via Vermont Ltd., with a global network of sales organizations to support the distribution of its designed giftware and collectibles to retail outlets. The Hamilton Group is a leader in direct response selling.

ANNUAL EARNINGS AND DIVIDENDS PER SHARE

	1994	1993	1992	1991	1990	1989	1988
Earnings Per Share	**2.25**	**1.00**	**2.32**	**2.22**	**2.55**	**2.23**	**1.96**
Dividends Per Share	**1.015**	**1.00**	**0.94**	**0.92**	**0.80**	**0.68**	**[1] 0.56**
Dividend Payout %	**45.1**	**N.M.**	**40.5**	**51.6**	**31.5**	**30.5**	**28.6**

[1] 2-for-1 stock split, 6/88.

ANNUAL FINANCIAL DATA

	1994	1993	1992	1991	1990	1989	1988
RECORD OF EARNINGS (IN THOUSANDS):							
Total Revenues	790,176	750,663	744,072	710,208	675,665	571,380	480,374
Costs and Expenses	701,967	676,757	652,243	623,131	580,506	484,365	399,529
Depreciation & Amort	7,657	8,354	8,396	7,940	7,649	6,725	6,660
Operating Profit	80,552	65,552	83,433	79,136	87,509	80,290	74,185
Income Bef Income Taxes	80,739	66,140	86,992	81,139	90,258	79,650	71,799
Income Taxes	36,684	33,007	40,276	36,086	39,191	35,027	31,159
Net Income	44,056	33,133	46,716	45,053	51,067	44,624	40,640
Aver. Shs. Outstg.	19,525	19,749	20,152	20,295	20,040	20,024	20,664
BALANCE SHEET (IN THOUSANDS):							
Cash and Cash Equivalents	19,352	60,726	42,270	52,221	51,827	43,790	65,632
Receivables, Net	140,697	123,018	107,366	105,713	88,600	75,453	53,154
Inventories	116,015	94,877	119,971	114,926	111,560	83,928	62,550
Gross Property	125,996	107,852	109,466	121,903	116,883	108,486	101,607
Accumulated Depreciation	68,037	63,177	59,388	63,144	56,960	52,948	45,494
Long-Term Debt	...	...	911	1,173	1,421	1,438	1,598
Net Stockholders' Equity	269,396	254,366	256,956	241,074	211,457	170,399	158,169
Total Assets	512,123	429,730	415,618	419,319	391,821	335,154	275,524
Total Current Assets	322,677	314,351	298,247	293,651	271,390	218,582	182,327
Total Current Liabilities	220,218	155,052	143,072	159,452	162,234	150,162	104,439
Net Working Capital	102,460	159,299	155,174	134,199	109,156	68,420	77,888
Year End Shares Outstg	19,151	19,392	19,774	19,791	19,550	19,365	19,953
STATISTICAL RECORD:							
Operating Profit Margin %	10.2	8.7	11.2	11.1	13.0	14.1	15.4
Book Value Per Share	14.07	13.12	10.00	9.19	8.08	5.96	6.12
Return on Equity %	16.4	13.0	18.2	18.7	24.2	26.2	25.7
Return on Assets %	8.6	7.7	11.2	10.7	13.0	13.3	14.8
Average Yield %	3.1	3.3	2.6	2.4	2.6	2.5	3.1
P/E Ratio	16.4-12.7	20.7-15.4	17.9-13.0	20.2-13.9	13.8-10.0	15.9-8.2	11.0-7.0
Price Range	37-28¾	34¾-25⅞	41⅝-30⅛	44¾-30¾	35¼-25⅝	35½-18⅜	21¾-13⅞

Statistics are as originally reported.

OFFICERS:
H.L. Tower, Chmn.
G.W. Seawright, Pres. & C.E.O.
A.G. Keirstead, Exec. V.P., Chief. Admin. Off., C.F.O. & Contr.
B.H. Wyatt, V.P., Gen. Couns. & Sec.
C.J. Mascaro, Treas.

INCORPORATED: MA, Jul., 1931

PRINCIPAL OFFICE: 333 Western Ave., Westfield, MA 01085

TELEPHONE NUMBER: (413) 562-3631

FAX: (413) 568-2820

NO. OF EMPLOYEES: 1,640

ANNUAL MEETING: In April

SHAREHOLDERS: 3,652

INSTITUTIONAL HOLDINGS:
No. of Institutions: 142
Shares Held: 12,440,972

REGISTRAR(S): Mellon Securities Trust Co., East Hartford, CT

TRANSFER AGENT(S): Mellon Securities Trust Co., East Hartford, CT

STANLEY WORKS

YIELD 3.5%
P/E RATIO 14.4

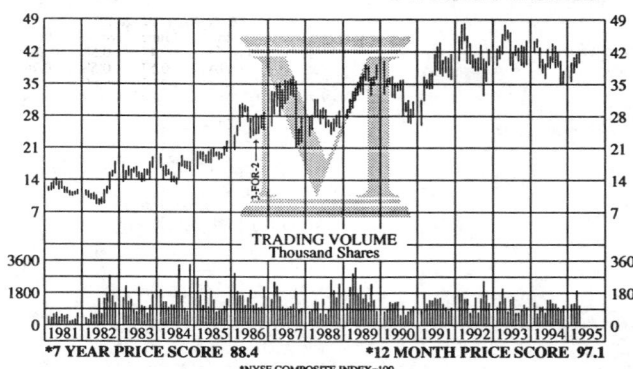

| *7 YEAR PRICE SCORE 88.4 | *12 MONTH PRICE SCORE 97.1 |

*NYSE COMPOSITE INDEX=100

INTERIM EARNINGS (Per Share):

Qtr.	Mar.	June	Sept.	Dec.
1991	0.38	0.66	0.66	0.61
1992		2.15		
1993	0.51	0.60	0.56	0.39
1994	0.57	0.75	0.72	0.76

INTERIM DIVIDENDS (Per Share):

Amt.	Decl.	Ex.	Rec.	Pay.
0.35Q	8/31/94	9/6/94	9/12/94	9/30/94
0.35Q	10/26	11/28	12/2	12/30
0.35Q	10/26	11/28	12/2	12/30
0.35Q	10/26	11/28	12/2	12/30
0.35Q	3/1/95	3/7/95	3/13/95	3/31/95

Indicated div.: $1.40*

CAPITALIZATION (12/31/94):

	($000)	(%)
Long-Term Debt	387,100	23.4
Deferred Income Tax	14,400	0.9
Common & Surplus	1,251,600	75.7
Total	1,653,100	100.0

DIVIDEND ACHIEVER STATUS:
Rank: 199   1984-94 Growth Rate: 8.7%
Total Years of Dividend Growth: 27

RECENT DEVELOPMENTS: For the twelve months ended 12/31/94, net income increased 35.3% to $125.3 million from $92.6 million, before an $8.5 million accounting charge, in 1993. Revenues were up 10.5% to $2.51 billion. Gross margins improved to 32.9% from 31.7%. Tools segment operating income climbed 37.3% to $217 million on a sales increase of 10.5% to $1.88 billion. Specialty Hardware sales and earnings rose 81.8% and 17.8%, respectively.

PROSPECTS: Improvement in gross margins will likely continue due to the successful transition of previously foreign-sourced fastening tools to U.S. in-house manufacture. Sales in European operations are being enhanced by unit volume gain and positive contributions from acquisitions. Meanwhile, U.S. sales are benefiting from strong internal growth. Future growth will be enhanced by new product developments and expansion into new geographic markets.

BUSINESS

STANLEY WORKS is a worldwide manufacturer and marketer of tools, hardware and specialty hardware products for consumer home improvement, professional and industrial use. The Tools segment which consists of consumer, industrial and engineered tools, includes Stanley Tools, Stanley Fastening Systems, National Hand Tool, Mac Tools, Stanley Air Tools and Hydraulic Tools, Stanley-Vidmar and Stanley-Proto. Hardware, includes Stanley Hardware, Acmetrack and Industrial Hardware. Specialty Hardware, consists of residential door systems and includes Stanley Door Systems and Magic-Door.

BUSINESS LINE ANALYSIS

(12/31/94)	Rev(%)	Inc(%)
Tools	75.0	79.1
Hardware	12.4	12.1
Specialty Hardware	12.6	8.8
Total	100.0	100.0

ANNUAL EARNINGS AND DIVIDENDS PER SHARE

	12/31/94	1/1/94	1/2/93	12/28/91	12/29/90	12/30/89	12/31/88
Earnings Per Share	2.80	2.06	2.15	① 2.31	2.53	2.71	2.40
Dividends Per Share	1.38	1.34	1.28	1.19	1.14	1.02	0.92
Dividend Payout %	49.3	65.1	55.8	51.5	45.1	37.6	38.3

① Before acctg. chg.

ANNUAL FINANCIAL DATA

RECORD OF EARNINGS (IN MILLIONS):

Total Revenues	2,510.9	2,273.1	2,217.7	1,962.2	1,976.7	1,971.5	1,909.0
Costs and Expenses	2,162.6	1,984.6	1,931.2	1,681.3	1,681.0	1,657.7	1,626.0
Depreciation & Amort	81.8	80.7	78.5	74.9	74.3	69.8	64.0
Operating Profit	826.9	720.1	735.8	668.4	684.4	693.2	656.3
Earn Bef Income Taxes	201.8	148.0	158.1	156.5	172.0	193.9	172.5
Income Taxes	76.5	55.4	60.0	61.4	65.4	76.2	69.0
Net Income	125.3	①92.6	98.1	②95.1	106.6	117.7	103.5
Aver. Shs. Outstg. (000)	44,775	44,935	45,703	43,266	42,192	43,378	43,109

① Before acctg. change dr$8,500,000. ② Before acctg. change dr$12,500,000.

BALANCE SHEET (IN MILLIONS):

Cash and Cash Equivalents	69.3	43.7	81.1	58.3	94.7	55.4	36.6
Receivables, Net	410.3	371.2	354.9	352.6	330.6	360.1	336.6
Inventories	369.2	308.1	302.0	299.6	291.8	313.2	308.0
Gross Property	1,128.6	1,119.0	1,088.8	1,045.5	979.4	918.8	849.0
Accumulated Depreciation	568.8	552.5	522.2	483.8	441.1	399.2	358.2
Long-Term Debt	387.1	377.2	438.0	396.7	398.1	416.4	339.4
Net Stockholders' Equity	1,251.6	1,203.9	1,233.9	1,257.7	902.3	891.1	736.4
Total Assets	1,701.1	1,576.9	1,607.6	1,547.9	1,493.8	1,491.2	1,405.2
Total Current Assets	888.5	758.6	778.7	743.9	744.2	759.7	710.5
Total Current Liabilities	421.5	357.1	329.9	308.9	282.4	283.7	266.5
Net Working Capital	467.0	401.5	448.8	435.0	461.8	476.0	443.9
Year End Shs Outstg (000)	44,449	44,696	45,439	45,241	41,176	43,017	42,790

STATISTICAL RECORD:

Operating Profit Margin %	10.6	9.1	9.4	10.5	11.2	12.4	11.5
Book Value Per Share	24.45	23.10	23.30	24.75	19.38	18.19	14.91
Return on Equity %	10.0	7.7	8.0	7.6	11.8	13.2	14.1
Return on Assets %	7.4	5.9	6.1	6.1	7.1	7.9	7.4
Average Yield %	3.5	3.2	3.3	3.4	3.4	3.1	3.3
P/E Ratio	16.0-12.5	23.2-18.4	22.4-15.1	19.0-11.3	15.8-10.4	14.5-10.1	13.2-9.8
Price Range	44⅞-34⅛	47⅞-37⅛	48⅛-32½		44-26	40-26⅜	39¼-27½	31¾-23⅝

Statistics are as originally reported.

OFFICERS:
R.H. Ayers, Chmn. & C.E.O.
R.A. Hunter, Pres. & C.O.O.
R. Huck, V.P.-Fin. & C.F.O.
S.S. Weddle, V.P., Gen. Couns. & Sec.

INCORPORATED: CT, Jul., 1852

PRINCIPAL OFFICE: 1000 Stanley Drive, New Britain, CT 06053

TELEPHONE NUMBER: (203) 225-5111

FAX: (203) 827-3911

NO. OF EMPLOYEES: 19,445 (avg.)

ANNUAL MEETING: In April

SHAREHOLDERS: 17,599

INSTITUTIONAL HOLDINGS:
No. of Institutions: 268
Shares Held: 23,290,062

REGISTRAR(S): Mellon Securities Trust Co., Hartford, CT

TRANSFER AGENT(S): Mellon Securities Trust Co., Hartford, CT

NYS SYMBOL STB
Rec. Pr. 41¾

STAR BANC CORP.

YIELD 3.8%
P/E RATIO 10.3

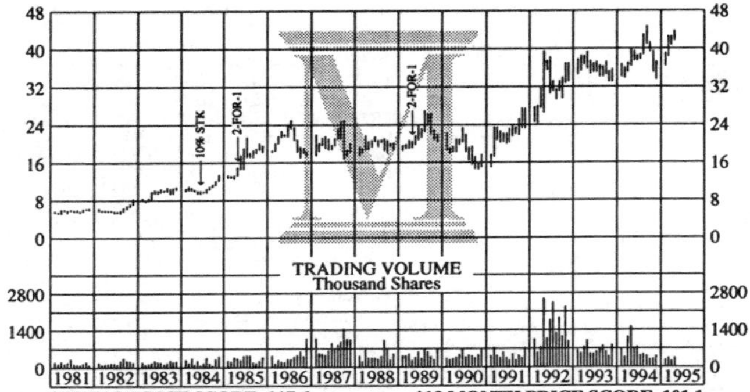

***7 YEAR PRICE SCORE 117.6** ***12 MONTH PRICE SCORE 101.1**

*NYSE COMPOSITE INDEX=100

INTERIM EARNINGS (Per Share):

Qtr.	Mar.	June	Sept.	Dec.
1992	0.59	0.67	0.68	0.63
1993	0.84	0.85	0.78	0.89
1994	0.93	0.95	1.00	1.02

INTERIM DIVIDENDS (Per Share):

Amt.	Decl.	Ex.	Rec.	Pay.
0.35Q	3/7/94	3/25/94	3/31/94	4/15/94
0.35Q	6/13	6/24	6/30	7/15
0.35Q	9/13	9/26	9/30	10/14
0.35Q	12/13	12/23	12/30	1/13/95
0.40Q	3/14/95	3/27/95	3/31/95	4/14

Indicated div.: $1.60*

CAPITALIZATION (12/31/94):

	($000)	(%)
Total Deposits	7,363,815	78.5
Total Debt	1,201,166	12.8
Preferred Stock	2,466	0.0
Common & Surplus	715,752	7.7
Loan Valuation Reserve	95,979	1.0
Total	9,379,178	100.0

DIVIDEND ACHIEVER STATUS:
Rank: 206 1984-94 Growth Rate: 8.3%
Total Years of Dividend Growth: 23

RECENT DEVELOPMENTS: For the year ended 12/31/94, net income advanced 16.3% to $116.6 million from $100.3 million in 1993. Results benefited from loan growth, higher fee income and improved credit quality; however, noninterest income increased 4%, primarily due to the acquisition of TransOhio Federal Savings Bank. Net interest income was $346.1 million versus $323.5 million a year earlier. Total loans were up by $955.2 million to $6.25 billion. The provision for loan losses was $24.4 million, down 26%.

PROSPECTS: The Company entered into an agreement to buy 24 branch offices and $680 million in deposits of the Ohio division of Household Bank, the consumer banking subsidiary of Household International. With this acquisition, STB will hold a 7% market share in the Columbus, OH market. STB became the third-largest bank in the Cleveland market with the acquisition of $1.1 billion in deposits and 47 branches of TransOhio Federal Savings Bank.

BUSINESS

STAR BANC CORPORATION is a $9.4 billion multi-state bank holding company headquartered in Cincinnati, Ohio. The merger of the ten independent subsidiaries, Star Bank, into three banks, one per state in Ohio, Kentucky, and Indiana, was completed in 1993. Star operates 253 banking offices. The Company's subsidiary banks serve the needs of business, industry, government entities, other financial institutions and individuals in all its market areas through a full range of consumer, commercial and trust financial products and investment services.

LOAN DISTRIBUTION

(12/31/94)	($000)	(%)
Commercial	2,079,804	32.9
Real Estate loans	2,378,661	37.6
Retail Loans	1,865,295	29.5
Total	6,323,760	100.0

ANNUAL EARNINGS AND DIVIDENDS PER SHARE

	1994	1993	1992	1991	1990	1989	1988
Earnings Per Share	**3.89**	**3.36**	**2.57**	**2.24**	**2.23**	**2.01**	**1.92**
Dividends Per Share	**1.34**	**1.13**	**1.03**	**0.99**	**0.94**	**[1] 0.865**	**0.81**
Dividend Payout %	**33.4**	**33.6**	**40.1**	**44.2**	**42.2**	**43.0**	**42.2**

[1] 2-for-1 stk split, 4/14/89

ANNUAL FINANCIAL DATA

	1994	1993	1992	1991	1990	1989	1988
RECORD OF EARNINGS (IN MILLIONS):							
Total Interest Income	569.7	518.2	541.4	576.8	586.8	563.9	467.1
Total Interest Expense	223.6	194.7	233.0	307.3	340.2	336.3	261.5
Net Interest Income	346.1	323.5	308.4	269.4	246.6	227.6	205.6
Credit Loss Provision	24.4	33.0	40.9	39.9	40.4	35.4	25.9
Net Income	116.6	100.3	76.1	65.8	64.9	58.0	[1] 55.4
Aver. Shs. Outstg. (000)	29,873	29,549	29,227	29,064	29,064	28,885	28,884
[1] Before acctg. change cr$3,066,000.							
BALANCE SHEET (IN MILLIONS):							
Cash & Due From Banks	429.5	387.8	434.8	326.9	395.3	399.4	326.9
Loans & Lse Financing, Net	6,153.6	5,211.3	4,914.1	4,784.6	4,493.8	4,210.3	3,834.2
Total Domestic Deposits	7,363.8	6,015.6	6,402.8	5,428.5	5,129.8	4,973.1	4,723.1
Long-term Debt	166.5	51.7	56.8	62.9	31.9	35.4	36.9
Net Stockholders' Equity	718.2	675.8	602.3	555.0	500.0	462.5	429.6
Total Assets	9,390.8	7,636.8	7,715.4	6,645.9	7,116.7	6,769.1	5,656.6
Year End Shs Outstg (000)	29,803	29,607	29,217	28,903	28,888	28,715	28,736
STATISTICAL RECORD:							
Return on Assets %	1.24	1.31	0.99	0.99	0.91	0.86	0.98
Return on Equity %	16.20	14.80	12.60	11.90	13.00	12.50	12.90
Book Value Per Share	24.02	22.33	20.09	18.58	17.31	16.11	14.95
Average Yield %	3.4	3.1	3.2	4.7	5.0	3.8	4.1
P/E Ratio	11.5-8.6	11.7-9.8	15.4-9.4	12.3-6.7	10.5-6.5	13.4-9.2	11.3-9.1
Price Range	44¾-33½	39⅜-33	39½-24¼	27½-15	23⅜-14½	27-18½	21¾-17½

Statistics are as originally reported.

OFFICERS:
J.A. Grundhofer, Chmn., Pres. & C.E.O.
D.M. Moffett, Exec. V.P. & C.F.O.

INCORPORATED: DE, Sep., 1973; reincorp., OH, 1988

PRINCIPAL OFFICE: Star Bank Center 425 Walnut St., Cincinnati, OH 45202

TELEPHONE NUMBER: (513) 632-4008
FAX: (513) 632-5512
NO. OF EMPLOYEES: 3,707
ANNUAL MEETING: In April
SHAREHOLDERS: 7,858 Com. Pfd. 98
INSTITUTIONAL HOLDINGS:
No. of Institutions: 111
Shares Held: 11,125,251

REGISTRAR(S):

TRANSFER AGENT(S): At Company's Office

NYS SYMBOL STT
Rec. Pr. 33½

STATE STREET BOSTON CORP.

YIELD 1.9%
P/E RATIO 12.5

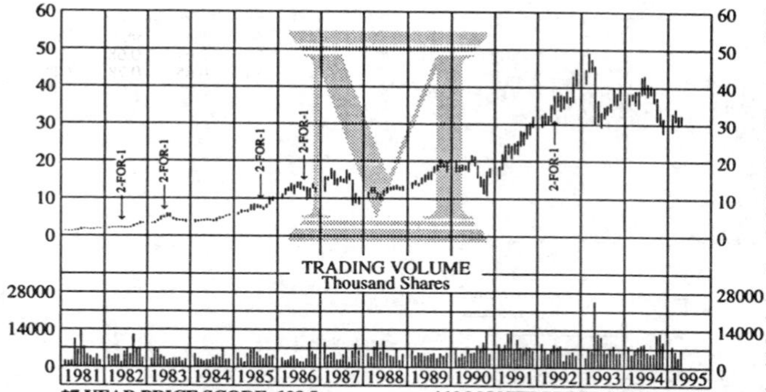

*7 YEAR PRICE SCORE 108.5 *12 MONTH PRICE SCORE 84.5

*NYSE COMPOSITE INDEX=100

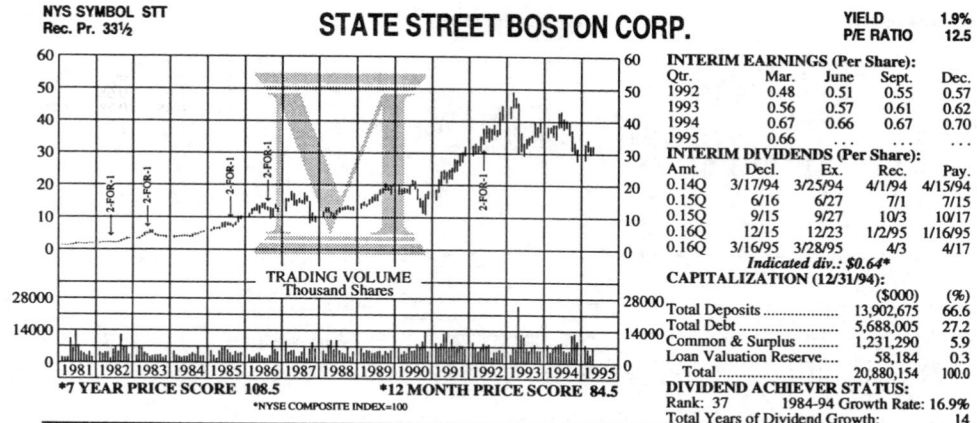

INTERIM EARNINGS (Per Share):

Qtr.	Mar.	June	Sept.	Dec.
1992	0.48	0.51	0.55	0.57
1993	0.56	0.57	0.61	0.62
1994	0.67	0.66	0.67	0.70
1995	0.66	...	...	...

INTERIM DIVIDENDS (Per Share):

Amt.	Decl.	Ex.	Rec.	Pay.
0.14Q	3/17/94	3/25/94	4/1/94	4/15/94
0.15Q	6/16	6/27	7/1	7/15
0.15Q	9/15	9/27	10/3	10/17
0.16Q	12/15	12/23	1/2/95	1/16/95
0.16Q	3/16/95	3/28/95	4/3	4/17

Indicated div.: $0.64*

CAPITALIZATION (12/31/94):

	($000)	(%)
Total Deposits	13,902,675	66.6
Total Debt	5,688,005	27.2
Common & Surplus	1,231,290	5.9
Loan Valuation Reserve	58,184	0.3
Total	20,880,154	100.0

DIVIDEND ACHIEVER STATUS:
Rank: 37 1984-94 Growth Rate: 16.9%
Total Years of Dividend Growth: 14

RECENT DEVELOPMENTS: For the year ended 12/31/94, net income was $207.4 million, up 15.3% from $179.8 million in 1993. Return on stockholders equity for 1994 was 17.5%. Results benefited from a 16% increase in net interest revenue to $367.2 million from $317.6 million the year before. Fee revenue rose 18% to $981.0 million from $833.4 million. As of 12/31/94, STT had more than $1.6 trillion in assets under custody and $160 billion under management. Net income for the quarter ended 12/31/94 was $53.3 million, up 11.7%. Total revenue for the quarter was $345.9 million, up $37.6 million from a year ago. This growth reflected new customers, and the use of additional and more complex services by existing customers. Net interest revenue advanced 13% to $93.9 million and fee revenue rose 11% to $247.7 million.

BUSINESS

STATE STREET BOSTON CORP. is a $21.7 billion bank holding company that carries on its business principally through its subsidiary, State Street Bank and Trust Company. The Company is a leading servicer of financial assets worldwide. State Street is the leading U.S. mutual fund custodian and the largest U.S. master trust/master custody bank. The Company is the leader in global custody for U.S. pension plans and the largest global custodian in Australia. State Street is the third-largest money-management firm in the U.S. and the largest international index firm in the world. The Company also provides a full range of commercial banking and capital markets services, as well as corporate trust, corporate stock transfer, defined contribution plan, planned gift management and personal trust services. Services are provided from offices in the United States, Canada, Grand Cayman, Netherlands Antilles, United Kingdom, France, Belgium, Luxembourg, Germany, United Arab Emirates, Hong Kong, Taiwan, Japan, Australia and New Zealand.

ANNUAL EARNINGS AND DIVIDENDS PER SHARE

	1994	1993	1992	1991	1990	1989	1988
Earnings Per Share	**2.70**	**2.36**	**2.10**	**1.86**	**1.59**	**1.42**	**1.26**
Dividends Per Share	**0.58**	**0.50**	**① 0.43**	**0.37**	**0.33**	**0.29**	**0.25**
Dividend Payout %	**21.5**	**21.2**	**20.5**	**19.9**	**20.8**	**20.4**	**19.9**

① 2-for-1 stk split, 5/14/92

ANNUAL FINANCIAL DATA

	1994	1993	1992	1991	1990	1989	1988
RECORD OF EARNINGS (IN MILLIONS):							
Total Interest Income	904.7	698.9	714.4	737.8	817.5	648.3	499.3
Total Interest Expense	537.5	381.3	432.1	464.2	546.7	431.3	299.7
Net Interest Income	367.2	317.6	282.3	273.6	270.8	217.0	199.6
Credit Loss Provision	11.6	11.3	12.2	60.0	45.7	19.4	15.6
Net Income	207.4	179.8	160.4	139.3	117.3	104.0	92.3
Aver. Shs. Outstg. (000)	76,851	76,193	76,235	74,969	73,888	73,314	73,686
BALANCE SHEET (IN MILLIONS):							
Cash & Due From Banks	1,004.9	1,469.4	1,284.5	1,016.8	1,403.1	1,225.1	781.0
Loans & Lse Financing, Net	3,175.0	2,625.9	1,945.8	1,839.4	2,054.1	2,414.7	2,128.8
Total Domestic Deposits	5,981.7	7,590.6	6,642.5	6,074.3	5,241.1	4,692.9	4,259.4
Total Foreign Deposits	7,920.9	5,427.2	4,417.6	2,657.1	2,416.6	1,485.2	1,129.0
Long-term Debt	127.5	128.9	145.8	147.0	112.4	114.6	123.2
Net Stockholders' Equity	1,231.3	1,105.0	953.1	816.6	695.1	597.2	505.6
Total Assets	21,729.5	18,720.1	16,489.8	15,046.3	11,650.9	9,983.0	8,372.0
Year End Shs Outstg (000)	76,475	75,874	75,061	74,440	73,098	72,054	70,048
STATISTICAL RECORD:							
Return on Assets %	0.95	0.96	0.97	0.93	1.01	1.04	1.10
Return on Equity %	16.80	16.30	16.80	17.10	16.90	17.40	18.30
Book Value Per Share	16.10	14.56	12.70	10.97	9.51	8.29	7.22
Average Yield %	1.6	1.3	1.2	1.6	2.0	1.7	2.1
P/E Ratio	16.0-10.2	20.8-12.4	21.4-13.9	17.3-8.3	13.6-6.9	14.4-9.0	11.0-7.8
Price Range	43⅛-27⅝	49⅛-29¼	44⅞-29¼	32⅛-15½	21⅝-11	20½-12¾	13¾-9¾

Statistics are as originally reported.

OFFICERS:
M.N. Carter, Chmn. & C.E.O.
D.A. Spina, Vice-Chmn., C.F.O. & Treas.

INCORPORATED: MA, Oct., 1969

PRINCIPAL OFFICE: 225 Franklin Street, Boston, MA 02110

TELEPHONE NUMBER: (617) 786-3000

NO. OF EMPLOYEES: 11,127

ANNUAL MEETING: In April

SHAREHOLDERS: 5,926

INSTITUTIONAL HOLDINGS:
No. of Institutions: 339
Shares Held: 54,011,953

REGISTRAR(S):

TRANSFER AGENT(S): State Street Bank & Trust Co., Boston, MA 02266

STEPAN CO.

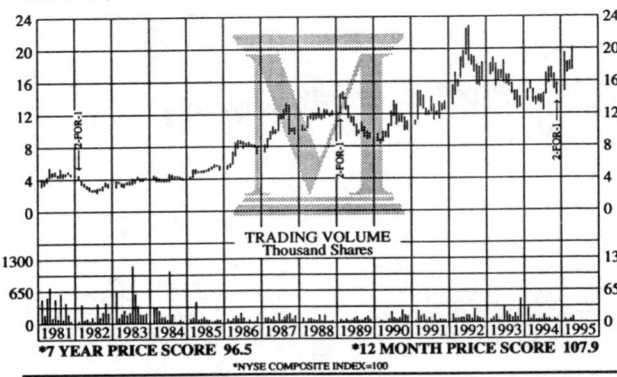

INTERIM EARNINGS (Per Share):

Qtr.	Mar.	June	Sept.	Dec.
1991	0.22	0.25	0.35	0.34
1992	0.37	0.38	0.38	d0.14
1993	0.45	0.31	0.29	d0.08
1994	0.17	0.38	0.38	0.34

INTERIM DIVIDENDS (Per Share):

Amt.	Decl.	Ex.	Rec.	Pay.
0.22Q	11/11/94	11/25/94	12/1/94	12/15/94
2-for-1	11/11	12/16	12/1	12/15
0.11Q	2/22/95	2/24/95	3/2/95	3/15/95
0.11Q	5/1	5/24	5/31	6/15

Indicated div.: $0.44

CAPITALIZATION (12/31/94):

	($000)	(%)
Long-Term Debt	89,795	38.4
Deferred Income Tax	32,976	14.1
Preferred Stock.................	19,980	8.5
Common & Surplus	91,322	39.0
Total	234,073	100.0

DIVIDEND ACHIEVER STATUS:
Rank: 165   1984-94 Growth Rate: 10.1%
Total Years of Dividend Growth: 28

*7 YEAR PRICE SCORE 96.5   *12 MONTH PRICE SCORE 107.9

*NYSE COMPOSITE INDEX=100

RECENT DEVELOPMENTS: For the year ended 12/31/94, net income increased 28% to $13.8 million from $10.8 million in the previous year. Net sales edged up 1% to $443.9 million from $438.8 million a year earlier. Operating expenses decreased 3% during 1994. A favorable impact was felt from insurance recoveries of $3.1 million relating to previously incurred legal and environmental costs. Net income for the quarter ended 12/31/94 was $3.6 million compared with a net

loss of $449,000 in the corresponding period of 1993. Net sales for the quarter advanced 11% to $113.6 million from $102.5 million a year earlier. Fourth quarter results benefited from higher phthalic anhydride sales volume and margins. Surfactants recorded higher quarterly earnings due to increased domestic surfactant sales of more profitable products.

BUSINESS

STEPAN COMPANY is a major manufacturer of basic and intermediate chemicals used in a broad range of industries. The Company is a leading merchant producer of surfactants, which are the key ingredient in consumer and industrial cleaning compounds. Stepan produces other specialty products which are often custom-made to meet individual needs. These include emulsifiers which facilitate spreading of insecticides and herbicides, and lubricant and cutting-oil ingredients. The Company is also a principal supplier of phthalic anhydride, a commodity chemical intermediate which is used in polyester resins, alkyd resins and plasticizers. Polyurethane foam systems sold by the Company are used in the expanding thermal insulation market primarily by the construction and refrigeration industries.

REVENUES

(12/31/94)	($000)	(%)
Surfactants.................	329,186	74.1
Polymers.....................	78,778	17.8
Specialty Products.....	35,984	8.1
Total	443,948	100.0

ANNUAL EARNINGS AND DIVIDENDS PER SHARE

	1994	1993	1992	1991	1990	1989	1988
Earnings Per Share	1.29	0.98	① 0.96	1.15	1.32	0.71	1.20
Dividends Per Share	③ 0.425	0.405	0.37	0.33	0.29	0.265	② 0.237
Dividend Payout %	32.9	41.3	38.7	28.7	22.0	37.3	19.9

① Before acctg. chg. ② 2-for-1 stk split, 12/88 ③ 2-for-1 stk split, 12/94

ANNUAL FINANCIAL DATA

RECORD OF EARNINGS (IN THOUSANDS):

	1994	1993	1992	1991	1990	1989	1988
Total Revenues	443,948	438,825	435,764	414,069	389,612	346,350	333,033
Costs and Expenses	385,365	383,896	381,341	367,611	342,976	311,620	292,575
Depreciation & Amort	28,935	27,679	23,914	21,108	19,391	17,061	15,393
Operating Profit	47,046	44,919	45,643	40,681	40,670	30,520	38,121
Income Bef Income Taxes	22,512	19,624	17,365	18,866	22,294	11,701	20,554
Income Taxes	8,667	8,848	6,942	6,319	7,803	3,861	7,126
Net Income	13,845	10,776	① 10,423	12,547	14,491	7,840	13,428
Aver. Shs. Outstg.	9,924	9,894	10,572	10,916	10,992	11,034	11,216

① Before acctg. change cr$5,406,000.

BALANCE SHEET (IN THOUSANDS):

	1994	1993	1992	1991	1990	1989	1988
Cash and Cash Equivalents	2,452	1,515	2,915	2,275	1,631	1,607	929
Receivables, Net	78,603	64,748	63,952	55,118	51,772	48,479	43,286
Inventories	45,464	48,918	47,778	43,955	39,894	30,432	26,278
Gross Property	417,654	378,828	353,999	322,260	288,764	251,526	218,372
Accumulated Depreciation	233,997	208,538	186,069	165,197	145,422	129,017	113,675
Long-Term Debt	89,795	89,660	90,505	89,759	77,326	68,568	45,369
Net Stockholders' Equity	111,302	104,217	99,506	90,866	82,698	70,741	66,790
Total Assets	324,948	300,488	297,080	271,442	246,992	216,059	185,601
Total Current Assets	129,371	119,160	118,625	104,005	95,976	83,799	72,743
Total Current Liabilities	80,456	70,591	74,360	62,033	57,033	46,139	44,245
Net Working Capital	48,915	48,569	44,265	41,972	38,943	37,660	28,498
Year End Shares Outstg	9,944	9,896	9,872	10,876	10,928	10,966	11,008

STATISTICAL RECORD:

	1994	1993	1992	1991	1990	1989	1988
Operating Profit Margin %	6.7	6.2	7.0	6.1	7.0	5.1	7.5
Book Value Per Share	9.18	8.51	8.05	8.35	7.57	6.45	6.07
Return on Equity %	12.4	10.3	10.5	13.8	17.5	11.1	20.1
Return on Assets %	4.3	3.6	3.5	4.6	5.9	3.6	7.2
Average Yield %	2.8	2.6	2.1	2.6	2.6	2.2	2.1
P/E Ratio	13.8-9.6	19.4-12.9	24.0-13.7	12.9-9.2	10.3-6.3	20.8-12.5	10.8-8.3
Price Range	17¾-12⅜	19-12⅝	22⅞-13⅛	14⅞-10⅝	13⅝-8⅜	14¾-8⅞	12⅞-9⅞

Statistics are as originally reported.

OFFICERS:
F.Q. Stepan, Chmn., Pres. & C.E.O.
J.W. Bartlett, V.P., Gen. Couns. & Corp. Sec.
W.J. Klein, V.P.-Fin.

INCORPORATED: IL, Jan., 1940; reincorp., DE, 1959

PRINCIPAL OFFICE: Edens & Winnetka Rd.'s, Northfield, IL 60093

TELEPHONE NUMBER: (708) 446-7500
FAX: (708) 501-2443
NO. OF EMPLOYEES: 1,265
ANNUAL MEETING: In May
SHAREHOLDERS: 1,792
INSTITUTIONAL HOLDINGS:
No. of Institutions: 29
Shares Held: 899,760

REGISTRAR(S): First Chicago Trust Co. of New York, New York, NY 10008

TRANSFER AGENT(S): First Chicago Trust Co. of New York, New York, NY 10008

STRAWBRIDGE & CLOTHIER

YIELD 5.8%
P/E RATIO 10.0

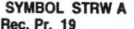

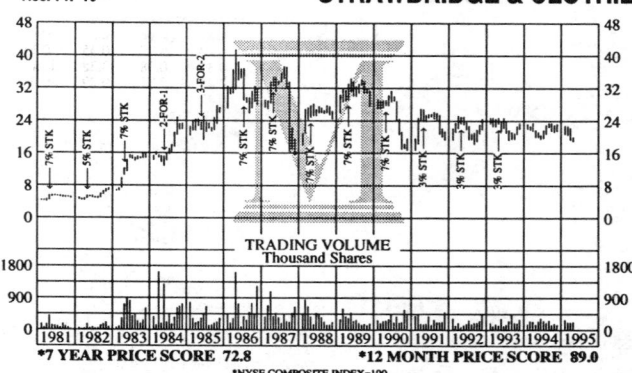

TRADING VOLUME
Thousand Shares

| 1981 | 1982 | 1983 | 1984 | 1985 | 1986 | 1987 | 1988 | 1989 | 1990 | 1991 | 1992 | 1993 | 1994 | 1995 |

*7 YEAR PRICE SCORE 72.8   *12 MONTH PRICE SCORE 89.0
*NYSE COMPOSITE INDEX=100

INTERIM EARNINGS (Per Share):

Qtr.	Apr.	July	Oct.	Jan.
1992-93	-------------	1.76	-------------	
1993-94	d0.41	d0.14	0.01	2.25
1994-95	d0.10	0.02	0.05	1.93

INTERIM DIVIDENDS (Per Share):

Amt.	Decl.	Ex.	Rec.	Pay.
0.275Q	3/23/94	3/28/94	4/4/94	5/2/94
0.275Q	6/22	6/28	7/5	8/1
0.275Q	9/21	9/27	10/3	11/1
0.275Q	12/21	12/27	1/3/95	2/1/95
0.275Q	3/22/95	3/28/95	4/3	5/1

Indicated div.: $1.10*

CAPITALIZATION (1/28/95):

	($000)	(%)
Long-Term Debt	161,442	34.7
Cap. Lease Oblig.	40,848	8.8
Common & Surplus	262,352	56.5
Total	464,642	100.0

DIVIDEND ACHIEVER STATUS:
Rank: 122   1984-94 Growth Rate: 11.8%
Total Years of Dividend Growth: 11

RECENT DEVELOPMENTS: For the year ended 1/28/95, net income was $20.0 million compared with $17.7 million a year earlier. Net sales increased 1.9% to $1.00 billion from $984.6 million the year before. As a percentage of sales, gross margin increased to 25.7% from 25.5% a year earlier. Selling, general and administrative expenses declined to 17.1% from 17.5% the year before. For the 13 weeks ended 1/28/95, net income was $20.3 million compared with $23.3 million a year earlier. Net sales increased 2.1% to $345.8 million from $338.8 million the year before. As a percentage of sales, gross margin declined to 27.8% from 29.0% a year earlier. Selling, general and administrative expenses declined to 14.5% of sales from 14.6% the year before. Additionally, the Company plans to invest approximately $36 million in new store growth and renovations of existing stores in 1995.

BUSINESS

STRAWBRIDGE & CLOTHIER operates 38 retail stores, including 13 department and 25 self-service Clover stores, which sell general merchandise in Philadelphia and the surrounding Delaware Valley area of Southeastern Pennsylvania, Southern New Jersey, and Northern Delaware. The Company grants credit to customers, substantially all of whom are residents of its trading area.

QUARTERLY DATA

(1/28/95)($000)	Rev	Inc
1st Quarter	208,303	(988)
2nd Quarter	222,894	244
3rd Quarter	226,559	526
4th Quarter	345,768	20,250

ANNUAL EARNINGS AND DIVIDENDS PER SHARE

	1/28/95	1/29/94	1/30/93	2/1/92	2/2/91	2/3/90	1/28/89
Earnings Per Share	1.92	1.71	1.76	1.34	1.72	2.76	
Dividends Per Share	1.10	1.084	1.052	1.022	0.974	② 0.91	② 0.818
Dividend Payout %	57.3	63.4	59.8	76.3	56.6	29.2	29.7

① 7% stk div, 5/11/89   ② 7% stk div, 5/12/88

ANNUAL FINANCIAL DATA

RECORD OF EARNINGS (IN MILLIONS):

Total Revenues	1,006.8	987.0	968.9	968.6	982.4	951.0	904.8
Costs and Expenses	917.3	905.7	885.3	888.8	895.3	844.9	810.6
Depreciation	29.6	28.8	28.3	28.7	27.9	24.6	22.1
Operating Profit	59.9	52.5	55.3	51.1	59.2	81.5	72.3
Earn Bef Income Taxes	30.1	26.8	27.2	20.7	28.6	51.7	45.0
Income Taxes	10.1	9.1	9.2	7.1	11.4	20.6	17.8
Net Income	20.0	17.7	① 18.0	13.6	17.2	31.2	27.3
Aver. Shs. Outstg. (000)	10,427	10,324	10,216	10,099	9,988	9,965	9,836

① Before acctg. change dr$16,850,000.

BALANCE SHEET (IN MILLIONS):

Cash and Cash Equivalents	1.6	2.9	5.4	2.8	1.3	1.9	3.4
Receivables, Net	165.9	202.8	184.1	173.2	162.6	159.8	165.1
Inventories	143.8	143.1	145.0	133.3	138.8	139.1	130.4
Gross Property	623.3	588.9	569.6	547.5	532.2	485.4	442.6
Accumulated Depreciation	315.1	288.6	262.4	234.7	210.2	184.2	163.2
Long-Term Debt	161.4	162.3	171.6	156.2	158.9	167.2	154.3
Capital Lease Obligations	40.8	43.6	52.0	55.5	59.4	59.2	63.8
Net Stockholders' Equity	262.4	252.2	243.3	251.2	245.0	235.8	212.0
Total Assets	639.8	663.1	653.9	632.0	645.6	618.5	593.3
Total Current Assets	322.5	356.2	342.5	314.3	312.3	307.5	305.4
Total Current Liabilities	117.2	146.6	130.0	129.7	140.8	119.1	126.5
Net Working Capital	205.3	209.6	212.5	184.6	171.5	188.4	178.9
Year End Shs Outstg (000)	10,461	10,386	9,958	10,256	9,618	9,171	9,100

STATISTICAL RECORD:

Operating Profit Margin %	6.0	5.3	5.7	5.3	6.0	8.6	8.0
Book Value Per Share	25.08	24.28	24.39	24.43	25.39	25.60	23.16
Return on Equity %	7.6	7.0	7.4	5.4	7.1	13.3	12.9
Return on Assets %	3.1	2.7	2.8	2.1	2.7	5.0	4.6
Average Yield %	5.1	4.9	4.8	4.7	4.0	3.0	3.6
P/E Ratio	12.2-10.2	14.5-11.3	14.3-10.4	20.1-12.5	18.2-9.7	11.0-8.3	10.2-6.5
Price Range	23½-19½	24¾-19¼	25¼-18¼	27-16¾	31⅜-16¾	34⅜-26	28⅛-17⅛

Statistics are as originally reported.

OFFICERS:
F.R. Strawbridge, III, Chrmn.
P.S. Strawbridge, Pres.
S.L. Strawbridge, V.P., Treas. & Sec.

INCORPORATED: PA, Feb., 1922

PRINCIPAL OFFICE: 801 Market St., Philadelphia, PA 19107-3199

TELEPHONE NUMBER: (215) 629-6000
FAX: (215) 629-7947
NO. OF EMPLOYEES: 12,710
ANNUAL MEETING: In May
SHAREHOLDERS: 5,668 Series A; 253 Series B;
INSTITUTIONAL HOLDINGS:
No. of Institutions: 77
Shares Held: 3,422,800

REGISTRAR(S):

TRANSFER AGENT(S): Mellon Bank, N.A., Pittsburgh, PA

NYS SYMBOL SVU
Rec. Pr. 27½

SUPERVALU INC.

YIELD 3.4%
P/E RATIO 45.1

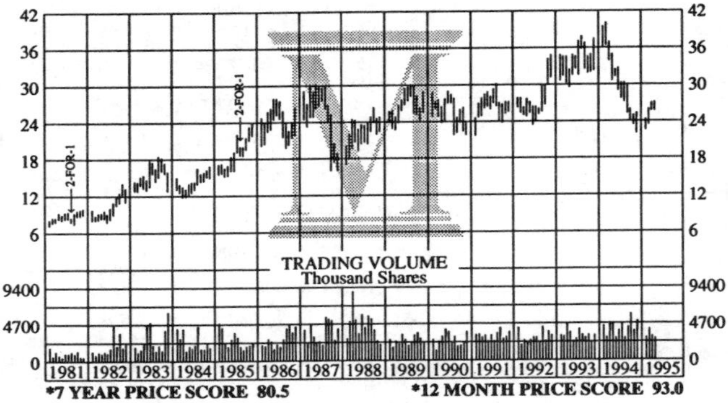
42
36
30
24
18
12
6
2-FOR-1
2-FOR-1
TRADING VOLUME
Thousand Shares
9400
4700
0
1981 1982 1983 1984 1985 1986 1987 1988 1989 1990 1991 1992 1993 1994 1995

*7 YEAR PRICE SCORE 80.5 *12 MONTH PRICE SCORE 93.0

*NYSE COMPOSITE INDEX=100

INTERIM EARNINGS (Per Share):

Qtr.	June	Sept.	Nov.	Feb.
1991-92	0.60	0.41	1.12	0.65
1992-93	----------------- 2.31 -----------------			
1993-94	0.71	0.51	0.63	0.73
1994-95	0.71	0.47	d1.18	0.61

INTERIM DIVIDENDS (Per Share):

Amt.	Decl.	Ex.	Rec.	Pay.
0.235Q	10/12/94	11/25/94	12/1/94	12/15/94
0.235Q	10/12	11/25	12/1	12/15
0.235Q	10/12	11/25	12/1	12/15
0.235Q	11/22/95	2/23/95	3/1/95	3/15/95
0.235Q	4/13	5/25	6/1	6/15

*Indicated div.: $0.94**

CAPITALIZATION (2/26/94):

	($000)	(%)
Long-Term Debt	2,060,756	56.2
Cap. Lease Oblig.	232,617	6.3
Deferred Income Tax	99,734	2.7
Preferred Stock	5,908	0.2
Common & Surplus	1,269,550	34.6
Total	3,668,565	100.0

DIVIDEND ACHIEVER STATUS:
Rank: 139 1984-94 Growth Rate: 11.0%
Total Years of Dividend Growth: 22

RECENT DEVELOPMENTS: For the quarter ended 12/3/94, SVU incurred a net loss, including restructuring and other charges, of $84.1 million compared with net income of $45.2 million in the equivalent period of the year before. Total restructuring charges were approximately $244.0 million and, as expected, were associated with the restructuring and/or disposition of certain retail operations. Sales advanced to $3.91 billion, an increase of 8%.

PROSPECTS: Although the Company has not fully realized the gains of its restructuring and consolidation initiatives, it plans to further reduce its retail holdings. Such dispositions will allow SVU to concentrate more resources on providing suppliers with more efficient distribution and logistics, and the most efficient methods of product promotion. Modest food cost inflation may permeate the near-term financial results.

BUSINESS

SUPERVALU INC. is the nation's leading distributor to independently-owned retail food stores and a major food retailer. The Company services over 4,350 retail food stores through 26 food distribution divisions located in 47 states, principally in the Midwest, Northwest, and Southwest regions of the U.S. SVU's retail support operation includes sales to corporate-owned stores and independent-owned food stores and the operations of several allied-service operations. The U.S. Retail Food operation includes company-owned and franchised Cub Food Stores. SVU owns approximately 297 retail food stores under the names of Cub Foods, Shop 'n Save, Laneco, and Scott's Foods.

BUSINESS LINE ANALYSIS

(2/26/94)($000)	Rev	Inc
First Quarter	4,875,784	51,084
Second Quarter	3,703,823	36,324
Third Quarter	3,670,298	45,238
Fourth Quarter	3,687,020	52,607

ANNUAL EARNINGS AND DIVIDENDS PER SHARE

	2/26/94	2/27/93	2/29/92	2/23/91	2/24/90	2/25/89	2/27/88
Earnings Per Share	**2.58**	**2.31**	**2.78**	**2.06**	**1.97**	**1.81**	**1.50**
Dividends Per Share	**0.91**	**0.83**	**0.705**	**0.63**	**0.56**	**0.47**	**0.43**
Dividend Payout %	**32.2**	**35.9**	**25.4**	**30.6**	**28.4**	**26.0**	**28.7**

ANNUAL FINANCIAL DATA

RECORD OF EARNINGS (IN MILLIONS):							
Total Revenues	15,936.9	12,568.0	10,632.3	11,612.4	11,136.0	10,296.3	9,371.7
Costs and Expenses	15,381.6	12,137.5	10,279.9	11,161.2	10,716.2	9,911.3	9,027.4
Depreciation & Amort	186.3	140.8	111.5	144.9	123.2	110.1	103.3
Operating Profit	1,413.5	1,036.6	824.7	1,195.0	1,116.4	1,023.8	905.2
Earn Bef Income Taxes	294.1	258.6	322.8	254.1	243.5	224.4	198.3
Income Taxes	108.8	94.1	115.2	99.0	95.7	86.9	86.5
Net Income	185.3	164.5	[1] 207.7	155.1	147.7	137.5	111.8
Aver. Shs. Outstg. (000)	71,817	71,341	74,700	75,165	74,972	74,785	74,634
[1] Before acctg. change dr$13,288,000.							
BALANCE SHEET (IN MILLIONS):							
Cash and Cash Equivalents	2.8	1.8	1.5	2.7	2.2	2.2	2.2
Receivables, Net	352.2	357.7	379.3	209.5	216.6	238.7	206.9
Inventories	1,113.9	1,134.1	745.1	901.4	833.2	779.0	698.4
Gross Property	2,195.9	2,061.1	1,471.0	1,931.0	1,725.4	1,549.4	1,340.4
Accumulated Depreciation	785.8	676.9	591.8	709.5	612.0	513.7	437.3
Long-Term Debt	2,060.8	2,224.1	396.2	382.4	387.9	399.7	389.5
Capital Lease Obligations	232.6	235.3	212.1	195.0	173.3	171.5	155.6
Net Stockholders' Equity	1,275.5	1,134.8	1,031.0	978.7	869.9	778.3	677.4
Total Assets	4,042.4	4,064.2	2,484.3	2,615.1	2,428.9	2,305.1	2,016.2
Total Current Assets	1,563.3	1,573.6	1,163.3	1,144.1	1,080.9	1,045.2	931.8
Total Current Liabilities	1,224.4	1,325.8	745.2	997.6	951.1	906.3	757.1
Net Working Capital	338.9	247.8	418.1	146.5	129.9	138.9	174.7
Year End Shs Outstg (000)	72,059	71,655	75,335	75,225	75,085	74,822	74,724
STATISTICAL RECORD:							
Operating Profit Margin %	2.3	2.3	2.3	2.6	2.7	2.7	2.6
Book Value Per Share	11.68	9.75	13.58	13.01	11.59	10.40	9.07
Return on Equity %	14.5	14.5	20.1	15.9	17.0	17.7	16.5
Return on Assets %	4.6	4.0	8.4	5.9	6.1	6.0	5.5
Average Yield %	2.5	2.9	2.7	2.5	2.1	2.2	1.9
P/E Ratio	14.7-11.4	15.1-10.1	10.9-7.8	14.1-10.6	15.3-11.5	14.6-9.4	20.3-10.7
Price Range	37⅞-29½	34⅞-23⅜	30¼-21⅝	29-21¾	30⅛-22⅝	26⅜-17	30⅜-16

Statistics are as originally reported.

OFFICERS:
M.W. Wright, Chmn., Pres. & C.E.O.
J.C. Girard, Exec. V.P. & C.F.O.
D.A. Cairns, V.P. & Treas.
T.H. Johnson, Sec.

INCORPORATED: DE, Dec., 1925

PRINCIPAL OFFICE: 11840 Valley View Road, Eden Prairie, MN 55344

TELEPHONE NUMBER: (612) 828-4000
FAX: (612) 828-8998
NO. OF EMPLOYEES: 42,500 (approx.)
ANNUAL MEETING: In June
SHAREHOLDERS: 8,230
INSTITUTIONAL HOLDINGS:
No. of Institutions: 315
Shares Held: 49,584,464

REGISTRAR(S): Norwest Bank Minnesota, N.A., South Saint Paul, MN

TRANSFER AGENT(S): Norwest Bank Minnesota, N.A., South Saint Paul, MN

ASE SYMBOL SGC
Rec. Pr. 12⅛

SUPERIOR SURGICAL MANUFACTURING CO., INC.

YIELD 3.0%
P/E RATIO 10.0

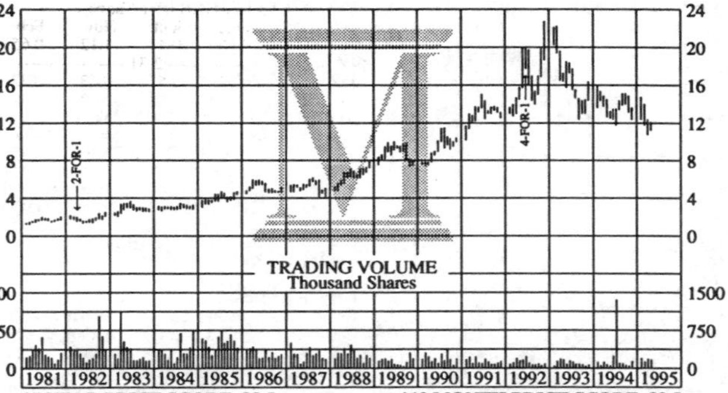

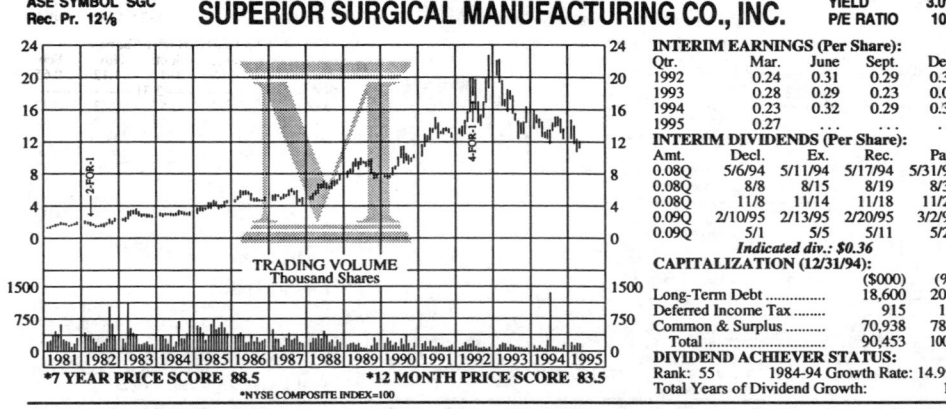

24
20
16
12
8
4
0
2-FOR-1
4-FOR-1
TRADING VOLUME
Thousand Shares
1500
750
0
1981 1982 1983 1984 1985 1986 1987 1988 1989 1990 1991 1992 1993 1994 1995

*7 YEAR PRICE SCORE 88.5 *12 MONTH PRICE SCORE 83.5

*NYSE COMPOSITE INDEX=100

INTERIM EARNINGS (Per Share):

Qtr.	Mar.	June	Sept.	Dec.
1992	0.24	0.31	0.29	0.31
1993	0.28	0.29	0.23	0.09
1994	0.23	0.32	0.29	0.33
1995	0.27	...	...	...

INTERIM DIVIDENDS (Per Share):

Amt.	Decl.	Ex.	Rec.	Pay.
0.08Q	5/6/94	5/11/94	5/17/94	5/31/94
0.08Q	8/8	8/15	8/19	8/30
0.08Q	11/8	11/14	11/18	11/29
0.09Q	2/10/95	2/13/95	2/20/95	3/2/95
0.09Q	5/1	5/5	5/11	5/23

Indicated div.: $0.36

CAPITALIZATION (12/31/94):

	($000)	(%)
Long-Term Debt	18,600	20.6
Deferred Income Tax	915	1.0
Common & Surplus	70,938	78.4
Total	90,453	100.0

DIVIDEND ACHIEVER STATUS:

Rank: 55 1984-94 Growth Rate: 14.9%

Total Years of Dividend Growth: 11

RECENT DEVELOPMENTS: For the year ended 12/31/94, SGC reported net income of $10.1 million, an increase of 30% from $7.7 million in 1993. Net sales increased 3.8% to $135.1 million from $130.1 million a year earlier. Earnings per share for the year were $1.17 compared with $0.89 in 1993. Net income for the quarter ended 12/31/94 was $2.8 million compared with $738,676 in the corresponding period of 1993. Net sales for the quarter were $34.0 million versus $32.4 million a year earlier.

PROSPECTS: The Company has announced that it has been advised that it is a target of a criminal investigation relating to a previously reported dispute involving alleged false statements and false claims purportedly made in connection with contracts ostensibly awarded by the U.S. Department of Veterans Affairs. The ultimate impact on the Company cannot be predicted, any amounts paid to the Federal government in connection with these matters may have a one-time material adverse effect on the results of operations.

BUSINESS

SUPERIOR SURGICAL MANUFACTURING COMPANY, INC. mnufactures and sells a wide range of uniforms, career apparel and accessories for the hospital and healthcare fields; hotels; fast food and other restaurants; and public safety, industrial, transportation and commercial markets.

ANNUAL EARNINGS AND DIVIDENDS PER SHARE

	1994	1993	1992	1991	1990	1989	1988
Earnings Per Share	**1.17**	**0.89**	**1.15**	**0.94**	**1.00**	**0.79**	**0.72**
Dividends Per Share	**0.32**	**0.28**	**[1] 0.25**	**0.22**	**0.18**	**0.15**	**0.125**
Dividend Payout %	**27.4**	**31.5**	**21.7**	**23.2**	**18.0**	**19.0**	**17.4**

[1] 4-for-1 stk split, 6/23/92

ANNUAL FINANCIAL DATA

	1994	1993	1992	1991	1990	1989	1988
RECORD OF EARNINGS (IN THOUSANDS):							
Total Revenues	135,067	130,127	128,666	117,503	123,002	113,754	112,389
Costs and Expenses	114,982	114,862	110,046	101,736	106,272	99,687	98,832
Depreciation & Amort	2,865	2,504	2,169	2,103	1,900	1,650	1,657
Operating Profit	17,221	15,011	16,451	13,664	14,830	12,417	11,900
Earn Bef Taxes on Income	16,261	12,119	15,864	12,840	13,755	11,360	11,190
Income Taxes	6,180	4,415	5,950	4,815	5,090	4,200	4,140
Net Income	10,081	7,704	9,914	8,025	8,665	7,160	7,050
Aver. Shs. Outstg.	8,646	8,693	8,648	8,500	8,644	9,072	9,807
BALANCE SHEET (IN THOUSANDS):							
Cash and Cash Equivalents	11,234	3,030	2,624	6,360	892	396	708
Receivables, Net	23,356	20,850	20,317	18,239	19,295	18,501	18,560
Inventories	40,992	39,633	38,860	33,914	33,861	32,488	30,617
Gross Property	45,999	38,497	32,424	28,000	26,557	26,243	23,590
Accumulated Depreciation	19,764	17,625	15,780	14,496	13,478	12,603	11,100
Long-Term Debt	18,600	4,200	4,955	7,110	8,946	9,416	10,382
Net Stockholders' Equity	70,938	68,568	63,082	54,659	47,686	44,327	40,319
Total Assets	104,864	87,168	80,585	74,471	69,193	66,968	64,498
Total Current Assets	76,457	64,201	62,231	59,250	54,504	51,779	50,451
Total Current Liabilities	12,161	11,105	10,878	11,376	11,262	11,825	12,397
Net Working Capital	64,296	53,097	51,353	47,874	43,242	39,953	38,054
Year End Shares Outstg	8,364	8,703	8,678	8,579	8,450	8,847	9,068
STATISTICAL RECORD:							
Operating Profit Margin %	12.7	9.8	12.8	11.6	12.1	10.9	10.6
Book Value Per Share	8.38	7.78	7.17	6.27	5.54	4.91	4.35
Return on Equity %	14.2	11.2	15.7	14.7	18.2	16.2	17.5
Return on Assets %	9.6	8.8	12.3	10.8	12.5	10.7	10.9
Average Yield %	2.3	1.6	1.4	1.7	1.9	1.7	2.0
P/E Ratio	13.7-10.0	25.0-13.9	19.8-11.1	16.1-10.8	11.5-7.4	12.7-9.3	11.1-6.6
Price Range	16-11¾	22¼-12⅜	22¾-12¾	15⅛-10⅛	11½-7⅜	10-7⅜	8-4¾

Statistics are as originally reported.

OFFICERS:
G.M. Benstock, Chmn. & C.E.O.
A.D. Schwartz, Co-Pres.
M. Benstock, Co-Pres.
J.W. Johansen, Sr. V.P., C.F.O., Treas. & Sec.

INCORPORATED: NY, 1922

PRINCIPAL OFFICE: 10099 Seminole Blvd. P O Box 4002, Seminole, FL 34642

TELEPHONE NUMBER: (813) 397-9611

FAX: (813) 391-5401

NO. OF EMPLOYEES: 1,900 (approx.)

ANNUAL MEETING: In May

SHAREHOLDERS: 620

INSTITUTIONAL HOLDINGS:
No. of Institutions: 29
Shares Held: 1,084,485

REGISTRAR(S): Chemical Bank, New York, NY

TRANSFER AGENT(S): Chemical Bank, New York, NY

SYSCO CORP.

YIELD 1.6%
P/E RATIO 21.9

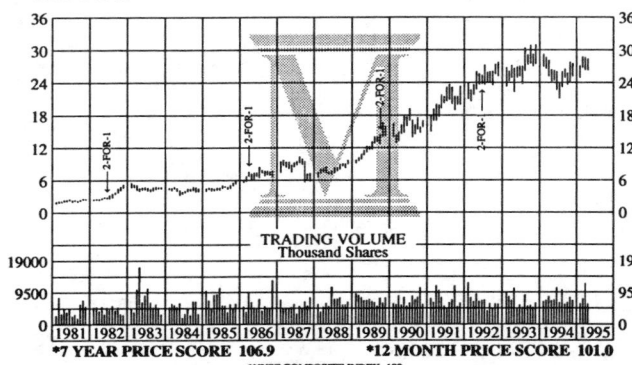

INTERIM EARNINGS (Per Share):

Qtr.	Sept.	Dec.	Mar.	June
1991-92	0.23	0.24	0.20	0.27
1992-93	---------------- 1.08 ----------------			
1993-94	0.26	0.30	0.25	0.37
1994-95	0.32	0.35	...	...

INTERIM DIVIDENDS (Per Share):

Amt.	Decl.	Ex.	Rec.	Pay.
0.09Q	2/9/94	4/25/94	4/29/94	5/13/94
0.09Q	5/11	7/25	7/29	8/12
0.09Q	9/2	10/24	10/28	11/18
0.11Q	11/4	1/23/95	1/27/95	2/17/95
0.11Q	2/8/95	4/24	4/28	5/12

*Indicated div.: $0.44**

CAPITALIZATION (7/2/94):

	($000)	(%)
Long-Term Debt	538,711	27.4
Deferred Income Tax	185,548	9.4
Common & Surplus	1,240,909	63.2
Total	1,965,168	100.0

DIVIDEND ACHIEVER STATUS:
Rank: 8   1984-94 Growth Rate: 23.1%
Total Years of Dividend Growth: 18

RECENT DEVELOPMENTS: For the thirteen weeks ended 12/31/94, net earnings rose by 14% to $63.5 million from $55.6 million in the equivalent period of the year before. Sales were $3.01 billion, up 13%. Favorable economic conditions and modest food cost inflation in the U.S. drove revenue and earnings higher. During the first six months of the year, net earnings rose by 18% to $121.9 million. Sales were $5.99 billion, an increase of 11%.

PROSPECTS: Sales will be enhanced by substantial new business from ARAMARK Corporation, Sysco's largest customer. Many foodservice operators, like ARAMARK, have been withdrawing from self-distribution to concentrate on basic business. Construction of new facilities, additions to storage capacity, fleet expansion and other investments will result in capital expenditures of between $150 million to $200 million in 1995.

BUSINESS

SYSCO CORPORATION is the largest marketer and distributor of foodservice products in America. Included among its customers are more than 245,000 restaurants, hotels, hospitals, schools and other institutions. The Company distributes entree items, dry and canned foods, fresh produce, beverages, dairy products and certain nonfood products. Through its SYGMA subsidiary, the Company serves pizza and hamburgers to fast-food chains and other limited menu chain restaurants. SYY has one Canadian facility in Vancouver, British Columbia. In fiscal 1994, the foodservice sales breakdown was: 60% restaurants; 13% hospitals and nursing homes; 7% schools; 6% hotels; and 14% other.

ANNUAL EARNINGS AND DIVIDENDS PER SHARE

	7/2/94	7/3/93	6/27/92	6/29/91	6/30/90	7/1/89	7/2/88
Earnings Per Share	1.18	1.08	0.93	0.84	0.73	0.60	① 0.45
Dividends Per Share	0.36	0.28	① 0.22	0.14	0.10	0.093	0.08
Dividend Payout %	30.5	25.9	23.7	16.7	13.8	15.5	17.8

① 2-for-1 stk split, 6/22/92 ② 100% stk dividend, payable 10/17/89

ANNUAL FINANCIAL DATA

RECORD OF EARNINGS (IN MILLIONS):

	7/2/94	7/3/93	6/27/92	6/29/91	6/30/90	7/1/89	7/2/88
Total Revenues	10,942.5	10,021.5	8,892.8	8,149.7	7,590.6	6,851.3	4,384.7
Costs and Expenses	10,420.4	9,545.0	8,474.8	7,765.1	7,240.8	6,545.1	4,195.8
Depreciation & Amort	120.0	107.7	99.5	92.2	84.4	76.8	45.0
Operating Profit	1,970.9	1,796.2	1,588.9	1,455.9	1,344.2	1,210.5	790.6
Earn Bef Income Taxes	367.6	332.0	281.7	250.9	216.1	176.9	129.4
Income Taxes	150.8	130.2	109.4	97.0	83.6	69.0	49.2
Net Income	216.8	201.8	172.2	153.8	132.5	107.9	86.9
Aver. Shs. Outstg. (000)	184,339	186,746	186,001	184,440	182,674	180,740	179,544

BALANCE SHEET (IN MILLIONS):

Cash and Cash Equivalents	86.7	68.8	74.4	70.2	56.0	55.5	35.6
Receivables, Net	894.5	799.4	660.3	600.6	548.3	518.1	336.7
Inventories	602.0	534.2	491.6	460.3	431.9	436.8	285.4
Gross Property	1,407.3	1,255.6	1,159.0	1,058.0	939.4	795.4	527.6
Accumulated Depreciation	590.1	495.7	424.6	358.9	303.5	253.4	194.4
Long-Term Debt	538.7	494.1	488.8	543.2	583.5	620.2	93.3
Net Stockholders' Equity	1,240.9	1,137.2	1,056.8	918.6	770.8	642.7	543.6
Total Assets	2,811.7	2,530.0	2,301.6	2,160.1	1,992.1	1,869.4	1,020.9
Total Current Assets	1,599.6	1,419.7	1,240.4	1,143.9	1,047.3	1,021.7	666.6
Total Current Liabilities	846.6	746.5	655.4	611.8	573.7	566.3	356.3
Net Working Capital	753.1	673.3	585.0	532.1	473.7	455.5	310.2
Year End Shs Outstg (000)	186,069	184,457	185,776	185,200	183,508	181,762	180,484

STATISTICAL RECORD:

Operating Profit Margin %	3.7	3.7	3.6	3.6	3.5	3.3	3.3
Book Value Per Share	5.24	4.72	4.25	3.48	2.73	2.01	3.01
Return on Equity %	17.5	17.7	16.3	16.7	17.2	16.8	16.0
Return on Assets %	7.7	8.0	7.5	7.1	6.6	5.8	8.5
Average Yield %	1.4	1.1	0.9	0.7	0.6	0.7	1.0
P/E Ratio	24.8-17.9	28.7-20.6	29.8-22.2	28.6-18.1	26.4-17.6	27.9-15.2	21.7-14.4
Price Range	29¼-21⅛	31-22¼	27¾-20⅝	23¾-15	19¼-12⅞	16¾-9⅛	9¾-6½

Statistics are as originally reported.

QUARTERLY DATA

(07/02/94)($000)	Rev	Inc
1st Quarter	2,709,874	48,060
2nd Quarter	2,665,882	55,563
3rd Quarter	2,684,854	45,694
4th Quarter	2,881,889	67,435

OFFICERS:
J.F. Woodhouse, Chmn.
B.M. Lindig, Pres. & C.E.O.
J.K. Stubblefield, Jr., Sr. V.P. & C.F.O.

INCORPORATED: DE, May, 1969

PRINCIPAL OFFICE: 1390 Enclave Parkway, Houston, TX 77077-2099

TELEPHONE NUMBER: (713) 584-1390

FAX: (713) 584-1245

NO. OF EMPLOYEES: 26,200

ANNUAL MEETING: In November

SHAREHOLDERS: 19,860

INSTITUTIONAL HOLDINGS:
No. of Institutions: 408
Shares Held: 110,853,879

REGISTRAR(S): First National Bank of Boston, Shareholder Services Division, Boston, MA

TRANSFER AGENT(S): First National Bank of Boston, Shareholder Services Division, Boston, MA

NYS SYMBOL TMB
Rec. Pr. 43¾

TAMBRANDS INC.

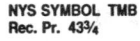

YIELD 4.0%
P/E RATIO 17.8

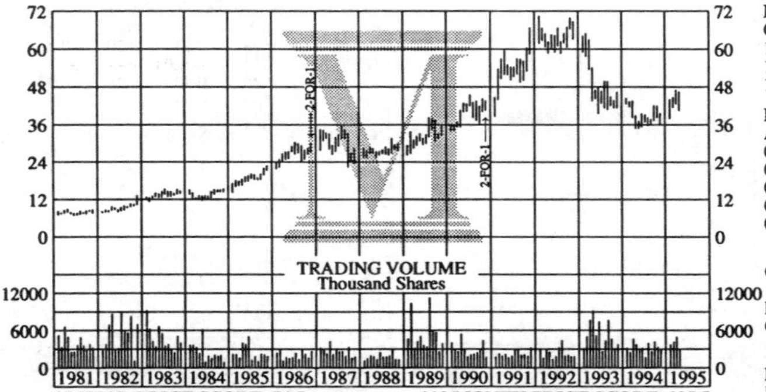
72
60
48
36
24
12
0
2-FOR-1
2-FOR-1
TRADING VOLUME
Thousand Shares
12000
6000
0
1981 1982 1983 1984 1985 1986 1987 1988 1989 1990 1991 1992 1993 1994 1995

*7 YEAR PRICE SCORE 74.5 *12 MONTH PRICE SCORE 105.5

*NYSE COMPOSITE INDEX=100

INTERIM EARNINGS (Per Share):

Qtr.	Mar.	June	Sept.	Dec.
1992	0.73	0.72	0.85	0.80
1993	0.82	d0.09	0.62	0.55
1994	0.58	0.54	0.68	0.62

INTERIM DIVIDENDS (Per Share):

Amt.	Decl.	Ex.	Rec.	Pay.
0.44Q	10/26/94	11/29/94	12/5/94	12/15/94
0.44Q	10/26	11/29	12/5	12/15
0.44Q	10/26	11/29	12/5	12/15
0.44Q	1/31/95	2/27/95	3/3/95	3/15/95
0.44Q	4/25	5/26	6/2	6/15

Indicated div.: $1.76*

CAPITALIZATION (12/31/94):

	($000)	(%)
Deferred Income Tax	21,450	20.7
Common & Surplus	82,014	79.3
Total	103,464	100.0

DIVIDEND ACHIEVER STATUS:
Rank: 206 1984-94 Growth Rate: 8.3%
Total Years of Dividend Growth: 43

RECENT DEVELOPMENTS: For the year ended 12/31/94, net income rose 21.7% to $89.7 million from $73.7 million, before an accounting change, for the prior year. Results for 1993 included a restructuring charge of $30.0 million. Net sales were $644.5 million, an increase of 5.4%. The higher sales reflected very strong U.S. unit volumes, aided by shipments of the newly introduced Tampax Satin Touch tampons. Gross profit margin as a percentage of sales was 68.0% in 1994.

PROSPECTS: Results will continue to be adversely affected by retailer and distributor efforts to reduce inventories. Prices are being pressured by highly competitive markets worldwide. Increased advertising and new products are being introduced in the feminine hygiene industry, which will intensify competitive conditions. Earnings will be constrained by higher marketing, selling and distribution expenses. Lower administrative expenses should help to offset the increases in other expenses.

BUSINESS

TAMBRANDS INC. (formerly Tampax), a leader in its field, is engaged in the manufacture and sale of feminine hygiene products, home diagnostics, cosmetics and other personal care products in various countries around the world. Brand names include Tampax and First Response. It has operating subsidiaries in Canada, the United Kingdom, Ireland, South Africa and France, and equity investments in companies operating in Spain and Mexico. The sales organization is made up of Tambrands employees, agents, brokers and distributors who create a unique distribution network covering over 150 countries. In 1994, foreign operations accounted for 41% of sales.

BUSINESS LINE ANALYSIS

(12/31/94)	Rev(%)	Inc(%)
United States	59.3	79.3
Europe	30.4	15.0
Other International	10.3	5.7
Total	100.0	100.0

ANNUAL EARNINGS AND DIVIDENDS PER SHARE

	1994	1993	1992	1991	1990	1989	1988
Earnings Per Share	**2.43**	**1.91**	**3.09**	**1.92**	**2.30**	**0.04**	**1.91**
Dividends Per Share	**1.70**	**1.56**	**1.40**	**1.24**	**[1] 1.11**	**1.035**	**0.975**
Dividend Payout %	**70.0**	**81.7**	**45.3**	**64.6**	**48.3**	**N.M.**	**50.9**

[1] 2-for-1 stk split,12/17/90

ANNUAL FINANCIAL DATA

	1994	1993	1992	1991	1990	1989	1988
RECORD OF EARNINGS (IN THOUSANDS):							
Total Revenues	644,513	611,465	684,113	660,722	631,511	583,408	563,347
Costs and Expenses	468,614	476,785	472,066	515,082	468,399	537,407	413,081
Depreciation & Amort	24,284	18,372	17,315	15,506	13,186	12,960	13,903
Operating Income	151,615	116,308	194,732	130,134	149,926	33,041	136,363
Earn Bef Income Taxes	141,751	118,652	191,863	131,825	154,696	30,859	134,017
Income Taxes	52,022	44,950	69,454	52,790	56,928	29,140	48,741
Net Income	89,729	[1] 73,702	[2] 122,409	79,035	97,768	1,719	85,276
Aver. Shs. Outstg.	36,992	38,632	39,640	41,216	42,524	44,571	44,580

[1] Before acctg. change dr$10,252,000. [2] Before acctg. change dr$1,009,000.

	1994	1993	1992	1991	1990	1989	1988
BALANCE SHEET (IN THOUSANDS):							
Cash and Cash Equivalents	13,876	15,298	23,785	72,712	100,297	115,401	87,525
Receivables, Net	156,372	149,937	98,639	99,963	92,474	82,778	101,922
Inventories	37,957	38,000	38,578	38,231	39,430	42,252	42,938
Gross Property	314,457	275,349	244,988	239,728	205,583	213,525	206,797
Accumulated Depreciation	120,142	94,953	86,801	104,051	95,884	95,894	76,381
Net Stockholders' Equity	82,014	115,025	168,206	222,873	249,175	284,456	352,930
Total Assets	454,854	436,743	372,981	390,266	381,029	411,002	465,306
Total Current Assets	252,915	248,107	197,202	234,396	250,212	249,456	238,689
Total Current Liabilities	203,160	186,381	184,310	152,865	116,900	112,819	83,265
Net Working Capital	49,755	61,726	12,892	81,531	133,312	136,637	155,424
Year End Shares Outstg	36,674	38,293	39,163	40,648	41,538	44,100	44,634
STATISTICAL RECORD:							
Operating Profit Margin %	23.5	19.0	28.5	19.7	23.7	5.7	24.2
Book Value Per Share	2.24	3.00	4.09	5.22	5.74	5.69	6.39
Return on Equity %	N.M.	64.1	72.8	35.5	39.2	0.6	24.2
Return on Assets %	19.7	16.9	32.8	20.3	25.7	0.4	18.3
Average Yield %	4.3	3.0	2.2	2.4	2.8	3.2	3.4
P/E Ratio	18.3-14.3	34.0-20.7	22.8-19.0	34.8-20.1	19.8-14.7	N.M	16.6-13.2
Price Range	44½-34¾	65-39½	70½-58⅝	66⅞-38⅝	45½-33¾	38¼-26⅜	31⅝-25¼

Statistics are as originally reported.

OFFICERS:
H.B. Wentz, Jr., Chmn.
E.T. Fogarty, Pres. & C.E.O.
R.F. Wright, Sr. V.P. & C.F.O.

INCORPORATED: DE, Mar., 1936

PRINCIPAL OFFICE: 777 Westchester Avenue, White Plains, NY 10604

TELEPHONE NUMBER: (914) 696-6000

NO. OF EMPLOYEES: 3,400 (approx.)

ANNUAL MEETING: In April

SHAREHOLDERS: 7,153

INSTITUTIONAL HOLDINGS:
No. of Institutions: 288
Shares Held: 30,765,202

REGISTRAR(S): First Chicago Trust Co. of New York, New York, NY 10008

TRANSFER AGENT(S): First Chicago Trust Co. of New York, New York, NY 10008

TCA CABLE TV, INC.

YIELD 1.9%
P/E RATIO 25.0

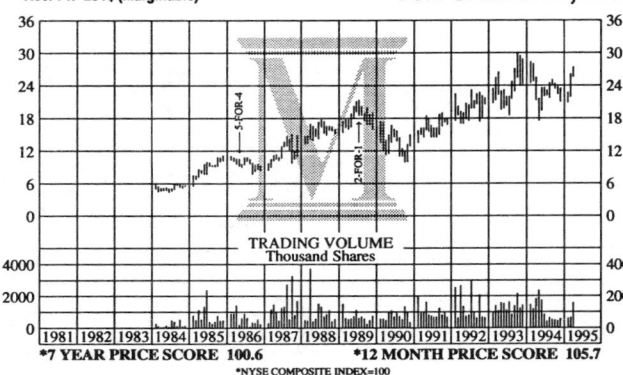

TRADING VOLUME
Thousand Shares

*7 YEAR PRICE SCORE 100.6   *12 MONTH PRICE SCORE 105.7
*NYSE COMPOSITE INDEX=100

INTERIM EARNINGS (Per Share):

Qtr.	Jan.	Apr.	July	Oct.
1990-91	0.08	0.08	0.09	0.10
1991-92	0.14	0.16	0.16	0.15
1992-93	0.19	0.21	0.20	0.23
1993-94	0.23	0.24	0.21	0.25
1994-95	0.31	...	...	...

INTERIM DIVIDENDS (Per Share):

Amt.	Decl.	Ex.	Rec.	Pay.
0.11Q	3/31/94	4/8/94	4/14/94	4/28/94
0.11Q	6/21	6/29	7/6	7/20
0.11Q	9/22	9/29	10/5	10/19
0.12Q	12/7	12/19	12/23	1/10/95
0.12Q	4/4/95	4/7/95	4/13/95	4/27

Indicated div.: $0.48

CAPITALIZATION (10/31/94):

	($000)	(%)
Long-Term Debt	126,447	47.6
Deferred Income Tax	40,000	15.1
Common & Surplus	98,897	37.3
Total	265,344	100.0

DIVIDEND ACHIEVER STATUS:
Rank: 7   1984-94 Growth Rate: 24.8%
Total Years of Dividend Growth: 12

RECENT DEVELOPMENTS: For the quarter ended 1/31/95, net income increased 34% to $7.7 million, or $0.31 per share, compared with $5.8 million, or $0.23 per share, before accounting changes, in the corresponding period of 1994. Revenues were $43.3 million, up 10% over the 1994 revenues of $39.3 million. Operating income before depreciation was $21.8 million, up 12% over the 1994 operating income before depreciation of $19.5 million. Results for the first quarter of last year were before a charge of $1.9 million, or $0.07 per share, for the cumulative effect of the Company's required adoption of SFAS No. 109. On March 3, 1995, TCAT announced that it would acquire the assets of the cable system serving 32,800 customers in San Angelo, TX, and nearby communities for $65.5 million.

BUSINESS

TCA CABLE TV, INC. is the nation's 25th largest multiple system cable television operator. The Company owns and operates 53 cable television systems and manages two additional systems owned by affiliated corporations. Formed in 1981 from the consolidation of corporations led by founder Robert M. Rogers since 1954, the Company serves 542,000 customers in Arkansas, Idaho, Louisiana, Mississippi, New Mexico and Texas. Its "classic" systems with an average size of 8,600 customer accounts are located in mostly rural markets, whose residents rely on cable to provide quality reception and service.

QUARTERLY DATA

(10/31/94)($000)	Rev	Inc
1st Quarter	39,279	3,864
2nd Quarter	39,848	5,763
3rd Quarter	41,078	5,354
4th Quarter	42,096	6,093

ANNUAL EARNINGS AND DIVIDENDS PER SHARE

	10/31/94	10/31/93	10/31/92	10/31/91	10/31/90	10/31/89	10/31/88
Earnings Per Share	0.93	0.83	0.61	0.35	0.20	0.20	0.40
Dividends Per Share	0.44	0.40	0.34	0.28	0.24	①0.20	0.16
Dividend Payout %	47.3	48.2	55.7	80.0	N.M.	44.4	40.5

① 2-for-1 stk split, 7/11/89

ANNUAL FINANCIAL DATA

RECORD OF EARNINGS (IN THOUSANDS):

Total Revenues	162,300	152,291	138,839	127,090	113,738	79,088	68,938
Costs and Expenses	82,712	74,622	68,439	61,708	53,055	37,987	33,979
Depreciation & Amort	33,636	33,330	32,805	34,007	32,110	18,050	15,611
Operating Income	45,952	44,340	37,594	31,374	28,574	23,052	19,347
Income Bef Income Taxes	37,867	33,690	24,671	13,868	8,219	18,022	15,669
Income Taxes	14,892	13,241	9,682	5,375	3,464	7,209	6,096
Net Income	①22,975	20,449	14,989	8,493	4,755	10,813	9,573
Aver. Shs. Outstg.	24,638	24,638	24,563	24,426	24,222	24,236	24,197

① Before acctg. change dr$1,900,000.

BALANCE SHEET (IN THOUSANDS):

Cash and Cash Equivalents	4,668	1,450	819	987	727	1,013	813
Receivables, Net	5,079	5,185	3,805	3,440	3,404	2,543	1,655
Gross Property	275,335	254,409	236,756	229,279	217,747	197,882	153,124
Accumulated Depreciation	162,750	147,999	132,075	119,649	97,373	76,733	66,397
Long-Term Debt	126,447	143,253	163,319	189,252	218,541	227,416	48,285
Net Stockholders' Equity	98,897	90,251	77,957	70,762	64,940	65,787	59,450
Total Assets	286,213	288,077	289,889	305,700	324,826	327,637	135,432
Total Current Assets	10,242	7,259	5,292	4,875	4,595	3,798	2,817
Total Current Liabilities	20,869	19,560	15,649	15,793	14,608	10,953	7,382
Net Working Capital	d10,627	d12,301	d10,357	d10,918	d10,013	d7,155	d4,565
Year End Shares Outstg	24,573	24,657	24,559	24,511	24,220	24,201	24,149

STATISTICAL RECORD:

Operating Profit Margin %	28.3	29.1	27.1	24.7	25.1	29.1	28.1
Return on Equity %	23.2	22.7	19.2	12.0	7.3	16.4	16.1
Return on Assets %	8.0	7.1	5.2	2.8	1.5	3.3	7.1
Average Yield %	1.6	1.6	1.7	1.7	1.8	1.1	1.0
P/E Ratio	30.5-18.8	36.3-22.3	38.1-27.9	54.3-38.6	87.5-49.4	47.5-34.2	44.4-33.1
Price Range	28⅜-17½	30⅛-18½	23¼-17	19-13½	17½-9⅞	21⅜-15⅜	17¾-13¼

Statistics are as originally reported.

OFFICERS:
R.M. Rogers, Chmn. & C.E.O.
F.R. Nichols, Pres. & C.O.O.
J.F. Taylor, V.P., C.F.O. & Treas.
M.S. Hensley, Sec.

INCORPORATED: TX, Dec., 1981

PRINCIPAL OFFICE: 3015 SSE Loop 323
P.O. Box 130489, Tyler, TX 75701

TELEPHONE NUMBER: (903) 595-3701

NO. OF EMPLOYEES: 991

ANNUAL MEETING: In March

SHAREHOLDERS: 2,950 (approx.)

INSTITUTIONAL HOLDINGS:
No. of Institutions: 134
Shares Held: 11,335,392

REGISTRAR(S): First Chicago Trust Co. of New York, New York, NY 10008

TRANSFER AGENT(S): First Chicago Trust Co. of New York, New York, NY 10008

TECO ENERGY, INC.

YIELD 4.8%
P/E RATIO 15.9

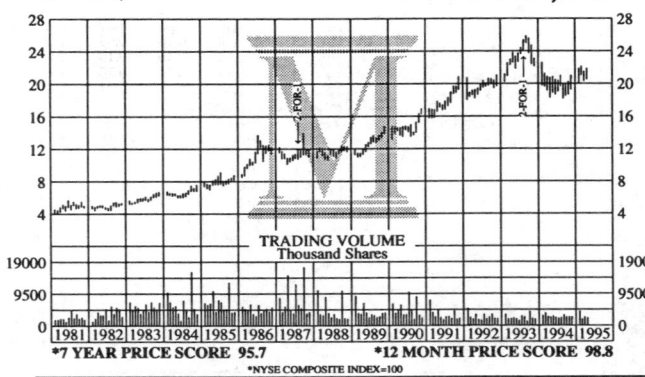

TRADING VOLUME
Thousand Shares

| | 1981 | 1982 | 1983 | 1984 | 1985 | 1986 | 1987 | 1988 | 1989 | 1990 | 1991 | 1992 | 1993 | 1994 | 1995 |

*7 YEAR PRICE SCORE 95.7   *12 MONTH PRICE SCORE 98.8
*NYSE COMPOSITE INDEX=100

INTERIM EARNINGS (Per Share):

Qtr.	Mar.	June	Sept.	Dec.
1992	0.23	0.31	0.47	0.30
1993	0.22	0.33	0.45	0.31
1994	0.29	0.36	0.47	0.20

INTERIM DIVIDENDS (Per Share):

Amt.	Decl.	Ex.	Rec.	Pay.
0.2525Q	7/19/94	7/26/94	8/1/94	8/15/94
0.2525Q	10/18	10/26	11/1	11/15
0.2525Q	1/17/95	1/26/95	2/1/95	2/15/95
0.265Q	4/19	4/25	5/1	5/15

Indicated div.: $1.01*

CAPITALIZATION (12/31/94):

	($000)	(%)
Long-Term Debt	1,023,881	39.1
Deferred Income Tax	457,422	17.4
Preferred Stock	54,956	2.1
Common & Surplus	1,084,221	41.4
Total	2,620,480	100.0
Current Debt	7,841	

DIVIDEND ACHIEVER STATUS:
Rank: 255   1984-94 Growth Rate: 6.3%
Total Years of Dividend Growth: 35

RECENT DEVELOPMENTS: For the quarter ended 12/31/94, net income before restructuring charges was $38.5 million compared with $35.4 million in the same period of 1993. Revenues rose slightly to $324.3 million. Revenues were affected by falling gas prices at TECO Coalbed Methane and lower volumes at TECO Transport. For the year ended 12/31/94, net income before restructuring charges was $168.6 million versus $150.3 million a year earlier.

PROSPECTS: Restructuring actions primarily at Tampa Electric should produce a much needed lift to earnings. In addition, Tampa's service area is showing signs of renewed economic vigor. The Company is trying to capitalize on its ever increasing diversified activities to boost future earnings growth. Higher demand for low-sulfer coal should also help bolster earnings. Capital expenditures are expected to be $1.1 billion during the period of 1995-1998.

BUSINESS

TECO ENERGY, INC., is a diversified, energy-related holding company. Tampa Electric generates, purchases, transmits, distributes and sells electric energy to more than 474,693 customers in a 2,000-square-mile area in West Central Florida. TECO Diversified, Inc. provides direction for several diversified, activities of TE. TECO Power Services is a wholesale power supplier. TECO Investments, Inc. invests capital in short- and long-term investments. TECO Finance, Inc. acts as the financing arm for all of TECO Energy's activities. TECO Coal produces and sells 3.5 million tons of coal annually.

BUSINESS LINE ANALYSIS

(12/31/94)	Rev(%)	Inc(%)
Regulated Electric	70.0	75.0
Other Energy		
Services	30.0	25.0
Total	100.0	100.0

ANNUAL EARNINGS AND DIVIDENDS PER SHARE

	1994	1993	1992	1991	1990	1989	1988
Earnings Per Share	1.32	1.30	1.30	1.28	1.22	1.18	1.07
Dividends Per Share	1.00	① 0.95	0.898	0.847	0.798	0.748	0.70
Dividend Payout %	75.8	73.0	69.0	66.5	65.1	63.6	65.7

① 2-for-1 stk split,08/31/93

ANNUAL FINANCIAL DATA

RECORD OF EARNINGS (IN MILLIONS):

	1994	1993	1992	1991	1990	1989	1988
Total Revenues	1,350.9	1,283.9	1,183.2	1,154.1	1,097.1	1,060.0	1,034.0
Depreciation	174.0	165.3	142.5	132.7	…	…	…
Maintenance	101.1	98.9	94.3	89.4	79.2	78.6	81.8
Prov for Fed Inc Taxes	45.8	55.0	56.5	53.3	63.1	70.5	60.0
Income From Operations	269.8	290.5	269.0	262.3	258.0	254.0	233.7
Interest Expense	77.1	76.1	64.5	65.0	59.5	57.0	60.3
Net Income	153.2	① 150.3	149.0	145.3	139.4	133.8	② 120.6
Aver. Shs. Outstg. (000)	115,923	115,340	114,611	113,922	113,664	113,549	113,413

① Before acctg. change cr$11,228,000. ② Before extra. item dr$6,293,000.

BALANCE SHEET (IN MILLIONS):

	1994	1993	1992	1991	1990	1989	1988
Gross Plant	4,095.7	3,846.1	3,638.7	3,286.2	2,881.1	2,668.9	2,557.6
Accumulated Depreciation	1,475.5	1,363.1	1,256.8	1,067.2	936.6	853.5	784.7
Prop, Plant & Equip, Net	2,620.3	2,483.0	2,381.9	2,219.0	1,944.6	1,815.4	1,772.8
Long-term Debt	1,023.9	1,043.2	1,048.5	907.9	762.9	674.8	684.0
Net Stockholders' Equity	1,139.2	1,082.5	1,010.7	946.3	885.5	938.4	900.6
Total Assets	3,312.2	3,127.8	3,024.3	2,833.6	2,513.0	2,386.8	2,314.6
Year End Shs Outstg (000)	116,199	115,621	114,966	114,219	113,697	113,597	113,496

STATISTICAL RECORD:

	1994	1993	1992	1991	1990	1989	1988
Book Value Per Share	9.33	8.89	8.31	7.80	7.30	7.72	7.29
Op. Inc/Net Pl %	10.3	11.7	11.3	11.8	13.3	14.0	13.2
Dep/Gr. Pl %	4.2	4.3	3.9	4.0	4.2	4.2	4.2
Accum. Dep/Gr. Pl %	36.0	35.4	34.5	32.5	32.5	32.0	30.7
Return on Equity %	13.4	13.9	14.7	15.4	15.7	14.4	13.7
Average Yield %	4.9	7.2	4.6	4.6	5.3	5.8	6.1
P/E Ratio	17.1-13.7	19.9-15.6	16.3-13.8	16.4-12.4	13.9-10.8	12.5-9.3	11.7-9.9
Price Range	22⅝-18⅛	25⅞-20¼	21⅛-18	20⅞-15¾	17-13⅛	14¾-11	12½-10⅝

Statistics are as originally reported.

OFFICERS:
T.L. Guzzle, Chmn. & C.E.O.
G.F. Anderson, Pres. & C.O.O.
A.D. Oak, Sr. V.P.-Fin., Treas. & C.F.O.
R.H. Kessel, V.P. & Sec.

INCORPORATED: FL, Jan., 1981

PRINCIPAL OFFICE: TECO Plaza 702 N. Franklin Street, Tampa, FL 33602

TELEPHONE NUMBER: (813) 228-4111

FAX: (813) 228-1670

NO. OF EMPLOYEES: 4,440

ANNUAL MEETING: In April

SHAREHOLDERS: 32,668

INSTITUTIONAL HOLDINGS:
No. of Institutions: 235
Shares Held: 45,860,950

REGISTRAR(S): First National Bank of Boston, Shareholder Services Division, Boston, MA

TRANSFER AGENT(S): First National Bank of Boston, Shareholder Services Division, Boston, MA

NYS SYMBOL TFX
Rec. Pr. 41¾

TELEFLEX, INC.

YIELD 1.5%
P/E RATIO 17.4

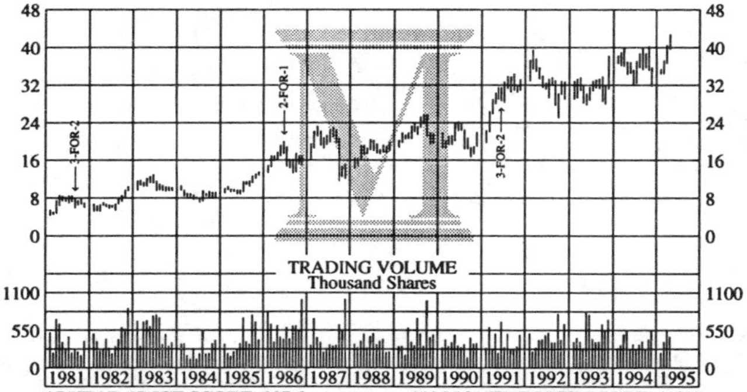

48
40
32
24
16
8
0
3-FOR-2
2-FOR-1
3-FOR-2
TRADING VOLUME
Thousand Shares
1100
550
0
1981 1982 1983 1984 1985 1986 1987 1988 1989 1990 1991 1992 1993 1994 1995

***7 YEAR PRICE SCORE 107.6** ***12 MONTH PRICE SCORE 103.4**

*NYSE COMPOSITE INDEX=100

INTERIM EARNINGS (Per Share):

Qtr.	Mar.	June	Sept.	Dec.
1991	0.45	0.47	0.35	0.50
1992	0.47	0.50	0.36	0.54
1993	0.50	0.54	0.34	0.57
1994	0.57	0.64	0.47	0.72

INTERIM DIVIDENDS (Per Share):

Amt.	Decl.	Ex.	Rec.	Pay.
0.135Q	11/8/94	11/8/94	11/15/94	12/15/94
0.135Q	11/8	11/8	11/15	12/15
0.135Q	11/8	11/8	11/15	12/15
0.135Q	2/6/95	2/17/95	2/24/95	3/15/95
0.155Q	4/28	5/19	5/25	6/15

Indicated div.: $0.62*

CAPITALIZATION (12/25/94):

	($000)	(%)
Long-Term Debt	190,499	35.2
Deferred Income Tax	41,593	7.7
Common & Surplus	309,024	57.1
Total	541,116	100.0

DIVIDEND ACHIEVER STATUS:

Rank: 69 1984-94 Growth Rate: 14.3%

Total Years of Dividend Growth: 17

RECENT DEVELOPMENTS: For the year ended 12/25/94, net income was $41.2 million, an increase of 22% from $33.7 million in the previous year. Total revenues rose to $812.7 million versus $666.8 million in the year before. Strong performance in the commercial and medical segments, which increased sales by 20% and 40%, respectively, offset the effects of a foundering commercial aviation market and decreased defense-related spending in the aerospace division.

PROSPECTS: Revenue and earnings will continue to benefit from the improving economies both domestically and abroad. However, higher interest rates in the U.S. may soften future demand for automobiles and limit earnings gains in TFX's commercial sector. Aerospace segment sales will remain soft due to the ongoing weakness in the aerospace controls and commercial aviation markets, and will offset strong gains in the commercial sector.

BUSINESS

TELEFLEX INC. designs, develops and manufactures a broad range of proprietary products for the automotive, aerospace, defense and medical markets. Aerospace Products and Services (25% of 1994 sales and 6% of operating profit) include the design and manufacture of precision mechanical electromechanical controls and systems; corrosion resistant coatings and repairs for gas turbine engines. Medical Products (31%, 36%) manufactures a broad range of disposable products for medical markets. Commercial Products (44%, 59%) develops mechanical, electrical and hydraulic controls for the automotive, pleasure marine and power equipment market.

BUSINESS LINE ANALYSIS

(12/27/94)	Rev(%)	Inc(%)
Commercial Products	43.9	58.5
Medical Products	31.1	35.6
Aerospace Prod & Services	25.0	5.9
Total	100.0	100.0

ANNUAL EARNINGS AND DIVIDENDS PER SHARE

	12/25/94	12/26/93	12/27/92	12/29/91	12/30/90	12/31/89	12/25/88
Earnings Per Share	2.35	1.95	1.87	1.77	1.73	1.63	1.48
Dividends Per Share	0.52	0.45	0.415	[1] 0.343	0.35	0.307	0.257
Dividend Payout %	22.1	23.1	22.2	19.4	20.2	18.8	17.3

[1] 5% stk div, 6/17/91

ANNUAL FINANCIAL DATA

	12/25/94	12/26/93	12/27/92	12/29/91	12/30/90	12/31/89	12/25/88
RECORD OF EARNINGS (IN THOUSANDS):							
Total Revenues	812,672	666,796	570,338	483,009	444,213	360,066	328,223
Costs and Expenses	698,301	571,949	484,650	405,506	371,750	301,034	274,573
Depreciation & Amort	33,019	28,071	21,556	18,404	17,154	12,908	11,046
Operating Profit	81,352	66,776	64,132	59,099	55,308	46,123	42,604
Income Before Taxes	62,991	52,310	48,650	45,334	42,907	39,237	36,379
Income Taxes	21,795	18,624	16,638	15,527	14,340	12,440	12,370
Net Income	41,196	33,686	[1] 32,012	29,807	28,567	26,797	24,009
Aver. Shs. Outstg.	17,530	17,267	17,132	16,850	16,476	16,403	16,244
[1] Before acctg. change cr$860,000.							
BALANCE SHEET (IN THOUSANDS):							
Cash and Cash Equivalents	24,094	11,255	36,331	24,503	44,267	18,383	33,173
Receivables, Net	183,745	143,489	116,818	105,081	87,841	82,034	67,046
Inventories	173,105	159,287	128,970	117,414	98,530	88,594	57,661
Gross Property	412,671	382,809	300,897	268,986	235,715	205,661	142,948
Accumulated Depreciation	148,354	121,389	101,305	90,187	76,129	59,543	48,120
Long-Term Debt	190,499	183,504	134,600	119,370	112,941	106,128	57,104
Net Stockholders' Equity	309,024	269,790	240,467	211,702	187,875	160,038	136,328
Total Assets	710,789	640,576	534,931	477,693	425,100	366,662	264,116
Total Current Assets	390,217	322,249	289,821	255,012	236,930	194,274	160,549
Total Current Liabilities	169,673	150,853	123,018	123,424	103,090	81,949	62,332
Net Working Capital	220,544	171,397	166,803	131,589	133,840	112,325	98,217
Year End Shares Outstg	17,277	17,084	16,876	16,630	16,417	16,213	16,051
STATISTICAL RECORD:							
Operating Profit Margin %	10.0	10.0	11.2	12.2	12.5	12.8	13.0
Book Value Per Share	17.89	15.79	14.25	12.73	11.44	9.87	8.49
Return on Equity %	13.3	12.5	13.3	14.1	15.2	16.7	17.6
Return on Assets %	5.8	5.3	6.0	6.2	6.7	7.3	9.1
Average Yield %	1.4	1.4	1.3	1.3	1.7	1.4	1.5
P/E Ratio	17.1-13.5	19.6-14.2	21.1-13.4	19.4-11.1	13.9-9.6	15.9-11.5	13.8-9.6
Price Range	40¼-31¾	38¼-27¾	39½-25	34⅜-19⅝	24⅛-16⅝	25⅞-18¾	20⅜-14¼

Statistics are as originally reported.

OFFICERS:
L.K. Black, Chmn. & C.E.O.
D.S. Boyer, Pres.
H.L. Zuber, Jr., V.P. & C.F.O.
S.K. Chance, V.P., General Couns. & Sec.

INCORPORATED: DE, 1943

PRINCIPAL OFFICE: 630 West Germantown Pike Suite 450, Plymouth Meeting, PA 19462

TELEPHONE NUMBER: (610) 834-6301

FAX: (610) 834-8228

NO. OF EMPLOYEES: 9,000 approx.

ANNUAL MEETING: In April

SHAREHOLDERS: 1,500 (approx.)

INSTITUTIONAL HOLDINGS:
No. of Institutions: 131
Shares Held: 8,668,752

REGISTRAR(S): Mellon Securities Trust Company, Ridgefield Park, NJ

TRANSFER AGENT(S): Mellon Securities Trust Company, Ridgefield Park, NJ

TELEPHONE & DATA SYSTEMS, INC.

YIELD 1.0%
P/E RATIO 28.1

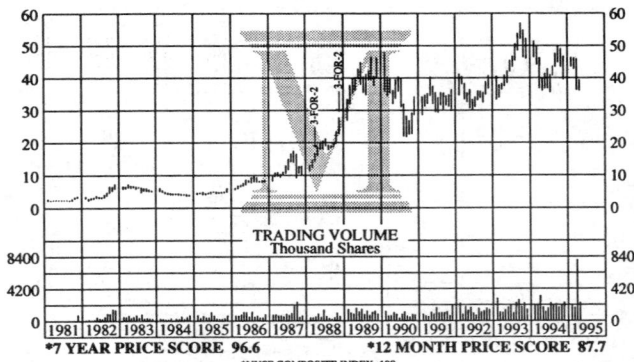

*7 YEAR PRICE SCORE 96.6   *12 MONTH PRICE SCORE 87.7
*NYSE COMPOSITE INDEX=100

INTERIM EARNINGS (Per Share):

Qtr.	Mar.	June	Sept.	Dec.
1992	0.35	0.16	0.15	0.26
1993	0.14	0.18	0.24	0.11
1994	0.18	0.26	0.31	0.36

INTERIM DIVIDENDS (Per Share):

Amt.	Decl.	Ex.	Rec.	Pay.
0.09Q	12/6/94	12/12/94	12/16/94	12/30/94
0.09Q	12/6	12/12	12/16	12/30
0.09Q	12/6	12/12	12/16	12/30
0.095Q	3/7/95	3/13/95	3/17/95	3/31/95

*Indicated div.: $0.38**

CAPITALIZATION (12/31/94):

	($000)	(%)
Long-Term Debt	536,509	22.3
Deferred Income Tax	85,390	3.5
Minority Interest	272,292	11.3
Preferred Stock	43,028	1.8
Common & Surplus	1,473,038	61.1
Total	2,410,257	100.0

DIVIDEND ACHIEVER STATUS:
Rank: 229   1984-94 Growth Rate: 7.5%
Total Years of Dividend Growth: 20

RECENT DEVELOPMENTS: For the year ended 12/31/94, net income before an accounting adjustment was $60.5 million, up 78.6% from $33.9 million in 1993. Revenues increased 31% to $730.8 million. Cellular telephone operations contributed 68.3% of the revenue increase, with telephone and radio paging contributing 22.1% and 9.6%, respectively. Cellular operation's results reflect system expansion and strong roaming revenue, while telephone operations benefited from acquisitions.

PROSPECTS: TDS's long-term outlook will be increasingly reliant on its cellular subsidiary's performance. The number of customers served by TDS's rapidly growing cellular subsidiary is closing the gap on the number of customers served by telephone operations. Moreover, the prospects for further cellular growth are very favorable. The Company is benefiting from new marketing strategies and improved economic conditions.

BUSINESS

TELEPHONE AND DATA SYSTEMS, INC. is a diversified telecommunications service company with local telephone, cellular telephone and radio paging operations. At December 31, 1994, the Company operated 96 telephone subsidiaries serving 392,500 access lines in rural and suburban areas; owned or had the right to acquire cellular interests representing approximately 25.2 million population equivalents and offered cellular telephone service through 207 majority-owned markets with 421,000 cellular telephones in service; and offered radio paging and related services with 652,800 pagers in service.

REVENUES

(12/31/94)	($000)	(%)
Telephone	306,341	41.9
Cellular Telephone	332,404	45.5
Radio Paging	92,065	12.6
Total	730,810	100.0

ANNUAL EARNINGS AND DIVIDENDS PER SHARE

	1994	1993	1992	1991	1990	1989	1988
Earnings Per Share	1.07	0.67	[1] [2]0.91	[3] 0.59	0.86	[4] 0.35	[4] 0.40
Dividends Per Share	0.36	0.34	0.32	0.30	0.28	0.26	[5]0.24
Dividend Payout %	33.6	50.8	35.2	50.8	32.6	74.3	60.0

[1] Before acctg. chg. & extraord. item [2] Before extraord. item [3] Before acctg. chg. [4] Before disc. oper. [5] 50% stk div, 3/17/88

ANNUAL FINANCIAL DATA

RECORD OF EARNINGS (IN MILLIONS):

	1994	1993	1992	1991	1990	1989	1988
Total Revenues	1,461.6	1,181.5	912.2	708.1	589.3	479.4	392.5
Costs and Expenses	460.2	393.5	303.1	236.7	184.6	158.3	122.2
Depreciation & Amort	161.8	127.5	99.0	76.8	62.9	53.3	44.1
Operating Income	108.8	69.7	54.1	40.5	47.1	28.2	30.0
Income Taxes	40.7	26.5	29.8	14.9	16.4	7.9	7.3
Net Income	59.8	33.9	[1] 38.5	16.1	27.2	11.1	[2] 10.6
Aver. Shs. Outstg. (000)	54,197	47,266	39,074	33,036	30,415	27,543	24,417

[1] Before extra. item dr$769,000. [2] Before disc. op. cr$731,000.

BALANCE SHEET (IN MILLIONS):

	1994	1993	1992	1991	1990	1989	1988
Cash and Cash Equivalents	45.9	74.9	58.9	54.8	73.6	64.0	53.9
Receivables, Net	110.3	80.8	64.5	51.3	36.6	37.8	29.5
Inventories	17.1	13.9	9.7	9.3	7.5	6.4	6.4
Gross Property	2,783.3	2,225.4	1,668.0	1,324.1	891.5	757.2	626.2
Accumulated Depreciation	629.7	487.1	392.5	326.9	266.9	243.1	205.0
Long-Term Debt	536.5	514.4	405.0	381.1	255.5	255.8	234.9
Net Stockholders' Equity	1,516.1	1,266.8	918.8	686.8	449.6	368.9	212.1
Total Assets	2,790.1	2,259.2	1,696.5	1,368.1	940.3	771.2	597.6
Total Current Assets	185.9	179.6	143.4	121.5	121.8	114.0	94.0
Total Current Liabilities	346.2	163.5	164.2	129.3	145.9	72.7	90.9
Net Working Capital	d160.3	16.0	d20.9	d7.8	d24.0	41.3	3.1
Year End Shs Outstg (000)	47,938	50,689	41,247	34,964	30,317	29,566	24,794

STATISTICAL RECORD:

	1994	1993	1992	1991	1990	1989	1988
Book Value Per Share	30.73	24.15	21.27	18.46	14.17	12.00	7.81
Return on Equity %	4.0	2.7	4.3	3.2	6.1	3.1	5.3
Average Yield %	0.8	0.8	0.9	0.9	0.8	0.7	1.2
P/E Ratio	48.1-33.2	85.1-49.6	45.3-33.1	68.4-43.5	55.8-25.3	N.M	69.4-28.1
Price Range	51½-35½	57-33¼	41¼-30⅛	40⅜-28½	48-21¾	46½-26⅞	27¾-11¼

Statistics are as originally reported.

OFFICERS:
L.T. Carlson, Chmn.
L.T. Carlson, Jr., Pres. & C.E.O.
M.L. Swanson, Exec. V.P.-Fin. & C.F.O.
R.D. Webster, V.P. & Treas.
M.G. Hron, Sec.

INCORPORATED: IA, Mar., 1968

PRINCIPAL OFFICE: 30 N. LaSalle Street Suite 4000, Chicago, IL 60602

TELEPHONE NUMBER: (312) 630-1900

NO. OF EMPLOYEES: 5,322

ANNUAL MEETING: In May

SHAREHOLDERS: 4,158 com., ser. A com., 106.

INSTITUTIONAL HOLDINGS:
No. of Institutions: 190
Shares Held: 32,003,902

REGISTRAR(S): Harris Trust & Savings Bank, Chicago, IL

TRANSFER AGENT(S): Harris Trust & Savings Bank, Chicago, IL

TEMPLE-INLAND INC.

YIELD 2.4%
P/E RATIO 15.3

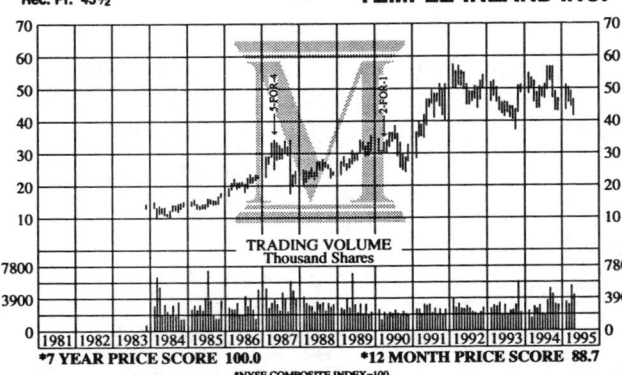

7 YEAR PRICE SCORE 100.0 **12 MONTH PRICE SCORE 88.7**

*NYSE COMPOSITE INDEX=100

INTERIM EARNINGS (Per Share):

Qtr.	Mar.	June	Sept.	Dec.
1992	---------------- 2.65 ----------------			
1993	0.50	0.38	0.21	0.12
1994	0.41	0.48	0.59	0.87

INTERIM DIVIDENDS (Per Share):

Amt.	Decl.	Ex.	Rec.	Pay.
0.27Q	11/7/94	11/25/94	12/1/94	12/15/94
0.27Q	11/7	11/25	12/1	12/15
0.27Q	11/7	11/25	12/1	12/15
0.27Q	2/3/95	2/23/95	3/1/95	3/15/95
0.27Q	5/5	5/25	6/1	6/15

Indicated div.: $1.08

CAPITALIZATION (12/31/94):

	($000)	(%)
Long-Term Debt	1,397,500	41.8
Deferred Income Tax	163,000	4.9
Common & Surplus	1,783,000	53.3
Total	3,343,500	100.0

DIVIDEND ACHIEVER STATUS:
Rank: 30   1984-94 Growth Rate: 17.7%
Total Years of Dividend Growth: 10

RECENT DEVELOPMENTS: For the twelve months ended 12/31/94, TIN reported net income of $131.4 million compared with $67.3 million, before an accounting credit of $50 million, in 1993. Revenues for the year advanced 7.4% to $2.94 billion. Manufacturing net sales were up 9.8% to $2.31 billion from $2.10 billion. Earnings in the corrugated container group improved to $102.0 million from $21.0 million and building products group earnings climbed 33.8% to $132.6 million.

PROSPECTS: TIN's building products group is benefiting from earnings growth in each of its manufacturing segments. Demand and prices for boxes remain strong, while inventories of containerboard are at low levels. However, costs for old corrugated containers have begun to rise. Losses continue to narrow in the bleached paperboard group. TIN expects this unit to return to profitability in 1995, following an extended outage, as it completes a mill expansion program.

BUSINESS

TEMPLE-INLAND is a holding company with interest in paper, packaging, building products and financial services. The Company operates through three subsidiaries: Inland Container Corporation, Temple-Inland Forest Products Corporation and Temple-Inland Financial Services. In addition, TIN manufactures bleached pulp and paperboard and a wide range of building products. Forest resources include approximately 1.9 million acres of timberland in Texas, Louisiana, Georgia and Alabama, including approximately 100,000 acres of leased lands.

REVENUES

(12/31/94)	$000	(%)
Corrugated Container	1,438,200	49.0
Bleached Paperboard.	299,400	10.2
Building Products......	549,300	18.7
Other Activities	19,200	0.6
Financial Services	631,400	21.5
Total	2,937,500	100.0

ANNUAL EARNINGS AND DIVIDENDS PER SHARE

	12/31/94	1/1/94	1/2/93	12/29/91	12/31/90	12/31/89	12/31/88
Earnings Per Share	2.35	1.21	2.65	2.51	4.20	3.75	3.58
Dividends Per Share	1.02	1.00	0.96	0.88	0.80	0.58	0.42
Dividend Payout %	43.4	82.7	72.7	35.1	19.0	15.5	11.7

ANNUAL FINANCIAL DATA

RECORD OF EARNINGS (IN MILLIONS):

	12/31/94	1/1/94	1/2/93	12/29/91	12/31/90	12/31/89	12/31/88
Total Revenues	2,938.0	2,735.9	2,713.2	2,507.2	2,401.2	1,901.2	1,767.8
Costs and Expenses	2,474.0	2,376.6	2,318.7	2,145.7	1,973.2	1,434.3	1,349.5
Depreciation & Depletion	208.0	196.9	172.3	161.6	139.8	126.5	114.0
Operating Income	256.0	162.4	222.1	199.9	288.1	340.4	304.3
Income Before Taxes	193.0	96.2	177.0	166.8	268.8	314.2	301.8
Income Taxes	61.8	28.9	30.1	28.4	36.3	106.8	102.6
Net Income	131.0	①67.4	146.9	138.4	232.5	207.4	199.2
Aver. Shs. Outstg. (000)	55,900	55,528	55,528	55,535	55,248	55,400	55,324	55,696
① Before acctg. change cr$50,000,000.							

BALANCE SHEET (IN MILLIONS):

	12/31/94	1/1/94	1/2/93	12/29/91	12/31/90	12/31/89	12/31/88
Cash and Cash Equivalents	4,279.0	4,572.2	5,389.7	4,643.3	1,545.0	343.5	16.2
Receivables, Net	244.0	198.5	214.1	641.2	1,603.8	1,579.9	376.5
Inventories	268.0	258.0	493.0	709.5	493.0	286.9	267.1	157.7
Gross Property	②2,671.0	②2,383.5	②2,228.0	②2,017.4	②1,792.7	②1,571.2	2,312.3
Long-Term Debt	1,397.5	1,121.0	1,063.4	940.2	595.5	429.2	417.8
Net Stockholders' Equity	1,783.0	1,700.2	1,632.6	1,531.5	1,439.3	1,258.9	1,095.8
Total Assets	12,251.0	11,959.1	10,765.5	10,068.5	7,834.5	6,390.1	2,164.0
Total Current Assets	5,339.0	6,323.0	6,707.1	6,340.6	4,718.1	3,834.0	565.1
Total Current Liabilities	8,118.0	8,087.1	7,161.7	6,696.8	5,014.0	3,979.7	214.0
Net Working Capital	d2,779.0	d1,764.1	d454.6	d356.2	d296.0	d145.7	351.0
Year End Shs Outstg (000)	56,019	55,481	55,251	54,914	54,589	54,850	55,166
② Net							

STATISTICAL RECORD:

	12/31/94	1/1/94	1/2/93	12/29/91	12/31/90	12/31/89	12/31/88
Operating Profit Margin %	8.7	5.9	8.2	8.0	12.0	17.9	17.2
Book Value Per Share	31.83	30.64	29.55	27.89	26.37	22.95	19.86
Return on Equity %	7.3	4.0	9.0	9.0	16.2	16.5	18.2
Return on Assets %	1.1	0.6	1.4	1.4	3.0	3.2	9.2
Average Yield %	2.0	2.3	2.0	2.2	2.5	2.0	1.7
P/E Ratio	24.1-18.3	43.4-30.8	21.7-16.6	20.5-11.4	9.2-5.7	9.5-6.2	7.9-5.6
Price Range	56¾-43	52½-37¼	57½-43⅞	51½-28½	38⅝-24⅛	35½-23⅜	28⅜-20⅛

Statistics are as originally reported.

OFFICERS:
C.J. Grum, Chmn. & C.E.O.
M.R. Warner, V.P., General Counsel & Sec.
D.W. Turpin, Treas.
K.M. Jastrow, II, C.F.O.

INCORPORATED: DE, 1983

PRINCIPAL OFFICE: 303 South Temple Drive, Diboll, TX 75941

TELEPHONE NUMBER: (409) 829-2211
FAX: (409) 829-3333
NO. OF EMPLOYEES: 15,000 (approx.)
ANNUAL MEETING: In May
SHAREHOLDERS: 8,081
INSTITUTIONAL HOLDINGS:
No. of Institutions: 295
Shares Held: 38,387,170

REGISTRAR(S): First Chicago Trust Co. of NY, New York, NY

TRANSFER AGENT(S): First Chicago Trust Co. of NY, New York, NY

TENNANT CO.

YIELD 2.8%
P/E RATIO 15.3

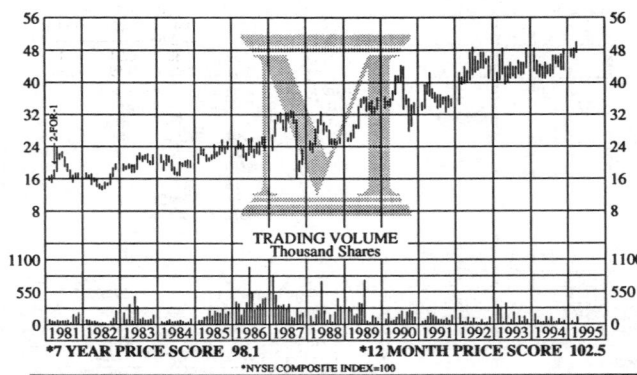

INTERIM EARNINGS (Per Share):

Qtr.	Mar.	June	Sept.	Dec.
1991	0.37	0.62	0.69	0.74
1992	0.50	0.66	0.65	0.93
1993	0.10	0.62	0.65	0.49
1994	0.54	0.86	0.79	1.01

INTERIM DIVIDENDS (Per Share):

Amt.	Decl.	Ex.	Rec.	Pay.
0.32Q	5/5/94	5/24/94	5/31/94	6/14/94
0.32Q	8/9	8/25	8/31	9/14
0.34Q	12/9	12/14	12/20	12/30
0.34Q	2/16/95	2/28/95	3/6/95	3/14/95

Indicated div.: $1.36

CAPITALIZATION (12/31/94):

	($000)	(%)
Long-Term Debt	6,300	6.1
Common & Surplus	96,249	93.9
Total	102,549	100.0

DIVIDEND ACHIEVER STATUS:

Rank: 295   1984-94 Growth Rate: 4.0%
Total Years of Dividend Growth: 22

RECENT DEVELOPMENTS: For the quarter ended 12/31/94, net income more than doubled to $4.9 million compared with $2.4 million in the corresponding quarter of 1993. Sales increased 25% to $81.2 million versus $65.0 million in the year-earlier period. Results for 1993 included a charge of $3.5 million pre-tax for restructuring. Profit from operations was $7.5 million, up 31% from 1993's operating profit before restructuring charges. For the year ended 12/31/94, net income was $15.7 million, up 72% from $9.1 million, including one-time charges, in 1993. Sales were up 27% to $281.7 million. Earnings growth was attributed to strong sales gains aided by improved economic conditions and new products, and the successful integration of the Castex acquisition. Industrial equipment and floor coatings sales were up 15% on a comparable basis with all key markets showing strong gains.

BUSINESS

TENNANT COMPANY is engaged in the manufacture and design of specialized industrial and commercial surface maintenance equipment and related products. The Company also markets replacement component parts for its equipment. The equipment manufactured includes gas, diesel or battery-powered sweepers, scrubbers and scarifiers. Accessories and floor-treating materials are also sold by the Company. Products are sold in more than 60 countries throughout the world. The equipment manufactured by the Company is generally used to clean and maintain commercial and industrial floors, roadways, parking areas and the like. Domestic manufacturing operations are carried on in a plant facility in Minneapolis, Minnesota. Operations overseas include Tennant N.V., a wholly-owned subsidiary in the Netherlands selling to customers throughout Europe; Equipamentos Tennant Limitada, a sales and manufacturing facility in Brazil; and Fuji-Tennant Ltd. a 50%-owned affiliate in Japan.

BUSINESS LINE ANALYSIS

(12/31/94)	Rev(%)	Inc(%)
North American.........	77.0	73.4
International	23.0	26.6
Total	100.0	100.0

ANNUAL EARNINGS AND DIVIDENDS PER SHARE

	1994	1993	1992	1991	1990	1989	1988
Earnings Per Share	3.20	1.86	① 2.68	2.42	① 3.17	2.87	② 2.18
Dividends Per Share	1.30	1.28	1.22	1.20	1.18	1.10	0.98
Dividend Payout %	40.6	68.8	45.5	49.6	37.2	38.3	45.0

① Before extraord. item & acctg. chg. ② Before extraord. item

ANNUAL FINANCIAL DATA

RECORD OF EARNINGS (IN THOUSANDS):

	1994	1993	1992	1991	1990	1989	1988
Total Revenues	281,685	221,002	214,863	198,575	211,503	197,078	183,888
Costs and Expenses	244,440	198,682	188,493	173,124	183,347	169,002	157,737
Depreciation & Amort	13,121	10,987	10,241	8,730	8,652	8,027	7,900
Profit From Operations	24,124	11,333	16,129	16,721	19,504	20,049	18,251
Profit Bef Income Taxes	24,081	12,928	17,993	18,521	19,878	23,804	19,700
Income Taxes	8,346	3,802	4,803	6,529	4,257	9,052	8,126
Net Income	15,735	9,126	① 13,190	11,992	② 15,621	14,752	③ 11,574
Aver. Shs. Outstg.	9,826	9,836	9,832	9,892	9,842	10,268	10,592

① Before extra. item cr$395,000. ② Before extra. item cr$590,000. ③ Before extra. item cr$1,689,000.

BALANCE SHEET (IN THOUSANDS):

	1994	1993	1992	1991	1990	1989	1988
Cash and Cash Equivalents	1,851	2,675	3,512	2,349	1,412	3,175	7,016
Receivables, Net	65,278	47,472	44,360	40,225	40,553	41,796	45,813
Inventories	30,985	22,893	25,805	22,533	24,440	22,668	20,865
Gross Property	122,384	111,131	104,874	94,131	91,242	84,397	74,233
Accumulated Depreciation	65,832	64,509	59,444	53,401	48,654	43,448	38,617
Long-Term Debt	6,300	1,103	3,107	1,853	1,995	2,568	2,401
Net Stockholders' Equity	96,249	84,093	84,850	76,613	73,164	74,050	77,998
Total Assets	182,834	128,624	128,988	111,644	116,234	117,627	117,813
Total Current Assets	98,810	73,752	74,741	66,028	67,065	70,325	79,222
Total Current Liabilities	66,065	30,847	30,340	32,864	40,386	36,987	33,657
Net Working Capital	32,745	42,905	44,401	33,164	26,679	33,338	45,565
Year End Shares Outstg	9,839	9,826	9,824	9,734	9,854	9,846	10,588

STATISTICAL RECORD:

	1994	1993	1992	1991	1990	1989	1988
Operating Profit Margin %	8.6	5.1	7.5	8.4	9.2	10.2	9.9
Book Value Per Share	7.82	8.38	8.64	7.87	7.42	7.52	7.37
Return on Equity %	16.3	10.9	15.5	15.7	21.4	19.9	14.8
Return on Assets %	8.6	7.1	10.2	10.7	13.4	12.5	9.8
Average Yield %	2.9	2.9	2.9	3.2	3.3	3.6	3.5
P/E Ratio	30.3-25.6	52.2-42.5	36.4-25.7	35.1-26.9	27.9-17.5	25.4-17.6	30.0-20.6
Price Range	48½-41	48½-39½	48¾-34½	42½-32½	44¼-27¾	36½-25¼	32¾-22½

Statistics are as originally reported.

OFFICERS:
R.L. Hale, Pres. & C.E.O.
J.M. Dolan, Sr. V.P., Gen. Couns. & Sec.
R.A. Snyder, V.P., Treas. & C.F.O.
B.J. Borgerding, Deputy General Counsel & Sec.

INCORPORATED: MN, Jan., 1909

PRINCIPAL OFFICE: 701 N. Lilac Dr. P.O. Box 1452, Minneapolis, MN 55440

TELEPHONE NUMBER: (612) 540-1200
FAX: (612) 540-1437
NO. OF EMPLOYEES: 1,916
ANNUAL MEETING: In May
SHAREHOLDERS: 3,000
INSTITUTIONAL HOLDINGS:
No. of Institutions: 57
Shares Held: 3,271,759

REGISTRAR(S): Norwest Bank Minnesota, N.A., St. Paul, MN

TRANSFER AGENT(S): Norwest Bank Minnesota, N.A., St. Paul, MN

TEXAS UTILITIES CO.

YIELD 9.1%
P/E RATIO 14.0

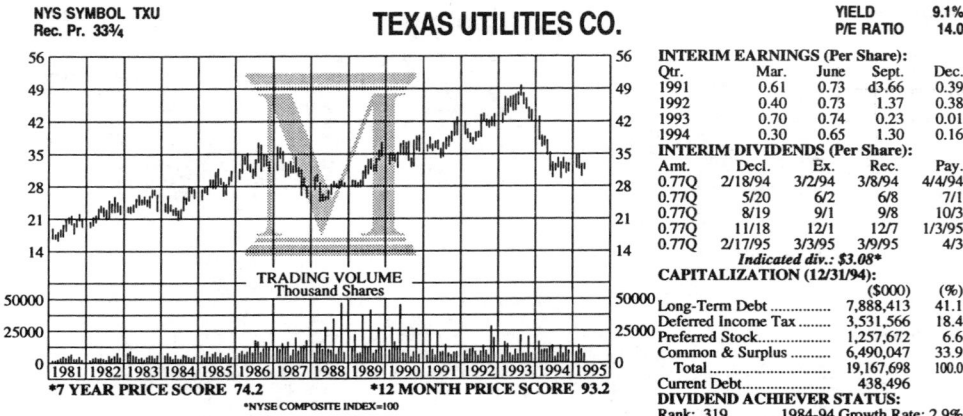

*7 YEAR PRICE SCORE 74.2   *12 MONTH PRICE SCORE 93.2
*NYSE COMPOSITE INDEX=100

INTERIM EARNINGS (Per Share):

Qtr.	Mar.	June	Sept.	Dec.
1991	0.61	0.73	d3.66	0.39
1992	0.40	0.73	1.37	0.38
1993	0.70	0.74	0.23	0.01
1994	0.30	0.65	1.30	0.16

INTERIM DIVIDENDS (Per Share):

Amt.	Decl.	Ex.	Rec.	Pay.
0.77Q	2/18/94	3/2/94	3/8/94	4/4/94
0.77Q	5/20	6/2	6/8	7/1
0.77Q	8/19	9/1	9/8	10/3
0.77Q	11/18	12/1	12/7	1/3/95
0.77Q	2/17/95	3/3/95	3/9/95	4/3

*Indicated div.: $3.08**

CAPITALIZATION (12/31/94):

	($000)	(%)
Long-Term Debt	7,888,413	41.1
Deferred Income Tax	3,531,566	18.4
Preferred Stock	1,257,672	6.6
Common & Surplus	6,490,047	33.9
Total	19,167,698	100.0
Current Debt	438,496	

DIVIDEND ACHIEVER STATUS:
Rank: 319   1984-94 Growth Rate: 2.9%
Total Years of Dividend Growth: 48

RECENT DEVELOPMENTS: For the quarter ended 12/31/94, net income was $35.6 million compared with $1.2 million in the corresponding quarter of 1993. Revenues were $1.23 billion, down 2%. The decline in revenues reflects milder than normal weather during the quarter. Earnings for 1993 were adversely affected by an adjustment to reflect a lower amout of rate relief granted than had been reflected in bonded rates.

PROSPECTS: Texas Utilities is trying to offset the effects of the disappointing rate decision through a new filing of strategic rates designed to retain existing commercial, industrial and wholesale load customers. Further steps being taken are interest charges being reduced through the refinancing or the retirement of high coupon debt and cost-containment measures to lower operating expenses.

BUSINESS

TEXAS UTILITIES CO. is the holding company of an electric system located entirely within the state of Texas. Its electric utility subsidiary, Texas Utilities Electric Co. generates and distributes in the north central, eastern and western parts of Texas, with a population estimated at 5,500,000, about one-third of the population of Texas. The territory includes the petroleum industry, banking, agriculture, and other commercial and industrial businesses. Other subsidiaries include: Texas Utilities Fuel Company (a natural gas pipeline system), Texas Utilities Mining Co., Texas Utilities Service (financial services), Basic Resources Inc., and Chaco Energy Co.

REVENUES

(12/31/94)	($000)	(%)
Residential	2,490,319	44.0
Commercial	1,707,306	30.1
Industrial	986,495	17.4
Government & Municipal	399,906	7.1
Other Electric	216,172	3.8
Other Operating	(136,655)	(2.4)
Total	5,663,543	100.0

ANNUAL EARNINGS AND DIVIDENDS PER SHARE

	1994	1993	1992	1991	1990	1989	1988
Earnings Per Share	2.40	1.66	①2.88	d1.98	4.40	4.44	4.00
Dividends Per Share	3.08	3.07	3.03	2.99	2.95	2.91	2.86
Dividend Payout %	N.M.	N.M.	N.M.	...	67.1	65.5	71.5

① Before acctg. chg.

ANNUAL FINANCIAL DATA

RECORD OF EARNINGS (IN MILLIONS):

	1994	1993	1992	1991	1990	1989	1988
Total Revenues	5,663.5	5,434.5	4,907.9	4,893.2	4,542.6	4,320.5	4,153.7
Depreciation & Amort	710.2	543.4	477.2	436.9	327.6	251.4	242.3
Maintenance	304.9	350.0	301.3	309.4	296.6	265.1	294.8
Income Taxes	317.0	322.1	171.1	120.1	113.9	144.1	129.1
Operating Income	1,331.6	1,186.9	1,163.3	1,135.7	1,083.5	1,032.8	953.3
Interest Expense	715.6	639.7	644.6	702.7	533.6	475.8	480.9
Net Income	542.8	368.7	①619.2	d410.0	850.8	779.1	642.7
Aver. Shs. Outstg. (000)	225,834	221,555	214,850	207,358	193,461	175,567	160,561

① Before acctg. change cr$80,907,000.

BALANCE SHEET (IN MILLIONS):

	1994	1993	1992	1991	1990	1989	1988
Gross Plant	22,692.5	22,413.4	21,685.7	20,593.9	20,715.3	19,137.0	17,391.1
Accumulated Depreciation	5,023.0	4,595.5	4,201.4	3,825.9	3,435.5	3,148.4	2,931.6
Prop, Plant & Equip, Net	17,669.5	17,817.9	17,484.3	16,768.0	17,279.8	15,988.6	14,459.5
Long-term Debt	7,888.4	8,379.8	7,932.0	7,951.1	7,380.6	6,416.9	6,342.5
Net Stockholders' Equity	7,747.7	8,050.9	7,918.8	7,717.2	8,262.3	7,667.0	6,879.4
Total Assets	20,893.4	21,518.1	19,428.6	18,792.8	18,651.0	17,219.2	16,057.6
Year End Shs Outstg (000)	225,841	224,345	217,316	210,700	196,970	183,189	169,009

STATISTICAL RECORD:

	1994	1993	1992	1991	1990	1989	1988
Book Value Per Share	28.74	29.29	30.33	29.82	34.66	34.56	33.38
Op. Inc/Net Pl %	7.5	6.7	6.7	6.8	6.3	6.5	6.6
Dep/Gr. Pl %	2.4	2.0	1.9	2.1	1.6	1.3	1.4
Accum. Dep/Gr. Pl %	22.1	20.5	19.4	18.6	16.6	16.5	16.9
Return on Equity %	7.4	4.8	8.3	...	10.9	10.6	9.8
Average Yield %	8.5	6.7	7.5	7.8	8.3	8.9	10.4
P/E Ratio	18.0-12.3	30.0-25.1	15.2-12.8	...	8.9-7.3	8.4-6.3	7.7-6.2
Price Range	43⅛-29⅝	49¾-41⅝	43¾-37	43-34⅛	39-32	37½-27¾	30⅝-24⅝

Statistics are as originally reported.

OFFICERS:
J.S. Farrington, Chmn. & Chief Exec.
E. Nye, Pres.

INCORPORATED: TX, Sep., 1945

PRINCIPAL OFFICE: 2001 Bryan Tower, Dallas, TX 75201

TELEPHONE NUMBER: (214) 812-4600

NO. OF EMPLOYEES: 10,798

ANNUAL MEETING: In May

SHAREHOLDERS: 107,048

INSTITUTIONAL HOLDINGS:
No. of Institutions: 576
Shares Held: 119,547,109

REGISTRAR(S): At Company's Office

TRANSFER AGENT(S): At Company's Office

TOMPKINS COUNTY TRUST CO.

YIELD 3.2%
P/E RATIO 13.2

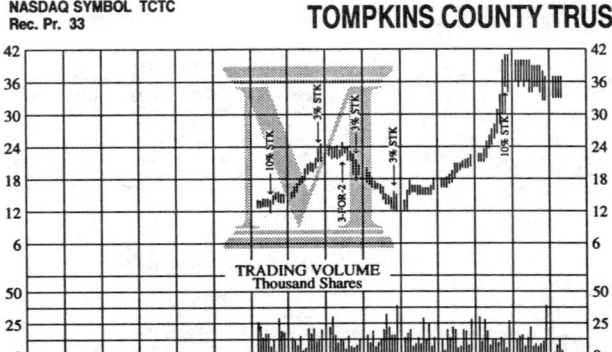

7 YEAR PRICE SCORE 128.4   *NYSE COMPOSITE INDEX=100*   **12 MONTH PRICE SCORE 92.0**

INTERIM EARNINGS (Per Share):

Qtr.	Mar.	June	Sept.	Dec.
1991	0.39	0.40	0.44	0.40
1992	0.52	0.52	0.57	0.61
1993	0.62	0.65	0.65	0.59
1994	0.62	0.64	0.68	0.58

INTERIM DIVIDENDS (Per Share):

Amt.	Decl.	Ex.	Rec.	Pay.
0.25Q	11/8/94	11/25/94	12/1/94	12/15/94
0.25Q	11/8	11/25	12/1	12/15
0.25Q	11/8	11/25	12/1	12/15
0.26Q	2/14/95	2/23/95	3/1/95	3/15/95
0.26Q	5/9	5/25	6/1	6/15

Indicated div.: $1.04

CAPITALIZATION (12/31/94):

	($000)	(%)
Total Deposits	345,776	67.5
Total Debt	114,238	22.3
Common & Surplus	47,817	9.3
Loan Valuation Reserve	4,654	0.9
Total	512,484	100.0

DIVIDEND ACHIEVER STATUS:
Rank: 40   1984-94 Growth Rate: 16.6%
Total Years of Dividend Growth: 12

RECENT DEVELOPMENTS: For the year ended 12/31/94, net income was $8.1 million, relatively unchanged from 1993. Total interest income was $35.7 million, up 3.8% from $34.4 million reported a year earlier. Net interest income was $22.8 million compared with $22.5 million in 1993. Total assets at 12/31/94 were $511.2 million, up 3.9%. The Bank's return on average equity was 17.2% and return of assets was 1.62%. In 1994, rising interest rates decreased net interest margin, which was offset by growth in loans and by reduced net loan losses. During 1994, the bank sold some securities from the investment portfolio in order to reinvest in higher yielding and/or shorter maturity securities. For the quarter ended 12/31/94, net income decreased 4.2% to $1.8 million from $1.9 million in the corresponding period of 1993. Total interest income for the quarter was $9.3 million compared with $8.6 million a year earlier. Net interest income increased slightly to $5.7 million from $5.6 million in 1993.

BUSINESS

TOMPKINS COUNTY TRUST COMPANY is a commercial bank chartered by the the State of New York. The bank serves as a depository of funds for individuals, corporations, organizations, institutions, and government entities. The bank serves as a source of credit for all qualified applicants and is also actively engaged in leasing and in exercising its trust powers. The Trust and Investment Management Department exercises fiduciary responsibility by managing individual accounts and estates.

LOAN DISTRIBUTION

(12/31/94)	($000)	(%)
Residential Real Estate	88,133	29.1
Commerical & Industrial	111,987	37.0
Consumer	67,315	22.3
Home Equity	20,985	6.9
Direct Lease Financing	11,225	3.7
All Other	2,767	1.0
Total	302,413	100.0

ANNUAL EARNINGS AND DIVIDENDS PER SHARE

	1994	1993	1992	1991	1990	1989	1988
Earnings Per Share	2.52	2.50	2.22	1.63	1.45	1.33	1.22
Dividends Per Share	1.00	[1] 0.96	0.709	0.582	[2] 0.515	[3] 0.438	[4] 0.392
Dividend Payout %	39.7	31.8	32.0	35.8	35.7	33.0	32.2

[1] 10% stk div,11/02/93   [2] 3% stk div, 12/1/90   [3] 3-for-2 stk split, 6/1/89   [4] 3% stk div, 12/1/88

ANNUAL FINANCIAL DATA

RECORD OF EARNINGS (IN THOUSANDS):

Total Interest Income	35,677	34,365	35,719	36,812	35,666	33,235	28,641
Total Interest Expense	12,911	11,887	13,982	18,405	19,509	18,072	14,851
Net Interest Income	22,765	22,478	21,738	18,407	16,157	15,162	13,790
Credit Loss Provision	768	1,207	2,048	1,391	997	547	492
Net Income	8,137	8,135	7,205	5,243	4,650	4,258	3,909
Aver. Shs. Outstg.	3,232	3,255	3,243	3,226	3,220	3,220	3,208

BALANCE SHEET (IN THOUSANDS):

Cash and Due From Banks	20,305	18,155	22,779	19,232	22,924	25,240	20,009
Loans & Lse Financing, Net	296,433	272,642	260,548	240,842	229,808	223,940	210,445
Total Domestic Deposits	345,776	350,446	337,280	331,157	298,295	286,470	268,928
Long-term Debt	12,000	12,000	...	...	...	...	...
Net Stockholders' Equity	47,817	47,402	39,775	34,372	30,879	27,896	24,768
Total Assets	511,162	492,155	459,291	576,537	498,449	449,614	337,986
Year End Shares Outstg	3,255	3,255	3,255	3,228	3,220	3,126	3,209

STATISTICAL RECORD:

Return on Assets %	1.59	1.65	1.57	0.91	0.93	0.95	1.16
Return on Equity %	17.00	17.20	18.10	15.30	15.10	15.30	15.80
Book Value Per Share	14.69	14.56	12.22	10.65	9.59	8.92	7.72
Average Yield %	2.8	3.1	3.6	3.8	3.2	2.1	2.0
P/E Ratio	15.9-12.9	16.4-8.4	10.1-7.4	11.1-7.5	13.9-8.4	18.7-13.3	20.2-11.8
Price Range	40-32½	41-21⅛	22½-16⅜	18⅛-12¼	20½-12¼	24⅞-17⅜	24⅜-14⅜

Statistics are as originally reported.

OFFICERS:
J.J. Byrnes, Chmn., Pres. & C.E.O.
R.D. Farr, Sr. V.P. & C.F.O.
J.W. Hulbert, V.P. & Sec.

PRINCIPAL OFFICE: The Commons P.O. Box 460, Ithaca, NY 14851

TELEPHONE NUMBER: (607) 273-3210
FAX: (607) 273-0024
NO. OF EMPLOYEES: 219
ANNUAL MEETING: In April
SHAREHOLDERS: 1,096
INSTITUTIONAL HOLDINGS:
No. of Institutions: 6
Shares Held: 94,414

REGISTRAR(S): The Bank of New York, New York, NY

TRANSFER AGENT(S): The Bank of New York, New York, NY

NYS SYMBOL TR
Rec. Pr. 65¾

TOOTSIE ROLL INDUSTRIES, INC.

YIELD 0.7%
P/E RATIO 19.2

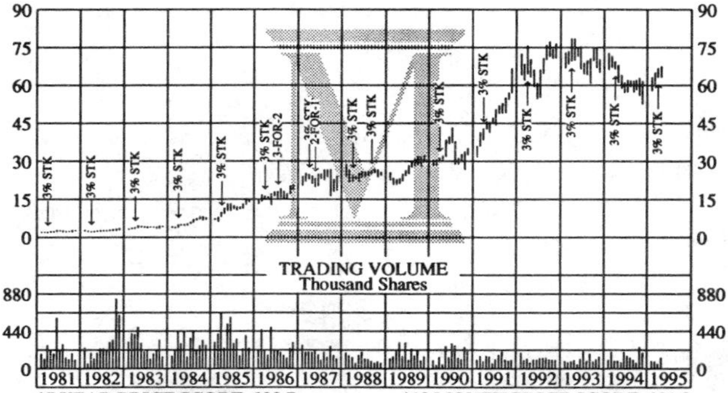

TRADING VOLUME
Thousand Shares

*7 YEAR PRICE SCORE 102.7 *12 MONTH PRICE SCORE 101.2

*NYSE COMPOSITE INDEX=100

INTERIM EARNINGS (Per Share):

Qtr.	Mar.	June	Sept.	Dec.
1991	0.46	0.50	1.08	0.50
1992	0.52	0.64	1.24	0.63
1993	0.62	0.68	1.33	0.65
1994	0.64	0.72	1.42	0.71

INTERIM DIVIDENDS (Per Share):

Amt.	Decl.	Ex.	Rec.	Pay.
0.11Q	6/1/94	6/17/94	6/23/94	7/12/94
0.11Q	9/12	9/21	9/27	10/12
0.11Q	12/7	12/16	12/22	1/12/95
0.11Q	2/21/95	3/6/95	3/10/95	4/11
3%	2/21	3/6	3/10	4/21

Indicated div.:$0.44

CAPITALIZATION (12/31/94):

	($000)	(%)
Long-Term Debt	7,500	2.9
Deferred Income Tax	7,716	3.0
Common & Surplus	240,461	94.1
Total	255,677	100.0

DIVIDEND ACHIEVER STATUS:
Rank: 51 1984-94 Growth Rate: 15.2%
Total Years of Dividend Growth: 31

RECENT DEVELOPMENTS: For the year ended 12/31/94, net income was $37.9 million compared with $35.4 million in 1993. Net sales rose 14% to $296.9 million. The record sales were attributed to a full year's sales of the chocolate and caramel brands acquired from Warner Lambert in October 1993 and increases in sales of many core Tootsie Roll products in 1994. Also, operating income improved 13% during the year due to effective cost-control programs.

PROSPECTS: The acquisition of several well-known brands of candy will strongly complement TR's existing product line. Despite temporarily declining margins, the Company will continue its aggressive promotional programs in order to enhance demand in all markets. Also, with plenty of cash on hand and a low level of debt, TR will continue investing in new products. Meanwhile, TR's sales and earnings will continue to benefit from established brand names and increased manufacturing efficiencies.

BUSINESS

TOOTSIE ROLL INDUSTRIES, INC. is engaged in the manufacture and sale of candy. Major products include: Tootsie Roll, Tootsie Roll Pops, Tootsie Pop Drops, Tootsie Flavor Rolls, Charms, and Blow-Pop lollipops. Other candy products include Tootsie Frooties, Cellas chocolate covered cherries, Junior Mints, Mason Dots and Mason Crows. In September 1988, TR acquired Charms Co. for approximately $65.0 million. The Company has manufacturing facilities in Chicago, New York, Covington, Tennessee and Mexico City.

REVENUES

(12/31/94)	($000)	(%)
United States	268,582	90.5
Mexico & Canada	28,350	9.5
Total	296,932	100.0

ANNUAL EARNINGS AND DIVIDENDS PER SHARE

	1994	1993	1992	1991	1990	1989	1988
Earnings Per Share	**3.40**	**3.27**	**2.95**	**[2] 2.45**	**2.08**	**1.85**	**1.52**
Dividends Per Share	**0.41**	**0.34**	**[1] 0.26**	**[3] 0.221**	**[4] 0.202**	**[5] 0.196**	**[6] 0.19**
Dividend Payout %	**12.1**	**10.0**	**8.8**	**9.1**	**9.7**	**10.5**	**12.4**

Note: 3%stk.div.4/21/95. [1] 3% stk div, 3/12/92 [2] Before acctg. chg. [3] 3% stk div, 3/12/91 [4] 3% stk div 4/25/90. [5] 3% stk. div., 4/89. [6] 3% stk div, 4/88.

ANNUAL FINANCIAL DATA

	1994	1993	1992	1991	1990	1989	1988
RECORD OF EARNINGS (IN THOUSANDS):							
Total Revenues	296,932	259,593	245,424	207,875	194,299	179,294	128,598
Costs and Expenses	234,238	204,566	196,226	165,376	157,534	140,253	101,212
Depreciation & Amort	10,478	8,814	6,071	5,202	5,696	5,133	3,626
Earnings From Operations	59,988	53,517	47,933	41,235	35,509	33,908	23,760
Earn Bef Income Taxes	61,167	57,710	51,922	44,174	37,119	33,206	25,481
Income Taxes	23,236	22,268	19,890	17,641	14,563	12,994	8,929
Net Income	37,931	35,442	32,032	[1] 26,533	22,556	20,212	16,552
Aver. Shs. Outstg.	10,848	10,840	10,848	10,854	10,856	10,858	10,860
[1] Before acctg. change dr$1,038,000.							
BALANCE SHEET (IN THOUSANDS):							
Cash and Cash Equivalents	62,370	56,203	88,942	65,313	36,758	18,492	16,820
Receivables, Net	24,255	22,750	12,889	13,035	16,207	12,061	11,381
Inventories	29,168	29,294	24,845	21,453	22,927	22,296	16,104
Gross Property	143,098	137,273	86,578	74,405	67,975	63,147	60,796
Accumulated Depreciation	57,450	50,574	44,766	40,386	35,876	32,240	29,240
Long-Term Debt	7,500	7,500	7,500	...	...	...	...
Net Stockholders' Equity	240,461	212,343	181,704	152,759	129,845	109,562	91,543
Total Assets	310,083	303,940	222,478	184,427	159,702	136,342	129,123
Total Current Assets	118,887	111,914	129,665	101,729	77,929	54,208	45,144
Total Current Liabilities	26,261	50,862	22,498	21,160	22,551	20,722	31,717
Net Working Capital	92,626	61,052	107,167	80,569	55,378	33,486	13,427
Year End Shares Outstg	10,848	10,840	10,536	10,853	10,856	10,858	10,860
STATISTICAL RECORD:							
Operating Profit Margin %	20.2	20.6	19.5	19.8	18.3	18.9	18.5
Book Value Per Share	13.07	10.24	12.96	9.79	7.56	5.55	3.77
Return on Equity %	15.8	16.7	17.6	17.4	17.4	18.4	18.1
Return on Assets %	12.2	11.7	14.4	14.4	14.1	14.8	12.8
Average Yield %	0.7	0.5	0.4	0.4	0.6	0.7	0.8
P/E Ratio	20.8-15.0	24.1-18.6	26.2-18.5	27.2-13.0	20.8-12.9	17.4-11.3	18.9-14.3
Price Range	72⅞-52⅜	78⅝-60¾	77⅜-54⅝	66⅝-31¾	43⅛-26¾	32¼-21	28⅞-21¾

Statistics are as originally reported.

OFFICERS:
M.J. Gordon, Chmn. & C.E.O.
E.R. Gordon, Pres. & C.O.O.
G.H. Ember, Jr., V.P.-Fin.
B.P. Bowen, Treas.
W. Touretz, Sec.

INCORPORATED: VA, Jun., 1919

PRINCIPAL OFFICE: 7401 South Cicero Ave., Chicago, IL 60629

TELEPHONE NUMBER: (312) 838-3400

NO. OF EMPLOYEES: 1,700 (approx.)

ANNUAL MEETING: In May

SHAREHOLDERS: 9,500 (approx.)

INSTITUTIONAL HOLDINGS:
No. of Institutions: 79
Shares Held: 2,397,051

REGISTRAR(S): Manufacturers Hanover Trust Co., New York, NY

TRANSFER AGENT(S): Manufacturers Hanover Trust Co., New York, NY

NYS SYMBOL TMK
Rec. Pr. 39⅛

TORCHMARK CORP.

YIELD		**2.9%**
P/E RATIO		**10.5**

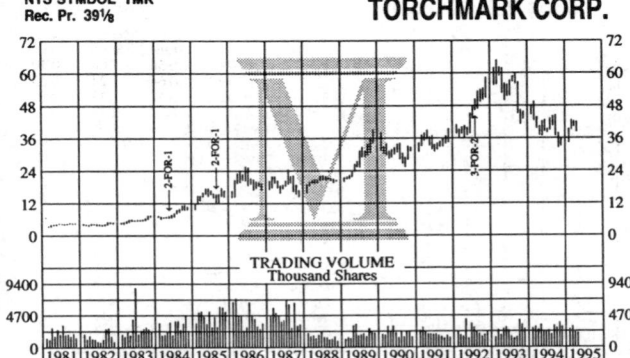

7 YEAR PRICE SCORE 87.8 **12 MONTH PRICE SCORE 98.0**
*NYSE COMPOSITE INDEX=100

INTERIM EARNINGS (Per Share):

Qtr.	Mar.	June	Sept.	Dec.
1991	0.75	0.77	0.80	0.81
1992	0.84	0.90	0.93	0.91
1993	0.68	1.05	0.86	1.16
1994	1.03	0.90	0.90	0.89

INTERIM DIVIDENDS (Per Share):

Amt.	Decl.	Ex.	Rec.	Pay.
0.28Q	5/13/94	7/11/94	7/8/94	8/1/94
0.28Q	7/28	10/3	10/9	11/1
0.28Q	11/4	12/30	1/6/95	2/1/95
0.28Q	3/6/95	4/3/95	4/7	5/1
0.28Q	5/9	7/5	7/7	8/1

*Indicated div.: $1.12**

CAPITALIZATION (12/31/94):

	($000)	(%)
Long-Term Debt	792,763	38.9
Common & Surplus	1,242,603	61.1
Total	2,035,366	100.0

DIVIDEND ACHIEVER STATUS:
Rank: 73   1984-94 Growth Rate: 14.1%
Total Years of Dividend Growth: 43

RECENT DEVELOPMENTS: For the year ended 12/31/94, net income was $269.0 million compared with $298.0 million for the prior year, a decrease of 9.7%. Total revenue was $1.9 billion, down 5.0% from $2.0 billion the year before. Life premiums grew 8.0% to $602.0 million and health premiums declined 4.0% to $769.0 million. Financial service revenue was relatively flat at $139.0 million. Life insurance sales were $150.0 million, up 17.0% while health insurance sales fell 31.0% to $121.0 million.

PROSPECTS: Businesses with consistent revenue and satisfactory profit margins will continue as the focal point of the earnings stream. The Company is emphasizing sales of protection life insurance over the more difficult and less profitable health insurance. The Company has introduced an attained-age product, along with a new group Medicare supplement plan, which should reverse the decline in Medicare supplement sales. Approval for the product is needed in a total of 38 states.

BUSINESS

TORCHMARK CORPORATION is a diversified insurance and financial services company. Through Liberty National Life Insurance Co., Globe Life & Accident Insurance Co., United American Insurance Co., Family Service Life Insurance Co., and other subsidiaries, TMK offers individual life and health insurance products. Liberty National Fire offers domestic and foreign reinsurance through off-shore subsidiaries. Waddell & Reed, Inc. offers financial planning services. Non-insurance operations include energy, asset management, real estate, oil and gas and equipment leases.

ANNUAL EARNINGS AND DIVIDENDS PER SHARE

	1994	1993	1992	1991	1990	1989	1988
Earnings Per Share	3.72	[1] 3.76	3.58	3.13	2.85	2.59	2.13
Dividends Per Share	1.12	1.081	[2] 1.066	1.00	0.933	0.833	0.733
Dividend Payout %	30.1	28.7	29.8	31.9	32.7	32.2	34.4

[1] Before acctg. chg. [2] 3-for-2 stk split, 8/20/92

ANNUAL FINANCIAL DATA

RECORD OF EARNINGS (IN MILLIONS):

	1994	1993	1992	1991	1990	1989	1988
Total Revenues	1,922.6	2,176.8	2,045.8	1,932.0	1,796.1	1,633.6	1,669.8
Costs and Expenses	1,459.3	1,668.2	1,572.3	1,501.0	1,397.4	1,261.3	1,346.9
Operating Profit	463.3	590.7	473.5	431.0	398.8	372.2	322.8
Inc Bef Income Tax & Eq In Subsids	386.9	441.4	417.9	380.8	352.5	324.1	282.0
Income Taxes	124.3	153.1	140.8	125.4	114.4	105.2	93.5
Net Income	268.9	[1] 279.6	265.5	246.5	229.2	211.3	180.1
Aver. Shs. Outstg. (000)	72,096	73,502	73,237	76,728	77,949	78,635	83,070

[1] Before acctg. change cr$18,403,000.

BALANCE SHEET (IN MILLIONS):

	1994	1993	1992	1991	1990	1989	1988
Cash and Cash Equivalents	115.5	236.6	139.3	175.0	737.9	648.7	477.9
Receivables, Net	290.9	209.7	181.0	144.4	126.1	153.9	122.1
Gross Property	103.8	80.5	183.1	174.2	92.7	78.4	68.8
Long-Term Debt	792.8	792.3	497.9	667.1	529.3	498.2	497.5
Net Stockholders' Equity	1,242.6	1,417.3	1,115.7	1,079.3	943.8	894.5	807.9
Total Assets	16,807.3	15,292.5	13,540.2	12,321.5	11,071.8	9,842.8	8,855.2
Total Current Assets	406.5	446.3	320.4	319.4	864.0	802.6	600.0
Total Current Liabilities	563.0	524.5	656.6	413.1	386.6	469.1	327.3
Net Working Capital	d156.6	d78.2	d336.3	d93.6	477.4	333.5	272.7
Year End Shs Outstg (000)	71,534	73,784	73,512	76,145	76,973	79,284	80,247

STATISTICAL RECORD:

	1994	1993	1992	1991	1990	1989	1988
Book Value Per Share	17.37	19.19	15.16	14.16	12.25	11.27	10.06
Return on Equity %	21.6	19.7	23.8	22.8	24.3	23.6	22.3
Return on Assets %	1.6	1.8	2.0	2.0	2.1	2.2	2.0
Average Yield %	2.7	2.0	2.3	2.8	2.9	2.8	3.8
P/E Ratio	13.3-8.7	17.2-10.9	16.3-10.1	12.6-9.9	13.4-8.9	15.1-7.7	10.5-7.5
Price Range	49½-32⅜	64¾-41⅛	58⅜-36	39½-30⅞	38¼-25⅜	39⅛-20	22⅜-15⅞

Statistics are as originally reported.

REVENUES

(12/31/94)	($000)	(%)
Premium Revenue	1,388,874	72.2
Net Investment Income	330,492	17.2
Financial Services Rev	139,276	7.2
Energy Operations	64,365	3.3
Other Revenue	450	0.1
Total	1,922,557	100.0

OFFICERS:
R.K. Richey, Chmn. & C.E.O.
C.B. Hudson, Chmn.-Insurance Operations
J.P. Bryan, Chmn. & C.E.O.-Torch Energy Advisors Inc.
K.A. Tucker, Vice-Chmn.
INCORPORATED: DE, Nov., 1979
PRINCIPAL OFFICE: 2001 Third Ave. South, Birmingham, AL 35233

TELEPHONE NUMBER: (205) 325-4200
NO. OF EMPLOYEES: 6,270
ANNUAL MEETING: In April
SHAREHOLDERS: 8,205
INSTITUTIONAL HOLDINGS:
No. of Institutions: 349
Shares Held: 39,378,543

REGISTRAR(S): First Chicago Trust Co. of New York, New York, NY 10008

TRANSFER AGENT(S): First Chicago Trust Co. of New York, New York, NY 10008

TRUSTMARK CORP.

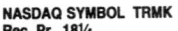

	YIELD	2.4%
	P/E RATIO	11.1

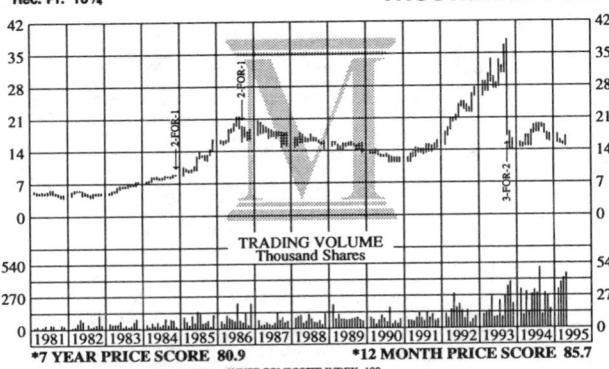

INTERIM EARNINGS (Per Share):

Qtr.	Mar.	June	Sept.	Dec.
1992	0.29	0.30	0.34	0.38
1993	0.39	0.46	0.41	0.40
1994	0.42	0.45	0.43	0.36

INTERIM DIVIDENDS (Per Share):

Amt.	Decl.	Ex.	Rec.	Pay.
0.10Q	7/14/94	8/26/94	9/1/94	9/15/94
0.1075Q	11/8	11/25	12/1	12/15
0.1075Q	11/8	11/25	12/1	12/15
0.1075Q	11/8	11/25	12/1	12/15
0.1075Q	2/14/95	2/23/95	3/1/95	3/15/95

*Indicated div.: $0.43**

CAPITALIZATION (12/31/94):

	($000)	(%)
Total Deposits	3,449,229	72.1
Total Debt	851,038	17.8
Common & Surplus	421,010	8.8
Loan Valuation Reserve	65,014	1.3
Total	4,786,291	100.0

DIVIDEND ACHIEVER STATUS:
Rank: 234   1984-94 Growth Rate: 7.4%
Total Years of Dividend Growth: 21

TRADING VOLUME
Thousand Shares

*7 YEAR PRICE SCORE 80.9   ***12 MONTH PRICE SCORE 85.7**
*NYSE COMPOSITE INDEX=100

RECENT DEVELOPMENTS: Net income for the year ended 12/31/94 was $55.0 million or $1.58 per share compared with $52.3 million or $1.55 per share for 1993. Deposits at 12/31/94 were $3.45 billion compared with $3.43 billion at 12/31/93. Total stockholders equity at 12/31/94 was $421.0 million. Total assets at year-end 1994 were $4.76 billion compared with $4.71 billion at the corresponding period of 1993. Total interest income for 1994 was $315.4 million, up 8.5% from $290.6 million in 1993. Net interest income for 1994 was $191.2 million compared with $181.6 million a year earlier. For the fourth quarter ended 12/31/94, net income was $12.5 million or $0.36 per share compared with $12.4 million or $0.36 per share for the same period last year.

BUSINESS

TRUSTMARK CORP. is a one-bank holding company which, through its subsidiaries, engages in the banking, real estate and consumer finance fields. The Corporation's principal operating subsidiary is Trustmark National Bank, which is the second largest bank in the state of Mississippi. Trustmark provides a full range of consumer banking services including checking accounts, NOW accounts, savings programs, other interest-bearing time accounts, personal and business loans, money transfers and safe deposit facilities. Trustmark also offers its customers the MasterCard and VISA credit cards.

LOAN DISTRIBUTION

(12/31/94)	($000)	(%)
Real Estate Loans	1,035,741	44.1
To Finance Agric Product	34,910	1.5
Commerical & Industrial	594,836	25.3
To Individuals	606,444	25.8
Oblig of States & Politic	50,033	2.1
For Purch or Carry Securs	1,840	0.2
Lease Fin Receiv & Other	23,761	1.0
Total	2,347,565	100.0

ANNUAL EARNINGS AND DIVIDENDS PER SHARE

	1994	1993	1992	1991	1990	1989	1988
Earnings Per Share	1.58	1.66	1.30	0.94	0.99	0.96	0.94
Dividends Per Share	0.4075	① 0.38	0.359	0.346	0.336	0.319	0.299
Dividend Payout %	25.8	22.9	27.6	36.9	34.1	33.4	32.0

① Adj for 3-for-1 stk split, 10/12/93

ANNUAL FINANCIAL DATA

RECORD OF EARNINGS (IN MILLIONS):

Total Interest Income	315.4	290.6	288.7	309.7	304.8	277.2	240.4
Total Interest Expense	124.3	109.0	128.7	174.3	187.9	172.4	140.3
Net Interest Income	191.2	181.6	160.0	135.3	116.8	104.8	100.1
Credit Loss Provision	2.8	17.6	24.1	25.2	15.1	11.5	9.4
Net Income	55.0	50.2	38.3	27.6	29.1	28.1	27.5

BALANCE SHEET (IN MILLIONS):

Cash & Due Fr Banks (non-int Bearing)	280.1	238.4	252.4	243.8	241.6	276.2	286.7
Loans & Lse Financing, Net	2,282.6	2,021.2	1,856.2	1,848.1	1,872.9	1,838.0	1,800.9
Total Domestic Deposits	3,449.2	3,189.2	3,196.9	3,160.7	3,065.6	2,570.3	2,421.8
Net Stockholders' Equity	421.0	358.6	295.4	267.7	250.3	231.2	212.5
Total Assets	4,763.4	4,432.0	4,085.1	3,878.4	3,754.5	3,165.7	2,947.0
Year End Shs Outstg (000)	34,911	31,173	29,476	29,476	29,476	29,476	29,476

STATISTICAL RECORD:

Return on Assets %	1.15	1.13	0.94	0.71	0.77	0.89	0.93
Return on Equity %	13.10	14.00	13.00	10.30	11.60	12.10	13.00
Book Value Per Share	12.06	11.50	10.02	9.08	8.49	7.84	7.21
Average Yield %	2.4	1.5	1.7	2.5	2.6	2.2	1.8
P/E Ratio	12.5-9.2	23.6-8.7	21.3-11.6	17.2-12.2	14.6-11.5	16.8-14.0	19.3-15.4
Price Range	19¾-14½	38-14	27⅝-15	16⅛-11⅜	14⅜-11⅜	16-13⅜	18-14⅜

Statistics are as originally reported.

OFFICERS:
F.R. Day, Chmn. & C.E.O.
H.M. Walker, Pres. & C.O.O.
D.R. Carter, Exec. V.P. & C.F.O.

INCORPORATED: MS, Aug., 1968

PRINCIPAL OFFICE: 248 E Capitol St P O Box 291, Jackson, MS 39201

TELEPHONE NUMBER: (601) 354-5111
FAX: (601) 949-2387
NO. OF EMPLOYEES: 2,206 (approx.)
ANNUAL MEETING: In March
SHAREHOLDERS: 4,200 (approx.)
INSTITUTIONAL HOLDINGS:
No. of Institutions: 34
Shares Held: 1,799,792

REGISTRAR(S): Trustmark National Bank, Jackson, MS

TRANSFER AGENT(S): Trustmark National Bank, Jackson, MS

TRW INC.

YIELD 2.7%
P/E RATIO 12.5

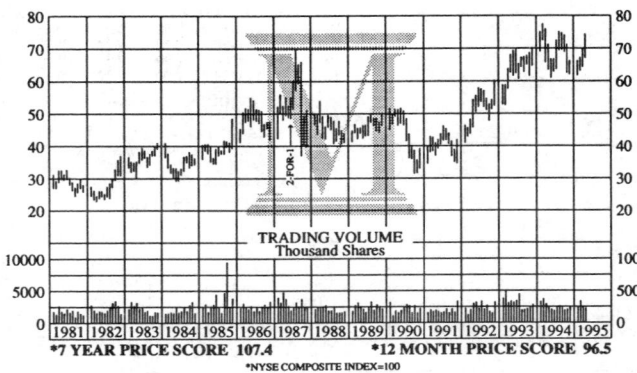

TRADING VOLUME Thousand Shares

1981 | 1982 | 1983 | 1984 | 1985 | 1986 | 1987 | 1988 | 1989 | 1990 | 1991 | 1992 | 1993 | 1994 | 1995

*7 YEAR PRICE SCORE 107.4　　***12 MONTH PRICE SCORE 96.5**

*NYSE COMPOSITE INDEX=100

INTERIM EARNINGS (Per Share):

Qtr.	Mar.	June	Sept.	Dec.
1992	d5.06	0.88	0.69	0.94
1993	0.79	0.85	0.77	0.98
1994	0.97	1.33	1.26	1.49

INTERIM DIVIDENDS (Per Share):

Amt.	Decl.	Ex.	Rec.	Pay.
0.47Q	4/27/94	5/9/94	5/13/94	6/15/94
0.50Q	7/27	8/8	8/12	9/15
0.50Q	10/26	11/4	11/11	12/15
0.50Q	12/14	2/6/95	2/10/95	3/15/95
0.50Q	4/26/95	5/8	5/12	6/15

Indicated div.: $2.00*

CAPITALIZATION (12/31/94):

	($000)	(%)
Long-Term Debt	694,000	24.3
Deferred Income Tax	269,000	9.4
Minority Interest	69,000	2.4
Preferred Stock	1,000	0.1
Common & Surplus	1,821,000	63.8
Total	2,854,000	100.0

DIVIDEND ACHIEVER STATUS:
Rank: 316　　1984-94 Growth Rate: 3.1%
Total Years of Dividend Growth: 23

RECENT DEVELOPMENTS: For the quarter ended 12/31/94, net earnings increased 57.5% to $100.2 million from $63.6 million for the same quarter in 1993. Sales rose 22% to $2.45 billion. Automotive sales went up 34.3% to $1.56 billion, benefiting from sales of air bags, seatbelts, steering systems and automotive electronics. Space and Defense sales rose 8.4% to $742.5 million. Information Systems and Services sales declined 9.9% to $139.8 million from $155.1 million.

PROSPECTS: Improved cost structures, processes and productivity should provide growth in sales and earnings. With expanded global presence, particularly in Europe, and a strong North American market, the Automotive division should continue to perform well. New technologies, namely automotive safety products, should help to maintain long-term strength in this division. TRW has won several contracts in Asia to meet its developing aerospace and electronics needs.

BUSINESS

TRW INC. provides high technology products and services primarily to the automotive, space and defense and information markets. Automotive products include steering, suspension, and occupant restraint systems, engine valves and valve train parts, electro-mechanical assemblies, fasteners, and automotive electronic products. Space & Defense designs and manufactures spacecraft and related equipment as well as software and systems engineering support services. Information Systems & Services include consumer estate and commercial credit services, plus real estate information systems.

BUSINESS LINE ANALYSIS

(12/31/94)	Rev(%)	Inc(%)
Automotive	62.5	57.1
Space & Defense	30.9	35.1
Info Systems & Services	6.6	7.8
Total	100.0	100.0

ANNUAL EARNINGS AND DIVIDENDS PER SHARE

	1994	1993	1992	1991	1990	1989	1988
Earnings Per Share	5.05	3.39	① 3.09	d2.30	3.39	4.31	4.29
Dividends Per Share	1.94	1.88	1.82	1.80	1.74	1.77	1.63
Dividend Payout %	38.4	55.5	58.9	...	51.3	41.1	38.0

① Before acctg. chg.

ANNUAL FINANCIAL DATA

RECORD OF EARNINGS (IN MILLIONS):

	1994	1993	1992	1991	1990	1989	1988
Total Revenues	9,087.0	7,948.0	8,311.0	7,913.0	8,169.0	7,340.0	6,982.0
Costs and Expenses	7,962.0	7,002.0	7,326.0	7,368.0	7,159.0	6,404.0	6,221.0
Depreciation & Amort	476.0	458.0	481.0	469.0	452.0	400.0	349.0
Operating Profit	1,061.0	873.0	868.0	765.0	860.0	781.0	637.0
Earn Bef Income Taxes	535.0	359.0	348.0	d129.0	343.0	399.0	420.0
Income Taxes	202.0	139.0	154.0	11.0	135.0	136.0	159.0
Net Income	333.0	① 220.0	② 194.0	d140.0	208.0	263.0	261.0
Aver. Shs. Outstg. (000)	65,800	64,700	62,300	61,200	61,900	61,900	60,500

① Before acctg. change dr$25,000,000. ② Before acctg. change dr$350,000,000.

BALANCE SHEET (IN MILLIONS):

Cash and Cash Equivalents	109.0	79.0	66.0	75.0	72.0	114.0	127.0
Receivables, Net	1,577.0	1,436.0	1,559.0	1,614.0	1,553.0	1,634.0	1,499.0
Inventories	470.0	410.0	422.0	512.0	530.0	480.0	419.0
Gross Property	5,556.0	5,120.0	5,052.0	5,010.0	4,734.0	4,127.0	3,733.0
Accumulated Depreciation	3,067.0	2,793.0	2,741.0	2,686.0	2,519.0	2,173.0	1,940.0
Long-Term Debt	694.0	870.0	941.0	1,213.0	1,042.0	1,063.0	863.0
Net Stockholders' Equity	1,822.0	1,534.0	1,416.0	1,685.0	1,907.0	1,749.0	1,566.0
Total Assets	5,636.0	5,336.0	5,458.0	5,635.0	5,555.0	5,259.0	4,442.0
Total Current Assets	2,215.0	1,994.0	2,116.0	2,262.0	2,237.0	2,295.0	2,105.0
Total Current Liabilities	1,986.0	1,826.0	2,012.0	1,982.0	1,947.0	1,794.0	1,396.0
Net Working Capital	229.0	168.0	104.0	280.0	290.0	501.0	709.0
Year End Shs Outstg (000)	64,900	64,100	62,900	61,600	60,800	60,600	60,200

STATISTICAL RECORD:

Operating Profit Margin %	7.1	6.1	6.1	1.0	6.8	7.3	5.9
Book Value Per Share	17.95	13.35	11.10	15.73	18.52	16.32	20.07
Return on Equity %	18.3	14.3	13.7	...	10.9	15.0	16.7
Return on Assets %	5.9	4.1	3.6	...	3.7	5.0	5.9
Average Yield %	2.8	3.1	3.6	4.5	4.2	3.9	3.4
P/E Ratio	15.3-12.1	20.7-15.5	19.5-13.3	...	15.3-9.3	11.6-9.6	12.6-9.5
Price Range	77½-61	70¼-52½	60¼-41	46¼-34½	51¾-31⅜	49⅞-41¼	54-40⅝

Statistics are as originally reported.

OFFICERS:
J.T. Gorman, Chmn. & C.E.O.
P.S. Hellman, Pres. & C.O.O.
M.A. Coyle, Exec. V.P., General Couns. & Sec.
R.D. Sugar, Exec. V.P. & C.F.O.

PRINCIPAL OFFICE: 1900 Richmond Road, Cleveland, OH 44124-3760

TELEPHONE NUMBER: (216) 291-7000
FAX: (216) 291-7758
NO. OF EMPLOYEES: 64,175
ANNUAL MEETING: In April
SHAREHOLDERS: 31,098
INSTITUTIONAL HOLDINGS:
No. of Institutions: 379
Shares Held: 35,003,407

REGISTRAR(S): First Chicago Trust Co. of New York, New York, NY 10008
National City Bank, Cleveland, OH 44114

TRANSFER AGENT(S): At Company's Office
First Chicago Trust Co. of New York, New York, NY 10008

NYS SYMBOL UEP
Rec. Pr. 36⅜

UNION ELECTRIC CO.

YIELD 6.7%
P/E RATIO 12.1

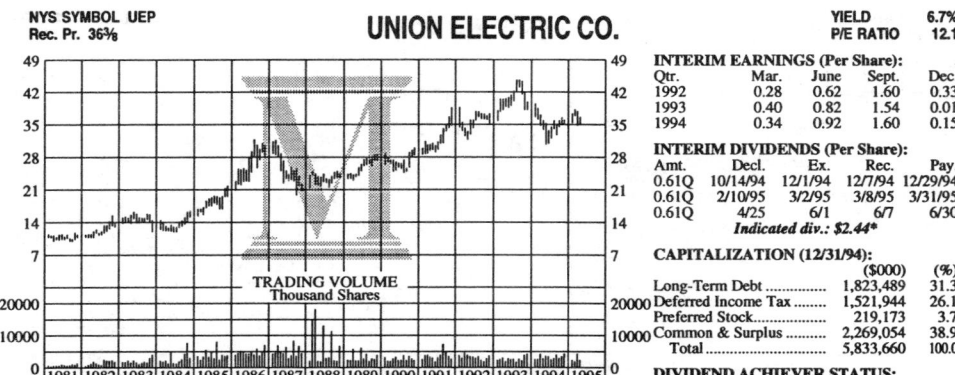

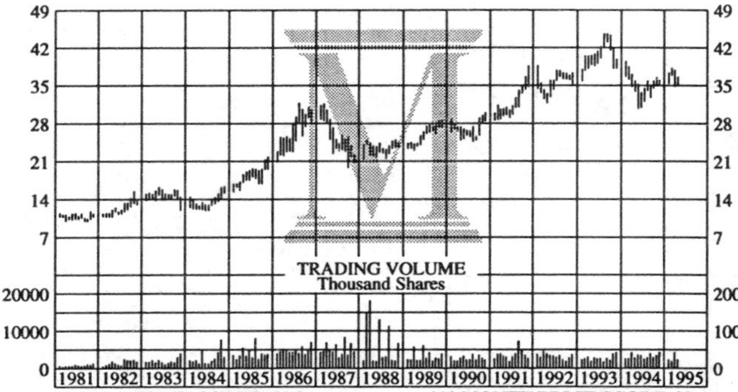
49
42
35
28
21
14
7
TRADING VOLUME
Thousand Shares
20000
10000
0
1981 1982 1983 1984 1985 1986 1987 1988 1989 1990 1991 1992 1993 1994 1995

***7 YEAR PRICE SCORE 91.0** ***12 MONTH PRICE SCORE 97.6**

*NYSE COMPOSITE INDEX=100

INTERIM EARNINGS (Per Share):

Qtr.	Mar.	June	Sept.	Dec.
1992	0.28	0.62	1.60	0.33
1993	0.40	0.82	1.54	0.01
1994	0.34	0.92	1.60	0.15

INTERIM DIVIDENDS (Per Share):

Amt.	Decl.	Ex.	Rec.	Pay.
0.61Q	10/14/94	12/1/94	12/7/94	12/29/94
0.61Q	2/10/95	3/2/95	3/8/95	3/31/95
0.61Q	4/25	6/1	6/7	6/30

Indicated div.: $2.44*

CAPITALIZATION (12/31/94):

	($000)	(%)
Long-Term Debt	1,823,489	31.3
Deferred Income Tax	1,521,944	26.1
Preferred Stock	219,173	3.7
Common & Surplus	2,269,054	38.9
Total	5,833,660	100.0

DIVIDEND ACHIEVER STATUS:
Rank: 311 1984-94 Growth Rate: 3.4%
Total Years of Dividend Growth: 19

RECENT DEVELOPMENTS: For the quarter ended 12/31/94, net income was $18.7 million compared with $4.8 million in the corresponding period of 1993. Revenues were $407.0 million, down 1%. Earnings benefited from the absence of a refueling at the Company's Callaway nuclear power plant and a rebounding local economy. For the year ended 12/31/94, net income was $320.8 million compared with $297.2 million a year earlier. Revenues were down slightly to $2.06 billion.

PROSPECTS: Earnings may be squeezed due to a scheduled refueling outage at the Callaway nuclear plant. However, the current cost-control program may offset some of the earnings pressure. The Company benefits from being one of the low cost producers of electricity, efficient operations, and strong cash flow. These attributes bode well for future earnings growth and enhance the Company's competitive position.

BUSINESS

UNION ELECTRIC COMPANY is engaged mainly in supplying electricity in and around St. Louis, East St. Louis, and Alton, Illinois and a small portion of southern Iowa. The Company also furnishes similar service in sections of central, northern and southeastern Missouri. In addition, UEP also provides gas, steam and water services. The 24,000-square mile service area, with a population of 2.7 million, is well diversified.

REVENUES

(12/31/94)	($000)	(%)
Residential	800,117	38.9
Commercial	705,505	34.3
Industrial	368,450	17.9
Other Electric Utilities	61,985	3.0
Miscellaneous	33,476	1.6
Gas	86,109	4.2
Other	474	0.1
Total	2,056,116	100.0

ANNUAL EARNINGS AND DIVIDENDS PER SHARE

	1994	1993	1992	1991	1990	1989	1988
Earnings Per Share	**3.01**	**2.77**	**2.83**	**3.01**	**2.74**	**2.61**	**2.56**
Dividends Per Share	**2.395**	**2.335**	**2.26**	**2.18**	**2.10**	**2.02**	**1.94**
Dividend Payout %	**79.6**	**84.3**	**79.9**	**72.4**	**76.6**	**77.4**	**75.8**

ANNUAL FINANCIAL DATA

	1994	1993	1992	1991	1990	1989	1988
RECORD OF EARNINGS (IN MILLIONS):							
Total Revenues	2,056.1	2,066.0	2,015.1	2,096.9	2,023.0	2,010.3	2,029.1
Depreciation & Amort	216.7	210.3	237.7	236.6	232.9	230.3	235.4
Maintenance	197.8	190.1	187.3	170.5	176.4	156.2	163.0
Income Taxes	206.4	179.5	179.7	222.7	192.2	203.4	194.2
Operating Income	450.2	411.3	412.0	482.8	457.5	466.5	484.2
Interest Expense	135.6	124.5	130.4	160.8	175.6	161.3	186.4
Net Income	320.8	297.2	302.7	321.5	294.2	285.6	291.6
Aver. Shs. Outstg. (000)	102,124	102,124	102,124	102,124	102,124	102,124	102,124
BALANCE SHEET (IN MILLIONS):							
Gross Plant	8,650.1	8,344.5	8,062.1	7,752.7	7,512.2	7,310.0	7,126.3
Accumulated Depreciation	3,305.6	3,079.5	2,860.7	2,634.1	2,391.5	2,192.2	1,974.4
Prop, Plant & Equip, Net	5,344.6	5,265.0	5,201.4	5,118.6	5,120.7	5,117.7	5,151.9
Long-term Debt	1,823.5	1,766.7	1,659.6	1,730.3	1,948.0	2,106.8	2,188.6
Net Stockholders' Equity	2,488.2	2,425.4	2,382.5	2,324.7	2,240.1	2,182.9	2,236.0
Total Assets	6,624.7	6,595.6	5,797.4	5,733.5	5,702.3	5,760.3	5,827.2
Year End Shs Outstg (000)	102,124	102,124	102,124	102,124	102,124	102,124	102,124
STATISTICAL RECORD:							
Book Value Per Share	22.22	21.60	21.19	20.62	19.79	19.14	18.56
Op. Inc/Net Pl %	8.4	7.8	7.9	9.4	8.9	9.1	9.4
Dep/Gr. Pl %	2.6	2.6	3.1	3.1	3.1	3.2	3.3
Accum. Dep/Gr. Pl %	38.2	36.9	35.5	34.0	31.8	30.0	27.7
Return on Equity %	12.9	12.3	12.7	13.8	13.1	13.1	13.4
Average Yield %	6.8	5.8	6.4	6.5	7.7	7.8	8.4
P/E Ratio	13.1-10.2	16.1-12.9	13.7-11.2	12.8-9.5	10.9-9.0	11.0-8.8	9.8-8.3
Price Range	39½-30¾	44⅝-35¾	38¼-31¾	38⅝-28½	30-24⅝	28⅝-23	25-21⅞

Statistics are as originally reported.

OFFICERS:
C.W. Mueller, Pres. & C.E.O.
D.E. Brandt, Sr. V.P.-Fin. & Corp. Services
J.E. Birdsong, Treas.
J.C. Thompson, Sec.

INCORPORATED: MO, Nov., 1922

PRINCIPAL OFFICE: 1901 Chouteau Avenue, Saint Louis, MO 63103

TELEPHONE NUMBER: (314) 621-3222

FAX: (314) 554-4075

NO. OF EMPLOYEES: 6,417

ANNUAL MEETING: In April

SHAREHOLDERS: 119,938 common.

INSTITUTIONAL HOLDINGS:
No. of Institutions: 299
Shares Held: 32,059,047

REGISTRAR(S): At Company's Office

TRANSFER AGENT(S): At Company's Office

UNITED CAROLINA BANCSHARES CORP.

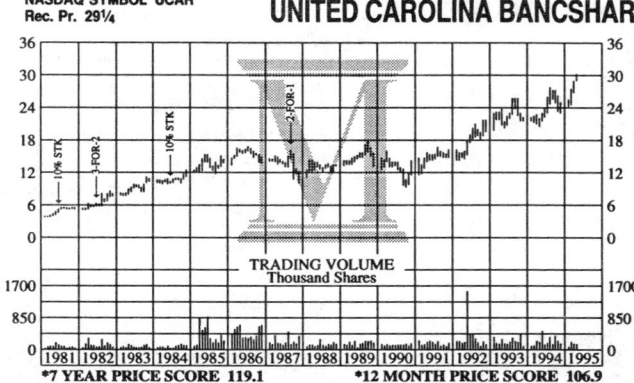

*7 YEAR PRICE SCORE 119.1   *12 MONTH PRICE SCORE 106.9

*NYSE COMPOSITE INDEX=100

INTERIM EARNINGS (Per Share):

Qtr.	Mar.	June	Sept.	Dec.
1992	0.48	0.51	0.52	0.50
1993	0.54	0.59	0.58	0.56
1994	0.61	0.64	0.64	0.20
1995	0.69	...	...	...

INTERIM DIVIDENDS (Per Share):

Amt.	Decl.	Ex.	Rec.	Pay.
0.20Q	4/14/94	4/25/94	4/29/94	5/6/94
0.22Q	7/22	7/28	8/3	8/10
0.22Q	10/13	10/25	10/31	11/8
0.22Q	1/18/95	1/25/95	1/31/95	2/7/95
0.25Q	4/13	4/24	4/28	5/8

Indicated div.: $1.00

CAPITALIZATION (12/31/94):

	($000)	(%)
Total Deposits	2,940,599	88.3
Total Debt	88,533	2.6
Common & Surplus	263,489	7.9
Loan Valuation Reserve	38,681	1.2
Total	3,331,302	100.0

DIVIDEND ACHIEVER STATUS:
Rank: 258   1984-94 Growth Rate: 6.2%
Total Years of Dividend Growth: 14

RECENT DEVELOPMENTS: For the fiscal year ended 12/31/94, income before the cumulative effects of changes in accounting methods was $30.1 million, down 7.8% from the $32.6 million earned in 1993. Results in 1994 were affected by an $11.9 million restructuring charge. Net interest income grew 13.4% to $144.8 million from $127.8 million as noninterest income increased a modest 4.2% from the prior year to $43.4 million. Operating expenses rose 8.4% to $125.7 million

from $116.0 million. The provision for loan losses was lowered 32.5% to $3.4 million. UCAR implemented a streamlining program that includes closing 15 branch offices and reducing its workforce by 235 full-time and 86 part-time positions. United Carolina Bank, a wholly-owned subsidiary, will purchase the deposits and certain assets worth about $200 million of 12 branch offices of Southern National and BB&T Financial.

BUSINESS

UNITED CAROLINA BANC-SHARES CORP. is a $3.3 billion bank holding company whose principal subsidiaries are United Carolina Bank and United Carolina Bank of South Carolina. The banks offer a wide variety of financial services to the retail and business sectors of North and South Carolina. UCB has 144 banking offices throughout 87 North Carolina and South Carolina communities.

ANNUAL EARNINGS AND DIVIDENDS PER SHARE

	1994	1993	1992	1991	1990	1989	1988
Earnings Per Share	2.05	2.27	2.01	1.65	1.43	1.74	1.65
Dividends Per Share	0.84	0.76	0.66	0.61	0.60	0.59	0.56
Dividend Payout %	41.0	33.5	32.8	37.0	42.0	33.9	33.9

ANNUAL FINANCIAL DATA

RECORD OF EARNINGS (IN MILLIONS):

	1994	1993	1992	1991	1990	1989	1988
Total Interest Income	231.9	201.0	208.0	230.0	237.3	229.1	199.0
Total Interest Expense	87.0	76.8	89.8	120.0	134.5	130.7	104.1
Net Interest Income	144.8	124.2	118.2	110.0	102.8	98.4	94.9
Credit Loss Provision	3.4	4.9	11.8	14.4	17.3	7.4	6.1
Net Income	① 30.1	② 31.7	28.0	23.0	19.9	24.2	22.9
Aver. Shs. Outstg. (000)	14,661	13,992	13,937	13,937	13,937	13,937	13,926

① Before acctg. change dr$316,000.   ② Before acctg. change cr$867,000.

BALANCE SHEET (IN MILLIONS):

	1994	1993	1992	1991	1990	1989	1988
Cash & Due Fr Banks-nonint Bearing	147.5	144.8	138.1	142.7	268.3	176.4	159.9
Loans & Lse Financing, Net	2,379.5	2,127.8	1,819.0	1,748.5	1,648.8	1,556.4	1,495.7
Total Domestic Deposits	2,940.6	2,736.8	2,481.5	2,372.3	2,358.4	2,229.1	2,014.2
Long-term Debt	2.3	1.4	0.4	1.7	3.0	3.9	4.8
Net Stockholders' Equity	263.5	245.0	222.4	203.4	185.1	174.2	159.2
Total Assets	3,331.6	3,258.4	3,443.5	3,162.2	3,126.1	2,988.8	2,598.1
Year End Shs Outstg (000)	14,700	14,023	13,958	13,937	13,937	13,937	13,937

STATISTICAL RECORD:

	1994	1993	1992	1991	1990	1989	1988
Return on Assets %	0.90	0.97	0.81	0.73	0.64	0.81	0.88
Return on Equity %	11.40	12.90	12.60	11.30	10.70	13.90	14.40
Book Value Per Share	17.92	17.47	15.93	14.59	13.28	12.50	11.42
Average Yield %	3.5	3.3	3.7	4.3	4.8	3.8	4.4
P/E Ratio	13.5-10.0	11.3-8.7	10.8-7.1	10.2-7.0	11.2-6.5	10.2-7.5	8.8-6.7
Price Range	27¾-20½	25¾-19¾	21¾-14¼	16¾-11½	16-9¼	17¾-13	14½-11

Statistics are as originally reported.

LOAN DISTRIBUTION

(12/31/94)	($000)	(%)
Real Estate	1,507,723	62.3
Commercial, Finl & Agric.	236,244	9.8
Loans to Indiv.	607,606	25.1
Other Loan & Lease Receiv.	67,573	2.8
Total	2,419,146	100.0

OFFICERS:
E.R. Sasser, Chmn., Pres. & C.E.O.
R.C. Monger, Exec. V.P. & C.F.O.
H.V. Hudson, Jr., Sec. & Gen. Counsel

INCORPORATED: NC, 1981

PRINCIPAL OFFICE: 127 West Webster Street, Whiteville, NC 28472

TELEPHONE NUMBER: (910) 642-5131

FAX: (910) 642-1452

NO. OF EMPLOYEES: 1,098

ANNUAL MEETING: In April

SHAREHOLDERS: 8,500 (approx.)

INSTITUTIONAL HOLDINGS:
No. of Institutions: 31
Shares Held: 2,079,216

REGISTRAR(S): United Carolina Bank, Whiteville, NC

TRANSFER AGENT(S): United Carolina Bank, Whiteville, NC

UNITED CITIES GAS CO.

YIELD	6.5%
P/E RATIO	13.5

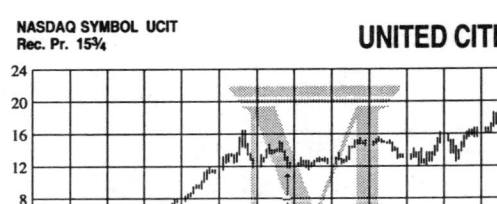

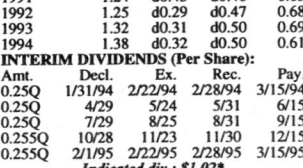

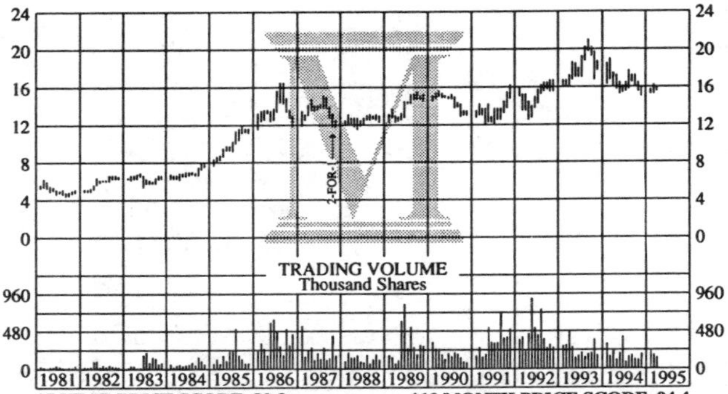

TRADING VOLUME
Thousand Shares

| 1981 | 1982 | 1983 | 1984 | 1985 | 1986 | 1987 | 1988 | 1989 | 1990 | 1991 | 1992 | 1993 | 1994 | 1995 |

*7 YEAR PRICE SCORE 89.3   *12 MONTH PRICE SCORE 94.4

*NYSE COMPOSITE INDEX=100

INTERIM EARNINGS (Per Share):

Qtr.	Mar.	June	Sept.	Dec.
1991	1.24	d0.45	d0.40	0.65
1992	1.25	d0.29	d0.47	0.68
1993	1.32	d0.31	d0.50	0.69
1994	1.38	d0.32	d0.50	0.61

INTERIM DIVIDENDS (Per Share):

Amt.	Decl.	Ex.	Rec.	Pay.
0.25Q	1/31/94	2/22/94	2/28/94	3/15/94
0.25Q	4/29	5/24	5/31	6/15
0.25Q	7/29	8/25	8/31	9/15
0.255Q	10/28	11/23	11/30	12/15
0.255Q	2/1/95	2/22/95	2/28/95	3/15/95

Indicated div.: $1.02*

CAPITALIZATION (12/31/94):

	($000)	(%)
Long-Term Debt	144,344	49.5
Deferred Income Tax	29,217	10.0
Common & Surplus	118,028	40.5
Total	291,589	100.0
Current Debt	6,068	

DIVIDEND ACHIEVER STATUS:

Rank: 300   1984-94 Growth Rate: 3.9%
Total Years of Dividend Growth: 13

RECENT DEVELOPMENTS: For the quarter ended 12/31/94, net income dropped 10% to $6.4 million, or $0.61 per share, compared with $7.1 million, or $0.69 per share, in the corresponding quater of 1993. Revenues declined 18% to $74.3 million versus $90.3 million for the same period a year earlier. For the year ended 12/31/94, net income was $12.1 million, or $1.16 per share, compared with $12.2 million, or $1.19 per share, in 1993. Revenues were $281.0 million,

down 2.3% from $287.5 million a year earlier. Earnings were pressured by temperatures throughout UCIT's service territory that ran approximately 10% warmer than normal during 1994 compared with weather that was approximately 3% colder than normal in 1993. The weather normalization adjustment clauses in effect in both Tennesse and Georgia played a role in stabilizing the Company's earnings in 1994.

BUSINESS

UNITED CITIES GAS COMPANY is primarily a distributor of natural and propane gas, operating in ten states and serving approximately 303,000 customers (283,000 natural gas and 20,000 propane). UCIT's natural gas business is conducted in eight states: Tennessee, Georgia, Illinois, South Carolina, Missouri, Virginia, Iowa and Kansas. Propane is distributed through UCIT's wholly-owned subsidiary, UCG Energy Corporation. The propane division of UCG Energy serves customers in Tennessee, North Carolina and Virginia. The subsidiary is engaged in other activities complementing the natural gas business through its rental and utility services divisions. United Cities Gas Storage Company provides UCIT and others with supplemental natural gas supplies through company-owned natural gas storage fields in Kentucky and Kansas.

ANNUAL EARNINGS AND DIVIDENDS PER SHARE

	1994	1993	1992	1991	1990	1989	1988
Earnings Per Share	1.16	1.19	1.07	0.97	0.44	1.52	1.24
Dividends Per Share	1.005	0.985	0.965	0.93	0.92	0.88	0.84
Dividend Payout %	86.6	83.2	90.2	95.9	N.M.	57.9	67.7

ANNUAL FINANCIAL DATA

RECORD OF EARNINGS (IN THOUSANDS):

Total Revenues	319,367	326,416	297,943	266,252	247,051	215,979	189,306
Depreciation & Amort	17,880	17,130	15,509	15,782	15,007	11,090	9,477
Maintenance	6,005	6,070	6,989	3,169	3,796	3,192	2,606
Prov for Fed Inc Taxes	2,294	1,835	2,117	1,488	754	1,612	1,307
Interest Expense	14,860	16,097	13,581	14,457	14,336	8,658	7,174
Net Income	12,093	12,150	10,218	7,875	3,373	10,310	7,224
Aver. Shs. Outstg.	10,409	10,197	9,459	8,000	7,238	6,572	5,218

BALANCE SHEET (IN THOUSANDS):

Gross Plant	474,343	442,287	412,576	388,265	366,445	326,199	220,043
Accumulated Depreciation	161,987	147,699	135,925	124,241	114,699	103,309	69,270
Prop, Plant & Equip, Net	312,356	294,588	276,651	264,024	251,746	222,890	150,773
Long-term Debt	144,344	151,843	157,734	127,430	96,521	78,230	64,719
Net Stockholders' Equity	118,028	111,888	106,206	87,305	72,601	75,407	55,516
Total Assets	421,200	401,520	373,682	368,257	340,648	307,160	199,036
Year End Shares Outstg	10,613	10,314	10,052	8,517	7,292	7,197	5,274

STATISTICAL RECORD:

Book Value Per Share	11.12	10.85	10.57	10.09	9.75	10.17	9.60
Dep/Gr. Pl %	3.7	3.7	3.7	4.0	4.0	3.4	4.3
Accum. Dep/Gr. Pl %	34.1	33.4	32.9	32.0	31.3	31.7	31.5
Return on Equity %	10.2	10.9	9.6	9.0	4.6	13.7	12.5
Average Yield %	5.9	5.3	6.6	6.6	6.5	6.3	6.8
P/E Ratio	16.4-12.9	17.6-13.4	15.7-11.7	16.8-12.4	35.5-29.3	10.2-8.1	10.6-9.3
Price Range	19-15	21-16	16¾-12½	16¼-12	15⅜-12⅞	15½-12¼	13⅛-11½

Statistics are as originally reported.

REVENUES

(12/31/94)	($000)	(%)
Residential	129,519	46.1
Commercial	73,376	26.1
Industrial	69,069	24.6
Other	1,813	0.6
Transportation	7,207	2.6
Total	280,984	100.0

OFFICERS:
D.C. Baum, Chmn.
G.C. Koonce, Pres. & C.E.O.
J.B. Ford, Sr. V.P. & Treas.
S.M. Hawkins, Sr. V.P. & Sec.
T.S. Hawkins, Jr., V.P.-Fin.

INCORPORATED: IL, Sep., 1929

PRINCIPAL OFFICE: 5300 Maryland Way, Brentwood, TN 37027

TELEPHONE NUMBER: (615) 373-5310

FAX: (615) 371-5053

NO. OF EMPLOYEES: 1,343

ANNUAL MEETING: In April

SHAREHOLDERS: 7,124

INSTITUTIONAL HOLDINGS:
No. of Institutions: 54
Shares Held: 1,887,847

REGISTRAR(S): Harris Trust & Savings Bank, Chicago, IL

TRANSFER AGENT(S): Harris Trust & Savings Bank, Chicago, IL

U.S. BANCORP

YIELD 3.7%
P/E RATIO 19.4

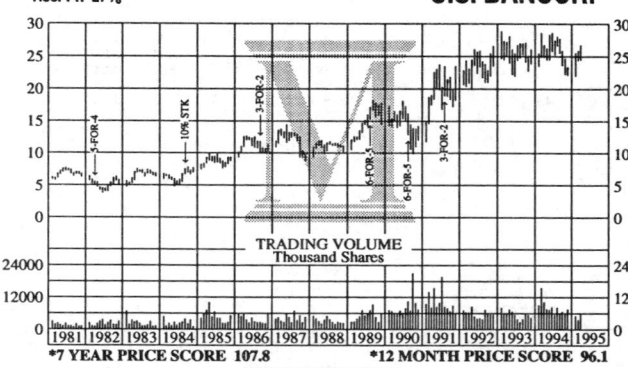

TRADING VOLUME
Thousand Shares

*NYSE COMPOSITE INDEX=100

| 1981 | 1982 | 1983 | 1984 | 1985 | 1986 | 1987 | 1988 | 1989 | 1990 | 1991 | 1992 | 1993 | 1994 | 1995 |

*7 YEAR PRICE SCORE 107.8   *12 MONTH PRICE SCORE 96.1

INTERIM EARNINGS (Per Share):

Qtr.	Mar.	June	Sept.	Dec.
1992	0.48	0.54	0.40	0.63
1993	0.59	0.61	0.63	0.64
1994	d0.32	0.49	0.60	0.63

INTERIM DIVIDENDS (Per Share):

Amt.	Decl.	Ex.	Rec.	Pay.
0.22Q	2/18/94	3/7/94	3/11/94	4/1/94
0.22Q	4/20	6/6	6/10	7/1
0.25Q	8/18	9/2	9/9	10/3
0.25Q	11/17	12/5	12/9	1/3/95
0.25Q	2/16/95	3/6/95	3/10/95	4/3

*Indicated div.: $1.00**

CAPITALIZATION (12/31/94):

	($000)	(%)
Total Deposits	15,048,366	70.1
Total Debt	4,343,414	20.2
Preferred Stock	150,000	0.7
Common & Surplus	1,627,285	7.6
Loan Valuation Reserve	305,802	1.4
Total	21,474,867	100.0

DIVIDEND ACHIEVER STATUS:
Rank: 108   1984-94 Growth Rate: 12.6%
Total Years of Dividend Growth: 35

RECENT DEVELOPMENTS: For the year ended 12/31/94, net income was $151.5 million, down 41% from the $257.9 million earned in 1993. Results for 1994 included a pre-tax restructuring charge of $100.0 million. Net interest income was $962.2 million versus $928.1 million a year earlier. Noninterest revenues declined 14.2% to $456.1 million. In August 1994, USBC sold most of its residential mortgage loan portfolio and 50 loan origination offices of its subsidi-

ary, U.S. Bancorp Mortage Company. Consequently, mortgage banking income is not comparable to prior years due to the impact of the sale. Noninterest expense, including the restructuring charge, was $1.10 billion compared with $982.8 million in 1993. The provision for loan losses was raised to $106.9 million from $92.9 million. Total assets were up slightly to $21.82 billion from $21.42 billion. Total deposits declined to $15.05 billion from $15.51 billion.

BUSINESS

U.S. BANCORP is a financial services holding company with assets of $21.8 billion. USBC's banking subsidiaries include U.S. Bank of Oregon, U.S. Bank of Washington, U.S. Bank of California, U.S. Bank of Nevada, and U.S. Bank of Idaho. These full service retail commercial banks operate through 176 locations in Oregon, 159 locations in Washington, 67 locations in Northern California, 28 locations in Nevada and 8 locations in Idaho. Other financial service businesses include U.S. Bancorp Corporate Banking Group, U.S. Bancorp Leasing & Financial, U.S. Bancorp Merchant Banking, U.S. Bancorp Mortgage Company, U.S. Bancorp National Products Group, and U.S. Bancorp Securities & Trust Group.

LOAN DISTRIBUTION

(12/31/94)	($000)	(%)
Commercial	7,384,600	47.3
Real Estate-		
Construction	667,200	4.3
Real Estate-Mortgage	2,946,500	18.9
Consumer	3,738,000	23.9
Foreign	49,800	0.3
Lease Financing	819,600	5.3
Total	15,605,700	100.0

ANNUAL EARNINGS AND DIVIDENDS PER SHARE

	1994	1993	1992	1991	1990	1989	1988
Earnings Per Share	1.40	2.47	[1] 2.05	2.01	2.04	1.69	1.40
Dividends Per Share	0.91	0.82	0.76	[2] 0.69	[3] 0.583	[4] 0.486	0.439
Dividend Payout %	65.0	34.4	37.1	34.3	28.6	28.7	31.4

[1] Before acctg. chg. [2] Adj for 3-for-2 stk split, 8/13/91 [3] 20% stk div, 9/14/90 [4] 20% stk div, 9/15/89

ANNUAL FINANCIAL DATA

RECORD OF EARNINGS (IN MILLIONS):

	1994	1993	1992	1991	1990	1989	1988
Total Interest Income	1,480.1	1,433.7	1,491.5	1,638.6	1,625.3	1,436.5	1,163.0
Total Interest Expense	517.9	505.6	631.1	869.3	966.3	832.9	635.5
Net Interest Income	962.2	928.1	860.4	769.3	659.1	603.6	527.5
Credit Loss Provision	106.9	92.9	114.5	125.4	102.8	83.8	69.2
Net Income	151.5	257.9	[1] 208.1	196.4	182.7	150.8	123.9
Aver. Shs. Outstg. (000)	99,448	99,327	98,650	97,640	89,697	89,097	88,626

[1] Before acctg. change dr$59,890,000.

BALANCE SHEET (IN MILLIONS):

	1994	1993	1992	1991	1990	1989	1988
Cash & Due From Banks	1,488.7	1,250.6	1,246.2	1,119.7	1,172.1	1,324.7	1,261.8
Loans & Lse Financing, Net	15,299.9	13,898.3	13,278.9	13,677.8	13,015.5	11,255.9	9,549.9
Total Domestic Deposits	15,048.4	15,510.7	15,425.3	13,316.4	12,533.9	11,432.2	10,167.7
Long-term Debt	994.9	1,051.6	1,329.2	1,214.1	666.3	603.0	624.8
Net Stockholders' Equity	1,777.3	1,818.2	1,631.3	1,411.9	1,196.5	1,053.7	943.8
Total Assets	21,816.4	21,415.5	20,741.1	18,875.2	17,613.1	16,975.4	14,383.4
Year End Shs Outstg (000)	98,138	99,476	99,068	98,194	90,498	89,310	88,797

STATISTICAL RECORD:

	1994	1993	1992	1991	1990	1989	1988
Return on Assets %	0.69	1.20	1.00	1.04	1.04	0.89	0.86
Return on Equity %	8.50	14.20	12.80	13.90	15.30	14.30	13.10
Book Value Per Share	16.58	16.77	14.95	14.38	13.22	11.80	10.63
Average Yield %	3.6	3.2	3.3	3.9	4.2	3.4	4.1
P/E Ratio	20.4-15.8	11.7-8.9	13.0-9.7	11.8-5.8	8.9-4.8	10.8-6.2	8.6-6.7
Price Range	28⅝-22⅛	28⅞-22	26⅝-19⅞	23¾-11¾	18⅛-9⅞	18¼-10½	12-9⅜

Statistics are as originally reported.

OFFICERS:
G.B. Cameron, Chmn., C.E.O. & C.O.O.
K.R. Kelly, Pres.
R.D. Geddes, Exec. V.P., Corp. Couns. & Sec.
T.P. Ducharme, Exec. V.P. & Treas.

INCORPORATED: OR, Sep., 1968

PRINCIPAL OFFICE: 111 S.W. Fifth Ave.
Suite 3500, Portland, OR 97204

TELEPHONE NUMBER: (503) 275-6111

NO. OF EMPLOYEES: 10,610 (approx.)

ANNUAL MEETING: In April

SHAREHOLDERS: 15,473

INSTITUTIONAL HOLDINGS:
No. of Institutions: 326
Shares Held: 49,556,757

REGISTRAR(S):

TRANSFER AGENT(S): First Chicago Trust Co. of New York, New York, NY 10008

NYS SYMBOL USW
Rec. Pr. 40¾

U S WEST, INC.

YIELD 5.3%
P/E RATIO 12.9

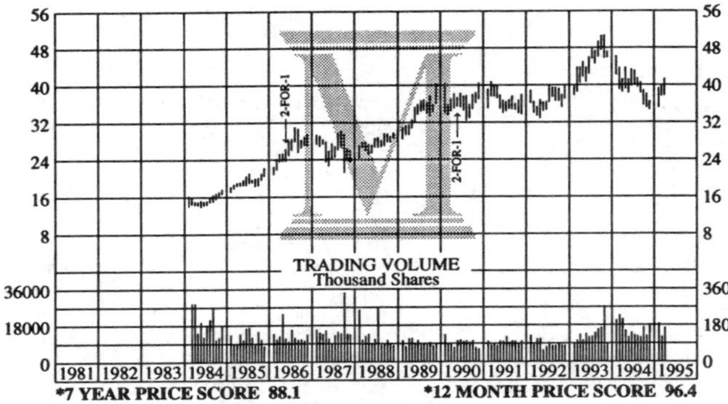

*7 YEAR PRICE SCORE 88.1 *12 MONTH PRICE SCORE 96.4

*NYSE COMPOSITE INDEX=100

INTERIM EARNINGS (Per Share):

Qtr.	Mar.	June	Sept.	Dec.
1991	0.73	0.70	0.63	d0.68
1992	0.77	0.71	0.65	0.73
1993	0.71	0.70	d0.90	0.62
1994	0.73	0.83	0.70	0.89

INTERIM DIVIDENDS (Per Share):

Amt.	Decl.	Ex.	Rec.	Pay.
0.535Q	4/1/94	4/14/94	4/20/94	5/2/94
0.535Q	7/8	7/14	7/20	8/1
0.535Q	10/7	10/14	10/20	11/1
0.535Q	12/2	1/13/95	1/20/95	2/1/95
0.535Q	4/7/95	4/12	4/19	5/1

*Indicated div.: $2.14**

CAPITALIZATION (12/31/94):

	($000)	(%)
Long-Term Debt	4,948,000	38.8
Cap. Lease Oblig.	153,000	1.2
Deferred Income Tax	231,000	1.8
Redeemable Pfd Stock	51,000	0.4
Common & Surplus	7,382,000	57.8
Total	12,765,000	100.0

DIVIDEND ACHIEVER STATUS:
Rank: 222 1984-94 Growth Rate: 7.7%
Total Years of Dividend Growth: 10

RECENT DEVELOPMENTS: For the year ended 12/31/94, income from continuing operations was $1.43 billion compared with $476.0 million, including restructuring charges of $610 million, in 1993. Revenues increased 6.4% to $10.95 billion. Earnings for 1994 include one-time gains of $197 million from the sale of certain assets. USW's core telecommunications business reported a 9.9% increase in earnings to $1.12 billion and access line growth of 4.0%.

PROSPECTS: Prospects for earnings growth are uncertain given the dilutive effects of USW's large aggressive investments in interactive services. The potential for these services is still unclear. USW acquired two cable-TV systems in the Atlanta area. Combined, the two systems have about 466,000 subscribers. The $1.2 billion acquisition was made with USW common stock, as well as cash and assumed debt.

BUSINESS

U S WEST INC. is one of the seven regional phone holding companies resulting from the AT&T breakup. Its major subsidiary is U S WEST Communications (formerly The Mountain States Telephone and Telegraph Co., Northwestern Bell Telephone Co. and Pacific Northwest Bell Telephone Co.). NewVector, 100%-owned, provides design, engineering and operation of mobile telecommunications systems. U S WEST International services the international business of U S WEST and its subsidiaries. U S WEST Marketing Resources Group, Inc. provides advertising and publishing, including publishing of directories. U S WEST Multimedia Group works with Time Warner and other partners to package voice, video and data services.

REVENUES

(12/31/94)	($000)	(%)
Local Service	4,067,000	37.1
Access Chges-Interstate	2,269,000	20.7
Access Chges-Intrastate	729,000	6.6
Long-Distance Network	1,329,000	12.1
Other Services	604,000	5.5
Publishing & Other	1,077,000	9.8
Developing Businesses	878,000	8.2
Total	10,953,000	100.0

ANNUAL EARNINGS AND DIVIDENDS PER SHARE

	1994	1993	1992	1991	1990	1989	1988
Earnings Per Share	3.14	1.13	(1) 2.86	1.38	3.11	3.01	3.09
Dividends Per Share	2.14	2.135	2.11	2.06	(2) 1.97	1.85	1.73
Dividend Payout %	68.2	N.M.	73.8	N.M.	63.3	61.5	56.1

(1) Before acctg. chg. (2) 2-for-1 stk split; 5/90

ANNUAL FINANCIAL DATA

	1994	1993	1992	1991	1990	1989	1988
RECORD OF EARNINGS (IN MILLIONS):							
Total Revenues	10,953.0	10,293.6	10,281.1	10,577.2	9,957.3	9,690.6	9,220.6
Costs and Expenses	6,394.0	7,066.4	5,986.6	7,156.9	5,679.4	5,784.8	5,432.1
Depreciation & Amort	2,052.0	1,954.5	1,890.1	1,876.1	1,844.9	1,712.4	1,760.2
Operating Profit	2,507.0	2,272.7	2,404.4	2,459.2	2,433.0	2,193.4	2,028.3
Income Bef Income Taxes	2,283.0	744.7	1,714.4	740.7	1,759.5	1,544.9	1,628.5
Income Taxes	857.0	268.8	535.0	187.3	560.6	434.2	496.8
Net Income	1,426.0	(1) 475.9	(2) 1,179.4	553.4	1,198.9	1,110.7	1,131.7
Aver. Shs. Outstg. (000)	453,316	419,365	412,518	401,332	386,012	369,098	366,854

(1) Before disc. op. dr$81,500,000; and extra. item dr$3,200,200,000. (2) Before acctg. change dr$1,793,400,000.

	1994	1993	1992	1991	1990	1989	1988
BALANCE SHEET (IN MILLIONS):							
Cash and Cash Equivalents	209.0	128.2	205.8	817.0	338.2	290.5	304.2
Receivables, Net	2,045.0	1,905.6	1,909.1	1,993.7	1,892.9	1,867.1	1,771.4
Inventories	189.0	192.7	196.6	219.1	246.5	262.6	214.3
Gross Property	31,014.0	29,161.4	28,383.0	27,159.5	26,850.5	25,750.4	24,346.3
Accumulated Depreciation	17,017.0	15,929.6	9,670.7	9,095.7	8,747.5	8,337.6	7,339.7
Long-Term Debt	4,948.0	5,422.7	6,736.9	7,629.2	7,175.3	7,247.9	6,465.9
Net Stockholders' Equity	7,433.0	5,861.2	8,267.9	9,587.4	9,239.6	8,071.3	7,785.6
Total Assets	23,204.0	20,679.7	27,963.6	27,854.1	27,050.2	25,425.9	22,415.9
Total Current Assets	2,766.0	2,499.8	2,670.0	3,395.1	2,815.1	2,775.8	2,514.0
Total Current Liabilities	6,014.0	4,981.5	5,124.8	4,849.4	4,321.0	4,069.2	3,330.7
Net Working Capital	d3,248.0	d2,481.7	d2,454.8	d1,454.3	d1,505.9	d1,293.4	d816.7
Year End Shs Outstg (000)	469,343	441,140	414,462	409,936	393,493	373,992	365,284
STATISTICAL RECORD:							
Book Value Per Share	11.77	12.12	19.95	23.39	23.48	21.58	21.31
Return on Equity %	19.3	8.1	14.3	5.8	13.0	13.8	14.5
Average Yield %	5.3	4.8	5.8	5.5	5.4	5.4	6.4
P/E Ratio	14.7-11.0	44.9-33.4	14.0-11.5	29.5-24.5	13.0-10.4	13.4-9.4	9.7-7.9
Price Range	46¼-34⅝	50¾-37¾	40-32⅞	40¾-33¾	40½-32⅜	40⅜-28⅜	29⅞-24⅜

Statistics are as originally reported.

OFFICERS:
R.D. McCormick, Chmn., Pres. & C.E.O.
J.M. Osterhoff, Exec. V.P. & C.F.O.
C.P. Russ, III, Exec. V.P., Gen. Counsel & Sec.
J.T. Anderson, V.P. & Treas.

PRINCIPAL OFFICE: 7800 East Orchard Road, Englewood, CO 80111

TELEPHONE NUMBER: (303) 793-6500
FAX: (303) 793-6354
NO. OF EMPLOYEES: 61,505
ANNUAL MEETING: In May
SHAREHOLDERS: 816,099
INSTITUTIONAL HOLDINGS:
No. of Institutions: 614
Shares Held: 172,852,135

REGISTRAR(S): Boston Financial Data Services, Quincy, MA

TRANSFER AGENT(S): Boston Financial Data Services, Quincy, MA

UNIVERSAL CORP.

YIELD 4.4%
P/E RATIO 25.4

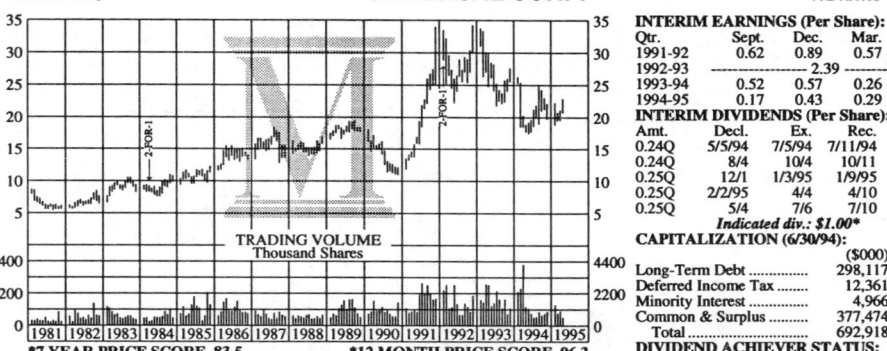

*7 YEAR PRICE SCORE 83.5   *12 MONTH PRICE SCORE 96.3

*NYSE COMPOSITE INDEX=100

INTERIM EARNINGS (Per Share):

Qtr.	Sept.	Dec.	Mar.	June
1991-92	0.62	0.89	0.57	Nil
1992-93	------------- 2.39 -------------			
1993-94	0.52	0.57	0.26	d0.26
1994-95	0.17	0.43	0.29	...

INTERIM DIVIDENDS (Per Share):

Amt.	Decl.	Ex.	Rec.	Pay.
0.24Q	5/5/94	7/5/94	7/11/94	8/8/94
0.24Q	8/4	10/4	10/11	11/7
0.25Q	12/1	1/3/95	1/9/95	2/6/95
0.25Q	2/2/95	4/4	4/10	5/8
0.25Q	5/4	7/6	7/10	8/7

*Indicated div.: $1.00**

CAPITALIZATION (6/30/94):

	($000)	(%)
Long-Term Debt	298,117	43.0
Deferred Income Tax	12,361	1.8
Minority Interest	4,966	0.7
Common & Surplus	377,474	54.5
Total	692,918	100.0

DIVIDEND ACHIEVER STATUS:
Rank: 219   1984-94 Growth Rate: 7.8%
Total Years of Dividend Growth: 24

RECENT DEVELOPMENTS: For the three months ended 12/31/94, net income slipped to $14.9 million from $20.2 million the year before. Sales increased 12% to $963.7 million. Domestically, tobacco earnings were down as the result of a shift in product mix to a lower margin business. Lower margins in Western Europe, economic pressures in Eastern Europe, and flat performance in Brazil offset higher year-over-year performance in Africa.

PROSPECTS: UVV's cost control and restructuring efforts are under way in its tobacco division. Operations in Eastern Europe are particularly sensitive, and are in the greatest need for review if that region is to become profitable. Further write-downs of inventories and obligations from customers may be necessary bto boost the Company's bottom line. Earnings from the agri-products section should be aided by the disposition of UVV's coffee operations.

BUSINESS

UNIVERSAL CORPORATION has operations in tobacco, lumber and building products and agri-products. UVV's primary subsidiary, Universal Leaf is the world's largest independent tobacco dealer, providing buying, processing, packing, storing and financing services for manufacturers of tobacco products. Lumber and building products operations involve distribution to the building and construction trade in Europe, and the manufacture of laminated wood products in the United States. Agri-products operations primarily involve the buying and selling of physical products such as rubber, tea, peanuts, sunflower seeds and vegetable oils. Title insurance operations were spun off in 1991.

BUSINESS LINE ANALYSIS

(6/30/94)	Rev(%)	Inc(%)
Tobacco	73.1	74.7
Lumber & Building Prods.	12.4	17.0
Agri-products	14.5	8.3
Total	100.0	100.0

ANNUAL EARNINGS AND DIVIDENDS PER SHARE

	6/30/94	6/30/93	6/30/92	6/30/91	6/30/90	6/30/89	6/30/88
Earnings Per Share	1.09	2.39	2.15	② 1.72	③ 1.11	1.60	1.78
Dividends Per Share	0.96	0.88	① 0.80	0.76	0.74	0.70	0.64
Dividend Payout %	88.1	36.8	37.2	44.2	66.7	43.9	36.0

① 2-for-1 stk split, 1/2/92   ② Before dicont oper. & extraord. item   ③ Before acctg. chg.

ANNUAL FINANCIAL DATA

RECORD OF EARNINGS (IN MILLIONS):

Total Revenues	2,975.1	3,047.2	2,989.0	2,896.5	2,815.1	2,920.3	2,429.0
Costs and Expenses	2,835.7	2,850.1	2,809.0	2,736.3	2,708.1	2,789.4	2,299.5
Depreciation	37.1	32.8	29.2	25.8	27.1	25.6	22.0
Operating Profit	119.7	164.3	150.9	134.3	79.9	105.3	107.4
Inc Bef Income Taxes & Other Items	43.8	118.2	101.1	76.3	46.2	75.7	74.9
Income Taxes	11.8	43.5	35.3	24.3	13.6	24.4	17.7
Net Income	9.2	80.2	70.7	① 56.4	② 37.1	54.0	60.7
Aver. Shs. Outstg. (000)	35,502	33,599	32,822	32,792	33,522	33,872	34,118

① Before disc. op. dr$32,350,000.   ② Before acctg. change cr$7,984,000.

BALANCE SHEET (IN MILLIONS):

Cash and Cash Equivalents	164.5	119.7	82.7	59.5	50.8	68.4	53.1
Receivables, Net	402.6	369.5	323.9	395.4	7.6	0.9	259.3
Inventories	588.4	569.3	544.3	406.1	356.1	279.3	267.5
Gross Property	539.1	524.2	446.9	408.2	385.5	341.9	313.2
Accumulated Depreciation	270.0	246.5	219.4	197.9	199.2	175.5	154.2
Long-Term Debt	298.1	281.8	190.2	160.0	144.3	85.2	88.1
Net Stockholders' Equity	377.5	417.9	301.7	389.8	397.1	386.4	356.9
Total Assets	1,667.0	1,562.0	1,261.4	1,275.6	887.0	784.8	1,006.6
Total Current Assets	1,186.0	1,086.9	970.5	877.5	433.3	361.4	610.2
Total Current Liabilities	868.0	786.4	697.2	341.6	452.9	438.2	429.0
Net Working Capital	318.0	300.5	273.3	535.9	d19.6	d76.9	181.2
Year End Shs Outstg (000)	35,001	35,632	32,863	32,778	32,880	33,862	33,928

STATISTICAL RECORD:

Operating Profit Margin %	3.4	5.4	5.0	4.6	2.8	3.6	4.4
Book Value Per Share	6.46	7.81	8.83	11.49	11.16	10.57	9.67
Return on Equity %	10.2	19.2	23.4	14.5	9.3	14.0	17.0
Return on Assets %	2.3	5.1	5.6	4.4	4.2	6.9	6.0
Average Yield %	4.4	3.2	2.8	3.3	5.1	3.9	4.1
P/E Ratio	24.1-16.1	14.1-9.1	15.9-10.3	19.8-6.9	16.3-9.9	12.2-10.3	9.5-7.9
Price Range	26¼-17½	33¾-21¾	34¼-22¼	34-11⅞	18⅛-11	19½-16½	16⅞-14

Statistics are as originally reported.

OFFICERS:
H.H. Harrell, Chmn. & C.E.O.
A.B. King, Pres. & C.O.O.
H.H. Roper, V.P. & C.F.O.

INCORPORATED: VA, Jan., 1918

PRINCIPAL OFFICE: Hamilton Street at Broad, Richmond, VA 23230

TELEPHONE NUMBER: (804) 359-9311
FAX: (804) 254-8594
NO. OF EMPLOYEES: 25,000 (approx.)
ANNUAL MEETING: In October
SHAREHOLDERS: 4,022
INSTITUTIONAL HOLDINGS:
No. of Institutions: 172
Shares Held: 25,685,968

REGISTRAR(S): Sovran Bank, N.A., Richmond, VA 23219

TRANSFER AGENT(S): Sovran Bank, N.A., Richmond, VA 23219

NYS SYMBOL USH
Rec. Pr. 38

USLIFE CORP.

YIELD 3.5%
P/E RATIO 9.0

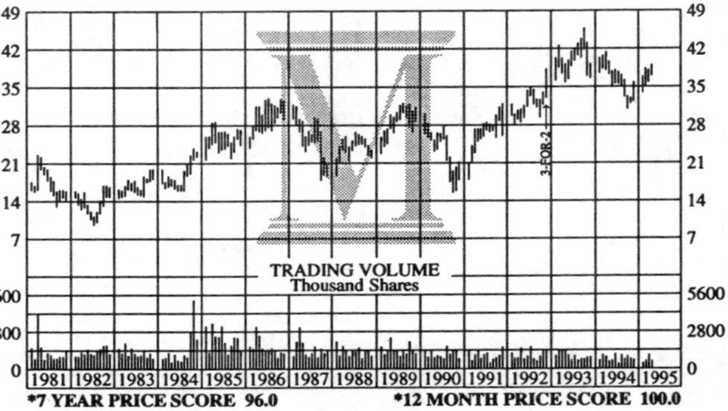

49
42
35
28
21
14
7
3-FOR-2
TRADING VOLUME
Thousand Shares
5600
2800
0
1981 1982 1983 1984 1985 1986 1987 1988 1989 1990 1991 1992 1993 1994 1995

*7 YEAR PRICE SCORE 96.0 *12 MONTH PRICE SCORE 100.0

*NYSE COMPOSITE INDEX=100

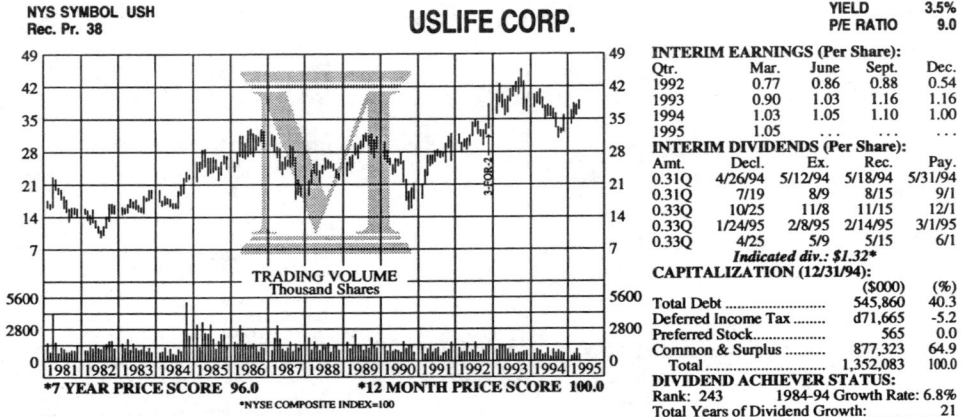

INTERIM EARNINGS (Per Share):

Qtr.	Mar.	June	Sept.	Dec.
1992	0.77	0.86	0.88	0.54
1993	0.90	1.03	1.16	1.16
1994	1.03	1.05	1.10	1.00
1995	1.05	...	...	...

INTERIM DIVIDENDS (Per Share):

Amt.	Decl.	Ex.	Rec.	Pay.
0.31Q	4/26/94	5/12/94	5/18/94	5/31/94
0.31Q	7/19	8/9	8/15	9/1
0.33Q	10/25	11/8	11/15	12/1
0.33Q	1/24/95	2/8/95	2/14/95	3/1/95
0.33Q	4/25	5/9	5/15	6/1

*Indicated div.: $1.32**

CAPITALIZATION (12/31/94):

	($000)	(%)
Total Debt	545,860	40.3
Deferred Income Tax	d71,665	-5.2
Preferred Stock	565	0.0
Common & Surplus	877,323	64.9
Total	1,352,083	100.0

DIVIDEND ACHIEVER STATUS:
Rank: 243 1984-94 Growth Rate: 6.8%
Total Years of Dividend Growth: 21

RECENT DEVELOPMENTS: In February 1995, the Company announced the formation of a new wholly-owned subsidiary, USLIFE Financial Institution Marketing Group, Inc. For the year ended 12/31/94, USH reported a modest decline in net income to $96.2 million or $4.18 per share from $97.2 million or $4.25 per share a year earlier. Total revenues increased 3.2% to $1.65 billion from $1.60 billion the year before.

PROSPECTS: The USLIFE Financial Institution Marketing Group was formed to coordinate the resources of the Company's three life insurance companies and its large credit life insurance group. The new company will direct its efforts toward the significant potential for new life insurance sales through financial institutions. Investment portfolio strength will continue as a major priority for the Company. The Company's core individual life insurance segment is performing well and is helping to boost revenues.

BUSINESS

USLIFE CORPORATION is a life insurance-based company. Growth has come through acquisitions and the forming of new operating units. With nationwide operations, USLIFE has three ordinary life insurance companies and a credit insurance group that provides individual and group life and health insurance. Other subsidiaries provide services to the life insurance companies. These subsidiaries are engaged in investment advisory, broker-dealer, real estate, data processing and administrative services.

PREMIUM INCOME

(12/31/94)	($000)	(%)
Life & Annuities	494,908	51.3
Accident & Health	470,570	48.7
Total	965,478	100.0

ANNUAL EARNINGS AND DIVIDENDS PER SHARE

	1994	1993	1992	1991	1990	1989	1988
Earnings Per Share	**4.18**	**4.25**	**[1] 3.05**	**3.22**	**2.85**	**3.09**	**2.54**
Dividends Per Share	**1.26**	**1.22**	**[2] 1.14**	**1.067**	**0.987**	**0.94**	**0.867**
Dividend Payout %	**30.1**	**28.7**	**37.4**	**33.1**	**34.7**	**30.5**	**34.1**

[1] Before acctg. chg. [2] 3-for-2 stk split,12/23/92

ANNUAL FINANCIAL DATA

	1994	1993	1992	1991	1990	1989	1988
RECORD OF EARNINGS (IN MILLIONS):							
Insurance Premiums	965.5	944.3	926.4	840.3	760.6	743.5	966.7
Total Interest Income	461.5	444.6	414.4	361.6	322.6	307.9	289.6
Total Revenues	1,651.2	1,600.0	1,529.5	1,382.9	1,235.6	1,200.2	1,279.1
Death & Other Benefits	727.6	737.3	740.9	686.9	622.0	595.6	606.2
Income Bef Income Taxes	147.0	151.6	104.3	111.0	103.5	120.5	94.8
Income Taxes	50.8	54.4	34.7	36.2	34.8	40.2	27.0
Gain on Sale Of Securities	...	...	...	...	...	...	3.1
Net Income	96.2	97.2	[1] 69.6	74.9	68.6	73.8	70.9
Aver. Shs. Outstg. (000)	23,020	22,871	22,723	23,136	23,979	25,833	26,463
[1] Before acctg. change dr$37,990,000.							
BALANCE SHEET (IN MILLIONS):							
Cash	51.9	60.3	74.6	76.5	76.5	72.7	70.5
Fixed Maturities	4,937.9	4,751.7	4,160.5	3,408.6	2,705.1	2,177.6	2,284.8
Equity Securities, At Mkt	4.6	9.2	19.5	23.8	25.3	25.9	29.4
Policy Loans	283.1	282.1	283.9	286.2	285.6	288.3	295.6
Mortgage Loans	319.6	361.1	388.4	434.1	442.1	449.2	416.6
Total Assets	7,004.3	6,740.2	6,095.3	5,329.3	4,573.3	4,336.4	4,145.3
Benefits and Claims	1,737.4	1,657.5	1,528.4	1,497.2	1,471.3	1,466.8	2,568.8
Net Stockholders' Equity	877.9	966.0	890.4	972.6	932.3	934.1	924.0
Year End Shs Outstg (000)	22,817	22,658	22,503	22,525	23,037	24,980	25,208
STATISTICAL RECORD:							
Book Value Per Share	38.45	42.61	39.54	43.02	40.27	37.17	36.23
Return on Equity %	11.0	10.1	7.8	7.7	7.4	8.6	7.7
Return on Assets %	1.4	1.4	1.1	1.4	1.5	1.9	1.7
Average Yield %	3.5	3.0	3.4	4.3	4.3	3.4	3.8
P/E Ratio	9.9-7.4	10.8-8.4	12.5-9.2	9.9-5.6	10.6-5.4	10.4-7.4	10.5-7.3
Price Range	41⅜-30⅞	45¾-35¾	38¼-28⅛	31⅞-17⅞	30⅛-15½	32⅛-22¾	26¾-18⅝

Statistics are as originally reported.

OFFICERS:
G.E. Crosby, Jr., Chmn. & C.E.O.
G.F. Henderson, Vice-Chmn. & C.F.O.
C.S. Ruisi, Vice-Chmn. & C.A.O.
W.A. Simpson, Pres. & C.E.O.

INCORPORATED: NY, Nov., 1966

PRINCIPAL OFFICE: 125 Maiden Lane, New York, NY 10038-4992

TELEPHONE NUMBER: (212) 709-6000
FAX: (212) 425-8010
NO. OF EMPLOYEES: 1,500 (approx.)
ANNUAL MEETING: In May
SHAREHOLDERS: 7,800 (approx.)
INSTITUTIONAL HOLDINGS:
No. of Institutions: 285
Shares Held: 16,659,649

REGISTRAR(S): Chemical Bank, New York, NY

TRANSFER AGENT(S): Chemical Bank, New York, NY

NYS SYMBOL UST
Rec. Pr. 29

UST, INC.

YIELD 4.5%
P/E RATIO 15.5

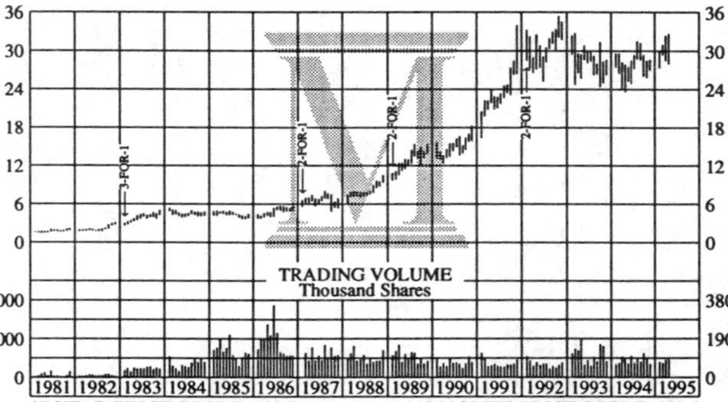

*7 YEAR PRICE SCORE 108.7 *12 MONTH PRICE SCORE 100.4

*NYSE COMPOSITE INDEX=100

INTERIM EARNINGS (Per Share):

Qtr.	Mar.	June	Sept.	Dec.
1992	0.31	0.35	0.38	0.36
1993	0.47	0.41	0.41	0.41
1994	0.42	0.48	0.48	0.49

INTERIM DIVIDENDS (Per Share):

Amt.	Decl.	Ex.	Rec.	Pay.
0.28Q	5/3/94	5/27/94	6/3/94	6/15/94
0.28Q	7/27	8/29	9/5	9/15
0.28Q	10/27	11/29	12/5	12/15
0.325Q	12/15	2/27/95	3/5/95	3/15/95
0.325Q	5/2/95	5/30	6/5	6/15

*Indicated div.:$1.30**

CAPITALIZATION (12/31/94):

	($000)	(%)
Long-Term Debt	125,000	25.4
Deferred Income Tax	5,065	1.0
Common & Surplus	361,669	73.6
Total	491,734	100.0

DIVIDEND ACHIEVER STATUS:
Rank: 17 1984-94 Growth Rate: 20.1%
Total Years of Dividend Growth: 24

RECENT DEVELOPMENTS: For the year ended 12/31/94, net earnings were $387.5 million, an increase of 11% from $349.0 million the year before. Revenue rose by 10% to $1.22 billion from $1.11 billion in the year before. Smokeless tobacco sales pushed the tobacco units sales higher year-over-year as the Company shipped 627.4 million cans. Net earnings for the quarter ended 12/31/94, rose 14% to $99.0 million. Revenue rose 12% to $322.1 million.

PROSPECTS: The Company should enjoy moderate near-term sales growth. Unit volume comparisons for moist smokeless tobacco are expected to return to positive levels in the near term, aided by UST's two flagship brands, Copenhagen and Skoal. However, UST will continue to face increased competition from private-label brands. Over the long term, sales may be constrained by federal and state initiatives to tax tobacco products and limit tobacco advertising.

BUSINESS

UST INC. is a holding company, and through its subsidiaries is a leading manufacturer of moist smokeless tobacco products with Copenhagen, Skoal, Skoal Bandits and Skoal Long Cut as principal brands. Other consumer products made and marketed by UST subsidiaries include premium wines from Washington State and California's Napa Valley, sold nationally under the Chateau Ste. Michelle, Columbia Crest, Conn Creek, and Villa Mt. Eden labels. UST also makes and markets pipes and imported pipe tobaccos, imported cigars, and other tobacco-related products, and is involved in a diverse mix of small businesses in other industries.

ANNUAL EARNINGS AND DIVIDENDS PER SHARE

	1994	1993	1992	1991	1990	1989	1988
Earnings Per Share	**1.87**	**1.71**	**1.41**	**1.18**	**0.98**	**0.82**	**0.71**
Dividends Per Share	**1.12**	**0.96**	**0.80**	[1] **0.66**	**0.55**	[2] **0.46**	**0.37**
Dividend Payout %	**59.9**	**56.1**	**56.7**	**66.0**	**56.0**	**56.4**	**52.5**

[1] 2-for-1 stk split,01/28/92 [2] 2-for-1 stk split, 1/27/89

ANNUAL FINANCIAL DATA

	1994	1993	1992	1991	1990	1989	1988
RECORD OF EARNINGS (IN MILLIONS):							
Total Revenues	1,223.0	1,110.4	1,044.4	907.3	764.7	682.5	618.5
Costs and Expenses	554.1	519.0	519.2	461.0	396.1	367.5	340.6
Depreciation & Amort	28.2	26.7	24.5	22.6	19.6	16.5	17.7
Operating Profit	640.7	564.8	789.5	680.8	572.9	497.0	444.0
Earn Bef Income Taxes	640.6	601.8	502.6	426.1	352.2	301.6	261.3
Income Taxes	253.1	214.8	190.1	160.2	128.9	111.1	99.1
Net Income	387.5	[1] 368.9	312.6	265.9	223.3	190.5	162.2
Aver. Shs. Outstg. (000)	207,504	215,719	222,033	225,130	227,667	233,305	230,416
[1] Before acctg. change dr$19,846,000.							
BALANCE SHEET (IN MILLIONS):							
Cash and Cash Equivalents	50.7	25.3	36.4	41.5	46.6	54.6	72.7
Receivables, Net	65.9	64.4	53.8	50.1	34.9	39.5	29.7
Inventories	237.7	215.6	213.5	193.7	169.9	168.8	174.8
Gross Property	489.3	472.9	423.9	406.1	380.7	347.6	327.8
Accumulated Depreciation	183.4	163.2	142.9	131.1	113.7	99.0	85.8
Long-Term Debt	125.0	40.0	...	...	3.1	6.8	21.8
Net Stockholders' Equity	361.7	463.0	516.6	482.9	473.9	482.3	453.3
Total Assets	741.2	706.2	674.0	656.5	622.6	636.3	598.0
Total Current Assets	381.9	335.0	330.2	305.4	265.9	279.6	291.0
Total Current Liabilities	160.8	106.6	22.1	26.9	21.9	24.2	23.7
Net Working Capital	221.2	228.4	308.1	278.6	244.0	255.4	267.3
Year End Shs Outstg (000)	195,940	196,290	211,037	210,980	212,983	218,204	219,960
STATISTICAL RECORD:							
Operating Profit Margin %	52.4	50.9	47.9	46.7	45.6	43.7	42.1
Book Value Per Share	1.80	2.30	2.45	2.29	2.22	2.21	2.06
Return on Equity %	N.M.	79.7	60.5	55.1	47.1	39.5	35.8
Return on Assets %	52.3	52.2	46.4	40.5	35.9	29.9	27.1
Average Yield %	4.1	3.4	2.6	2.6	3.6	3.7	4.5
P/E Ratio	16.8-12.6	19.2-14.3	25.1-17.9	28.8-13.9	18.6-12.6	19.0-12.0	14.8-8.6
Price Range	31½-23⅝	32¾-24⅜	35⅝-25¼	34-16⅜	18¼-12⅜	15⅜-9¾	10½-6⅛

Statistics are as originally reported.

OFFICERS:
V.A. Gierer, Jr., Chmn., C.E.O. & Pres.
J.J. Bucchignano, Exec. V.P. & C.F.O.
J.P. Nelson, Sr. V.P. & Sec.
J.D. Harris, Treas.

INCORPORATED: DE, Dec., 1986

PRINCIPAL OFFICE: 100 West Putnam Ave., Greenwich, CT 06830

TELEPHONE NUMBER: (203) 661-1100

NO. OF EMPLOYEES: 3,724 (avg.)

ANNUAL MEETING: In May

SHAREHOLDERS: 13,621

INSTITUTIONAL HOLDINGS:
No. of Institutions: 562
Shares Held: 105,011,041

REGISTRAR(S): First National Bank of Boston, Shareholder Services Division, Boston, MA

TRANSFER AGENT(S): First National Bank of Boston, Shareholder Services Division, Boston, MA

UTILICORP UNITED INC.

YIELD 6.2%
P/E RATIO 13.2

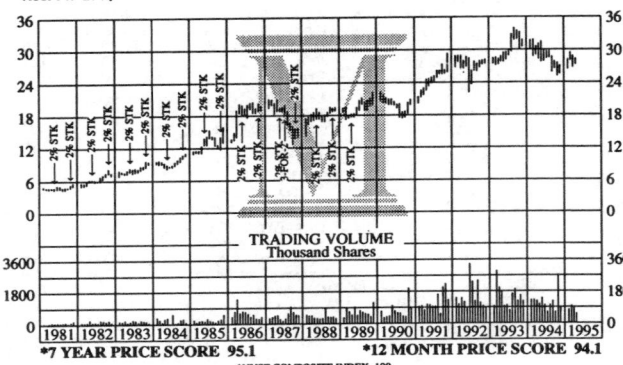

TRADING VOLUME
Thousand Shares

| | 1981 | 1982 | 1983 | 1984 | 1985 | 1986 | 1987 | 1988 | 1989 | 1990 | 1991 | 1992 | 1993 | 1994 | 1995 |

*7 YEAR PRICE SCORE 95.1   ***12 MONTH PRICE SCORE 94.1**
*NYSE COMPOSITE INDEX=100

INTERIM EARNINGS (Per Share):

Qtr.	Mar.	June	Sept.	Dec.
1991	0.95	0.15	0.36	0.75
1992	0.77	d0.23	0.10	0.68
1993	0.87	0.13	0.22	0.76
1994	0.88	0.15	0.31	0.76

INTERIM DIVIDENDS (Per Share):

Amt.	Decl.	Ex.	Rec.	Pay.
0.42Q	5/4/94	5/13/94	5/19/94	6/12/94
0.43Q	8/3	8/15	8/19	9/12
0.43Q	11/2	11/14	11/18	12/12
0.43Q	2/1/95	2/13/95	2/17/95	3/12/95
0.43Q	5/3	5/15	5/19	6/12

Indicated div.: $1.72*

CAPITALIZATION (12/31/94):

	($000)	(%)
Long-Term Debt	976,900	44.2
Deferred Income Tax	300,400	13.6
Preferred Stock	25,400	1.2
Common & Surplus	906,800	41.0
Total	2,209,500	100.0

DIVIDEND ACHIEVER STATUS:
Rank: 165   1984-94 Growth Rate: 10.1%
Total Years of Dividend Growth: 37

RECENT DEVELOPMENTS: For the quarter ended 12/31/94, net income was relatively flat at $33.6 million compared with $33.3 million in the corresponding period of 1993. Revenues rose 4.3% to $449.7 million. For the year ended 12/31/94, net income was $94.4 million versus $86.4 million a year earlier. Revenues were $1.51 billion, down 3.6%. The improvement for the year reflects increased contributions from non-regulated and overseas businesses and improved efficiencies at the Company's largest electric generation facility.

PROSPECTS: The recently acquired business segments, the gas distribution systems and several non-regulated power generation projects, should provide further earnings growth. The Company's geographically diverse service territory is helping it achieve growth of 6% in its service area. UCU's strategy to diversify with overseas investments in other utilities should boost earnings and revenues. These investments, in the United Kingdom and New Zealand, carry greater risks than other investments that have been made.

BUSINESS

UTILICORP UNITED INC. provides electric and gas utility service to nearly 1 million customers in eight states and one Canadian province. Utility divisions include: Missouri Public Service; Kansas Public Service; Peoples Natural Gas; Northern Minnesota Utilities; West Virginia Power; Michigan Gas Utilities; West-Plains Energy; and its Canadian subsidiary West Kootenay Power, B.C. Virtually all of UCU's U.S. electric power generation is coal or gas-fired, and all of its Canadian generation is hydroelectric. The Company does not operate nuclear power plants. Aquila Energy, a wholly owned subsidiary, is one of the nation's largest independent marketers of natural gas. Utilco Group, another wholly-owned subsidiary, owns and operates independent electric generating projects.

BUSINESS LINE ANALYSIS

(12/31/94)	Rev(%)	Inc(%)
Electric Opers	36.8	54.3
Gas Opers	40.8	26.8
Energy Related		
Business	22.4	18.9
Total	100.0	100.0

ANNUAL EARNINGS AND DIVIDENDS PER SHARE

	1994	1993	1992	1991	1990	1989	1988
Earnings Per Share	2.08	1.95	1.32	2.23	2.13	2.04	1.98
Dividends Per Share	1.70	1.62	1.60	1.54	1.46	1.413 [1]	1.028 [2]
Dividend Payout %	81.7	83.1	N.M.	69.1	68.5	69.3	51.9

[1] 2% stk div, 3/89 [2] 2% stk div, 12/88 & 6/88

ANNUAL FINANCIAL DATA

RECORD OF EARNINGS (IN MILLIONS):

	1994	1993	1992	1991	1990	1989	1988
Total Revenues	1,514.6	1,571.6	1,298.9	1,075.2	894.4	731.9	672.8
Depreciation & Amort	147.1	74.5	66.1	53.9	49.2	44.2	38.9
Maintenance	49.3	47.2	40.5	37.1	29.2	31.7	29.8
Prov for Fed Inc Taxes	...	...	...	...	...	21.7	18.5
Income From Operations	230.5	152.2	169.0	188.8	145.0	86.9	77.2
Interest Expense	102.3	100.1	99.1	81.7	58.9	49.4	38.9
Net Income	94.4	86.4	52.9	73.5	58.9	48.3	40.9
Aver. Shs. Outstg. (000)	43,970	40,740	34,930	29,390	23,968	20,863	19,420

BALANCE SHEET (IN MILLIONS):

Gross Plant	2,556.6	2,445.2	2,220.7	2,087.8	1,590.5	1,479.2	1,199.0
Accumulated Depreciation	923.0	865.0	767.2	721.8	506.5	475.7	386.2
Prop, Plant & Equip, Net	1,633.6	1,580.2	1,453.5	1,366.0	1,084.0	1,003.5	812.9
Long-term Debt	976.9	1,009.7	890.8	928.1	667.6	437.6	358.0
Net Stockholders' Equity	932.2	935.6	756.2	767.4	588.4	474.9	357.1
Total Assets	3,111.1	2,850.5	2,552.8	2,402.2	1,844.6	1,466.9	1,124.9
Year End Shs Outstg (000)	44,600	42,021	35,422	34,456	28,088	22,763	20,723

STATISTICAL RECORD:

Book Value Per Share	20.33	20.27	18.66	19.45	17.49	16.58	15.54
Op. Inc/Net Pl %	14.1	9.6	11.6	13.8	13.4	8.7	9.5
Dep/Gr. Pl %	5.5	3.0	3.0	2.6	3.1	3.0	3.2
Accum. Dep/Gr. Pl %	36.1	35.4	34.5	34.6	31.8	32.2	32.2
Return on Equity %	10.1	9.2	7.0	9.6	10.0	10.2	11.4
Average Yield %	6.0	5.3	6.3	6.2	7.3	7.2	6.1
P/E Ratio	15.3-12.1	17.4-13.9	22.0-16.8	13.2-9.0	10.5-8.2	10.9-8.4	9.9-7.1
Price Range	31⅞-25⅛	34-27⅛	29-22⅛	29⅜-20⅛	22⅜-17⅜	22¼-17⅛	19⅝-14⅛

Statistics are as originally reported.

OFFICERS:
R.C. Green, Jr., Chmn., Pres. & C.E.O.
J.R. Baker, Vice-Chmn.
D.J. Wolf, V.P., Corp. Sec. & Treas.

INCORPORATED: MO, Apr., 1950; reincorp., DE, Apr., 1987

PRINCIPAL OFFICE: 3000 Commerce Tower 911 Main, Kansas City, MO 64105

TELEPHONE NUMBER: (816) 421-6600
FAX: (816) 691-3591
NO. OF EMPLOYEES: 4,683 (approx.)
ANNUAL MEETING: In May
SHAREHOLDERS: 37,255
INSTITUTIONAL HOLDINGS:
No. of Institutions: 164
Shares Held: 9,863,669

REGISTRAR(S): First Chicago Trust Co. of New York, New York, NY 10008
First National Bank of Chicago, Chicago, IL 60670

TRANSFER AGENT(S): First Chicago Trust Co. of New York, New York, NY 10008
United Missouri Bank, N.A., Kansas City, MO 64141-0064

VALLEY RESOURCES, INC.

YIELD 6.9%
P/E RATIO 12.7

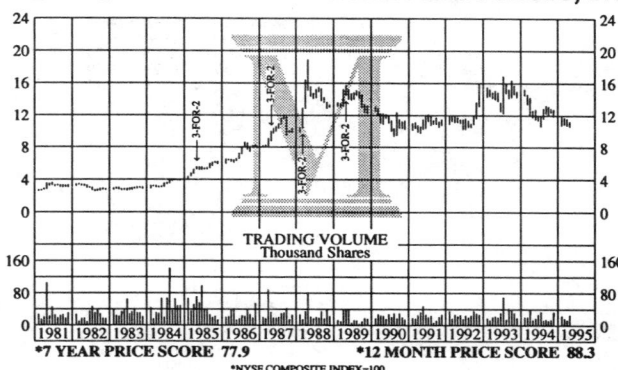

*7 YEAR PRICE SCORE 77.9   ***12 MONTH PRICE SCORE 88.3**

*NYSE COMPOSITE INDEX=100

INTERIM EARNINGS (Per Share):

Qtr.	Nov.	Feb.	May	Aug.
1991-92	d0.07	0.58	0.34	d0.12
1992-93	d0.01	0.69	0.41	d0.21
1993-94	d0.09	0.81	0.37	d0.18
1994-95	d0.17	0.56	...	...

INTERIM DIVIDENDS (Per Share):

Amt.	Decl.	Ex.	Rec.	Pay.
0.175Q	3/15/94	3/25/94	3/31/94	4/15/94
0.175Q	6/21	6/24	6/30	7/15
0.175Q	9/20	9/26	9/30	10/15
0.175Q	12/13	12/23	12/30	1/15/95
0.18Q	3/21/95	3/27/95	3/31/95	4/15

Indicated div.: $0.72*

CAPITALIZATION (8/31/94):

	($000)	(%)
Long-Term Debt	27,035	40.3
Cap. Lease Oblig.	1,747	2.6
Deferred Income Tax	12,255	18.3
Common & Surplus	26,036	38.8
Total	67,073	100.0
Current Debt	1,140	

DIVIDEND ACHIEVER STATUS:
Rank: 238   1984-94 Growth Rate: 7.2%
Total Years of Dividend Growth: 14

RECENT DEVELOPMENTS: For the quarter ended 2/28/95, net income fell 30.1% to $2.4 million from $3.4 million in corresponding 1994 quarter. Earnings for the 1995 quarter declined due to the adverse effect the warm winter had on utility and propane operations. Operating revenues totaled $27.0 million compared with $31.6 million in the year-earlier quarter, a decrease of 14.6%. Operating income was $3.2 million, down 22.1% from $4.1 million in the prior-year quarter. For the six months ended 2/28/95, net income dropped 45.7% to $1.6 million from $3.0 million for the same period in 1994. Operating revenue was $41.7 million, down 11.8% from $47.3 million the year before. Results for the six months were negatively affected by warmer weather in the second quarter, partially offset by improvements in nonutility operations.

BUSINESS

VALLEY RESOURCES, INC. is a holding company that has seven wholly-owned subsidiaries. Valley Gas Company is a regulated natural gas distribution company. Valley Appliance and Merchandising Company is a merchandising and appliance rental company. Valley Propane, Inc. is a retail propane company. Morris Merchants, Inc. is a wholesale distributor of franchised lines in plumbing and heating contractor supply and other energy related business. Bristol & Warren Gas Company is a regulated natural gas distribution company. New England Gas Company is a retail propane company. Rhode Island Development and Exploration Company is an inactive company.

REVENUES

(8/31/94)	($000)	(%)
Utility Gas Revenues.	65,324	78.2
Nonutility Revenues..	18,229	21.8
Total	83,553	100.0

ANNUAL EARNINGS AND DIVIDENDS PER SHARE

	8/31/94	8/31/93	8/31/92	8/31/91	8/31/90	8/31/89	8/31/88
Earnings Per Share	0.91	0.89	0.74	0.56	0.80	0.78	0.72
Dividends Per Share	0.695	0.67	0.635	0.615	0.59	①0.553	②0.533
Dividend Payout %	76.4	75.3	85.8	N.M.	73.8	70.9	75.1

① 3-for-2 stk split, 4/15/89   ② 3-for-2 stk. split, 1/88 & 4/87.

ANNUAL FINANCIAL DATA

RECORD OF EARNINGS (IN THOUSANDS):

Total Revenues	83,553	77,286	67,144	59,990	61,408	59,686	56,440
Depreciation	2,473	2,304	1,771	1,594	1,506	1,385	1,265
Maintenance	1,485	1,497	1,369	1,260	1,237	1,202	1,495
Prov for Fed Inc Taxes	1,313	1,400	955	652	1,202	1,223	896
Operating Income	6,501	6,084	4,898	3,791	4,718	4,431	4,050
Interest Expense	2,902	2,610	2,051	1,812	1,743	1,695	1,631
Net Income	3,826	3,727	3,115	2,358	3,209	2,982	2,711
Aver. Shs. Outstg.	4,206	4,203	4,201	4,200	4,036	3,823	3,778

BALANCE SHEET (IN THOUSANDS):

Gross Plant	73,636	69,219	63,881	52,521	48,843	46,153	42,626
Accumulated Depreciation	23,473	21,177	19,520	15,948	14,832	13,831	13,549
Prop, Plant & Equip, Net	50,163	48,042	44,361	36,573	34,011	32,322	29,077
Long-term Debt	28,782	29,427	17,585	15,509	15,046	15,620	14,792
Net Stockholders' Equity	26,036	24,943	24,018	23,600	23,648	18,280	18,091
Total Assets	91,069	80,795	75,865	60,166	54,444	49,673	46,032
Year End Shares Outstg	4,213	4,213	4,213	4,213	4,213	4,213	3,843

STATISTICAL RECORD:

Book Value Per Share	6.18	5.92	5.70	5.60	5.61	4.76	4.73
Op. Inc/Net Pl %	13.0	12.7	11.0	10.4	13.9	13.7	13.9
Dep/Gr. Pl %	3.4	3.3	2.8	3.0	3.1	3.0	3.0
Accum. Dep/Gr. Pl %	31.9	30.6	30.6	30.4	30.4	30.0	31.8
Return on Equity %	14.7	14.9	13.0	10.0	13.6	16.3	15.1
Average Yield %	5.4	4.6	4.9	5.6	5.2	4.0	3.7
P/E Ratio	16.8-11.7	19.0-13.8	21.5-13.9	21.7-17.4	16.4-11.7	20.2-15.7	26.2-13.7
Price Range	15¼-10⅝	16⅞-12¼	15⅞-10¼	12⅛-9¾	13⅛-9⅜	15¾-12¼	18⅞-9⅞

Statistics are as originally reported.

OFFICERS:
C.H. Goss, Chmn. & C.E.O.
A.P. Degen, Pres. & C.O.O.
K.W. Hogan, Sr. V.P., Treas. & Sec.

INCORPORATED: RI, Oct., 1979

PRINCIPAL OFFICE: 1595 Mendon Road, Cumberland, RI 02864

TELEPHONE NUMBER: (401) 334-1188
FAX: (401) 333-3527
NO. OF EMPLOYEES: 251
ANNUAL MEETING: In December
SHAREHOLDERS: 2,847
INSTITUTIONAL HOLDINGS:
No. of Institutions: 15
Shares Held: 562,433

REGISTRAR(S): State Street Bank and Trust Co., Boston, MA

TRANSFER AGENT(S): State Street Bank and Trust Co., Boston, MA

NYS SYMBOL VAL
Rec. Pr. 35½

VALSPAR CORP.

YIELD 1.7%
P/E RATIO 16.6

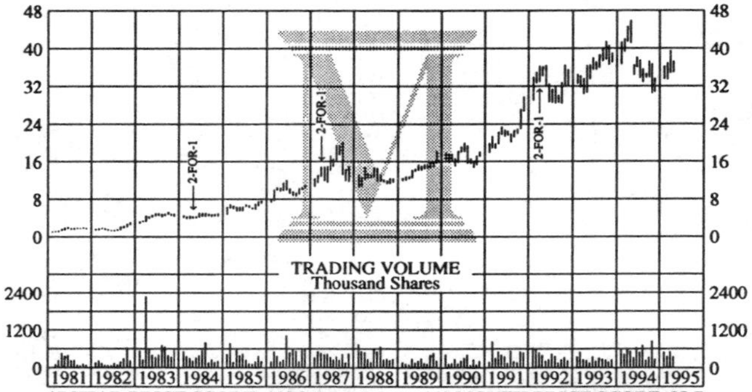

*7 YEAR PRICE SCORE 113.9 *12 MONTH PRICE SCORE 98.7

*NYSE COMPOSITE INDEX=100

INTERIM EARNINGS (Per Share):

Qtr.	Jan.	Apr.	July	Oct.
1991-92	0.16	0.42	0.52	0.47
1992-93	0.16	0.47	0.66	0.56
1993-94	0.20	0.65	0.67	0.57
1994-95	0.25	...	...	...

INTERIM DIVIDENDS (Per Share):

Amt.	Decl.	Ex.	Rec.	Pay.
stock	4/4/94	5/2/94	4/15/94	4/29/94
0.13Q	6/16	6/27	7/1	7/15
0.13Q	8/17	9/26	9/30	10/14
0.15Q	12/14	12/23	12/30	1/13/95
0.15Q	2/22/95	3/27/95	3/31/95	4/14

Indicated div.: $0.60

CAPITALIZATION (10/28/94):

	($000)	(%)
Long-Term Debt	35,334	16.5
Deferred Income Tax	4,758	2.2
Common & Surplus	174,120	81.3
Total	214,212	100.0

DIVIDEND ACHIEVER STATUS:
Rank: 27 1984-94 Growth Rate: 17.9%
Total Years of Dividend Growth: 16

RECENT DEVELOPMENTS: For the three months ended 1/27/95, net income increased 26.0% to $5.4 million from $4.3 million in the comparable period of 1994. Sales for the quarter advanced 9.0% to $161.4 million, compared with $148.0 million a year ago. Results for the 1994 period included the results of McWhorter Technologies, which was spun-off in April 1994, and a $2.5 million charge from the write-down of a plant. The Company experienced strong sales performances in each of its major businesses.

PROSPECTS: Three new plants will provide VAL with a strong basis for sales and earnings growth. Rapid growth at VAL's Color Corporation subsidiary is being supported by the start-up of a new colorant plant in Kentucky. A new consumer coatings plant in North Carolina, currently in the start-up process, will boost supply capabilities in the Southeast. Production at a new resin plant in Illinois is expected to begin in mid-1994. The Company will also benefit from international expansion.

BUSINESS

THE VALSPAR CORPORATION is a major domestic manufacturer of paints and related coatings. The Company's products include latex and oil-based paints, stains, and varnishes sold through dealers primarily to the do-it-yourself market; packaging coatings for the food and beverage industries; industrial and protective coatings sold to a broad range of original equipment manufacturers; and specialty products, including resins, colorants, floor coatings and industrial maintenance and marine coatings. Operations are carried out through four divisions: Consumer Coatings, Industrial Coatings, Packaging Coatings, and Special Products Division. Valspar operates 19 manufacturing plants in North America and licenses its technology worldwide.

REVENUES

(10/28/94)	($000)	(%)
Consumer Coatings	243,923	31.0
Industrial Coatings	180,975	23.0
Packaging Coatings	196,712	25.0
Special Products	165,238	21.0
Total	786,848	100.0

ANNUAL EARNINGS AND DIVIDENDS PER SHARE

	10/28/94	10/29/93	10/30/92	10/25/91	10/26/90	10/27/89	10/28/88
Earnings Per Share	2.08	1.85	1.57	1.27	1.22	1.04	0.82
Dividends Per Share	0.52	0.44	[1] 0.36	0.30	0.26	0.22	0.20
Dividend Payout %	25.0	23.8	22.9	23.7	21.2	21.2	24.5

[1] 2-for-1 stk split, 3/30/92

ANNUAL FINANCIAL DATA

	10/28/94	10/29/93	10/30/92	10/25/91	10/26/90	10/27/89	10/28/88
RECORD OF EARNINGS (IN THOUSANDS):							
Total Revenues	786,848	693,678	683,485	632,562	568,108	528,447	482,350
Costs and Expenses	688,806	603,742	603,531	560,700	504,181	470,209	433,837
Depreciation & Amort	19,115	20,621	19,793	18,896	15,119	13,975	12,759
Operating Profit	78,927	69,315	60,161	52,966	69,158	62,300	52,944
Income Bef Income Taxes	75,817	65,632	56,869	45,776	44,104	38,425	29,384
Income Taxes	30,333	25,450	22,451	18,100	17,373	15,191	11,089
Net Income	45,484	40,182	34,418	27,676	26,731	23,234	18,295
Aver. Shs. Outstg.	21,823	21,691	21,973	21,862	21,854	22,330	22,488
BALANCE SHEET (IN THOUSANDS):							
Cash and Cash Equivalents	2,364	1,637	1,780	1,211	1,503	1,323	1,921
Receivables, Net	111,907	105,505	92,198	88,048	75,102	77,987	64,540
Inventories	82,430	68,390	70,726	72,355	77,370	68,338	64,900
Gross Property	208,293	207,168	190,097	179,742	179,369	143,454	126,085
Accumulated Depreciation	101,265	104,029	89,092	80,924	72,748	60,767	52,433
Long-Term Debt	35,334	7,890	10,684	27,299	45,888	36,475	38,539
Capital Lease Obligations	...	...	...	3,398	3,568	3,726	3,873
Net Stockholders' Equity	174,120	196,518	169,377	147,896	128,707	112,698	99,895
Total Assets	363,368	336,798	321,618	319,367	302,806	261,103	232,974
Total Current Assets	220,899	197,480	184,711	182,173	167,094	159,607	139,782
Total Current Liabilities	134,798	113,481	127,211	124,107	110,895	96,088	79,088
Net Working Capital	86,101	83,999	57,500	58,066	56,199	63,519	60,694
Year End Shares Outstg	21,582	21,506	21,612	21,769	21,748	22,044	22,394
STATISTICAL RECORD:							
Operating Profit Margin %	10.0	10.0	8.8	8.4	8.6	8.4	7.4
Book Value Per Share	8.07	9.14	7.84	6.79	5.92	5.11	4.46
Return on Equity %	26.1	20.4	20.3	18.7	20.8	20.6	18.3
Return on Assets %	12.5	11.9	10.7	8.7	8.8	8.9	7.9
Average Yield %	1.4	1.2	1.1	1.3	1.5	1.5	1.6
P/E Ratio	22.1-14.7	22.4-16.4	23.2-18.1	23.4-14.1	16.4-12.1	17.5-11.4	18.2-13.1
Price Range	45⅞-30½	41½-30⅜	36½-28⅜	29¾-17⅞	20-14¾	18¼-11⅞	14¾-10⅝

Statistics are as originally reported.

OFFICERS:
C.A. Wurtele, Chmn. & C.E.O.
R.M. Rompala, Pres.
P.C. Reyelts, V.P.-Fin.
B.J. Eppel, Treas.

INCORPORATED: DE, Dec., 1934

PRINCIPAL OFFICE: 1101 Third Street South, Minneapolis, MN 55415

TELEPHONE NUMBER: (612) 332-7371
FAX: (612) 375-7723
NO. OF EMPLOYEES: 2,500 (approx.)
ANNUAL MEETING: In February
SHAREHOLDERS: 1,903
INSTITUTIONAL HOLDINGS:
No. of Institutions: 91
Shares Held: 13,467,767

REGISTRAR(S): Mellon Securities Trust Co., New York, NY

TRANSFER AGENT(S): Mellon Financial Securities, New York, NY

NYS SYMBOL VFC
Rec. Pr. 52¼

VF CORP.

YIELD 2.6%
P/E RATIO 12.2

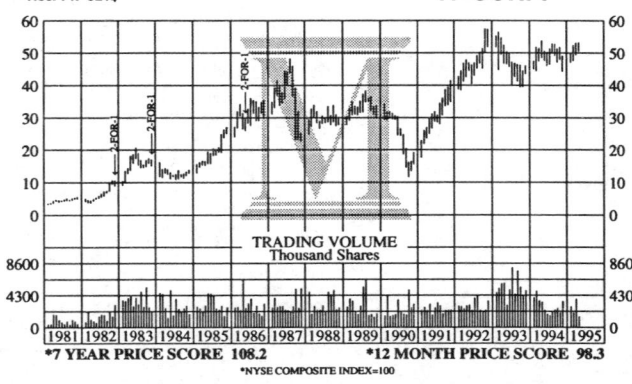

TRADING VOLUME
Thousand Shares

| 1981 | 1982 | 1983 | 1984 | 1985 | 1986 | 1987 | 1988 | 1989 | 1990 | 1991 | 1992 | 1993 | 1994 | 1995 |

*7 YEAR PRICE SCORE 108.2   *12 MONTH PRICE SCORE 98.3

*NYSE COMPOSITE INDEX=100

INTERIM EARNINGS (Per Share):

Qtr.	Mar.	June	Sept.	Dec.
1993	0.83	0.85	1.18	0.94
1994	0.81	0.90	1.34	1.15
1995	0.89	...	...	...

INTERIM DIVIDENDS (Per Share):

Amt.	Decl.	Ex.	Rec.	Pay.
0.34Q	10/19/94	12/5/94	12/9/94	12/19/94
0.34Q	10/19	12/5	12/9	12/19
0.34Q	10/19	12/5	12/9	12/19
0.34Q	2/14/95	3/6/95	3/10/95	3/20/95
0.34Q	4/18	6/6	6/9	6/19

*Indicated div.: $1.36**

CAPITALIZATION (12/31/94):

	($000)	(%)
Long-Term Debt	497,227	20.9
Cap. Lease Oblig.	19,473	0.8
Deferred Income Tax	64,830	2.8
Redeemable Pfd Stock	62,195	2.6
Common & Surplus	1,734,009	72.9
Total	2,377,734	100.0

DIVIDEND ACHIEVER STATUS:
Rank: 179   1984-94 Growth Rate: 9.7%
Total Years of Dividend Growth: 22

RECENT DEVELOPMENTS: For the year ended 12/31/94, net income was $274.5 million, a gain of 11.4% over $246.4 million for the prior year. Net sales totaled $4.97 billion compared with $4.32 billion a year earlier, an increase of 15.1%. The Company's jeanswear, intimate apparel, decorated knitwear and playwear business groups reported improved sales and operating income in 1994, with record sales achieved by Wrangler, Lee, Vanity Fair, Bassett-Walker, Healthtex, JanSport and Red Kap.

PROSPECTS: VFC will continue to realize greater efficiencies as a result of the reorganization of the Company into five new business groups. VFC is now better positioned to take advantage of growth opportunities. Continued strong performances from the jeanswear division are more than offsetting a recent softening in licensed sports apparel markets. VFC will hold a majority share in a joint venture with a Chinese manufacturer to market Lee jeans in the southern province of Guangdong.

BUSINESS

VF CORP. is one of the world's largest publicly-held apparel companies, competing primarily in the jeanswear, decorated knitwear, intimate apparel, playwear and specialty apparel categories. Apparel is manufactured and marketed under the following brands: jeanswear-Lee, Wrangler, Rustler, Riders and Marithe & Francois Girbaud; casual/sportswear-Lee, Jantzen and JanSport; intimate apparel-Vanity Fair, Vassarette and Barbizon; occupational apparel-Red Kap and WorkWear; and children's apparel-Healthtex. Jeanswear is manufactured and marketed internationally under the Lee and Wrangler brands, and intimate apparel is marketed under various labels.

BUSINESS LINE ANALYSIS

(12/31/94)	Rev(%)	Inc(%)
Jeanswear	51.2	64.5
Decorated Knitwear	12.5	5.6
Intimate Apparel	14.6	10.5
Playwear	7.4	6.3
Specialty Apparel	14.3	13.1
Total	100.0	100.0

ANNUAL EARNINGS AND DIVIDENDS PER SHARE

	12/31/94	1/1/94	1/2/93	1/4/92	12/29/90	12/30/89	12/31/88
Earnings Per Share	4.20	3.80	3.97	2.75	1.35	2.72	2.55
Dividends Per Share	1.30	1.22	1.11	1.02	1.00	0.91	0.85
Dividend Payout %	31.0	32.1	27.5	37.1	74.1	33.5	33.3

ANNUAL FINANCIAL DATA

RECORD OF EARNINGS (IN MILLIONS):

Total Revenues	4,971.7	4,320.4	3,824.4	2,952.4	2,612.6	2,532.7	2,516.1
Costs and Expenses	4,274.4	3,762.8	3,286.8	2,572.1	2,324.4	2,146.9	2,141.2
Depreciation & Amort	158.5	125.8	108.3	76.3	80.9	72.9	70.3
Operating Income	538.8	431.8	429.4	304.1	207.3	312.9	304.6
Income Bef Income Taxes	455.7	400.0	375.8	263.2	143.1	283.7	274.9
Income Taxes	181.1	153.6	138.7	101.9	62.0	107.7	101.3
Net Income	274.5	246.4	237.0	161.3	81.1	176.0	173.7
Aver. Shs. Outstg. (000)	64,620	64,011	58,608	57,152	57,122	64,803	68,165

BALANCE SHEET (IN MILLIONS):

Cash and Cash Equivalents	59.7	151.6	86.3	162.3	62.0	36.2	86.7
Receivables, Net	661.7	550.0	514.8	353.3	314.0	320.0	266.4
Inventories	801.3	778.8	742.5	537.0	436.7	507.5	422.8
Gross Property	1,403.9	1,250.0	1,241.6	1,041.1	954.3	877.3	792.5
Accumulated Depreciation	636.8	537.3	530.5	464.1	417.1	363.4	310.2
Long-Term Debt	497.2	527.6	767.6	583.2	585.1	637.5	302.3
Net Stockholders' Equity	1,796.2	1,610.7	1,217.9	1,002.6	888.1	819.8	1,095.4
Total Assets	3,335.6	2,877.3	2,712.4	2,126.9	1,852.8	1,889.8	1,759.9
Total Current Assets	1,551.2	1,500.2	1,365.6	1,071.1	824.2	873.5	786.5
Total Current Liabilities	912.3	659.8	684.0	510.8	351.5	325.1	231.0
Net Working Capital	638.8	840.3	681.6	560.3	472.8	548.5	555.4
Year-end Shs Outstg (000)	64,165	64,489	59,519	57,700	57,013	57,986	68,255

STATISTICAL RECORD:

Operating Profit Margin %	10.8	10.0	11.2	10.3	7.9	12.4	12.1
Book Value Per Share	12.82	15.07	10.07	8.94	6.94	6.69	9.46
Return on Equity %	15.8	15.9	20.5	17.2	9.9	21.5	15.9
Return on Assets %	8.2	8.6	8.7	7.6	4.4	9.3	9.9
Average Yield %	2.7	2.5	2.3	3.5	4.4	2.8	2.9
P/E Ratio	12.8-10.5	14.9-10.4	14.5-9.7	15.1-6.4	25.4-8.6	14.1-10.2	13.3-9.7
Price Range	53¾-44¼	56½-39½	57½-38½	41½-17⅝	34¼-11⅝	38⅛-27¾	33⅞-24¾

Statistics are as originally reported.

OFFICERS:
L.R. Pugh, Chmn. & C.E.O.
M.J. McDonald, Pres. & C.O.O.
G.G. Johnson, V.P.-Fin. & C.F.O.
F.C. Pickard, III, V.P. & Treas.
INCORPORATED: PA, Dec., 1889
PRINCIPAL OFFICE: 1047 North Park Road, Wyomissing, PA 19610

TELEPHONE NUMBER: (610) 378-1151
FAX: (610) 375-9371
NO. OF EMPLOYEES: 72,247
ANNUAL MEETING: In April
SHAREHOLDERS: 8,238
INSTITUTIONAL HOLDINGS:
No. of Institutions: 316
Shares Held: 48,537,079

REGISTRAR(S): First Chicago Trust Co. of New York, New York, NY 10008

TRANSFER AGENT(S): First Chicago Trust Co. of New York, New York, NY 10008

WACHOVIA CORP.

YIELD 3.7%
P/E RATIO 11.0

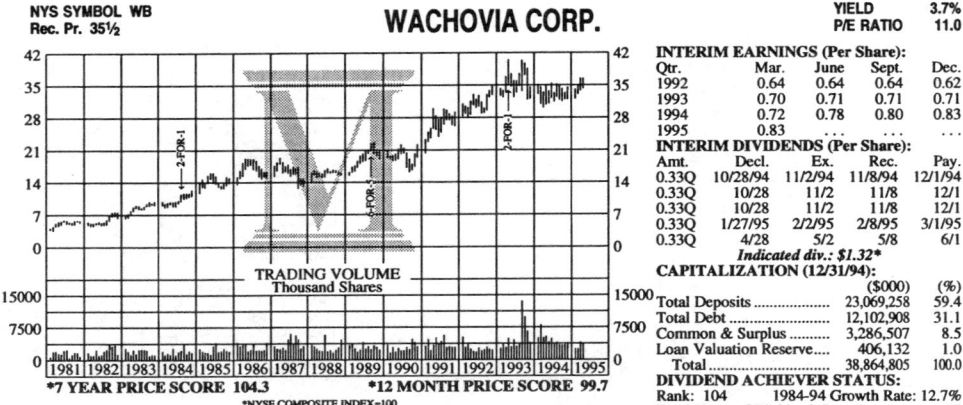

*7 YEAR PRICE SCORE 104.3   *12 MONTH PRICE SCORE 99.7

*NYSE COMPOSITE INDEX=100

TRADING VOLUME Thousand Shares

INTERIM EARNINGS (Per Share):

Qtr.	Mar.	June	Sept.	Dec.
1992	0.64	0.64	0.64	0.62
1993	0.70	0.71	0.71	0.71
1994	0.72	0.78	0.80	0.83
1995	0.83	...	...	...

INTERIM DIVIDENDS (Per Share):

Amt.	Decl.	Ex.	Rec.	Pay.
0.33Q	10/28/94	11/2/94	11/8/94	12/1/94
0.33Q	10/28	11/2	11/8	12/1
0.33Q	10/28	11/2	11/8	12/1
0.33Q	1/27/95	2/2/95	2/8/95	3/1/95
0.33Q	4/28	5/2	5/8	6/1

Indicated div.: $1.32*

CAPITALIZATION (12/31/94):

	($000)	(%)
Total Deposits	23,069,258	59.4
Total Debt	12,102,908	31.1
Common & Surplus	3,286,507	8.5
Loan Valuation Reserve	406,132	1.0
Total	38,864,805	100.0

DIVIDEND ACHIEVER STATUS:
Rank: 104   1984-94 Growth Rate: 12.7%
Total Years of Dividend Growth: 17

RECENT DEVELOPMENTS: Net income for the year ended 12/31/94 was $539.1 million, an increase of 9.5% from the $492.1 million earned in 1993. Strong loan growth, cost-control efforts and reduced credit costs were cited as reasons for results. Net interest income was $1.32 billion, up a modest 3.1% from the prior year's $1.28 billion. Average earning assets rose $3.00 billion or 10.1% while average loans grew $2.67 billion or 12.4%. Other income was $607.8 million, down 3.2% from $627.6 million.

PROSPECTS: Wachovia began a management-efficiency review recently. The Company will review all core business units in an effort to eliminate duplication and improve operating efficiency. Wachovia has put its $9.1 billion mortgage servicing portfolio up for sale, citing that the mortgage servicing business does not fit in with long-term growth plans. However, the Company will continue to originate residential mortgage loans. The robust economic climate of the Southeast bodes well for near-term earnings.

BUSINESS

WACHOVIA CORPORATION is one of the largest interstate bank holding companies in the Southeast. Its principal banking subsidiaries are Wachovia Bank of Georgia, N.A., Wachovia Bank of North Carolina, N.A., and Wachovia Bank of South Carolina, N.A. The Company operates 493 full-service banking offices in cities throughout Georgia, North Carolina and South Carolina. In addition to full-service banking, Wachovia offers investment banking, mortgage banking and a line of several other businesses to customers.

LOAN DISTRIBUTION

(12/31/94)	($000)	(%)
Commercial	10,187,478	39.3
Retail	7,402,626	28.6
Real Estate	7,857,764	30.3
Lease Financing - net	188,521	0.7
Foreign	254,415	1.1
Total	25,890,804	100.0

ANNUAL EARNINGS AND DIVIDENDS PER SHARE

	1994	1993	1992	1991	1990	1989	1988
Earnings Per Share	3.13	2.83	2.51	1.34	2.14	1.94	1.80
Dividends Per Share	1.23	1.11	① 1.00	0.92	0.82	② 0.698	0.584
Dividend Payout %	39.3	39.2	39.8	68.7	38.6	36.0	32.3

① Adj for 2-for-1 stk split, 3/1/93 ② 20% stk div, 8/31/89

ANNUAL FINANCIAL DATA

RECORD OF EARNINGS (IN MILLIONS):

	1994	1993	1992	1991	1990	1989	1988
Total Interest Income	2,362.3	2,122.8	2,222.1	2,637.0	2,137.2	2,092.1	1,718.4
Total Interest Expense	1,038.4	839.0	967.0	1,467.8	1,320.4	1,321.5	982.5
Net Interest Income	1,323.9	1,283.8	1,255.1	1,169.2	816.8	770.6	735.9
Credit Loss Provision	71.8	92.7	119.4	293.0	86.5	62.2	61.3
Net Income	539.1	492.1	433.2	229.5	297.2	269.0	244.3
Aver. Shs. Outstg. (000)	172,339	173,941	172,641	171,481	139,910	139,024	134,944

BALANCE SHEET (IN MILLIONS):

Cash & Due From Banks	2,670.1	2,529.5	2,627.9	2,475.6	3,080.1	2,737.3	2,749.2
Loans & Lse Financing, Net	25,484.7	22,572.7	20,706.1	20,257.4	16,432.9	15,102.0	13,561.7
Total Domestic Deposits	22,153.4	22,545.3	22,856.7	22,602.0	17,713.3	16,911.1	15,915.8
Total Foreign Deposits	915.9	807.1	518.8	404.3	499.1	475.5	576.2
Long-term Debt	4,790.5	2,960.5	1,196.9	170.8	113.1	171.0	178.7
Net Stockholders' Equity	3,286.5	3,017.9	2,774.8	2,484.4	1,928.7	1,739.9	1,557.3
Total Assets	39,188.0	36,525.8	33,366.5	33,158.3	26,270.8	24,049.5	21,815.2
Year End Shs Outstg (000)	170,934	171,376	171,471	170,646	139,357	128,803	137,618

STATISTICAL RECORD:

Return on Assets %	1.38	1.35	1.30	0.69	1.13	1.12	1.12
Return on Equity %	16.40	16.30	15.60	9.20	15.40	15.50	15.70
Book Value Per Share	19.23	17.61	16.18	14.56	13.84	13.51	11.32
Average Yield %	3.7	3.1	3.2	3.7	4.3	3.6	3.8
P/E Ratio	11.3-9.6	14.3-11.3	13.8-11.3	22.4-15.1	10.4-7.6	11.7-8.0	9.4-7.7
Price Range	35⅜-30⅛	40½-31⅞	34¾-28¼	30-20¼	22¼-16¼	22¾-15½	17-13⅞

Statistics are as originally reported.

OFFICERS:
J.G. Medlin, Jr., Chmn.
L.M. Baker, Jr., Pres. & C.E.O.
R.B. Roberts, Exec. V.P. & Treas.
R.S. McCoy, Jr., Exec. V.P. & C.F.O.

INCORPORATED: NC, Jul., 1985

PRINCIPAL OFFICE: 301 N. Main Street P.O. Box 3099, Winston-Salem, NC 27150

TELEPHONE NUMBER: (910) 770-5000

NO. OF EMPLOYEES: 15,602

ANNUAL MEETING: In April

SHAREHOLDERS: 579

INSTITUTIONAL HOLDINGS:
No. of Institutions: 345
Shares Held: 79,893,105

REGISTRAR(S): Wachovia Bank & Trust Co., N.A., Winston-Salem, NC 27102

TRANSFER AGENT(S): Wachovia Bank & Trust Co., N.A., Winston-Salem, NC 27102

WAL-MART STORES, INC.

YIELD 0.8%
P/E RATIO 20.8

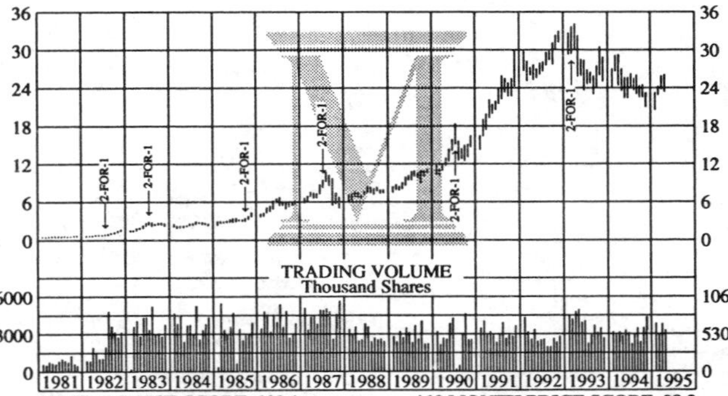

7 YEAR PRICE SCORE 100.1   *NYSE COMPOSITE INDEX=100   **12 MONTH PRICE SCORE 98.3**

INTERIM EARNINGS (Per Share):

Qtr.	Apr.	July	Oct.	Jan.
1991-92	0.14	0.15	0.16	0.26
1992-93	------------- 0.87 -------------			
1993-94	0.20	0.22	0.23	0.38
1994-95	0.22	0.25	0.26	0.45

INTERIM DIVIDENDS (Per Share):

Amt.	Decl.	Ex.	Rec.	Pay.
0.0425Q	6/2/94	6/7/94	6/13/94	7/8/94
0.0425Q	8/11	8/30	9/6	10/3
0.0425Q	11/10	11/29	12/5	1/5/95
0.05Q	3/9/95	3/15/95	3/21/95	4/14

Indicated div.: $0.20

CAPITALIZATION (1/31/95):

	($000)	(%)
Long-Term Debt	7,871,000	34.5
Cap. Lease Oblig.	1,838,000	8.0
Deferred Income Tax	411,000	1.8
Common & Surplus	12,726,000	55.7
Total	22,846,000	100.0

DIVIDEND ACHIEVER STATUS:

Rank: 4   1984-94 Growth Rate: 28.5%
Total Years of Dividend Growth: 13

RECENT DEVELOPMENTS: For the year ended 1/31/95, net income was $2.68 billion compared with $2.33 billion a year ago. Sales advanced 22.5% to $82.49 billion. As a percentage of sales, selling, general and administrative expenses increased to 15.6% from 15.3% a year ago. For the quarter ended 1/31/95, net income was $1.03 billion versus $868.0 million a year ago. Sales increased 20.1% to $24.45 billion.

PROSPECTS: Despite a slower growth rate than in previous years, and continued intense competition, Wal-Mart will continue to aggressively expand. Plans for fiscal 1995 call for the addition of 100 stores each to the domestic Discount Store and Supercenter divisions. Internationally, Wal-Mart plans to develop 50 to 60 stores in Mexico, Canada, Brazil and Argentina and 10 new clubs in the Sam's division.

BUSINESS

WAL-MART STORES, INC., as of 1/31/95, operated 2,256 discount department stores (including 143 Supercenter stores) and 428 Sam's Wholesale Clubs in 49 states, Puerto Rico and Canada. WMT also operates 72 Mexican units and 3 Hong Kong Value Clubs. Wal-Mart stores are designed to be one-stop shopping centers which provide a wide assortment of merchandise to satisfy most of the clothing, home recreational and convenience needs of the family. Supercenters combine food, general merchandise, and services including pharmacy, dry cleaning, portrait studios, photo finishing, hair salons, and optical shops. WMT also operates McLane and Western, a specialty distribution subsidiary, serving over 30,000 convenience stores and independent grocers.

QUARTERLY DATA

(01/31/95)($000)	Rev	Inc
1st Quarter	17,686,000	498,000
2nd Quarter	19,942,000	565,000
3rd Quarter	20,418,000	588,000
4th Quarter	24,448,000	1,030,000

ANNUAL EARNINGS AND DIVIDENDS PER SHARE

	1/31/95	1/31/94	1/31/93	1/31/92	1/31/91	1/31/90	1/31/89
Earnings Per Share	1.17	1.02	0.87	0.70	0.57	0.48	0.37
Dividends Per Share	0.16	0.16	①0.10	0.081	②0.066	0.052	0.04
Dividend Payout %	13.9	14.1	11.5	11.6	11.7	10.8	10.1

① 2-for-1 stk split,02/26/93 ② 2-for-1 stk split; 7/90

ANNUAL FINANCIAL DATA

RECORD OF EARNINGS (IN MILLIONS):

Total Revenues	83,412.0	67,985.0	55,985.0	44,290.0	32,863.0	25,986.0	20,786.0
Costs and Expenses	77,374.0	62,928.0	51,847.0	40,995.0	30,305.0	23,871.0	19,111.0
Depreciation & Amort	1,070.0	849.0	649.0	475.0	347.0	269.0	214.0
Operating Profit	17,826.0	14,541.0	11,810.0	9,504.0	7,363.0	5,916.0	4,729.0
Income Bef Income Taxes	4,262.0	3,691.0	3,166.0	2,553.0	2,043.0	1,708.0	1,325.0
Income Taxes	1,581.0	2,716.0	2,342.0	1,888.0	1,504.0	1,264.0	976.0
Net Income	2,681.0	2,333.0	1,995.0	1,608.0	1,291.0	1,076.0	837.0

BALANCE SHEET (IN MILLIONS):

Cash and Cash Equivalents	45.0	20.0	12.0	31.0	13.0	13.0	13.0
Receivables, Net	900.0	898.0	837.0	1,100.0	545.0	235.0	242.0
Inventories	14,064.0	11,014.0	9,268.0	7,384.0	5,809.0	4,428.0	3,351.0
Gross Property	19,237.0	15,859.0	11,848.0	8,140.0	5,995.0	4,402.0	3,391.0
Accumulated Depreciation	3,363.0	2,683.0	2,056.0	1,707.0	1,285.0	972.0	729.0
Long-Term Debt	7,871.0	6,156.0	3,073.0	1,722.0	740.0	185.0	184.0
Capital Lease Obligations	1,838.0	1,804.0	1,772.0	1,556.0	1,159.0	1,087.0	1,009.0
Net Stockholders' Equity	12,726.0	10,753.0	8,760.0	6,990.0	5,366.0	3,965.0	3,008.0
Total Assets	32,819.0	26,441.0	20,564.0	15,442.0	11,387.0	8,199.0	6,361.0
Total Current Assets	15,338.0	12,114.0	10,197.0	8,575.0	6,415.0	4,713.0	3,632.0
Total Current Liabilities	9,973.0	7,406.0	6,755.0	5,004.0	3,990.0	2,846.0	2,067.0
Net Working Capital	5,365.0	4,708.0	3,442.0	3,571.0	2,425.0	1,867.0	1,565.0
Year End Shs Outstg (000)	2,297,000	2,299,000	2,300,000	2,298,000	2,285,000	2,265,000	2,262,000

STATISTICAL RECORD:

Operating Profit Margin %	6.0	6.2	6.2	6.4	6.7	7.1	7.0
Book Value Per Share	5.54	4.68	3.81	3.04	2.35	1.75	1.31
Return on Equity %	21.1	21.7	22.8	23.0	24.1	27.1	27.8
Return on Assets %	8.2	8.8	9.7	10.4	11.3	13.1	13.2
Average Yield %	0.3	0.40.55	0.4	0.5	0.6	0.5	
P/E Ratio	25.0-17.9	33.5-22.5	37.9-28.9	42.9-20.4	32.2-17.8	23.4-15.6	23.0-16.6
Price Range	29¼-21	34⅛-23	33-25⅛	30-14¼	18⅜-10⅛	11¼-7½	8½-6⅛

Statistics are as originally reported.

OFFICERS:
S.R. Walton, Chmn.
D.D. Glass, Pres. & C.E.O.
P.R. Carter, Exec. V.P. & C.F.O.
R. K. Rhoads, Sr. V.P., Gen Coun. & Sec.

INCORPORATED: DE, Oct., 1969

PRINCIPAL OFFICE: 702 Southwest 8th St, Bentonville, AR 72716

TELEPHONE NUMBER: (501) 273-4000

NO. OF EMPLOYEES: 622,000 (approx.)

ANNUAL MEETING: In June

SHAREHOLDERS: 259,286

INSTITUTIONAL HOLDINGS:
No. of Institutions: 738
Shares Held: 345,463,181

REGISTRAR(S): Boatmen's Trust Co,, St. Louis, MO

TRANSFER AGENT(S): Boatmen's Trust Co. St. Louis, MO

WALGREEN CO.

YIELD 1.7%
P/E RATIO 18.9

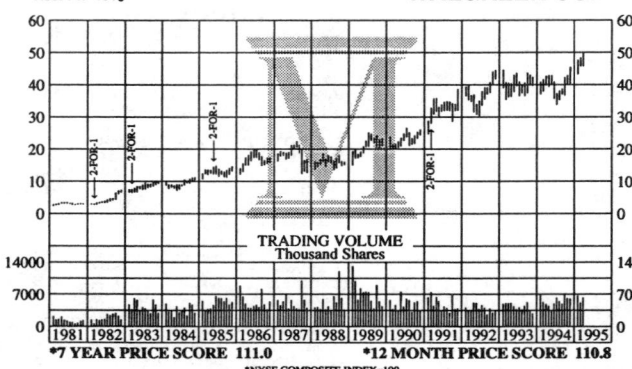

TRADING VOLUME
Thousand Shares

*7 YEAR PRICE SCORE 111.0   *12 MONTH PRICE SCORE 110.8
*NYSE COMPOSITE INDEX=100

INTERIM EARNINGS (Per Share):

Qtr.	Nov.	Feb.	May	Aug.
1991-92	0.29	0.62	0.46	0.41
1992-93	----------------	1.98	----------------	
1993-94	0.36	0.79	0.57	0.56
1994-95	0.44	0.90	...	...

INTERIM DIVIDENDS (Per Share):

Amt.	Decl.	Ex.	Rec.	Pay.
0.17Q	4/13/94	5/16/94	5/20/94	6/11/94
0.17Q	7/13	8/16	8/22	9/12
0.195Q	10/12	11/7	11/14	12/12
0.195Q	1/11/95	2/15/95	2/22/95	3/11/95
0.195Q	4/12	5/16	5/22	6/12

*Indicated div.: $0.78**

CAPITALIZATION (8/31/94):

	($000)	(%)
Deferred Income Tax	173,649	9.9
Common & Surplus	1,573,640	90.1
Total	1,747,289	100.0

DIVIDEND ACHIEVER STATUS:
Rank: 77   1984-94 Growth Rate: 14.0%
Total Years of Dividend Growth: 19

RECENT DEVELOPMENTS: For the quarter ended 11/30/94, net income was $54.0 million compared with $44.2 million a year earlier. Net sales increased 13.6% to $2.41 billion. Comparable store sales increased 7.8%, despite continued low inflation in pharmaceuticals and general merchandise. The increase in earnings was aided by strong sales in the pharmacy and self-service merchandise areas. Gross margin declined to 27.6% of sales from 27.8% in the prior-year.

PROSPECTS: The Company should continue to grow with the aid of new store openings and increased demand for prescriptions. Capital spending is expected to reach $300 million in fiscal 1995 with most of this targeted for new stores and high technology systems. WAG's expansion program in fiscal 1995 calls for the opening of 200 full-service drugstores, including new market entries into the Seattle/Tacoma area.

BUSINESS

WALGREEN CO. is the largest retail drugstore chain in the United States. At 12/31/94, the Company operated 2,017 drugstores located in 30 states and Puerto Rico. Forty-five percent of stores are located in Florida, Illinois and Texas. These stores serve more than 1.8 million customers a day and average over $4.7 million in annual sales per unit, or $473 per square foot. Walgreen drugstores are served by eight major distribution centers and five photo-processing plants. Pharmacy comprised 41% of fiscal 1994 total sales; general merchandise, 24%; nonprescription drugs, 13%; liquor and beverages, 9%; cosmetics and toiletries, 9%; and tobacco, 4%.

QUARTERLY DATA

(8/31/94) ($000)	Rev	Inc
1st Quarter	2,117,954	44,213
2nd Quarter	2,498,537	97,615
3rd Quarter	2,335,961	71,018
4th Quarter	2,282,526	69,083

ANNUAL EARNINGS AND DIVIDENDS PER SHARE

	8/31/94	8/31/93	8/31/92	8/31/91	8/31/90	8/31/89	8/31/88
Earnings Per Share	2.28	[1] 1.98	1.78	1.58	1.41	1.25	1.05
Dividends Per Share	0.705	0.62	0.54	[2] 0.475	0.415	0.355	0.31
Dividend Payout %	30.9	31.3	30.3	30.1	29.3	28.4	29.5

[1] Before acctg. chg.   [2] 2-for-1 stk split,02/04/91

ANNUAL FINANCIAL DATA

RECORD OF EARNINGS (IN MILLIONS):

	8/31/94	8/31/93	8/31/92	8/31/91	8/31/90	8/31/89	8/31/88
Total Revenues	9,235.0	8,294.8	7,475.0	6,733.0	6,047.5	5,380.1	4,883.5
Costs and Expenses	8,661.2	7,784.0	7,024.4	6,327.6	5,692.9	5,062.9	4,599.9
Depreciation & Amort	118.1	104.7	92.1	84.3	70.4	63.8	59.4
Operating Profit	2,620.5	2,335.8	2,097.2	1,903.9	1,691.1	1,531.6	1,414.5
Earn Bef Inc Tax Provision	458.4	399.7	353.0	311.9	280.9	243.8	209.0
Income Taxes	176.5	154.4	132.4	117.0	106.3	89.6	79.9
Net Income	281.9	[1] 245.3	220.6	195.0	174.6	154.2	129.1
Aver. Shs. Outstg. (000)	123,646	123,770	123,671	123,582	123,393	123,287	123,162

[1] Before acctg. change dr$23,623,000.

BALANCE SHEET (IN MILLIONS):

Cash and Cash Equivalents	108.4	121.3	225.6	135.1	213.9	225.5	209.7
Receivables, Net	193.9	139.3	136.1	132.4	97.6	93.4	76.1
Inventories	1,263.4	1,094.0	994.2	912.0	828.0	728.5	655.4
Gross Property	1,597.2	1,380.5	1,258.3	1,154.6	993.0	831.0	757.6
Accumulated Depreciation	511.8	453.2	402.0	345.3	295.9	252.1	220.7
Long-Term Debt	...	...	18.7	123.0	146.7	150.1	172.1
Net Stockholders' Equity	1,573.6	1,378.8	1,233.3	1,081.2	947.2	823.4	712.6
Total Assets	2,908.7	2,535.2	2,373.6	2,094.6	1,913.6	1,681.1	1,511.9
Total Current Assets	1,672.8	1,463.1	1,438.8	1,247.4	1,187.0	1,083.0	974.3
Total Current Liabilities	1,050.7	883.5	889.3	683.8	632.3	544.9	488.6
Net Working Capital	622.1	579.6	549.6	563.6	554.8	538.1	485.7
Year End Shs Outstg (000)	123,071	123,071	123,071	123,071	123,048	123,033	123,028

STATISTICAL RECORD:

Operating Profit Margin %	4.9	4.9	4.8	4.8	4.7	4.7	4.6
Book Value Per Share	12.79	11.20	10.02	8.78	7.70	6.69	5.79
Return on Equity %	17.9	17.8	17.9	18.0	18.4	18.7	18.1
Return on Assets %	9.7	9.7	9.3	9.3	9.1	9.2	8.5
Average Yield %	1.8	1.6	1.4	1.5	1.8	1.8	1.9
P/E Ratio	19.9-14.8	22.5-17.9	25.0-17.1	24.4-15.7	18.9-14.2	20.1-12.0	17.9-13.0
Price Range	45⅜-33¾	44⅝-35⅜	44½-30⅜	38⅝-24¾	26⅝-20	25⅛-15	18¾-13⅝

Statistics are as originally reported.

OFFICERS:
C.R. Walgreen, III, Chmn. & C.E.O.
C.D. Hunter, Vice Chmn. & C.F.O.
L.D. Jorndt, Pres. & C.O.O.
J.A. Oettinger, V.P., Gen. Couns. & Sec.
W.L. Earnest, V.P. & Treas.

INCORPORATED: IL, Feb., 1909

PRINCIPAL OFFICE: 200 Wilmot Rd.,
Deerfield, IL 60015

TELEPHONE NUMBER: (708) 940-2500

NO. OF EMPLOYEES: 42,000 full-time
(approx.); 19,900 part-time (approx.)

ANNUAL MEETING: In January

SHAREHOLDERS: 29,910

INSTITUTIONAL HOLDINGS:
No. of Institutions: 409
Shares Held: 59,450,683

REGISTRAR(S): Harris Trust & Savings
Bank, Chicago, IL

TRANSFER AGENT(S): Harris Trust &
Savings Bank, Chicago, IL

WALLACE COMPUTER SERVICES, INC.

YIELD 2.2%
P/E RATIO 15.3

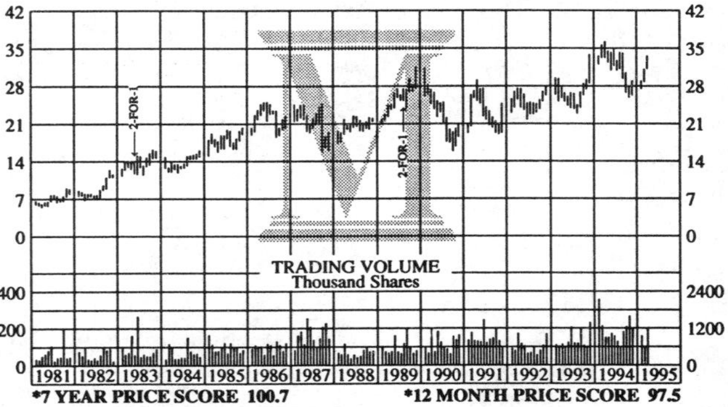

TRADING VOLUME
Thousand Shares

| 1981 | 1982 | 1983 | 1984 | 1985 | 1986 | 1987 | 1988 | 1989 | 1990 | 1991 | 1992 | 1993 | 1994 | 1995 |

*7 YEAR PRICE SCORE 100.7   *12 MONTH PRICE SCORE 97.5

*NYSE COMPOSITE INDEX=100

INTERIM EARNINGS (Per Share):

Qtr.	Oct.	Jan.	Apr.	July
1991-92	0.41	0.49	0.43	0.43
1992-93	---------- 1.84 ----------			
1993-94	0.50	0.58	0.52	0.53
1994-95	0.52	0.60	...	...

INTERIM DIVIDENDS (Per Share):

Amt.	Decl.	Ex.	Rec.	Pay.
0.16Q	3/9/94	5/25/94	6/1/94	6/20/94
0.16Q	6/8	8/26	9/1	9/20
0.185Q	11/9	11/25	12/1	12/20
0.185Q	1/26/95	2/23/95	3/1/95	3/20/95
0.185Q	3/8	5/25	6/1	6/20

Indicated div.: $0.74

CAPITALIZATION (7/31/94):

	($000)	(%)
Long-Term Debt	23,500	5.1
Deferred Income Tax	22,183	4.9
Common & Surplus	410,139	90.0
Total	455,822	100.0

DIVIDEND ACHIEVER STATUS:

Rank: 110   1984-94 Growth Rate: 12.4%
Total Years of Dividend Growth: 23

RECENT DEVELOPMENTS: For the quarter ended 1/31/95, net income increased 5% to $13.4 million from $12.8 million in the same period a year ago. Net sales rose 15% to $176.2 million from $153.1 million in the year-earlier period. The Company reported improved earnings compared with the second quarter of the year before, primarily due to strong sales growth from each product group. WCS increased paper prices to offset the higher paper costs.

PROSPECTS: Sales growth will be driven by label products and the Colorforms division. Operations should benefit from capacity expansion in North Carolina and Georgia. The Company will also build a new plant in Kentucky. Margins will be enhanced by cost-containment efforts and improved manufacturing efficiencies. However, these gains will be partially offset by anticipated increases in paper prices.

BUSINESS

WALLACE COMPUTER SER-VICES is engaged primarily in the computer services and supply industry. The Company provides its customers with a full line of products and services in the business forms, commercial printing, computer labels, machine ribbons, computer hardware and software, and computer accessory supplies market. Principal products include the design, manufacture and sale of business forms, industrial and consumer catalogues, directories and price lists, pressure-sensitive labels, and one-time carbon paper and carbon inks. The Company also markets accessory supplies, computer software, tax and utility billing forms, and computer and business machine ribbons.

QUARTERLY DATA

(7/31/94)($000)	Rev	Inc
1st Quarter...............	144,510	11,651
2nd Quarter...............	153,122	12,833
3rd Quarter	141,472	11,576
4th Quarter...............	149,069	11,871

ANNUAL EARNINGS AND DIVIDENDS PER SHARE

	7/31/94	7/31/93	7/31/92	7/31/91	7/31/90	7/31/89	7/31/88
Earnings Per Share	2.13	1.84	1.76	1.63	1.86	1.76	1.53
Dividends Per Share	0.665	0.595	0.55	0.51	① 0.47	0.415	② 0.348
Dividend Payout %	31.2	32.3	31.3	31.3	25.3	23.6	22.8

① 2-for-1 stk split, 8/1/89 ② 2-for-1 stk split; 8/89.

ANNUAL FINANCIAL DATA

RECORD OF EARNINGS (IN THOUSANDS):

Total Revenues	588,173	545,315	511,572	458,840	448,700	429,008	383,045
Costs and Expenses	483,537	454,129	428,155	387,226	374,851	358,746	321,218
Depreciation & Amort	33,006	30,299	28,580	22,454	18,403	16,953	14,390
Operating Profit	71,630	60,887	54,837	49,160	55,446	53,309	47,437
Income Bef Income Taxes	73,856	62,379	59,780	53,860	60,854	56,542	48,631
Income Taxes	26,588	21,209	20,325	18,851	21,299	19,675	17,021
Net Income	① 47,268	41,170	39,455	35,009	39,555	36,867	31,610
Aver. Shs. Outstg.	22,193	22,348	22,418	21,526	21,278	21,007	20,748

① Before acctg. change cr$663,000.

BALANCE SHEET (IN THOUSANDS):

Cash and Cash Equivalents	76,998	46,930	55,119	52,325	54,402	60,922	78,824
Receivables, Net	95,178	92,775	89,193	75,630	69,085	64,604	59,762
Inventories	69,543	68,690	56,038	53,534	59,327	50,613	52,072
Gross Property	432,244	398,846	371,035	315,810	277,790	230,911	205,089
Accumulated Depreciation	199,382	170,975	145,691	123,459	105,360	91,278	78,034
Long-Term Debt	23,500	25,210	25,959	19,790	20,155	20,465	20,830
Net Stockholders' Equity	410,139	368,146	355,564	308,809	279,446	244,080	211,001
Total Assets	538,592	480,722	467,142	399,093	375,203	331,830	331,176
Total Current Assets	248,226	213,104	205,200	184,331	186,556	179,164	193,286
Total Current Liabilities	64,794	55,167	52,954	42,941	48,958	40,946	36,735
Net Working Capital	183,432	157,937	152,246	141,390	137,598	138,218	156,551
Year End Shares Outstg	22,393	22,061	22,606	21,722	21,433	21,169	20,912

STATISTICAL RECORD:

Operating Profit Margin %	12.2	11.2	10.7	10.7	12.4	12.4	12.4
Book Value Per Share	17.61	15.95	15.00	14.15	12.97	11.46	10.02
Return on Equity %	11.5	11.2	11.1	11.3	14.2	15.1	15.0
Return on Assets %	8.8	8.6	8.4	8.8	10.5	11.1	9.5
Average Yield %	2.1	2.1	2.2	2.1	2.0	1.6	1.8
P/E Ratio	17.0-12.1	18.4-12.4	15.9-12.4	17.9-11.7	16.9-8.5	17.9-11.9	14.7-11.3
Price Range	36¼-25⅞	33⅞-22⅞	28-21¾	29⅛-19	31½-15⅞	31½-21	22½-17¼

Statistics are as originally reported.

OFFICERS:
T. Dimitriou, Chmn.
R.J. Cronin, Pres. & C.E.O.
M.J. Halloran, V.P. & C.F.O.
M.T. Quane, Treas.
M.T. Laudizio, Corp. Sec.

INCORPORATED: DE, Jun., 1963

PRINCIPAL OFFICE: 4600 West Roosevelt Road, Hillside, IL 60162

TELEPHONE NUMBER: (312) 626-2000

NO. OF EMPLOYEES: 3,530

ANNUAL MEETING: In November

SHAREHOLDERS: 3,985

INSTITUTIONAL HOLDINGS:
No. of Institutions: 161
Shares Held: 15,688,807

REGISTRAR(S): Harris Trust & Savings Bank, Chicago, IL

TRANSFER AGENT(S): Harris Trust & Savings Bank, Chicago, IL

WARNER-LAMBERT CO.

YIELD 3.3%
P/E RATIO 15.2

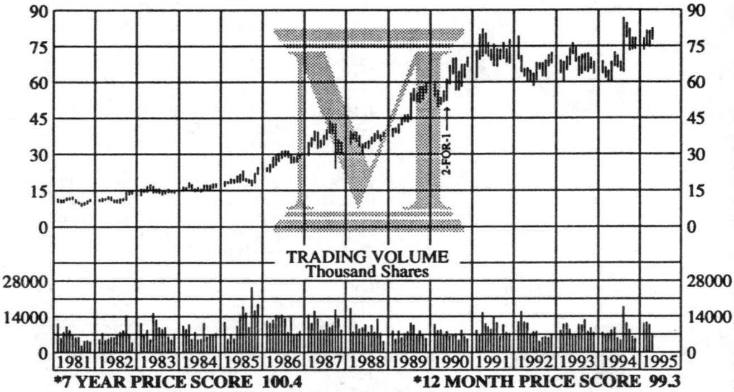

7 YEAR PRICE SCORE 100.4   **12 MONTH PRICE SCORE 99.3**
*NYSE COMPOSITE INDEX=100

INTERIM EARNINGS (Per Share):

Qtr.	Mar.	June	Sept.	Dec.
1991	1.04	1.15	1.07	d2.21
1992	1.22	1.32	1.22	1.02
1993	1.35	1.40	1.16	d1.46
1994	1.42	1.47	1.26	1.02

INTERIM DIVIDENDS (Per Share):

Amt.	Decl.	Ex.	Rec.	Pay.
0.61Q	4/26/94	5/2/94	5/6/94	6/10/94
0.61Q	7/26	8/1	8/5	9/9
0.61Q	10/25	10/31	11/4	12/9
0.65Q	1/24/95	1/30/95	2/3/95	3/10/95
0.65Q	4/25	5/1	5/5	6/9

*Indicated div.: $2.60**

CAPITALIZATION (12/31/94):

	($000)	(%)
Long-Term Debt	535,200	22.6
Minority Interest	21,300	0.9
Common & Surplus	1,816,400	76.5
Total	2,372,900	100.0

DIVIDEND ACHIEVER STATUS:
Rank: 104   1984-94 Growth Rate: 12.7%
Total Years of Dividend Growth: 42

RECENT DEVELOPMENTS: For the year ended 12/31/94, net income amounted to $694.0 million compared with $285.0 million, before an accounting adjustment, the previous year. Sales were up 10.8% to $6.42 billion from $5.79 billion in 1993. The prior-year results included an after-tax restructuring charge of $360.4 million. Consumer Sector sales advanced 18% to $4.34 billion due in part to alliances and acquisitions. Pharmaceutical Sector sales fell 2% to $2.08 billion.

PROSPECTS: The Company will make an initial capital investment of approximately $30 million over the next three years to establish a joint venture confectionery-products operation in China. The plant will be located in Guangzhou, near Hong Kong, and will produce Halls, Chiclets and Clorets. Sales of Zantac, for the treatment of episodic heartburn, will benefit from an OTC marketing clearance in the United Kingdom.

BUSINESS

WARNER LAMBERT COMPANY develops, manufactures and markets ethical pharmaceuticals and non-prescription health care products. Non-prescription health care products include Benadryl antiallergy medication, Lubriderm skin lotion, Rolaids antacid, Efferdent denture cleanser, Halls cough tablets, and Listerine. Other products include Schick razors and blades, Tetra pet care products and empty gelatin capsules for pharmaceutical use.

BUSINESS LINE ANALYSIS

(12/31/94)	Rev(%)	Inc(%)
Consumer Health		
Care	46.3	42.1
Confectionery	21.3	15.6
Pharmaceutical	32.4	42.3
Total	100.0	100.0

ANNUAL EARNINGS AND DIVIDENDS PER SHARE

	1994	1993	1992	1991	1990	1989	1988
Earnings Per Share	5.17	2.11	4.78	① 1.05	3.61	3.05	2.50
Dividends Per Share	2.44	2.28	2.04	1.76	② 1.52	1.28	1.08
Dividend Payout %	47.2	N.M.	42.7	N.M.	42.1	42.0	43.2

① Before acctg. chg. ② 2-for-1 stk split; 5/90

ANNUAL FINANCIAL DATA

RECORD OF EARNINGS (IN MILLIONS):

	1994	1993	1992	1991	1990	1989	1988
Total Revenues	6,416.8	5,793.7	5,597.6	5,166.6	4,773.8	4,272.0	3,970.3
Costs and Expenses	5,224.3	5,333.9	4,608.7	4,751.4	3,904.7	3,520.0	3,267.4
Depreciation & Amort	181.4	170.4	155.6	135.5	119.7	104.8	96.4
Operating Profit	1,467.1	1,279.5	1,306.8	1,246.9	1,128.7	956.0	865.9
Income Before Income Tax	1,005.3	318.5	858.2	221.5	680.7	591.6	538.3
Income Taxes	219.1	67.0	214.5	80.7	195.8	178.9	198.0
Net Income	694.0	① 140.8	643.7	② 140.8	484.9	412.7	340.3
Aver. Shs. Outstg. (000)	134,100	135,000	134,717	134,441	134,330	135,336	136,070

① Before acctg. change cr$46,000,000. ② Before acctg. change dr$106,000,000.

BALANCE SHEET (IN MILLIONS):

	1994	1993	1992	1991	1990	1989	1988
Cash and Cash Equivalents	465.1	440.5	718.4	535.7	306.1	252.5	176.6
Receivables, Net	1,096.0	890.8	752.8	650.5	634.4	532.8	525.2
Inventories	636.2	476.5	424.6	418.5	412.8	374.3	381.4
Gross Property	3,167.6	2,834.2	2,546.1	2,323.5	2,127.9	1,884.2	1,761.6
Accumulated Depreciation	1,321.6	1,234.9	1,039.0	973.5	826.5	751.7	708.6
Long-Term Debt	535.2	546.2	564.6	447.9	306.8	303.4	318.2
Net Stockholders' Equity	1,816.4	1,389.6	1,528.5	1,170.7	1,402.3	1,129.8	998.6
Total Assets	5,532.8	4,828.1	4,077.4	3,602.0	3,261.3	2,859.8	2,702.8
Total Current Assets	2,515.3	2,218.7	2,176.3	1,843.7	1,558.6	1,366.5	1,264.5
Total Current Liabilities	2,353.4	2,015.9	1,333.3	1,249.9	1,100.7	1,031.3	1,025.2
Net Working Capital	161.9	202.8	843.0	593.8	457.9	335.2	239.3
Year End Shs Outstg (000)	134,595	134,140	135,340	134,594	134,341	134,842	160,330

STATISTICAL RECORD:

	1994	1993	1992	1991	1990	1989	1988
Operating Profit Margin %	15.8	5.0	14.9	5.4	15.7	15.1	15.3
Book Value Per Share	10.67	8.02	10.14	7.52	9.24	7.34	5.30
Return on Equity %	38.2	20.5	42.1	12.0	34.6	36.5	34.1
Return on Assets %	12.5	5.9	15.8	3.9	14.9	14.4	12.6
Average Yield %	3.3	3.3	3.0	2.4	2.5	2.6	3.1
P/E Ratio	16.8-11.6	36.2-28.3	16.6-12.2	78.3-58.8	19.5-13.7	19.5-12.2	15.9-12.0
Price Range	86¾-60	76⅜-59¾	79¼-58⅜	82¼-61¾	70⅜-49⅝	59⅜-37¼	39¾-30

Statistics are as originally reported.

OFFICERS:
M.R. Goodes, Chmn. & C.E.O.
L.J. De Vink, Pres. & C.O.O.
E.J. Larini, V.P. & C.F.O.
W.S. Woodson, V.P. & Treas.
R.G. Paltiel, Sec.
INCORPORATED: DE, Nov., 1920
PRINCIPAL OFFICE: 201 Tabor Rd., Morris Plains, NJ 07950-2693

TELEPHONE NUMBER: (201) 540-2000
NO. OF EMPLOYEES: 36,000 (approx.)
ANNUAL MEETING: In April
SHAREHOLDERS: 43,000 (approx.)
INSTITUTIONAL HOLDINGS:
No. of Institutions: 702
Shares Held: 85,947,022

REGISTRAR(S): First Chicago Trust Co. of New York, New York, NY 10008

TRANSFER AGENT(S): First Chicago Trust Co. of New York, New York, NY 10008

NYS SYMBOL WGL
Rec. Pr. 38⅛

WASHINGTON GAS LIGHT CO.

YIELD 5.9%
P/E RATIO 13.4

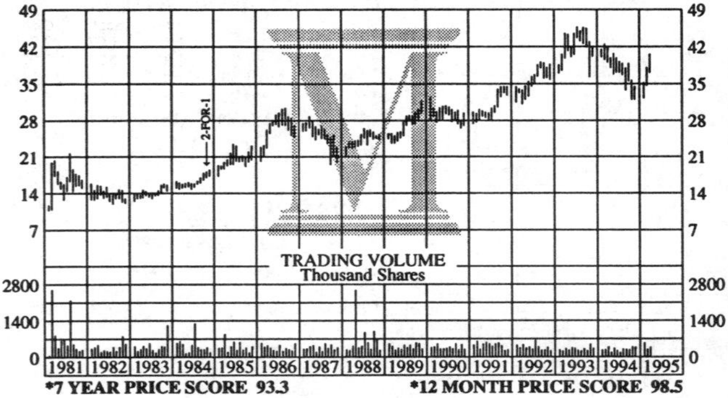

*7 YEAR PRICE SCORE 93.3 *12 MONTH PRICE SCORE 98.5
*NYSE COMPOSITE INDEX=100

INTERIM EARNINGS (Per Share):

Qtr.	Dec.	Mar.	June	Sept.
1990-91	1.22	1.95	d0.29	d0.59
1991-92	1.24	2.14	d0.15	d0.69
1992-93	----------	2.62	----------	
1993-94	1.44	2.62	d0.50	d0.71

INTERIM DIVIDENDS (Per Share):

Amt.	Decl.	Ex.	Rec.	Pay.
0.555Q	6/29/94	7/6/94	7/12/94	8/1/94
0.555Q	9/28	10/4	10/11	11/1
0.555Q	12/14	1/4/95	1/10/95	2/1/95
0.56Q	3/29/95	4/4	4/10	5/1

Indicated div.:$2.24*

CAPITALIZATION (9/30/94):

	($000)	(%)
Long-Term Debt	342,270	34.3
Deferred Income Tax	140,391	14.1
Preferred Stock	28,498	2.9
Common & Surplus	485,504	48.7
Total	996,663	100.0
Current Debt	8,560	

DIVIDEND ACHIEVER STATUS:
Rank: 303 1984-94 Growth Rate: 3.8%
Total Years of Dividend Growth: 18

RECENT DEVELOPMENTS: For the quarter ended 12/31/94, net income was $27.7 million compared with $30.3 million for the corresponding period of 1993. Operating revenues dropped 10% to $242.9 million versus $271.2 million for the same quarter a year earlier. Results for the current quarter were adversely affected by weather that was 23% warmer than for the same period in the prior year and 14.5% warmer than normal.

PROSPECTS: The Company is proposing an innovative rate design and market pricing to help increase shareholder value. The proposal will be accomplished through providing new service offerings, improving productivity, and cost-effectively increasing customers and sales. The Company's service area is experiencing higher conversion rates, which should provide higher earnings in the future.

BUSINESS

WASHINGTON GAS LIGHT CO. distributes natural gas to Washington D.C. and adjoining areas through three divisions: District of Columbia Natural Gas, Maryland Natural Gas, and Northern Virginia Natural Gas. WGL also has five active subsidiaries: Shenandoah Gas, Frederick Gas and Hampshire Gas, which provide gas service to areas in Virginia and West Virginia; Crab Run Gas, which is involved in the exploration and development of natural gas prospects; and Washington Resources Group, which conducts the Company's non-gas investments including real estate, energy-related services and equity holdings in emerging growth companies. Consolidated gas sales for 1994 were: 54.9% residential, 30.5% commercial and industrial, 10.7% interruptible and 2.4% interruptible-electric generation, transportation 0.2%.

QUARTERLY DATA

(9/30/94)($000)	Rev	Inc
1st Quarter	271,222	30,252
2nd Quarter	410,184	54,958
3rd Quarter	130,907	10,129
4th Quarter	102,550	14,622

ANNUAL EARNINGS AND DIVIDENDS PER SHARE

	9/30/94	9/30/93	9/30/92	9/30/91	9/30/90	9/30/89	9/30/88
Earnings Per Share	**2.83**	**2.62**	**2.53**	**2.28**	**2.51**	**2.43**	**2.52**
Dividends Per Share	**2.21**	**2.17**	**2.13**	**2.085**	**2.02**	**1.94**	**1.86**
Dividend Payout %	**78.1**	**82.8**	**84.2**	**91.4**	**80.5**	**79.8**	**73.8**

Note: 2-for-1stk.split,5/1/95.

ANNUAL FINANCIAL DATA

RECORD OF EARNINGS (IN MILLIONS):							
Total Revenues	914.9	894.3	746.2	697.9	735.5	755.6	698.0
Depreciation & Amort	49.0	42.7	42.7	36.1	36.1	32.8	29.4
Maintenance	35.8	33.5	31.4	30.9	32.3	31.4	30.0
Prov for Fed Inc Taxes	37.3	34.6	31.5	26.9	29.3	26.8	25.3
Operating Income	92.3	86.0	82.2	70.8	75.7	68.7	65.6
Interest Expense	32.1	29.1	28.0	27.4	28.3	25.1	22.8
Net Income	60.5	55.1	52.2	46.4	50.2	47.3	45.1
Aver. Shs. Outstg. (000)	20,918	20,522	20,122	19,777	19,478	18,907	17,021
BALANCE SHEET (IN MILLIONS):							
Gross Plant	1,516.2	1,405.3	1,313.5	1,240.4	1,186.1	1,108.7	1,037.6
Accumulated Depreciation	521.2	484.2	449.0	419.3	402.8	379.7	361.3
Prop, Plant & Equip, Net	995.0	921.1	864.5	821.1	783.3	729.0	676.2
Long-term Debt	342.3	347.7	294.5	263.0	279.6	296.8	252.5
Net Stockholders' Equity	514.0	486.6	461.7	441.0	427.5	410.1	411.2
Total Assets	1,333.0	1,194.7	1,065.7	1,013.9	967.5	924.0	922.5
Year End Shs Outstg (000)	21,093	20,752	20,308	19,944	19,614	19,352	17,148
STATISTICAL RECORD:							
Book Value Per Share	23.02	22.07	21.33	20.68	20.33	19.71	22.30
Op. Inc/Net Pl %	9.3	9.3	9.5	8.6	9.7	9.4	9.7
Dep/Gr. Pl %	2.9	2.8	2.8	2.9	3.0	3.0	2.8
Accum. Dep/Gr. Pl %	34.4	34.5	34.2	33.8	34.0	34.2	34.8
Return on Equity %	11.8	11.3	11.3	10.5	11.7	11.5	11.0
Average Yield %	5.9	5.3	6.1	6.7	6.8	7.0	7.8
P/E Ratio	15.0-11.3	17.5-13.8	15.5-12.3	15.1-12.0	12.9-10.6	13.1-9.7	10.5-8.4
Price Range	42½-32	45¾-36¼	39⅛-31⅛	34½-27⅜	32½-26½	31¾-23⅝	26½-21⅛

Statistics are as originally reported.

OFFICERS:
P.J. Maher, Chmn. & C.E.O.
J.H. DeGraffenreidt, Jr., Pres. & C.O.O.
J.M. Schepis, Sr. V.P. & C.F.O.
E.M. Arnold, Treas.
D.V. Pope, Sec.

INCORPORATED: DC, Mar., 1957

PRINCIPAL OFFICE: 1100 H Street, N.W., Washington, DC 20080

TELEPHONE NUMBER: (703) 750-4440

FAX: (202) 624-6196

NO. OF EMPLOYEES: 2,647

ANNUAL MEETING: In February

SHAREHOLDERS: 24,843

INSTITUTIONAL HOLDINGS:
No. of Institutions: 128
Shares Held: 4,695,020

REGISTRAR(S): Riggs National Bank of Washington, D.C., 808 17th Street, N.W., Suite 240, Washington, DC 20006-3950

TRANSFER AGENT(S): Riggs National Bank of Washington, D.C., 808 17th Street, N.W., Suite 240, Washington, DC 20006-3950

WASHINGTON REAL ESTATE INVESTMENT TRUST

YIELD 6.2%
P/E RATIO 18.5

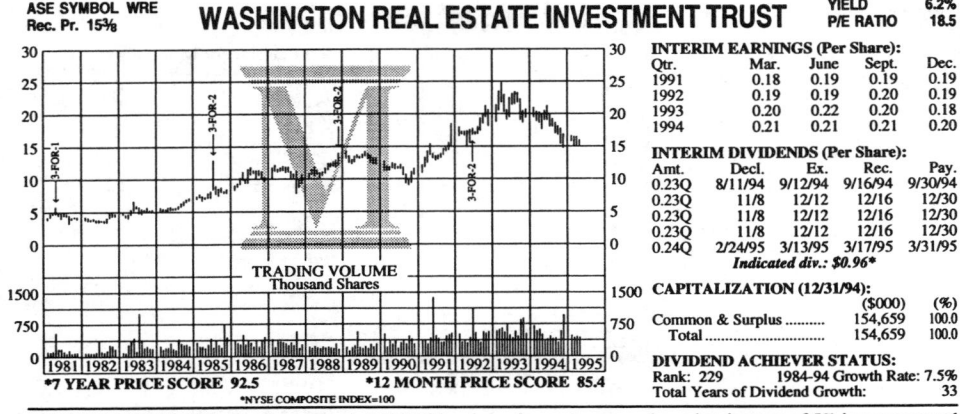

INTERIM EARNINGS (Per Share):

Qtr.	Mar.	June	Sept.	Dec.
1991	0.18	0.19	0.19	0.19
1992	0.19	0.19	0.20	0.19
1993	0.20	0.22	0.20	0.18
1994	0.21	0.21	0.21	0.20

INTERIM DIVIDENDS (Per Share):

Amt.	Decl.	Ex.	Rec.	Pay.
0.23Q	8/11/94	9/12/94	9/16/94	9/30/94
0.23Q	11/8	12/12	12/16	12/30
0.23Q	11/8	12/12	12/16	12/30
0.23Q	11/8	12/12	12/16	12/30
0.24Q	2/24/95	3/13/95	3/17/95	3/31/95

Indicated div.: $0.96*

TRADING VOLUME
Thousand Shares

1981|1982|1983|1984|1985|1986|1987|1988|1989|1990|1991|1992|1993|1994|1995

*7 YEAR PRICE SCORE 92.5   ***12 MONTH PRICE SCORE 85.4**

NYSE COMPOSITE INDEX=100

CAPITALIZATION (12/31/94):

	($000)	(%)
Common & Surplus	154,659	100.0
Total	154,659	100.0

DIVIDEND ACHIEVER STATUS:
Rank: 229   1984-94 Growth Rate: 7.5%
Total Years of Dividend Growth: 33

RECENT DEVELOPMENTS: For the year ended 12/31/94, net income was $23.1 million compared with $22.5 million, before a gain on sale of real estate of $741,217, for the corresponding period of 1993. Rental revenue advanced 15.6% to $45.5 million from $39.4 million a year earlier. Revenues were bolstered by the office building group achieving an increase of 34% in revenues and 36% in operating income, mostly due to the acquisition of buildings. The shop-

ping center group showed an increase of 5% in revenues and 3% in operating income, due to the acquisition of the Shoppes at Foxchase in June of 1994. WRE's business center group showed a 17% increase in revenues and a 15% increase in operating income, due to the acquisition of the Charleston business center and major occupancy increases at the Fullerton and Port Royal properties, which were offset by a vacancy increase at the V Street property.

BUSINESS

WASHINGTON R.E. INVESTMENT TRUST is a self-administered qualified equity real estate investment trust. The Trust's business consists of the ownership of income-producing real estate properties principally in the Washington, D.C. metropolitan area. Upon the purchase of a property, WRE begins a program of improving real estate to increase the value and to improve the operations with the goals of generating higher rental income and reducing expenses. The Trust currently owns a diversified portfolio consisting of eleven shopping centers, thirteen office buildings, five high-rise apartment buildings and eight business centers. WRE's principal objective is to invest in high quality, real estate in prime locations and to monitor closely the management of these properties, which includes active leasing and ongoing capital improvement programs.

ANNUAL EARNINGS AND DIVIDENDS PER SHARE

	1994	1993	1992	1991	1990	1989	1988
Earnings Per Share	0.82	0.80	0.76	0.75	0.69	0.64	0.56
Dividends Per Share	0.92	0.89	① 0.836	0.787	0.733	0.68	② 0.633
Dividend Payout %	N.M.	N.M.	N.M.	N.M.	N.M.	N.M.	N.M.

① 3-for-2 stk split, 6/1/92   ② 3-for-2 stk split, 12/88.

ANNUAL FINANCIAL DATA

RECORD OF EARNINGS (IN THOUSANDS):

Total Revenues	45,511	39,375	34,132	33,311	30,233	27,678	25,713
Costs and Expenses	17,247	14,648	13,138	12,850	12,165	11,526	10,876
Depreciation	3,978	3,656	3,422	3,321	3,108	3,015	2,753
Operating Profit	24,287	21,071	17,753	17,141	14,961	13,138	12,084
Net Income	23,122	23,247	20,429	18,386	16,122	14,266	11,573
Aver. Shs. Outstg.	28,243	28,223	26,910	24,708	23,223	22,269	20,664

BALANCE SHEET (IN THOUSANDS):

Cash and Cash Equivalents	2,736	18,044	55,565	40,862	14,173	27,598	4,228
Receivables, Net	2,207	2,473	1,498	1,562	1,121	933	998
Long-Term Debt	...	...	1,115	11,329	12,379	12,012	12,463
Net Stockholders' Equity	154,659	157,348	159,027	119,944	90,621	91,479	61,564
Total Assets	178,806	162,011	185,673	135,741	106,955	106,518	76,511
Total Current Assets	8,217	24,005	60,369	45,524	18,066	30,500	7,203
Total Current Liabilities	25,665	5,981	26,618	5,387	4,851	3,886	3,359
Net Working Capital	d17,448	18,023	33,751	40,138	13,215	26,614	3,844
Year End Shares Outstg	28,243	28,228	28,211	25,594	23,765	23,217	20,667

STATISTICAL RECORD:

Return on Equity %	15.0	14.8	12.8	15.3	17.8	15.6	18.8
Return on Assets %	12.9	14.4	11.0	13.6	15.1	13.4	15.1
Book Value Per Share	5.48	5.57	5.64	4.69	3.81	3.94	2.98
Average Yield %	5.1	4.1	4.6	5.4	6.7	5.1	5.3
P/E Ratio	25.9-18.0	30.9-23.3	28.0-19.6	24.7-14.5	18.5-13.2	22.5-19.1	25.0-17.9
Price Range	21¼-14¾	24¾-18⅝	21¼-14⅞	18½-10⅞	12¾-9⅛	14⅜-12¼	14-10

Statistics are as originally reported.

QUARTERLY DATA

(12/31/94)($000)	Rev	Inc
1st Quarter	11,312	5,805
2nd Quarter	10,759	5,828
3rd Quarter	11,759	5,847
4th Quarter	11,681	5,643

OFFICERS:
A.A. Birney, Chmn.
E.B. Cronin, Pres. & C.E.O.
L.E. Finger, V.P. & C.F.O.
B.H. Dorsey, Sec. & Gen. Couns.

INCORPORATED: DC, Nov., 1960

PRINCIPAL OFFICE: 10400 Connecticut Avenue, Kensington, MD 20895

TELEPHONE NUMBER: (301) 929-5900

FAX: (301) 929-5910

NO. OF EMPLOYEES: 25

ANNUAL MEETING: In June

SHAREHOLDERS: 32,000 (approx.)

INSTITUTIONAL HOLDINGS:
No. of Institutions: 77
Shares Held: 4,392,229

REGISTRAR(S): American Stock Transfer & Trust Co., 40 Wall Street, New York, NY 10005

TRANSFER AGENT(S): American Stock Transfer & Trust Co., 40 Wall Street, New York, NY 10005

WAUSAU PAPER MILLS CO.

YIELD 1.1%
P/E RATIO 17.0

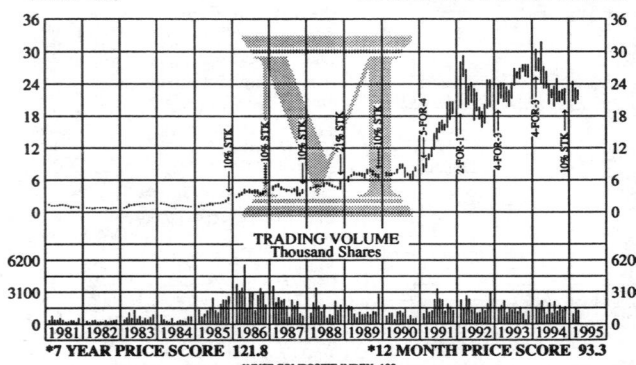

TRADING VOLUME
Thousand Shares

*7 YEAR PRICE SCORE 121.8   *12 MONTH PRICE SCORE 93.3
*NYSE COMPOSITE INDEX=100

INTERIM EARNINGS (Per Share):

Qtr.	Nov.	Feb.	May	Aug.
1991-92	0.38	0.32	0.40	0.40
1992-93	0.30	0.32	0.44	0.40
1993-94	0.38	0.31	0.42	0.42
1994-95	0.29	0.24	...	...

INTERIM DIVIDENDS (Per Share):

Amt.	Decl.	Ex.	Rec.	Pay.
0.06Q	5/27/94	6/13/94	6/17/94	7/1/94
0.06Q	8/15	9/12	9/16	10/3
10%	12/19	12/28	1/4/95	1/17/95
0.0625Q	12/19	12/28	1/4	1/17
0.0625Q	2/15/95	3/7/95	3/13	4/3

Indicated div.: $0.25

CAPITALIZATION (8/31/94):

	($000)	(%)
Long-Term Debt	30,270	10.9
Deferred Income Tax	31,945	11.5
Common & Surplus	214,818	77.6
Total	277,033	100.0

DIVIDEND ACHIEVER STATUS:
Rank: 16   1984-94 Growth Rate: 20.2%
Total Years of Dividend Growth: 10

RECENT DEVELOPMENTS: For the quarter ended 2/28/95, net earnings decreased 21.9% to $7.1 million from $9.1 million in the corresponding 1993 period. Net sales advanced 21.9% to $119.1 million, compared with $97.7 million the previous year. Earnings before taxes dropped 21.1% to $11.6 million from $14.7 million. Shipments made during the quarter jumped 16% over the prior-year period to 95,100 tons. The decline in earnings was attributed to the significant rise in the price of market pulp. The Company's pulp costs for the second quarter of fiscal 1995 were $18 million higher than the prior-year amount. WSAU will continue to face rising pulp costs as further price increases have been scheduled for June 1995. For the six months ended 12/31/94, net earnings declined 22.1% to $15.7 million from $20.2 million in the comparable 1993 period. Sales grew 18.9% to $245.4 million.

BUSINESS

WAUSAU PAPER MILLS COMPANY manufactures and sells paper. WSAU is presently organized into a small corporate staff consisting of principal executive officers and two operating divisions, the Rhinelander Division, which consists of Rhinelander Paper Company, Inc.; and the Printing and Writing Division. The Printing and Writing Division manufactures fine printing, writing and specialty papers, which are sold to paper distributors and converters throughout the United States and Canada. Typical end uses for these fine papers include printed advertising, office papers and converted products such as items as announcements and greeting card envelopes. The Rhinelander Division manufactures lightweight, dense, technical specialty papers, which are sold directly to converters. Typical end uses are pressure-sensitive products, medical packaging, food packaging and multiple laminated products. Small volumes of yeast and lignosulfonates are also manufactured from pulping liquors purchased from other paper companies. These products are sold for use as food additives and for other end uses. Wausau Papers International, Inc. acts as a commissioned sales agent for the export sales of WSAU.

ANNUAL EARNINGS AND DIVIDENDS PER SHARE

	8/31/94	8/31/93	8/31/92	8/31/91	8/31/90	8/31/89	8/31/88
Earnings Per Share	1.56	②1.43	1.49	1.13	0.59	0.78	0.60
Dividends Per Share	①0.24	③0.211	④0.169	⑤0.127	⑥0.114	⑦0.099	⑧0.071
Dividend Payout %	15.4	14.7	17.2	14.9	25.7	16.9	15.8

Note: 10%stk.div.1/17/95. ① Adj for 4-for-3 stk split, 01/10/94 ② Before acctg. chg. ③ 33.3% stk div,01/14/93 ④ 2-for-1 stk split, 1/17/92 ⑤ 5-for-4 stk split,01/14/91 ⑥ 10% stk div, 1/12/90 ⑦ 10% stk div, 1/13/89 ⑧ 10% stk div, 1/88

ANNUAL FINANCIAL DATA

RECORD OF EARNINGS (IN THOUSANDS):

Total Revenues	426,504	381,816	370,935	350,361	339,935	317,097	284,240
Costs and Expenses	338,879	303,461	294,761	286,827	302,793	277,672	251,993
Deprec, Depl & Amort	17,635	15,445	13,760	13,344	11,590	7,686	7,274
Operating Profit	69,990	62,910	62,414	50,190	25,552	31,739	24,973
Earn Bef Income Taxes	68,052	61,771	61,309	47,025	24,170	32,212	24,376
Income Taxes	26,000	23,400	21,300	16,550	8,300	11,300	8,371
Net Income	①42,052	②38,371	40,009	30,475	15,870	20,912	16,005
Aver. Shs. Outstg.	26,929	26,948	27,932	26,928	26,885	26,757	26,753

① Before acctg. change cr$1,000,000. ② Before acctg. change dr$15,750,000.

BALANCE SHEET (IN THOUSANDS):

Cash and Cash Equivalents	3,214	2,624	1,984	3,495	1,994	1,914	10,575
Receivables, Net	42,040	36,176	32,832	29,823	29,834	26,809	25,182
Inventories	60,222	59,659	37,196	29,535	22,242	19,961	23,188
Gross Property	380,250	339,147	288,582	258,581	235,172	193,081	135,822
Accumulated Depreciation	133,178	117,308	102,397	90,123	77,856	67,838	60,632
Long-Term Debt	30,270	42,712	22,695	30,727	55,364	37,487	15,835
Net Stockholders' Equity	214,818	183,139	165,989	130,034	104,382	92,411	74,797
Total Assets	361,389	329,583	266,592	240,306	216,527	178,086	137,549
Total Current Assets	105,934	98,921	72,510	63,324	54,750	49,382	59,623
Total Current Liabilities	46,056	41,914	38,172	43,663	31,251	28,389	29,881
Net Working Capital	59,878	57,007	34,338	19,661	23,499	20,993	29,742
Year End Shares Outstg	26,858	26,891	26,863	26,857	26,859	26,762	24,315

STATISTICAL RECORD:

Operating Profit Margin %	16.4	16.5	16.8	14.3	7.5	10.0	8.8
Book Value Per Share	8.00	6.81	6.18	4.84	3.89	3.45	3.07
Return on Equity %	19.6	21.0	24.1	23.4	15.2	22.6	21.4
Return on Assets %	11.6	11.6	15.0	12.7	7.3	11.7	11.6
Average Yield %	1.5	1.2	1.0	1.1	1.8	1.7	1.7
P/E Ratio	22.4-13.9	21.3-15.2	21.7-11.8	20.0-7.3	16.8-11.2	11.5-8.0	10.8-7.7
Price Range	35-21¾	30⅜-21¾	32¼-17½	22¾-8¼	10-6⅝	9-6¼	6½-4⅝

Statistics are as originally reported.

OFFICERS:
S.W. Orr, Jr., Chmn. & C.E.O.
D.D. King, Pres. & C.O.O.
S.A. Schmidt, V.P.-Fin., Sec. & Treas.

INCORPORATED: WI, 1899

PRINCIPAL OFFICE: One Clark's Island P.O.
Box 1408, Wausau, WI 54402-1408

TELEPHONE NUMBER: (715) 845-5266

FAX: (715) 848-2652

NO. OF EMPLOYEES: 1,695

ANNUAL MEETING: In December

SHAREHOLDERS: 1,941

INSTITUTIONAL HOLDINGS:
No. of Institutions: 143
Shares Held: 15,370,040

REGISTRAR(S):

TRANSFER AGENT(S): Harris Trust & Savings Bank, Chicago, IL

WEIS MARKETS, INC.

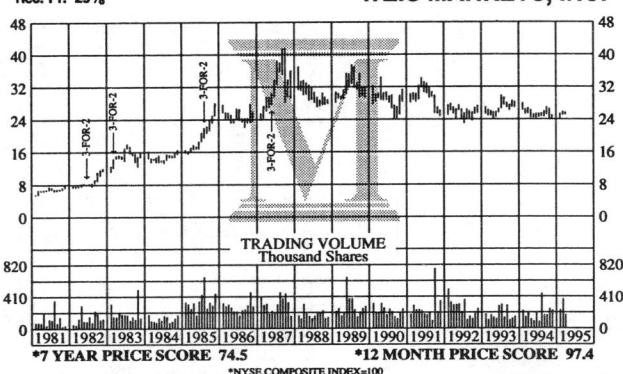

7 YEAR PRICE SCORE 74.5　　**12 MONTH PRICE SCORE 97.4**
*NYSE COMPOSITE INDEX=100

TRADING VOLUME
Thousand Shares

INTERIM EARNINGS (Per Share):

Qtr.	Mar.	June	Sept.	Dec.
1992	0.42	0.41	0.41	0.39
1993	0.43	0.41	0.39	0.44

INTERIM DIVIDENDS (Per Share):

Amt.	Decl.	Ex.	Rec.	Pay.
0.18Q	4/4/94	5/9/94	5/13/94	5/27/94
0.19Q	7/5	8/8	8/12	8/26
0.19Q	10/27	11/7	11/14	11/28
0.19Q	1/26/95	2/6/95	2/10/95	2/24/95
0.19Q	4/4	5/8	5/12	5/26

*Indicated div.: $0.76**

CAPITALIZATION (12/31/94):

	($000)	(%)
Deferred Income Tax	17,495	2.2
Minority Interest	d85	0.0
Common & Surplus	762,380	97.8
Total	779,790	100.0

DIVIDEND ACHIEVER STATUS:
Rank: 170　　1984-94 Growth Rate: 9.9%
Total Years of Dividend Growth: 20

RECENT DEVELOPMENTS: For the year ended 12/31/94, net income was $76.2 million compared with $73.0 million a year earlier. Net sales increased 8.0% to $1.56 billion from $1.44 billion the year before. During the year, WMK acquired six supermarkets located in Eastern Pennsylvania from King's Supermarkets. Additionally, the Company's 80%-owned subsidiary, Superpetz, acquired five pet supply stores located in Georgia and South Carolina from Pet Owners Warehouse.

PROSPECTS: Increased price competition from grocery stores and warehouse clubs will affect near-term earnings. As a result of this price competition, WMK will likely focus on offering everyday low prices and lowering promotional expenses. Meanwhile, Weis plans to continue with its store expansion program, remodeling about 8 existing stores and opening four new supermarkets in the near term.

BUSINESS

WEIS MARKETS, INC. operates 149 supermarkets in Pennsylvania, New Jersey, New York, Maryland, Virginia and West Virginia. Many of WMK's 1,800 different private label products are supplied by the Company's ice cream manufacturing plant, fresh meat processing plant, milk processing plant, and delicatessen kitchen. Distribution centers located in Sunbury and Milton, PA are served by a Company-owned fleet of tractor trailers. WMK conducts food service operations through its wholly-owned Weis Food Service subsidiary which distributes frozen foods and grocery items to restaurants and institutions. Full-service pharmacy departments are located in 66 WMK markets. The Company also operates 10 Superpetz stores and one Amity House restaurant

ANNUAL EARNINGS AND DIVIDENDS PER SHARE

	12/31/94	12/25/93	12/26/92	12/28/91	12/29/90	12/30/89	12/31/88
Earnings Per Share	1.75	1.66	1.63	1.81	1.93	1.91	1.82
Dividends Per Share	0.74	0.70	0.68	0.64	0.60	0.56	0.50
Dividend Payout %	42.3	42.2	41.7	35.4	31.1	29.3	27.5

ANNUAL FINANCIAL DATA

RECORD OF EARNINGS (IN MILLIONS):

	12/31/94	12/25/93	12/26/92	12/28/91	12/29/90	12/30/89	12/31/88
Total Revenues	1,556.7	1,441.1	1,289.2	1,294.3	1,271.8	1,239.3	1,189.2
Costs and Expenses	1,446.1	1,332.5	1,187.4	1,181.7	1,151.9	1,117.2	1,069.0
Depreciation & Amort	30.6	29.0	26.4	25.1	23.2	22.0	19.6
Income From Operations	80.0	79.7	75.4	87.5	96.7	100.1	100.6
Income Bef Income Taxes	117.2	113.7	110.2	124.2	132.3	134.0	129.9
Income Taxes	40.9	40.7	38.6	43.6	45.5	47.6	47.3
Net Income	76.2	73.0	☐71.7	80.6	86.8	86.4	82.6
Aver. Shs. Outstg. (000)	43,662	43,827	43,979	44,503	45,050	45,338	45,514

☐ Before acctg. change cr$1,046,000.

BALANCE SHEET (IN MILLIONS):

Cash and Cash Equivalents	457.0	467.2	420.6	408.6	391.4	356.1	318.1
Receivables, Net	26.5	20.4	25.9	21.1	13.8	12.1	10.5
Inventories	130.0	111.8	97.7	92.3	87.7	85.3	81.7
Gross Property	542.4	496.5	450.3	422.1	388.1	369.6	336.3
Accumulated Depreciation	297.2	271.2	245.8	223.0	201.0	182.4	163.1
Net Stockholders' Equity	762.4	738.1	680.3	647.4	610.1	567.3	509.8
Total Assets	892.1	844.5	761.5	734.5	693.9	655.6	595.7
Total Current Assets	617.8	605.8	552.4	530.2	503.3	464.7	418.7
Total Current Liabilities	112.3	92.6	68.8	73.8	71.6	77.1	76.6
Net Working Capital	505.4	513.2	483.6	456.5	431.7	387.6	342.2
Year End Shs Outstg (000)	43,484	43,796	43,832	44,216	44,730	45,307	45,418

STATISTICAL RECORD:

Operating Profit Margin %	5.1	5.5	5.9	6.8	7.6	8.1	8.5
Book Value Per Share	16.86	16.55	15.41	14.53	13.56	12.44	11.14
Return on Equity %	10.0	9.9	10.5	12.4	14.2	15.2	16.2
Return on Assets %	8.5	8.6	9.4	11.0	12.5	13.2	13.9
Average Yield %	2.9	2.6	2.7	2.2	2.0	1.7	1.6
P/E Ratio	16.0-13.6	18.0-14.5	17.1-14.1	18.9-13.7	17.8-12.6	19.6-14.7	20.3-14.8
Price Range	28-23⅞	29⅞-24	27⅞-23	34¼-24¾	34⅜-24¼	37½-28⅛	37-27

Statistics are as originally reported.

QUARTERLY DATA

(12/31/94)($000)	Rev	Inc
1st Quarter	372,626	17,398
2nd Quarter	368,467	17,808
3nd Quarter	377,197	18,733
4rd Quarter	438,373	22,310

OFFICERS:
R.F. Weis, Chmn. & Treas.
N.S. Rich, Pres.
W.R. Mills, V.P.-Fin. & Sec.

INCORPORATED: PA, Dec., 1924

PRINCIPAL OFFICE: 1000 S. Second Street, Sunbury, PA 17801

TELEPHONE NUMBER: (717) 286-4571

NO. OF EMPLOYEES: 16,500 (approx.)

ANNUAL MEETING: In April

SHAREHOLDERS: 8,800 (approx.)

INSTITUTIONAL HOLDINGS:
No. of Institutions: 63
Shares Held: 21,421,099

REGISTRAR(S): American Stock Transfer Co., New York, NY

TRANSFER AGENT(S): American Stock Transfer Co., New York, NY

ASE SYMBOL WSC
Rec. Pr. 119

WESCO FINANCIAL CORP.

YIELD	0.9%
P/E RATIO	44.7

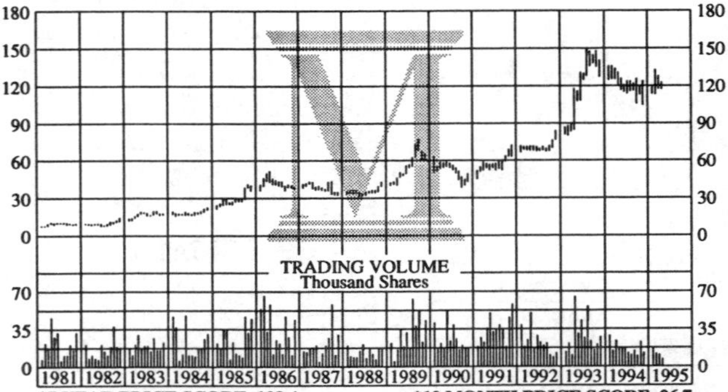

180
150
120
90
60
30
0
TRADING VOLUME
Thousand Shares
70
35
0
1981 1982 1983 1984 1985 1986 1987 1988 1989 1990 1991 1992 1993 1994 1995

*7 YEAR PRICE SCORE 128.4 *12 MONTH PRICE SCORE 96.7

*NYSE COMPOSITE INDEX=100

INTERIM EARNINGS (Per Share):

Qtr.	Mar.	June	Sept.	Dec.
1991	0.90	1.52	0.96	0.77
1992	0.75	0.84	0.73	d1.62
1993	0.90	0.51	0.43	0.79
1994	0.85	0.82	0.95	0.04

INTERIM DIVIDENDS (Per Share):

Amt.	Decl.	Ex.	Rec.	Pay.
0.245Q	3/25/94	5/5/94	5/11/94	6/8/94
0.245Q	7/21	8/4	8/10	9/7
0.245Q	9/21	11/3	11/9	12/7
0.255Q	1/19/95	2/2/95	2/8/95	3/8/95
0.255Q	3/16	5/4	5/10	6/7

Indicated div.: $1.02

CAPITALIZATION (12/31/94):

	($000)	(%)
Long-Term Debt	37,557	5.2
Common & Surplus	678,147	94.8
Total	715,704	100.0

DIVIDEND ACHIEVER STATUS:
Rank: 275 1984-94 Growth Rate: 5.4%
Total Years of Dividend Growth: 23

RECENT DEVELOPMENTS: For the year ended 12/31/94, net income increased 1.5% to $19.0 million compared with $18.7 million, before an accounting adjustment, the previous year. Revenues declined 18.7% to $95.5 million from $117.4 million. Costs and expenses fell 20.2% to $74.7 million from $93.6 million. The lower costs and expenses allowed the Company to post an earnings gain on significantly reduced revenues. The decline in revenues was partly attributable to a relatively low volume of insurance and reinsurance premiums. Insurance premiums earned declined to $1.1 million from $12.2 million in the previous year. Separately, Wesco's financial condition remains very strong with a moderate level of long-term debt on the balance sheet and solid cash flows from operations. However, unexpected changes in the rate of inflation could adversely affect the insurance business because premium rates are set well in advance of the incurrence of related costs.

BUSINESS

WESCO FINANCIAL CORPORATION's principal businesses, conducted by wholly owned subsidiaries, are the property and casualty insurance business (Wesco-Financial Insurance Company) and the steel service center business (Precision Steel Warehouse, Inc.). Precision Steel operates a steel service center business at two locations: one in Franklin Park, IL and the other operated by a wholly-owned subsidiary in Charlotte, NC. Since 1973, WSC has been 80.1% owned by Blue Chip Stamps, a wholly owned subsidiary of Berkshire Hathaway Inc. Therefore, Wesco and its subsidiaries are controlled by Blue Chip Stamps and Berkshire. The Company discontinued its Mutual Savings and Loan Association after disposing of its savings accounts and most of its real estate loans in October of 1993.

BUSINESS LINE ANALYSIS

(12/31/94)	Rev(%)	Inc(%)
Insurance	27.6	74.6
Industrial....................	65.5	20.2
Other..........................	6.9	5.2
Total	100.0	100.0

ANNUAL EARNINGS AND DIVIDENDS PER SHARE

	1994	1993	1992	1991	1990	1989	1988
Earnings Per Share	**2.66**	**2.63**	**0.70**	**4.15**	**3.57**	**4.26**	**4.22**
Dividends Per Share	**0.98**	**0.94**	**0.90**	**0.86**	**0.82**	**0.78**	**0.74**
Dividend Payout %	**36.8**	**35.7**	**N.M.**	**20.7**	**23.0**	**18.3**	**17.5**

ANNUAL FINANCIAL DATA

	1994	1993	1992	1991	1990	1989	1988
RECORD OF EARNINGS (IN THOUSANDS):							
Total Revenues	95,458	117,358	131,815	132,846	122,641	168,395	186,213
Costs and Expenses	71,601	86,307	101,069	93,444	92,093	131,271	148,224
Operating Profit	32,857	31,051	30,746	39,402	30,548	37,124	37,989
Income Bef Income Taxes	20,765	23,741	25,874	34,629	25,790	33,185	34,938
Income Taxes	1,793	5,046	20,873	5,107	361	2,851	4,849
Net Income	18,972	[1] 18,695	5,001	29,522	25,429	30,334	30,089
Aver. Shs. Outstg.	7,120	7,120	7,120	7,120	7,120	7,120	7,120
[1] Before acctg. change cr$1,023,000.							
BALANCE SHEET (IN THOUSANDS):							
Cash and Cash Equivalents	15,800	5,230	123,705	41,849	84,020	55,096	42,703
Receivables, Net	6,501	6,962	14,145	11,989	12,961	13,050	15,355
Gross Property	14,279	13,907	14,354	14,310	8,545	8,352	8,055
Long-Term Debt	37,557	37,896	55,119	55,429	55,726	56,011	31,786
Net Stockholders' Equity	678,147	626,087	411,714	406,363	308,978	281,496	238,588
Total Assets	961,761	915,155	864,959	871,129	744,081	737,505	706,264
Total Current Assets	22,301	12,192	137,850	53,838	96,981	68,146	58,058
Total Current Liabilities	191,858	180,722	323,540	339,693	300,115	301,344	290,161
Net Working Capital	d169,557	d168,530	d185,690	d285,855	d203,134	d233,198	d232,103
Year End Shares Outstg	7,120	7,120	7,120	7,120	7,120	7,120	7,120
STATISTICAL RECORD:							
Book Value Per Share	95.25	87.93	57.83	57.07	43.40	39.54	33.51
Return on Equity %	2.8	3.0	1.2	7.3	8.2	10.8	12.6
Return on Assets %	2.0	2.0	0.6	3.4	3.4	4.1	4.3
Average Yield %	0.8	0.8	1.2	1.5	1.6	1.3	2.0
P/E Ratio	51.1-39.3	56.9-30.4	N.M	17.4-10.8	17.8-10.6	18.1-9.4	10.2-7.5
Price Range	136-104½	149¾-80	83⅞-66⅜	72⅜-45	63½-38	77¼-40⅛	42⅞-31⅝

Statistics are as originally reported.

OFFICERS:
C.T. Munger, Chmn.
R.H. Bird, Pres.
J.L. Jacobson, V.P. & C.F.O.
M. Patrick, Sec.

INCORPORATED: DE, Mar., 1959

PRINCIPAL OFFICE: 301 East Colorado Boulevard Suite 300, Pasadena, CA 91101

TELEPHONE NUMBER: (818) 585-6700

NO. OF EMPLOYEES: 260 (approx.)

ANNUAL MEETING: In May

SHAREHOLDERS: 825 (approx.)

INSTITUTIONAL HOLDINGS:
No. of Institutions: 45
Shares Held: 6,247,079

REGISTRAR(S): Chemical Bank, New York, NY

TRANSFER AGENT(S): Chemical Bank, New York, NY

WESTERN RESOURCES, INC.

YIELD   6.4%
P/E RATIO   11.2

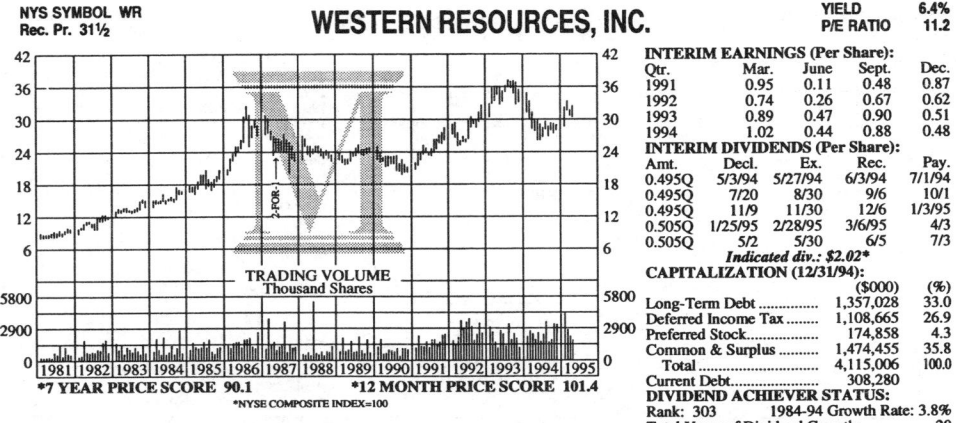

*7 YEAR PRICE SCORE 90.1   ***12 MONTH PRICE SCORE 101.4**

*NYSE COMPOSITE INDEX=100

INTERIM EARNINGS (Per Share):

Qtr.	Mar.	June	Sept.	Dec.
1991	0.95	0.11	0.48	0.87
1992	0.74	0.26	0.67	0.62
1993	0.89	0.47	0.90	0.51
1994	1.02	0.44	0.88	0.48

INTERIM DIVIDENDS (Per Share):

Amt.	Decl.	Ex.	Rec.	Pay.
0.495Q	5/3/94	5/27/94	6/3/94	7/1/94
0.495Q	7/20	8/30	9/6	10/1
0.495Q	11/9	11/30	12/6	1/3/95
0.505Q	1/25/95	2/28/95	3/6/95	4/3
0.505Q	5/2	5/30	6/5	7/3

Indicated div.: $2.02*

CAPITALIZATION (12/31/94):

	($000)	(%)
Long-Term Debt	1,357,028	33.0
Deferred Income Tax	1,108,665	26.9
Preferred Stock	174,858	4.3
Common & Surplus	1,474,455	35.8
Total	4,115,006	100.0
Current Debt	308,280	

DIVIDEND ACHIEVER STATUS:
Rank: 303   1984-94 Growth Rate: 3.8%
Total Years of Dividend Growth: 20

RECENT DEVELOPMENTS: For the quarter ended 12/31/94, net income dropped 4.7% to $33.4 million from $35.0 million in the same period of 1993. Revenues were $359.2 million, down 29.6%. For the year ended 12/31/94, net income was $187.4 million versus $177.4 million a year earlier. Earnings reflect above average sales growth, continued successful cost savings by employees, and the sale of the Missouri natural gas properties.

PROSPECTS: Future prospects look favorable due to the outlook in sales growth resulting from the Company's unregulated activities and the development of the Mid Continent Market Center, WR's newest natural gas transportation and marketing venture. In addition, the economy in WR's service area continues to strengthen. Cash flow has improved significantly due to the acquisition of Kansas Gas and Electric Company.

BUSINESS

WESTERN RESOURCES, INC. (formerly The Kansas Power and Light Company) is a combination electric and natural gas public utility engaged in the generation, transmission, distribution and sale of electric energy in Kansas and the purchase transmission, distribution, transportation and sale of natural gas in Kansas, Missouri and Oklahoma. In March 1992, the Company acquired The Kansas Gas and Electric Company under a merger agreement for approximately $1 billion in which KG&E became a wholly-owned subsidiary of WR. KG&E provides electric service to over 250,000 retail customers in the Southeast quarter of Kansas.

BUSINESS LINE ANALYSIS

(12/31/94)	Rev(%)	Inc(%)
Natural Gas	30.7	6.0
Electric	69.3	94.0
Total	100.0	100.0

ANNUAL EARNINGS AND DIVIDENDS PER SHARE

	1994	1993	1992	1991	1990	1989	1988
Earnings Per Share	2.82	2.76	2.20	① 1.91	2.25	2.05	2.25
Dividends Per Share	1.97	1.93	1.89	② 2.025	1.79	1.75	1.703
Dividend Payout %	69.9	69.9	85.9	N.M.	79.6	85.4	75.7

① Before acctg. chg.   ② Includes special $0.18 dividend.

ANNUAL FINANCIAL DATA

RECORD OF EARNINGS (IN MILLIONS):

	1994	1993	1992	1991	1990	1989	1988
Total Revenues	1,617.9	1,909.4	1,556.2	1,162.2	1,149.8	1,127.6	1,166.1
Depreciation & Amort	151.6	164.4	144.0	85.7	76.8	73.3	70.4
Maintenance	113.2	117.8	101.6	60.5	57.8	58.4	55.1
Prov for Fed Inc Taxes	76.5	62.4	34.9	24.5	24.6	27.3	36.4
Operating Income	269.5	292.1	239.2	129.6	132.0	125.5	130.4
Interest Expense	116.0	140.2	135.5	60.7	61.4	53.6	50.2
Net Income	187.4	177.4	127.9	① 72.3	79.6	72.8	79.8
Aver. Shs. Outstg. (000)	61,618	59,294	52,272	34,566	34,566	34,566	34,566

① Before acctg. change cr$17,360,000.

BALANCE SHEET (IN MILLIONS):

	1994	1993	1992	1991	1990	1989	1988
Gross Plant	6,088.5	6,331.9	6,125.6	2,552.6	2,441.8	2,324.9	2,187.2
Accumulated Depreciation	1,790.3	1,821.7	1,682.8	826.1	761.6	701.0	642.3
Prop, Plant & Equip, Net	4,298.3	4,510.2	4,442.8	1,726.4	1,680.2	1,623.8	1,544.9
Long-term Debt	1,357.0	1,524.0	1,926.0	586.6	590.2	545.9	548.5
Net Stockholders' Equity	1,649.3	1,597.0	1,424.7	771.3	661.0	646.7	637.9
Total Assets	5,189.6	5,412.0	5,523.6	2,120.1	2,016.0	1,959.0	1,777.5
Year End Shs Outstg (000)	61,618	61,618	58,046	34,566	34,566	34,566	34,566

STATISTICAL RECORD:

	1994	1993	1992	1991	1990	1989	1988
Book Value Per Share	23.93	23.08	21.51	18.59	18.25	17.80	17.51
Op. Inc/Net PI %	6.3	6.5	5.4	7.5	7.9	7.7	8.4
Dep/Gr. PI %	2.8	2.9	2.6	3.4	3.1	3.2	3.2
Accum. Dep/Gr. PI %	29.4	28.8	27.5	32.4	31.2	30.2	29.4
Return on Equity %	12.5	12.3	10.0	10.8	12.1	11.4	12.7
Average Yield %	6.6	5.7	6.5	8.2	8.0	7.4	6.9
P/E Ratio	12.4-9.3	13.5-11.0	14.8-11.4	14.9-10.9	11.2-8.8	12.4-10.5	12.0-9.9
Price Range	34⅞-26⅛	37¼-30⅜	32⅝-25⅛	28½-20¾	25⅛-19¾	25⅜-21⅝	27-22¼

Statistics are as originally reported.

OFFICERS:
J.E. Hayes, Jr., Chmn., Pres. & C.E.O.
S.L. Kitchen, Exec. V.P. & C.F.O.

INCORPORATED: KS, Mar., 1924

PRINCIPAL OFFICE: 818 Kansas Ave., Topeka, KS 66612-1217

TELEPHONE NUMBER: (913) 575-6300

NO. OF EMPLOYEES: 5,192

ANNUAL MEETING: In May

SHAREHOLDERS: 45,902

INSTITUTIONAL HOLDINGS:
No. of Institutions: 217
Shares Held: 21,799,631

REGISTRAR(S): Chemical Bank, New York, NY

TRANSFER AGENT(S): Chemical Bank, New York, NY

WEYCO GROUP, INC.

YIELD   2.5%
P/E RATIO   11.5

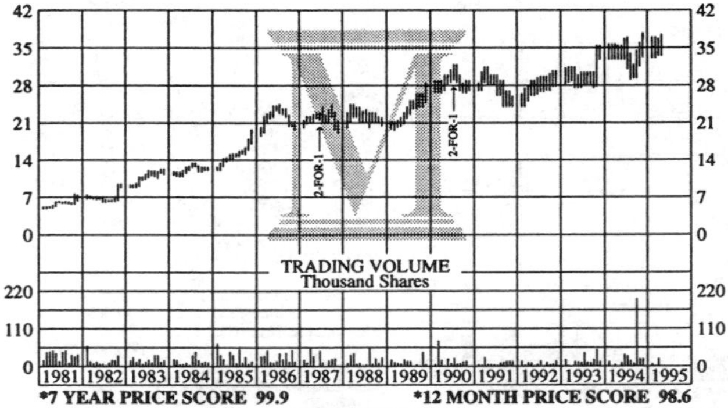

INTERIM EARNINGS (Per Share):

Qtr.	Mar.	June	Sept.	Dec.
1991	0.18	0.29	0.67	1.23
1992	0.61	0.47	0.70	1.32
1993	0.54	0.61	0.59	0.58
1994	0.60	0.30	0.94	1.14

INTERIM DIVIDENDS (Per Share):

Amt.	Decl.	Ex.	Rec.	Pay.
0.20Q	5/18/94	5/25/94	6/1/94	7/1/94
0.20Q	7/27	8/26	9/1	10/1
0.20Q	11/7	11/25	12/1	1/2/95
0.20Q	1/25/95	2/28/95	3/6/95	4/1
0.21Q	4/25	5/25	6/1	7/1

Indicated div.: $0.84

CAPITALIZATION (12/31/94):

	($000)	(%)
Common & Surplus	59,427	100.0
Total	59,427	100.0

DIVIDEND ACHIEVER STATUS:
Rank: 170   1984-94 Growth Rate: 9.9%
Total Years of Dividend Growth: 14

*7 YEAR PRICE SCORE 99.9   ***12 MONTH PRICE SCORE 98.6**
*NYSE COMPOSITE INDEX=100

RECENT DEVELOPMENTS: For the year ended 12/31/94, net income increased 25.9% to $6.2 million compared with $4.9 million, before the cumulative effect of an accounting change, the previous year. Sales fell 6.1% to $114.7 million from $122.1 million. The sales decline was primarily attributable to the closing of leased departments and Company stores in the retail division. The smaller retail division is principally the result of a terminated lease agreement with a major department store chain. Retail sales decreased 37.6% to $24.5 million. Moreover, same-store retail sales fell 6.4%. However, wholesale sales climbed 8.8% to $90.2 million. The improved wholesale results reflect a 12.8% increase in the number of pairs of shoes shipped. This volume gain was partially offset by a 6% decline in the average price per pair. The lower price per pair was attributable to strong consumer demand for lower priced casual shoes.

BUSINESS

WEYCO GROUP, INC. and its subsidiaries engage in the manufacture, purchase and distribution of men's footwear. The Company distributes a broad line of quality men's dress and casual shoes. These shoes are sold under various brand names, the better known ones being "Nunn-Bush", "Brass Boot", "Stacy Adams", and "Weyenberg". The Company and a subsidiary, Nunn-Bush Shoe Company, market their footwear through shoe stores, clothing stores and department stores across the United States. The retail division consists of 13 Brass Boot stores and 28 other Company stores and leased departments.

ANNUAL EARNINGS AND DIVIDENDS PER SHARE

	1994	1993	1992	1991	1990	1989	1988
Earnings Per Share	2.98	2.32	3.10	2.37	3.02	2.95	2.32
Dividends Per Share	0.80	0.76	0.68	0.62	① 0.55	0.45	0.38
Dividend Payout %	26.9	27.7	21.9	26.2	18.2	15.3	16.4

① 2-for-1 stk split; 7/1990

ANNUAL FINANCIAL DATA

RECORD OF EARNINGS (IN THOUSANDS):

	1994	1993	1992	1991	1990	1989	1988
Total Revenues	114,719	122,144	139,462	140,940	148,495	138,868	126,295
Costs and Expenses	104,100	113,809	128,282	132,292	137,202	128,232	117,505
Depreciation	1,226	1,203	1,325	1,184	1,171	944	1,172
Earnings From Operations	9,392	7,131	9,855	7,464	10,122	9,692	7,618
Earn Bef Prov for Inc Taxes	10,066	7,716	10,493	8,368	10,584	10,237	8,138
Income Taxes	3,887	2,808	3,924	3,258	4,035	3,852	3,044
Net Income	6,179	① 4,908	6,569	5,110	6,549	6,385	5,094
Aver. Shs. Outstg.	2,077	2,117	2,120	2,158	2,166	2,167	2,197

① Before acctg. change cr$880,000.

BALANCE SHEET (IN THOUSANDS):

	1994	1993	1992	1991	1990	1989	1988
Cash and Cash Equivalents	32,694	26,536	25,659	20,021	8,843	6,604	8,740
Receivables, Net	18,958	20,853	20,633	22,313	20,796	24,183	20,055
Inventories	10,737	17,050	16,496	22,654	26,827	24,985	18,226
Gross Property	9,232	8,966	9,402	8,784	9,047	9,766	9,357
Accumulated Depreciation	4,658	4,106	4,821	5,213	5,072	5,489	5,682
Net Stockholders' Equity	59,427	62,335	57,745	52,986	50,235	44,969	39,799
Total Assets	72,827	74,915	71,848	71,660	63,147	62,142	52,130
Total Current Assets	62,454	64,996	62,808	64,988	56,466	55,772	47,021
Total Current Liabilities	9,486	9,132	11,094	15,132	9,524	14,066	10,345
Net Working Capital	52,968	55,864	51,714	49,856	46,942	41,705	36,675
Year End Shares Outstg	1,894	2,132	2,114	2,125	2,166	2,176	2,176

STATISTICAL RECORD:

	1994	1993	1992	1991	1990	1989	1988
Operating Profit Margin %	8.2	5.8	7.1	5.3	6.8	7.0	6.0
Book Value Per Share	31.38	29.24	27.32	24.93	23.19	20.67	18.29
Return on Equity %	10.4	7.9	11.4	9.6	13.0	14.2	12.8
Return on Assets %	8.5	6.6	9.1	7.1	10.4	10.3	9.8
Average Yield %	2.4	2.4	2.5	2.2	1.9	1.9	1.7
P/E Ratio	12.7-9.7	15.3-11.9	9.9-7.7	13.3-10.1	10.6-8.8	9.7-6.6	10.6-8.6
Price Range	37¾-29	35½-27½	30¾-24	31½-24	32-26½	28½-19½	24½-20

Statistics are as originally reported.

OFFICERS:
T.W. Florsheim, Chmn. & C.E.O.
R. Feitler, Pres. & C.O.O.
J. Wittkowske, Treas. & Sec.

INCORPORATED: WI, Jun., 1906

PRINCIPAL OFFICE: 234 E. Reservoir Ave.
P.O. Box 1188, Milwaukee, WI 53201

TELEPHONE NUMBER: (414) 263-8800

NO. OF EMPLOYEES: 525 (approx.)

ANNUAL MEETING: In April

SHAREHOLDERS: 550 (approx.)

INSTITUTIONAL HOLDINGS:
No. of Institutions: 32
Shares Held: 590,447

REGISTRAR(S): American Stock Transfer & Trust Co., New York, NY

TRANSFER AGENT(S): American Stock Transfer & Trust Co., New York, NY

NYS SYMBOL WIC
Rec. Pr. 27⅛

WICOR, INC.

YIELD 5.9%
P/E RATIO 15.5

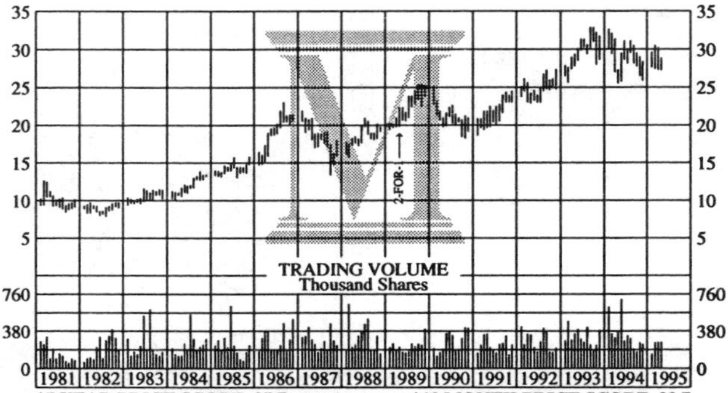

*7 YEAR PRICE SCORE 97.7 *12 MONTH PRICE SCORE 93.7

*NYSE COMPOSITE INDEX=100

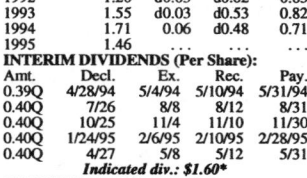

INTERIM EARNINGS (Per Share):

Qtr.	Mar.	June	Sept.	Dec.
1992	1.20	d0.03	d0.62	0.85
1993	1.55	d0.03	d0.53	0.82
1994	1.71	0.06	d0.48	0.71
1995	1.46	...	...	...

INTERIM DIVIDENDS (Per Share):

Amt.	Decl.	Ex.	Rec.	Pay.
0.39Q	4/28/94	5/4/94	5/10/94	5/31/94
0.40Q	7/26	8/8	8/12	8/31
0.40Q	10/25	11/4	11/10	11/30
0.40Q	1/24/95	2/6/95	2/10/95	2/28/95
0.40Q	4/27	5/8	5/12	5/31

*Indicated div.: $1.60**

CAPITALIZATION (12/31/94):

	($000)	(%)
Long-Term Debt	161,669	32.1
Deferred Income Tax	50,509	10.0
Common & Surplus	291,468	57.9
Total	503,646	100.0
Current Debt	116,537	

DIVIDEND ACHIEVER STATUS:
Rank: 307 1984-94 Growth Rate: 3.6%
Total Years of Dividend Growth: 11

RECENT DEVELOPMENTS: For the quarter ended 12/31/94, net income dropped 10% to $12.0 million compared with $13.4 million the previous year. Revenues were $210.0 million, down 10% from $233.8 million the year before. Gas sales were depressed by weather that was 25% warmer than normal and 18% warmer than the period a year earlier. As a result, Wisconsin Gas reported earnings of $8.8 million, down from $12.2 million in 1993.

PROSPECTS: WICOR's manufacturing subsidiaries, Sta-Rite Industries, Inc. and SHURflo Pump Manufacturing Co., are starting to pump profits into the Company through an expanded international sales presence. In addition, Wisconsin Gas' strong growth outlook, due to a healthy state economy, coupled with favorable regulatory climate will aid earnings growth. Additionally, opportunities to promote natural gas vehicles and gas-fired cogeneration should boost revenues.

BUSINESS

WICOR, INC. is a holding company for Wisconsin Gas Company, the state's largest distributor of natural gas, and Sta-Rite Industries, a worldwide manufacturer of pumps and filters. Wisconsin Gas serves 460,000 customers in 416 communities throughout the state. Sta-Rite Industries, Inc. is a leading manufacturer of pumps and other water-processing equipment. Sta-Rite markets its products in the United States and worldwide on six continents. In July of 1993, the Company acquired SHURflo Pump Manufacturing Co. SHURflo is a leader in small, high-performance pumps.

BUSINESS LINE ANALYSIS

(12/31/94)	Rev(%)	Inc(%)
Gas Distribution	64.1	57.0
Manufacturing	35.9	43.0
Total	100.0	100.0

ANNUAL EARNINGS AND DIVIDENDS PER SHARE

	1994	1993	1992	1991	1990	1989	1988
Earnings Per Share	1.99	1.82	0.86	1.54	[2] 1.04	2.40	2.46
Dividends Per Share	1.58	1.54	[1] 1.50	1.46	1.42	[3] 1.37	1.32
Dividend Payout %	79.4	84.6	N.M.	94.8	N.M.	57.1	53.7

[1] Bef acctg chge [2] Before extraord. item [3] 2-for-1 stk split, 4/89.

ANNUAL FINANCIAL DATA

	1994	1993	1992	1991	1990	1989	1988
RECORD OF EARNINGS (IN THOUSANDS):							
Total Revenues	867,755	849,528	704,905	681,708	659,779	710,601	754,187
Depreciation & Amort	47,097	43,738	26,650	24,759	34,790	22,030	20,612
Oper Inc Fr Contin Opers	66,610	63,951	49,393	49,022	41,455	69,680	67,424
Interest Expense	16,698	17,428	17,980	16,554	18,064	17,419	16,537
Net Income	33,174	29,313	[1] 20,469	21,527	[2] 14,323	32,657	33,750
Aver. Shs. Outstg.	16,708	16,096	14,589	13,988	13,755	13,615	13,452

[1] Before acctg. change dr$7,965,000. [2] Before disc. op. dr$5,524,000.

	1994	1993	1992	1991	1990	1989	1988
BALANCE SHEET (IN THOUSANDS):							
Gross Plant	822,684	777,704	757,364	690,087	654,850	653,984	623,839
Accumulated Depreciation	407,121	377,004	369,162	342,316	318,614	347,440	322,717
Prop, Plant & Equip, Net	415,563	400,700	388,202	347,771	336,236	306,544	301,122
Long-term Debt	161,669	165,230	164,001	168,154	127,683	122,453	132,137
Net Stockholders' Equity	291,468	270,276	235,762	235,486	230,169	238,028	221,341
Total Assets	930,708	933,726	809,896	668,691	637,856	607,956	553,452
Year End Shares Outstg	16,918	16,407	14,821	14,464	13,829	13,686	13,542
STATISTICAL RECORD:							
Book Value Per Share	17.23	16.47	15.91	16.28	16.64	17.39	16.34
Op. Inc/Net Pl %	16.0	16.0	12.7	14.1	12.3	22.7	22.4
Dep/Gr. Pl %	3.6	3.6	3.5	3.6	3.7	3.4	3.3
Accum. Dep/Gr. Pl %	49.5	48.5	48.7	49.6	48.7	53.1	51.7
Return on Equity %	11.4	10.8	8.7	9.1	6.2	13.7	15.2
Average Yield %	5.4	5.3	6.0	6.8	6.5	6.1	7.2
P/E Ratio	16.4-12.8	18.1-14.1	19.6-16.3	15.9-12.1	24.3-17.5	10.6-8.1	8.5-6.4
Price Range	32⅝-25½	32⅞-25⅝	27⅜-22⅞	24½-18⅝	25¼-18¼	25½-19⅜	20⅞-15⅝

Statistics are as originally reported.

OFFICERS:
G.E. Wardeberg, Chmn., Pres. & C.E.O.
J.P. Wenzler, Treas. & C.F.O.
R.A. Nuernberg, Secretary

INCORPORATED: WI, Feb., 1980

PRINCIPAL OFFICE: 626 East Wisconsin Avenue, Milwaukee, WI 53201

TELEPHONE NUMBER: (414) 291-7026

FAX: (414) 291-7025

NO. OF EMPLOYEES: 3,214

ANNUAL MEETING: In April

SHAREHOLDERS: 16,517

INSTITUTIONAL HOLDINGS:
No. of Institutions: 112
Shares Held: 5,169,206

REGISTRAR(S): Chemical Bank, New York, NY

TRANSFER AGENT(S): Chemical Bank, New York, NY

WILMINGTON TRUST CORP.

YIELD 4.3%
P/E RATIO 14.0

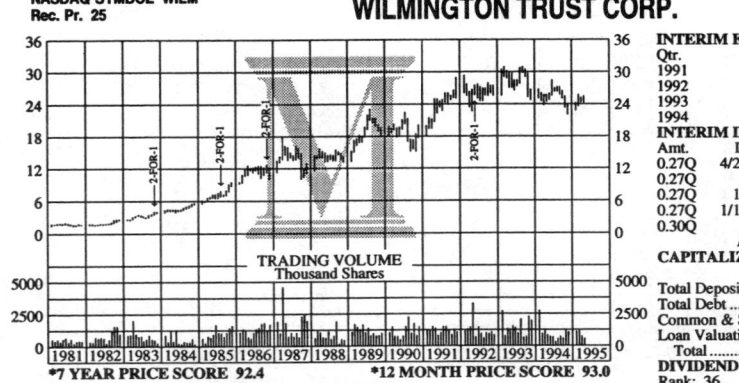

*7 YEAR PRICE SCORE 92.4   *12 MONTH PRICE SCORE 93.0
*NYSE COMPOSITE INDEX=100

INTERIM EARNINGS (Per Share):

Qtr.	Mar.	June	Sept.	Dec.
1991	0.46	0.50	0.53	0.54
1992	0.47	0.51	0.56	0.56
1993	0.53	0.55	0.59	0.57
1994	0.58	0.60	0.59	0.60

INTERIM DIVIDENDS (Per Share):

Amt.	Decl.	Ex.	Rec.	Pay.
0.27Q	4/21/94	4/26/94	5/2/94	5/16/94
0.27Q	7/21	7/26	8/1	8/15
0.27Q	10/20	10/26	11/1	11/15
0.27Q	1/19/95	1/26/95	2/1/95	2/15/95
0.30Q	4/20	4/25	5/1	5/15

Indicated div.: $1.08

CAPITALIZATION (12/31/94):

	($000)	(%)
Total Deposits	3,308,750	70.2
Total Debt	934,807	19.9
Common & Surplus	418,222	8.9
Loan Valuation Reserve	48,669	1.0
Total	4,710,448	100.0

DIVIDEND ACHIEVER STATUS:
Rank: 36   1984-94 Growth Rate: 17.0%
Total Years of Dividend Growth: 13

RECENT DEVELOPMENTS: Net income for the fiscal year ended 12/31/94 was $85.2 million compared with $82.8 million for the year ended 12/31/93. Total assets advanced to $4.74 billion from $4.64 billion as net loans were $3.23 billion versus $2.99 billion a year earlier. Total deposits decreased slightly to $3.31 billion from $3.39 billion. Net interest income climbed up a modest 5% to $184.3 million while noninterest or other income was flat at $113.1 million compared with $113.7 million the year before. Trust and investment management fees totaled $82.5 million, an increase of 5.4% from $78.3 million. The Company recorded a $2.2 million loss on securities transactions versus a gain of $268,000 in the prior year. The provision for loan losses was reduced by 52% from the year before to $4.6 million. Other expense increased by 6% to $172.0 million from $161.8 million the year before.

BUSINESS

WILMINGTON TRUST CORP. and its subsidiaries, with assets of $4.7 billion, provide a full range of banking and related services to individual and corporate customers in the Delaware area. A general and commercial and retail banking business with normal banking services including acceptance of demand, savings and time deposits and the making of various types of loans. The Company operates 65 branches in Wilmington, New Castle County, Kent County and Sussex County, Delaware, one branch in West Chester, Pennsylvania and three trust offices in Florida. It offers a full range of trust, custody and investment services to institutions and individuals, including a family of mutual funds, portfolio management and precious metals storage. The bank also provides discount brokerage, insurance and travel services.

LOAN DISTRIBUTION

(12/31/93)	($000)	(%)
Commercial, Finan & Agri	922,499	30.3
Real Estate-Construction	122,329	4.0
Mortgage-Commercial	651,011	21.4
Mortgage-Residential	609,031	20.0
Install To Individuals	734,916	24.3
Total	3,039,786	100.0

ANNUAL EARNINGS AND DIVIDENDS PER SHARE

	1994	1993	1992	1991	1990	1989	1988
Earnings Per Share	2.37	2.24	2.09	2.04	1.90	1.70	1.49
Dividends Per Share	1.06	0.975	① 0.88	0.795	0.72	0.59	0.46
Dividend Payout %	44.7	43.8	42.1	39.0	37.9	34.7	30.9

① 2-for-1 stk split, 5/18/92

ANNUAL FINANCIAL DATA

RECORD OF EARNINGS (IN MILLIONS):

	1994	1993	1992	1991	1990	1989	1988
Total Interest Income	309.0	291.6	318.0	335.6	342.8	308.5	247.0
Total Interest Expense	123.6	116.1	150.3	191.4	212.0	186.7	140.6
Net Interest Income	185.5	175.5	167.7	144.3	130.9	121.8	106.4
Credit Loss Provision	4.6	9.5	13.0	13.3	10.5	10.3	10.3
Net Income	85.2	82.8	① 78.8	71.9	67.0	59.4	51.8
Aver. Shs. Outstg. (000)	35,990	37,029	37,765	35,352	35,302	35,904	34,820

① Before acctg. change dr$14,749,000.

BALANCE SHEET (IN MILLIONS):

	1994	1993	1992	1991	1990	1989	1988
Cash & Due From Banks	203.5	186.3	210.1	203.4	195.6	224.9	194.5
Obligs Of State & Political Subdiviss	...	69.3	93.2	93.1	89.2	83.4	84.5
Loans & Lse Financing, Net	3,231.4	2,986.2	2,950.2	2,723.2	2,567.5	2,337.3	2,014.4
Total Domestic Deposits	3,308.8	3,391.4	3,274.2	3,046.2	2,853.0	2,613.3	2,291.1
Net Stockholders' Equity	418.2	395.2	377.2	345.7	296.0	257.6	228.0
Total Assets	4,742.4	4,637.8	4,284.6	4,061.3	3,834.3	3,702.7	2,982.1
Year End Shs Outstg (000)	35,449	36,308	37,273	35,582	35,194	34,598	34,960

STATISTICAL RECORD:

	1994	1993	1992	1991	1990	1989	1988
Return on Assets %	1.80	1.78	1.84	1.77	1.75	1.60	1.74
Return on Equity %	20.40	20.90	20.90	20.80	22.60	23.10	22.70
Book Value Per Share	11.80	10.88	10.12	9.72	8.41	7.44	6.52
Average Yield %	4.2	3.5	3.4	3.4	3.8	3.2	3.4
P/E Ratio	12.0-9.3	13.8-11.0	14.1-10.8	14.2-8.8	11.8-8.0	13.6-7.8	10.6-7.7
Price Range	28½-22	31-24¾	29⅜-22⅝		29-18	22½-15⅛	23⅛-13¼	15¾-11½

Statistics are as originally reported.

OFFICERS:
L.W. Quill, Chmn., Pres. & C.E.O.
T.T. Cecala, Exec. V.P. & C.F.O.
R.V. Harra, Jr., Exec. V.P. & Treas.
T.P. Collins, V.P. & Sec.

INCORPORATED: DE, Mar., 1901

PRINCIPAL OFFICE: Wilmington Trust Center Rodney Square North 1100 North Market St., Wilmington, DE 19890-0001

TELEPHONE NUMBER: (302) 651-1000

NO. OF EMPLOYEES: 2,254

ANNUAL MEETING: In April

SHAREHOLDERS: 8,866

INSTITUTIONAL HOLDINGS:
No. of Institutions: 155
Shares Held: 13,283,678

REGISTRAR(S): At Company's Office

TRANSFER AGENT(S): At Company's Office

WINN-DIXIE STORES, INC.

YIELD 2.8%
P/E RATIO 18.8

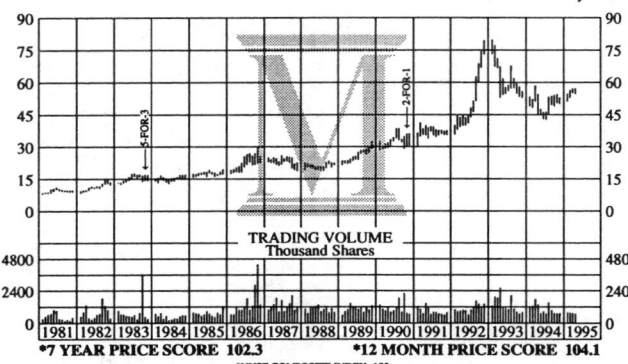

TRADING VOLUME
Thousand Shares

| 1981 | 1982 | 1983 | 1984 | 1985 | 1986 | 1987 | 1988 | 1989 | 1990 | 1991 | 1992 | 1993 | 1994 | 1995 |

*7 YEAR PRICE SCORE 102.3   *12 MONTH PRICE SCORE 104.1

*NYSE COMPOSITE INDEX=100

INTERIM EARNINGS (Per Share):

Qtr.	Sept.	Jan.	Apr.	June
1991-92	0.35	0.70	0.70	1.07
1992-93	------------ 3.11 ------------			
1993-94	0.48	0.85	0.70	0.87
1994-95	0.54	...	...	...

INTERIM DIVIDENDS (Per Share):

Amt.	Decl.	Ex.	Rec.	Pay.
0.13M	1/3/95	2/9/95	2/15/95	3/1/95
0.13M	1/3	3/9	3/15	4/3
0.13M	4/3	4/10	4/17	5/1
0.13M	4/3	5/9	5/15	6/1
0.13M	4/3	6/13	6/15	7/3

Indicated div.: $1.56

CAPITALIZATION (6/29/94):

	($000)	(%)
Cap. Lease Oblig...............	85,374	7.5
Common & Surplus	1,057,461	92.5
Total	1,142,835	100.0

DIVIDEND ACHIEVER STATUS:
Rank: 255   1984-94 Growth Rate: 6.3%
Total Years of Dividend Growth: 51

RECENT DEVELOPMENTS: For the 16 weeks ended 1/11/95, net income was $67.5 million compared with $63.8 million a year earlier. Net sales increased 4.6% to $3.54 billion. Average store sales rose 6.1% and identical store sales rose 2.7%. As a percentage of sales, gross profit increased to 22.9% from 22.7% a year earlier. For the 28 weeks ended 1/11/95, net income increased to $107.5 million, up 7.8% from $99.7 million a year earlier. Net sales increased 4.8% to $6.13 billion.

PROSPECTS: With a capital expenditure budget of $600 million, Winn-Dixie is committed to expanding the average size of its stores. Expansion plans call for the opening of approximately 64 new stores and the enlarging or remodeling of 64 existing stores through mid-1995. These larger store formats, with expanded specialty departments and continued cost control measures should contribute to sales and margin growth. Meanwhile, continued dividend growth is anticipated.

BUSINESS

WINN-DIXIE STORES, INC., with stores in thirteen southeastern and southwestern states and the Bahamas, is the fifth largest food retailer in the U.S. in terms of sales. Winn-Dixie offers a broad line of groceries, meats, seafood, fresh produce, deli/bakery, pharmaceuticals and general merchandise items. As of 1/11/95, the Company operated 1,158 stores, totaling 41.0 million square feet, of which half are larger than 35,000 square feet. Winn-Dixie also operates support facilities, including 16 distribution centers, 27 processing and manufactring plants, and a truck delivery fleet. The Davis family owns about 40% of the Company's common stock.

QUARTERLY DATA

(6/29/94)($000)	Rev	Inc
1st Quarter.................	2,464,440	35,951
2nd Quarter.................	3,380,986	63,781
3rd Quarter.................	2,651,491	52,032
4th Quarter.................	2,585,252	64,353

ANNUAL EARNINGS AND DIVIDENDS PER SHARE

	6/29/94	6/30/93	6/24/92	6/26/91	6/27/90	6/28/89	6/29/88
Earnings Per Share	2.90	3.11	[1] 2.82	2.20	1.93	1.68	1.44
Dividends Per Share	1.49	1.37	1.25	[2] 1.13	1.028	0.973	0.943
Dividend Payout %	51.4	44.1	42.6	51.4	53.3	57.9	65.7

[1] Before acctg. chg. [2] 2-for-1 stk split, 10/31/90

ANNUAL FINANCIAL DATA

RECORD OF EARNINGS (IN MILLIONS):

	6/29/94	6/30/93	6/24/92	6/26/91	6/27/90	6/28/89	6/29/88
Total Revenues	11,082.2	10,831.5	10,337.3	10,074.3	9,744.5	9,151.1	9,007.7
Costs and Expenses	10,660.1	10,441.0	9,976.7	9,792.8	9,497.5	8,909.6	8,760.7
Depreciation & Amort	157.4	141.1	126.9	113.4	118.1	136.0	161.9
Operating Income	264.7	249.4	233.8	168.2	128.9	105.5	85.2
Earn Bef Income Taxes	348.5	363.7	328.0	259.0	224.2	197.9	168.8
Income Taxes	132.4	127.3	111.6	88.1	71.7	63.3	52.1
Net Income	216.1	236.4	[1] 216.4	170.9	152.5	134.5	116.7
Aver. Shs. Outstg. (000)	74,644	74,956	76,805	77,826	79,037	80,064	81,344

[1] Before acctg. change dr$20,485,000.

BALANCE SHEET (IN MILLIONS):

Cash and Cash Equivalents	31.5	107.8	203.7	102.5	198.1	128.2	132.4
Receivables, Net	171.9	162.6	124.0	98.8	69.7	65.4	57.8
Inventories	1,058.9	1,041.5	948.3	924.3	848.4	784.7	753.3
Gross Property	2,049.3	1,892.4	1,789.5	1,691.9	1,589.0	1,514.5	1,476.9
Accumulated Depreciation	1,342.5	1,305.8	1,260.4	1,198.2	1,152.6	1,087.8	1,048.0
Long-Term Debt	...	...	...	...	...	...	24.2
Capital Lease Obligations	85.4	87.2	90.3	96.9	83.4	72.4	63.1
Net Stockholders' Equity	1,057.5	985.0	952.2	860.0	813.2	783.2	726.3
Total Assets	2,146.6	2,062.6	1,977.4	1,817.5	1,732.7	1,575.1	1,514.0
Total Current Assets	1,361.2	1,413.2	1,363.5	1,202.6	1,168.7	1,031.0	988.9
Total Current Liabilities	873.2	868.5	812.7	766.8	742.3	634.8	631.2
Net Working Capital	488.0	544.7	550.8	435.8	426.4	396.2	357.7
Year End Shs Outstg (000)	74,176	74,956	76,851	77,129	78,314	79,862	79,814

STATISTICAL RECORD:

Operating Profit Margin %	2.4	2.3	2.3	1.7	1.3	1.2	0.9
Book Value Per Share	14.26	13.14	12.39	11.15	10.38	9.81	9.10
Return on Equity %	20.4	24.0	22.7	19.9	18.8	17.2	16.1
Return on Assets %	10.1	11.5	10.9	9.4	8.8	8.5	7.7
Average Yield %	3.0	2.1	2.1	3.2	3.1	3.6	4.5
P/E Ratio	20.1-14.7	25.6-17.0	28.2-12.7	18.8-13.5	20.0-14.7	19.3-12.8	16.3-13.0
Price Range	58⅜-42⅝	79¾-52¾	79½-35¾	41¼-29¾	38⅝-28⅜	32½-21½	23½-18¾

Statistics are as originally reported.

OFFICERS:
A.D. Davis, Chmn. & C.E.O.
J. Kufeldt, Pres.
D.H. Bragin, Treas.
J.W. Dixon, Sec.

INCORPORATED: FL, Dec., 1928

PRINCIPAL OFFICE: 5050 Edgewood Court, Jacksonville, FL 32205

TELEPHONE NUMBER: (904) 783-5000
NO. OF EMPLOYEES: 40,000 (full-time); 72,000 (part-time).
ANNUAL MEETING: In October
SHAREHOLDERS: 39,226
INSTITUTIONAL HOLDINGS:
No. of Institutions: 201
Shares Held: 14,143,669

REGISTRAR(S): American Transtech, Inc., Jacksonville, FL

TRANSFER AGENT(S): American Transtech, Inc., Jacksonville, FL

NYS SYMBOL WEC
Rec. Pr. 27¾

WISCONSIN ENERGY CORP.

YIELD 5.3%
P/E RATIO 17.2

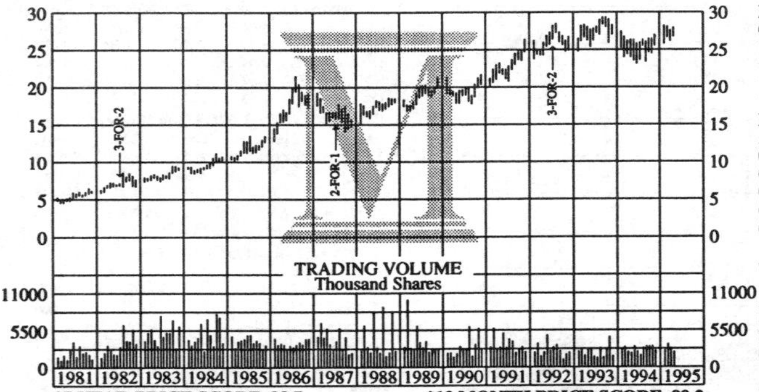

3-FOR-2
2-FOR-1
3-FOR-2
TRADING VOLUME
Thousand Shares
1981 1982 1983 1984 1985 1986 1987 1988 1989 1990 1991 1992 1993 1994 1995

*7 YEAR PRICE SCORE 93.7 *12 MONTH PRICE SCORE 99.2

*NYSE COMPOSITE INDEX=100

INTERIM EARNINGS (Per Share):

Qtr.	Mar.	June	Sept.	Dec.
1991	0.54	0.36	0.50	0.48
1992	0.53	0.30	0.37	0.46
1993	0.56	0.28	0.46	0.52
1994	0.21	0.40	0.48	0.58

INTERIM DIVIDENDS (Per Share):

Amt.	Decl.	Ex.	Rec.	Pay.
0.3525Q	4/27/94	5/3/94	5/9/94	6/1/94
0.3525Q	7/27	8/2	8/8	9/1
0.3525Q	10/26	11/2	11/8	12/1
0.3525Q	1/25/95	2/2/95	2/8/95	3/1/95
0.3675Q	4/27	5/2	5/8	6/1

Indicated div.: $1.47*

CAPITALIZATION (12/31/94):

	($000)	(%)
Long-Term Debt	1,283,686	35.4
Deferred Income Tax	569,695	15.7
Preferred Stock	30,451	0.8
Common & Surplus	1,744,566	48.1
Total	3,628,398	100.0
Current Debt	32,531	

DIVIDEND ACHIEVER STATUS:
Rank: 248 1984-94 Growth Rate: 6.5%
Total Years of Dividend Growth: 33

RECENT DEVELOPMENTS: For the quarter ended 12/31/94, net income was $63.1 million compared with $55.2 million last year. Revenues were $431.7 million, down 3.7% from $448.3 million a year earlier. Earnings were higher due to a 7.5% reduction in operating expenses. For the twelve months ended 12/31/94, net income was $180.9 million, including a restructuring charge, versus $190.1 million a year earlier. Comparisons were made with restated prior-year figures.

PROSPECTS: Near-term profits are being pressured by the restructuring program, which will better position WEC in the changing energy marketplace. The cost savings from reduced operation and maintenance expenses will be recognized by the end of 1995. These cost-cutting efforts will likely eliminate the need to raise rates for the next several years. Growth in revenues will likely come from conversions, new construction, or the addition of new natural gas franchise territory.

BUSINESS

WISCONSIN ENERGY CORP. is the holding company for Wisconsin Electric Power Co. and Wisconsin Natural Gas Co. and five non-utility subsidiaries. Wisconsin Electric is an electric utility operating in southeastern, east central and northern Wisconsin and in the Upper Peninsula of Michigan. Wisconsin Natural distributes and sells natural gas within the service territory of Wisconsin Electric.

REVENUES

(12/31/94)	($000)	(%)
Electric	1,404,562	80.6
Gas	324,349	18.6
Steam	14,281	0.8
Total	1,742,192	100.0

ANNUAL EARNINGS AND DIVIDENDS PER SHARE

	1994	1993	1992	1991	1990	1989	1988
Earnings Per Share	1.67	1.81	1.67	1.87	1.85	1.92	1.82
Dividends Per Share	1.396	1.341	[1] 1.285	1.223	1.157	1.087	1.01
Dividend Payout %	83.6	74.1	76.9	65.3	62.6	56.6	55.5

[1] 3-for-2 stk split, 7/1/92

ANNUAL FINANCIAL DATA

	1994	1993	1992	1991	1990	1989	1988
RECORD OF EARNINGS (IN MILLIONS):							
Total Revenues	1,742.2	1,643.7	1,551.8	1,538.9	1,442.5	1,493.4	1,540.7
Depreciation	177.6	165.3	162.7	146.7	144.7	141.8	129.8
Maintenance	124.6	155.2	149.6	142.2	133.7	150.4	171.3
Income Taxes	104.4	101.9	93.5	103.7	96.8	110.4	105.4
Operating Income	263.3	262.6	238.9	251.3	241.2	264.0	260.2
Interest Expense	108.0	101.8	89.4	84.9	82.6	85.2	85.0
Net Income	180.9	188.5	169.7	189.3	186.7	194.0	183.2
Aver. Shs. Outstg. (000)	108,025	104,240	101,744	101,037	101,037	101,037	100,530
BALANCE SHEET (IN MILLIONS):							
Gross Plant	5,075.2	4,773.4	4,462.9	4,169.5	3,977.0	3,805.3	3,676.1
Accumulated Depreciation	2,134.5	1,964.3	1,834.2	1,703.5	1,603.4	1,745.5	1,650.7
Prop, Plant & Equip, Net	2,940.7	2,809.1	2,628.7	2,466.0	2,373.6	2,059.8	2,025.4
Long-term Debt	1,283.7	1,286.2	1,210.4	1,093.6	990.4	1,003.7	1,044.3
Net Stockholders' Equity	1,775.0	1,686.5	1,641.8	1,550.4	1,484.7	1,414.8	1,330.7
Total Assets	4,408.3	4,223.1	3,744.6	3,503.7	3,361.0	3,003.0	2,849.2
Year End Shs Outstg (000)	108,940	105,320	103,093	101,037	101,037	101,037	101,037
STATISTICAL RECORD:							
Book Value Per Share	16.01	15.67	14.97	14.35	13.70	13.01	12.18
Op. Inc/Net Pl %	9.0	9.3	9.1	10.2	10.2	12.8	12.8
Dep/Gr. Pl %	3.5	3.5	3.6	3.5	3.6	3.7	3.5
Accum. Dep/Gr. Pl %	42.1	41.2	41.1	40.9	40.3	45.9	44.9
Return on Equity %	10.2	11.2	10.8	12.8	13.2	14.4	14.5
Average Yield %	5.5	5.0	4.9	5.3	5.9	5.7	6.0
P/E Ratio	16.5-13.8	16.2-13.7	17.1-14.2	14.1-10.7	11.7-9.6	11.1-8.7	10.2-8.2
Price Range	27½-23⅛	29⅜-24¾	28½-23¾	26⅜-20	21⅝-17¾	21⅜-16¾	18⅝-15

Statistics are as originally reported.

OFFICERS:
R.A. Abdoo, Chmn., Pres. & C.E.O.
J.W. Boston, Vice-Chmn.
J.H. Goetsch, V.P. & Sec.
J.G. Remmel, V.P., Treas. & C.F.O.

INCORPORATED: WI, Jun., 1981

PRINCIPAL OFFICE: 231 West Michigan Street P.O. Box 2949, Milwaukee, WI 53201

TELEPHONE NUMBER: (414) 221-2100

NO. OF EMPLOYEES: 4,801 full-time; 114 part-time

ANNUAL MEETING: In May

SHAREHOLDERS: 85,255

INSTITUTIONAL HOLDINGS:
No. of Institutions: 280
Shares Held: 32,528,729

REGISTRAR(S): First Chicago Trust Co. of New York, New York, NY 10008

TRANSFER AGENT(S): First Chicago Trust Co. of New York, New York, NY 10008
At Company's Office

WITCO CORP.

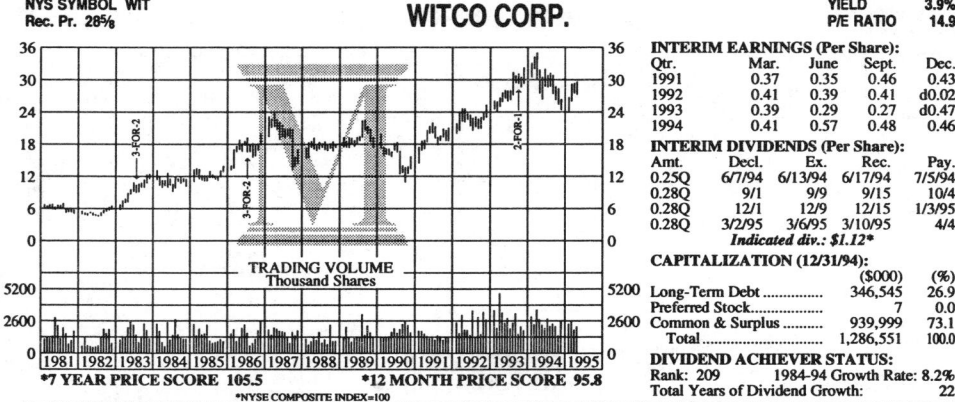

*7 YEAR PRICE SCORE 105.5   ***12 MONTH PRICE SCORE 95.8**
*NYSE COMPOSITE INDEX=100

INTERIM EARNINGS (Per Share):

Qtr.	Mar.	June	Sept.	Dec.
1991	0.37	0.35	0.46	0.43
1992	0.41	0.39	0.41	d0.02
1993	0.39	0.29	0.27	d0.47
1994	0.41	0.57	0.48	0.46

INTERIM DIVIDENDS (Per Share):

Amt.	Decl.	Ex.	Rec.	Pay.
0.25Q	6/7/94	6/13/94	6/17/94	7/5/94
0.28Q	9/1	9/9	9/15	10/4
0.28Q	12/1	12/9	12/15	1/3/95
0.28Q	3/2/95	3/6/95	3/10/95	4/4

Indicated div.: $1.12*

CAPITALIZATION (12/31/94):

	($000)	(%)
Long-Term Debt	346,545	26.9
Preferred Stock	7	0.0
Common & Surplus	939,999	73.1
Total	1,286,551	100.0

DIVIDEND ACHIEVER STATUS:
Rank: 209   1984-94 Growth Rate: 8.2%
Total Years of Dividend Growth: 22

RECENT DEVELOPMENTS: For the year ended 12/31/94, net income was $107.1 million compared with net income, including non-recurring net charges of $68.0 million, of $19.8 million in the year before. Non-recurring items in 1994 included a $3.1 million gain on the sale of WIT's metal finishing and metal working operations. Sales reached a record $2.22 billion, an increase of 4% versus $2.14 billion in the previous year, despite the disposition of two businesses during the year.

PROSPECTS: WIT continues to concentrate on its core areas of specialty chemicals and petroleum products. The Company plans to reach its goal of $5 billion in sales by the year 2000 through an aggressive acquisition program that will expand its core businesses. WIT must work to recoupe slight losses incurred in the previous year as a result of increased raw material costs, but a new pricing structure should aid in that goal.

BUSINESS

WITCO CORP. is a manufacturer of specialty chemical and petroleum products and engineered materials with 59 plants in twelve countries. Specialty chemicals include organic chemicals, epoxy plasticizers and stabilizers, all raw materials for the plastics industry, detergent products, and mining and distribution of diatomaceous earth. Specialty petroleum products include white oils, petrolatums and petroleum sulfonates. Two refineries primarily produce lubricating oils sold under private label brands as well as under the Kendall and Amalie names.

BUSINESS LINE ANALYSIS

(12/31/94)	Rev(%)	Inc(%)
Chemical	59.7	62.8
Petroleum	33.9	28.2
Diversified products	6.4	9.0
Total	100.0	100.0

ANNUAL EARNINGS AND DIVIDENDS PER SHARE

	1994	1993	1992	1991	1990	1989	1988
Earnings Per Share	1.92	0.46	1.19	1.61	1.48	0.80	⑤ 1.53
Dividends Per Share	1.03	① 0.94	② 0.92	0.89	0.86	0.805	0.695
Dividend Payout %	53.6	N.M.	77.3	55.5	58.3	N.M.	45.6

① 2-for-1 stk split,10/06/93   ② Bef acctg chge   ⑤ Before acctg. chg.

ANNUAL FINANCIAL DATA

RECORD OF EARNINGS (IN MILLIONS):

	1994	1993	1992	1991	1990	1989	1988
Total Revenues	2,234.7	2,151.2	1,738.2	1,641.1	1,650.9	1,609.0	1,590.9
Costs and Expenses	1,944.6	1,879.9	1,545.8	1,449.5	1,477.6	1,433.3	1,410.2
Depreciation & Amort	105.1	102.5	76.2	67.6	60.1	52.7	48.8
Operating Profit	185.0	168.9	116.2	123.9	113.2	123.1	131.9
Inc Bef Fed & Fgn Income Taxes	164.8	33.3	82.1	109.8	105.8	53.4	115.5
Income Taxes	57.7	13.6	28.2	36.3	37.9	18.4	43.9
Net Income	107.1	19.8	① 53.9	73.5	68.0	35.0	② 71.6
Aver. Shs. Outstg. (000)	56,378	54,866	49,801	49,212	49,702	50,674	50,498

① Before acctg. change dr$14,690,000.   ② Before acctg. change cr$20,289,000.

BALANCE SHEET (IN MILLIONS):

	1994	1993	1992	1991	1990	1989	1988
Cash and Cash Equivalents	197.2	183.1	134.4	139.3	116.4	213.4	194.4
Receivables, Net	395.5	340.9	329.2	250.2	261.4	245.4	251.2
Inventories	258.4	227.5	249.7	162.8	166.5	155.0	156.4
Gross Property	1,416.0	1,318.1	1,287.9	991.9	964.9	864.2	823.3
Accumulated Depreciation	696.0	621.7	566.7	517.2	493.8	447.0	422.3
Long-Term Debt	346.5	496.3	173.1	179.1	230.2	235.5	240.7
Net Stockholders' Equity	940.0	713.4	614.3	625.7	587.5	571.6	578.3
Total Assets	1,919.3	1,839.0	1,811.8	1,198.3	1,178.9	1,139.3	1,114.6
Total Current Assets	896.8	792.6	747.3	576.8	562.9	635.9	635.0
Total Current Liabilities	345.2	341.3	769.0	255.9	203.8	179.7	195.8
Net Working Capital	551.6	451.2	d21.6	320.9	359.1	456.2	439.3
Year End Shs Outstg (000)	56,147	50,500	44,456	43,554	43,304	45,054	44,812

STATISTICAL RECORD:

	1994	1993	1992	1991	1990	1989	1988
Operating Profit Margin %	8.3	7.8	6.7	7.6	6.9	7.6	8.3
Book Value Per Share	13.33	9.83	8.20	12.77	11.88	12.29	12.50
Return on Equity %	11.4	2.8	8.8	11.7	11.6	6.1	12.4
Return on Assets %	5.6	1.1	3.0	6.1	5.8	3.1	6.4
Average Yield %	3.5	3.3	4.1	4.9	5.6	4.0	4.0
P/E Ratio	18.2-12.7	70.1-52.2	21.3-16.8	13.7-9.0	13.6-7.4	28.3-21.7	12.7-10.1
Price Range	35-24⅜	32¼-24	25⅜-20	22-14½	20-10⅞	22⅝-17⅜	19¼-15⅜

Statistics are as originally reported.

OFFICERS:
W.R. Toller, Chmn. & C.E.O.
W.E. Mahoney, Vice-Chmn. & C.O.O.
M.D. Fullwood, Exec. V.P. & C.F.O.
D. McCoy, V.P., Gen. Couns. & Sec.
J.M. Rutledge, V.P. & Treas.
INCORPORATED: DE, Jun., 1958
PRINCIPAL OFFICE: One American Lane, Greenwich, CT 06831-2559

TELEPHONE NUMBER: (203) 552-2263
FAX: (203) 552-2864
NO. OF EMPLOYEES: 7,955
ANNUAL MEETING: In April
SHAREHOLDERS: 203 pfd.; 4,991 com.
INSTITUTIONAL HOLDINGS:
No. of Institutions: 169
Shares Held: 15,516,087

REGISTRAR(S): First Chicago Trust Co. of New York, New York, NY 10008

TRANSFER AGENT(S): First Chicago Trust Co. of New York, New York, NY 10008

NYS SYMBOL WMX
Rec. Pr. 28

WMX TECHNOLOGIES INC.

YIELD 2.1%
P/E RATIO 17.3

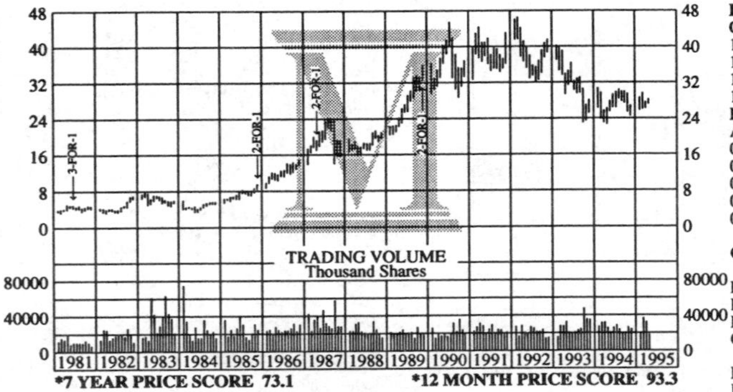

48
40
32
24
16
8
0
3-FOR-1
2-FOR-1
2-FOR-1
2-FOR-1
TRADING VOLUME
Thousand Shares
80000
40000
0
1981 1982 1983 1984 1985 1986 1987 1988 1989 1990 1991 1992 1993 1994 1995

*7 YEAR PRICE SCORE 73.1 *12 MONTH PRICE SCORE 93.3

*NYSE COMPOSITE INDEX=100

INTERIM EARNINGS (Per Share):

Qtr.	Mar.	June	Sept.	Dec.
1991	0.34	0.42	0.42	0.05
1992	0.39	0.66	0.44	0.37
1993	0.41	0.45	d0.26	0.34
1994	0.34	0.42	0.44	0.42

INTERIM DIVIDENDS (Per Share):

Amt.	Decl.	Ex.	Rec.	Pay.
0.15Q	1/28/94	3/17/94	3/23/94	4/7/94
0.15Q	5/13	6/16	6/22	7/7
0.15Q	8/9	9/15	9/21	10/6
0.15Q	11/15	12/15	12/21	1/5/95
0.15Q	1/30/95	3/16/95	3/22/95	4/6

Indicated div.: $0.60*

CAPITALIZATION (12/31/94):

	($000)	(%)
Long-Term Debt	6,044,411	47.3
Deferred Income Tax	665,677	5.2
Minority Interest	1,536,165	12.0
Common & Surplus	4,540,981	35.5
Total	12,787,234	100.0

DIVIDEND ACHIEVER STATUS:
Rank: 14 1984-94 Growth Rate: 20.6%
Total Years of Dividend Growth: 18

RECENT DEVELOPMENTS: For the year ended 12/31/94, net income increased 73.2% to $784.4 million from $452.8 million, including special charges of $550 million, in 1993. Revenues advanced 10.5% to $10.10 billion, compared with $9.14 billion the prior year. SG & A expenses increased 5.0% to $1.18 billion. WMX's solid waste subsidiary turned in a strong performance due to greater waste volumes, better pricing and improved commodities markets for recycled materials.

PROSPECTS: Although solid waste volumes are on the rise, hazardous waste volumes continue to decline. The Company is considering using idle capacity at its hazardous waste facilities to handle non-hazardous materials. WMX continues with efforts to simplify its organizational structure. Chemical Waste Management is now a 100%-owned subsidiary and WMX has propsed to acquire the remaining shares of Rust International that are publicly held.

BUSINESS

WMX TECHNOLOGIES, INC. (formerly Waste Management, Inc.) provides solid and hazardous waste services, energy recovery and environmental technologies and engineering resources. WMX currently includes nine independently managed business organizations. They are Waste Management of North America's East, Mideast, South and West groups, constituting its solid waste recycling, collection and disposal operations; four publicly traded, majority-owned subsidiaries, Chemical Waste Management, 100%-owned, Wheelabrator, 56%-owned, and Waste Management International, 56%-owned; and Rust International Inc., which provides consulting, engineering and construction services. Another group, WMX Technology & Services, Inc., consists of WMX's corporate headquarters staff.

REVENUES

(12/31/94)	($000)	(%)
Solid Waste	5,117,871	48.8
Hazardous Waste	649,581	6.2
Eng., Constr., Ind & rel	1,682,907	16.0
Water Treat. & Air Qual.	1,324,567	12.6
International Waste Mgmt.	1,710,862	16.4
Total	9,708,848	100.0

ANNUAL EARNINGS AND DIVIDENDS PER SHARE

	1994	1993	1992	1991	1990	1989	1988
Earnings Per Share	**1.62**	**0.93**	**[1] 1.86**	**1.23**	**[2] 1.49**	**1.22**	**1.02**
Dividends Per Share	**0.60**	**0.56**	**0.48**	**0.40**	**0.34**	**[3] 0.27**	**0.21**
Dividend Payout %	**37.0**	**60.2**	**25.8**	**32.5**	**22.8**	**22.1**	**20.5**

[1] Before acctg. chges [2] Before extraord. item [3] 2-for-1 stk split, 12/89

ANNUAL FINANCIAL DATA

	1994	1993	1992	1991	1990	1989	1988
RECORD OF EARNINGS (IN MILLIONS):							
Total Revenues	10,097.3	9,135.6	8,661.0	7,550.9	6,034.4	4,458.9	3,565.6
Costs and Expenses	8,218.6	8,025.1	7,213.7	6,372.3	4,818.9	3,208.4	2,455.7
Depreciation & Amort	714.1	796.7	714.1	592.8	501.3	394.8	301.7
Operating Profit	1,777.8	1,566.1	1,590.1	1,413.0	1,168.0	855.7	808.3
Income Bef Income Taxes	1,379.2	809.2	1,398.4	1,027.9	1,173.2	850.7	746.3
Income Taxes	594.8	356.4	477.2	421.6	463.9	288.5	282.1
Net Income	784.4	452.8	[1] 921.2	606.3	[2] 709.3	562.1	464.2
Aver. Shs. Outstg. (000)	484,144	485,374	493,948	493,167	476,580	459,727	453,710

[1] Before acctg. change dr$71,139,000. [2] Before extra. item dr$24,547,000.

	1994	1993	1992	1991	1990	1989	1988
BALANCE SHEET (IN MILLIONS):							
Cash and Cash Equivalents	141.6	126.4	68.1	222.1	232.7	106.8	54.1
Receivables, Net	2,837.5	2,558.5	2,421.0	1,670.2	1,249.6	745.9	587.9
Inventories	194.6	148.0	126.6	114.5	105.9	58.4	54.5
Gross Property	12,789.0	11,804.9	10,382.7	8,846.7	7,454.4	4,931.1	3,685.9
Accumulated Depreciation	3,503.2	3,035.4	2,624.5	2,147.2	1,737.4	1,272.0	991.2
Long-Term Debt	6,044.4	6,145.6	4,312.5	3,783.0	3,139.6	1,503.8	1,270.3
Net Stockholders' Equity	4,541.0	4,159.5	4,319.6	4,133.1	3,673.0	2,738.0	2,179.2
Total Assets	17,973.6	16,657.8	14,529.1	12,683.9	10,518.2	6,405.2	4,878.5
Total Current Assets	3,523.5	3,170.9	2,923.3	2,256.2	1,904.8	1,086.1	826.5
Total Current Liabilities	3,179.7	2,677.6	2,379.6	2,114.0	1,916.0	1,242.2	744.6
Net Working Capital	343.8	493.3	543.7	142.2	d11.1	d156.1	81.9
Year End Shs Outstg (000)	496,387	483,453	490,177	493,621	488,665	465,782	453,200
STATISTICAL RECORD:							
Operating Profit Margin %	17.5	11.1	15.8	14.8	19.4	19.2	22.7
Book Value Per Share	1.51	1.44	3.14	3.30	3.70	3.72	2.96
Return on Equity %	17.3	10.9	21.3	14.7	19.3	20.5	21.3
Return on Assets %	4.4	2.7	6.3	4.8	6.7	8.8	9.5
Average Yield %	2.2	1.8	1.2	1.0	0.9	1.0	1.1
P/E Ratio	19.0-14.0	43.3-24.7	25.1-17.2	36.1-26.5	30.5-19.2	29.4-16.7	21.0-15.4
Price Range	30¾-22⅝	40¼-23	46⅝-32	44⅜-32⅝	45½-28⅝	35⅞-20⅜	21⅜-15¾

Statistics are as originally reported.

OFFICERS:
D.L. Buntrock, Chmn. & C.E.O.
P.B. Rooney, Pres. & C.O.O.
J.E. Koenig, Sr. V.P., C.F.O. & Treas.
H.A. Getz, V.P., Sec. & Gen. Coun.

INCORPORATED: DE, Sep., 1968

PRINCIPAL OFFICE: 3003 Butterfield Rd., Oak Brook, IL 60521

TELEPHONE NUMBER: (708) 572-8800
FAX: (708) 572-3094
NO. OF EMPLOYEES: 74,400 (approx.)
ANNUAL MEETING: In May
SHAREHOLDERS: 65,000 (approx.)
INSTITUTIONAL HOLDINGS:
No. of Institutions: 959
Shares Held: 262,308,363

REGISTRAR(S): Harris Trust & Savings Bank, Chicago, IL

TRANSFER AGENT(S): Harris Trust & Savings Bank, Chicago, IL

NYS SYMBOL WPH
Rec. Pr. 28½

WPL HOLDINGS, INC.

YIELD 6.8%
P/E RATIO 13.4

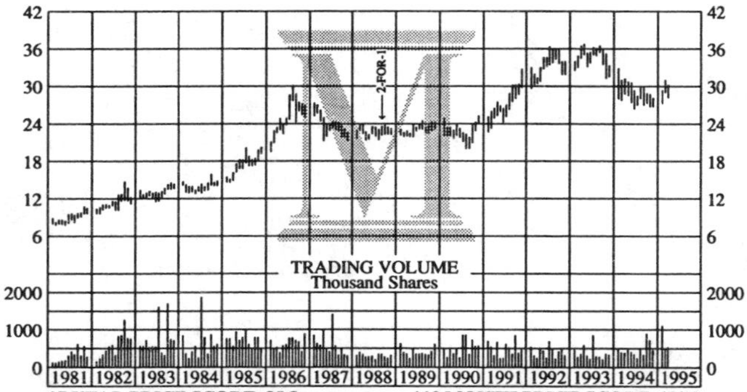

***7 YEAR PRICE SCORE 85.8** ***12 MONTH PRICE SCORE 100.0**

*NYSE COMPOSITE INDEX=100

INTERIM EARNINGS (Per Share):

Qtr.	Mar.	June	Sept.	Dec.
1992	0.69	0.26	0.45	0.71
1993	0.71	0.24	0.44	0.73
1994	0.87	0.33	0.50	0.43

INTERIM DIVIDENDS (Per Share):

Amt.	Decl.	Ex.	Rec.	Pay.
0.48Q	4/15/94	4/25/94	4/29/94	5/14/94
0.48Q	7/13	7/25	7/29	8/15
0.48Q	10/19	10/25	10/31	11/15
0.485Q	1/18/95	1/25/95	1/31/95	2/15/95
0.485Q	4/12	4/24	4/28	5/15

Indicated div.: $1.94*

CAPITALIZATION (12/31/94):

	($000)	(%)
Long-Term Debt	448,110	32.7
Deferred Income Tax	264,807	19.3
Preferred Stock	59,963	4.4
Common & Surplus	597,798	43.6
Total	1,370,678	100.0
Current Debt	124,308	

DIVIDEND ACHIEVER STATUS:
Rank: 289 1984-94 Growth Rate: 4.3%
Total Years of Dividend Growth: 22

RECENT DEVELOPMENTS: For the quarter ended 12/31/94, net income dropped 40% to $13.3 million compared with $22.3 million in the corresponding period of 1993. Revenues slid 3% to $209.4 million versus $215.9 million a year earlier. Lower earnings reflect a combination of early retirement and severance program costs as well as unseasonably mild winter weather. For the year ended 12/31/94, net income was $65.3 million, up 4% from $62.5 million in 1993. Revenues advanced 6% to $816.2 million.

PROSPECTS: Results will benefit from improved economic conditions and cost-containment measures instituted in 1994. The Company plans to build three 86-megawatt combustion turbines over the next five years, which should increase the need for external financing. WPH, one of the lowest overall in generation costs in its region, is well positioned to compete in its market place and ward off competition. The Company expects to have a new rate structure by the end of the year and has requested a $3.5 million increase in water and natural gas rates.

BUSINESS

WPL HOLDINGS, INC. is a diversified holding company for Wisconsin Power and Light, an electric energy utility, and Heartland Development, a non-utility business dealing with telecommunications and real estate development. Wisconsin Power and Light provides electric energy, natural gas and water to 376,600 customers in a 16,000-square-mile area in south-central Wisconsin. WP&L generating mix of its major power plants include coal, nuclear and hydroelectric power. Heartland Development is an unregulated, non-utility business engaged in three major areas: environmental consulting and engineering, affordable housing and energy technology.

REVENUES

(12/31/94)	($000)	(%)
Electric	531,747	65.2
Gas	139,646	17.1
Other	144,766	17.7
Total	816,159	100.0

ANNUAL EARNINGS AND DIVIDENDS PER SHARE

	1994	1993	1992	1991	1990	1989	1988
Earnings Per Share	**2.13**	**2.11**	**2.11**	**2.43**	**2.23**	**1.93**	**2.18**
Dividends Per Share	**1.92**	**1.90**	**1.86**	**1.80**	**1.74**	**1.68**	**[1] 1.62**
Dividend Payout %	**90.1**	**90.1**	**88.2**	**74.1**	**78.0**	**87.0**	**74.3**

[1] 2-for-1 stk split, 9/88.

ANNUAL FINANCIAL DATA

	1994	1993	1992	1991	1990	1989	1988
RECORD OF EARNINGS (IN MILLIONS):							
Total Revenues	816.2	773.1	651.7	648.8	618.5	604.8	600.9
Depreciation	81.5	69.1	59.5	53.0	55.3	54.6	52.3
Maintenance	41.2	44.8	45.1	42.9	41.7	40.6	39.8
Prov for Fed Inc Taxes	35.4	25.1	22.6	31.8	28.5	26.9	31.2
Operating Income	130.0	126.2	116.2	131.0	126.3	116.2	120.9
Interest Expense	36.7	37.0	37.6	34.8	32.1	29.3	29.3
Net Income	65.3	62.5	57.0	64.9	59.5	51.5	57.9
Aver. Shs. Outstg. (000)	30,671	29,681	27,043	26,730	26,663	26,663	26,528
BALANCE SHEET (IN MILLIONS):							
Gross Plant	2,198.3	2,119.0	1,968.3	1,819.6	1,694.3	1,633.1	1,553.1
Accumulated Depreciation	808.9	779.8	728.4	681.0	640.5	739.6	695.7
Prop, Plant & Equip, Net	1,389.5	1,339.1	1,239.9	1,138.5	1,053.8	893.5	857.4
Long-term Debt	448.1	425.1	417.8	367.5	360.2	321.2	323.2
Net Stockholders' Equity	657.8	642.9	540.9	517.7	497.0	483.9	477.3
Total Assets	1,805.9	1,761.9	1,556.9	1,376.3	1,251.7	1,047.4	1,026.2
Year End Shs Outstg (000)	30,774	30,439	27,313	26,785	26,663	26,663	26,663
STATISTICAL RECORD:							
Book Value Per Share	19.43	19.15	17.61	17.09	16.39	15.90	15.65
Op. Inc/Net Pl %	9.4	9.4	9.4	11.5	12.0	13.0	14.1
Dep/Gr. Pl %	3.7	3.3	3.0	2.9	3.3	3.3	3.4
Accum. Dep/Gr. Pl %	36.8	36.8	37.0	37.4	37.8	45.3	44.8
Return on Equity %	9.9	9.7	10.5	12.5	12.0	10.6	12.1
Average Yield %	6.5	5.6	5.6	6.5	7.7	7.2	7.2
P/E Ratio	15.4-12.4	17.4-14.8	17.2-14.0	13.5-9.3	11.3-9.0	12.7-11.3	11.0-9.7
Price Range	32⅞-26⅜	36¾-31¼	36⅜-29⅝	32¾-22⅝	25¼-20	24½-21⅞	23⅞-21¼

Statistics are as originally reported.

OFFICERS:
E.B. Davis, Jr., Pres. & C.E.O.
E.M. Gleason, V.P., Treas. & Sec.

INCORPORATED: WI, Apr., 1981

PRINCIPAL OFFICE: 222 West Washington Avenue, Madison, WI 53703

TELEPHONE NUMBER: (608) 252-3311
NO. OF EMPLOYEES: 2,391
ANNUAL MEETING: In May
SHAREHOLDERS: 37,049 (approx.)
INSTITUTIONAL HOLDINGS:
No. of Institutions: 108
Shares Held: 4,763,972

REGISTRAR(S): At Company's Office

TRANSFER AGENT(S): At Company's Office

NYS SYMBOL WPS
Rec. Pr. 28⅞

WPS RESOURCES CORP.

YIELD 6.3%
P/E RATIO 13.1

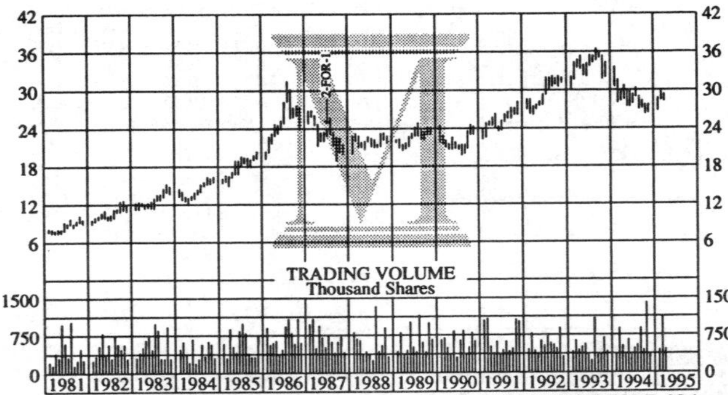

*7 YEAR PRICE SCORE 89.1 *12 MONTH PRICE SCORE 98.1
*NYSE COMPOSITE INDEX=100

INTERIM EARNINGS (Per Share):

Qtr.	Mar.	June	Sept.	Dec.
1992	0.77	0.30	0.50	0.78
1993	0.85	0.45	0.66	0.51
1994	0.90	0.31	0.54	0.46

INTERIM DIVIDENDS (Per Share):

Amt.	Decl.	Ex.	Rec.	Pay.
0.455Q	10/17/94	11/23/94	11/30/94	12/20/94
0.455Q	2/9/95	2/22/95	2/28/95	3/19/95
0.455Q	4/13	5/24	5/31	6/20

*Indicated div.: $1.82**

CAPITALIZATION (12/31/94):

	($000)	(%)
Long-Term Debt	309,945	32.1
Deferred Income Tax	158,811	16.4
Preferred Stock	51,200	5.3
Common & Surplus	446,540	46.2
Total	966,496	100.0
Current Debt	12,500	

DIVIDEND ACHIEVER STATUS:
Rank: 295 1984-94 Growth Rate: 4.0%
Total Years of Dividend Growth: 36

RECENT DEVELOPMENTS: For the year ended 12/31/94, net income was $52.7 million compared with $58.9 million in the corresponding period of 1993. Revenues were $673.8 million, down 1% from $680.6 million a year earlier. Revenues were affected by the Public Service Commission of Wisconsin lowering the Company's ROE from 12.3% to 11.3%. Electric operating revenues decreased $12.4 million, or 2.5% due to a 4.2% reduction in retail rate.

PROSPECTS: As a low cost producer, WPS intends to remain focused on the energy business by capitalizing on the changing market place and by building on its core competencies to provide the best value in energy to its customers. WPS received a two-year rate order from Public Service Commission of Wisconsin which became effective 1/1/95. This rate order decreased electric retail rates by 2.6% and kept retail gas rates at current levels.

BUSINESS

WPS RESOURCES CORP. (formerly Wisconsin Public Service Corp.) supplies electricity and gas services in north-central and north-eastern Wisconsin and an adjacent part of upper Michigan. Included in the service area are the cities of Green Bay, Sheboygan, Oshkosh and Wausau. The area is balanced between industry, agriculture, dairying and recreation. About 34% of electric revenues come from residential customers; 53% from commercial & industrial; and 13% other. The Company purchases most of its supply of natural gas from ANR Pipeline Company and makes spot markets purchases for the remainder. WPS' primary 1994 generation mix was 62.8% steam; 14.5% nuclear; 2.6% hydro; and 20.1% purchased and other.

ANNUAL EARNINGS AND DIVIDENDS PER SHARE

	1994	1993	1992	1991	1990	1989	1988
Earnings Per Share	2.21	2.47	2.35	2.23	2.00	1.98	2.28
Dividends Per Share	1.80	1.76	1.72	1.68	1.64	1.60	1.56
Dividend Payout %	81.4	71.3	73.2	75.3	82.0	80.8	68.4

ANNUAL FINANCIAL DATA

	1994	1993	1992	1991	1990	1989	1988
RECORD OF EARNINGS (IN MILLIONS):							
Total Revenues	673.8	680.6	634.8	623.5	589.0	585.8	604.3
Depreciation	56.4	60.6	58.6	55.7	55.4	53.1	50.5
Maintenance	50.0	51.6	46.4	48.2	44.3	43.4	43.4
Income Taxes	29.5	27.7	23.1	22.0	20.8	21.0	26.6
Operating Income	105.8	83.7	79.1	75.0	70.8	70.3	77.2
Interest Expense	25.1	25.8	26.6	24.8	24.9	23.8	23.0
Net Income	52.7	62.2	58.0	54.2	49.0	49.1	56.4
Aver. Shs. Outstg. (000)	23,897	23,888	23,350	22,889	22,889	23,087	23,201
BALANCE SHEET (IN MILLIONS):							
Gross Plant	1,710.3	1,644.9	1,595.5	1,506.2	1,588.2	1,513.0	1,448.0
Accumulated Depreciation	846.5	801.1	748.4	695.6	759.2	834.8	779.8
Prop, Plant & Equip, Net	863.8	843.9	847.1	810.6	829.0	678.3	668.3
Long-term Debt	309.9	314.2	321.5	332.9	273.3	255.3	256.3
Net Stockholders' Equity	497.7	485.7	464.4	420.5	423.3	425.0	424.5
Total Assets	1,217.3	1,198.8	1,145.6	1,073.5	1,028.8	877.0	843.4
Year End Shs Outstg (000)	23,897	23,897	23,846	22,889	22,889	22,889	23,201
STATISTICAL RECORD:							
Book Value Per Share	18.69	18.18	17.33	16.13	16.26	16.30	16.00
Op. Inc/Net Pl %	12.3	9.9	9.3	9.3	8.5	10.4	11.6
Dep/Gr. Pl %	3.3	3.7	3.7	3.7	3.5	3.5	3.5
Accum. Dep/Gr. Pl %	49.5	48.7	46.9	46.2	47.8	55.2	53.8
Return on Equity %	10.6	12.8	12.5	12.9	11.6	11.6	13.4
Average Yield %	1.5	5.3	5.9	6.7	7.4	7.1	7.2
P/E Ratio	15.2-11.9	14.8-12.2	13.7-11.1	12.7-10.0	12.3-9.9	12.6-10.4	10.3-8.8
Price Range	33⅝-26¼	36½-30⅛	32¼-26⅛	28¼-22¼	24⅝-19¾	24⅞-20½	23⅜-20

Statistics are as originally reported.

BUSINESS LINE ANALYSIS

(12/31/94)	Rev(%)	Inc(%)
Electric	71.4	90.2
Gas	28.6	9.8
Total	100.0	100.0

OFFICERS:
D.A. Bollom, Pres. & C.E.O.
D.P. Bittner, Sr. V.P.-Fin.
R.H. Knuth, Asst. V.P. & Sec.
R.G. Baeten, Treasurer

INCORPORATED: WI, Jul., 1883

PRINCIPAL OFFICE: 700 North Adams Street P.O. Box 19001, Green Bay, WI 54307-9001

TELEPHONE NUMBER: (414) 433-1445
FAX: (414) 433-1526
NO. OF EMPLOYEES: 2,603
ANNUAL MEETING: In May
SHAREHOLDERS: 25,240 common; 3,577, pfd.
INSTITUTIONAL HOLDINGS:
No. of Institutions: 139
Shares Held: 6,112,499

REGISTRAR(S): First Wisconsin Trust Co., Milwaukee, WI

TRANSFER AGENT(S): First Wisconsin Trust Co., Milwaukee, WI

NYS SYMBOL WWY
Rec. Pr. 43⅜

WRIGLEY (WM.) JR. CO.

YIELD 1.3%
P/E RATIO 21.9

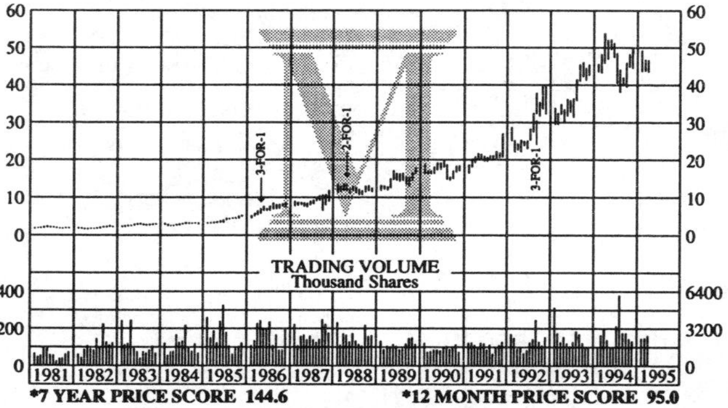

*7 YEAR PRICE SCORE 144.6 *12 MONTH PRICE SCORE 95.0
*NYSE COMPOSITE INDEX=100

INTERIM EARNINGS (Per Share):

Qtr.	Mar.	June	Sept.	Dec.
1991	0.27	0.33	0.30	0.20
1992	0.32	0.38	0.35	0.22
1993	0.36	0.46	0.42	0.26
1994	0.65	0.50	0.53	0.30

INTERIM DIVIDENDS (Per Share):

Amt.	Decl.	Ex.	Rec.	Pay.
0.12Q	6/8/94	7/11/94	7/15/94	8/1/94
0.12Q	8/17	10/7	10/14	11/1
0.44Sp	10/25	12/9	12/15	12/31
0.14Q	10/25	1/9/95	1/13/95	2/1/95
0.14Q	3/9/95	4/10	4/17	5/1

Indicated div.: $0.56*

CAPITALIZATION (12/31/94):

	($000)	(%)
Deferred Income Tax	15,760	2.2
Common & Surplus	688,470	97.8
Total	704,230	100.0

DIVIDEND ACHIEVER STATUS:
Rank: 20 1984-94 Growth Rate: 19.2%
Total Years of Dividend Growth: 14

RECENT DEVELOPMENTS: For the year ended 12/31/94, net income was $230.5 million compared with $174.9 million in 1993. Results for 1994 include a net gain of $24.8 million from the sale of some property in Singapore in the first quarter. Revenues increased 12% to $1.60 billion, primarily due to higher volumes worldwide. Also, selected selling price increases benefited results as well. During 1994, consolidated unit volumes of chewing gum advanced 9% from 1993 levels.

PROSPECTS: Selective price increases and new marketing initiatives should boost near-term earnings growth. WWY's newest chewing gum, Winterfresh, has received favorable customer response, and should contribute modestly to overall volumes. Meanwhile, WWY will continue its expansion program in Indonesia, Thailand and Mexico. In Europe, sugar-free brands such as Orbit and Extra should continue to produce strong volume growth, especially in France and England.

BUSINESS

WM. WRIGLEY JR. CO. is the world's largest chewing gum producer. Wrigley brands are produced in 12 factories around the world and sold in more than 100 countries. Main brands are Wrigley's Spearmint, Doublemint, Juicy Fruit, Big Red, Extra, and Freedent plus Hubba Bubba bubble gum. All other businesses account for less than 10% of combined revenues, operating profit and assets. Wrigley operates plants in Chicago, IL, Santa Cruz, CA and Gainesville, GA, plus others in Europe, Asia, Africa and Australia. U.S. wholly-owned subsidiaries are Amurol Products Co., Four-Ten Corp., L.A. Dreyfus Co. and Northwestern Flavors, Inc. Wrigley has also expanded distribution into Hungary, and Yugoslavia, where it also has wholly-owned subsidiaries.

GEOGRAPHIC DATA

(12/31/94)	Rev(%)	Inc(%)
North America...........	54.8	49.9
Europe	33.5	30.3
Asia, Pacific & Other	11.7	19.8
Total	100.0	100.0

ANNUAL EARNINGS AND DIVIDENDS PER SHARE

	1994	1993	1992	1991	1990	1989	1988
Earnings Per Share	**1.98**	**1.50**	**[1] 0.42**	**1.09**	**1.00**	**0.90**	**0.73**
Dividends Per Share	**0.90**	**0.75**	**[2] 0.62**	**0.55**	**0.493**	**0.453**	**[3] 0.363**
Dividend Payout %	**45.5**	**50.0**	**N.M.**	**50.3**	**49.5**	**50.4**	**50.0**

[1] Before acctg. chg. [2] 3-for-1 stk split,09/16/92 [3] 2-for-1 stk. split, 4/88 & 4/86.

ANNUAL FINANCIAL DATA

	1994	1993	1992	1991	1990	1989	1988
RECORD OF EARNINGS (IN MILLIONS):							
Total Revenues	1,661.3	1,440.4	1,301.3	1,159.8	1,123.5	1,010.7	902.0
Costs and Expenses	1,265.4	1,125.5	1,038.0	921.7	907.3	814.8	737.5
Depreciation	41.1	34.6	29.8	28.7	26.9	24.6	23.2
Operating Profit	963.8	823.3	728.8	652.0	614.6	558.9	509.5
Earn Bef Income Taxes	353.3	278.8	232.3	208.0	188.3	170.4	140.7
Income Taxes	122.7	103.9	83.7	79.4	70.9	64.3	53.5
Net Income	230.5	174.9	[1] 148.6	128.7	117.4	106.1	87.2
Aver. Shs. Outstg. (000)	116,358	116,511	117,055	117,517	117,743	118,035	120,309
[1] Before acctg. change dr$7,278,000.							
BALANCE SHEET (IN MILLIONS):							
Cash and Cash Equivalents	230.2	189.8	182.5	144.9	114.2	108.7	114.7
Receivables, Net	138.5	118.2	95.9	92.5	85.9	76.8	60.7
Inventories	221.1	176.8	155.8	155.5	147.8	122.4	93.4
Gross Property	638.5	550.9	513.4	486.5	457.1	416.8	387.8
Accumulated Depreciation	349.0	311.0	291.3	285.1	268.2	244.9	232.6
Net Stockholders' Equity	688.5	575.2	498.9	463.4	401.4	343.0	308.5
Total Assets	978.8	815.3	711.4	625.1	563.7	498.6	440.4
Total Current Assets	623.3	502.3	448.6	403.4	357.0	307.9	268.8
Total Current Liabilities	209.9	159.2	149.5	127.3	127.3	147.9	125.2
Net Working Capital	413.4	343.1	299.1	276.0	229.7	160.0	143.7
Year End Shs Outstg (000)	116,209	116,400	116,834	117,418	117,507	117,876	119,196
STATISTICAL RECORD:							
Operating Profit Margin %	21.4	19.5	17.9	18.1	16.9	16.9	15.7
Book Value Per Share	5.92	4.94	4.27	3.95	3.42	2.91	2.59
Return on Equity %	33.5	30.4	29.8	27.8	29.2	30.9	28.3
Return on Assets %	23.6	21.5	20.9	20.6	20.8	21.3	19.8
Average Yield %	2.0	2.0	2.0	2.5	2.9	3.0	3.0
P/E Ratio	27.2-19.3	30.8-19.7	31.4-17.4	24.8-15.0	19.8-14.6	19.9-13.2	18.7-14.6
Price Range	53⅞-38⅛	46⅛-29½	39⅞-22⅛	27-16⅜	19¾-14⅝	17⅞-11⅞	13⅝-10⅝

Statistics are as originally reported.

OFFICERS:
W. Wrigley, Pres. & C.E.O.
W.M. Piet, V.P.-Corporate Affairs & Sec.
D. Petrovich, V.P. & Treas.

INCORPORATED: DE, Oct., 1927

PRINCIPAL OFFICE: Wrigley Building 410 North Michigan Avenue, Chicago, IL 60611

TELEPHONE NUMBER: (312) 644-2121
FAX: (312) 644-7879
NO. OF EMPLOYEES: 7,000
ANNUAL MEETING: In March
SHAREHOLDERS: 24,078
INSTITUTIONAL HOLDINGS:
No. of Institutions: 232
Shares Held: 11,083,317

REGISTRAR(S): First Chicago Trust Co. of New York, New York, NY 10008

TRANSFER AGENT(S): First Chicago Trust Co. of New York, New York, NY 10008